2020
U.S. Master
Tax Guide®

SPECIAL EDITION

Wolters Kluwer Editorial Staff Publication

Access the Latest Tax Developments

A special webpage created by Wolters Kluwer for the *U.S. Master Tax Guide®* will keep you up-to-date with legislative developments affecting the 2019 tax year. Visit *CCHCPELink.com/TaxUpdates* to find the information you'll need to keep *U.S. Master Tax Guide* your first source for practical tax guidance.

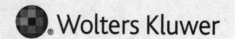

This publication is designed to provide accurate and authoritative information in regard to the subject matter covered. It is sold with the understanding that the publisher is not engaged in rendering legal, accounting, or other professional service. If legal advice or other expert assistance is required, the services of a competent professional person should be sought.

ISBN: 978-0-8080-5418-4

2700 Lake Cook Road
Riverwoods, IL 60015
800 248 3248
CCHCPELink.com

No claim is made to original government works; however, within this Product or Publication, the following are subject to CCH Incorporated's copyright: (1) the gathering, compilation, and arrangement of such government materials; (2) the magnetic translation and digital conversion of data, if applicable; (3) the historical, statutory and other notes and references; and (4) the commentary and other materials.

Do not send returns to the above address. If for any reason you are not satisfied with your book purchase, it can easily be returned within 30 days of shipment. Please go to *support.cch.com/returns* to initiate your return. If you require further assistance with your return, please call: (800) 344-3734 M-F, 8 a.m. – 6 p.m CT.

Printed in the United States of America

SUSTAINABLE FORESTRY INITIATIVE

Certified Sourcing
www.sfiprogram.org
SFI-01681

Preface

Income taxation in the United States has been around for over 100 years. From the very beginning, Wolters Kluwer was there and is still setting the standard as the number one quick reference resource for tax professionals. Wolters Kluwer is proud to serve the tax professional community with this special edition of the *U.S. Master Tax Guide* ®. This edition of the industry standard explains the complex set of tax rules and is designed to provide fast and reliable answers to tax questions affecting individuals and businesses. In all, 29 chapters contain comprehensive, timely, and precise explanations of the ever-changing federal income tax rules for individuals, businesses, estates, and trusts.

The Special Edition covers the Families First Coronavirus Response Act (P.L. 116-127) and the Coronavirus Aid, Relief, and Economic Security (CARES) Act (P.L. 116-136), both passed in response to the COVID-19 (coronavirus) pandemic affecting individuals and businesses in the United States and across the globe. It also covers the deluge of IRS and other administrative guidance issued in the wake of these two bills, as well as the unprecedented delay in income tax return filing and payment. Also reflected in this Special Edition is the Further Consolidated Appropriations Act, 2020 (P.L. 116-94), which contained the SECURE Act, which made significant changes to the rules governing retirement funding and distributions, and the Taxpayer Certainty and Disaster Tax Relief Act of 2019, which extended through 2020 many taxpayer friendly deductions and credits.

As in previous editions, major legislative provisions are reflected throughout the *Guide*, while important non-legislative tax developments are conveniently highlighted at ¶ 3. The *Guide* also comes complete with many timesaving features that help practitioners quickly and easily determine how particular tax items and situations should be treated (see the following page for a listing and description of these "Key Features").

The tax world has been very busy in the few months since the last publication of the *U.S. Master Tax Guide* ®, and this Special Edition comes just at the right time, ready to provide all the guidance you will need to complete 2019 returns.

April 2020

Key Features

In addition to 29 chapters of tax law explanations, the *U.S. Master Tax Guide*® provides a wealth of information in the pages that lead up to Chapter 1. Some of these timesaving tools and features are described below, listed by paragraph location.

OVERVIEW (¶ 1-6): The Overview division contains informative features available to facilitate research and dealing with clients, including the following.

- "AGI Phaseout Thresholds," includes a number of tax items subject to phaseout restrictions.
- "Where to File Returns," a listing of income tax return mailing addresses.
- "2020 Tax Calendar," shows the filing dates for 2019 tax returns and tax payments throughout 2020.

TAX RATES (¶ 11-53): This section contains the 2019 and 2020 tax rate schedules for individuals and estates and trusts, the corporate tax rate schedule and related rates, and the estate and gift tax rate schedule, as well as a listing of key excise tax rates.

CHECKLISTS (¶ 63-65): A collection of checklists designed to provide tax return preparers with quick references to assist in answering common questions regarding IRS forms to use, information returns, and types of payments.

SPECIAL TAX TABLES (¶ 83-88): This is a collection of often-used interest rates and percentages including:

- Applicable Federal Rates (AFRs)
- Adjusted Applicable Federal Rates
- Federal Long-Term Tax-Exempt Rates
- Low-Income Housing Credit percentages

ADDITIONAL FORMATS: To provide flexibility for users, the *Guide* is available in a softbound print edition and an e-Book version. The *Guide* is also available on CCH® Answer-Connect, Wolters Kluwer's industry-leading research platform that combines the quick-reference ease and reliability of the *Guide* with current primary sources including the Internal Revenue Code, Income Tax Regulations, cases, IRS rulings, and more.

Wolters Kluwer Tax and Accounting

EDITORIAL STAFF

DETAILED TABLE OF CONTENTS

Filing 2019 Returns
OVERVIEW

¶ 1 Introduction

For 103 years, the *U.S. Master Tax Guide* ® has been the tax professional's best friend. A handy reference that goes anywhere, does not need electricity, and gives quick and simple answers to a wide array of tough tax questions. It has been there through the '86 Act, Taxpayer Bill of Rights, EGTRRA, the Fiscal Cliff, and, in more recent memory, the Tax Cuts and Jobs Act.

In December of 2017, the Tax Cuts and Jobs Act was signed into law. The massive tax legislation had an unprecedented impact on taxpayers of all types. Wolters Kluwer took an unprecedented action: for the first time in more than 100 years, we published a special edition of the *U.S. Master Tax Guide* ® to help you understand the new law. That special edition took everything we knew for the prior tax law and augmented it with everything changed by the landmark tax legislation.

Now, for the second time in our history, we are printing a special edition of the *U.S. Master Tax Guide* ® in response to the unprecedented COVID-19 crisis. Since March of 2020, the COVID-19 pandemic has impacted every aspect of life around the world. In order to help slow the spread of the virus, as well as to stabilize an economy ground to a halt by the shutdown of businesses across the country, Congress passed two major bills: the Families First Coronavirus Response Act (P.L. 116-127) and the Coronavirus Aid, Relief, and Economic Security (CARES) Act (P.L. 116-136).

While the scope of these two bills, from a federal income tax standpoint, pales in comparison to the Tax Cuts and Jobs Act, there is one significant way in which they are more important: they take effect immediately. Significant portions of the bills not only impact the 2019 tax year, they even go back to the 2018 tax year.

This fact, coupled with the IRS, as well as state taxing authorities across the United States, taking the heretofore unthinkable step of postponing the filing of tax returns, means that a special edition of the *U.S. Master Tax Guide* ® is more necessary than ever.

Inside, you will find the same Wolters Kluwer explanations of the federal income tax laws that you have come to appreciate, but all enhanced by the changes made by the federal response to this crisis. The government responses to these unprecedented times may be on a level never seen before, but the response by Wolters Kluwer is exactly what you have come to expect. A steady partner ready to help you weather any storm.

¶ 2 Income Tax Filing Deadline Changes Due to COVID-19

Below are the income tax payment and filing deadlines provided by the IRS and state taxing authorities due to the COVID-19 (coronavirus) crisis, as of April 21, 2020.

Wolters Kluwer	CCH® Answer*Connect*
Income Tax Filing Deadline Changes Due to Coronavirus/COVID-19 Pandemic as of 4/21/20	
Jurisdiction	**Relief Guidance**
Federal	7/15 for all taxpayers with income tax returns and estimated tax payments due on or after 4/1 and before 7/15, including returns, payments, quarterly estimated tax payments, and other specified forms
Alabama	7/15 for individual/corporate income tax returns/payments/estimated tax payments due 4/15
Alaska	7/15 payment due date for corporate income/estimated payments due on or after 4/15 and before 7/15; return due 8/14
Arizona	7/15 for filing and paying state individual, corporate and fiduciary income taxes
Arkansas	7/15 for personal income/S corporation/fiduciary/partnership/composite returns/payments due 4/15
California	7/15 for all personal income tax and corporate tax returns/payments/estimated tax payments
Colorado	7/15 for all corporate and personal income tax payments, including estimated payments, with original due dates between April 15, 2020, and July 15, 2020
Connecticut	7/15 for personal income tax filing/payment; 6/15 for corporation/unrelated business taxes filing/payment; 4/15 for pass-through entity taxes filing & 6/15 payment
Delaware	7/15 for all taxpayers with income tax returns due 4/15; estimated payments due 4/15
DC	7/15 for income/fiduciary/partnership/franchise tax returns due 4/15; est. payments unchanged
Florida	Florida does not tax income
Georgia	7/15 for all taxpayers with income tax returns due 4/15
Hawaii	7/20 for income tax returns/payments due 4/20 through 6/20
Idaho	6/15 for income tax return filing and payment
Illinois	7/15 for all corporations/trusts/individual income tax return filings/payments
Indiana	7/15 for all taxpayers with income tax returns due 4/15
Iowa	7/31 for filing/payment of income, franchise, moneys and credits taxes due 3/19 -- 7/31
Kansas	7/15 for corporate/fiduciary/individual income tax returns/payments; penalties and interest waived for Q1 estimated taxes due 4/15 paid by 7/15
Kentucky	7/15 fo filing/payment corporation/partnership/LLC/individual income tax/estimated payments due on 4/15 and before 7/15
Louisiana	7/15 for corporate/personal/franchise tax returns/payments due in April and May
Maine	7/15 for corporate and personal income tax return filing and payment
Maryland	7/15 for corporate/personal income tax filing/payment, and first/second quarter estimated payments
Massachusetts	7/15 for personal income/estate/trust/partnership composite return/payment due 4/15; estimated payments due 4/15, 6/15
Michigan	7/15 for all state income tax returns/payments due 4/15-7/14; 7/31 for all state income tax returns/payments due 4/30-7/30; 7/15 of 7/31 for all city income tax returns/payments due 4/15 or 4/30, respectively, or as otherwise indicated by each city

Minnesota	7/15 for Individual income tax returns/payments
Mississippi	5/15 for corporate/personal income taxes
Missouri	7/15 for corporate and individual income tax return/payments
Montana	7/15 for individual and fiduciary income tax return filing/payment including Q1 estimated payments
Nebraska	7/15 for corporate/individual/fiduciary income tax and estimated returns/payments due 4/15
Nevada	Nevada does not tax income
New Hampshire	6/15 for BPT/BET/I&D taxpayer earning under certain thresholds for returns due 4/15; safe harbors
New Jersey	7/15 announced, not adopted yet, for corporate and personal income tax returns and payments due 4/15
New Mexico	7/15 for corporate and personal income tax returns and payments due 4/15 -- 7/15
New York	7/15 for individual/corporate/fiduciary returns/payments/estimated payments due 4/15
New York City	Penalties waived for late-filed business/excise tax returns due 3/16 -- 4/25
North Carolina	7/15 for corporate/individual/Scorp/partnership/fiduciary income/franchise returns due 4/15
North Dakota	7/15 for income tax returns/payments/quarterly estimated payments due on or after 4/1 and before 7/15
Ohio	7/15 for individual income/school district income/pass-through entity/municipal net profit (managed by state) taxes returns/payments due 4/15
Oklahoma	7/15 for all taxpayers with income tax returns due 4/15
Oregon	7/15 personal/corporate excise/income payments/filing. Fiscal year returns/payments due after 5/15 & 2020 estimated payments unchanged
Pennsylvania	7/15 for personal/S corporation/partnership/fiduciary income tax returns/payments due 4/15 and certain 2020 estimated payments; 8/14 for corporation returns and payments due May 15
Rhode Island	7/15 for all corporate/personal income/fiduciary/pass-through/withholding/insurance premiums returns/payments due 4/15
South Carolina	7/15 for income tax returns/payments/quarterly estimated payments due on or after 4/1 and before 7/15
South Dakota	South Dakota does not tax income
Tennessee	7/15 "Hall income tax"/franchise/excise tax returns/payments/quarterly estimated payments due 4/15
Texas	Texas does not tax income
Utah	7/15 for all corporate and personal income tax returns due 4/15
Vermont	7/15 for personal/corporate/fiduciary income filings/payments/estimated payments due 4/15
Virginia	6/1 for income tax payments/estimated payments due from 4/1 to 6/1
Washington	Washington does not tax income
West Virginia	7/15 for C corporation/individual/fiduciary income tax filing/payment; estimated payments due 4/15, 6/15
Wisconsin	7/15 for income tax payments/estimated income tax payments/returns due on or after 4/1 and before 7/15
Wyoming	Wyoming does not tax income

¶ 3 What's New on 2019 Returns

The *U.S. Master Tax Guide* ® reflects all of the important administrative and judicial developments of 2019, including final regulations, major court decisions, and important rulings of the Internal Revenue Service. Following are highlights of the changes in 2019 with the greatest impact on individuals and businesses.

Individuals

Income levels at which individuals must file income tax returns have increased for 2019 . . . . ¶ 101

"Kiddie" tax amount is $2,200 for 2019 . . . . ¶ 115

The basic standard deduction amounts for 2019 are $24,400 for married filing jointly and surviving spouses, $18,350 for head of household filers, and $12,200 for married filing separately and single filers . . . . ¶ 131

The deduction for each personal and dependent exemption is $0 for 2019 . . . . ¶ 133

The itemized deduction of medical and dental expenses is limited to 10 percent of the taxpayer's adjusted gross income (AGI) for 2019 . . . . ¶ 1015

The itemized deduction of state and local taxes is limited to $10,000 ($5,000 if married filing separately) for 2019 . . . . ¶ 1026

Business Expenses

The standard mileage rate for all business use of a car is 58 cents per mile for 2019 . . . . ¶ 947

Per diem rates under the high-low method of substantiating travel expenses are $297 for high-cost localities and $200 for low-cost localities for travel after September 30, 2019 . . . . ¶ 954A

Depreciation, Amortization and Depletion

The maximum Code Sec. 179 deduction is $1,020,000 for 2019 . . . . ¶ 1208

The Code Sec. 179 investment limitation is $2,550,000 for 2019 . . . . ¶ 1208

Tax Credits

The education tax credits (American Opportunity and lifetime learning) are $2,500 and $2,000, respectively, ... ¶ 1403

The child tax credit is $2,000 for a qualifying child under age 17 and $500 for any other dependent. The refundable portion of the credit for qualifying children under age 17 is limited to $1,400 for 2019 . . . . ¶ 1405

For 2019, the maximum earned income credit for eligible taxpayers with no qualifying children is $529, with one qualifying child is $3,526, with two qualifying children is $5,828, and with three or more qualifying children is $6,557 . . . . ¶ 87, ¶ 1422

Retirement Plans

The contribution limit for traditional and Roth IRAs is $6,000 for 2019, with a maximum catch-up contribution limit of $1,000 for individuals age 50 and over . . . . ¶ 2155, ¶ 2171

The limit on elective deferrals to a 401(k) retirement plan is $19,000 for 2019, with a maximum catch-up contribution limit of $6,000 for individuals age 50 and over . . . . ¶ 2121

Withholding

The 2019 OASDI wage base for FICA and self-employment tax
purposes is $132,900 . . . . ¶ 47, ¶ 49, ¶ 2648, ¶ 2670
The 2019 wage threshold for "Nanny Tax" reporting is $2,100 . . . . ¶ 2652

Estate, Gifts and Generation-Skipping Transfer Tax

The applicable exclusion amount for estate and gift taxes is
$11,400,000 for 2019 providing an applicable credit amount
against the taxes of $4,505,800 . . . . ¶ 2910, ¶ 2934
The annual exclusion amount for gifts made in 2019 is $15,000,
with an annual maximum of $30,000 per donee for spouses
who use gift-splitting . . . . ¶ 2905

¶ 4 AGI Phaseout Thresholds

Adjusted gross income (AGI) levels in excess of certain phaseout thresholds limit the following deductions, credits, and other tax benefits. This chart provides the beginning point for the 2019 thresholds and the ending point of the phaseout, where applicable.

Tax Item	Taxpayers Affected	Phaseout—Begin	Phaseout—End
Floor on Itemized Medical Expenses Deduction	all taxpayers	7.5% of AGI	N/A
Itemized Deduction of Casualty Loss	all taxpayers	10% of AGI	N/A
	taxpayers with net disaster losses	0% of AGI	N/A
Child Tax Credit*	married filing jointly	$400,000	phaseout varies by taxpayer
	single, head of household, married filing separately	$200,000	phaseout varies by taxpayer
Dependent Care Credit	married filing jointly, single, head of household	35% credit if AGI not over $15,000	20% credit if AGI over $43,000
Elderly and Disabled Credit	married filing jointly	$10,000	$20,000 if one qualifying spouse; $25,000 if two qualifying spouses
	single, head of household married filing separately	$7,500 $5,000	$17,500 $12,500
Adoption Credit*	all filers	$211,160	$251,160
Adoption Assistance Programs*	all filers	$211,160	$251,160
Earned Income Credit	joint filers, no child	$14,450	$21,370
	married filing jointly, one child	$24,820	$46,884
	married filing jointly, two children	$24,820	$52,493
	married filing jointly, three or more children	$24,820	$55,952
	single, head of household, surviving spouse, no child	$8,650	$15,570
	single, head of household, surviving spouse, one child	$19,030	$41,094
	single, head of household, surviving spouse, two children	$19,030	$46,703
	single, head of household, surviving spouse, three or more children	$19,030	$50,162
American Opportunity Credit*	married filing jointly	$160,000	$180,000
	single, head of household	$80,000	$90,000
Lifetime Learning Credit*	married filing jointly single, head of household	$116,000 $58,000	$136,000 $68,000
Student Loan Interest Deduction*	married filing jointly	$140,000	$170,000
	single, head of household	$70,000	$85,000

Tax Item	Taxpayers Affected	Phaseout—Begin	Phaseout—End
Savings Bonds Interest Exclusion*	married filing jointly	$121,600	$151,600
	single, head of household	$81,100	$96,100
Coverdell Education Savings Accounts*	married filing jointly	$190,000	$220,000
	single, head of household, married filing separately	$95,000	$110,000
IRA Deduction* (for active participant in employer plan)	married filing jointly (both spouses active participants)	$103,000	$123,000
	married (contributing spouse not active participant, but other spouse is)	$193,000	$203,0000
	single, head of household	$64,000	$74,000
	married filing separately	$0	$10,000
Roth IRA Contribution*	married filing jointly	$193,000	$203,000
	single, head of household	$122,000	$137,000
	married filing separately	$0	$10,000
Rental Real Estate Passive Losses	married filing jointly, single, head of household	$100,000	$150,000
	married filing separately	$50,000	$75,000

* Modified AGI, as defined by the relevant Code sections, is used instead of AGI.

¶ 5 Where to File Paper Returns

Individuals. Listed below are the mailing addresses to use for filing an individual tax return on Form 1040 for the 2019 tax year, whether it is self-prepared or prepared by a tax professional (¶ 2513). Individual taxpayers and tax professionals may also consult the IRS website https://www.irs.gov/uac/where-to-file-paper-tax-returns-with-or-without-a-payment or the Where to File Interactive Chart on CCH® AnswerConnect for the most current mailing addresses. The first two lines of the address should be Department of the Treasury, Internal Revenue Service, but no street address is needed.

If you are filing **Form 1040** and are located in:	*And are not enclosing a payment, mail your return to:*	*And are enclosing a payment, mail your return to:*
Alabama, North Carolina, South Carolina	Kansas City, MO 64999-0002	P.O. Box 1214 Charlotte, NC 28201-1214
Alaska, California, Hawaii, Washington	Fresno, CA 93888-0002	P.O. Box 7704 San Francisco, CA 94120-7704
Arizona, Colorado, Idaho, Kansas, Montana, Nebraska, New Mexico, Nevada, North Dakota, Oregon, South Dakota, Utah, Wyoming	Ogden, UT 84201-0002	P.O. Box 802501 Cincinnati, OH 45280-2501
Arkansas, Georgia, Indiana, Iowa, Kentucky, Missouri, New Jersey, Oklahoma, Tennessee, Virginia	Kansas City, MO 64999-0002	P.O. Box 931000 Louisville, KY 40293-1000
Connecticut, District of Columbia, Maryland, Rhode Island, West Virginia	Ogden, UT 84201-0002	P.O. Box 931000 Louisville, KY 40293-1000
Delaware, Maine, Massachusetts, New Hampshire, New York, Vermont	Kansas City, MO 64999-0002	P.O. Box 37008 Hartford, CT 06176-7008
Florida, Louisiana, Mississippi, Texas	Austin, TX 73301-0002	P.O. Box 1214 Charlotte, NC 28201-1214
Illinois, Michigan, Minnesota, Ohio, Wisconsin	Fresno, CA 93888-0002	P.O. Box 802501 Cincinnati, OH 45280-2501
Pennsylvania	Ogden, UT 84201-0002	P.O. Box 37008 Hartford, CT 06176-7008

If you are filing **Form 1040** and are located in:	*And are not enclosing a payment, mail your return to:*	*And are enclosing a payment, mail your return to:*
A foreign country, U.S. possession or territory*, or use an APO or FPO address, or file Form 2555 or 4563, or are a dual-status alien	Austin, TX 73301-0215 USA	P.O. Box 1303 Charlotte, NC 28201-1303 USA

* For residents of American Samoa, Puerto Rico, Guam, the U.S. Virgin Islands, or the Northern Mariana Islands, see IRS Pub. 570 for the filing requirements for both U.S. possessions and Federal income tax returns along with a list of addresses of where to file each type of return.

Corporations and Partnerships. A corporation or partnership should file Form 1120 or Form 1065 in accordance with the "Where to File" addresses listed in the instructions to the forms. A corporation or partnership is "located in" the place where it has its principal place of business or principal office or agency. If a corporation or partnership is without a principal office or agency or principal place of business in the United States, returns are to be filed with the Internal Revenue Service Center in Ogden, Utah.

Estates and Trusts. A fiduciary of an estate or trust, including the fiduciary of a charitable or split interest trust or of a pooled income fund, generally should file Form 1041 in accordance with the instructions to the form. A fiduciary is "located in" the place where he or she resides or has his or her principal place of business.

Private Delivery Services (PDSs). Certain private delivery services designated by the IRS are available to meet the timely mailed as timely filing/paying rule for tax returns and payments. The designated private delivery services can be found at the IRS website https://www.irs.gov/uac/private-delivery-services-pds.

¶5

¶ 6 2020 Tax Calendar

Each date shown below is the last day for filing the return or making the payment of tax indicated. For income tax returns, the due dates apply to calendar-year taxpayers only. Employment tax due dates are determined on a calendar-year basis for all taxpayers. **If any statutory due date falls on a Saturday, Sunday, or legal holiday, the due date is the next succeeding day that is not a Saturday, Sunday, or legal holiday (national, District of Columbia, or statewide in the state where the return is to be filed).**

This day 2020	Tax Return Due Dates
Jan. 15th—	**Estimated Tax.** Final installment of 2019 estimated tax (Form 1040-ES) by individuals unless income tax return is filed with final payment by January 31, 2020. Payment in full of estimated tax by farmers and fishermen unless income tax returns are filed by March 2, 2020.
	Final installment of 2019 estimated tax (Form 1041-ES) by trusts, calendar-year estates, and certain residuary trusts in existence more than two years, unless Form 1041 is filed and taxes are paid in full by January 31, 2020.
Jan. 31st—	**Employers' Taxes.** Employers of nonagricultural and nonhousehold employees file return on Form 941 for withheld income and FICA taxes in last quarter of 2019.[1]
	Employers of agricultural workers must file the annual Form 943 to report income and FICA taxes withheld on 2019 wages.[1]
	Employers must file Form 940, annual return of federal unemployment (FUTA) taxes, for 2019.[1]
	Withholding. Employees' statements (Form W-2 and Form 1099-R) for amounts withheld in 2019 to be furnished by employer to employees. Copy A of Form W-2 (together with transmittal Form W-3) must be filed with the Social Security Administration, whether filed electronically or on paper.
	Individuals. Individuals, other than farmers and fishermen, who owed, but did not pay, estimated tax on January 15 must file final 2019 income tax return (Form 1040 or Form 1040-SR) and pay tax in full to avoid late payment penalty.
	Trusts and Estates. Trusts, as well as estates and certain residuary trusts in existence more than two years, that owed but did not pay estimated tax on January 15 must file final 2019 income tax return (Form 1041) and pay tax in full to avoid late payment penalty.

This day 2020

Tax Return Due Dates

Information Returns. Annual statements must be furnished to recipients of: gambling winnings (Form W-2G); dividends and liquidating distributions (Form 1099-DIV); interest, including interest on bearer certificates of deposit (Form 1099-INT); patronage dividends (Form 1099-PATR); original issue discount (Form 1099-OID); certain government payments, including unemployment compensation and state and local tax refunds of $10 or more (Form 1099-G); royalty payments of $10 or more, rent or other business payments of $600 or more, prizes and awards of $600 or more, crop insurance proceeds of $600 or more, fishing boat proceeds, medical and health care payments of $600 or more, nonemployee compensation payments in box 7 (Form 1099-MISC); debt canceled by certain financial entities including financial institutions, credit unions, and Federal Government agencies of $600 or more (Form 1099-C); distributions from retirement or profit-sharing plans, IRAs, SEPs, or insurance contracts (Form 1099-R); payments received from a third-party settlement entity (Form 1099-K). See ¶ 64 for a chart of information returns and due dates.

Businesses, tax-exempt organizations, and educational institutions that receive certain payments must furnish annual statements to payors of: $600 or more of mortgage interest (Form 1098); $600 or more of student loan interest (Form 1098-E); qualified tuition and expenses (Form 1098-T). See ¶ 64 for a chart of information returns and due dates.

Information called for on Form 8300 must be provided to each payer in a transaction of more than $10,000 in cash at any time during 2019. Form 8300 must be filed with the IRS by the 15th day after the date of the transaction.

Partnerships must provide a copy of Form 8308 to the transferor and transferee in any exchange of a partnership interest that involved unrealized receivables or substantially appreciated inventory items. Form 8308 must be filed with the IRS with a partnership's income tax return for the year in which the exchange took place.

Trustees or issuers of IRAs or SEPs must provide participants with a statement of the account's value and required minimum distribution (RMD), if applicable, on Form 5498. Participants and the IRS must be provided with IRA plan contribution information by July 15.

Feb. 18th— **Information Returns.** Annual statements must be furnished to recipients of proceeds from broker and barter exchange transactions (Form 1099-B); proceeds from real estate transactions of $600 or more (Form 1099-S); broker payments of $10 or more in lieu of dividends or tax-exempt interest, and gross proceeds paid to an attorney (Form 1099-MISC).

Individuals. Last day for filing Form W-4 by employees who wish to claim exemption from withholding of income tax for 2020.

Feb. 28th— **Information Returns.** Annual 1099 series returns (together with transmittal Form 1096) for paper filings (March 31 if filing electronically) must be filed with the IRS to report payments to recipients who received Form 1099 on January 31 or February 18, as indicated above.

This day 2020	**Tax Return Due Dates**

Businesses, tax-exempt organizations, and educational institutions that receive certain payments must file with the IRS (together with transmittal Form 1096) for paper filings (March 31 if filing electronically); Form 1098 for $600 or more of mortgage interest received; Form 1098-E for $600 or more student loan interest received; and Form 1098-T for payments of qualified tuition and expenses. See ¶ 64 for a chart of information returns and due dates.

Withholding. Form W-2G and Form 1099-R for 2019 "A" copies (together with transmittal Form 1096) for paper filings (March 31 if filing electronically) must be filed with the IRS.

Mar. 2nd— **Individuals.** Last day for farmers and fishermen who owed, but did not pay, estimated tax on January 15 to file a 2019 calendar-year income tax return (Form 1040 or Form 1040-SR) and pay tax in full to avoid late payment penalty.

Mar. 16th— **Partnerships.** Last day for filing income tax return for calendar-year partnership (Form 1065) and providing each partner with a copy of Schedule K-1. Returns for fiscal-year partnerships are due on the 15th day of the 3rd month after the close of the tax year but returns otherwise due on or after April 1, 2020, and before July 15, 2020, are now due July 15, 2020.

Last day for calendar-year U.S. partnerships to file application (Form 7004) for automatic six-month extension to file 2019 income tax return.

Last day for calendar-year partnerships to file an amended return (Form 1065X) for 2016.

S Corporations. Last day for filing income tax return for calendar-year S corporation (Form 1120-S) and to provide each shareholder with a copy of Schedule K-1. Returns for fiscal-year S corporations are due on the 15th day of the 3rd month after the close of the tax year but returns otherwise due on or after April 1, 2020, and before July 15, 2020, are now due July 15, 2020.

Last date for filing application (Form 7004) by S corporations for automatic six-month extension to file 2019 income tax return.

Last date for filing Form 2553 to elect to be treated as an S corporation beginning with calendar year 2020. The penalty for filing the election late is to postpone treatment as an S corporation until calendar year 2021.

Withholding. File returns on Form 1042 and Form 1042-S to report tax withheld at the source from nonresident aliens, foreign corporations, foreign partnerships and foreign fiduciaries of a trust or estate.

ABLE Accounts. Trustees of ABLE accounts must furnish a copy of Form 5498-QA to participants. ABLE account information must be reported to the IRS by July 15.

Mar. 31st— **Information Returns—Electronic Filing.** Due date for filing Form 1099 series (for reporting certain payments made) and Form 1098 series (for reporting receipt of certain payments) with the IRS electronically. See ¶ 64 for a chart of information returns and due dates.

Withholding—Electronic Filing. Last day for filing Form W-2G with the IRS if filing electronically.

This day 2020   **Tax Return Due Dates**

Apr. 30th—   **Employers' Taxes.** Employers of nonagricultural and nonhousehold employees must file return on Form 941 to report income tax withholding and FICA taxes for the first quarter of 2020.[2]

July 15th—   **Individuals.** Income tax and self-employment tax returns of individuals for calendar year 2019 and income tax returns of calendar-year decedents who died in 2019 (Form 1040 or Form 1040-SR) are due. Fiscal-year individuals must file returns by the 15th day of the 4th month after the close of the tax year but returns otherwise due on or after April 1, 2020, and before July 15, 2020, are now due July 15, 2020.

Last day for calendar-year individuals to file application (Form 4868) for automatic three-month extension to file 2019 income tax return. Last day for fiscal-year individuals to file application for an automatic extension for the 2019 tax year income tax return otherwise due on or after April 1, 2020, and before July 15, 2020.

Individuals' information returns (Form 5471) with respect to foreign corporations, to be filed with Form 1040.

Last day for individuals to file amended income tax returns (Form 1040-X) for the calendar year 2016.

Last day for nonresident alien individuals not subject to withholding to file income tax return (Form 1040-NR) for calendar year 2019 or file Form 4868 for automatic five-month extension.

Estimated Tax. Calendar-year corporations pay first and second installments of 2020 estimated income taxes (Form 1120-W). Fiscal-year corporations make payments on the 15th day of the 4th, 6th, 9th, and 12th months of the tax year but payments otherwise due on or after April 1, 2020, and before July 15, 2020, are now due July 15, 2020.

Payment of first and second installments of 2020 estimated income taxes (Form 1040-ES) by calendar-year individuals, other than farmers and fishermen. Estimated tax payments for fiscal-year individuals are due on the 15th day of the 4th, 6th, and 9th months of the tax year and the 1st month of the following tax year but payments otherwise due on or after April 1, 2020, and before July 15, 2020, are now due July 15, 2020.

Trusts and calendar-year estates and certain residuary trusts in existence more than two years must make first and second payments of estimated taxes for 2020 (Form 1041-ES). Fiscal-year estates make payments on the 15th day of the 4th, 6th, and 9th months of the fiscal year and the 1st month of the following fiscal year but payments otherwise due on or after April 1, 2020, and before July 15, 2020, are now due July 15, 2020.

Nonresident aliens who have no wages subject to U.S. withholding must make first payment of 2020 estimated tax (Form 1040-ES (NR)).

This day 2020

Tax Return Due Dates

Corporations. Due date of 2019 income tax returns (Form 1120) for calendar-year C corporations, including domestic corporations or foreign corporations with offices in the United States (Form 1120-F). Fiscal-year C corporations with a U.S. office generally must file by the 15th day of the 4th month following the close of the tax year but returns otherwise due on or after April 1, 2020, and before July 15, 2020, are now due July 15, 2020. C corporations with a fiscal tax year ending on June 30, however, must file their returns by the 15th day of the 3rd month following the close of the tax year but returns otherwise due on or after April 1, 2020, and before July 15, 2020, are now due July 15, 2020.

Last date for filing application (Form 7004) by calendar-year C corporations for automatic three-month extension to file 2019 income tax return.

Form 5452 for reporting nondividend corporate distributions made to shareholders during calendar year 2019 should be filed by calendar-year corporations with their income tax return. Fiscal-year corporations file Form 5452 with their income tax return for the first fiscal year ending after the calendar year in which distributions were made.

Calendar-year corporations must file 2019 information return (Form 5471) with respect to foreign corporations. Fiscal-year corporations file form with income tax return.

Last date for a calendar-year corporation to file an amended income tax return (Form 1120X) for the calendar year 2016.[3]

Last day for calendar-year foreign corporation that does not maintain an office or place of business in United States to file income tax return (Form 1120-F) for calendar year 2019. Fiscal-year foreign corporations without offices in the United States must file by the 15th day of the 6th month following the close of the tax year but returns otherwise due on or after April 1, 2020, and before July 15, 2020, are now due July 15, 2020.

Last day for calendar-year foreign corporations without offices in the United States to file application (Form 7004) for automatic five-month extension of time to file 2019 income tax return.

Trusts and Estates. Fiduciary income tax return (Form 1041) for calendar year 2019. Fiscal-year estates must file returns by the 15th day of the 4th month following the close of the tax year but returns otherwise due on or after April 1, 2020, and before July 15, 2020, are now due July 15, 2020.

Last day for calendar-year estates and trusts to file application (Form 7004) for automatic 2½-month extension of time to file 2019 income tax return (Form 1041). Last day for fiscal-year estates and trusts to file application for an automatic extension for the 2019 tax year income tax return otherwise due on or after April 1, 2020, and before July 15, 2020.

Last day for estates and trusts to file amended tax returns (Form 1041) for calendar year 2016.

This day 2020   **Tax Return Due Dates**

Exempt Organizations. Annual information return (Form 990) for 2019 by calendar-year organizations exempt or claiming exemption from tax under Code Sec. 501 or Code Sec. 4947(a)(1). Fiscal-year organizations must file by the 15th day of the 5th month after the close of the accounting period but returns otherwise due on or after April 1, 2020, and before July 15, 2020, are now due July 15, 2020.

Calendar-year private foundations and Code Sec. 4947(a) trusts treated as private foundations must file Form 990-PF, and private foundations must pay the first quarter installment of estimated excise tax on net investment income or tax on unrelated business income. Fiscal-year organizations must file by the 15th day of the 5th month after the close of the foundation's tax year but payments otherwise due on or after April 1, 2020, and before July 15, 2020, are now due July 15, 2020.

Calendar-year Code Sec. 501(a) organizations with unrelated business income must file income tax return on Form 990-T. Fiscal-year organizations must file by the 15th day of the 5th month following close of the tax year but returns otherwise due on or after April 1, 2020, and before July 15, 2020, are now due July 15, 2020. File Form 8868 for an automatic four-month extension to file Form 990-T.

Last day for calendar-year exempt organizations to file application (Form 8868) for automatic four-month extension of time to file Form 990 for the 2019 tax year.

Information Returns. Annual information return (Form 1041-A) for complex trusts claiming charitable deductions under Code Sec. 642(c) and annual information return (Form 5227) for charitable remainder trusts, pooled income funds, and Code Sec. 4947(a)(2) trusts (split-interest trusts) must be filed.

Last day for trustees of a trust to file application (Form 8868) for automatic three-month extension of time to file Form 1041-A or Form 5227 for the 2019 tax year.

Trustees must report contributions, including rollover contributions, to any IRA, SEP, SIMPLE, or Roth IRA, as well as Roth conversions, IRA recharacterizations, and the fair market value (FMV) of the account to the IRS and to participants (Form 5498). Participants of IRAs and SEPs must be provided statement of account's fair market value and required minimum distribution by January 31, 2020.

Trustees must report contributions, including rollover contributions, to Coverdell ESAs (Form 5498-ESA) and ABLE accounts (Form 5498-QA) to the IRS. Report Coverdell ESA contributions to the beneficiary. ABLE account contributions must be reported to the beneficiary by March 16.

Trustees must report to the IRS and participants (Form 5498-SA) contributions to a health savings account (HSA), including transfers and rollovers, or Archer medical savings account (MSA) and the fair market value of an HSA, Archer MSA, or Medicare Advantage MSA.

This day 2020	**Tax Return Due Dates**

July 31st— **Employers' Taxes.** Employers of nonagricultural and nonhousehold employees must file return on Form 941 to report income tax withholding and FICA taxes for the second quarter of 2020.[4]

Sept. 15th— **Estimated Tax.** Payment of third installment of 2020 estimated tax by calendar-year corporations (Form 1120-W).

Payment of third installment of 2020 estimated tax by individuals (Form 1040-ES), other than farmers and fishermen, by trusts and by estates (Form 1041-ES), and certain residuary trusts in existence more than two years. Nonresident aliens who have no wages subject to U.S. withholding must make second payment of 2020 estimated tax (Form 1040-ES (NR)).

Exempt Organizations. Last day for exempt calendar-year farmers' cooperatives to file 2019 income tax returns (Form 1120-C). Fiscal-year cooperatives must file by the 15th day of the 9th month following the close of the tax year but returns otherwise due on or after April 1, 2020, and before July 15, 2020, are now due July 15, 2020. An automatic six-month extension of the filing date may be obtained by filing Form 7004.

Partnerships. Last day for filing 2019 Form 1065 for calendar-year partnerships that obtained an automatic six-month filing extension.

S Corporations. Last day for filing 2019 Form 1120-S for calendar-year S corporations that obtained an automatic six-month filing extension.

Oct. 1st— **Trusts and Estates.** Last day for filing 2019 Form 1041 for calendar-year estates and trusts that obtained an automatic 2½-month filing extension.

Oct. 15th— **Individuals.** Last day for filing 2019 income tax return (Form 1040 or Form 1040-SR) by calendar-year individuals who obtained a three-month filing extension.

C Corporations. Last day for filing 2019 income tax return by calendar-year C corporations (Form 1120) that obtained an automatic three-month filing extension using Form 7004.

Nov. 2nd— **Employers' Taxes.** Employers of nonagricultural and nonhousehold employees must file return on Form 941 to report income tax withholding and FICA taxes for the third quarter of 2020.[5]

Dec. 15th— **Estimated Tax.** Payment of last installment of 2020 estimated tax by calendar-year corporations (Form 1120-W).

This day 2021	

Jan. 15th— **Estimated Tax.** Final installment of 2020 estimated tax (Form 1040-ES) by individuals unless income tax return is filed with final payment by February 1, 2021. Payment in full of estimated tax by farmers and fishermen unless income tax returns are filed by March 1, 2021. Nonresident aliens who have no wages subject to U.S. withholding must make final installment of 2020 estimated tax (Form 1040-ES (NR)).

Final installment of 2020 estimated tax (Form 1041-ES) by trusts, calendar-year estates, and certain residuary trusts in existence more than two years, unless Form 1041 is filed and taxes are paid in full by February 1, 2021.

This day 2021

Feb. 1st—   **Individuals.** Final income tax return for 2020 by calendar-year individuals (Form 1040 or Form 1040-SR) and by trusts and estates (Form 1041) in existence more than two years who owed but did not pay 2020 estimated tax otherwise due January 15.

Employers' Taxes. Employers of nonagricultural and nonhousehold employees must file return on Form 941 to report income tax withholding and FICA taxes for the fourth quarter of 2020.[6]

[1] If timely deposits in full payment of tax due were made, the due date for Form 940, Form 941, and Form 943 is February 10, 2020.

[2] If timely deposits in full payment of taxes due were made, the due date for Form 941 is May 11, 2020.

[3] Fiscal-year corporations generally must file within three years of the date the original return was due.

[4] If timely deposits in full payment of taxes due were made, the due date for Form 941 is August 10, 2020.

[5] If timely deposits in full payment of taxes due were made, the due date for Form 941 is November 10, 2020.

[6] If timely deposits in full payment of taxes due were made, the due date for Form 941 is February 10, 2021.

EMPLOYMENT TAX DEPOSITS

Income Tax Withholding, FICA Taxes, Backup Withholding. Employment taxes are withheld income tax, FICA contributions, and backup withholding on reportable payments. Generally, an employer must make either MONTHLY or SEMIWEEKLY deposits during a calendar year based upon the aggregate amount of employment taxes paid during the "lookback" period. The lookback period for each calendar year is the 12-month period that ended the preceding June 30. Thus, an employer's obligation to make deposits in 2020 will be based upon the aggregate employment taxes paid during the period July 1, 2018, through June 30, 2019 (¶ 2651). New employers are considered to have an aggregate tax liability of zero for any calendar quarter in which the employer did not exist.

Monthly Deposits. Monthly deposits are required if the aggregate amount of employment taxes reported by the employer for the lookback period is $50,000 or less. Monthly deposits are due on the 15th day of the following month in which the payments were made.

Semiweekly Deposits. An employer is a semiweekly depositor for the entire calendar year if the aggregate amount of employment taxes during the lookback period exceeds $50,000. Further, a monthly depositor will become a semiweekly depositor on the first day after the employer becomes subject to the Next-Day Rule, discussed later. Semiweekly deposits are generally due on either Wednesday or Friday—depending upon the timing of the employer's pay period. Employers with payment dates, i.e., paydays, that fall on Wednesday, Thursday, or Friday must deposit the employment taxes on or before the following Wednesday. Employers with payment dates that fall on Saturday, Sunday, Monday, or Tuesday must make their deposit on or before the following Friday. An employer will always have three business days in which to make the deposit. Thus, if any of the three weekdays following the close of a semiweekly period is a holiday, then the employer will have an additional business day in which to make the deposit.

Next-Day Rule. If an employer has accumulated $100,000 or more of undeposited employment taxes, then the taxes must be deposited by the close of the next banking day.

Federal Unemployment (FUTA) Taxes. The calendar year is divided into four quarters for purposes of determining when deposits of federal unemployment tax (FUTA) are necessary. The periods end on March 31, June 30, September 30, and December 31. If the employer's FUTA tax liability is $500 or less, then the employer does not have to deposit the tax; instead, the amount may be carried forward and added to the liability for the next quarter to determine if a deposit is required. If the employer owes more than $500 in undeposited FUTA tax at the end of a quarter (including any FUTA tax carried forward from an earlier quarter), then the tax owed must be deposited by the end of the next month by either an electronic funds transfer through the Electronic Federal Tax Payment System (EFTPS) directly or at an EFTPS financial institution.

Schedules and Tables

TAX RATES

TAX RATE SCHEDULES FOR 2019 AND 2020

NOTE. The 2019 Tax Rate Schedules reproduced below are based on the rate changes and inflation adjustments to the tax brackets released by the IRS (Code Sec. 1(j); Rev. Proc. 2018-57). The 2020 Tax Rate Schedules reproduced below are based on the rate changes and inflation adjustments to the tax brackets released by the IRS (Rev. Proc. 2019-44).

The 2019 and 2020 tax rate schedules for single individuals are at ¶ 11; for married individuals filing jointly and surviving spouses, see ¶ 13; for married individuals filing separately, see ¶ 15; for heads of households, see ¶ 17; and for estates and nongrantor trusts, see ¶ 19.

¶ 11 SCHEDULE X: Single Individuals

2019

Taxable Income Over	But Not Over	Pay	+	% on Excess	of the amount over—
$0—	$9,700	$0		10%	$0
9,700—	39,475	970.00		12	9,700
39,475—	84,200	4,543.00		22	39,475
84,200—	160,725	14,382.50		24	84,200
160,725—	204,100	32,748.50		32	160,725
204,100—	510,300	46,628.50		35	204,100
510,300—	. . . . . .	153,798.50		37	510,300

2020

Taxable Income Over	But Not Over	Pay	+	% on Excess	of the amount over—
$0—	$9,875	$0		10%	$0
9,875—	40,125	987.50		12	9,875
40,125—	85,525	4,617.50		22	40,125
85,525—	163,300	14,605.50		24	85,525
163,300—	207,350	33,271.50		32	163,300
207,350—	518,400	47,367.50		35	207,350
518,400—	. . . . . .	156,235.00		37	518,400

¶ 13 SCHEDULE Y-1: Married Filing Jointly and Surviving Spouses

2019

Taxable Income Over	But Not Over	Pay	+	% on Excess	of the amount over—
$0—	$19,400	$0		10%	$0
19,400—	78,950	1,940.00		12	19,400
78,950—	168,400	9,086.00		22	78,950
168,400—	321,450	28,765.00		24	168,400
321,450—	408,200	65,497.00		32	321,450
408,200—	612,350	93,257.00		35	408,200
612,350—	. . . . . .	164,709.50		37	612,350

2020

Taxable Income Over	But Not Over	Pay	+	% on Excess	of the amount over—
$0—	$19,750	$0		10%	$0
19,750—	80,250	1,975.00		12	19,750
80,250—	171,050	9,235.00		22	80,250
171,050—	326,600	29,211.00		24	171,050
326,600—	414,700	66,543.00		32	326,600
414,700—	622,050	94,735.00		35	414,700
622,050—	. . . . . .	167,307.50		37	622,050

¶ 15 SCHEDULE Y-2: Married Individuals Filing Separately

2019

Taxable Income Over	But Not Over	Pay	+	% on Excess	of the amount over—
$0—	$9,700	$0		10%	$0
9,700—	39,475	970.00		12	9,700
39,475—	84,200	4,543.00		22	39,475
84,200—	160,725	14,382.50		24	84,200
160,725—	204,100	32,748.50		32	160,725
204,100—	306,175	46,628.50		35	204,100
306,175—	. . . . . .	82,354.75		37	306,175

2020

Taxable Income Over	But Not Over	Pay	+	% on Excess	of the amount over—
$0—	$9,875	$0		10%	$0
9,875—	40,125	987.50		12	9,875
40,125—	85,525	4,617.50		22	40,125
85,525—	163,300	14,605.50		24	85,525
163,300—	207,350	33,271.50		32	163,300
207,350—	311,025	47,367.50		35	207,350
311,025—	. . . . . .	83,653.75		37	311,025

¶ 17 SCHEDULE Z: Heads of Households

2019

Taxable Income Over	But Not Over	Pay	+	% on Excess	of the amount over—
$0—	$13,850	$0		10%	$0
13,850—	52,850	1,385.00		12	13,850
52,850—	84,200	6,065.00		22	52,850
84,200—	160,700	12,962.00		24	84,200
160,700—	204,100	31,322.00		32	160,700
204,100—	510,300	45,210.00		35	204,100
510,300—	. . . . . .	152,380.00		37	510,300

2020

Taxable Income Over	But Not Over	Pay	+	% on Excess	of the amount over—
$0—	$14,100	$0		10%	$0
14,100—	53,700	1,410.00		12	14,100
53,700—	85,500	6,162.00		22	53,700
85,500—	163,300	13,158.00		24	85,500
163,300—	207,350	31,830.00		32	163,300
207,350—	518,400	45,926.00		35	207,350
518,400—	. . . . . .	154,793.50		37	518,400

¶ 19 Income Tax Rate Schedule for Estates and Nongrantor Trusts

2019

Taxable Income Over	But Not Over	Pay	+	% on Excess	of the amount over—
$0—	$2,600	$0		10%	$0
2,600—	9,300	260.00		24	2,600
9,300—	12,750	1,868.00		35	9,300
12,750—	. . . . . .	3,075.50		37	12,750

2020

Taxable Income Over	But Not Over	Pay	+	% on Excess	of the amount over—
$0—	$2,600	$0		10%	$0
2,600—	9,450	260.00		24	2,600
9,450—	12,950	1,904.00		35	9,450
12,950—	. . . . . .	3,129.00		37	12,950

¶ 20 2019 Tax Computation Worksheet

2019 Tax Computation Worksheet—Line 12a

See the instructions for line 12a to see if you must use the worksheet below to figure your tax.

Note. If you are required to use this worksheet to figure the tax on an amount from another form or worksheet, such as the Qualified Dividends and Capital Gain Tax Worksheet, the Schedule D Tax Worksheet, Schedule J, Form 8615, or the Foreign Earned Income Tax Worksheet, enter the amount from that form or worksheet in column (a) of the row that applies to the amount you are looking up. Enter the result on the appropriate line of the form or worksheet that you are completing.

Section A—Use if your filing status is **Single**. Complete the row below that applies to you.

Taxable income. If line 11b is—	(a) Enter the amount from line 11b	(b) Multiplication amount	(c) Multiply (a) by (b)	(d) Subtraction amount	Tax. Subtract (d) from (c). Enter the result here and on the entry space on line 12a.
At least $100,000 but not over $160,725	$	× 24% (0.24)	$	$ 5,825.50	$
Over $160,725 but not over $204,100	$	× 32% (0.32)	$	$ 18,683.50	$
Over $204,100 but not over $510,300	$	× 35% (0.35)	$	$ 24,806.50	$
Over $510,300	$	× 37% (0.37)	$	$ 35,012.50	$

Section B—Use if your filing status is **Married filing jointly** or **Qualifying widow(er)**. Complete the row below that applies to you.

Taxable income. If line 11b is—	(a) Enter the amount from line 11b	(b) Multiplication amount	(c) Multiply (a) by (b)	(d) Subtraction amount	Tax. Subtract (d) from (c). Enter the result here and on the entry space on line 12a.
At least $100,000 but not over $168,400	$	× 22% (0.22)	$	$ 8,283.00	$
Over $168,400 but not over $321,450	$	× 24% (0.24)	$	$ 11,651.00	$
Over $321,450 but not over $408,200	$	× 32% (0.32)	$	$ 37,367.00	$
Over $408,200 but not over $612,350	$	× 35% (0.35)	$	$ 49,613.00	$
Over $612,350	$	× 37% (0.37)	$	$ 61,860.00	$

Section C—Use if your filing status is **Married filing separately**. Complete the row below that applies to you.

Taxable income. If line 11b is—	(a) Enter the amount from line 11b	(b) Multiplication amount	(c) Multiply (a) by (b)	(d) Subtraction amount	Tax. Subtract (d) from (c). Enter the result here and on the entry space on line 12a.
At least $100,000 but not over $160,725	$	× 24% (0.24)	$	$ 5,825.50	$
Over $160,725 but not over $204,100	$	× 32% (0.32)	$	$ 18,683.50	$
Over $204,100 but not over $306,175	$	× 35% (0.35)	$	$ 24,806.50	$
Over $306,175	$	× 37% (0.37)	$	$ 30,930.00	$

Section D—Use if your filing status is **Head of household**. Complete the row below that applies to you.

Taxable income. If line 11b is—	(a) Enter the amount from line 11b	(b) Multiplication amount	(c) Multiply (a) by (b)	(d) Subtraction amount	Tax. Subtract (d) from (c). Enter the result here and on the entry space on line 12a.
At least $100,000 but not over $160,700	$	× 24% (0.24)	$	$ 7,246.00	$
Over $160,700 but not over $204,100	$	× 32% (0.32)	$	$ 20,102.00	$
Over $204,100 but not over $510,300	$	× 35% (0.35)	$	$ 26,225.00	$
Over $510,300	$	× 37% (0.37)	$	$ 36,431.00	$

Need more information or forms? Visit IRS.gov.   **-74-**

¶20

2019 TAX TABLE—INDIVIDUALS

¶ 25 2019 Tax Table for Use with Form 1040

☐ The Tax Table that follows is for use with Form 1040.

2019 TAX TABLE   Based on Taxable Income. For persons with taxable incomes of less than $100,000.

Read down the income columns of the tax table until you find the line covering the taxable income shown on line 11b of Form 1040. Then read across that income line until you find the column heading that describes your filing status. Enter the tax found there on line 12a of Form 1040.

2019 Tax Table

See the instructions for line 12a to see if you must use the Tax Table below to figure your tax.

Sample Table

At Least	But Less Than	Single	Married filing jointly*	Married filing sepa-rately	Head of a house-hold
			Your tax is—		
25,200	25,250	2,833	2,639	2,833	2,750
25,250	25,300	2,839	2,645	2,839	2,756
25,300	25,350	2,845	(2,651)	2,845	2,762
25,350	25,400	2,851	2,657	2,851	2,768

Example. Mr. and Mrs. Brown are filing a joint return. Their taxable income on Form 1040, line 11b, is $25,300. First, they find the $25,300–25,350 taxable income line. Next, they find the column for married filing jointly and read down the column. The amount shown where the taxable income line and filing status column meet is $2,651. This is the tax amount they should enter in the entry space on Form 1040, line 12a.

If line 11b (taxable income) is—		And you are—				If line 11b (taxable income) is—		And you are—				If line 11b (taxable income) is—		And you are—			
At least	But less than	Single	Married filing jointly *	Married filing sepa-rately	Head of a house-hold	At least	But less than	Single	Married filing jointly *	Married filing sepa-rately	Head of a house-hold	At least	But less than	Single	Married filing jointly *	Married filing sepa-rately	Head of a house-hold
		Your tax is—						**Your tax is—**						**Your tax is—**			
0	5	0	0	0	0	**1,000**						**2,000**					
5	15	1	1	1	1												
15	25	2	2	2	2	1,000	1,025	101	101	101	101	2,000	2,025	201	201	201	201
25	50	4	4	4	4	1,025	1,050	104	104	104	104	2,025	2,050	204	204	204	204
50	75	6	6	6	6	1,050	1,075	106	106	106	106	2,050	2,075	206	206	206	206
75	100	9	9	9	9	1,075	1,100	109	109	109	109	2,075	2,100	209	209	209	209
100	125	11	11	11	11	1,100	1,125	111	111	111	111	2,100	2,125	211	211	211	211
125	150	14	14	14	14	1,125	1,150	114	114	114	114	2,125	2,150	214	214	214	214
150	175	16	16	16	16	1,150	1,175	116	116	116	116	2,150	2,175	216	216	216	216
175	200	19	19	19	19	1,175	1,200	119	119	119	119	2,175	2,200	219	219	219	219
200	225	21	21	21	21	1,200	1,225	121	121	121	121	2,200	2,225	221	221	221	221
225	250	24	24	24	24	1,225	1,250	124	124	124	124	2,225	2,250	224	224	224	224
250	275	26	26	26	26	1,250	1,275	126	126	126	126	2,250	2,275	226	226	226	226
275	300	29	29	29	29	1,275	1,300	129	129	129	129	2,275	2,300	229	229	229	229
300	325	31	31	31	31	1,300	1,325	131	131	131	131	2,300	2,325	231	231	231	231
325	350	34	34	34	34	1,325	1,350	134	134	134	134	2,325	2,350	234	234	234	234
350	375	36	36	36	36	1,350	1,375	136	136	136	136	2,350	2,375	236	236	236	236
375	400	39	39	39	39												
400	425	41	41	41	41	1,375	1,400	139	139	139	139	2,375	2,400	239	239	239	239
425	450	44	44	44	44	1,400	1,425	141	141	141	141	2,400	2,425	241	241	241	241
						1,425	1,450	144	144	144	144	2,425	2,450	244	244	244	244
450	475	46	46	46	46	1,450	1,475	146	146	146	146	2,450	2,475	246	246	246	246
475	500	49	49	49	49	1,475	1,500	149	149	149	149	2,475	2,500	249	249	249	249
500	525	51	51	51	51	1,500	1,525	151	151	151	151	2,500	2,525	251	251	251	251
525	550	54	54	54	54	1,525	1,550	154	154	154	154	2,525	2,550	254	254	254	254
550	575	56	56	56	56	1,550	1,575	156	156	156	156	2,550	2,575	256	256	256	256
575	600	59	59	59	59	1,575	1,600	159	159	159	159	2,575	2,600	259	259	259	259
600	625	61	61	61	61	1,600	1,625	161	161	161	161	2,600	2,625	261	261	261	261
625	650	64	64	64	64												
650	675	66	66	66	66	1,625	1,650	164	164	164	164	2,625	2,650	264	264	264	264
675	700	69	69	69	69	1,650	1,675	166	166	166	166	2,650	2,675	266	266	266	266
						1,675	1,700	169	169	169	169	2,675	2,700	269	269	269	269
700	725	71	71	71	71	1,700	1,725	171	171	171	171	2,700	2,725	271	271	271	271
725	750	74	74	74	74	1,725	1,750	174	174	174	174	2,725	2,750	274	274	274	274
750	775	76	76	76	76												
775	800	79	79	79	79	1,750	1,775	176	176	176	176	2,750	2,775	276	276	276	276
800	825	81	81	81	81	1,775	1,800	179	179	179	179	2,775	2,800	279	279	279	279
						1,800	1,825	181	181	181	181	2,800	2,825	281	281	281	281
825	850	84	84	84	84	1,825	1,850	184	184	184	184	2,825	2,850	284	284	284	284
850	875	86	86	86	86	1,850	1,875	186	186	186	186	2,850	2,875	286	286	286	286
875	900	89	89	89	89												
900	925	91	91	91	91	1,875	1,900	189	189	189	189	2,875	2,900	289	289	289	289
925	950	94	94	94	94	1,900	1,925	191	191	191	191	2,900	2,925	291	291	291	291
						1,925	1,950	194	194	194	194	2,925	2,950	294	294	294	294
950	975	96	96	96	96	1,950	1,975	196	196	196	196	2,950	2,975	296	296	296	296
975	1,000	99	99	99	99	1,975	2,000	199	199	199	199	2,975	3,000	299	299	299	299

(Continued)

* This column must also be used by a qualifying widow(er).

¶25

2019 Tax Table — *Continued*

If line 11b (taxable income) is—		And you are—				If line 11b (taxable income) is—		And you are—				If line 11b (taxable income) is—		And you are—			
At least	But less than	Single	Married filing jointly *	Married filing separately	Head of a household	At least	But less than	Single	Married filing jointly *	Married filing separately	Head of a household	At least	But less than	Single	Married filing jointly *	Married filing separately	Head of a household
		Your tax is—						Your tax is—						Your tax is—			
3,000						**6,000**						**9,000**					
3,000	3,050	303	303	303	303	6,000	6,050	603	603	603	603	9,000	9,050	903	903	903	903
3,050	3,100	308	308	308	308	6,050	6,100	608	608	608	608	9,050	9,100	908	908	908	908
3,100	3,150	313	313	313	313	6,100	6,150	613	613	613	613	9,100	9,150	913	913	913	913
3,150	3,200	318	318	318	318	6,150	6,200	618	618	618	618	9,150	9,200	918	918	918	918
3,200	3,250	323	323	323	323	6,200	6,250	623	623	623	623	9,200	9,250	923	923	923	923
3,250	3,300	328	328	328	328	6,250	6,300	628	628	628	628	9,250	9,300	928	928	928	928
3,300	3,350	333	333	333	333	6,300	6,350	633	633	633	633	9,300	9,350	933	933	933	933
3,350	3,400	338	338	338	338	6,350	6,400	638	638	638	638	9,350	9,400	938	938	938	938
3,400	3,450	343	343	343	343	6,400	6,450	643	643	643	643	9,400	9,450	943	943	943	943
3,450	3,500	348	348	348	348	6,450	6,500	648	648	648	648	9,450	9,500	948	948	948	948
3,500	3,550	353	353	353	353	6,500	6,550	653	653	653	653	9,500	9,550	953	953	953	953
3,550	3,600	358	358	358	358	6,550	6,600	658	658	658	658	9,550	9,600	958	958	958	958
3,600	3,650	363	363	363	363	6,600	6,650	663	663	663	663	9,600	9,650	963	963	963	963
3,650	3,700	368	368	368	368	6,650	6,700	668	668	668	668	9,650	9,700	968	968	968	968
3,700	3,750	373	373	373	373	6,700	6,750	673	673	673	673	9,700	9,750	973	973	973	973
3,750	3,800	378	378	378	378	6,750	6,800	678	678	678	678	9,750	9,800	979	978	979	978
3,800	3,850	383	383	383	383	6,800	6,850	683	683	683	683	9,800	9,850	985	983	985	983
3,850	3,900	388	388	388	388	6,850	6,900	688	688	688	688	9,850	9,900	991	988	991	988
3,900	3,950	393	393	393	393	6,900	6,950	693	693	693	693	9,900	9,950	997	993	997	993
3,950	4,000	398	398	398	398	6,950	7,000	698	698	698	698	9,950	10,000	1,003	998	1,003	998
4,000						**7,000**						**10,000**					
4,000	4,050	403	403	403	403	7,000	7,050	703	703	703	703	10,000	10,050	1,009	1,003	1,009	1,003
4,050	4,100	408	408	408	408	7,050	7,100	708	708	708	708	10,050	10,100	1,015	1,008	1,015	1,008
4,100	4,150	413	413	413	413	7,100	7,150	713	713	713	713	10,100	10,150	1,021	1,013	1,021	1,013
4,150	4,200	418	418	418	418	7,150	7,200	718	718	718	718	10,150	10,200	1,027	1,018	1,027	1,018
4,200	4,250	423	423	423	423	7,200	7,250	723	723	723	723	10,200	10,250	1,033	1,023	1,033	1,023
4,250	4,300	428	428	428	428	7,250	7,300	728	728	728	728	10,250	10,300	1,039	1,028	1,039	1,028
4,300	4,350	433	433	433	433	7,300	7,350	733	733	733	733	10,300	10,350	1,045	1,033	1,045	1,033
4,350	4,400	438	438	438	438	7,350	7,400	738	738	738	738	10,350	10,400	1,051	1,038	1,051	1,038
4,400	4,450	443	443	443	443	7,400	7,450	743	743	743	743	10,400	10,450	1,057	1,043	1,057	1,043
4,450	4,500	448	448	448	448	7,450	7,500	748	748	748	748	10,450	10,500	1,063	1,048	1,063	1,048
4,500	4,550	453	453	453	453	7,500	7,550	753	753	753	753	10,500	10,550	1,069	1,053	1,069	1,053
4,550	4,600	458	458	458	458	7,550	7,600	758	758	758	758	10,550	10,600	1,075	1,058	1,075	1,058
4,600	4,650	463	463	463	463	7,600	7,650	763	763	763	763	10,600	10,650	1,081	1,063	1,081	1,063
4,650	4,700	468	468	468	468	7,650	7,700	768	768	768	768	10,650	10,700	1,087	1,068	1,087	1,068
4,700	4,750	473	473	473	473	7,700	7,750	773	773	773	773	10,700	10,750	1,093	1,073	1,093	1,073
4,750	4,800	478	478	478	478	7,750	7,800	778	778	778	778	10,750	10,800	1,099	1,078	1,099	1,078
4,800	4,850	483	483	483	483	7,800	7,850	783	783	783	783	10,800	10,850	1,105	1,083	1,105	1,083
4,850	4,900	488	488	488	488	7,850	7,900	788	788	788	788	10,850	10,900	1,111	1,088	1,111	1,088
4,900	4,950	493	493	493	493	7,900	7,950	793	793	793	793	10,900	10,950	1,117	1,093	1,117	1,093
4,950	5,000	498	498	498	498	7,950	8,000	798	798	798	798	10,950	11,000	1,123	1,098	1,123	1,098
5,000						**8,000**						**11,000**					
5,000	5,050	503	503	503	503	8,000	8,050	803	803	803	803	11,000	11,050	1,129	1,103	1,129	1,103
5,050	5,100	508	508	508	508	8,050	8,100	808	808	808	808	11,050	11,100	1,135	1,108	1,135	1,108
5,100	5,150	513	513	513	513	8,100	8,150	813	813	813	813	11,100	11,150	1,141	1,113	1,141	1,113
5,150	5,200	518	518	518	518	8,150	8,200	818	818	818	818	11,150	11,200	1,147	1,118	1,147	1,118
5,200	5,250	523	523	523	523	8,200	8,250	823	823	823	823	11,200	11,250	1,153	1,123	1,153	1,123
5,250	5,300	528	528	528	528	8,250	8,300	828	828	828	828	11,250	11,300	1,159	1,128	1,159	1,128
5,300	5,350	533	533	533	533	8,300	8,350	833	833	833	833	11,300	11,350	1,165	1,133	1,165	1,133
5,350	5,400	538	538	538	538	8,350	8,400	838	838	838	838	11,350	11,400	1,171	1,138	1,171	1,138
5,400	5,450	543	543	543	543	8,400	8,450	843	843	843	843	11,400	11,450	1,177	1,143	1,177	1,143
5,450	5,500	548	548	548	548	8,450	8,500	848	848	848	848	11,450	11,500	1,183	1,148	1,183	1,148
5,500	5,550	553	553	553	553	8,500	8,550	853	853	853	853	11,500	11,550	1,189	1,153	1,189	1,153
5,550	5,600	558	558	558	558	8,550	8,600	858	858	858	858	11,550	11,600	1,195	1,158	1,195	1,158
5,600	5,650	563	563	563	563	8,600	8,650	863	863	863	863	11,600	11,650	1,201	1,163	1,201	1,163
5,650	5,700	568	568	568	568	8,650	8,700	868	868	868	868	11,650	11,700	1,207	1,168	1,207	1,168
5,700	5,750	573	573	573	573	8,700	8,750	873	873	873	873	11,700	11,750	1,213	1,173	1,213	1,173
5,750	5,800	578	578	578	578	8,750	8,800	878	878	878	878	11,750	11,800	1,219	1,178	1,219	1,178
5,800	5,850	583	583	583	583	8,800	8,850	883	883	883	883	11,800	11,850	1,225	1,183	1,225	1,183
5,850	5,900	588	588	588	588	8,850	8,900	888	888	888	888	11,850	11,900	1,231	1,188	1,231	1,188
5,900	5,950	593	593	593	593	8,900	8,950	893	893	893	893	11,900	11,950	1,237	1,193	1,237	1,193
5,950	6,000	598	598	598	598	8,950	9,000	898	898	898	898	11,950	12,000	1,243	1,198	1,243	1,198

(Continued)

* This column must also be used by a qualifying widow(er).

- 63 -

Need more information or forms? Visit IRS.gov.

¶25

2019 Tax Table — *Continued*

12,000

If line 11b (taxable income) is—		And you are—			
At least	But less than	Single	Married filing jointly *	Married filing separately	Head of a household
		Your tax is—			
12,000	12,050	1,249	1,203	1,249	1,203
12,050	12,100	1,255	1,208	1,255	1,208
12,100	12,150	1,261	1,213	1,261	1,213
12,150	12,200	1,267	1,218	1,267	1,218
12,200	12,250	1,273	1,223	1,273	1,223
12,250	12,300	1,279	1,228	1,279	1,228
12,300	12,350	1,285	1,233	1,285	1,233
12,350	12,400	1,291	1,238	1,291	1,238
12,400	12,450	1,297	1,243	1,297	1,243
12,450	12,500	1,303	1,248	1,303	1,248
12,500	12,550	1,309	1,253	1,309	1,253
12,550	12,600	1,315	1,258	1,315	1,258
12,600	12,650	1,321	1,263	1,321	1,263
12,650	12,700	1,327	1,268	1,327	1,268
12,700	12,750	1,333	1,273	1,333	1,273
12,750	12,800	1,339	1,278	1,339	1,278
12,800	12,850	1,345	1,283	1,345	1,283
12,850	12,900	1,351	1,288	1,351	1,288
12,900	12,950	1,357	1,293	1,357	1,293
12,950	13,000	1,363	1,298	1,363	1,298

13,000

At least	But less than	Single	Married filing jointly *	Married filing separately	Head of a household
13,000	13,050	1,369	1,303	1,369	1,303
13,050	13,100	1,375	1,308	1,375	1,308
13,100	13,150	1,381	1,313	1,381	1,313
13,150	13,200	1,387	1,318	1,387	1,318
13,200	13,250	1,393	1,323	1,393	1,323
13,250	13,300	1,399	1,328	1,399	1,328
13,300	13,350	1,405	1,333	1,405	1,333
13,350	13,400	1,411	1,338	1,411	1,338
13,400	13,450	1,417	1,343	1,417	1,343
13,450	13,500	1,423	1,348	1,423	1,348
13,500	13,550	1,429	1,353	1,429	1,353
13,550	13,600	1,435	1,358	1,435	1,358
13,600	13,650	1,441	1,363	1,441	1,363
13,650	13,700	1,447	1,368	1,447	1,368
13,700	13,750	1,453	1,373	1,453	1,373
13,750	13,800	1,459	1,378	1,459	1,378
13,800	13,850	1,465	1,383	1,465	1,383
13,850	13,900	1,471	1,388	1,471	1,388
13,900	13,950	1,477	1,393	1,477	1,394
13,950	14,000	1,483	1,398	1,483	1,400

14,000

At least	But less than	Single	Married filing jointly *	Married filing separately	Head of a household
14,000	14,050	1,489	1,403	1,489	1,406
14,050	14,100	1,495	1,408	1,495	1,412
14,100	14,150	1,501	1,413	1,501	1,418
14,150	14,200	1,507	1,418	1,507	1,424
14,200	14,250	1,513	1,423	1,513	1,430
14,250	14,300	1,519	1,428	1,519	1,436
14,300	14,350	1,525	1,433	1,525	1,442
14,350	14,400	1,531	1,438	1,531	1,448
14,400	14,450	1,537	1,443	1,537	1,454
14,450	14,500	1,543	1,448	1,543	1,460
14,500	14,550	1,549	1,453	1,549	1,466
14,550	14,600	1,555	1,458	1,555	1,472
14,600	14,650	1,561	1,463	1,561	1,478
14,650	14,700	1,567	1,468	1,567	1,484
14,700	14,750	1,573	1,473	1,573	1,490
14,750	14,800	1,579	1,478	1,579	1,496
14,800	14,850	1,585	1,483	1,585	1,502
14,850	14,900	1,591	1,488	1,591	1,508
14,900	14,950	1,597	1,493	1,597	1,514
14,950	15,000	1,603	1,498	1,603	1,520

15,000

At least	But less than	Single	Married filing jointly *	Married filing separately	Head of a household
15,000	15,050	1,609	1,503	1,609	1,526
15,050	15,100	1,615	1,508	1,615	1,532
15,100	15,150	1,621	1,513	1,621	1,538
15,150	15,200	1,627	1,518	1,627	1,544
15,200	15,250	1,633	1,523	1,633	1,550
15,250	15,300	1,639	1,528	1,639	1,556
15,300	15,350	1,645	1,533	1,645	1,562
15,350	15,400	1,651	1,538	1,651	1,568
15,400	15,450	1,657	1,543	1,657	1,574
15,450	15,500	1,663	1,548	1,663	1,580
15,500	15,550	1,669	1,553	1,669	1,586
15,550	15,600	1,675	1,558	1,675	1,592
15,600	15,650	1,681	1,563	1,681	1,598
15,650	15,700	1,687	1,568	1,687	1,604
15,700	15,750	1,693	1,573	1,693	1,610
15,750	15,800	1,699	1,578	1,699	1,616
15,800	15,850	1,705	1,583	1,705	1,622
15,850	15,900	1,711	1,588	1,711	1,628
15,900	15,950	1,717	1,593	1,717	1,634
15,950	16,000	1,723	1,598	1,723	1,640

16,000

At least	But less than	Single	Married filing jointly *	Married filing separately	Head of a household
16,000	16,050	1,729	1,603	1,729	1,646
16,050	16,100	1,735	1,608	1,735	1,652
16,100	16,150	1,741	1,613	1,741	1,658
16,150	16,200	1,747	1,618	1,747	1,664
16,200	16,250	1,753	1,623	1,753	1,670
16,250	16,300	1,759	1,628	1,759	1,676
16,300	16,350	1,765	1,633	1,765	1,682
16,350	16,400	1,771	1,638	1,771	1,688
16,400	16,450	1,777	1,643	1,777	1,694
16,450	16,500	1,783	1,648	1,783	1,700
16,500	16,550	1,789	1,653	1,789	1,706
16,550	16,600	1,795	1,658	1,795	1,712
16,600	16,650	1,801	1,663	1,801	1,718
16,650	16,700	1,807	1,668	1,807	1,724
16,700	16,750	1,813	1,673	1,813	1,730
16,750	16,800	1,819	1,678	1,819	1,736
16,800	16,850	1,825	1,683	1,825	1,742
16,850	16,900	1,831	1,688	1,831	1,748
16,900	16,950	1,837	1,693	1,837	1,754
16,950	17,000	1,843	1,698	1,843	1,760

17,000

At least	But less than	Single	Married filing jointly *	Married filing separately	Head of a household
17,000	17,050	1,849	1,703	1,849	1,766
17,050	17,100	1,855	1,708	1,855	1,772
17,100	17,150	1,861	1,713	1,861	1,778
17,150	17,200	1,867	1,718	1,867	1,784
17,200	17,250	1,873	1,723	1,873	1,790
17,250	17,300	1,879	1,728	1,879	1,796
17,300	17,350	1,885	1,733	1,885	1,802
17,350	17,400	1,891	1,738	1,891	1,808
17,400	17,450	1,897	1,743	1,897	1,814
17,450	17,500	1,903	1,748	1,903	1,820
17,500	17,550	1,909	1,753	1,909	1,826
17,550	17,600	1,915	1,758	1,915	1,832
17,600	17,650	1,921	1,763	1,921	1,838
17,650	17,700	1,927	1,768	1,927	1,844
17,700	17,750	1,933	1,773	1,933	1,850
17,750	17,800	1,939	1,778	1,939	1,856
17,800	17,850	1,945	1,783	1,945	1,862
17,850	17,900	1,951	1,788	1,951	1,868
17,900	17,950	1,957	1,793	1,957	1,874
17,950	18,000	1,963	1,798	1,963	1,880

18,000

At least	But less than	Single	Married filing jointly *	Married filing separately	Head of a household
18,000	18,050	1,969	1,803	1,969	1,886
18,050	18,100	1,975	1,808	1,975	1,892
18,100	18,150	1,981	1,813	1,981	1,898
18,150	18,200	1,987	1,818	1,987	1,904
18,200	18,250	1,993	1,823	1,993	1,910
18,250	18,300	1,999	1,828	1,999	1,916
18,300	18,350	2,005	1,833	2,005	1,922
18,350	18,400	2,011	1,838	2,011	1,928
18,400	18,450	2,017	1,843	2,017	1,934
18,450	18,500	2,023	1,848	2,023	1,940
18,500	18,550	2,029	1,853	2,029	1,946
18,550	18,600	2,035	1,858	2,035	1,952
18,600	18,650	2,041	1,863	2,041	1,958
18,650	18,700	2,047	1,868	2,047	1,964
18,700	18,750	2,053	1,873	2,053	1,970
18,750	18,800	2,059	1,878	2,059	1,976
18,800	18,850	2,065	1,883	2,065	1,982
18,850	18,900	2,071	1,888	2,071	1,988
18,900	18,950	2,077	1,893	2,077	1,994
18,950	19,000	2,083	1,898	2,083	2,000

19,000

At least	But less than	Single	Married filing jointly *	Married filing separately	Head of a household
19,000	19,050	2,089	1,903	2,089	2,006
19,050	19,100	2,095	1,908	2,095	2,012
19,100	19,150	2,101	1,913	2,101	2,018
19,150	19,200	2,107	1,918	2,107	2,024
19,200	19,250	2,113	1,923	2,113	2,030
19,250	19,300	2,119	1,928	2,119	2,036
19,300	19,350	2,125	1,933	2,125	2,042
19,350	19,400	2,131	1,938	2,131	2,048
19,400	19,450	2,137	1,943	2,137	2,054
19,450	19,500	2,143	1,949	2,143	2,060
19,500	19,550	2,149	1,955	2,149	2,066
19,550	19,600	2,155	1,961	2,155	2,072
19,600	19,650	2,161	1,967	2,161	2,078
19,650	19,700	2,167	1,973	2,167	2,084
19,700	19,750	2,173	1,979	2,173	2,090
19,750	19,800	2,179	1,985	2,179	2,096
19,800	19,850	2,185	1,991	2,185	2,102
19,850	19,900	2,191	1,997	2,191	2,108
19,900	19,950	2,197	2,003	2,197	2,114
19,950	20,000	2,203	2,009	2,203	2,120

20,000

At least	But less than	Single	Married filing jointly *	Married filing separately	Head of a household
20,000	20,050	2,209	2,015	2,209	2,126
20,050	20,100	2,215	2,021	2,215	2,132
20,100	20,150	2,221	2,027	2,221	2,138
20,150	20,200	2,227	2,033	2,227	2,144
20,200	20,250	2,233	2,039	2,233	2,150
20,250	20,300	2,239	2,045	2,239	2,156
20,300	20,350	2,245	2,051	2,245	2,162
20,350	20,400	2,251	2,057	2,251	2,168
20,400	20,450	2,257	2,063	2,257	2,174
20,450	20,500	2,263	2,069	2,263	2,180
20,500	20,550	2,269	2,075	2,269	2,186
20,550	20,600	2,275	2,081	2,275	2,192
20,600	20,650	2,281	2,087	2,281	2,198
20,650	20,700	2,287	2,093	2,287	2,204
20,700	20,750	2,293	2,099	2,293	2,210
20,750	20,800	2,299	2,105	2,299	2,216
20,800	20,850	2,305	2,111	2,305	2,222
20,850	20,900	2,311	2,117	2,311	2,228
20,900	20,950	2,317	2,123	2,317	2,234
20,950	21,000	2,323	2,129	2,323	2,240

* This column must also be used by a qualifying widow(er).

(Continued)

Need more information or forms? Visit IRS.gov.

TAX RATES

2019 Tax Table — *Continued*

If line 11b (taxable income) is— At least	But less than	And you are— Single	Married filing jointly *	Married filing separately	Head of a household
		Your tax is—			
21,000					
21,000	21,050	2,329	2,135	2,329	2,246
21,050	21,100	2,335	2,141	2,335	2,252
21,100	21,150	2,341	2,147	2,341	2,258
21,150	21,200	2,347	2,153	2,347	2,264
21,200	21,250	2,353	2,159	2,353	2,270
21,250	21,300	2,359	2,165	2,359	2,276
21,300	21,350	2,365	2,171	2,365	2,282
21,350	21,400	2,371	2,177	2,371	2,288
21,400	21,450	2,377	2,183	2,377	2,294
21,450	21,500	2,383	2,189	2,383	2,300
21,500	21,550	2,389	2,195	2,389	2,306
21,550	21,600	2,395	2,201	2,395	2,312
21,600	21,650	2,401	2,207	2,401	2,318
21,650	21,700	2,407	2,213	2,407	2,324
21,700	21,750	2,413	2,219	2,413	2,330
21,750	21,800	2,419	2,225	2,419	2,336
21,800	21,850	2,425	2,231	2,425	2,342
21,850	21,900	2,431	2,237	2,431	2,348
21,900	21,950	2,437	2,243	2,437	2,354
21,950	22,000	2,443	2,249	2,443	2,360
22,000					
22,000	22,050	2,449	2,255	2,449	2,366
22,050	22,100	2,455	2,261	2,455	2,372
22,100	22,150	2,461	2,267	2,461	2,378
22,150	22,200	2,467	2,273	2,467	2,384
22,200	22,250	2,473	2,279	2,473	2,390
22,250	22,300	2,479	2,285	2,479	2,396
22,300	22,350	2,485	2,291	2,485	2,402
22,350	22,400	2,491	2,297	2,491	2,408
22,400	22,450	2,497	2,303	2,497	2,414
22,450	22,500	2,503	2,309	2,503	2,420
22,500	22,550	2,509	2,315	2,509	2,426
22,550	22,600	2,515	2,321	2,515	2,432
22,600	22,650	2,521	2,327	2,521	2,438
22,650	22,700	2,527	2,333	2,527	2,444
22,700	22,750	2,533	2,339	2,533	2,450
22,750	22,800	2,539	2,345	2,539	2,456
22,800	22,850	2,545	2,351	2,545	2,462
22,850	22,900	2,551	2,357	2,551	2,468
22,900	22,950	2,557	2,363	2,557	2,474
22,950	23,000	2,563	2,369	2,563	2,480
23,000					
23,000	23,050	2,569	2,375	2,569	2,486
23,050	23,100	2,575	2,381	2,575	2,492
23,100	23,150	2,581	2,387	2,581	2,498
23,150	23,200	2,587	2,393	2,587	2,504
23,200	23,250	2,593	2,399	2,593	2,510
23,250	23,300	2,599	2,405	2,599	2,516
23,300	23,350	2,605	2,411	2,605	2,522
23,350	23,400	2,611	2,417	2,611	2,528
23,400	23,450	2,617	2,423	2,617	2,534
23,450	23,500	2,623	2,429	2,623	2,540
23,500	23,550	2,629	2,435	2,629	2,546
23,550	23,600	2,635	2,441	2,635	2,552
23,600	23,650	2,641	2,447	2,641	2,558
23,650	23,700	2,647	2,453	2,647	2,564
23,700	23,750	2,653	2,459	2,653	2,570
23,750	23,800	2,659	2,465	2,659	2,576
23,800	23,850	2,665	2,471	2,665	2,582
23,850	23,900	2,671	2,477	2,671	2,588
23,900	23,950	2,677	2,483	2,677	2,594
23,950	24,000	2,683	2,489	2,683	2,600

If line 11b (taxable income) is— At least	But less than	And you are— Single	Married filing jointly *	Married filing separately	Head of a household
		Your tax is—			
24,000					
24,000	24,050	2,689	2,495	2,689	2,606
24,050	24,100	2,695	2,501	2,695	2,612
24,100	24,150	2,701	2,507	2,701	2,618
24,150	24,200	2,707	2,513	2,707	2,624
24,200	24,250	2,713	2,519	2,713	2,630
24,250	24,300	2,719	2,525	2,719	2,636
24,300	24,350	2,725	2,531	2,725	2,642
24,350	24,400	2,731	2,537	2,731	2,648
24,400	24,450	2,737	2,543	2,737	2,654
24,450	24,500	2,743	2,549	2,743	2,660
24,500	24,550	2,749	2,555	2,749	2,666
24,550	24,600	2,755	2,561	2,755	2,672
24,600	24,650	2,761	2,567	2,761	2,678
24,650	24,700	2,767	2,573	2,767	2,684
24,700	24,750	2,773	2,579	2,773	2,690
24,750	24,800	2,779	2,585	2,779	2,696
24,800	24,850	2,785	2,591	2,785	2,702
24,850	24,900	2,791	2,597	2,791	2,708
24,900	24,950	2,797	2,603	2,797	2,714
24,950	25,000	2,803	2,609	2,803	2,720
25,000					
25,000	25,050	2,809	2,615	2,809	2,726
25,050	25,100	2,815	2,621	2,815	2,732
25,100	25,150	2,821	2,627	2,821	2,738
25,150	25,200	2,827	2,633	2,827	2,744
25,200	25,250	2,833	2,639	2,833	2,750
25,250	25,300	2,839	2,645	2,839	2,756
25,300	25,350	2,845	2,651	2,845	2,762
25,350	25,400	2,851	2,657	2,851	2,768
25,400	25,450	2,857	2,663	2,857	2,774
25,450	25,500	2,863	2,669	2,863	2,780
25,500	25,550	2,869	2,675	2,869	2,786
25,550	25,600	2,875	2,681	2,875	2,792
25,600	25,650	2,881	2,687	2,881	2,798
25,650	25,700	2,887	2,693	2,887	2,804
25,700	25,750	2,893	2,699	2,893	2,810
25,750	25,800	2,899	2,705	2,899	2,816
25,800	25,850	2,905	2,711	2,905	2,822
25,850	25,900	2,911	2,717	2,911	2,828
25,900	25,950	2,917	2,723	2,917	2,834
25,950	26,000	2,923	2,729	2,923	2,840
26,000					
26,000	26,050	2,929	2,735	2,929	2,846
26,050	26,100	2,935	2,741	2,935	2,852
26,100	26,150	2,941	2,747	2,941	2,858
26,150	26,200	2,947	2,753	2,947	2,864
26,200	26,250	2,953	2,759	2,953	2,870
26,250	26,300	2,959	2,765	2,959	2,876
26,300	26,350	2,965	2,771	2,965	2,882
26,350	26,400	2,971	2,777	2,971	2,888
26,400	26,450	2,977	2,783	2,977	2,894
26,450	26,500	2,983	2,789	2,983	2,900
26,500	26,550	2,989	2,795	2,989	2,906
26,550	26,600	2,995	2,801	2,995	2,912
26,600	26,650	3,001	2,807	3,001	2,918
26,650	26,700	3,007	2,813	3,007	2,924
26,700	26,750	3,013	2,819	3,013	2,930
26,750	26,800	3,019	2,825	3,019	2,936
26,800	26,850	3,025	2,831	3,025	2,942
26,850	26,900	3,031	2,837	3,031	2,948
26,900	26,950	3,037	2,843	3,037	2,954
26,950	27,000	3,043	2,849	3,043	2,960

If line 11b (taxable income) is— At least	But less than	And you are— Single	Married filing jointly *	Married filing separately	Head of a household
		Your tax is—			
27,000					
27,000	27,050	3,049	2,855	3,049	2,966
27,050	27,100	3,055	2,861	3,055	2,972
27,100	27,150	3,061	2,867	3,061	2,978
27,150	27,200	3,067	2,873	3,067	2,984
27,200	27,250	3,073	2,879	3,073	2,990
27,250	27,300	3,079	2,885	3,079	2,996
27,300	27,350	3,085	2,891	3,085	3,002
27,350	27,400	3,091	2,897	3,091	3,008
27,400	27,450	3,097	2,903	3,097	3,014
27,450	27,500	3,103	2,909	3,103	3,020
27,500	27,550	3,109	2,915	3,109	3,026
27,550	27,600	3,115	2,921	3,115	3,032
27,600	27,650	3,121	2,927	3,121	3,038
27,650	27,700	3,127	2,933	3,127	3,044
27,700	27,750	3,133	2,939	3,133	3,050
27,750	27,800	3,139	2,945	3,139	3,056
27,800	27,850	3,145	2,951	3,145	3,062
27,850	27,900	3,151	2,957	3,151	3,068
27,900	27,950	3,157	2,963	3,157	3,074
27,950	28,000	3,163	2,969	3,163	3,080
28,000					
28,000	28,050	3,169	2,975	3,169	3,086
28,050	28,100	3,175	2,981	3,175	3,092
28,100	28,150	3,181	2,987	3,181	3,098
28,150	28,200	3,187	2,993	3,187	3,104
28,200	28,250	3,193	2,999	3,193	3,110
28,250	28,300	3,199	3,005	3,199	3,116
28,300	28,350	3,205	3,011	3,205	3,122
28,350	28,400	3,211	3,017	3,211	3,128
28,400	28,450	3,217	3,023	3,217	3,134
28,450	28,500	3,223	3,029	3,223	3,140
28,500	28,550	3,229	3,035	3,229	3,146
28,550	28,600	3,235	3,041	3,235	3,152
28,600	28,650	3,241	3,047	3,241	3,158
28,650	28,700	3,247	3,053	3,247	3,164
28,700	28,750	3,253	3,059	3,253	3,170
28,750	28,800	3,259	3,065	3,259	3,176
28,800	28,850	3,265	3,071	3,265	3,182
28,850	28,900	3,271	3,077	3,271	3,188
28,900	28,950	3,277	3,083	3,277	3,194
28,950	29,000	3,283	3,089	3,283	3,200
29,000					
29,000	29,050	3,289	3,095	3,289	3,206
29,050	29,100	3,295	3,101	3,295	3,212
29,100	29,150	3,301	3,107	3,301	3,218
29,150	29,200	3,307	3,113	3,307	3,224
29,200	29,250	3,313	3,119	3,313	3,230
29,250	29,300	3,319	3,125	3,319	3,236
29,300	29,350	3,325	3,131	3,325	3,242
29,350	29,400	3,331	3,137	3,331	3,248
29,400	29,450	3,337	3,143	3,337	3,254
29,450	29,500	3,343	3,149	3,343	3,260
29,500	29,550	3,349	3,155	3,349	3,266
29,550	29,600	3,355	3,161	3,355	3,272
29,600	29,650	3,361	3,167	3,361	3,278
29,650	29,700	3,367	3,173	3,367	3,284
29,700	29,750	3,373	3,179	3,373	3,290
29,750	29,800	3,379	3,185	3,379	3,296
29,800	29,850	3,385	3,191	3,385	3,302
29,850	29,900	3,391	3,197	3,391	3,308
29,900	29,950	3,397	3,203	3,397	3,314
29,950	30,000	3,403	3,209	3,403	3,320

(Continued)

* This column must also be used by a qualifying widow(er).

Need more information or forms? Visit IRS.gov.

¶25

2019 Tax Table — *Continued*

TAX RATES

30,000 / 31,000 / 32,000

If line 11b (taxable income) is— At least	But less than	Single	Married filing jointly *	Married filing separately	Head of a household
30,000					
30,000	30,050	3,409	3,215	3,409	3,326
30,050	30,100	3,415	3,221	3,415	3,332
30,100	30,150	3,421	3,227	3,421	3,338
30,150	30,200	3,427	3,233	3,427	3,344
30,200	30,250	3,433	3,239	3,433	3,350
30,250	30,300	3,439	3,245	3,439	3,356
30,300	30,350	3,445	3,251	3,445	3,362
30,350	30,400	3,451	3,257	3,451	3,368
30,400	30,450	3,457	3,263	3,457	3,374
30,450	30,500	3,463	3,269	3,463	3,380
30,500	30,550	3,469	3,275	3,469	3,386
30,550	30,600	3,475	3,281	3,475	3,392
30,600	30,650	3,481	3,287	3,481	3,398
30,650	30,700	3,487	3,293	3,487	3,404
30,700	30,750	3,493	3,299	3,493	3,410
30,750	30,800	3,499	3,305	3,499	3,416
30,800	30,850	3,505	3,311	3,505	3,422
30,850	30,900	3,511	3,317	3,511	3,428
30,900	30,950	3,517	3,323	3,517	3,434
30,950	31,000	3,523	3,329	3,523	3,440
31,000					
31,000	31,050	3,529	3,335	3,529	3,446
31,050	31,100	3,535	3,341	3,535	3,452
31,100	31,150	3,541	3,347	3,541	3,458
31,150	31,200	3,547	3,353	3,547	3,464
31,200	31,250	3,553	3,359	3,553	3,470
31,250	31,300	3,559	3,365	3,559	3,476
31,300	31,350	3,565	3,371	3,565	3,482
31,350	31,400	3,571	3,377	3,571	3,488
31,400	31,450	3,577	3,383	3,577	3,494
31,450	31,500	3,583	3,389	3,583	3,500
31,500	31,550	3,589	3,395	3,589	3,506
31,550	31,600	3,595	3,401	3,595	3,512
31,600	31,650	3,601	3,407	3,601	3,518
31,650	31,700	3,607	3,413	3,607	3,524
31,700	31,750	3,613	3,419	3,613	3,530
31,750	31,800	3,619	3,425	3,619	3,536
31,800	31,850	3,625	3,431	3,625	3,542
31,850	31,900	3,631	3,437	3,631	3,548
31,900	31,950	3,637	3,443	3,637	3,554
31,950	32,000	3,643	3,449	3,643	3,560
32,000					
32,000	32,050	3,649	3,455	3,649	3,566
32,050	32,100	3,655	3,461	3,655	3,572
32,100	32,150	3,661	3,467	3,661	3,578
32,150	32,200	3,667	3,473	3,667	3,584
32,200	32,250	3,673	3,479	3,673	3,590
32,250	32,300	3,679	3,485	3,679	3,596
32,300	32,350	3,685	3,491	3,685	3,602
32,350	32,400	3,691	3,497	3,691	3,608
32,400	32,450	3,697	3,503	3,697	3,614
32,450	32,500	3,703	3,509	3,703	3,620
32,500	32,550	3,709	3,515	3,709	3,626
32,550	32,600	3,715	3,521	3,715	3,632
32,600	32,650	3,721	3,527	3,721	3,638
32,650	32,700	3,727	3,533	3,727	3,644
32,700	32,750	3,733	3,539	3,733	3,650
32,750	32,800	3,739	3,545	3,739	3,656
32,800	32,850	3,745	3,551	3,745	3,662
32,850	32,900	3,751	3,557	3,751	3,668
32,900	32,950	3,757	3,563	3,757	3,674
32,950	33,000	3,763	3,569	3,763	3,680

33,000 / 34,000 / 35,000

If line 11b (taxable income) is— At least	But less than	Single	Married filing jointly *	Married filing separately	Head of a household
33,000					
33,000	33,050	3,769	3,575	3,769	3,686
33,050	33,100	3,775	3,581	3,775	3,692
33,100	33,150	3,781	3,587	3,781	3,698
33,150	33,200	3,787	3,593	3,787	3,704
33,200	33,250	3,793	3,599	3,793	3,710
33,250	33,300	3,799	3,605	3,799	3,716
33,300	33,350	3,805	3,611	3,805	3,722
33,350	33,400	3,811	3,617	3,811	3,728
33,400	33,450	3,817	3,623	3,817	3,734
33,450	33,500	3,823	3,629	3,823	3,740
33,500	33,550	3,829	3,635	3,829	3,746
33,550	33,600	3,835	3,641	3,835	3,752
33,600	33,650	3,841	3,647	3,841	3,758
33,650	33,700	3,847	3,653	3,847	3,764
33,700	33,750	3,853	3,659	3,853	3,770
33,750	33,800	3,859	3,665	3,859	3,776
33,800	33,850	3,865	3,671	3,865	3,782
33,850	33,900	3,871	3,677	3,871	3,788
33,900	33,950	3,877	3,683	3,877	3,794
33,950	34,000	3,883	3,689	3,883	3,800
34,000					
34,000	34,050	3,889	3,695	3,889	3,806
34,050	34,100	3,895	3,701	3,895	3,812
34,100	34,150	3,901	3,707	3,901	3,818
34,150	34,200	3,907	3,713	3,907	3,824
34,200	34,250	3,913	3,719	3,913	3,830
34,250	34,300	3,919	3,725	3,919	3,836
34,300	34,350	3,925	3,731	3,925	3,842
34,350	34,400	3,931	3,737	3,931	3,848
34,400	34,450	3,937	3,743	3,937	3,854
34,450	34,500	3,943	3,749	3,943	3,860
34,500	34,550	3,949	3,755	3,949	3,866
34,550	34,600	3,955	3,761	3,955	3,872
34,600	34,650	3,961	3,767	3,961	3,878
34,650	34,700	3,967	3,773	3,967	3,884
34,700	34,750	3,973	3,779	3,973	3,890
34,750	34,800	3,979	3,785	3,979	3,896
34,800	34,850	3,985	3,791	3,985	3,902
34,850	34,900	3,991	3,797	3,991	3,908
34,900	34,950	3,997	3,803	3,997	3,914
34,950	35,000	4,003	3,809	4,003	3,920
35,000					
35,000	35,050	4,009	3,815	4,009	3,926
35,050	35,100	4,015	3,821	4,015	3,932
35,100	35,150	4,021	3,827	4,021	3,938
35,150	35,200	4,027	3,833	4,027	3,944
35,200	35,250	4,033	3,839	4,033	3,950
35,250	35,300	4,039	3,845	4,039	3,956
35,300	35,350	4,045	3,851	4,045	3,962
35,350	35,400	4,051	3,857	4,051	3,968
35,400	35,450	4,057	3,863	4,057	3,974
35,450	35,500	4,063	3,869	4,063	3,980
35,500	35,550	4,069	3,875	4,069	3,986
35,550	35,600	4,075	3,881	4,075	3,992
35,600	35,650	4,081	3,887	4,081	3,998
35,650	35,700	4,087	3,893	4,087	4,004
35,700	35,750	4,093	3,899	4,093	4,010
35,750	35,800	4,099	3,905	4,099	4,016
35,800	35,850	4,105	3,911	4,105	4,022
35,850	35,900	4,111	3,917	4,111	4,028
35,900	35,950	4,117	3,923	4,117	4,034
35,950	36,000	4,123	3,929	4,123	4,040

36,000 / 37,000 / 38,000

If line 11b (taxable income) is— At least	But less than	Single	Married filing jointly *	Married filing separately	Head of a household
36,000					
36,000	36,050	4,129	3,935	4,129	4,046
36,050	36,100	4,135	3,941	4,135	4,052
36,100	36,150	4,141	3,947	4,141	4,058
36,150	36,200	4,147	3,953	4,147	4,064
36,200	36,250	4,153	3,959	4,153	4,070
36,250	36,300	4,159	3,965	4,159	4,076
36,300	36,350	4,165	3,971	4,165	4,082
36,350	36,400	4,171	3,977	4,171	4,088
36,400	36,450	4,177	3,983	4,177	4,094
36,450	36,500	4,183	3,989	4,183	4,100
36,500	36,550	4,189	3,995	4,189	4,106
36,550	36,600	4,195	4,001	4,195	4,112
36,600	36,650	4,201	4,007	4,201	4,118
36,650	36,700	4,207	4,013	4,207	4,124
36,700	36,750	4,213	4,019	4,213	4,130
36,750	36,800	4,219	4,025	4,219	4,136
36,800	36,850	4,225	4,031	4,225	4,142
36,850	36,900	4,231	4,037	4,231	4,148
36,900	36,950	4,237	4,043	4,237	4,154
36,950	37,000	4,243	4,049	4,243	4,160
37,000					
37,000	37,050	4,249	4,055	4,249	4,166
37,050	37,100	4,255	4,061	4,255	4,172
37,100	37,150	4,261	4,067	4,261	4,178
37,150	37,200	4,267	4,073	4,267	4,184
37,200	37,250	4,273	4,079	4,273	4,190
37,250	37,300	4,279	4,085	4,279	4,196
37,300	37,350	4,285	4,091	4,285	4,202
37,350	37,400	4,291	4,097	4,291	4,208
37,400	37,450	4,297	4,103	4,297	4,214
37,450	37,500	4,303	4,109	4,303	4,220
37,500	37,550	4,309	4,115	4,309	4,226
37,550	37,600	4,315	4,121	4,315	4,232
37,600	37,650	4,321	4,127	4,321	4,238
37,650	37,700	4,327	4,133	4,327	4,244
37,700	37,750	4,333	4,139	4,333	4,250
37,750	37,800	4,339	4,145	4,339	4,256
37,800	37,850	4,345	4,151	4,345	4,262
37,850	37,900	4,351	4,157	4,351	4,268
37,900	37,950	4,357	4,163	4,357	4,274
37,950	38,000	4,363	4,169	4,363	4,280
38,000					
38,000	38,050	4,369	4,175	4,369	4,286
38,050	38,100	4,375	4,181	4,375	4,292
38,100	38,150	4,381	4,187	4,381	4,298
38,150	38,200	4,387	4,193	4,387	4,304
38,200	38,250	4,393	4,199	4,393	4,310
38,250	38,300	4,399	4,205	4,399	4,316
38,300	38,350	4,405	4,211	4,405	4,322
38,350	38,400	4,411	4,217	4,411	4,328
38,400	38,450	4,417	4,223	4,417	4,334
38,450	38,500	4,423	4,229	4,423	4,340
38,500	38,550	4,429	4,235	4,429	4,346
38,550	38,600	4,435	4,241	4,435	4,352
38,600	38,650	4,441	4,247	4,441	4,358
38,650	38,700	4,447	4,253	4,447	4,364
38,700	38,750	4,453	4,259	4,453	4,370
38,750	38,800	4,459	4,265	4,459	4,376
38,800	38,850	4,465	4,271	4,465	4,382
38,850	38,900	4,471	4,277	4,471	4,388
38,900	38,950	4,477	4,283	4,477	4,394
38,950	39,000	4,483	4,289	4,483	4,400

Your tax is—

* This column must also be used by a qualifying widow(er).

(Continued)

Need more information or forms? Visit IRS.gov.   - 66 -

¶25

2019 Tax Table — Continued

If line 11b (taxable income) is— At least	But less than	Single	Married filing jointly *	Married filing separately	Head of a household
39,000					
39,000	39,050	4,489	4,295	4,489	4,406
39,050	39,100	4,495	4,301	4,495	4,412
39,100	39,150	4,501	4,307	4,501	4,418
39,150	39,200	4,507	4,313	4,507	4,424
39,200	39,250	4,513	4,319	4,513	4,430
39,250	39,300	4,519	4,325	4,519	4,436
39,300	39,350	4,525	4,331	4,525	4,442
39,350	39,400	4,531	4,337	4,531	4,448
39,400	39,450	4,537	4,343	4,537	4,454
39,450	39,500	4,543	4,349	4,543	4,460
39,500	39,550	4,554	4,355	4,554	4,466
39,550	39,600	4,565	4,361	4,565	4,472
39,600	39,650	4,576	4,367	4,576	4,478
39,650	39,700	4,587	4,373	4,587	4,484
39,700	39,750	4,598	4,379	4,598	4,490
39,750	39,800	4,609	4,385	4,609	4,496
39,800	39,850	4,620	4,391	4,620	4,502
39,850	39,900	4,631	4,397	4,631	4,508
39,900	39,950	4,642	4,403	4,642	4,514
39,950	40,000	4,653	4,409	4,653	4,520
40,000					
40,000	40,050	4,664	4,415	4,664	4,526
40,050	40,100	4,675	4,421	4,675	4,532
40,100	40,150	4,686	4,427	4,686	4,538
40,150	40,200	4,697	4,433	4,697	4,544
40,200	40,250	4,708	4,439	4,708	4,550
40,250	40,300	4,719	4,445	4,719	4,556
40,300	40,350	4,730	4,451	4,730	4,562
40,350	40,400	4,741	4,457	4,741	4,568
40,400	40,450	4,752	4,463	4,752	4,574
40,450	40,500	4,763	4,469	4,763	4,580
40,500	40,550	4,774	4,475	4,774	4,586
40,550	40,600	4,785	4,481	4,785	4,592
40,600	40,650	4,796	4,487	4,796	4,598
40,650	40,700	4,807	4,493	4,807	4,604
40,700	40,750	4,818	4,499	4,818	4,610
40,750	40,800	4,829	4,505	4,829	4,616
40,800	40,850	4,840	4,511	4,840	4,622
40,850	40,900	4,851	4,517	4,851	4,628
40,900	40,950	4,862	4,523	4,862	4,634
40,950	41,000	4,873	4,529	4,873	4,640
41,000					
41,000	41,050	4,884	4,535	4,884	4,646
41,050	41,100	4,895	4,541	4,895	4,652
41,100	41,150	4,906	4,547	4,906	4,658
41,150	41,200	4,917	4,553	4,917	4,664
41,200	41,250	4,928	4,559	4,928	4,670
41,250	41,300	4,939	4,565	4,939	4,676
41,300	41,350	4,950	4,571	4,950	4,682
41,350	41,400	4,961	4,577	4,961	4,688
41,400	41,450	4,972	4,583	4,972	4,694
41,450	41,500	4,983	4,589	4,983	4,700
41,500	41,550	4,994	4,595	4,994	4,706
41,550	41,600	5,005	4,601	5,005	4,712
41,600	41,650	5,016	4,607	5,016	4,718
41,650	41,700	5,027	4,613	5,027	4,724
41,700	41,750	5,038	4,619	5,038	4,730
41,750	41,800	5,049	4,625	5,049	4,736
41,800	41,850	5,060	4,631	5,060	4,742
41,850	41,900	5,071	4,637	5,071	4,748
41,900	41,950	5,082	4,643	5,082	4,754
41,950	42,000	5,093	4,649	5,093	4,760

If line 11b (taxable income) is— At least	But less than	Single	Married filing jointly *	Married filing separately	Head of a household
42,000					
42,000	42,050	5,104	4,655	5,104	4,766
42,050	42,100	5,115	4,661	5,115	4,772
42,100	42,150	5,126	4,667	5,126	4,778
42,150	42,200	5,137	4,673	5,137	4,784
42,200	42,250	5,148	4,679	5,148	4,790
42,250	42,300	5,159	4,685	5,159	4,796
42,300	42,350	5,170	4,691	5,170	4,802
42,350	42,400	5,181	4,697	5,181	4,808
42,400	42,450	5,192	4,703	5,192	4,814
42,450	42,500	5,203	4,709	5,203	4,820
42,500	42,550	5,214	4,715	5,214	4,826
42,550	42,600	5,225	4,721	5,225	4,832
42,600	42,650	5,236	4,727	5,236	4,838
42,650	42,700	5,247	4,733	5,247	4,844
42,700	42,750	5,258	4,739	5,258	4,850
42,750	42,800	5,269	4,745	5,269	4,856
42,800	42,850	5,280	4,751	5,280	4,862
42,850	42,900	5,291	4,757	5,291	4,868
42,900	42,950	5,302	4,763	5,302	4,874
42,950	43,000	5,313	4,769	5,313	4,880
43,000					
43,000	43,050	5,324	4,775	5,324	4,886
43,050	43,100	5,335	4,781	5,335	4,892
43,100	43,150	5,346	4,787	5,346	4,898
43,150	43,200	5,357	4,793	5,357	4,904
43,200	43,250	5,368	4,799	5,368	4,910
43,250	43,300	5,379	4,805	5,379	4,916
43,300	43,350	5,390	4,811	5,390	4,922
43,350	43,400	5,401	4,817	5,401	4,928
43,400	43,450	5,412	4,823	5,412	4,934
43,450	43,500	5,423	4,829	5,423	4,940
43,500	43,550	5,434	4,835	5,434	4,946
43,550	43,600	5,445	4,841	5,445	4,952
43,600	43,650	5,456	4,847	5,456	4,958
43,650	43,700	5,467	4,853	5,467	4,964
43,700	43,750	5,478	4,859	5,478	4,970
43,750	43,800	5,489	4,865	5,489	4,976
43,800	43,850	5,500	4,871	5,500	4,982
43,850	43,900	5,511	4,877	5,511	4,988
43,900	43,950	5,522	4,883	5,522	4,994
43,950	44,000	5,533	4,889	5,533	5,000
44,000					
44,000	44,050	5,544	4,895	5,544	5,006
44,050	44,100	5,555	4,901	5,555	5,012
44,100	44,150	5,566	4,907	5,566	5,018
44,150	44,200	5,577	4,913	5,577	5,024
44,200	44,250	5,588	4,919	5,588	5,030
44,250	44,300	5,599	4,925	5,599	5,036
44,300	44,350	5,610	4,931	5,610	5,042
44,350	44,400	5,621	4,937	5,621	5,048
44,400	44,450	5,632	4,943	5,632	5,054
44,450	44,500	5,643	4,949	5,643	5,060
44,500	44,550	5,654	4,955	5,654	5,066
44,550	44,600	5,665	4,961	5,665	5,072
44,600	44,650	5,676	4,967	5,676	5,078
44,650	44,700	5,687	4,973	5,687	5,084
44,700	44,750	5,698	4,979	5,698	5,090
44,750	44,800	5,709	4,985	5,709	5,096
44,800	44,850	5,720	4,991	5,720	5,102
44,850	44,900	5,731	4,997	5,731	5,108
44,900	44,950	5,742	5,003	5,742	5,114
44,950	45,000	5,753	5,009	5,753	5,120

If line 11b (taxable income) is— At least	But less than	Single	Married filing jointly *	Married filing separately	Head of a household
45,000					
45,000	45,050	5,764	5,015	5,764	5,126
45,050	45,100	5,775	5,021	5,775	5,132
45,100	45,150	5,786	5,027	5,786	5,138
45,150	45,200	5,797	5,033	5,797	5,144
45,200	45,250	5,808	5,039	5,808	5,150
45,250	45,300	5,819	5,045	5,819	5,156
45,300	45,350	5,830	5,051	5,830	5,162
45,350	45,400	5,841	5,057	5,841	5,168
45,400	45,450	5,852	5,063	5,852	5,174
45,450	45,500	5,863	5,069	5,863	5,180
45,500	45,550	5,874	5,075	5,874	5,186
45,550	45,600	5,885	5,081	5,885	5,192
45,600	45,650	5,896	5,087	5,896	5,198
45,650	45,700	5,907	5,093	5,907	5,204
45,700	45,750	5,918	5,099	5,918	5,210
45,750	45,800	5,929	5,105	5,929	5,216
45,800	45,850	5,940	5,111	5,940	5,222
45,850	45,900	5,951	5,117	5,951	5,228
45,900	45,950	5,962	5,123	5,962	5,234
45,950	46,000	5,973	5,129	5,973	5,240
46,000					
46,000	46,050	5,984	5,135	5,984	5,246
46,050	46,100	5,995	5,141	5,995	5,252
46,100	46,150	6,006	5,147	6,006	5,258
46,150	46,200	6,017	5,153	6,017	5,264
46,200	46,250	6,028	5,159	6,028	5,270
46,250	46,300	6,039	5,165	6,039	5,276
46,300	46,350	6,050	5,171	6,050	5,282
46,350	46,400	6,061	5,177	6,061	5,288
46,400	46,450	6,072	5,183	6,072	5,294
46,450	46,500	6,083	5,189	6,083	5,300
46,500	46,550	6,094	5,195	6,094	5,306
46,550	46,600	6,105	5,201	6,105	5,312
46,600	46,650	6,116	5,207	6,116	5,318
46,650	46,700	6,127	5,213	6,127	5,324
46,700	46,750	6,138	5,219	6,138	5,330
46,750	46,800	6,149	5,225	6,149	5,336
46,800	46,850	6,160	5,231	6,160	5,342
46,850	46,900	6,171	5,237	6,171	5,348
46,900	46,950	6,182	5,243	6,182	5,354
46,950	47,000	6,193	5,249	6,193	5,360
47,000					
47,000	47,050	6,204	5,255	6,204	5,366
47,050	47,100	6,215	5,261	6,215	5,372
47,100	47,150	6,226	5,267	6,226	5,378
47,150	47,200	6,237	5,273	6,237	5,384
47,200	47,250	6,248	5,279	6,248	5,390
47,250	47,300	6,259	5,285	6,259	5,396
47,300	47,350	6,270	5,291	6,270	5,402
47,350	47,400	6,281	5,297	6,281	5,408
47,400	47,450	6,292	5,303	6,292	5,414
47,450	47,500	6,303	5,309	6,303	5,420
47,500	47,550	6,314	5,315	6,314	5,426
47,550	47,600	6,325	5,321	6,325	5,432
47,600	47,650	6,336	5,327	6,336	5,438
47,650	47,700	6,347	5,333	6,347	5,444
47,700	47,750	6,358	5,339	6,358	5,450
47,750	47,800	6,369	5,345	6,369	5,456
47,800	47,850	6,380	5,351	6,380	5,462
47,850	47,900	6,391	5,357	6,391	5,468
47,900	47,950	6,402	5,363	6,402	5,474
47,950	48,000	6,413	5,369	6,413	5,480

* This column must also be used by a qualifying widow(er).

(Continued)

- 67 - *Need more information or forms? Visit IRS.gov.*

¶25

2019 Tax Table — *Continued*

48,000 – 50,000

If line 11b (taxable income) is—		And you are—			
At least	But less than	Single	Married filing jointly *	Married filing separately	Head of a household
		Your tax is—			
48,000	48,050	6,424	5,375	6,424	5,486
48,050	48,100	6,435	5,381	6,435	5,492
48,100	48,150	6,446	5,387	6,446	5,498
48,150	48,200	6,457	5,393	6,457	5,504
48,200	48,250	6,468	5,399	6,468	5,510
48,250	48,300	6,479	5,405	6,479	5,516
48,300	48,350	6,490	5,411	6,490	5,522
48,350	48,400	6,501	5,417	6,501	5,528
48,400	48,450	6,512	5,423	6,512	5,534
48,450	48,500	6,523	5,429	6,523	5,540
48,500	48,550	6,534	5,435	6,534	5,546
48,550	48,600	6,545	5,441	6,545	5,552
48,600	48,650	6,556	5,447	6,556	5,558
48,650	48,700	6,567	5,453	6,567	5,564
48,700	48,750	6,578	5,459	6,578	5,570
48,750	48,800	6,589	5,465	6,589	5,576
48,800	48,850	6,600	5,471	6,600	5,582
48,850	48,900	6,611	5,477	6,611	5,588
48,900	48,950	6,622	5,483	6,622	5,594
48,950	49,000	6,633	5,489	6,633	5,600
49,000	49,050	6,644	5,495	6,644	5,606
49,050	49,100	6,655	5,501	6,655	5,612
49,100	49,150	6,666	5,507	6,666	5,618
49,150	49,200	6,677	5,513	6,677	5,624
49,200	49,250	6,688	5,519	6,688	5,630
49,250	49,300	6,699	5,525	6,699	5,636
49,300	49,350	6,710	5,531	6,710	5,642
49,350	49,400	6,721	5,537	6,721	5,648
49,400	49,450	6,732	5,543	6,732	5,654
49,450	49,500	6,743	5,549	6,743	5,660
49,500	49,550	6,754	5,555	6,754	5,666
49,550	49,600	6,765	5,561	6,765	5,672
49,600	49,650	6,776	5,567	6,776	5,678
49,650	49,700	6,787	5,573	6,787	5,684
49,700	49,750	6,798	5,579	6,798	5,690
49,750	49,800	6,809	5,585	6,809	5,696
49,800	49,850	6,820	5,591	6,820	5,702
49,850	49,900	6,831	5,597	6,831	5,708
49,900	49,950	6,842	5,603	6,842	5,714
49,950	50,000	6,853	5,609	6,853	5,720
50,000	50,050	6,864	5,615	6,864	5,726
50,050	50,100	6,875	5,621	6,875	5,732
50,100	50,150	6,886	5,627	6,886	5,738
50,150	50,200	6,897	5,633	6,897	5,744
50,200	50,250	6,908	5,639	6,908	5,750
50,250	50,300	6,919	5,645	6,919	5,756
50,300	50,350	6,930	5,651	6,930	5,762
50,350	50,400	6,941	5,657	6,941	5,768
50,400	50,450	6,952	5,663	6,952	5,774
50,450	50,500	6,963	5,669	6,963	5,780
50,500	50,550	6,974	5,675	6,974	5,786
50,550	50,600	6,985	5,681	6,985	5,792
50,600	50,650	6,996	5,687	6,996	5,798
50,650	50,700	7,007	5,693	7,007	5,804
50,700	50,750	7,018	5,699	7,018	5,810
50,750	50,800	7,029	5,705	7,029	5,816
50,800	50,850	7,040	5,711	7,040	5,822
50,850	50,900	7,051	5,717	7,051	5,828
50,900	50,950	7,062	5,723	7,062	5,834
50,950	51,000	7,073	5,729	7,073	5,840

51,000 – 53,000

If line 11b (taxable income) is—		And you are—			
At least	But less than	Single	Married filing jointly *	Married filing separately	Head of a household
		Your tax is—			
51,000	51,050	7,084	5,735	7,084	5,846
51,050	51,100	7,095	5,741	7,095	5,852
51,100	51,150	7,106	5,747	7,106	5,858
51,150	51,200	7,117	5,753	7,117	5,864
51,200	51,250	7,128	5,759	7,128	5,870
51,250	51,300	7,139	5,765	7,139	5,876
51,300	51,350	7,150	5,771	7,150	5,882
51,350	51,400	7,161	5,777	7,161	5,888
51,400	51,450	7,172	5,783	7,172	5,894
51,450	51,500	7,183	5,789	7,183	5,900
51,500	51,550	7,194	5,795	7,194	5,906
51,550	51,600	7,205	5,801	7,205	5,912
51,600	51,650	7,216	5,807	7,216	5,918
51,650	51,700	7,227	5,813	7,227	5,924
51,700	51,750	7,238	5,819	7,238	5,930
51,750	51,800	7,249	5,825	7,249	5,936
51,800	51,850	7,260	5,831	7,260	5,942
51,850	51,900	7,271	5,837	7,271	5,948
51,900	51,950	7,282	5,843	7,282	5,954
51,950	52,000	7,293	5,849	7,293	5,960
52,000	52,050	7,304	5,855	7,304	5,966
52,050	52,100	7,315	5,861	7,315	5,972
52,100	52,150	7,326	5,867	7,326	5,978
52,150	52,200	7,337	5,873	7,337	5,984
52,200	52,250	7,348	5,879	7,348	5,990
52,250	52,300	7,359	5,885	7,359	5,996
52,300	52,350	7,370	5,891	7,370	6,002
52,350	52,400	7,381	5,897	7,381	6,008
52,400	52,450	7,392	5,903	7,392	6,014
52,450	52,500	7,403	5,909	7,403	6,020
52,500	52,550	7,414	5,915	7,414	6,026
52,550	52,600	7,425	5,921	7,425	6,032
52,600	52,650	7,436	5,927	7,436	6,038
52,650	52,700	7,447	5,933	7,447	6,044
52,700	52,750	7,458	5,939	7,458	6,050
52,750	52,800	7,469	5,945	7,469	6,056
52,800	52,850	7,480	5,951	7,480	6,062
52,850	52,900	7,491	5,957	7,491	6,071
52,900	52,950	7,502	5,963	7,502	6,082
52,950	53,000	7,513	5,969	7,513	6,093
53,000	53,050	7,524	5,975	7,524	6,104
53,050	53,100	7,535	5,981	7,535	6,115
53,100	53,150	7,546	5,987	7,546	6,126
53,150	53,200	7,557	5,993	7,557	6,137
53,200	53,250	7,568	5,999	7,568	6,148
53,250	53,300	7,579	6,005	7,579	6,159
53,300	53,350	7,590	6,011	7,590	6,170
53,350	53,400	7,601	6,017	7,601	6,181
53,400	53,450	7,612	6,023	7,612	6,192
53,450	53,500	7,623	6,029	7,623	6,203
53,500	53,550	7,634	6,035	7,634	6,214
53,550	53,600	7,645	6,041	7,645	6,225
53,600	53,650	7,656	6,047	7,656	6,236
53,650	53,700	7,667	6,053	7,667	6,247
53,700	53,750	7,678	6,059	7,678	6,258
53,750	53,800	7,689	6,065	7,689	6,269
53,800	53,850	7,700	6,071	7,700	6,280
53,850	53,900	7,711	6,077	7,711	6,291
53,900	53,950	7,722	6,083	7,722	6,302
53,950	54,000	7,733	6,089	7,733	6,313

54,000 – 56,000

If line 11b (taxable income) is—		And you are—			
At least	But less than	Single	Married filing jointly *	Married filing separately	Head of a household
		Your tax is—			
54,000	54,050	7,744	6,095	7,744	6,324
54,050	54,100	7,755	6,101	7,755	6,335
54,100	54,150	7,766	6,107	7,766	6,346
54,150	54,200	7,777	6,113	7,777	6,357
54,200	54,250	7,788	6,119	7,788	6,368
54,250	54,300	7,799	6,125	7,799	6,379
54,300	54,350	7,810	6,131	7,810	6,390
54,350	54,400	7,821	6,137	7,821	6,401
54,400	54,450	7,832	6,143	7,832	6,412
54,450	54,500	7,843	6,149	7,843	6,423
54,500	54,550	7,854	6,155	7,854	6,434
54,550	54,600	7,865	6,161	7,865	6,445
54,600	54,650	7,876	6,167	7,876	6,456
54,650	54,700	7,887	6,173	7,887	6,467
54,700	54,750	7,898	6,179	7,898	6,478
54,750	54,800	7,909	6,185	7,909	6,489
54,800	54,850	7,920	6,191	7,920	6,500
54,850	54,900	7,931	6,197	7,931	6,511
54,900	54,950	7,942	6,203	7,942	6,522
54,950	55,000	7,953	6,209	7,953	6,533
55,000	55,050	7,964	6,215	7,964	6,544
55,050	55,100	7,975	6,221	7,975	6,555
55,100	55,150	7,986	6,227	7,986	6,566
55,150	55,200	7,997	6,233	7,997	6,577
55,200	55,250	8,008	6,239	8,008	6,588
55,250	55,300	8,019	6,245	8,019	6,599
55,300	55,350	8,030	6,251	8,030	6,610
55,350	55,400	8,041	6,257	8,041	6,621
55,400	55,450	8,052	6,263	8,052	6,632
55,450	55,500	8,063	6,269	8,063	6,643
55,500	55,550	8,074	6,275	8,074	6,654
55,550	55,600	8,085	6,281	8,085	6,665
55,600	55,650	8,096	6,287	8,096	6,676
55,650	55,700	8,107	6,293	8,107	6,687
55,700	55,750	8,118	6,299	8,118	6,698
55,750	55,800	8,129	6,305	8,129	6,709
55,800	55,850	8,140	6,311	8,140	6,720
55,850	55,900	8,151	6,317	8,151	6,731
55,900	55,950	8,162	6,323	8,162	6,742
55,950	56,000	8,173	6,329	8,173	6,753
56,000	56,050	8,184	6,335	8,184	6,764
56,050	56,100	8,195	6,341	8,195	6,775
56,100	56,150	8,206	6,347	8,206	6,786
56,150	56,200	8,217	6,353	8,217	6,797
56,200	56,250	8,228	6,359	8,228	6,808
56,250	56,300	8,239	6,365	8,239	6,819
56,300	56,350	8,250	6,371	8,250	6,830
56,350	56,400	8,261	6,377	8,261	6,841
56,400	56,450	8,272	6,383	8,272	6,852
56,450	56,500	8,283	6,389	8,283	6,863
56,500	56,550	8,294	6,395	8,294	6,874
56,550	56,600	8,305	6,401	8,305	6,885
56,600	56,650	8,316	6,407	8,316	6,896
56,650	56,700	8,327	6,413	8,327	6,907
56,700	56,750	8,338	6,419	8,338	6,918
56,750	56,800	8,349	6,425	8,349	6,929
56,800	56,850	8,360	6,431	8,360	6,940
56,850	56,900	8,371	6,437	8,371	6,951
56,900	56,950	8,382	6,443	8,382	6,962
56,950	57,000	8,393	6,449	8,393	6,973

(Continued)

* This column must also be used by a qualifying widow(er).

¶25

2019 Tax Table — *Continued*

If line 11b (taxable income) is— At least	But less than	And you are— Single	Married filing jointly *	Married filing separately	Head of a household
		Your tax is—			
57,000					
57,000	57,050	8,404	6,455	8,404	6,984
57,050	57,100	8,415	6,461	8,415	6,995
57,100	57,150	8,426	6,467	8,426	7,006
57,150	57,200	8,437	6,473	8,437	7,017
57,200	57,250	8,448	6,479	8,448	7,028
57,250	57,300	8,459	6,485	8,459	7,039
57,300	57,350	8,470	6,491	8,470	7,050
57,350	57,400	8,481	6,497	8,481	7,061
57,400	57,450	8,492	6,503	8,492	7,072
57,450	57,500	8,503	6,509	8,503	7,083
57,500	57,550	8,514	6,515	8,514	7,094
57,550	57,600	8,525	6,521	8,525	7,105
57,600	57,650	8,536	6,527	8,536	7,116
57,650	57,700	8,547	6,533	8,547	7,127
57,700	57,750	8,558	6,539	8,558	7,138
57,750	57,800	8,569	6,545	8,569	7,149
57,800	57,850	8,580	6,551	8,580	7,160
57,850	57,900	8,591	6,557	8,591	7,171
57,900	57,950	8,602	6,563	8,602	7,182
57,950	58,000	8,613	6,569	8,613	7,193
58,000					
58,000	58,050	8,624	6,575	8,624	7,204
58,050	58,100	8,635	6,581	8,635	7,215
58,100	58,150	8,646	6,587	8,646	7,226
58,150	58,200	8,657	6,593	8,657	7,237
58,200	58,250	8,668	6,599	8,668	7,248
58,250	58,300	8,679	6,605	8,679	7,259
58,300	58,350	8,690	6,611	8,690	7,270
58,350	58,400	8,701	6,617	8,701	7,281
58,400	58,450	8,712	6,623	8,712	7,292
58,450	58,500	8,723	6,629	8,723	7,303
58,500	58,550	8,734	6,635	8,734	7,314
58,550	58,600	8,745	6,641	8,745	7,325
58,600	58,650	8,756	6,647	8,756	7,336
58,650	58,700	8,767	6,653	8,767	7,347
58,700	58,750	8,778	6,659	8,778	7,358
58,750	58,800	8,789	6,665	8,789	7,369
58,800	58,850	8,800	6,671	8,800	7,380
58,850	58,900	8,811	6,677	8,811	7,391
58,900	58,950	8,822	6,683	8,822	7,402
58,950	59,000	8,833	6,689	8,833	7,413
59,000					
59,000	59,050	8,844	6,695	8,844	7,424
59,050	59,100	8,855	6,701	8,855	7,435
59,100	59,150	8,866	6,707	8,866	7,446
59,150	59,200	8,877	6,713	8,877	7,457
59,200	59,250	8,888	6,719	8,888	7,468
59,250	59,300	8,899	6,725	8,899	7,479
59,300	59,350	8,910	6,731	8,910	7,490
59,350	59,400	8,921	6,737	8,921	7,501
59,400	59,450	8,932	6,743	8,932	7,512
59,450	59,500	8,943	6,749	8,943	7,523
59,500	59,550	8,954	6,755	8,954	7,534
59,550	59,600	8,965	6,761	8,965	7,545
59,600	59,650	8,976	6,767	8,976	7,556
59,650	59,700	8,987	6,773	8,987	7,567
59,700	59,750	8,998	6,779	8,998	7,578
59,750	59,800	9,009	6,785	9,009	7,589
59,800	59,850	9,020	6,791	9,020	7,600
59,850	59,900	9,031	6,797	9,031	7,611
59,900	59,950	9,042	6,803	9,042	7,622
59,950	60,000	9,053	6,809	9,053	7,633
60,000					
60,000	60,050	9,064	6,815	9,064	7,644
60,050	60,100	9,075	6,821	9,075	7,655
60,100	60,150	9,086	6,827	9,086	7,666
60,150	60,200	9,097	6,833	9,097	7,677
60,200	60,250	9,108	6,839	9,108	7,688
60,250	60,300	9,119	6,845	9,119	7,699
60,300	60,350	9,130	6,851	9,130	7,710
60,350	60,400	9,141	6,857	9,141	7,721
60,400	60,450	9,152	6,863	9,152	7,732
60,450	60,500	9,163	6,869	9,163	7,743
60,500	60,550	9,174	6,875	9,174	7,754
60,550	60,600	9,185	6,881	9,185	7,765
60,600	60,650	9,196	6,887	9,196	7,776
60,650	60,700	9,207	6,893	9,207	7,787
60,700	60,750	9,218	6,899	9,218	7,798
60,750	60,800	9,229	6,905	9,229	7,809
60,800	60,850	9,240	6,911	9,240	7,820
60,850	60,900	9,251	6,917	9,251	7,831
60,900	60,950	9,262	6,923	9,262	7,842
60,950	61,000	9,273	6,929	9,273	7,853
61,000					
61,000	61,050	9,284	6,935	9,284	7,864
61,050	61,100	9,295	6,941	9,295	7,875
61,100	61,150	9,306	6,947	9,306	7,886
61,150	61,200	9,317	6,953	9,317	7,897
61,200	61,250	9,328	6,959	9,328	7,908
61,250	61,300	9,339	6,965	9,339	7,919
61,300	61,350	9,350	6,971	9,350	7,930
61,350	61,400	9,361	6,977	9,361	7,941
61,400	61,450	9,372	6,983	9,372	7,952
61,450	61,500	9,383	6,989	9,383	7,963
61,500	61,550	9,394	6,995	9,394	7,974
61,550	61,600	9,405	7,001	9,405	7,985
61,600	61,650	9,416	7,007	9,416	7,996
61,650	61,700	9,427	7,013	9,427	8,007
61,700	61,750	9,438	7,019	9,438	8,018
61,750	61,800	9,449	7,025	9,449	8,029
61,800	61,850	9,460	7,031	9,460	8,040
61,850	61,900	9,471	7,037	9,471	8,051
61,900	61,950	9,482	7,043	9,482	8,062
61,950	62,000	9,493	7,049	9,493	8,073
62,000					
62,000	62,050	9,504	7,055	9,504	8,084
62,050	62,100	9,515	7,061	9,515	8,095
62,100	62,150	9,526	7,067	9,526	8,106
62,150	62,200	9,537	7,073	9,537	8,117
62,200	62,250	9,548	7,079	9,548	8,128
62,250	62,300	9,559	7,085	9,559	8,139
62,300	62,350	9,570	7,091	9,570	8,150
62,350	62,400	9,581	7,097	9,581	8,161
62,400	62,450	9,592	7,103	9,592	8,172
62,450	62,500	9,603	7,109	9,603	8,183
62,500	62,550	9,614	7,115	9,614	8,194
62,550	62,600	9,625	7,121	9,625	8,205
62,600	62,650	9,636	7,127	9,636	8,216
62,650	62,700	9,647	7,133	9,647	8,227
62,700	62,750	9,658	7,139	9,658	8,238
62,750	62,800	9,669	7,145	9,669	8,249
62,800	62,850	9,680	7,151	9,680	8,260
62,850	62,900	9,691	7,157	9,691	8,271
62,900	62,950	9,702	7,163	9,702	8,282
62,950	63,000	9,713	7,169	9,713	8,293
63,000					
63,000	63,050	9,724	7,175	9,724	8,304
63,050	63,100	9,735	7,181	9,735	8,315
63,100	63,150	9,746	7,187	9,746	8,326
63,150	63,200	9,757	7,193	9,757	8,337
63,200	63,250	9,768	7,199	9,768	8,348
63,250	63,300	9,779	7,205	9,779	8,359
63,300	63,350	9,790	7,211	9,790	8,370
63,350	63,400	9,801	7,217	9,801	8,381
63,400	63,450	9,812	7,223	9,812	8,392
63,450	63,500	9,823	7,229	9,823	8,403
63,500	63,550	9,834	7,235	9,834	8,414
63,550	63,600	9,845	7,241	9,845	8,425
63,600	63,650	9,856	7,247	9,856	8,436
63,650	63,700	9,867	7,253	9,867	8,447
63,700	63,750	9,878	7,259	9,878	8,458
63,750	63,800	9,889	7,265	9,889	8,469
63,800	63,850	9,900	7,271	9,900	8,480
63,850	63,900	9,911	7,277	9,911	8,491
63,900	63,950	9,922	7,283	9,922	8,502
63,950	64,000	9,933	7,289	9,933	8,513
64,000					
64,000	64,050	9,944	7,295	9,944	8,524
64,050	64,100	9,955	7,301	9,955	8,535
64,100	64,150	9,966	7,307	9,966	8,546
64,150	64,200	9,977	7,313	9,977	8,557
64,200	64,250	9,988	7,319	9,988	8,568
64,250	64,300	9,999	7,325	9,999	8,579
64,300	64,350	10,010	7,331	10,010	8,590
64,350	64,400	10,021	7,337	10,021	8,601
64,400	64,450	10,032	7,343	10,032	8,612
64,450	64,500	10,043	7,349	10,043	8,623
64,500	64,550	10,054	7,355	10,054	8,634
64,550	64,600	10,065	7,361	10,065	8,645
64,600	64,650	10,076	7,367	10,076	8,656
64,650	64,700	10,087	7,373	10,087	8,667
64,700	64,750	10,098	7,379	10,098	8,678
64,750	64,800	10,109	7,385	10,109	8,689
64,800	64,850	10,120	7,391	10,120	8,700
64,850	64,900	10,131	7,397	10,131	8,711
64,900	64,950	10,142	7,403	10,142	8,722
64,950	65,000	10,153	7,409	10,153	8,733
65,000					
65,000	65,050	10,164	7,415	10,164	8,744
65,050	65,100	10,175	7,421	10,175	8,755
65,100	65,150	10,186	7,427	10,186	8,766
65,150	65,200	10,197	7,433	10,197	8,777
65,200	65,250	10,208	7,439	10,208	8,788
65,250	65,300	10,219	7,445	10,219	8,799
65,300	65,350	10,230	7,451	10,230	8,810
65,350	65,400	10,241	7,457	10,241	8,821
65,400	65,450	10,252	7,463	10,252	8,832
65,450	65,500	10,263	7,469	10,263	8,843
65,500	65,550	10,274	7,475	10,274	8,854
65,550	65,600	10,285	7,481	10,285	8,865
65,600	65,650	10,296	7,487	10,296	8,876
65,650	65,700	10,307	7,493	10,307	8,887
65,700	65,750	10,318	7,499	10,318	8,898
65,750	65,800	10,329	7,505	10,329	8,909
65,800	65,850	10,340	7,511	10,340	8,920
65,850	65,900	10,351	7,517	10,351	8,931
65,900	65,950	10,362	7,523	10,362	8,942
65,950	66,000	10,373	7,529	10,373	8,953

(Continued)

* This column must also be used by a qualifying widow(er).

Need more information or forms? Visit IRS.gov.

2019 Tax Table — *Continued*

66,000

At least	But less than	Single	Married filing jointly *	Married filing separately	Head of a household
66,000	66,050	10,384	7,535	10,384	8,964
66,050	66,100	10,395	7,541	10,395	8,975
66,100	66,150	10,406	7,547	10,406	8,986
66,150	66,200	10,417	7,553	10,417	8,997
66,200	66,250	10,428	7,559	10,428	9,008
66,250	66,300	10,439	7,565	10,439	9,019
66,300	66,350	10,450	7,571	10,450	9,030
66,350	66,400	10,461	7,577	10,461	9,041
66,400	66,450	10,472	7,583	10,472	9,052
66,450	66,500	10,483	7,589	10,483	9,063
66,500	66,550	10,494	7,595	10,494	9,074
66,550	66,600	10,505	7,601	10,505	9,085
66,600	66,650	10,516	7,607	10,516	9,096
66,650	66,700	10,527	7,613	10,527	9,107
66,700	66,750	10,538	7,619	10,538	9,118
66,750	66,800	10,549	7,625	10,549	9,129
66,800	66,850	10,560	7,631	10,560	9,140
66,850	66,900	10,571	7,637	10,571	9,151
66,900	66,950	10,582	7,643	10,582	9,162
66,950	67,000	10,593	7,649	10,593	9,173

67,000

At least	But less than	Single	Married filing jointly *	Married filing separately	Head of a household
67,000	67,050	10,604	7,655	10,604	9,184
67,050	67,100	10,615	7,661	10,615	9,195
67,100	67,150	10,626	7,667	10,626	9,206
67,150	67,200	10,637	7,673	10,637	9,217
67,200	67,250	10,648	7,679	10,648	9,228
67,250	67,300	10,659	7,685	10,659	9,239
67,300	67,350	10,670	7,691	10,670	9,250
67,350	67,400	10,681	7,697	10,681	9,261
67,400	67,450	10,692	7,703	10,692	9,272
67,450	67,500	10,703	7,709	10,703	9,283
67,500	67,550	10,714	7,715	10,714	9,294
67,550	67,600	10,725	7,721	10,725	9,305
67,600	67,650	10,736	7,727	10,736	9,316
67,650	67,700	10,747	7,733	10,747	9,327
67,700	67,750	10,758	7,739	10,758	9,338
67,750	67,800	10,769	7,745	10,769	9,349
67,800	67,850	10,780	7,751	10,780	9,360
67,850	67,900	10,791	7,757	10,791	9,371
67,900	67,950	10,802	7,763	10,802	9,382
67,950	68,000	10,813	7,769	10,813	9,393

68,000

At least	But less than	Single	Married filing jointly *	Married filing separately	Head of a household
68,000	68,050	10,824	7,775	10,824	9,404
68,050	68,100	10,835	7,781	10,835	9,415
68,100	68,150	10,846	7,787	10,846	9,426
68,150	68,200	10,857	7,793	10,857	9,437
68,200	68,250	10,868	7,799	10,868	9,448
68,250	68,300	10,879	7,805	10,879	9,459
68,300	68,350	10,890	7,811	10,890	9,470
68,350	68,400	10,901	7,817	10,901	9,481
68,400	68,450	10,912	7,823	10,912	9,492
68,450	68,500	10,923	7,829	10,923	9,503
68,500	68,550	10,934	7,835	10,934	9,514
68,550	68,600	10,945	7,841	10,945	9,525
68,600	68,650	10,956	7,847	10,956	9,536
68,650	68,700	10,967	7,853	10,967	9,547
68,700	68,750	10,978	7,859	10,978	9,558
68,750	68,800	10,989	7,865	10,989	9,569
68,800	68,850	11,000	7,871	11,000	9,580
68,850	68,900	11,011	7,877	11,011	9,591
68,900	68,950	11,022	7,883	11,022	9,602
68,950	69,000	11,033	7,889	11,033	9,613

69,000

At least	But less than	Single	Married filing jointly *	Married filing separately	Head of a household
69,000	69,050	11,044	7,895	11,044	9,624
69,050	69,100	11,055	7,901	11,055	9,635
69,100	69,150	11,066	7,907	11,066	9,646
69,150	69,200	11,077	7,913	11,077	9,657
69,200	69,250	11,088	7,919	11,088	9,668
69,250	69,300	11,099	7,925	11,099	9,679
69,300	69,350	11,110	7,931	11,110	9,690
69,350	69,400	11,121	7,937	11,121	9,701
69,400	69,450	11,132	7,943	11,132	9,712
69,450	69,500	11,143	7,949	11,143	9,723
69,500	69,550	11,154	7,955	11,154	9,734
69,550	69,600	11,165	7,961	11,165	9,745
69,600	69,650	11,176	7,967	11,176	9,756
69,650	69,700	11,187	7,973	11,187	9,767
69,700	69,750	11,198	7,979	11,198	9,778
69,750	69,800	11,209	7,985	11,209	9,789
69,800	69,850	11,220	7,991	11,220	9,800
69,850	69,900	11,231	7,997	11,231	9,811
69,900	69,950	11,242	8,003	11,242	9,822
69,950	70,000	11,253	8,009	11,253	9,833

70,000

At least	But less than	Single	Married filing jointly *	Married filing separately	Head of a household
70,000	70,050	11,264	8,015	11,264	9,844
70,050	70,100	11,275	8,021	11,275	9,855
70,100	70,150	11,286	8,027	11,286	9,866
70,150	70,200	11,297	8,033	11,297	9,877
70,200	70,250	11,308	8,039	11,308	9,888
70,250	70,300	11,319	8,045	11,319	9,899
70,300	70,350	11,330	8,051	11,330	9,910
70,350	70,400	11,341	8,057	11,341	9,921
70,400	70,450	11,352	8,063	11,352	9,932
70,450	70,500	11,363	8,069	11,363	9,943
70,500	70,550	11,374	8,075	11,374	9,954
70,550	70,600	11,385	8,081	11,385	9,965
70,600	70,650	11,396	8,087	11,396	9,976
70,650	70,700	11,407	8,093	11,407	9,987
70,700	70,750	11,418	8,099	11,418	9,998
70,750	70,800	11,429	8,105	11,429	10,009
70,800	70,850	11,440	8,111	11,440	10,020
70,850	70,900	11,451	8,117	11,451	10,031
70,900	70,950	11,462	8,123	11,462	10,042
70,950	71,000	11,473	8,129	11,473	10,053

71,000

At least	But less than	Single	Married filing jointly *	Married filing separately	Head of a household
71,000	71,050	11,484	8,135	11,484	10,064
71,050	71,100	11,495	8,141	11,495	10,075
71,100	71,150	11,506	8,147	11,506	10,086
71,150	71,200	11,517	8,153	11,517	10,097
71,200	71,250	11,528	8,159	11,528	10,108
71,250	71,300	11,539	8,165	11,539	10,119
71,300	71,350	11,550	8,171	11,550	10,130
71,350	71,400	11,561	8,177	11,561	10,141
71,400	71,450	11,572	8,183	11,572	10,152
71,450	71,500	11,583	8,189	11,583	10,163
71,500	71,550	11,594	8,195	11,594	10,174
71,550	71,600	11,605	8,201	11,605	10,185
71,600	71,650	11,616	8,207	11,616	10,196
71,650	71,700	11,627	8,213	11,627	10,207
71,700	71,750	11,638	8,219	11,638	10,218
71,750	71,800	11,649	8,225	11,649	10,229
71,800	71,850	11,660	8,231	11,660	10,240
71,850	71,900	11,671	8,237	11,671	10,251
71,900	71,950	11,682	8,243	11,682	10,262
71,950	72,000	11,693	8,249	11,693	10,273

72,000

At least	But less than	Single	Married filing jointly *	Married filing separately	Head of a household
72,000	72,050	11,704	8,255	11,704	10,284
72,050	72,100	11,715	8,261	11,715	10,295
72,100	72,150	11,726	8,267	11,726	10,306
72,150	72,200	11,737	8,273	11,737	10,317
72,200	72,250	11,748	8,279	11,748	10,328
72,250	72,300	11,759	8,285	11,759	10,339
72,300	72,350	11,770	8,291	11,770	10,350
72,350	72,400	11,781	8,297	11,781	10,361
72,400	72,450	11,792	8,303	11,792	10,372
72,450	72,500	11,803	8,309	11,803	10,383
72,500	72,550	11,814	8,315	11,814	10,394
72,550	72,600	11,825	8,321	11,825	10,405
72,600	72,650	11,836	8,327	11,836	10,416
72,650	72,700	11,847	8,333	11,847	10,427
72,700	72,750	11,858	8,339	11,858	10,438
72,750	72,800	11,869	8,345	11,869	10,449
72,800	72,850	11,880	8,351	11,880	10,460
72,850	72,900	11,891	8,357	11,891	10,471
72,900	72,950	11,902	8,363	11,902	10,482
72,950	73,000	11,913	8,369	11,913	10,493

73,000

At least	But less than	Single	Married filing jointly *	Married filing separately	Head of a household
73,000	73,050	11,924	8,375	11,924	10,504
73,050	73,100	11,935	8,381	11,935	10,515
73,100	73,150	11,946	8,387	11,946	10,526
73,150	73,200	11,957	8,393	11,957	10,537
73,200	73,250	11,968	8,399	11,968	10,548
73,250	73,300	11,979	8,405	11,979	10,559
73,300	73,350	11,990	8,411	11,990	10,570
73,350	73,400	12,001	8,417	12,001	10,581
73,400	73,450	12,012	8,423	12,012	10,592
73,450	73,500	12,023	8,429	12,023	10,603
73,500	73,550	12,034	8,435	12,034	10,614
73,550	73,600	12,045	8,441	12,045	10,625
73,600	73,650	12,056	8,447	12,056	10,636
73,650	73,700	12,067	8,453	12,067	10,647
73,700	73,750	12,078	8,459	12,078	10,658
73,750	73,800	12,089	8,465	12,089	10,669
73,800	73,850	12,100	8,471	12,100	10,680
73,850	73,900	12,111	8,477	12,111	10,691
73,900	73,950	12,122	8,483	12,122	10,702
73,950	74,000	12,133	8,489	12,133	10,713

74,000

At least	But less than	Single	Married filing jointly *	Married filing separately	Head of a household
74,000	74,050	12,144	8,495	12,144	10,724
74,050	74,100	12,155	8,501	12,155	10,735
74,100	74,150	12,166	8,507	12,166	10,746
74,150	74,200	12,177	8,513	12,177	10,757
74,200	74,250	12,188	8,519	12,188	10,768
74,250	74,300	12,199	8,525	12,199	10,779
74,300	74,350	12,210	8,531	12,210	10,790
74,350	74,400	12,221	8,537	12,221	10,801
74,400	74,450	12,232	8,543	12,232	10,812
74,450	74,500	12,243	8,549	12,243	10,823
74,500	74,550	12,254	8,555	12,254	10,834
74,550	74,600	12,265	8,561	12,265	10,845
74,600	74,650	12,276	8,567	12,276	10,856
74,650	74,700	12,287	8,573	12,287	10,867
74,700	74,750	12,298	8,579	12,298	10,878
74,750	74,800	12,309	8,585	12,309	10,889
74,800	74,850	12,320	8,591	12,320	10,900
74,850	74,900	12,331	8,597	12,331	10,911
74,900	74,950	12,342	8,603	12,342	10,922
74,950	75,000	12,353	8,609	12,353	10,933

Your tax is— applies to the Single / Married filing jointly * / Married filing separately / Head of a household columns.

(Continued)

* This column must also be used by a qualifying widow(er).

Need more information or forms? Visit IRS.gov.　　- 70 -

¶25

2019 Tax Table — *Continued*

If line 11b (taxable income) is—		And you are—			
At least	But less than	Single	Married filing jointly *	Married filing separately	Head of a household
		Your tax is—			

75,000

At least	But less than	Single	Married filing jointly *	Married filing separately	Head of a household
75,000	75,050	12,364	8,615	12,364	10,944
75,050	75,100	12,375	8,621	12,375	10,955
75,100	75,150	12,386	8,627	12,386	10,966
75,150	75,200	12,397	8,633	12,397	10,977
75,200	75,250	12,408	8,639	12,408	10,988
75,250	75,300	12,419	8,645	12,419	10,999
75,300	75,350	12,430	8,651	12,430	11,010
75,350	75,400	12,441	8,657	12,441	11,021
75,400	75,450	12,452	8,663	12,452	11,032
75,450	75,500	12,463	8,669	12,463	11,043
75,500	75,550	12,474	8,675	12,474	11,054
75,550	75,600	12,485	8,681	12,485	11,065
75,600	75,650	12,496	8,687	12,496	11,076
75,650	75,700	12,507	8,693	12,507	11,087
75,700	75,750	12,518	8,699	12,518	11,098
75,750	75,800	12,529	8,705	12,529	11,109
75,800	75,850	12,540	8,711	12,540	11,120
75,850	75,900	12,551	8,717	12,551	11,131
75,900	75,950	12,562	8,723	12,562	11,142
75,950	76,000	12,573	8,729	12,573	11,153

76,000

At least	But less than	Single	Married filing jointly *	Married filing separately	Head of a household
76,000	76,050	12,584	8,735	12,584	11,164
76,050	76,100	12,595	8,741	12,595	11,175
76,100	76,150	12,606	8,747	12,606	11,186
76,150	76,200	12,617	8,753	12,617	11,197
76,200	76,250	12,628	8,759	12,628	11,208
76,250	76,300	12,639	8,765	12,639	11,219
76,300	76,350	12,650	8,771	12,650	11,230
76,350	76,400	12,661	8,777	12,661	11,241
76,400	76,450	12,672	8,783	12,672	11,252
76,450	76,500	12,683	8,789	12,683	11,263
76,500	76,550	12,694	8,795	12,694	11,274
76,550	76,600	12,705	8,801	12,705	11,285
76,600	76,650	12,716	8,807	12,716	11,296
76,650	76,700	12,727	8,813	12,727	11,307
76,700	76,750	12,738	8,819	12,738	11,318
76,750	76,800	12,749	8,825	12,749	11,329
76,800	76,850	12,760	8,831	12,760	11,340
76,850	76,900	12,771	8,837	12,771	11,351
76,900	76,950	12,782	8,843	12,782	11,362
76,950	77,000	12,793	8,849	12,793	11,373

77,000

At least	But less than	Single	Married filing jointly *	Married filing separately	Head of a household
77,000	77,050	12,804	8,855	12,804	11,384
77,050	77,100	12,815	8,861	12,815	11,395
77,100	77,150	12,826	8,867	12,826	11,406
77,150	77,200	12,837	8,873	12,837	11,417
77,200	77,250	12,848	8,879	12,848	11,428
77,250	77,300	12,859	8,885	12,859	11,439
77,300	77,350	12,870	8,891	12,870	11,450
77,350	77,400	12,881	8,897	12,881	11,461
77,400	77,450	12,892	8,903	12,892	11,472
77,450	77,500	12,903	8,909	12,903	11,483
77,500	77,550	12,914	8,915	12,914	11,494
77,550	77,600	12,925	8,921	12,925	11,505
77,600	77,650	12,936	8,927	12,936	11,516
77,650	77,700	12,947	8,933	12,947	11,527
77,700	77,750	12,958	8,939	12,958	11,538
77,750	77,800	12,969	8,945	12,969	11,549
77,800	77,850	12,980	8,951	12,980	11,560
77,850	77,900	12,991	8,957	12,991	11,571
77,900	77,950	13,002	8,963	13,002	11,582
77,950	78,000	13,013	8,969	13,013	11,593

78,000

At least	But less than	Single	Married filing jointly *	Married filing separately	Head of a household
78,000	78,050	13,024	8,975	13,024	11,604
78,050	78,100	13,035	8,981	13,035	11,615
78,100	78,150	13,046	8,987	13,046	11,626
78,150	78,200	13,057	8,993	13,057	11,637
78,200	78,250	13,068	8,999	13,068	11,648
78,250	78,300	13,079	9,005	13,079	11,659
78,300	78,350	13,090	9,011	13,090	11,670
78,350	78,400	13,101	9,017	13,101	11,681
78,400	78,450	13,112	9,023	13,112	11,692
78,450	78,500	13,123	9,029	13,123	11,703
78,500	78,550	13,134	9,035	13,134	11,714
78,550	78,600	13,145	9,041	13,145	11,725
78,600	78,650	13,156	9,047	13,156	11,736
78,650	78,700	13,167	9,053	13,167	11,747
78,700	78,750	13,178	9,059	13,178	11,758
78,750	78,800	13,189	9,065	13,189	11,769
78,800	78,850	13,200	9,071	13,200	11,780
78,850	78,900	13,211	9,077	13,211	11,791
78,900	78,950	13,222	9,083	13,222	11,802
78,950	79,000	13,233	9,092	13,233	11,813

79,000

At least	But less than	Single	Married filing jointly *	Married filing separately	Head of a household
79,000	79,050	13,244	9,103	13,244	11,824
79,050	79,100	13,255	9,114	13,255	11,835
79,100	79,150	13,266	9,125	13,266	11,846
79,150	79,200	13,277	9,136	13,277	11,857
79,200	79,250	13,288	9,147	13,288	11,868
79,250	79,300	13,299	9,158	13,299	11,879
79,300	79,350	13,310	9,169	13,310	11,890
79,350	79,400	13,321	9,180	13,321	11,901
79,400	79,450	13,332	9,191	13,332	11,912
79,450	79,500	13,343	9,202	13,343	11,923
79,500	79,550	13,354	9,213	13,354	11,934
79,550	79,600	13,365	9,224	13,365	11,945
79,600	79,650	13,376	9,235	13,376	11,956
79,650	79,700	13,387	9,246	13,387	11,967
79,700	79,750	13,398	9,257	13,398	11,978
79,750	79,800	13,409	9,268	13,409	11,989
79,800	79,850	13,420	9,279	13,420	12,000
79,850	79,900	13,431	9,290	13,431	12,011
79,900	79,950	13,442	9,301	13,442	12,022
79,950	80,000	13,453	9,312	13,453	12,033

80,000

At least	But less than	Single	Married filing jointly *	Married filing separately	Head of a household
80,000	80,050	13,464	9,323	13,464	12,044
80,050	80,100	13,475	9,334	13,475	12,055
80,100	80,150	13,486	9,345	13,486	12,066
80,150	80,200	13,497	9,356	13,497	12,077
80,200	80,250	13,508	9,367	13,508	12,088
80,250	80,300	13,519	9,378	13,519	12,099
80,300	80,350	13,530	9,389	13,530	12,110
80,350	80,400	13,541	9,400	13,541	12,121
80,400	80,450	13,552	9,411	13,552	12,132
80,450	80,500	13,563	9,422	13,563	12,143
80,500	80,550	13,574	9,433	13,574	12,154
80,550	80,600	13,585	9,444	13,585	12,165
80,600	80,650	13,596	9,455	13,596	12,176
80,650	80,700	13,607	9,466	13,607	12,187
80,700	80,750	13,618	9,477	13,618	12,198
80,750	80,800	13,629	9,488	13,629	12,209
80,800	80,850	13,640	9,499	13,640	12,220
80,850	80,900	13,651	9,510	13,651	12,231
80,900	80,950	13,662	9,521	13,662	12,242
80,950	81,000	13,673	9,532	13,673	12,253

81,000

At least	But less than	Single	Married filing jointly *	Married filing separately	Head of a household
81,000	81,050	13,684	9,543	13,684	12,264
81,050	81,100	13,695	9,554	13,695	12,275
81,100	81,150	13,706	9,565	13,706	12,286
81,150	81,200	13,717	9,576	13,717	12,297
81,200	81,250	13,728	9,587	13,728	12,308
81,250	81,300	13,739	9,598	13,739	12,319
81,300	81,350	13,750	9,609	13,750	12,330
81,350	81,400	13,761	9,620	13,761	12,341
81,400	81,450	13,772	9,631	13,772	12,352
81,450	81,500	13,783	9,642	13,783	12,363
81,500	81,550	13,794	9,653	13,794	12,374
81,550	81,600	13,805	9,664	13,805	12,385
81,600	81,650	13,816	9,675	13,816	12,396
81,650	81,700	13,827	9,686	13,827	12,407
81,700	81,750	13,838	9,697	13,838	12,418
81,750	81,800	13,849	9,708	13,849	12,429
81,800	81,850	13,860	9,719	13,860	12,440
81,850	81,900	13,871	9,730	13,871	12,451
81,900	81,950	13,882	9,741	13,882	12,462
81,950	82,000	13,893	9,752	13,893	12,473

82,000

At least	But less than	Single	Married filing jointly *	Married filing separately	Head of a household
82,000	82,050	13,904	9,763	13,904	12,484
82,050	82,100	13,915	9,774	13,915	12,495
82,100	82,150	13,926	9,785	13,926	12,506
82,150	82,200	13,937	9,796	13,937	12,517
82,200	82,250	13,948	9,807	13,948	12,528
82,250	82,300	13,959	9,818	13,959	12,539
82,300	82,350	13,970	9,829	13,970	12,550
82,350	82,400	13,981	9,840	13,981	12,561
82,400	82,450	13,992	9,851	13,992	12,572
82,450	82,500	14,003	9,862	14,003	12,583
82,500	82,550	14,014	9,873	14,014	12,594
82,550	82,600	14,025	9,884	14,025	12,605
82,600	82,650	14,036	9,895	14,036	12,616
82,650	82,700	14,047	9,906	14,047	12,627
82,700	82,750	14,058	9,917	14,058	12,638
82,750	82,800	14,069	9,928	14,069	12,649
82,800	82,850	14,080	9,939	14,080	12,660
82,850	82,900	14,091	9,950	14,091	12,671
82,900	82,950	14,102	9,961	14,102	12,682
82,950	83,000	14,113	9,972	14,113	12,693

83,000

At least	But less than	Single	Married filing jointly *	Married filing separately	Head of a household
83,000	83,050	14,124	9,983	14,124	12,704
83,050	83,100	14,135	9,994	14,135	12,715
83,100	83,150	14,146	10,005	14,146	12,726
83,150	83,200	14,157	10,016	14,157	12,737
83,200	83,250	14,168	10,027	14,168	12,748
83,250	83,300	14,179	10,038	14,179	12,759
83,300	83,350	14,190	10,049	14,190	12,770
83,350	83,400	14,201	10,060	14,201	12,781
83,400	83,450	14,212	10,071	14,212	12,792
83,450	83,500	14,223	10,082	14,223	12,803
83,500	83,550	14,234	10,093	14,234	12,814
83,550	83,600	14,245	10,104	14,245	12,825
83,600	83,650	14,256	10,115	14,256	12,836
83,650	83,700	14,267	10,126	14,267	12,847
83,700	83,750	14,278	10,137	14,278	12,858
83,750	83,800	14,289	10,148	14,289	12,869
83,800	83,850	14,300	10,159	14,300	12,880
83,850	83,900	14,311	10,170	14,311	12,891
83,900	83,950	14,322	10,181	14,322	12,902
83,950	84,000	14,333	10,192	14,333	12,913

(Continued)

* This column must also be used by a qualifying widow(er).

¶25

2019 Tax Table — Continued

84,000 / 85,000 / 86,000

If line 11b (taxable income) is—		And you are—			
At least	But less than	Single	Married filing jointly *	Married filing separately	Head of a household
		Your tax is—			
84,000					
84,000	84,050	14,344	10,203	14,344	12,924
84,050	84,100	14,355	10,214	14,355	12,935
84,100	84,150	14,366	10,225	14,366	12,946
84,150	84,200	14,377	10,236	14,377	12,957
84,200	84,250	14,389	10,247	14,389	12,968
84,250	84,300	14,401	10,258	14,401	12,980
84,300	84,350	14,413	10,269	14,413	12,992
84,350	84,400	14,425	10,280	14,425	13,004
84,400	84,450	14,437	10,291	14,437	13,016
84,450	84,500	14,449	10,302	14,449	13,028
84,500	84,550	14,461	10,313	14,461	13,040
84,550	84,600	14,473	10,324	14,473	13,052
84,600	84,650	14,485	10,335	14,485	13,064
84,650	84,700	14,497	10,346	14,497	13,076
84,700	84,750	14,509	10,357	14,509	13,088
84,750	84,800	14,521	10,368	14,521	13,100
84,800	84,850	14,533	10,379	14,533	13,112
84,850	84,900	14,545	10,390	14,545	13,124
84,900	84,950	14,557	10,401	14,557	13,136
84,950	85,000	14,569	10,412	14,569	13,148
85,000					
85,000	85,050	14,581	10,423	14,581	13,160
85,050	85,100	14,593	10,434	14,593	13,172
85,100	85,150	14,605	10,445	14,605	13,184
85,150	85,200	14,617	10,456	14,617	13,196
85,200	85,250	14,629	10,467	14,629	13,208
85,250	85,300	14,641	10,478	14,641	13,220
85,300	85,350	14,653	10,489	14,653	13,232
85,350	85,400	14,665	10,500	14,665	13,244
85,400	85,450	14,677	10,511	14,677	13,256
85,450	85,500	14,689	10,522	14,689	13,268
85,500	85,550	14,701	10,533	14,701	13,280
85,550	85,600	14,713	10,544	14,713	13,292
85,600	85,650	14,725	10,555	14,725	13,304
85,650	85,700	14,737	10,566	14,737	13,316
85,700	85,750	14,749	10,577	14,749	13,328
85,750	85,800	14,761	10,588	14,761	13,340
85,800	85,850	14,773	10,599	14,773	13,352
85,850	85,900	14,785	10,610	14,785	13,364
85,900	85,950	14,797	10,621	14,797	13,376
85,950	86,000	14,809	10,632	14,809	13,388
86,000					
86,000	86,050	14,821	10,643	14,821	13,400
86,050	86,100	14,833	10,654	14,833	13,412
86,100	86,150	14,845	10,665	14,845	13,424
86,150	86,200	14,857	10,676	14,857	13,436
86,200	86,250	14,869	10,687	14,869	13,448
86,250	86,300	14,881	10,698	14,881	13,460
86,300	86,350	14,893	10,709	14,893	13,472
86,350	86,400	14,905	10,720	14,905	13,484
86,400	86,450	14,917	10,731	14,917	13,496
86,450	86,500	14,929	10,742	14,929	13,508
86,500	86,550	14,941	10,753	14,941	13,520
86,550	86,600	14,953	10,764	14,953	13,532
86,600	86,650	14,965	10,775	14,965	13,544
86,650	86,700	14,977	10,786	14,977	13,556
86,700	86,750	14,989	10,797	14,989	13,568
86,750	86,800	15,001	10,808	15,001	13,580
86,800	86,850	15,013	10,819	15,013	13,592
86,850	86,900	15,025	10,830	15,025	13,604
86,900	86,950	15,037	10,841	15,037	13,616
86,950	87,000	15,049	10,852	15,049	13,628

87,000 / 88,000 / 89,000

If line 11b (taxable income) is—		And you are—			
At least	But less than	Single	Married filing jointly *	Married filing separately	Head of a household
		Your tax is—			
87,000					
87,000	87,050	15,061	10,863	15,061	13,640
87,050	87,100	15,073	10,874	15,073	13,652
87,100	87,150	15,085	10,885	15,085	13,664
87,150	87,200	15,097	10,896	15,097	13,676
87,200	87,250	15,109	10,907	15,109	13,688
87,250	87,300	15,121	10,918	15,121	13,700
87,300	87,350	15,133	10,929	15,133	13,712
87,350	87,400	15,145	10,940	15,145	13,724
87,400	87,450	15,157	10,951	15,157	13,736
87,450	87,500	15,169	10,962	15,169	13,748
87,500	87,550	15,181	10,973	15,181	13,760
87,550	87,600	15,193	10,984	15,193	13,772
87,600	87,650	15,205	10,995	15,205	13,784
87,650	87,700	15,217	11,006	15,217	13,796
87,700	87,750	15,229	11,017	15,229	13,808
87,750	87,800	15,241	11,028	15,241	13,820
87,800	87,850	15,253	11,039	15,253	13,832
87,850	87,900	15,265	11,050	15,265	13,844
87,900	87,950	15,277	11,061	15,277	13,856
87,950	88,000	15,289	11,072	15,289	13,866
88,000					
88,000	88,050	15,301	11,083	15,301	13,880
88,050	88,100	15,313	11,094	15,313	13,892
88,100	88,150	15,325	11,105	15,325	13,904
88,150	88,200	15,337	11,116	15,337	13,916
88,200	88,250	15,349	11,127	15,349	13,928
88,250	88,300	15,361	11,138	15,361	13,940
88,300	88,350	15,373	11,149	15,373	13,952
88,350	88,400	15,385	11,160	15,385	13,964
88,400	88,450	15,397	11,171	15,397	13,976
88,450	88,500	15,409	11,182	15,409	13,988
88,500	88,550	15,421	11,193	15,421	14,000
88,550	88,600	15,433	11,204	15,433	14,012
88,600	88,650	15,445	11,215	15,445	14,024
88,650	88,700	15,457	11,226	15,457	14,036
88,700	88,750	15,469	11,237	15,469	14,048
88,750	88,800	15,481	11,248	15,481	14,060
88,800	88,850	15,493	11,259	15,493	14,072
88,850	88,900	15,505	11,270	15,505	14,084
88,900	88,950	15,517	11,281	15,517	14,096
88,950	89,000	15,529	11,292	15,529	14,108
89,000					
89,000	89,050	15,541	11,303	15,541	14,120
89,050	89,100	15,553	11,314	15,553	14,132
89,100	89,150	15,565	11,325	15,565	14,144
89,150	89,200	15,577	11,336	15,577	14,156
89,200	89,250	15,589	11,347	15,589	14,168
89,250	89,300	15,601	11,358	15,601	14,180
89,300	89,350	15,613	11,369	15,613	14,192
89,350	89,400	15,625	11,380	15,625	14,204
89,400	89,450	15,637	11,391	15,637	14,216
89,450	89,500	15,649	11,402	15,649	14,228
89,500	89,550	15,661	11,413	15,661	14,240
89,550	89,600	15,673	11,424	15,673	14,252
89,600	89,650	15,685	11,435	15,685	14,264
89,650	89,700	15,697	11,446	15,697	14,276
89,700	89,750	15,709	11,457	15,709	14,288
89,750	89,800	15,721	11,468	15,721	14,300
89,800	89,850	15,733	11,479	15,733	14,312
89,850	89,900	15,745	11,490	15,745	14,324
89,900	89,950	15,757	11,501	15,757	14,336
89,950	90,000	15,769	11,512	15,769	14,348

90,000 / 91,000 / 92,000

If line 11b (taxable income) is—		And you are—			
At least	But less than	Single	Married filing jointly *	Married filing separately	Head of a household
		Your tax is—			
90,000					
90,000	90,050	15,781	11,523	15,781	14,360
90,050	90,100	15,793	11,534	15,793	14,372
90,100	90,150	15,805	11,545	15,805	14,384
90,150	90,200	15,817	11,556	15,817	14,396
90,200	90,250	15,829	11,567	15,829	14,408
90,250	90,300	15,841	11,578	15,841	14,420
90,300	90,350	15,853	11,589	15,853	14,432
90,350	90,400	15,865	11,600	15,865	14,444
90,400	90,450	15,877	11,611	15,877	14,456
90,450	90,500	15,889	11,622	15,889	14,468
90,500	90,550	15,901	11,633	15,901	14,480
90,550	90,600	15,913	11,644	15,913	14,492
90,600	90,650	15,925	11,655	15,925	14,504
90,650	90,700	15,937	11,666	15,937	14,516
90,700	90,750	15,949	11,677	15,949	14,528
90,750	90,800	15,961	11,688	15,961	14,540
90,800	90,850	15,973	11,699	15,973	14,552
90,850	90,900	15,985	11,710	15,985	14,564
90,900	90,950	15,997	11,721	15,997	14,576
90,950	91,000	16,009	11,732	16,009	14,588
91,000					
91,000	91,050	16,021	11,743	16,021	14,600
91,050	91,100	16,033	11,754	16,033	14,612
91,100	91,150	16,045	11,765	16,045	14,624
91,150	91,200	16,057	11,776	16,057	14,636
91,200	91,250	16,069	11,787	16,069	14,648
91,250	91,300	16,081	11,798	16,081	14,660
91,300	91,350	16,093	11,809	16,093	14,672
91,350	91,400	16,105	11,820	16,105	14,684
91,400	91,450	16,117	11,831	16,117	14,696
91,450	91,500	16,129	11,842	16,129	14,708
91,500	91,550	16,141	11,853	16,141	14,720
91,550	91,600	16,153	11,864	16,153	14,732
91,600	91,650	16,165	11,875	16,165	14,744
91,650	91,700	16,177	11,886	16,177	14,756
91,700	91,750	16,189	11,897	16,189	14,768
91,750	91,800	16,201	11,908	16,201	14,780
91,800	91,850	16,213	11,919	16,213	14,792
91,850	91,900	16,225	11,930	16,225	14,804
91,900	91,950	16,237	11,941	16,237	14,816
91,950	92,000	16,249	11,952	16,249	14,828
92,000					
92,000	92,050	16,261	11,963	16,261	14,840
92,050	92,100	16,273	11,974	16,273	14,852
92,100	92,150	16,285	11,985	16,285	14,864
92,150	92,200	16,297	11,996	16,297	14,876
92,200	92,250	16,309	12,007	16,309	14,888
92,250	92,300	16,321	12,018	16,321	14,900
92,300	92,350	16,333	12,029	16,333	14,912
92,350	92,400	16,345	12,040	16,345	14,924
92,400	92,450	16,357	12,051	16,357	14,936
92,450	92,500	16,369	12,062	16,369	14,948
92,500	92,550	16,381	12,073	16,381	14,960
92,550	92,600	16,393	12,084	16,393	14,972
92,600	92,650	16,405	12,095	16,405	14,984
92,650	92,700	16,417	12,106	16,417	14,996
92,700	92,750	16,429	12,117	16,429	15,008
92,750	92,800	16,441	12,128	16,441	15,020
92,800	92,850	16,453	12,139	16,453	15,032
92,850	92,900	16,465	12,150	16,465	15,044
92,900	92,950	16,477	12,161	16,477	15,056
92,950	93,000	16,489	12,172	16,489	15,068

(Continued)

* This column must also be used by a qualifying widow(er).

Need more information or forms? Visit IRS.gov.

¶25

2019 Tax Table — Continued

93,000

At least	But less than	Single	Married filing jointly *	Married filing separately	Head of a household
			Your tax is—		
93,000	93,050	16,501	12,183	16,501	15,080
93,050	93,100	16,513	12,194	16,513	15,092
93,100	93,150	16,525	12,205	16,525	15,104
93,150	93,200	16,537	12,216	16,537	15,116
93,200	93,250	16,549	12,227	16,549	15,128
93,250	93,300	16,561	12,238	16,561	15,140
93,300	93,350	16,573	12,249	16,573	15,152
93,350	93,400	16,585	12,260	16,585	15,164
93,400	93,450	16,597	12,271	16,597	15,176
93,450	93,500	16,609	12,282	16,609	15,188
93,500	93,550	16,621	12,293	16,621	15,200
93,550	93,600	16,633	12,304	16,633	15,212
93,600	93,650	16,645	12,315	16,645	15,224
93,650	93,700	16,657	12,326	16,657	15,236
93,700	93,750	16,669	12,337	16,669	15,248
93,750	93,800	16,681	12,348	16,681	15,260
93,800	93,850	16,693	12,359	16,693	15,272
93,850	93,900	16,705	12,370	16,705	15,284
93,900	93,950	16,717	12,381	16,717	15,296
93,950	94,000	16,729	12,392	16,729	15,308

94,000

At least	But less than	Single	Married filing jointly *	Married filing separately	Head of a household
94,000	94,050	16,741	12,403	16,741	15,320
94,050	94,100	16,753	12,414	16,753	15,332
94,100	94,150	16,765	12,425	16,765	15,344
94,150	94,200	16,777	12,436	16,777	15,356
94,200	94,250	16,789	12,447	16,789	15,368
94,250	94,300	16,801	12,458	16,801	15,380
94,300	94,350	16,813	12,469	16,813	15,392
94,350	94,400	16,825	12,480	16,825	15,404
94,400	94,450	16,837	12,491	16,837	15,416
94,450	94,500	16,849	12,502	16,849	15,428
94,500	94,550	16,861	12,513	16,861	15,440
94,550	94,600	16,873	12,524	16,873	15,452
94,600	94,650	16,885	12,535	16,885	15,464
94,650	94,700	16,897	12,546	16,897	15,476
94,700	94,750	16,909	12,557	16,909	15,488
94,750	94,800	16,921	12,568	16,921	15,500
94,800	94,850	16,933	12,579	16,933	15,512
94,850	94,900	16,945	12,590	16,945	15,524
94,900	94,950	16,957	12,601	16,957	15,536
94,950	95,000	16,969	12,612	16,969	15,548

95,000

At least	But less than	Single	Married filing jointly *	Married filing separately	Head of a household
95,000	95,050	16,981	12,623	16,981	15,560
95,050	95,100	16,993	12,634	16,993	15,572
95,100	95,150	17,005	12,645	17,005	15,584
95,150	95,200	17,017	12,656	17,017	15,596
95,200	95,250	17,029	12,667	17,029	15,608
95,250	95,300	17,041	12,678	17,041	15,620
95,300	95,350	17,053	12,689	17,053	15,632
95,350	95,400	17,065	12,700	17,065	15,644
95,400	95,450	17,077	12,711	17,077	15,656
95,450	95,500	17,089	12,722	17,089	15,668
95,500	95,550	17,101	12,733	17,101	15,680
95,550	95,600	17,113	12,744	17,113	15,692
95,600	95,650	17,125	12,755	17,125	15,704
95,650	95,700	17,137	12,766	17,137	15,716
95,700	95,750	17,149	12,777	17,149	15,728
95,750	95,800	17,161	12,788	17,161	15,740
95,800	95,850	17,173	12,799	17,173	15,752
95,850	95,900	17,185	12,810	17,185	15,764
95,900	95,950	17,197	12,821	17,197	15,776
95,950	96,000	17,209	12,832	17,209	15,788

96,000

At least	But less than	Single	Married filing jointly *	Married filing separately	Head of a household
			Your tax is—		
96,000	96,050	17,221	12,843	17,221	15,800
96,050	96,100	17,233	12,854	17,233	15,812
96,100	96,150	17,245	12,865	17,245	15,824
96,150	96,200	17,257	12,876	17,257	15,836
96,200	96,250	17,269	12,887	17,269	15,848
96,250	96,300	17,281	12,898	17,281	15,860
96,300	96,350	17,293	12,909	17,293	15,872
96,350	96,400	17,305	12,920	17,305	15,884
96,400	96,450	17,317	12,931	17,317	15,896
96,450	96,500	17,329	12,942	17,329	15,908
96,500	96,550	17,341	12,953	17,341	15,920
96,550	96,600	17,353	12,964	17,353	15,932
96,600	96,650	17,365	12,975	17,365	15,944
96,650	96,700	17,377	12,986	17,377	15,956
96,700	96,750	17,389	12,997	17,389	15,968
96,750	96,800	17,401	13,008	17,401	15,980
96,800	96,850	17,413	13,019	17,413	15,992
96,850	96,900	17,425	13,030	17,425	16,004
96,900	96,950	17,437	13,041	17,437	16,016
96,950	97,000	17,449	13,052	17,449	16,028

97,000

At least	But less than	Single	Married filing jointly *	Married filing separately	Head of a household
97,000	97,050	17,461	13,063	17,461	16,040
97,050	97,100	17,473	13,074	17,473	16,052
97,100	97,150	17,485	13,085	17,485	16,064
97,150	97,200	17,497	13,096	17,497	16,076
97,200	97,250	17,509	13,107	17,509	16,088
97,250	97,300	17,521	13,118	17,521	16,100
97,300	97,350	17,533	13,129	17,533	16,112
97,350	97,400	17,545	13,140	17,545	16,124
97,400	97,450	17,557	13,151	17,557	16,136
97,450	97,500	17,569	13,162	17,569	16,148
97,500	97,550	17,581	13,173	17,581	16,160
97,550	97,600	17,593	13,184	17,593	16,172
97,600	97,650	17,605	13,195	17,605	16,184
97,650	97,700	17,617	13,206	17,617	16,196
97,700	97,750	17,629	13,217	17,629	16,208
97,750	97,800	17,641	13,228	17,641	16,220
97,800	97,850	17,653	13,239	17,653	16,232
97,850	97,900	17,665	13,250	17,665	16,244
97,900	97,950	17,677	13,261	17,677	16,256
97,950	98,000	17,689	13,272	17,689	16,268

98,000

At least	But less than	Single	Married filing jointly *	Married filing separately	Head of a household
98,000	98,050	17,701	13,283	17,701	16,280
98,050	98,100	17,713	13,294	17,713	16,292
98,100	98,150	17,725	13,305	17,725	16,304
98,150	98,200	17,737	13,316	17,737	16,316
98,200	98,250	17,749	13,327	17,749	16,328
98,250	98,300	17,761	13,338	17,761	16,340
98,300	98,350	17,773	13,349	17,773	16,352
98,350	98,400	17,785	13,360	17,785	16,364
98,400	98,450	17,797	13,371	17,797	16,376
98,450	98,500	17,809	13,382	17,809	16,388
98,500	98,550	17,821	13,393	17,821	16,400
98,550	98,600	17,833	13,404	17,833	16,412
98,600	98,650	17,845	13,415	17,845	16,424
98,650	98,700	17,857	13,426	17,857	16,436
98,700	98,750	17,869	13,437	17,869	16,448
98,750	98,800	17,881	13,448	17,881	16,460
98,800	98,850	17,893	13,459	17,893	16,472
98,850	98,900	17,905	13,470	17,905	16,484
98,900	98,950	17,917	13,481	17,917	16,496
98,950	99,000	17,929	13,492	17,929	16,508

99,000

At least	But less than	Single	Married filing jointly *	Married filing separately	Head of a household
			Your tax is—		
99,000	99,050	17,941	13,503	17,941	16,520
99,050	99,100	17,953	13,514	17,953	16,532
99,100	99,150	17,965	13,525	17,965	16,544
99,150	99,200	17,977	13,536	17,977	16,556
99,200	99,250	17,989	13,547	17,989	16,568
99,250	99,300	18,001	13,558	18,001	16,580
99,300	99,350	18,013	13,569	18,013	16,592
99,350	99,400	18,025	13,580	18,025	16,604
99,400	99,450	18,037	13,591	18,037	16,616
99,450	99,500	18,049	13,602	18,049	16,628
99,500	99,550	18,061	13,613	18,061	16,640
99,550	99,600	18,073	13,624	18,073	16,652
99,600	99,650	18,085	13,635	18,085	16,664
99,650	99,700	18,097	13,646	18,097	16,676
99,700	99,750	18,109	13,657	18,109	16,688
99,750	99,800	18,121	13,668	18,121	16,700
99,800	99,850	18,133	13,679	18,133	16,712
99,850	99,900	18,145	13,690	18,145	16,724
99,900	99,950	18,157	13,701	18,157	16,736
99,950	100,000	18,169	13,712	18,169	16,748

$100,000
or over
use the Tax
Computation
Worksheet

* This column must also be used by a qualifying widow(er).

Need more information or forms? Visit IRS.gov.

¶25

CORPORATION INCOME TAX RATES

¶ 33 Corporate Income Tax Rates Before 2018

For tax years beginning after December 31, 2017, corporations are subject to a flat 21-percent rate on taxable income (¶ 219). For tax years beginning before 2018, corporations are generally subject to the tax rates in the table below on taxable income (Code Sec. 11(b), prior to amendment by the Tax Cuts and Jobs Act (P.L. 115-97)).

Taxable Income				% on	of the amount
Over	But Not Over	Pay	+	Excess	over—
$0—	$50,000	$0		15%	$0
50,000—	75,000	7,500		25	50,000
75,000—	100,000	13,750		34	75,000
100,000—	335,000	22,250		39	100,000
335,000—	10,000,000	113,900		34	335,000
10,000,000—	15,000,000	3,400,000		35	10,000,000
15,000,000—	18,333,333	5,150,000		38	15,000,000
18,333,333—	. . . .			35	0

The regular corporate income tax rates apply to:

 • a controlled group of corporations as though the group is one corporation (¶ 289);

 • a foreign corporation that is effectively connected with a U.S. trade or business (¶ 2425), but the income of a foreign that is not effectively connected with a U.S. trade or business is taxed at a rate of 30 percent unless a lower tax rate is provided under a income tax treaty (¶ 2431);

 • a regulated investment company's (RIC) investment company taxable income (¶ 2303);

 • a real estate investment trust's (REIT) real estate investment trust taxable income (¶ 2329);

 • an insurance company's taxable income (¶ 2370 and ¶ 2378);

For tax years beginning before January 1, 2018, taxable income of certain personal service corporations is taxed at a flat rate of 35 percent (¶ 219) and personal holding companies are subject to a 20 percent tax on a corporation's undistributed personal holding company income (¶ 275) in addition to regular corporate income taxes.

ESTATE AND GIFT TAXES

¶ 40 Unified Transfer Tax Rate Schedule

Estate and gift transfer taxes are designed to form a unified transfer tax system on the transfer of property at death and during a taxpayer's life (¶ 2901). The maximum tax rate is 40 percent for applicable transfers made after December 31, 2012 (Code Sec. 2001). The unified tax rate schedule is as follows:

Unified Transfer Tax Rate Schedule After 2012

Column A	Column B	Column C	Column D
Taxable amount over	Taxable amount not over	Tax on amount in column A	Rate of tax on excess over amount in column A
$0	$10,000	$0	18 %
10,000	20,000	1,800	20
20,000	40,000	3,800	22
40,000	60,000	8,200	24
60,000	80,000	13,000	26
80,000	100,000	18,200	28
100,000	150,000	23,800	30
150,000	250,000	38,800	32
250,000	500,000	70,800	34
500,000	750,000	155,800	37
750,000	1,000,000	248,300	39
1,000,000	. . . .	345,800	40

¶ 41 Transfer Tax Credits, Exclusions, and Exemptions

An applicable credit amount (previously known as the unified credit) applies to both estate and gift tax, and it is the amount of tentative tax that would be imposed on an amount equal to the applicable exclusion amount (¶ 2910 and ¶ 2934). The applicable credit is subtracted from any estate or gift tax owed, and any applicable credit used against gift tax in one year reduces the amount of credit that can be used against estate or gift tax in a later year. The basic exclusion amount is adjusted annually for inflation.

Applicable Credit and Basic Exclusion Amounts

Year	Applicable Credit Amount	Basic Exclusion Amount
2012	1,772,800	5,120,000
2013	2,045,800	5,250,000
2014	2,081,800	5,340,000
2015	2,117,800	5,430,000
2016	2,125,800	5,450,000
2017	2,141,800	5,490,000
2018	4,417,800	11,180,000
2019	4,505,800	11,400,000

Gift Tax Annual Exclusion. There is an annual exclusion of $15,000 per donee for gifts made in 2019, with an annual maximum of $30,000 per donee for spouses who use gift-splitting (¶ 2905). If the donor's spouse is not a U.S. citizen, an annual exclusion of $155,000 in 2019 is allowed for present interest gifts to the spouse that would qualify for the marital deduction if the spouse were a U.S. citizen.

Nonresident Aliens. The annual gift tax exclusion is available to nonresident alien donors. Where permitted by treaty, the estate of a nonresident alien is allowed a credit equal to the unified credit available to a U.S. citizen multiplied by the percentage of the decedent's entire gross estate situated in the United States (¶ 2940). In computing the credit, property is not treated as situated in the United States if such property is exempt from tax under any treaty. The estate of a resident of a U.S. possession is entitled to a unified credit equal to the greater of $13,000 or $46,800 multiplied by the percentage of the decedent's gross estate situated in the United States (Code Sec. 2102). With respect to the gift tax, no portion of the unified credit may be used as a credit against gift taxes payable on lifetime transfers by a nonresident alien.

Generation-Skipping Transfers. An exemption amount is provided for each person making generation-skipping transfers (¶ 2943). The exemption may be allocated by a transferor (or the transferor's executor) to property transferred at any time but, once made, is irrevocable. The exemption amount is indexed annually for inflation and is the same as the applicable credit schedule above.

OTHER TAXES

¶ 47 Self-Employment Taxes

A tax rate of 15.3 percent is imposed on net earnings from self-employment. The rate consists of a 12.4 percent component for Social Security (old-age, survivors, and disability insurance (OASDI)) and a 2.9 percent component for Medicare hospital insurance (HI). For 2019, the OASDI rate applies to net earnings from self-employment up to the OASDI wage base of $132,900. The Medicare rate applies to all net earnings in 2019 (¶ 2664). The Medicare rate is increased by 0.9 percent to 3.8 percent for net earnings from self-employment in excess of $200,000 ($250,000 if married filing jointly; $125,000 if married filing separately). In the case of a joint return, the additional 0.9 percent tax for Medicare is imposed on the combined net earnings of both spouses. For 2020, the OASDI rate applies to net earnings from self-employment up to the OASDI wage base of $137,700. The Medicare rate applies to all net earnings in 2020.

¶ 49 Employment Taxes

FICA Taxes. Under the Federal Insurance Contributions Act (FICA), taxes are imposed on both employers and employees on wages paid to the employee for Social Security (old-age, survivors, and disability insurance (OASDI)), and Medicare hospital insurance (HI) (¶ 2648). The tax rate on both the employer's and the employee's portion of wages is 7.65 percent (15.3 percent total), consisting of a 6.2 percent rate for OASDI and a 1.45 percent rate for Medicare. For 2019, the OASDI rate for employers and employees applies only to wages up to the OASDI wage base of $132,900. The Medicare rate applies to all wages in 2019. The Medicare rate on the employee's portion of wages is increased 0.9 percent to 2.35 percent for wages in excess of $200,000 ($250,000 if married filing jointly; $125,000 if married filing separately). In the case of a joint return, the additional 0.9 percent tax for Medicare is imposed on the combined income of both spouses. For 2020, the OASDI rate applies to wages up to the OASDI wage base of $137,700. The Medicare rate applies to all wages in 2020.

Unemployment Compensation. Under the Federal Unemployment Tax Act (FUTA), a tax is imposed on the first $7,000 of wages paid to a covered employee by an employer who employs one or more persons in covered employment in each of 20 days in a year, each day being in a different week, or who has a payroll for covered employment of at least $1,500 in a calendar quarter in the current or preceding calendar year (¶ 2649). The FUTA tax rate is 6.0 percent for wages paid during the year. Since employers are allowed credits against the FUTA rate through participation in state unemployment insurance laws, the net FUTA rate actually paid by most employers is 0.6 percent, except when credit reductions are in effect in a state. The unemployment tax also applies to any person who paid total cash wages of $1,000 or more to a household employee during any calendar quarter in the current or preceding calendar year.

Railroad Retirement Tax. The Railroad Retirement and Survivors' Improvement Act provides benefits similar to those as under Social Security and Medicare. Tier I benefits are financed by taxes on employers and employees equal to those under FICA. The tax rate on the employer's and the employee's portion of wages for the calendar year is 7.65 percent (15.3 percent total), consisting of a 6.2 percent rate for OASDI and a 1.45 percent rate for Medicare. The OASDI rate for employers and employees applies only to wages up to the OASDI wage base of $132,900 for 2019 and $137,700 for 2020. The Medicare rate applies to all wages in 2019 and 2020. The Medicare rate on the employee's portion of wages is increased 0.9 percent to 2.35 percent for wages in excess of $200,000 ($250,000 if married filing jointly; $125,000 if married filing separately). In the case of a joint return, the additional 0.9 percent tax for Medicare is imposed on the combined income of both spouses.

Tier II benefits are also available equivalent to a private pension plan and financed with employers and employees contributing a certain percentage of pay toward the system to finance benefits. For calendar year 2019, a tier II tax rate of 13.1 percent for employers and 4.9 percent for employees is imposed on annual compensation within a compensation base of $98,700. For calendar year 2020, a tier II tax rate of 13.1 percent for employers and 4.9 percent for employees is imposed on annual compensation within a compensation base of $102,300.

TAX RATES

¶ 53 Excise Taxes

Identified below are various excise taxes.

FUELS
Gasoline
Gasoline (per gallon) . . . . 18.4¢
Diesel fuel, biodiesel, and kerosene
Diesel fuel (except if used on a farm for farming purposes)
    (per gallon) . . . . 24.4¢
Diesel fuel for use in trains (per gallon) . . . . 24.3¢
Diesel-water fuel emulsions (per gallon) . . . . 19.8¢
Kerosene (except if used in a farm for farming purposes)
    (per gallon) . . . . 24.4¢
B-100 (100 percent biodiesel) (per gallon) . . . . 24.4¢
Special fuels
Alternative fuel (per gallon) . . . . 18.4¢
Liquefied petroleum gas (LPG) . . . . 18.3¢
"P Series" fuels . . . . 18.4¢
Compressed natural gas (CNG) (per energy equivalent of a
    gallon of gasoline) . . . . 18.3¢
Liquefied hydrogen . . . . 18.4¢
Any liquid fuel derived from coal (including peat) through
    the Fischer-Tropsch process (per gallon) . . . . 24.4¢
Liquid fuel derived from biomass (per gallon) . . . . 24.4¢
Liquefied natural gas (LNG) (per gallon) . . . . 24.3¢
Liquefied gas derived from biomass (per gallon) . . . . 18.4¢
Qualified ethanol produced from coal (per gallon) . . . . 18.4¢
Qualified methanol produced from coal (per gallon) . . . . 18.4¢
Partially exempt ethanol produced from natural gas (per
    gallon) . . . . 11.4¢
Partially exempt methanol produced from natural gas (per
    gallon) . . . . 9.25¢
Fuel used on inland waterways
Inland waterways fuel use tax (per gallon) . . . . 29.1¢
Aviation fuels
Per P.L. 116-136, there is an excise tax holiday period
    beginning after March 27, 2020, and ending before
    January 1, 2021, for kerosene used in commercial aviation.
    Kerosene used in commercial aviation (when removed
    from a refinery or terminal directly into the fuel tank of an
    aircraft) (per gallon) . . . . 4.4¢
Kerosene used in noncommercial aviation (when removed
    from a refinery or terminal directly into the fuel tank of an
    aircraft) (per gallon) . . . . 21.9¢
Noncommercial aviation gasoline (per gallon) . . . . 19.4¢
Fuel used in fractional aircraft ownership program flights
    (per gallon) . . . . 14.1¢ surtax
Crude oil
Crude oil (per barrel) . . . . 9¢
Fuel credits
Second generation biofuel (per gallon) . . . . $1.01 credit until 2021
Biodiesel and biodiesel mixtures (per gallon) . . . . $1.00 credit until 2023
Agri-biodiesel (per gallon) . . . . $1.00 credit until 2023
Agri-biodiesel if benefited from the small agri-biodiesel
    producer credit (per gallon) . . . . $1.10 credit until 2023

Renewable diesel and renewable diesel mixtures (per
gallon) . . . . $1.00 credit until 2023
Alternative fuel (as defined in Code Sec. 6426(d)(2)) (per
gallon) . . . . 50¢ credit until 2021 (including
for liquefied hydrogen)

HEAVY TRUCKS, TRAILERS

Truck chassis or body (that is suitable for use with a vehicle
in excess of 33,000 lbs. gross vehicle weight) . . . . 12% of retail price
Trailer and semitrailer chassis or body (that is suitable for
use with a trailer or semitrailer in excess of 26,000 lbs.
gross vehicle weight) . . . . 12% of retail price
Parts and accessories installed on taxable vehicles within 6
months after being placed in service (when cost of parts
or accessories exceeds $1,000) . . . . 12% of retail price

HIGHWAY-TYPE TIRES

Tires with load capacity of 3,500 lbs. or less . . . . No tax
Tires with load capacity over 3,500 lbs. . . . . 9.45¢ for each 10 lbs. of tire load
capacity over 3,500 lbs.
Super single tires designed for steering . . . . 9.45¢ for each 10 lbs. of tire load
capacity over 3,500 lbs.
Super single tires not designed for steering . . . . 4.725¢ for each 10 lbs. of tire
load capacity over 3,500 lbs.
Biasply tires . . . . 4.725¢ for each 10 lbs. of tire
load capacity over 3,500 lbs.

GAS GUZZLER TAX

Mileage ratings per gallon of at least 22.5 . . . . $ 0
Mileage ratings per gallon of at least 21.5 but less than 22.5 1,000
Mileage ratings per gallon of at least 20.5 but less than 21.5 1,300
Mileage ratings per gallon of at least 19.5 but less than 20.5 1,700
Mileage ratings per gallon of at least 18.5 but less than 19.5 2,100
Mileage ratings per gallon of at least 17.5 but less than 18.5 2,600
Mileage ratings per gallon of at least 16.5 but less than 17.5 3,000
Mileage ratings per gallon of at least 15.5 but less than 16.5 3,700
Mileage ratings per gallon of at least 14.5 but less than 15.5 4,500
Mileage ratings per gallon of at least 13.5 but less than 14.5 5,400
Mileage ratings per gallon of at least 12.5 but less than 13.5 6,400
Mileage ratings per gallon of less than 12.5 7,700

FACILITIES AND SERVICES
Communications
Local telephone service and teletypewriter service 3%
Transportation by air
Per P.L. 116-136, there is an excise tax holiday period
beginning after March 27, 2020, and ending before
January 1, 2021, for certain aviation excise taxes.
Domestic passenger tickets . . . . 7.5% plus $4.30 (from 1/1/2020
to 12/31/2020) for each flight
segment (excepting segments to
or from rural airports)
Alaska and Hawaii passenger tickets (amount per person
per departure) (from 1/1/2020 to 12/31/2020) $9.50
International passenger tickets (amount per person for each
arrival and for each departure) (from 1/1/2020 to
12/31/2020) . . . . generally $18.90

¶53

Air freight waybill 6.25%
Transportation by water
Persons $3.00
Port use tax on imports (harbor maintenance tax) . . . . 0.125% of cargo value

ALCOHOL TAXES

Per P.L. 116-136, distilled spirits removed after December 31, 2019, and before January 1, 2021, which are used in or contained in certain hand sanitizers are temporarily exempt from excise tax.

Distilled spirits (per gallon for 2018, 2019 and 2020) . . . . $2.70 per proof gallon on the first 100,000 proof gallons of distilled spirits; $13.34 for all proof gallons on the next 22,130,000 (after the first 100,000 proof gallons); and $13.50 for amounts over 22,230,000 proof gallons

Distilled spirits (per gallon for 2021) $13.50
Beer (per barrel—31 gallons or less) for 2018, 2019 and 2020
. . . .$16 per barrel on the first six million barrels; $18 per barrel over six million barrels
Beer (per barrel—31 gallons or less) for 2021 . . . . $18, generally
First 60,000 barrels removed during calendar year by U.S. brewer producing not more than 2 million barrels during year (per barrel, for 2018, 2019 and 2020) $3.50
First 60,000 barrels removed during calendar year by U.S. brewer producing not more than 2 million barrels during year (per barrel, for 2021) $7
Wines
Not more than 16% alcohol (per gallon) for 2018, 2019 and 2020 . . . . $1.07
Not more than 14% alcohol (per gallon) for 2021 . . . . $1.07
More than 16 to 21% alcohol (per gallon) for 2018, 2019 and 2020 . . . . $1.57
More than 14 to 21% alcohol (per gallon) for 2021 . . . . $1.57
More than 21 to 24% alcohol (per gallon) $3.15
More than 24% alcohol (per gallon) . . . . See Distilled spirits above
Artificially carbonated wines (per gallon) $3.30
Champagne and other sparkling wines (per gallon) $3.40
Hard cider (per gallon) $0.226

TOBACCO TAXES
Cigars weighing not more than 3 lbs. (per 1,000) $50.33
Cigars weighing more than 3 lbs. . . . . 52.75% of sales price, not to exceed 40.26 cents per cigar
Cigarettes weighing not more than 3 lbs. (per 1,000) $50.33
Cigarettes weighing more than 3 lbs. (per 1,000) $105.69
Cigarette papers (per 50 papers) . . . . 3.15¢
Cigarette tubes (per 50 tubes) . . . . 6.30¢
Snuff (per pound) $1.51
Chewing tobacco (per pound) . . . . 50.33¢
Pipe tobacco (per pound) . . . . $2.8311 cents
Roll-your-own tobacco (per pound) $24.78

WAGERING TAXES

State authorized wagers placed with bookmakers and lottery
operators .... 0.25% of wager amt.
Unauthorized wagers placed with bookmakers and lottery
operators .... 2% of wager amt.
License fee on state authorized persons accepting wagers
(per year, per person) $50
License fee on unauthorized persons accepting wagers (per
year, per person) $500

HIGHWAY MOTOR VEHICLE USE TAX

Vehicles of less than 55,000 lbs. .... No tax
Vehicles of 55,000 lbs.—75,000 lbs. (per year) .... $100 per year + $22 for each
1,000 lbs. (or fraction thereof)
over 55,000 lbs.
Vehicles over 75,000 lbs. (per year) $550

FIREARMS

Transfer taxes (per firearm) .... $5 (concealable weapons) or
$200
Occupational taxes (per year) .... $1,000 (importers or
manufacturers), or $500
(dealers, small importers and
manufacturers)
Pistols and revolvers .... 10% of sales price
Firearms other than pistols and revolvers .... 11% of sales price
Ammunition (shells and cartridges) .... 11% of sales price

OTHER TAXES

Electric outboard motors .... 3% of sales price
Fishing tackle boxes .... 3% of sales price
Sport fishing equipment .... 10% of sales price
Bows with a peak draw weight of at least 30 pounds .... 11% of sales price
Quivers, broadheads, points .... 11% of sales price
Arrow shafts .... 52¢ per shaft (from 1/1/2020 to
12/31/2020)
Coal—underground mines .... $1.10 per ton, not to exceed 4.4%
of sales price
Coal—surface mines .... 55¢ per ton, not to exceed 4.4%
of sales price
Vaccines .... 75¢ per dose on taxable
vaccines
Indoor tanning services .... 10% of amount paid
Casualty insurance and indemnity, fidelity and surety bonds
(per dollar of premium paid) .... 4¢
Life insurance, sickness and accident policies, and annuity
contracts (per dollar of premium paid) .... 1¢
Reinsurance of taxable contracts above (per dollar of
premium paid) .... 1¢

Preparing Income Tax Returns

CHECKLISTS

¶ 63 Checklist for Forms

The following chart lists key forms in use by the IRS and provides paragraph references to the main discussions of those forms in the 2019 *U.S. Master Tax Guide*®.

Form	Paragraph reference	Form	Paragraph reference
56	¶ 2747	966	¶ 211; ¶ 2259; ¶ 2261; ¶ 2565
433-A	¶ 2723		
433-B	¶ 2723	970	¶ 1565; ¶ 1571
637	¶ 1465I	972	¶ 259
656	¶ 2723	973	¶ 259
656-L	¶ 2723	976	¶ 2317
673	¶ 2408	982	¶ 855
706	¶ 2912; ¶ 2938; ¶ 2944	990	¶ 537; ¶ 625; ¶ 2503; ¶ 2509
706, Schedule A	¶ 2912		
706, Schedule A-1	¶ 2922	990, Schedule B	¶ 625
706, Schedule B	¶ 2912	990, Schedule C	¶ 613
706, Schedule C	¶ 2912	990-BL	¶ 625
706, Schedule D	¶ 2915	990-EZ	¶ 537; ¶ 625; ¶ 2503; ¶ 2509
706, Schedule E	¶ 2919		
706, Schedule F	¶ 2912	990-PF	¶ 631; ¶ 633; ¶ 2503; ¶ 2509
706, Schedule G	¶ 2914		
706, Schedule H	¶ 2918	990-T	¶ 658; ¶ 1465HA; s¶ 2503
706, Schedule I	¶ 2917		
706, Schedule J	¶ 2925	990-W	¶ 633; ¶ 658
706, Schedule K	¶ 2925	1023	¶ 602; ¶ 623
706, Schedule L	¶ 2925	1024	¶ 692
706, Schedule M	¶ 2926	1024-A	¶ 692
706, Schedule O	¶ 2932	1028	¶ 698
706, Schedule Q	¶ 2934	1040	¶ 105; ¶ 107
706, Schedule R	¶ 2944	1040, Schedule 1	¶ 105
706, Schedule R-1	¶ 2944	1040, Schedule 2	¶ 105
706-A	¶ 2922	1040, Schedule 3	¶ 105
706-CE	¶ 2934	1040, Schedule A	¶ 1014; ¶ 1015; ¶ 1021; ¶ 1043; ¶ 1058; ¶ 1079; ¶ 1095; ¶ 1121; ¶ 1123
706-GS(D)	¶ 2944		
706-GS(T)	¶ 2944		
706-NA	¶ 2940		
708	¶ 2948	1040, Schedule B	¶ 724; ¶ 730; ¶ 734; ¶ 863
709	¶ 2910; ¶ 2944		
712	¶ 2915	1040, Schedule C	¶ 1006
843	¶ 1413; ¶ 2759; ¶ 2813; ¶ 2838	1040, Schedule D	¶ 113; ¶ 1007; ¶ 1736
		1040, Schedule E	¶ 762; ¶ 763; ¶ 785; ¶ 1006A
851	¶ 295		
866	¶ 2721	1040, Schedule EIC	¶ 1422
870	¶ 2712	1040, Schedule F	¶ 767; ¶ 769; ¶ 1006
906	¶ 2721	1040, Schedule H	¶ 2652
911	¶ 2707	1040, Schedule J	¶ 767
926	¶ 2492; ¶ 2565	1040, Schedule R	¶ 1402
940	¶ 2650	1040, Schedule SE	¶ 767; ¶ 1027; ¶ 2664
941	¶ 1465J; ¶ 2650	1040-C	¶ 2411
943	¶ 2650	1040-ES	¶ 125; ¶ 127
944	¶ 2650	1040-NR	¶ 2425
945	¶ 2645; ¶ 2650	1040-NR-EZ	¶ 2425
965	¶ 2488C	1040-PR	¶ 2501
		1040-SR	¶ 105
		1040-SS	¶ 2501

Form	Paragraph reference
1040-V	¶ 2525
1040-X	¶ 107; ¶ 1145; ¶ 2759
1041	¶ 510; ¶ 1145; ¶ 2503; ¶ 2509
1041, Schedule I	¶ 190; ¶ 192; ¶ 516
1041, Schedule J	¶ 567
1041, Schedule K-1	¶ 510
1041-A	¶ 537
1041-ES	¶ 511
1041-N	¶ 2396; ¶ 2565
1041-QFT	¶ 575
1041-T	¶ 511
1042	¶ 2455; ¶ 2469; ¶ 2473
1042-S	¶ 2455; ¶ 2469; ¶ 2473
1042-T	¶ 2455
1045	¶ 1145; ¶ 2773
1065	¶ 406; ¶ 604; ¶ 2503; ¶ 2509
1065, Schedule D	¶ 1758
1065, Schedule K-1	¶ 406; ¶ 431
1066	¶ 2343
1066, Schedule Q	¶ 2344; ¶ 2361
1094-B	¶ 2567
1094-C	¶ 2567
1095-A	¶ 1431
1095-B	¶ 2567
1095-C	¶ 2567
1098	¶ 1047; ¶ 1048A; ¶ 2565
1098-C	¶ 627; ¶ 1070A; ¶ 2565
1098-E	¶ 1011; ¶ 2565
1098-F	¶ 972; ¶ 2565
1098-MA	¶ 2565
1098-Q	¶ 2565
1098-T	¶ 1011A; ¶ 1403; ¶ 2565
1099-A	¶ 2565
1099-B	¶ 785; ¶ 1975; ¶ 1980; ¶ 2565
1099-C	¶ 2565
1099-DIV	¶ 733; ¶ 2565
1099-G	¶ 722; ¶ 769; ¶ 2565
1099-H	¶ 1432; ¶ 2565
1099-INT	¶ 724; ¶ 2565
1099-K	¶ 2565
1099-LS	¶ 807; ¶ 2565
1099-MISC	¶ 785; ¶ 2565
1099-OID	¶ 1952; ¶ 2565
1099-PATR	¶ 768; ¶ 2565
1099-Q	¶ 867; ¶ 869; ¶ 2565
1099-QA	¶ 2565
1099-R	¶ 839; ¶ 2149; ¶ 2151; ¶ 2565
1099-S	¶ 1705; ¶ 2565
1099-SA	¶ 2035; ¶ 2037; ¶ 2565
1099-SB	¶ 807; ¶ 2565
1116	¶ 1461; ¶ 2475; ¶ 2476; ¶ 2479
1118	¶ 2475; ¶ 2476; ¶ 2479
1120	¶ 211; ¶ 2503; ¶ 2509
1120, Schedule PH	¶ 275
1120, Schedule UTP	¶ 2501
1120-C	¶ 698
1120-F	¶ 2425
1120-FSC	¶ 2501
1120-H	¶ 699
1120-IC-DISC	¶ 2501
1120-L	¶ 2370
1120-ND	¶ 2501
1120-PC	¶ 2501

Form	Paragraph reference
1120-POL	¶ 696
1120-REIT	¶ 2326; ¶ 2329
1120-RIC	¶ 2301; ¶ 2303
1120-S	¶ 306; ¶ 351; ¶ 2503; ¶ 2509
1120-S, Schedule D	¶ 1758
1120-S, Schedule K-1	¶ 309; ¶ 351
1120-SF	¶ 2501
1120X	¶ 1145; ¶ 2759
1122	¶ 295
1127	¶ 2537
1128	¶ 1513
1138	¶ 1145; ¶ 2773
1139	¶ 1145; ¶ 2773
1310	¶ 180
2063	¶ 2411
2106	¶ 941; ¶ 941A; ¶ 941D; ¶ 941E; ¶ 942; ¶ 1095; ¶ 1215
2120	¶ 147
2210	¶ 125
2210-F	¶ 125
2220	¶ 241
2350	¶ 107; ¶ 2509
2438	¶ 2305; ¶ 2329
2439	¶ 1430; ¶ 2305; ¶ 2329
2441	¶ 1401
2553	¶ 306
2555	¶ 2401; ¶ 2403; ¶ 2408
2848	¶ 2708A
3115	¶ 1221; ¶ 1529
3468	¶ 1465A; ¶ 1465B; ¶ 1465C; ¶ 1465D; ¶ 1465E; ¶ 1465F
3520	¶ 567; ¶ 588; ¶ 2565
3520-A	¶ 588; ¶ 2493; ¶ 2565
3800	¶ 1465
3903	¶ 1073; ¶ 1075
3921	¶ 2565
3922	¶ 2565
4070	¶ 717; ¶ 2605
4070A	¶ 717
4136	¶ 1429
4137	¶ 717
4255	¶ 1465A; ¶ 1779
4361	¶ 2667
4419	¶ 2503
4466	¶ 247
4562	¶ 481; ¶ 904; ¶ 987; ¶ 1201; ¶ 1208; ¶ 1214; ¶ 1774
4563	¶ 2414
4626	¶ 239
4684	¶ 1121; ¶ 1123; ¶ 1125; ¶ 1131; ¶ 1713
4720	¶ 590A; ¶ 610; ¶ 614; ¶ 617; ¶ 635; ¶ 637
4768	¶ 2938
4797	¶ 1208; ¶ 1211; ¶ 1713; ¶ 1747; ¶ 1779; ¶ 1797
4868	¶ 107; ¶ 2509
4876-A	¶ 2498
4952	¶ 1057
4970	¶ 567
4972	¶ 2143
5213	¶ 1195
5227	¶ 537; ¶ 590; ¶ 593
5304-SIMPLE	¶ 2181

Form	Paragraph reference
5305-SEP	¶ 2189
5305-SIMPLE	¶ 2181
5329	¶ 2127; ¶ 2151; ¶ 2155; ¶ 2161; ¶ 2169; ¶ 2173
5405	¶ 1424
5471	¶ 2487; ¶ 2565
5498	¶ 2155; ¶ 2565
5498-ESA	¶ 2565
5498-QA	¶ 2565
5498-SA	¶ 2565
5500	¶ 2137
5500-EZ	¶ 2137
5500-SF	¶ 2137
5558	¶ 2137
5695	¶ 1441; ¶ 1442
5713	¶ 2496
5735	¶ 1462
5768	¶ 613
5884	¶ 1465G
5884-A	¶ 1465P
5884-C	¶ 1465G
6198	¶ 1155; ¶ 2450
6251	¶ 190; ¶ 192
6252	¶ 1801
6478	¶ 1465I
6765	¶ 1465J
6781	¶ 1947; ¶ 1948
7004	¶ 351; ¶ 406; ¶ 510; ¶ 2455; ¶ 2509
8023	¶ 2265
8027	¶ 2565; ¶ 2605
8082	¶ 415
8275	¶ 2856; ¶ 2858; ¶ 2863
8275-R	¶ 2856; ¶ 2858; ¶ 2863
8282	¶ 627; ¶ 2565
8283	¶ 627; ¶ 1070A; ¶ 1071; ¶ 2565
8288	¶ 2442
8288-A	¶ 2442
8300	¶ 2565
8332	¶ 139A
8379	¶ 163
8396	¶ 1406
8453	¶ 2503
8508	¶ 2503; ¶ 2565
8582	¶ 1169
8582-CR	¶ 1169
8586	¶ 1465K
8594	¶ 1620; ¶ 1743
8596	¶ 2565
8596-A	¶ 2565
8606	¶ 2160; ¶ 2165; ¶ 2173; ¶ 2177
8609	¶ 1465K
8611	¶ 1465K
8612	¶ 2329
8615	¶ 115
8621	¶ 2490
8689	¶ 2416
8697	¶ 1551
8716	¶ 1501
8752	¶ 1501
8801	¶ 1409
8802	¶ 2450
8804	¶ 2509
8806	¶ 2565
8809	¶ 2455; ¶ 2565
8809-I	¶ 2471

Form	Paragraph reference
8810	¶ 1169
8811	¶ 2343
8812	¶ 1405
8814	¶ 115
8815	¶ 863
8818	¶ 863
8820	¶ 1465S
8822	¶ 2711
8822-B	¶ 2711
8824	¶ 1721; ¶ 1732
8825	¶ 1169
8826	¶ 1465M
8827	¶ 1237; ¶ 1409
8828	¶ 1406
8829	¶ 961; ¶ 964
8832	¶ 201; ¶ 306; ¶ 402A
8833	¶ 2450
8835	¶ 1465N
8839	¶ 1407; ¶ 2063
8840	¶ 2409
8843	¶ 2409
8844	¶ 1465O; ¶ 1799B
8845	¶ 1465Q
8846	¶ 1465R
8849	¶ 1429
8850	¶ 1465G
8853	¶ 2037
8854	¶ 2412; ¶ 2565
8855	¶ 516
8857	¶ 162
8859	¶ 1408
8862	¶ 1403; ¶ 1405; ¶ 1422
8863	¶ 1403
8864	¶ 1465X
8865	¶ 2487; ¶ 2494
8866	¶ 1229
8867	¶ 173; ¶ 1403; ¶ 1405; ¶ 1422; ¶ 2807
8868	¶ 2509
8869	¶ 304
8871	¶ 696
8872	¶ 696
8874	¶ 1465T
8875	¶ 2340
8878	¶ 2517
8879	¶ 2517
8880	¶ 1404
8881	¶ 1465U
8882	¶ 1465V
8885	¶ 1432
8886	¶ 2592; ¶ 2594
8886-T	¶ 619
8888	¶ 2155; ¶ 2759
8889	¶ 2035
8893	¶ 415
8898	¶ 2414
8899	¶ 627; ¶ 1062A; ¶ 2565
8900	¶ 1465W
8903	¶ 312; ¶ 431A; ¶ 980A
8904	¶ 1465KK
8906	¶ 1465Z
8908	¶ 1465CC
8910	¶ 1446
8911	¶ 1455
8912	¶ 1471
8915-A	¶ 2129
8915-B	¶ 2129
8917	¶ 1011A

¶63

Form	Paragraph reference
8918	¶ 2593
8919	¶ 2602
8923	¶ 1465GG
8925	¶ 804; ¶ 2565
8927	¶ 2317
8928	¶ 322; ¶ 2015
8932	¶ 1465II
8933	¶ 1465JJ
8936	¶ 1451
8937	¶ 1980
8938	¶ 2572
8940	¶ 607; ¶ 623; ¶ 649
8941	¶ 1465HA
8944	¶ 2503
8945	¶ 2517
8946	¶ 2517
8948	¶ 2503
8949	¶ 1007; ¶ 1705; ¶ 1713; ¶ 1735; ¶ 1741; ¶ 1760; ¶ 1905; ¶ 1907; ¶ 1911
8952	¶ 2602
8955-SSA	¶ 2137
8957	¶ 2471
8958	¶ 711
8959	¶ 2648; ¶ 2664
8960	¶ 117
8962	¶ 1431
8965	¶ 119
8966	¶ 2471

Form	Paragraph reference
8971	¶ 1633; ¶ 2938
8974	¶ 1465J
8990	¶ 937
8991	¶ 2489
8992	¶ 2488B
8993	¶ 2488B
8996	¶ 1799E
9465	¶ 2529
SS-4	¶ 2579; ¶ 2652
SS-5	¶ 2579
SS-8	¶ 2602
T	¶ 1772
W-2	¶ 2565; ¶ 2650; ¶ 2655
W-2G	¶ 2642
W-3	¶ 2650; ¶ 2565
W-4	¶ 2616; ¶ 2619; ¶ 2632; ¶ 2634; ¶ 2637
W-4P	¶ 2643
W-4S	¶ 2604
W-4V	¶ 2629
W-7	¶ 2579
W-7A	¶ 2579
W-8BEN	¶ 2431; ¶ 2455
W-8BEN-E	¶ 2455
W-8ECI	¶ 2429; ¶ 2455
W-8EXP	¶ 2455
W-8IMY	¶ 2455
W-9	¶ 2455; ¶ 2579
W-12	¶ 2517

¶ 64 Guide to Information Returns

The following chart lists information returns in use by the IRS. It provides reportable payment types and amounts, as well as the due dates for filing the returns with the IRS and for providing statements to a payee or other person.

(If any date shown falls on a Saturday, Sunday, or legal holiday, the due date is the next business day.)

				Due Date	
Form	**Title**	**What To Report**	**Amounts To Report**	**To IRS**	**To Recipient (unless indicated otherwise)**
1042-S	Foreign Person's U.S. Source Income Subject to Withholding	Income such as interest, dividends, royalties, pensions and annuities, etc., and amounts withheld for nonresident aliens and foreign corporations. Also, distributions of effectively connected income by publicly traded partnerships or nominees.	See form instructions	March 15	March 15
1097-BTC	Bond Tax Credit	Tax credit bond credits to shareholders.	All amounts	February 28*	On or before the 15th day of the 2nd calendar month after the close of the calendar month in which the credit is allowed
1098	Mortgage Interest Statement	Mortgage interest (including points) and certain mortgage insurance premiums received in the course of a trade or business from individuals and reimbursements of overpaid interest.	$600 or more	February 28*	(To Payer/ Borrower) January 31
1098-C	Contributions of Motor Vehicles, Boats, and Airplanes	Information regarding a donated motor vehicle, boat, or airplane.	Gross proceeds of more than $500	February 28*	(To Donor) 30 days from date of sale or contribution
1098-E	Student Loan Interest Statement	Student loan interest received in the course of a trade or business.	$600 or more	February 28*	January 31
1098-F	Fines, Penalties and Other Amounts	Statement furnished by a government or governmental entity regarding a court order or agreement with respect to a violation or potential violation of law.	All amounts required to be paid	January 31	January 31
1098-MA	Mortgage Assistance Payments	Assistance payments paid to homeowners from funds allocated from the Housing Finance Authority Innovation Fund for the Hardest Hit Housing Markets (HFA Hardest Hit Fund) or the Emergency Homeowner's Loan Program.	All amounts	February 28	January 31

				Due Date	
Form	Title	What To Report	Amounts To Report	To IRS	To Recipient (unless indicated otherwise)
1098-Q	Qualified Longevity Annuity Contract Information	Status of a contract that is intended to be a qualifying longevity annuity contract (QLAC), defined in section A-17 of Reg. § 1.401(a)(9)-6, that is purchased or held under any plan, annuity, or account described in Code Secs. 401(a), 403(a), 403(b), or 408 (other than a Roth IRA) or eligible governmental plan under Code Sec. 457(b).	All amounts	February 28	January 31
1098-T	Tuition Statement	Qualified tuition and related expenses, reimbursements or refunds, and scholarships or grants (optional).	See instructions	February 28*	January 31
1099-A	Acquisition or Abandonment of Secured Property	Information about the acquisition or abandonment of property that is security for a debt for which you are the lender.	All amounts	February 28*	(To Borrower) January 31
1099-B	Proceeds From Broker and Barter Exchange Transactions	Sales or redemptions of securities, futures transactions, commodities, and barter exchange transactions (including payments reported pursuant to an election described in Reg. § 1.1471-4(d)(5)(i)(A) or reported as described in Reg. § 1.1471-4(d)(2)(iii)(A)).	All amounts	February 28*	February 15**
1099-C	Cancellation of Debt	Cancellation of a debt owed to a financial institution, the Federal Government, a credit union, RTC, FDIC, NCUA, a military department, the U.S. Postal Service, the Postal Rate Commission, or any organization having a significant trade or business of lending money.	$600 or more	February 28*	January 31
1099-CAP	Changes in Corporate Control and Capital Structure	Information about cash, stock, or other property from an acquisition of control or the substantial change in capital structure of a corporation.	Over $1,000	February 28*	(To Shareholders) January 31, (To Clearing Organization) January 5

Form	Title	What To Report	Amounts To Report	To IRS	To Recipient (unless indicated otherwise)
				Due Date	
1099-DIV	Dividends and Distributions	Distributions, such as dividends, capital gain distributions, or nontaxable distributions, that were paid on stock and liquidation distributions (including distributions reported pursuant to an election described in Reg. § 1.1471-4(d)(5)(i)(A) or reported as described in Reg. § 1.1471-4(d)(2)(iii)(A)).	$10 or more, except $600 or more for liquidations	February 28*	January 31**
1099-G	Certain Government Payments	Unemployment compensation, state and local income tax refunds, agricultural payments, and taxable grants.	$10 or more for refunds and unemployment	February 28*	January 31
1099-INT	Interest Income	Interest income (including payments reported pursuant to an election described in Reg. § 1.1471-4(d)(5)(i)(A) or reported as described in Reg. § 1.1471-4(d)(2)(iii)(A)); market discount subject to an election under Code Sec. 1278(b).	$10 or more ($600 or more in some cases)	February 28*	January 31**
1099-K	Payment Card and Third Party Network Transactions	Payment card transactions.	All amounts	February 28*	January 31
		Third party network transactions.	$20,000 or more **and** 200 or more transactions	February 28*	January 31
1099-LS	Reportable Life Insurance Sale	Payments made in a reportable policy sale.	All amounts	February 28*	(To recipients) February 15, (To Issuers) Date specified in Prop. Reg. § 1.6050Y-2(d)(2)
1099-LTC	Long-Term Care and Accelerated Death Benefits	Payments under a long-term care insurance contract and accelerated death benefits paid under a life insurance contract or by a viatical settlement provider.	All amounts	February 28*	January 31
1099-MISC	Miscellaneous Income	Rent or royalty payments; prizes and awards that are not for services, such as winnings on TV or radio shows (including payments reported pursuant to an election described in Reg. § 1.1471-4(d)(5)(i)(A) or reported as described in Reg. § 1.1471-4(d)(2)(iii)(A)).	$600 or more, except $10 or more for royalties	February 28*	January 31**

CHECKLISTS

¶64

Form	Title	What To Report	Amounts To Report	Due Date To IRS	Due Date To Recipient (unless indicated otherwise)
	(Also, use to report direct sales of $5,000 or more of consumer goods for resale.)	Payments to crew members by owners or operators of fishing boats including payments of proceeds from sale of catch.	All amounts	February 28*	January 31**
		Code Sec. 409A income from nonqualified deferred compensation plans (NQDCs).	All amounts	February 28*	January 31**
		Payments to a physician, physicians' corporation, or other supplier of health and medical services. Issued mainly by medical assistance programs or health and accident insurance plans.	$600 or more	February 28*	January 31**
		Fish purchases paid in cash for resale.	$600 or more	February 28*	January 31**
		Crop insurance proceeds.	$600 or more	February 28*	January 31**
		Substitute dividends and tax-exempt interest payments reportable by brokers.	$10 or more	February 28*	February 15**
		Gross proceeds paid to attorneys.	$600 or more	February 28*	February 15**
		A U.S. account for FATCA purposes to which no payments were made during the year that are reportable on any applicable Form 1099 (or a U.S. account to which payments were made during the year that do not reach the applicable reporting threshold for any applicable Form 1099) reported pursuant to an election described in Reg. § 1.1471-4(d)(5)(i)(A).	All amounts (including $0)	February 28*	January 31**
1099-NEC	Nonemployee Compensation	Payments for services performed for a trade or business by people not treated as its employees (including payments reported pursuant to an election described in Reg. § 1.1471-4(d)(5)(i)(A) or reported as described in Reg. § 1.1471-4(d)(2)(iii)(A)). Examples: fees to subcontractors or directors and golden parachute payments.	$600 or more	January 31	January 31

Form	Title	What To Report	Amounts To Report	Due Date To IRS	To Recipient (unless indicated otherwise)
1099-OID	Original Issue Discount	Original issue discount (including amounts reported pursuant to an election described in Reg. § 1.1471-4(d)(5)(i)(A) or reported as described in Reg. § 1.1471-4(d)(2)(iii)(A)); market discount subject to an election under Code Sec. 1278(b).	$10 or more	February 28*	January 31**
1099-PATR	Taxable Distributions Received From Cooperatives	Distributions from cooperatives passed through to their patrons including any domestic production activities deduction and certain pass-through credits.	$10 or more	February 28*	January 31
1099-Q	Payments From Qualified Education Programs (Under Sections 529 and 530)	Earnings from qualified tuition programs and Coverdell ESAs.	All amounts	February 28*	January 31
1099-QA	Distributions from ABLE Accounts	Distributions from ABLE accounts.	All amounts	February 28	January 31
1099-R	Distributions From Pensions, Annuities, Retirement or Profit-Sharing Plans, IRAs, Insurance Contracts, etc.	Distributions from retirement or profit-sharing plans, any IRA, insurance contracts, and IRA recharacterizations (including payments reported pursuant to an election described in Reg. § 1.1471-4(d)(5)(i)(B) or reported as described in Reg. § 1.1471-4(d)(2)(iii)(A)).	$10 or more	February 28*	January 31
1099-S	Proceeds From Real Estate Transactions	Gross proceeds from the sale or exchange of real estate and certain royalty payments.	Generally, $600 or more	February 28*	February 15
1099-SA	Distributions From an HSA, Archer MSA, or Medicare Advantage MSA	Distributions from an HSA, Archer MSA, or Medicare Advantage MSA.	All amounts	February 28*	January 31
1099-SB	Seller's Investment in Life Insurance Contract	Seller's investment in a life insurance contract as determined by the issuer.	All amounts	February 28*	February 15
3921	Exercise of an Incentive Stock Option Under Code Sec. 422(b)	Transfer of stock pursuant to the exercise of an incentive stock option under Code Sec. 422(b).	All amounts	February 28*	January 31

Form	Title	What To Report	Amounts To Report	Due Date To IRS	To Recipient (unless indicated otherwise)
3922	Transfer of Stock Acquired Through an Employee Stock Purchase Plan Under Code Sec. 423(c)	Transfer of stock acquired through an employee stock purchase plan under Code Sec. 423(c).	All amounts	February 28*	January 31
5498	IRA Contribution Information	Contributions (including rollover contributions) to any individual retirement arrangement (IRA) including a SEP, SIMPLE, and Roth IRA; Roth conversions; IRA recharacterizations; and the fair market value (FMV) of the account.	All amounts	May 31***	(To Participant) For FMV/RMD Jan 31; For contributions, May 31***
5498-ESA	Coverdell ESA Contribution Information	Contributions (including rollover contributions) to a Coverdell ESA.	All amounts	May 31	April 30
5498-QA	ABLE Account Contribution Information	Contributions (including rollover contributions) to an ABLE account.	All amounts	May 31***	March 15***
5498-SA	HSA, Archer MSA, or Medicare Advantage MSA Information	Contributions to an HSA (including transfers and rollovers) or Archer MSA and the FMV of an HSA, Archer MSA, or Medicare Advantage MSA.	All amounts	May 31***	(To Participant) May 31***
W-2	Wage and Tax Statement	Wages, tips, other compensation; Social Security, Medicare, and withheld income taxes. Include bonuses, vacation allowances, severance pay, certain moving expense payments, some kinds of travel allowances, and third-party payments of sick pay.	See separate instructions	(TO SSA) January 31	(To Employee) January 31
W-2G	Certain Gambling Winnings	Gambling winnings from horse racing, dog racing, jai alai, lotteries, keno, bingo, slot machines, sweepstakes, wagering pools, poker tournaments, etc.	Generally, $600 or more; $1,200 or more from bingo or slot machines; $1,500 or more from keno	February 28*	January 31

+ **Note:** If any payments for nonemployee compensation are reported in box 7, the due date is January 31 for both paper and electronic returns.

* The due date is March 31 if filed electronically.

** The due date is March 15 for reporting by trustees and middlemen of widely-held financial investment trusts (WHFITs).

*** The due date is July 15, 2020, for the 2019 calendar year if otherwise due on or after April 1, 2020, and before July 15, 2020.

¶ 65 Checklist for Types of Payments

The following chart lists common payments and the forms used to file and report them. It is not a complete list of all payments, and the absence of a payment from the list does not indicate that the payment is not reportable.

Type of Payment	Report on Form	Type of Payment	Report on Form
ABLE accounts:		Fees, employee	W-2
Contributions	5498-QA	Fees, nonemployee	1099-NEC
Distributions	1099-QA	Fishing boat crew members proceeds	1099-MISC
Abandonment	1099-A		
Accelerated death benefits	1099-LTC	Fish purchases for cash	1099-MISC
Acquisition of control	1099-CAP	Foreclosures	1099-A
Agriculture payments	1099-G	Foreign persons' income	1042-S
Allocated tips	W-2	401(k) contributions	W-2
Alternate TAA payments	1099-G	404(k) dividend	1099-DIV
Annuities	1099-R	Gambling winnings	W-2G
Archer MSAs:		Golden parachute, employee	W-2
Contributions	5498-SA	Golden parachute, nonemployee	1099-NEC
Distributions	1099-SA	Grants, taxable	1099-G
Attorney, fees and gross proceeds	1099-MISC	Health care services	1099-MISC
Auto reimbursements, employee	W-2	Health savings accounts:	
Auto reimbursements, nonemployee	1099-NEC	Contributions	5498-SA
Awards, employee	W-2	Distributions	1099-SA
Awards, nonemployee	1099-NEC	Income attributable to domestic	
Barter exchange income	1099-B	production activities, deduction for	1099-PATR
Bond tax credit	1097-BTC	Income tax refunds, state and local	1099-G
Bonuses, employee	W-2	Indian gaming profits paid to tribal	
Bonuses, nonemployee	1099-NEC	members	1099-MISC
Broker transactions	1099-B	Interest income	1099-INT
Cancellation of debt	1099-C	Interes, tax-exempt	1099-INT
Capital gain distributions	1099-DIV	Interest, mortgage	1098
Car expenses, employee	W-2	IRA contributions	5498
Car expenses, nonemployee	1099-NEC	IRA distributions	1099-R
Changes in capital structure	1099-CAP	Life insurance contract distributions	1099-R,
Charitable gift annuities	1099-R		1099-LTC
Commissions, employee	W-2	Liquidation, distributions in	1099-DIV
Commissions, nonemployee	1099-NEC	Loans, distribution from pension plan	1099-R
Commodities transactions	1099-B	Long-term care benefits	1099-LTC
Compensation, employee	W-2	Medicare Advantage MSAs:	
Compensation, nonemployee	1099-MISC	Contributions	5498-SA
Contributions of motor vehicles, boats,		Distributions	1099-SA
and airplanes	1098-C	Medical services	1099-MISC
Cost of current life insurance protection		Mileage, employee	W-2
	1099-R	Mileage, nonemployee	1099-NEC
Coverdell ESA contributions	5498-ESA	Military retirement	1099-R
Coverdell ESA distributions	1099-Q	Mortgage assistance payments	1098-MA
Crop insurance proceeds	1099-MISC	Mortgage interest	1098
Damages	1099-MISC	Moving expense	W-2
Death benefits	1099-R	Nonemployee compensation	1099-NEC
Debt cancellation	1099-C	Nonqualified deferred compensation:	
Dependent care payments	W-2	Beneficiary	1099-R
Direct rollovers	1099-Q,	Employee	W-2
	1099-R,	Nonemployee	1099-NEC
	5498	Original issue discount (OID)	1099-OID
Direct sales of consumer products for		Tax-exempt OID	1099-OID
resale	1099-MISC	Patronage dividends	1099-PATR
Directors' fees	1099-MISC	Payment card transactions	1099-K
Discharge of indebtedness	1099-C	Pensions	1099-R
Dividends	1099-DIV	Points	1098
Donation of motor vehicle	1098-C	Prizes, employee	W-2
Education loan interest	1098-E	Prizes, nonemployee	1099-NEC
Employee business expense		Profit-sharing plan	1099-R
reimbursement	W-2	Punitive damages	1099-MISC
Employee compensation	W-2	Qualified longevity annuity contract	1098-Q
Excess deferrals, excess contributions,		Qualified plan distributions	1099-R
distributions of	1099-R	Qualified tuition program payments	1099-Q
Exercise of incentive stock option		Real estate transactions	1099-S
under Code Sec. 422(b)	3921		

CHECKLISTS

Type of Payment	Report on Form	Type of Payment	Report on Form
Recharacterized IRA contributions . .	1099-R, 5498	Severance pay	W-2
		Sick pay	W-2
Refund, state and local tax	1099-G	SIMPLE contributions	W-2, 5498
Rents	1099-MISC	SIMPLE distributions	1099-R
Reportable policy sale	1099-LS	Student loan interest	1098-E
Retirement	1099-R	Substitute payments in lieu of dividends	
Roth conversion IRA contributions .	5498	or tax-exempt interest	1099-MISC
Roth conversion IRA distributions . .	1099-R	Supplemental unemployment	W-2
Roth IRA contributions	5498	Tax refunds, state and local	1099-G
Roth IRA distributions	1099-R	Third-party network payments	1099-K
Royalties	1099-MISC, 1099-S	Tips	W-2
		Traditional IRA contributions	5498
Timber, pay-as-cut contract	1099-S	Traditional IRA distributions	1099-R
Sales:		Transfer of stock acquired through an	
Real estate	1099-S	employee stock purchase plan under	
Securities	1099-B	Code Sec. 423(c)	3922
Code Sec. 1035 exchange	1099-R	Tuition	1098-T
Seller's investment in life insurance		Unemployment benefits	1099-G
contract	1099-SB	Vacation allowance, employee	W-2
SEP contributions	W-2, 5498	Vacation allowance, nonemployee . .	1099-NEC
SEP distributions	1099-R	Wages	W-2

SPECIAL TAX TABLES

¶ 83 Applicable Federal Rates

Following are the monthly applicable federal interest rates for January 2019 through May 2020 published by the IRS for purposes of testing imputed interest in below-market interest loans (¶ 795) and debt-for-property transactions (¶ 1954). The rates are also relevant under the golden parachute rules (¶ 907) and for testing interest in connection with deferred payments for the use of property (¶ 1859).

In the case of below-market interest loans that are demand or gift loans, an amount deemed the "foregone" interest is treated as transferred from the lender to the borrower and retransferred by the borrower to the lender as interest. In order to simplify the computation of such foregone interest, the IRS prescribes a "blended annual rate," which is 2.42% on loans for the calendar year 2019.

		Period for Compounding			
		Annual	*Semiannual*	*Quarterly*	*Monthly*
January 2019					
	Short-Term				
	AFR	2.72	2.70	2.69	2.68
110%	AFR	2.99	2.97	2.96	2.95
120%	AFR	3.27	3.24	3.23	3.22
130%	AFR	3.54	3.51	3.49	3.48
	Mid-Term				
	AFR	2.89	2.87	2.86	2.85
110%	AFR	3.18	3.16	3.15	3.14
120%	AFR	3.47	3.44	3.43	3.42
130%	AFR	3.76	3.73	3.71	3.70
150%	AFR	4.36	4.31	4.29	4.27
175%	AFR	5.08	5.02	4.99	4.97
	Long-Term				
	AFR	3.15	3.13	3.12	3.11
110%	AFR	3.47	3.44	3.43	3.42
120%	AFR	3.80	3.76	3.74	3.73
130%	AFR	4.11	4.07	4.05	4.04

		Period for Compounding			
		Annual	Semiannual	Quarterly	Monthly
February 2019					
	Short-Term				
	AFR	2.57	2.55	2.54	2.54
110%	AFR	2.83	2.81	2.80	2.79
120%	AFR	3.08	3.06	3.05	3.04
130%	AFR	3.35	3.32	3.31	3.30
	Mid-Term				
	AFR	2.63	2.61	2.60	2.60
110%	AFR	2.89	2.87	2.86	2.85
120%	AFR	3.15	3.13	3.12	3.11
130%	AFR	3.42	3.39	3.38	3.37
150%	AFR	3.96	3.92	3.90	3.89
175%	AFR	4.62	4.57	4.54	4.53
	Long-Term				
	AFR	2.91	2.89	2.88	2.87
110%	AFR	3.21	3.18	3.17	3.16
120%	AFR	3.50	3.47	3.46	3.45
130%	AFR	3.80	3.76	3.74	3.73
March 2019					
	Short-Term				
	AFR	2.55	2.53	2.52	2.52
110%	AFR	2.80	2.78	2.77	2.76
120%	AFR	3.06	3.04	3.03	3.02
130%	AFR	3.32	3.29	3.28	3.27
	Mid-Term				
	AFR	2.59	2.57	2.56	2.56
110%	AFR	2.85	2.83	2.82	2.81
120%	AFR	3.10	3.08	3.07	3.06
130%	AFR	3.37	3.34	3.33	3.32
150%	AFR	3.90	3.86	3.84	3.83
175%	AFR	4.55	4.50	4.47	4.46
	Long-Term				
	AFR	2.91	2.89	2.88	2.87
110%	AFR	3.21	3.18	3.17	3.16
120%	AFR	3.50	3.47	3.46	3.45
130%	AFR	3.80	3.76	3.74	3.73
April 2019					
	Short-Term				
	AFR	2.52	2.50	2.49	2.49
110%	AFR	2.77	2.75	2.74	2.73
120%	AFR	3.02	3.00	2.99	2.98
130%	AFR	3.28	3.25	3.24	3.23
	Mid-Term				
	AFR	2.55	2.53	2.52	2.52
110%	AFR	2.80	2.78	2.77	2.76
120%	AFR	3.06	3.04	3.03	3.02
130%	AFR	3.32	3.29	3.28	3.27
150%	AFR	3.84	3.80	3.78	3.77
175%	AFR	4.48	4.43	4.41	4.39
	Long-Term				
	AFR	2.89	2.87	2.86	2.85
110%	AFR	3.18	3.16	3.15	3.14
120%	AFR	3.47	3.44	3.43	3.42
130%	AFR	3.76	3.73	3.71	3.70

¶83

		Period for Compounding			
		Annual	Semiannual	Quarterly	Monthly
May 2019					
	Short-Term				
	AFR	2.39	2.38	2.37	2.37
110%	AFR	2.64	2.62	2.61	2.61
120%	AFR	2.88	2.86	2.85	2.84
130%	AFR	3.11	3.09	3.08	3.07
	Mid-Term				
	AFR	2.37	2.36	2.35	2.35
110%	AFR	2.62	2.60	2.59	2.59
120%	AFR	2.85	2.83	2.82	2.81
130%	AFR	3.09	3.07	3.06	3.05
150%	AFR	3.57	3.54	3.52	3.51
175%	AFR	4.17	4.13	4.11	4.09
	Long-Term				
	AFR	2.74	2.72	2.71	2.70
110%	AFR	3.01	2.99	2.98	2.97
120%	AFR	3.29	3.26	3.25	3.24
130%	AFR	3.57	3.54	3.52	3.51
June 2019					
	Short-Term				
	AFR	2.37	2.36	2.35	2.35
110%	AFR	2.62	2.60	2.59	2.59
120%	AFR	2.85	2.83	2.82	2.81
130%	AFR	3.09	3.07	3.06	3.05
	Mid-Term				
	AFR	2.38	2.37	2.36	2.36
110%	AFR	2.63	2.61	2.60	2.60
120%	AFR	2.86	2.84	2.83	2.82
130%	AFR	3.10	3.08	3.07	3.06
150%	AFR	3.59	3.56	3.54	3.53
175%	AFR	4.19	4.15	4.13	4.11
	Long-Term				
	AFR	2.76	2.74	2.73	2.72
110%	AFR	3.03	3.01	3.00	2.99
120%	AFR	3.32	3.29	3.28	3.27
130%	AFR	3.59	3.56	3.54	3.53
July 2019					
	Short-Term				
	AFR	2.13	2.12	2.11	2.11
110%	AFR	2.34	2.33	2.32	2.32
120%	AFR	2.56	2.54	2.53	2.53
130%	AFR	2.78	2.76	2.75	2.74
	Mid-Term				
	AFR	2.08	2.07	2.06	2.06
110%	AFR	2.29	2.28	2.27	2.27
120%	AFR	2.50	2.48	2.47	2.47
130%	AFR	2.71	2.69	2.68	2.68
150%	AFR	3.13	3.11	3.10	3.09
175%	AFR	3.65	3.62	3.60	3.59
	Long-Term				
	AFR	2.50	2.48	2.47	2.47
110%	AFR	2.75	2.73	2.72	2.71
120%	AFR	3.00	2.98	2.97	2.96
130%	AFR	3.25	3.22	3.21	3.20

SPECIAL TABLES

Period for Compounding

		Annual	Semiannual	Quarterly	Monthly
August 2019					
	Short-Term				
	AFR	1.91	1.90	1.90	1.89
110%	AFR	2.10	2.09	2.08	2.08
120%	AFR	2.29	2.28	2.27	2.27
130%	AFR	2.49	2.47	2.46	2.46
	Mid-Term				
	AFR	1.87	1.86	1.86	1.85
110%	AFR	2.06	2.05	2.04	2.04
120%	AFR	2.24	2.23	2.22	2.22
130%	AFR	2.43	2.42	2.41	2.41
150%	AFR	2.81	2.79	2.78	2.77
175%	AFR	3.29	3.26	3.25	3.24
	Long-Term				
	AFR	2.33	2.32	2.31	2.31
110%	AFR	2.57	2.55	2.54	2.54
120%	AFR	2.80	2.78	2.77	2.76
130%	AFR	3.04	3.02	3.01	3.00
September 2019					
	Short-Term				
	AFR	1.85	1.84	1.84	1.83
110%	AFR	2.03	2.02	2.01	2.01
120%	AFR	2.22	2.21	2.20	2.20
130%	AFR	2.40	2.39	2.38	2.38
	Mid-Term				
	AFR	1.78	1.77	1.77	1.76
110%	AFR	1.96	1.95	1.95	1.94
120%	AFR	2.13	2.12	2.11	2.11
130%	AFR	2.31	2.30	2.29	2.29
150%	AFR	2.68	2.66	2.65	2.65
175%	AFR	3.12	3.10	3.09	3.09
	Long-Term				
	AFR	2.21	2.20	2.19	2.19
110%	AFR	2.43	2.42	2.41	2.41
120%	AFR	2.66	2.64	2.63	2.63
130%	AFR	2.88	2.86	2.85	2.84
October 2019					
	Short-Term				
	AFR	1.69	1.68	1.68	1.67
110%	AFR	1.86	1.85	1.85	1.84
120%	AFR	2.03	2.02	2.01	2.01
130%	AFR	2.19	2.18	2.17	2.17
	Mid-Term				
	AFR	1.51	1.50	1.50	1.50
110%	AFR	1.66	1.65	1.65	1.64
120%	AFR	1.81	1.80	1.80	1.79
130%	AFR	1.96	1.95	1.95	1.94
150%	AFR	2.26	2.25	2.24	2.24
175%	AFR	2.65	2.63	2.62	2.62
	Long-Term				
	AFR	1.86	1.85	1.85	1.84
110%	AFR	2.05	2.04	2.03	2.03
120%	AFR	2.23	2.22	2.21	2.21
130%	AFR	2.42	2.41	2.40	2.40

	Period for Compounding			
	Annual	Semiannual	Quarterly	Monthly

November 2019

Short-Term

		Annual	Semiannual	Quarterly	Monthly
	AFR	1.68	1.67	1.67	1.66
110%	AFR	1.85	1.84	1.84	1.83
120%	AFR	2.01	2.00	2.00	1.99
130%	AFR	2.18	2.17	2.16	2.16

Mid-Term

		Annual	Semiannual	Quarterly	Monthly
	AFR	1.59	1.58	1.58	1.57
110%	AFR	1.75	1.74	1.74	1.73
120%	AFR	1.91	1.90	1.90	1.89
130%	AFR	2.06	2.05	2.04	2.04
150%	AFR	2.38	2.37	2.36	2.36
175%	AFR	2.79	2.77	2.76	2.75

Long-Term

		Annual	Semiannual	Quarterly	Monthly
	AFR	1.94	1.93	1.93	1.92
110%	AFR	2.13	2.12	2.11	2.11
120%	AFR	2.33	2.32	2.31	2.31
130%	AFR	2.53	2.51	2.50	2.50

December 2019

Short-Term

		Annual	Semiannual	Quarterly	Monthly
	AFR	1.61	1.60	1.60	1.59
110%	AFR	1.77	1.76	1.76	1.75
120%	AFR	1.93	1.92	1.92	1.91
130%	AFR	2.09	2.08	2.07	2.07

Mid-Term

		Annual	Semiannual	Quarterly	Monthly
	AFR	1.69	1.68	1.68	1.67
110%	AFR	1.86	1.85	1.85	1.84
120%	AFR	2.03	2.02	2.01	2.01
130%	AFR	2.19	2.18	2.17	2.17
150%	AFR	2.54	2.52	2.51	2.51
175%	AFR	2.96	2.94	2.93	2.92

Long-Term

		Annual	Semiannual	Quarterly	Monthly
	AFR	2.09	2.08	2.07	2.07
110%	AFR	2.30	2.29	2.28	2.28
120%	AFR	2.52	2.50	2.49	2.49
130%	AFR	2.72	2.70	2.69	2.68

January 2020

Short-Term

		Annual	Semiannual	Quarterly	Monthly
	AFR	1.60	1.59	1.59	1.58
110%	AFR	1.76	1.75	1.75	1.74
120%	AFR	1.92	1.91	1.91	1.90
130%	AFR	2.08	2.07	2.06	2.06

Mid-Term

		Annual	Semiannual	Quarterly	Monthly
	AFR	1.69	1.68	1.68	1.67
110%	AFR	1.86	1.85	1.85	1.84
120%	AFR	2.03	2.02	2.01	2.01
130%	AFR	2.19	2.18	2.17	2.17
150%	AFR	2.54	2.52	2.51	2.51
175%	AFR	2.96	2.94	2.93	2.92

Long-Term

		Annual	Semiannual	Quarterly	Monthly
	AFR	2.07	2.06	2.05	2.05
110%	AFR	2.28	2.27	2.26	2.26
120%	AFR	2.49	2.47	2.46	2.46
130%	AFR	2.70	2.68	2.67	2.67

SPECIAL TABLES

Period for Compounding			
Annual	*Semiannual*	*Quarterly*	*Monthly*

February 2020

Short-Term

	Annual	Semiannual	Quarterly	Monthly
AFR	1.59	1.58	1.58	1.57
110% AFR	1.75	1.74	1.74	1.73
120% AFR	1.91	1.90	1.90	1.89
130% AFR	2.06	2.05	2.04	2.04

Mid-Term

AFR	1.75	1.74	1.74	1.73
110% AFR	1.92	1.91	1.91	1.90
120% AFR	2.10	2.09	2.08	2.08
130% AFR	2.27	2.26	2.25	2.25
150% AFR	2.63	2.61	2.60	2.60
175% AFR	3.07	3.05	3.04	3.03

Long-Term

AFR	2.15	2.14	2.13	2.13
110% AFR	2.36	2.35	2.34	2.34
120% AFR	2.59	2.57	2.56	2.56
130% AFR	2.80	2.78	2.77	2.76

March 2020

Short-Term

AFR	1.50	1.49	1.49	1.49
110% AFR	1.65	1.64	1.64	1.63
120% AFR	1.80	1.79	1.79	1.78
130% AFR	1.95	1.94	1.94	1.93

Mid-Term

AFR	1.53	1.52	1.52	1.52
110% AFR	1.68	1.67	1.67	1.66
120% AFR	1.83	1.82	1.82	1.81
130% AFR	1.99	1.98	1.98	1.97
150% AFR	2.29	2.28	2.27	2.27
175% AFR	2.68	2.66	2.65	2.65

Long-Term

AFR	1.93	1.92	1.92	1.91
110% AFR	2.12	2.11	2.10	2.10
120% AFR	2.31	2.30	2.29	2.29
130% AFR	2.52	2.50	2.49	2.49

April 2020

Short-Term

AFR	0.91	0.91	0.91	0.91
110% AFR	1.00	1.00	1.00	1.00
120% AFR	1.09	1.09	1.09	1.09
130% AFR	1.18	1.18	1.18	1.18

Mid-Term

AFR	0.99	0.99	0.99	0.99
110% AFR	1.09	1.09	1.09	1.09
120% AFR	1.19	1.19	1.19	1.19
130% AFR	1.29	1.29	1.29	1.29
150% AFR	1.50	1.49	1.49	1.49
175% AFR	1.74	1.73	1.73	1.72

Long-Term

AFR	1.44	1.43	1.44	1.44
110% AFR	1.58	1.57	1.57	1.56
120% AFR	1.73	1.72	1.72	1.71
130% AFR	1.87	1.86	1.86	1.85

		Period for Compounding			
		Annual	*Semiannual*	*Quarterly*	*Monthly*
May 2020					
	Short-Term				
	AFR	0.25	0.25	0.25	0.25
110%	AFR	0.28	0.28	0.28	0.28
120%	AFR	0.30	0.30	0.30	0.30
130%	AFR	0.33	0.33	0.33	0.33
	Mid-Term				
	AFR	0.58	0.58	0.58	0.58
110%	AFR	0.64	0.64	0.64	0.64
120%	AFR	0.70	0.70	0.70	0.70
130%	AFR	0.75	0.75	0.75	0.75
150%	AFR	0.87	0.87	0.87	0.87
175%	AFR	1.02	1.02	1.02	1.02
	Long-Term				
	AFR	1.15	1.15	1.15	1.15
110%	AFR	1.27	1.27	1.27	1.27
120%	AFR	1.38	1.38	1.38	1.38
130%	AFR	1.51	1.50	1.50	1.50

SPECIAL TABLES

¶83

¶ 84 Adjusted Applicable Federal Rates

Code Sec. 1288 provides that, in determining original issue discount on tax-exempt obligations, an adjustment must be made to the applicable federal rates (¶ 83) to take into account the tax exemption for interest on the obligations.

Adjusted Applicable Federal Rates

January 2019

	Annual Compounding	SemiAnnual Compounding	Quarterly Compounding	Monthly Compounding
Short-term rate	2.06%	2.05%	2.04%	2.04%
Mid-term rate	2.19%	2.18%	2.17%	2.17%
Long-term rate	2.39%	2.38%	2.37%	2.37%

February 2019

	Annual Compounding	SemiAnnual Compounding	Quarterly Compounding	Monthly Compounding
Short-term rate	1.95%	1.94%	1.94%	1.93%
Mid-term rate	1.99%	1.98%	1.98%	1.97%
Long-term rate	2.20%	2.19%	2.18%	2.18%

March 2019

	Annual Compounding	SemiAnnual Compounding	Quarterly Compounding	Monthly Compounding
Short-term rate	1.93%	1.92%	1.92%	1.91%
Mid-term rate	1.96%	1.95%	1.95%	1.94%
Long-term rate	2.20%	2.19%	2.18%	2.18%

April 2019

	Annual Compounding	SemiAnnual Compounding	Quarterly Compounding	Monthly Compounding
Short-term rate	1.91%	1.90%	1.90%	1.89%
Mid-term rate	1.93%	1.92%	1.92%	1.91%
Long-term rate	2.19%	2.18%	2.17%	2.17%

May 2019

	Annual Compounding	SemiAnnual Compounding	Quarterly Compounding	Monthly Compounding
Short-term rate	1.82%	1.81%	1.81%	1.80%
Mid-term rate	1.80%	1.79%	1.79%	1.78%
Long-term rate	2.08%	2.07%	2.06%	2.06%

June 2019

	Annual Compounding	SemiAnnual Compounding	Quarterly Compounding	Monthly Compounding
Short-term rate	1.80%	1.79%	1.79%	1.78%
Mid-term rate	1.81%	1.80%	1.80%	1.79%
Long-term rate	2.09%	2.08%	2.07%	2.07%

July 2019

	Annual Compounding	SemiAnnual Compounding	Quarterly Compounding	Monthly Compounding
Short-term rate	1.62%	1.61%	1.61%	1.60%
Mid-term rate	1.58%	1.57%	1.57%	1.56%
Long-term rate	1.89%	1.88%	1.88%	1.87%

August 2019

	Annual Compounding	SemiAnnual Compounding	Quarterly Compounding	Monthly Compounding
Short-term rate	1.45%	1.44%	1.44%	1.44%
Mid-term rate	1.41%	1.41%	1.41%	1.41%
Long-term rate	1.77%	1.76%	1.76%	1.75%

September 2019

	Annual Compounding	SemiAnnual Compounding	Quarterly Compounding	Monthly Compounding
Short-term rate	1.40%	1.40%	1.40%	1.40%
Mid-term rate	1.34%	1.34%	1.34%	1.34%
Long-term rate	1.68%	1.67%	1.67%	1.66%

October 2019

	Annual Compounding	SemiAnnual Compounding	Quarterly Compounding	Monthly Compounding
Short-term rate	1.28%	1.28%	1.28%	1.28%
Mid-term rate	1.14%	1.14%	1.14%	1.14%
Long-term rate	1.40%	1.40%	1.40%	1.40%

November 2019

	Annual Compounding	SemiAnnual Compounding	Quarterly Compounding	Monthly Compounding
Short-term rate	1.27%	1.27%	1.27%	1.27%
Mid-term rate	1.20%	1.20%	1.20%	1.20%
Long-term rate	1.48%	1.47%	1.47%	1.47%

December 2019

	Annual Compounding	SemiAnnual Compounding	Quarterly Compounding	Monthly Compounding
Short-term rate	1.21%	1.21%	1.21%	1.21%
Mid-term rate	1.28%	1.28%	1.28%	1.28%
Long-term rate	1.59%	1.58%	1.58%	1.57%

January 2020

	Annual Compounding	SemiAnnual Compounding	Quarterly Compounding	Monthly Compounding
Short-term rate	1.21%	1.21%	1.21%	1.21%
Mid-term rate	1.28%	1.28%	1.28%	1.28%
Long-term rate	1.57%	1.56%	1.56%	1.55%

February 2020

	Annual Compounding	SemiAnnual Compounding	Quarterly Compounding	Monthly Compounding
Short-term rate	1.20%	1.20%	1.20%	1.20%
Mid-term rate	1.32%	1.32%	1.32%	1.32%
Long-term rate	1.63%	1.62%	1.62%	1.61%

March 2020

	Annual Compounding	SemiAnnual Compounding	Quarterly Compounding	Monthly Compounding
Short-term rate	1.13%	1.13%	1.13%	1.13%
Mid-term rate	1.15%	1.15%	1.15%	1.15%
Long-term rate	1.47%	1.46%	1.46%	1.46%

April 2020

	Annual Compounding	SemiAnnual Compounding	Quarterly Compounding	Monthly Compounding
Short-term rate	0.69%	0.69%	0.69%	0.69%
Mid-term rate	0.75%	0.75%	0.75%	0.75%
Long-term rate	1.09%	1.09%	1.09%	1.09%

May 2020

	Annual Compounding	SemiAnnual Compounding	Quarterly Compounding	Monthly Compounding
Short-term rate	0.19%	0.19%	0.19%	0.19%
Mid-term rate	0.44%	0.44%	0.44%	0.44%
Long-term rate	0.87%	0.87%	0.87%	0.87%

SPECIAL TABLES

¶84

¶ 85 Federal Long-Term Tax-Exempt Rates

Code Sec. 382 provides that the long-term tax-exempt rate for purposes of net operating loss carryforwards shall be the highest of the adjusted federal long-term rates (¶ 84) for the three months ending with the month in which the particular ownership change occurs. Each rate below is the highest for the 3-month period.

Long-Term Tax-Exempt Rates

Month	Rate
January 2019	2.51%
February 2019	2.51%
March 2019	2.39%
April 2019	2.20%
May 2019	2.20%
June 2019	2.19%
July 2019	2.09%
August 2019	2.09%
September 2019	1.89%
October 2019	1.77%
November 2019	1.68%
December 2019	1.59%
January 2020	1.59%
February 2020	1.63%
March 2020	1.63%
April 2020	1.63%
May 2020	1.47%

¶ 86 Applicable Credit Percentages for Low-Income Housing

Code Sec. 42 provides that applicable credit percentages for low-income housing are to be computed so that the present value of the 10 annual credit amounts at the beginning of the 10-year credit period equals either 70% or 30% of the qualified basis of the low-income units in a project. The discount rate for determining the present value in these computations is a rate equal to 72% of the average of the month's AFR for mid-term and long-term obligations. The applicable credit percentage for new construction or rehabilitation expenditures not federally subsidized is indicated under the 70% rate column. The applicable credit percentage for subsidized construction or rehabilitation expenditures and the acquisition of existing housing is indicated under the 30% rate column. See ¶ 1465K.

Applicable Credit Percentages for Low-Income Housing

Month	70% Rate	30% Rate
January 2019	7.70%	3.30%
February 2019	7.64%	3.27%
March 2019	7.63%	3.27%
April 2019	7.63%	3.27%
May 2019	7.59%	3.25%
June 2019	7.59%	3.25%
July 2019	7.53%	3.23%
August 2019	7.48%	3.21%
September 2019	7.46%	3.20%
October 2019	7.39%	3.17%
November 2019	7.40%	3.17%
December 2019	7.43%	3.19%
January 2020	7.43%	3.18%
February 2020	7.45%	3.19%
March 2020	7.40%	3.17%
April 2020	7.28%	3.12%
May 2020	7.20%	3.08%

¶ 87 Earned Income Credit

The earned income credit tables are used in conjunction with the Form 1040 and Schedule EIC. The Schedule EIC must be filed with the taxpayer's tax return in order to claim the earned income credit. The credit, as computed on the EIC Worksheet found in the Form 1040 instructions, is entered on the appropriate line of Form 1040.

2019 Earned Income Credit (EIC) Table
Caution. This is **not** a tax table.

1. To find your credit, read down the "At least - But less than" columns and find the line that includes the amount you were told to look up from your EIC Worksheet.

2. Then, go to the column that includes your filing status and the number of qualifying children you have. Enter the credit from that column on your EIC Worksheet.

Example. If your filing status is single, you have one qualifying child, and the amount you are looking up from your EIC Worksheet is $2,455, you would enter $842.

If the amount you are looking up from the worksheet is–		And your filing status is– Single, head of household, or qualifying widow(er) and the number of children you have is–			
At least	But less than	0	1	2	3
2,400	2,450	186	825	970	1,091
2,450	2,500	189	842	990	1,114

If the amount you are looking up from the worksheet is–		And your filing status is–							
		Single, head of household, or qualifying widow(er) and you have–				Married filing jointly and you have–			
At least	But less than	0	1	2	3	0	1	2	3
		Your credit is–				Your credit is–			
$1	$50	$2	$9	$10	$11	$2	$9	$10	$11
50	100	6	26	30	34	6	26	30	34
100	150	10	43	50	56	10	43	50	56
150	200	13	60	70	79	13	60	70	79
200	250	17	77	90	101	17	77	90	101
250	300	21	94	110	124	21	94	110	124
300	350	25	111	130	146	25	111	130	146
350	400	29	128	150	169	29	128	150	169
400	450	33	145	170	191	33	145	170	191
450	500	36	162	190	214	36	162	190	214
500	550	40	179	210	236	40	179	210	236
550	600	44	196	230	259	44	196	230	259
600	650	48	213	250	281	48	213	250	281
650	700	52	230	270	304	52	230	270	304
700	750	55	247	290	326	55	247	290	326
750	800	59	264	310	349	59	264	310	349
800	850	63	281	330	371	63	281	330	371
850	900	67	298	350	394	67	298	350	394
900	950	71	315	370	416	71	315	370	416
950	1,000	75	332	390	439	75	332	390	439
1,000	1,050	78	349	410	461	78	349	410	461
1,050	1,100	82	366	430	484	82	366	430	484
1,100	1,150	86	383	450	506	86	383	450	506
1,150	1,200	90	400	470	529	90	400	470	529
1,200	1,250	94	417	490	551	94	417	490	551
1,250	1,300	98	434	510	574	98	434	510	574
1,300	1,350	101	451	530	596	101	451	530	596
1,350	1,400	105	468	550	619	105	468	550	619
1,400	1,450	109	485	570	641	109	485	570	641
1,450	1,500	113	502	590	664	113	502	590	664
1,500	1,550	117	519	610	686	117	519	610	686
1,550	1,600	120	536	630	709	120	536	630	709
1,600	1,650	124	553	650	731	124	553	650	731
1,650	1,700	128	570	670	754	128	570	670	754
1,700	1,750	132	587	690	776	132	587	690	776
1,750	1,800	136	604	710	799	136	604	710	799
1,800	1,850	140	621	730	821	140	621	730	821
1,850	1,900	143	638	750	844	143	638	750	844
1,900	1,950	147	655	770	866	147	655	770	866
1,950	2,000	151	672	790	889	151	672	790	889
2,000	2,050	155	689	810	911	155	689	810	911
2,050	2,100	159	706	830	934	159	706	830	934
2,100	2,150	163	723	850	956	163	723	850	956
2,150	2,200	166	740	870	979	166	740	870	979
2,200	2,250	170	757	890	1,001	170	757	890	1,001
2,250	2,300	174	774	910	1,024	174	774	910	1,024
2,300	2,350	178	791	930	1,046	178	791	930	1,046
2,350	2,400	182	808	950	1,069	182	808	950	1,069
2,400	2,450	186	825	970	1,091	186	825	970	1,091
2,450	2,500	189	842	990	1,114	189	842	990	1,114
2,500	2,550	193	859	1,010	1,136	193	859	1,010	1,136
2,550	2,600	197	876	1,030	1,159	197	876	1,030	1,159
2,600	2,650	201	893	1,050	1,181	201	893	1,050	1,181
2,650	2,700	205	910	1,070	1,204	205	910	1,070	1,204
2,700	2,750	208	927	1,090	1,226	208	927	1,090	1,226
2,750	2,800	212	944	1,110	1,249	212	944	1,110	1,249

If the amount you are looking up from the worksheet is–		And your filing status is–							
		Single, head of household, or qualifying widow(er) and you have–				Married filing jointly and you have–			
At least	But less than	0	1	2	3	0	1	2	3
		Your credit is–				Your credit is–			
2,800	2,850	216	961	1,130	1,271	216	961	1,130	1,271
2,850	2,900	220	978	1,150	1,294	220	978	1,150	1,294
2,900	2,950	224	995	1,170	1,316	224	995	1,170	1,316
2,950	3,000	228	1,012	1,190	1,339	228	1,012	1,190	1,339
3,000	3,050	231	1,029	1,210	1,361	231	1,029	1,210	1,361
3,050	3,100	235	1,046	1,230	1,384	235	1,046	1,230	1,384
3,100	3,150	239	1,063	1,250	1,406	239	1,063	1,250	1,406
3,150	3,200	243	1,080	1,270	1,429	243	1,080	1,270	1,429
3,200	3,250	247	1,097	1,290	1,451	247	1,097	1,290	1,451
3,250	3,300	251	1,114	1,310	1,474	251	1,114	1,310	1,474
3,300	3,350	254	1,131	1,330	1,496	254	1,131	1,330	1,496
3,350	3,400	258	1,148	1,350	1,519	258	1,148	1,350	1,519
3,400	3,450	262	1,165	1,370	1,541	262	1,165	1,370	1,541
3,450	3,500	266	1,182	1,390	1,564	266	1,182	1,390	1,564
3,500	3,550	270	1,199	1,410	1,586	270	1,199	1,410	1,586
3,550	3,600	273	1,216	1,430	1,609	273	1,216	1,430	1,609
3,600	3,650	277	1,233	1,450	1,631	277	1,233	1,450	1,631
3,650	3,700	281	1,250	1,470	1,654	281	1,250	1,470	1,654
3,700	3,750	285	1,267	1,490	1,676	285	1,267	1,490	1,676
3,750	3,800	289	1,284	1,510	1,699	289	1,284	1,510	1,699
3,800	3,850	293	1,301	1,530	1,721	293	1,301	1,530	1,721
3,850	3,900	296	1,318	1,550	1,744	296	1,318	1,550	1,744
3,900	3,950	300	1,335	1,570	1,766	300	1,335	1,570	1,766
3,950	4,000	304	1,352	1,590	1,789	304	1,352	1,590	1,789
4,000	4,050	308	1,369	1,610	1,811	308	1,369	1,610	1,811
4,050	4,100	312	1,386	1,630	1,834	312	1,386	1,630	1,834
4,100	4,150	316	1,403	1,650	1,856	316	1,403	1,650	1,856
4,150	4,200	319	1,420	1,670	1,879	319	1,420	1,670	1,879
4,200	4,250	323	1,437	1,690	1,901	323	1,437	1,690	1,901
4,250	4,300	327	1,454	1,710	1,924	327	1,454	1,710	1,924
4,300	4,350	331	1,471	1,730	1,946	331	1,471	1,730	1,946
4,350	4,400	335	1,488	1,750	1,969	335	1,488	1,750	1,969
4,400	4,450	339	1,505	1,770	1,991	339	1,505	1,770	1,991
4,450	4,500	343	1,522	1,790	2,014	343	1,522	1,790	2,014
4,500	4,550	346	1,539	1,810	2,036	346	1,539	1,810	2,036
4,550	4,600	350	1,556	1,830	2,059	350	1,556	1,830	2,059
4,600	4,650	354	1,573	1,850	2,081	354	1,573	1,850	2,081
4,650	4,700	358	1,590	1,870	2,104	358	1,590	1,870	2,104
4,700	4,750	361	1,607	1,890	2,126	361	1,607	1,890	2,126
4,750	4,800	365	1,624	1,910	2,149	365	1,624	1,910	2,149
4,800	4,850	369	1,641	1,930	2,171	369	1,641	1,930	2,171
4,850	4,900	373	1,658	1,950	2,194	373	1,658	1,950	2,194
4,900	4,950	377	1,675	1,970	2,216	377	1,675	1,970	2,216
4,950	5,000	381	1,692	1,990	2,239	381	1,692	1,990	2,239
5,000	5,050	384	1,709	2,010	2,261	384	1,709	2,010	2,261
5,050	5,100	388	1,726	2,030	2,284	388	1,726	2,030	2,284
5,100	5,150	392	1,743	2,050	2,306	392	1,743	2,050	2,306
5,150	5,200	396	1,760	2,070	2,329	396	1,760	2,070	2,329
5,200	5,250	400	1,777	2,090	2,351	400	1,777	2,090	2,351
5,250	5,300	404	1,794	2,110	2,374	404	1,794	2,110	2,374
5,300	5,350	407	1,811	2,130	2,396	407	1,811	2,130	2,396
5,350	5,400	411	1,828	2,150	2,419	411	1,828	2,150	2,419
5,400	5,450	415	1,845	2,170	2,441	415	1,845	2,170	2,441
5,450	5,500	419	1,862	2,190	2,464	419	1,862	2,190	2,464
5,500	5,550	423	1,879	2,210	2,486	423	1,879	2,210	2,486
5,550	5,600	426	1,896	2,230	2,509	426	1,896	2,230	2,509

(Continued)

SPECIAL TABLES

¶87

82   U.S. Master Tax Guide

Earned Income Credit (EIC) Table - *Continued*   (Caution. This is not a tax table.)

At least	But less than	Single 0	1	2	3	Married 0	1	2	3
5,600	5,650	430	1,913	2,250	2,531	430	1,913	2,250	2,531
5,650	5,700	434	1,930	2,270	2,554	434	1,930	2,270	2,554
5,700	5,750	438	1,947	2,290	2,576	438	1,947	2,290	2,576
5,750	5,800	442	1,964	2,310	2,599	442	1,964	2,310	2,599
5,800	5,850	446	1,981	2,330	2,621	446	1,981	2,330	2,621
5,850	5,900	449	1,998	2,350	2,644	449	1,998	2,350	2,644
5,900	5,950	453	2,015	2,370	2,666	453	2,015	2,370	2,666
5,950	6,000	457	2,032	2,390	2,689	457	2,032	2,390	2,689
6,000	6,050	461	2,049	2,410	2,711	461	2,049	2,410	2,711
6,050	6,100	465	2,066	2,430	2,734	465	2,066	2,430	2,734
6,100	6,150	469	2,083	2,450	2,756	469	2,083	2,450	2,756
6,150	6,200	472	2,100	2,470	2,779	472	2,100	2,470	2,779
6,200	6,250	476	2,117	2,490	2,801	476	2,117	2,490	2,801
6,250	6,300	480	2,134	2,510	2,824	480	2,134	2,510	2,824
6,300	6,350	484	2,151	2,530	2,846	484	2,151	2,530	2,846
6,350	6,400	488	2,168	2,550	2,869	488	2,168	2,550	2,869
6,400	6,450	492	2,185	2,570	2,891	492	2,185	2,570	2,891
6,450	6,500	495	2,202	2,590	2,914	495	2,202	2,590	2,914
6,500	6,550	499	2,219	2,610	2,936	499	2,219	2,610	2,936
6,550	6,600	503	2,236	2,630	2,959	503	2,236	2,630	2,959
6,600	6,650	507	2,253	2,650	2,981	507	2,253	2,650	2,981
6,650	6,700	511	2,270	2,670	3,004	511	2,270	2,670	3,004
6,700	6,750	514	2,287	2,690	3,026	514	2,287	2,690	3,026
6,750	6,800	518	2,304	2,710	3,049	518	2,304	2,710	3,049
6,800	6,850	522	2,321	2,730	3,071	522	2,321	2,730	3,071
6,850	6,900	526	2,338	2,750	3,094	526	2,338	2,750	3,094
6,900	6,950	529	2,355	2,770	3,116	529	2,355	2,770	3,116
6,950	7,000	529	2,372	2,790	3,139	529	2,372	2,790	3,139
7,000	7,050	529	2,389	2,810	3,161	529	2,389	2,810	3,161
7,050	7,100	529	2,406	2,830	3,184	529	2,406	2,830	3,184
7,100	7,150	529	2,423	2,850	3,206	529	2,423	2,850	3,206
7,150	7,200	529	2,440	2,870	3,229	529	2,440	2,870	3,229
7,200	7,250	529	2,457	2,890	3,251	529	2,457	2,890	3,251
7,250	7,300	529	2,474	2,910	3,274	529	2,474	2,910	3,274
7,300	7,350	529	2,491	2,930	3,296	529	2,491	2,930	3,296
7,350	7,400	529	2,508	2,950	3,319	529	2,508	2,950	3,319
7,400	7,450	529	2,525	2,970	3,341	529	2,525	2,970	3,341
7,450	7,500	529	2,542	2,990	3,364	529	2,542	2,990	3,364
7,500	7,550	529	2,559	3,010	3,386	529	2,559	3,010	3,386
7,550	7,600	529	2,576	3,030	3,409	529	2,576	3,030	3,409
7,600	7,650	529	2,593	3,050	3,431	529	2,593	3,050	3,431
7,650	7,700	529	2,610	3,070	3,454	529	2,610	3,070	3,454
7,700	7,750	529	2,627	3,090	3,476	529	2,627	3,090	3,476
7,750	7,800	529	2,644	3,110	3,499	529	2,644	3,110	3,499
7,800	7,850	529	2,661	3,130	3,521	529	2,661	3,130	3,521
7,850	7,900	529	2,678	3,150	3,544	529	2,678	3,150	3,544
7,900	7,950	529	2,695	3,170	3,566	529	2,695	3,170	3,566
7,950	8,000	529	2,712	3,190	3,589	529	2,712	3,190	3,589
8,000	8,050	529	2,729	3,210	3,611	529	2,729	3,210	3,611
8,050	8,100	529	2,746	3,230	3,634	529	2,746	3,230	3,634
8,100	8,150	529	2,763	3,250	3,656	529	2,763	3,250	3,656
8,150	8,200	529	2,780	3,270	3,679	529	2,780	3,270	3,679
8,200	8,250	529	2,797	3,290	3,701	529	2,797	3,290	3,701
8,250	8,300	529	2,814	3,310	3,724	529	2,814	3,310	3,724
8,300	8,350	529	2,831	3,330	3,746	529	2,831	3,330	3,746
8,350	8,400	529	2,848	3,350	3,769	529	2,848	3,350	3,769
8,400	8,450	529	2,865	3,370	3,791	529	2,865	3,370	3,791
8,450	8,500	529	2,882	3,390	3,814	529	2,882	3,390	3,814
8,500	8,550	529	2,899	3,410	3,836	529	2,899	3,410	3,836
8,550	8,600	529	2,916	3,430	3,859	529	2,916	3,430	3,859
8,600	8,650	529	2,933	3,450	3,881	529	2,933	3,450	3,881
8,650	8,700	527	2,950	3,470	3,904	529	2,950	3,470	3,904
8,700	8,750	524	2,967	3,490	3,926	529	2,967	3,490	3,926
8,750	8,800	520	2,984	3,510	3,949	529	2,984	3,510	3,949
8,800	8,850	516	3,001	3,530	3,971	529	3,001	3,530	3,971
8,850	8,900	512	3,018	3,550	3,994	529	3,018	3,550	3,994
8,900	8,950	508	3,035	3,570	4,016	529	3,035	3,570	4,016
8,950	9,000	505	3,052	3,590	4,039	529	3,052	3,590	4,039
9,000	9,050	501	3,069	3,610	4,061	529	3,069	3,610	4,061
9,050	9,100	497	3,086	3,630	4,084	529	3,086	3,630	4,084
9,100	9,150	493	3,103	3,650	4,106	529	3,103	3,650	4,106
9,150	9,200	489	3,120	3,670	4,129	529	3,120	3,670	4,129
9,200	9,250	485	3,137	3,690	4,151	529	3,137	3,690	4,151
9,250	9,300	482	3,154	3,710	4,174	529	3,154	3,710	4,174
9,300	9,350	478	3,171	3,730	4,196	529	3,171	3,730	4,196
9,350	9,400	474	3,188	3,750	4,219	529	3,188	3,750	4,219
9,400	9,450	470	3,205	3,770	4,241	529	3,205	3,770	4,241
9,450	9,500	466	3,222	3,790	4,264	529	3,222	3,790	4,264
9,500	9,550	462	3,239	3,810	4,286	529	3,239	3,810	4,286
9,550	9,600	459	3,256	3,830	4,309	529	3,256	3,830	4,309
9,600	9,650	455	3,273	3,850	4,331	529	3,273	3,850	4,331
9,650	9,700	451	3,290	3,870	4,354	529	3,290	3,870	4,354
9,700	9,750	447	3,307	3,890	4,376	529	3,307	3,890	4,376
9,750	9,800	443	3,324	3,910	4,399	529	3,324	3,910	4,399
9,800	9,850	439	3,341	3,930	4,421	529	3,341	3,930	4,421
9,850	9,900	436	3,358	3,950	4,444	529	3,358	3,950	4,444
9,900	9,950	432	3,375	3,970	4,466	529	3,375	3,970	4,466
9,950	10,000	428	3,392	3,990	4,489	529	3,392	3,990	4,489
10,000	10,050	424	3,409	4,010	4,511	529	3,409	4,010	4,511
10,050	10,100	420	3,426	4,030	4,534	529	3,426	4,030	4,534
10,100	10,150	417	3,443	4,050	4,556	529	3,443	4,050	4,556
10,150	10,200	413	3,460	4,070	4,579	529	3,460	4,070	4,579
10,200	10,250	409	3,477	4,090	4,601	529	3,477	4,090	4,601
10,250	10,300	405	3,494	4,110	4,624	529	3,494	4,110	4,624
10,300	10,350	401	3,511	4,130	4,646	529	3,511	4,130	4,646
10,350	10,400	397	3,526	4,150	4,669	529	3,526	4,150	4,669
10,400	10,450	394	3,526	4,170	4,691	529	3,526	4,170	4,691
10,450	10,500	390	3,526	4,190	4,714	529	3,526	4,190	4,714
10,500	10,550	386	3,526	4,210	4,736	529	3,526	4,210	4,736
10,550	10,600	382	3,526	4,230	4,759	529	3,526	4,230	4,759
10,600	10,650	378	3,526	4,250	4,781	529	3,526	4,250	4,781
10,650	10,700	374	3,526	4,270	4,804	529	3,526	4,270	4,804
10,700	10,750	371	3,526	4,290	4,826	529	3,526	4,290	4,826
10,750	10,800	367	3,526	4,310	4,849	529	3,526	4,310	4,849
10,800	10,850	363	3,526	4,330	4,871	529	3,526	4,330	4,871
10,850	10,900	359	3,526	4,350	4,894	529	3,526	4,350	4,894
10,900	10,950	355	3,526	4,370	4,916	529	3,526	4,370	4,916
10,950	11,000	352	3,526	4,390	4,939	529	3,526	4,390	4,939
11,000	11,050	348	3,526	4,410	4,961	529	3,526	4,410	4,961
11,050	11,100	344	3,526	4,430	4,984	529	3,526	4,430	4,984
11,100	11,150	340	3,526	4,450	5,006	529	3,526	4,450	5,006
11,150	11,200	336	3,526	4,470	5,029	529	3,526	4,470	5,029
11,200	11,250	332	3,526	4,490	5,051	529	3,526	4,490	5,051
11,250	11,300	329	3,526	4,510	5,074	529	3,526	4,510	5,074
11,300	11,350	325	3,526	4,530	5,096	529	3,526	4,530	5,096
11,350	11,400	321	3,526	4,550	5,119	529	3,526	4,550	5,119
11,400	11,450	317	3,526	4,570	5,141	529	3,526	4,570	5,141
11,450	11,500	313	3,526	4,590	5,164	529	3,526	4,590	5,164
11,500	11,550	309	3,526	4,610	5,186	529	3,526	4,610	5,186
11,550	11,600	306	3,526	4,630	5,209	529	3,526	4,630	5,209
11,600	11,650	302	3,526	4,650	5,231	529	3,526	4,650	5,231
11,650	11,700	298	3,526	4,670	5,254	529	3,526	4,670	5,254
11,700	11,750	294	3,526	4,690	5,276	529	3,526	4,690	5,276
11,750	11,800	290	3,526	4,710	5,299	529	3,526	4,710	5,299
11,800	11,850	286	3,526	4,730	5,321	529	3,526	4,730	5,321
11,850	11,900	283	3,526	4,750	5,344	529	3,526	4,750	5,344
11,900	11,950	279	3,526	4,770	5,366	529	3,526	4,770	5,366
11,950	12,000	275	3,526	4,790	5,389	529	3,526	4,790	5,389
12,000	12,050	271	3,526	4,810	5,411	529	3,526	4,810	5,411
12,050	12,100	267	3,526	4,830	5,434	529	3,526	4,830	5,434
12,100	12,150	264	3,526	4,850	5,456	529	3,526	4,850	5,456
12,150	12,200	260	3,526	4,870	5,479	529	3,526	4,870	5,479
12,200	12,250	256	3,526	4,890	5,501	529	3,526	4,890	5,501
12,250	12,300	252	3,526	4,910	5,524	529	3,526	4,910	5,524
12,300	12,350	248	3,526	4,930	5,546	529	3,526	4,930	5,546
12,350	12,400	244	3,526	4,950	5,569	529	3,526	4,950	5,569
12,400	12,450	241	3,526	4,970	5,591	529	3,526	4,970	5,591
12,450	12,500	237	3,526	4,990	5,614	529	3,526	4,990	5,614
12,500	12,550	233	3,526	5,010	5,636	529	3,526	5,010	5,636
12,550	12,600	229	3,526	5,030	5,659	529	3,526	5,030	5,659
12,600	12,650	225	3,526	5,050	5,681	529	3,526	5,050	5,681
12,650	12,700	221	3,526	5,070	5,704	529	3,526	5,070	5,704
12,700	12,750	218	3,526	5,090	5,726	529	3,526	5,090	5,726
12,750	12,800	214	3,526	5,110	5,749	529	3,526	5,110	5,749

(Continued)

¶87

Earned Income Credit (EIC) Table - Continued   (**Caution.** This is **not** a tax table.)

If the amount you are looking up from the worksheet is—		Single, head of household, or qualifying widow(er) and you have—				Married filing jointly and you have—				If the amount you are looking up from the worksheet is—		Single, head of household, or qualifying widow(er) and you have—				Married filing jointly and you have—			
At least	But less than	0	1	2	3	0	1	2	3	At least	But less than	0	1	2	3	0	1	2	3
		Your credit is—				Your credit is—						Your credit is—				Your credit is—			
12,800	12,850	210	3,526	5,130	5,771	529	3,526	5,130	5,771	16,000	16,050	0	3,526	5,828	6,557	409	3,526	5,828	6,557
12,850	12,900	206	3,526	5,150	5,794	529	3,526	5,150	5,794	16,050	16,100	0	3,526	5,828	6,557	405	3,526	5,828	6,557
12,900	12,950	202	3,526	5,170	5,816	529	3,526	5,170	5,816	16,100	16,150	0	3,526	5,828	6,557	401	3,526	5,828	6,557
12,950	13,000	199	3,526	5,190	5,839	529	3,526	5,190	5,839	16,150	16,200	0	3,526	5,828	6,557	397	3,526	5,828	6,557
13,000	13,050	195	3,526	5,210	5,861	529	3,526	5,210	5,861	16,200	16,250	0	3,526	5,828	6,557	394	3,526	5,828	6,557
13,050	13,100	191	3,526	5,230	5,884	529	3,526	5,230	5,884	16,250	16,300	0	3,526	5,828	6,557	390	3,526	5,828	6,557
13,100	13,150	187	3,526	5,250	5,906	529	3,526	5,250	5,906	16,300	16,350	0	3,526	5,828	6,557	386	3,526	5,828	6,557
13,150	13,200	183	3,526	5,270	5,929	529	3,526	5,270	5,929	16,350	16,400	0	3,526	5,828	6,557	382	3,526	5,828	6,557
13,200	13,250	179	3,526	5,290	5,951	529	3,526	5,290	5,951	16,400	16,450	0	3,526	5,828	6,557	378	3,526	5,828	6,557
13,250	13,300	176	3,526	5,310	5,974	529	3,526	5,310	5,974	16,450	16,500	0	3,526	5,828	6,557	374	3,526	5,828	6,557
13,300	13,350	172	3,526	5,330	5,996	529	3,526	5,330	5,996	16,500	16,550	0	3,526	5,828	6,557	371	3,526	5,828	6,557
13,350	13,400	168	3,526	5,350	6,019	529	3,526	5,350	6,019	16,550	16,600	0	3,526	5,828	6,557	367	3,526	5,828	6,557
13,400	13,450	164	3,526	5,370	6,041	529	3,526	5,370	6,041	16,600	16,650	0	3,526	5,828	6,557	363	3,526	5,828	6,557
13,450	13,500	160	3,526	5,390	6,064	529	3,526	5,390	6,064	16,650	16,700	0	3,526	5,828	6,557	359	3,526	5,828	6,557
13,500	13,550	156	3,526	5,410	6,086	529	3,526	5,410	6,086	16,700	16,750	0	3,526	5,828	6,557	355	3,526	5,828	6,557
13,550	13,600	153	3,526	5,430	6,109	529	3,526	5,430	6,109	16,750	16,800	0	3,526	5,828	6,557	352	3,526	5,828	6,557
13,600	13,650	149	3,526	5,450	6,131	529	3,526	5,450	6,131	16,800	16,850	0	3,526	5,828	6,557	348	3,526	5,828	6,557
13,650	13,700	145	3,526	5,470	6,154	529	3,526	5,470	6,154	16,850	16,900	0	3,526	5,828	6,557	344	3,526	5,828	6,557
13,700	13,750	141	3,526	5,490	6,176	529	3,526	5,490	6,176	16,900	16,950	0	3,526	5,828	6,557	340	3,526	5,828	6,557
13,750	13,800	137	3,526	5,510	6,199	529	3,526	5,510	6,199	16,950	17,000	0	3,526	5,828	6,557	336	3,526	5,828	6,557
13,800	13,850	133	3,526	5,530	6,221	529	3,526	5,530	6,221	17,000	17,050	0	3,526	5,828	6,557	332	3,526	5,828	6,557
13,850	13,900	130	3,526	5,550	6,244	529	3,526	5,550	6,244	17,050	17,100	0	3,526	5,828	6,557	329	3,526	5,828	6,557
13,900	13,950	126	3,526	5,570	6,266	529	3,526	5,570	6,266	17,100	17,150	0	3,526	5,828	6,557	325	3,526	5,828	6,557
13,950	14,000	122	3,526	5,590	6,289	529	3,526	5,590	6,289	17,150	17,200	0	3,526	5,828	6,557	321	3,526	5,828	6,557
14,000	14,050	118	3,526	5,610	6,311	529	3,526	5,610	6,311	17,200	17,250	0	3,526	5,828	6,557	317	3,526	5,828	6,557
14,050	14,100	114	3,526	5,630	6,334	529	3,526	5,630	6,334	17,250	17,300	0	3,526	5,828	6,557	313	3,526	5,828	6,557
14,100	14,150	111	3,526	5,650	6,356	529	3,526	5,650	6,356	17,300	17,350	0	3,526	5,828	6,557	309	3,526	5,828	6,557
14,150	14,200	107	3,526	5,670	6,379	529	3,526	5,670	6,379	17,350	17,400	0	3,526	5,828	6,557	306	3,526	5,828	6,557
14,200	14,250	103	3,526	5,690	6,401	529	3,526	5,690	6,401	17,400	17,450	0	3,526	5,828	6,557	302	3,526	5,828	6,557
14,250	14,300	99	3,526	5,710	6,424	529	3,526	5,710	6,424	17,450	17,500	0	3,526	5,828	6,557	298	3,526	5,820	6,557
14,300	14,350	95	3,526	5,730	6,446	529	3,526	5,730	6,446	17,500	17,550	0	3,526	5,828	6,557	294	3,526	5,828	6,557
14,350	14,400	91	3,526	5,750	6,469	529	3,526	5,750	6,469	17,550	17,600	0	3,526	5,828	6,557	290	3,526	5,828	6,557
14,400	14,450	88	3,526	5,770	6,491	529	3,526	5,770	6,491	17,600	17,650	0	3,526	5,828	6,557	286	3,526	5,828	6,557
14,450	14,500	84	3,526	5,790	6,514	527	3,526	5,790	6,514	17,650	17,700	0	3,526	5,828	6,557	283	3,526	5,828	6,557
14,500	14,550	80	3,526	5,810	6,536	524	3,526	5,810	6,536	17,700	17,750	0	3,526	5,828	6,557	279	3,526	5,828	6,557
14,550	14,600	76	3,526	5,828	6,557	520	3,526	5,828	6,557	17,750	17,800	0	3,526	5,828	6,557	275	3,526	5,828	6,557
14,600	14,650	72	3,526	5,828	6,557	516	3,526	5,828	6,557	17,800	17,850	0	3,526	5,828	6,557	271	3,526	5,828	6,557
14,650	14,700	68	3,526	5,828	6,557	512	3,526	5,828	6,557	17,850	17,900	0	3,526	5,828	6,557	267	3,526	5,828	6,557
14,700	14,750	65	3,526	5,828	6,557	508	3,526	5,828	6,557	17,900	17,950	0	3,526	5,828	6,557	264	3,526	5,828	6,557
14,750	14,800	61	3,526	5,828	6,557	505	3,526	5,828	6,557	17,950	18,000	0	3,526	5,828	6,557	260	3,526	5,828	6,557
14,800	14,850	57	3,526	5,828	6,557	501	3,526	5,828	6,557	18,000	18,050	0	3,526	5,828	6,557	256	3,526	5,828	6,557
14,850	14,900	53	3,526	5,828	6,557	497	3,526	5,828	6,557	18,050	18,100	0	3,526	5,828	6,557	252	3,526	5,828	6,557
14,900	14,950	49	3,526	5,828	6,557	493	3,526	5,828	6,557	18,100	18,150	0	3,526	5,828	6,557	248	3,526	5,828	6,557
14,950	15,000	46	3,526	5,828	6,557	489	3,526	5,828	6,557	18,150	18,200	0	3,526	5,828	6,557	244	3,526	5,828	6,557
15,000	15,050	42	3,526	5,828	6,557	485	3,526	5,828	6,557	18,200	18,250	0	3,526	5,828	6,557	241	3,526	5,828	6,557
15,050	15,100	38	3,526	5,828	6,557	482	3,526	5,828	6,557	18,250	18,300	0	3,526	5,828	6,557	237	3,526	5,828	6,557
15,100	15,150	34	3,526	5,828	6,557	478	3,526	5,828	6,557	18,300	18,350	0	3,526	5,828	6,557	233	3,526	5,828	6,557
15,150	15,200	30	3,526	5,828	6,557	474	3,526	5,828	6,557	18,350	18,400	0	3,526	5,828	6,557	229	3,526	5,828	6,557
15,200	15,250	26	3,526	5,828	6,557	470	3,526	5,828	6,557	18,400	18,450	0	3,526	5,828	6,557	225	3,526	5,828	6,557
15,250	15,300	23	3,526	5,828	6,557	466	3,526	5,828	6,557	18,450	18,500	0	3,526	5,828	6,557	221	3,526	5,828	6,557
15,300	15,350	19	3,526	5,828	6,557	462	3,526	5,828	6,557	18,500	18,550	0	3,526	5,828	6,557	218	3,526	5,828	6,557
15,350	15,400	15	3,526	5,828	6,557	459	3,526	5,828	6,557	18,550	18,600	0	3,526	5,828	6,557	214	3,526	5,828	6,557
15,400	15,450	11	3,526	5,828	6,557	455	3,526	5,828	6,557	18,600	18,650	0	3,526	5,828	6,557	210	3,526	5,828	6,557
15,450	15,500	7	3,526	5,828	6,557	451	3,526	5,828	6,557	18,650	18,700	0	3,526	5,828	6,557	206	3,526	5,828	6,557
15,500	15,550	3	3,526	5,828	6,557	447	3,526	5,828	6,557	18,700	18,750	0	3,526	5,828	6,557	202	3,526	5,828	6,557
15,550	15,600	*	3,526	5,828	6,557	443	3,526	5,828	6,557	18,750	18,800	0	3,526	5,828	6,557	199	3,526	5,828	6,557
15,600	15,650	0	3,526	5,828	6,557	439	3,526	5,828	6,557	18,800	18,850	0	3,526	5,828	6,557	195	3,526	5,828	6,557
15,650	15,700	0	3,526	5,828	6,557	436	3,526	5,828	6,557	18,850	18,900	0	3,526	5,828	6,557	191	3,526	5,828	6,557
15,700	15,750	0	3,526	5,828	6,557	432	3,526	5,828	6,557	18,900	18,950	0	3,526	5,828	6,557	187	3,526	5,828	6,557
15,750	15,800	0	3,526	5,828	6,557	428	3,526	5,828	6,557	18,950	19,000	0	3,526	5,828	6,557	183	3,526	5,828	6,557
15,800	15,850	0	3,526	5,828	6,557	424	3,526	5,828	6,557	19,000	19,050	0	3,526	5,828	6,557	179	3,526	5,828	6,557
15,850	15,900	0	3,526	5,828	6,557	420	3,526	5,828	6,557	19,050	19,100	0	3,519	5,819	6,547	176	3,526	5,828	6,557
15,900	15,950	0	3,526	5,828	6,557	417	3,526	5,828	6,557	19,100	19,150	0	3,511	5,808	6,536	172	3,526	5,828	6,557
15,950	16,000	0	3,526	5,828	6,557	413	3,526	5,828	6,557	19,150	19,200	0	3,503	5,797	6,526	168	3,526	5,828	6,557

* If the amount you are looking up from the worksheet is at least $15,550 but less than $15,570, and you have no qualifying children, your credit is $1.
If the amount you are looking up from the worksheet is $15,570 or more, and you have no qualifying children, you can't take the credit.

(Continued)

- 48 -   *Need more information or forms? Visit IRS.gov.*

SPECIAL TABLES

¶87

Earned Income Credit (EIC) Table - *Continued* (**Caution.** This is **not** a tax table.)

If the amount you are looking up from the worksheet is–		Single, head of household, or qualifying widow(er) and you have–				Married filing jointly and you have–			
At least	But less than	0	1	2	3	0	1	2	3
		Your credit is–				Your credit is–			
19,200	19,250	0	3,495	5,787	6,515	164	3,526	5,828	6,557
19,250	19,300	0	3,487	5,776	6,505	160	3,526	5,828	6,557
19,300	19,350	0	3,479	5,766	6,494	156	3,526	5,828	6,557
19,350	19,400	0	3,471	5,755	6,484	153	3,526	5,828	6,557
19,400	19,450	0	3,463	5,745	6,473	149	3,526	5,828	6,557
19,450	19,500	0	3,455	5,734	6,463	145	3,526	5,828	6,557
19,500	19,550	0	3,447	5,724	6,452	141	3,526	5,828	6,557
19,550	19,600	0	3,439	5,713	6,442	137	3,526	5,828	6,557
19,600	19,650	0	3,431	5,703	6,431	133	3,526	5,828	6,557
19,650	19,700	0	3,423	5,692	6,421	130	3,526	5,828	6,557
19,700	19,750	0	3,415	5,682	6,410	126	3,526	5,828	6,557
19,750	19,800	0	3,407	5,671	6,400	122	3,526	5,828	6,557
19,800	19,850	0	3,399	5,661	6,389	118	3,526	5,828	6,557
19,850	19,900	0	3,391	5,650	6,379	114	3,526	5,828	6,557
19,900	19,950	0	3,383	5,640	6,368	111	3,526	5,828	6,557
19,950	20,000	0	3,375	5,629	6,357	107	3,526	5,828	6,557
20,000	20,050	0	3,367	5,618	6,347	103	3,526	5,828	6,557
20,050	20,100	0	3,359	5,608	6,336	99	3,526	5,828	6,557
20,100	20,150	0	3,351	5,597	6,326	95	3,526	5,828	6,557
20,150	20,200	0	3,343	5,587	6,315	91	3,526	5,828	6,557
20,200	20,250	0	3,335	5,576	6,305	88	3,526	5,828	6,557
20,250	20,300	0	3,327	5,566	6,294	84	3,526	5,828	6,557
20,300	20,350	0	3,319	5,555	6,284	80	3,526	5,828	6,557
20,350	20,400	0	3,311	5,545	6,273	76	3,526	5,828	6,557
20,400	20,450	0	3,303	5,534	6,263	72	3,526	5,828	6,557
20,450	20,500	0	3,295	5,524	6,252	68	3,526	5,828	6,557
20,500	20,550	0	3,287	5,513	6,242	65	3,526	5,828	6,557
20,550	20,600	0	3,279	5,503	6,231	61	3,526	5,828	6,557
20,600	20,650	0	3,271	5,492	6,221	57	3,526	5,828	6,557
20,650	20,700	0	3,263	5,482	6,210	53	3,526	5,828	6,557
20,700	20,750	0	3,255	5,471	6,200	49	3,526	5,828	6,557
20,750	20,800	0	3,247	5,461	6,189	46	3,526	5,828	6,557
20,800	20,850	0	3,239	5,450	6,178	42	3,526	5,828	6,557
20,850	20,900	0	3,231	5,439	6,168	38	3,526	5,828	6,557
20,900	20,950	0	3,223	5,429	6,157	34	3,526	5,828	6,557
20,950	21,000	0	3,215	5,418	6,147	30	3,526	5,828	6,557
21,000	21,050	0	3,207	5,408	6,136	26	3,526	5,828	6,557
21,050	21,100	0	3,199	5,397	6,126	23	3,526	5,828	6,557
21,100	21,150	0	3,191	5,387	6,115	19	3,526	5,828	6,557
21,150	21,200	0	3,183	5,376	6,105	15	3,526	5,828	6,557
21,200	21,250	0	3,175	5,366	6,094	11	3,526	5,828	6,557
21,250	21,300	0	3,167	5,355	6,084	7	3,526	5,828	6,557
21,300	21,350	0	3,159	5,345	6,073	3	3,526	5,828	6,557
21,350	21,400	0	3,151	5,334	6,063	*	3,526	5,828	6,557
21,400	21,450	0	3,143	5,324	6,052	0	3,526	5,828	6,557
21,450	21,500	0	3,135	5,313	6,042	0	3,526	5,828	6,557
21,500	21,550	0	3,127	5,303	6,031	0	3,526	5,828	6,557
21,550	21,600	0	3,119	5,292	6,021	0	3,526	5,828	6,557
21,600	21,650	0	3,111	5,281	6,010	0	3,526	5,828	6,557
21,650	21,700	0	3,103	5,271	5,999	0	3,526	5,828	6,557
21,700	21,750	0	3,095	5,260	5,989	0	3,526	5,828	6,557
21,750	21,800	0	3,087	5,250	5,978	0	3,526	5,828	6,557
21,800	21,850	0	3,079	5,239	5,968	0	3,526	5,828	6,557
21,850	21,900	0	3,071	5,229	5,957	0	3,526	5,828	6,557
21,900	21,950	0	3,063	5,218	5,947	0	3,526	5,828	6,557
21,950	22,000	0	3,055	5,208	5,936	0	3,526	5,828	6,557
22,000	22,050	0	3,047	5,197	5,926	0	3,526	5,828	6,557
22,050	22,100	0	3,039	5,187	5,915	0	3,526	5,828	6,557
22,100	22,150	0	3,031	5,176	5,905	0	3,526	5,828	6,557
22,150	22,200	0	3,023	5,166	5,894	0	3,526	5,828	6,557
22,200	22,250	0	3,015	5,155	5,884	0	3,526	5,828	6,557
22,250	22,300	0	3,007	5,145	5,873	0	3,526	5,828	6,557
22,300	22,350	0	2,999	5,134	5,863	0	3,526	5,828	6,557
22,350	22,400	0	2,991	5,124	5,852	0	3,526	5,828	6,557
22,400	22,450	0	2,983	5,113	5,842	0	3,526	5,828	6,557
22,450	22,500	0	2,975	5,102	5,831	0	3,526	5,828	6,557
22,500	22,550	0	2,967	5,092	5,820	0	3,526	5,828	6,557
22,550	22,600	0	2,959	5,081	5,810	0	3,526	5,828	6,557
22,600	22,650	0	2,951	5,071	5,799	0	3,526	5,828	6,557
22,650	22,700	0	2,943	5,060	5,789	0	3,526	5,828	6,557
22,700	22,750	0	2,935	5,050	5,778	0	3,526	5,828	6,557
22,750	22,800	0	2,927	5,039	5,768	0	3,526	5,828	6,557
22,800	22,850	0	2,919	5,029	5,757	0	3,526	5,828	6,557
22,850	22,900	0	2,911	5,018	5,747	0	3,526	5,828	6,557
22,900	22,950	0	2,903	5,008	5,736	0	3,526	5,828	6,557
22,950	23,000	0	2,895	4,997	5,726	0	3,526	5,828	6,557
23,000	23,050	0	2,887	4,987	5,715	0	3,526	5,828	6,557
23,050	23,100	0	2,879	4,976	5,705	0	3,526	5,828	6,557
23,100	23,150	0	2,871	4,966	5,694	0	3,526	5,828	6,557
23,150	23,200	0	2,863	4,955	5,684	0	3,526	5,828	6,557
23,200	23,250	0	2,855	4,945	5,673	0	3,526	5,828	6,557
23,250	23,300	0	2,847	4,934	5,663	0	3,526	5,828	6,557
23,300	23,350	0	2,839	4,923	5,652	0	3,526	5,828	6,557
23,350	23,400	0	2,831	4,913	5,641	0	3,526	5,828	6,557
23,400	23,450	0	2,823	4,902	5,631	0	3,526	5,828	6,557
23,450	23,500	0	2,815	4,892	5,620	0	3,526	5,828	6,557
23,500	23,550	0	2,807	4,881	5,610	0	3,526	5,828	6,557
23,550	23,600	0	2,800	4,871	5,599	0	3,526	5,828	6,557
23,600	23,650	0	2,792	4,860	5,589	0	3,526	5,828	6,557
23,650	23,700	0	2,784	4,850	5,578	0	3,526	5,828	6,557
23,700	23,750	0	2,776	4,839	5,568	0	3,526	5,828	6,557
23,750	23,800	0	2,768	4,829	5,557	0	3,526	5,828	6,557
23,800	23,850	0	2,760	4,818	5,547	0	3,526	5,828	6,557
23,850	23,900	0	2,752	4,808	5,536	0	3,526	5,828	6,557
23,900	23,950	0	2,744	4,797	5,526	0	3,526	5,828	6,557
23,950	24,000	0	2,736	4,787	5,515	0	3,526	5,828	6,557
24,000	24,050	0	2,728	4,776	5,505	0	3,526	5,828	6,557
24,050	24,100	0	2,720	4,766	5,494	0	3,526	5,828	6,557
24,100	24,150	0	2,712	4,755	5,483	0	3,526	5,828	6,557
24,150	24,200	0	2,704	4,744	5,473	0	3,526	5,828	6,557
24,200	24,250	0	2,696	4,734	5,462	0	3,526	5,828	6,557
24,250	24,300	0	2,688	4,723	5,452	0	3,526	5,828	6,557
24,300	24,350	0	2,680	4,713	5,441	0	3,526	5,828	6,557
24,350	24,400	0	2,672	4,702	5,431	0	3,526	5,828	6,557
24,400	24,450	0	2,664	4,692	5,420	0	3,526	5,828	6,557
24,450	24,500	0	2,656	4,681	5,410	0	3,526	5,828	6,557
24,500	24,550	0	2,648	4,671	5,399	0	3,526	5,828	6,557
24,550	24,600	0	2,640	4,660	5,389	0	3,526	5,828	6,557
24,600	24,650	0	2,632	4,650	5,376	0	3,526	5,828	6,557
24,650	24,700	0	2,624	4,639	5,368	0	3,526	5,828	6,557
24,700	24,750	0	2,616	4,629	5,357	0	3,526	5,828	6,557
24,750	24,800	0	2,608	4,618	5,347	0	3,526	5,828	6,557
24,800	24,850	0	2,600	4,608	5,336	0	3,526	5,828	6,557
24,850	24,900	0	2,592	4,597	5,326	0	3,517	5,816	6,545
24,900	24,950	0	2,584	4,587	5,315	0	3,509	5,806	6,534
24,950	25,000	0	2,576	4,576	5,304	0	3,501	5,795	6,524
25,000	25,050	0	2,568	4,565	5,294	0	3,493	5,785	6,513
25,050	25,100	0	2,560	4,555	5,283	0	3,485	5,774	6,503
25,100	25,150	0	2,552	4,544	5,273	0	3,477	5,764	6,492
25,150	25,200	0	2,544	4,534	5,262	0	3,469	5,753	6,482
25,200	25,250	0	2,536	4,523	5,252	0	3,461	5,743	6,471
25,250	25,300	0	2,528	4,513	5,241	0	3,453	5,732	6,461
25,300	25,350	0	2,520	4,502	5,231	0	3,445	5,722	6,450
25,350	25,400	0	2,512	4,492	5,220	0	3,437	5,711	6,440
25,400	25,450	0	2,504	4,481	5,210	0	3,429	5,701	6,429
25,450	25,500	0	2,496	4,471	5,199	0	3,421	5,690	6,419
25,500	25,550	0	2,488	4,460	5,189	0	3,413	5,680	6,408
25,550	25,600	0	2,480	4,450	5,178	0	3,405	5,669	6,397

* If the amount you are looking up from the worksheet is at least $21,350 but less than $21,370, and you have no qualifying children, your credit is $1.
If the amount you are looking up from the worksheet is $21,370 or more, and you have no qualifying children, you can't take the credit.

(Continued)

Need more information or forms? Visit IRS.gov. - 49 -

¶87

Earned Income Credit (EIC) Table - *Continued*   (**Caution.** This is **not** a tax table.)

If the amount you are looking up from the worksheet is–		Single, head of household, or qualifying widow(er) and you have–				Married filing jointly and you have–			
At least	But less than	0	1	2	3	0	1	2	3
		Your credit is–				Your credit is–			
25,600	25,650	0	2,472	4,439	5,168	0	3,397	5,658	6,387
25,650	25,700	0	2,464	4,429	5,157	0	3,389	5,648	6,376
25,700	25,750	0	2,456	4,418	5,147	0	3,381	5,637	6,366
25,750	25,800	0	2,448	4,408	5,136	0	3,373	5,627	6,355
25,800	25,850	0	2,440	4,397	5,125	0	3,365	5,616	6,345
25,850	25,900	0	2,432	4,386	5,115	0	3,357	5,606	6,334
25,900	25,950	0	2,424	4,376	5,104	0	3,349	5,595	6,324
25,950	26,000	0	2,416	4,365	5,094	0	3,341	5,585	6,313
26,000	26,050	0	2,408	4,355	5,083	0	3,333	5,574	6,303
26,050	26,100	0	2,400	4,344	5,073	0	3,325	5,564	6,292
26,100	26,150	0	2,392	4,334	5,062	0	3,317	5,553	6,282
26,150	26,200	0	2,384	4,323	5,052	0	3,309	5,543	6,271
26,200	26,250	0	2,376	4,313	5,041	0	3,301	5,532	6,261
26,250	26,300	0	2,368	4,302	5,031	0	3,293	5,522	6,250
26,300	26,350	0	2,360	4,292	5,020	0	3,285	5,511	6,240
26,350	26,400	0	2,352	4,281	5,010	0	3,277	5,501	6,229
26,400	26,450	0	2,344	4,271	4,999	0	3,269	5,490	6,218
26,450	26,500	0	2,336	4,260	4,989	0	3,261	5,479	6,208
26,500	26,550	0	2,328	4,250	4,978	0	3,253	5,469	6,197
26,550	26,600	0	2,320	4,239	4,968	0	3,245	5,458	6,187
26,600	26,650	0	2,312	4,228	4,957	0	3,237	5,448	6,176
26,650	26,700	0	2,304	4,218	4,946	0	3,229	5,437	6,166
26,700	26,750	0	2,296	4,207	4,936	0	3,221	5,427	6,155
26,750	26,800	0	2,288	4,197	4,925	0	3,213	5,416	6,145
26,800	26,850	0	2,280	4,186	4,915	0	3,205	5,406	6,134
26,850	26,900	0	2,272	4,176	4,904	0	3,197	5,395	6,124
26,900	26,950	0	2,264	4,165	4,894	0	3,189	5,385	6,113
26,950	27,000	0	2,256	4,155	4,883	0	3,181	5,374	6,103
27,000	27,050	0	2,248	4,144	4,873	0	3,173	5,364	6,092
27,050	27,100	0	2,240	4,134	4,862	0	3,165	5,353	6,082
27,100	27,150	0	2,232	4,123	4,852	0	3,157	5,343	6,071
27,150	27,200	0	2,224	4,113	4,841	0	3,149	5,332	6,061
27,200	27,250	0	2,216	4,102	4,831	0	3,141	5,322	6,050
27,250	27,300	0	2,208	4,092	4,820	0	3,133	5,311	6,039
27,300	27,350	0	2,200	4,081	4,810	0	3,126	5,300	6,029
27,350	27,400	0	2,192	4,071	4,799	0	3,118	5,290	6,018
27,400	27,450	0	2,184	4,060	4,789	0	3,110	5,279	6,008
27,450	27,500	0	2,176	4,049	4,778	0	3,102	5,269	5,997
27,500	27,550	0	2,168	4,039	4,767	0	3,094	5,258	5,987
27,550	27,600	0	2,160	4,028	4,757	0	3,086	5,248	5,976
27,600	27,650	0	2,152	4,018	4,746	0	3,078	5,237	5,966
27,650	27,700	0	2,144	4,007	4,736	0	3,070	5,227	5,955
27,700	27,750	0	2,136	3,997	4,725	0	3,062	5,216	5,945
27,750	27,800	0	2,128	3,986	4,715	0	3,054	5,206	5,934
27,800	27,850	0	2,120	3,976	4,704	0	3,046	5,195	5,924
27,850	27,900	0	2,112	3,965	4,694	0	3,038	5,185	5,913
27,900	27,950	0	2,104	3,955	4,683	0	3,030	5,174	5,903
27,950	28,000	0	2,096	3,944	4,673	0	3,022	5,164	5,892
28,000	28,050	0	2,088	3,934	4,662	0	3,014	5,153	5,882
28,050	28,100	0	2,080	3,923	4,652	0	3,006	5,142	5,871
28,100	28,150	0	2,072	3,913	4,641	0	2,998	5,132	5,860
28,150	28,200	0	2,064	3,902	4,631	0	2,990	5,121	5,850
28,200	28,250	0	2,056	3,892	4,620	0	2,982	5,111	5,839
28,250	28,300	0	2,048	3,881	4,610	0	2,974	5,100	5,829
28,300	28,350	0	2,040	3,870	4,599	0	2,966	5,090	5,818
28,350	28,400	0	2,032	3,860	4,588	0	2,958	5,079	5,808
28,400	28,450	0	2,024	3,849	4,578	0	2,950	5,069	5,797
28,450	28,500	0	2,016	3,839	4,567	0	2,942	5,058	5,787
28,500	28,550	0	2,008	3,828	4,557	0	2,934	5,048	5,776
28,550	28,600	0	2,001	3,818	4,546	0	2,926	5,037	5,766
28,600	28,650	0	1,993	3,807	4,536	0	2,918	5,027	5,755
28,650	28,700	0	1,985	3,797	4,525	0	2,910	5,016	5,745
28,700	28,750	0	1,977	3,786	4,515	0	2,902	5,006	5,734
28,750	28,800	0	1,969	3,776	4,504	0	2,894	4,995	5,724
28,800	28,850	0	1,961	3,765	4,494	0	2,886	4,985	5,713
28,850	28,900	0	1,953	3,755	4,483	0	2,878	4,974	5,703
28,900	28,950	0	1,945	3,744	4,473	0	2,870	4,963	5,692
28,950	29,000	0	1,937	3,734	4,462	0	2,862	4,953	5,681
29,000	29,050	0	1,929	3,723	4,452	0	2,854	4,942	5,671
29,050	29,100	0	1,921	3,713	4,441	0	2,846	4,932	5,660
29,100	29,150	0	1,913	3,702	4,430	0	2,838	4,921	5,650
29,150	29,200	0	1,905	3,691	4,420	0	2,830	4,911	5,639
29,200	29,250	0	1,897	3,681	4,409	0	2,822	4,900	5,629
29,250	29,300	0	1,889	3,670	4,399	0	2,814	4,890	5,618
29,300	29,350	0	1,881	3,660	4,388	0	2,806	4,879	5,608
29,350	29,400	0	1,873	3,649	4,378	0	2,798	4,869	5,597
29,400	29,450	0	1,865	3,639	4,367	0	2,790	4,858	5,587
29,450	29,500	0	1,857	3,628	4,357	0	2,782	4,848	5,576
29,500	29,550	0	1,849	3,618	4,346	0	2,774	4,837	5,566
29,550	29,600	0	1,841	3,607	4,336	0	2,766	4,827	5,555
29,600	29,650	0	1,833	3,597	4,325	0	2,758	4,816	5,545
29,650	29,700	0	1,825	3,586	4,315	0	2,750	4,806	5,534
29,700	29,750	0	1,817	3,576	4,304	0	2,742	4,795	5,524
29,750	29,800	0	1,809	3,565	4,294	0	2,734	4,784	5,513
29,800	29,850	0	1,801	3,555	4,283	0	2,726	4,774	5,502
29,850	29,900	0	1,793	3,544	4,273	0	2,718	4,763	5,492
29,900	29,950	0	1,785	3,534	4,262	0	2,710	4,753	5,481
29,950	30,000	0	1,777	3,523	4,251	0	2,702	4,742	5,471
30,000	30,050	0	1,769	3,512	4,241	0	2,694	4,732	5,460
30,050	30,100	0	1,761	3,502	4,230	0	2,686	4,721	5,450
30,100	30,150	0	1,753	3,491	4,220	0	2,678	4,711	5,439
30,150	30,200	0	1,745	3,481	4,209	0	2,670	4,700	5,429
30,200	30,250	0	1,737	3,470	4,199	0	2,662	4,690	5,418
30,250	30,300	0	1,729	3,460	4,188	0	2,654	4,679	5,408
30,300	30,350	0	1,721	3,449	4,178	0	2,646	4,669	5,397
30,350	30,400	0	1,713	3,439	4,167	0	2,638	4,658	5,387
30,400	30,450	0	1,705	3,428	4,157	0	2,630	4,648	5,376
30,450	30,500	0	1,697	3,418	4,146	0	2,622	4,637	5,366
30,500	30,550	0	1,689	3,407	4,136	0	2,614	4,627	5,355
30,550	30,600	0	1,681	3,397	4,125	0	2,606	4,616	5,344
30,600	30,650	0	1,673	3,386	4,115	0	2,598	4,605	5,334
30,650	30,700	0	1,665	3,376	4,104	0	2,590	4,595	5,323
30,700	30,750	0	1,657	3,365	4,094	0	2,582	4,584	5,313
30,750	30,800	0	1,649	3,355	4,083	0	2,574	4,574	5,302
30,800	30,850	0	1,641	3,344	4,072	0	2,566	4,563	5,292
30,850	30,900	0	1,633	3,333	4,062	0	2,558	4,553	5,281
30,900	30,950	0	1,625	3,323	4,051	0	2,550	4,542	5,271
30,950	31,000	0	1,617	3,312	4,041	0	2,542	4,532	5,260
31,000	31,050	0	1,609	3,302	4,030	0	2,534	4,521	5,250
31,050	31,100	0	1,601	3,291	4,020	0	2,526	4,511	5,239
31,100	31,150	0	1,593	3,281	4,009	0	2,518	4,500	5,229
31,150	31,200	0	1,585	3,270	3,999	0	2,510	4,490	5,218
31,200	31,250	0	1,577	3,260	3,988	0	2,502	4,479	5,208
31,250	31,300	0	1,569	3,249	3,978	0	2,494	4,469	5,197
31,300	31,350	0	1,561	3,239	3,967	0	2,486	4,458	5,187
31,350	31,400	0	1,553	3,228	3,957	0	2,478	4,448	5,176
31,400	31,450	0	1,545	3,218	3,946	0	2,470	4,437	5,165
31,450	31,500	0	1,537	3,207	3,936	0	2,462	4,426	5,155
31,500	31,550	0	1,529	3,197	3,925	0	2,454	4,416	5,144
31,550	31,600	0	1,521	3,186	3,915	0	2,446	4,405	5,134
31,600	31,650	0	1,513	3,175	3,904	0	2,438	4,395	5,123
31,650	31,700	0	1,505	3,165	3,893	0	2,430	4,384	5,113
31,700	31,750	0	1,497	3,154	3,883	0	2,422	4,374	5,102
31,750	31,800	0	1,489	3,144	3,872	0	2,414	4,363	5,092
31,800	31,850	0	1,481	3,133	3,862	0	2,406	4,353	5,081
31,850	31,900	0	1,473	3,123	3,851	0	2,398	4,342	5,071
31,900	31,950	0	1,465	3,112	3,841	0	2,390	4,332	5,060
31,950	32,000	0	1,457	3,102	3,830	0	2,382	4,321	5,050
32,000	32,050	0	1,449	3,091	3,820	0	2,374	4,311	5,039
32,050	32,100	0	1,441	3,081	3,809	0	2,366	4,300	5,029
32,100	32,150	0	1,433	3,070	3,799	0	2,358	4,290	5,018
32,150	32,200	0	1,425	3,060	3,788	0	2,350	4,279	5,008
32,200	32,250	0	1,417	3,049	3,778	0	2,342	4,269	4,997
32,250	32,300	0	1,409	3,039	3,767	0	2,334	4,258	4,986
32,300	32,350	0	1,401	3,028	3,757	0	2,327	4,247	4,976
32,350	32,400	0	1,393	3,018	3,746	0	2,319	4,237	4,965
32,400	32,450	0	1,385	3,007	3,736	0	2,311	4,226	4,955
32,450	32,500	0	1,377	2,996	3,725	0	2,303	4,216	4,944
32,500	32,550	0	1,369	2,986	3,714	0	2,295	4,205	4,934
32,550	32,600	0	1,361	2,975	3,704	0	2,287	4,195	4,923
32,600	32,650	0	1,353	2,965	3,693	0	2,279	4,184	4,913
32,650	32,700	0	1,345	2,954	3,683	0	2,271	4,174	4,902
32,700	32,750	0	1,337	2,944	3,672	0	2,263	4,163	4,892
32,750	32,800	0	1,329	2,933	3,662	0	2,255	4,153	4,881

(Continued)

SPECIAL TABLES

Need more information or forms? Visit IRS.gov.

¶87

Earned Income Credit (EIC) Table - *Continued* (**Caution.** This is **not** a tax table.)

If the amount you are looking up from the worksheet is–		Single, head of household, or qualifying widow(er) and you have–				Married filing jointly and you have–			
At least	But less than	0	1	2	3	0	1	2	3
		Your credit is–				Your credit is–			
32,800	32,850	0	1,321	2,923	3,651	0	2,247	4,142	4,871
32,850	32,900	0	1,313	2,912	3,641	0	2,239	4,132	4,860
32,900	32,950	0	1,305	2,902	3,630	0	2,231	4,121	4,850
32,950	33,000	0	1,297	2,891	3,620	0	2,223	4,111	4,839
33,000	33,050	0	1,289	2,881	3,609	0	2,215	4,100	4,829
33,050	33,100	0	1,281	2,870	3,599	0	2,207	4,089	4,818
33,100	33,150	0	1,273	2,860	3,588	0	2,199	4,079	4,807
33,150	33,200	0	1,265	2,849	3,578	0	2,191	4,068	4,797
33,200	33,250	0	1,257	2,839	3,567	0	2,183	4,058	4,786
33,250	33,300	0	1,249	2,828	3,557	0	2,175	4,047	4,776
33,300	33,350	0	1,241	2,817	3,546	0	2,167	4,037	4,765
33,350	33,400	0	1,233	2,807	3,535	0	2,159	4,026	4,755
33,400	33,450	0	1,225	2,796	3,525	0	2,151	4,016	4,744
33,450	33,500	0	1,217	2,786	3,514	0	2,143	4,005	4,734
33,500	33,550	0	1,209	2,775	3,504	0	2,135	3,995	4,723
33,550	33,600	0	1,202	2,765	3,493	0	2,127	3,984	4,713
33,600	33,650	0	1,194	2,754	3,483	0	2,119	3,974	4,702
33,650	33,700	0	1,186	2,744	3,472	0	2,111	3,963	4,692
33,700	33,750	0	1,178	2,733	3,462	0	2,103	3,953	4,681
33,750	33,800	0	1,170	2,723	3,451	0	2,095	3,942	4,671
33,800	33,850	0	1,162	2,712	3,441	0	2,087	3,932	4,660
33,850	33,900	0	1,154	2,702	3,430	0	2,079	3,921	4,650
33,900	33,950	0	1,146	2,691	3,420	0	2,071	3,910	4,639
33,950	34,000	0	1,138	2,681	3,409	0	2,063	3,900	4,628
34,000	34,050	0	1,130	2,670	3,399	0	2,055	3,889	4,618
34,050	34,100	0	1,122	2,660	3,388	0	2,047	3,879	4,607
34,100	34,150	0	1,114	2,649	3,377	0	2,039	3,868	4,597
34,150	34,200	0	1,106	2,638	3,367	0	2,031	3,858	4,586
34,200	34,250	0	1,098	2,628	3,356	0	2,023	3,847	4,576
34,250	34,300	0	1,090	2,617	3,346	0	2,015	3,837	4,565
34,300	34,350	0	1,082	2,607	3,335	0	2,007	3,826	4,555
34,350	34,400	0	1,074	2,596	3,325	0	1,999	3,816	4,544
34,400	34,450	0	1,066	2,586	3,314	0	1,991	3,805	4,534
34,450	34,500	0	1,058	2,575	3,304	0	1,983	3,795	4,523
34,500	34,550	0	1,050	2,565	3,293	0	1,975	3,784	4,513
34,550	34,600	0	1,042	2,554	3,283	0	1,967	3,774	4,502
34,600	34,650	0	1,034	2,544	3,272	0	1,959	3,763	4,492
34,650	34,700	0	1,026	2,533	3,262	0	1,951	3,753	4,481
34,700	34,750	0	1,018	2,523	3,251	0	1,943	3,742	4,471
34,750	34,800	0	1,010	2,512	3,241	0	1,935	3,731	4,460
34,800	34,850	0	1,002	2,502	3,230	0	1,927	3,721	4,449
34,850	34,900	0	994	2,491	3,220	0	1,919	3,710	4,439
34,900	34,950	0	986	2,481	3,209	0	1,911	3,700	4,428
34,950	35,000	0	978	2,470	3,198	0	1,903	3,689	4,418
35,000	35,050	0	970	2,459	3,188	0	1,895	3,679	4,407
35,050	35,100	0	962	2,449	3,177	0	1,887	3,668	4,397
35,100	35,150	0	954	2,438	3,167	0	1,879	3,658	4,386
35,150	35,200	0	946	2,428	3,156	0	1,871	3,647	4,376
35,200	35,250	0	938	2,417	3,146	0	1,863	3,637	4,365
35,250	35,300	0	930	2,407	3,135	0	1,855	3,626	4,355
35,300	35,350	0	922	2,396	3,125	0	1,847	3,616	4,344
35,350	35,400	0	914	2,386	3,114	0	1,839	3,605	4,334
35,400	35,450	0	906	2,375	3,104	0	1,831	3,595	4,323
35,450	35,500	0	898	2,365	3,093	0	1,823	3,584	4,313
35,500	35,550	0	890	2,354	3,083	0	1,815	3,574	4,302
35,550	35,600	0	882	2,344	3,072	0	1,807	3,563	4,291
35,600	35,650	0	874	2,333	3,062	0	1,799	3,552	4,281
35,650	35,700	0	866	2,323	3,051	0	1,791	3,542	4,270
35,700	35,750	0	858	2,312	3,041	0	1,783	3,531	4,260
35,750	35,800	0	850	2,302	3,030	0	1,775	3,521	4,249
35,800	35,850	0	842	2,291	3,019	0	1,767	3,510	4,239
35,850	35,900	0	834	2,280	3,009	0	1,759	3,500	4,228
35,900	35,950	0	826	2,270	2,998	0	1,751	3,489	4,218
35,950	36,000	0	818	2,259	2,988	0	1,743	3,479	4,207
36,000	36,050	0	810	2,249	2,977	0	1,735	3,468	4,197
36,050	36,100	0	802	2,238	2,967	0	1,727	3,458	4,186
36,100	36,150	0	794	2,228	2,956	0	1,719	3,447	4,176
36,150	36,200	0	786	2,217	2,946	0	1,711	3,437	4,165
36,200	36,250	0	778	2,207	2,935	0	1,703	3,426	4,155
36,250	36,300	0	770	2,196	2,925	0	1,695	3,416	4,144
36,300	36,350	0	762	2,186	2,914	0	1,687	3,405	4,134
36,350	36,400	0	754	2,175	2,904	0	1,679	3,395	4,123

If the amount you are looking up from the worksheet is–		Single, head of household, or qualifying widow(er) and you have–				Married filing jointly and you have–			
At least	But less than	0	1	2	3	0	1	2	3
		Your credit is–				Your credit is–			
36,400	36,450	0	746	2,165	2,893	0	1,671	3,384	4,112
36,450	36,500	0	738	2,154	2,883	0	1,663	3,373	4,102
36,500	36,550	0	730	2,144	2,872	0	1,655	3,363	4,091
36,550	36,600	0	722	2,133	2,862	0	1,647	3,352	4,081
36,600	36,650	0	714	2,122	2,851	0	1,639	3,342	4,070
36,650	36,700	0	706	2,112	2,840	0	1,631	3,331	4,060
36,700	36,750	0	698	2,101	2,830	0	1,623	3,321	4,049
36,750	36,800	0	690	2,091	2,819	0	1,615	3,310	4,039
36,800	36,850	0	682	2,080	2,809	0	1,607	3,300	4,028
36,850	36,900	0	674	2,070	2,798	0	1,599	3,289	4,018
36,900	36,950	0	666	2,059	2,788	0	1,591	3,279	4,007
36,950	37,000	0	658	2,049	2,777	0	1,583	3,268	3,997
37,000	37,050	0	650	2,038	2,767	0	1,575	3,258	3,986
37,050	37,100	0	642	2,028	2,756	0	1,567	3,247	3,976
37,100	37,150	0	634	2,017	2,746	0	1,559	3,237	3,965
37,150	37,200	0	626	2,007	2,735	0	1,551	3,226	3,955
37,200	37,250	0	618	1,996	2,725	0	1,543	3,216	3,944
37,250	37,300	0	610	1,986	2,714	0	1,535	3,205	3,933
37,300	37,350	0	602	1,975	2,704	0	1,528	3,194	3,923
37,350	37,400	0	594	1,965	2,693	0	1,520	3,184	3,912
37,400	37,450	0	586	1,954	2,683	0	1,512	3,173	3,902
37,450	37,500	0	578	1,943	2,672	0	1,504	3,163	3,891
37,500	37,550	0	570	1,933	2,661	0	1,496	3,152	3,881
37,550	37,600	0	562	1,922	2,651	0	1,488	3,142	3,870
37,600	37,650	0	554	1,912	2,640	0	1,480	3,131	3,860
37,650	37,700	0	546	1,901	2,630	0	1,472	3,121	3,849
37,700	37,750	0	538	1,891	2,619	0	1,464	3,110	3,839
37,750	37,800	0	530	1,880	2,609	0	1,456	3,100	3,828
37,800	37,850	0	522	1,870	2,598	0	1,448	3,089	3,818
37,850	37,900	0	514	1,859	2,588	0	1,440	3,079	3,807
37,900	37,950	0	506	1,849	2,577	0	1,432	3,068	3,797
37,950	38,000	0	498	1,838	2,567	0	1,424	3,058	3,786
38,000	38,050	0	490	1,828	2,556	0	1,416	3,047	3,776
38,050	38,100	0	482	1,817	2,546	0	1,408	3,036	3,765
38,100	38,150	0	474	1,807	2,535	0	1,400	3,026	3,754
38,150	38,200	0	466	1,796	2,525	0	1,392	3,015	3,744
38,200	38,250	0	458	1,786	2,514	0	1,384	3,005	3,733
38,250	38,300	0	450	1,775	2,504	0	1,376	2,994	3,723
38,300	38,350	0	442	1,764	2,493	0	1,368	2,984	3,712
38,350	38,400	0	434	1,754	2,482	0	1,360	2,973	3,702
38,400	38,450	0	426	1,743	2,472	0	1,352	2,963	3,691
38,450	38,500	0	418	1,733	2,461	0	1,344	2,952	3,681
38,500	38,550	0	410	1,722	2,451	0	1,336	2,942	3,670
38,550	38,600	0	403	1,712	2,440	0	1,328	2,931	3,660
38,600	38,650	0	395	1,701	2,430	0	1,320	2,921	3,649
38,650	38,700	0	387	1,691	2,419	0	1,312	2,910	3,639
38,700	38,750	0	379	1,680	2,409	0	1,304	2,900	3,628
38,750	38,800	0	371	1,670	2,398	0	1,296	2,889	3,618
38,800	38,850	0	363	1,659	2,388	0	1,288	2,879	3,607
38,850	38,900	0	355	1,649	2,377	0	1,280	2,868	3,597
38,900	38,950	0	347	1,638	2,367	0	1,272	2,857	3,586
38,950	39,000	0	339	1,628	2,356	0	1,264	2,847	3,575
39,000	39,050	0	331	1,617	2,346	0	1,256	2,836	3,565
39,050	39,100	0	323	1,607	2,335	0	1,248	2,826	3,554
39,100	39,150	0	315	1,596	2,324	0	1,240	2,815	3,544
39,150	39,200	0	307	1,585	2,314	0	1,232	2,805	3,533
39,200	39,250	0	299	1,575	2,303	0	1,224	2,794	3,523
39,250	39,300	0	291	1,564	2,293	0	1,216	2,784	3,512
39,300	39,350	0	283	1,554	2,282	0	1,208	2,773	3,502
39,350	39,400	0	275	1,543	2,272	0	1,200	2,763	3,491
39,400	39,450	0	267	1,533	2,261	0	1,192	2,752	3,481
39,450	39,500	0	259	1,522	2,251	0	1,184	2,742	3,470
39,500	39,550	0	251	1,512	2,240	0	1,176	2,731	3,460
39,550	39,600	0	243	1,501	2,230	0	1,168	2,721	3,449
39,600	39,650	0	235	1,491	2,219	0	1,160	2,710	3,439
39,650	39,700	0	227	1,480	2,209	0	1,152	2,700	3,428
39,700	39,750	0	219	1,470	2,198	0	1,144	2,689	3,418
39,750	39,800	0	211	1,459	2,188	0	1,136	2,678	3,407
39,800	39,850	0	203	1,449	2,177	0	1,128	2,668	3,396
39,850	39,900	0	195	1,438	2,167	0	1,120	2,657	3,386
39,900	39,950	0	187	1,428	2,156	0	1,112	2,647	3,375
39,950	40,000	0	179	1,417	2,145	0	1,104	2,636	3,365

(Continued)

¶87

Earned Income Credit (EIC) Table - *Continued*   (Caution. This is **not** a tax table.)

If the amount you are looking up from the worksheet is—		Single, head of household, or qualifying widow(er) and you have—				Married filing jointly and you have—			
At least	But less than	0	1	2	3	0	1	2	3
		Your credit is—				Your credit is—			
40,000	40,050	0	171	1,406	2,135	0	1,096	2,626	3,354
40,050	40,100	0	163	1,396	2,124	0	1,088	2,615	3,344
40,100	40,150	0	155	1,385	2,114	0	1,080	2,605	3,333
40,150	40,200	0	147	1,375	2,103	0	1,072	2,594	3,323
40,200	40,250	0	139	1,364	2,093	0	1,064	2,584	3,312
40,250	40,300	0	131	1,354	2,082	0	1,056	2,573	3,302
40,300	40,350	0	123	1,343	2,072	0	1,048	2,563	3,291
40,350	40,400	0	115	1,333	2,061	0	1,040	2,552	3,281
40,400	40,450	0	107	1,322	2,051	0	1,032	2,542	3,270
40,450	40,500	0	99	1,312	2,040	0	1,024	2,531	3,260
40,500	40,550	0	91	1,301	2,030	0	1,016	2,521	3,249
40,550	40,600	0	83	1,291	2,019	0	1,008	2,510	3,238
40,600	40,650	0	75	1,280	2,009	0	1,000	2,499	3,228
40,650	40,700	0	67	1,270	1,998	0	992	2,489	3,217
40,700	40,750	0	59	1,259	1,988	0	984	2,478	3,207
40,750	40,800	0	51	1,249	1,977	0	976	2,468	3,196
40,800	40,850	0	43	1,238	1,966	0	968	2,457	3,186
40,850	40,900	0	35	1,227	1,956	0	960	2,447	3,175
40,900	40,950	0	27	1,217	1,945	0	952	2,436	3,165
40,950	41,000	0	19	1,206	1,935	0	944	2,426	3,154
41,000	41,050	0	11	1,196	1,924	0	936	2,415	3,144
41,050	41,100	0	*	1,185	1,914	0	928	2,405	3,133
41,100	41,150	0	0	1,175	1,903	0	920	2,394	3,123
41,150	41,200	0	0	1,164	1,893	0	912	2,384	3,112
41,200	41,250	0	0	1,154	1,882	0	904	2,373	3,102
41,250	41,300	0	0	1,143	1,872	0	896	2,363	3,091
41,300	41,350	0	0	1,133	1,861	0	888	2,352	3,081
41,350	41,400	0	0	1,122	1,851	0	880	2,342	3,070
41,400	41,450	0	0	1,112	1,840	0	872	2,331	3,059
41,450	41,500	0	0	1,101	1,830	0	864	2,320	3,049
41,500	41,550	0	0	1,091	1,819	0	856	2,310	3,038
41,550	41,600	0	0	1,080	1,809	0	848	2,299	3,028
41,600	41,650	0	0	1,069	1,798	0	840	2,289	3,017
41,650	41,700	0	0	1,059	1,787	0	832	2,278	3,007
41,700	41,750	0	0	1,048	1,777	0	824	2,268	2,996
41,750	41,800	0	0	1,038	1,766	0	816	2,257	2,986
41,800	41,850	0	0	1,027	1,756	0	808	2,247	2,975
41,850	41,900	0	0	1,017	1,745	0	800	2,236	2,965
41,900	41,950	0	0	1,006	1,735	0	792	2,226	2,954
41,950	42,000	0	0	996	1,724	0	784	2,215	2,944
42,000	42,050	0	0	985	1,714	0	776	2,205	2,933
42,050	42,100	0	0	975	1,703	0	768	2,194	2,923
42,100	42,150	0	0	964	1,693	0	760	2,184	2,912
42,150	42,200	0	0	954	1,682	0	752	2,173	2,902
42,200	42,250	0	0	943	1,672	0	744	2,163	2,891
42,250	42,300	0	0	933	1,661	0	736	2,152	2,880
42,300	42,350	0	0	922	1,651	0	729	2,141	2,870
42,350	42,400	0	0	912	1,640	0	721	2,131	2,859
42,400	42,450	0	0	901	1,630	0	713	2,120	2,849
42,450	42,500	0	0	890	1,619	0	705	2,110	2,838
42,500	42,550	0	0	880	1,608	0	697	2,099	2,828
42,550	42,600	0	0	869	1,598	0	689	2,089	2,817
42,600	42,650	0	0	859	1,587	0	681	2,078	2,807
42,650	42,700	0	0	848	1,577	0	673	2,068	2,796
42,700	42,750	0	0	838	1,566	0	665	2,057	2,786
42,750	42,800	0	0	827	1,556	0	657	2,047	2,775
42,800	42,850	0	0	817	1,545	0	649	2,036	2,765
42,850	42,900	0	0	806	1,535	0	641	2,026	2,754
42,900	42,950	0	0	796	1,524	0	633	2,015	2,744
42,950	43,000	0	0	785	1,514	0	625	2,005	2,733
43,000	43,050	0	0	775	1,503	0	617	1,994	2,723
43,050	43,100	0	0	764	1,493	0	609	1,983	2,712
43,100	43,150	0	0	754	1,482	0	601	1,973	2,701
43,150	43,200	0	0	743	1,472	0	593	1,962	2,691
43,200	43,250	0	0	733	1,461	0	585	1,952	2,680
43,250	43,300	0	0	722	1,451	0	577	1,941	2,670
43,300	43,350	0	0	711	1,440	0	569	1,931	2,659
43,350	43,400	0	0	701	1,429	0	561	1,920	2,649
43,400	43,450	0	0	690	1,419	0	553	1,910	2,638
43,450	43,500	0	0	680	1,408	0	545	1,899	2,628
43,500	43,550	0	0	669	1,398	0	537	1,889	2,617
43,550	43,600	0	0	659	1,387	0	529	1,878	2,607
43,600	43,650	0	0	648	1,377	0	521	1,868	2,596
43,650	43,700	0	0	638	1,366	0	513	1,857	2,586
43,700	43,750	0	0	627	1,356	0	505	1,847	2,575
43,750	43,800	0	0	617	1,345	0	497	1,836	2,565
43,800	43,850	0	0	606	1,335	0	489	1,826	2,554
43,850	43,900	0	0	596	1,324	0	481	1,815	2,544
43,900	43,950	0	0	585	1,314	0	473	1,804	2,533
43,950	44,000	0	0	575	1,303	0	465	1,794	2,522
44,000	44,050	0	0	564	1,293	0	457	1,783	2,512
44,050	44,100	0	0	554	1,282	0	449	1,773	2,501
44,100	44,150	0	0	543	1,271	0	441	1,762	2,491
44,150	44,200	0	0	532	1,261	0	433	1,752	2,480
44,200	44,250	0	0	522	1,250	0	425	1,741	2,470
44,250	44,300	0	0	511	1,240	0	417	1,731	2,459
44,300	44,350	0	0	501	1,229	0	409	1,720	2,449
44,350	44,400	0	0	490	1,219	0	401	1,710	2,438
44,400	44,450	0	0	480	1,208	0	393	1,699	2,428
44,450	44,500	0	0	469	1,198	0	385	1,689	2,417
44,500	44,550	0	0	459	1,187	0	377	1,678	2,407
44,550	44,600	0	0	448	1,177	0	369	1,668	2,396
44,600	44,650	0	0	438	1,166	0	361	1,657	2,386
44,650	44,700	0	0	427	1,156	0	353	1,647	2,375
44,700	44,750	0	0	417	1,145	0	345	1,636	2,365
44,750	44,800	0	0	406	1,135	0	337	1,625	2,354
44,800	44,850	0	0	396	1,124	0	329	1,615	2,343
44,850	44,900	0	0	385	1,114	0	321	1,604	2,333
44,900	44,950	0	0	375	1,103	0	313	1,594	2,322
44,950	45,000	0	0	364	1,092	0	305	1,583	2,312
45,000	45,050	0	0	353	1,082	0	297	1,573	2,301
45,050	45,100	0	0	343	1,071	0	289	1,562	2,291
45,100	45,150	0	0	332	1,061	0	281	1,552	2,280
45,150	45,200	0	0	322	1,050	0	273	1,541	2,270
45,200	45,250	0	0	311	1,040	0	265	1,531	2,259
45,250	45,300	0	0	301	1,029	0	257	1,520	2,249
45,300	45,350	0	0	290	1,019	0	249	1,510	2,238
45,350	45,400	0	0	280	1,008	0	241	1,499	2,228
45,400	45,450	0	0	269	998	0	233	1,489	2,217
45,450	45,500	0	0	259	987	0	225	1,478	2,207
45,500	45,550	0	0	248	977	0	217	1,468	2,196
45,550	45,600	0	0	238	966	0	209	1,457	2,185
45,600	45,650	0	0	227	956	0	201	1,446	2,175
45,650	45,700	0	0	217	945	0	193	1,436	2,164
45,700	45,750	0	0	206	935	0	185	1,425	2,154
45,750	45,800	0	0	196	924	0	177	1,415	2,143
45,800	45,850	0	0	185	913	0	169	1,404	2,133
45,850	45,900	0	0	174	903	0	161	1,394	2,122
45,900	45,950	0	0	164	892	0	153	1,383	2,112
45,950	46,000	0	0	153	882	0	145	1,373	2,101
46,000	46,050	0	0	143	871	0	137	1,362	2,091
46,050	46,100	0	0	132	861	0	129	1,352	2,080
46,100	46,150	0	0	122	850	0	121	1,341	2,070
46,150	46,200	0	0	111	840	0	113	1,331	2,059
46,200	46,250	0	0	101	829	0	105	1,320	2,049
46,250	46,300	0	0	90	819	0	97	1,310	2,038
46,300	46,350	0	0	80	808	0	89	1,299	2,028
46,350	46,400	0	0	69	798	0	81	1,289	2,017

* If the amount you are looking up from the worksheet is at least $41,050 but less than $41,094, and you have one qualifying child, your credit is $3.
If the amount you are looking up from the worksheet is $41,094 or more, and you have one qualifying child, you can't take the credit.

(Continued)

Need more information or forms? Visit IRS.gov.

SPECIAL TABLES

¶87

Earned Income Credit (EIC) Table - *Continued*   **(Caution.** This is **not** a tax table.)

If the amount you are looking up from the worksheet is–		Single, head of household, or qualifying widow(er) and you have–				Married filing jointly and you have–			
At least	But less than	0	1	2	3	0	1	2	3
		Your credit is–				Your credit is–			
46,400	46,450	0	0	59	787	0	73	1,278	2,006
46,450	46,500	0	0	48	777	0	65	1,267	1,996
46,500	46,550	0	0	38	766	0	57	1,257	1,985
46,550	46,600	0	0	27	756	0	49	1,246	1,975
46,600	46,650	0	0	16	745	0	41	1,236	1,964
46,650	46,700	0	0	6	734	0	33	1,225	1,954
46,700	46,750	0	0	0	724	0	25	1,215	1,943
46,750	46,800	0	0	0	713	0	17	1,204	1,933
46,800	46,850	0	0	0	703	0	9	1,194	1,922
46,850	46,900	0	0	0	692	0	*	1,183	1,912
46,900	46,950	0	0	0	682	0	0	1,173	1,901
46,950	47,000	0	0	0	671	0	0	1,162	1,891
47,000	47,050	0	0	0	661	0	0	1,152	1,880
47,050	47,100	0	0	0	650	0	0	1,141	1,870
47,100	47,150	0	0	0	640	0	0	1,131	1,859
47,150	47,200	0	0	0	629	0	0	1,120	1,849
47,200	47,250	0	0	0	619	0	0	1,110	1,838
47,250	47,300	0	0	0	608	0	0	1,099	1,827
47,300	47,350	0	0	0	598	0	0	1,088	1,817
47,350	47,400	0	0	0	587	0	0	1,078	1,806
47,400	47,450	0	0	0	577	0	0	1,067	1,796
47,450	47,500	0	0	0	566	0	0	1,057	1,785
47,500	47,550	0	0	0	555	0	0	1,046	1,775
47,550	47,600	0	0	0	545	0	0	1,036	1,764
47,600	47,650	0	0	0	534	0	0	1,025	1,754
47,650	47,700	0	0	0	524	0	0	1,015	1,743
47,700	47,750	0	0	0	513	0	0	1,004	1,733
47,750	47,800	0	0	0	503	0	0	994	1,722
47,800	47,850	0	0	0	492	0	0	983	1,712
47,850	47,900	0	0	0	482	0	0	973	1,701
47,900	47,950	0	0	0	471	0	0	962	1,691
47,950	48,000	0	0	0	461	0	0	952	1,680
48,000	48,050	0	0	0	450	0	0	941	1,670
48,050	48,100	0	0	0	440	0	0	930	1,659
48,100	48,150	0	0	0	429	0	0	920	1,648
48,150	48,200	0	0	0	419	0	0	909	1,638
48,200	48,250	0	0	0	408	0	0	899	1,627
48,250	48,300	0	0	0	398	0	0	888	1,617
48,300	48,350	0	0	0	387	0	0	878	1,606
48,350	48,400	0	0	0	376	0	0	867	1,596
48,400	48,450	0	0	0	366	0	0	857	1,585
48,450	48,500	0	0	0	355	0	0	846	1,575
48,500	48,550	0	0	0	345	0	0	836	1,564
48,550	48,600	0	0	0	334	0	0	825	1,554
48,600	48,650	0	0	0	324	0	0	815	1,543
48,650	48,700	0	0	0	313	0	0	804	1,533
48,700	48,750	0	0	0	303	0	0	794	1,522
48,750	48,800	0	0	0	292	0	0	783	1,512
48,800	48,850	0	0	0	282	0	0	773	1,501
48,850	48,900	0	0	0	271	0	0	762	1,491
48,900	48,950	0	0	0	261	0	0	751	1,480
48,950	49,000	0	0	0	250	0	0	741	1,469
49,000	49,050	0	0	0	240	0	0	730	1,459
49,050	49,100	0	0	0	229	0	0	720	1,448
49,100	49,150	0	0	0	218	0	0	709	1,438
49,150	49,200	0	0	0	208	0	0	699	1,427

If the amount you are looking up from the worksheet is–		Single, head of household, or qualifying widow(er) and you have–				Married filing jointly and you have–			
At least	But less than	0	1	2	3	0	1	2	3
		Your credit is–				Your credit is–			
49,200	49,250	0	0	0	197	0	0	688	1,417
49,250	49,300	0	0	0	187	0	0	678	1,406
49,300	49,350	0	0	0	176	0	0	667	1,396
49,350	49,400	0	0	0	166	0	0	657	1,385
49,400	49,450	0	0	0	155	0	0	646	1,375
49,450	49,500	0	0	0	145	0	0	636	1,364
49,500	49,550	0	0	0	134	0	0	625	1,354
49,550	49,600	0	0	0	124	0	0	615	1,343
49,600	49,650	0	0	0	113	0	0	604	1,333
49,650	49,700	0	0	0	103	0	0	594	1,322
49,700	49,750	0	0	0	92	0	0	583	1,312
49,750	49,800	0	0	0	82	0	0	572	1,301
49,800	49,850	0	0	0	71	0	0	562	1,290
49,850	49,900	0	0	0	61	0	0	551	1,280
49,900	49,950	0	0	0	50	0	0	541	1,269
49,950	50,000	0	0	0	39	0	0	530	1,259
50,000	50,050	0	0	0	29	0	0	520	1,248
50,050	50,100	0	0	0	18	0	0	509	1,238
50,100	50,150	0	0	0	8	0	0	499	1,227
50,150	50,200	0	0	0	**	0	0	488	1,217
50,200	50,250	0	0	0	0	0	0	478	1,206
50,250	50,300	0	0	0	0	0	0	467	1,196
50,300	50,350	0	0	0	0	0	0	457	1,185
50,350	50,400	0	0	0	0	0	0	448	1,175
50,400	50,450	0	0	0	0	0	0	436	1,164
50,450	50,500	0	0	0	0	0	0	425	1,154
50,500	50,550	0	0	0	0	0	0	415	1,143
50,550	50,600	0	0	0	0	0	0	404	1,132
50,600	50,650	0	0	0	0	0	0	393	1,122
50,650	50,700	0	0	0	0	0	0	383	1,111
50,700	50,750	0	0	0	0	0	0	372	1,101
50,750	50,800	0	0	0	0	0	0	362	1,090
50,800	50,850	0	0	0	0	0	0	351	1,080
50,850	50,900	0	0	0	0	0	0	341	1,069
50,900	50,950	0	0	0	0	0	0	330	1,059
50,950	51,000	0	0	0	0	0	0	320	1,048
51,000	51,050	0	0	0	0	0	0	309	1,038
51,050	51,100	0	0	0	0	0	0	299	1,027
51,100	51,150	0	0	0	0	0	0	288	1,017
51,150	51,200	0	0	0	0	0	0	278	1,006
51,200	51,250	0	0	0	0	0	0	267	996
51,250	51,300	0	0	0	0	0	0	257	985
51,300	51,350	0	0	0	0	0	0	246	975
51,350	51,400	0	0	0	0	0	0	236	964
51,400	51,450	0	0	0	0	0	0	225	953
51,450	51,500	0	0	0	0	0	0	214	943
51,500	51,550	0	0	0	0	0	0	204	932
51,550	51,600	0	0	0	0	0	0	193	922
51,600	51,650	0	0	0	0	0	0	183	911
51,650	51,700	0	0	0	0	0	0	172	901
51,700	51,750	0	0	0	0	0	0	162	890
51,750	51,800	0	0	0	0	0	0	151	880
51,800	51,850	0	0	0	0	0	0	141	869
51,850	51,900	0	0	0	0	0	0	130	859
51,900	51,950	0	0	0	0	0	0	120	848
51,950	52,000	0	0	0	0	0	0	109	838

* If the amount you are looking up from the worksheet is at least $46,850 but less than $46,884, and you have one qualifying child, your credit is $3.
If the amount you are looking up from the worksheet is $46,884 or more, and you have one qualifying child, you can't take the credit.

** If the amount you are looking up from the worksheet is at least $50,150 but less than $50,162, and you have three qualifying children, your credit is $1.
If the amount you are looking up from the worksheet is $50,162 or more, and you have three qualifying children, you can't take the credit

(Continued)

¶87

Earned Income Credit (EIC) Table - *Continued*   (**Caution.** This is **not** a tax table.)

If the amount you are looking up from the worksheet is–		Single, head of household, or qualifying widow(er) and you have–				Married filing jointly and you have–			
At least	But less than	0	1	2	3	0	1	2	3
		Your credit is–				Your credit is–			
52,000	52,050	0	0	0	0	0	0	99	827
52,050	52,100	0	0	0	0	0	0	88	817
52,100	52,150	0	0	0	0	0	0	78	806
52,150	52,200	0	0	0	0	0	0	67	796
52,200	52,250	0	0	0	0	0	0	57	785
52,250	52,300	0	0	0	0	0	0	46	774
52,300	52,350	0	0	0	0	0	0	35	764
52,350	52,400	0	0	0	0	0	0	25	753
52,400	52,450	0	0	0	0	0	0	14	743
52,450	52,500	0	0	0	0	0	0	*	732
52,500	52,550	0	0	0	0	0	0	0	722
52,550	52,600	0	0	0	0	0	0	0	711
52,600	52,650	0	0	0	0	0	0	0	701
52,650	52,700	0	0	0	0	0	0	0	690
52,700	52,750	0	0	0	0	0	0	0	680
52,750	52,800	0	0	0	0	0	0	0	669
52,800	52,850	0	0	0	0	0	0	0	659
52,850	52,900	0	0	0	0	0	0	0	648
52,900	52,950	0	0	0	0	0	0	0	638
52,950	53,000	0	0	0	0	0	0	0	627
53,000	53,050	0	0	0	0	0	0	0	617
53,050	53,100	0	0	0	0	0	0	0	606
53,100	53,150	0	0	0	0	0	0	0	595
53,150	53,200	0	0	0	0	0	0	0	585
53,200	53,250	0	0	0	0	0	0	0	574
53,250	53,300	0	0	0	0	0	0	0	564
53,300	53,350	0	0	0	0	0	0	0	553
53,350	53,400	0	0	0	0	0	0	0	543
53,400	53,450	0	0	0	0	0	0	0	532
53,450	53,500	0	0	0	0	0	0	0	522
53,500	53,550	0	0	0	0	0	0	0	511
53,550	53,600	0	0	0	0	0	0	0	501
53,600	53,650	0	0	0	0	0	0	0	490
53,650	53,700	0	0	0	0	0	0	0	480
53,700	53,750	0	0	0	0	0	0	0	469
53,750	53,800	0	0	0	0	0	0	0	459
53,800	53,850	0	0	0	0	0	0	0	448
53,850	53,900	0	0	0	0	0	0	0	438
53,900	53,950	0	0	0	0	0	0	0	427
53,950	54,000	0	0	0	0	0	0	0	416

If the amount you are looking up from the worksheet is–		Single, head of household, or qualifying widow(er) and you have–				Married filing jointly and you have–			
At least	But less than	0	1	2	3	0	1	2	3
		Your credit is–				Your credit is–			
54,000	54,050	0	0	0	0	0	0	0	406
54,050	54,100	0	0	0	0	0	0	0	395
54,100	54,150	0	0	0	0	0	0	0	385
54,150	54,200	0	0	0	0	0	0	0	374
54,200	54,250	0	0	0	0	0	0	0	364
54,250	54,300	0	0	0	0	0	0	0	353
54,300	54,350	0	0	0	0	0	0	0	343
54,350	54,400	0	0	0	0	0	0	0	332
54,400	54,450	0	0	0	0	0	0	0	322
54,450	54,500	0	0	0	0	0	0	0	311
54,500	54,550	0	0	0	0	0	0	0	301
54,550	54,600	0	0	0	0	0	0	0	290
54,600	54,650	0	0	0	0	0	0	0	280
54,650	54,700	0	0	0	0	0	0	0	269
54,700	54,750	0	0	0	0	0	0	0	259
54,750	54,800	0	0	0	0	0	0	0	248
54,800	54,850	0	0	0	0	0	0	0	237
54,850	54,900	0	0	0	0	0	0	0	227
54,900	54,950	0	0	0	0	0	0	0	216
54,950	55,000	0	0	0	0	0	0	0	206
55,000	55,050	0	0	0	0	0	0	0	195
55,050	55,100	0	0	0	0	0	0	0	185
55,100	55,150	0	0	0	0	0	0	0	174
55,150	55,200	0	0	0	0	0	0	0	164
55,200	55,250	0	0	0	0	0	0	0	153
55,250	55,300	0	0	0	0	0	0	0	143
55,300	55,350	0	0	0	0	0	0	0	132
55,350	55,400	0	0	0	0	0	0	0	122
55,400	55,450	0	0	0	0	0	0	0	111
55,450	55,500	0	0	0	0	0	0	0	101
55,500	55,550	0	0	0	0	0	0	0	90
55,550	55,600	0	0	0	0	0	0	0	79
55,600	55,650	0	0	0	0	0	0	0	69
55,650	55,700	0	0	0	0	0	0	0	58
55,700	55,750	0	0	0	0	0	0	0	48
55,750	55,800	0	0	0	0	0	0	0	37
55,800	55,850	0	0	0	0	0	0	0	27
55,850	55,900	0	0	0	0	0	0	0	16
55,900	55,950	0	0	0	0	0	0	0	6
55,950	55,952	0	0	0	0	0	0	0	0

* If the amount you are looking up from the worksheet is at least $52,450 but less than $52,493, and you have two qualifying children, your credit is $5.
If the amount you are looking up from the worksheet is $52,493 or more, and you have two qualifying children, you can't take the credit.

Need more information or forms? Visit IRS.gov.

SPECIAL TABLES

¶87

¶ 88 Average Itemized Deductions

For those taxpayers who itemize their deductions on Schedule A of Form 1040, the following chart should be of special interest. Based on preliminary statistics for 2017 returns, the chart shows the average deductions of taxpayers for tax year 2017 for interest (¶ 1043), taxes (¶ 1021), medical and dental expenses (¶ 1015), and charitable contributions (¶ 1058). While it may be interesting for those who itemize their deductions to compare them with these average figures, the chart should *not* be considered as indicating amounts that would be allowed by the IRS. In any case, taxpayers must be able to substantiate claimed itemized deductions.

Individual Income Tax Returns, Preliminary Data, Tax Year 2017, Table 1 (Source: *Winter 2019 Statistics of Income (SOI) Bulletin*).

PRELIMINARY AVERAGE ITEMIZED DEDUCTIONS FOR TAX YEAR 2017 BY ADJUSTED GROSS INCOME RANGES

Adjusted Gross Income Ranges	Medical Expenses	Taxes	Interest	Charitable Contributions
Under $ 15,000	$9,163	$3,740	$6,209	$1,550
$ 15,000 to $ 30,000	9,197	3,454	6,501	2,490
$ 30,000 to $ 50,000	8,452	4,263	6,302	2,889
$ 50,000 to $ 100,000	9,429	6,559	7,119	3,454
$ 100,000 to $ 200,000	11,442	11,452	8,751	4,371
$ 200,000 to $ 250,000	17,397	18,280	11,057	5,638
$ 250,000 or more	32,062	51,301	16,241	22,484

Chapter 1

INDIVIDUALS

Income Tax Return

See CCH® AnswerConnect: *Who Must File an Individual Income Tax Return* for more information on this topic.

101. Who Must File an Individual Tax Return. A federal income tax return (¶ 105) generally must be filed each tax year by a U.S. citizen or resident alien whose gross income equals or exceeds a threshold amount based on his or her filing status (Code Sec. 6012; IRS Pub. 17). In the case of married individuals filing jointly, the filing threshold applies to the couple's combined gross income, but only if the couple shares the same household at the close of the tax year, neither spouse files a separate return, and neither spouse is a dependent of another taxpayer (e.g., a married student supported by a parent).

For tax years 2018 through 2025, the filing threshold of an individual generally is the standard deduction amount for the tax year (¶ 131). This includes the additional standard deduction for an individual age 65 or older, but not the additional standard deduction for an individual who is blind. However, the IRS requires married individuals filing separately to file a return if their gross income is at least $5, regardless of age. The filing threshold for tax years beginning in 2019 is:

Single	$12,200
Single, 65 or older	13,850
Married filing separately	5
Married filing jointly	24,400
Married filing jointly, one spouse 65 or older	25,700
Married filing jointly, both spouses 65 or older	27,000
Head of household	18,350
Head of household, 65 or older	20,000
Qualifying widow(er) (surviving spouse)	24,400
Qualifying widow(er) (surviving spouse), 65 or older	25,700

For tax years beginning before 2018 and after 2025, the filing threshold for an individual other than a dependent is the sum of the standard deduction and the personal exemption deduction (¶ 133). This includes the additional standard deduction for an individual age 65 or older, but not the additional standard deduction for an individual who is blind.

Dependents. A child or other individual who can be claimed as a dependent (¶ 137) is subject to different filing thresholds based on earned or unearned income for the tax year (Code Sec. 6012(a)(1)(C)). A dependent who is neither age 65 or older, nor blind, must file a return for the 2019 tax year if he or she has:

- unearned income over $1,100 ($1,100 for 2020),

- earned income over $12,200 ($12,400 for 2020), or

- gross income more than the larger of $1,100 or earned income up to $11,850, plus $350 for 2019 ($1,100, $12,050, and $350, respectively, for 2020).

¶101

If the dependent is either age 65 or older, or blind, the filing thresholds include the additional standard deduction amounts. A married dependent must also file a return if he or she has gross income of at least $5 and his or her spouse files a separate return and itemizes deductions.

Earned income of a dependent includes salaries, wages, tips, professional fees, and taxable scholarship and fellowship grants. Unearned income includes investment-type income, such as taxable interest, ordinary dividends, capital gain distributions, unemployment compensation, taxable Social Security benefits, pensions, annuities, and distributions of unearned income from a trust.

The parent of a child who is subject to the kiddie tax and who has income only from interest or dividends may elect to report the child's income on the parent's return (¶ 115). The child will then *not* have to file a return. If a guardian or other person is charged with the care of a minor, a minor's property, or a person under a disability, the return for the individual should be filed by the responsible person, unless already filed by the individual or some other person (¶ 504).

Return Requirement. If the filing threshold is met, then a return must be filed even if no tax is due. If the filing threshold is *not* met, then a return should be filed if a tax refund or any refundable credit is available (for example, child tax credit or earned income credit). A return is also required if the taxpayer is liable for:

- alternative minimum tax (AMT) calculated on Form 6251 (¶ 190);

- additional tax on a qualified retirement plan or individual retirement account (IRA) calculated on Form 5329 (¶ 2169);

- household employment taxes calculated on Schedule H (Form 1040) (¶ 2652);

- Social Security and Medicare (FICA) taxes on tip income not reported to an employer, as calculated on Form 4137 (¶ 717), or on wages received from an employer who did not withhold the taxes, as calculated on Form 8919;

- uncollected Social Security, Medicare, or Railroad Retirement Tax Act (RRTA) taxes on tips reported to an employer or on group-term life insurance;

- additional taxes on a health savings account (HSA) (¶ 2035) or Archer medical savings account (MSA) (¶ 2037) calculated on Form 5329;

- the net investment income tax (NIIT) calculated on Form 8960 (¶ 117) or Additional Medicare Tax calculated on Form 8959 (¶ 2648);

- the recapture of any of the following: first-time homebuyer credit (¶ 1424), investment credit (¶ 1465A), low-income housing credit (¶ 1465K), Indian employment credit (¶ 1465Q), new markets credit (¶ 1465T), employer-provided child care credit (¶ 1465V), alternative motor vehicle credit (¶ 1446), alternative fuel vehicle refueling property credit (¶ 1455), qualified plug-in electric drive motor vehicle credit (¶ 1451), or on the disposition of a home purchased with a federally subsidized mortgage;

- net earnings from self-employment for the year are at least $400 (¶ 2664);

- wages of $108.28 or more were earned from a church or qualified church-controlled organization that is exempt from employer FICA taxes (¶ 2601);

- advance payments of the premium assistance tax credit (¶ 1431) or health care coverage tax credit (¶ 1432) were received; or

- the taxpayer is a U.S. shareholder that is required to include his or her pro rata share of income of a deferred foreign income corporation, and has elected to pay the net liability in installments (¶ 2488C).

Any person who is required to file an income tax return must report on that return the amount of tax-exempt interest received or accrued during the tax year (¶ 724) (Code Sec. 6012(d)).

105. Individual Income Tax Return (Form 1040). An individual whose gross income equals or exceeds a threshold amount for the tax year (¶ 101) must file a federal income tax return using Form 1040 or Form 1040-SR even if no income tax is due. Even if the filing threshold is not met, a return should be filed if the individual owes any additional taxes, or to claim a tax refund or certain refundable credits. The return may serve as a joint return or separate return for married individuals (¶ 152). The return generally must be filed by April 15 of the following calendar year, but the due date is automatically extended to July 15, 2020, for the 2019 tax year as a result of the COVID-19 (coronavirus) crisis (¶ 107).

Form 1040 is a double-sided page that contains taxpayer and dependent information, as well as basic income amounts (for example, W-2 wages, pension distributions, dividends) and the income tax calculation. Form 1040-SR may be used an individual who is age 65 or older for tax years beginning in 2019. The form is almost identical to Form 1040 except with larger font sizes and no color contrasts to make it easier to read.

There are three additional schedules a taxpayer may need to use depending on his or her situation for tax years beginning in 2019 (this is reduced from the six additional schedules used for tax years beginning in 2018):

- Schedule 1 is used to report additional sources of income from other forms and adjustments to gross income (i.e., "above-the-line" deductions) (¶ 1005);

- Schedule 2 is used to report liability for certain additional income taxes, including alternative minimum tax (AMT), self-employment tax, unreported social security and Medicare taxes, household employment taxes, additional taxes on IRAs and other retirement plans, the additional Medicare tax, and net investment income tax (NIIT); and

- Schedule 3 is used to report certain nonrefundable tax credits and other tax payments including estimated taxes and refundable tax credits.

An individual may also need to file any necessary schedules or forms as needed (e.g., Schedule A for itemized deductions, etc.). An individual's return generally is not required to be filed electronically, unless prepared and filed by a specified tax return preparer (¶ 2503).

For tax years beginning before 2018, an individual may file alternative forms in lieu of Form 1040 if certain filing conditions are met. Form 1040A is a shorter form for an individual with less than $100,000 of taxable income, who does not itemize deductions and does not claim certain tax credits. Form 1040EZ is a simplified form for an individual with taxable income of less than $100,000 who does not claim any dependents or any adjustments to gross income. Form 1040A or Form 1040EZ may not be filed for tax years beginning after 2017.

IRS Computation of Tax. Any taxpayer who files an individual tax return by the due date can have the IRS compute the tax, as well as the earned income credit or elderly and disabled credit under certain conditions (IRS Pub. 17).

107. Due Date for Individual Income Tax Return (Form 1040). The due date for an individual to file an income tax return using Form 1040 or Form 1040-SR is generally the 15th day of the fourth month following the close of the tax year (April 15 in the case of a calendar-year taxpayer) (¶ 2505) (Code Sec. 6072(a); Reg. § 1.6072-1). If the due date falls on Saturday, Sunday, or legal holiday, the return is due on the next business day (¶ 2549). An individual's return generally is not required to be filed electronically, unless prepared and filed by a specified tax return preparer (¶ 2503). The due date for filing any federal income tax return, including Form 1040 or Form 1040-SR, otherwise due on or after April 1, 2020, and before July 15, 2020, is automatically extended to July 15, 2020, in response to the COVID-19 (coronavirus) crisis (Notice 2020-23, amplifying Notice 2020-18).

Filing Extensions. An individual generally may obtain an automatic six-month extension (until October 15) to file Form 1040 or Form 1040SR by filing Form 4868 on or before the normal due date of the return (¶ 2509) (Code Sec. 6081(a); Reg. § 1.6081-1). The extension of the filing deadline to July 15, 2020, for returns otherwise due on or after April 1, 2020, and before July 15, 2020, is automatic and an individual does not need to file Form 4868 or call the IRS to receive it. An individual that needs more time to file his or her return after July 15, 2020, may request an additional extension by filing Form 4868 by July 15, 2020, but the extension may not go beyond the original statutory or regulatory extension date (for example, October 15, 2020, for a calendar year taxpayer).

The extension of time for filing a return generally does not extend the time for payment of any tax due, and penalties and interest may apply (¶ 2529) (Code Sec. 6151; Reg. § 1.6151-1). However, the deadline for making federal income tax payments with Form 1040 or Form 1040-SR, including payments of tax on self-employment income and estimated taxes (¶ 127) is also extended to July 15, 2020, if otherwise due on or after April 1, 2020, and before July 15, 2020 (Notice 2020-23, amplifying Notice 2020-18). Penalties and interest for failure to file returns or pay taxes otherwise due on or after April 1, 2020, and before July 15, 2020, will not accrue until July 16, 2020.

Living Outside the United States. A U.S. citizen or resident alien living outside the United States generally must file Form 1040 or Form 1040-SR by the 15th day of the sixth month after the close of the tax year (June 15 in the case of a calendar-year taxpayer) (Code Sec. 6072(c); Reg. § 1.6072-1(c)). The filing deadline is automatically extended to July 15, 2020, as a result of the COVID-19 (coronavirus) crisis for any return otherwise due on or after April 1, 2020, and before July 15, 2020 (Notice 2020-23, amplifying Notice 2020-18).

The extended due date (June 15 generally, July 15, 2020, for the 2019 tax year) applies if the individual lives and has a main place of business or post of duty outside the United States and Puerto Rico, or the individual is in military or naval service duty outside the United States and Puerto Rico. Similarly, a nonresident alien who has wages not subject to withholding generally must file a return by the 15th day of the 6th month after the close of the tax year (July 15, 2020, for the 2019 tax year). The extension to June 15 (July 15, 2020 for the 2019 tax year) runs concurrently with the automatic six-month extension. The maximum extension is only six months (October 15 for a calendar-year individual), unless the individual files Form 2350 to qualify for the foreign earned income or foreign housing exclusion.

Decedent. The final income tax return of a decedent for a fractional part of a year is due on the same date as would apply had the taxpayer lived the entire year (¶ 180).

Amended Return. An individual may correct an error in a return, without incurring interest or penalties, by filing an amended return (Form 1040-X) and paying any additional tax due on or before the last day prescribed for filing the original return.

109. Taxpayer Identification Number (TIN) for Individuals. An individual filing any income, employment, or excise tax return, as well as any statement or other document, must include his or her own taxpayer identification number (TIN) (Code Sec. 6109(a); Reg. § 301.6109-1). This is generally the individual's Social Security number (SSN), Individual Taxpayer Identification Number (ITIN), or Adoption Taxpayer Identification Number (ATIN) (¶ 2579).

If the return, statement, or other document is made with respect to another person, then the other person's TIN also must be included. For example, a taxpayer must provide TINs for qualifying children on his or her return to claim a dependent (¶ 133), the child and dependent care credit (¶ 1401), the child tax credit (¶ 1405), the adoption credit (¶ 1407), and the earned income tax credit (¶ 1422). In the case of the earned income credit and child tax credit, the TIN must be issued before the due date of the taxpayer's return. The parent of any child to whom the kiddie tax rules apply must provide his or her TIN to the child for inclusion on the child's tax return (¶ 115).

A penalty is imposed for each failure by a taxpayer to include his or her identifying number on a return, statement, or other document unless he or she can show that the failure was due to reasonable cause (¶ 2833). Failure to include a correct TIN is treated as a mathematical or clerical error, as are instances in which the information provided differs from the information on file with the IRS that is obtained from the Social Security Administration (Code Sec. 6213(g)(2)).

Computation of Tax Liability

See CCH® AnswerConnect: *Computation of Taxable Income of Individuals* for more information on this topic.

111. Taxable Income of Individuals. An individual generally computes federal income tax liability for a tax year by multiplying his or her taxable income by the applicable income tax rate and subtracting allowable tax credits. The computation of taxable income starts with the taxpayer's gross income (¶ 701), from which certain deductions are subtracted to determine the taxpayer's adjusted gross income (AGI) (¶ 1005) (Code Sec. 63).

After AGI is determined, certain other deductions are subtracted from the taxpayer's AGI to determine his or her taxable income. This includes either the standard deduction (¶ 131) or the taxpayer's itemized deductions (¶ 1014), any deduction for qualified business income (QBI) for tax years beginning after 2017 and before 2026 (¶ 980P), and the deduction for personal and dependency exemptions for tax years beginning before January 1, 2018 (¶ 133).

After taxable income is determined, the taxpayer's gross tax liability is generally computed by applying the appropriate tax rates based on the taxpayer's filing status (single, married filing jointly, head of household, surviving spouse, or married filing separately). Subject to certain exceptions, a taxpayer *must* use either the tax rate tables or tax schedules issued by the IRS to compute his or her income tax liability (¶ 113).

From gross tax liability, the individual subtracts nonrefundable tax credits he or she may claim such as the American opportunity credit, lifetime learning credit, or the child tax credit. Any other taxes not based on taxable income are added to his or her liability including self-employment taxes, net investment income tax (NIIT), and taxes on certain distributions from health savings accounts (HSAs), qualified tuition plans (529 plans), Coverdell accounts, or retirement plans. The taxpayer is then entitled to reduce his or her final tax liability by any payments of taxes and refundable tax credits. For the first tax years beginning in 2020, this includes the Recovery Rebate Credit provided in response to the COVID-19 (coronavirus) crisis for which advance payments are made during 2020 as economic impact payments (¶ 1420).

113. Income Tax Rates and Tables for Individuals. An individual determines his or her income tax liability by applying the appropriate tax rate to his or her taxable income (¶ 111). There are seven tax rates for an individual with each rate applied to a different level of taxable income (Code Sec. 1(i) and (j)). The seven graduated tax rates are 10, 12, 22, 24, 32, 35, and 37 percent for tax years beginning in 2018 through 2025. The seven graduated tax rates are 10, 15, 25, 28, 33, 35, and 39.6 for tax years beginning before 2018 and after 2025. The income levels at which the seven tax brackets apply depend on the taxpayer's filing status and are adjusted annually for inflation (Rev. Proc. 2018-18).

An individual generally uses either the tax rate tables or tax schedules issued by the IRS to compute his or her income tax liability (Code Sec. 3). A taxpayer uses:

- the tax tables produced by the IRS (¶ 25) if his or her taxable income is less than $100,000;

- the Tax Computation Worksheet in the Instructions to Form 1040 (¶ 20) if his or her taxable income is $100,000 or more.

The Tax Computation Worksheet is based on the tax rate schedules at ¶ 11 if single or unmarried, ¶ 13 if married filing jointly or surviving spouse, ¶ 15 if married filing separately, and ¶ 17 if head of household. An individual may *not* use the tax tables if he or she files a short-period return because of a change in his or her annual accounting period (¶ 1507).

Capital Gains and Qualified Dividends. An individual's capital gains and qualified dividend income may be subject to a reduced rate of tax depending on the type of gain, the taxpayer's taxable income, and the taxpayer's regular income tax rate (¶ 1736). The tax on capital gains and qualified dividends is calculated on the Qualified Dividends and

1

INDIVIDUALS

¶113

Capital Gain Tax Worksheet in the Instructions to Form 1040 or the Schedule D Tax Worksheet in the Instructions to Schedule D (Form 1040), whichever applies.

Kiddie Tax. If a child's investment income exceeds a threshold amount, then he or she is subject to the kiddie tax on their net unearned income (¶ 115). For tax years beginning in 2018 and 2019, kiddie tax liability on net unearned income is calculated using the tax brackets and rates for estates and trusts but the taxpayer may elect to use the rules applicable for tax years beginning after 2019. For tax years beginning after 2019, kiddie tax liability is calculated using the tax rate of the child's parents (allocable parental tax). A child subject to kiddie tax uses Form 8615 to calculate the tax.

Foreign Earned Income. An individual who excludes foreign earned income and housing expenses from gross income (¶ 2402 and ¶ 2403) applies the tax rates as if the exclusion has not been claimed. The taxpayer uses the Foreign Earned Income Tax Worksheet in the Form 1040 Instructions to calculate the individual's income tax liability for this purpose.

115. Kiddie Tax on Unearned Income of Child. A child's income tax liability is generally computed in the same manner as for any other individual taking into account the limits on the standard deduction (¶ 131) and personal exemptions (¶ 135), if applicable. If the child's investment income exceeds a threshold amount ($2,200 for 2019 and $2,200 for 2020), then he or she also is subject to "kiddie tax" on their net unearned income (Code Sec. 1(g) and (j)(4), prior to being stricken by the Setting Every Community Up for Retirement Enhancement Act of 2019 (SECURE Act) (P.L. 116-94); Rev. Proc. 2018-57; Rev. Proc. 2019-44).

Form 8615 is used to figure the kiddie tax. For tax years beginning in 2018 and 2019, kiddie tax liability is calculated using the tax brackets and rates for estates and trusts (¶ 19). However, a taxpayer may elect to calculate kiddie tax liability using the rules applicable for tax years beginning before 2018 and after 2019. The election is made by including a statement directly on the return or as an attachment. In either case, the kiddie tax applies only if it results in a higher tax than would apply at the child's normal tax rate.

For tax years beginning before 2018 and after 2019, kiddie tax liability on net unearned income is calculated using the tax rate of the child's parents if it would result in a higher tax liability. For this purpose, the child computes the increase in tax that would result from adding the net unearned income of the child to his or her parent's taxable income (allocable parental tax). Special rules apply for parents with more than one child or who are married filing separately, divorced, or legally separated.

Who is Subject to Kiddie Tax. A child is subject to the kiddie tax if:

- the child is required to file a tax return and he or she does not file a joint return for the year;

- the child's unearned or investment income is more than $2,200 for 2019 ($2,200 for 2020);

- either parent of the child is alive at the end of the year; and

- the child is:

    — under age 18 at the end of the tax year;

    — age 18 at the end of the tax year and does not provide more than one-half of his or her own support with earned income; or

    — at least age 19 and under age 24 at the end of the tax year, a full-time student, and does not provide more than one-half of his or her own support with earned income.

The kiddie tax rules apply regardless of whether or not the child is a dependent of the parent. A child for this purpose includes adopted children and stepchildren as long as one of the child's parents is alive at the end of the tax year.

A child's unearned income is generally all income *other than* salaries, wages, and other payments received for work. Unearned income includes taxable interest, divi-

¶115

dends, capital gains, social security and pension payments, taxable scholarships, certain distributions from trusts, and unemployment compensation. It also includes income produced by property the child obtained with earned income or by gift. It does not include nontaxable income.

Parent's Election. The parents of a child may elect to include on their return the unearned income of a child to avoid the kiddie tax. The election is made by filing Form 8814 and can only be made if:

- the child is required to file a tax return and would otherwise be subject to the kiddie tax;

- the child's only income for the tax year is from interest and dividends, including Alaska Permanent Fund dividends;

- the income was more than $1,100 but less than $11,000 for 2019 ($1,100 and $11,000 for 2020, respectively);

- no estimated tax payments were made for the year in the child's name and Social Security number, including any overpayment of tax from the previous tax year; and

- the child is not subject to backup withholding.

If the election is made, the child does not have to file a tax return or make estimated tax payments for the tax year. The income of the child is added to the electing parent's income with some adjustments. A separate Form 8814 must be filed for each child of the parents.

117. Net Investment Income Tax. An individual is subject to a 3.8 percent tax on the lesser of:

- net investment income for the tax year, or

- modified adjusted gross income (AGI) for the tax year exceeding a threshold amount ($250,000 if married filing jointly, $200,000 if single or head of household, and $125,000 if married filing separately) (Code Sec. 1411; Reg. § 1.1411-2).

The net investment income tax (NIIT) is calculated using Form 8960. The NIIT is an addition to the regular income tax liability, and is taken into account for purposes of calculating estimated tax payments and underpayment penalties (¶ 125). It applies to all U.S. citizens and resident aliens, as well as estates and trusts (¶ 517). It does not apply to a nonresident alien. If a U.S. citizen or resident alien is married to a nonresident alien and does not elect to file a joint return (¶ 2410), then he or she is treated as married filing separately for purposes of determining application of the NIIT.

Net investment income is the excess of the sum of the following items, less any otherwise allowable deductions properly allocable to such income or gain (Reg. § 1.1411-4):

- gross income from interest, dividends, annuities, royalties, rents, and substitute interest and dividend payments, but not to the extent the income is derived in the ordinary course of an active trade or business;

- other gross income from a passive activity (¶ 1169) or from a trade or business of trading in financial instruments or commodities; and

- net gain included in computing taxable income that is attributable to the disposition of property, but not to the extent the property was held in an active trade or business.

Any item that is excluded from gross income for regular income tax purposes is also excluded from net investment income and modified AGI (for example, excludable gain on the sale of a taxpayer's personal residence, veterans' benefits, and tax-exempt bond interest).

Net investment income generally does not include income and gain derived in the ordinary course of a trade or business, unless the trade or business is a passive activity or that of a trader of financial instruments or commodities. If an individual owns or engages in a trade or business directly (or indirectly through a disregarded entity), the determination of whether gross income is derived in a trade or business is made at the individual level. If an individual owns an interest in a trade or business through one or more pass-through entities such as a partnership or S corporation, the determination of whether gross income is derived in a passive activity is made at the owner level. The determination of whether gross income is derived in the trade or business of trading in financial instruments or commodities is made at the entity level.

Similar rules apply for determining whether net gain is attributable to property held in a trade or business. For purposes of determining net gain, a disposition is a sale, exchange, transfer, conversion, cash settlement, cancellation, termination, lapse, expiration, or other disposition. Net gain cannot be less than zero, and losses from dispositions of capital assets are allowed to offset gains, unless the asset's disposition is subject to the NIIT. The $3,000 deduction ($1,500 if married filing separately) for capital losses (¶ 1752) may not be taken against losses on capital assets but may be taken against other net investment income. Losses deductible under Code Sec. 165, including losses attributable to casualty, theft, and abandonment or other worthlessness (¶ 1101), are applied to calculate net gains. Any excess losses are applied as properly allocable deductions against investment income.

Property held in a trade or business generally does not include an interest in a partnership or stock in an S corporation, so gain from the disposition of the interest or stock is usually treated as net gain. However, special rules apply upon the disposition of an active interest in a partnership or S corporation (Prop. Reg. § 1.1411-7).

The NIIT rules might cause a taxpayer to reconsider the way he or she previously grouped activities for passive activity loss purposes under Code Sec. 469. Thus, a taxpayer subject to the NIIT is provided a one-time election to regroup activities under Code Sec. 469 to allow for realignment of grouped activities to properly reflect the interaction of the passive activity rules and income for NIIT purposes (¶ 1175). Further, regrouping may be done on an amended return if the taxpayer was not subject to NIIT on the original return (Reg. § 1.469-11(b)(3)(iv)).

Net investment income includes any income, gain, or loss that is attributable to an investment of working capital (Reg. § 1.1411-6). Net investment income does not include a distribution from qualified employee benefit plans or arrangements, including: a qualified pension, profit sharing, and stock-bonus plan; qualified annuity plan under Code Sec. 403(a) or (b); a traditional or Roth IRA; or a Code Sec. 457 plan of a government or tax-exempt organization (Reg. § 1.1411-8). However, a distribution from a qualified plan or arrangement that is includible in gross income is taken into account for determining the taxpayer's modified AGI in the NIIT calculation.

Special rules are provided for self-employed individuals (Reg. § 1.1411-9) and controlled foreign corporations and passive foreign investment companies (Reg. § 1.1411-10).

119. Individual Health Care Coverage Mandate. An individual is subject to a penalty for failing to maintain minimum essential health care coverage for each month of a tax year beginning before January 1, 2019 (Code Sec. 5000A; Reg. § 1.5000A-1; Notice 2018-84). The penalty (referred to as a shared responsibility payment) is reported on the individual's income tax return for the year, and includes the penalty for the taxpayer's spouse if filing jointly, and any dependent claimed on the return. The penalty is calculated using the worksheets in the Instructions to Form 8965 and for any month is the lesser of:

- the monthly national average premium for bronze-level coverage offered through a Health Benefit Exchange (Marketplace) (for 2018, $283 per individual and $1,415 for a family with five or more members; for 2017, $272 per individual and $1,360 for a family with five or more members) (Rev. Proc. 2018-43; Rev. Proc. 2017-48); or

- 1/12 of the greater of: 2.5 percent of the taxpayer's household income over his or her filing threshold or a flat dollar amount ($695 per adult and $347.50 per child, but limited to 300 percent of the amount).

Applicable Individual. An applicable individual is subject to the penalty unless he or she has a coverage exemption. Form 8965 is used to report a coverage exemption granted by an Exchange or claim an exemption on the tax return. An individual is exempt from the penalty if any of the following apply:

- coverage is unaffordable, meaning the individual's required contribution for coverage under an employer-sponsored plan or the lowest cost bronze plan available through an Exchange exceeds a percentage of his or her household income (8.05 percent for 2018; 8.16 percent for 2017;) (Rev. Proc. 2017-36; Rev. Proc. 2016-24);

- the individual has household income below the threshold for filing an income tax return for the tax year (¶ 101);

- the individual lacked minimum essential coverage for a continuous period of less than three months (short coverage gap) without regard to the calendar year, but only the first lapsed period during the year is counted; or

- the individual experiences a hardship with respect to the capability to obtain coverage under a qualified health plan and either receives a hardship exemption certificate from an Exchange or as provided by the IRS (e.g., residing in state that did not expand Medicaid eligibility) (Notice 2019-5; Notice 2017-14; Notice 2014-76).

An individual is also not subject to the penalty for failing to maintain minimum essential coverage if he or she is: (1) a member of an Indian tribe (¶ 1465Q); (2) a member of a religious sect or division who has obtained a religious conscience exemption to Social Security taxes; (3) a member of a tax-exempt health-care sharing ministry; (4) an individual who is not U.S. citizen or national, or not lawfully present in the United States; and (5) an individual who is incarcerated unless waiting for disposition of charges.

Minimum Essential Coverage. Minimum essential coverage means health care coverage under a government-sponsored program (Medicare, Medicaid, CHIP, etc.), an eligible employer-sponsored plan, a health insurance plan offered in the individual market, a group health plan in which the individual was enrolled on March 23, 2010, an eligible expatriate health plan (for plans issued or modified on or after July 1, 2015), or any other coverage recognized by the IRS. If an applicable individual, spouse, or dependent had minimum essential coverage during the calendar year, the provider of that coverage is required to provide Form 1094-A, Form 1095-B, or Form 1095-C listing the individuals who were enrolled in the coverage and the months of coverage.

Minimum essential coverage does not include health insurance coverage that consists of excepted benefits, such as accident or disability benefits, liability insurance, workers compensation, credit-only insurance, automobile medical payments, or coverage for on-site medical clinics. Certain government-sponsored limited benefit coverage (e.g., line of duty coverage for inactive service members, Medicaid coverage for the medically needy, etc.) does not constitute minimum essential coverage.

If benefits are provided under a separate policy, certificate, or insurance contract, then excepted benefits also include: (1) limited scope dental or vision benefits, benefits for long-term care, nursing home care, home health care, community-based care, or any combination thereof, and other similar limited benefits; (2) coverage only for a specified disease or illness; (3) hospital indemnity or other fixed indemnity insurance; and (4) Medicare supplemental health insurance, coverage supplemental to the medical and dental coverage provided to military personnel, and similar supplemental coverage provided for coverage under a group health plan.

125. Estimated Taxes for Individuals. An individual may need to pay a portion of his or her tax liability through estimated tax payments over the course of the tax year rather than when his or her income tax return is filed. Estimated taxes are generally used to pay tax on income that is not subject to withholding and if the amount of tax being withheld from wages or other income is not enough. Estimated taxes not only cover the individual's liability for income tax but also liability for self-employment taxes, the 3.8 percent net investment income tax (¶ 117), the 0.9 percent Additional Medicare Tax (¶ 2648), and income from an estate, trust, partnership, and S corporation.

The Code does not directly impose an obligation to pay estimated taxes, but it does impose a penalty (addition to tax) for failure to pay enough tax either through withholding or estimated taxes (Code Sec. 6654; Notice 2019-25; Notice 2019-11). If an individual expects to owe at least $1,000 in taxes after subtracting withholding and refundable tax credits, the penalty may be avoided if he or she makes required installment payments of estimated taxes. A required installment is 25 percent of the lesser of:

- 90 percent of the tax shown on the individual's tax return for the current year (80 percent for an individual required to make 2018 estimated payments on or before January 15, 2019); or

- 100 percent of the tax shown on the prior year's return (110 percent in the case of an individual with adjusted gross income in excess of $150,000 or $75,000 if married filing separately), unless the prior year was not a 12-month period.

An individual uses Form 1040-ES to figure and pay his or her required estimated income tax payments for the tax year. Taxes withheld from wages or other income are treated as payments of estimated tax for this purpose. A lower required installment payment may be made if the individual annualizes tax at the end of each payment period based on a reasonable estimate of income, deductions, and tax credits. The annualized income installment method may be use if the taxpayer does not receive income evenly throughout the year.

Each required installment of estimated income taxes generally must be paid by its due date regardless of whether an individual uses the regular or annualized installment method to calculate. This is generally the 15th day of the fourth, sixth, and ninth months of the tax year and the 1st month of the following tax year (April 15, June 15, September 15, and January 1 for a calendar-year taxpayer) (¶ 127). Special rules apply for farmers and fishermen.

The due date of any required installment calculated on Form 1040-ES and otherwise due on or after April 1, 2020, and before July 15, 2020, is automatically extended to July 15, 2020, as a result of the COVID-19 (coronavirus) crisis (Notice 2020-23, amplifying Notice 2020-18). The extension is automatic, and an individual does not need to file any form or call the IRS to receive it. Penalties and interest for failure to pay the required installment payments otherwise due on or after April 1, 2020, and before July 15, 2020, will not accrue until July 16, 2020.

Married Taxpayers. Married individuals may make joint estimated tax payments unless they are legally separated under a divorce decree or separate maintenance agreement, either spouse is a nonresident alien, or the spouses have different tax years. Individuals who cannot make joint estimated tax payments must apply the estimated tax rules to their separate estimated income. If married individuals make joint estimated tax payments or separate estimated payments, it does not affect their ability to file an income tax return jointly or separately (Reg. § 1.6654-2(e)(5)).

Household Employees. An employer of domestic workers who fails to satisfy FICA and FUTA withholding obligations (¶ 2652) through regular estimated tax payments or increased tax withholding from their own wages, may be liable for estimated tax penalties (IRS Pub. 926).

Exceptions to Penalty. A U.S. citizen or resident alien is not subject to the penalty for failing to pay estimated taxes if he or she had no tax liability for the preceding tax year, provided the year was a 12-month period. The penalty may also be waived under certain other circumstances or hardship, or following an individual's retirement or disability (Code Sec. 6654(e)).

Calculation of Penalty. The penalty for underpayment of estimated taxes is computed on Form 2210 and attached to the individual's income tax return; farmers and fishermen use Form 2210-F. If the form is not completed and attached to the individual's return, the IRS will compute the penalty for the taxpayer. If the IRS computes the penalty, it will investigate any reason why the penalty should be waived.

¶125

127. Estimated Tax Payment Due Dates for Individuals. The due dates for required installment payments of estimated taxes by an individual (¶ 125) are generally divided into four payment periods (Code Sec. 6654(c)(2)). This is generally the 15th day of the fourth, sixth, and ninth months of the tax year and the 1st month of the following tax year (April 15, June 15, September 15, and January 1 for a calendar-year taxpayer). If the due date falls on a Saturday, Sunday, or legal holiday in the District of Columbia (¶ 2549), the individual has until the next succeeding business day to make the payment. Special rules apply to farmers and fisherman.

The due date of any required installment calculated on Form 1040-ES and otherwise due on or after April 1, 2020, and before July 15, 2020, is automatically extended to July 15, 2020, as a result of the COVID-19 (coronavirus) crisis (Notice 2020-23, amplifying Notice 2020-18). The extension is automatic, and an individual does not need to file any form or call the IRS to receive it. Penalties and interest for failure to pay taxes will not accrue until July 16, 2020. Thus, a calendar-year individual is required to pay estimated income tax for the 2020 tax year as follows:

Installment	Due date
First and Second	July 15, 2020
Third	September 15, 2020
Fourth	January 15, 2021

The fourth (last) tax installment for the tax year does not need to be made by the normal due date if the taxpayer files Form 1040 or Form 1040-SR and pays the balance of the tax on or before January 31 of the following calendar year, or for a fiscal year on or before the last day of the month following the close of the fiscal year. However, filing a final 2019 return by January 31, 2020, with payment of any tax due does not avoid an addition to tax for underpayment of any of the first three installments that were due for the year (Code Sec. 6654(h); IRS Pub. 505).

If an individual is not liable for estimated tax for the 2020 tax year on March 31, 2020, but his or her tax situation changes so that he or she becomes liable for estimated tax at some point after March 31, then the individual must make estimated tax payments as follows:

- If the individual becomes required to pay estimated tax after March 31 and before June 1, then he or she should pay 50 percent of estimated tax on or before July 15, 2020, 25 percent on September 15, 2020, and 25 percent on January 15, 2021.

- If the individual becomes required to pay estimated tax after May 31 and before September 1, then he or she should pay 75 percent of estimated tax on or before September 15, 2020, and 25 percent on January 15, 2021.

- If the individual becomes required to pay estimated tax after August 31, then he or she should pay 100 percent of estimated tax by January 15, 2021 (Form 1040-ES; IRS Pub. 505).

Farmer or Fisherman. An individual who expects to receive at least two-thirds of his or her gross income for the tax year from farming or fishing, or who received at least two-thirds of gross income for the previous tax year from farming or fishing, may pay estimated tax for the year in one installment on the last installment due date (January 15, 2020, for the 2019 tax year; January 15, 2021, for the 2020 tax year). The entire amount of the estimated tax for the tax year generally must be paid at that time. The payment date may be ignored if the farmer or fisherman files his or her income tax return for the year and pays the entire tax due by March 1.

The penalty for underpayment of estimated tax does not apply unless a farmer or fisherman underpays the tax by more than one-third (Code Sec. 6654(i); IRS Pub. 505). If a joint return is filed, a farmer or fisherman must consider his or her spouse's gross income in determining if at least two-thirds of gross income is from farming or fishing.

Nonresident Alien. A nonresident alien who does *not* have wages subject to federal income tax withholding must pay estimated taxes for 2020 in three installments (July 15, 2020, September 15, 2020, and January 15, 2021). Fifty percent of the annual payment must be made on the first installment due date and 25 percent on each of the remaining two installment due dates (Code Sec. 6654(j); Notice 2020-23, amplifying Notice 2020-18).

Standard Deduction and Exemptions

See CCH® AnswerConnect: *Standard Deduction* and *Personal and Dependency Exemptions* for more information on this topic.

131. Standard Deduction. An individual may elect to claim a standard deduction or itemize deductions (¶ 1014) in calculating taxable income (¶ 111), whichever will result in a higher deduction. The standard deduction is the sum of the basic standard deduction amount, plus an additional standard deduction amount if the taxpayer is age 65 or older, blind, or both (Code Sec. 63(c)). Some individuals also may claim an additional amount for certain net disasters losses.

Basic Standard Deduction. The basic standard deduction amount varies according to the taxpayer's filing status and is adjusted annually for inflation. The basic standard deduction amount for 2019 is (Rev. Proc. 2018-57):

Filing status	2019
Married filing jointly and surviving spouses	$24,400
Head of household filers	18,350
Married filing separately	12,200
Single filers	12,200

The basic standard deduction amount for 2020 is (Rev. Proc. 2019-44):

Filing status	2020
Married filing jointly and surviving spouses	$24,800
Head of household filers	18,650
Married filing separately	12,400
Single filers	12,400

Dependents. A taxpayer who can be claimed as a dependent on another taxpayer's return (¶ 137) is limited to a smaller standard deduction regardless of whether the individual actually is claimed as a dependent. The dependent's basic standard deduction may not exceed the greater of:

- $1,100 for 2019 ($1,100 for 2020); or

- the sum of $350 and the individual's earned income, up to the applicable standard deduction amount (e.g., for single filers: $12,200 for 2019 and $12,400 for 2020).

The limit applies to the basic standard deduction and not to any additional amount for elderly or blind taxpayers. A taxable scholarship or fellowship grant (¶ 865) is considered earned income for this purpose (IRS Pub. 501).

Aged and/or Blind Taxpayers. An individual who is age 65 or older, blind, or both, at the end of the tax year receives an additional standard deduction amount that is added to the basic standard deduction shown in the table above (Code Sec. 63(f), Prop. Reg. § 1.63-3; Reg. § 1.151-1; Rev. Proc. 2018-57; Rev. Proc. 2019-44). The additional amount is:

- $1,300 for 2019 ($1,300 for 2020) if married filing jointly, married filing separately, or surviving spouse; and

- $1,650 for 2019 ($1,650 for 2020) if single, unmarried, or head of household.

Two additional standard deduction amounts are allowed to an individual who is both over 65 and blind at the end of the tax year. Thus, married individuals filing jointly, both of whom are over 65 and blind, can claim four additional standard deduction amounts.

A taxpayer claiming the additional standard deduction must be either age 65, blind, or both, before the close of the tax year. An individual who reaches age 65 on January 1st of any year is deemed to have reached that age on the preceding December 31st. A taxpayer claiming the additional amount for blindness must obtain a certified statement from a doctor or registered optometrist. The statement should be kept with the taxpayer's records and must state either that: (1) the individual cannot see better than

¶131

20/200 in the better eye with glasses or contact lenses; or (2) the individual's field of vision is 20 degrees or less.

A married individual filing separately may claim the additional amounts for a spouse who had no gross income for the year and was not claimed as a dependent by another taxpayer (Code Sec. 151(b)). A taxpayer who claims as a dependent an individual who is either age 65 or older, blind, or both may *not* claim the additional standard deduction amounts for that individual.

Taxpayers Ineligible for Standard Deduction. If married individuals file separate returns, both spouses should either itemize deductions or claim the standard deduction. If one spouse itemizes and the other does not, the non-itemizing spouse's standard deduction amount is zero ($-0-), even if that spouse is age 65 or older, or blind, or both. This rule does not apply if one spouse qualifies to file as head-of-household. A zero standard deduction amount also applies to an individual with a short tax year, as well as a nonresident alien, estate, trust, common trust fund, and partnership (Code Sec. 63(c)(6)). A taxpayer who itemizes even though his or her itemized deductions are less than the standard deduction must check the box on the last line of Schedule A (Form 1040) to make this election.

Net Disaster Losses. An individual may claim an additional standard deduction amount for a net disaster loss reported on Form 4684 in computing regular taxable income and alternative minimum tax (AMT) liability (¶ 1131). A net disaster loss is the excess of personal casualty losses over personal casualty gains in the designated disaster areas for: a qualified federal disaster declared between January 1, 2018, and February 18, 2020; the California wildfires of 2017; Hurricanes Harvey, Irma, or Maria in 2017; or a federally declared disaster in 2016 (Act Secs. 201 and 204(b) of the Taxpayer Certainty and Disaster Tax Relief Act of 2019 (P.L. 116-94); Act Sec. 20104(b) of the Bipartisan Budget Act of 2018 (P.L. 115-123); Act Sec. 11028(c) of the Tax Cuts and Jobs Act (P.L. 115-97); Act Secs. 501 and 504(b)(1) of the Disaster Tax Relief and Airport and Airway Extension Act of 2017 (P.L. 115-63)).

133. Personal and Dependency Exemption Amount. For tax years beginning before 2018 and after 2025, an individual may claim a personal exemption deduction (¶ 135) and an exemption deduction for each dependent claimed on his or her tax return (¶ 137). The exemption amount is adjusted annually for inflation and is $4,050 for 2017 (Code Sec. 151(d); Rev. Proc. 2016-55).

The exemption amount is zero (-$0-) for tax years beginning in 2018 through 2025. No deduction may be claimed for personal and dependency exemptions during these years, but the rules for determining who is a dependent of the taxpayer are applicable for claiming other tax benefits (e.g., child tax credit). In determining who is a dependent for these other tax benefits, the exemption amount is $4,200 for 2019 and $4,300 for 2020 (Rev. Proc. 2018-57; Rev. Proc. 2019-44).

For tax years beginning before 2018 and after 2025, a taxpayer whose adjusted gross income (AGI) exceeds an applicable threshold amount based on filing status must reduce the amount of his or her otherwise allowable exemption deduction. The applicable threshold amounts are also adjusted annually for inflation.

135. Personal Exemption. For tax years beginning before 2018 and after 2025, an individual may claim a personal exemption deduction on Form 1040 for himself or herself in calculating taxable income equal to the exemption amount for the year ($4,050 for 2017; $0 for 2018 through 2025) (¶ 133) on his or her tax return (Code Sec. 151(b); Reg. § 1.151-1; Prop. Reg. § 1.151-1). No personal exemption may be claimed by an individual who is eligible to be claimed as a dependent on another taxpayer's return (¶ 137). For example, a student who works part-time during the year may *not* claim a personal exemption on a return if any other taxpayer (i.e., a parent) is *entitled* to claim him or her as a dependent on a return. If a dependent who is not allowed his or her own personal exemption has gross income in an amount not exceeding $1,050 in 2017, he or she will *not* be taxed on that amount and need *not* file an income tax return for the year (¶ 101).

Married individuals may claim two personal exemptions for tax years before 2018 and after 2025 if filing a joint return, even if one spouse has no income. If spouses file a joint return, neither can be claimed as a dependent on the return of any other taxpayer. If married individuals file separate returns (or one qualifies as head of household), each spouse must claim his or her own personal exemption on their respective return. However, if one of the spouses has no gross income and is *not* the dependent of another taxpayer, then the spouse with gross income may claim the personal exemption for the other spouse on his or her separate return. A married taxpayer who files a separate return may *not* claim two exemptions for his or her spouse, one as a spouse and one as a dependent.

Death or Divorce. If a married individual dies during a tax year beginning before 2018 and after 2025, and his or her surviving spouse files a joint return (¶ 152), the surviving spouse may claim the personal exemption for the deceased spouse unless he or she remarries during the same tax year. The determination of the survivor's filing status is made at the time of the spouse's death, rather than at the end of his or her tax year. If the surviving spouse remarries before the end of the tax year, his or her marital status is determined on the last day of the tax year. If a taxpayer and his or her spouse divorce or are declared legally separated, then the taxpayer cannot claim the exemption for the former spouse (IRS Pub. 17 (2017)).

Resident and Nonresident Aliens. A resident alien may claim his or her own personal exemption for tax years beginning before 2018 and after 2025. If a resident alien files a joint return, he or she may also claim a personal exemption for his or her spouse. However, the filing of a joint return is *not* permissible if either spouse was a nonresident alien at any time during the tax year unless the taxpayer elects to be treated as a resident alien (¶ 2410) (Code Sec. 6013(a)(1); Reg. § 1.6013-1(b)).

137. Dependency Exemption. For tax years beginning before 2018 and after 2025, an individual may claim an exemption deduction in calculating taxable income for each dependent claimed on his or her tax return (Code Sec. 151(c); Reg. § 1.151-1; Prop. Reg. § 1.151-1). The exemption amount is adjusted annually for inflation and is $4,050 for 2017 (¶ 133).

The exemption amount is zero (-$0-) for tax years beginning in 2018 through 2025. No deduction may be claimed for dependency exemptions during these years, but the rules for determining who is a dependent of the taxpayer are applicable for claiming other tax benefits. In determining who is a dependent for these other tax benefits, the exemption amount is $4,200 for 2019 and $4,300 for 2020 (Rev. Proc. 2018-57; Rev. Proc. 2019-44).

A dependent is defined as an individual who is a qualifying child (¶ 137A) or qualifying relative (¶ 137B) of the taxpayer for the year (Code Sec. 152; Prop. Reg. § 1.152-1). The following general requirements must be met with respect to both a qualifying child and qualifying relative to be claimed as a dependent:

• The taxpayer claiming the dependent must include the dependent's taxpayer identification number (TIN) (¶ 109) on his or her return (Code Sec. 151(e)).

• The dependent must be a U.S. citizen or national, or a resident of the United States, Canada, or Mexico for some part of the year, but an exception may apply to certain adopted children of the taxpayer.

• A dependent cannot claim any dependent on his or her own return.

• A married individual cannot be claimed as a dependent if he or she files a joint return with his or her spouse, unless the joint return was only filed as a claim for refund of estimated or withheld taxes and neither spouse would have a tax liability if they had filed separately.

Special rules apply for claiming a dependent child whose parents are divorced or legally separated (¶ 139A). Also, tie-breaking rules apply to claim a dependent if a child meets the requirements to be a qualifying child of more than one taxpayer (¶ 139).

If a parent is barred from claiming a child as a dependent because that child fails to meet either the qualifying child or qualifying relative requirements, the child may claim a personal exemption before 2018 and after 2025 on his or her own return. Also a dependent, whether a qualifying child or a qualifying relative, who has earned income on which tax has been withheld should file a return even though he or she is claimed as a dependent by another. The return will serve as a claim for refund of the tax withheld if the dependent incurs no tax liability (¶ 2670). If a dependent child of the taxpayer has earned income or unearned income in excess of the filing threshold amounts (¶ 101), a return must be filed whether or not the child is claimed as a dependent.

In a community property state (¶ 710), if a child's support is derived from community income, he or she may be claimed as a dependent by either spouse on a separate return by agreement. A single exemption amount before 2018 and after 2025 may *not* be divided between them (IRS Pub. 555 (2016)).

137A. Qualifying Child Definition. An individual may claim a qualifying child as a dependent (¶ 137) on his or her return for purposes of certain tax benefits (e.g., child tax credit). The following requirements must be met for an individual to be considered a qualifying child of the taxpayer (Code Sec. 152(c) and (f); Prop. Reg. § 1.152-2).

- *Relationship.* The individual must bear one of the following relationships to the taxpayer:

    — a son, daughter, stepson, stepdaughter, or a descendant of such child; or

    — a brother, sister, stepbrother, stepsister, or a descendant of such relative.

    The relationship test includes foster and adopted children. An eligible foster child is a child who is placed with the taxpayer by an authorized placement agency or by a decree issued by the courts. An eligible adopted child includes both a legally adopted child and a child legally placed for adoption (Prop. Reg. § 1.152-1(b)).

- *Age.* The individual must be younger than the taxpayer, and either under the age of 19 at the end of the calendar year, or under the age of 24 at the end of the calendar year and a full-time student. An individual who is totally and permanently disabled (¶ 1402) at any time during the year satisfies the age requirement regardless of his or her age. An individual is a full-time student if enrolled or registered for at least part of five calendar months in a year at a qualified educational institution or on-farm training program.

- *Residency or Abode.* The individual must have the same principal place of abode as the taxpayer for more than one-half of the year. Temporary absences for illness, school, vacation, or military service may count as time living with the taxpayer. Special rules apply in the case of a child of divorced or separated parents (¶ 139A). A child who is born or dies during the tax year is considered living with the taxpayer for the entire year if the taxpayer's home was the child's home for the entire time he or she was alive (Prop. Reg. § 1.152-4(c) and (d)). A special rule also applies for kidnapped or missing children (Prop. Reg. § 1.152-4(e)).

- *Support.* The individual must *not* provide more than one-half of his or her own support for the year (¶ 147). For this purpose, if the individual is the taxpayer's child and a full-time student, amounts received as scholarships are not considered support.

- *Joint Return.* The individual cannot have filed a joint return with his or her spouse except as a claim for refund.

A child who is a qualifying child of divorced or separated parents generally may be claimed as a dependent of the parent who has primary custody, but the custodial parent may waive claiming the dependent (¶ 139A). If an individual may be claimed as a qualifying child of two or more taxpayers, they may decide between themselves who will clam the individual as a dependent. If the taxpayers cannot agree, certain tie-breaking rules apply (¶ 139).

If the individual fails to meet all the requirements to be considered a qualifying child, the individual may still be claimed as a dependent if he or she meets all the requirements for a qualifying relative (¶ 137B).

137B. Qualifying Relative Definition. An individual may claim a qualifying relative as a dependent (¶ 137) on his or her return for purposes of certain tax benefits (e.g., child tax credit). The following requirements must be met for an individual to be considered a qualifying relative of the taxpayer (Code Sec. 152(d) and (f); Prop. Reg. § 1.152-3).

- *Relationship.* The individual must bear one of the following relationships to the taxpayer (a relationship does not terminate due to divorce or death of a spouse):

    — a child, stepchild, adopted child, eligible foster child, or a descendant of such child (see ¶ 137A for the definition of adopted and foster child; a special rule also applies for kidnapped or missing children (Prop. Reg. § 1.152-4(e));

    — a brother, sister, stepbrother, stepsister, half brother, or half sister;

    — a parent, grandparent, or other direct ancestor (other than foster parent), as well as any stepparent;

    — a brother or sister of the taxpayer's parent (aunt or uncle), and any son or daughter of the taxpayer's brother or sister (niece or nephew);

    — a son-in-law, daughter-in-law, father-in-law, mother-in-law, brother-in-law or sister-in-law; or

    — an individual who, for the entire year, has the same principal place of abode as the taxpayer and is a member of the taxpayer's household (temporary absences for illness, school, vacation, or military service are permitted).

- *Gross Income.* The individual's gross income for the calendar year must be less than the exemption amount for the year ($4,200 for 2019 and $4,300 for 2020) (¶ 133). Gross income includes all income in the form of money, property, and services that is not exempt from tax. Deductions are not taken into account. Thus, it includes gross sales, rents, share of partnership gross income, etc., without reduction for expenses or determining net income. Any income excludable from the claimed dependent's gross income (e.g. tax-exempt interest) is disregarded, as well as income received by a permanently and totally disabled individual at a sheltered workshop school.

- *Support.* Over one-half of the individual's total support for that calendar year must have been furnished by the taxpayer (¶ 147). If an individual provides more than one-half of his or her own support for the tax year, then generally no taxpayer can meet the support test and the individual cannot be a qualifying relative.

- *Not A Qualifying Child.* The individual must *not* be the qualifying child of the taxpayer or of any other taxpayer for the tax year (¶ 137A). An unrelated child who lives with, and is supported by a taxpayer, may be claimed as a qualifying relative if the other individual for whom the child is a qualifying child does not file a return or files a return solely to claim a refund (Prop. Reg. § 1.152-3(e); Notice 2008-5)

A child who is a qualifying relative of divorced or separated parents generally may be claimed as a dependent of the parent who has primary custody, but the custodial parent may waive claiming the dependent (¶ 139A).

139. Tie-Breaking Rules for Claiming Qualifying Child as Dependent. An individual may meet the requirements to be a qualifying child of more than one taxpayer (¶ 137A), but generally only one taxpayer can claim the individual as a dependent (¶ 137). If an individual may be claimed as a qualifying child by two or more taxpayers, the taxpayers generally may decide between themselves who may claim the child as a dependent.

If the taxpayers cannot agree and more than one taxpayer is entitled to claim the individual as a qualifying child, regardless of whether a return is filed and the qualifying child is claimed, the IRS will disallow all but one of the claims based on the following tie-breaking rules (Code Sec. 152(c)(4); Prop. Reg. § 1.152-2(g); Notice 2006-86):

- If only one of the taxpayers is the child's parent, then the child is the qualifying child of the parent.

- If the child's parents do not file a joint return, then the child is the qualifying child of the parent with whom the child lived the longest during the year.

- If the child resided with both parents equally during the year and the parents do not file a joint return, then the child is the qualifying child of the parent with the highest adjusted gross income (AGI).

- If none of the taxpayers claiming the child is the child's parent, then the child is the qualifying child of the person with the highest AGI.

- If the parents may claim the child as a qualifying child, but do not actually do so, then the child may be the qualifying child of any other taxpayer but only if the other taxpayer's AGI is higher than the AGI of either parent. In the case of parents who file jointly, their AGI is divided equally to make this determination.

When applying the tie-breaking rules, the taxpayer is allowed to claim the child as a dependent for purposes of claiming a dependency exemption before 2018 and after 2025 (¶ 137), head-of-household filing status (¶ 173), the child tax credit (¶ 1405), the dependent care credit (¶ 1401), the earned income credit (¶ 1422), and the exclusion for dependent care benefits (¶ 2065). The tax benefits cannot be divided among the taxpayers.

See ¶ 139A for separate tie-breaker rules for divorced and separated parents.

139A. Dependent of Divorced or Separated Parents. A child who is a qualifying child (¶ 137A) or qualifying relative (¶ 137B) of divorced or separated parents generally may be claimed as a dependent of the parent who has primary custody of the child for the calendar year. The custodial parent is determined by the number of nights that the child resided with the parent (Code Sec. 152(e); Reg. § 1.152-4; Prop. Reg. § 1.152-5(e)). If the child spends an equal amount of time with each parent, the parent with the higher adjusted gross income (AGI) is allowed to claim the child as a dependent.

The custodial parent may waive claiming the dependent, and the child may be claimed as a dependent of the noncustodial parent if all of the following requirements are met:

- the parents are divorced or legally separated under a decree of divorce or separate maintenance, separated under a written separation agreement, or lived apart at all times during the last six months of the calendar year, including parents who were never married and who do not live together;

- one or both parents provided more than one-half of the child's total support for the calendar year determined without regard to any multiple support agreement (¶ 147); if a parent has remarried, support received from the parent's spouse is treated as received from the parent (Code Sec. 152(d)(5));

- one or both parents have legal custody of the child for more than one-half of the calendar year; and

- the custodial parent makes a written declaration on Form 8332 that he or she will not claim the child as a dependent and the noncustodial parent attaches the declaration to his or her original or amended return for each year the dependent is claimed.

If all of the above requirements are met, the noncustodial parent may claim the child as a dependent for purposes of the dependency exemption before 2018 and after 2025 (¶ 137), the child tax credit (¶ 1405), and any education credits attributable to educational expenses made for the child by the noncustodial parent (¶ 1403). Even if the custodial parent waives claiming the dependent, the custodial parent may still claim the child as a dependent for purposes of the head of household filing status (¶ 173), earned

¶139A

income credit (¶ 1422), dependent care credit (¶ 1401), and the exclusion of dependent care benefits (¶ 2065) (Reg. § 1.152-4(f); Notice 2006-86).

Also, so long as the first three requirements listed above are met, regardless of whether the custodial parent waives claiming the dependent, if the child is the qualifying child or qualifying relative of one of the parents, he or she can be treated as a dependent of both parents for purposes of:

- the child's receipt of benefits under a parent's employer-provided health care plan (¶ 2015);

- contributions to an accident or health plan by a parent's employer on behalf of the child (¶ 2013);

- the child's use of a fringe benefit that qualifies as a no-additional-cost service or qualified employee discount (¶ 2087 and ¶ 2088, respectively);

- the child's deductible medical expense (¶ 1015); and

- the child's qualified medical expenses paid from distributions from a health savings account (HSA) (¶ 2035) or Archer medical savings account (MSA) (¶ 2037) that are excludable from gross income (Rev. Proc. 2008-48).

147. Support Test for Dependent. An individual may be claimed as dependent by a taxpayer only if: (1) the individual does not provide over one-half of his or her own support in the calendar year in order to be the taxpayer's qualifying child (¶ 137A), or (2) the taxpayer furnishes over one-half of the individual's support for the calendar year in order to be the taxpayer's qualifying relative (¶ 137B). If an individual provides one-half of his or her own support for the calendar year, then no other taxpayer can claim that individual as a dependent except in the case of certain divorced parents (¶ 139A).

Multiple Support Agreement. An exception also applies for a qualifying relative if there is a multiple support agreement between two or more taxpayers who provide more than 50 percent of the dependent's support for the tax year, but no one person provides at least 50 percent of the support (Code Sec. 152(d)(3); Reg. § 1.152-3; Prop. Reg. § 1.152-3(d)(4)). In that case, a taxpayer who provided at least 10 percent of the dependent's support is treated as providing more than 50 percent of the support if the other taxpayers who provided at least 10 percent of the support waive any claim to the dependent for the calendar year by written declaration. The taxpayer who claims the dependent must keep these signed statements for his or her record. Form 2120 identifying each of the other persons who agreed not to claim the dependent must be attached to the return of the taxpayer claiming the dependent.

Support Defined. Support includes amounts spent to provide food, shelter, clothing, medical and dental care, education, transportation, and similar necessities. Expenses not directly related to any one member of a household, such as the cost of food for the household, must be divided among the members of the household. Support does not include the individual's income, Social Security, or Medicare taxes paid from the individual's own income or assets, or life insurance premiums, funeral expenses, or scholarships received. In addition, alimony payments are not treated as payments by the payor for the support of any dependent. In the case of remarriage, a child's support that is provided by a parent's spouse is treated as provided by the parent (Code Sec. 152(d)(5) and (f)(5); Prop. Reg. § 1.152-4(a); IRS Pub. 501).

In determining support for a dependent for a calendar year, the amount of support provided by a taxpayer or by the dependent themselves is generally compared to the total amount of the dependent's support from all sources, including amounts that are excludable from gross income such as tax-exempt interest. The amount of any item of support is the amount of expense paid or incurred to furnish the item of support, except for property or lodging in which case the amount of the item of support is the fair market value of the item. An amount paid in a calendar year after the calendar year in which the liability is incurred is treated as paid in the year of payment.

Governmental payments and subsidies provided to the needy are generally considered support provided by a third party (i.e., provided by the state). Examples include low-income housing assistance, foster care maintenance payments, adoption assistance benefits, payments of Temporary Assistance for Needy Families (TANF), and Supplemental Nutrition Assistance Program (SNAP) benefits. Governmental payments and subsidies that are used by the recipient to support another person are considered support of that other person provided by the recipient, rather than support provided by the state. For example, if a mother receives TANF and uses the TANF payments to support her children, the mother is treated as having provided that support.

Medical insurance premiums are treated as support, including premiums for Medicare Parts A, B, C, and D. Medical insurance proceeds are not treated as items of support and are disregarded in determining the amount of the individual's support. Similarly, services provided to an individual under the medical and dental care provisions of the Armed Forces Act are not treated as support and are disregarded in determining the amount of the individual's support.

Filing Status

See CCH® AnswerConnect: *Tax Filing Status for Individuals* for more information on this topic.

152. Married Filing Jointly Filing Status. Married individuals may elect to file a joint return if they are married on the last day of the tax year, use the same tax year, agree to file jointly, and neither is a nonresident alien during the tax year. Spouses may file a joint return even though one spouse has no income or deductions (Code Sec. 6013; Reg. § 1.6013-1). Both spouses generally must sign a joint return but exceptions are provided if one spouse cannot sign due to disease, injury, or mental incompetence, or because the spouse is serving in a combat zone, qualified hazardous duty area, or contingency operation. Once a joint return has been filed for a tax year, the spouses generally may not elect to file separate returns for that year after the due date of the return.

If a spouse dies during the year, the taxpayers are considered married for the whole year. The surviving spouse may elect to file a joint return for the decedent's final year unless he or she remarries before the end of the tax year (¶ 180). However, the executor or administrator of the decedent's estate may elect to change from a joint to a separate return within one year of the due date of the return.

Items of gross income, deductions, and credits of both spouses are combined on a joint return and the tax is computed on the spouses' aggregate taxable income. The tax calculated on a joint return is usually lower than the combined tax than if the spouses filed separately (¶ 154) because certain tax benefits may not be claimed if married filing separately (¶ 156). The spouses are jointly and severally liable for the tax due on a joint return (¶ 162).

Marital Status. Whether a marriage is recognized for federal tax purposes depends on state law. If taxpayers are married in compliance with the laws of the state in which they are married, then the marriage is recognized for federal tax purposes, even if they later reside in another state. This includes common law and same-sex marriages. A marriage conducted in a foreign jurisdiction is also recognized if that marriage would be recognized in at least one state, possession, or territory of the United States, regardless of where the individuals are domiciled. A marriage for federal tax purposes does not include registered domestic partnerships, civil unions, or other similar relationships recognized under state law that are not denominated as a marriage under that state's law (Reg. § 301.7701-18; Rev. Rul. 58-66).

If married persons are not living together on the last day of the tax year, they may still file a joint return if they are *not* legally separated under a decree of divorce or separate maintenance on that date (Reg. § 1.6013-4). Spouses who are separated under an interlocutory decree of divorce are considered married and entitled to file a joint return until the decree becomes final. However, certain married individuals living apart may file separate returns as heads of households (¶ 173).

Nonresident Alien. A U.S. citizen or resident alien married to a nonresident alien generally must file as married filing separately. The couple may file a joint return if the nonresident alien elects to be taxed as a resident alien (¶ 2410).

¶152

Spouse in Combat Zone. Spouses of military personnel serving in a combat zone and missing in action may file a joint return for any tax year until the tax year beginning two years after the termination of combat activities in the combat zone (Code Sec. 6013(f)).

154. Married Filing Separately Filing Status. A married individual may elect to file separately rather than filing a joint return with his or her spouse (¶ 152). A married taxpayer generally is required to file separately if his or her spouse uses a different tax year or if the spouse does not agree to file a joint return. Also, the taxpayer may file as head of household if he or she is considered unmarried, lives apart from his or her spouse for the last six months of the tax year, and meets certain other requirements (¶ 173). Spouses that file separate returns will generally have a higher combined tax than spouses that file a joint return because certain tax benefits may not be claimed if married filing separately (¶ 156).

If married individuals file separate returns for a tax year, they can change filing status and elect to make a joint return for that year by filing an amended return on Form 1040-X within three years of the due date for the separate return (without regard to extensions) (Code Sec. 6013(b)). A separate return for this purpose includes a return filed claiming married filing separately, single, or head of household filing status. All payments, credits, refunds, or other repayments relating to the separate returns are applied to the joint return. Any election made on a separate return must also be made on the joint return if the election would have been irrevocable on an original joint return. The change to a joint return cannot be made in certain circumstances.

Once a joint return has been filed for a tax year, the spouses may *not* elect to file separate returns for that year after the due date of the return. However, if either spouse dies during the tax year, the executor or administrator of the decedent's estate may elect to change from a joint to a separate return within one year of the due date of the return (¶ 180).

156. Joint Return v. Separate Return. Generally, it is more beneficial for married taxpayers to file a joint return (¶ 152) as differences in the tax rate brackets for joint and separate returns result in higher tax rates for married individuals filing separately. Unlike with separate returns, taxable income (¶ 111) on a joint return is the entire taxable income amount of the couple. Although there are two taxpayers on the joint return, income and deductions on a joint return are computed on an aggregate basis (Reg. § 1.6013-4).

> **Example:** For 2019, Joe has taxable income in the amount of $30,000, and his wife, Trisha, has taxable income in the amount of $39,600. If they elect to file a joint return, they will not be subject to the 22-percent tax rate because their combined taxable income of $69,600 does not exceed the $78,950 threshold amount for 2019 (¶ 13). If they elect to file separate returns, Trisha's taxable income exceeds the threshold for the 22 percent bracket ($39,475) by $125 for the year (¶ 15).

Spouses who file separate returns generally have a higher combined tax because the standard deduction is one-half the amount allowed on joint return (¶ 131), and if one spouse itemizes deductions the other spouse must also itemize deductions. A married individual filing separately also may *not* claim the earned income credit (¶ 1422), the child and dependent care credit (¶ 1401), the educational credits (¶ 1403), the elderly or permanently disabled (¶ 1402), the credit or exclusion for adoption expenses (¶ 1407), and the exclusion of any interest income from qualified U.S. savings bonds used for higher education expenses (¶ 863).

There are circumstances under which married taxpayers might reduce their tax liability by filing separate returns. Because taxpayers who file joint returns are jointly and severally liable for the tax on the return, filing separately may be preferable if one spouse does not want to be held liable for the other spouse's tax liability. For example, a spouse whose medical expenses are high, but not high enough to exceed the adjusted gross income (AGI) threshold reported on a joint return, may exceed the AGI threshold on a separate return (¶ 1015).

Actual tax comparisons should be made using both joint and separate returns if there is doubt as to which return produces a more favorable result. Considerations other than tax savings might enter into the decision to file a separate rather than a joint return.

162. Innocent Spouse Relief from Joint Return. Married individuals filing joint returns are liable jointly and individually for the entire amount of tax, penalties, and interest arising from the return (¶ 152). Relief from joint liability is generally available under three circumstances to an electing spouse: liability relief (commonly referred to as innocent spouse relief), separation of liability relief, or equitable relief (Code Sec. 6015, as amended by the Taxpayer First Act (P.L. 116-25)).

A spouse must generally request one of these types of relief on Form 8857 within two years of the IRS beginning collection of a tax deficiency or assessment. Equitable relief requests may be requested within the limitations period for filing any claim for refund (¶ 2763) or for the collection of tax (¶ 2735). If a joint filer is denied any type of innocent spouse relief, he or she may petition the Tax Court for review in addition to any other remedy provided by law. The due date for performing certain time-sensitive actions, including requesting innocent spouse relief, otherwise due on or after April 1, 2020, and before July 15, 2020, is automatically extended to July 15, 2020, in response to the COVID-19 (coronavirus) crisis (Notice 2020-23; Rev. Proc. 2018-58). Taxpayers in community property states who file separate returns may be able to avoid liability for deficiencies attributable to community income under a special "innocent spouse" provision (¶ 711).

Innocent Spouse Relief. To qualify for innocent spouse relief, the electing taxpayer must:

- file a joint return for the tax year that has an understatement of tax due to erroneous items of the other spouse;

- establish that at the time of signing the tax return the taxpayer did not know, or have reason to know, there was an understatement of tax; and

- show that it would be unfair to hold the innocent spouse liable for the understatement of tax, taking into account all the facts and circumstances (Code Sec. 6015(b)).

A key element for the IRS in granting innocent spouse relief is whether the electing spouse received any substantial benefits, or later was divorced or separated from, or deserted by, the other spouse.

Separation of Liability Relief. Alternatively, a spouse may elect to obtain relief by separation of liabilities (Code Sec. 6015(c)). To qualify, an individual must have filed a joint return, and either:

- is no longer married to, or is legally separated from, the spouse with whom the joint return was filed, or

- must *not* have been a member of the same household with the other spouse for a 12-month period ending on the date of the filing of Form 8857.

The burden of proof for determining income and deductions is on the taxpayer who elects relief under separation of liability.

Equitable Relief. If an individual fails to qualify for either of the first two types of relief, he or she may still obtain relief from joint liability by electing equitable relief (Code Sec. 6015(f); Rev. Proc. 2013-34). The taxpayer must show that, under all the facts and circumstances, it would be unfair to be held liable for the understatement or underpayment of taxes.

163. Injured Spouse Relief from Joint Return. If married taxpayers file a joint return (¶ 152) and one spouse owes certain past-due amounts (e.g., child support, alimony, student loans), all or part of the tax overpayment shown on the joint return may be used to satisfy the past-due debt. The nonobligated spouse may be considered an injured spouse and entitled to a refund of his or her part of the overpayment if he or she:

- is not required to pay the past-due amount;

- received and reported income such as wages, taxable interest, etc., on the joint return; and

- made and reported payments on the joint return, including withheld federal income taxes or estimated taxes (Financial Management Service Reg. § 285.3).

The injured spouse should file Form 8379 either with the married couple's jointly filed return (with "Injured Spouse" in the upper left corner) or by itself if filing after the joint return has already been filed. A separate Form 8379 must be filed for each tax year. An injured spouse claim is different from an innocent spouse relief from joint liability (¶ 162).

173. Head of Household Filing Status. An individual who qualifies to file as head of household is generally entitled to a higher standard deduction (¶ 131) and lower tax rates than a single individual (Code Sec. 2(b)). A taxpayer qualifies as head of household if:

- he or she is unmarried or considered unmarried, and not a surviving spouse (¶ 175) on the last day of the tax year;

- maintains a household by paying more than one-half the cost of keeping up a home; and

- a qualifying individual lived with the taxpayer in the home for more than one-half of the year, unless the person is the taxpayer's dependent parent.

Qualifying Individual. A qualifying individual includes a qualifying child that is a dependent of the taxpayer (¶ 137A) determined without regard to the rules for divorced parents (¶ 139A). A child is not a qualifying individual if the child is married at the close of the taxpayer's tax year and (1) files a joint return with his or her spouse, or (2) is not a U.S. citizen, national, or a resident of the United States, Canada, or Mexico. For this purpose, an adopted child or a foster child, as defined under the qualifying child rules, is treated as the taxpayer's child by blood.

A qualifying individual also includes any other person who is a qualifying relative of the taxpayer and claimed as a dependent (¶ 137B)). However, the taxpayer must be related to the individual for this purpose. A taxpayer cannot claim head of household status with respect to an individual who is the taxpayer's dependent only because the individual is part of the taxpayer's household or is claimed as a dependent under a multiple support agreement (¶ 147).

An individual qualifies for head of household status if a *separate* household is maintained for a parent for the tax year. The separate household must be the parent's principal place of abode, and the parent must qualify as the child's dependent. A parent's principal place of abode can include residence in a rest home or home for the aged. An institutionalized or hospitalized dependent, other than a parent, may also qualify a taxpayer as head of a household if the taxpayer can prove that the taxpayer's home was the principal place of abode of the dependent, even though the dependent may never return home because of the nature of the infirmity.

Marital Status. The marital status of an individual is determined at the end of a tax year. A taxpayer is considered to be unmarried at the end of a tax year if he or she is legally separated from his or her spouse under a decree of divorce or separate mainte-nance at the close of the tax year, or his or her spouse was a nonresident alien at any time during the tax year. A taxpayer under an interlocutory decree of divorce is not legally separated. A widow or widower may not use the head of household rates in those tax years in which he or she qualifies as a surviving spouse (¶ 175).

A married taxpayer will be considered unmarried and eligible for head of household status if the taxpayer's spouse was not a member of the household for the last six months of the year and if the household is the principal place of abode of a child that the taxpayer is entitled to claim as a dependent (Code Secs. 2(c) and 7703(b)). The taxpayer is eligible for head-of-household status even if the taxpayer waived the right to claim the dependent (¶ 139A). A nonresident alien who is considered unmarried may not use the head of household tax rate but must use the tax rate schedule for single individuals (Reg. § 1.2-2(b)(6)).

¶173

Maintains Household. An individual taxpayer maintains a household if: (1) the taxpayer furnishes, with funds attributable to him or her, more than 50 percent the cost of maintaining the home during the tax year; and (2) at least one of the qualifying individuals lives there for more than 50 percent of the year except for temporary absence. An exemption is made for institutionalized or hospitalized dependents. Birth or death of a qualifying individual during the year will not disqualify the taxpayer as the head of a household if the individual lived in the household during the part of the year when he or she was alive (Code Sec. 2(b)(1); Reg. § 1.2-2(c)).

The cost of maintaining a household includes the expenses incurred for the mutual benefit of the occupants by reason of its use as the principal place of abode. This includes property taxes, mortgage interest, rent, utility charges, upkeep and repairs, property insurance, food consumed on the premises, and other household expenses. It does not include the cost of clothing, education, medical treatment, vacations, life insurance, transportation, food consumed off the premises, or the value of services rendered by the taxpayer or by any person who qualifies the taxpayer as head of a household (Reg. § 1.2-2(d)).

Paid Preparer's Due Diligence. A paid tax return preparer is subject to a penalty if he or she fails to comply with certain due diligence requirements for any return claiming head of household filing status. This may include completing and submitting Form 8867 with the taxpayer's return or claim for refund (¶ 2807).

175. Surviving Spouse Filing Status. A surviving spouse who is a widow or widower with a dependent child may continue to use the tax rates and standard deduction for married individuals filing a joint return for two tax years following the year of death of his or her spouse (Code Sec. 2(a); Reg. § 1.2-2(a)). To qualify as a surviving spouse, the taxpayer must:

- have been entitled to file a joint return with the deceased spouse for the year or his or her death (whether or not a joint return was actually filed for that year);

- not remarry during the tax year of the spouse's death or the following two tax years; and

- maintain a household (¶ 173) for the entire tax year that is the principal place of abode of a child, adopted child, or stepchild (but not foster child) whom the taxpayer is entitled to claim as a dependent (¶ 137).

An individual qualifying as a surviving spouse may not file a joint return, but does compute tax liability using the tax rates and standard deduction applicable to joint filers. For example, a surviving spouse may generally use the joint return rates and standard deduction for 2019 if his or her spouse died in 2017 or 2018. Also, a surviving spouse may not claim any personal or dependent exemptions before 2018 and after 2025 other than his or her own personal exemption and those of the dependents for whom the household is maintained.

A taxpayer does not qualify as a surviving spouse for the tax year in which his or her spouse dies. Thus, the taxpayer may file a joint return for that year with the executor or administrator of the deceased spouse's estate (¶ 180). A surviving spouse who continues to meet all of the above requirements is entitled to claim the head of household filing status (¶ 173) after the two-year period following the year of death of his or her spouse.

176. Single or Unmarried Filing Status. An individual who is not married or considered unmarried at the end of the tax year files his or her income tax return as single or unmarried if he or she does not qualify as a head of household (¶ 173) or surviving spouse (¶ 175). (Code Sec. 1(c)). A taxpayer's marital status is generally determined on the last day of his or her tax year, unless the taxpayer's spouse dies during the tax year (¶ 180). For example, an individual who is legally divorced or legally separated under state law on the last day of the tax year is considered as unmarried for the entire tax year and may file as single.

Decedent's Final Return

180. Decedent's Final Income Tax Return. An income tax return must be filed for a deceased person who would have been required to file a return if he or she were still alive during the tax year (¶ 101) (Code Sec. 6012; IRS Pub. 559). The final return covers a short year, including the part of the year up to the date of death. The final income tax return of a decedent is due by the date on which the return would have been due had death not occurred. This is generally 15th day of the fourth month following the close of the tax year (April 15 in the case of a calendar-year taxpayer) but for the 2019 tax year, the filing deadline is automatically extended to July 15, 2020, as a result of the COVID-19 (coronavirus) crisis (¶ 107) (Notice 2020-23, amplifying Notice 2020-18). The word "DECEASED," the decedent's name, and the date of death should be written across the top of the decedent's final return.

The return for the decedent must be filed by his or her administrator, executor, or any other person charged with responsibility for the decedent's affairs. The personal representative can file a joint return for the decedent and the surviving spouse. The surviving spouse alone can file the joint return if no personal representative has been appointed before the due date for filing the return for the year of death. A joint return may also be filed for the year preceding death if the decedent died after the close of the preceding tax year and before filing the return for that year. A final joint return with the decedent may not be filed if the surviving spouse remarried before the end of the year of the decedent's death (Reg. § 1.6013-1(d); IRS Pub. 559).

A court-appointed personal representative may revoke an election to file a joint return previously made by the surviving spouse by filing a separate return for the decedent within one year from the due date of the return (including extensions). In that case, the joint return made by the surviving spouse is regarded as the separate return of that spouse by excluding the decedent's items and refiguring the tax liability.

If a refund is due, the personal representative must attach to the return either Form 1310 or a copy of the court certificate showing his or her appointment. A surviving spouse filing a joint return with the decedent can claim the refund without attaching Form 1310.

182. Income in Respect of Decedent (IRD). If a cash-basis taxpayer dies, only income actually or constructively received up to the date of death is included in the decedent's final return (¶ 180). If the decedent was on the accrual basis of accounting, income accrued up to the date of death is included in the final return. Income that accrues *only because of death* is not included (Code Sec. 451; Reg. § 1.451-1(b)).

Income to which a decedent was entitled but which is not properly includible in the decedent's gross income for the tax year ending on the date of death or an earlier year is known as income in respect of a decedent (IRD). Items of IRD are *not* includible in the final return of the decedent, but instead are includible in the gross income of the decedent's estate or other person who acquires the right to receive the income from the decedent by bequest, devise, or inheritance (Code Sec. 691(a); Reg. § 1.691(a)-2; Reg. § 1.691(a)-3).

IRD retains the character it would have had in the hands of the decedent. Thus, if the income would have been capital gain, exempt income, or interest to the decedent, it is the same kind of income to the recipient. The depreciation recapture rules under Code Secs. 1245 and 1250 apply to sales or other dispositions of property (¶ 1779) if that income is treated as income on the decedent's final return or as IRD. These rules do not apply to transfers of depreciable property at death (Code Secs. 1245(b)(2) and 1250(d)(2)).

Installment Obligations. Any installment obligation acquired from a decedent is treated as an item of IRD if the decedent had been reporting the profit of the obligation on the installment basis (Code Sec. 691(a)(4); Reg. § 1.691(a)-5). If, however, the obligor of the installment obligation acquires the uncollected obligation, then the decedent's estate is considered to have made a taxable disposition of the installment obligation. Thus, any previously unreported gain is recognized by the decedent's estate. This rule also applies if the obligation is canceled because of the death of the payee or if the estate allows the obligation to become unenforceable because it is canceled by the executor.

184. Deductions in Respect of Decedent (DRD). If a cash-basis taxpayer dies, only expenses actually paid up to the date of death are deductible on the decedent's final return (¶ 180). If the decedent was on the accrual basis, expenses accrued up to the date of death are also deductible on the final return but only if the expenses do not accrue solely as a result of the taxpayer's death (Code Sec. 461(b); Reg. § 1.461-1(b)).

Expenses for medical care of the decedent, paid out of his or her estate within one year from the date of death, are deductible on the decedent's final income tax return (Reg. § 1.213-1(d)). The estate must attach a statement, in duplicate, to the decedent's return waiving the right to claim the deduction on the estate tax return.

Business expenses, income-producing expenses, interest, and taxes for which the decedent was liable but which were not properly allowable as a deduction on his or her last return are known as deductions in respect of decedent (DRD). Items of DRD, as well as the foreign tax credit, are not deductible on the final return of the decedent, but instead may be deducted by the decedent's estate or the person who by reason of the decedent's death acquires—subject to such obligation—an interest in property of the decedent (Code Sec. 691(b); Reg. § 1.691(b)-1). The percentage depletion deduction is allowed only to the person who receives the income in respect of the decedent to which the deduction relates.

186. Income Tax Deduction for Estate Taxes. If a person includes in gross income an item of income that had accrued as of the date of death of a decedent or prior successive decedents, so that it was included in the valuation of the estate for estate tax purposes, that person may take a corresponding deduction for income tax purposes based on the estate tax attributable to the net value of the income item (Code Sec. 691(c); Reg. § 1.691(c)-1). This deduction is taken by individuals on Form 1040 and by estates and trusts on Form 1041 but only as a miscellaneous itemized deduction (¶ 1095). In the case of any generation-skipping transfer tax imposed on a taxable termination or a direct skip as a result of the death of the transferor, an income tax deduction is available for the portion of this tax attributable to items of gross income that were not properly includible in the gross income of the trust before the date of such termination.

Alternative Minimum Tax (AMT)

See CCH® AnswerConnect: *Alternative Minimum Tax (AMT)* for more information on this topic.

190. Alternative Minimum Tax (AMT) for Individuals, Estates, & Trusts. An individual, estate, or trust is subject to the alternative minimum tax (AMT) in addition to regular income tax liability (Code Sec. 55). A taxpayer's AMT for a tax year is the excess of the taxpayer's tentative minimum tax over regular tax. A taxpayer's regular tax for the tax year is regular income tax liability (¶ 1415) reduced by the foreign tax credit used for regular income tax purposes (¶ 1461). It does not include any increase in tax due to the recapture of the investment tax credit (¶ 1465A) or the low-income housing credit (¶ 1465K). The income averaging rules for farmers and fishermen also do not apply when determining regular tax liability (¶ 767).

Tentative minimum tax is equal to 26 percent of the taxpayer's alternative minimum taxable income (AMTI) up to a certain threshold amount, plus 28 percent of any AMTI in excess of the threshold amount. For tax years beginning in 2019, the threshold amount is $194,800 ($97,400 if married filing separately) (Rev. Proc. 2018-57). For tax years beginning in 2020, the threshold amount is $197,900 ($98,950 if married filing separately) (Rev. Proc. 2019-44).

AMTI is the taxpayer's regular taxable income increased by AMT tax preference items (¶ 194) and modified by AMT adjustments (¶ 196). A certain amount of AMTI is exempt from tax (¶ 192). A taxpayer also may claim the AMT foreign tax credit in computing its tentative minimum tax (¶ 2475). Subject to limits, AMT liability may also be reduced by nonrefundable personal credits (¶ 1415) and general business credits

1

INDIVIDUALS

(¶ 1465). Individuals use Form 6251 to compute AMT. Estates and trusts use Schedule I (Form 1041).

Net Capital Gain and Qualified Dividends. The taxation of net capital gains and qualified dividends for AMT purposes is the same as for regular income tax purposes (¶ 1736 and ¶ 1738), including the netting of capital gains and losses into separate tax-rate groups (¶ 1739). However, the capital gain or loss amounts may differ from the regular tax amounts because of AMT tax preferences and adjustments affecting the basis of capital assets in computing AMTI.

AMT and Kiddie Tax. A child who is subject to the kiddie tax (¶ 115) is also subject to the AMT and computes tentative minimum tax in the same manner as any individual taxpayer. Thus, all adjustments and preferences apply, and AMT liability on the child's net unearned income is computed under the rules that apply to other individuals except that the child's exemption amount is limited. A child's AMT exemption amount and AMT liability do not depend on his or her parent's AMTI or AMT exemption amount.

Partners and S Corporation Shareholders. A taxpayer who is a partner or S corporation shareholder computes AMT liability separately by taking into account his or her share of partnership or S corporation income and deductions. Special rules apply to partners of an electing large partnership using a simplified pass-through system for tax years beginning before 2018 (¶ 482). Partnerships and S corporations are not subject to the AMT.

192. AMTI of Individuals, Estates, and Trusts. The alternative minimum taxable income (AMTI) of an individual, estate, or trust for alternative minimum tax (AMT) purposes (¶ 190) is the taxpayer's regular taxable income modified by AMT tax preference items and various AMT adjustments (Code Sec. 55(b)(2); Reg. § 1.55-1). These are items of deductions, exclusions, and income that are either recomputed or not allowed for in calculating AMTI (¶ 194 and ¶ 196). A taxpayer may avoid having some deductions classified as AMT preferences or adjustments if it elects to capitalize the expenses and deduct them ratably for regular tax purposes (circulation expenditures, research and experimental expenditures, mining exploration and development costs, intangible drilling costs) (Code Sec. 59(e)).

AMT Exemption. A certain amount of AMTI is exempt from AMT, adjusted annually for inflation (Code Sec. 55(d)). The AMT exemption amounts are phased out or reduced 25 percent for each $1 of the excess of the taxpayer's AMTI over certain threshold amounts, also adjusted annually for inflation. Married individuals filing separately must also increase AMTI by 25 cents for every $1 by which it exceeds the phased-out level up to an overall increase of the exemption amount. Individuals use Form 6251 to compute AMT. Estates and trusts use Schedule I (Form 1041).

Individuals. The AMT exemption amount for individuals for tax years beginning in 2019 is $111,700 if married filing jointly or surviving spouse, $71,700 if single or head of household, and $55,850 if married filing separately (Rev. Proc. 2018-57). The threshold amount for phaseout or reduction of the AMT exemption amount in 2019 is $1,020,600 if married filing jointly or surviving spouse, and $510,300 if single, head of household, or married filing separately. Thus, the AMT exemption amount is completely phased out in 2019 when AMTI reaches $1,467,400 if married filing jointly or surviving spouse, $797,100 if single or head of household, and $733,700 if married filing separately.

The AMT exemption amount for individuals for tax years beginning in 2020 is $113,400 if married filing jointly or surviving spouse, $72,900 if single or head of household, and $56,700 if married filing separately (Rev. Proc. 2019-44). The threshold amount for phaseout or reduction of the AMT exemption amount in 2020 is $1,036,800 if married filing jointly or surviving spouse, and $518,400 if single, head of household, or married filing separately. Thus, the AMT exemption amount is completely phased out in 2020 when AMTI reaches $1,490,400 if married filing jointly or surviving spouse, $810,000 if single or head of household filer, and $745,200 if married filing separately.

Estates and Trusts. The AMT exemption amount for estates and trusts is $25,000 for 2019 and $25,400 for 2020. In the case of a portion of electing small business trusts (ESBTs) (¶ 304) that is treated as a separate trust, the AMT exemption amount is zero for any tax year (Code Sec. 641(c)(2)(B)). The threshold amount for phaseout or reduction of the AMT exemption amount for estates or trusts is $83,500 for 2019 and $84,800 for 2020. Thus, the AMT exemption amount is completely phased out for estates and trusts when AMTI reaches $183,500 for 2019 and $186,400 for 2020.

AMT Exemption for Minor Child. A child who is subject to the kiddie tax (¶ 115) is subject to the AMT and computes tentative minimum tax in the same manner as any other individual. For tax years beginning in 2018 through 2025, the AMTI exemption for a child subject to the kiddie tax is the same as for any other individual (for example, $71,700 for single individual in 2019) (Code Sec. 55(d)(4)(A), as amended by the Setting Every Community Up for Retirement Enhancement Act of 2019 (SECURE Act) (P.L. 116-94)). For tax years beginning before 2018 and after 2025, the AMTI exemption amount of a child subject to the kiddie tax is limited to the sum of the child's earned income for the year, plus a threshold amount ($7,500 for 2017) (Code Sec. 59(j)).

AMTI and Losses. The passive activity loss limitations generally apply in determining a taxpayer's AMTI with certain modifications (Code Sec. 58). The limitations on the deductibility of other losses, including the at-risk rules (¶ 1155), partnership losses claimed by partners (¶ 425), and S corporation losses claimed by shareholders (¶ 321) also apply (Code Sec. 59(h)). These limitations are applied separately, taking into account all AMT tax preferences and adjustments. Thus, the amount of losses suspended and carried over may differ for AMT and regular tax purposes. A taxpayer cannot deduct any losses from tax-shelter farming activities.

194. AMT Tax Preference Items. A taxpayer's regular taxable income is increased by certain tax preference items in determining alternative minimum taxable income (AMTI) for the tax year (¶ 192) (Code Sec. 57). Tax preference items include the following:

- Seven percent of any gain realized on the sale of qualified small business stock and excluded from gross income under Code Sec. 1202 is treated as a tax preference item if the taxpayer acquired the stock before September 28, 2010 (¶ 1905).

- Tax-exempt interest (less any related expenses) on certain tax-exempt private activity bonds issued after August 7, 1986, is a tax preference item (except for bonds issued in 2009 and 2010).

- If the taxpayer is not an independent oil and gas producer, the amount by which the depletion deduction (¶ 1380) exceeds the adjusted basis of the property interest at the end of a tax year is a tax preference item.

- If a taxpayer deducts intangible drilling costs (IDCs) (¶ 989), the difference between the amount allowed as a deduction and the amount that would have been deductible if the costs had been capitalized and ratably amortized over a 120-month period is a tax preference item to the extent it exceeds 65 percent of the taxpayer's net income from oil, gas, and geothermal properties. An independent producer is not subject to this rule, but its AMTI may not be reduced by more than 40 percent of the AMTI that would otherwise be determined if the taxpayer took the IDC tax preference into account and did not compute an alternative tax net operating loss deduction (¶ 196). A taxpayer may avoid the classification of IDCs as a tax preference item by electing to capitalize the expenses and deduct them over a 60-month period for regular income tax purposes (Code Sec. 59(e)).

- The accelerated depreciation of real property, leased personal property, leased recovery property, and pollution control facilities placed in service before 1987 is treated as a tax preference item to the extent that it was a preference item under prior law, unless the taxpayer elected to apply the modified accelerated cost recovery system (MACRS) to the property for regular tax purposes.

196. AMT Adjustments for Individuals, Estates, and Trusts. An individual, estate, or trust must make a number of adjustments to various tax items in calculating alternative minimum taxable income (AMTI) (¶ 192) as compared to how they are

¶196

calculated for regular tax liability (Code Sec. 56, as amended by the Taxpayer Certainty and Disaster Tax Relief Act of 2019 (P.L. 116-94)).

Taxes. Itemized deductions for state, local, and foreign taxes (¶ 1021) are not allowed for AMT other than any generation-skipping transfer taxes on income distributions. Tax refunds are not included in AMTI even though the recovered taxes are included in gross income for regular tax purposes.

Medical Expenses. The itemized deduction for medical expenses is calculated for the alternative minimum tax (AMT) the same as for regular tax liability (i.e., to the extent they exceed 7.5 percent of AGI percent of AGI) (¶ 1015).

Home Mortgage Interest. The itemized deduction for home mortgage interest (¶ 1047) is allowed for AMT, except that it is limited to interest paid on acquisition debt for a house, apartment, condominium, or mobile home (qualified housing interest).

Investment Interest. Investment interest expenses are deductible for AMT to the same extent as regular tax liability (¶ 1057). However, investment interest does not include qualified housing interest for AMT purposes even if it is otherwise allocable to property held for investment. In addition, tax-exempt interest on private activity bonds is included in investment income for AMT purposes, and interest expended to carry the bonds is included in investment interest expenses.

Miscellaneous Itemized Deductions. The miscellaneous itemized deductions subject to the two-percent of AGI limit (¶ 1079) are not allowed for AMT purposes.

Standard Deduction. The standard deduction (¶ 131) is not allowed in computing AMTI, including the additional standard deduction for elderly and blind taxpayers. However, an additional standard deduction amount may be claimed in computing AMTI for net disaster losses arising from: a qualified federal disaster declared between January 1, 2018, and February 18, 2020; the California wildfires of 2017; Hurricanes Harvey, Irma, or Maria, in 2017; or a federally declared disaster in 2016 (¶ 1131).

Personal Exemptions. Personal and dependency exemption deductions (¶ 133) may not be claimed against AMTI, including the personal exemption deduction allowed to a decedent's estate or a trust (¶ 534).

Incentive Stock Options. An individual does not recognize gain or loss for regular tax purposes when an incentive stock option (ISO) is granted or exercised (¶ 1925). However, an adjustment is made for AMT purposes by the amount that the stock's fair market value exceeds the option price at the time it is freely transferable and not subject to a substantial risk of forfeiture. This generally occurs when the option is exercised, but the taxpayer may make a Code Sec. 83(b) election to take the AMT adjustment into account when the stock is received (¶ 713).

There is no AMT adjustment if the option is exercised and the stock is disposed of in the same tax year. The basis of the stock acquired is increased for AMT purposes by the amount of the AMT adjustment unless the stock is nontransferable and subject to a substantial risk of forfeiture. Although the exercise of an ISO can trigger an AMT liability, a taxpayer may be able to recover the liability through the AMT credit in future years (¶ 1409).

Depreciation. Assets other than section 1250 property placed in service after 1998 are generally depreciated for AMT purposes over the modified accelerated cost recovery system (MACRS) class life using 150-percent declining balance method (¶ 1243). The class lives for AMT are listed in Rev. Proc. 87-56. For assets placed in service before 1999, depreciation is refigured for AMT using the alternative depreciation system (ADS). No AMT adjustment of depreciation is required for: residential rental property placed in service after 1998; nonresidential real property with a class life of 27.5 years or more placed in service after 1998 that is depreciated for the regular tax using the straight line method; any qualified property that is or was eligible for bonus depreciation or special depreciation allowance (¶ 1237); any portion of property expensed under Code Sec. 179 (¶ 1208); motion picture films, videotapes, or sound recordings; and certain public utility property, qualified Indian reservation property, qualified revitalization expenditures, and natural gas gathering lines.

¶196

Net Operating Losses (NOLs). The alternative tax NOL (ATNOL) is generally computed in the same manner as for regular tax purposes (¶ 1145) except that all AMT adjustments and preferences are taken into account first. The ATNOL may not offset more than 90 percent of AMTI, determined without regard to the ATNOL deduction and the domestic production activities deduction for tax years beginning before 2018. Unused ATNOLs are carried over similar to regular NOLs (¶ 1149) except the amount of ATNOLs carried over is reduced by 90 percent of the AMTI for any year to which they are carried, whether or not the taxpayer is liable for the AMT in that year.

Disposition of Property. Certain AMT adjustments are taken into account in determining property's adjusted basis for AMT purposes (e.g., depreciation, incentive stock options, etc.). Thus, gain or loss from the disposition of the property may be different for AMT purposes than for regular tax purposes. The difference is a negative adjustment in calculating AMTI if the AMT gain is less than the regular tax gain, the AMT loss is more than the regular tax loss, or there is an AMT loss and a regular tax gain.

Passive Activity and Loss Limits. The limits on losses that apply for regular tax purposes also apply for AMT purposes with certain modifications (¶ 192). This includes the limit on passive activities, at-risk activities, partnership losses claimed by partners, and S corporation losses claimed by shareholders. The limits are applied separately, taking into account all AMT adjustments and preferences first. A taxpayer cannot deduct any losses from tax-shelter farming activities (Code Sec. 59(h)).

Long-Term Contracts. A taxpayer must use the percentage-of-completion method of accounting (¶ 1551) to determine AMTI from long-term contracts (other than home construction contracts). The percentage-of-completion is determined using simplified cost allocation procedures for construction contracts of certain small contractors if the contract has an estimated duration of less than two years.

Mining Costs. Mining exploration and development costs that are expensed or amortized for regular tax liability purposes (¶ 987 and ¶ 988) are amortized over a 10-year period for AMT purposes. If a tax loss is incurred from a mine, the deduction is the lesser of the loss allowed for the costs had they remained capitalized or all expenses that have been capitalized but not yet amortized.

Research, Experimental, and Circulation Costs. Research and experimental costs that are expensed for regular tax purposes (¶ 979) are amortized over a 10-year period for AMT purposes. The adjustment applies only to an individual who does not materially participate (¶ 1165) in the activity that generated the expenses. Circulation costs that are expensed for regular tax purposes (¶ 971) are amortized for over a three-year period for AMT purposes. The adjustment applies to any individual, as well as any personal holding company before 2018 (¶ 277). If a loss is sustained on property that generated the research, experimental, or circulation expenses, a deduction is allowed equal to the lesser of the unamortized expenses or the amount that would be allowed as a loss had the expenses remained capitalized.

Other Adjustments. Additional AMT adjustments must be made for: items passed through an estate, trust, partnership, or S corporation and reported on the individual's Schedule K-1; certain patronage distributions received by a cooperative; income from certain installment sales before 1987; and pollution control facilities.

1

INDIVIDUALS

Chapter 2

CORPORATIONS

Corporate Formation

See CCH® AnswerConnect: *Choice of Entity* and *Section 351 Transfers to Controlled Corporations and Contributions to Capital* for more information on this topic.

201. How Organizations Are Taxed. A corporation, like any business entity, is formed by one or more persons to conduct a business venture and divide profits among investors (Reg. §§ 301.7701-2 and 301.7701-3). A corporation files a charter or articles of incorporation in a state, in a U.S. possession, with a foreign government (¶ 2425), or (in certain cases) with the U.S. government. It prepares bylaws, has its business affairs overseen by a board of directors, and issues stock.

Under the check-the-box regulations (¶ 402A), entities formed under a corporation statute are automatically classified as corporations and may not elect to be treated as any other kind of entity; other entities are allowed to elect corporate status on Form 8832. Thus, an entity that is a partnership or limited liability company (¶ 402B) under the laws of the state in which it is formed may elect to be taxed as a C corporation or an S corporation under the Code. However, a partnership that is publicly traded is taxed as a corporation unless 90 percent or more of its gross income consists of qualifying passive-type income (Code Sec. 7704; Reg. §§ 1.7704-1 and 1.7704-3).

For tax purposes, the predominant forms of business enterprises are C corporations, S corporations (¶ 301), partnerships (¶ 401), and sole proprietorships. These different forms are treated differently under federal tax law and care should be taken in choosing the appropriate entity for the business. Although many of the Code's provisions apply to all of these entities, some areas of the law are specially tailored for each type. The classification of an entity will have a lingering tax impact throughout the entity's existence.

Of the types of business organizations, income earned in a C corporation is generally subject to the toughest tax bite, as the earnings are taxed twice. First, a *corporate* income tax is imposed on the corporation's net earnings (¶ 219). Then, after the earnings are distributed to shareholders as dividends, each shareholder must pay taxes separately on its share of the dividends (¶ 733). A corporation can reduce, or even eliminate, its federal income tax liability by distributing its income as salary to shareholder-employees who actually perform valuable services for the corporation (¶ 713). Although this can reduce taxation at the corporate level, employees who receive payments from a corporation in exchange for services must still pay tax on the amount received as salary or wages.

This scheme of taxation differs radically from that applied to partnerships, limited liability companies, S corporations, and sole proprietorships. These entities generally do not pay an entity-level tax on their earnings. There is no income tax on partnerships (¶ 404) or limited liability companies (¶ 402B) treated as partnerships for federal tax purposes. Nor (in most cases) is there an S corporation income tax (¶ 319) or sole proprietorship income tax. Rather, the owners or members of these entities are taxed on their share of the entity's earnings. Also, for tax years beginning after 2017, and before 2026, noncorporate taxpayers may deduct up to 20 percent of domestic qualified business income received from a partnership, S corporation, or sole proprietorship (¶ 980P).

203. Tax-Free Contributions in Exchange for Stock. A corporation is formed by the transfer of money or property from shareholders to the corporate entity in return for corporate stock. If one or more shareholders transfer money or property to a corporation solely in exchange for stock of that corporation, and if the shareholders control the corporation immediately after the exchange, neither the shareholders nor the corporation recognize any gain or loss (Code Secs. 351(a) and 1032).

To be considered in "control," the transferring shareholders—as a group—must own, immediately after the exchange: (1) at least 80 percent of the total combined voting power of all classes of stock entitled to vote, and (2) at least 80 percent of the total number of shares of all other classes of stock (Code Sec. 368(c)). The exchanges need not actually be simultaneous to avoid nonrecognition of gain (Reg. § 1.351-1(a)(1)). Rather, all that is required is a situation where the rights of the parties have been previously defined and the execution of the agreement proceeds in an orderly manner.

Money or property transferred to a controlled corporation generally includes all property, tangible or intangible, with certain limitations (Code Sec. 351(d)). Stock issued for services, indebtedness of the corporation that is not evidenced by a security, or interest on indebtedness of the corporation that accrued on or after the beginning of the transferor's holding period for the debt are not considered issued in return for property.

Shareholders can be individuals, estates, trusts, partnerships, or other corporations (Reg. § 1.351-1(a)(1)). However, the rules permitting tax-free transfers to a corporation in exchange for corporate stock do not apply if the transferee corporation is an investment company (Code Sec. 351(e)(1)).

If the transferor owners receive additional property along with the stock when they transfer property to the corporation, the transfer can still qualify as a contribution to a controlled corporation described in Code Sec. 351 (Code Sec. 351(b); Reg. § 1.351-2(a)). The shareholders are taxed on any additional property received ("boot"). Thus, gain is recognized, but only to the extent of the cash received plus the fair market value of the additional property received. No loss is recognized on the transfer.

Assumption of Liabilities. If property transferred in what would otherwise be a Code Sec. 351 tax-free transaction is subject to liabilities, the acceptance of the transfer or the assumption of the liabilities does not prevent the transaction from being tax free (Code Sec. 357). This rule does not apply if the principal purpose of the transfer is tax avoidance or if liabilities assumed by the transferee exceed the transferor's basis in the property.

Bankruptcy. A debtor must recognize gain or loss upon its transfer of assets to a controlled corporation pursuant to a plan approved by a bankruptcy court (other than a reorganization plan) in which the stock is exchanged (Code Sec. 351(e)(2)). Essentially, the transaction is treated as if the property had first been transferred to the creditors and then transferred by them to the controlled corporation. If less than all the stock is transferred to creditors, only a proportionate share of the gain or loss must be recognized. Both the basis of the stock and of the assets are adjusted for the gain or loss recognized on the transfer to the corporation. Note that this rule does not apply to a transfer by one corporation to another corporation in a bankruptcy case. Instead, the transfer is considered a Code Sec. 368(a)(1)(G) reorganization and its tax consequences are determined accordingly (¶ 2247).

Treatment by Corporation. Contributions to a corporation's capital are generally excluded from the corporation's gross income, except for (1) contributions in aid of construction or any other contribution as a customer or potential customer (such as in the case of a regulated utility), and (2) contributions by a governmental entity or civic group other than as a shareholder (Code Sec. 118; Reg. § 1.118-2).

Reporting Requirements. If a person is a significant transferor and receives stock of a corporation in exchange for property in a Code Sec. 351 transaction, then the person and the corporation must each attach to their tax return a complete statement of all the facts pertinent to the exchange, including:

- the name and employer identification number (if any) of the transferee corporation (for the significant transferor's statement), or the name and taxpayer identification number (if any) of every significant transferor (for the transferee corporation's statement);
- the date(s) of the transfer(s) of assets;
- effective generally for exchanges occurring before March 28, 2016, the aggregate fair market value and basis of the assets transferred by the significant transferor (for the significant transferor's statement) or received by the transferee corporation (for the transferee corporation's statement);
- effective generally for exchanges occurring on or after March 28, 2016, the fair market value and basis of the property transferred by the significant transferor (for the significant transferor's statement) or received by the transferee corporation (for the transferee corporation's statement) in the exchange, determined immediately before the transfer and aggregated as follows:

 — importation property transferred in a loss importation transaction (a transaction subject to the anti-loss importation rule of Code Sec. 362(e)(1));

 — loss duplication property transferred in a loss duplication transaction (a transaction subject to the anti-loss duplication rule of Code Sec. 362(e)(2));

 — property with respect to which any gain or loss is recognized on the transfer (without regard to whether such property is also identified above); and

 — property not described above.

- the date and control number of any private letter ruling(s) issued by the IRS in connection with the Code Sec. 351 exchange (Reg. § 1.351-3).

The transferee corporation does not have to file a statement if a significant transferor's statement that includes the required information is attached to the same return for the same Code Sec. 351 exchange. For this purpose, a significant transferor is a person that owns, immediately after the exchange, at least five percent of the corporation's outstanding stock if the stock owned is publicly traded, or at least one percent of the corporation's outstanding stock if the stock owned is not publicly traded.

Return and Paying of Tax

See CCH® AnswerConnect: *Filing Corporate Income Tax Return and Paying Tax* for more information on this topic.

211. C Corporation Income Tax Return. A C corporation must file an income tax return using Form 1120 series, even if it has no income or no tax is due (Code Sec. 6012(a)(2); Reg. § 1.6012-2). The return must be filed electronically if the corporation has assets of $10 million or more and is required to file at least 250 returns during the calendar year (¶ 2503).

Form 1120 series generally must be filed on or before the 15th day of the *fourth* month following the close of the corporation's tax year (April 15 for a calendar-year corporation) (Code Sec. 6072; Reg. § 1.6072-2(a)). A C corporation with a fiscal tax year ending on June 30 and beginning before January 1, 2026, must file a return on or before the 15th day of the *third* month following the close of its tax year. If the last day of a corporation's tax year does not end on the last day of a month (as in the case of a dissolved corporation whose tax year ends on the date of dissolution), the return is due on or before the 15th day of the third or fourth full month (as applicable) following the date of dissolution. A corporation is generally entitled to an automatic extension of *six* months for filing its return (*seven* months in the case of a C corporation with a fiscal year ending on June 30 and beginning before January 1, 2026) (¶ 2509).

The due date for filing any federal income tax return, including Form 1120 series, otherwise due on or after April 1, 2020, and before July 15, 2020, is automatically extended to July 15, 2020, in response to the COVID-19 (coronavirus) crisis (Notice 2020-23, amplifying Notice 2020-18). The extension is automatic and a corporation does not need to file Form 7004 or call the IRS to receive it. Penalties and interest for failure to file a return or pay taxes as a result of the extension will not accrue until July 16, 2020. A corporation that needs more time to file its return after July 15, 2020, may request an additional extension by filing Form 7004 by July 15, 2020, but the extension may not go beyond the original statutory or regulatory extension date (for example, October 15, 2020, for a calendar year taxpayer).

A corporation's tax year generally may be a calendar year or fiscal year (¶ 1501), but restrictions apply to the choice of tax years by S corporations, personal service corporations, REITs, or REMICs. A corporation's return generally may not cover a period of more than a year except that a corporation may elect to use an annual filing period that fluctuates between 52 and 53 weeks (¶ 1505). A return may cover less than a year (i.e., short period) if a corporation was formed or dissolved during the year. For example, if a corporation elects the calendar year method but starts operations on August 1, it must report income from August 1 to December 31. If a calendar-year corporation dissolves on June 30, it must file a short-period return covering the period from January 1 to June 30. In addition to filing its regular income tax return, a corporation that has adopted a resolution to dissolve itself or liquidate all or part of its stock must file Form 966 (Code Sec. 6043; Reg. § 1.6043-1).

215. Due Date for Payment of Corporate Taxes. The due date for the payment of a corporation's taxes is generally the same as the due date for the filing of a return, without regard to filing extensions—the 15th day of the *fourth* month (the 15th day of the third month for returns of a C corporation with a fiscal year ending on June 30 and beginning before January 1, 2026) that follows the close of its tax year (¶ 211) (Code Sec. 6151).

A corporation that anticipates a tax liability of $500 or more must estimate its taxes and make quarterly estimated tax payments using electronic fund transfers. If the liability exceeds the total estimated payments, the corporation must pay the remaining amount by the due date of its return. Failure to pay estimated taxes may be penalized (¶ 241). A corporation may file for an extension of time to file returns or to pay taxes (¶ 2509 and ¶ 2537).

The due date for a C corporation to make federal income tax payments with its return (¶ 211) is automatically extended to July 15, 2020, in response to the COVID-19 (coronavirus) crisis if the payment was otherwise due on or after April 1, 2020, and before July 15, 2020 (Notice 2020-23, amplifying Notice 2020-18). The extension applies to both a calendar-year and fiscal-year corporation. It also applies to any quarterly estimated income tax payments calculated on or submitted Form 1120-W. The extension is automatic and a taxpayer does not need to file an application or call the IRS to receive it. Penalties and interest for failure to file a return or pay taxes as a result of the extension will not accrue until July 16, 2020. The extension does not extend the time to pay federal income taxes beyond July 15, 2020.

Computation of Tax Liability

See CCH® AnswerConnect: *Corporate Taxation* for more information on this topic.

219. Corporate Income Tax Rates. For tax years beginning after December 31, 2017, a corporation is subject to a flat 21-percent rate on taxable income (Code Sec. 11(b)). For tax years beginning before 2018, a corporation is generally subject to the tax rates in the table below based on its taxable income.

If taxable income is:					
Over—	*But not over—*	*Tax is—*			*Of the amt. over—*
$0	$50,000			15%	$0
50,000	75,000	$7,500	+	25%	50,000
75,000	100,000	13,750	+	34%	75,000
100,000	335,000	22,250	+	39%	100,000
335,000	10,000,000	113,900	+	34%	335,000
10,000,000	15,000,000	3,400,000	+	35%	10,000,000
15,000,000	18,333,333	5,150,000	+	38%	15,000,000
18,333,333	—			35%	0

A corporation with a fiscal year that includes January 1, 2018, calculates its federal income tax for the year by using a blended tax rate determined under the Code Sec. 15 tax proration rules. More specifically, a corporation determines its tax for such a fiscal year by:

(1) calculating its tax for the entire tax year using the graduated corporate income tax rates in effect for tax years beginning before 2018;

(2) calculating its tax for the tax year using the 21-percent rate for tax years beginning after 2017;

(3) proportioning each tax amount in (1) and (2) based on the number of days in the tax year when the different rates were in effect; and

(4) adding the two amounts determined in (3).

The sum of these two amounts is the corporation's income tax for the fiscal year that includes January 1, 2018 (Notice 2018-38).

Qualified Personal Service Corporations. For tax years beginning after 2017, the flat 21-percent corporate income tax rate also applies to qualified personal service corporations. A qualified personal service corporation performs services in the fields of health, law, engineering, architecture, accounting (including the preparation of tax returns), actuarial science, the performing arts, or consulting. Substantially all of the stock of a personal service corporation is held by employees, retired employees, or their estates (¶ 273) (Code Secs. 11(b) and 448(d)(2)). For tax years beginning before 2018, the normal graduated corporate income tax rates do not apply to qualified personal service corporations; instead, all the income of a qualified personal service corporation is taxed at a special flat 35-percent rate.

Foreign Corporations. A foreign corporation is taxed at regular U.S. corporate rates on most income that is effectively connected with a U.S. trade or business (¶ 2429) and subject to a flat 30-percent withholding tax on U.S.-source fixed or determinable income that is not effectively connected (¶ 2431). Tax treaties between the U.S. and foreign countries may provide for lower rates or exemptions from taxation.

Additional Taxes. For tax years beginning before 2018, a corporation having tax preference items may be subject to the alternative minimum tax (AMT) in addition to the regular corporate income tax (¶ 239). A corporation is exempt from the AMT in tax years beginning before 2018 if it is the corporation's first year or it is a small corporation with average annual gross receipts for the three-tax-year period (or portion thereof) ending before the current tax year not in excess of $7.5 million. The $7.5-million amount is reduced to $5 million for the corporation's first three-tax-year period. The corporate AMT is repealed for tax years beginning after 2017.

Certain corporations used by their shareholders for the purpose of avoiding taxes might also be subject to the accumulated earnings tax (¶ 251) or the personal holding company tax (¶ 275).

Alternative Tax on Net Capital Gain and Certain Timber Gains. For tax years beginning before 2018, if a corporation has a net capital gain for the year, it must pay an alternative tax at a maximum tax rate of 35 percent if the alternative tax is less than the regular income tax. The alternative tax rate is applied to the lesser of the corporation's net capital gain or its taxable income (Code Sec. 1201(a), prior to being stricken by the Tax Cuts and Jobs Act (P.L. 115-97)). The alternative tax on net capital gain is repealed for tax years beginning after 2017.

In addition, for tax years beginning in 2016 and 2017, a 23.8-percent alternative tax rate applies to corporations on the portion of a corporation's taxable income that consists of qualified timber gain (Code Sec. 1201(b), prior to being stricken by P.L. 115-97; Act Sec. 40310 of the Bipartisan Budget Act of 2018 (P.L. 115-123)). The tax is equal to the sum of (1) 23.8 percent of the least of qualified timber gain, net capital gain, or taxable income, plus (2) 35 percent of any excess of taxable income over the sum of the amounts for which a tax was determined under former Code Sec. 1201(a)(1) and the 23.8-percent computation. Qualified timber gain is the net gain from the sale or exchange of timber described in Code Sec. 631(a) (cutting of standing timber) and Code Sec. 631(b) (disposal of timber with a retained economic interest or outright sale). The special rate applies only to timber that has been held for more than 15 years.

221. Corporate Taxable Income. The corporate tax rate (¶ 219) is applied to a corporation's taxable income, which is the corporation's gross income for the year minus allowable deductions (Code Sec. 11). The principal items of corporation income include gross sales receipts, dividends and interest received, rent and royalty income, and capital gains. The common deductions for a corporation include compensation paid to officers and workers, expenses for repairs and maintenance of property, taxes, licenses, interest paid, depreciation and depletion, advertising, and deductible amounts paid to pension and profit-sharing plans and employee benefit programs. In addition, a corporation may be entitled to special deductions for dividends received from other corporations (¶ 223), affiliates (¶ 229), and foreign corporations (¶ 231), as well as deductions for organizational expenses (¶ 237) and domestic production activities (for tax years beginning before 2018) (¶ 980A).

A corporation generally must use the accrual method of accounting to determine when income and expenses are reported (¶ 1515) (Code Sec. 448). However, the cash basis of accounting may be used by a qualified personal service corporation (¶ 219), a corporation engaged in a farming business (¶ 1519), and a corporation whose average annual gross receipts do not exceed a threshold amount for the three tax years preceding the current tax year ($26 million for 2019 and 2020). Securities dealers must use the mark-to-market method of accounting (¶ 1903).

223. Dividends Received from Other Corporations. A corporation may claim a deduction from gross income for dividends received from a domestic corporation that is subject to income tax (Code Sec. 243). The deduction is:

- 50 percent (70 percent for tax years beginning before 2018) of dividends from a corporation if the recipient corporation owns less than 20 percent of the distributing corporation;

- 65 percent (80 percent for tax years beginning before 2018) of dividends received from a 20-percent-owned corporation—a corporation having at least 20 percent (but generally less than 80 percent) of its stock owned by the recipient corporation;

- 100 percent of qualifying dividends received from members of the same affiliated group (generally, 80-percent-or-more common ownership) to which the recipient corporation belongs (¶ 229); and

- 100 percent of dividends received by a small business investment company (¶ 2392).

These rules also apply to dividends received from a foreign corporation that are paid out of the earnings and profits of a taxable domestic predecessor corporation (¶ 231). Domestic corporations are allowed a 100-percent deduction ("participation exemption deduction") for the foreign-source portion of dividends received after 2017 from specified 10-percent owned foreign corporations (¶ 231).

Aggregate Limitation. The aggregate amount of dividends-received deductions that may be taken by a corporation is limited to 50 percent (70 percent for tax years beginning before 2018), and 65 percent (80 percent for tax years beginning before 2018) in the case of 20-percent-owned corporations, of the corporation's taxable income. For this purpose, taxable income is computed without regard to any net operating loss deduction, the domestic production activities deduction (for tax years beginning before 2018), the qualified business income deduction (for tax years beginning after 2017), the dividends-received deduction, the participation exemption deduction (for dividends received after 2017), the deduction for foreign-derived intangible income (FDII) and global intangible low-taxed income (GILTI) (for tax years beginning after 2017), capital loss carryback, or adjustment for nontaxed portions of extraordinary dividends received.

The aggregate limitation is applied first with respect to any deductible dividends received from 20-percent owned corporations and then separately for deductible dividends received from less-than-20-percent owned corporations (after reducing taxable income by the deductible dividends received from 20-percent owned corporations), but it does not apply for the year if the full deduction results in a net operating loss (Code Sec. 246(b)). Also, it does not apply in the case of dividends received by a small business investment company.

The dividends-received deduction is not allowed in computing the accumulated earnings tax (¶ 251) or the tax on personal holding companies (¶ 275). The deduction is allowed to a resident foreign corporation, as well as to a domestic corporation. No deduction is allowed for dividends received from a corporation exempt from income tax (including an exempt farmers' cooperative) during the tax year or the preceding year (Code Sec. 246(a)).

Holding Period. The dividends-received deduction is only allowed if the underlying stock is held for at least 46 days during the 91-day period beginning on the date 45 days before the ex-dividend date of the stock (Code Sec. 246(c)). If the stock is cumulative preferred stock with an arrearage of dividends, it must be held at least 91 days during the 181-day period beginning on the date 90 days before the ex-dividend date.

The ex-dividend date is the first day the stock trades without a buyer having a right to an announced dividend and, to account for the delay needed to accommodate settlement, is normally two business days before the record date (the day when the company determines who is the record owner of the stock). A person who buys stock on the trading day before the ex-dividend date will receive a dividend, while a person who buys the stock on the ex-dividend date will not. A one-year holding period requirement applies for purposes of the participation exemption deduction for the foreign-source portion of dividends received after 2017 from specified 10-percent owned foreign corporations (¶ 231).

The holding period is reduced for any period during which the taxpayer's risk of loss with respect to the stock is diminished because the taxpayer:

- has an option to sell, is under an obligation to sell, or has made (and not closed) a short sale of substantially identical stock or securities;

- is the grantor of an option to purchase substantially identical stock or securities; or

- has reduced the risk loss by virtue of holding one or more other positions with respect to substantially similar or related property.

Debt-Financed Portfolio Stock. The dividends-received deduction is reduced for dividends received from debt-financed portfolio stock by a percentage related to the amount of debt incurred to purchase such stock. The deduction is calculated by multiplying the difference between 100 percent and the average portfolio indebtedness by 50 percent (70 percent for tax years beginning before 2018), or 65 percent (80 percent for tax years beginning before 2018) in the case of 20-percent-owned corporations (Code Sec. 246A). Any required reduction is limited to the amount of the interest deduction allocable to the related dividend. In addition, the reduction does not apply to dividends that are eligible for the 100-percent dividends-received deduction for qualifying dividends received from a member of an affiliated group, and dividends received from a small business investment company.

Other Limitations. Capital gain dividends from a regulated investment company (RIC) or real estate investment trust (REIT), and distributions that are a return of capital, do not qualify for the dividends-received deduction (Code Sec. 243(d)). Additionally, the deduction is not allowed to the extent that the taxpayer is under an obligation (pursuant to a short sale or otherwise) to make related payments with respect to positions in substantially similar or related property (Code Sec. 246(c)(1)(B)).

227. Debt-Equity Rules. For instruments issued by a corporation and advances made to a corporation, a question can arise as to whether such instruments and advances are treated as bona fide debt of the corporation or as an equity interest in the corporation. If they are treated as a bona fide debt, the corporation can deduct interest payments as a business expense and the shareholders can receive principal payments as a tax-free return of capital. However, if they are treated as stock, the corporation cannot deduct payments made with respect to such instruments.

The Code lists five factors that may be considered in making the debt-equity determination (Code Sec. 385):

- if there is a written, unconditional promise to pay on demand or on a specified date a sum certain in money in return for an adequate consideration in money or money's worth, and to pay a fixed rate of interest;

- if there is subordination to or preference over any indebtedness of the corporation;

- the ratio of debt to equity of the corporation;

- if there is convertibility into the stock of the corporation; and

- the relationship between holdings of stock in the corporation and holdings of the interest in question.

The courts have developed other guidelines to be used in making a debt-equity determination (*Stinnett's Pontiac Service, Inc.*, CA-11, 84-1 USTC ¶ 9406).

The Treasury Department is authorized to make loans, loan guarantees, and other investments in the aggregate of up to $500 billion to provide liquidity to eligible businesses, states, and municipalities related to losses incurred as a result of the COVID-19 (coronavirus) crisis (Act Sec. 4003 of the Coronavirus Aid, Relief, and Economic Security (CARES) Act (P.L. 116-136)). Any emergency relief loan made by or guaranteed by the Treasury Department under the program is treated as debt for federal tax purposes.

Code Sec. 385 Debt-Equity Regulations. Final and temporary regulations under Code Sec. 385 address related-party debt and recharacterize related-party debt as stock in certain situations (Reg. §§ 1.385-1 and 1.385-3; Temp. Reg. §§ 1.385-3T and 1.385-4T).

The Code Sec. 385 regulations generally apply to debt instruments issued between related corporations that are members of an expanded group. An expanded group is defined by reference to the term affiliated group in Code Sec. 1504(a), subject to certain modifications, and generally includes all corporations connected to a common parent that owns, directly or indirectly, 80 percent of the vote or value of each such corporation.

Foreign issuers, S corporations, non-controlled regulated investment companies (RICs), and non-controlled real estate investment trusts (REITs) are excluded from the application of the Code Sec. 385 regulations. In addition, the regulations generally do not apply to debt instruments issued by partnerships, but contain certain anti-abuse provisions intended to prevent the use of controlled partnerships to avoid the rules. Intercompany obligations issued between members of a consolidated group are also outside the scope of these regulations.

The debt recharacterization rules of the Code Sec. 385 regulations recharacterize a purported debt instrument as stock if the instrument is issued between expanded group members as part of a transaction that does not finance new investment in the operations of the issuer (Reg. § 1.385-3 and Temp. Reg. §§ 1.385-3T and 1.385-4T). Subject to a variety of exceptions for more ordinary course transactions, the debt recharacterization rules apply to instruments distributed from a U.S. issuer to a parent corporation, or other highly-related entity. The debt recharacterization rules also apply to the use of instruments, other than certain qualified short-term debt instruments, to fund acquisitions of related-party stock and internal asset reorganizations, as well as multi-step transactions that have an economically similar result.

A taxpayer can exclude the first $50 million of debt that otherwise would be recharacterized as stock under these rules. The debt recharacterization rules generally do not apply to debt instruments issued by dealers in securities or by regulated financial or insurance companies. Other exceptions, such as a subsidiary stock exception, an earnings and profits exception, and a net equity contribution exception, also apply. Debt instruments issued before April 5, 2016, are not subject to the debt recharacterization rules.

The IRS intends to issue proposed regulations modifying the debt recharacterization rules to make these rules more streamlined and targeted (Advance Notice of Proposed Rulemaking (NPRM) REG-123112-19). The proposed debt recharacterization regulations would apply to tax years beginning on or after the date on which the proposed regulations are published as final regulations. In addition, since the temporary debt recharacterization regulations (Temp. Reg. §§ 1.385-3T and 1.385-4T) expired on October 13, 2019, taxpayers may rely, until further notice, on Prop. Reg. §§ 1.385-3 and 1.385-4 (Notice of Proposed Rulemaking (NPRM) REG-130314-16) that cross-reference the temporary regulations, provided that taxpayers consistently apply these rules in their entirety.

229. 100-Percent Dividends-Received Deduction for Affiliates. Affiliated corporations are allowed a 100-percent dividends-received deduction for qualifying dividends received from members of the affiliated group (Code Sec. 243). A qualifying dividend is any dividend received by a corporation that is a member of the same affiliated group as the corporation distributing it.

If the affiliated group includes at least one life insurance company, no dividend by any member of the group is treated as qualified unless a special election is in effect for the tax year in which the dividend is received. If any member of an affiliated group elects the foreign tax credit, then all members of the group that pay or accrue foreign taxes must elect the credit in order for any dividend paid by a member of the group to qualify for the 100-percent dividends-received deduction.

231. Dividends from Foreign Corporations. A domestic corporation is entitled to a deduction equal to 50 percent (70 percent for tax years beginning before 2018), or 65 percent (80 percent for tax years beginning before 2018) in the case of 20-percent-owned corporations (¶ 223), of the U.S.-source portion of dividends received from a foreign corporation that is at least 10 percent owned, by vote and value, by the domestic corporation (Code Secs. 243 and 245(a)).

The U.S.-source portion of a dividend is the amount that bears the same ratio to the dividend as undistributed U.S. earnings bear to total undistributed earnings. U.S. earnings include (1) income of the foreign corporation that is effectively connected with a U.S. trade or business and that is subject to U.S. income tax, or (2) dividends received from 80-percent-or-more-owned (directly or indirectly) domestic corporations (Code Sec. 245(a)(5)). For this purpose, dividends received from regulated investment companies (RICs) and real estate investment trusts (REITs) are not treated as dividends received from domestic corporations (Code Sec. 245(a)(12)).

A 100-percent dividends-received deduction is allowed to a domestic corporation for dividends paid by a wholly owned foreign subsidiary out of its earnings and profits for the tax year (Code Sec. 245(b)). All of the foreign subsidiary's gross income must be effectively connected with a U.S. trade or business.

Debt-Financed Portfolio Stock. Any reduction in the dividends-received deduction resulting from the rules concerning debt-financed portfolio stock (¶ 223) must be computed before applying the above ratios.

Participation Exemption Deduction. A domestic corporation is allowed a 100 percent deduction ("participation exemption deduction") for the foreign-source portion of dividends received after December 31, 2017, from specified 10-percent owned foreign corporations (Code Sec. 245A). A specified 10-percent owned foreign corporation is any foreign corporation (other than a passive foreign investment company (¶ 2490) that is not also a controlled foreign corporation (CFC) (¶ 2487)) with respect to which any domestic corporation is a U.S. shareholder. A U.S. shareholder is a U.S. person that owns at least 10 percent (by vote or value) of the foreign corporation's stock (Code Sec. 245A(b)).

The foreign-source portion of any dividend from a specified 10-percent owned foreign corporation is the amount that bears the same ratio to the dividend as (1) the undistributed foreign earnings of the specified 10-percent owned foreign corporation, bears to (2) the total undistributed earnings of that corporation. Undistributed earnings are the earnings and profits of a specified 10-percent owned foreign corporation as of the close of the tax year of the specified 10-percent owned foreign corporation in which the dividend is distributed that are not reduced by dividends distributed during that tax year. Undistributed foreign earnings of a specified 10-percent owned foreign corporation are the portion of the undistributed earnings of that corporation that is not attributable to:

- the corporation's income that is effectively connected with the conduct of a trade or business within the United States, and subject to U.S. income tax, or

- any dividend received (directly or through a wholly owned foreign corporation) from an 80-percent owned (by vote or value) domestic corporation (Code Sec. 245A(c)).

No foreign tax credit or deduction is allowed for any taxes paid or accrued (or treated as paid or accrued) with respect to a dividend that qualifies for the participation exemption deduction (Code Sec. 245A(d)).

The participation exemption deduction is not available for the following:

- any dividend received by a U.S. shareholder from a CFC if the dividend is an amount received from a CFC for which a participation exemption deduction would otherwise be allowed and for which the CFC received a deduction (or other tax benefit) with respect to any income, war profits, or excess profits taxes imposed by any foreign country or U.S. possession ("hybrid dividend") (Code Sec. 245A(e); Reg. § 1.245A(e)-1; Proposed Reg. § 1.245A(e)-1);

¶231

- any amount that is treated as a dividend pursuant to the Code Sec. 1291(d)(2)(B) deemed dividend election (Code Sec. 245A(f));
  - dividends received from tax-exempt organizations and tax-exempt farmers' cooperative associations (Code Sec. 246(a)).

In applying the holding period rules for the dividends-received deduction (¶ 223) to the participation exemption deduction, the stock must be held for at least 366 days during the 731-day period beginning on the date 365 days before the ex-dividend date of the stock (Code Sec. 246(c)(5)).

Temporary regulations limit the availability of the participation exemption deduction in situations where the deduction effectively eliminates subpart F income (¶ 2488) or global intangible low-taxed income (GILTI) (¶ 2488B) from the U.S. tax system (Temporary Reg. § 1.245A-5T).

237. Organizational Expenditures of Corporations. A corporation may elect to deduct up to $5,000 of any organizational expenses it incurs in the tax year in which it begins business (Code Sec. 248; Reg. § 1.248-1). A taxpayer is deemed to have made an election to deduct and amortize organizational expenses in the tax year in which the active trade or business to which the expenditures relate begins. A taxpayer may choose to forego the deemed election by clearly electing to capitalize its organizational expenditures on a timely filed federal income tax return, including extensions, for the tax year in which the active trade or business to which the expenditures relate begins. The $5,000 deducted for organizational expenses must be reduced by the amount by which the expenses exceed $50,000. Any remaining balance of organizational expenditures that are not immediately deductible must be amortized over a 180-month period.

Organizational expenditures are those that are (1) connected directly with the creation of the corporation, (2) chargeable to capital account, and (3) of a character that would be amortizable over the life of the corporation if its life were limited by its charter. They include expenses of temporary directors and organizational meetings, state fees for incorporation privileges, accounting service costs incident to organization, and legal service expenditures, such as for drafting of documents, minutes of organizational meetings, and terms of the original stock certificates.

Expenditures connected with issuing or selling stock or with the transfer of assets to a corporation are not amortizable. Instead, such costs must be netted against the proceeds of the stock sale. Pre-opening or start-up expenses, such as employee training, advertising, and expenses of lining up suppliers or potential customers, are not organizational expenses, but may be amortizable as start-up expenditures (¶ 904). Likewise, corporate expenditures that are incurred in investigating the creation or acquisition of an active trade or business or in creating such a trade or business do not qualify for amortization as organizational expenses, but may qualify as start-up expenses (Rev. Rul. 99-23).

239. Alternative Minimum Tax (AMT) for Corporations. The alternative minimum tax (AMT) for corporations is repealed for tax years beginning after 2017 (Code Sec. 55(a)). Any unused minimum tax credit of a corporation can be recovered as a refundable credit in tax years beginning in 2018 and 2019. The refundable credit amount is equal to 50 percent (100 percent for tax years beginning in 2019) of the excess of the minimum tax credit for the tax year, over the amount allowable for the year against regular tax liability. Corporations can elect to take the entire refundable credit amount in tax years beginning in 2018. In this case, the regular tax liability limitation does not apply (Code Sec. 53(e), as amended by the Coronavirus Aid, Relief, and Economic Security (CARES) Act (P.L. 116-136)). If a corporation has a short tax year, then the refundable credit amount for that year is prorated based on the number of days in the short year compared to 365 days.

For tax years beginning before 2018, a corporation may be subject to the AMT in addition to the regular corporate income tax. The AMT is imposed only if the corporation's tentative minimum tax (TMT) exceeds the corporation's regular tax liability for tax years beginning before 2018. The AMT for a corporation is 20 percent of alternative minimum taxable income (AMTI) (Code Sec. 55, prior to amendment by the Tax Cuts and Jobs Act (P.L. 115-97)). A corporation can claim the AMT foreign tax credit (¶ 2475) and general business credits (¶ 1465) against AMT liability. Corporate AMT is calculated on Form 4626.

2 CORPORATIONS

A corporation with a fiscal year that includes January 1, 2018, calculates the AMT using a blended tax rate under the Code Sec. 15 tax proration rules. The repeal of the corporate AMT for tax years beginning after 2017 is a change in the TMT rate from 20 percent to zero for purposes of applying the tax proration rules. As a result, a tentative TMT is computed by applying the 20-percent TMT rate prior to the change, and a tentative TMT is computed by applying the zero percent TMT rate resulting from the repeal of the corporate AMT. The corporation's TMT for the tax year that includes January 1, 2018, is the sum of that proportion of each tentative TMT which the number of days in each period bears to the number of days in the entire tax year (Notice 2018-38).

Exemption for Small Corporations. For tax years beginning before 2018, a corporation is exempt from the AMT if its average gross receipts do not exceed $7.5 million for the three previous tax years. The threshold is $5 million for a corporation's first three-year-period of existence, except that a corporation is generally treated as exempt in its first year of existence regardless of its gross receipts. Any reference to the corporation includes its predecessor and any related corporation for this purpose. If a corporation ceases to be a small corporation, it cannot qualify as such for any subsequent tax year.

AMTI of Corporations. For tax years beginning before 2018, a corporation's AMTI is generally the corporation's regular taxable income modified by AMT tax preference items and various AMT adjustments. These are items of deductions, exclusions, and income that are either recomputed or not allowed in calculating AMTI (e.g., depreciation, depletion, net operating losses (NOLs), adjusted current earnings (ACE), tax-exempt interest from certain tax-exempt private activity bonds) (Code Sec. 56, prior to amendment by P.L. 115-97, and Code Sec. 57). A corporation can exempt up to $40,000 of AMTI from AMT, but the exemption is phased out if the corporation's AMTI exceeds $150,000 (Code Sec. 55(d)(2), prior to amendment by P.L. 115-97).

A corporation can avoid having some deductions classified as AMT preferences or adjustments if it elects to capitalize the expenses and deducts them ratably for regular tax purposes (e.g., circulation expenditures, mining exploration and development costs, intangible drilling costs) (Code Sec. 59, prior to amendment by P.L. 115-97). AMT tax preference items and adjustments have to be apportioned between a regulated investment company (RIC) (¶ 2301) or real estate investment trust (REIT) (¶ 2326), and its shareholders and holders of beneficial interests. Special rules also apply to Blue Cross and Blue Shield organizations and shipping companies contributing to Merchant Marine capital constructions funds.

Corporate Preference Cutbacks. For tax years beginning before 2018, the tax benefit a corporation derived from certain tax preferences generally must be reduced or cut back 20 or 30 percent before the calculation of AMTI (Code Secs. 59(f), prior to being stricken by P.L. 115-97, and 291).

Estimated Tax

See CCH® AnswerConnect: *Corporate Estimated Tax Payments* for more information on this topic.

241. Penalty for Underpayment of Corporate Estimated Tax. A corporation must estimate its income tax liability for the current tax year and pay four quarterly estimated tax installments using electronic fund transfers during that year (Code Sec. 6655). Any underpayment of a required installment results in a penalty (addition to tax) on the amount of the underpayment for the period of underpayment. The penalty is based on current interest rates (¶ 2838). The period of underpayment generally begins with the due date of the underpaid installment and ends with the earlier of (1) the date that the underpayment is satisfied, or (2) the 15th day of the fourth month after the close of the tax year, except for certain fiscal year corporations (¶ 211). Each estimated tax payment is credited against unpaid installments in the order in which they are required to be paid. The due date of any required installment due on or after April 1, 2020, and before July 15, 2020, is automatically extended to July 15, 2020, as a result of the COVID-19 (coronavirus) crisis (¶ 243) (Notice 2020-23, amplifying Notice 2020-18). The penalty for any underpayment, as well as interest, will not accrue until July 16, 2020, as a result of the extension.

No penalty applies if the tax shown on the return, or the actual tax if no return is filed, is less than $500. If there is an underpayment, the taxpayer may use Form 2220 to determine if the penalty applies and, if so, the amount of the penalty. However, a corporation is not required to file the form, as the IRS will determine any penalty owed and notify the corporation of the amount due (Instructions to Form 2220).

What is the Tax? The tax liabilities to which corporate estimated tax applies are: (1) the corporate income tax (¶ 219), the alternative tax on corporate capital gains (for tax years beginning before 2018) (¶ 1738), or the income tax imposed on insurance companies (¶ 2370), whichever applies; (2) the alternative minimum tax (for tax years beginning before 2018) (¶ 239); (3) the base erosion tax under Code Sec. 59A (for tax years beginning after 2017) (¶ 2489); and (4) the tax on gross transportation income of foreign corporations (Code Sec. 887). For this purpose, the 30-percent tax on fixed, determinable, annual or periodic income of a foreign corporation not effectively connected with a U.S. business is considered a corporate income tax (¶ 2431). The total expected tax liability is reduced by the sum of the credits against tax. Special rules apply for estimating the book income adjustment by corporations that use the annualization method to calculate estimated tax liability (¶ 245).

243. Time and Amount of Corporate Estimated Tax Payments. The due dates for required installment payments of estimated taxes by corporation are generally divided into four payment period (Code Sec. 6655). This is generally the 15th day of the fourth, sixth, ninth, and twelfth months of the tax year (April 15, June 15, September 15, and December 1 for a calendar-year taxpayer). If any due date falls on a Saturday, Sunday, or legal holiday (¶ 2549), the payment is due on the first following business day. Corporations required to deposit taxes must transfer their tax deposits electronically from their accounts to the IRS's general account (Reg. § 31.6302-1(h)).

The due date of any required installment calculated on Form 1120-W and due on or after April 1, 2020, and before July 15, 2020, is automatically extended to July 15, 2020, as a result of the COVID-19 (coronavirus) crisis (Notice 2020-23, amplifying Notice 2020-18). The extension is automatic, and a corporation does not need to file any form or call the IRS to receive it. Penalties and interest for failure to pay taxes will not accrue until July 16, 2020, as a result of the extension. The extension does not extend the time to pay estimated income tax beyond July 15, 2020.

To avoid a penalty for underpayment of estimated taxes (¶ 241), each estimated tax installment must equal at least 25 percent of the lesser of:

- 100 percent of the tax shown on the current year's tax return or of the actual tax if no return is filed, or

- 100 percent of the tax shown on the corporation's return for the preceding tax year, provided a positive tax liability was shown and the preceding tax year consisted of 12 months (Code Sec. 6655(d)) (but see special limitation on certain large corporations, below).

A lower installment amount may be paid if it is shown that use of an annualized income method or, for corporations with seasonal incomes, an adjusted seasonal method would result in a lower required installment (¶ 245).

Example: The X Corporation, a calendar-year taxpayer, estimates at the end of March that its federal income tax for the current tax year would be $800,000. Accordingly, it pays $200,000 [25% of ($800,000 × 100%)] of estimated tax by April 15, and another $200,000 by June 15. At the end of August, a recalculation shows that its tax for the year is expected to be $1 million. Assuming that there is no later change in the estimated tax, the estimated tax installments for September and December are computed as follows:

Estimated tax required to be paid by 9/15 [75% of ($1 million × 100%)]	$750,000
Less payments made in April and June	$400,000
Payment due in September	$350,000
Payment due in December [25% of ($1 million × 100%)]	$250,000
Total estimated tax payments	$1,000,000

Large Corporations. A large corporation—one with taxable income of at least $1 million in any one of the three immediately preceding tax years—is prohibited from using its prior year's tax liability, *except* in determining the first installment of its tax year

(Code Sec. 6655(d)(2) and (g)(2)). Any reduction in a large corporation's first install-ment as a result of using the prior year's tax must be recaptured in the corporation's second installment. In applying the $1-million test, taxable income is computed without regard to net operating loss carryovers or capital loss carrybacks. Also, a controlled group of corporations (¶ 291) must divide a single $1-million amount among its members.

Corporations with $1 Billion in Assets. Corporations with $1 billion or more in assets are required to make larger and smaller estimated tax payments in certain months in 2017 (Act Sec. 4 of the Amendment to Africa Growth and Opportunity Act (P.L. 112-163)). Specifically, for a payment due in July, August, or September of 2017, the amount due is 100.25 percent of the estimated tax the taxpayer would otherwise be required to pay. For a payment in October, November, or December of 2017, the amount due is 99.75 percent of the amount that would otherwise be due.

245. Annualized and Seasonal Installment Methods of Corporations. A corpora-tion may make a lower required installment payment of estimated taxes (¶ 243) where its annualized income installment or adjusted seasonal installment is less than the regular amount of the required installment. The annualized income installment is the product of the tax on the corporation's taxable income for the corresponding portion of the tax year on an annualized basis, and reduced by all prior required installments for the tax year (Code Sec. 6655(e); Reg. § 1.6655-2). Taxable income includes the corpora-tion's modified taxable income for the Code Sec. 59A base erosion tax for tax years beginning after 2017 (¶ 2489) and alternative minimum taxable income for tax years beginning before 2018 (¶ 239).

A corporation can choose between using the standard monthly periods or either of two optional monthly periods. An election to use either of the two optional monthly periods is effective only for the year of election. The election must be made on or before the date required for the first installment payment.

Installment	Standard Monthly Periods	Optional Monthly Periods #1	Optional Monthly Periods #2
1st	first 3 months	first 2 months	first 3 months
2nd	first 3 months	first 4 months	first 5 months
3rd	first 6 months	first 7 months	first 8 months
4th	first 9 months	first 10 months	first 11 months

To annualize income, multiply the income for the applicable period by 12 and divide by the number of months in the period. A corporation that uses the annualization method and switches to another method during the same tax year must, in its first installment under the new method, recapture 100 percent of any reduction achieved in the earlier installments.

Adjusted Seasonal Installments. Adjusted seasonal installments may be used only if the average of the corporation's taxable income for the same six-month period in the three preceding years was 70 percent or more of annual taxable income. An adjusted seasonal installment is the excess (if any) of 100 percent of the amount determined by following the four steps set forth below, over the aggregate amount of all prior required installments for the tax year. The steps are as follows:

- take the taxable income for the portion of the tax year up to the month in which the installment is due (filing month);
- divide this amount by the base period percentage for such months;
- determine the tax on the result; and
- multiply the tax by the base period percentage for the filing month and all preceding months during the tax year.

For any period of months, the base period percentage is the average percentage that the taxable income for the corresponding months in each of the three preceding tax years bears to the taxable income for those years (Code Sec. 6655(e)(3); Reg. § 1.6655-3).

247. Refund of Estimated Tax Overpayment by Corporations. A corporation may apply for a refund of an overpayment of estimated tax immediately after the close of its tax year if its overpayment is at least 10 percent of the expected tax liability and amounts to at least $500. Overpayment, for this purpose, is the excess of the estimated tax paid over what the corporation expects its final income tax liability to be at the time the application is filed. The application generally must be filed by the 15th day of the fourth month after the close of the tax year, except for certain fiscal year corporations (¶ 211), and before the day on which the corporation files its income tax return for the tax year for which a quick refund is requested (Code Sec. 6425; Reg. § § 1.6425-1—1.6425-3). The taxpayer should file Form 4466. An extension of time to file Form 1120 will not extend the time for filing Form 4466. However, the filing of a claim for refund or credit otherwise due on or after April 1, 2020, and before July 15, 2020, is automatically extended to July 15, 2020 (Notice 2020-23, amplifying Notice 2020-18). The extension is automatic, and the taxpayer does not need to file any form or otherwise contact the IRS to receive. The extension does not provide relief for the time period for filing a refund claim if that period expired before April 1, 2020.

Accumulated Earnings Tax

See CCH® AnswerConnect: *Accumulated Earnings Tax* for more information on this topic.

251. Accumulated Earnings Tax. In addition to being liable for regular income taxes, a corporation (other than a personal holding company (¶ 277), tax-exempt organization (¶ 601), and passive foreign investment company (¶ 2490)) may be liable for the accumulated earnings tax. The tax is in the form of a penalty and applies if a corporation is formed or used for the purpose of avoiding the imposition of income tax upon its shareholders by permitting its earnings or profits to accumulate instead of being distributed (Code Secs. 531 and 532). A corporation is presumed to be availed of for a tax avoidance purpose if its earnings are accumulated beyond the reasonable needs of its business (¶ 265). The tax may be imposed on a corporation without regard to the number of shareholders, so it applies to both closely held and publicly held corporations.

The accumulated earnings tax is 20 percent of the corporation's accumulated taxable income (¶ 253) (Code Sec. 531). There is no particular form that a corporation files to compute the tax. Instead, the IRS enforces the tax by reaching a conclusion whether enough dividends were paid during the tax year based on the corporation's filed income tax return. Interest on any underpayment is computed from the date the corporation's tax return is due without regard to extensions (¶ 211) (Code Sec. 6601(b)(3)).

253. Accumulated Taxable Income. The accumulated earnings tax (¶ 251) is imposed on a corporation's accumulated taxable income for the tax year. Accumulated taxable income is the corporation's taxable income with certain adjustments, and minus the sum of the dividends-paid deduction (¶ 259) and the accumulated earnings credit (¶ 261). The adjustments to taxable income include the following:

- A deduction is allowed for federal income taxes, as well as for income, war, and excess profits taxes of foreign countries and U.S. possessions (to the extent not allowed as deductions in computing taxable income) accrued during the tax year, regardless of the accounting method used. The deduction will not include any accumulated earnings tax or personal holding company tax paid.

- Charitable contributions for the tax year are deductible without regard to the 10-percent-of-taxable-income limitation (¶ 927).

- No deduction is allowed for dividends received from other corporations (¶ 223).

- The net operating loss deduction is not allowed.

- A corporation (other than a mere holding company or investment company) is allowed a deduction for net capital losses incurred for the tax year determined without regard to capital loss carryovers. However, the deduction is reduced by the lesser of (1) the capital gains deducted in earlier years that have not already been used in a previous year to reduce the capital loss reduction, or (2) the corporation's accumulated earnings and profits at the close of the preceding year.

- A deduction is allowed for net capital gains for the year taking into account capital loss carryovers, reduced by the taxes attributable to them. In the case of a foreign corporation, only net capital gains that are effectively connected with the conduct of a trade or business within the United States and that are not exempt under treaty are taken into account.

- No capital loss carryback or carryover is allowed.

- A controlled foreign corporation (CFC) is allowed to deduct the amount of its subpart F income that is required to be included in the income of its U.S. shareholders (¶ 2488). However, if the corporation would otherwise calculate its accumulated taxable income on a gross basis, then the corporation's deduction must be reduced by any deduction that may have reduced a U.S. shareholder's income inclusion (Code Sec. 535; Reg. § 1.535-2).

Although exempt interest income is excludable from accumulated taxable income for purposes of determining the accumulated earnings tax base, it is considered for purposes of determining whether earnings and profits have been accumulated beyond the reasonable needs of the business (¶ 265) (Rev. Rul. 70-497).

Holding or Investment Companies. If a corporation is a mere holding or investment company, then in determining its accumulated taxable income: (1) net capital losses may not be deducted, (2) net short-term capital gains are deductible only to the extent of any capital loss carryovers, and (3) accumulated earnings and profits cannot be less than they would have been had the rules in (1) and (2) been applied in computing earnings and profits (Code Sec. 535(b)(8)).

Foreign Corporations. A foreign corporation is subject to U.S. income tax on U.S. source income, including the accumulated earnings tax (¶ 2425). Thus, foreign source income is generally excluded from accumulated taxable income. However, if 10 percent or more of the earnings and profits of any foreign corporation is derived from U.S. sources, then any distribution out of such earnings and profits (and any interest payment) retains its character as U.S.-source income upon receipt by a U.S.-owned foreign corporation (Code Sec. 535(d)). A U.S.-owned foreign corporation is any foreign corporation in which 50 percent or more of voting power or total value is held directly or indirectly by U.S. persons.

259. Dividends-Paid Deduction for Accumulated Earnings Tax. Dividends paid by a regulated investment company (RIC), real estate investment trust (REIT), personal holding company, and corporation subject to the accumulated earnings tax are deductible in determining accumulated taxable income (¶ 253) (Code Sec. 561). The deduction is the sum of dividends paid during the tax year, consent dividends, and, in the case of a personal holding company, dividends carried over from the two preceding tax years (¶ 275).

The deduction is unaffected by the taxpayer's accounting method, but rather is based upon the amount of dividends actually paid by the corporation and received by the shareholder. A corporation subject to the accumulated earnings tax is required, and a personal holding company may elect, to deduct dividends paid the 15th day of the fourth month following the close of the tax year (on or before the 15th day of the third month following the close of a tax year beginning on or before December 31, 2025, in the case of a corporation with a fiscal tax year ending on June 30) (Code Sec. 563). The due date for performing certain time-sensitive actions, including paying dividends within a three ½-month period, otherwise due on or after April 1, 2020, and before July 15, 2020, is automatically extended to July 15, 2020, in response to the COVID-19 (coronavirus) crisis (Notice 2020-23; Rev. Proc. 2018-58).

The dividends-paid deduction may be claimed for any payment that is a distribution of property to shareholders with respect to their stock and paid out of earnings and profits (¶ 747) (Code Sec. 562). For a personal holding company, however, the deduction is up to the amount of undistributed personal holding company income, regardless of its earnings and profits (Code Sec. 316(b)(2)(A)). Except in the case of a publicly offered RIC or a publicly offered REIT, no deduction is allowed for preferential dividends. On the other hand, distributions in complete liquidation of a corporation other than a personal holding company are included as part of the deduction. Distributions in complete liquidation of a personal holding company can be included depending on whether the distributee is a noncorporate or corporate shareholder. For a RIC, the deduction is computed without regard to capital gain dividends and exempt-interest dividends (¶ 2303). For a REIT, the deduction is computed without regard to excluded net income from foreclosure property (¶ 2329).

¶259

Consent Dividend. A consent dividend is any dividend that a shareholder agrees to include in taxable income, even though the corporation does not make an actual distribution (Code Sec. 565). The consent dividend is treated as paid by the corporation on the last day of its tax year and immediately contributed as paid-in capital by the shareholder. A consent dividend may be paid only with respect to consent stock, which is either common stock or preferred stock with unlimited participation; thus, the consent dividend must not be a preferential dividend. Shareholders consent on Form 972, which the corporation includes with Form 973 when filing its return to claim the dividends-paid deduction for consent dividends.

261. Accumulated Earnings Credit. For a corporation other than a holding or investment company, the accumulated earnings credit allowed in computing accumulated taxable income (¶ 253) is an amount equal to the part of the earnings and profits of the tax year retained for the reasonable needs of the business, reduced by the net capital gain (which is itself reduced by the amount of income tax attributable to it). A minimum amount of $250,000 ($150,000 for personal service corporations (¶ 219)) may be accumulated from past and present earnings combined by all corporations, including holding or investment companies. This minimum amount is the only credit allowable to a holding or investment company (Code Sec. 535(c)). Only one $250,000 accumulated earnings credit is allowed to a controlled group of corporations (¶ 291) (Code Sec. 1561(a)). The single credit is to be divided equally among the corporations, unless the regulations allow an unequal allocation.

263. Basis of Liability for Accumulated Earnings Tax. Although the accumulated earnings tax is computed as a percentage of the corporation's accumulated taxable income (¶ 253), liability for the tax hinges on whether the corporation was formed or availed of to avoid the income tax on income otherwise receivable by its shareholders. A corporation can be subject to the accumulated earnings tax for a year in which it has accumulated taxable income on hand even though, because of a stock redemption, no earnings and profits were accumulated for the tax year (*GPD, Inc.*, CA-6, 75-1 USTC ¶ 9142).

The courts have shifted the focus of attention from earnings and profits to liquidity (*Smoot Sand & Gravel Corp.*, CA-4, 60-1 USTC ¶ 9241). The reason for this change in emphasis is that the earnings-and-profits figure often is no indication of the funds available to the corporation to meet its business needs and pay dividends to its shareholders. Whether a corporation can be subjected to the accumulated earnings tax is therefore determined by comparing the reasonable needs of its business (¶ 265) to its total liquid assets at the end of the year. Liquid assets include the corporation's cash and marketable securities.

265. Reasonable Needs of the Business for Accumulation of Income. In order to justify an accumulation of income (¶ 251), a corporation must have a reasonable business need for it and a definite plan for its use. Since a corporation is given a credit (¶ 261) for its reasonable business needs (including reasonably anticipated needs) in figuring the accumulated earnings tax, the resolution of most disputes hinges on this issue (¶ 267).

The Code does not contain a comprehensive definition of reasonable business needs. However, a number of acceptable and unacceptable grounds for accumulating income are listed in the regulations (Code Sec. 537(b); Reg. § 1.537-2). Acceptable grounds include: (1) business expansion and plant replacement; (2) acquisition of a business through purchase of stock or assets; (3) debt retirement; (4) working capital; and (5) investments or loans to suppliers or customers necessary to the maintenance of the corporation's business. The self-insurance of product liability risks is also a business need for which earnings and profits may be accumulated to a reasonable extent.

Unacceptable grounds include: (1) loans to shareholders and expenditures for their personal benefit; (2) loans to relatives or friends of shareholders or to others who have no reasonable connection with the business; (3) loans to a commonly controlled corporation; (4) investments that are not related to the business; and (5) accumulations to provide against unrealistic hazards.

Courts have used an operating-cycle approach to determine the amount of working capital a corporation needs. An operating cycle consists of an inventory cycle (conversion of cash and raw materials into inventory), a receivables cycle (conversion of inventory into accounts receivable and cash), and, possibly a credit cycle (accounts payable turnover) (*Bardahl Mfg. Corp.*, Dec. 27,494(M), 24 TCM 1030).

A stock redemption under Code Sec. 303 to pay death taxes and expenses (¶ 745) and a redemption of stock in order to bring a private foundation within the 20-percent excess business holdings limit (¶ 640) are good cause for an accumulation of income (Code Sec. 537(a)). Although other types of stock redemptions are not accorded this certainty, accumulations to redeem a minority interest (or the interest of one of two 50-percent stockholders) have been approved where they would eliminate dissent, would prevent the minority interest from falling into hostile hands, or were an essential ingredient of an employee incentive plan. Court decisions in this area show that except in rare circumstances, the redemption of a majority interest is not good cause for accumulating income (*Wilcox Manufacturing Co., Inc.*, Dec. 35,936(M), 38 TCM 378).

267. Burden of Proof of Reasonable Business Needs for Accumulation of Income. On the issue of whether a corporation has accumulated income in excess of the reasonable needs of its business (¶ 265), the burden of proof in the Tax Court is on the government in two instances (Code Sec. 534; Reg. § 1.534-2). First, the burden is on the government if, in advance of a formal deficiency notice, it does not notify the corporation by certified or registered mail of its intention to assess a deficiency based in whole or in part on the accumulated earnings tax or fails to state the tax years at issue. Second, in the event of such notification, the burden falls on the government if the corporation responds within 60 days with a statement of the grounds on which it relies to establish the reasonableness of all or any part of its accumulation of income. In other courts, the burden of proof is wholly on the corporation.

269. Tax Avoidance Intent for Accumulated Earnings Tax. One of the conditions that must exist before a corporation can be subject to the accumulated earnings tax (¶ 251) is an intent to avoid the income tax on its shareholders (Code Sec. 533). If the corporation accumulates income beyond the reasonable needs of its business (or if it is a mere holding or investment company), a presumption of tax avoidance intent arises. This presumption can be overcome by showing that tax avoidance was not one of the purposes of the accumulation of income (*Donruss Co.*, 69-1 USTC ¶ 9167; *Shaw-Walker*, 69-1 USTC ¶ 9198).

Personal Service Corporation

273. Personal Service Corporations. A personal service corporation (PSC) is a corporation that furnishes personal services performed by employee-owners (Code Secs. 269A and 280H; Prop. Reg. § 1.269A-1(a)). An employee-owner is an employee who owns, directly or indirectly, more than 10 percent of the outstanding stock of the corporation on any day during the corporation's tax year.

The IRS may allocate income, deductions, credits, exclusions, or other allowances between the PSC and its employee-owners in order to prevent tax evasion or avoidance or to clearly reflect the income of both if: (1) substantially all of the services of a PSC are performed for, or on behalf of, one other corporation, partnership, or other entity, and (2) the principal purpose for forming or using the PSC is the avoidance or evasion of income tax by reducing the income of any employee-owner or securing the benefit of any expense, deduction, credit, exclusion or other allowance that would not otherwise be available. The purpose of evading or avoiding income tax can be shown by a reduction in the tax liability of, or the increase of tax benefits to, an employee-owner or by any other increase in tax benefits. Code Sec. 280H restricts the amount that can be deducted by a PSC for amounts paid to owners if the corporation has elected a noncalendar tax year.

Personal Holding Company

See CCH® AnswerConnect: *Personal Holding Company* for more information on this topic.

275. Tax on Personal Holding Companies. In addition to being liable for regular income taxes, a corporation that is a personal holding company (¶ 277) will be liable for a separate tax on its undistributed personal holding company income (¶ 281). The personal holding company tax is designed to prevent individuals from establishing a corporation to receive and hold investment income or compensation so that it would be taxed at a lower rate (i.e., "incorporated pocketbooks").

The personal holding company tax is 20 percent of a corporation's undistributed personal holding company income and is calculated on Schedule PH (Form 1120) (Code Sec. 541; Reg. § 1.541-1). Undistributed personal holding company income is computed by making the following adjustments to the corporation's taxable income, not just its personal holding company income (Code Sec. 545):

• A deduction is allowed for federal income taxes, as well as for income, war, and excess profits taxes of foreign countries and U.S. possessions (to the extent not allowed as deductions in computing taxable income) accrued during the tax year, regardless of the accounting method used. The deduction does not include any accumulated earnings tax or personal holding company tax paid.

• Charitable contributions for the tax year are deductible but the contribution base for individuals (¶ 1059) must be used, rather than the contribution for corporations (¶ 927).

• No deduction is allowed for dividends received from other corporations (¶ 223).

• The net operating loss deduction is not allowed.

• A deduction is allowed for net capital gains for the year, reduced by the taxes attributable to them. In the case of a foreign corporation, only net capital gains that are effectively connected with the conduct of a trade or business within the United States and that are not exempt under treaty are taken into account.

• Any deduction for ordinary and necessary business expenses, as well as depreciation, attributable to the operation and maintenance of property owned or operated by the corporation is limited to the aggregate rental income or other compensation earned from the property, unless the corporation shows that the compensation received was the highest available, the property was held in a bona fide business operated for profit, and either there was a reasonable expectation of a profit or the property was necessary for carrying on the corporation's business.

After these adjustments are made, the dividends-paid deduction is deducted from the adjusted taxable income (¶ 259). The amount of deduction for a personal holding company includes a dividend carryover from the two preceding tax years (Code Sec. 564). The carryover is the excess of the dividends paid in the two preceding years over the income for such years. Any remaining balance is the corporation's undistributed personal holding company income.

277. Personal Holding Company Defined. A personal holding company is any corporation in which at least 60 percent of adjusted ordinary gross income for the tax year is personal holding company income (¶ 281), and at any time during the last half of the tax year more than 50 percent in value of its outstanding stock is owned, directly or indirectly, by or for not more than five individuals (¶ 285) (Code Sec. 542; Reg. §§ 1.542-1—1.542-3). For this purpose, individuals include: a qualified pension, profit-sharing, or stock bonus plan (¶ 2101); a supplemental unemployment benefit (SUB) trust (¶ 692); a private foundation (¶ 631); or part of a trust permanently set aside or used exclusively for charitable purposes (¶ 537).

Certain corporations are exempt from the personal holding company tax (¶ 275), even though they meet the income and stock ownership qualifications (Code Sec. 542(c)). These include tax-exempt corporations (¶ 601); banks or domestic building and loan associations (¶ 2383); certain lending and finance companies that meet gross income, deduction, and loan tests; life insurance companies (¶ 2370); surety companies; corporations in bankruptcy or similar proceedings (unless the purpose of the proceedings is to avoid the personal holding company tax); and foreign corporations. A small business investment company (¶ 2392) is exempt from personal holding company tax if it is licensed by the Small Business Administration, but not if any shareholder of the company owns directly or indirectly a five-percent-or-more proprietary interest in a small business concern to which the investment company provides funds, or five percent or more in value of outstanding stock of such a concern.

281. Personal Holding Company Income. Personal holding company income for purposes of the personal holding company tax (¶ 275) means the portion of the adjusted ordinary gross income that consists of (Code Sec. 543):

- dividends (other than dividends received by a U.S. shareholder from a controlled foreign corporation), interest, royalties (other than mineral, oil and gas, copyright, or computer software royalties), and annuities (such income does not, however, include interest received by a broker or dealer in connection with any securities or money market instruments held as inventory or primarily for sale to customers, margin accounts, or any financing for a customer secured by securities or money market instruments);

- rents, unless they constitute 50 percent or more of the adjusted ordinary gross income, and unless the sum of dividends paid during the tax year, dividends paid after the close of the tax year but considered paid on the last day of the year, and consent dividends (¶ 259), equals or exceeds the amount by which personal holding company income exceeds 10 percent of the ordinary gross income;

- mineral, oil, and gas royalties, unless (1) they constitute 50 percent or more of the adjusted ordinary gross income, (2) the other personal holding company income for the tax year is not more than 10 percent of the ordinary gross income, and (3) the ordinary and necessary business expense deductions, other than compensation for personal services rendered by shareholders, are 15 percent or more of adjusted ordinary gross income;

- copyright royalties, unless (1) apart from royalties derived from the works of shareholders, they make up 50 percent or more of the ordinary gross income, (2) personal holding company income for the tax year (not taking into account copyright royalties and dividends in any corporation in which the taxpayer owns at least 50 percent of all classes of voting stock and at least 50 percent of the value of all classes of stock) is 10 percent or less of the ordinary gross income, and (3) ordinary and necessary business expense deductions, other than compensation for personal services rendered by shareholders and deductions for royalties, equal or exceed 25 percent of the amount by which the ordinary gross income exceeds the sum of royalties paid or accrued and depreciation allowed;

- rents from the distribution and exhibition of produced films (i.e., rents from a film interest acquired before the film production was substantially complete) unless such rents are 50 percent or more of the ordinary gross income;

- amounts received as compensation for the use of, or right to use, tangible property of the corporation where, at any time during the tax year, 25 percent or more in value of the outstanding stock of the corporation is owned, directly or indirectly, by or for an individual entitled to the use of the property, whether such right is obtained directly from the corporation or by means of a sublease or other arrangement (but this provision applies only if the corporation's other personal holding company income, computed with certain adjustments, for the tax year is more than 10 percent of its ordinary gross income);

- amounts received by a corporation from contracts for personal services, including gain from the sale or other disposition thereof, if (1) some person other than the corporation has the right to designate (by name or by description) the individual who is to perform the services or if the individual who is to perform the services is designated (by name or by description) in the contract and (2) at some time during the tax year 25 percent or more in value of the outstanding stock of the corporation is owned, directly or indirectly, by or for the individual who has performed, is to perform, or may be designated (by name or by description) as the one to perform such services; and

- income required to be reported by a corporate beneficiary under the income tax provisions relating to estates and trusts.

Active Business Computer Software Royalties. Active business computer software royalties received in connection with the licensing of computer software are excluded from personal holding company income (Code Sec. 543(d)). To qualify for the exclusion: (1) the royalties must be derived by a corporation actively engaged in the trade or business of developing, manufacturing, or producing computer software; (2) the royalties must make up at least 50 percent of the corporation's gross income; (3) business and research expenses relating to the royalties must equal or exceed 25 percent of ordinary gross income; and (4) dividends must equal or exceed the excess of personal holding company income over 10 percent of ordinary gross income. If one member of an

¶281

affiliated group receives software royalties, it will be treated as having met the above requirements if another member meets the requirements.

283. Adjusted Ordinary Gross Income of Personal Holding Company. In determining whether 60 percent or more of a corporation's adjusted ordinary gross income is personal holding company income (¶ 281), the following adjustments must be made to ordinary gross income (Code Sec. 543(b)(2)):

- Rental income must be reduced by deductions for depreciation and amortization, property taxes, interest, and rents paid that are attributable to such income.

- Income from mineral, oil, and gas royalties and from working interests in oil and gas wells must be reduced by deductions for depreciation, amortization and depletion, property and severance taxes, interest, and rents paid that are attributable to such income.

- Interest on U.S. bonds held for sale by a dealer who is making a primary market for these obligations, and interest on condemnation awards, judgments, and tax refunds, must be excluded.

- Rent received from the lease of tangible personal property manufactured by a taxpayer engaged in substantial manufacturing or production of property of the same type must be reduced by deductions for depreciation and amortization, taxes, rent, and interest paid that are attributable to such income.

All capital gains are excluded in determining whether the 60-percent test has been met because it is based on adjusted ordinary gross income.

285. Constructive Ownership of Personal Holding Company. The following constructive ownership rules apply in determining if (1) a corporation is a personal holding company (¶ 277), (2) amounts received under a personal service contract are personal holding company income (¶ 281), (3) copyright royalties are personal holding company income, or (4) compensation for the use of property is personal holding company income (Code Sec. 544; Reg. § 1.544-1):

- Stock owned, directly or indirectly, by or for a corporation, partnership, estate, or trust is considered owned proportionately by its shareholders, partners, or beneficiaries.

- An individual is considered to own the stock owned, directly or indirectly, by or for his or her family (brothers and sisters (whole or half blood), spouse, ancestors, and lineal descendants), or by or for his or her partner.

- If any person has an option to acquire stock, such stock is considered owned by such person. An option to acquire an option, and each one of a series of such options, is regarded as an option to acquire stock.

- Stock constructively owned by a corporation, partnership, estate, or trust will be reattributed to its owners or beneficiaries so that they are treated as constructive owners of the stock. However, stock constructively and not actually owned by an individual will not be reattributed.

- Outstanding securities convertible into stock (whether or not during the tax year) are considered outstanding stock, but only if the effect of the inclusion of all such securities is to make the corporation a personal holding company.

287. Deficiency Dividend Deduction for Personal Holding Company Tax. If a deficiency is determined in the personal holding company tax (¶ 275), the corporation may then distribute dividends and, in redetermining the undistributed personal holding company income, reduce or eliminate the deficiency by means of a deduction for deficiency dividends in the amount of the dividends so paid (Code Sec. 547; Reg. § § 1.547-1—1.547-7). The distribution must be made within 90 days after the deficiency determination. Claim for the deduction must be filed within 120 days of the determination.

Controlled Corporate Groups

See CCH® AnswerConnect: *Multiple Corporations and Controlled Groups* for more information on this topic.

289. Allocation of Tax Benefits of Certain Controlled Corporations. A controlled group of corporations (¶ 291) is allowed one $250,000 accumulated earnings credit (¶ 261), which must be divided equally among the corporations, unless an unequal allocation is allowed by the regulations (Code Sec. 1561). For tax years beginning before 2018, controlled groups are also allowed one set of graduated income tax brackets for regular income tax purposes (¶ 219) and one $40,000 exemption amount for alternative minimum tax (AMT) purposes (¶ 239). Each of these items is to be allocated equally among the members of the group unless they all consent to a different apportionment (Code Sec. 1561, prior to amendment by P.L. 115-97). For tax years beginning after 2017, the graduated corporate income tax rate structure is replaced by a 21-percent flat corporate income tax rate (¶ 219) and the corporate AMT is repealed.

Dividends-Received Deduction. If a parent-subsidiary controlled group is also an affiliated group, a 100-percent dividends-received deduction may be taken with respect to dividends paid from one member to another (¶ 223).

291. Controlled Group of Corporations. There are three types of controlled corporate groups—parent-subsidiary, brother-sister, and combined groups (Code Sec. 1563(a)). A parent-subsidiary controlled group exists if: (1) one or more chains of corporations are connected through stock ownership with a common parent corporation; (2) 80 percent or more of the voting power or value of the stock of each corporation in the group other than the parent is owned by one or more corporations in the group; and (3) the common parent owns at least 80 percent of the voting power or value of the stock of one of the other corporations in the group (not counting stock owned directly by other members).

A brother-sister controlled group exists if five or fewer persons (individuals, estates, or trusts) own stock possessing more than 50 percent of the total combined voting power of all classes of stock entitled to vote, or more than 50 percent of the total value of all stock, taking into account the stock ownership of each person only to the extent the person owns stock in each corporation.

A combined group consists of three or more corporations, each of which is a member of either a parent-subsidiary controlled group or a brother-sister controlled group, and at least one of which is the common parent of a parent-subsidiary group and also is a member of a brother-sister group.

293. Controlled Group of Corporations—Expenses, Interest, and Losses. Controlled groups of corporations are subject to the related-party transaction rules of Code Sec. 267 (¶ 1717), under which controlled members must use a matching rule that defers the deductibility of an expense or interest by a payor until the payment is included in the payee's income (Code Sec. 267(a)(2)). Also, losses on sales between members of a controlled group must be deferred until the property is sold to an unrelated person (Code Sec. 267(f)). The loss-deferral rule does not apply, however, to sales to a domestic international sales corporation (DISC) (¶ 2498), to sales of inventory in the ordinary course of business if one of the parties is a foreign corporation, or to loan repayment losses attributable to foreign currency value reductions.

Consolidated Returns

See CCH® AnswerConnect: *Consolidated Returns* for more information on this topic.

295. Consolidated Returns. An affiliated group of corporations may file a consolidated income tax return for the tax year instead of filing separate returns (Code Sec. 1501). An affiliated group is one or more chains of includible corporations connected through stock ownership with a common parent corporation that is an includible corporation if:

- the common parent directly owns stock possessing at least 80 percent of the total voting power of at least one of the other includible corporations and has a value equal to at least 80 percent of the total value of the stock of the corporation; and

- stock meeting the 80-percent test in each includible corporation other than the common parent is owned directly by one or more of the other includible corporations (Code Sec. 1504(a)).

A consolidated return may be filed only if all corporations that were members of the affiliated group *at any time* during the tax year consent prior to the last day for filing the return. The making of a consolidated return is such consent. The common parent corporation, when filing a consolidated return, must attach Form 851. In addition, for the

¶291

first year a consolidated return is filed, each subsidiary must attach a Form 1122 (consent to be included in the consolidated return) (Code Sec. 1501; Reg. § 1.1502-75(b)). A subsidiary may be treated as if it filed a Form 1122, even though it failed to do so, if the affiliated group meets certain requirements (Rev. Proc. 2014-24).

The following corporations may not file consolidated returns (Code Sec. 1504(b)):

- tax-exempt corporations (¶ 601), except that such organizations may be affiliated with other such organizations at least one of which is organized only to hold title for exempt organizations and from which the others derive income;

- life insurance companies (¶ 2370), except for those included in the group at the election of the common parent (Code Sec. 1504(c));

- foreign corporations, except for Canadian or Mexican subsidiaries for which the common parent makes an election to treat them as domestic corporations includible in the consolidated group (Code Sec. 1504(d));

- regulated investment companies (RICs) and real estate investment trusts (REITs) (but see ¶ 2340 for circumstances in which a REIT may treat income and deductions of a qualified subsidiary as its own);

- domestic international sales corporations (DISCs); and

- S corporations.

297. Advantages and Disadvantages of Consolidated Returns. The advantages of filing a consolidated income tax return (¶ 295) include: (1) offsetting operating losses of one company against the profits of another (see the rule for dual resident companies, following); (2) offsetting capital losses of one company against the capital gains of another (subject to a limitation on pre-acquisition losses of newly acquired corporations (¶ 2285)); (3) avoidance of tax on intercompany distributions; (4) deferral of income on intercompany transactions; (5) use by the corporate group of the excess of one member's foreign tax credit over its limitation; and (6) designation of the parent corporation (or another corporation in certain cases) as an agent of the group for all tax purposes.

The disadvantages include: (1) the effect on later years' returns; (2) deferral of losses on intercompany transactions; (3) additional bookkeeping required to keep track of deferred intercompany transactions; (4) intercompany profit in inventories still within the group must be reflected in annual inventory adjustments; (5) possible elimination of foreign tax credits if the limiting fraction is diminished because of lack of foreign income on the part of some members; and (6) possible accumulated earnings tax liability (¶ 251) when the consolidated accumulated earnings and profits of the group exceed the minimum credit amount.

Dual Resident Companies. If a U.S. corporation is subject to foreign tax on its worldwide income, or on a residence basis as opposed to a source basis, any net operating loss it incurs in a year can only offset the taxable income of any other member of a U.S. affiliated group to the extent the loss is not used to offset the income of any foreign corporation. The general prohibition against the domestic use of such dual consolidated loss is subject to certain exceptions (Code Sec. 1503(d); Reg. § § 1.1503(d)-1—1.1503(d)-8).

Preferred Dividends. Income out of which a member of an affiliated group, other than a common parent, distributes preferred dividends to a nonmember may not be offset by the group's net operating losses or capital losses (Code Sec. 1503(f)). Taxes on that income may not be offset by most group tax credits.

Golden Parachutes. All members of an affiliated group are treated as a single corporation when determining excessive payments that are contingent on a change in corporate control (¶ 907) (Code Sec. 280G(d)(5)).

Chapter 3
S CORPORATIONS

S Corporation Status

See CCH® AnswerConnect: *S Corporation Elections* and *Corporations Qualifying as S Corporations* for more information on this topic.

301. S Corporations — Generally. An S corporation is a corporation that elects (¶ 303) and is eligible (¶ 304) to choose S corporation status and whose shareholders consent to the corporation's election (¶ 306). An S corporation generally does not pay any income tax (with exceptions discussed in ¶ 335 and following). Instead, the corporation's income and deductions are passed through to its shareholders. The shareholders must then report the income and deductions on their own income tax returns.

To the extent the S corporation rules do not apply, S corporations are governed by the regular (C corporation) corporate tax rules. Thus, while the taxation of income earned by, and the allocation of losses incurred by, S corporations closely parallel the taxation of partnerships with respect to items of income and loss, S corporations generally are treated as regular corporations for purposes of the rules relating to corporate distributions, redemptions, liquidations, and reorganizations, as well as contributions of capital by shareholders (Code Sec. 1371).

303. Corporations Eligible to Elect S Corporation Status. To qualify as an S corporation, a corporation must be a "small business corporation" and meet all of the following requirements (Code Sec. 1361; Reg. § 1.1361-1(b)):

- The entity must be a domestic corporation that is organized under the laws of a state or U.S. territory, or a domestic eligible entity (i.e., a partnership or limited liability company (LLC)) that elects to be taxed as a corporation under the check-the-box rules (Reg. §§ 1.1361-1(c) and 301.7701-3).

- The corporation's shareholders must be individuals, estates, certain trusts, and certain tax-exempt organizations (¶ 304). Partnerships and corporations cannot be shareholders.

- Only U.S. citizens or residents can be shareholders.

- The corporation can have only one class of stock (¶ 305).

Some corporations cannot be small business corporations, including (Code Sec. 1361(b)(2)):

- a financial institution that uses the reserve method of accounting;

- an insurance company taxed under subchapter L of the Code (¶ 2370); or

- a domestic international sales corporation (DISC) or former DISC.

An existing domestic eligible entity that is treated as a partnership for tax purposes can change its tax status and elect to be taxed as an S corporation. In other words, provided requirements that apply to check-the-box elections and S corporations are met, the entity may elect to change from a partnership to a corporation and also file an S election. It will not have an intervening C year between the partnership tax year and the S tax year, so long as the check-the-box and S elections are effective on the same date and both sets of deadlines are met (Rev. Rul. 2009-15).

100-Shareholder Limitation. An S corporation can have no more than 100 shareholders (Code Sec. 1361(b)(1)(A) and (c)). However, two or more shareholders can count as only one shareholder if they are related in particular ways. For example, two spouses (and their estates) are counted as a single shareholder. In addition, all qualifying members of a family are treated as one shareholder. A family is defined as a common ancestor and his or her lineal descendants, plus the spouses (or former spouses) of the common ancestor and the descendants. The common ancestor can be no more than six generations removed from the youngest shareholder who is treated as a member of the family on the latest of: (1) the date the S corporation election is made (¶ 306); (2) the earliest date that a family member first holds stock in the corporation; or (3) October 22, 2004. Legally adopted children, children lawfully placed for legal adoption, and eligible foster children are treated as the children of the adoptive or foster parent. The estate of a family member is also treated as a member of the family.

304. Eligible S Corporation Shareholders. All shareholders of an S corporation must be individuals, estates, certain specified trusts, or certain tax-exempt organizations (Code Sec. 1361(b)(1)(B)). Partnerships and C corporations are not eligible to hold stock in an S corporation. A limited liability company (LLC) with a single, individual member that is taxed as a disregarded entity can be a shareholder, with the owner treated as the owner of the S corporation stock. However, a single-member LLC that checks the box to be taxed as a C corporation may not hold stock in an S corporation. A taxpayer who holds only restricted bank director stock is not considered a shareholder for determining whether an S corporation has an ineligible shareholder (Code Sec. 1361(f)).

Trusts. Trusts eligible to hold S corporation shares include grantor trusts (where the grantor is regarded as the shareholder) and voting trusts (where each beneficiary is treated as the shareholder) (Code Sec. 1361(c)(2); Reg. § 1.1361-1(h)).

A trust that qualifies as a traditional or Roth individual retirement arrangement (IRA) is generally not an eligible S corporation shareholder (*Taproot Administrative Services, Inc.*, CA-9, 2012-1 USTC ¶ 50,256; Rev. Rul. 92-73). An IRA, however, may hold stock in a bank or depository holding company that is an S corporation if the IRA held the stock as of October 22, 2004 (Code Sec. 1361(c)(2)(A)(vi)). The IRA can also sell the stock to the IRA beneficiary within 120 days after the corporation makes the S corporation election without violating the prohibited transaction rules.

A testamentary trust that receives S corporation stock under the terms of a will is an eligible S corporation shareholder for two years after the stock is transferred (Reg. § 1.1361-1(h)(1)(iv)). A charitable remainder trust is not an eligible S corporation shareholder (Rev. Rul. 92-48).

ESBTs. An electing small business trust (ESBT) can be an S corporation shareholder so long as all of its beneficiaries are individuals, estates, or organizations eligible to accept charitable contributions under Code Sec. 170 (other than a political entity) (Code Sec. 1361(c)(2)(A)(v), (c)(2)(B)(v)), and (e)). ESBTs also cannot have any interest acquired by purchase (i.e., acquired with a cost basis).

To qualify as an ESBT, the trustee must file an election by signing and filing a statement with the IRS service center where the S corporation files its income tax return (Reg. § 1.1361-1(m)). The election statement must identify the trust, its potential current beneficiaries, the S corporations in which the trust currently owns stock, and the first date on which the trust owned the stock. It must include words identifying it as an ESBT election statement, the effective date of the election, and representations that the trust qualifies as an ESBT and that all potential current beneficiaries are eligible shareholders. A trust is treated as an ESBT as of the effective date of the election. Once effective, the election applies to the tax year in which it is made and all subsequent tax years unless it is revoked with IRS consent. Some types of trusts are not permitted to be ESBTs. Ineligible trust types include qualified subchapter S trusts (see following), any trust that is exempt from income tax, and charitable remainder unitrusts (CRUTs) and charitable remainder annuity trusts (CRATs).

The deadline for filing the ESBT election is two months and 16 days (one day longer than the S election deadline) from the earliest date the trust needs to qualify. However, the due date for performing certain time-sensitive actions, including the election to be a ESBT, otherwise due on or after April 1, 2020, and before July 15, 2020, is automatically extended to July 15, 2020, in response to the COVID-19 (coronavirus) crisis (Notice 2020-23; Rev. Proc. 2018-58).

Each potential current beneficiary of an ESBT is treated as a shareholder. For any period in which there is no potential current beneficiary, the trust itself is treated as the shareholder. A potential current beneficiary is a person who is entitled to a distribution from the trust or may receive a distribution at the discretion of any person. Any person who may benefit from a power of appointment is not a potential current beneficiary if the power has not been exercised. If the potential current beneficiaries of an ESBT would disqualify an entity from S corporation status, the ESBT has a grace period of one year to dispose of its stock in the S corporation, thereby avoiding disqualification. Effective January 1, 2018, a potential current beneficiary of a shareholder ESBT may be a nonresident alien without causing the loss of S corporation status (Code Sec. 1361(c)(2)(B)(v)).

QSSTs. A qualified subchapter S trust (QSST) may be an S corporation shareholder if the beneficiary elects to be treated as owner of the stock (Code Sec. 1361(d); Reg. § 1.1361-1(j)). A QSST must own stock in at least one S corporation and must distribute all of its income to one individual who is a U.S. citizen or resident. The QSST beneficiary is taxed on all items of income, loss, deduction, and credit attributable to the S corporation stock held by the QSST. However, the QSST and not the beneficiary is treated as the owner of the S corporation stock in determining the tax consequences of the trust's disposition of the S corporation stock. In addition, the terms of the QSST must provide:

- there may be only one income beneficiary at any time (but successive income beneficiaries are permitted);

- trust corpus may be distributed only to the income beneficiary;

- each income interest must end no later than the death of the income beneficiary; and

- if the trust ends at any time during the life of the income beneficiary, it must distribute all of its assets to the beneficiary.

The deadline for filing the QSST election is two months and 16 days (one day longer than the S election deadline) from the earliest date the trust needs to qualify. The election is effective for up to two months and 15 days before the election date. A separate election must be made with respect to each corporation the stock of which is held by the trust and must be made by each successive income beneficiary. The due date for performing certain time-sensitive actions, including the election to be a QSST, otherwise due on or after April 1, 2020, and before July 15, 2020, is automatically extended to July 15, 2020, in response to the COVID-19 (coronavirus) crisis (Notice 2020-23; Rev. Proc. 2018-58). The election may be revoked only with the consent of the IRS.

Exempt Organizations as Shareholders. Certain tax-exempt organizations can be S corporation shareholders: qualified pension, profit-sharing, and stock bonus plans; charitable organizations; and Code Sec. 501(c)(3) organizations.

QSSS. Even though a corporation generally cannot be an S corporation shareholder, an S corporation is permitted to own a qualified subchapter S subsidiary (QSSS or QSub) (Code Sec. 1361(b)(3)). This includes any domestic corporation that qualifies as an S corporation and is 100 percent owned by an S corporation parent that elects to treat it as a QSSS. A QSSS is not taxed as a separate corporation, and all of its tax items are treated as belonging to the parent. Form 8869 is used to elect QSub treatment for wholly-owned corporate subsidiaries.

305. Single Class of Stock Requirement for S Corporation Status. An S corporation may have only one class of stock outstanding. The shares must confer identical rights to distribution and liquidation proceeds (Code Sec. 1361(b)(1)(D) and (c)(5); Reg. § 1.1361-1(l)). Differences in voting rights are permitted. In addition, a corporate obligation that qualifies as "straight debt" is not considered a second class of stock. Buy-sell and redemption agreements restricting transferability of the stock are generally disregarded in determining whether the corporation has a single class of stock.

Stock of an S corporation does not include stock received for the performance of services that is substantially nonvested, unless the holder has made a Code Sec. 83(b) election to include the value of the stock in income (Reg. § 1.1361-1(b)(3)). However, stock warrants, call options, or other similar rights to purchase stock (collectively, "options") generally are treated as stock of the corporation if the options are substantially certain to be exercised at a strike price substantially below fair market value. This rule does not apply if the option was issued:

- to a commercial lender;
- in connection with the performance of services, provided the option is nontransferable and does not have a readily ascertainable fair market value when issued (¶ 713); or
- at a strike price that is at least 90 percent of the stock's fair market value (Reg. § 1.1361-1(l)(4)(iii)).

In addition, restricted bank director stock is not taken into account as outstanding stock in applying the provisions of subchapter S (Code Sec. 1361(f)(1)). Accordingly, it is not treated as a second class of stock in the S corporation.

306. Election of S Corporation Status. The election of S corporation status must be made on Form 2553 by a qualified corporation (¶ 303), with the unanimous consent of the shareholders, on or before the 15th day of the 3rd month of its tax year in order for the election to be effective beginning with the year when made (Code Sec. 1362(a), (b), and (c); Reg. § 1.1362-6). However, the due date for performing certain time-sensitive actions, including the election to be an S corporation by filing Form 2553, otherwise due on or after April 1, 2020, and before July 15, 2020, is automatically extended to July 15, 2020, in response to the COVID-19 (coronavirus) crisis (Notice 2020-23; Rev. Proc. 2018-58).

The corporation must meet all of the eligibility requirements for the pre-election portion of the tax year, and all persons who were shareholders during the pre-election portion also must consent to the election. If these requirements are not met during the pre-election period, the election becomes effective the following year. A domestic eligible entity (¶ 402A) may file both its check-the-box and S elections simply by filing Form 2553. It does not need to file Form 8832. The two elections will apply as of the same effective date (Reg. § 301.7701-3(c)(1)(v)(C)).

Late Elections. A simplified procedure is available for obtaining relief from a late or invalid S corporation election, electing small business trust (ESBT) election, qualified subchapter S trust (QSST) election, or qualified subchapter S subsidiary (QSub) election (¶ 304). Relief is generally available if a request for relief is filed within three years and 75 days after the date on which the election is intended to be effective (Rev. Proc. 2013-30). An entity may request relief for a late S corporation election by filing with the applicable IRS service center:

- a properly completed Form 2553 with Form 1120-S for the corporation's current tax year;
- a properly completed Form 2553 with a Form 1120-S for one of the corporation's late-filed prior-year Form 1120-S; or
- a properly completed Form 2553 submitted independently of Form 1120-S.

The simplified procedure for requesting late-election relief also applies where a domestic eligible entity has failed to timely file both its S corporation election and its election to be treated as a corporation under the check-the-box rules (¶ 402A). An entity that obtains relief under the simplified procedure is treated as having made both an election to be classified as an association taxable as a corporation and an S corporation election as of the same date.

Community Property. Shareholders in community property states are also eligible for automatic relief for late S elections if their spouses did not file timely shareholder consents (Rev. Proc. 2004-35). To qualify for relief, the S corporation election must be invalid solely because the spouse's signature is missing from the election form. Shareholders must alert the IRS that they are seeking relief under Rev. Proc. 2004-35 and identify the number of shares they own as of the date of the election. Each spouse must sign a separate statement indicating his or her consent to the election.

307. Termination of S Corporation Status. S corporation status is automatically terminated if any event occurs that would prohibit the corporation from making the election in the first place (Code Sec. 1362(d)(2); Reg. § 1.1362-2(b)). The election is ended as of the date on which the disqualifying event occurs. Also, if a corporation has accumulated earnings and profits as of the end of three consecutive years, and the corporation's passive investment income exceeds 25 percent of its gross receipts in each of those three years, its S election is terminated beginning with the following tax year (Code Sec. 1362(d)(3); Reg. § 1.1362-2(c)). For this purpose, dividends received by an S corporation from a C corporation subsidiary of which the S corporation owns 80 percent or more of stock are not treated as passive investment income to the extent the dividends are attributable to the earnings and profits derived from the active conduct of a trade or business.

An S corporation election may be revoked with the consent of shareholders holding more than 50 percent of the outstanding shares of stock (voting and nonvoting) on the day the revocation is made. A revocation may designate a prospective effective date (Code Sec. 1362(d)(1); Reg. § 1.1362-2(a)). If no date is specified, a revocation made on or before the 15th day of the 3rd month of a corporation's tax year is effective on the first day of the tax year. A revocation made after this date is effective on the first day of the following tax year. However, the due date for performing certain time-sensitive actions, including revocation of an election of S corporation status, otherwise due on or after April 1, 2020, and before July 15, 2020, is automatically extended to July 15, 2020, in response to the COVID-19 (coronavirus) crisis (Notice 2020-23; Rev. Proc. 2018-58).

If an election is terminated or revoked, the corporation may not re-elect S corporation status without IRS consent until the 5th year after the year in which the termination or revocation became effective (Code Sec. 1362(g); Reg. § 1.1362-5). An S corporation whose status as a qualified subchapter S subsidiary (QSSS or QSub) (¶ 304) has ended also cannot elect to be treated as a QSub until the 5th year after the year in which the termination was effective (Code Sec. 1361(b)(3)(D)).

In addition to formally filing an election to terminate S corporation status, an S corporation can simply create a situation that bars it from being an S corporation. This can help it avoid any delay in the effective date of the termination. For instance, S corporation status terminates immediately if the corporation creates another corporation and transfers one share of S corporation stock to the new corporation, because corporations cannot be S corporation shareholders.

Reorganizations. A corporation's subchapter S election does not terminate merely because it is a party to a reorganization (¶ 2221) if it continues to meet the S corporation eligibility requirements (Rev. Rul. 71-266). Typically, this issue arises because the reorganization results in an ineligible shareholder owning stock of the S corporation. For example, the IRS ruled that the S election of a corporation that was acquired by another corporation in a stock-for-stock B reorganization terminated on the date of acquisition. On the other hand, the IRS has ruled that A, C, and F reorganizations did not cause the S elections of the respective corporations to terminate when all owners of the corporations after the transaction were eligible S corporation shareholders.

Frequently, reorganizations can involve transfers of the same corporate stock several times to different parties as part of the transaction. The intermediate parties may be deemed to hold the stock only for an instant before transferring it to its ultimate holder. The question arises whether a corporation's subchapter S election terminates where one or more of these intermediate parties is not an eligible S corporation shareholder. This issue is not addressed by the Code or regulations. However, the IRS has privately ruled that having shareholders who acquire a corporation's stock only to immediately transfer it to another party does not cause the corporation's S election to terminate (LTR 200453007 and LTR 9010042).

Correction of Inadvertent Terminations. If a corporation's subchapter S election is inadvertently terminated or invalid when made, and the corporation makes a timely correction, the IRS can waive the termination or can permit the election (Code Sec. 1362(f); Reg. § 1.1362-4). The IRS can also provide a waiver where an election to treat family members as one shareholder or to treat a corporation as a QSub is invalid when made or inadvertently terminated. To obtain a waiver, the corporation must correct any condition that either barred it from qualifying as a subchapter S corporation or otherwise made an election invalid, and must obtain any required shareholder consents. All shareholders must also agree to make such adjustments as may be required by the IRS.

Election to End Tax Year. If a shareholder terminates his or her interest in an S corporation and all affected shareholders consent to the termination, the tax year can be treated as two tax years, the first of which ends on the date of termination (Code Sec.

1377(a)(2)). Affected shareholders include the shareholder whose interest is terminated and all shareholders to whom that shareholder has transferred shares during the tax year.

S Corporation Shareholders

See CCH® AnswerConnect: *Treatment of S Corporation Shareholders* for more information on this topic.

309. Taxation of S Corporation Shareholders. Each shareholder of an S corporation separately accounts for his or her pro rata share of corporate items of income, deduction, loss, and credit in his or her tax year in which the corporation's tax year ends (Code Sec. 1366(a); Reg. §§ 1.1366-1(a) and 1.1377-1). Certain items must be separately stated if they could affect the shareholder's individual tax liability (¶ 320). A shareholder's share of each item generally is based on the number of shares held on each day of the corporation's tax year.

The character of an item included in a shareholder's pro rata share of S corporation income is generally determined as if the item were realized directly from the source from which the corporation realized it, or incurred in the same manner in which the corporation incurred it, subject to exceptions (Code Sec. 1366(b); Reg. § 1.1366-1(b)). Thus, when income passes through from the S corporation to the shareholder, the character of that income passes through as well. For example, if an S corporation makes a charitable contribution to a qualifying organization, a shareholder's pro rata share of the S corporation's charitable contribution is characterized as made to a qualifying organization.

Similarly, if an S corporation has capital gain on the sale or exchange of a capital asset, a shareholder's pro rata share of that gain is also characterized as a capital gain, regardless of whether the shareholder is otherwise a dealer in that type of property. However, this rule does not apply if the S corporation is formed or availed of for a principal purpose of selling or exchanging contributed property that, in the hands of the shareholder, would not have produced capital gain if sold or exchanged by the shareholder.

The same exception applies when the S corporation is formed or availed of for a principal purpose of selling or exchanging contributed property that, in the hands of a shareholder, would have produced capital loss if sold or exchanged by the shareholder. Any loss recognized by the corporation is treated as a capital loss to the extent that, immediately before the contribution, the adjusted basis of the property in the hands of the shareholder exceeded the fair market value of the property.

Duty of Consistency. A shareholder of an S corporation must treat a subchapter S item in a manner consistent with the treatment of that item on the S corporation's return (Code Sec. 6037). Any shareholder who does not treat the item consistently must file a statement identifying the inconsistency.

At-Risk and Passive Activity Rules. The at-risk rules disallow losses that exceed an investor's amount at risk (¶ 1155). Generally, the amount at risk is the amount of investment that an investor could lose. The at-risk rules apply to all individuals, including S corporation shareholders, and are applied at the shareholder level (Code Sec. 465). The at-risk amount is determined at the close of the S corporation's tax year. Thus, an S corporation shareholder who realizes that his or her at-risk amount is low, and wishes to deduct an anticipated S corporation net loss, can make additional contributions to the corporation.

Likewise, passive activity loss (PAL) rules generally are applied at the shareholder level (¶ 1169) (Code Sec. 469). However, several determinations that affect the application of the PAL rules must be made at the corporate level. For example, the determination of whether an activity constitutes a trade or business, as opposed to a rental activity, is made at the corporate level. The distinction between portfolio and nonportfolio income is also made at the corporate level. This information is conveyed via the Schedule K-1 (Form 1120-S) that is provided to the shareholder by the corporation. The shareholder then uses the information to apply the PAL and at-risk limitations when preparing his or her individual tax return.

Since a qualified subchapter S trust (QSST) (¶ 304) is treated as the shareholder when it disposes of S corporation stock, the application of the at-risk and PAL rules would normally be determined at the trust level, not the beneficiary level. However, to ensure that the beneficiary can take disallowed losses on the QSST's disposition of the stock, the at-risk and passive activity loss rules apply as if the beneficiary disposed of the stock (Code Sec. 1361(d)(1)(C)).

Small Business Stock. Since S corporations are not entitled to ordinary loss treatment from the sale of qualified small business stock under Code Sec. 1244 (¶ 1911), and the character of loss items passes through to shareholders, S corporation shareholders cannot claim ordinary losses incurred by the S corporation from the sale of qualified small business stock (*V.D. Rath*, Dec. 49,266, 101 TC 196). However, if the S corporation stock itself is qualified small business stock, shareholders may claim ordinary loss deductions if all the requirements are met.

310. Qualified Business Income Deduction for S Corporation Shareholders. For tax years beginning after 2017, an S corporation shareholder may deduct up to 20 percent of certain domestic qualified business income from an S corporation for a tax year (¶ 980P). The deduction is applied at the shareholder level. Each shareholder must take into account his or her pro rata share of each qualified item of income, gain, deduction, and loss (Code Sec. 199A).

Regulations provide that an S corporation that directly engages in a qualified trade or business reports qualified items on the owner's K-1. The S corporation uses an attachment to the K-1 to report qualified items that are passed through from a lower-tier entity, as well as qualified REIT dividends and publicly traded partnership (PTP) income or loss. Any items that are not reported are presumed to be zero (Reg. § 1.199A-6(b)(3)). The deduction does not affect the adjusted basis of a shareholder's stock in an S corporation, or an S corporation's accumulated adjustments account (Reg. § 1.199A-1(e)(1)).

312. Domestic Production Activities of S Corporation Shareholders. An S corporation may not claim the domestic production activities deduction (DPAD) available only for tax years beginning before 2018 (¶ 980A). Instead, the deduction is determined at the shareholder level (Code Sec. 199(d)(1), prior to repeal by the Tax Cuts and Jobs Act (P.L. 115-97); Reg. § 1.199-5(c)). Generally, each shareholder computes the deduction separately on Form 8903 by aggregating his or her pro rata share of qualified production activity (QPA) items of the S corporation (i.e., income, expenses) with his or her share of QPA items from other sources. The shareholder does not have to be directly engaged in the S corporation's trade or business to claim the deduction on the basis of his or her share of QPA items. In determining the deduction, the activities of an S corporation are not attributed to its shareholders (or vice-versa) (Reg. § 1.199-5(g)). However, limited exceptions apply to expanded affiliated groups and to the production of qualified films.

314. Net Investment Income Tax (NIIT) for S Corporations. Individuals, trusts, and estates are subject to a 3.8-percent tax on the lesser of their net investment income for the tax year or the excess of their modified adjusted gross income (MAGI) for the tax year over a threshold amount (¶ 117). S corporations are not subject to the net investment income (NII) tax, but S corporation shareholders may be subject to the tax on income items related to their investments in the corporation.

Allocations of Net Investment Income (NII). NII generally includes income and gain from passive activities. It does not include gross income derived in the ordinary course of a trade or business. Thus, income from a trade or business conducted by the S corporation in which the shareholder actively participates is not NII to the shareholder (Reg. § 1.1411-4(b)(2)). However, income from a trade or business that is a passive activity with respect to the shareholder is included in the shareholder's NII. In other words, the shareholder's distributive share of income earned by the S corporation that would be NII had it been earned directly by the shareholder is NII to the shareholder. In addition, if the S corporation is engaged in the trade or business of trading in financial instruments or commodities, the income or loss from that trade or business is excluded from the shareholder's NII without regard to whether the shareholder is engaged in the trade or business.

Dispositions of S Corporation Stock. Net gain or loss upon the disposition of S corporation stock is NII only to the extent it would be taken into account as such by the shareholder if all S corporation property were sold at fair market value immediately before the disposition (Code Sec. 1411(c)(4); Prop. Reg. §1.1411-7). Specifically, gain or loss from property used in the S corporation's trade or business is excluded from NII, unless the trade or business is a passive activity with respect to the shareholder or involves trading in financial instruments or commodities.

315. Basis in S Corporation Stock. An S corporation shareholder's basis in the stock is determined under the same rules that apply to C corporation shareholders. Thus, the original basis of purchased stock is the shareholder's purchase price (the money or the fair market value of any property given in exchange for the stock) (Code Sec. 1012). Stock acquired by gift normally carries over the donor's basis (¶ 1630). The basis of stock acquired from a decedent is its fair market value on the date of the decedent's death or, if elected, on the alternate valuation date (¶ 1633). While the corporation is an S corporation, each shareholder must make adjustments to the stock (¶ 317).

Similarly, the rules providing for contributions to controlled corporations under Code Sec. 351 (¶ 203) and tax-free corporate reorganizations under Code Sec. 368 (¶ 2209) generally apply to S corporations (Code Sec. 1371). Thus, the basis of stock received under a tax-free reorganization is equal to the transferor's basis in the property transferred plus any gain realized, and minus the fair market value of the boot received and any loss recognized in the transaction.

Stock for Services. An S corporation may grant stock to an employee or other service provider as part of a compensation package. Typically, in a stock-for-services arrangement, an employee may receive the stock at a particular price or for nothing, with the rights to the stock becoming vested only after a number of years of employment. The stock usually appreciates between the time of the transfer and the vesting point. The difference between the amount that the employee pays for the S stock and the fair market value of the stock when the employee's rights to the stock are vested must be included in the employee's ordinary gross income (¶ 713). The S corporation may claim a compensation deduction for the amount the employee includes in income in the year the employee includes it.

317. Adjustments to Basis in S Corporation Stock. An S corporation shareholder's basis in the stock (¶ 315) is *increased* by the shareholder's portion of:

- income items, including tax-exempt income, that are separately computed and passed through to the shareholder;

- the income of the corporation that is not separately computed; and

- the excess of the corporation's deductions for depletion (¶ 1384) over the basis of the property subject to depletion (Code Sec. 1367(a)(1); Reg. § 1.1367-1(b)).

A shareholder's basis is *decreased* by the portion of:

- distributions that are not includible in the shareholder's income (¶ 309);

- all loss and deduction items that are separately stated and passed through to the shareholder (but see the later discussion with respect to charitable contributions of appreciated property);

- the corporation's nonseparately computed loss;

- any expense not deductible in computing the corporation's taxable income and not properly chargeable to its capital account; and

- the shareholder's deduction for depletion with respect to oil and gas wells to the extent that it does not exceed his or her proportionate share of the adjusted basis of such property (Code Sec. 1367(a)(2); Reg. § 1.1367-1(c)).

If a shareholder's stock basis is reduced to zero, the remaining net decrease attributable to losses and deductions reduces any basis in debt the corporation owes to the shareholder (¶ 318). Distributions may not be applied against basis in debt. Any net increase in basis in a subsequent year restores the basis of debt before it may increase the shareholder's stock basis.

Generally, stock basis adjustments are determined as of the close of the corporation's tax year, and the adjustments are effective as of that date. However, if a shareholder disposes of stock during the corporation's tax year, the adjustments with respect to that stock are effective immediately before the disposition (Reg. § 1.1367-1(d)). An adjustment for a nontaxable item is determined for the tax year in which the item would have been includible or deductible under the corporation's method of accounting for federal income tax purposes if the item had been subject to federal income taxation.

Charitable Deductions. A shareholder's reduction of basis in S corporation stock because of the corporation's charitable contribution of property equals the shareholder's pro rata share of the adjusted basis of the contributed property (Code Sec. 1367(a)(2)). The amount of the contribution is generally the fair market value of the property, reduced by the amount of gain that would have resulted if the donor had sold the contributed property for its fair market value at the time of the contribution (¶ 1062).

Cancellation of Debt. An S corporation's discharge of debt income that is excluded from income (¶ 855) is not taken into account as an item of income that flows through to any shareholder (¶ 309). Thus, it does not increase a shareholder's basis in S corporation stock (Code Sec. 108(d)(7)(A); Reg. § 1.108-7(d)).

318. Basis in S Corporation Debt. For purposes of deducting S corporation losses, a shareholder has basis in certain debts of the S corporation to the shareholder (Code Sec. 1366(d)(1)(B); Reg. § 1.1366-2(a)(2)). The debt in question must run directly to the shareholder and represent a bona fide debt of the S corporation. Federal tax principles generally determine whether debt is bona fide, based on all relevant facts and circumstances. Unlike a partner in a partnership, an S corporation shareholder does not receive basis or an increase in basis for the corporation's debt to an outside lender. A shareholder's mere guaranty of the S corporation's debt to a third party also does not increase the shareholder's basis, including acting as a surety, accommodation party, or in any similar capacity relating to the loan.

The basis that a shareholder has in debt owed to that shareholder by the S corporation must be adjusted like the shareholder's basis in stock. Adjustments to stock are calculated before the basis in debt is affected (Code Sec. 1367(b)(2); Reg. § 1.1367-2). If decreases relating to losses, deductions, noncapital, nondeductible expenses, and certain oil and gas depletion deductions have reduced stock basis to zero, any excess is applied to reduce debt basis. Any debt by the corporation to the shareholder that has been satisfied by the corporation, disposed of, or forgiven by the shareholder during the tax year, and is not held by the shareholder at the close of that year is not subject to basis reduction.

Generally, the adjustments to debt basis are made as of the close of the tax year. However, if the shareholder terminates his or her interest in the corporation during the tax year the adjustments in basis to debt are applied with respect to any S corporation debt held by the shareholder immediately before the termination of the shareholder's interest in the corporation. If there is a reduction in the shareholder's basis in S corporation debt, any net increase in any subsequent tax year is applied first to the restoration of that reduction before any increase is applied to stock basis.

319. Taxable Income of S Corporation. An S corporation must compute its taxable income to determine the amount of income, gain, loss, deduction and credit passed through to its shareholders (¶ 309) (Code Sec. 1363(b)). Computation of an S corporation's taxable income parallels the computation of the taxable income of an individual, except that organizational expenditures may be amortized (¶ 237) and the reduction in certain corporate tax benefits (¶ 239) is applied if the S corporation was a C corporation for any of its three immediately preceding tax years. Moreover, certain deductions allowed to individuals, such as those for charitable contributions, medical expenses, alimony, net operating losses, and personal exemptions for tax years before 2018 and after 2025, are not allowed to the S corporation when calculating taxable income. Certain items must be separately stated when passed through to shareholders (¶ 320).

Items from a year in which the corporation was not an S corporation cannot be carried over to a year that it is an S corporation (Code Sec. 1371(b)). Also, no carryforward or carryback arises at the corporate level in a tax year for which a corporation is an S corporation. However, a tax year for which a corporation is an S corporation is treated as a tax year for purposes of determining the number of tax years to which an item may be carried back or carried forward. Thus, while the item remains intact during the time the corporation is an S corporation, those years count for any carryforward period applicable to the item.

320. Separately Stated Items of S Corporation Income. Certain items of an S corporation's taxable income (¶ 319) must be separately stated (Code Sec. 1363(b)).

These items must be reported and computed separately from items that can be combined. Items that must be separately stated include, but are not limited to:

- net income or loss from rental activities, including rental real estate activities;
- portfolio income or loss and expenses related to portfolio income or loss;
- Code Sec. 1231 net gain or loss;
- charitable contributions, grouped by the percentage limitations of Code Sec. 170(b);
- Code Sec. 179 expense deductions;
- the low-income housing credit;
- investment interest expense;
- tax preference and adjustment items needed to compute shareholders' alternative minimum tax;
- gains and losses from wagering transactions;
- medical, dental, etc., expenses;
- itemized deductions;
- capital gain or loss grouped by applicable holding periods;
- foreign taxes paid or accrued;
- tax-exempt income; and
- passive activity items for each of the corporation's activities (Code Sec. 1366(a)(1)(A); Reg. § 1.1366-1(a)).

Each shareholder must also take into account his or her pro rata share of the nonseparately computed income or loss of the S corporation. Nonseparately computed income or loss is the corporation's gross income less the deductions allowed to the corporation, determined by excluding any item requiring separate computation.

Nonbusiness Bad Debts. An S corporation may claim a nonbusiness bad debt deduction (¶ 1143) in the same manner as an individual. Accordingly, an S corporation that incurs a nonbusiness bad debt must separately state the debt as a short-term capital loss (Rev. Rul. 93-36). On the other hand, partially or wholly worthless business debts are included in nonseparately stated S corporation income or loss (¶ 1135).

321. Limits on S Corporation Deductions. A shareholder's currently deductible share of an S corporation's losses and deductions for any tax year is limited to the total of his or her adjusted basis in the corporation's stock (¶ 315) and any bona fide debt the S corporation owes to the shareholder (¶ 318) (Code Sec. 1366(d)).

An S corporation's itemized deductions are separately stated items (¶ 320). Thus, the two percent of adjusted gross income floor on miscellaneous itemized deductions for tax years beginning before 2018 and after 2025 (¶ 1079) applies at the shareholder level rather than at the S corporation level (Temp. Reg. § 1.67-2T(b)(1)). Shareholders take into account separately their pro rata share of the corporation's miscellaneous itemized deductions, add them to their other individual miscellaneous deductions.

The election to expense the cost of Code Sec. 179 property (¶ 1208) is made at the S corporation level (Reg. § 1.179-1(h)). The dollar, investment, and taxable income limitations apply at both the S corporation and shareholder levels (Code Sec. 179(d)(8); Reg. § 1.179-2).

Charitable Deductions. If an S corporation makes a charitable contribution of property, each shareholder reduces stock basis by his or her pro rata share of the S corporation's adjusted basis in the contributed property (Code Sec. 1367(a)(2)). The stock basis limitation on deductions does not apply to a charitable contribution of appreciated property to the extent the shareholder's pro rata share of the contribution exceeds the shareholder's pro rata share of the adjusted basis of the property (Code Secs. 1366(d)(4) and 1367(a)(2)).

Suspended Losses and Deductions. If the amount of a shareholder's loss or deduction is limited for a tax year, the excess is treated, for that individual shareholder, as incurred by the S corporation in the next tax year and may be carried forward until used by that shareholder (Code Sec. 1366(d)(2)). Disallowed losses and deductions may be transferred only to the shareholder's current or former spouse when the S corporation stock is transferred between spouses or incident to divorce in a nontaxable transaction (¶ 1734).

If the shareholder's losses or deductions are limited for the last tax year in which the corporation is an S corporation, the excess is treated as incurred by the shareholder on the last day of the corporation's post-termination transition period (¶ 329) (Code Sec. 1366(d)(3)). The excess amount cannot exceed the shareholder's adjusted basis of the stock in the corporation, determined at the close of the last day of the post-termination transition period. The losses or deductions taken into account during this period reduce the shareholder's basis of stock in the corporation. Losses of an S corporation that are suspended under the at-risk rules (¶ 1155) are carried forward to the post-termination period.

322. Employee Benefits Provided to S Corporation Shareholders. The tax treatment of fringe benefits (¶ 2085) paid to owner-employees of an S corporation is different from the tax treatment for other employees (Code Sec. 1372). Fringe benefits paid to S corporation employees who are not shareholders, or who own two percent or less of the outstanding S corporation stock, are excluded from gross income. They can be excluded from the employees' taxable wages and are deductible as fringe benefits by the corporation. On the other hand, owner-employees owning more than two percent of the S corporation stock are not treated as employees for fringe benefit purposes, and their fringe benefits may be included in gross income. In other words, more-than-two-percent shareholders are treated like partners in a partnership (¶ 421).

Health Insurance Expenses. An owner-employee who owns more than two percent of the S corporation stock can deduct 100 percent of the amount paid for medical insurance for himself or herself, a spouse, and dependents under a plan established by the S corporation (Code Sec. 162(l)(1) and (5); Notice 2008-1). The S corporation must either pay the plan's premium payments itself or must reimburse the shareholder for the payments.

For purposes of the deduction, a more-than-two-percent shareholder's wages from the S corporation are treated as the shareholder's earned income. No deduction is allowed in excess of an individual's earned income (within the meaning of Code Sec. 401(c)) derived from the trade or business with respect to which the plan providing the health insurance is established.

Note that reimbursement plans are generally no longer in compliance with group health plan rules and may incur an excise tax of $100 per day per affected employee (Code Sec. 4980D). However, under transition relief, two-percent shareholder-employee arrangements of S corporations are not subject to the excise tax and are not required to file Form 8928 solely as a result of having such an arrangement (Notice 2015-17). Until the IRS issues further guidance, the deduction rules discussed previously continue to apply.

Tax Treatment of Distributions

See CCH® AnswerConnect: *Distributions of Cash and Property to S Corporation Shareholders* for more information on this topic.

323. S Corporation Distributions. Distributions of cash or property received by a shareholder from an S corporation are taxable depending on whether the corporation has earnings and profits (Code Sec. 1368; Reg. § 1.1368-1). An S corporation generally has no earnings and profits unless attributable to tax years when the corporation was not an S corporation. An S corporation may also succeed to the earnings and profits of an acquired or merged corporation.

For an S corporation without earnings and profits, distributions are treated first as a nontaxable return of capital to the extent of the shareholder's basis in stock, and then as gain from the sale or exchange of property. For an S corporation with earnings and profits, unless an election is made to distribute the earnings and profits as dividends (¶ 333), distributions are treated as:

- a nontaxable return of capital, to the extent of the corporation's accumulated adjustments account (AAA) (¶ 325);

- dividends, to the extent of the S corporation's accumulated earnings and profits;

- a nontaxable return of capital, to the extent of the shareholder's remaining stock basis; and

- gain from the sale or exchange of property.

Before applying these rules, the shareholder's stock basis and the AAA are adjusted for the corporate items passed through from the corporate tax year during which the distribution is made.

If an employee stock ownership plan (ESOP) holds S corporation shares that are employer securities, and the ESOP takes out a loan to purchase the employer securities, the prohibited transaction rules do not apply to S corporation distributions that are used to repay the loan, and the plan's status as an ESOP is not jeopardized (Code Sec. 4975(f)(7)).

325. Accumulated Adjustments Account of S Corporation. The accumulated adjustments account (AAA) is used to compute the tax effect of distributions made by an S corporation with accumulated earnings and profits (¶ 323) (Code Sec. 1368(e); Reg. § 1.1368-2). The AAA is generally a measure of the corporation's accumulated gross income, less expenses, that has not been distributed. The AAA is zero on the first day of a corporation's first S corporation tax year. It is *increased* by:

- all corporate income items (excluding tax-exempt income items) that are separately stated and passed through to shareholders (¶ 320);

- nonseparately computed corporate income; and

- the excess of deductions for depletion over the basis of the property subject to depletion.

The AAA is *decreased* by:

- certain nontaxable corporate distributions;

- all loss and deduction items of the corporation that are separately stated and passed through (other than items that are not deductible in computing taxable income and not properly chargeable to capital account);

- the nonseparately computed loss of the corporation;

- the nondeductible amounts that are unrelated to the production of tax-exempt income; and

- the amount of the shareholder's deduction for oil and gas depletion.

An S corporation's AAA is not increased by tax-exempt income, and it is not decreased by an expense related to the tax-exempt income. For example, premiums that an S corporation pays on an employer-owned life insurance contract (COLI) that names the S corporation as a beneficiary, do not reduce the S corporation's AAA. Nor is the AAA increased by death benefits received by the corporation under the policy that meets one of the exceptions for COLI (¶ 804) (Rev. Rul. 2008-42).

No adjustment is made for federal taxes that arose when the corporation was a C corporation. Because the AAA may become negative, the account becomes positive only after the negative balance is restored by later income (Code Sec. 1368(e)(1)(A); Reg. § 1.1368-2). The amount in the AAA as of the close of a tax year is determined without regard to any net negative adjustment for the tax year. A negative adjustment occurs in any tax year in which negative adjustments to the account exceed increases to the account.

Distributions received by an S corporation shareholder in a stock redemption that is treated as a Code Sec. 301 distribution are treated as distributions that reduce the S corporation's AAA (Rev. Rul. 95-14). For a distribution in redemption of an S corporation's stock, if the redemption is treated as an exchange under Code Sec. 302 or 303, the AAA is decreased by an amount determined by multiplying the account balance by the number of shares redeemed and dividing the product by the total number of shares outstanding. This adjustment is made before the distribution rules are applied (Code Sec. 1368(e)(1)(B)).

The AAA relates only to the most recent continuous period in which the corporation has been an S corporation. However, the period does not include tax years beginning before January 1, 1983 (Code Sec. 1368(e)(2); Reg. § 1.1368-2(a)). If corporate distributions during a tax year exceed the amount in the AAA at the end of that year, the balance of the account is allocated among distributions in proportion to their respective sizes (¶ 329) (Code Sec. 1368(c)).

329. Post-Termination Distributions by S Corporations. If a corporation terminates its election to be an S corporation, it has the opportunity for a limited period of time to unfreeze the income that was previously taxed to shareholders under the pass-through rules but that was not actually distributed. Specifically, any cash distribution by the corporation with respect to its stock during the post-termination transition period is applied against and reduces the adjusted basis of the stock to the extent that the amount of the distribution does not exceed the accumulated adjustments account (AAA) (¶ 325) (Code Secs. 1371(e) and 1377(b)). A distribution in redemption of shareholder stock during this period also reduces the corporation's remaining AAA (Rev. Rul. 2019-13).

The post-termination transition period is:

- the period beginning on the day after the last day of the corporation's last tax year as an S corporation and ending on the later of: (i) the day that is one year after such last day, or (ii) the due date for filing the return for the last tax year as an S corporation including extensions;

- the 120-day period beginning on the date of any determination under an audit of the taxpayer that follows the termination of the corporation's S election and adjusts a subchapter S item of income, loss, or deduction of the corporation arising during the S period (Code Sec. 1368(e)(2)); and

- the 120-day period beginning on the date of a determination that the corporation's S election had ended for a previous tax year.

Any AAA that is not exhausted by the end of the post-termination transition period disappears. Distributions made thereafter are taxed under the usual C corporation rules—first, as a distribution of current earnings and profits; next, as a distribution of accumulated earnings and profits; then, as a return of capital to the extent of the shareholder's basis; and, finally, as a capital gain. Because the AAA is always reflected in the basis of the shareholder's stock, failure to exhaust it during the transition period moves it, in effect, below current and accumulated earnings and profits in the priority system for distributions. The grace period for post-termination distributions applies only to cash distributions. It does not apply to noncash distributions. A noncash distribution is taxed under the usual C corporation rules.

Code Sec. 481 Adjustments. Any Code Sec. 481(a) adjustment resulting from an accounting method change that is attributable to an eligible S corporation's revocation of its S corporation election during the two-year period beginning on December 22, 2017, is taken into account ratably over a six-year period (Code Sec. 481(d); Prop. Reg. § 1.481-5). If an eligible terminated S corporation (ETSC) distributes money after the post-termination transition period, the AAA is allocated to such distribution. The distribution is chargeable to accumulated earnings and profits in the same ratio as the amount of such AAA bears to the amount of such earnings and profits (Code Sec. 1371(f); Prop. Reg. § 1.1371-1).

333. S Corporation Election to Distribute Earnings. An S corporation can avoid the priority system (¶ 323) for distributions by electing to treat distributions as dividends (Code Sec. 1368(e)(3); Reg. § 1.1368-1(f)(2)). An S corporation might elect to treat a distribution as a taxable dividend if it wants to avoid a termination of its S status on account of excess passive investment income. All shareholders who receive a distribution during the tax year must consent to this treatment. An electing corporation is not required to distribute its entire accumulated adjustments account (AAA) (¶ 325) at the end of its tax year before it can pay a dividend.

Taxation of S Corporations

See CCH® AnswerConnect: *Taxation of S Corporations* and *Built In Gains Tax* for more information on this topic.

335. Taxation of S Corporation. Since an S corporation is a pass-through entity (¶ 301 and ¶ 309), it is generally not subject to federal income taxes. However, an S corporation may be liable for the following corporate-level tax liabilities and is required to make estimated tax payments attributable to them:

- the tax imposed on built-in gains or capital gains (¶ 337);

- the tax on excess net passive income (¶ 341);

- the recapture of the investment credit on the disposition of property placed in service before 1985; and

- the recapture of benefits from using the last-in, first-out (LIFO) inventory method of accounting upon conversion to an S corporation (¶ 339) (Code Sec. 6655(g)(4)).

If the S corporation was incorporated after 1982, immediately became an S corporation, and has no earnings or profits, only the capital gains tax applies. If the S corporation was incorporated and elected S corporation status before 1987, the tax on built-in gains does not apply.

337. Tax on Built-In Gains of S Corporation. A corporate-level tax ("built-in gains tax") is imposed on S corporations that dispose of assets that appreciated in value during tax years when the corporation was a C corporation (Code Sec. 1374). The built-in gains tax applies only to corporations that made S corporation elections after 1986. However, a tax imposed on certain capital gains of S corporations applies to corporations that made S elections before 1987.

An S corporation may be liable for tax on its built-in gains if:

- it was a C corporation before making its S corporation election;

- it has a net recognized built-in gain within the recognition period; and

- the net recognized built-in gain for the tax year does not exceed the net unrealized built-in gain minus the net recognized built-in gain for prior years in the recognition period, to the extent that such gains were subject to tax.

Net recognized built-in gain is the lesser of: (1) the amount that would be the taxable income of the S corporation if only recognized built-in gains and recognized built-in losses were taken into account, or (2) the corporation's taxable income. Any net recognized built-in gain that is not subject to the built-in gains tax due to the net income limitation is carried forward (Code Sec. 1374(d)(2); Reg. § 1.1374-2). The amount of recognized built-in gain passed through and taxed to shareholders is reduced by the tax imposed on the built-in gain and paid by the S corporation (Code Sec. 1366(f)(2)).

A recognized built-in loss is any loss recognized during the recognition period on the disposition of any asset to the extent that the S corporation establishes that: (1) the asset was held by the S corporation at the beginning of its first tax year as an S corporation; and (2) the loss is not greater than the excess of the adjusted basis of the asset at the beginning of the corporation's first tax year as an S corporation, over the fair market value of the asset at that time.

Recognition Period. The recognition period for net built-in gain is the five-year period beginning on the first day on which the corporation is an S corporation (Code Sec. 1374(d)(7); Reg. § 1.1374-1(d)). For example, if the first day of the recognition period is July 12, 2015, the last day of the recognition period is July 11, 2020. If the S corporation sells an asset within the recognition period under the installment method (¶ 1801), all the payments received (whether within the recognition period or not) are treated as received in the tax year of the sale. The recognition period applies separately with respect to any asset acquired in a carryover basis transaction (Code Sec. 1374(d)(8)).

Amount of Tax. The built-in gains tax is computed by applying the highest corporate income tax rate to the S corporation's net recognized built-in gain for the tax year. The amount of the net recognized built-in gain is taxable income. However, any net operating loss carryforward arising in a tax year in which the corporation was a C corporation is allowed as a deduction against the net recognized built-in gain of the S corporation. Capital loss carryforwards may also be used to offset recognized built-in gains (Code Sec. 1374(b) and (d); Reg. § 1.1374-5). Furthermore, business tax credit carryovers of an S corporation arising in a tax year in which the corporation was a C corporation can offset the built-in gains tax of the S corporation (Code Sec. 1374(b)(3)(B); Reg. § 1.1374-6).

339. LIFO Recapture by S Corporation. A C corporation that maintains its inventory using the last-in, first-out (LIFO) method (¶ 1565) for its last tax year before an S corporation election becomes effective must include in gross income a LIFO recapture amount when it converts to S corporation status (Code Sec. 1363(d); Reg. § 1.1363-2).

LIFO recapture is also required for transfers of inventory from a C corporation to an S corporation in a tax-free reorganization. The LIFO recapture amount is the amount, if any, by which the amount of the inventory assets using the first-in, first-out (FIFO) method (¶ 1564) exceeds the inventory amount of such assets under the LIFO method.

The tax attributable to the inclusion in income of any LIFO recapture amount is payable by the corporation in four equal installments. The first payment is due on or before the due date of the corporate tax return for the electing corporation's last tax year as a C corporation. The three subsequent installments are due on or before the respective due dates of the S corporation's returns for the three succeeding tax years. No interest is payable on these installments if they are paid by the respective due dates.

341. Passive Investment Income of S Corporation. An S corporation with accumulated earnings and profits and total passive investment income totaling more than 25 percent of gross receipts is subject to an income tax computed by multiplying the corporation's excess net passive income by the highest corporate income tax rate (Code Sec. 1375; Reg. § 1.1375-1). Passive investment income is gross receipts derived from royalties, rents, dividends, annuities, and interest (excluding interest on installment sales of inventory to customers and gross receipts from certain lending and financing businesses) (Code Sec. 1362(d)(3)(C); Reg. § 1.1362-2(c)(5)).

Income derived by an S corporation in the ordinary course of its trade or business is generally excluded from the definition of passive investment income. For an S corporation bank (including a bank holding company and a depository institution holding company), passive investment income does not include interest earned by the bank or any dividends received on assets that the bank is required to hold. The exception for assets applies to stock in the Federal Reserve Bank, the Federal Home Loan Bank, or the Federal Agriculture Mortgage Bank, and participation certificates issued by a Federal Intermediate Credit Bank.

Excess net passive income is the amount that bears the same ratio to net passive income as the amount of passive investment income that exceeds 25 percent of gross receipts bears to passive investment income (Code Sec. 1375(b); Reg. § 1.1375-1(b)). Net passive income is passive investment income reduced by any allowable deduction directly connected with the production of such income except for the net operating loss (NOL) deduction (¶ 1145) and the special deductions allowed to corporations in computing taxable income (¶ 221—¶ 237). Excess net passive income cannot exceed the corporation's taxable income for the tax year computed without regard to any NOL deduction and without regard to the special deductions allowed to corporations, other than the deduction for organizational expenditures (¶ 237).

Passive investment income is determined without taking into account any recognized built-in gain or loss during the recognition period (¶ 337). This means that S corporations without earnings and profits cannot be taxed on excess net passive income if they have no taxable income. This can happen if the corporation has NOLs and income from passive investments. The tax is not merely carried over. Instead, there is no tax due if during the year the corporation did not have taxable income.

The tax on excess net passive income reduces each item of passive income by the amount of tax attributable to it, and thereby reduces the amount of passive investment income that each shareholder must take into account in computing gross income (Code Sec. 1366(f)(3)).

The only credits allowable against the passive investment income tax are those for certain uses of gasoline and special fuels (¶ 1429) (Code Sec. 1375(c); Reg. § 1.1375-1(c)).

The IRS may waive the tax on excess net passive income if the S corporation establishes: (1) that it made a good-faith determination that it had no C corporation earnings and profits at the close of the tax year; and (2) within a reasonable time after determining that it did have C corporation earnings and profits at the close of the tax year, those earning and profits were distributed (Code Sec. 1375(d); Reg. § 1.1375-1(d)).

349. Foreign Income of S Corporation. Foreign taxes paid by an S corporation pass through to shareholders who can elect to treat them as deductions or credits on their individual returns (Code Sec. 1373). An S corporation is treated as a partnership rather than a corporation. Therefore, for purposes of the indirect foreign tax credit— available in tax years beginning before 2018—for taxes paid by a foreign corporation with an S corporation shareholder, neither the S corporation nor its own shareholders could claim the indirect foreign tax credit (¶ 2475). The foreign loss recapture rules apply to an S corporation that previously passed foreign losses through to the shareholders and subsequently terminates its S corporation status. For the purpose of computing the amount of foreign losses that must be recaptured, the making or termination of an S corporation election is treated as a disposition of a trade or business.

Returns and Tax Year

See CCH® AnswerConnect: *S Corporation Return Requirements* for more information on this topic.

351. S Corporation Return (Form 1120-S). An S corporation is required to file Form 1120-S for each tax year that the election to be treated as an S corporation is in effect (¶ 303), regardless of whether the corporation has taxable income for that year (Reg. § 1.6012-2(h)). The return must be filed electronically if the corporation has assets of $10 million or more, and if the corporation is required to file at least 250 returns during a calendar year before 2021 (¶ 2503).

Form 1120-S is due on or before the 15th day of the third month following the close of the tax year (March 15th for a calendar-year S corporation) (Code Sec. 6072(b); Reg. § 1.6072-2(a)). An S corporation may obtain an automatic six-month extension of time to file its return by filing Form 7004 on or before the due date of its Form 1120-S (Reg. § 1.6081-3(a)).

The due date for filing any federal income tax return, including Form 1120-S, otherwise due on or after April 1, 2020, and before July 15, 2020, is automatically extended to July 15, 2020, in response to the COVID-19 (coronavirus) crisis (Notice 2020-23, amplifying Notice 2020-18). The extension is automatic and an S corporation does not need to file Form 7004 or call the IRS to receive it. Penalties and interest for failure to file a return or pay taxes as a result of the extension will not accrue until July 16, 2020. An S corporation that needs more time to file its return after July 15, 2020, may request an additional extension by filing Form 7004 by July 15, 2020, but the extension may not go beyond the original statutory or regulatory extension date (for example, November 15, 2020 for a fiscal year S corporation with a return normally due date of May 15, 2020).

An S corporation must provide to each shareholder a copy of the information shown on Schedule K-1 (Form 1120-S). The information must be provided on or before the day the corporation files Form 1120-S (Code Sec. 6037(b)).

An S corporation that fails to timely file any required return may be subject to penalties (¶ 353).

353. Failure to File Penalties for S Corporations. An S corporation that fails to timely file Form 1120-S (¶ 351) (or files an incomplete return) is liable for a penalty on a per shareholder, per month basis for a maximum of twelve months, unless reasonable cause is shown (Code Sec. 6699). The penalty is adjusted annually for inflation, and is $200 for returns required to be filed in 2019 ($205 for 2020) (Rev. Proc. 2017-58; Rev. Proc. 2018-57). An S corporation may not contest the penalty assessment in the Tax Court but can pay the entire penalty and then sue for a refund. An S corporation may also be subject to penalties for failure to furnish Schedules K-1 (Form 1120-S) to its shareholders (¶ 2823) (Code Sec. 6722).

355. Tax Year of S Corporation. The tax year of an S corporation must be a permitted year. Permitted years include the calendar year, a tax year elected under Code Sec. 444 (¶ 1501), a 52-53 week tax year ending with reference to the calendar year or a tax year elected under Code Sec. 444, or any other tax year for which the corporation establishes a business purpose to the satisfaction of the IRS (Reg. § 1.1378-1(a)). The procedures for an S corporation to establish a business purpose are contained in Rev. Proc. 2006-46.

An S corporation may elect to have a tax year other than its required tax year. Generally, this election may be made only if the deferral period of the tax year elected is not longer than three months. The S corporation makes this election by filing Form 8716 (¶ 1501). If such an election is made, the S corporation may be required to make certain tax payments.

Chapter 4
PARTNERSHIPS

Choice of Entity

See CCH® AnswerConnect: *Choice of Entity* for more information on this topic.

401. Partnership Defined. A partnership includes a syndicate, group, pool, joint venture, or other unincorporated organization that carries on any business, financial operation, or venture, and that is not a trust, estate, or corporation within the meaning of the Code (Code Sec. 761). A noncorporate entity with at least two members can be classified under the check-the-box rules (¶ 402A) either as a partnership or as an association taxable as a corporation. A noncorporate entity with one member can be taxed either as a corporation or as a sole proprietorship (Reg. § 301.7701-3).

401A. Limited Partnerships. A limited partnership is a partnership (¶ 401) that has one or more general partners and one or more limited partners. Limited partnerships are formed under the limited partnership laws of each state. Unlike general partnerships in which all the partners are responsible for partnership liabilities, limited partners are not responsible for partnership liabilities beyond the amount of their investments. In addition, under state law, limited partners cannot participate in partnership management.

401B. Limited Liability Partnerships. Limited liability partnerships (LLPs) are partnerships (¶ 401) that are generally used by professionals such as accountants, attorneys, and doctors. An LLP is a general partnership in which each individual partner remains liable for his or her own liabilities as well as the liabilities arising out of the wrongful acts or omissions of those over whom the partner has supervisory duties. For this reason, they are sometimes used for large professional partnerships with hundreds of partners scattered over the country or even on different continents.

Each state and the District of Columbia have LLP-enabling legislation. Some states provide members of LLPs only limited protection from partnership liabilities, such as protection that is limited to malpractice claims against other partners. Other states offer full protection from liabilities, including the partnership's contractual liabilities. These are called "full shield" states.

As a practical matter, LLPs are most often used to give liability protection to partners in an existing partnership. The conversion of an existing partnership to an LLP does not create a new partnership, as the IRS has ruled that the registration of a general partnership as a registered LLP does not cause a termination of the partnership (¶ 410) (Rev. Rul. 95-55). In such a case, the partnership must continue to use the same method of accounting used before its registration as an LLP. Each partner's total percentage interest in the partnership's profits, losses, and capital remains the same after the registration.

¶401

Limited Liability Limited Partnerships. Some states have passed legislation allowing limited liability limited partnerships (LLLPs). These entities operate like a traditional limited partnership, but the general partner also has the limited personal liability of a partner in a limited liability partnership.

402. Exclusion from Partnership Provisions. In two situations, an entity that would otherwise be considered a partnership (¶ 401) may elect to not be treated as a partnership or not have all or part of the partnership rules under Subchapter K of the Code apply. One situation is where the income of the partners can be adequately determined without partnership-level computation. The second situation is in the case of certain partnerships that consist solely of a married couple.

Unincorporated organizations may elect not to be taxed as partnerships if they are used either for investment purposes only or for the joint production, extraction, or use—but not the sale—of property under an operating agreement (Code Sec. 761(a)). The exclusion also can be used by securities dealers for a short period for the purpose of underwriting, selling, or distributing a particular issue of securities. However, the members of an unincorporated organization can elect the exclusion only if the members' incomes can be determined without first computing partnership taxable income.

An unincorporated organization may choose to be completely or only partially excluded from the partnership provisions. However, the IRS does not allow an organization making the partial election to be excluded from the tax-year conformity rules (¶ 416) or from the limitations on the allowance of losses (¶ 425) (Rev. Rul. 57-215).

Qualified Joint Ventures. A trade or business co-owned by a married couple who file a joint return may elect to be taxed as a qualified joint venture instead of a partnership for federal tax purposes (Code Sec. 761(f)). A qualified joint venture is a joint venture involving the conduct of a trade or business if: (1) the only members of the joint venture are a married couple, (2) both spouses materially participate in the trade or business, and (3) both spouses elect to have the qualified joint venture provision apply. The IRS takes the position that qualified joint ventures include only businesses that are owned and operated by spouses as co-owners, and do not include businesses that are run as a state-law entity, such as a limited liability company (IRS Pub. 1635).

All items of income, gain, loss, deduction, and credit from a qualified joint venture are divided between the spouses in accordance with their respective interests in the venture. Each spouse takes into account his or her respective share of these items as a sole proprietor. Each spouse should account for his or her respective share on a separate Schedule C (Form 1040) or Schedule F (Form 1040). Each spouse may also need to file Schedule SE (Form 1040) for self-employment tax purposes.

402A. Check-the-Box Regulations. Any business entity not required to be treated as a corporation for federal tax purposes may choose its own classification (Reg. § 301.7701-3). An entity with two or more members can be classified either as a partnership or as an association taxed as a corporation. An entity with only one member can choose to be taxed as a corporation or it can be disregarded as an entity separate from its owner. An entity uses Form 8832 to elect how it will be classified for federal tax purposes.

Domestic entities with two or more members that do not file an election have a default classification of partnership. A single-member limited liability company (SMLLC) cannot elect partnership status because a partnership, by definition, has two or more partners (¶ 401). A domestic entity with one member that does not elect to be taxed as a corporation is considered a disregarded entity; it is ignored and the taxpayer is treated as a sole proprietorship. Thus, a domestic LLC will be taxed as a partnership or disregarded entity unless it files an election to be taxed as a corporation. An election on Form 8832 not to be taxed as a partnership applies to all Code provisions and is different from the election under Code Sec. 761, which removes an entity from some or all parts of Subchapter K of the Code (¶ 402).

Foreign Business Entities. The check-the-box rules apply somewhat differently to foreign business organizations. Entities listed in Reg. § 301.7701-2(b)(8) are considered

¶402A

corporations and are not eligible to be partnerships under the check-the-box rules. Any other foreign entity may be taxed as either a corporation or partnership (or a disregarded entity if it has one owner). A foreign business entity where all owners have limited liability will generally be treated as a corporation unless it elects to be taxed as a partnership. A foreign business entity where one or more owners has unlimited liability will generally be taxed as a partnership unless it elects to be taxed as a corporation. Thus, the foreign equivalent of an LLC (such as a German *GmbH*), in which all members have limited liability, will be taxed as a corporation unless it elects to be taxed as a partnership. The default classification for foreign and domestic entities existing before January 1, 1997, is the classification the entity claimed immediately prior to that date.

Note that the term "limited liability" is not precisely defined by the regulations, and whether the IRS would consider a given foreign law as providing limited liability for all members of an entity may be uncertain. It will usually be easier and safer for practitioners to file an election under the check-the-box rules for a foreign entity than to determine what its default classification would be.

402B. Limited Liability Companies. A state-registered limited liability company (LLC) can be taxed as a partnership for federal income tax purposes. However, its members, like corporate shareholders, are not personally liable for the entity's debts or liabilities. Under the check-the-box rules (¶ 402A), an LLC can choose partnership status to avoid taxation at the entity level as an association taxed as a corporation.

Unlike limited partners, LLC members may participate in management without risking personal liability for company debts. In addition, no limitations are placed on the number of owners of LLCs taxed as partnerships. Contrast this to S corporations, which have a maximum number of shareholders (¶ 303). There is also no limitation on the different types of owners of LLCs. S corporations may generally only have U.S. resident individuals or certain types of trusts as shareholders. Additional advantages of LLCs over S corporations include the ability to make disproportionate allocations and distributions (Code Sec. 704) and to distribute appreciated property to members without the recognition of gain (Code Sec. 731(b)). Members may also exchange appreciated property for membership interests without the recognition of gain or loss (Code Sec. 721).

Conversion from Partnership to LLC. A conversion of a partnership into an LLC that is taxed as a partnership for federal income tax purposes is treated as a nontaxable partnership-to-partnership conversion (Rev. Rul. 95-37). The conversion is treated as a contribution of assets to the new partnership (¶ 443) and does not result in gain or loss to the partners. The tax results are the same whether the LLC is formed in the same state as the former partnership or a different state. Upon a conversion, the tax year of the converting partnership does not close with respect to any of the partners, and the resulting LLC does not need to obtain a new taxpayer identification number.

Conversion from C Corporation to LLC. The conversion of an existing C corporation into an LLC taxed as a partnership is generally treated as a liquidation of the corporation and thus a taxable event for both the corporation and the shareholders (Code Sec. 7701; LTR 9701029). The possible tax hit diminishes the attractiveness of existing corporate entities converting to LLCs. This is especially true if the corporation holds appreciated property. Only a corporation with little or no net worth and shareholders with bases exceeding the amount of any distribution can escape this tax result. The conversion can be accomplished in one of two ways: (1) the assets of the corporation can be contributed to the LLC in return for membership interests, which are then distributed to the shareholders in liquidation of the corporation; or (2) the corporation can distribute its assets in complete liquidation, and the shareholders can then contribute their undivided interests in the assets to the LLC in exchange for membership interests.

Conversion from S Corporation to LLC. For an S corporation to convert to an LLC taxed as a partnership, it must undergo the same process as a C corporation discussed above. However, unlike a C corporation, when an S corporation distributes appreciated assets to its shareholders in exchange for their stock, there is no double tax. Because the S corporation is a flow-through entity, the gain incurred at the corporate level passes

¶402B

through to the shareholders and is generally included in income on the shareholder's tax return.

Any gain recognized by the shareholder as a result of the gain attributable to the liquidating distribution increases the shareholder's stock basis. The shareholder's increased basis then reduces the amount of gain recognized, or increases the amount of loss recognized. Thus, with the exception of the built-in gains tax (¶ 337), there is a single level of taxation. Although, with an S corporation, there is usually only this one level of taxation, rather than the two levels of taxation for the C corporation, this single level of current taxation may still be enough to dissuade an S corporation from converting to an LLC.

Series LLCs. Several states permit the creation of separate series within an LLC. The debts and other liabilities of each series are enforceable only against that series. Each series is recognized as a distinct entity for state law purposes and each series can have its own separate business purposes. A series can be terminated without affecting the other series of the LLC. Under proposed regulations, effective when finalized, each series of a series organization (such as a series LLC) would be treated for federal tax purposes as an entity formed under local law, regardless of whether local law actually treats the series as a separate entity (Prop. Reg. § 301.7701-1(a)(5)).

Publicly Traded Partnerships

403. Publicly Traded Partnerships. A publicly traded partnership (PTP) is a partnership with interests traded on an established securities market or readily tradable on a secondary market (or substantial equivalent), including master limited partnerships. A PTP is taxed as a corporation unless 90 percent or more of its gross income is derived from qualifying passive income sources—interest, dividends, rents from real property, gain from the disposition of real property, mining and natural resource income, and gain from the disposition of capital assets or section 1231 property held for the production of such income (Code Sec. 7704).

A partnership that was publicly traded on December 17, 1987, continues to be treated as a partnership rather than a corporation if it meets certain conditions. Specifically, a grandfather rule exempts electing 1987 partnerships from corporate treatment if: the partnership existed as a PTP or was treated as having existed as a PTP on December 17, 1987; elected to continue its partnership status; and does not add a substantial new line of business (Reg. § 1.7704-2). A grandfathered electing 1987 partnership must pay an annual 3.5-percent tax on gross income from the conduct of an active business.

Partnership-Level Issues

See CCH® AnswerConnect: *Partnerships* for more information on this topic.

404. Partners, Not Partnership, Subject to Tax. A partnership generally does not pay federal income tax. Instead, items of partnership income, gain, loss, deduction, and credit flow through to the partners who are taxed on their distributive shares of partnership taxable income. Thus, a partnership is a tax-reporting entity that must file an annual partnership return (¶ 406). In determining federal income tax, a partner must take into account his or her distributive share of partnership income or loss for the year, as well as his or her distributive share of certain separately stated items (¶ 431) of partnership income, gain, loss, deduction, or credit. A partner's distributive share of partnership items is includible on his or her individual income tax return (or corporate income tax return for corporate partners) for his or her tax year in which the partnership tax year ends (Code Sec. 706(a)).

A partner is generally not taxed on distributions of cash, marketable securities, and property received from the partnership, except to the extent that any money and marketable securities distributed exceeds the partner's adjusted basis in his or her partnership interest immediately before the distribution (¶ 453). Taxable gain can also result from distributions of property that were contributed to a partnership with a built-in gain (where property has a fair market value in excess of its adjusted basis) and from property distributions that are characterized as sales and exchanges (¶ 432).

A 3.8-percent net investment income (NII) tax applies to individuals, estates, and trusts, but not to partnerships (¶ 117) (Code Sec. 1411). Income from trades or businesses conducted by partnerships is not considered net investment income. Income from a trade or business that is a passive activity with respect to the partner is included in the partner's net investment income. Thus, the partner's distributive share of income earned by a partnership that would otherwise be net investment income in the hands of the partner is considered net investment income to the partner.

406. Partnership Return (Form 1065). A partnership is generally required to file Form 1065 for each partnership tax year to report the income, gains, losses, deductions, credits, etc., from the operation of the partnership (Code Sec. 6031(a); Reg. § 1.6031(a)-1). This includes a foreign partnership unless it has no income effectively connected with a U.S. trade or business and no U.S. partners at any time during the partnership's tax year.

Form 1065 is generally due on or before the 15th day of the *third* month following the close of the tax year (March 15 for a calendar-year partnership) (Code Sec. 6072(b); Reg. § 1.6031(a)-1(e)(2)). IRS regulations may require a partnership to file Form 1065 electronically if the partnership files a certain number of returns during the calendar year (¶ 2503). However, a partnership with more than 100 partners is always required to file its return electronically.

The return may be signed by any one of the partners or, in the case of a limited liability company (LLC), any one of the members (Code Sec. 6063; Instructions to Form 1065). Form 7004 is used by a partnership to apply for an automatic *six-month* filing extension of Form 1065 (Reg. § 1.6081-2).

A partnership that fails to timely file Form 1065 or files an incomplete return for the tax year is liable for a penalty of $205 for returns required to be filed in 2020 ($210 for returns required to be filed in 2021), per month or fraction of a month up to a maximum of 12 months (Code Sec. 6698; Rev. Proc. 2018-57; Rev. Proc. 2019-44). The penalty amount is multiplied by the total number of partners in the partnership during any part of the tax year for which the return is due. No penalty will be imposed if the failure is due to a reasonable cause and not willful neglect. The penalty is waived for filing Schedule K-1 with the partnership return without reporting negative tax basis capital account information for a tax year beginning in 2018 (Notice 2019-20). Certain domestic partnerships with 10 or fewer partners do not have to pay the penalty if all partners have fully reported their distributive shares on timely filed income tax returns (Rev. Proc. 84-35).

The due date for filing any federal income tax return, including Form 1065, otherwise due on or after April 1, 2020, and before July 15, 2020, is automatically extended to July 15, 2020, in response to the COVID-19 (coronavirus) crisis (Notice 2020-23, amplifying Notice 2020-18). The extension is automatic and a partnership does not need to file Form 7004 or call the IRS to receive it. Penalties and interest for failure to file a return or pay taxes as a result of the extension will not accrue until July 16, 2020. A partnership that needs more time to file its return after July 15, 2020, may request an additional extension by filing Form 7004 by July 15, 2020, but the extension may not go beyond the original statutory or regulatory extension date (for example, November 15, 2020, for a fiscal year partnership with a normal return due date of May 15).

Schedule K-1s. A partnership required to file Form 1065 for the tax year generally must furnish each partner with a Schedule K-1 (Form 1065) on or before the due date for Form 1065 (Code Sec. 6031(b); Temp. Reg. § 1.6031(b)-1T(a); Rev. Proc. 2012-17). Schedule K-1 can be provided in an electronic format to partners, but the partnership must first obtain their consent.

The Schedule K-1 reports to each partner its distributive share of partnership income, gain, loss, deduction, or credit. It must also report any additional information necessary to enable the partner to determine the correct income tax treatment of a partnership item. For partnership tax years beginning in 2019, the partnership must report each partner's capital account using any available method, including tax basis, Code Sec. 704(b) book, or GAAP. It must also report negative tax basis capital accounts on a partner-by-partner basis. The partnership must include a statement identifying the method it used to report a partner's capital account. For partnership tax years beginning *after* 2019, the partnership must report partners' shares of partnership capital on the tax basis method (Notice 2019-66).

The partnership may be subject to penalties for failure to furnish Schedule K-1 to its partners (¶ 2823). The penalty is waived if incurred as a result of failing to report negative tax basis capital account information for a tax year beginning in 2018 (Notice 2019-20).

Effective for returns filed for partnership tax years beginning after December 31, 2017, Schedule K-1s generally may not be amended by the partnership after the due date of Form 1065 unless the partnership elects to apply the post-2017 audit adjustment rules at the partner level. However, a special allowance for the issue of amended Schedules K-1 to benefit from the retroactive provisions of the Coronavirus Aid, Response, and Economic Stability Act (P.L. 116-136) is available. (¶ 413).

410. Changes in Ownership Interests of Partnerships. The tax year of a partnership closes with respect to a partner whose entire interest in the partnership ends, whether by a sale of the entire interest or otherwise (Code Sec. 706(c)(2)(A)). The sale of a portion of a partnership interest does not result in the closing of the partnership's tax year with respect to the selling partner.

In the case of a sale, exchange, gift, or liquidation of a partner's entire interest in a partnership, the partnership "closes the books" as to that partner (Code Sec. 706(c)(2)(A); Reg. § 1.706-1(c)(2)). In this case, the date of the disposition of the partnership interest is treated *as to the withdrawing partner* as if it is the close of the tax year. That partner's share of the partnership tax items is then determined as of that date, and the partner must include his or her share of partnership tax items in income for the tax year in which his or her partnership interest ends.

A partnership does not have to make an interim closing of the books. Instead, a retiring partner's share of income may, by agreement among the partners, be estimated by taking a pro rata portion of the amount of such items the partner would have included in income had he or she remained a partner until the end of the partnership tax year. The prorated amount may be based on the portion of the tax year that has elapsed prior to the sale, exchange, or liquidation, or may be determined under any other method that is reasonable.

Technical Terminations. For partnership tax years beginning before 2018, a partnership was considered to terminate if, within a 12-month period, there was a sale or exchange of 50 percent or more of the total interests in partnership capital and profits (Code Sec. 708(b)(1), prior to amendment by the Tax Cuts and Jobs Act (P.L. 115-97)).

Changes in Partnership Interests During Tax Year. If there is a change in any partner's interest in the partnership (for instance, because of the retirement of a partner, entry of a new partner, or simply a change in the allocations of partnership items), each remaining partner's distributive share must take into account the varying interests during the partnership tax year (Code Sec. 706(d); Reg. § § 1.706-1 and 1.706-4; Prop. Reg. § 1.706-4). The varying interests rule generally may be satisfied either by using an interim closing of the books or by prorating income, losses, etc., for the entire year. Special rules apply with respect to cash-basis items and tiered partnerships.

If there is a change in any partner's interest in the partnership, the distributive shares of certain cash-method items are determined by assigning the appropriate portion of each item to each day to which it is attributable, and then by allocating the daily portions among the partners in proportion to their interests in the partnership at the close of each day. For this purpose, cash-method items are interest, taxes, payments for services or for the use of property, and any other item specified in the regulations.

Cash-method items deductible or includible within the tax year but attributable to a time period before the beginning of the tax year (for example, payment during the tax year for services performed in the prior tax year) are assigned to the first day of the tax year. If persons to whom such items are allocable are no longer partners on the first day of the tax year, then their portion of the items must be capitalized by the partnership and allocated to the basis of partnership assets (¶ 459). Cash-method items attributable to periods following the close of the tax year (for example, properly deductible prepaid expenses) are assigned to the last day of the tax year.

In the case of changes in a partner's interest in an upper-tier partnership that has an ownership interest in a lower-tier partnership, each partner's distributive share of any items of the upper-tier partnership attributable to the lower-tier partnership is determined by: (1) assigning the appropriate portion of each of these items to the appropriate days of the upper-tier partnership's tax year on which the upper-tier partnership is a partner in the lower-tier partnership; and (2) allocating the assigned portion among the partners in proportion to their interests in the upper-tier partnership as of the close of each day.

413. Partnership Audits and Adjustments (Post-2017). Effective for returns filed for partnership tax years beginning after December 31, 2017, a single set of rules for auditing partnerships and their partners at the partnership level applies, replacing the TEFRA audit rules (¶ 415) and the rules for electing large partnerships (¶ 482). A partnership could elect to apply the post-2017 audit rules to returns filed for partnership tax years beginning after November 2, 2015, and before January 1, 2018 (Reg. § 301.9100-22).

Under the post-2017 audit rules, the IRS will examine any partnership-related item or amount that is relevant in determining the income tax liability of any person and any partners' distributive shares of the items for a particular year of the partnership (reviewed year). Any adjustments (including penalties) are taken into account by the partnership and not the individual partners in the year the audit or any judicial review is completed (adjustment year) (Code Secs. 6221 and 6241(2)).

Partnerships with 100 or fewer qualifying partners for whom a Schedule K-1 (Form 1065) is required to be provided (including each statement S corporation partners must furnish to shareholders) may opt out of these rules and be audited under the rules applicable to individuals. The election to opt out is made on a timely filed return (including extensions) for the tax year to which the election applies, and is revocable only with the consent of the IRS. The election is made by the partnership, and is generally binding on all partners, but does not bind any partnership in which the electing partnership is a partner (Reg. § 301.6221(b)-1).

A partner must generally treat on its income tax return any partnership-related item in a manner consistent with the treatment of that item on the partnership return (Code Sec. 6222; Reg. § 301.6222-1). Any underpayment of tax attributable to failure to meet the consistency requirement is treated as if the underpayment were due to a mathematical or clerical error. An additional tax will not be assessed for a failure to meet the consistency requirement if certain notification requirements are met. However, accuracy-related and fraud penalties may apply if the partner disregards the requirement.

A partnership must designate a person with substantial presence in the United States as the partnership representative (replacing the concept of tax-matter partner under the TEFRA rules) (Code Sec. 6223; Reg. § § 301.6223-1 and 301.6223-2). A partnership may designate itself as its own partnership representative, or may designate a disregarded entity. In either case, a representative that is an entity must have substantial presence in the United States and also appoint a designated individual that has substantial presence in the United States to act on the entity's behalf as partnership representative. The IRS may select a representative if none is selected by the partnership. The partnership representative has the sole authority to act on behalf of the partnership for purposes of the partnership audit rules and all partners are bound by the representative's actions.

Partnership Adjustments. If the IRS adjusts any partnership-related item relevant to determining the tax liability of any person (regardless of whether it appears on the partnership's return), the partnership must pay an imputed underpayment in the adjustment year based on the highest rate of tax in effect for the reviewed year (Code Sec. 6225; Reg. § 301.6225-1). The IRS may modify the imputed underpayment in certain situations (for example, where a partner files an amended return or is a tax-exempt entity). No deduction is permitted for the imputed underpayment (Code Sec. 6241(4)). If a partnership ceases to exist before a partnership adjustment takes effect, the adjustment is taken into account by the former partners under IRS regulations (Code Sec. 6241(7)).

As an alternative to paying an imputed underpayment, a partnership may elect within 45 days of the date of the notice of final partnership adjustment (FPA) to apply any adjustments at the partner level rather than at the partnership level. If the "push-out" election is made, then no assessment, levy, or collection proceeding will be made against the partnership for the imputed underpayment (Code Sec. 6226; Reg. § 301.6226-1). In a push-out election, the partnership must furnish to each partner for the reviewed year an adjusted Schedule K-1 indicating the partner's share of any partnership adjustment associated with the imputed underpayment to which the election relates (Reg. § 301.6226-2). Penalties and additions to tax arising due to the adjustment continue to be determined at the partnership level, but interest on the imputed underpayment passed through to a partner is computed at the partner level (Code Sec. 6233). Special rules regarding the application of the election, reporting, and the determination of interest on imputed underpayments apply to partners that are partnerships or S corporations (i.e., tiered structures).

As under the pre-2018 audit rules, a partnership may file an administrative adjustment request (AAR) for one or more partnership-related items for the tax year (Code Sec. 6227; Reg. § 301.6227-1). Any administrative adjustment is taken into account in the year the request is made by the partnership, or in the year the request is made by the partnership and partners if the election not to apply the adjustment at the partnership level is made.

A partnership operating under the post-2017 rules does not have to file an AAR to benefit from the provisions of the Coronavirus Aid, Response, and Economic Stability Act (P.L. 116-136) applied retroactively for the 2018 and 2019 tax years, such as the allowance of bonus depreciation for qualified improvement property (¶ 1237), or the delayed application of the limitations on excess business losses (¶ 1190) or the deduction of business interest (¶ 937) (Rev. Proc. 2020-23). Partnerships that have already filed a Form 1065 and Schedule K-1 for 2018 or 2019 prior to April 8, 2020, can instead file an amended Form 1065 for 2018 or 2019 and furnish amended Schedules K-1 to partners. In order to qualify for the relief, the Form 1065 must have the "Amended Return" box checked and have "FILED PURSUANT TO REV PROC 2020-23" at the top of the amended return, and amended Schedules K-1 must have a statement attached with the same notation at the top. Partnerships under examination for 2018 or 2019 that wish to take advantage of this relief must provide notice and a copy of the amended return to the revenue agent coordinating the examination prior to or contemporaneously with the filing of the amended Form 1065. Partnerships that already filed an AAR for 2018 or 2019 should use prepare the amended Form 1065 using items as adjusted by the AAR, and not the items as reported in the original return.

Administrative Procedures. The IRS is required to provide to the partnership and partnership representative notice of proceedings and adjustments (Code Sec. 6231). Any imputed underpayment with respect to any partnership adjustment is treated as if it were a tax imposed for assessment and collection purposes, subject to certain restrictions. Any failure to pay an imputed underpayment within 10 days of notice and demand results in interest at five percentage points above the federal short-term rate and the possible assessment on each partner of a tax equal to the partner's share of the underpayment amount (including penalties and interest) (Code Sec. 6232). Within 90 days after the date on which a notice of final partnership adjustment is mailed, the partnership may petition for readjustment with the proper court (Code Secs. 6234 and 6241(5)). The statute of limitations for making adjustments for any partnership tax year is generally three years, but may be extended if there is a modification of an imputed underpayment or a notice of proposed partnership adjustment issued by the IRS (Code Sec. 6235).

415. Partnership Audits and Adjustments (Pre-2018). Effective for returns filed for partnership tax years beginning before January 1, 2018, the determination of the tax treatment of partnership items is generally made at the partnership level in a single administrative partnership proceeding. The Tax Equity and Fiscal Responsibility Act of 1982 (P.L. 97-248) provides rules (TEFRA audit rules) governing proceedings that must be conducted at the partnership level for the assessment and collection of tax deficiencies or for tax refunds arising out of the partners' distributive shares of partnership items (Code Secs. 6221—6233, prior to amendment by the Bipartisan Budget Act of 2015 (P.L. 114-74)). See also ¶ 482 for special rules that applied to electing large partnerships with 100 or more partners.

The TEFRA audit rules, as well as the electing large partnership rules, are repealed for returns filed for partnership tax years beginning after December 31, 2017 (Act Sec. 1101 of P.L. 114-74). In their place, a single set of rules applies for partnership audits and adjustments at the partnership level. A partnership could elect to apply the new audit rules to returns filed for partnership tax years beginning after November 2, 2015. See ¶ 413 for the post-2017 partnership audit rules.

Under the pre-2018 TEFRA audit rules, notice of the beginning of administrative proceedings and the resulting final partnership administrative adjustment (FPAA) must be given to all partners whose names and addresses are furnished to the IRS, except those with less than a one-percent interest in partnerships that have more than 100 partners (Code Sec. 6223, prior to amendment by P.L. 114-74). A group of partners having an aggregate profits interest of five percent or more may request notice to be mailed to a designated partner.

Each partnership should have a tax matters partner (TMP) who receives notice on behalf of small partners not entitled to notice and who keeps all of the partners informed of all administrative and judicial proceedings at the partnership level (Code Sec. 6231, prior to amendment by P.L. 114-74). The TMP is either the general partner designated as such by the partnership or, in the absence of a designation, the general partner with the largest interest in partnership profits for the relevant tax year. Settlement agreements may be entered into between the TMP and the IRS that bind the parties to the agreement, and may extend to other partners who request to enter into consistent settlement agreements (Code Sec. 6224, prior to amendment by P.L. 114-74).

Consistency Requirement. Each partner is required to treat partnership items on his or her return in a manner consistent with the treatment of such items on the partnership return (Code Sec. 6222, prior to amendment by P.L. 114-74). A partner may be penalized for intentionally disregarding this requirement. The consistency requirement may be waived if the partner files Form 8082 identifying the inconsistency or shows that it resulted from an incorrect schedule furnished by the partnership.

The IRS may apply entity-level audit procedures when it appears from the return that such procedures should apply. The IRS's determination will stand even if it later proves to be erroneous (Code Sec. 6231(g), prior to amendment by P.L. 114-74).

Innocent Spouse Relief. Innocent spouse relief is available with respect to partnership-level proceedings (Code Sec. 6230, prior to amendment by P.L. 114-74). If the spouse of a partner in a partnership subject to the TEFRA audit rules asserts that the innocent spouse rules apply with respect to a liability attributable to any adjustment to a partnership item, the spouse may file with the IRS a request for an abatement of the assessment. The spouse must file the request within 60 days after the notice of a computational adjustment has been mailed by the IRS. Upon receipt of the request, the IRS must abate the assessment. If the IRS chooses to reassess the abated tax, it then has 60 days after the date of the abatement in which to make any reassessment. In such a scenario, the regular deficiency procedures apply.

If the taxpayer claiming innocent spouse relief files a Tax Court petition under Code Sec. 6213 with respect to the request for abatement, the Tax Court can determine only whether the innocent spouse requirements have in fact been satisfied. For purposes of this determination, the treatment of the TEFRA partnership items under the settlement, the FPAA, or the court decision (whichever is appropriate) that gave rise to the liability in question is conclusive.

Small Partnership Exception. The TEFRA audit rules do not apply to partnerships with 10 or fewer partners if each partner is an individual U.S. resident, C corporation, or estate, and each partner's share of any partnership item is the same as his or her distributive share of every other partnership item. However, these small partnerships may elect to have the TEFRA audit rules apply using Form 8893 (Code Sec. 6231(a)(1)(B), prior to amendment by P.L. 114-74). The partnership also can allocate items without jeopardizing its exemption from the TEFRA audit rules. Once a small partnership elects to have the TEFRA rules apply, the election cannot be revoked without IRS consent.

416. Partnership's Required Tax Year. A partnership generally cannot have a tax year other than its majority-interest tax year (Code Sec. 706(b); Reg. § 1.706-1). This is the tax year that, on each testing day, constitutes the tax year of one or more partners having an aggregate interest in partnership profits and capital of more than 50 percent. The testing day is the first day of the partnership's tax year (determined without regard to the majority-interest rule). A partnership that changes to a majority-interest tax year is generally not required to change to another tax year for the two tax years following the year of change.

If the partnership has no majority-interest tax year, then its tax year must be the same as the tax year of all of the partnership's principal partners (partners who individually own five percent or more of the partnership's profits or capital). Partnerships that are unable to determine a tax year under either of the foregoing methods must adopt a tax year that results in the least aggregate deferral of income to the partners. A partnership may avoid the tax year rules if it can establish a business purpose for selecting a different tax year.

Code Sec. 444 Election. Certain partnerships are permitted to make an election to have a tax year other than the normally required tax year (Code Sec. 444). For any tax year for which an election is made, a partnership generally must make a required payment that is intended to represent the tax on the income deferred through the use of a tax year other than a required year (¶ 1501) (Code Sec. 7519; Temp. Reg. § 1.7519-2T(a)(4)(ii)).

417. Partnership Taxable Income. A partnership is generally not subject to tax (¶ 404). Instead, the partnership's taxable income passes through to its partners (Code Sec. 701). Each partner generally must account for his or her distributive share of partnership taxable income in computing income tax. The partnership reports to each partner his or her share of partnership tax items on Schedule K-1 (Form 1065).

A partner's basis in his or her partnership interest is increased by his or her distributive share of partnership taxable income, while the partner's basis generally decreases by the amount distributed to the partner by the partnership. Thus, if a partnership distributes all of its taxable income by the end of the partnership tax year, the basis of each partner's interest in the partnership does not change (Code Secs. 705 and 731(a)).

The taxable income of a partnership is computed in the same manner as that of an individual except that the following deductions and carryovers are not allowed to a partnership:

- the deduction for personal exemptions (not available for tax years after 2017 and before 2026) (¶ 133);

- the deduction for foreign taxes (note that the taxes are allocated to the partners as separately stated items);

- the net operating loss deduction (which is determined at the partner level, not the partnership level) (¶ 1145);

- the deduction for charitable contributions (which is allocated to the partners as a separately stated item) (¶ 1058);

¶417

- individuals' itemized deductions (medical expenses, etc. (¶ 1014));
- the capital loss carryover (which is determined at the partner level, not the partnership level) (¶ 1754);
- the domestic production activities deduction for tax years beginning before 2018 (¶ 431A); and
- depletion deductions with respect to oil and gas wells (which are allocated to the partners as separately stated items) (¶ 1380) (Code Sec. 703(a); Reg. § 1.703-1).

Certain items of gain, loss, etc. also must be separately stated (¶ 431).

418. Partnership Anti-Abuse Regulations. Regulations give the IRS power to recast transactions that attempt to use the partnership provisions for tax-avoidance purposes (Reg. § 1.701-2). Under the rules, a partnership must be *bona fide* and each partnership transaction must be entered into for a substantial business purpose. The form of each transaction must be respected under substance-over-form rules. In addition, the tax consequences to each partner of partnership operations and transactions must accurately reflect the partners' economic agreement and clearly reflect each partner's income. Whether there is a principal purpose of substantially reducing the present value of the partners' aggregate tax liability is determined at the partnership level.

In abusive situations, the IRS can treat a partnership as the aggregate of its partners, in whole or in part, to carry out the purpose of any Code provision or regulation. However, to the extent that a Code provision or regulation prescribes treatment of the partnership as an entity and the treatment and ultimate tax results are clearly contemplated by the provision, the IRS will not recast a transaction.

419. Elections by Partnerships. Most elections affecting the computation of income derived from a partnership must be made by the partnership. Thus, elections as to methods of accounting, methods of computing depreciation, the Code Sec. 179 expensing election, the election not to use the installment sales provision, the option to expense intangible drilling and development costs, and similar elections must be made by the partnership and must apply to all partners, insofar as partnership transactions are concerned (Reg. § 1.703-1(b)). In the case of an involuntary conversion of partnership property, the partnership must purchase replacement property and elect nonrecognition of gain treatment (Rev. Rul. 66-191).

Individual partners may make elections to: (1) use as a credit or as a deduction their distributive shares of foreign taxes of the partnership, (2) deduct or capitalize their shares of the partnership's mining exploration expenditures, and (3) reduce basis in connection with discharge of indebtedness under Code Sec. 108 (Code Sec. 703(b)).

421. Guaranteed Payments to Partners. Any fixed or guaranteed payments to partners for services or the use of capital made without regard to partnership income are treated as paid to a nonpartner for purposes of computing partnership gross income and business expense deductions (¶ 432). Thus, guaranteed payments are regarded as ordinary income to the recipient and deductible by the partnership if they are ordinary and necessary business expenses (¶ 901) (Code Sec. 707(c); Reg. § § 1.707-1(c) and 1.707-4). This rule applies only to the extent that the amounts paid are in fact guaranteed payments determined without regard to the income of the partnership. The partner must report the payments on his or her return for the tax year within, or with which ends, the partnership year in which the partnership deducted the payments as paid or accrued under its method of accounting.

> **Example 1:** In the AB partnership, Ann is the managing partner and is entitled to receive a fixed annual payment of $100,000 for her services, without regard to the income of the partnership. Her distributive share of partnership profit and loss is 10 percent. After deducting her guaranteed payment, the partnership has $300,000 ordinary income. Ann must include $130,000 ($100,000 guaranteed payment plus $30,000 distributive share) as ordinary income for her tax year within, or with which ends, the partnership tax year. If the partnership had shown a $100,000

loss after deduction of Ann's guaranteed payment, her guaranteed payment ($100,000) would be reported as income, and her $10,000 distributive share of the loss, subject to the limitations on partnership losses (¶ 425), would be taken into account on her individual tax return.

If a partner is entitled to a minimum payment and the percentage of profits is less than the minimum payment, the guaranteed payment is the difference between the minimum payment and the distributive share of the profits determined before the deduction of the minimum payment. Only the amount of the guaranteed payment may qualify as a deductible business expense of the partnership.

Example 2: The AB partnership agreement provides that Ann is to receive 30% of partnership income before taking into account any guaranteed payments, but not less than $100,000. The income of the partnership is $600,000, and Ann is entitled to $180,000 (30% of $600,000) as her distributive share. Because her distributive share exceeds the minimum amount that was guaranteed, no part of the $180,000 is a guaranteed payment. If the partnership had income of only $200,000, Ann's distributive share would have been $60,000 (30% of $200,000), and the remaining $40,000 payable to Ann would have been a guaranteed payment.

A partner who receives a guaranteed salary payment is not regarded as an employee of the partnership for the purpose of withholding of income or Social Security taxes, or for pension plans. The guaranteed salary is includible in self-employment income for the purpose of the self-employment tax along with the partner's share of ordinary income or loss of the partnership (Reg. § 1.707-1(c); Rev. Rul. 56-675).

Fringe Benefits. The value of fringe benefits (¶ 2085) provided to a partner for services rendered in the capacity as a partner is generally treated as a guaranteed payment (Code Sec. 162(l); Rev. Rul. 91-26). As such, the value of the benefit is generally deductible by the partnership as an ordinary and necessary business expense; and the value of the benefit is included in the partner's gross income unless specifically excluded under another Code provision. Thus, a payment of premiums by a partnership for a partner's health or accident insurance is generally deductible by the partnership and included in the partner's gross income. As an alternative, a partnership may choose to account for premiums paid for a partner's insurance by reducing that partner's distributions. In this case, the premiums are not deductible by the partnership and all partners' distributive shares are unaffected by payment of the premiums. A partner can deduct 100 percent of the cost of the health insurance premiums paid on his or her behalf.

Partnership Losses

See CCH® AnswerConnect: *Determination of Partner's Distributive Share* for more information on this topic.

425. Partnership Loss Limited to Partner's Basis. The amount of partnership loss (including capital loss) that a partner may recognize is limited to the amount of the adjusted basis (before reduction by the current year's loss) of the partner's interest in the partnership at the end of the partnership tax year in which the loss occurred. For tax years beginning after 2017, the partner's distributive share of foreign taxes paid and charitable contributions (except to the extent that the fair market value of contributed property exceeds its basis) is taken into account in determining the basis limitation (Code Sec. 704(d)(3); Reg. § 1.704-1(d)). Any disallowed loss is carried forward to, and may be deducted by the partner in, subsequent partnership tax years to the extent that his or her basis exceeds zero before deducting the loss. Techniques that have been used to increase a partner's basis so that he or she can deduct losses that otherwise would be unavailable include making additional contributions to the capital of the partnership (¶ 443) and increasing the partner's share of partnership liabilities (¶ 447). A partner's recognition of losses may be further limited to the amount the partner has at risk in partnership activities (¶ 426), and the amount of passive-activity income (¶ 427).

426. Partners and At-Risk Rules. A partners' deduction for partnership losses for any tax year is generally limited to the amount the partner has at risk in the partnership for the year (¶ 1155). Thus, the at-risk limits apply at the partner level, and not the partnership level (Code Sec. 465; Temp. Reg. § 1.469-2T(d)(6)). A partner is not at risk for any portion of a partnership liability for which he or she has no personal liability. The at-risk loss limitation rules are applied after taking into account the basis limitation for partners' losses (¶ 425), but before taking into account the limitations that apply to computing any passive activity loss for the year (¶ 427).

Real Estate Exception. The at-risk rules generally apply to the holding of property in the same manner as they apply to other activities (Code Sec. 465(b)(6)). An exception applies to the holding of real estate. A taxpayer is at risk with respect to qualified nonrecourse financing that is secured by the real property used in the activity of holding real estate. Thus, lending provided by any person actively and regularly engaged in the business of lending money is qualified nonrecourse financing. This generally includes banks, savings and loan associations, credit unions, insurance companies regulated under federal, state, or local law, or pension trusts.

Qualified nonrecourse financing includes a loan made by any federal, state, or local government or a governmental entity, or a loan that is guaranteed by any federal, state, or local government. Convertible debt cannot be treated as qualified nonrecourse financing. Qualified nonrecourse financing also can be provided by a related person (generally, family members, fiduciaries, and corporations, or partnerships in which a person has at least a 10-percent interest) if the financing from the related person is commercially reasonable and on substantially the same terms as loans involving unrelated persons.

427. Partnerships and Passive Activity Loss Rules. A partner's deduction for partnership losses for any tax year is generally limited by the passive activity rules (¶ 1169), which apply at the partner level to his or her share of any loss or credit attributable to a passive activity of the partnership (Code Sec. 469). The passive activity limits are applied to a partner only after taking into account the basis limitation for the partners' losses (¶ 425) and the at-risk limits (¶ 426), and before taking into account the limit on excess business losses for tax years beginning in 2021 through 2025 (¶ 1190).

A partnership may engage in both passive and nonpassive activities. For example, a partnership may engage in business that is a passive activity of its limited partners (who normally do not participate in the management of a limited partnership), and it may also have investment assets that produce portfolio income (not a passive activity). Thus, a partner who disposes of his or her interest in a partnership must allocate any gain or loss among the various activities of the partnership in order to determine the amount that is passive gain or loss and the amount that is nonpassive gain or loss. The allocation is generally made in accordance with the relative value of the partnership's assets.

To allow a partner to make these calculations, a partnership must report separately a partner's share of income, losses, and credits from each of its trade or business activities, rental real estate activities, and rental activities other than rental real estate. The separate activities must be reported on a statement attached to the Schedule K-1 (Form 1065) provided to the partner (Instructions to Form 1065). A partnership's portfolio income, which is excluded from passive income, must also be separately reported.

A passive activity of a partner generally is: (1) a trade or business activity in which the partner does not materially participate, or (2) any rental activity. Except as otherwise provided, an interest in an activity as a limited partner in a limited partnership is not one in which the partner materially participates (Temp. Reg. § 1.469-5T(e)). If a partnership reports amounts from more than one activity on a partner's Schedule K-1 and one or more of the activities is passive to the partner, the partnership must attach a statement detailing the income, losses, deductions, and credits from each passive activity, and identify the line of Schedule K-1 on which that amount is included.

427A. Net Operating Loss (NOL) Deduction of Partners. The benefit of the net operating loss deduction (¶ 1145) is not allowed to the partnership but is allowed to its partners (Reg. § 1.702-2). For purposes of determining net operating loss, each partner takes into account his or her distributive share of income, gain, loss, deduction, and credit of the partnership as if each item were realized directly from the source from which it was realized by the partnership, or incurred in the same manner as it was incurred by the partnership.

Partner's Distributive Share of Partnership Items

See CCH® AnswerConnect: *Partnership Income* and *Partnership Distributions* for more information on this topic.

428. Allocations of Partnership Items Under Partnership Agreement. A partner's distributive share of income, gain, loss, deduction, or credit is generally determined by the partnership agreement. Allocations of any partnership item must have substantial economic effect (Code Sec. 704(b); Reg. § 1.704-1(b)). If a partnership agreement does not provide for the allocation of partnership items or if partnership allocations lack substantial economic effect, the partner's distributive share is determined according to his or her interest in the partnership.

Economic Effect. Allocations have economic effect if they are consistent with the underlying economic arrangement of the partners. For example, a limited partner who has no risk under the partnership agreement other than his or her initial capital contribution ordinarily may not be allocated losses attributable to a partnership recourse liability to the extent such losses exceed the capital contribution. Recourse losses ordinarily must be allocated to the partners (usually the general partners) who bear the ultimate burden of discharging the partnership's liability. A partnership's nonrecourse deductions—those attributable to liabilities of the partnership for which no partner bears personal liability, such as a mortgage secured only by a building and the land on which it is located—are deemed to lack economic effect and must be allocated according to the partners' interests in the partnership (¶ 448).

Partnership allocations may be deemed to have substantial economic effect if the requirements of *optional* safe harbor provisions are met. Under the safe harbor, a partnership generally must maintain its "book" capital accounts as set out by Reg. § 1.704-1 and make tax allocations consistent with the capital accounts. A second safe harbor in Reg. § 1.704-2 applies to the allocation of nonrecourse deductions.

Substantiality. The economic effect of an allocation is generally considered substantial if there is a reasonable possibility that the allocation will substantially affect the dollar amounts to be received by the partners from the partnership, independent of tax consequences.

Contributed Property. Income, gain, loss, and deductions attributable to property contributed to a partnership by a partner must be allocated among the partners to take into account the variation between the property's fair market value and its basis to the partnership at the time of contribution (Code Sec. 704(c)). The partnership's basis in the contributed property at the time of contribution in exchange for a partnership interest is *carryover basis*—that is, the basis of the property in the hands of the contributing partner. Any built-in gain or loss with respect to the contributed property must be allocated to the contributing partner. A similar rule applies to contributions by cash-method partners of accounts payable and other accrued but unpaid items.

When allocating tax items to property contributed to a partnership, three reasonable allocation methods are permitted—the traditional method, the traditional method with curative allocations, and the remedial allocation method (Reg. § 1.704-3). If a U.S. person contributes certain property with built-in gain to a partnership that has a foreign partner related to the transferor, then gain will be recognized unless the partnership adopts the gain deferral method (GDM) with respect to the property (Code Sec. 721(c); Reg. § 1.721(c)-2 and 1.721(c)-3).

Special rules also prevent use of allocations to improperly shift the tax consequences associated with contributed property among partners in a partnership (Reg. § 1.704-3(a)(10)). Under the anti-abuse rule, an allocation method is not reasonable if the property contribution and the corresponding allocation of tax items regarding the property are made with a view to shifting the tax consequences of built-in gain or loss among the partners in a manner that substantially reduces the present value of the partners' aggregate tax liability (¶ 418). Also, the distribution of built-in gain or loss property to partners other than the contributing partner within seven years of its contribution to the partnership may result in the recognition of gain or loss to the contributing partner (¶ 453).

430. Disproportionate Partnership Distributions. Disproportionate distribution rules apply if an actual or constructive distribution to a partner changes his or her proportionate interest in a partnership's unrealized receivables or inventory. The purpose of these rules is to prevent conversion of ordinary income to capital gain on the distribution or a change in share of unrealized receivables or substantially appreciated inventory.

A disproportionate distribution is treated as a sale or exchange of the receivables or inventory items from the partnership to the partner (Code Sec. 751(b) and 751(f)). This results in ordinary income rather than capital gain. These rules cannot be avoided through the use of tiered partnerships. Sale or exchange treatment does not apply to a distribution of property that the distributee contributed to the partnership or to payments to a retiring partner or a successor in interest of a deceased partner.

Although the substantially appreciated inventory test was dropped for most appreciated inventory in the case of a sale or exchange of a partnership interest (¶ 434), it remains in effect for disproportionate distributions from a partnership to its partners. Inventory is considered to be substantially appreciated if its fair market value exceeds the partnership's basis in the property by 120 percent or more. The inventory need not appreciate in value after the partnership acquired it to satisfy the 120-percent test (Reg. § 1.751-1(d)(1)).

431. Separate Reporting of Partnership Items. Each partner of a partnership must account separately for his or her distributive share of the following partnership items on his or her tax return (Code Sec. 702; Reg. § 1.702-1):

- short-term capital gains and losses;

- long-term capital gains and losses;

- gains and losses from sales or exchanges of property used in a trade or business or subject to involuntary conversion (¶ 1747);

- charitable contributions (¶ 1061);

- dividends for which there is a dividends-received deduction (¶ 223);

- taxes paid or accrued to foreign countries and to U.S. possessions (¶ 2475);

- taxable income or loss, exclusive of items requiring separate computation; and

- other items required to be stated separately either by Reg. § 1.702-1 or because separate statement could affect the income tax liability of any partner, including:

— recovery of bad debts, prior taxes, and delinquency amounts;

— gains and losses from wagering transactions (¶ 785);

— soil and water conservation expenditures (¶ 982);

— deductible investment expenses (¶ 1085);

— medical and dental expenses (¶ 1015);

— alimony payments (¶ 771);

— amounts paid to cooperative housing corporations (¶ 1040);

— intangible drilling and development costs (¶ 989);

— alternative minimum tax adjustments and tax preference items (¶ 194 and ¶ 196);

— investment tax credit recapture (¶ 1465A);

— recapture of mining exploration expenditures (¶ 987);

— information necessary for partners to compute oil and gas depletion allowances (¶ 1380);

— cost of recovery property being currently expensed (¶ 1208);

— work opportunity tax credit (¶ 1465G);

— biofuel producer credit (¶ 1465I);

— net earnings from self-employment (¶ 2670);

— investment interest (¶ 1057);

— income or loss to the partnership on certain distributions of unrealized receivables and inventory items to a partner (¶ 453);

— any items subject to a special allocation under the partnership agreement (¶ 428);

— contributions (and the deductions for contributions) made on a partner's behalf to qualified retirement plans (¶ 2115 and ¶ 2117);

— income and expenses from domestic production activities for tax years beginning before 2018 (¶ 431A); and

— income, gain, and losses for purposes of the deduction for qualified business income (¶ 431B).

The need for a separate statement of various partnership items gives rise to the separate reporting of these items on Form 1065 and Schedule K-1.

Partnerships that regularly carry on a trade or business are required to furnish to tax-exempt partners a separate statement of items of unrelated business taxable income (Code Sec. 6031(d)).

431A. Domestic Production Activities by Partnerships. A partnership cannot claim the deduction for qualified domestic production activities, which is available for tax years beginning before 2018 (¶ 980A). Instead, the deduction is determined at the partner level (Code Sec. 199(d)(1), prior to repeal by the Tax Cuts and Jobs Act (P.L. 115-97); Reg. § 1.199-5(b)). Each partner generally computes its deduction separately on Form 8903 by aggregating its proportionate share of qualified production activity (QPA) items of the partnership (i.e., income, expenses) with its share of QPA items from other sources. The partner does not have to be directly engaged in the partnership's trade or business to claim the deduction on the basis of its share of QPA items.

A partner will not be treated as directly conducting the QPA of the partnership (and vice versa) with respect to property transferred between the parties (Reg. § 1.199-5(g)). For example, if a partner manufactures qualified production property within the United States and then contributes the property to the partnership, which subsequently sells, licenses, leases, or otherwise disposes of the property, then the income derived by the partnership will not qualify as domestic production gross receipts (DPGR). A limited exception is provided for certain qualifying oil and gas partnerships and expanded affiliated groups.

Allocation of Items. QPA items of a partnership are allocated to each partner like any other tax item (¶ 428). This includes special allocations of QPA items, subject to the rules of Reg. § 1.704-1(b), including the rules for determining substantial economic effect. A partner's distributive share of expenses allocable to the partnership's QPA must be taken into account even if the partnership has no taxable income. If a partner is unable to claim a loss or deduction for regular tax purposes (i.e., at-risk, passive loss, or basis limitations), then the loss or deduction cannot be taken into account in computing the Code Sec. 199 deduction. The amount of any loss or deduction is subject to proportionate reduction if it is only partially allowed for regular tax purposes. Also, a loss or deduction that is temporarily disallowed for regular tax purposes may be used in computing the Code Sec. 199 deduction in the tax year in which the loss or deduction is allowed for regular tax purposes.

Instead of taking into account its distributive share of each QPA item of the partnership, a partner may compute its deduction by combining its distributive share of the partnership's qualified production activities income (QPAI) and W-2 wages with its QPAI and W-2 wages from other sources. This option applies only if the partnership has elected to use the small business overall method for allocating costs, expenses, and other deductions to its DPGR (¶ 980G). A partner's share of QPAI from a partnership may be less than zero under this method.

Special rules apply to 20-percent partners of partnerships engaged in film or television production (Code Sec. 199(d)(1)(A)(iv), prior to repeal by P.L. 115-97).

Sale of Partnership Interest. Gain or loss recognized on the sale of a partnership interest is not be taken into account by a partner in computing its QPAI (Reg. § 1.199-5(f)). This is because the sale of the partnership interest does not reflect the realization of DPGR by the entity. However, if the taxpayer receives a distribution of unrealized receivables or partnership inventory for its entire partnership interest (Code Sec. 751 property (¶ 434 and ¶ 436)), then any gain or loss that would be attributable to the sale or other disposition of such assets which would give rise to QPAI may be taken into account by the partner.

W-2 Wage Limitation. A partner computes the W-2 wage limitation for the domestic production activities deduction by aggregating its share of W-2 wages from the partnership allocable to DPGR with its W-2 wages allocable to DPGR from other sources.

431B. Qualified Business Income Deduction for Partners. For tax years beginning after 2017, a partner may deduct up to 20 percent of certain domestic qualified business income (QBI) from a partnership for a tax year (¶ 980P) (Code Sec. 199A). The deduction is applied at the partner level. Each partner must take into account his or her allocable share of each qualified item of income, gain, deduction, and loss. Further, each partner is treated as having W-2 wages and unadjusted basis immediately after acquisition of qualified property for the tax year, in an amount equal to his or her allocable share of the partnership's W-2 wages and unadjusted basis for the tax year as determined in the regulations. The partner's share of W-2 wages is determined in the same manner as the partner's share of wage expenses. The partner's share of the unadjusted basis of qualified property is determined in the same manner as the partner's allocable share of depreciation.

432. Members' Dealings with Own Partnership. Transactions between a partnership and partner may be deemed to be between a partnership and a nonpartner under certain circumstances (Code Sec. 707(a)). This rule prevents the use of disguised payments to circumvent the requirement that a partnership capitalize certain expenses (such as syndication and organization expenses).

Disguised Sales or Payments for Services. A transaction is treated as if it occurred between a partnership and a nonpartner for income tax purposes if:

> • a partner performs services for a partnership or transfers property to a partnership;

> • there is a related direct or indirect allocation and distribution to the partner; and

> • the performance of the partner's service (or the partner's transfer of property) and the allocation and distribution, when viewed together, are properly characterized as a transaction that occurred between the partnership and the partner acting as a nonpartner (Code Sec. 707).

If this rule applies to a transaction, then the allocation and distribution made by the partnership to the partner is recharacterized as a payment for services or property. In this case, the payment must be capitalized where required or otherwise treated in a manner consistent with its recharacterization. The partners' shares of taxable income or loss must then be redetermined.

Whether a transfer constitutes a disguised sale depends on the facts and circumstances. However, contributions and distributions made within a two-year period are presumed to be a sale, while those transactions occurring more than two years apart are presumed not to be a sale (Reg. § 1.707-3(c) and (d)). Under proposed regulations, effective when finalized, the primary factor in determining whether a payment is a disguised payment for services is whether the payment is subject to significant entrepreneurial risk (Prop. Reg. § 1.707-2). Exceptions to the disguised sale rules are provided for guaranteed payments for capital, reasonable preferred returns, operating cash flow distributions, and reimbursements of preformation capital expenditures, subject to certain limitations. On or after October 5, 2016, a partner is permitted limited aggregation of property for purposes of applying the limitations for reimbursements of capital expenditures (Reg. § 1.707-4).

A "qualified liability" of a partner is a type of liability that meets certain requirements set forth in regulations, and includes certain liabilities that were not incurred in anticipation of a partner's transfer of property to the partnership (Reg. § 1.707-5(a)(6)(i)). If a transfer of property by a partner to a partnership is not treated as part of a disguised sale, any assumption of a qualified liability by a partnership in connection with the transfer is not treated as part of a sale (Reg. § 1.707-5(a)(5)(i)).

The transfer of a nonqualified liability from a partner to a partnership is treated as a transfer of consideration to the partner to the extent of the excess of the amount of the liability over the partner's share of that liability immediately after the transfer (Reg. § 1.707-5(a)). A partner's share of a partnership's recourse liability equals the partner's share of the liability under Code Sec. 752. A partner's share of a partnership's nonrecourse liability is determined by applying the same percentage used to determine the partner's share of the excess nonrecourse liability.

If a partner's transfer of property to a partnership is treated as a sale only because of the partnership's assumption of a *nonqualified* liability, the partnership's assumption of a *qualified* liability may escape being treated as consideration if the *nonqualified* liability is small enough. This means that the *nonqualified* liability must be the lesser of 10 percent of the total amount of all qualified liabilities the partnership assumes or $1 million.

Transactions Between Controlled Partnerships. Special rules also apply to controlled partnerships. No loss deduction is allowed from a sale or exchange of property (other than an interest in the partnership) between a partnership and a person whose interest in the partnership's capital *or* profits is more than 50 percent. A loss deduction is also not allowed if the sale or exchange is between two partnerships in which the same persons own more than 50 percent of the capital or profits interests (Code Sec. 707(b)). In either case, if one of the purchasers or transferees realizes gain on a later sale, the gain is taxable only to the extent it exceeds the amount of the disallowed loss attributable to the property sold. Gain recognized on transactions involving controlled partnerships is treated as ordinary income if the property sold or exchanged is not a capital asset in the hands of the transferee.

Code Sec. 267 disallows deductions for losses from the sale or exchange of property between related persons, including a partnership and a corporation controlled by the same persons (¶ 1717). This loss-denial rule does not apply to a transaction between a partnership and a partner, where the disguised sales rules apply instead. The rule does apply, however, to a transaction between a partnership and a person who, with respect to a partner, is a related person under Code Sec. 267(b) (Reg. § 1.267(b)-1(b)). In addition to the disallowance of losses, accrued interest and expense deductions are not deductible until paid if the amount giving rise to the deduction is owed to a related cash-method taxpayer. For purposes of this rule, a partnership and persons holding interests in the partnership (actually or constructively) or persons related (under Code Sec. 267(b) or 707(b)(1)) to actual or constructive partners are treated as related persons (¶ 905 and ¶ 1540B) (Code Sec. 267(e)(1)).

Sale and Purchase of Partnership Interest

See CCH® AnswerConnect: *Sale and Purchase of a Partnership Interest* and *Death and Retirement of a Partner* for more information on this topic.

434. Sale or Exchange of Partnership Interests. The sale or exchange of a partnership interest is generally treated as the sale of a single capital asset rather than a sale of each of the underlying partnership properties (Code Sec. 741). The amount of gain or loss is based on the partner's basis in the partnership interest and the amount realized on the sale (Code Sec. 721). Ordinary income or loss may be recognized under the constructive sale rules if the partner receives a disproportionate distribution of partnership unrealized receivables or inventory (¶ 430). In addition, the sale or exchange of a partnership interest is distinguishable from the liquidation or redemption of a partner's entire interest in a partnership (¶ 435). A three-year holding period applies to a taxpayer's net long-term capital gain from the sale or disposition of an "applicable partnership interest" (i.e., carried interest) for tax years beginning after 2017 (¶ 442).

Sale or Exchange by Foreign Persons. Gain or loss from the sale or exchange of a partnership interest by a nonresident alien or foreign corporation after November 27, 2017, is effectively connected with a U.S. trade or business (¶ 2429) to the extent the transferor would have effectively connected gain or loss had the partnership sold all of its assets at fair market value on the disposition date (Code Secs. 864(c)(8) and 1446(f); Proposed Reg. § 1.864(c)(8)-1; Notice 2018-29; Notice 2018-8). The transferee of the partnership interest must withhold 10 percent of the amount realized on a sale or exchange after December 31, 2017, unless the transferor certifies that it is not a nonresident alien or foreign corporation.

Abandonment of Partnership Interests. If a partner abandons or forfeits a partnership interest, a loss may be recognized equal to the partner's basis in the partnership interest. Thus, a partner with a zero basis in its partnership interest is not allowed an abandonment loss. If the partnership has liabilities, the abandoning partner is deemed to have received a distribution from the partnership when relieved of the liabilities. In that case, the partner's loss is the basis in the partnership interest less any liabilities of which the partner is relieved. If there are no partnership liabilities of which the partner is relieved, the abandoning partner has an ordinary loss because no sale or exchange has taken place (*B.P. Citron*, Dec. 47,513, 97 TC 200; *G.G. Gannon*, Dec. 18,304, 16 TC 1134). If there are partnership liabilities of which the abandoning partner is relieved, the resulting gain or loss is a capital gain or loss (*A.O. Stilwell*, Dec. 27,950, 46 TC 247). Even a *de minimis* actual or deemed distribution generally results in capital loss treatment to the partner. Capital loss also occurs if the transaction is, in substance, a sale or exchange (Rev. Rul. 93-80).

Net Investment Income. For purposes of the 3.8-percent net investment income (NII) tax, net gain or loss upon the disposition of a partnership interest is considered NII only to the extent it would be taken into account by the partner if all partnership property were sold at fair market value immediately before the disposition (¶ 117) (Code Sec. 1411).

Unrealized Receivables and Inventory. A partner recognizes ordinary income or loss on any portion of a sale of a partnership interest that is attributable to his or her share of the partnership's unrealized receivables and inventory (¶ 436) (Code Sec. 751(a); Reg. § 1.751-1(a)(2)). The gain is measured by the portion of the selling price attributable to unrealized receivables and inventory, and the partner's basis in the assets. The partner's basis is the basis the partner's share of partnership unrealized receivables and inventory would have if these assets were distributed to the partner in a current distribution. Capital gain or loss is determined by subtracting the partner's remaining basis from the rest of the amount realized (Reg. § 1.741-1(a)).

435. Liquidation or Redemption of Partnership Interests. If a partner's entire interest in a partnership is liquidated or redeemed, he or she recognizes gain to the extent any money or marketable securities received exceeds his or her basis in the partnership interest immediately before the distribution (Code Sec. 731(a)(1) and (c)). If only partnership property is received as part of the liquidating distribution, then no gain is recognized except to the extent provided for payments to retiring partners (¶ 438) and unrealized receivables and inventory (¶ 436). The partner's basis in any distributed partnership property received is equal to his or her partnership interest, less the amount of money and marketable securities received (¶ 456).

A partner recognizes loss from a distribution in liquidation of his or her entire partnership interest if no property other than money, unrealized receivables, or inventory is distributed to the partner. The loss is equal to the excess of the partner's basis in the partnership interest over the sum of (1) the amount of money received, and (2) the basis of the distributed receivables and inventory (Code Sec. 731(a)(2)).

> **Example:** Martin has an adjusted basis in his partnership interest of $100,000. He retires from the partnership and receives a distribution in liquidation of his share of partnership property. This includes $50,000 cash and inventory with a basis to him of $30,000. Martin can recognize a loss of $20,000, his basis minus the money received and his basis in the inventory distributed to him ($100,000 − ($50,000 + $30,000) = $20,000).

If a partner receives money or property in exchange for any part of his or her partnership interest, the amount attributable to the partner's share of the partnership's unrealized receivables or inventory items results in ordinary income or loss. This treatment applies to the unrealized receivables portion of the payments to a retiring partner or successor in interest of a deceased partner only if that part is not treated as paid in exchange for partnership property. The rationale behind this rule is that the inventory or the accounts receivable would give rise to ordinary income had the partnership interest not been sold. If the partner does not sell the distributed inventory items within five years from the date of distribution, the gain can be recognized as a capital gain (Code Sec. 735(a)(2)). For this purpose, inventory does not include real estate or depreciable trade or business property (¶ 436) (Code Sec. 735(c)(1)).

For exchanges of partnership interests involving unrealized receivables or inventory, the partnership must file an information return describing the exchange, and must furnish statements to each party (Reg. § 1.6050K-1).

436. Unrealized Receivables and Inventory Items of Partnerships. Unrealized receivables of a partnership include any rights to payment for services, or for goods that are not capital assets, to the extent that such rights have not been included in gross income under the partnership's method of accounting (Code Sec. 751(c); Reg. § 1.751-1(c)). This classification generally relates to cash-method partnerships that have acquired a contractual or legal right to income for goods or services. It usually does not apply to an accrual-method partnership because the partnership has already included unrealized receivables in gross income.

Unrealized receivables also includes certain property to the extent of the amount of gain that would have been realized and recharacterized or recaptured as ordinary income by the partnership if it had sold the property at its fair market value at the time of the sale or exchange of the partnership interest being considered. The types of property covered (e.g., depreciable personal property and real property) are listed in the flush language of Code Sec. 751(c). Concerning payments in liquidation of a retiring or deceased partner's interest, this property is not treated as an unrealized receivable (¶ 438).

"Inventory items" of a partnership is defined more broadly than the term itself might suggest (Code Sec. 751(d); Reg. § 1.751-1(d)(2)). It includes not only inventory, but also any other assets that would not be treated either as capital assets or section 1231 assets (generally, depreciable property and land used in a trade or business) if they were sold by the partnership (or by the partner, if he or she had held them). Thus, the term might include a copyright or artistic work, accounts receivable for services and inventory, or any unrealized receivables.

Distributions of inventory made in exchange for all or a part of a partner's interest in other partnership property, including money, are governed by the "substantially appreciated" rule (¶ 430) (Code Sec. 751(b); Reg. § 1.751-1(d)). Thus, gain from such distributions is taxed as ordinary income if the fair market value of the partnership's inventory exceeds 120 percent of its adjusted basis.

438. Payments to Retired Partner or Deceased Partner's Successor. Payments made by a partnership in liquidation of the interest of a retiring or deceased partner are considered distributions by the partnership to the extent that the payments are in exchange for the partner's interest in partnership property. Otherwise, they are considered a distributive share of partnership income or guaranteed payment (Code Secs. 736

and 761(d)). This rule does not apply if the estate or other successor in interest of a deceased partner continues as a partner in its own right under local law (Reg. §1.736-1(a)(1)). In addition, it applies only to payments made by the partnership and not to transactions such as the sale of a partnership interest between the partners.

Under Code Sec. 731, distributions are generally nontaxable except to the extent that money distributed exceeds the partner's adjusted basis in his or her partnership interest (¶453); that excess is treated as capital gain. However, all gain relating to inventory is treated as being from the sale of a noncapital asset (¶436). The partners' valuation of a retiring or deceased partner's interest in partnership property in an arm's-length agreement is presumptively correct, but that presumption may be rebutted (Reg. §1.736-1(b)(1)).

Payments for unrealized receivables and goodwill are treated as distributive shares of partnership income or as guaranteed payments if: (1) capital is not a material income-producing factor, and (2) the retiring or deceased partner was a general partner (Code Sec. 736(b)(2) and (3)). The payments are deductible by the partnership. If these two requirements are not met, payments for goodwill may be treated as payments for partnership property that do not create a deduction for the partnership. Payments for goodwill can be treated as payments for property if: (1) the goodwill was originally purchased by the partnership or otherwise acquired in a transaction resulting in a cash basis to the partnership, *or* (2) the partnership agreement calls for a reasonable payment for goodwill.

The payments result in capital gain or loss to the extent of the partnership's basis in the goodwill. In fixing the amount attributable to goodwill, an amount arrived at under an arm's-length agreement generally is accepted by the IRS. A formula approach involving the capitalization of earnings in excess of a fair market rate of return on the partnership's net tangible assets may be used, but only where there is no better approach for making such a determination (Rev. Rul. 68-609).

Amounts not considered as distributions by the partnership made for an interest in the partnership property are treated as either distributive shares of partnership income or guaranteed payments (Code Sec. 736(a)). If the payments are determined by reference to partnership income, they are taxed as a distributive share to the recipient; if not, they are treated as guaranteed payments (¶421). Accordingly, if the payments consist of a percentage of partnership profits, they reduce the distributive shares of income of the remaining partners. If they are guaranteed payments, the effect is the same because they are deductible as business expenses in determining partnership taxable income. In either event, the payments are treated as ordinary income in the hands of the recipient partner.

Example 1: Partnership ABC is a personal service partnership and its balance sheet is as follows:

	Assets			Liabilities and Capital	
	Adjusted basis	Market value		Adjusted basis	Market value
Cash	$130,000	$130,000	Liabilities .	$30,000	$30,000
Accounts			Capital:		
receivable . .	0	300,000	A	100,000	210,000
Capital and Sec.			B	100,000	210,000
1231 assets .	200,000	230,000	C	100,000	210,000
Total	$330,000	$660,000	Total .	$330,000	$660,000

General Partner A retires from the partnership in accordance with an agreement under which his share of liabilities (⅓ of $30,000) is assumed. In addition, he is to receive $90,000 in the year of retirement, plus $100,000 in each of the two succeeding years, for a total of $300,000 (including his $10,000 share of liabilities) for his partnership interest. The value of A's interest in the partnership's section 736(b) property is $120,000 (⅓ of $360,000, which is the sum of $130,000 cash and $230,000, the fair market value of section 1231 assets). The accounts receivable are not included in A's interest in partnership property because A is a general partner in a partnership in which capital is not a material income-producing factor. Assuming that the basis of A's interest is $110,000 ($100,000, the basis of his capital investment, plus $10,000, his share of partnership liabilities), he realizes a capital gain of $10,000 on the sale of his interest in partnership property. The $180,000 balance to be received by him is treated as guaranteed payments taxable as ordinary income.

The $100,000 that A receives in each of the three years would ordinarily be allocated as follows: $40,000 as payment for A's interest in section 736(b) property ($120,000/$300,000 × $100,000) and the balance of $60,000 as guaranteed payments. While the $10,000 capital gain is normally recognized in the first year, A may elect to prorate the gain over the three-year period.

Example 2: Assume the same facts as in Example 1 above, except that the agreement provides for payments to A for three years of a percentage of annual income instead of a fixed amount. As a result, all payments received by A are treated as payments for A's interest in partnership property until he has received $120,000. After that, the payments are treated as a distributive share of partnership income to A (Reg. § 1.736-1(b)(7)).

For income tax purposes, a retired partner or a deceased partner's successor is treated as a partner until his or her interest has been completely liquidated (Reg. § 1.736-1(a)(6)).

440. Partner Receiving Income In Respect of a Decedent. All payments to the successor of a deceased partner under Code Sec. 736(a)—that is, payments made in liquidation of a deceased partner's interest and considered as a distributive share or guaranteed payment (¶ 438)—are income in respect of a decedent (Code Sec. 753; Reg. § 1.753-1). The payments are taxed to the recipient when received to the extent that they are not properly includible in the short tax year ending with the decedent's death (¶ 182). The estate or heir of a deceased partner is also treated as receiving income in respect of a decedent to the extent that amounts are received from an outsider in exchange for rights to future payments by the partnership representing distributive shares or guaranteed payments.

442. Capital Gain Holding Period for Partners with Carried Interests. Effective for tax years beginning after 2017, a three-year holding period applies to certain net long-term capital gain with respect to any applicable partnership interest (i.e., "carried interest") held by the taxpayer at any time during the tax year (Code Sec. 1061). Specifically, the taxpayer's net-long term capital gain from the applicable interest is treated as short-term capital gain—taxed at ordinary income tax rates—unless the interest is held for at least three years. This rule will apply notwithstanding Code Sec. 83 and any section 83(b) election in effect.

An applicable partnership interest is any interest in a partnership that is transferred to or held by the taxpayer in connection with the performance of services by the taxpayer or a related person in any applicable trade of business, even if the taxpayer made contributions to the partnership. It does not include (1) any interest in a partnership held by a corporation, or (2) any capital interest in the partnership that provides the taxpayer with a right to share in partnership capital based on the amount of capital contributed or the value of the interest subject to tax under Code Sec. 83 when the interest is received or vested.

An "applicable trade or business" is one whose regular business activity consists of (1) raising or returning capital, and (2) either investing in or disposing of specified assets, or developing specified assets (i.e., securities, commodities, investment real estate, etc.). The IRS plans to issue regulations clarifying that partnership interests held by S corporations are subject to the extended three-year holding period (Notice 2018-18).

If a taxpayer transfers an applicable partnership interest to a related person, the taxpayer must include in gross income as short-term capital gain the taxpayer's net long-term capital gain attributable to the sale or exchange of an asset held for less than three years as is allocable to the interest. The amount included as short-term capital gain on the transfer is reduced by the amount treated as short-term capital gain under the general rule, meaning that amounts are not double-counted.

Partnership Contributions, Distributions, and Basis

See CCH® AnswerConnect: *Contribution to Partnership, Liabilities of Partners and Partnerships,* and *Partnership Distributions* for more information on this topic.

443. Contribution to Partnership. No gain or loss is recognized by either a partnership or any of its partners upon a contribution of property to the partnership in exchange for a partnership interest (Code Sec. 721(a); Reg. §1.721-1). This is true whether the contribution is made to an existing partnership or to a newly formed partnership. However, a partner must recognize any gain realized on the transfer of appreciated property to a partnership that would be treated as an investment company if the partnership were incorporated (Code Secs. 707(c) and 721(b)). Further, the value of a capital interest in a partnership that is transferred to a partner in exchange for his or her services is taxable to the partner as ordinary income if the interest is not subject to a substantial risk of forfeiture (¶ 713) (Reg. §1.721-1(b)). The receipt of a profits interest in exchange for services rendered is not taxable as ordinary income (Rev. Proc. 93-27, clarified by Rev. Proc. 2001-43; Notice of Proposed Rulemaking (NPRM) REG-115452-14).

If a U.S. person contributes certain property with built-in gain to a partnership that has a foreign partner related to the transferor, then gain will be recognized unless the gain deferral method (GDM) is applied with respect to the property (Code Sec. 721(c); Reg. §§1.721(c)-2 and 1.721(c)-3). Under a *de minimis* exception, nonrecognition of gain continues to apply if the sum of all built-in gain property contributed to the partnership during the tax year does not exceed $1 million.

Basis of Partner's Interest. The basis of a partner's interest acquired by a contribution of property is the amount of the money contributed, plus the adjusted basis to the contributing partner of any property contributed (Code Sec. 722). If a partner receives a partnership interest as compensation for services rendered or to be rendered, and this results in taxable income to the incoming partner, then the income is added to the basis of the partnership interest (Reg. §1.722-1). If the contributed property is subject to debt, or if liabilities of the partner are assumed by the partnership, the basis of the contributing partner's interest is reduced by the portion of the debt assumed by the other partners (¶ 447) (Code Sec. 752). The assumption of the partner's debt by others is treated as a distribution of money to the partner and as a contribution of money by those assuming the debt.

Basis of Property to Partnership. The basis to the partnership of property contributed by a partner is the adjusted basis of such property in the hands of the contributing partner at the time of the contribution—*carryover basis*—and any gain the partner recognized on the transfer (Code Sec. 723). However, a federal court of appeals has held that the basis of a nonbusiness asset (e.g., a personal automobile) converted to a business asset upon contribution to a partnership was its fair market value at the time of contribution (*L.Y.S. Au*, CA-9, 64-1 USTC ¶ 9447). The holding period of a contributed asset includes the period during which it was held by the contributing partner (Reg. §1.723-1).

Only the contributing partner may take into account any built-in loss. In determining items allocated to the noncontributing partners, the basis of the contributed property is the property's fair market value at the time of contribution (Code Sec. 704(c)(1)(C)). Proposed regulations effective for partnership contributions occurring on or after the regulations are finalized would clarify that the basis adjustment is initially equal to the built-in loss associated with the property and then is adjusted in a manner generally similar to basis adjustments on transfers of partnership interests (¶ 467) (Prop. Reg. §1.704-3(f)).

Contributions of Unrealized Receivables, Inventory, and Capital Loss Property. Unrealized receivables and inventory items contributed by the partner to the partnership retain their ordinary income character in the hands of the partnership (Code Sec. 724). That is, unrealized receivables remain ordinary income property up to the time of disposal by the partnership, and inventory items remain ordinary income property for the five-year period beginning on the date of contribution. In addition, a partner's contribution of

¶443

property with a built-in capital loss results in retention of the property's capital loss status in the hands of the partnership to the extent of built-in loss for the five-year period beginning on the date of contribution.

To keep partnerships from dodging these rules through the exchange of contributed unrealized receivables, inventory items, or capital loss property in a nonrecognition transaction (or series of transactions), the rule applies to any substituted basis property resulting from the exchange. It does not apply to any stock in a C corporation received in an exchange of property for stock if the contributor is in control following the exchange (Code Secs. 351 and 735(c)(2)). For this purpose, control is at least 80 percent of the total combined voting power of all classes of stock entitled to vote and at least 80 percent of the total number of shares of all other classes of stock of the corporation (Code Sec. 368(c)).

445. Increases and Decreases in Basis of Partner's Interest. The basis of a partner's interest in a partnership (¶ 443) is *increased* by his or her distributive share of partnership taxable income, the partnership's tax-exempt income, and the excess of partnership deductions for depletion over the basis to the partnership of the depletable property (Code Sec. 705). The basis of the partner's interest in a partnership is *decreased* (but not below zero) by distributions to the partner from the partnership (¶ 453). In addition, the partner's basis is also *decreased* by the sum of the partner's share of partnership losses and partnership expenditures not deductible in computing its taxable income and not chargeable to capital account, and the partner's depletion deduction for oil and gas wells. Distributions are taken into account before losses in adjusting the partner's interest basis (Rev. Rul. 66-94).

Example: Partner A of ABC partnership has an $80,000 basis for her partnership interest. During the tax year, she receives cash distributions of $50,000, and her share of the partnership's losses is $40,000. Her interest is adjusted as follows:

Basis at beginning of year................	$80,000	
Less cash distributions..................	50,000	$30,000
Less share of losses ($40,000) but only to the extent that the basis is not reduced below zero		30,000
Adjusted basis for interest		0

Because basis is decreased by distributions received before reduction by A's share of partnership losses, no gain is recognized on the cash distribution. However, $10,000 of A's share of partnership loss is disallowed and carried forward to subsequent tax years (¶ 425).

The basis of partnership interests may also be determined by reference to proportionate shares of the adjusted basis of partnership property that would be distributable if the partnership were to be terminated. This alternative rule is available only in limited circumstances: if a partner cannot practicably apply the general rule, or when the IRS approves (Code Sec. 705(b); Reg. § 1.705-1(b)).

For determining a partner's basis in his or her partnership interest, or for figuring gain or loss on a distribution, advances or drawings of money or property against a partner's distributive share of income are treated as current distributions made on the last day of the partnership's tax year (Reg. § 1.731-1(a)(1)(ii)). Money received by a partner under an obligation to repay the partnership is not a distribution but is a loan that is treated as a transaction between the partnership and a nonpartner (Reg. §§ 1.707-1(a) and 1.731-1(c)(2)).

447. Partnership Liabilities Treated as Distributions or Contributions. Any increase in a partner's share of partnership liabilities, including a partner's assumption of partnership liabilities or receipt of partnership property subject to a liability (limited to the fair market value of the encumbered property) is treated as a contribution of money that increases a partner's basis in his or her interest (¶ 445) (Code Secs. 722 and 752(a)). A decrease in a partner's share of partnership liabilities is treated as a distribution of money by the partnership, which decreases the distributee partner's basis in his or her partnership interest (but not below zero) (Code Secs. 733 and 752(b)). When a partner's basis has been reduced to zero, the deemed distributions can result in taxable gain (¶ 453).

448. Allocation of Partnership Liabilities. Partners' shares of partnership liabilities (and corresponding allocations of basis) depend upon whether the liability is "recourse" or "nonrecourse." Separate rules apply in the case of nonrecourse debts of the partnership if a partner is the lender or has guaranteed repayment of the debt.

Recourse Liabilities. Liabilities are recourse to the extent that a partner bears the economic risk of loss if the liability is not satisfied by the partnership. Recourse liabilities are allocated in accordance with the partners' economic risk of loss (Reg. § 1.752-2(a)). Economic risk of loss is generally borne by a partner to the extent that he or she must make a contribution to the partnership (including the obligation to restore a deficit capital account) or pay a creditor if all partnership assets, including money, were deemed worthless and all partnership liabilities were due and payable (Reg. § 1.752-2(b)(1)). Thus, a limited partner cannot be allocated recourse liabilities in excess of his or her capital contribution and future contribution obligations unless he or she has agreed to restore any deficit in his or her capital account or to indemnify other partners for their debts with respect to a liability.

Recourse liabilities must be allocated to a partner if a related person bears the risk of loss for the liability (Reg. § 1.752-4(b)). A partner does not bear the economic risk of loss if he or she is entitled to reimbursement from other partners or the partnership—for example, through an indemnification agreement or a state law right to subrogation (Reg. § 1.752-2(b)(5)). A partner or related person generally does not bear the economic risk of loss with respect to a bottom-dollar payment obligation (BDPO). A BDPO is generally defined as an obligation other than one in which the partner or related person is liable for the full amount of a payment obligation to the extent that any amount of a partnership liability is not otherwise satisfied (Reg. § 1.752-2(b)(3)(ii)).

Nonrecourse Liabilities. Nonrecourse liabilities are liabilities for which no partner bears the economic risk of loss—for example, a mortgage on an office building that is secured only by a lien on the building and on the rents, but with no personal obligation to repay the loan on the part of any of the owners. Such liabilities are generally shared by the partners in a manner that correlates with their allocations of deductions attributable to the liabilities (¶ 428). A partner's share of nonrecourse liabilities of a partnership equals the sum of:

- the partner's share of partnership minimum gain;

- the amount of any taxable gain that would be allocated to the partner if the partnership disposed of all partnership property subject to one or more nonrecourse liabilities of the partnership in full satisfaction of the liabilities and no other consideration; and

- the partner's share of the excess nonrecourse liabilities as determined in accordance with the partner's share of partnership profits (Reg. § 1.752-3(a)).

Although excess nonrecourse liabilities are allocated in accordance with the partners' respective profits interests, the partnership agreement may state the partners' interests for purposes of sharing nonrecourse liabilities, provided that the stated sharing ratios are reasonably consistent with the allocation of significant items of partnership income or gain among the partners. Because no partner bears the economic risk of loss for nonrecourse liabilities, limited partners may be allocated shares of such liabilities (and the basis in such liabilities) in amounts exceeding their total capital contribution obligations.

Partner Nonrecourse Loans and Guarantees. A partner who lends money to the partnership on a nonrecourse basis bears the economic risk of loss for the liability. Likewise, a partner who guarantees an otherwise nonrecourse liability bears the risk of loss to the extent of his or her guarantee (Reg. § 1.752-2(d)(2)).

A loss incurred on the abandonment or worthlessness of a partnership interest is an ordinary loss if sale or exchange treatment does not apply. If there is an actual or deemed distribution to the partner, or if the transaction is otherwise in substance a sale or exchange, the partner's loss is a capital loss except where the partner receives a disproportionate distribution of partnership unrealized receivables or inventory (¶ 430). A deemed distribution includes the relief from partnership debts in which the abandoning partner shares. As with other losses, the partners must establish the finality and uncollectibility of the loss (Reg. § 1.165-1(d)).

453. Gain or Loss on Distribution to Partners. The income of a partnership is taxable to the partners in accordance with their distributive shares of partnership taxable income (¶ 428). It does not matter when or if the income is actually distributed to the partners, but distributions to partners decrease the partners' bases for their partnership interests (¶ 445).

> **Example 1:** A partner contributes $100,000 to the capital of a partnership. During the first year, his share of the partnership taxable income is $25,000, but only $10,000 of this amount is actually distributed to him. The $25,000 taxable income increases his basis to $125,000, and the $10,000 distribution decreases it to $115,000.

No gain or loss is recognized by a partnership on a distribution of property to a partner, including money (Code Sec. 731(b); Reg. § 1.731-1(b)). However, a partnership may have to recognize gain or loss on the distribution of unrealized receivables or substantially appreciated inventory items that is treated as a sale or exchange of property between the partnership and the distributee partner (¶ 436).

A partner recognizes gain on the distribution of property from the partnership, but only to the extent any money or marketable securities received exceeds his or her basis in the partnership immediately before the distribution (Code Sec. 731(a)(1) and (c)). This rule applies both to current distributions and distributions in liquidation of a partner's entire interest in the partnership. If only partnership property is received by the partner, then no gain is recognized except to the extent provided for payments to retiring partners (¶ 438) and unrealized receivables and inventory (¶ 436). The partner's basis in any property received is equal to the basis of his or her partnership interest, less the amount of money and marketable securities received (¶ 456).

> **Example 2:** Partner A purchases a partnership interest for $100,000. During the first year, A receives a cash distribution of $100,000 and a distribution of property with a fair market value of $30,000. He recognizes no gain on the distributions since the amount of money distributed does not exceed A's basis for his partnership interest ($100,000). If he had received a cash distribution of $130,000, he would have recognized a $30,000 gain.

No loss is recognized by a partner on the distribution of property from the partnership, except in liquidation of the partner's entire interest in the partnership, and then only if the distribution is limited to money, unrealized receivables, and inventory (¶ 435). The loss is equal to the excess of the partner's basis in the partnership interest over the sum of the amount of money received plus the basis of the distributed receivables and inventory (Code Sec. 731(a)(2)).

> **Example 3:** A partner whose basis for his partnership interest is $100,000 retires from the partnership, receiving $50,000 in cash, and inventory items having a basis to the partnership of $30,000. The taxpayer has a capital loss of $20,000.

A distribution of property encumbered by a liability may cause a partner's share of partnership liabilities to decrease, resulting in a deemed distribution of money to that partner (¶ 447). For instance, if a partner receives a distribution of property subject to a secured liability, the liability becomes a personal liability of the distributee partner, and there is a decrease in the liabilities of all other partners who had been allocated a share of the liability. These partners must decrease the bases in their partnership interests in

¶453

the amount of their deemed distributions (but not below zero), and any amounts deemed distributed in excess of their respective bases are taxable as capital gain.

The nonrecognition rules of Code Sec. 731 may not apply if, within a short period before or after property is contributed to a partnership, there is a distribution of either: (1) other partnership property to the contributing partner, or (2) the contributed property to another partner (Code Sec. 707(a)(2)(B); Reg. § 1.731-1(c)(3)). If the distribution is made in order to effect an exchange of property between the partnership and a partner, or between two or more partners, then the transaction is treated as an exchange and the disguised sale rules (¶ 432) may apply. There is a presumption that distributions made within two years of a contribution are made as part of a sale arrangement (Reg. § § 1.707-3(c) and § 1.707-4). The presumption can be rebutted if the facts and circumstances clearly establish that there is no sale.

A partner who contributes property to a partnership may have to recognize gain or loss if the contributed property is distributed by the partnership to another partner within seven years (¶ 454).

454. Partnership Distribution of Contributed Property. A partner who contributes property to a partnership may have to recognize gain or loss if the contributed property is distributed by the partnership to another partner within seven years (Code Sec. 704(c)). The gain or loss recognized is limited to the difference between the property's tax basis and its fair market value at the time of contribution. Upon distribution of the property within the seven-year period, the precontributed gain or loss recognized is equal to the amount that would have been allocated to the contributing partner had the partnership sold the property rather than distributed it to a partner. Appropriate adjustments must be made to the basis of the contributing partner's partnership interest and to the basis of the distributed property to reflect any gain or loss recognized (¶ 445 and ¶ 456).

The recognition rule does not apply if the property is distributed to the contributing partner (or its successor). Also, the rule does not apply with respect to certain distributions made as part of an exchange of like-kind property (¶ 1721).

A similar rule may cause a partner contributing appreciated property to recognize precontribution gain if the partner receives a distribution of other partnership property (except money or marketable securities) within a seven-year period (Code Sec. 737(b)). Precontribution gain must be recognized to the extent that it exceeds the partner's basis for his or her partnership interest at the time the distribution is received.

456. Basis of Property Distributed to Partner. The basis of property received in a distribution from a partnership other than in liquidation of a partner's interest is ordinarily the same as the basis in the hands of the partnership immediately prior to distribution (Code Sec. 732(a)). In no case may the basis of property in the hands of the partner exceed the basis of his or her partnership interest reduced by the amount of money distributed to the partner in the same transaction.

> **Example 1:** A partner has a basis of $100,000 for his partnership interest. He receives a nonliquidating distribution of $40,000 in cash and property with a basis to the partnership of $80,000. The basis to the partner of the distributed property is $60,000 ($100,000 minus $40,000). The partnership can recover the $20,000 difference by making the election to adjust the basis of its remaining assets to take up the unused basis (¶ 459).

The basis of property distributed *in liquidation* of a partner's interest is the basis of the distributee's partnership interest less any money received in the same transaction (Code Sec. 732(b)).

A distributee partner's basis adjustment is allocated among distributed assets, first to unrealized receivables and inventory items in an amount equal to the partnership's basis in each property (Code Sec. 732(c)). For this purpose, unrealized receivables includes any property the sale of which would create ordinary income (Code Sec. 751(c))—for example, depreciation-recapture property. However, the amount of unrealized receivables is limited to that amount that would be treated as ordinary income if the property were sold at fair market value.

Basis is allocated first to the extent of each distributed property's adjusted basis to the partnership. Any remaining basis adjustment that is an increase is allocated among properties with unrealized appreciation in proportion to their respective amounts of unrealized appreciation (to the extent of each property's appreciation) and then in proportion to their respective fair market values.

> **Example 2:** A partnership has two assets, a tractor and a steam shovel. Both assets are distributed to a partner whose adjusted basis in his partnership interest is $550,000. The tractor has a basis to the partnership of $50,000 and a fair market value of $400,000. The steam shovel has a basis to the partnership of $100,000 and a fair market value of $100,000. Basis is first allocated to the tractor in the amount of $50,000 and to the steam shovel in the amount of $100,000 (their adjusted bases to the partnership). The remaining basis adjustment is an increase of $400,000 (the partner's $550,000 basis minus the partnership's total basis of $150,000 in the distributed assets). Basis is then allocated to the tractor in the amount of $350,000, its unrealized appreciation, with no allocation to the steam shovel attributable to unrealized appreciation because its fair market value equals the partnership's adjusted basis. The remaining basis adjustment of $50,000 is allocated in the ratio of the assets' fair market values, which are $40,000 to the tractor (for a total basis of $440,000) and $10,000 to the steam shovel (for a total basis of $110,000).

If the remaining basis adjustment is a decrease, it is allocated among properties with unrealized depreciation in proportion to their respective amounts of unrealized depreciation (to the extent of each property's depreciation), and then in proportion to their respective adjusted bases, taking into account the adjustments already made. Accordingly, a partner's substituted basis in distributed partnership property is allocated among multiple properties based on the fair market value of the distributed properties.

Optional Basis Adjustments. If a partner has acquired his or her partnership interest (1) by purchase from a former partner or another partner, or (2) from a deceased partner, then the partner can elect to have a special basis adjustment for property (other than money) received in a distribution from the partnership within two years after the partnership interest was acquired (Code Sec. 732(d)). This can be done if the partnership has not already made an election to have the special basis adjustment apply to its assets. The partner's election accomplishes substantially the same result as if the partnership had made the election. The special basis adjustment is the difference between the amount paid for the partnership interest and the partner's share of the adjusted basis of partnership assets.

The special basis adjustment applies to property received in current distributions as well as to distributions in complete liquidation of the partner's interest. If the partner makes the election when a distribution of depreciable or depletable property is received, the amount of the adjustment is not diminished by any depletion or depreciation on that portion of the basis of partnership property that arises from the special basis adjustment (Reg. § 1.732-1(d)(1)(iv)). Depletion or depreciation on that portion for the period before distribution is allowed or allowable only if the partnership made the election.

If a transferee-partner wishes to make the election, it must be made on his or her tax return for the year of the distribution if the distribution includes any property subject to depreciation, depletion, or amortization. If the distribution does not include any such property, the election may be made with the return for any tax year not later than the first tax year in which the basis of the distributed property is pertinent in determining income tax.

Distributions of Stock to a Corporate Partner. A basis reduction to the assets of a corporation is required if stock in that corporation is distributed by a partnership to a corporate partner. The reduction applies if: (1) after the distribution, the corporate partner controls the distributed corporation; and (2) the partnership's adjusted basis in the stock of the distributed corporation immediately before the distribution is greater than the corporate partner's adjusted basis in the stock immediately after the distribution (Code Sec. 732(f); Reg. § 1.732-3(a)).

¶456

For purposes of applying this rule, when corporations that are members of the same consolidated group are partners in the same partnership, the bases in the corporations' partnership interests may be aggregated (Reg. § 1.732-3(b)).

Certain distributions of stock of a corporation to a corporate partner can have the effect of eliminating gain in the stock of the distributed corporation while avoiding a Code Sec. 732(f) basis step-down for the distributed corporation's property. These are termed "gain elimination transactions." They can occur when such distributions fall outside the literal language of Code Sec. 732(f) because the corporate partner is not in control of the distributed corporation immediately after the distribution. The regulations, however, apply Code Sec. 732(f) to gain elimination transactions (Reg. § 1.732-3(c)).

459. Optional Adjustment to Basis of Partnership Assets. If the basis of distributed assets in the hands of the distributee partner is less than the basis of the assets in the hands of the partnership (¶ 456), there may be an "unused" basis. The partnership may elect to adjust the basis of its remaining assets to take up this unused basis (¶ 470) (Code Secs. 734, 754, and 755).

If gain is recognized by a partner because of a distribution of money (¶ 453), a similar increase in the partnership's basis of its remaining assets may be made. If the election is made, the partnership may have to decrease the basis of its remaining assets. The decrease would be required for the excess of the basis of distributed assets to the partner over the basis that the partnership had for those assets, in the event of a distribution in liquidation of a partner's interest. Decrease would also be required to the extent that any distribution to a partner resulted in loss to the partner. Loss results to the partner only if the distribution terminates the partner's interest and if the distribution generally consists only of money, unrealized receivables, and inventories.

Example: An equal three-person partnership has the following assets:

	Partnership's Basis	Fair Market Value
Cash	$120,000	$120,000
Land	60,000	120,000
Securities	90,000	120,000
Total	$270,000	$360,000

If a partner retires and the partnership pays him $120,000 for the fair market value of his partnership interest, the partnership is really distributing $40,000 as his pro rata share of the partnership's cash and paying him $80,000 for his ⅓ interest in the land and securities. However, the retiring partner's share of the partnership's basis for these properties totals only $50,000. Therefore, the partnership, if it wishes to reflect the $30,000 excess cost, may elect to adjust the basis of the land and securities.

A partnership is barred from increasing the adjusted basis of remaining property following a distribution of an interest in another partnership if the other partnership has not made a consistent Code Sec. 754 election. In other words, tiered partnerships must make consistent elections.

The allocation of any increase or decrease in basis is made among the various partnership assets or categories of assets (Code Sec. 755). These rules generally contemplate that the allocation will be made first to like-kind assets and will reduce the difference between fair market value and basis of each asset adjusted.

No allocation of basis decrease may be made to stock of a corporate partner. The basis decrease must be allocated to other partnership property. The partnership recognizes gain to the extent the decrease in basis exceeds the basis of the other partnership assets.

462. Character of Gain or Loss on Disposition of Distributed Property. A partner recognizes ordinary gain or loss on the disposition of unrealized receivables or inventory items distributed by the partnership (¶ 436), regardless of whether the property has substantially appreciated in value (Code Sec. 735; Reg. § 1.735-1). In the case of inventory items, this rule applies only if the sale takes place within five years of the date of distribution. If the sale takes place after the five-year period, gain may be treated as capital gain if the assets are capital assets in the hands of the partner at that time.

If a partner disposes of distributed unrealized receivables or inventory items in a nonrecognition transaction (or series of transactions), these rules apply to treat gain or loss on the substituted basis property as ordinary income or loss, except in the case of stock in a C corporation received in a Code Sec. 351 exchange. The House Committee Report to the Deficit Reduction Act of 1984 (P.L. 98-369) states the intention that the basis-tainting rules regarding distributed property apply only for the period during which the underlying rules as to character of gain or loss under Code Sec. 735 would apply if the property were not disposed of in a nonrecognition transaction. For example, if an inventory item was distributed by the partnership, and the partner subsequently disposed of it in a nonrecognition transaction, ordinary income treatment would apply to any substitute basis property only for the duration of the five-year period beginning on the date of the original distribution.

467. Adjustment of Basis on Sale of Partnership Interest. The transfer of a partnership interest by a partner generally does not affect the basis of partnership assets. However, the partnership may elect to adjust the basis of partnership assets to reflect the difference between the partner's basis for his or her partnership interest (generally, the purchase price) and his or her proportionate share of the adjusted basis of all partnership property (his or her share of the partnership's adjusted basis in the partnership property). The election applies only to the transferee partner and applies where there is a transfer of an interest in a partnership by sale or exchange or upon the death of a partner, but not upon the contribution of property (including money) to the partnership (Code Sec. 743; Reg. § 1.743-1(a)).

Basis adjustments must be made to undistributed partnership property, regardless of the existence of a Code Sec. 754 election, any time there is a transfer of a partnership interest and there is a substantial built-in loss, meaning that immediately after the transfer the partnership's adjusted basis in partnership property exceeds the fair market value (FMV) of the property by more than $250,000. In addition, for transfers after December 31, 2017, there is a substantial built-in loss if the transferee partner would be allocated a loss of more than $250,000 under a hypothetical sale of partnership assets for cash equal to the assets' FMV (Code Sec. 743(a) and (d)).

The amount of the increase or decrease is an adjustment affecting only the transferee partner (Code Sec. 743(b)). In addition, a partner's proportionate share of the adjusted basis of partnership property is determined in accordance with his or her interest in partnership capital. However, if an agreement on contributed property is in effect, the agreement must be taken into account in determining a partner's proportionate share.

A Code Sec. 743 basis adjustment is mandatory in the case of a transferred partnership interest with a substantial built-in loss. A substantial built-in loss exists if the partnership's adjusted basis in the property is more than $250,000 over the fair market value. An electing investment partnership is excepted from this rule. It will not be treated as having a substantial built-in loss; therefore, it is not required to make basis adjustments to partnership property (Code Sec. 743(e)(1)).

The basis adjustment must be allocated among the partnership assets or categories of assets (¶ 459).

470. Election for Partnership Basis Adjustment. A partnership makes a basis adjustment or section 754 election (¶ 459 and ¶ 467) by filing an election statement with the partnership's timely-filed tax return. Under proposed regulations that taxpayers can rely on, the signature requirement for the election has been eliminated (Prop. Reg. § 1.754-1(b)(1)). The election applies to all property distributions and transfers of partnership interests taking place in the year of the election and in all later partnership tax years until revoked. The election cannot be made for distributions or for transfers only. The IRS may, but is not required to, grant extensions of time to file the election.

¶470

A section 754 election may be revoked only by the partnership. The application for permission to revoke must be filed within 30 days after the close of the partnership tax year to which the revocation applies. Valid reasons for revocation include: (1) a change in the nature of the partnership's business; (2) a substantial increase in the partnership's assets; (3) a change in the character of partnership assets; or (4) an increased frequency of retirements or shifts of partnership interests resulting in an increased administrative burden on the partnership in tracking the adjustments. If the purpose of the revocation is primarily to avoid stepping down the basis of partnership assets upon a transfer or distribution, the application for revocation will be denied.

Family Partnerships

474. Family Partnerships. The family partnership is a common device for splitting income among family members and having more income taxed in the lower tax brackets. A person is recognized as a partner for income tax purposes if he or she owns a capital interest in a partnership in which capital is a material income-producing factor, whether or not the partnership interest was acquired by gift from another person (Code Sec. 761(b); Reg. § 1.704-1(e)). If capital is *not* a material income-producing factor, a partnership resulting from a gift of an interest might be disregarded as an invalid attempt to assign income.

In any event, if all the income is attributable to the personal efforts of the donor, the donor is taxed on the entire income. In addition, the donee's distributive share of income must be proportionate to his or her capital interest, and his or her control over the partnership must be consistent with his or her status as partner. Family limited partnerships are also used for estate planning purposes (¶ 2903).

Organization, Syndication, Start-Up Costs

See CCH® AnswerConnect: *Deduction for Partnership Organizational and Syndication Expenditures* for more information on this topic.

477. Partnership Syndication and Organization Fees. No deduction is generally allowed a partnership or a partner for the costs of organizing a partnership (organization fees) or of selling partnership interests (syndication fees) (with certain exceptions) (¶ 481) (Code Sec. 709; Reg. § 1.709-1). Guaranteed payments (¶ 421) made to partners for their services in organizing a partnership are capital expenditures and are not deductible by the partnership.

A partnership may elect to deduct up to $5,000 in organizational expenses, generally in the same manner as start-up expenditures. The $5,000 amount is reduced (but not below zero) by the amount by which the organizational expenditures exceed $50,000. The remainder of the organizational expenditures may be amortized ratably over a 180-month period, beginning with the month the active trade or business begins. The partnership is deemed to have made an election to deduct and amortize such expenses for the tax year in which begins the active trade or business to which the expenditures relate. A partnership may choose to forgo the deemed election by affirmatively electing to capitalize its organizational expenditures on a timely filed federal income tax return, including extensions, for the tax year in which begins the active trade or business to which the expenditures relate.

A new partnership formed after a technical termination (¶ 410) must continue amortizing organizational expenses over the remainder of the amortization period originally established by the terminating partnership (Reg. § 1.708-1(b)(6)).

481. Partnership Start-Up Expenditures. Taxpayers that pay or incur start-up costs for a trade or business and who subsequently enter the trade or business can elect to expense up to $5,000 of the costs (¶ 904). The $5,000 deduction amount is reduced dollar for dollar when the start-up expenses exceed $50,000. The balance of start-up expenses (if any) are amortized over a period of not less than 180 months, starting with the month in which the business begins (Code Sec. 195; Reg. § 1.195-1(b)). The election must be made on Form 4562 no later than the date (including extensions) for filing the return for the tax year in which the business begins or is acquired. Taxpayers that do not make the election must capitalize the expenses.

In the case of start-up expenses incurred by the partnership itself and for which an election is made, the amortization deduction is taken into account in computing partnership income. In the case of qualifying investigatory expenses incurred in connection with acquiring a partnership interest, the deduction is taken by the partner who has incurred the expenses. A new partnership formed after a technical termination (¶ 410) must continue amortizing start-up expenses over the remainder of the amortization period originally established by the terminating partnership (Reg. § 1.708-1(b)(6)).

Electing Large Partnerships

482. Simplified Reporting for Electing Large Partnerships. A partnership with 100 or more members in the preceding tax year may elect large partnership status for returns filed for tax years beginning before January 1, 2018. Partnerships making this election combine most items of partnership income, deduction, credit, and loss at the partnership level, and pass through net amounts to the partners (Code Secs. 771—777). Special modifications apply to partnerships engaged in oil and gas activities, and to partnerships with residual interests in real estate mortgage investment conduits (REMICs). Service partnerships and commodity pools generally are unable to elect large partnership treatment. Electing large partnerships are subject to audit and procedural rules separate from the general TEFRA audit rules.

The taxable income of an electing large partnership for returns filed for tax years beginning before January 1, 2018, is computed in the same manner as for an individual, except that certain items are separately stated, and specified modifications apply (Code Sec. 773). For example, miscellaneous itemized deductions are not separately reported to the partners, and in place of the two-percent floor, 70 percent of the itemized deductions are disallowed at the partnership level. The remaining 30 percent is allowed at the partnership level in determining the large partnership's taxable income and is not subject to the two-percent floor at the partner level. Tax credits other than the low-income housing credit, the rehabilitation credit, and the credit for producing fuel from nonconventional sources are reported as a single item. Credit recapture also is recognized at the partnership level.

For electing large partnerships, the netting of capital gains and losses for returns filed for tax years beginning before January 1, 2018, occurs at the partnership level (Code Sec. 773). Passive activity items are separated from capital gains stemming from partnership portfolio income. Each partner separately takes into account the partner's distributive shares of net capital gain or net capital loss for passive activity and portfolio items. Any partnership gains and losses under Code Sec. 1231 (¶ 1747) are netted at the partnership level. Net gain is treated as long-term capital gain, and any net loss is treated as ordinary loss and consolidated with the partnership's other taxable income.

The TEFRA audit rules that normally apply to partnerships for returns filed for partnership tax years beginning before January 1, 2018, do not apply to electing large partnerships (¶ 415). An electing large partnership, like other partnerships, appoints a representative to handle IRS matters (Code Sec. 6255(b)). Unlike under the TEFRA rules, the representative does not have to be a partner. In addition, only the partnership, and not the individual partners, receives notice of partnership adjustments (Code Sec. 6245(b)). Only the partnership has the right to appeal the adjustment (Code Sec. 6247(a)). After a partnership-level adjustment, prior-year partners and prior tax years generally are not affected. Instead, the adjustments generally are passed through to current partners, but prior years can be affected if there has been a partnership dissolution or a finding that the shares of a distribution to partners were erroneous.

The electing large partnerships rules, as well as the TEFRA audit rules, are repealed for returns filed for partnership tax years beginning after December 31, 2017, and a single set of rules applies for partnership audits and adjustments (Act Sec. 1101 of the Bipartisan Budget Act of 2015 (P.L. 114-74)). A partnership may elect to apply the new rules for returns filed for partnership tax years beginning after November 2, 2015. See ¶ 413 for a discussion of the post-2017 partnership audit rules as well as the election to apply those rules earlier.

Chapter 5

TRUSTS □ ESTATES

Trusts and Estates as Taxable Entities

See CCH® AnswerConnect: *Income Taxation of Trusts and Estates* for more information on this topic.

501. Trust, Estate, and Fiduciary Defined. A trust is a separate taxable entity for federal income tax purposes. A trust usually involves an arrangement created either by a will upon the creator's death or by a trust instrument that may take effect during the creator's life (Reg. § 301.7701-4(a)). Under either arrangement, a trustee takes title to the property in order to protect or conserve it for beneficiaries. Usually, the beneficiaries merely accept the trust's benefits. However, even if the beneficiaries are the persons who planned or created it, the trust will still be recognized as a separate taxable entity if its purpose is to vest the trustee with the responsibility to protect and preserve property on behalf of beneficiaries who cannot share in the discharge of this responsibility.

Federal tax law provides specific guidelines for what constitutes a business trust or investment trust (¶ 502) and a liquidating trust (¶ 503). Some types of trusts are governed by special tax rules, such as grantor trusts (¶ 571), charitable trusts (¶ 590), and common trust funds (¶ 595). Decedents' estates are also considered separate taxable entities for income tax purposes during the period of administration (¶ 507). Other types of estates are discussed at ¶ 504—¶ 506.

Fiduciaries. Trustees, executors, and certain receivers are considered fiduciaries. A fiduciary is a person who occupies a position of special confidence toward another, who holds in trust property in which another person has the beneficial title or interest, or who receives and controls income of another (Reg. § 301.7701-6). However, a person who is an agent of another person is not necessarily a fiduciary for federal income tax purposes, even though a fiduciary relationship may be said to exist for state law purposes. For example, if a person receives income as an agent, intermediary debtor, or conduit, and the income is paid over to another, the agent is not considered a fiduciary for tax purposes. The fiduciary is responsible for computing the entity's income tax liability and paying the resulting tax (¶ 510), and may be personally liable for any tax delinquencies if others are paid in preference to the IRS (¶ 512).

Small Business Trusts. An electing small business trust (ESBT) is a special kind of trust permitted to be a shareholder in an S corporation. An ESBT has no beneficiaries other than individuals or estates eligible to be S corporation shareholders, except that charitable organizations may hold contingent remainder interests. The portion of any ESBT that consists of stock in one or more S corporations is treated as a separate trust (¶ 304 and ¶ 516).

Qualified Domestic Trusts. A qualified domestic trust (QDOT) is a trust that meets certain requirements and is subject to a special estate tax. Property that is transferred from a decedent who is a U.S. citizen or resident to a nonresident alien spouse does not qualify for the usual estate tax marital deduction unless it is transferred from the decedent to a QDOT (¶ 2926).

Foreign Trusts and Estates. A foreign trust is a trust that (1) no court within the United States can exercise primary supervision over the trust's administration (court

¶501

test), and (2) no U.S. person has the authority to control all of the trust's substantial decisions (control test). A foreign estate is an estate whose income, from non-U.S. sources that is not effectively connected with the conduct of a trade or business in the United States (¶ 2431), is not includible in gross income for federal income tax purposes (Code Sec. 7701(a)(30) and (31); Reg. §301.7701-7).

502. Business and Investment Trusts. A business or commercial trust is a trust created as a means of carrying on a profit-making business, usually using capital or property supplied by the beneficiaries (Reg. §301.7701-4(b)). The trustees or other designated persons are, in effect, managers of the undertaking, whether appointed or controlled by the beneficiaries. This arrangement is treated for federal tax purposes as an association that may be taxed as a corporation or partnership, and is distinguishable from the type of trust that is a separate taxable entity (¶ 501). The fact that the trust property is not supplied by beneficiaries is not sufficient in itself to avoid the trust being classified and taxed as a business entity.

An investment trust may also be taxed as an association, rather than a trust, if there is a power under the trust agreement to vary the investment of the certificate holders (Reg. §301.7701-4(c)). However, if this power is lacking, the arrangement is taxed as a trust. Unit investment trusts, as defined in the Investment Company Act of 1940, that are set up to hold shares of regulated investment companies (RICs) for investors are also not taxed as trusts. Instead, their income is taxed directly to the investors (Reg. §1.851-7).

503. Liquidating Trusts. A liquidating trust formed for the primary purpose of liquidating and distributing the assets transferred to it is taxed as a trust, and not as an association, despite the possibility of profit (Reg. §301.7701-4(d)). All activities of the trust must be reasonably necessary for, and consistent with, accomplishing the primary purpose of liquidation and distribution. If the liquidation is unreasonably prolonged, or if the liquidation purpose becomes so obscured by business activities that the declared purpose of liquidation can be considered lost or abandoned, the arrangement is no longer a liquidating trust.

504. Estate of Minor, Incompetent, or Person Under a Disability. The estate of a minor, incompetent person, or other person under a disability is not a taxable entity separate from the person for whom the fiduciary (¶ 501) is acting (Reg. §1.641(b)-2(b)). Therefore, the estate of such a person is not required to file Form 1041.

A guardian is generally required to file a tax return as an agent for a minor or legally disabled person if the individual would otherwise be required to file a return (Code Sec. 6012(b)(2); Reg. §1.6012-3(b)(3)). However, a minor can file a return for himself or herself or have someone else file it, relieving the guardian of this obligation. For the tax year during which an incompetent person is declared competent and the fiduciary is discharged, the former incompetent person must file the tax return.

An agent filing a return for another person should file Form 2848, granting power of attorney, with the taxpayer's return (Reg. §1.6012-1(a)(5)). If an agent is used, both the agent and the taxpayer for whom the return is made may be liable for penalties for erroneous, false, or fraudulent returns. One spouse may execute a valid return on behalf of his or her mentally incompetent or disabled spouse prior to appointment of a legal guardian without a formal power of attorney (Rev. Rul. 56-22).

505. Bankruptcy Estate of Individual Debtor. Property held by a trustee in bankruptcy for an individual under Chapter 7 (liquidation) or Chapter 11 (business reorganization) of the Bankruptcy Code is considered the estate of the debtor (Code Sec. 1398). The estate is treated as a separate taxable entity unless the bankruptcy case is dismissed.

The fiduciary of a Chapter 7 or Chapter 11 bankruptcy estate is obligated to file the estate's return. If the bankruptcy plan creates a liquidating trust, the fiduciary must file the trust's return (Code Sec. 6012(b)(4)). Form 1041 must be filed if the bankruptcy estate has gross income for the tax year of at least the basic standard deduction amount for a married individual filing separately ($12,200 for 2019 and $12,400 for 2020), plus the personal exemption amount ($0 for 2018 through 2025) (Code Sec. 6012(a)(8)). The tax year for which the fiduciary files a return begins on the date of the bankruptcy petition filing. The return may be for a calendar year or fiscal year. A trustee in bankruptcy has

¶505

no authority to file a return on Form 1040 for a bankrupt individual. The individual must file an individual return.

Taxable income for bankruptcy estates is computed in the same manner as an individual, but the tax rates for a married individual filing separately apply (¶ 15) (Code Sec. 1398(c); Instructions to Form 1041). If a bankruptcy estate does not itemize deductions, it can claim the standard deduction available for a married individual filing separately (¶ 131).

A separate taxable entity is not created when a case is brought under Chapter 13 of the Bankruptcy Code, which involves adjustment of debts of an individual with regular income. A separate taxable entity also is not created when an individual is in receivership (Reg. § 1.641(b)-2(b)).

506. Bankruptcy Estate of Partnership or Corporate Debtor. The commencement of bankruptcy proceedings for a partnership or corporation does not create a separate taxable entity (Code Sec. 1399). Thus, there is no obligation imposed on the bankruptcy trustee to file a Form 1041 on behalf of the estate. A receiver, trustee, or assignee who by court order has possession or holds title to substantially of the property or business of a corporation must file the income tax return for the corporation on Form 1120 (Reg. § 1.6012-3(b)(4)). The receiver, trustee, or assignee must file the return whether or not it is operating the property or business of the corporation. A receiver in charge of only *a small part* of the property of a corporation, such as a receiver in mortgage foreclosure proceedings, need not file the return. Bankrupt partnerships must file their returns on Form 1065.

507. Termination of Trusts and Estates. An estate is recognized as a taxable entity only during the period of administration or settlement (i.e., the period actually required by the executor or administrator to perform the ordinary duties of administration, such as collection of assets, payment of debts and legacies, etc.) (Reg. § 1.641(b)-3(a)). This is true whether the period is longer or shorter than that specified under local law for estate settlement. However, estate administration may not be unduly prolonged.

The estate is considered terminated for federal tax purposes after the expiration of a reasonable period for the performance of administration duties. It may also expire when all estate assets have been distributed except for a reasonable amount set aside in good faith for the payment of contingent liabilities and expenses. If the estate has joined in making a valid election to treat a qualified revocable trust as part of the estate (¶ 516), then it does not terminate prior to the end of the election period.

A trust is recognized as a taxable entity until the trust property has been distributed to successors, plus a reasonable time after this event as is necessary for the trustee to complete trust administration (Reg. § 1.641(b)-3(b)). A trust is also considered terminated when all the assets have been distributed except for a reasonable amount set aside in good faith to pay contingent liabilities and expenses (other than a claim by a beneficiary in that capacity).

Once an estate or trust is considered terminated for tax purposes, its gross income, deductions, and credits subsequent to termination are considered to be the gross income, deductions, and credits of the persons who succeed to the property (Reg. § 1.641(b)-3(d)).

Fiduciary Return and Payment of Tax

See CCH® AnswerConnect: *Trust and Estate Filing Requirements and Other Compliance Issues for Form 1041* for more information on this topic.

510. Return of Trust or Estate by Fiduciary (Form 1041). A fiduciary must file a return on Form 1041 or Form 1040-NR for an estate or trust if:

- the estate has gross income of $600 or more for the tax year;

- the trust (other than a trust exempt under Code Sec. 501(a)) has any taxable income, or gross income of at least $600 regardless of the amount of taxable income;

- any beneficiary of the estate or trust is a nonresident alien (unless the trust is exempt under Code Sec. 501(a)); or

- an individual's bankruptcy estate under Chapter 7 or Chapter 11 of the Bankruptcy Code has gross income for the tax year of at least the basic standard deduction amount for a married individual filing separately ($12,200 for 2019 and $12,400 for 2020), plus the personal exemption amount ($0 for 2018 through 2025) (¶ 505) (Code Sec. 6012(a); Reg. § 1.6012-3; Instructions to Form 1041).

If there is more than one fiduciary, the return can be filed by any one of them. However, if an estate has both domiciliary and ancillary representatives, each representative must file a return. A trustee of two or more trusts must file a separate return for each trust, even though the trusts were created by the same grantor for the same beneficiaries. Two or more trusts may be treated as one trust under certain circumstances (¶ 515).

Form 1041 generally must be filed on or before the 15th day of the *fourth* month following the close of the tax year (Code Sec. 6072(a)). An automatic extension of *five-and-a-half months* is provided by filing Form 7004 on or before the normal due date of the return, and making a proper estimate of the amount of tax due for the tax year (Reg. § 1.6081-6). The automatic extension period is *six months* for an individual's Chapter 7 or 11 bankruptcy estate (¶ 505) or for a qualified funeral trust (¶ 575). The automatic extension does not extend the time for payment of any tax due on the return. In addition, the extension to file does not extend the time for a beneficiary of the estate or trust to file its income tax return or to pay any tax on the beneficiary's return. Form 1041 generally is not required to be filed electronically, unless prepared and filed by a specified tax return preparer (¶ 2503).

The due date for filing any federal income tax return, including Form 1041, otherwise due on or after April 1, 2020, and before July 15, 2020, is automatically extended to July 15, 2020, in response to the COVID-19 (coronavirus) crisis (Notice 2020-23, amplifying Notice 2020-18). The extension is automatic and a trust does not need to file Form 7004 or call the IRS to receive it. Penalties and interest for failure to file a return or pay taxes as a result of the extension will not accrue until July 16, 2020. A trust that needs more time to file its return after July 15, 2020, may request an additional extension by filing Form 7004 by July 15, 2020, but the extension may not go beyond the original statutory or regulatory extension date.

The fiduciary of an estate or trust need not file a copy of the will or trust instrument with the estate or trust income tax return unless requested by the IRS (Reg. § 1.6012-3(a)(2)). If requested, the fiduciary should file a copy (including any amendments), accompanied by a written declaration of truth and completeness and a statement indicating the provisions of the will or trust instrument that determine the extent to which estate or trust income is taxable to the estate or trust, the beneficiaries, or the grantor.

An estate or trust that is obligated to file an income tax return must furnish a copy of Schedule K-1 (Form 1041) to each beneficiary (1) who receives a distribution from the estate or trust for the year, or (2) to whom any item with respect to the tax year is allocated (Code Sec. 6034A). This statement must contain the information required to be shown on the return and be furnished on or before the date on which the return is to be filed. A copy must also be attached to Form 1041 (Instructions to Form 1041). A penalty may be assessed for each failure to file or furnish a correct information return (¶ 2816) or payee statement (¶ 2823).

Accounting Period. When filing its first return, an estate may choose the same accounting period as the decedent, or it may choose a calendar tax year or fiscal tax year. If it chooses the decedent's accounting period, its first return will be for a short period to cover the unexpired term of the decedent's regular tax year (Code Secs. 441 and 443). An exemption of $600 is allowed on a short-period return, without proration (¶ 534) (Reg. § 1.443-1(a)(2)). However, if the estate gets approval from the IRS to change the accounting period, the exemption on the short-period return must be prorated (Reg. § 1.443-1(b)(1)(v)).

A trust (other than a trust exempt from tax under Code Sec. 501 and a charitable trust under Code Sec. 4947(a)) must adopt a calendar tax year (Code Sec. 644). Thus, a trust must generally file Form 1041 on or before April 15 following the close of the tax year, unless the due date falls on a weekend or holiday (¶ 2549). An existing trust that is required to change its tax year must annualize any income earned in the short year. A trust must obtain IRS approval to change its annual accounting period to its required (calendar) tax year (¶ 1513).

Payment of Tax. The entire income tax liability of an estate or trust must be paid on or before the due date for its return (Code Sec. 6151). An estate that has been in existence for more than two years, and a new or existing trust, must pay estimated tax in the same manner as an individual (¶ 511).

511. Payment of Estimated Tax by Trust or Estate. Estates and trusts are generally required to make quarterly estimated tax payments in the same manner as individuals (¶ 125). However, estates and grantor trusts that receive the residue of a probate estate under the grantor's will are only required to make estimated tax payments for tax years that end two or more years after the decedent's death (Code Sec. 6654(l)).

Estates or trusts with a short tax year generally must pay installments of tax on or before the 15th day of the fourth, sixth and ninth months of the tax year, and the 15th day of the first month of the following tax year (¶ 127). The amount of each installment in a short tax year is determined by dividing the required annual payment by the number of payments required for that year (Notice 87-32).

The due date of any required installment calculated on Form 1041-ES and due on or after April 1, 2020, and before July 15, 2020, is automatically extended to July 15, 2020, as a result of the COVID-19 (coronavirus) crisis (Notice 2020-23, amplifying Notice 2020-18). The extension is automatic, and an estate or trust does not need to file any form or call the IRS to receive it. Penalties and interest for failure to pay taxes will not accrue until July 16, 2020, as a result of the extension. The extension does not extend the time to pay estimated income tax beyond July 15, 2020.

Estates and trusts generally have 45 days (rather than the 15 days allowed individuals) to compute the payments under the estimated tax annualization rules. The payment due dates are unchanged (Code Sec. 6654(l)). First-time filers must file Form 1041-ES, which includes vouchers to be included with quarterly payments. After the first payment, the IRS should provide pre-printed vouchers. A fiduciary paying estimated tax for more than one trust should submit a separate Form 1041-ES and a separate check for each trust. However, a fiduciary may submit a single check for multiple trusts if a separate estimated tax voucher is submitted for each trust (Announcement 87-32).

The trustee of a trust, or the fiduciary of an estate whose tax year is reasonably expected to be its last tax year, may elect to treat any or all of an estimated tax payment as a payment made by the beneficiary and credited toward the beneficiary's tax liability (Code Sec. 643(g)). If elected, the payment is not treated as an estimated tax payment made by the estate or trust. The election is made on Form 1041-T and must be filed on or before the 65th day after the close of the tax year (generally March 6, 2020, for the 2019 calendar year). However, the due date for performing certain time-sensitive actions, including making the election to treat estimated taxes as paid by the beneficiary, otherwise due on or after April 1, 2020, and before July 15, 2020, is automatically extended to July 15, 2020, in response to the COVID-19 (coronavirus) crisis (Notice 2020-23; Rev. Proc. 2018-58).

512. Personal Liability of Fiduciary. Any fiduciary (other than a trustee acting under the Bankruptcy Code) who pays any debt due by the decedent or the estate, in whole or in part, before federal tax obligations are satisfied becomes personally liable for the tax of the estate to the extent of such payments (Reg. § 1.641(b)-2; 31 U.S.C. § 3713). The fiduciary is not liable for amounts paid out for debts that have priority over the federal taxes due and owing on the estate, such as a decedent's funeral expenses or probate administration costs. Further, an executor or administrator who pays other debts is not personally liable unless the executor or administrator has either personal knowledge of a tax due the United States or knowledge that would put a reasonably prudent person on notice that such tax debts exist (*L.K. New*, Dec. 28,568, 48 TC 671). Discharge of the fiduciary does not terminate the fiduciary's personal liability for the payment of other debts of the estate without satisfying prior tax claims.

Taxation of Trusts and Estates

See CCH® AnswerConnect: *Income Taxation of Trusts and Estates* for more information on this topic.

514. Income Taxation of Trusts and Estates. An estate or trust is a separate taxable entity (¶ 501). Its entire income for its tax year generally must be reported on Form 1041, which must be filed by the fiduciary (¶ 510). If income is required to be distributed currently or is properly distributed to a beneficiary, the estate or trust is regarded as a conduit with respect to that income. It is allowed a deduction for the portion of gross income that is currently distributable to the beneficiaries or is properly paid or credited to them (¶ 542—¶ 545). The beneficiaries are generally taxed on the part of the income currently distributed, and the estate or trust is taxed on the portion that it has accumulated. The income allocated to a beneficiary retains the same character in the beneficiary's hands that it had in the hands of the estate or trust (Reg. § § 1.652(b)-1 and 1.662(b)-1).

For purposes of the income taxation of estates and nongrantor trusts, the term income (without specifying gross income, taxable income, undistributed net income, or distributable net income) refers to income of the estate or trust for the tax year determined under the terms of its governing instrument and applicable local law. Thus, it is income as it would be computed in an accounting to the court having jurisdiction over the estate or trust (Code Sec. 643(b); Reg. § 1.643(b)-1). Trust provisions that depart fundamentally from concepts of income and principal are not recognized for tax purposes. An allocation of amounts between income and principal pursuant to applicable local law will be respected if local law provides for a reasonable apportionment between the income and remainder beneficiaries of the trust's total return for the year, including ordinary income, tax-exempt income, capital gains, and appreciation.

Income items of an estate or trust are discussed at ¶ 520—¶ 527. Ordinary deductions of an estate or trust are discussed at ¶ 528—¶ 536. The charitable contribution deduction is discussed at ¶ 537—¶ 538. The deduction for distributions to beneficiaries and the concept of distributable net income (DNI) are discussed at ¶ 542—¶ 549. The treatment of tax credits of an estate or trust is discussed at ¶ 540.

515. Multiple Trusts Treated as One Trust. One grantor may create several trusts, and the income may be taxed separately for each trust. If there is intent to create separate trusts for multiple beneficiaries, the fact that the corpus of each trust is kept in one fund will not necessarily defeat the grantor's intent. Although it is not necessary to divide the corpus physically in order to carry out the intent of the parties, it is necessary to comply literally with the terms of the trust instrument in other respects (*United States Trust Co. of New York*, SCt, 36-1 USTC ¶ 9040).

Two or more trusts, however, will be treated as one trust if (1) the trusts have substantially the same grantor or grantors and substantially the same primary beneficiary or beneficiaries, and (2) a principal purpose of the trusts is the avoidance of income tax (Code Sec. 643(f)). A special safe-harbor provision applies to any trust that was irrevocable on March 1, 1984, except to the extent that corpus is contributed to the trust after that date.

516. Computation of Tax for Trust and Estates. An estate or trust computes its tax liability by using the separate estate and trust income tax rate schedule at ¶ 19. The taxable income of an estate or trust for purposes of regular income tax is determined by subtracting from its gross income (¶ 520) allowable deductions (¶ 528), amounts distributable to beneficiaries (to the extent of distributable net income (DNI)) (¶ 543), and the proper exemption amount (¶ 534) (Code Sec. 641; Reg. § § 1.641(a)-1 and 1.641(b)-1).

The alternative minimum tax (AMT) of an estate or trust (¶ 190) is computed by determining DNI under the general rules for regular income tax liability, subject to adjustments under the minimum tax rules. The AMT is computed on Part III of Schedule I (Form 1041). Grantor trusts and employees' trusts are subject to special tax treatment (¶ 571 and ¶ 2101).

Qualified Revocable Trusts. A trustee of a qualified revocable trust (QRT) and the executor, if any, of a decedent's estate may join in an election to treat the revocable trust as part of the estate (Code Sec. 645; Reg. § 1.645-1). A QRT is any trust or portion of a trust that, on the date of the decedent's death, is treated as owned by the decedent as grantor by reason of a power to revoke the trust (¶ 582), but without regard to powers held by the decedent's spouse (¶ 578). The election allows the revocable trust to enjoy certain income tax treatment that would otherwise be accorded only to the decedent's estate, such as claiming the unlimited deduction for amounts permanently set aside for charity without first actually paying the amount (¶ 537), waiving the active participation requirement under the passive loss rules for two years after the decedent's death (¶ 1165), and qualifying for amortization of reforestation expenditures (¶ 530).

The election is made on Form 8855, which must be filed by the due date (including extensions) of the Form 1041 for the first tax year of the related estate or filing trust. The election period begins on the date of the decedent's death, and ends on the earlier of the day on which both the trust and related estate have distributed all of their assets, or the day before the applicable date, which is either (1) two years after the date of death, if no federal estate tax return is required, or (2) six months after the final determination of estate tax liability, if a federal estate tax return must be filed. The due date for filing any federal income tax return, including Form 1041 and Form 8855, otherwise due on or after April 1, 2020, and before July 15, 2020, is automatically extended to July 15, 2020, in response to the COVID-19 (coronavirus) crisis. This delay also applies to any time-sensitive acts for which the deadline would fall during the affected period, including an election to treat a QRT as part of an estate on Form 8855 (Notice 2020-23, amplifying Notice 2020-18; Rev. Proc. 2018-58).

Electing Small Business Trust. An electing small business trust (ESBT) (¶ 501) is taxed in a different manner than other trusts (Code Sec. 641(c); Reg. § 1.641(c)-1). First, the portion of the ESBT that consists of stock in one or more S corporations is treated as a separate trust for purposes of computing the income tax attributable to the S corporation stock held by the trust. This portion of the trust's income is taxed at the highest rate imposed on estates and trusts, and includes:

- the items of income, loss, deduction, or credit allocated to the trust as an S corporation shareholder;

- gain or loss from the sale of the S corporation stock;

- any state or local income taxes and administrative expenses of the trust properly allocable to the S corporation stock; and

- any interest expense paid or accrued on debt incurred to acquire S corporation stock.

Capital losses are allowed in computing an ESBT's income only to the extent of capital gains. Moreover, no deduction is allowed for amounts distributed to beneficiaries except as described above. No additional deductions or credits are allowed. Also, the ESBT's income is not included in the DNI of the trust and, therefore, is not included in the beneficiaries' income. Furthermore, no item relating to the S corporation stock is apportioned to any beneficiary. The trust's AMT exemption amount is zero. Special rules apply upon termination of all or a part of the ESBT (¶ 304).

For tax years beginning after 2017, an ESBT's charitable deduction is determined by the rules that apply to individual donors (¶ 1058), not by the rules that generally apply to trusts (¶ 537). Further, for the temporary 60-percent limit on cash contributions to certain charitable organizations (¶ 1059), the ESBT's adjusted gross income (AGI) is generally calculated in the same way it is for individuals. However, deductions for costs which are paid or incurred in connection with the trust's administration and would not have been incurred were the property not held in the trust are allowable in arriving at AGI (Code Sec. 641(c)(2)(E)).

Special rules apply for calculating the 3.8-percent net investment income tax (¶ 517) of an ESBT (Reg. § 1.1411-3(c)).

A nonresident alien may be a potential current beneficiary (PCB) of a shareholder electing small business trust (ESBT) without causing the loss of S corporation status (see ¶ 304). Nonresident alien PCBs are prevented from avoiding U.S. tax on certain types of S corporation income when these nonresident aliens are owners of grantor trusts electing to be ESBTs. The S corporation income is reallocated to the S corporation portion of the ESBT if that income otherwise would have been allocated to a nonresident alien deemed owner under the grantor trust rules (Reg. § 1.641(c)-1). Essentially, the S Corporation income is taxed at the trust level instead of the beneficiary level.

Gifts from Expatriates. A domestic trust that receives property, directly or indirectly, by gift, devise, bequest, or inheritance from a covered expatriate (¶ 2412) after the date of expatriation must pay a tax equal to the value of such covered gift or bequest multiplied by the greater of the highest federal estate tax rate or the highest federal gift tax rate in effect. Similarly, a covered gift or bequest made to a foreign trust (¶ 501) is subject to the tax, but only at the time a distribution of income or principal is made to a U.S. citizen or resident from the trust that is attributable to the covered gift or bequest. A foreign trust can elect to be treated as a domestic trust for these purposes. The election can be revoked with IRS consent (¶ 2948).

517. Net Investment Income Tax of Trusts and Estates. An estate or trust is liable for a 3.8-percent net investment income tax (NIIT) on the lesser of: (1) its undistributed net investment income for the tax year, or (2) any excess of its adjusted gross income (AGI) (¶ 528) over the dollar amount at which the highest tax bracket for estates and trusts begins for the tax year ($12,750 for 2019 and $12,950 for 2020) (Code Sec. 1411(a)(2); Reg. § 1.1411-3). An estate or trust's undistributed net investment income is its net investment income (¶ 117) reduced by distributions of net investment income to beneficiaries, and by deductions for amounts of net investment income paid or permanently set aside for a charitable purpose (¶ 537).

The NIIT does not apply to several types of trusts, including:

- trusts that are exempt from federal income taxes;

- trusts whose unexpired interests are devoted to one or more charitable purposes described in Code Sec. 170(c)(2)(B);

- grantor trusts (¶ 571);

- electing Alaska Native Settlement Trusts (¶ 2396);

- cemetery perpetual care funds under Code Sec. 642(i); and

- any other trust, fund, or account that is statutorily exempt from federal income tax (Code Sec. 1411(e)(2); Reg. § 1.1411-3(b)).

The tax applies to individual debtors' Chapter 7 and Chapter 11 bankruptcy estates (¶ 505). The tax does not apply to foreign trusts or foreign estates (¶ 501), but does apply to distributions of current year income by foreign trusts or foreign estates to their U.S. beneficiaries (Reg. § 1.1411-3(e)(3)).

520. Gross Income of Trusts and Estates. The gross income of an estate or trust is generally determined in the same manner as that of an individual (Code Sec. 641(b); Reg. § 1.641(a)-2). It includes all items of income received during the tax year, including:

- income accumulated in trust for the benefit of unborn or unascertained persons or persons with contingent interests;

- income accumulated or held for future distribution under the terms of the will or trust;

- income that is to be distributed currently by the fiduciary to the beneficiaries, and income collected by the guardian of an infant that is to be held or distributed as the court may direct;

- income received by the estate of a deceased person during the period of administration or settlement of the estate; and

- income that, at the discretion of the fiduciary, may be either distributed to the beneficiaries or accumulated.

Although all the items above are includible in gross income, the tax liability may rest on either the estate or trust as a separate entity or on the beneficiary (¶ 542).

The allocation of income and deductions between a decedent's estate and the surviving spouse in community property states depends on state community property laws. In most states, the surviving spouse is taxed on one-half of the income flowing from the community property of the estate (Rev. Rul. 55-726).

522. Real Estate Income of Estates. State law determines whether income from real estate during the period of administration is taxable to the decedent's estate or to the heirs or devisees (¶ 520). The IRS has ruled that if state law provides that real property is subject to administration, income derived from the property is taxable to the estate even though legal title may pass directly to the heirs or devisees. However, if the administrator is not entitled to possession or control of real property, income from the property is taxable to the heirs or devisees and not to the estate. Even if the property is not subject to the administrator's control, all or a part of the gain from a sale of property is taxable to the estate to the extent that the property was sold, under state law, to raise funds for its administration (Rev. Rul. 57-133; Rev. Rul. 59-375).

523. Personal Property Income of Estates. Income from personal property, including a gain from the sale or exchange of such property, is taxable to the estate (¶ 520). This is because title to personal property vests in the administrator or executor immediately upon appointment and does not pass to the heirs or legatees until the estate is fully administered and distribution is ordered or approved by the courts, and notwithstanding the fact that the basis of the property distributed relates back to the date of the decedent's death (Rev. Rul. 57-133).

524. Sale of Property by Trusts and Estates. The gain or loss realized on the sale of property acquired by an estate, trust, or beneficiary is determined under special basis rules, the applicability of which depends on how the property was acquired and the nature of the property sold (¶ 1601 and ¶ 1701).

526. Gain on Transfer of Property to Beneficiary. Gain or loss is generally realized by an estate or trust, or by the other beneficiaries, on the distribution of property in kind that satisfies a beneficiary's right to receive a specific dollar amount, specific property other than the property distributed, or other income if income is required to be distributed currently (Reg. § 1.661(a)-2(f)). A special rule generally limits gain recognized on transfers to qualified heirs of property for which a special use valuation election under Code Sec. 2032A was made (¶ 2922) (Code Sec. 1040).

For purposes of the rule limiting gain on transfers to qualified heirs of special use valuation property, a marital deduction trust (¶ 2926) comprising a portion of the residuary estate and measured by a percentage of the value of the adjusted gross estate is considered as being provided for in a fixed dollar amount (Rev. Rul. 60-87). Upon a distribution of property to such a trust, the estate realizes gain or loss equal to the difference between the property's fair market value at the distribution date and its federal estate tax value.

Distribution of a stated percentage of trust corpus to the beneficiary before termination of the trust is not considered a satisfaction of a trust obligation for a definite amount of cash or equivalent value in property. Instead, it is treated as a partial distribution of a share of the trust principal. Thus, there is no sale or exchange, and neither the trustee nor the beneficiary realizes taxable income (Rev. Rul. 55-117). However, a trustee or executor may elect to recognize gain or loss on the distribution of noncash property to a beneficiary as if the property had been sold to the beneficiary at its fair market value (Code Sec. 643(e)(3)). The election is made on the return for the year of distribution and applies to all distributions made by the estate or trust during its entire tax year. Thus, an election to recognize gain or loss cannot be made separately for each distribution. See ¶ 566 for gain recognition on certain property distributions to expatriates.

In the event the election is made, the beneficiary's basis in the distributed property is the estate's or trust's adjusted basis just prior to the distribution, adjusted by the gain or loss recognized by the estate or trust. If the election is not made, the beneficiary's basis is the same as the trust's or estate's, and any gain or loss is recognized by the beneficiary when the beneficiary disposes of the property.

527. Income of Foreign Trusts and Estates. For purposes of computing the taxable income of a foreign estate or foreign trust (¶ 501), the estate or trust is treated as a nonresident alien individual who is not present in the United States at any time (¶ 2409 and ¶ 2425) (Code Sec. 641(b)).

The estate of a nonresident alien is taxed on its income received from U.S. sources, including capital gains and dividends (Rev. Rul. 68-621). The estate is allowed a deduction for distributions to both nonresident aliens and U.S. beneficiaries to the extent that these distributions are not in excess of its distributable net income (¶ 545). The portion of the distribution allocated to capital gains is not includible in the gross income of nonresident alien beneficiaries if they have not resided in the United States for a period of at least 183 days (¶ 2435). However, the portion of a distribution that represents dividends is includible in the gross income of nonresident alien beneficiaries. The fiduciary must withhold U.S. taxes from these dividend distributions at the statutory rate or the applicable treaty rate.

528. Deductions of Trusts and Estates—Generally. An estate or trust is generally allowed the same deductions as an individual in computing taxable income (Code Sec. 641(b); Reg. § 1.641(b)-1). However, the standard deduction available to an estate or trust is zero (Code Sec. 63(c)(6)(D)). In addition, special rules govern the computation of certain deductions and the allocation of deductions between the beneficiaries and the estate or trust (¶ 529—¶ 538). Further, the estate or trust is permitted to claim a deduction for certain distributions to beneficiaries (¶ 544 and ¶ 545). The overall limit on itemized deductions for an individual for tax years before 2018 and after 2025 (¶ 1014) does not apply to an estate and trust (Code Sec. 68(e)).

Miscellaneous Deductions. An estate or trust may claim certain miscellaneous itemized deductions without regard to the two-percent-of-adjusted-gross-income (AGI) limit (¶ 1095) (Code Sec. 67(e); Notice 2018-61). The AGI of an estate or trust is computed in the same manner as for individuals (¶ 1005), except that the following deductions are allowed in determining AGI: administration expenses that would not have been incurred had property not been held by an estate or trust; the personal exemption deduction allowed to an estate and trust (¶ 534); and any distribution to beneficiaries (¶ 544 and ¶ 545).

No other miscellaneous itemized deductions may be claimed in 2018 through 2025 (¶ 1079). For tax years beginning before 2018 and after 2025, certain miscellaneous itemized deductions of an estate or trust may only be claimed to the extent of they exceed two percent of the taxpayer's AGI. The IRS is authorized to apply the two-percent AGI floor at the beneficiary level, rather than the entity level, with respect to a simple trust. The IRS intends to issue regulations on the ability of beneficiaries to claim the excess deductions of an estate or and trust upon termination for tax years 2018 through 2025.

The U.S. Supreme Court has ruled that only estate or trust administration expenses that would be uncommon, unusual, or unlikely for a hypothetical individual to incur are not subject to the two-percent floor (*M.J. Knight, Trustee,* SCt, 2008-1 USTC ¶ 50,132). These types of costs would not "commonly" or "customarily" be incurred by individuals. Hence, investment advisory fees incurred by an estate or trust are generally subject to the two-percent AGI floor before 2018. Expenses incurred in administering a bankruptcy estate are fully deductible from gross income (CCA 200630016).

Regulations consistent with *Knight* provide that a cost is subject to the two-percent floor to the extent that it commonly or customarily would be incurred by a hypothetical individual holding the same property (Reg. § 1.67-4(a)). Rules are provided for four specific categories of costs: ownership costs, tax preparation fees, investment advisory fees, and appraisal fees. Fees for investment advice are generally subject to the two-percent floor, but certain incremental costs of investment advice beyond the amount normally charged to an individual investor are not. A single fee or commission (a "bundled fee") paid by an estate or nongrantor trust must be allocated between the costs that are subject to the two-percent floor and those that are not (Reg. § 1.67-4(c)). The allocation can be made using any reasonable method. Taxpayers are not required to determine the portion of a bundled fiduciary fee that is subject to the two-percent floor. Instead, taxpayers may deduct 100 percent of the bundled fiduciary fee without regard to the two-percent floor (Reg. § 1.67-4(d); Notice 2011-37).

Qualified Business Income Deduction. An estate and trust can claim the qualified business income deduction (¶ 980P) for tax years beginning after December 31, 2017. Rules similar to those in effect on December 1, 2017, for the domestic production activities deduction (¶ 536) apply for apportioning W-2 wages and unadjusted basis of qualified property between fiduciaries and beneficiaries (Code Sec. 199A(f)(1)(B)). Final regulations provide special rules for applying Code Sec. 199A to estates and trusts and establish anti-abuse rules that apply specifically to the use of a multiple nongrantor trust (Reg. § § 1.199A-6(d) and 1.643(f)-1). Under Code Sec. 199A, the threshold amount is determined at the trust level. Taxpayers could avoid the threshold limit by dividing the assets among multiple trusts, so that each trust would be able to claim its own threshold amount. Reg. § 1.643(f)-1 provides that, for multiple trust arrangements entered into or modified after August 16, 2018, that have substantially the same grantor(s) and primary beneficiary(ies), and if a principal purpose is tax avoidance, will be treated as a single trust. Spouses are treated as one person for purposes of this rule (T.D. 9847).

> **Comment:** In light of comments received, however, the final regulations removed the definition of "principal purpose" and the accompanying examples. The IRS is taking this issue under advisement. In the meantime, the position of the IRS is that treatment under Reg. § 1.643(f)-1 may be made based on the statute and guidance regarding that provision in the legislative history of Code Sec. 643(f).

> Proposed regulations, upon which taxpayers may rely, provide rules for separate shares and charitable remainder unitrusts and their beneficiaries (Proposed Reg. §§ 1.199A-6(d)(iii) and (v)).

529. Deductible Expenses of Trusts and Estates. An estate or trust is generally allowed deductions for any ordinary and necessary expenses incurred in carrying on a trade or business (¶ 901), in the production of income or the management or conservation of income-producing property (¶ 1085), or in connection with the determination, collection, or refund of any tax. Reasonable amounts paid or incurred by a fiduciary on account of administration, including fiduciary fees and litigation expenses, are deductible as well. Such expenses are deductible even if the estate or trust is not engaged in a trade or business, unless the expenses were for the production or collection of tax-exempt income (Reg. § 1.212-1(i)).

Deductions are not allowed for: (1) expenses that are allocable to one or more classes of income exempt from tax (other than interest income); or (2) any amount relating to expenses for the production of income that is allocable to tax-exempt interest income (¶ 970). The IRS allows a deduction for an executor's or administrator's commissions, as paid or accrued, except the portion allocable to tax-exempt income (Rev. Rul. 58-53).

Alimony Payments. An estate can deduct the value of periodic alimony payments it makes under the rules regarding deductions for distributions to beneficiaries (Rev. Rul. 67-304).

> **Comment:** However, note that alimony payments are no longer deductible generally with respect to divorce or separation agreements entered into or modified after December 31, 2018.

Double Deductions Prohibited. Amounts deductible as administration expenses or losses for estate tax (¶ 2925) or generation-skipping transfer tax (¶ 2942) purposes may not also be deducted or offset against the sales price of property in determining gain or loss (i.e., selling expenses) for income tax purposes by the estate or any other person (Code Sec. 642(g); Reg. § 1.642(g)-1). However, the estate can deduct such items for income tax purposes if it files a statement (in duplicate) that the items have not been claimed as deductions for estate tax purposes and that all rights to deduct them for such purposes are waived.

A deduction or portion of a deduction may be allowed for income tax purposes if the appropriate statement is filed, while another deduction or portion is allowed for estate tax purposes (Reg. § 1.642(g)-2). Deductions for taxes, interest, business expenses, and other items accrued *at the decedent's date of death* are allowed as a deduction for estate tax purposes as claims against the estate, and are also allowed as a deduction in respect of a decedent for income tax purposes. However, the estate cannot take an income tax deduction for the decedent's medical and dental expenses that it has paid. These expenses can only be claimed on the estate tax return or the decedent's final income tax return (¶ 1015).

530. Depreciation and Depletion Deductions of Trusts and Estates. Depreciation and depletion deductions must be apportioned between an estate or trust and its beneficiaries (Code Secs. 167(d), 611(b), and 642(e); Reg. §§ 1.167(h)-1, 1.611-1(c), and 1.642(e)-1). Different rules govern estates and trusts.

For a trust, the allowable deduction for depreciation or depletion is generally apportioned between the income beneficiaries and the trustee on the basis of the trust income allocable to each. However, if the trust instrument or local law requires or permits the trustee to maintain a reserve for depreciation or depletion, the deduction is first allocated to the trustee to the extent that income is set aside for the reserve. Any excess is apportioned between the income beneficiaries and the trust on the basis of the trust income allocable to each. No effect is given to any allocation that gives any beneficiary or trustee a share of the deduction greater than a pro rata share of the trust income.

For an estate, the depreciation or depletion allowance is apportioned between the estate and the heirs, legatees, and devisees on the basis of the income from the property allocable to each.

Section 179 Election. Although an estate or trust is entitled to take MACRS depreciation on qualified assets, neither can make a Code Sec. 179 election to expense depreciable business assets (¶ 1208) (Code Sec. 179(d)(4)).

Reforestation Expenditures. Estates can elect to expense reforestation expenditures and amortize any excess expenditures (¶ 1360) (Code Sec. 194). Trusts cannot elect the expense deduction but can elect to amortize such expenditures. Total reforestation expenditures incurred must be apportioned between the income beneficiaries and the fiduciary. Amounts apportioned to a beneficiary must be taken into account in determining the dollar limit on the reforestation expenditures that the beneficiary can expense.

531. Losses and Bad Debt Deductions of Trusts and Estates. An estate or trust can deduct losses from a trade or business or from transactions entered into for profit (¶ 1101). Similarly, the rules governing nonbusiness casualty and theft losses (¶ 1121) apply to an estate or trust. Thus, after the $100-per-occurrence floor has been satisfied, losses in excess of nonbusiness casualty and theft gains are deductible to the extent that they exceed 10 percent of the adjusted gross income (AGI) of the estate or trust. Special rules apply for certain qualified disasters that occurred in 2016 or 2017. For this purpose, an estate's or trust's administration expenses are allowable as a deduction in computing its AGI (Code Sec. 165(h)(4)(C)). The deduction for nonbusiness casualty losses incurred in tax years 2018 through 2025 is limited to losses attributable to federally declared disaster.

A nonbusiness casualty or theft loss sustained or discovered during the settlement of an estate is deductible on the estate's income tax return only if it has not been allowed for estate tax purposes (Code Sec. 165(h)(4)(D); Reg. §§1.165-7(c) and 1.165-8(b)). A statement to this effect should be filed with the return for the year for which the deduction is claimed.

Net Operating Losses. An estate or trust is allowed a deduction for net operating losses (NOLs) (¶ 1145) (Reg. §1.642(d)-1). However, an estate cannot deduct an NOL (or a capital loss (¶ 1752)) sustained by a decedent during the decedent's last tax year (Rev. Rul. 74-175). These losses must be deducted on the decedent's final return. In addition, in computing gross income and deductions for the NOL calculation, a trust must not take into account income and deductions attributable to the grantor or any substantial owner under the grantor trust rules (¶ 571). Also, an estate or trust cannot claim the deductions for charitable contributions (¶ 537) and distributions to beneficiaries (¶ 544 and ¶ 545) in calculating NOLs.

Bad Debts. An estate or trust is entitled to claim bad debt deductions under the rules governing individuals (¶ 1135).

Passive Losses. The passive activity loss rules (¶ 1165) apply to estates and trusts, but not grantor trusts (¶ 1173).

532. Deduction of Taxes by Trusts and Estates. An estate or trust is entitled to the same deductions for taxes as individuals (¶ 1021). In addition, an estate or trust is permitted an offset of the allocable federal estate tax against income in respect of a decedent (¶ 186). The portion of state income taxes allocable to exempt income, other than exempt interest income, is not deductible (¶ 970). The portion of state income taxes attributable to exempt interest income and to income subject to federal income tax is deductible (Rev. Rul. 61-86).

533. Deduction of Interest by Trusts and Estates. Interest paid or accrued during the tax year is deductible by an estate or trust under the same rules that apply to individuals (¶ 1043) (Code Sec. 163). However, there are a number of important differences. For example, interest owed and accrued at the death of the decedent can be deducted on the estate's income tax return as a deduction in respect of the decedent for the tax year in which the interest is paid. If the interest accrues after the decedent's death, it may be claimed as either an estate tax deduction or an income tax deduction (¶ 529).

Interest is not deductible by an estate or trust on a debt incurred, or continued, to purchase or carry obligations the interest on which is wholly exempt from federal income taxes (¶ 970). Personal interest of an estate or trust is also nondeductible (¶ 1043). Further, the deduction for investment interest may not exceed net investment income for the tax year (Code Sec. 163(d)). Net capital gain attributable to the disposition of property held for investment is generally excluded from investment income for purposes of computing this limitation. However, a special election is available to increase net capital gain includible in investment income by reducing the amount eligible for capital gain treatment (¶ 1057).

534. Personal Exemption Amount of Trusts and Estates. An estate can claim a personal exemption of $600 in determining its taxable income (Code Sec. 642(b); Reg. § 1.642(b)-1). A simple trust (¶ 542)—one that is required to distribute all of its income currently—is allowed an exemption of $300. A complex trust is entitled to a $100 exemption. If a final distribution of assets has been made during the year, all income of the estate or trust must be reported as distributed to the beneficiaries, without reduction for the amount claimed for the exemption (¶ 535).

A qualified disability trust, whether taxed as a simple or complex trust, can claim an exemption in the amount available to an unmarried individual who is not a surviving spouse or head of a household (¶ 133) (Code Sec. 642(b)(2)(C)). The exemption amount is adjusted annually for inflation and is $4,200 for 2019 and $4,300 for 2020 (Rev. Proc. 2018-57; Rev. Proc. 2019-44).

535. Loss Carryovers and Excess Deductions of Trusts and Estates. A beneficiary succeeding to the property of an estate or trust can deduct a net operating loss (NOL) carryover (¶ 1149 and ¶ 1153), a capital loss carryover (¶ 562 and ¶ 1754), and deductions in excess of gross income for the year in which the estate or trust terminates (Code Sec. 642(h); Reg. § § 1.642(h)-1—1.642(h)-5). Excess deductions on termination of an estate or trust are allowed only in computing taxable income and must be taken into account in computing the beneficiary's tax preference items. Such deductions may not be used in computing adjusted gross income. In computing excess deductions, the deductions for personal exemptions and amounts set aside for charitable purposes are disregarded. The deduction is claimed as an itemized deduction or capital loss (depending on its nature) on the beneficiary's tax return filed for the year in which the estate or trust terminates.

An individual debtor's bankruptcy estate (¶ 505) succeeds to certain tax attributes of the debtor, including any NOL carryover (Code Sec. 1398(g)). The tax attributes that become part of the estate are determined as of the first day of the debtor's tax year in which the bankruptcy case commences. If any carryback year of the estate is a tax year before the estate's first tax year, the carryback is taken into account in the tax year of the debtor that corresponds to such carryback year and may offset the pre-bankruptcy income of the debtor (Code Sec. 1398(j)(2)(A)). If the estate closes on the issuance of a final decree, the debtor succeeds to the same attributes as the estate, including any unused NOL carryover (Code Sec. 1398(i)). The debtor, however, cannot carry an unused NOL carryback from a tax year that ended after commencement of the bankruptcy case to a tax year that precedes the tax year in which the bankruptcy case was commenced (Code Sec. 1398(j)(2)(B)).

536. Domestic Production Activities Deduction of Trusts and Estates. For tax years beginning before 2018, an estate or nongrantor trust, and the beneficiaries of the estate or trust, may claim the deduction for domestic production activities (¶ 980A) (Code Sec. 199(d)(1)(B), prior to repeal by the Tax Cuts and Jobs Act (P.L. 115-97); Reg. § 1.199-5(e)). In computing the deduction, an estate or trust apportions W-2 wages, domestic production gross receipts (DPGR), cost of goods sold allocable to DPGR, and expenses, losses and deductions properly allocable to DPGR between the beneficiaries and the fiduciary, and among the beneficiaries. The nine-percent applicable percentage limitation on the deduction is applied to the lesser of the estate's or trust's qualified production activities income (QPAI) or its adjusted gross income (AGI), as determined under the AGI computation rules for estates and trusts (¶ 528).

The estate or trust calculates each beneficiary's share (as well as the estate's or trust's own share, if any) of the estate's or trust's QPAI and W-2 wages at the estate or trust level. The QPAI and W-2 wages are allocated to each beneficiary based on the relative proportion of the estate's or trust's distributable net income (DNI) for the tax year that is distributed or required to be distributed to the beneficiary, or retained by the estate or trust (¶ 542 and ¶ 543). If the estate or trust has no DNI for the tax year, QPAI and W-2 wages are allocated entirely to the estate or trust.

Each beneficiary computes his or her DPAD deduction by combining their share of QPAI and W-2 wages from the estate or trust with their share of QPAI and W-2 wages from other sources. When determining its total QPAI and W-2 wages from such other sources, the beneficiary does not take into account the items allocated from the estate or trust. The beneficiary's share of W-2 wages from the estate or trust is determined under the law applicable to pass-through entities based on the beginning date of the estate's or trust's tax year, not the beneficiary's tax year (Reg. § 1.199-5(e)(3)).

Grantor Trust. For a grantor trust (¶ 571), the owner computes its QPAI with respect to the owned portion of the trust as if that QPAI had been generated by activities performed directly by the owner (Reg. § 1.199-5(d)). Similarly, for purposes of the wage limitation (¶ 980C), the owner takes into account its share of the trust's W-2 wages that are attributable to the owned portion of the trust. The nongrantor trust provisions (discussed above) do not apply to the owned portion of the trust.

537. Charitable Deductions of Trusts and Estates—Generally. Estates and complex trusts are allowed an unlimited charitable deduction for amounts paid to recognized charities (¶ 1061) out of gross income (other than unrelated business income of a trust) under the terms of the governing instrument during the tax year (Code Sec. 642(c)). For example, amounts bequeathed to charity that are paid out of corpus under state law are not deductible from income as charitable contributions or as distributions to beneficiaries (Rev. Rul. 71-285). However, payments in compromise of bequests to charity are deductible (Rev. Rul. 59-15). See ¶ 538 for limitations on the charitable deduction for estates and trusts.

The trustee or administrator may elect to treat charitable payments made during the year following the close of a tax year as having been paid in the earlier year for deduction purposes (Code Sec. 642(c)(1); Reg. § 1.642(c)-1(b)). The election must be made no later than the time, including extensions, prescribed by law for filing the income tax return for the tax year in which payment is made. The election is binding for the tax year for which it is made and may not be revoked after the time for making the election has expired.

Estates may also claim an unlimited deduction for amounts of gross income permanently set aside for charitable purposes (Reg. § 1.642(c)-2). The income must be permanently set aside for a purpose specified in Code Sec. 170(c) or it must be used exclusively for: (1) religious, charitable, scientific, literary, or educational purposes; (2) the prevention of cruelty to children or animals; or (3) the establishment, acquisition, maintenance, or operation of a nonprofit public cemetery. For most complex trusts, the unlimited deduction for gross income that is permanently set aside for charitable purposes does not apply.

A provision in a governing instrument or local law that specifically identifies the source out of which amounts are to be paid, permanently set aside, or used for charitable purposes must have economic effect independent of income tax consequences in order to be respected for federal tax purposes (Reg. § 1.642(c)-3(b)(2)).

Pooled income funds (¶ 593) may claim a set-aside deduction only for gross income attributable to gain from the sale of a long-term capital asset that is permanently set aside for the benefit of the charity (Reg. § 1.642(c)-2(c)). No deduction is allowed with respect to gross income of the fund that is (1) attributable to income other than net long-term capital gains or (2) earned with respect to amounts transferred to the fund before August 1, 1969. The investment and accounting requirements applicable to trusts also apply to pooled income funds.

5

TRUSTS/ESTATES

The charitable deduction is normally computed on Schedule A (Form 1041). However, pooled income funds claiming the set-aside deduction for long-term capital gain and nonexempt charitable trusts under Code Sec. 4947(a)(1) treated as private foundations (¶ 631) must compute their deduction on a separate schedule. Also, a nonexempt charitable trust not treated as a private foundation must file Form 990 or Form 990-EZ in addition to Form 1041 if its gross receipts are normally more than $50,000. However, the trust may file Form 990 or Form 990-EZ to satisfy its Form 1041 filing requirement if it has zero taxable income (¶ 625).

Every trust claiming a charitable deduction for amounts permanently set aside (other than nonexempt charitable trusts under Code Sec. 4947(a)(1), and split-interest trusts under Code Sec. 4947(a)(2)) is required to file an information return on Form 1041-A generally by April 15 following the close of the trust's calendar year (Code Sec. 6034). However, the due date for performing certain time-sensitive actions, including the date for filing Form 1041-A, otherwise due on or after April 1, 2020, and before July 15, 2020, is automatically extended to July 15, 2020, in response to the COVID-19 (coronavirus) crisis (Notice 2020-23; Rev. Proc. 2018-58). Form 1041-A does not have to be filed if the trust must distribute all of its income for the tax year (a simple trust). Split-interest trusts (pooled income funds (¶ 593), charitable remainder trusts (¶ 590), and charitable lead trusts (¶ 2932)) file their information return on Form 5227.

Both the trust and the trustee can be liable for a penalty of $10 per day for returns to be filed in 2019, up to a maximum of $5,000, for failure to timely file Form 1041-A ($10 for return to be filed 2020) (Code Sec. 6652(c)(2) and (7); Rev. Proc. 2018-18; Rev. Proc. 2018-57). A split-interest trust that fails to timely file or to provide the required information on Form 5227 can be liable for a penalty of $20 per day for returns to be filed in 2019, up to a maximum of $10,000 ($20 per day, up to a maximum of $10,500 for 2020). For returns to be filed in 2019, if the split-interest trust's gross income exceeds $261,500, the penalty is $100 per day, up to a maximum of $52,000 (for 2020, $105 per day, up to a maximum of $53,000 if the split-interest trust's gross income exceeds $266,500). An additional penalty may be assessed against the person required to file the return if he or she knowingly fails to file it. Criminal penalties also apply for willful failure to file a return and filing a false or fraudulent return (Reg. § 1.6034-1(d)).

538. Limitations on Charitable Deductions of Trusts. A trust is not entitled to an unlimited charitable deduction (¶ 537) for income that is allocable to its unrelated business income for the tax year (Code Secs. 642(c)(4) and 681(a); Reg. § § 1.642(c)-3(d), 1.681(a)-1, and 1.681(a)-2). The unrelated business income of a trust is computed in much the same manner as the unrelated business taxable income (UBTI) of a tax-exempt organization (¶ 655 and ¶ 687). However, in computing unrelated business income, a trust can claim deductions for payments to charities, subject to the percentage limitations applicable to individuals' charitable deductions (¶ 1058).

Charitable deductions are not allowed for otherwise deductible gifts to an organization upon which a tax has been imposed for termination of private foundation status, unless the IRS has abated the tax (¶ 649) (Code Sec. 508(d)(1) and (3)). General contributors will be denied deductions after the organization is notified of the loss of its private foundation status. Substantial contributors (¶ 635) will be denied deductions in the year in which action is taken to terminate the organization's private foundation status.

If a charitable contribution consists of gain from the sale of qualified small business stock (section 1202 stock) held for more than five years (¶ 1905), the charitable deduction amount must be adjusted for any gain excluded from gross income (Code Sec. 642(c)(4)).

Deductions are also denied for contributions to any private foundation, nonexempt charitable trust, or split-interest trust as defined in Code Sec. 4947 that fails to meet the governing instrument requirements for private foundations (Code Sec. 508(d)(2)). Deductions for gifts and bequests to any organization are disallowed during the period that the organization fails to notify the IRS that it is claiming exempt status as a charitable organization (¶ 623). Churches, organizations with gross receipts of $5,000 or less, and certain other organizations designated by the IRS are exempt from the notification requirements. Charitable deductions are also disallowed for bequests and gifts to a foreign private foundation after the IRS notifies it that it has engaged in a prohibited transaction, or for a year in which such an organization loses its exempt status for engaging in such a transaction (Code Sec. 4948(c)(4)).

State or Local Tax Benefits. A taxpayer that makes a charitable contribution after August 27, 2018, must reduce the amount of any charitable contribution deduction by any state or local tax (SALT) credit or deduction received or expected to be received. An exception exists if the SALT credit is 15 percent or less of the contribution or the SALT deduction does not exceed the contribution (¶ 1061). The reduction in the charitable contribution deduction applies to a trust or decedent's estate if it makes a payment of gross income to charitable organization, and the trust or estate receives or expects to receive a SALT benefit in consideration for such payment (Reg. § 1.642(c)-3(g)).

540. Income Tax Credits of Trusts and Estates. The tax credits allowed to individuals are generally allowed to estates and trusts in computing income tax liability (Reg. § 1.641(b)-1). The credits typically must be apportioned between the estate or trust and the beneficiaries on the basis of the income allocable to each. However, the foreign tax credit (¶ 1461) is allocated according to the proportionate share of the foreign taxes (Code Sec. 642(a); Reg. § 1.642(a)(2)-1).

The general business tax credit is a limited nonrefundable credit against income tax that is claimed after all other nonrefundable credits are claimed (¶ 1465). The amount of the general business tax credit may not exceed the net income tax minus the greater of the tentative minimum tax or 25 percent of the net regular tax liability over $25,000. For estates and trusts, the $25,000 amount must be reduced to an amount that bears the same ratio to $25,000 as the portion of the income of the estate or trust that is not allocated to the beneficiaries bears to the total income of the estate or trust (Code Sec. 38(c)(6)(D)). Any unused credit can be carried back one year and forward 20 years (Code Sec. 39).

Estates and trusts are also entitled to claim various refundable tax credits, including the credit for federal income tax withheld on wages and backup withholding (¶ 1421 and ¶ 2645), the credit for taxes paid on undistributed capital gain of a regulated investment company (¶ 1430), and the credit for federal excise taxes paid on fuels (¶ 1429).

Income Distribution Deduction

See CCH® AnswerConnect: *Income Taxation of Trusts and Estates* for more information on this topic.

542. Simple v. Complex Trust. The deduction allowed to simple trusts (¶ 544) and to estates and complex trusts (¶ 545) for distributions to beneficiaries is determined by reference to distributable net income (DNI) (¶ 543).

A simple trust is a trust that: (1) is required to distribute all of its income currently whether or not distributions of current income are in fact made; and (2) does not allow any amount to be paid or set aside for charitable contributions (Code Sec. 651; Reg. § 1.651(a)-1). A trust may be a simple trust even though, under local law or the governing trust instrument, capital gains must be allocated to corpus. The income required to be distributed in order for the trust to qualify as a simple trust is the income determined under local law and the governing instrument (Code Sec. 643(b); Reg. § 1.643(b)-1). This will generally include only ordinary income because capital gains under most trust instruments and state laws are considered corpus. A trust will lose its classification as a simple trust (but not its $300 exemption) for any year during which it distributes corpus (¶ 544). Thus, a trust can never be a simple trust during the year of termination or in a year of partial liquidation (Reg. § 1.651(a)-3).

A complex trust is any trust other than a simple trust described above (Reg. § 1.661(a)-1). The same rules that apply to complex trusts generally also apply to estates.

Loans by Foreign Trusts. A foreign trust (¶ 501) will not be treated as a simple trust if it makes a loan of cash, cash equivalents, or marketable securities to, or permits the uncompensated use of any other trust property by, a grantor or beneficiary who is a U.S. person or a party related to such a grantor or beneficiary (Code Sec. 643(i)). The amount of the loan or the fair market value of the property's use is treated as a distribution by the trust for purposes of the distribution deduction (¶ 545), the gross income of trust beneficiaries (¶ 556), and the treatment of excess trust distributions (¶ 567). For trust property other than a loan of cash or marketable securities, distribution treatment does not apply if the trust is paid the fair market value for the property's use within a reasonable time period. Any subsequent transaction between the trust and the original borrower regarding the loan principal—such as the complete or partial repayment, satisfaction, cancellation, or discharge of the loan—or the return of the property used is disregarded.

543. Distributable Net Income (DNI). The deductions allowable to an estate or trust for amounts paid or credited to beneficiaries (¶ 544 and ¶ 545) are limited to the entity's distributable net income (DNI). The entity's DNI may also limit the amount of the distribution taxable to the beneficiary (¶ 554) and it is a factor in applying the conduit rule (¶ 559).

The DNI of an estate or trust generally consists of the same items of gross income and deductions that make up the taxable income of the estate or trust. There are important modifications:

- no deduction is allowed for distributions to beneficiaries;
- the deduction for the personal exemption is disallowed (¶ 534);
- tax-exempt interest on state and local bonds is included, reduced by amounts that would be deductible but for the disallowance of deductions on expenses and interest related to tax-exempt income;
- for a foreign trust (¶ 501), gross income from outside the United States (reduced by amounts which would be deductible but for the disallowance of deductions on expenses related to tax-exempt income) and within the United States is included;
- capital gains are excluded if they are allocable to corpus and are not (1) paid, credited, or required to be distributed to any beneficiary during the tax year, or (2) paid, permanently set aside, or to be used for a charitable purpose (¶ 537);
- capital losses are excluded except to the extent of their use in determining the amount of capital gains paid, credited, or required to be distributed to any beneficiary during the tax year; and
- in the case of a simple trust, extraordinary dividends or taxable stock dividends that the fiduciary, acting in good faith, allocates to corpus are excluded (Code Sec. 643(a); Reg. § § 1.643(a)-0—1.643(a)-7).

The DNI of the estate or trust is determined by taking into account a net operating loss (NOL) deduction (¶ 531 and ¶ 556) (Rev. Rul. 61-20). However, the exclusion of gain from the sale or exchange of qualified small business stock (section 1202 stock) held for more than five years (¶ 1905) is not taken into account (Code Sec. 643(a)(3)).

544. Deduction for Distributions to Beneficiaries of a Simple Trust. A simple trust (¶ 542) may deduct the amount of income that the trustee is under a duty to distribute currently to beneficiaries, even if the trustee makes the actual distribution after the close of the tax year (Code Sec. 651; Reg. § § 1.651(a)-2 and 1.651(b)-1). If other amounts are distributed—such as a payment from corpus to meet the terms of an annuity payable from income or corpus—the complex trust rules apply for that year, except that the $300 personal exemption (¶ 534) is still allowed (Reg. § 1.642(b)-1). If the income required to be distributed exceeds distributable net income (DNI), the distribution deduction is limited to DNI (¶ 543), computed without including tax-exempt income and related deductions.

545. Deduction for Distributions to Beneficiaries of Complex Trusts and Estates. An estate or complex trust (¶ 542) may deduct any amount of income for the tax year that is required to be distributed currently to beneficiaries (Code Sec. 661(a); Reg. § 1.661(a)-2). This includes any amount required to be distributed that may be paid out of income or corpus, to the extent that it is in fact paid out of income. An estate or complex trust may also deduct any other amounts properly paid or credited or required to be distributed in the tax year, including amounts distributable at the discretion of the fiduciary and a distribution in kind. The amount to be taken into account in determining the deduction depends on whether the estate or trust elected to recognize gain on a noncash distribution of property in kind (¶ 526). In no case may the deduction exceed the distributable net income (DNI) of the estate or trust (¶ 543).

¶543

Special provisions exclude from the estate's or trust's distribution deduction any unlimited charitable contribution (¶ 537), and certain gifts or bequests of a specific sum of money or specific property if paid or distributed all at once or in not more than three installments (¶ 556 and ¶ 564) (Code Sec. 663(a); Reg. §§ 1.663(a)-1 and 1.663(a)-2). Also, an estate or trust cannot include in the distribution deduction for the current tax year an amount deemed distributed to a beneficiary in a prior tax year (Reg. § 1.663(a)-3).

If a will is silent, state law determines whether income or gain during the period of estate administration is properly paid or credited to a legatee (Rev. Rul. 71-335). Also, a testamentary trustee can be a legatee or beneficiary for the purpose of a taxable distribution (*G.W. Crawford Estate*, CA-3, 44-1 USTC ¶ 9110).

If estate or trust income is of varying types, the distribution deduction is treated as consisting of the same proportion of each class of items entering into the DNI calculation as the total of each class bears to total DNI (Code Sec. 661(b); Reg. § 1.661(b)-1). However, items will be allocated in accordance with a trust instrument or local law providing for a different method of allocation. No deduction is allowed to the estate or trust for the part of a beneficiary's distribution that consists of DNI that is not included in the gross income of the estate or trust, such as tax-exempt interest income (Code Sec. 661(c); Reg. § 1.661(c)-1).

In applying the above rule, all deductions entering into the computation of DNI (including charitable contributions) are allocated among the different types of income that make up the DNI in the following manner (Reg. §§ 1.652(b)-3 and 1.661(b)-2):

(1) The deductions *directly* attributable to an income class are allocated to that income. For example, real estate taxes, repairs, the trustee's share of depreciation, fire insurance premiums, etc., would be allocated to rental income.

(2) The deductions *not directly* attributable to a specific income class (such as trustee's commissions, safe deposit box rental, and state income and personal property taxes) may be allocated to any income item (including capital gains) included in computing DNI. However, a trust with nontaxable income must allocate a portion of these deductions to nontaxable income.

(3) Any excess deductions from step (1) may be assigned to any other class of income (including capital gains) in the manner described in step (2). However, excess deductions attributable to tax-exempt income may not be offset against any other class of income. Also, excess deductions from a passive activity (¶ 1169) cannot be allocated to income from a nonpassive activity, or to portfolio income earned by the estate or trust (Instructions to Form 1041).

For purposes of the computation, the unlimited charitable deduction (¶ 537) is first allocated ratably among all classes of income entering into DNI before any other expenses, unless a different allocation is specified by the governing instrument or local law (Reg. §§ 1.643(a)-5 and 1.661(b)-2). The charitable deduction is allocated by multiplying it by a ratio: the numerator is the amount of each single class of income, and the denominator is the total of all income classes. See ¶ 559 for examples of allocations.

546. Complex Trust's and Estate 65-Day Election. The fiduciary of an estate or complex trust can elect annually to treat any distribution or any portion of a distribution to a beneficiary made within the first 65 days following the end of a tax year as having been distributed in the prior year (Code Sec. 663(b); Reg. §§ 1.663(b)-1 and 1.663(b)-2). The election is made on Form 1041, is irrevocable for the year involved, and is binding for that year only. The amount to which the election can apply is the greater of: (1) the estate's or trust's income (¶ 514); or (2) distributable net income (DNI) (¶ 543) for the tax year, reduced by any amounts paid, credited, or required to be distributed during the tax year other than those amounts that are subject to the 65-day election. There is no 65-day election for distributions of accumulated income (¶ 567).

548. Annuities Distributable from Income or Corpus. In the case of recurring distributions, payments by an estate or trust (where the amounts to be distributed, paid, or credited are a charge upon the corpus *or* the income) are generally taxable to the beneficiary and deductible by the estate or trust, to the extent that they are made from income (Code Sec. 661(a)(1); Reg. § 1.661(a)-2(b)).

549. Widow(er)'s Allowance. A widow(er)'s or dependent's statutory allowance or award for support during administration of the estate is deductible by an estate if it is paid pursuant to a court order or decree or under local law (Reg. § 1.661(a)-2(e)). The allowance can be paid from either income or principal, but the deduction is limited to the estate's distributable net income (DNI) for the year (¶ 543). Such payments are includible in the recipient's income to the extent of his or her share of the estate's DNI (Reg. § § 1.662(a)-2(c) and 1.662(a)-3(b)). The allowance is treated as a distribution to a beneficiary, even if it is considered to be a debt of the estate rather than a payment to a beneficiary under local law (Rev. Rul. 75-124).

Taxation of Beneficiaries

See CCH® AnswerConnect: *Income Taxation of Trusts and Estates* for more information on this topic.

554. Taxation of Simple Trust Beneficiary. A beneficiary of a simple trust (¶ 542) must include in gross income the income that is required to be distributed currently to the beneficiary (¶ 514), whether or not it is actually distributed during the tax year, up to the amount of distributable net income (DNI) (¶ 543) (Code Sec. 652; Reg. § § 1.652(a)-1—1.652(b)-3). If the income required to be distributed exceeds DNI, only a proportionate share of each item is includible in the beneficiary's income.

Each income item retains the same character (such as rent, dividends, etc.) that it had in the hands of the trust, and is treated as consisting of the same proportion of each class of items entering into the DNI calculation as the total of each class bears to total DNI, unless the trust instrument specifically allocates a particular type of income to a particular beneficiary. Deductions reflected in the computation of DNI are allocated among the various types of income (¶ 545). On termination of a trust, unused loss carryovers and excess deductions of the trust are allowed to certain beneficiaries (¶ 535). The amounts reported on the beneficiary's return must be consistent with the amounts reported on the trust return (¶ 2823) (Code Sec. 6034A(c)).

Net Investment Income Tax. For purposes of determining the 3.8-percent net investment income tax (¶ 117), net investment income includes a beneficiary's share of DNI to the extent that the character of such income constitutes gross income from certain income items (e.g., interest, dividends, annuities, royalties, rents, gross income from a passive trade or business or from a trader's financial instrument trading business, etc.) or net gain attributable to the disposition of certain property, with further computations for the trust's undistributed net investment income (¶ 517) (Reg. § 1.1411-4(e)(1)).

556. Taxation of Beneficiary of Complex Trust or Estate. A beneficiary of a complex trust (¶ 542) or a decedent's estate must include in gross income the income that is required to be distributed currently to the beneficiary (¶ 514), whether or not it is actually distributed during the tax year, plus any other amounts that are properly paid, credited, or required to be distributed to the beneficiary for the year (Code Sec. 662; Reg. § 1.662(a)-1). If a fiduciary elects to treat a distribution to a beneficiary made in the year as an amount paid in a prior year (¶ 546), the amount covered by the election is included in the beneficiary's income for the year for which the trust takes the deduction. Special rules also apply to distributions by certain trusts out of accumulated income (¶ 567).

If the amount of income required to be distributed currently to all beneficiaries exceeds distributable net income (DNI) (¶ 543) (computed without the charitable deduction (¶ 537)), then each beneficiary includes in income an amount that bears the same ratio to DNI as the amount of income required to be distributed currently to the beneficiary bears to the amount required to be distributed currently to all beneficiaries (Reg. § 1.662(a)-2(b)).

If the sum of income required to be distributed currently, plus other amounts properly paid, credited, or required to be distributed, exceeds DNI, then the beneficiary includes such other amounts in gross income only to the extent that DNI exceeds income required to be distributed currently (Reg. § 1.662(a)-3(c)). If the other amounts are paid, credited, or required to be distributed to more than one beneficiary, each beneficiary includes in gross income his or her proportionate share of such other amounts includible in gross income. The beneficiary's proportionate share is the amount which bears the same ratio to DNI (after subtracting income required to be distributed currently) as the other amounts distributed to the beneficiary bear to the other amounts distributed to all beneficiaries. The amount to be used in determining the beneficiary's share of estate or trust income depends on whether the estate or trust elected to recognize gain on the distribution (¶ 526).

Any amount which, under a will or trust instrument, is used in full or partial discharge or satisfaction of a legal obligation of any person is included in that person's gross income as though the amount was directly distributed to him or her as a beneficiary (Reg. § 1.662(a)-4). A legal obligation includes an obligation to support another person only if it is not affected by the adequacy of the dependent's own resources. The amount of trust income included in the gross income of a person obligated to support a dependent is limited by the extent of the person's legal obligation under local law. For example, in the case of a parent's obligation to support his or her child, to the extent that the support obligation (including education) is determined under local law by the family's station in life and the means of the parent, it is determined without consideration of the trust income in question. This rule does not pertain to alimony payments (¶ 771) or income of an alimony trust (¶ 775).

If a net operating loss carryback of the estate or trust (¶ 531) reduces the DNI of the estate or trust for the prior tax year to which the NOL is carried, the beneficiary's tax liability for the prior year may be recomputed based upon the revised DNI of the estate or trust (Rev. Rul. 61-20).

In allocating the various types of income to the beneficiaries, the amount reflected in DNI is determined first. It is charged with directly related expenses and a proportionate part of other expenses, including the unlimited charitable deduction (¶ 537) to the extent it is chargeable to income of the current year (Reg. §§ 1.662(b)-1 and 1.662(b)-2). Each beneficiary's share of income paid, credited, or required to be distributed to the beneficiary is then multiplied by fractions, for each class of income. The numerator is the amount of such income included in DNI (whether the aggregate is more or less than the DNI), and the denominator is the total DNI (¶ 545). However, if the governing instrument specifies or local law requires a different allocation, such allocation is to be followed. See ¶ 559 for examples of the computations.

Special provisions exclude certain amounts from the beneficiary's gross income (and from the estate's or trust's distribution deduction) (Code Sec. 663(a); Reg. §§ 1.663(a)-1, 1.663(a)-2, and 1.663(a)-3). Any amount paid, permanently set aside, or to be used for charitable purposes and allowable for the unlimited charitable deduction (¶ 537) cannot be part of the distribution deduction or treated as an amount distributed for purposes of determining the beneficiary's gross income. Additionally, amounts deemed to be distributed to a beneficiary in a *prior* tax year cannot be deducted by the estate or trust, and are not included in the beneficiary's gross income for the current tax year. Certain gifts or bequests of a specific sum of money or specific property if paid or distributed all at once or in not more than three installments are also excluded (¶ 564).

On termination of an estate or trust, unused loss carryovers and excess deductions of the estate or trust are allowed to certain beneficiaries (¶ 535).

The amounts reported on the beneficiary's return must be consistent with the amounts reported on the estate or trust return (¶ 2823) (Code Sec. 6034A(c)).

Net Investment Income Tax. For purposes of determining the 3.8-percent net investment income tax (¶ 117), net investment income includes a beneficiary's share of DNI to the extent that the character of such income constitutes gross income from certain income items (e.g., interest, dividends, annuities, royalties, rents, gross income from a passive trade or business or from a trader's financial instrument trading business, etc.) or net gain attributable to the disposition of certain property, with further computations for the estate's or trust's undistributed net investment income (¶ 517) (Reg. § 1.1411-4(e)(1)).

557. Separate Shares as Separate Trusts and Estates. If an estate or trust has two or more beneficiaries and is to be administered in well-defined and separate shares, the shares must be treated as separate estates or trusts in determining the amount of distributable net income (DNI) allocable to the beneficiaries (¶ 554 and ¶ 556) (Code Sec. 663(c); Reg. §§ 1.663(c)-1—1.663(c)-5). This rule limits the tax liability of a beneficiary on a distribution of income and corpus where the income is being accumulated for

5

TRUSTS/ESTATES

the benefit of another beneficiary. The separate-share treatment is mandatory, not elective. A trustee or an executor must apply it even if separate and independent accounts are not maintained for each share, or if assets are not physically segregated.

The separate-share rule does not affect situations in which a single trust instrument creates not one, but several separate trusts, as opposed to separate shares in the same trust. It also does not apply to trusts that provide for successive interests (e.g., a trust that provides a life estate to A and remainder to B).

The treatment of separate shares as separate estates or trusts applies *only* for determining DNI in computing the distribution deduction allowable to the estate or trust and the amount includible in the income of the beneficiary. It cannot be applied to obtain more than one deduction for the personal exemption or to split the income of the estate or trust into several shares so as to be taxed at a lower-bracket rate.

559. How the Complex Trust Rules Operate. The examples below illustrate computations of distributable net income (DNI) (¶ 543), the distributive share of a beneficiary (¶ 544 and ¶ 545), and the taxable income of a complex trust. No "throwback" distributions (¶ 567) are involved.

Example 1: Trust income: A complex trust has the following items of income in 2019:

Dividends	$16,000
Taxable interest	10,000
Exempt interest	10,000
Rent	4,000
Long-term capital gain allocable to corpus	6,000

The trust has expenses as follows:

Expenses directly allocable to rent	$2,000
Commissions allocable to income	3,000
Commissions allocable to corpus	1,500

On these facts, the trust would have income of $40,000 (¶ 514). The income items consist of dividends, taxable interest, exempt interest and rent. No expenses or charges against income or corpus are subtracted; only receipts treated as income under local law and the governing instrument are counted (e.g., rent). Also, the long-term capital gain is excluded from this income in order to apply the conduit rule (as illustrated in Example 3) because it is not income under local law. It is, however, included in the taxable income computation.

Example 2: Distributable net income: In computing the trust's DNI, the net amount of tax-exempt interest is added to the net income of the trust (after subtracting any charitable contribution). The net amount of tax-exempt interest is the full amount of such interest minus any expenses directly allocable to it and a proportionate part of all general expenses such as commissions.

As indicated in Example 1, there are $4,500 in general expenses (i.e., expenses not directly allocable to rental income), so 25 percent ($10,000/$40,000) of $4,500, or $1,125, is allocated to the exempt interest ($10,000), leaving a net of $8,875. This $1,125 must also be excluded from the deductions claimed by the trust as an expense indirectly related to the production of exempt interest income and therefore disallowed by Code Sec. 265 (¶ 970). Accordingly, DNI is $33,500, computed as follows:

Dividends		$16,000
Taxable interest		10,000
Exempt interest ($10,000 less $1,125 allocable to exempt interest)		8,875
Rent		4,000
Total		$38,875
Deductions:		
Rent expense	$2,000	
Commissions ($4,500 less $1,125 allocable to exempt interest)	3,375	5,375
Distributable net income		$33,500

Example 3: Taxable income of beneficiary: There is one beneficiary to whom the trustee must distribute $20,000 under the terms of the trust instrument.

The first step in computing the amount taxable to the beneficiary is to determine the extent to which each income item is reflected in DNI, allocating expenses to the various items. Those allocable to exempt interest have already been reflected in the $8,875 figure carried into DNI in Example 2, so no further allocation of that item is needed. Allocation is needed for dividends, rent, and taxable interest income, but this allocation does not have to be proportionate.

Expenses directly related to any source or type of income must be allocated directly to that income, but general expenses can be allocated to any taxable income the taxpayer wishes when computing DNI as long as no deficit is created for any item. In this example, it is assumed the trustee allocates all general expenses to taxable interest. Accordingly, the trustee charges the entire $3,375 of general expenses to the taxable interest ($10,000) so that the $33,500 DNI, for the purpose of applying the conduit rule, is deemed to have been derived from:

Rent	$2,000
Taxable interest	6,625
Dividends	16,000
Tax-exempt interest	8,875
	$33,500

The total corresponds to the DNI and is only an intermediate or identification step. Because the amounts actually distributable are less than the amount of DNI, the next step is to multiply each of the above amounts by $20,000/$33,500 to determine what part of each is taxable to the beneficiary and deductible by the trust. Using these figures (the same result could be obtained by determining $2,000/$33,500 of $20,000, $6,625/$33,500 of $20,000, and so on), the apportionment is as follows:

Rent	$1,194.03
Taxable interest	3,955.22
Dividends	9,552.24
Tax-exempt interest	5,298.51
	$20,000.00

The beneficiary's share of income and deductions is reported on Schedule K-1 (Form 1041). The beneficiary will omit the $5,298.51 tax-exempt interest in reporting income from the trust. The $1,194.03 rent, $9,552.24 dividend, and $3,955.22 taxable interest income should be reported on the beneficiary's Form 1040.

Example 4: Taxable income of the trust: The trust is allowed a deduction for the amount required to be distributed currently up to the amount of its DNI, but not for any portion that consists of tax-exempt income. The deduction for distributions, therefore, is $14,701.49 ($20,000 minus $5,298.51). Taxable income of the trust is then computed as follows:

Dividends	$16,000.00	
Taxable Interest	10,000.00	
Rent	4,000.00	
Long-term capital gain	6,000.00	$36,000.00
Less:		
Expenses allocable to rent	$2,000.00	
Commissions allocable to income ($3,000 minus the 25% [$750] allocable to exempt interest)	2,250.00	
Commissions allocable to corpus ($1,500 minus the 25% [$375] allocable to exempt interest)	1,125.00	
Distribution to beneficiary	14,701.49	
Exemption	100.00	20,176.49
Taxable income		$15,823.51

562. Capital Gain or Loss of Trusts and Estates. Capital gains, whether long or short term, are generally *excluded* from distributable net income (DNI) (i.e., are taxed to an estate or trust) to the extent allocated to corpus and not:

- paid, credited, or required to be distributed to any beneficiary during the tax year, or

- paid, permanently set aside, or to be used for a charitable purpose (Code Sec. 643(a)(3); Reg. § 1.643(a)-3).

Capital gains are *included* in DNI to the extent they are:

- allocated to income,

- allocated to corpus but consistently treated by the fiduciary as part of a distribution to a beneficiary, or

- allocated to corpus but actually distributed to a beneficiary or used by the fiduciary in determining the amount that is distributed or required to be distributed to a beneficiary (¶ 543).

A net capital loss of an estate or trust will reduce the taxable income of the estate or trust, but no part of the loss is deductible by the beneficiaries. If the estate or trust distributes all of its income, the capital loss will not result in a tax benefit for the year of the loss. Losses from the sale or exchange of capital assets are first netted at the trust level against any capital gains, except for capital gains utilized by the fiduciary in determining the amount to be distributed to a particular beneficiary (Reg. § 1.643(a)-3(d)). On termination of an estate or trust, any unused capital loss carryover of the estate or trust is available to the beneficiaries (¶ 535).

564. Gift or Bequest by Trusts and Estates. An estate or trust may not deduct as a distribution to a beneficiary, and a beneficiary does not include in income, a gift or bequest of a specific sum of money or specific property that is paid or credited in three installments or less (Code Sec. 663(a)(1); Reg. § 1.663(a)-1). However, an amount will *not* be treated as an excluded gift or bequest if the governing instrument provides that the specific sum is payable only from the income of the estate or trust. The following are also *not* treated as an excluded gift or bequest of a sum of money or specific property:

- an annuity, or periodic gifts of specific property in lieu of or having the effect of an annuity;

- a residuary estate or the corpus of a trust; and

- a gift or bequest paid in a lump sum or in three installments or less, if required by the governing instrument to be paid in more than three installments.

In determining the number of installments, gifts or bequests of articles of personal use (e.g., personal and household effects, cars, etc.) are disregarded. Also disregarded are transfers of specific real estate, title to which passes directly from the decedent to the devisee under local law.

565. Beneficiary's Tax Year Different From Trust's or Estate's. If a beneficiary has a different tax year from that of an estate or complex trust (¶ 542), the amount included in the beneficiary's gross income is based on the distributable net income (DNI) of the estate or trust (¶ 543) and the amounts paid, credited, or required to be distributed to the beneficiary for any tax year or years of the estate or trust ending with or within his or her tax year (Code Sec. 662(c); Reg. § 1.662(c)-1). Similarly, if a beneficiary of a simple trust has a tax year different from that of the trust, the amount that the beneficiary includes in gross income must be based on the amount of the trust's income for any tax year or years ending with or within his or her tax year (Code Sec. 652(c); Reg. § 1.652(c)-1).

566. Distributions to Expatriates by Nongrantor Trusts. If a covered expatriate (¶ 2412) is a beneficiary of a nongrantor trust on the day before the individual's expatriation date, and receives a direct or indirect distribution of any property from the trust, the trustee must deduct and withhold 30 percent of the taxable portion of the distribution (Code Sec. 877A(f)). Additionally, if the fair market value of the property distributed exceeds the adjusted basis in the hands of the trust, the trust must recognize gain as if the property were sold to the expatriate at its fair market value.

The taxable portion of the distribution is the portion that would be includible in the covered expatriate's gross income had the expatriate continued to be subject to tax as a U.S. citizen or resident. A nongrantor trust is the portion of any trust that the individual is not considered the owner under the grantor trust rules (¶ 571) as determined immediately before the beneficiary's expatriation date.

The withholding rules apply in a manner similar to those that apply to nonresident aliens (¶ 2455), but the distribution item is not subject to the nonresident alien withholding tax itself or the withholding tax on wages (¶ 2601). Further, the covered expatriate is treated as having waived any claim to a withholding reduction under any treaty with the United States, unless the expatriate agrees to other treatment that the IRS deems appropriate. Items subject to withholding are taxed according to the rules that apply to nonresident aliens (¶ 2429 and ¶ 2431).

567. "Throwback" of Accumulated Income. Special "throwback rules" generally apply to trust distributions made in tax years beginning before August 6, 1997 (Code Secs. 665—668). Although the throwback rules have been repealed for most trusts, they continue to apply to trusts created before March 1, 1984, that would be treated as multiple trusts under Code Sec. 643(f), and to foreign trusts (¶ 501) and domestic trusts that were once treated as foreign trusts.

The throwback rules are designed to prevent the accumulation of trust income by a complex or accumulation trust over a period of years with a distribution to a beneficiary only in low-income years. The rules have the effect of carrying back to preceding years any distributions in excess of distributable net income (DNI) (¶ 543) for the distribution year and taxing them to the beneficiaries as if they were distributed in the year the income was accumulated by the trust. This additional income is taxed to the beneficiary in the year that the beneficiary receives the accumulation distribution, but the beneficiary's tax liability is computed on Form 4970 under special rules.

Beneficiaries who receive the accumulation distribution from a foreign trust report it and the partial tax on Form 3520. Schedule J (Form 1041) is used to determine the amount, the year, and the character of the additional distributions taxable to beneficiaries under the throwback rules. The trustee must give a copy of Part IV of Schedule J to each beneficiary. The beneficiary is allowed an offset or credit against the partial tax for the proportionate part of the trust's tax for the prior year, thus eliminating any double tax on the income. Beneficiaries of estates are not subject to the throwback rules.

Grantor Trusts

See CCH® AnswerConnect: *Grantor Trusts: Definitions and Rules* for more information on this topic.

571. Grantor Trust Rules. Under the grantor trust rules, a person (i.e., the grantor) who transfers property to a trust and retains certain powers or interests (¶ 576—¶ 584) is treated as the owner of the trust property for income tax purposes (Code Sec. 671). As a result, the income, deductions, and credits attributable to the trust are included in determining the grantor's taxable income to the extent of the owned portion of the trust. For income tax purposes, conversion of a nongrantor trust to a grantor trust is not a transfer of the property held by the nongrantor trust to the owner of the grantor trust, so the owner is not required to recognize gain (CCA 200923024).

Family Trusts. Income-producing property is often conveyed in trust for the benefit of a family member in an effort to split any income generated by the property or to otherwise lessen the original owner's tax liability. However, there must be an actual transfer of property to accomplish the desired tax savings. It is not enough to transfer income generated by the property. The limitations of the grantor trust rules also prevent a taxpayer from escaping tax on the income from property if the taxpayer in effect remains the property owner by retaining control over the trust. For example, a "family estate" trust (i.e., a trust to which an individual transfers personal assets and the right to income in exchange for the beneficial enjoyment of such assets and compensation) is taxed as a grantor trust (Rev. Rul. 75-257).

The grantor's assignment of lifetime services or salary to the trust is not recognized for income tax purposes. Such trusts are deemed a "nullity" for income tax purposes and their income is taxable to the persons who created them. This principle deprives a grantor of any possible refuge in the technicalities of the grantor trust provisions. Expenses incurred in setting up family estate trusts are not deductible under Code Sec. 212 (*S.H. Epp*, Dec. 39,016, 78 TC 801). Intra-family transfers of income-producing property also cannot be used to reduce income tax liability by shifting income from the parents' higher tax bracket to their child's generally lower tax bracket. Under the kiddie tax rules, if the net unearned income of the child exceeds an annual inflation-adjusted amount, it is taxed at the parents' top marginal rate (¶ 115).

Net Investment Income Tax. A grantor trust is not subject to the 3.8-percent net investment income tax (¶ 117 and ¶ 517) (Reg. §1.1411-3(b)(1)). Instead, for purposes of calculating the net investment income of the grantor or other person who is taxable on trust income (¶ 585), each item of income or deduction included in computing his or her taxable income under the grantor trust rules must be treated as if it had been received by, or paid to, the grantor or other person.

575. Funeral Trusts. A qualified funeral trust (QFT) is a nonforeign funeral trust that elects not to be treated as a grantor trust (¶ 571), so that the income tax on the annual earnings of the trust is payable by the trustee (Code Sec. 685). A QFT is generally an arrangement that would otherwise be treated as a grantor trust, under which an individual purchases funeral services or necessary property for himself or herself, or for another individual, from a funeral home prior to death and funds the purchase via contributions. There are no dollar limitations on contributions to a QFT, but the contributions must be held, invested, and reinvested by the trust solely to make payments for funeral services or property upon the individual's or the other trust beneficiaries' death.

If the election is made, the income tax rate schedule generally applicable to estates and trusts (¶ 19) is applied to the trust by treating each beneficiary's interest as a separate trust. However, the trust is not entitled to a personal exemption (¶ 534). The trustee's election must be made separately for each such separate trust. No gain or loss is recognized by a purchaser of a funeral trust contract as a result of any payment from the trust to the purchaser due to the cancellation of the contract.

The trustee elects QFT status by filing Form 1041-QFT. The election must be filed no later than the due date (with extensions) for filing the trust income tax return for the year of election. The election applies to each trust reported in the QFT return. The trustee can use the form to file for a single QFT or multiple QFTs having the same trustee. The election may be made for the trust's first eligible year or for any subsequent year. Once made, the election cannot be revoked without IRS consent.

576. Trusts With Reversionary Interest in Grantor. A grantor is considered to be the owner of any portion of a trust (¶ 571) in which the grantor or the grantor's spouse (¶ 578) has a reversionary interest in either the trust corpus or income if the value of the interest exceeds five percent of the value of that portion of the trust (Code Sec. 673). The value of the interest is measured as of the inception of the portion of the trust in which the grantor holds an interest. In determining whether the grantor's reversionary interest exceeds the five-percent threshold, the maximum exercise of discretion in the grantor's favor is assumed. Any postponement of the reacquisition or enjoyment of the interest is considered to be a new transfer in trust. However, no trust income is included in the grantor's income that would not have been included absent postponement. In addition, a grantor is exempt from the reversionary interest rule if the interest takes effect only upon the death of a beneficiary who is a minor lineal descendant of the grantor (under age 21) and if the beneficiary has the entire present interest in all or part of the trust.

578. Powers Held by Grantor's Spouse. A grantor is treated as holding any power or interest in a trust (¶ 571) that is held by a person who was the grantor's spouse at the time the power or interest was created, or who became the grantor's spouse after creation of the power or interest (but only with respect to periods that the individual was the grantor's spouse) (Code Sec. 672(e)). Thus, the grantor trust rules cannot be avoided by having the spouse of the grantor possess prohibited powers or interests (e.g., spousal remainder trusts). Individuals who are legally separated under a decree of divorce or separate maintenance are not considered to be married for this purpose.

579. Power to Control Beneficial Enjoyment. A grantor of a trust (¶ 571) is taxed on trust income if the grantor or the grantor's spouse (¶ 578) retains the power to control the beneficial enjoyment of trust property or income without the consent of an adverse party (e.g., power to change beneficiaries or to change remainder interests) (Code Sec. 674; Reg. §1.674(a)-1). There are a number of exceptions to this rule including, but not limited to:

- an unexercised power to apply income to support a dependent (¶ 137);
- power to allocate income among charitable beneficiaries;
- power to distribute corpus limited by a reasonably definite standard; and
- power to withhold income temporarily (Reg. §§1.674(b)-1—1.674(d)-2).

581. Retention of Administrative Powers. The grantor of a trust (¶ 571) is taxed on trust income if the grantor or the grantor's spouse (¶ 578) retains administrative powers enabling the grantor to obtain, by dealings with the trust, financial benefits that would not be available in an arm's-length transaction (Code Sec. 675; Reg. §1.675-1). For example, if the grantor or his or her spouse borrows trust corpus or income at any time during a tax year, the grantor is taxed on the trust income for that entire year, even if the grantor repays the loan with interest during the same year (Rev. Rul. 86-82).

582. Power to Revoke Trust. If a grantor creates a trust (¶ 571) and reserves a right to revoke it, the income of the trust is treated as the grantor's income (Code Sec. 676; Reg. §§1.676(a)-1 and 1.676(b)-1). The trust income is not taxed to the grantor if the power can only affect the beneficial enjoyment of the income after the occurrence of an event such that the grantor would not be treated as the owner if the power were a reversionary interest (¶ 576). However, the grantor may be treated as the owner after the event occurs unless the power to revoke is then relinquished.

584. Income for Grantor's Benefit. The grantor of a trust (¶ 571) is taxed on trust income that is or may be accumulated for or distributed to the grantor or the grantor's spouse, or used to pay life insurance premiums on either the grantor's or the spouse's life (except for policies irrevocably payable to charities) (Code Sec. 677; Reg. §§1.677(a)-1 and 1.677(b)-1). To the extent that trust income may be used in satisfaction of the grantor's legal obligation to support a beneficiary (such as a child, but not a spouse), it is regarded as distributable to the grantor.

If the discretion to so use the income is not in the grantor acting as such, but in another person (for example, the trustee or the grantor acting as trustee or co-trustee), then that income is includible in the grantor's gross income only to the extent that it is actually used for the beneficiary's support or maintenance. In addition, any capital gain under state law that is added to trust corpus is taxable to the grantor if the corpus reverts to the grantor upon termination of the trust (Reg. §§1.671-3(b)(2) and 1.677(a)-1(f); Rev. Rul. 58-242; Rev. Rul. 75-267).

585. Income Taxable to Person Other Than Grantor. A person other than the grantor of a trust (¶ 571), including a beneficiary, may be taxed on the trust's income if that person has a power, exercisable alone, to vest trust corpus or income in himself or herself (Code Sec. 678; Reg. §§1.678(a)-1—1.678(d)-1). For example, if a father establishes a trust for the benefit of his children, but the trust provides that the grantor's brother may take trust property at any time, the brother is treated as the owner and trust income is taxed to him. This rule does not apply if the power is renounced or disclaimed within a reasonable period. It also does not apply to a power over income as originally granted or later modified, if the grantor of the trust or a transferor to a foreign trust (¶ 588) is treated as the trust owner under the other grantor trust rules.

A U.S. person who is a beneficiary of a trust is treated as the grantor to the extent that the beneficiary transferred property, directly or indirectly and for less than adequate consideration, to a foreign person who otherwise would have been treated as the owner under the grantor trust rules (Code Sec. 672(f)(5)).

586. Return for Grantor Trust. Items of income, deduction, or credit that are treated as belonging to a trust grantor or another person (¶ 571) are generally not reported by the trust on Form 1041 (Reg. §1.671-4). Instead, these items are reflected on the income tax return of the grantor (or other person who is taxable on the trust income). A separate statement should be attached to Form 1041 stating the name, taxpayer identification number, and address of the person to whom the income is taxable, and setting forth the income, deductions, and credits. However, there are other optional reporting methods available to certain types of grantor trusts. Widely held fixed investment trusts have specific information reporting requirements (Reg. §1.671-5).

588. Foreign Grantor Trust Rules. Any U.S. person transferring property to a foreign trust (¶ 501) (other than certain employee benefit plans and charitable trusts) that has a U.S. beneficiary will be treated as the owner of that portion of the trust attributable to the property transferred (Code Sec. 679). The IRS can presume that the trust has a U.S. beneficiary unless the transferor submits to the IRS any information required regarding the transfer. The transferor must also demonstrate that:

- under the terms of the trust, no part of the trust's income or corpus may be paid or accumulated during the tax year to or for the benefit of a U.S. person, even if that person's interest is contingent on a future event; and

- no part of the trust's income or corpus could be paid to or for the benefit of a U.S. person if the trust were terminated at any time during the tax year.

The transferor must ensure that the trust satisfies certain reporting requirements, and submit any information the IRS may require regarding the foreign trust (Code Secs. 6048(b) and 6677(a)). A foreign trust with at least one U.S. owner must file Form 3520-A in order for the U.S. owner to satisfy its annual information reporting requirements. The U.S. grantor trust rules (¶ 571) generally do not apply to any portion of a trust that would otherwise be deemed to be owned by a foreign person (Code Sec. 672(f)). A U.S. person who is treated as the owner of a foreign trust under the grantor trust rules (¶ 571) must file Form 3520.

Charitable Remainder Trust (CRT)

See CCH® AnswerConnect: *Charitable Remainder Trust (CRT)* for more information on this topic.

590. Charitable Remainder Trusts. If there is a noncharitable income beneficiary of a trust, gifts of remainder interests qualify for a charitable contribution deduction only if the trust is a charitable remainder annuity trust (CRAT) or a charitable remainder unitrust (CRUT) (Code Sec. 664; Reg. §§ 1.664-1, 1.664-2 and 1.664-3). Charitable contribution deductions are denied for gifts of remainder interests in all other types of trusts. However, if the donor gives *all* the interests in a trust to charity, the above rules do not apply, and a deduction is allowable (¶ 1070).

Qualification. An *annuity trust* is a trust from which a sum certain or a specified amount is to be paid to the income beneficiary (Code Sec. 664(d)(1); Reg. §§ 1.664-1 and 1.664-2). The specified amount cannot be less than five percent or more than 50 percent of the initial net fair market value of all property placed in trust, and it must be paid at least annually to the income beneficiary. Furthermore, the value of the charitable remainder interest must be at least 10 percent of the initial net fair market value of all of the property placed in trust. There are several provisions designed to provide relief to trusts that do not meet the 10-percent test. In addition, under the "probability of exhaustion" test, no charitable deduction is allowed if there is a greater than five percent probability that the life beneficiary or beneficiaries will survive exhaustion of the CRAT assets. The IRS has provided a sample provision that can be used as an alternative to satisfying the probability of exhaustion test, applicable to trusts created on or after August 8, 2016 (Rev. Proc. 2016-42). No contributions can be made to a CRAT after the initial contribution, and the governing instrument must contain a prohibition against future contributions.

A *unitrust* is a trust that specifies that the income beneficiary is to receive annual payments based on a fixed percentage of the net fair market value of the trust's assets as determined each year (Code Sec. 664(d)(2); Reg. §§ 1.664-1 and 1.664-3). The fixed percentage cannot be less than five percent or more than 50 percent of the net fair market value of the trust's assets for the year. However, a qualified CRUT may provide for the distribution each year of five percent of the net fair market value of its assets or the amount of the trust income, whichever is lower. For this purpose, trust income excludes capital gains, and trust assets must be valued annually. The payment requirement may not be discretionary with the trustee. Additional contributions can be made to a unitrust. For most transfers in trust, the value of the charitable remainder interest with respect to each contribution to the unitrust must be at least 10 percent of the net fair market value of such contributed property as of the date the property is contributed to the trust. If an additional contribution would cause the trust to fail the 10-percent remainder test, then the contribution is treated as a transfer to a separate trust under regulations. Other provisions may provide relief to trusts that fail to meet the 10-percent test.

In the case of the early termination of a net income only charitable remainder unitrust (NICRUT) or a net income with make-up CRUT (NIMCRUT), the remainder interest is computed on the basis that an amount equal to five percent of the net fair market value of the trust assets (or a greater amount, if required by the trust instrument) is to be distributed each year, with any net income limit to be disregarded (Code Sec. 664(e)).

CRATs and CRUTs cannot have noncharitable remainder interests. The remainder interests generally must pass to a charity upon the termination of the last income interest, and the trust instrument must contain a provision that determines how the final payment of a specified distribution is to be made. However, a charitable trust may make certain limited qualified gratuitous transfers of qualified employer securities to an employee stock ownership plan (ESOP) without adversely affecting the status of the charitable remainder trust.

To avoid the possible disqualification of a charitable remainder trust due to a surviving spouse's right of election against the grantor spouse's estate under state law, the IRS created a safe harbor requiring the surviving spouse to irrevocably waive the right (Rev. Proc. 2005-24). Until further guidance is published, the IRS will disregard the existence of a right of election *without* requiring a waiver, but only if the surviving spouse does not exercise the right (Notice 2006-15).

There may be more than one noncharitable income beneficiary, either concurrently or successively, and the income interest may be a life estate or for a term of years not in excess of 20 years. However, a contingency clause may be placed in the trust instrument providing that the noncharitable interest is to terminate and the charitable remainder interest is to be accelerated upon the happening of an event, such as the remarriage of the noncharitable beneficiary (Code Sec. 664(f)). The income beneficiary can receive only a specified or fixed amount from the trust, and the trustee cannot have additional power to invade corpus or to alter, amend, or revoke the trust for the benefit of the noncharitable income beneficiary. The trustee cannot be restricted from investing in income-producing assets (Reg. § 1.664-1(a)(3)).

Division of Trust. The IRS has provided guidelines for dividing a CRAT or a CRUT into two or more separate and equal trusts without violating the charitable remainder trust requirements (Rev. Rul. 2008-41).

Reporting. A CRAT or CRUT does not file Form 1041, but instead is required to file Form 5227. In addition, the fiduciary of a CRAT or CRUT may be required to file other returns regarding the excise tax on unrelated business taxable income (¶ 590A), and the excise taxes on private foundations that apply to charitable remainder trusts (¶ 591). Form 5227 must generally be filed on or before the 15th day of the fourth month following the close of the tax year of the trust (Rev. Proc. 83-32). However, the due date for performing certain time-sensitive actions, including the deadline for filing Form 5227, otherwise due on or after April 1, 2020, and before July 15, 2020, is automatically extended to July 15, 2020, in response to the COVID-19 (coronavirus) crisis (Notice 2020-23; Rev. Proc. 2018-58).

590A. Taxation of Charitable Remainder Trust. A charitable remainder annuity trust (CRAT) or a charitable remainder unitrust (CRUT) (¶ 590) is generally exempt from income tax (Code Sec. 664(c); Reg. § 1.664-1). However, if a CRAT or CRUT has unrelated business taxable income (UBTI) (¶ 670), it is subject to a 100-percent excise tax on its UBTI, but will retain its tax-exempt status. The excise tax is treated as paid from corpus, and trust income that is UBTI is income of the trust for purposes of determining the character of distributions made to beneficiaries (¶ 590B). The tax is reported on Form 4720, which must be filed by the due date for Form 5227 (¶ 590). The rule preventing the IRS from filing an additional deficiency notice once a taxpayer files a Tax Court petition challenging the deficiency also applies to this tax. In addition to the tax on UBTI, a charitable remainder trust may be subject to the income and excise taxes imposed on private foundations (¶ 591).

590B. Treatment of Charitable Remainder Trust Beneficiaries. Under either a charitable remainder annuity trust (CRAT) or a charitable remainder unitrust (CRUT) (¶ 590), the amount paid to a beneficiary is considered as having the following characteristics in the beneficiary's hands: (1) ordinary income to the extent of the trust's

¶590B

ordinary income for the tax year and its undistributed ordinary income from prior years; (2) capital gains to the extent of the trust's capital gains for the tax year and its undistributed capital gains, determined on a cumulative net basis, for prior years; (3) other income (including tax-exempt interest) to the extent of the trust's other income for the tax year and its undistributed other income from prior years; and (4) a distribution of trust corpus (Code Sec. 664(b); Reg. §§ 1.664-1—1.664-4).

Items within the ordinary income and capital gains categories are assigned to different subcategories based on the federal income tax rate applicable to each type of income within the category. Categories of income that are taxed at the same rate can be combined into a single class if the tax rate will not change in the future. If the tax rate is temporary, then the categories must be maintained as separate groups (Reg. § 1.664-1(d)(1)).

The characterizations of income items distributed or deemed distributed at any time during the tax year of the charitable remainder trust are determined as of the end of the tax year. Distributions are subject to the tax rate applicable to the income class from which the distribution is derived, not the tax rate applicable when the income was received by the trust. Gains and losses of long-term capital gain classes are netted prior to netting short-term capital loss against any class of long-term capital gain.

Net Investment Income Tax. While CRATs and CRUTs are not subject to the 3.8-percent net investment income tax (¶ 517), special rules apply for calculating the tax applicable to CRAT and CRUT distributions to beneficiaries (Reg. § 1.1411-3(d)).

591. Private Foundation Rules Applicable to Charitable Trusts. The income and excise taxes imposed on private foundations extend to all nonexempt charitable trusts with certain modifications (Code Sec. 4947). First, a nonexempt trust that devotes all of its unexpired interests to charitable, religious, educational, and other purposes that enable contributors to obtain a charitable deduction is treated as a private foundation (¶ 631). Thus, it may be subject to the excise taxes on: investment income (¶ 633), self-dealing (¶ 635), failure to distribute income (¶ 637), excess business holdings (¶ 640), investments that jeopardize charitable purposes (¶ 642), and certain taxable expenditures (lobbying, electioneering, etc.) (¶ 644). For this purpose, unexpired interests include life or term income interests, interests in trust corpus, and remainder interests.

Second, a nonexempt trust that does not devote all of its unexpired interests to charitable purposes (split-interest trust) is subject to the excise taxes on self-dealing, excess business holdings, investments that jeopardize charitable purposes, and certain taxable expenditures (lobbying, electioneering, etc.) as if it were a private foundation. However, the taxes apply to income to be paid to trust beneficiaries under the terms of the trust instrument only if the trust was a charitable remainder annuity trust (CRAT) or charitable remainder unitrust (CRUT) (¶ 590). The taxes do not, in any event, apply to amounts in trust for which a deduction is not allowable if segregated from deductible amounts.

In addition, the taxes on excess business holdings and investments that jeopardize charitable purposes do not apply to a split-interest trust if: (1) the charity is only an income beneficiary and its beneficial interest is no more than 60 percent of the value of the trust property; or (2) the charity's only interest in the trust is as a remainderman. Split-interest trusts are treated like private foundations with regard to the rules on governing instruments and the tax on involuntary termination of status for repeated or willful violations (¶ 631 and ¶ 649).

The excise tax on investment income and failure to distribute income do not apply to split-interest trusts under any circumstances.

593. Pooled Fund Arrangements. A pooled income fund is generally a trust to which a person transfers an irrevocable remainder interest in property for the benefit of a public charity while retaining an income interest in the property for the life of one or more beneficiaries living at the time of the transfer (Code Sec. 642(c)(5); Reg. § 1.642(c)-5). Income, estate, and gift tax charitable contribution deductions are allowed for the value of remainder interests in property transferred to a pooled income fund (Code Sec. 642(c)(3)). To protect the value of depreciable property that will pass to the charitable remainderman, the governing instrument of the pooled income fund must provide for the creation of a depreciation reserve (Rev. Rul. 92-81). In addition, the fund:

- must commingle all property contributed to it;

- cannot invest in tax-exempt securities; and

- must be maintained by the recipient charity with no donor or income beneficiary acting as a trustee. The charity does not have to act as trustee of the fund.

Each person who has an income interest resulting from a transfer of property to the fund must be paid an annual income based on the fund's yearly rate of return (i.e., the trust cannot accumulate income for any beneficiary). A pooled income fund's method of calculating its yearly rate of return must be supported by a full statement attached to the fund's annual income tax return. The fund and its beneficiaries are taxable under the rules applicable to trusts, except that the grantor trust rules (¶ 571) do not apply. In addition to its income tax return, a pooled income fund must file an annual information return on Form 5227 regarding its charitable deductions (¶ 537).

595. Common Trust Fund. Each participant in a common trust fund (¶ 2389) must report its share of the taxable income of the fund, whether or not distributed or distributable. The taxable income of a common trust fund is computed in much the same manner as an individual's taxable income, except that:

- the charitable contribution deduction is not allowed;

- gains and losses from the sale or exchange of capital assets must be segregated, and the fund cannot benefit from capital loss carryovers;

- ordinary taxable income or net loss is computed without regard to capital gains or losses; and

- the net operating loss deduction is not allowed (Code Sec. 584).

5

TRUSTS/ESTATES

Chapter 6

EXEMPT ORGANIZATIONS

Overview

601. Overview of Tax-Exempt Organizations. A variety of organizations may qualify for exemption from federal income taxation. The most common basis for exempt status is as a charitable organization under Code Sec. 501(c)(3) (¶ 602). Charitable organizations can be either publicly supported or private foundations. While all charitable organizations are subject to limitations on how they operate, private foundations may be subject to excise taxes for engaging in prohibited activities (¶ 631). In addition to charitable organizations under Code Sec. 501(c)(3), there are a number of organizations that qualify for exempt status if they have a socially beneficial purpose (¶ 692). Regardless of how an entity qualifies as a tax-exempt organization, it may still be subject to federal income tax on any business income not related to its exempt purpose (¶ 655) and any income arising from debt-financed property (¶ 687). All tax-exempt organizations are also subject to various reporting requirements, such as annual information reporting (¶ 625), involvement in tax shelter transactions (¶ 619), and other disclosure requirements (¶ 627).

Code Sec. 501(c)(3) Organizations

602. Charitable Organizations Under Code Sec. 501(c)(3). Code Sec. 501 provides that various classes of nonprofit organizations may be exempt from federal income tax unless they are feeder organizations (¶ 694) or they engage in certain prohibited transactions. The most common basis for invoking tax-exempt status falls under the broad exemption of Code Sec. 501(c)(3) for religious, charitable, scientific, literary, and educational organizations (collectively referred to as charitable organizations). Charitable organizations are generally either public charities or private foundations (¶ 631). Among other benefits, exempt status conferred by Code Sec. 501(c)(3) allows a public charity to receive tax-deductible contributions from its donors (¶ 627 and ¶ 1061). Any corporation, community chest, fund, trust, or foundation may qualify for the exemption. Application for recognition of Code Sec. 501(c)(3) federal tax-exempt status is made on Form 1023 (¶ 623).

To qualify for tax-exempt status under Code Sec. 501(c)(3), the entity must be organized and operated exclusively for religious (¶ 604), charitable, scientific, educational, or literary purposes; prevention of cruelty to children or animals; promotion of amateur sports competition; or testing for public safety. What constitutes a charitable purpose is interpreted broadly and may include purposes beyond those explicitly stated in Code Sec. 501(c)(3). For example, a charitable purpose can include: providing relief to the poor or disadvantaged; the advancement of education, religion, or science; or lessening the burdens of government through the promotion of social welfare or other community development (Reg. § 1.501(c)(3)-1(d)). An educational organization can include a childcare center whose services are available to the general public (Code Sec. 501(k)). Regardless of an entity's charitable purpose, it must meet certain organizational, operational, and private benefit tests to qualify as a tax-exempt charitable organization.

Organizational Test. The organizational test requires that the entity's articles of organization specifically limit its purpose to one or more exempt purposes, including that its assets are dedicated to an exempt purpose (Reg. § 1.501(c)(3)-1(b)). The articles of organization also must not expressly permit the organization to carry on activities that do not further the organization's exempt purpose, except where the nonexempt activities are an insubstantial part of the organization's activities. For example, the articles of organization must not allow more than an insubstantial part of the organization's activities to consist of carrying on propaganda or attempting to influence legislation (¶ 613); or authorize the organization to directly or indirectly participate or intervene in any political campaign on behalf of or in opposition to any candidate for public office (¶ 614). Whether an organization meets the organizational requirement is determined exclusively from the language of the articles of organization and not from the activities conducted by the organization. For this purpose, "articles of organization" include trust instruments, corporate charters, articles of association, or any other written instrument that created an organization.

Operational Test. The operational test requires an entity to be operated exclusively for one or more exempt purposes. This means the organization engages primarily in activities that accomplish one or more of its exempt purposes (Reg. § 1.501(c)(3)-1(c)). Only an insubstantial part of the entity's activities may be in the furtherance of nonexempt purposes. Whether an organization has a substantial nonexempt purpose is determined by taking into account all facts and circumstances, including the size and extent of all of the organization's activities. If the entity is an "action organization," then it will *not* be considered as operated exclusively for an exempt purpose. An entity is an action organization if it devotes a substantial part of its activities to attempting to influence legislation or if it participates in political campaigns. However, if an organization fails the operational test because it is an action organization, it may still qualify for tax-exempt status as a social welfare organization under Code Sec. 501(c)(4) (¶ 692). If a charitable organization provides commercial-type insurance as an insubstantial part of its activities, then the insurance activity will be treated as an unrelated trade or business (¶ 655) (Code Sec. 501(m) and (n)).

An entity will not be considered as operating exclusively for exempt purposes if any part of its net earnings inure to the benefit of private shareholders or individuals. A private shareholder or individual is any person having a personal and private interest in the activities of the organization, such as founders of the organization, employees, board members, or family members of officers, employees, etc. The inurement prohibition does not prohibit all payments to a private shareholder or individual but instead is directed at payments that are made for purposes other than as reasonable compensation for goods or services (¶ 617).

Private Benefit Test. An organization is not organized or operated exclusively for charitable purposes unless it serves a public rather than an outside private interest (as opposed to inside interests addressed by the inurement prohibition under the operation test). The question of private benefit often arises in situations in which a charitable organization enters into partnerships and other joint ventures with for-profit entities. The charitable organization can form such ventures and still satisfy the operational test only if it is permitted to act exclusively in furtherance of its exempt purpose and only incidentally for the benefit of the for-profit partners (Rev. Rul. 98-15). In addition, the for-profit party cannot be allowed to control or use the charitable organization's activities or assets for its own benefit unless the control or use is incidental.

Charitable Hospitals. In addition to the requirements that apply to all Code Sec. 501(c)(3) organizations, each hospital organization operated by a charitable organization is subject to the following four requirements on a facility-by-facility basis:

- each facility must conduct and implement a community health needs assessment;

- each facility must adopt, implement, and widely publicize a written financial assistance policy;

- each facility may not bill patients who qualify for financial assistance more than the amount generally billed to insured patients; and

- the facility (or affiliates) may not undertake extraordinary collection actions against patients (Code Sec. 501(r); Reg. §§1.501(r)-0). If a hospital organization fails to meet the community health needs assessment requirement, an excise tax of $50,000 for any applicable year is imposed (Code Sec. 4959).

The IRS has provided procedures that a charitable hospital organization may use to correct and disclose certain failures to meet the requirements (Rev. Proc. 2015-21).

604. Churches and Religious Organizations. A church or religious organization is exempt from federal income tax and eligible to receive tax-deductible contributions if it meets the Code Sec. 501(c)(3) requirements (¶ 602). The term "church" is not specifically defined in the Code, but is used in its generic sense as a place of worship including, for example, mosques and synagogues. It also includes conventions or associations of churches, as well as integrated auxiliaries of a church. For this purpose, a convention or association of churches is a cooperative undertaking by churches of the same or differing denominations (Rev. Rul. 74-224). The fact that the convention or association may extend membership to individuals and those individuals have voting rights will not cause it to lose exempt status (Code Sec. 7701(n)).

It is important to distinguish churches from other religious organizations. To balance the need for the IRS to combat efforts on the part of some individuals and organizations to use churches to avoid taxes, and the equally important need to protect legitimate churches from undue IRS interference in their activities, the Code and regulations contain detailed rules governing when the IRS may inquire into or examine the activities of a "church" (Code Sec. 7611; Reg. §301.7611-1; Prop. Reg. §301.7611-1). Religious organizations that are not churches may still be eligible for tax-exempt status, including nondenominational ministries, interdenominational and ecumenical organizations, and other entities whose principal purpose is the study or advancement of religion (IRS Pub. 1828). Unlike churches, however, religious organizations that want to be tax exempt must apply to the IRS for tax-exempt status by filing Form 1023 (¶ 623).

A religious or apostolic association that does not meet the requirements to be a Code Sec. 501(c)(3) organization may nonetheless qualify as exempt from federal income taxation if it has a common or community treasury. The exemption applies even if the association engages in business for the common good of its members, provided that the members include in their gross income their pro rata share of the association's taxable income as dividends received, whether distributed or not (Code Sec. 501(d); Reg. §1.501(d)-1). There is no official exemption application form for this purpose but the association must file Form 1065 each tax year for information purposes (Temp. Reg. §1.6033-2(e)).

607. Supporting Organizations of Charitable Organization. A charitable organization under Code Sec. 501(c)(3) that carries out its exempt purpose by providing support to other tax-exempt organizations (usually public charities) (¶ 602) is considered a public charity rather than a private foundation (¶ 631). To qualify as a supporting organization, an organization must not only meet the requirements to be a charitable organization under Code Sec. 501(c)(3), but must also be:

- organized and operated exclusively for the benefit of, to perform the functions of, or to carry out the purposes of, a public charity (organizational and operational tests);

- operated or controlled by a public charity (relationship test); and

- not controlled either directly or indirectly by a disqualified person (¶ 635), other than a foundation manager or publicly supported charity (lack of control test) (Code Sec. 509(a)(3)).

To satisfy the relationship test, a supporting organization must hold one of three close relationships with the supported organization (Reg. §1.509(a)-4; Prop. Reg. §1.509(a)-4). In a Type I relationship, the supported organization must exercise a substantial degree of control over the programs, activities, and policies of the supporting organization (comparable to a parent-subsidiary relationship). In a Type II relationship, there must be common control or supervision by persons controlling or supervising both the supporting organization and the supported organization (comparable to brother-sister corporations). In a Type III relationship, the supporting organization must be operated in connection with the supported organization by being responsive to its needs and demands, and by being significantly involved in its operations to the point that the supported organization is dependent upon the supporting organization for the type of support it provides. Regardless of whether these relationship requirements are met, if a Type I or Type III organization supports an organization that is controlled by a donor, then the supporting organization will be treated as a private foundation rather than as a public charity (Code Sec. 509(f)(2)).

A number of special rules also apply to Type III supporting organizations. Each tax year, a Type III organization must provide each supported organization with any information that may be required by the IRS to ensure that the relationship requirements of being a Type III organization are met (Code Sec. 509(f)(1)). This may include the Type III organization's annual information return (Form 990), any tax return filed (Form 990-T), and any annual report. In addition, a Type III organization may not be operated in connection with any public charity that is organized outside the United States. Similarly, a trust will not be considered to be a Type III organization *solely* based on the fact that it is a charitable trust under state law, the public charity is a beneficiary of the trust, and the public charity has the power to enforce the trust terms (Act Sec. 1241(c) of the Pension Protection Act of 2006 (P.L. 109-280)).

Tax-exempt organizations use Form 8940 to request determinations about a change in type of supporting organization.

610. Donor Advised Funds. A Code Sec. 501(c)(3) charitable organization (other than a private foundation) may establish a donor advised fund that is a separate account where contributions made by a donor to the organization under which the donor (or person appointed by the donor) reasonably expects to provide nonbinding advice regarding distributions or investments (Code Sec. 4966(d)(2)). The donor may be entitled to a charitable deduction for contributions to a donor advised fund (¶ 1061), but only if the sponsoring organization legally owns and controls the contributions.

For this purpose, a donor advised fund does not include any fund that only makes distributions to a single identified organization or governmental entity. It also does not include a fund that allows the donor to provide advice as to which individuals receive grants for travel, study, or similar purposes through a committee that is appointed by the sponsoring organization that is not controlled by a donor or group of donors with advisory privileges and under which all grants are made on an objective and nondiscriminatory basis. The IRS has discretionary authority to exempt a fund or account from treatment as a donor advised fund. The charitable organization must provide information to the IRS when it applies for tax-exempt status (¶ 623) whether it maintains or intends to maintain the donor advised fund, and the manner in which it plans to operate those funds (Code Sec. 508(f)).

Taxable Distributions. An excise tax is imposed on any taxable distribution from a donor advised fund that is any distribution to a natural person or other person for a purpose other than an exempt purpose under Code Sec. 501(c)(3) (¶ 602) (Code Sec. 4966; Rev. Proc. 2018-32). It also includes any distribution to a disqualified supporting organization (¶ 607), unless the sponsoring organization exercises responsibility for the distribution. A taxable distribution does not include any distribution to a 50-percent organization (¶ 1059), to the sponsoring organization, or to another donor advised fund. The excise tax is 20 percent of the distribution and is imposed on the sponsoring organization. A separate five-percent excise tax is imposed on any fund manager who knowingly agrees to the distribution (up to $10,000 per distribution). A fund manager includes any officer, director, or trustee of the sponsoring organization, as well as an employee having authority with respect to the distribution. Fund managers who knowingly participate in the transaction are jointly and severally liable for the five-percent tax. The taxes on both the sponsoring organization and the fund manager are reported on Form 4720. The IRS has discretionary authority to abate both taxes (¶ 647).

6

EXEMPT ORGS

Prohibited Benefits. An excise tax is also imposed if a donor advised fund makes a distribution to any person that results (directly or indirectly) in a more-than-incidental benefit to the donor, donor advisor, member of the donor's family, or any entity in which the donor holds more than a 35-percent ownership interest (Code Sec. 4967; Notice 2017-73). The tax is 125 percent of the benefit received and is imposed on the donor, donor advisor, and related persons who recommended the distribution or received the prohibited benefit. A tax of 10 percent of the benefit (up to $10,000) is also imposed on fund managers who agreed to make a distribution knowing it would confer a more-than-incidental benefit. All persons liable for the taxes are jointly and severally liable. If the taxes are imposed, the IRS has discretionary authority to abate them (¶ 647). Neither tax will be imposed if the distribution is subject to tax as an excess benefit transaction (¶ 617). Also, a donor advised fund is treated as a private foundation for purposes of the excise tax on excess business holdings (¶ 640).

613. Limitations on Lobbying Activities by Charitable Organization. An organization that otherwise qualifies as a Code Sec. 501(c)(3) charitable organization is denied tax-exempt status if: (1) a *substantial* part of its activities consists of carrying on propaganda or attempting to influence legislation; or (2) it participates or intervenes in any political campaign on behalf of, or in opposition to, any candidate for public office (Code Sec. 501(h); Reg. § 1.501(h)-1). If a charitable organization engages in substantial legislative activity or participates in any political campaign, then it is an action organization (¶ 602) and not operated exclusively for one or more exempt purposes (Reg. § 1.501(c)(3)-1(c)(3)).

There are no specific guidelines as to what constitutes *substantial* legislative activities for this purpose; instead it is determined on the facts and circumstances of each case. However, the IRS has issued guidance of the facts and circumstances to be evaluated in determining whether or not a Code Sec. 501(c)(3) organization has participated or intervened in a political campaign for public office (Rev. Rul. 2007-41). If the organization has made a political expenditure, it will be subject to an excise tax (¶ 614).

As an alternative to the substantial part test, a charitable organization may elect on Form 5768 a sliding scale limitation on expenditures to objectively determine its permissible level of lobbying activities (Code Sec. 501(h); Reg. § 1.501(h)-2). The election can be made at any time during the organization's tax year. It is effective for the entire tax year and all succeeding years until revoked. A charitable organization may make this election unless it is: a church or a convention or association of churches (¶ 604), private foundation (¶ 631), or supporting organization (¶ 607) for social welfare organizations, labor unions, trade associations, and organizations that test for public safety (¶ 692).

The basic permitted level for lobbying expenditures (but not grassroots lobbying) is 20 percent of the first $500,000 of the electing organization's exempt-purpose expenditures for the year, 15 percent of the second $500,000, 10 percent of the third $500,000, and five percent of any additional expenditures with a maximum annual limitation of $1 million (Code Sec. 4911). In the case of so-called grassroots lobbying—attempts to influence the public on legislative matters—the basic permitted level is limited to 25 percent of the general lobbying level described above. An excise tax of 25 percent is imposed on any excess lobbying expenditures above these limits. In addition, if an organization's lobbying expenditures normally—on an average over a four-year period—exceed 150 percent of these limits (computed on Schedule C (Form 990)), the organization will lose its tax-exempt status (Reg. § 1.501(h)-3).

614. Excise Tax on Political Expenditures of Charitable Organizations. A 10-percent excise tax is imposed on a Code Sec. 501(c)(3) organization for each political expenditure made during the tax year (Code Sec. 4955). For this purpose, a political expenditure is generally defined as any amount paid or incurred by the organization in connection with any participation or intervention in any political campaign on behalf of (or in opposition to) any candidate for public office (¶ 613). A separate 2.5-percent excise tax (up to $5,000) is imposed on any organization manager who agrees to the making of the expenditure if the manager knows that it is a political expenditure, unless the agreement is not willful and due to reasonable cause. An organization manager includes a director, officer, trustee, or any individual with comparable responsibilities.

If the political expenditure is not corrected within the taxable period, then a second-tier excise tax is imposed on the organization equal to 100 percent of the amount of the expenditure. Organization managers who refuse to agree to all or part of the correction are also subject to a second-tier tax of 50 percent of the amount of the expenditure (up to $10,000). If more than one manager is liable for either the first- or second-tier taxes, then each manager is jointly and severally liable for them. The taxable period is the period beginning on the date on which the taxable expenditure is made and ending on the earlier of the date on which a deficiency notice for the first-tier tax is mailed or it is assessed. A correction of a political expenditure means the foundation takes all reasonable means to recover the expenditure to the extent possible and establishes safeguards to prevent future political expenditures. If full recovery is not possible, then the foundation must take whatever corrective action is prescribed by the IRS. Both the first and second levels of taxes may be abated under certain circumstances (¶ 647). The organization's taxes are reported on Form 4720.

616. Excess Executive Compensation of Tax-Exempt Organizations. An applicable tax-exempt organization is subject to a 21-percent excise tax on the sum of wages paid to a covered employee in excess of $1 million within a tax year and any excess parachute payments paid to a covered employee (Code Sec. 4960: Notice 2019-9). An applicable tax-exempt organization is any tax-exempt organization under Code Sec. 501(a), a farmers' cooperative, a political organization, or an organization that has income accruing to a state, territory, District of Columbia, or any political subdivision that is derived from a public utility and excluded from gross income.

A covered employee includes any current or former employee of the applicable tax-exempt organization who is one of the five highest compensated employees for the current tax year, or a covered employee of the organization (or any predecessor organization) for any tax year beginning after 2017. Wages for this purpose are considered paid if no substantial risk of forfeiture exists including any compensation deferred under a nonqualified deferred compensation plan required to be included in the recipient's gross income. The wages of a covered employee includes not only compensation paid by an applicable tax-exempt organization, but also any compensation paid to that employee for employment by any related organization of the applicable tax-exempt organization in that same tax year. Wages do not include any designated Roth contributions and wages paid to a licensed medical professional (doctor, nurse, or veterinarian) for the performance of medical or veterinary services. Any remuneration that is not deductible due to the $1 million limit on deductible compensation under Code Sec. 162(m) is not included in determining the total wages of a covered employee (¶ 906).

617. Excess Benefit Transactions of Charitable Organizations. An excise tax is imposed on any excess benefit transaction involving a charitable organization under Code Sec. 501(c)(3) other than a private foundation (¶ 631), a social welfare organization under Code Sec. 501(c)(4) (¶ 692), or a qualified nonprofit health insurance issuer under Code Sec. 501(c)(29) (Code Sec. 4958). The tax may be applied instead of, or in addition to, the organization being disqualified as an exempt organization due to the prohibition on private inurement (¶ 602). An excess benefit transaction is any transaction in which an economic benefit is provided to a disqualified person by the organization that exceeds any consideration given. It also includes any grant, loan, or other payment from a donor advised fund (¶ 610) or qualified supporting organization (¶ 607) to a disqualified person.

The tax is imposed on the disqualified person and is 25 percent of the amount of the excess benefit or the amount of the grant, loan, or other compensation received from a donor advised fund or qualified supporting organization. A manager of the exempt organization who knowingly participates in the transaction is subject to a separate excise tax of 10 percent, up to $20,000 per act. Managers who knowingly participate in the transaction are jointly and severally liable for the 10-percent tax. A manager will not be liable if participation is not willful and due to reasonable cause. For this purpose, a manager includes a director, officer, trustee, and any other individual of the exempt organization with comparable responsibilities.

If the excess benefit is not corrected within the taxable period (¶ 614), then a second-tier excise tax is imposed on the disqualified person equal to 200 percent of the amount of the excess benefit, grant, loan, or other payment. If more than one person is liable for either the first- or second-tier taxes on disqualified persons, then these persons are jointly and severally liable for them. The taxes on disqualified persons and organization managers are reported on Form 4720. Both levels of taxes may be abated under certain circumstances (¶ 647). In addition, private foundations are subject to different sanctions (¶ 635).

Disqualified Persons. For this purpose, a disqualified person is a person who is in a position to exercise substantial influence over the affairs of the exempt organization (including a qualified supporting organization), regardless of the individual's title. Certain family members and entities in which a disqualified person holds at least a 35-percent ownership interest are also treated as disqualified persons. In the case of any donor advised fund, a disqualified person includes any donor, donor advisor, and investment advisor to the fund, as well as any family member or any entity controlled by such persons. A disqualified person with respect to a qualified supporting organization includes any substantial contributor (¶ 635), family member of a substantial contributor, or a 35-percent controlled entity.

619. Involvement of Tax-Exempt Entities in Tax Shelter Transactions. A tax-exempt entity that is a party to a prohibited tax shelter transaction (¶ 2591), or that becomes a party to a subsequently listed transaction at any time during the tax year, is generally subject to an excise tax on a percentage of the entity's net income or proceeds attributable to the prohibited transaction (Code Sec. 4965). The rate of tax depends on whether the exempt entity *knew or had reason to know* that the transaction was a prohibited tax shelter transaction at the time it became a party to the transaction. Any manager of a tax-exempt entity who approves or otherwise causes the exempt entity to be a party to a prohibited tax shelter transaction at any time during the tax year, and knew or had reason to know that the transaction was a prohibited tax shelter transaction, must pay a separate excise tax for each approval.

A tax-exempt entity for this purpose includes any tax-exempt organization under Code Sec. 501(c) or religious organization under Code Sec. 501(d), including any charitable organization, and any qualified retirement plan, individual retirement account (IRA), health savings account (HSA), Archer medical savings account (MSA), qualified tuition plan, and ABLE account. The tax-exempt entity must disclose that it is a party to a prohibited tax shelter transaction on Form 8886-T, as well as the identity of any other parties (including both taxable and tax-exempt parties) to the transaction that are known by the entity (Code Sec. 6033(a)(2); Reg. § 1.6033-5). The entity or certain entity managers may be liable for a penalty if the disclosure requirement is not met (Code Sec. 6652(c)(3)).

620. Excise Tax on Investment Income of Private Colleges and Universities. An applicable educational institution is subject to a 1.4 percent excise tax on its net investment income for the tax year (Code Sec. 4968; Prop. Reg. § 53.4968-1; Notice 2018-55). Net investment income of the institution is defined the same as for the excise tax on net investment income of a private foundation (¶ 633) and generally includes gross investment income and net capital gain, less the ordinary and necessary business expenses incurred for the production or collection of gross investment income. For this purpose, the assets and net investment income of any related organization are treated as assets and net investment income of the institution.

An applicable educational institution is any private educational institution that has at least 500 tuition-paying students during the preceding tax year, more than 50 percent of the tuition-paying students are from the United States, and the aggregate fair market value of its assets at the end of the preceding tax year is at least $500,000 per student (not including assets used directly in carrying out the institution's exempt purpose). The number of students of an institution is based on the daily average number of full-time students attending the institution, with part-time students being taken into account on a full-time student equivalent basis.

Clarification and standardization of the rules for determining the excise tax applicable to the net investment income of certain private colleges and universities under Code Sec. 4968 have been proposed (Proposed Reg. § 53.4968-1).

623. Application and Modification of Tax-Exempt Status by Charitable Organizations. A charitable organization seeking exempt status under Code Sec. 501(c)(3) generally must file an application for exemption on Form 1023 or Form 1023-EZ within 15 months from the end of the month that it is organized (Code Sec. 508; Reg. § 1.508-1; Rev. Proc. 2020-5; Rev. Proc. 2020-8). However, the due date for performing certain time-sensitive actions, including filing an application for exemption on Form 1023, otherwise due on or after April 1, 2020, and before July 15, 2020, is automatically extended to July 15, 2020, in response to the COVID-19 (coronavirus) crisis (Notice 2020-23; Rev. Proc. 2018-58).

Form 1023 generally must be filed electronically if submitted after January 31, 2020. Form 1023-EZ may be used by organizations with gross receipts of $50,000 or less and assets of $250,000 or less. An organization that fails to file a timely notice will not qualify for exempt status for any period prior to the date actual notice is given. The IRS generally will not require a new exemption application from a domestic Code Sec. 501(c)(3) that changes its form or place of organization (i.e., restructuring) (Rev. Proc. 2018-15).

A second notification is required to be included on the application if the organization wants to claim public charity status. An organization that fails to notify the IRS of public charity status will be presumed to be a private foundation (¶ 631). An organization is a publicly supported organization qualifying for public charity status in its first five years if it can reasonably be expected to receive the requisite public support during the period (Reg. § 1.170A-9(f)(4)(v)).

Organizations that are not required to file an application for exempt status or notification of public charity status include: (1) any organization (other than a private foundation) whose annual gross receipts normally do not exceed $5,000; (2) a church and its affiliates; (3) any subordinate organization (other than a private foundation) covered by a group exemption of a parent; and (4) certain nonexempt charitable trusts (¶ 591) (Reg. § 1.508-1(a)(3)). In order for the organization to establish its exemption with the IRS and receive a determination letter, it should file the appropriate information return as proof of its exemption (¶ 625) (Reg. § 1.508-1(a)(4)).

The IRS will issue a favorable determination letter or exemption ruling if the organization's application and supporting documents establish that it meets the particular requirements under which it is claiming tax-exempt status (Rev. Proc. 2020-5). A ruling may also be modified or revoked by the IRS at any time (Reg. § 601.201(n)(6)). A revocation generally occurs prospectively but a retroactive revocation may occur where (1) the IRS was not fully or correctly informed as to the material facts on which the exemption ruling was based, or (2) there have been material changes in law or fact after the original ruling was issued.

If an organization receives an unfavorable exemption ruling, or its exempt status is revoked, it may seek judicial review only after it has exhausted all administrative remedies with the IRS. If an adverse ruling is issued (or if the IRS fails to issue a ruling), the organization can seek a declaratory judgment that it qualifies for exempt status (Code Sec. 7428). If the organization has actually begun operations before it receives an adverse ruling (or its exempt status is revoked retroactively), it may either pay the taxes on its activities it thought were exempt then file for a refund, or it can protest the assessment of any taxes in the Tax Court. An organization whose tax-exempt status has been revoked because it did not file annual information returns for three consecutive years (¶ 625) can apply for reinstatement of its status (Rev. Proc. 2020-5).

Tax-exempt organizations use Form 8940 to request determinations (other than initial exemption applications) about their tax-exempt status. These determinations include advance approval for foundation set-asides and scholarship approvals, change in type of supporting organization, and termination of foundation status.

625. Annual Information Return for Tax-Exempt Organizations. All tax-exempt organizations are generally required to file an annual information return with the IRS, including organizations whose application for exemption is pending, as well as nonexempt charitable trusts (¶ 591) (Code Sec. 6033; Reg. § 1.6033-2). For most organizations, the return is filed on or before the 15th day of the *fifth* month following the close of the organization's tax year on Form 990, Form 990-EZ, or Form 990-N, depending on its gross receipts and total assets. An automatic *six-month* extension is available (Reg. § 1.6081-9). The due date for performing certain time-sensitive actions, including filing Form 990 series, otherwise due on or after April 1, 2020, and before July 15, 2020, is automatically extended to July 15, 2020, in response to the COVID-19 (coronavirus) crisis (Notice 2020-23; Rev. Proc. 2018-58). Effective for tax years beginning after July 1, 2019, a tax-exempt organization must file its annual information return on Form 990 electronically (¶ 2503).

Other forms may be required for certain organizations: private foundations file Form 990-PF (¶ 631), farmers' cooperatives file Form 1120-C (¶ 698), religious and apostolic organizations file Form 1065 (¶ 604), and black lung benefits trusts file Form 990-BL. Organizations that exclude exempt function income from their gross income may be required to file a variation of Form 1120 in lieu of, or in addition to, Form 990 or Form 990-EZ, such as political organizations, which file Form 1120-POL (¶ 696), and certain homeowner associations, which file Form 1120-H (¶ 699).

Exempt organizations that are not required to file Form 990 or Form 990-EZ, regardless of gross receipts and total assets, include: any organization, other than a private foundation or supporting organization (¶ 607), that has annual gross receipts of $50,000 or less; any church, including its integrated auxiliary, and convention or association of churches (¶ 604); an exclusively religious activity of a religious order; church-sponsored mission societies; governmental units exempt from taxation; corporations organized under an act of Congress; certain schools affiliated with a church or religious order; and certain foreign or U.S. possession organizations (Code Sec. 6033(a)(3); Reg. § 1.6033-2(g)(1); Rev. Proc. 2011-15). An exempt organization that is not required to file Form 990 or Form 990-EZ because its annual gross receipts normally do not exceed $50,000 is still required to file an annual information return electronically on Form 990-N (Code Sec. 6033(i); Reg. § 1.6033-6; Rev. Proc. 2011-15).

Information Required. Form 990 and Form 990-EZ require an exempt organization to provide information on its finances, governance, compliance with certain federal tax filings and requirements, compensation paid to certain persons, exempt and nonexempt activities, and, in the case of a charitable hospital, the needs identified in its community health needs assessments and a copy of its audited financial statements (Code Sec. 6033(b)). Additional schedules and information are required to be completed depending upon the activities and type of the organization. For example, a charitable organization under Code Sec. 501(c)(3) must include information on its lobbying activities (¶ 613) and any donor advised funds (¶ 610) it sponsors (Code Sec. 6033(e) and (k)). A qualified nonprofit health insurance issuer under Code Sec. 501(c)(29) must include information on the amount of reserves on hand, and the amount of reserves required by each state in which the issuer is licensed to issue qualified health plans (Code Sec. 6033(m)). If an organization was tax-exempt for any of its last five tax years preceding its dissolution, liquidation, termination, or substantial contraction, then it must also include on Form 990 or Form 990-EZ information relating to that event (Code Sec. 6043(b); Reg. § 1.6043-3(b)). Organizations exempt from reporting information on their dissolution or termination include churches, organizations other than private foundations with $5,000 or less in annual gross receipts, and other organizations specified in the regulations.

Under Rev. Proc. 2018-38, many tax-exempt organizations were no longer required to report the names and addresses of contributors on Form 990, Schedule B, when filing their information returns for tax years ending on or after December 31, 2018, for donations above certain applicable thresholds. However, Rev. Proc. 2018-38 was overturned by a federal district court for failing to follow the notice and comment procedures required by the Administrative Procedure Act (APA). The IRS subsequently proposed amendments to regulations under Code Sec. 6033 that would effectively change the reporting requirements to align with Rev. Proc. 2018-38, but those proposed amendments are not yet effective (Proposed Reg. § 1.6033-2; (NPRM) REG-102508-16). Code Sec. 6652(c)(1)(A) imposes penalties for failure to include any required information. Under Code Sec. 6652(c)(5), the penalty is not imposed if it is shown that the failure was due to reasonable cause. Notice 2019-47 provides that the IRS will consider there to be a reasonable cause based on reliance on Rev. Proc. 2018-38 for any organizations that file Forms 990, 990-EZ, or 990-PF and did not include on their 2018 information return such donor information as Rev. Proc. 2018-38 indicated was not required.

Disclosure. Tax-exempt organizations, including private foundations, must make available for public inspection, at the organization's principal, regional, and district offices (having three or more employees) during regular business hours, its three most recent annual information returns, as well as a copy of its application for exemption. Charitable organizations must also make available for public inspection any returns related to the organization's unrelated business taxable income (¶ 670) filed in the previous three tax years (Code Sec. 6104; Reg. § 301.6104(d)-3). Organizations do not have to honor requests if they reasonably believe that the request is part of a harassment campaign. Requests may be made either in person or in writing. Copies of an organization's Form 990 must be furnished immediately for requests made in person and within 30 days of written requests. Organizations are permitted to charge a reasonable fee for reproduction and mailing costs. An exempt organization can comply with these disclosure requirements by posting information on its website.

Penalties. A penalty is imposed on each tax-exempt organization that fails to file an annual information return, files a late return without reasonable cause, or fails to file the information return on dissolution or substantial contraction (Code Sec. 6652(c)(1) and (7)). The penalty is adjusted annually for inflation and is $20 per day for returns to be filed in 2019 ($20 per day for 2020). The maximum penalty for one return is $10,000 for returns to be filed in 2019 ($10,500 for 2019) or five percent of the organization's gross receipts for the year, whichever is less (Rev. Proc. 2018-18; Rev. Proc. 2018-57).

The penalty is $100 per day for returns to be filed in 2019 ($105 per day for 2020), up to a maximum for any return of $52,000 ($53,000 for 2020) for an exempt organization with gross receipts in excess of $1,046,500 ($1,067,000 for 2020). An additional penalty of $10 a day for returns to be filed in 2019 ($10 per day for 2020), up to a maximum $5,000 on any return ($5,000 for 2020), is imposed on any officer, trustee, employee, etc., who fails to file the return without reasonable cause after requested by the IRS. There is no monetary penalty on an organization that is required to file Form 990-N but fails to do so.

If an organization fails to file an annual return for three consecutive years, its exempt status is automatically revoked (Code Sec. 6033(j), as amended by the Taxpayer First Act (P.L. 116-25)). The revocation is preconditioned on the IRS providing written notice to the organization after it has failed to timely file for two consecutive years after December 31, 2019. An organization whose tax-exempt status has been revoked because it did not file annual information returns for three consecutive years can apply for reinstatement of its status (Rev. Proc. 2020-5).

Failure to comply with the public disclosure requirements results in a penalty of $20 per day for returns to be filed in 2019 ($20 per day for 2020), with a maximum of $10,000 (maximum of $10,500 for 2020) (Code Sec. 6652(c)(1)(C)). There is no maximum penalty for failure to disclose the organization's exemption application. The penalty for a willful failure to comply with the public disclosure requirements is $5,000 for each return or application (Code Sec. 6685).

627. Other Reporting and Disclosure Requirements of Tax-Exempt Organizations. A tax-exempt organization, other than a private foundation (¶ 631), has a number of other filing requirements in addition to filing an application for tax-exempt status (¶ 623) and annual information returns (¶ 625).

Nondeductible Contributions. A tax-exempt organization that is not eligible to receive deductible charitable contributions, such as a lobbying group, political action committee, labor union, trade association, social club, and political organization (¶ 692 and ¶ 1061), must disclose this fact in a conspicuous and easily recognizable format in its fundraising solicitations (Code Secs. 6113 and 6710). Violation of this requirement without reasonable cause will subject an organization to a penalty of $1,000 per day of solicitation (up to $10,000 for any calendar year). A larger penalty will apply if the failure was intentional.

Quid Pro Quo Contributions. A charitable organization is required to inform donors in a written statement that quid pro quo contributions in excess of $75 are deductible only to the extent that the contributions exceed the value of goods or services provided by the organization (Code Secs. 6115 and 6714). Failure to make the required disclosure subjects the organization to a penalty of $10 per contribution unless due to reasonable cause. A quid pro quo contribution is any payment made partly as a contribution to the organization and partly in consideration for goods or services provided by the organization (e.g., fundraising dinners and auctions).

Donated Vehicles. A charitable organization is required to provide a donor of a motor vehicle, boat, or airplane with a contemporaneous written acknowledgment of the donation using Form 1098-C, including a certification of the organization's use or sale of the vehicle (¶ 1070A). A donee organization that fails to provide the acknowledgment or that provides a fraudulent acknowledgment will be subject to a penalty (Code Sec. 6720).

Donated Intellectual Property. A charitable organization that receives or accrues net income during a tax year from a qualified intellectual property contribution must file an information return on Form 8899 and provide a copy to the donor (¶ 1062A). The return is required for any tax year that occurs during the 10-year period beginning on the date of the contribution and if the legal life of the donated property has not expired. The organization will be subject to a penalty for failure to file the return (¶ 2816).

Dispositions of Donated Property. A charitable organization is required to file a donee information return on Form 8282 if it sells or otherwise disposes of any charitable deduction property within three years after it is donated to the organization (Code Sec. 6050L(a)). Charitable donation property is any property (other than cash or public securities) for which the donor claims a charitable contribution deduction of more than $5,000 and for which the organization signed an acknowledgment on Form 8283. The organization will be subject to a penalty for failure to file the return (¶ 2816).

Private Foundations

631. Private Foundations. A charitable organization under Code Sec. 501(c)(3) is either a public charity or private foundation (¶ 602). A public charity is an organization that has broad public support or that actively functions in a supporting relationship to such an organization. A private foundation typically is funded by one individual, family, or corporation. Thus, a private foundation is any Code Sec. 501(c)(3) organization *other than*:

- a charitable deduction donee listed in Code Sec. 170(b)(1)(A) (¶ 1059);

- a publicly supported organization receiving more than ⅓ of its annual support from members and the public, and not more than ⅓ of its support from investment income and unrelated business income (¶ 655);

- a qualified supporting organization (¶ 607); or

- an organization operated for public safety testing (Code Sec. 509; Reg. § 1.509(a)-3).

An organization that fails the public support test for two consecutive years will be treated as a private foundation as of the beginning of the second year of failure for certain purposes. The organization will be treated as a private foundation for all purposes beginning the first day of the third consecutive year.

Like all Code Sec. 501(c)(3) organizations, a private foundation must provide notice to the IRS to be tax-exempt (¶ 623). Even if notice is provided, a private foundation will be denied tax-exempt status unless its governing instrument specifically prohibits it from accumulating income (¶ 637), engaging in certain prohibited activities including acts of self-dealing (¶ 635), retaining excess business holdings (¶ 640), making investments that jeopardize its charitable purpose (¶ 642), or making certain taxable expenditures (¶ 644) (Code Sec. 508(e)). All private foundations must also file an annual information return on Form 990-PF reporting gross income, receipts, disbursements, etc. (¶ 625). If at any time during the tax year the foundation has at least $5,000 of assets, it must also include information on its assets, managers, and grants or contributions made during the year (Code Sec. 6033(c); Reg. § 1.6033-3).

633. Investment Income of Private Foundations. A 1.39 percent excise tax (two percent for tax years beginning before December 21, 2020) is imposed on the net investment income of a private foundation (¶ 631) for each tax year (Code Sec. 4940, as amended by the Tax Certainty and Disaster Tax Relief Act (P.L. 116-94)). For tax years beginning before December 21, 2020, the tax is reduced to one percent if the foundation satisfies certain requirements as to the amount of charitable distributions it made during the year and if it was not liable for the excise tax on undistributed income (¶ 637) in any of the preceding five tax years. The excise tax is reported on the foundation's annual return, Form 990-PF.

Estimated payments of the foundation's liability for the tax, as well as its unrelated business taxable income (UBTI) (¶ 670), are computed on Form 990-W. The first-quarter installment is due by the 15th day of the fifth month following the foundation's tax year (May 15 for calendar year foundations) (Code Sec. 6655(g)(3)). The due date of any required installment calculated on Form 990-W and due on or after April 1, 2020, and before July 15, 2020, is automatically extended to July 15, 2020, as a result of the COVID-19 (coronavirus) crisis (Notice 2020-23, amplifying Notice 2020-18). The extension is automatic, and an organization does not need to file any form or call the IRS to receive it. Penalties and interest for failure to pay taxes will not accrue until July 16, 2020, as a result of the extension. The extension does not extend the time to pay estimated income tax beyond July 15, 2020.

The net investment income of a private foundation generally includes the foundation's gross investment income and net capital gain, less the ordinary and necessary business expenses incurred for the production or collection of gross investment income. Gross investment income includes interest, dividends, rents, royalties, and payments with respect to securities loans, as well as any similar source of income such as income from annuities and notional principal contracts. It does not include income to the extent it is taken into account as UBTI, including any gain or loss from the sale or disposition of property (no capital loss carryovers or carrybacks are allowed).

The tax on investment income does not apply to an exempt operating foundation. This is any operating foundation that has been publicly supported for at least 10 years, has at all times during the tax year been governed by representatives at least 75 percent of whom represent the public, and has had at no time during the tax year an officer who is a disqualified individual. For this purpose, a disqualified individual is a substantial contributor to the foundation, an owner of more than 20 percent of a business or trust that is a substantial contributor, or a member of the family of any of the preceding. An operating foundation is a foundation that spends at least 85 percent of the lesser of its adjusted net income or its minimum investment return in carrying on its exempt activities (Code Sec. 4942(j)(3); Reg. § 53.4942(b)-1). A nonoperating private foundation is generally a grantmaking organization that does not operate its own charitable program.

635. Prohibitions on Self-Dealing by Private Foundations. Certain acts of self-dealing are prohibited between a disqualified person and a private foundation (¶ 631) (Code Sec. 4941). This includes the sale or exchange of property, loans or other extensions of credit, the furnishing of goods or services, payments of compensation, or the transfer of income or assets to the disqualified person. It does not include the pro rata division of a trust that qualifies as a charitable remainder trust (¶ 590) into two separate trusts (Rev. Rul. 2008-41). For this purpose, a disqualified person includes:

- a substantial contributor (any person who contributes more than $5,000 if that amount is more than two percent of the total contributions received by the foundation before the end of its tax year);

- a foundation manager, including an officer, director, or trustee;

- the owner of more than 20 percent of a corporation, partnership, trust, or other enterprise that is a substantial contributor;

- a member of the family of any of the preceding (including spouse, ancestor, child, grandchild, great grandchild, or spouse of any of these descendants);

- a corporation, trust, estate, or partnership more than 35 percent of which is owned or held by any of the preceding; and

- a government official (Code Sec. 4946).

The disqualified person is subject to a 10-percent excise tax on the amount involved in any act of self-dealing for each year in the taxable period. Any foundation manager who knowingly participates in the self-dealing act is subject to a five-percent excise tax on the amount involved, but only if participation was willful and not due to reasonable cause. A second-level tax of 200 percent (50 percent on the manager) applies if the prohibited act is not corrected within the taxable period. For this purpose, the taxable period begins on the date the self-dealing act occurs and ends on the earliest of: (1) the date the deficiency notice for the first-level tax is mailed; (2) the date the first-level tax is assessed; or (3) the date the act of self-dealing is completely corrected (Code Sec. 4941(e)). The maximum tax imposed on a foundation manager is $20,000 per act for each level of tax. The IRS has discretionary authority to abate both levels of tax for the manager and the disqualified person (¶ 647). However, a third-level tax may be imposed or the foundation's status may be terminated (¶ 649) if there are repeated or flagrant acts of self-dealing (Code Sec. 6684). The initial excise tax on an act of self-dealing is reported on Form 4720.

637. Undistributed Income of Private Foundations. A private foundation (¶ 631) other than an operating foundation (¶ 633) is required to annually distribute its minimum investment return for the tax year. This is five percent of the foundation's net investment assets adjusted for certain taxes and loan repayments. Failure to do so will cause the foundation to be subject to an excise tax of 30 percent of any undistributed income (Code Sec. 4942). Undistributed income is the amount by which the minimum investment return of the foundation exceeds the amount of qualifying distributions made during the tax year. Qualifying distributions include distributions to public charities and private operating foundations, and payments for expenses and assets used for charitable purposes. It does not generally include payments made by the nonoperating private foundation to a supporting organization (¶ 607).

If the foundation fails to make the necessary distributions within the taxable period, then a second-level tax will be imposed equal to 100 percent of the undistributed income. The taxable period is the period that begins on the first day of the tax year, and ends on the earlier of: (1) the date the deficiency notice for the initial tax is mailed, or (2) the date it is assessed. The IRS has discretionary authority to abate both levels of tax (¶ 647). However, a third-level tax may be imposed or the foundation's status may be terminated (¶ 649) if there are repeated or flagrant acts of failure to distribute income (Code Sec. 6684). The initial excise tax on undistributed income is reported on Form 4720.

640. Excess Business Holdings of Private Foundations. A private foundation (¶ 631) is allowed to own a certain amount of business enterprises jointly with disqualified persons (¶ 635) but is subject to a 10-percent excise tax on any excess business holdings during the tax year (Code Sec. 4943). If the excess business holdings are not divested within the taxable period (¶ 637), then a second-level tax of 200 percent is imposed. The permitted amount of business ownership that a private foundation and disqualified person may have in any enterprise that is not substantially related to the exempt purposes of the foundation is generally 20 percent. If third parties have effective control of the business enterprise, then the limit is 35 percent. Special rules apply to certain grandfathered holdings. The IRS has discretionary authority to abate both levels of tax (¶ 647). However, a third-level tax may be imposed or the foundation's status may be terminated (¶ 649) if there are repeated or flagrant acts of excess business holdings

(Code Sec. 6684). An exception to the tax is provided for certain philanthropic business holdings (i.e. independently operated business enterprises that pay all after-tax profits to the private foundation).

The excise tax on excess business holdings will apply to donor advised funds (¶ 610) and certain qualified supporting organizations (¶ 607). In applying the tax to donor advised funds, a disqualified person is defined as any donor, a member of the donor's family, or a 35-percent controlled entity. A qualified supporting organization will be subject to the excess business holdings tax only if it is a Type III supporting organization, or a Code Sec. 501(c)(3) organization that meets the organizational and operational test of a qualified supporting organization and it is not controlled by a disqualified person. For this purpose, a disqualified person with respect to the supporting organization is any person with substantial influence over the organization (or any family member of such a person), as well as any substantial contributor, family member of a substantial contributor, or 35-percent controlled entity.

642. Investments Jeopardizing Exempt Purpose of Private Foundations. A 10-percent excise tax is imposed on any investment of a private foundation (¶ 631) that jeopardizes the foundation's exempt status (Code Sec. 4944; Reg. § 53.4944-1). A jeopardizing investment is generally one that shows a lack of reasonable business care and prudence in providing for the foundation's short- and long-term financial needs. Examples of investments that will be closely scrutinized include trading in securities on margin, trading in commodity futures, investing in working interests in oil and gas wells, and selling short. Investments made by a private foundation that are not program-related investments (PRIs) but are made at least partially for charitable purposes are not jeopardizing investments (Reg. § 53.4944-3; Notice 2015-62).

A 10-percent excise tax is also imposed on any foundation manager who knowingly participates in such an investment (up to $10,000 per investment), unless the participation is not willful but due to reasonable cause. A second-level tax of 25 percent is imposed on the foundation if the jeopardy situation is not corrected within the taxable period (¶ 637). Any foundation manager who refuses to agree to part or all of the correction will be subject to a second-level tax of five percent of the investment (up to $20,000). If more than one foundation manager is liable for either level of tax, then all such managers are jointly and severally liable for them. The IRS has discretionary authority to abate both levels of tax (¶ 647). However, a third-level tax may be imposed on either the foundation or a manager, or the foundation's status may be terminated (¶ 649), if there are repeated or flagrant acts of jeopardizing investments (Code Sec. 6684).

644. Lobbying and Other Prohibited Expenditures of Private Foundations. A private foundation (¶ 631) is subject to a 20-percent excise tax on the amount of any taxable expenditure made during the tax year. Any foundation manager who, without reasonable cause, willfully agrees to the expenditure knowing it is improper is subject to a five-percent excise tax on the expenditure (up to $10,000) (Code Sec. 4945). A taxable expenditure generally includes any amount paid by the foundation for legislative or political purposes, or any grant to an individual for travel, study, or other similar purpose (unless made under objective standards). It also includes any grant to any organization unless the grantee organization is a public charity, qualified supporting organization (¶ 607), exempt operating foundation (¶ 633), or the nonoperating private foundation exercises responsibility for the expenditure of the grant. A taxable expenditure does not include the pro rata division of a trust that qualifies as a charitable remainder trust (¶ 590) into two separate trusts (Rev. Rul. 2008-41).

A second-level tax of 100 percent is imposed on the foundation if the taxable expenditure is not corrected within the taxable period (¶ 637). Any foundation manager who refuses to agree to part or all of the correction will be subject to a second-level tax of 50 percent of the investment (up to $20,000). If more than one foundation manager is liable for either level of tax, then all such managers are jointly and severally liable for them. The IRS has discretionary authority to abate both levels of tax for the foundation or the manager (¶ 647). However, a third-level tax may be imposed or the foundation's

6

EXEMPT ORGS

status may be terminated (¶ 649) if there are repeated or flagrant acts of taxable expenditures (Code Sec. 6684).

647. Abatement of Certain Taxes on Tax-Exempt Organizations. The IRS has discretionary authority not to assess certain first-tier excise taxes imposed on tax-exempt organizations, or to abate such taxes if already assessed, or to provide a credit or refund if the tax is already collected. The IRS will exercise this authority only if the violation giving rise to the imposition of the excise tax in question was due to reasonable cause and not willful neglect, and is corrected within the correction period (Code Sec. 4962).

First-tier excise taxes to which this relief may apply include: all of the excise taxes imposed on private foundations and disqualified persons (¶ 631), except for the tax on acts of self-dealing (¶ 635); the excise tax on the lobbying and political activities of public charities (¶ 614); the excise tax on excess benefit transactions (¶ 617); and the excise taxes on taxable distributions and prohibited benefits from donor advised funds (¶ 610). The IRS may withhold or abate an assessment of any second-tier excise taxes if the taxable event in question is corrected voluntarily during the correction period (Code Sec. 4961). The correction period begins on the date of the taxable event and ends 90 days after the deficiency notice for the second-tier tax is mailed (Code Sec. 4963).

649. Termination of Private Foundation Status. The status of any organization as a private foundation (¶ 631) may be terminated voluntarily or involuntarily (Code Sec. 507). A voluntary termination requires the foundation to notify the IRS of its plan to terminate. An involuntary termination occurs when the IRS notifies the foundation of the intent to terminate its status because of willful repeated violations or a willful and flagrant violation giving rise to excise taxes on the foundation. In either case, the private foundation must pay a termination tax equal to the lesser of: (1) the aggregate amount of tax benefits received by the foundation and any of its substantial contributors (¶ 635) since its inception resulting from its exempt status under Code Sec. 501(c)(3); or (2) the value of its net assets. The pro rata division of a trust that qualifies as a charitable remainder trust (¶ 590) into two separate trusts does not terminate private foundation status or cause the termination tax to apply (Rev. Rul. 2008-41).

The IRS may abate a portion or all of the termination tax if, prior to providing notice to the IRS of its voluntary termination, the foundation distributes all of its net assets to another private foundation or public charity described in Code Sec. 170(b)(1)(A) (¶ 1059) that has been in existence for at least five years immediately before the distribution. Under these circumstances, the transfer of assets is not a termination of the foundation's status. Instead, the foundation retains its status until it gives actual notice of its termination to the IRS. When notice is provided after all net assets are transferred, then the termination tax will be zero (but the distributions may give rise to excise taxes). The termination tax may also be abated if the foundation becomes a public charity within 12 months or it actually operates as a public charity for at least five years. However, notice of termination must be provided to the IRS prior to the beginning of the 12-month or five-year termination period.

A tax-exempt organization uses Form 8940 to request determinations about termination of foundation status.

Unrelated Business Taxable Income

655. Tax-Exempt Organizations Subject to Unrelated Business Income Tax. Although a variety of nonprofit organizations with charitable or socially beneficial purposes may be granted tax-exempt status under Code Sec. 501, they are still subject to a tax on unrelated business income (¶ 658) (Code Sec. 511). Unrelated business income is income from a trade or business regularly carried on by the exempt organization (¶ 664) that is not substantially related (¶ 667) to the organization's exempt purposes (Code Sec. 512).

All types of exempt organizations, except government instrumentalities (other than colleges or universities) and federally licensed businesses or educational institutions sponsored by a religious order, are subject to the tax (Reg. § 1.511-2; Reg. § 1.511-2(e)).

¶647

Additionally, title-holding companies may be exempt from tax on unrelated business income if the holding corporation and the payee organization file a consolidated return.

658. Unrelated Business Income Tax Rate and Payment. A tax-exempt organization subject to the unrelated business income tax (¶ 655) is taxed on its unrelated business taxable income (UBTI) (¶ 670) at the income tax rates for a corporation or trust (Code Sec. 511(a)). The alternative minimum tax (AMT) (¶ 190) also applies to a corporation before 2018 and trust for any tax year for tax preference items used in the computation of organization's UBTI.

Returns are made on Form 990-T for each tax year that the organization has gross income of $1,000 or more from an unrelated trade or business. The form is filed at the same time as the organization's annual information return (¶ 625) (Reg. § 1.6012-2(e)). Effective for tax years beginning after July 1, 2019, Form 990-T must be filed electronically (Code Sec. 6011(h), as added by the Taxpayer First Act (P.L. 116-25)). Transition relief is provided for up to two year for certain small organizations and other organizations designated by the IRS. Estimated payments of the exempt organization's liability for UBTI are computed on Form 990-W. The first-quarter installment is due by the 15th day of the fifth month following the organization's tax year (May 15 for calendar year organizations) (Code Sec. 6655(g)(3)).

The due date of any required installment calculated on Form 990-W and due on or after April 1, 2020, and before July 15, 2020, is automatically extended to July 15, 2020, as a result of the COVID-19 (coronavirus) crisis (Notice 2020-23, amplifying Notice 2020-18). The extension is automatic, and an organization does not need to file any form or call the IRS to receive it. Penalties and interest for failure to pay taxes will not accrue until July 16, 2020, as a result of the extension. The extension does not extend the time to pay estimated income tax beyond July 15, 2020.

664. Business Regularly Carried on by Tax-Exempt Organizations. The unrelated business taxable income (UBTI) of a tax-exempt organization (¶ 670) is its gross income from any unrelated trade or business *regularly* carried on by the organization, minus any deductions for expenses related to the trade or business (¶ 682) (Code Sec. 512(a); Reg. § § 1.512(a)-1 and 1.513-1(c)). An exempt organization with more than one unrelated trade or business must calculate UBTI separately for each trade or business without regard to the specific $1,000 deduction (Code Sec. 512(a)(6)).

A trade or business generally includes any activity carried on for the production of income from selling goods or performing services. In determining whether a trade or business is regularly carried on, the frequency and continuity with which an activity is pursued is judged with comparable commercial activities of nonexempt organizations. In the case of a social club, voluntary employees' beneficiary association (VEBA), or an organization for the payment of supplemental unemployment benefits (SUB) (¶ 692), UBTI is subject to tax only to the extent that it is not set aside for the purposes that constitute the basis for the organization's exemption (i.e., exempt function income) (Code Sec. 512(a)(3); Reg. § 1.512(a)-5; Prop. Reg. § 1.512(a)-5).

667. Business Unrelated to Exempt Function of Tax-Exempt Organizations. The unrelated business taxable income (UBTI) of a tax-exempt organization (¶ 670) includes any income from a business *not substantially related* to the organization's exempt purpose (Code Sec. 513; Reg. § 1.513-1). A business activity is not substantially related to an organization's exempt purpose if it does not contribute importantly to accomplishing that purpose (other than through the production of funds). Whether an activity contributes importantly depends on the facts, including the size and extent of the activities involved in relation to the exempt function they serve.

A number of activities will *not* be considered an unrelated trade or business, including any trade or business that:

- has substantially all the work in carrying on the business performed for the organization without compensation;
- is carried on by a Code Sec. 501(c)(3) organization or governmental college or university primarily for the convenience of its members, students, etc.;

¶667

- consists of selling merchandise, substantially all of which has been received by the organization as gifts or contributions;

- is a qualified entertainment activity or a qualified convention and trade show activity (¶ 685) (Code Sec. 513(d));

- in the case of a public charity hospital, performs services that a tax-exempt cooperative hospital organization may perform (¶ 699) (Code Sec. 513(e));

- consists of conducting any bingo games if the games are conducted in accordance with local law and do not compete with profit-making businesses (Code Sec. 513(f));

- in the case of a mutual or cooperative telephone or electric company, engages in qualified pole rentals (Code Sec. 513(g));

- includes exchanging or renting member donor lists between exempt organizations or distributing low-cost articles ($11.10 for 2019 and $11.20 for 2020) incidental to the solicitation of charitable contributions (Code Sec. 513(h); Rev. Proc. 2018-57; Rev. Proc. 2019-44); or

- involves soliciting and receiving qualified sponsorship payment (Code Sec. 513(i)) (¶ 685).

670. Unrelated Business Taxable Income Defined. The unrelated business taxable income (UBTI) of a tax-exempt organization is its gross income from any unrelated trade or business regularly carried on (¶ 664 and ¶ 667), less the deductions directly connected with the trade or business (¶ 682) (Code Sec. 512). An exempt organization with more than one unrelated trade or business must calculate UBTI separately for each trade or business without regard to the specific $1,000 deduction and the UBTI of any particular trade or business cannot be less than zero (Code Sec. 512(a)(6)). The IRS has provided guidance for determining when unrelated businesses should be treated separately or as parts of the same unrelated business for this purpose (Notice 2018-67).

The following income items (and any related deductions) are generally excluded from the calculation of UBTI: dividends, interest, annuities and royalties (¶ 673); rents from real property or incidental rents from personal property leased with real property (¶ 676); gains or losses from the disposition of property other than stock in trade (¶ 679); certain research income; certain amounts received from controlled entities and foreign corporations; income of a mutual or cooperative electric company derived from the sale of electricity from its members; and gains or losses on the disposition of qualified brownfield sites. Annual dues not exceeding $169 for 2019 ($171 for 2020) that are paid to an exempt agricultural or horticultural organization are also excluded from UBTI (Rev. Proc. 2018-57; Rev. Proc. 2019-44).

An exempt organization's UBTI calculation must include its share of income and deductions from an unrelated trade or business conducted by a partnership (including a publicly traded partnership) or S corporation in which it is a partner or shareholder. If the tax year of the organization differs from the partnership's, then the amounts used to calculate UBTI will be based on the income and deductions of the partnership in the tax year that ends within the tax year of the exempt organization. In addition, the organization's share of S corporation income and deductions must be included regardless of whether they would normally be excluded from UBTI (dividends, interest, royalties, etc.).

Fringe Benefits. UBTI does not include the nondeductible amount of certain fringe benefit expenses for any tax year. The Tax Cuts and Jobs Act (P.L. 115-97) increased UBTI by fringe benefits if paid or incurred in tax years beginning after 2017, unless directly connected with an unrelated trade or business regularly carried on by the organization. This included qualified transportation fringe benefits (¶ 2091), any parking facility used in connection with qualified parking, and any on-premises athletic facility (¶ 2094). This addition to UBTI has been repealed with the result being as if it was never enacted (Code Sec. 512(a)(7), stricken by the Tax Certainty and Disaster Tax Relief Act (P.L. 116-94)).

673. Unrelated Business Taxable Income—Investment Income. The unrelated business taxable income (UBTI) of a tax-exempt organization (¶ 670) generally does *not* include investment income such as dividends, interest, annuities, royalties, payments with respect to securities loans, amounts received or accrued as consideration for entering into agreements to make loans, and income derived from notional principal contracts, as well as income from ordinary investments that are substantially similar (Code Sec. 512(b); Reg. § 1.512(b)-1(a)). Royalties for this purpose include amounts paid to an exempt organization for use of its name, trademarks, and other intellectual property rights in connection with the sale of merchandise or services (Rev. Rul. 81-178). If an exempt organization provides active services in relation to marketing products or services associated with its name or other rights, the income may not be excluded as royalty income. The exclusion for investment income also does not apply to income from debt-financed property (¶ 687).

Membership Organizations. Special rules apply to certain membership organizations including a social and recreational club, voluntary employees' beneficiary association (VEBA), or a supplemental unemployment compensation benefit trust (SUB) (¶ 692). Unlike other exempt organizations, these organizations cannot exclude investment income from UBTI and losses from nonexempt activities cannot generally be used to offset investment income. However, gross income does not include exempt function income, which is income from dues, fees, and charges for providing facilities and services for members, dependents, and guests, as well as income set aside for charitable purposes or by a VEBA to provide insurance benefits (Code Sec. 512(a)(3)). An exclusion also applies for gain such organizations realize on the sale of assets used in pursuing their exempt function to the extent the proceeds are reinvested (within a four-year period) in other assets for such purposes. A title-holding corporation whose income is payable to a membership organization will be treated as the exempt organization for this purpose.

To prevent bypassing these limitations through termination of tax-exempt status, a *nonexempt* social club or other membership organization operated primarily to furnish goods or services to members may deduct the cost of furnishing these goods, services, insurance, etc., only to the extent of membership-related income (Code Sec. 277). A nonexempt social club or VEBA is also not allowed to claim the corporate dividends-received deduction (¶ 223).

Look-Through Rules. If an exempt organization receives or accrues a payment of interest, annuity, royalty or rent (but not a dividend) from an entity that it controls, then the payment is includible in the organization's UBTI to the extent it either reduces the net unrelated business income of the controlled entity or increases its net unrelated losses (Code Sec. 512(b)(13)). Any payment made pursuant to a binding written contract in effect on August 17, 2006 (or renewal of such a contract), is included in UBTI only to the extent it exceeds the amount of the payment if it were made as if the parties were not related (i.e., arms-length transaction).

A valuation misstatement penalty applies to excess payments that are included in UBTI. In addition, the exempt organization must report the payments from a controlled entity on its annual return (Code Sec. 6033(h)). The threshold of control of a subsidiary that triggers UBTI is having more than 50-percent ownership (more than 50 percent of stock by vote or value in a corporation, or more than 50 percent of a profits, capital, or beneficial interest of a partnership or other entity). The constructive ownership rules of Code Sec. 318 apply for this purpose (¶ 743).

676. Unrelated Business Taxable Income—Rents. The unrelated business taxable income (UBTI) of a tax-exempt organization (¶ 670) does *not* include amounts received from the rental of real property. It also does not include rents from personal property leased with real property so long as they are incidental in relation to the total amount of rents under the lease (10 percent or less of total rents from all leased property) (Code Sec. 512(b)(3); Reg. § 1.512(b)-1(c)).

6

EXEMPT ORGS

Rents are taxable if they are:

- rents from real property leased with personal property if more than 50 percent of the rent is attributable to the personal property;

- rents from both real and personal property if the amount of the rents depends on the income or profits derived by any person from the leased property (other than an amount based on a fixed percentage of gross receipts or sales); and

- unrelated income from debt-financed property (¶ 687).

Payments for the use or occupancy of rooms and other space (for example, in a hotel, boarding house, storage facility) where services are also provided primarily for the occupant's convenience and are not those customarily rendered in rental for occupancy only (such as maid service) are not rents from real property.

679. Unrelated Business Taxable Income—Gains and Losses. The unrelated business taxable income (UBTI) of a tax-exempt organization (¶ 670) does *not* include gains or losses from the sale, exchange, or other disposition (including involuntary conversions and casualties) of property *other than*:

- stock in trade or other property of a kind properly includible in inventory;

- property held primarily for sale to customers in the ordinary course of a trade or business; or

- timber cutting that the organization has elected to consider as a sale or exchange (Code Sec. 512(b)(5); Reg. § 1.512(b)-1(d)).

The exclusion also applies to all gains or losses recognized in connection with the organization's investment activities from the lapse or termination of options to buy and sell securities (whether or not written by the organization), as well as options to buy or sell real property. The exclusion does not apply to gains from the sale or other disposition of debt-financed property (¶ 687). Gains from certain pension plan investments in property of troubled financial institutions are also excluded (Code Sec. 512(b)(16)).

682. Unrelated Business Taxable Income—Deductions. A tax-exempt organization is entitled to deduct all ordinary and necessary business expenses *directly connected* with carrying on an unrelated trade or business (¶ 667) in computing unrelated business taxable income (UBTI) (¶ 670). A deduction must have a proximate and primary relationship to carrying on the particular trade or business to be directly connected with the conduct of the unrelated trade or business. Expenses attributable to an exempt activity generally are not deductible unless:

- the unrelated business exploits the exempt activity;

- the business is of a type normally carried on for profit by a taxable organization; and

- the exempt activity is of a type normally carried on by a taxable organization in carrying on its business.

If facilities or personnel are used for both exempt functions and the conduct of an unrelated business, expenses must be allocated on a reasonable basis (Code Sec. 512(a) and (b)(12); Reg. § 1.512(a)-1).

An exempt organization is also allowed a specific deduction of $1,000, as well as the deduction for charitable contributions allowed to corporations (¶ 927), and net operating losses (NOLs) (¶ 1145). The charitable contribution deduction is allowed whether or not directly connected with the carrying on of the trade or business but is limited to 10 percent of the organization's UBTI, computed without regard to the contributions deduction (Code Sec. 512(b)(10)). An exempt trust that is subject to the unrelated business income tax at trust rates generally is allowed a deduction for charitable contributions in the same amounts as allowed for individuals (¶ 1058). With respect to the NOL deduction, the deduction must only reflect taxable business income, and carryovers and items attributable to exempt income and expenses are disregarded (Code Sec. 512(b)(6)).

685. Advertising, Sponsorships, and Trade Shows. The sale of advertising in a periodical, journal, or magazine of a tax-exempt organization is considered an unrelated business of the organization (¶ 667) that exploits an exempt activity if the advertising activity is regularly carried on (¶ 664) (Reg. § 1.512(a)-1(d) and (f)). An activity such as advertising does not lose its identity as a trade or business merely because it is carried on within a larger complex of other activities which may or may not be related to the organization's exempt purpose (Reg. § 1.513-1(b)). As a result, advertising revenue is used in computing the organization's unrelated business taxable income (UBTI) (¶ 670) but may be offset by the expenses directly related to the advertising business activity. If facilities and personnel are both used to carry on exempt activities and unrelated advertising, the expenses must be allocated on a reasonable basis.

For this purpose, income realized by an exempt organization from the sponsorship of a public event will generally constitute advertising services. However, the solicitation and receipt of qualified sponsorship payments by an exempt organization is not an unrelated business, and the payments are excluded from computing UBTI (Code Sec. 513(i); Reg. § 1.513-4). A qualified sponsorship payment is any payment by a payor engaged in a trade or business that does not expect any substantial return from the exempt organization other than the use or acknowledgment of the payor's name, logo, or product lines in connection with the activities of the tax-exempt organization. A qualified sponsorship payment does *not* include any payment:

- for advertising the payor's product or services, including messages that contain qualitative or comparative language, price information, an endorsement, or an inducement to purchase, sell, or use the payor's products and services;

- contingent upon factors indicating the degree of public exposure at one or more events (attendance, broadcast ratings);

- that entitles the payor to the use or acknowledgment of the business name, logo, or product lines in the exempt organization's publication; or

- made in connection with a qualified convention or trade show activity—a convention or trade show conducted by a charitable organization (¶ 602), social welfare program, labor organization, or business league (¶ 692) that has as one of its purposes the promotion of interest in the products and services of the industry in general, or the education of the attendees regarding new developments or products and services related to the exempt activities of the organizations (Reg. § 1.513-3).

Taxable Income from Debt-Financed Property

687. Unrelated Debt-Financed Income of Tax-Exempt Organizations. A percentage of income from debt-financed property must be included in a tax-exempt organization's unrelated business taxable income (UBTI) (¶ 670) regardless of whether the organization is engaged in a trade or business (Code Sec. 514(a); Reg. § 1.514(a)-1). The percentage included in UBTI is the same percentage (not to exceed 100 percent) as the average acquisition indebtedness on the property (¶ 689) for the tax year divided by the average amount of the adjusted basis of the property. Deductions with respect to each debt-financed property are allowed by applying the same percentage to expenses related to the property, except for any deduction resulting from the carryback or carryover of net capital losses (¶ 1752).

Debt-financed property for this purpose generally means any property held to produce income, including gain from its disposition (for example, rental real estate, corporate stock, etc.) on which there is an acquisition indebtedness at any time during the tax year (or preceding 12 months if the property is disposed of during the tax year) (Code Sec. 514(b); Reg. § 1.514(b)-1(a)). Certain property, however, is not debt-financed property even if it is held to produce income (¶ 691).

689. Acquisition Indebtedness on Debt-Financed Property of Tax-Exempt Organizations. For any debt-financed property of a tax-exempt organization (¶ 687), acquisition indebtedness is the outstanding amount of principal debt:

- incurred to acquire or improve property;

- incurred before the acquisition or improvement if it would not have been incurred but for the acquisition or improvement; and

- incurred after acquisition or improvement if it would not have been incurred but for the acquisition or improvement and was reasonably foreseeable at the time (Code Sec. 514(c); Reg. § 1.514(c)-1).

If property is acquired subject to a mortgage, the amount of the mortgage (or similar lien) is considered acquisition indebtedness, even if the organization does not assume or agree to pay the debt. However, if mortgaged property is received by bequest or devise (or by gift under certain circumstances), the debt is not treated as an acquisition indebtedness for 10 years from the date of acquisition. A lien for taxes or assessments under state law will be treated similar to a mortgage to the extent the amount becomes due and the organization has an opportunity to pay it.

Acquisition indebtedness does not include debt that was incurred by an exempt organization in the exercise of its exempt purpose. Generally, it also does not include debt incurred by certain qualified organizations (qualified employee benefits trust; an exempt school; exempt title-holding company; retirement income account of church plan) in acquiring or improving real property. Annuities may be excluded from the definition of acquisition indebtedness, as well as certain obligations insured by the Federal Housing Administration or incurred by a small business investment company (¶ 2392).

691. Exceptions to Debt-Financed Property of Tax-Exempt Organizations. The following types of property are excluded from the definition of debt-financed property of a tax-exempt organization (¶ 687):

(1) property substantially all the use of which (85 percent or more) is related to the exercise or performance of the organization's tax-exempt function (special rules apply to real property used as a medical clinic);

(2) property to the extent that its income is subject to tax as income from carrying on an unrelated trade or business, but if any gain on disposition of the property is not included in unrelated business taxable income (¶ 655), it may be income from debt-financed property (¶ 679);

(3) property to the extent that its income is from certain research activities and is excluded from gross income of an unrelated trade or business;

(4) property to the extent it is used in a business where substantially all of the work of carrying on the business is performed without compensation, the Code Sec. 501(c)(3) organization carrying on the business does so primarily for the convenience of members, students, patients, etc., or the business consists of selling merchandise substantially all of which has been received as contributions; and

(5) certain brownfield site property to the extent the gain or loss from its sale or exchange would be excluded from gross income of an unrelated trade or business (Code Sec. 514(b); Reg. § 1.514(b)-1).

For (1), (3), and (4) above, property use by a related organization is taken into account in determining use of a tax-exempt organization. In addition, special rules apply to life income contracts and real property located in the neighborhood of other property owned and used for exempt purposes by the tax-exempt organization.

Other Tax-Exempt Organizations

692. Alternative Tax-Exempt Organizations Under Code Sec. 501(c). In addition to charitable organizations (¶ 602), Code Sec. 501 exempts other types of nonprofit organizations from federal income tax unless they are feeder organizations (¶ 694). Among the most common are civic leagues and social welfare organizations, business leagues, social and recreation clubs, and fraternal beneficiary societies. Contributions to these organizations are generally *not* deductible as charitable contributions. An organization described in this section files an application for exemption on Form 1024 (unless otherwise noted) and an annual information return on Form 990 (¶ 625).

Social Welfare Organizations and Civic Leagues. A civic league or organization is exempt from federal income taxes if it is not organized for profit and is operated *exclusively* for the promotion of social welfare (Code Sec. 501(c)(4)). This includes a local association of employees if the membership is limited to the employees of a designated employer in a particular municipality and whose net earnings are devoted exclusively to charitable, educational, or recreational purposes. An exemption is not allowed if any part of the net earnings of the civic league or organization inures to the benefit of any private shareholder or individual (¶ 602). If the organization provides an excess benefit to certain persons, an excise tax may be imposed (¶ 617).

A civic league or organization is considered to be operated exclusively for the promotion of social welfare if it *primarily* engages in promoting the common good and general welfare of the community (for example, volunteer fire departments or community associations) (¶ 699). Promoting social welfare does not include participation or intervention in the political campaign of any candidate for office. In addition, the promotion of social welfare does not include the operation of a social club for the benefit of its members or carrying on a business similar to for-profit organizations (Reg. § 1.501(c)(4)-1). This includes providing commercial-type insurance unless it is an insubstantial part of the organization's activities, in which case the activity will be treated as an unrelated trade or business (¶ 655) (Code Sec. 501(m) and (n)).

A Code Sec. 501(c)(4) organization generally is required to notify the IRS on Form 8976 that it is operating as a 501(c)(4) organization within 60 days of being established (Code Sec. 506; Reg. § 1.506-1). However, the due date for performing certain time-sensitive actions, including notification of operation as a 501(c)(4) organization on Form 8976, otherwise due on or after April 1, 2020, and before July 15, 2020, is automatically extended to July 15, 2020, in response to the COVID-19 (coronavirus) crisis (Notice 2020-23; Rev. Proc. 2018-58).

A $20 per-day penalty (up to maximum of $5,000) is imposed for failure to provide the notification. The IRS may also provide a written demand for notification (Code Sec. 6652(c)(4)). The organization must include with its first annual information return filed after submitting the notification: (1) the name, address, and taxpayer identification number of the organization; (2) the date on which, and the state or other jurisdiction under the laws of which, the organization was organized; and (3) a statement of the purpose of the organization (Code Sec. 6033(f)(2)). Effective January 16, 2018, a 501(c)(4) social welfare organization must file Form 1024-A with the IRS for determination of tax-exempt status (Rev. Proc. 2018-10).

Labor, Agricultural, and Horticultural Organizations. A qualifying labor, agricultural, or horticultural organization is tax-exempt if: (1) no net earnings of the organization inure to the benefit of any member; and (2) it has as its objective the betterment of the conditions of those engaged in such pursuits, the improvement of the grade of their products, and the development of a higher degree of efficiency in their respective occupations (Code Sec. 501(c)(5); Reg. § 1.501(c)(5)-1). This does not include administration of any type of retirement plan. A qualifying labor organization is generally an association of workers such as a labor union. An agricultural or horticultural organization is involved with raising livestock, forestry, harvesting crops or aquatic resources, the cultivation of useful or ornamental plants, and similar pursuits (Code Sec. 501(g); IRS Pub. 557).

Business Leagues. A business league, chamber of commerce, real estate board, board of trade, or professional football league is tax-exempt if it is not organized for profit and no part of its net earnings inures to the benefit of any private shareholder or individual (Code Sec. 501(c)(6); Reg. § 1.501(c)(6)-1). A business league is an association of persons having some common business interest, having a purpose to promote the common interest, and not engaging in a regular business of a kind ordinarily carried on for profit. For example, an association engaged in furnishing information to prospective investors is not a business league because its activities do not further any common business interest.

6

EXEMPT ORGS

¶692

Social Clubs. A social club or similar organization is exempt from federal income taxes if it is organized and operated exclusively for pleasure, recreation, and other nonprofitable purposes and no part of its net earnings inures to the benefit of any person having an interest in the activities of the organization (Code Sec. 501(c)(7); Reg. § 1.501(c)(7)-1; IRS Pub. 557). Membership in the club must be limited, but personal contact, commingling, and fellowship must exist between the members. In addition, the club's charter, bylaws, other governing instrument, or any written policy statement must not provide for discrimination against any person on the basis of race, color, or religion (Code Sec. 501(i)). A club that in good faith limits its membership to the members of a particular religion to further the teachings or principles of that religion will not be considered as discriminating on the basis of religion. The restriction on religious discrimination does not apply to an auxiliary club of a fraternal beneficiary society if that society limits its membership to the members of a particular religion.

A social club is generally only exempt if it is supported solely by membership fees, dues, and assessments. The club cannot be engaged in any business activities, such as making its facilities available to the public or by selling real estate, timber, or other products. However, a club may receive up to 35 percent of its gross income, including investment income, from sources outside of its membership. Up to 15 percent of the gross receipts may be derived from the use of the club's facilities or services by the public, or from other activities not furthering social or recreational purposes for members. If an organization has outside income that is more than these limits, all the facts and circumstances will be taken into account in determining whether the organization qualifies for exempt status (IRS Pub. 557).

Fraternal Beneficiary Societies. A fraternal beneficiary society, order, or association is exempt from federal income taxes if: (1) it operates under the lodge system for the exclusive benefit of the members of a fraternity itself operating under the lodge system; and (2) it provides for the payment of life, sickness, accident, or other benefits to the members of such society, order, or association or their dependents (Code Sec. 501(c)(8)). Contributions by an individual to a fraternal beneficiary society are deductible as charitable contributions if the gift is used exclusively for religious, charitable, scientific, literary, or educational purposes, or for the prevention of cruelty to children or animals (¶ 1061). A domestic fraternal society, order, or association that operates under the lodge system but does not provide for the payment of life, sickness, accident, or other benefits may nonetheless qualify for exemption if its net earnings are devoted exclusively to religious, charitable, scientific, literary, educational, and fraternal purposes (Code Sec. 501(c)(10)).

Other Nonprofit Organizations. Other nonprofit organizations that may be exempt from federal income taxes under Code Sec. 501(c) include:

- corporations organized under an Act of Congress (Code Sec. 501(c)(1));

- title-holding corporations for exempt organizations (Code Sec. 501(c)(2) and (25));

- voluntary employees' beneficiary associations (VEBAs) providing life, sickness, accident, and other benefits to members or their dependents or beneficiaries (Code Secs. 501(c)(9) and 505);

- local teachers' retirement fund associations (Code Sec. 501(c)(11));

- local benevolent life insurance associations, mutual or cooperative electric, irrigation, and telephone companies that collect at least 85 percent of income from members for the sole purpose of meeting losses and expenses (Code Sec. 501(c)(12));

- cemetery companies (Code Sec. 501(c)(13));

- state-chartered credit unions and mutual reserve funds (Code Sec. 501(c)(14));

- mutual insurance companies or associations (other than life insurance) (Code Sec. 501(c)(15));

- corporations used to finance crop operations (¶ 698) (Code Sec. 501(c)(16));

- supplemental unemployment benefit (SUB) trusts (Code Sec. 501(c)(17));

- employee-funded pension trusts created before June 25, 1959 (Code Sec. 501(c)(18));

- posts or organizations for veterans, members of the armed services, and their families (Code Sec. 501(c)(19));

- black lung benefit trusts (Code Sec. 501(c)(21));

- domestic trusts set up to pay for withdrawal liability from multiemployer pension plans under ERISA (Code Sec. 501(c)(22));

- veterans organizations created before 1880 (Code Sec. 501(c)(23));

- trusts set up by a corporation in connection with the termination of its pension, profit sharing, or stock bonus plan (Code Sec. 501(c)(24));

- state-sponsored high-risk health coverage organizations (Code Sec. 501(c)(26));

- state-sponsored workers' compensation reinsurance organizations (Code Sec. 501(c)(27));

- the National Railroad Retirement Investment Trust (Code Sec. 501(c)(28));

- a qualified nonprofit health insurance issuer under the Consumer Operated and Oriented Plan (CO-OP) program established by the Secretary of Health and Human Services (Code Sec. 501(c)(29)); and

- a reinsurance entity established or entered into a contract with by a state government to collect payments and make payments to the health insurance issuers that cover high-risk individuals in the individual market during the three-year period beginning January 1, 2014 (Act Sec. 1341(a) of P.L. 111-148).

694. Feeder Organizations. An organization whose primary purpose is to operate a trade or business, with all the profits paid to one or more tax-exempt entities, is known as a feeder organization (Code Sec. 502; Reg. § 1.502-1). The fact that the income is turned over to a tax-exempt organization does not entitle the feeder organization to tax-exempt status. A feeder organization is subject to tax unless its activities are an integral part of the exempt activities of the parent organization. A trade or business of a feeder organization does *not* include:

- rentals if the rents received would not be subject to the unrelated business income tax (¶ 655);

- any trade or business if substantially all the work of carrying on the trade or business is performed by unpaid individuals or volunteers; or

- any trade or business that sells merchandise, substantially all of which has been donated or contributed.

696. Political Organizations. A political organization is generally considered tax exempt to the extent that it is organized and operated to accept contributions and make expenditures for influencing the selection, nomination, election, or appointment of any individual to public office (Code Sec. 527). Examples of political organizations include political parties; federal, state, or local candidate committees; political action committees (PACs); and certain newsletters and segregated funds. The exempt function income of a political organization consists solely of contributions of money or property, membership dues or fees, and proceeds from a political fundraising event or the sale of political campaign materials. Any other income received (less deductions not related to exempt functions) is taxed at the income tax rate for corporations, except that for tax years beginning before 2018, the organization is subject to the alternative tax on net capital gains. In calculating its taxable income, a political organization is permitted a $100 deduction, but it will not be allowed a net operating loss deduction (¶ 1145), a dividends received deduction (¶ 223), or other special deductions allowed to corporations (¶ 221).

A political organization that is exempt from tax is nevertheless required to file an income tax return Form 1120-POL for any year that is has taxable income (Code Sec. 6012(a)(6)). Political organizations with $25,000 or more of gross receipts ($100,000 for certain state or local organizations) must also file an annual information return on Form 990 or Form 990-EZ (Code Sec. 6033(g)). All political organizations must notify the IRS electronically on Form 8871 of their existence within 24 hours of establishment or 30 days after any material change (Code Sec. 527(i)). They must also provide periodic reports on Form 8872 of the contributions they receive and their expenditures (Code Sec. 527(j)). The due date for performing certain time-sensitive actions, including notifications provided on Forms 8871 and 8872, otherwise due on or after April 1, 2020, and before July 15, 2020, is automatically extended to July 15, 2020, in response to the COVID-19 (coronavirus) crisis (Notice 2020-23; Rev. Proc. 2018-58).

Organizations do not have to meet these two requirements if they have gross receipts of less than $25,000, are already required to file similar reports with the Federal Election Commission, or are certain state or local political organizations. Failure to provide notification will result in all income (including exempt function income) being taxed. In addition, failure to provide periodic reports will result in all undisclosed contributions and expenditures being taxed. A safe harbor is provided that waives the amounts due for failing to comply with the reporting requirements due to reasonable cause but not willful neglect (Rev. Proc. 2007-27). The public disclosure of all returns and forms filed by a political organization is required (Code Sec. 6104).

698. Farmers' Cooperatives. A cooperative (or federation of cooperatives) of farmers, fruit growers, and persons engaged in similar pursuits may qualify for tax-exempt status if the cooperative is organized and operated to market the members' products and return to them net proceeds, or purchase supplies and equipment for the use of members at cost plus expenses (Code Sec. 521; Reg. § 1.521-1). The cooperative can deal with nonmembers, so long as the business does not account for more than 15 percent of all of its business. Application for exemption is filed on Form 1028.

A farmers' association that has capital stock will not be denied exemption if: (1) the dividend rate is fixed at the legal rate of interest for the state of incorporation or eight percent (whichever is greater), and (2) substantially all of the stock is owned by producers who market their products or purchase their supplies through the association. A farmers' cooperative will also not be denied exemption if it computes its net earnings by offsetting certain earnings and losses in determining any amount available for distribution to patrons (Code Sec. 1388(j)(1)).

An exempt farmers' cooperatives and nonexempt corporation operating on a cooperative basis must file Form 1120-C to report its taxable income and is taxed at the income tax rate for corporations, except that for tax years beginning before 2018 the organization is subject to the alternative tax on net capital gains (Code Secs. 1381 and 1382; Reg. § 1.1382-3). In computing taxable income, all cooperatives are allowed certain deductions from gross income in addition to other deductions allowed to corporations (¶ 221). For example, an exempt farmers' cooperative is permitted a deduction for any dividends paid on capital stock, for amounts paid on a patronage basis arising from certain non-patronage earnings, and for amounts paid in redemption of certain nonqualified written notices of allocation. In addition, all cooperatives are allowed a deduction for any patronage dividend paid or allocated to its members during the tax year. A patronage dividend is an amount paid to a member:

- on the basis of quantity or value of business done with the cooperative;

- under an obligation of the cooperative to pay such amount, if the obligation existed before the cooperative received the amount paid; and

- which is determined by reference to the net earnings of the cooperative from business done with or for its members. However, net earnings will not be reduced by amounts paid as dividends on capital stock to the extent that the dividends are in addition to amounts otherwise payable to patrons (Code Sec. 1388(a)).

699. Additional Tax-Exempt Organizations. There are a number of organizations other than charitable (¶ 602) and social (¶ 692) that may be exempt from federal income taxes, including homeowners' associations, credit counseling organizations, and cooperative service organizations.

Homeowners' Association. A homeowners' association formed to own and maintain common areas and enforce covenants to preserve the appearance of a development may qualify as a tax-exempt social welfare organization under Code Sec. 501(c)(4) (¶ 692). A homeowners' association that is not exempt as a social welfare organization and that is either a condominium management, real estate management, or timeshare association, may nonetheless elect to exclude certain exempt function income from its gross income, including membership dues, fees, and assessments from member-owners (Code Sec. 528). Electing associations are taxed at a flat rate of 30 percent (32 percent for timeshare associations) on both ordinary income and capital gains that are nonexempt. Form 1120-H is used by the association to make the election for each tax year and to report annual taxable income.

Credit Counseling Organizations. An organization that provides credit counseling services as a substantial purpose may not qualify as a tax-exempt organization unless it qualifies as a Code Sec. 501(c)(3) charitable or educational organization, or a Code Sec. 501(c)(4) social welfare organization (Code Sec. 501(q)). In addition, the organization:

- must provide services tailored to customers' specific needs;
- must not refuse to provide services to customers due to inability to pay or ineligibility for debt management plan enrollment;
- make no loans to customers;
- have a reasonable fee policy and must not pay or receive referral fees;
- have limited ownership of related service providers; and
- have independent board members with public interests.

Cooperative Hospital Service Organizations. A cooperative hospital service organization is exempt from federal income taxation if it performs specifically listed services for two or more patron hospitals that are tax exempt under Code Sec. 501(c)(3), or if it is owned and operated by the federal government or by a state or local government (Code Sec. 501(e)). Services that may be performed include data processing, purchasing (including purchasing insurance on a group basis, such as malpractice and general liability insurance), laboratory, billing and collection (including the purchase of patron accounts receivable on a recourse basis), food, personnel, and clinical services. It does not include laundry services (*HCSC-Laundry*, SCt, 81-1 USTC ¶ 9202). A cooperative arrangement formed and controlled by a group of exempt educational organizations for the collective investment of their funds may also qualify for tax-exempt status (Code Sec. 501(f)). These organizations qualify for exemption only if all of the relevant requirements of Code Sec. 501(c)(3) are also satisfied.

6

EXEMPT ORGS

Chapter 7

INCOME

Gross Income Defined

See CCH® AnswerConnect: *Gross Income* for more information on this topic.

701. Gross Income Defined. Gross income for federal income tax purposes means all income from whatever source derived, except for those items specifically excluded by the Code (Code Sec. 61; Reg. § 1.61-1). A nonexclusive list of specific items that are included in gross income is provided in Code Sec. 61 and includes:

- compensation for services, including fees, commissions, fringe benefits, and similar items (¶ 713);
- gross income from business (¶ 759 and ¶ 767);
- gains from dealings in property (¶ 1701);
- interest (¶ 724);
- rents (¶ 762);
- royalties (¶ 763);
- dividends (¶ 733);
- alimony or separate maintenance payments generally made under a divorce or separation agreement executed before 2019 (¶ 771);
- annuities (¶ 817);
- income from life insurance and endowment contracts (Reg. § 1.61-10);
- pensions (¶ 718);
- income from the discharge of indebtedness (¶ 855);
- a partner's share of partnership income (¶ 404);
- income in respect of a decedent (¶ 182); and
- income from an interest in an estate or trust (¶ 554 and ¶ 556).

Although nearly every type of accession to wealth appears to fall within this comprehensive definition, income items should be checked against the specific exclusions in Code Secs. 101—140 (¶ 801). See ¶ 847 and ¶ 849 for the income tax treatment of gifts and inheritances of property.

702. Determining Income. Court decisions have developed a concept of "income" that is quite different from the layman's concept. The U.S. Supreme Court has defined income as an undeniable accession to wealth, clearly realized, and over which the taxpayer has complete dominion (*Glenshaw Glass Co.*, SCt, 55-1 USTC ¶ 9308). Further, the Supreme Court pointed out that it has repeatedly given a liberal construction to this broad definition of what constitutes gross income in recognition of Congress's intent to tax all gain unless specifically exempted. In addition to those items specifically excludable from gross income by law (¶ 801), certain other items are not considered income.

Return of Capital. A return of capital, such as repayment of a loan, is not income unless the loan has been previously deducted as a bad debt, resulting in a tax benefit (*J.M. Smith*, CA-9, 70-1 USTC ¶ 9327). Similarly, car pool reimbursements are not income even if only one person provides the car and does the driving (Rev. Rul. 55-555).

Damages. Damages, other than punitive damages, that compensate an injured person for personal physical injuries or physical sickness are excludable from gross income (¶ 852). Damages received for personal nonphysical injuries, such as employment discrimination or injury to reputation, are generally taxable. Interest on a judgment, including mandatory prejudgment interest, is generally includible in income (IRS Pub. 525). See ¶ 759 for treatment of damages awarded for business claims.

Attorney Fees and Court Costs. Court costs and attorney fees paid in connection with an action based on unlawful discrimination under federal law, as well as certain other claims (i.e., whistleblower actions), are deductible from gross income in determining adjusted gross income (¶ 1093).

Governmental Assistance. Many types of government assistance payments are not included in income if they are for the promotion of general welfare. For example, rental assistance payments made by the Department of Housing and Urban Development under the National Housing Act and relocation payments made under the Housing and Community Development Act of 1974 are nontaxable. However, payments made by individuals or other nongovernmental entities are not considered payments for the general welfare and are taxable (IRS Pub. 525).

Gift v. Income. The characterization of a payment or transfer as either a gift or taxable income must be made on a case-by-case basis (*M. Duberstein*, SCt, 60-2 USTC ¶ 9515). For example, the value of a "gift" transferred to a business friend for furnishing the names of potential customers is taxable compensation (¶ 849).

Strike and Lockout Benefits. Strike benefits received from a labor union may be treated as nontaxable gifts if the benefits are paid in the form of food, clothing, and rent and are: (1) given to both member and nonmember strikers, (2) dependent upon individual need, (3) dependent on the unavailability of unemployment compensation or local public assistance, and (4) given without conditions. The fact that benefits are paid only to union members is not, of itself, determinative as to taxability (*A. Kaiser*, SCt, 60-2 USTC ¶ 9517).

Unrealized Appreciation. Unrealized appreciation in the value of property is not income (*Baldwin Locomotive Works*, CA-3, 1 USTC ¶ 2).

Ownership of Income

See CCH® AnswerConnect: *Gross Income* and *Residents of Community Property States* for more information on this topic.

704. Tax Liability for Income. In the vast majority of cases, the taxpayer's identity is clear. The taxpayer is simply the person who is legally entitled to receive income. Thus, an individual who receives wages for services is the person who must pay income tax on the wages. Under certain circumstances, however, a person may be taxed on income that is paid to another in an anticipatory assignment of income (¶ 705). Special rules also affect the treatment of unearned income of a minor (¶ 115), income from property held in joint tenancy (¶ 709), and income of taxpayers living in community property states (¶ 710).

705. Assignment of Income. Generally, an individual can escape tax on income from property only if the individual makes a valid gift or assignment of the income-producing property itself, as distinguished from an assignment of the income. For example, an individual who gave his spouse the legally enforceable right to receive the future income generated by his law practice was still taxable on that income (*G.C. Earl*, SCt, 2 USTC ¶ 496). Similarly, an individual who gave his son interest coupons, which were detached from bonds that he owned, was liable for the tax on the interest accrued before the gift and later paid to his son (*P.R.G. Horst*, SCt, 40-2 USTC ¶ 9787). See ¶ 115 for the taxation of the unearned income of minor and certain dependent children.

709. Joint Tenancy and Tenancy in Common. If property is held in joint tenancy with a right of survivorship, income from the property, including gain or loss upon its sale, is divided between the owners to the extent that each is entitled under state law to share in the income. There must be evidence that the joint ownership was bona fide and not used merely as a tax-avoidance scheme. These rules also apply to tenants in common (*D.L. Edmonds*, CA-9, 37-1 USTC ¶ 9245).

710. Community Property Income—Generally. In community property states (Arizona, California, Idaho, Louisiana, Nevada, New Mexico, Texas, Washington, and Wisconsin), property acquired by a married couple during their marriage while they reside in the state is generally regarded as owned by the spouses together, each owning an undivided interest in the whole property. Similarly, income from the property is divided equally between the spouses.

Although each state has exceptions in classifying income as separate income or community income, the general rule is that salaries, wages, and other compensation for the services of either or both of the spouses, as well as income from community real and personal property, are community income; but it does not follow in every state that income from separate property is separate income. The states also differ in their treatment of property acquired by inheritance or intestate succession. The IRS can disallow the benefits of any community property law to a spouse for any income that the spouse treats as his or hers alone if that spouse fails to notify the other spouse of the nature and amount of the income before the due date, including extensions, for filing the return for the tax year in which the income was derived (Code Sec. 66(b); Reg. § 1.66-3).

Same-Sex Married Couples and Registered Domestic Partners. A marriage of two individuals is recognized for federal tax purposes if the marriage would be recognized by the state, possession, or territory of the United States in which the marriage was entered into, regardless of where the individuals are domiciled. A marriage conducted in a foreign jurisdiction will also be recognized for federal tax purposes if that marriage would be recognized in at least one state, possession, or territory of the United States, regardless of where the individuals are domiciled. Thus, legally married same-sex couples are recognized as married for federal tax purposes, and the terms "spouse", "husband", and "wife" mean an individual lawfully married to another individual, regardless of sex (Reg. § 301.7701-18).

A marriage for federal tax purposes does not include registered domestic partnerships, civil unions, or other similar relationships recognized under state law that are not denominated as a marriage under that state's law. Nonetheless, registered domestic partners in Nevada, Washington, or California generally must follow state community property laws (CCA 201021050; IRS Pub. 555). Thus, each partner must report one-half of the combined community income on his or her federal income tax return.

711. Community Property Income—Joint v. Separate Return. If spouses residing in a community property state file separate returns (¶ 710), each must report one-half of the community income (Reg. § 1.66-1). In Idaho, Louisiana, Texas, and Wisconsin, income from the separate property of a spouse is community income, with one-half being allocable to each spouse. In the other community property states, income from separate property is separate income. Each spouse filing a separate return must use Form 8958 to allocate income, deductions, credits, and other return amounts between the spouses (IRS Pub. 555). It is usually more beneficial to file a joint return (¶ 152). There are some situations, however, when filing separate returns may be beneficial for married spouses (¶ 156).

Nonresident Alien Spouse. A U.S. citizen or resident alien who is married to a nonresident alien may elect to file a joint return if both agree to be taxed on their worldwide income (¶ 2410). If the couple does not make this election and has community income, any community income that is earned income, trade or business income, partnership income, or income from separate property is treated as the separate income of the spouse associated with the income item (¶ 2438) (Code Sec. 879).

Separated Spouses. The usual community property rules do not apply to spouses living apart from each other if:

- they are separated for the entire calendar year;
- they file separate returns;
- either or both spouses have community earned income; and
- they do not transfer between each other more than a *de minimis* amount of the earned income before the end of the calendar year (Code Sec. 66(a); Reg. § 1.66-2).

Instead, their community income is treated as if one of the spouses is a nonresident alien and they did not elect to file a joint return.

Innocent Spouse Relief. Spouses in community property states who file separate returns may be able to avoid liability for deficiencies attributable to community income under special "innocent spouse" rules (Code Sec. 66(c), Reg. § 1.66-4). These are separate from the innocent spouse relief provided to married taxpayers filing joint returns (¶ 162). A requesting spouse may receive relief ("traditional relief") under the special rules if the community income would be properly treated as income of the nonrequesting spouse under the Code Sec. 879 rules (¶ 2438) and the requesting spouse did not know or have reason to know of the omitted item of community income. If the requirements of traditional relief are not met, the IRS may still provide relief from a tax liability or deficiency arising from the community income item if failure to do so would be inequitable

Salaries, Wages, and Benefits

See CCH® AnswerConnect: *Gross Income* for more information on this topic.

713. Compensation for Personal Services Includible in Gross Income. All compensation for personal services, no matter what the form of payment, is includible in gross income (Code Sec. 61(a); Reg. § 1.61-2). Wages, salaries, commissions, bonuses, fringe benefits that do not qualify for statutory exclusions, tips, payments based on a percentage of profits, rewards, directors' fees, jury fees, election officials' fees, retirement pay and pensions, and other forms of compensation are includible in gross income in the year received and not in the year earned, unless the taxpayer reports income on an accrual basis (¶ 1515). Under the claim-of-right doctrine, payments must be included in gross income if the taxpayer receives them without restriction under a claim of right (¶ 1543).

Compensation is income even though the amount is not fixed in advance, as in the case of marriage fees, baptismal offerings, and similar sums received by a member of the clergy. A year-end bonus is usually taxable, particularly if based on salary or length of service. Severance pay and vacation pay are also taxable as compensation. The value of a nominally valued item (turkey, ham, etc.) distributed to an employee on holidays is *not* reportable income even though the employer is entitled to deduct the cost as a business expense. However, a distribution of cash, a gift certificate or gift card, or a similar item of value readily convertible to cash, must be included in the employee's income (IRS Pub. 525).

The amount of compensation included in the taxpayer's gross income is the gross amount before any reductions for withheld income tax or social security taxes, union dues, insurance, or other deductions by the employer. Even if the employer is denied a deduction for the compensation paid to the extent it is unreasonable (¶ 906), the employee must include the amount received in income (as a dividend, rent, amount received for property, or other income, depending on the circumstances). In absence of evidence to justify another treatment of excessive compensation, the amount is treated as payment for personal services and included in the employee's gross income (Reg. § 1.162-8). Compensation for the personal services of a child are included in the child's gross income, even if the compensation is or must be received by the parent rather than the child (¶ 115).

7

INCOME

¶713

Restricted Property Transfers. If stock or other property is given as compensation for services instead of cash, the fair market value (FMV) of the property is generally included in the taxpayer's gross income unless the property is subject to a substantial risk of forfeiture (Code Sec. 83; Reg. § 1.61-2(d), Reg. § 1.83-1). The FMV of the property included in income becomes its basis to the employee. If the property is sold to the employee for less than its market value, the difference between the amount paid and the value of the property is also income. A qualified employee of a privately held company may elect to defer including in gross income the amount of income attributable to a qualified equity grant (¶ 1933).

If compensation for services is paid in property, the FMV of the property at the time of receipt must be included in gross income (Reg. § 1.61-2(d)). A note received in payment for services, and not merely as security for the payment, comes within this rule and its FMV must be included in income. A portion of each payment received under the note is excludable from gross income as a recovery of capital.

If the stock or other property is subject to a substantial risk of forfeiture, no amount is included in income until the year that the property becomes substantially vested as the result of the removal of the risk of forfeiture. However, any income (e.g., a dividend) from property that is subject to a substantial risk of forfeiture, or from the right to use such property, is included in income as compensation when received (Rev. Proc. 80-11; Rev. Proc. 83-38). Property is substantially vested when it is either (1) transferable to another person who is not required to give up the property or its value if the substantial risk of forfeiture occurs, or (2) no longer subject to a substantial risk of forfeiture (Code Sec. 83(c)(1); Reg. § 1.83-3).

A substantial risk of forfeiture exists if the right to the property is conditioned on (1) the future performance or refraining from performance of substantial services by any person, or (2) the occurrence of a condition related to a purpose of the transfer if the possibility of forfeiture is substantial. A substantial risk of forfeiture may be established *only* by the two conditions described above. In determining whether a substantial risk of forfeiture exists due to a condition related to the purpose of the transfer, the likelihood that the forfeiture event will occur and that the forfeiture will be enforced must both be considered. Except as provided in Reg. § 1.83-3(j) or (k), transfer restrictions do not create a substantial risk of forfeiture if the restriction is violated, even if the violation results in forfeiture of property or in liability for damages, penalties, or fees.

A taxpayer who receives property subject to a substantial risk of forfeiture may elect to include its FMV, less any amount paid for it, in gross income in the year the property is received ("section 83(b) election") (Code Sec. 83(b); Reg. § 1.83-2; Rev. Proc. 2012-29). Once the value of the property is included in income, any subsequent appreciation is not taxed as compensation to the person who performed the services. If the property is forfeited after the election is made and before it is substantially vested, the forfeiture is treated as a sale or exchange on which a loss is realized, equal to any excess of the amount paid for the property minus any amount realized upon the forfeiture. The election is made by filing a written statement with the IRS center where the tax return is filed generally no later than 30 days after the date the property was transferred. However, the due date for performing certain time-sensitive actions, including making the section 83(b) election, otherwise due on or after April 1, 2020, and before July 15, 2020, is automatically extended to July 15, 2020, in response to the COVID-19 (coronavirus) crisis (Notice 2020-23). The IRS has provided sample language that may be used for making the election, as well as examples of the tax consequences of the election. Once made, the election can be revoked only with the consent of the IRS. As an alternative to the 83(b) election, a qualified employee of a privately held company may elect to defer including in gross income the amount of income attributable to a qualified equity grant (¶ 1933).

Stock Options. Nonstatutory stock options (NSOs) are discussed at ¶ 1923. Incentive stock options (ISOs) are discussed at ¶ 1925 and ¶ 1927. Employee stock purchase plans (ESPPs) are discussed at ¶ 1929 and ¶ 1931.

Employee Benefits. Compensation for personal services includes any benefits an employer provides to an employee that are not otherwise excludable from gross income

(Reg. § 1.61-21). Some excludable employee benefits may be provided to an employee through the employer's cafeteria plan (¶ 2045) and may include:

- amounts received under employer-financed accident and health plans (¶ 2015);

- employer contributions to provide the accident and health benefits (¶ 2013);

- employer contributions to a health savings account (HSA) (¶ 2035), Archer medical savings account (MSA) (¶ 2037), health reimbursement arrangement (HRA) (¶ 2039), or flexible spending arrangement (FSA) (¶ 2041);

- premiums for group-term life insurance to the extent coverage does not exceed $50,000 (¶ 2055);

- qualified adoption expenses reimbursed under an employer adoption assistance program (¶ 2063);

- child and dependent care assistance benefits (¶ 2065);

- educational assistance benefits (¶ 2067);

- employee achievement awards to the extent deductible by the employer (¶ 2069);

- qualified moving expense reimbursements for tax years beginning before 2018 (¶ 2092); and

- certain other fringe benefits (¶ 2085).

Employer-Provided Vehicle. An employee who uses an employer-provided vehicle for more than *de minimis* personal use receives a taxable fringe benefit from the employer. The amount includible in an employee's wages is determined by the fair market value of the vehicle's availability (¶ 2059).

Vacation and Club Expenses. The portion of an employee's vacation, athletic club, or health resort expenses that is paid by the employer is taxable to the employee (IRS Pub. 525).

Occupational Disability or Insurance Benefit. Compensation received under a workers' compensation act for personal injuries or sickness and amounts received under a policy of accident and health insurance are excludable from gross income (¶ 851).

716. Social Security or Railroad Retirement Benefits. A portion of a taxpayer's social security benefits or an equivalent portion of tier 1 railroad retirement benefits may be taxable (Code Sec. 86). The amount includible in gross income is the lesser of 50 percent of the annual benefits received or 50 percent of the excess of the taxpayer's provisional income over a specified base amount. If the taxpayer's provisional income exceeds an adjusted base amount, up to 85 percent of the benefits may be included (discussed below). The Instructions to Form 1040 contain a worksheet for computing the taxable amount.

Provisional income is the taxpayer's modified adjusted gross income (MAGI), plus 50 percent of the social security or tier 1 railroad retirement benefits received. MAGI is the taxpayer's AGI (¶ 1005), plus any tax-exempt interest received. AGI is determined without including any social security benefits or equivalent railroad retirement benefits, and without subtracting the following items from gross income: interest income from U.S. savings bonds used to finance higher education (¶ 863), amounts paid under an employer's adoption assistance program (¶ 2063), the domestic production activities deduction for tax years beginning before 2018 (¶ 980A), deductible student loan interest (¶ 1011), deductible tuition and related expenses before 2021 (¶ 1011A), foreign earned income and foreign housing expenses attributable to living and working abroad (¶ 2402), and certain income of bona fide residents of U.S. possessions (¶ 2414) or Puerto Rico (¶ 2415). The base amount is: $32,000 for joint filers; $0 if married filing separately and the taxpayer lived with his or her spouse at any time during the tax year; and $25,000 for married individuals filing separately who live apart from their spouse for the entire year and individuals filing as single or head-of-household.

> **Example 1:** John and Jane Mapes have AGI of $24,000 for 2019. John, who is retired, receives social security benefits of $7,200 per year. The couple also

receives $6,000 a year from a mutual fund that invests solely in tax-exempt municipal bonds. On their joint return for 2019, the couple make the following computation to determine how much, if any, of John's social security benefits must be included in their gross income:

(1) Adjusted gross income	$24,000
(2) Plus: All tax-exempt interest	6,000
(3) Modified adjusted gross income	30,000
(4) Plus: 50% of social security benefits	3,600
(5) Provisional income	33,600
(6) Less: Base amount	32,000
(7) Excess above base amount	1,600
(8) 50% of excess above base amount	800
(9) 50% of social security benefits	3,600
(10) Amount includible in gross income (lesser of (8) or (9)) . .	800

Social security benefits are the monthly benefits under Title II of the Social Security Act (Code Sec. 86(d)(1)). Supplemental security income (SSI, commonly known as disability) payments are authorized by Title XVI of the Social Security Act, and thus are *not* included in gross income. Although tier 2 railroad retirement benefits are not taken into account under the above rules, these benefits are taxed in the same manner as benefits paid under qualified retirement plans (Code Sec. 72(r)).

85-Percent Inclusion. Up to 85 percent of an individual's social security benefits or tier 1 railroad retirement benefits may be includible in gross income. This affects taxpayers whose provisional income exceeds the adjusted base amount, which is: $44,000 for married taxpayers filing jointly; $0 for married taxpayers filing separately and not living apart during the entire tax year; and $34,000 for all other taxpayers (Code Sec. 86(c)(2)).

Those who exceed the appropriate adjusted base amount must include in gross income the lesser of: (1) 85 percent of social security benefits, or (2) the sum of 85 percent of the excess of provisional income over the adjusted base amount, plus the smaller of: (a) the amount that would otherwise be includible if the second threshold did not apply (i.e., the amount calculated under the 50-percent rules discussed previously), or (b) 50 percent of the difference of the adjusted base amount over the base amount (i.e., $6,000 for joint filers; $0 for married filing separately and not living apart from their spouse; $4,500 for all other taxpayers).

Example 2: Assume the same facts as in Example 1 above, except that the Mapes' provisional income is increased from $33,600 to $53,600. The includible amount is determined as follows:

(1) Provisional income	$53,600
(2) Adjusted base amount	44,000
(3) Excess of (1) over (2)	9,600
(4) 85% of amount in (3)	8,160
(5) Amount otherwise includible: lesser of (a) 50% of benefits received ($3,600) or (b) 50% of the excess of provisional income minus base amount ($10,800)	3,600
(6) 50% of adjusted base amount minus base amount (for joint filers)	6,000
(7) Lesser of (5) or (6)	3,600
(8) Sum of amounts in (4) and (7)	11,760
(9) 85% of social security benefits	6,120
(10) Amount includible in gross income (lesser of (8) or (9)) . .	6,120

Individual Retirement Account (IRA) Contributions. Employed individuals who are covered by a retirement plan and receiving social security benefits must make a special computation to determine the allowable IRA deduction amount (¶ 2157).

¶716

717. Tip Income. Tip income generally is includible in the recipient's gross income. Tips are amounts paid freely by a customer to a person providing a service, such as amounts received by cab drivers, waiters, barbers, hotel, railroad, and cruise ship employees, etc. (Reg. § 1.61-2(a)(1)). In the absence of proof of the actual amount of tips received, tip income may be reconstructed on the basis of average tips in a given locality for a given type of service.

An employee who receives tips may use Form 4070A, which should be retained with the individual's tax records, to maintain a daily record of his or her tips. Cash, check, and credit card tips totalling $20 or more per month are reported to the employer on Form 4070 or a similar statement by the 10th day of the following month in which they are received. Forms 4070A and 4070 are available in IRS Pub. 1244. An employer may also allow tips to be reported electronically (Reg. § 31.6053-1; IRS Pub. 531).

Form 4137 is used to compute an employee's liability for Social Security and Medicare taxes on monthly tips of $20 or more that were not reported to the employer or on tips allocated by a large food and beverage establishment. Social Security and Medicare taxes on reported tip income that an employer failed to withhold are shown on Form W-2 and reported as an additional tax on the tipped employee's income tax return. Noncash tips and tips of less than $20 per month are not subject to Social Security and Medicare tax, but these amounts are subject to income tax and must be reported on the employee's return.

See ¶ 2605 regarding the duty to report tips monthly to employer on Form 4070, ¶ 2606 regarding the employer's withholding requirements, and ¶ 1465R regarding an employer credit for its portion of Social Security taxes on employee cash tips.

718. Pension Income. Pension payments are made to a retired employee and generally represent compensation for past services rendered (Reg. § 1.61-11). Payments from pension plans that do not represent return of investment and payments that result from tax-free contributions generally are included in the recipient's income. See ¶ 2101 and ¶ 2141 for the rules governing qualified retirement and pension plans.

719. Salary Payments to Employee's Survivor. The IRS and the Tax Court have generally taken the position that salary payments made to the surviving spouse of a deceased employee are taxable income, while several U.S. Courts of Appeal have viewed the payments as tax-free gifts (*M.E. Jensen*, CA-5, 75-1 ustc ¶ 9377). Unpaid salary owed to a taxpayer at the time of his or her death is typically treated as income in respect of a decedent (¶ 182).

722. Unemployment Compensation. Unemployment compensation benefits are fully includible in the recipient's gross income (Code Sec. 85; Reg. § 1.85-1; IRS Pub. 525). If an employee makes nondeductible contributions to a governmental unemployment compensation program, amounts the employee receives under the program are not unemployment compensation until he or she has recovered the total amount of nondeductible contributions. Payments to laid-off employees from company-financed supplemental unemployment benefit plans (also referred to as "guaranteed annual wage" plans) constitute taxable income to the employees in the year received. Payors report unemployment compensation on Form 1099-G.

723. Deferred Compensation. Not all compensation is paid in the year services are rendered. Some may be deferred to a later year. There are two types of deferred compensation arrangements—funded and unfunded.

Funded Arrangements. If deferred compensation is contributed to a trust or is used to purchase an annuity or other insurance contract, the arrangement is funded and a participant may be subject to tax on his or her portion of the trust's income (¶ 2199).

Unfunded Arrangements. If the deferral takes the form of an employer's unsecured promise (i.e., not represented by a note) to pay compensation for current services at some time in the future, and if the employee uses the cash method of accounting, the amount promised is not includible in the employee's gross income until it is received or made available (¶ 906) (Rev. Rul. 60-31, modified by Rev. Rul. 64-279 and Rev. Rul. 70-435). This rule is not altered merely because the employee agrees with the employer in advance to receive compensation on a deferred basis, so long as the agreement is made before the taxpayer obtains an unqualified and unconditional right to the compensation (*J.F. Oates,* CA-7, 53-2 USTC ¶ 9596).

Unfunded Plans of State and Local Governments and Other Tax-Exempt Organizations. The treatment of unfunded deferred compensation plans is modified for participants in plans maintained by state and local governments and other tax-exempt organizations other than churches and qualified church-controlled organizations (see ¶ 2193) (Code Sec. 457). For distributions from an eligible nongovernment plan, the deferred compensation is includible in income only when received by, or unconditionally made available to, a participant. For distributions from an eligible government plan, the deferred compensation is included in gross income only when actually paid. If a plan is not an eligible plan, the present value of the deferred compensation is includible in gross income for the first tax year in which there is no substantial risk of forfeiture, and the tax treatment of any amount made available to a participant is determined under the annuity rules.

Unfunded Plans of Taxable Employers. An unfunded plan of a taxable employer is not subject to the limitations that apply to a tax-exempt employer. As a practical matter, however, a taxable employer's unfunded plan is limited to providing benefits in excess of those permitted under qualified plans or benefits for highly compensated and managerial employees. This is because any other unfunded deferred compensation plan of a taxable employer would be subject to participation, vesting, funding, and fiduciary standards of the Employee Retirement Income Security Act of 1974 (ERISA) (P.L. 93-406) (ERISA Secs. 4(b)(5), 201(2), 301(a)(3), and 401(a)(1)). See ¶ 2197 and ¶ 2199 for the rules of nonqualified deferred compensation plans.

Interest Income

See CCH® AnswerConnect: *Interest Income* for more information on this topic.

724. Interest Income. A taxpayer generally must include in gross income interest received or accrued (Code Sec. 61(a)(4); Reg. § 1.61-7). Exceptions exist for interest on tax-exempt state or municipal bonds, including qualified private activity bonds (¶ 729), interest on U.S. savings bonds used to pay qualified educational expenses (¶ 863), and certain interest received to recovery property from the IRS (¶ 889). See ¶ 730 for interest on U.S. obligations. An individual generally must report dividends and interest in excess of $1,500 on Schedule B (Form 1040).

A cash-basis taxpayer recognizes interest income in the year payment is actually or constructively received (¶ 1515). An accrual-basis taxpayer recognizes interest income in the year in which all events have occurred that fix the right to receive the amount of interest income, and the amount of the interest can be determined with reasonable accuracy. For example, interest on a certificate of deposit must generally be reported as income in the year in which the interest is paid or credited to the taxpayer's account, even if there is a penalty for early withdrawal (Rev. Rul. 80-157, amplified by Rev. Rul. 82-42). A depositor can deduct any penalty imposed for early withdrawal in the year of forfeiture in arriving at adjusted gross income (¶ 1111).

Increments in value of growth savings certificates are taxable in the year that the increase occurs because the certificate holder has a present right to redeem the certificate (Rev. Rul. 66-44). Any increment in the value of life insurance or annuity due to prepaid premiums or premium deposits is income when made available to the policyholder for withdrawal or when credited against premiums payable (Rev. Rul. 65-199). Interest on a judgment is taxable even if the underlying award is nontaxable (*M. Brabson,* CA-10, 96-1 ustc ¶ 50,038).

If a bond with defaulted interest coupons is bought "flat" (i.e., the price covers both principal and unpaid interest), any interest received that was in default on the date of purchase is not taxable but is a return of capital. If the bond is sold, this amount must be applied to reduce the basis. Interest received for a period that *follows* the date of purchase is taxable in full (Reg. § 1.61-7(c)).

Holders of bonds or other obligations issued at a discount may be required to include in gross income a portion of the discount as imputed interest in each year the obligation is held, even though no interest corresponding to the amount is paid or accrued during the period (¶ 1952). Holders of notes or other debt instruments that were issued in exchange for property or services may be required to include imputed interest in gross income if no interest is provided in the debt instrument or the rate of interest is less than the applicable federal rate (AFR) (¶ 1954). Other loans bearing interest at less than the AFR may also result in imputed interest income to the lender (¶ 795).

State and Local Bonds; Tax Credit Bonds. The federal government provides financial assistance to state and local governmental agencies by excluding from the recipient's gross income the interest on certain tax-exempt state and local bonds. Bond interest is not excludible, however, if it is derived from certain state or local bonds that are nonqualified private activity bonds (¶ 729), bonds that have not been issued in registered form, arbitrage bonds, hedge bonds, federally guaranteed bonds, or advance refunding bonds issued after 2017 (Code Secs. 103, 148, and 149).

The federal government also authorized governments and certain other entities to issue tax credit bonds for tax years beginning before 2018. A tax credit bond essentially provides the issuer with a tax-free loan. Instead of interest payments, the bond holders receive a tax credit on their federal income tax at the specified credit rate, and the issuer only has to repay the principal (¶ 1471). The bond holders must include the credit amount in income, then claim the credit against tax on their return. In effect, the holders usually receive the same net amount from the credit as they would receive in interest from a conventional state or local bond.

"Thank You" Points. A depositor who received airline tickets by redeeming "thank you" award points from a bank for making a deposit or maintaining a balance in his account received something "in the nature of interest" that constituted gross income (*P.H. Shankar*, Dec. 60,001, 143 TC 140).

726. Interest on Foreclosed Mortgaged Property. If a taxpayer forecloses on a mortgage and purchases the property at a foreclosure sale by bidding on the property for the full amount of the mortgage plus accrued unpaid interest, taxable income is realized in the amount of the accrued interest even if the fair market value (FMV) of the property is less than the principal due on the mortgage (*Midland Mutual Life Ins. Co.*, SCt, 37-1 USTC ¶ 9114). Some courts have applied this rule to *voluntary* conveyances by the mortgagor in consideration for the cancellation of the principal and interest of the mortgage. However, there is no interest income in a voluntary conveyance if the property is worth less than the principal of the loan. Nor is any taxable income realized if only the principal of the mortgage is bid on. See ¶ 1841 for repossessions of real property.

If a creditor bids on a property for a debt, a loss may be deductible if the property is worth less than the debt. Any such loss must take into account the basis and FMV of the property bid on, and therefore a loss may exist even though the creditor bid on the property for more than the debt (*Hadley Falls Trust Co.*, CA-1, 40-1 USTC ¶ 9352). The FMV of the mortgaged property is presumed to be the amount bid on, in the absence of clear and convincing proof to the contrary (Reg. § 1.166-6). See ¶ 1135 for the bad debt deduction and ¶ 1139 for discussion of secured bad debt.

Seller-Provided Financing. A taxpayer who receives or accrues qualified residence interest (¶ 1047) from seller-provided financing must include on his or her income tax return the name, address and taxpayer identification number of the person from whom the interest was received or accrued (Code Sec. 6109(h)). Failure to provide this information exposes the taxpayer to information reporting penalties (¶ 2833).

728. Bond Transaction Between Interest Dates. If a bond is sold between interest dates, part of the sales price represents the interest earned up to the date of sale. The seller reports that portion as interest income in the year of the sale (Reg. § 1.61-7(d)). Because the buyer has paid for the accrued interest as part of the sales price, if the interest is paid later it is a return of capital that reduces the buyer's basis in the bond, rather than taxable interest income, except to the extent it exceeds the amount paid the

7 INCOME

seller (Reg. § 1.61-7(c)). This interest adjustment has no effect on the cost of the bond and no connection with the adjustment for amortizable bond premium (¶ 1967).

729. Interest on Private Activity Bonds. Although interest on obligations of a state or local government is generally excludable from gross income (¶ 724), interest is generally not tax free when it is derived from a private activity bond that does not qualify for tax exemption (Code Sec. 103(b)). A private activity bond is part of a state or local government bond issue in which: (1) more than 10 percent of the bond proceeds is to be used for a private business use; and (2) more than 10 percent of the payment of principal or interest is secured by an interest in property to be used for a private business use or payments for such property, or is to be derived from payments for property or borrowed money used for a private business use. Part of an issue may also qualify as a private activity bond if the amount of the bond proceeds to be used to make or finance loans to persons other than government units exceeds the lesser of five percent of the proceeds or $5 million (Code Sec. 141; IRS Pub. 550). Certain bonds issued by a governmental unit to fund the acquisition of existing electric and gas generation and transmission systems are generally treated as private activity bonds.

Private activity bonds that *do* qualify for tax exemption include exempt facility bonds, qualified mortgage bonds, qualified veterans' mortgage bonds, qualified small-issue bonds, qualified student loan bonds, qualified redevelopment bonds, and qualified Code Sec. 501(c)(3) bonds. Qualified private activity bonds must meet the applicable volume cap requirements of Code Sec. 146 and the applicable requirements of Code Sec. 147. Exempt facility bonds may include enterprise zone facility bonds, Midwestern disaster area bonds issued before 2013, Hurricane Ike disaster area bonds issued before 2013, New York Liberty bonds issued before 2012, Gulf Opportunity Zone (GO Zone) bonds issued before 2012, and recovery zone facility bonds issued before 2011. Qualified mortgage bonds may include Midwestern disaster area bonds issued before 2013, Hurricane Ike disaster area bonds issued before 2013, and GO Zone bonds issued before 2012 and treated as qualified mortgage bonds. Qualified small issue bonds include tribal manufacturing facility bonds.

Tax Preference Items. Tax-exempt interest on private activity bonds is ordinarily considered a tax preference for purposes of the alternative minimum tax (AMT) (Code Sec. 57(a)(5)). Thus, the amount of interest received is taken into account in computing alternative minimum taxable income (AMTI) for AMT purposes (¶ 192). However, exempt interest is *not* a tax preference item on qualified 501(c)(3) bonds, New York Liberty bonds, GO Zone bonds, Midwestern disaster area bonds, or Hurricane Ike disaster area bonds, as well as the following bonds issued after July 30, 2008: certain exempt facility bonds, qualified mortgage bonds, or qualified veterans' mortgage bonds. Additionally, exempt interest on private activity bonds issued in 2009 or 2010 is *not* treated as a tax preference item.

730. Interest on U.S. Savings Bonds. Interest on all obligations of the United States and its agencies and instrumentalities (i.e., U.S. Treasury bills, notes, and bonds) issued after February 28, 1941, is subject to federal taxes to the same extent as private obligations (Reg. § § 1.61-7(b)(2) and (3)). An accrual basis taxpayer reports interest on U.S. savings bonds each year as it accrues. A cash basis taxpayer generally reports U.S. savings bond interest in the year received (¶ 1515). Series HH and H bonds, which the U.S. Treasury no longer issues, were issued at face value, and interest was paid every six months. Paper Series EE and Series E bonds are issued at a discount, and interest is payable on redemption. Electronic Series EE bonds and inflation-indexed Series I bonds are issued at face value, and accrued interest is payable at maturity (IRS Pub. 550).

For a cash basis taxpayer, none of the interest on Series EE, E, or I bonds is taxable until the earlier of (1) the year the bonds are cashed in or disposed, or (2) the year they mature. The taxpayer *may*, however, elect to report the interest income on these bonds each year as it accrues (Code Sec. 454; Reg. § 1.454-1(a); IRS Pub. 550).

Trades for Series H or HH bonds are no longer allowed. When such trades were available, taxable income was not recognized if Series EE or E bonds on which interest reporting was postponed were traded for Series HH or H bonds, unless cash was received in the trade. Any cash received was taxed to the extent of interest earned on the Series EE or E bonds. When the Series HH or H bonds mature, or, when they are disposed of prior to maturity, the difference between their redemption value and cost is reported as interest income. Cost is the amount paid for the Series EE or E bonds plus any additional amount paid for the Series HH or H bonds. A taxpayer could have elected to treat all previously unreported accrued interest on Series EE or E bonds traded for Series HH bonds as income in the year of the trade (IRS Pub. 550).

Individuals generally report interest income from U.S. savings bonds on Schedule B (Form 1040). An individual who redeems a qualified U.S. savings bond and uses the interest to pay certain higher education expenses may be able to exclude from gross income some or all of the interest redeemed (¶ 863).

Dividend Income

See CCH® AnswerConnect: *Taxation of Dividends* for more information on this topic.

733. Dividend Income. Dividends on stock that are paid out of the corporation's earnings and profits (¶ 747), whether in the form of cash or other property, are generally included in the shareholder's gross income (Code Secs. 61(a)(7), 301, and 316). The amount included for a cash dividend is the amount of the cash. If the dividend is in both cash and noncash property, the amount of the dividend is the amount of the cash plus the fair market value (FMV) of the property distributed (¶ 735). Special rules apply to distributions received by 20-percent corporate shareholders (Code Sec. 301(e)).

Dividends are generally taxed as ordinary income. However, qualified dividend income received by an individual, estate, or trust is taxed at capital gains rates. Qualified dividend income is defined as dividends received during the tax year from a domestic corporation or qualified foreign corporation (Code Sec. 1(h)(11)). The capital gains rate for individuals and estates and trusts is 20, 15, and 0 percent depending on the taxpayer's taxable income (¶ 1736). Individuals, estates, and trusts subject to the 20-percent capital gains rate, as well as the higher amounts subject to the 15-percent rate, may also be subject to the net investment income tax of 3.8 percent, which brings the capital gains rate for higher-income taxpayers to 23.8 percent or 18.8 percent (¶ 117).

Corporate stock dividends passed through to investors by a regulated investment company (RIC), partnership, real estate investment trust (REIT), or held by a common trust fund are also eligible for the reduced rate assuming the distribution would otherwise be classified as qualified dividend income. Investments in tax-deferred retirement vehicles such as regular IRAs, 401(k)s, and deferred annuities receive no benefit from the rate reduction. Distributions from these accounts are taxed at ordinary income tax rates even if the funds represent dividends paid on the stocks held in the account. The reduced tax rates also do not apply to dividends paid by corporations such as credit unions, mutual insurance companies, farmers' cooperatives, nonprofit voluntary employee benefit associations (VEBAs), mutual savings banks, building and loan associations, and certain stock owned for short terms. Special rules apply to Code Sec. 306 stock (¶ 739).

Holding Period. To qualify for the lower rate on qualified dividend income, shareholders must hold the stock from which the dividend is paid for more than 60 days in the 121-day period beginning 60 days before the ex-dividend date. The ex-dividend date is the date following the record date on which the corporation finalizes the list of shareholders who will receive the dividend.

733A. Stock Dividends and Stock Rights. A stockholder's gross income generally does not include the value of stock received as a stock dividend from a corporation (Code Sec. 305(a); Reg. § § 1.305-1—1.305-8). However, the following distributions by a corporation of its stock or stock rights are taxed as a dividend (¶ 733):

- distributions in lieu of money (Reg. § 1.305-2);
- disproportionate distributions (Reg. § 1.305-3);
- convertible preferred stock and debentures (Reg. § 1.305-6);
- distributions of common and preferred stock (Reg. § 1.305-4);

7

INCOME

¶733A

- certain transactions increasing a shareholder's proportionate interest (Reg. § 1.305-7); and

- dividends on preferred stock, unless the limited exception applies (Reg. § 1.305-5).

An increase in the conversion ratio of convertible preferred stock made solely to account for stock dividends or stock splits on the stock into which the convertible stock can be converted is tax free.

The basis of the stock, stock rights, or fractional shares acquired in a nontaxable distribution is an allocable portion of the basis of the stock on which the distribution was made. To determine the basis of the stock received in a tax-free distribution, the shareholder allocates a part of the basis of the stock previously held to the new stock or stock rights. The basis is allocated between the old stock and the new stock or stock rights in proportion to the fair market values of each on the date of the distribution, not the record date (Code Sec. 307; Reg. § 1.307-1). If the fair market value of rights received in the distribution is less than 15 percent of the fair market value of the old stock, the shareholder takes a basis of zero in the stock rights unless the shareholder elects to allocate a portion of the basis of the old stock in a statement attached to a timely filed return for the year in which the rights were received. An election, once made, is irrevocable (Reg. § 1.307-2).

A corporate shareholder that receives an extraordinary dividend generally reduces its basis of the stock (but not below zero) by the nontaxed portion of the dividend. There is an exception if the corporation held the stock for more than two years before the dividend announcement. An extraordinary dividend is a dividend that equals or exceeds 10 percent (five percent in the case of stock preferred as to dividends) of the shareholder's adjusted basis in the stock (Code Sec. 1059).

733B. Corporate Debt v. Equity. Factors used to determine whether a corporation has issued a debt or equity instrument include the source of the payments made to the holder and whether there is an unconditional promise to pay a sum certain together with a fixed rate of interest. For instruments issued after October 24, 1992, the corporate issuer's characterization of the nature of the instrument made at the time of issuance is binding upon the corporation and all the holders, but not the IRS. Interest holders are not bound, however, by the issuer's characterization if they disclose any inconsistent treatment on their tax returns (Code Sec. 385(c)).

The IRS closely scrutinizes debt instruments that contain a combination of debt and equity characteristics (Notice 94-47). Of particular interest are instruments that contain equity features such as an unreasonably long maturity or an ability to repay principal with the issuer's stock. No deduction is allowed for any interest paid or accrued on a "disqualified debt instrument" issued after June 8, 1997 (Code Sec. 163(l)). A disqualified debt instrument means any debt that is payable in equity of the issuer or a related party, or equity held by the issuer or any related party in any other person, but only if:

(1) a substantial portion of the principal or interest is required to be paid or converted, or at the issuer's or related party's option is payable in, or convertible into, equity of the issuer or any other person;

(2) a substantial portion of the principal or interest is required to be determined, or may be determined at the option of the issuer or a related party, by reference to the value of equity of the issuer or any other person; or

(3) the debt is part of an arrangement reasonably expected to result in a transaction described in (1) or (2).

An exception to the "no deduction" rule applies for certain instruments issued by dealers in securities.

The IRS also examines corporate transactions designed to produce interest deductions with respect to a related issuance of stock and to provide companies with significant tax advantages in satisfying their equity capital requirements (Notice 94-48). The overall substance of an arrangement whereby a corporation creates a partnership that issues notes to investors and uses most of its capital to buy stock of the corporation is viewed by the IRS as merely an issuance of preferred stock by the corporation. Thus, such a corporation could not deduct an allocable portion of interest expense on the note without an offsetting inclusion of dividend income.

734. When Is a Dividend Received. A dividend on corporate stock is taxable when it is unqualifiedly made subject to the demand of the shareholder (Code Sec. 301; Reg. § 1.301-1(b)). For cash-method shareholders, this generally occurs when payment is actually received. For accrual-method shareholders, this occurs when the dividend is constructively received or at the time of declaration. As an exception to the constructive receipt rule, a dividend is taxable when the check is actually received, even though it may be dated and mailed in an earlier tax year, unless the recipient requested delivery by mail in order to delay recognition of income. Therefore, both accrual and cash basis taxpayers essentially may use the cash method for including dividends in income and must report the income as received (Prop. Reg. § 1.301-1).

A shareholder who voluntarily repays a legally declared and distributed dividend receives dividend income and is subject to tax on that income (*St. Regis Paper Co.*, CA-2, 46-2 ustc ¶ 9383). Also, dividends paid by regulated investment companies (RICs) are not always taxable when received (¶ 2323). Individuals must report dividends and interest in excess of $1,500 on Schedule B (Form 1040).

735. Dividend Paid in Property. If any part of a dividend of corporation stock (¶ 733) is paid in a form other than cash, the property received must be included in gross income at its fair market value (FMV) at the date of distribution, regardless of whether it is the same date on which the distribution is includible in gross income (Code Sec. 301(b)(1) and (3)). If property is distributed to a corporate shareholder, the adjusted basis of the property in the hands of the distributing corporation at the time of the distribution, plus any gain recognized by the distributing corporation, is substituted for the FMV of the property if the adjusted basis is less than the FMV.

The amount of income realized on a distribution is reduced, but not below zero, by the amount of any liability to which property is subject or which is assumed by the shareholder (Code Sec. 301(b)(2); Reg. § 1.301-1). The basis of property received in a distribution is the FMV of the property (Code Sec. 301(d)).

If a distribution is paid in property having an FMV in excess of the corporation's earnings and profits, the dividend is limited to accumulated and current earnings and profits. The portion of the distribution that is not a dividend is applied to reduce the basis of the stock. If the amount of the nondividend distribution exceeds the basis of the stock, the excess is treated as a gain from the sale or exchange of property (Code Sec. 301(c)).

736. Gain or Loss to Corporation on Nonliquidating Distributions. A corporation generally does not recognize gain or loss on the distribution of its stock, stock rights, or corporate property to its shareholders (Code Sec. 311(a)). A corporation generally must recognize gain, however, when it distributes appreciated property to its shareholders in any ordinary, nonliquidating distribution to the extent that the fair market value (FMV) of the property exceeds its adjusted basis (Code Sec. 311(b)). See ¶ 2257 for gain or loss rules applicable to corporations on liquidating distributions.

739. Sale or Disposition of Section 306 Stock. Code Sec. 306 is designed to prevent shareholders from receiving nontaxable stock dividends or stock distribution from a corporation in connection with a reorganization, and disposing of the stock to avoid dividend income (¶ 733) (Code Sec. 306). This is accomplished by denying capital gain treatment when the stockholder disposes of section 306 stock. Section 306 stock includes:

- stock other than common stock received as a tax-free stock dividend,

- stock other than common stock received in certain tax-free divisions or reorganizations, and

- stock, including common stock, with a substituted or carryover basis determined by reference to other section 306 stock.

If section 306 stock is redeemed by a corporation (¶ 742), the amount realized by a shareholder is considered a distribution of property and treated as ordinary income or a taxable distribution to the extent that it is made out of earnings and profits (¶ 733 and ¶ 747). If section 306 stock is sold or disposed of by a shareholder other than by a redemption, the amount realized by the shareholder is ordinary income to the extent that it is not more than the amount that would have been realized as a dividend if, instead of the stock, the corporation had distributed cash equal to the fair market value of the stock. Thus, it would be ordinary income up to the stockholder's share of the amount of earnings and profits of the corporation available for distribution. Section 306 stock is not subject to these rules under certain circumstances (¶ 740).

740. Special Rules and Exceptions for Code Sec. 306 Stock. A holder of section 306 stock of a corporation (¶ 739) is not subject to the ordinary income recognition rule for a transfer of the stock if the disposition occurs as part of a transaction that cannot be used to bail out earnings and profits. The rules governing gain realized on section 306 stock do not apply to a disposition (Code Sec. 306(b)):

- if it is not a redemption,

    — that is not made, directly or indirectly, to a related person under the constructive ownership rules, and

    — that terminates the entire stock interest of the shareholder in the corporation, including stock constructively owned;

- if it is a complete redemption of all the stock held in the corporation by the shareholder or in redemption of stock held by a shareholder who is not a corporation and in partial liquidation of the distributing corporation;

- if it is redeemed in a complete liquidation of the corporation;

- to the extent that gain or loss to the shareholder is not recognized with respect to the disposition; or

- if the IRS is satisfied that the distribution of the stock and the disposition or redemption, simultaneously or previously, of the stock on which the distribution was made were not in pursuance of a plan having federal income tax avoidance as one of its principal purposes.

The sale of new preferred stock to an employees' trust, however, was held not to be within the scope of Code Sec. 306(a) (Rev. Rul. 56-223).

Stock Redemptions

See CCH® AnswerConnect: *Stock Redemptions* for more information on this topic.

742. Redemption of Stock as a Dividend. If a corporation cancels or redeems its stock in a way that makes the action equivalent to a dividend distribution (¶ 747), the amount received by the shareholder that is paid out of earnings and profits is a taxable dividend (Reg. § 1.302-1). Whether a distribution in connection with a cancellation or redemption of stock is equivalent to a taxable dividend depends on the facts and circumstances in each case.

A cancellation or redemption of a part of the stock, pro rata among all the shareholders, generally results in a dividend distribution (Reg. § 1.302-2). A redemption is treated as an exchange of stock rather than as a dividend if the redemption:

- is substantially disproportionate with respect to the shareholder;

- terminates the shareholder's entire interest in the corporation;

- is not substantially equivalent to a dividend;

- is made to a noncorporate shareholder and in partial liquidation of the redeeming corporation; or

- is stock of a publicly offered regulated investment company (RIC) if the redemption is based upon the stockholder's demand and the RIC issues only stock that is redeemable upon such demand (Code Sec. 302(b)).

Amounts received by a shareholder in a distribution in complete liquidation of a corporation are not equivalent to the distribution of a taxable dividend (Code Sec. 331).

A distribution is substantially disproportionate as to a shareholder if, after the redemption, the shareholder owns less than 50 percent of the combined voting power of all classes of voting stock and there is an exchange of stock but not a dividend. Further, the ratio of the shareholder's holdings of voting stock after the redemption to all the voting stock must be less than 80 percent of the ratio of the voting stock the shareholder owned immediately before the redemption to the entire voting stock in the corporation. The stockholder's ownership of common stock, whether voting or nonvoting, after and before redemption must also meet the 80-percent test (Reg. § 1.302-3).

Stock Redemption Expenses. A corporation cannot deduct any amount paid or incurred in connection with any redemption of its stock or the stock of any related person (¶ 432 and ¶ 1717). This restriction does not apply to deductions for interest paid or accrued within the tax year on indebtedness, deductions for dividends paid in connection with the redemption of stock in a RIC, or deductions for amounts properly allocable to indebtedness and amortized over the term of the debt (Code Sec. 162(k)).

743. Constructive Ownership of Stock. The constructive ownership rules provide that stock owned by certain individuals or entities that are related to a shareholder is deemed owned by that shareholder for certain provisions relating to corporate distributions and adjustments.

An individual is treated as owning stock owned, directly or indirectly, by (1) a spouse if not legally separated under a decree of divorce or separate maintenance, and (2) children, including adopted children, grandchildren, and parents (Code Sec. 318(a)(1); Reg. §§ 1.318-1, 1.318-2). Stock constructively owned by an individual under the family attribution rule is not treated as owned by that individual for the purpose of applying the constructive stock ownership rule to make another the owner of such stock (Reg. § 1.318-4).

Stock owned directly or indirectly by or for a partnership, S corporation, or estate is considered as being owned proportionately by the partners, S corporation shareholders, or beneficiaries. Stock owned directly or indirectly by or for a partner, S corporation shareholder, or beneficiary is treated as being owned by the partnership, S corporation, or estate (Code Sec. 318(a)(2) and (3)).

Stock owned directly or indirectly by or for a trust is considered as being owned by its beneficiaries in proportion to their actuarial interests in the trust. Stock owned directly or indirectly by or for a beneficiary of a trust is considered as being owned by the trust. However, a contingent beneficial interest of not more than five percent of the value of the trust property is not taken into account (Code Sec. 318(a)(2) and (3); Reg. § 1.318-2).

If 50 percent or more in value of the stock in a corporation is owned directly or indirectly by or for any person, that person is considered as owning the stock owned directly or indirectly by or for the corporation in the proportion that the value of the stock the person owns bears to the value of all the stock in the corporation. The corporation, on the other hand, is considered as owning the stock owned directly or indirectly by or for any person holding 50 percent or more in value of its stock directly or indirectly (Code Sec. 318(a)(2)(C) and (a)(3)(C)).

744. Redemption of Stock Through Use of Related Corporations. If stock of an issuing corporation is acquired by a corporation that is controlled by the issuing corporation, the amount paid for the stock is a dividend by the issuing corporation provided that it is a redemption that would be considered a taxable dividend (¶ 742).

Also, when the stock of one corporation is sold to a related corporation (i.e., brother-sister corporations), the sale proceeds are considered as distributed in redemption of the stock of the corporation that bought it. If the sales are related, it is immaterial whether they are made simultaneously (Reg. § 1.304-2). Whether the sales are related is determined upon the facts and circumstances surrounding all the sales. To the extent that a redemption involving related corporations is treated as a distribution under Code Sec. 301, the transferor and the acquiring corporation are treated as if the transferor had transferred the stock involved to the acquiring corporation in exchange for stock of the acquiring corporation, in a Code Sec. 351(a) nontaxable contribution of capital, and then the acquiring corporation had redeemed the stock it was deemed to have issued (Code Sec. 304(a)(1)).

745. Redemption of Stock to Pay Estate Taxes and Expenses. A distribution of property by a corporation in redemption of its stock that has been included in the gross estate of a decedent for estate tax purposes can qualify as a sale or exchange of the stock. The amount of the distribution qualifying for this treatment is limited to the sum of the estate, generation-skipping transfer (GST), inheritance, legacy, and succession taxes on the estate, including interest, plus the funeral and administration expenses allowable as deductions from the gross estate for federal estate tax purposes (Code Sec. 303). See ¶ 2901 for discussion of the estate tax and GST tax.

The redemption must have been made after the decedent's death and not later than 90 days after the period of limitations on assessment of the federal estate tax, which is three years after the return is filed. If a petition for redetermination of an estate tax deficiency has been filed with the Tax Court, the redemption period is extended for 60 days after the decision of the Tax Court becomes final. A distribution made more than 60 days after the decision of the Tax Court becomes final can be timely, provided it is made within 90 days after expiration of the three-year period.

In order for the redemption not to be treated as a taxable dividend, the value of the decedent's stock in the redeeming corporation must exceed 35 percent of the gross estate, after the deductions for allowable funeral and administration expenses and losses. The shares must be redeemed from a person whose interest in the estate is reduced by payment of estate, generation-skipping transfer, inheritance, and succession taxes or funeral and administration expenses.

If stock in a corporation is the subject of a generation-skipping transfer occurring at the same time and as a result of the death of an individual, the tax imposed on the transfer is treated as an estate tax for purposes of the redemption rules. The period of distribution is measured from the date of the generation-skipping transfer, and the relationship of stock to the decedent's estate is measured with reference solely to the amount of the generation-skipping transfer.

Corporate Earnings and Profits

See CCH® AnswerConnect: *Corporate Earnings and Profits* for more information on this topic.

747. Source of Dividend Distributions. A distribution received by a shareholder from a corporation must be paid out of earnings and profits of the distributing corporation (¶ 748) to be subject to income tax as a dividend (¶ 733). A dividend is any distribution made by a corporation to its shareholders out of its earnings and profits accumulated after February 28, 1913, or out of the earnings and profits of the current tax year, computed as of the close of the tax year without diminution by reason of any distributions made during the tax year, and without regard to the amount of the earnings and profits at the time the distribution was made (Code Sec. 316; Reg. § 1.316-1). Even if there is an operating deficit at the beginning of the year, total dividends paid are taxable to the extent of earning and profits of the corporation for the *entire* year.

In order to determine the source of a distribution, consideration should be given to: (1) the earnings and profits of the tax year; (2) the earnings and profits accumulated since February 28, 1913, but only in the case when, and to the extent that, the distributions made during the tax year are not regarded as out of the earnings and profits of that year; (3) the earnings and profits accumulated before March 1, 1913, only after all of the earnings and profits of the tax year and all the earnings and profits accumulated since February 28, 1913, have been distributed; and (4) sources other than earnings and profits only after the earnings and profits have been distributed (Reg. § 1.316-2).

If the current year's earnings and profits are sufficient to cover all distributions made during the year, each distribution is a taxable dividend. If the year's cash distributions exceed current earnings and profits, a part of the earnings and profits must be allocated proportionately to each distribution, on the basis of the following formula: distribution × (current earnings and profits ÷ total distributions). The remaining portion of each distribution not covered by current earnings and profits is then treated as a taxable dividend to the extent of accumulated earnings and profits. If these are not sufficient to cover the remaining portion of any distribution, they are to be applied against each distribution in chronological order until exhausted.

748. Computation of Earnings and Profits. In computing earnings and profits of a corporation for the year, all income that is exempt from tax must be included, as well as all items includible in gross income (Reg. § 1.312-6). Thus, exempt income such as life insurance proceeds and fully tax-exempt interest on state or municipal obligations is included. Similarly, cancellation of indebtedness income and intercorporate dividends are included. A loss for a preceding year cannot be used to decrease the earnings and profits of the current tax year.

The starting point for the computation of earnings and profits is the corporation's taxable income, which is then adjusted to more accurately reflect true economic income available for distribution. This involves the different treatment of certain items from their treatment for tax purposes, including depreciation (¶ 755), depletion, certain reserves, and other items. Gain or loss from a sale or other disposition of property is also generally included in earnings and profits at the time and to the extent that it is recognized for tax purposes (Reg. § 1.312-7). There are numerous exceptions to this general rule and the corporation's earnings and profits are very unlikely to be the same as the corporation's taxable income. For example, income from installment sales is treated differently than earnings and profits (¶ 756). In addition, some items that are required to be capitalized for income tax purposes are deducted in the computation of earnings and profits (Rev. Rul. 60-123).

The general rule on the distribution of property, including cash, by a corporation is that the earnings and profits for future distributions are reduced by the amount of money distributed, the principal amount of any obligations of the corporation distributed, and the adjusted basis of any other property distributed (Reg. § 1.312-1). If appreciated property is distributed with respect to stock, earnings and profits must be increased by the amount of the gain realized upon the distribution even if the gain is not recognized for purposes of computing taxable income. There are special rules for distributions to 20-percent corporate shareholders (¶ 733).

Nontaxable stock dividends or stock rights (¶ 733A) do not reduce earnings and profits. The same rule applies to distributions of the stock or securities, or rights to acquire stock or securities, of other corporations and distributions of property or money when they were nontaxable to the recipient when made (Code Sec. 312(d)).

751. Redemptions and Earnings and Profits. A corporation that distributes amounts in redemption of its stock can reduce its post-February 28, 1913, accumulated earnings and profits only by the ratable share of those earnings and profits attributable to the redeemed stock (¶ 747) (Code Sec. 312(n)(7)).

752. Effect of Reorganization on Earnings and Profits. If a corporate reorganization results in no recognized gain or loss, the company's life as a continuing venture does not stop, so that what were earnings and profits of the original company remain, for purposes of distribution of dividend, earnings and profits of the continuing corporation (¶ 747) (*R.L. Putnam*, CA-1, 45-1 USTC ¶ 9319).

755. Effect of Depreciation on Earnings and Profits. Depreciation claimed on the corporation's income tax return that exceeds the straight-line method increases the corporation's current earnings and profits (¶ 747) (Code Sec. 312(k); Reg. § 1.312-15). For tangible property placed in service in tax years beginning after 1986, the alternative MACRS method is used to compute depreciation in order to determine the corporation's earnings and profits (¶ 1247). For depreciable assets first placed in service after 1980, but before 1987, the adjustment to earnings and profits for depreciation is determined under the straight-line ACRS, using extended recovery periods (¶ 1252). For assets placed in service before 1981, the amount of the depreciation deduction for the purpose of computing earnings and profits is generally the amount allowable under the tradi-

¶755

tional straight-line method, although a corporation that uses the permissible non-accelerated depreciation method (e.g., the machine-hour method) can use that method for earnings and profits purposes.

Bonus depreciation (¶ 1237) is not allowable for purposes of computing earnings and profits. However, an amount that can be deducted under certain provisions can be deducted ratably over a period of five years in computing earnings and profits, beginning with the year the amount is otherwise deductible. This includes property that can be expensed under Code Sec. 179 (¶ 1208), sulfur regulation compliance under Code Sec. 179B, the cost of refinery property deducted under Code Sec. 179C, the cost of energy-efficient property deducted under Code Sec. 179D (¶ 1286), and the cost of advanced mine safety equipment deducted under Code Sec. 179E (¶ 989A).

756. Effect of Installment Sales on Earnings and Profits. A corporation that sells property on the installment method of accounting (¶ 1801) is treated for earnings and profits purposes as if it had not used the installment method (¶ 747) (Code Sec. 312(n)(5)).

757. Effect of LIFO Reserve Changes on Earnings and Profits. A corporation's earnings and profits (¶ 747) generally must be increased or decreased by the amount of any change in the corporation's "LIFO recapture amount" at the end of each tax year (Code Sec. 312(n)(4)). The LIFO recapture amount is the amount, if any, by which the inventory amount of the inventory assets under the first-in, first-out (FIFO) method (¶ 1564) exceeds the inventory amount of the inventory assets under the last-in, first-out (LIFO) method (¶ 1565).

Business Income

759. Business Income or Profit. Gross income of a taxpayer includes "gross income derived from business," which is usually the same as gross profit, *not* gross receipts (Code Sec. 61(a)(2); Reg. § 1.61-3(a)). Gross profit is the total receipts from sales minus the cost of the goods sold, plus investment income and income from other sources. In the case of most mercantile businesses, cost of goods sold includes the purchase price of the article sold plus delivery costs, warehousing, etc. In a manufacturing firm it includes the entire factory cost—materials, direct labor, and factory overhead, including depreciation attributable to manufacturing processes—applicable to goods manufactured and sold. Gross income derived from business is determined without subtracting selling expenses, losses, or other items not ordinarily used in computing costs of goods sold, as well as amounts paid for bribes, kickbacks, fines, or penalties for which a business deduction would not be allowed (¶ 972). Cost of goods sold should be determined according to the accounting method consistently used by the taxpayer (¶ 1515).

Damages for Lost Profit or Capital. Damage awards and amounts received in settlement of claims for business injuries that represent compensation for lost profits are included in gross income and taxable as ordinary income. This includes proceeds from business interruption insurance, liquidated damages, and awards for breach of contract. Damages received for injury to goodwill are a nontaxable return of capital to the extent they do not exceed the taxpayer's basis in goodwill (*Phoenix Coal Co.*, CA-2, 56-1 USTC ¶ 9366). Similarly, compensation for injury to, or loss of, capital is a nontaxable return of capital to the extent of basis. Any excess is treated as capital gain if received for damage to a capital asset. Punitive damages, such as treble damages under antitrust laws, are taxable ordinary income (Reg. § 1.61-14(a)). See ¶ 852 for damages arising out of employment discrimination claims.

Rents and Royalties

See CCH® AnswerConnect: *Gross Income: Taxable Rents and Royalties* for more information on this topic.

762. Rental Income. Amounts received or accrued as rents in payment for the use of property must be included in gross income (Code Sec. 61(a)(5); Reg. § 1.61-8). The payment by a lessee of any expenses of a lessor is generally considered additional rental income to the lessor (¶ 765). Consideration received by the lessor for cancellation of a lease is in substitution for rental payments and not a return of capital. Any reduction in the value of property due to cancellation of a lease is a deductible loss only when fixed by a closed transaction (*W.M. Hort*, SCt, 41-1 USTC ¶ 9354). Rental activities are generally treated as passive activities (¶ 1181).

For individuals, expenses attributable to property held for the production of rents are deductible in computing adjusted gross income (AGI) (¶ 1006A). An individual lessor generally reports rental real estate income and expenses on Schedule E (Form 1040), but Schedule C (Form 1040) is used if the taxpayer provided significant services to the real property lessee. In addition, Schedule C is used to report income and expenses from the rental of personal property if the taxpayer is in the business of renting personal property. If the taxpayer is not in the business of renting personal property, the income is reported as other income on Form 1040 and the expenses are reported as an adjustment to AGI (Instructions to Form 1040).

See ¶ 966 for special rules for the rental of the taxpayer's residence or vacation home.

763. Royalty Income. Royalties from copyrights on literary, musical, or artistic works and similar property or from a patent on an invention are includible in gross income (Code Sec. 61(a)(6); Reg. § 1.61-8(a)). Royalties received from oil, gas, or other mineral properties are also includible in gross income. See ¶ 1772 for the treatment of royalties on the disposition of an interest in timber, coal, and iron ore. See ¶ 1380 for the depletion allowance for royalties.

For individuals, expenses attributable to property held for the production of royalties are deductible in computing adjusted gross income (AGI) (¶ 1006A). Royalty income and expenses are generally reported on Schedule E (Form 1040), but Schedule C (Form 1040) is used to report royalties received by the holder of an operating oil, gas, or mineral interest, and by self-employed writers, inventors, artists, etc.

764. Improvements by Lessee. Ordinarily, on the termination of a lease, a lessor of real property excludes any income derived from improvements made on the property by the lessee (Code Sec. 109; Reg. § 1.109-1). This exclusion applies to improvements that revert to the lessor upon expiration of a lease as well as to those acquired by the lessor upon forfeiture of a lease prior to the end of the full term. If the improvements represent a liquidation-in-kind of lease rentals, the exclusion does not apply to the extent that the improvements represent such liquidation.

If the lessee makes improvements in lieu of paying rent, the lessor has rental income to the extent of the fair market value of the improvements in the year they are made (Reg. § § 1.61-8(c) and 1.109-1). This treatment of lessee improvements depends on the parties' intention, which may be indicated by the lease terms or the surrounding circumstances.

Construction Allowances. A retail tenant with a lease of 15 years or less that receives a construction allowance of cash or rent reductions from the lessor does not include the allowance in gross income if the tenant uses it for construction or improvement of nonresidential real property that is part of the retail space and used in the tenant's trade or business (Code Sec. 110(a); Reg. § 1.110-1). The lessor must depreciate the improvement as MACRS nonresidential real property (¶ 1234 and ¶ 1240). If the improvement is disposed or abandoned at the termination of the lease, the lessor may claim a gain or loss by reference to the remaining adjusted basis of the improvement (¶ 1109).

765. Lessor's Obligations Paid by Lessee. If a lessee pays any of the lessor's expenses, such as property taxes, the payment is additional rental income to the lessor (Reg. § 1.61-8(c)). If the taxes paid are income to the lessor, they may be treated as if paid by the lessor in determining their deductibility (¶ 986). If a lessee agrees to pay, in lieu of rent, a dividend on the lessor's stock or interest on its mortgages, the payments are rental income to the lessor.

Farming Income

See CCH® AnswerConnect: *Farm and Fishing Income* for more information on this topic.

767. Farming Income. Income from farming is treated the same way as income from any other business (¶ 759). Every individual, partnership, or corporation that cultivates, operates, or manages a farm for gain or profit, either as owner or tenant, is designated as a farmer (Reg. § 1.61-4(d)). A person who cultivates or operates a farm for recreation or pleasure, and who experiences a continual net loss from year to year, generally lacks a profit motive and may not deduct the losses (¶ 1195).

An individual engaged in farming for profit must file Schedule F (Form 1040) to report income and expenses from the farming activity. An individual farmer must also file Schedule SE (Form 1040) for computing earnings from self-employment (¶ 2676). A partnership engaged in farming must file Schedule F along with Form 1065. An estate or trust engaged in farming must file Schedule F along with Form 1041. A corporation engaged in farming must file the appropriate Form 1120.

Cash Basis. The general rules for cash-basis taxpayers also apply to a farmer on the cash basis (¶ 1515). A cash-basis farmer does not use inventories. Instead, the taxpayer includes in gross income all cash and the value of merchandise or other property received from the sale of livestock and produce that have been raised, profits from the sale of livestock or other items that have been purchased, amounts received from breeding fees, rental fees, and other incidental farm income. All subsidy or conservation payments treated as income, and income received from all other sources are also included in gross income (Reg. § 1.61-4).

A cash-basis farmer may defer recognition of gain from the sale of a crop delivered in one year until the following year if a valid contract (deferred payment contract) with the purchaser or the purchaser's agent prohibits payment until the following year, but not if the payment is deferred merely at the seller's request. If the sales contract states that the farmer has the right to the proceeds of the sale from the purchaser at any time after delivery of the item, the farmer must include the sales price in gross income in the year of the sale, regardless of when payment is received (IRS Pub. 225).

Profit from the sale of livestock or other items purchased by a farmer is computed by deducting the cost from the sales price. For the sale of animals that originally were purchased as draft or work animals, or for breeding or dairy purposes and not for resale, the profit is the difference between the sale price and the depreciated basis of the animal sold (Reg. § 1.61-4(a)).

A cash-basis farmer who receives insurance proceeds as a result of destruction or damage to crops may elect to include the proceeds in income in the year after the year of damage if the farmer can show that the income from the crops would normally have been reported in the following year. This includes payments received under the Agricultural Act of 1949, Title II of the Disaster Assistance Act of 1988, or Title I of the Disaster Assistance Act of 1989 as a result of damage to crops caused by drought, flood, or other natural disaster, or the inability to plant crops because of such a natural disaster (Code Sec. 451(f); Reg. § 1.451-6; Rev. Rul. 91-55).

A cash-method farmer who is forced to sell more livestock than usual due to drought, flood, or other weather-related conditions in an area designated as eligible for assistance by the federal government, may elect to be taxed on the forced sale income (gain that normally would not have been realized in the year of the forced sale) in the following year if the farmer can show that, under usual business practices, the additional animals would not have been sold except for the weather-related condition (Code Sec. 451(g); Reg. § 1.451-7).

Accrual Method. A farmer on the accrual method (¶ 1515) must use inventories taken at the start and the end of the tax year (Reg. § 1.61-4(b)). Although many farmers may use the cash method, the accrual method of accounting is required for certain farming corporations and partnerships (¶ 1519), and for all farming tax shelters including farming syndicates (¶ 1521). Gross profit of a farmer on the accrual basis is calculated by:

- adding the inventory value of livestock and other products on hand at the end of the year, plus the amount received from the sale of livestock and other products during the year, miscellaneous income items (i.e., breeding fees, rental fees, other incidental farm income), all subsidy or conservation payments treated as income, and gross income from all other sources, and

- subtracting from that total the sum of the inventory value of livestock and products on hand at the beginning of the year and the cost of livestock and products purchased during the year, but not livestock held for draft, dairy, or breeding purposes, unless they are included in inventory.

Livestock raised or purchased for sale must be inventoried (¶ 1569). Livestock purchased for draft, breeding, or dairy purposes and not for sale may be inventoried. Alternatively, they may be treated as capital assets subject to depreciation if the farmer uses that method consistently from year to year. If inventoried livestock is sold, its cost must not be taken as an additional deduction in computing taxable income, because the cost is reflected in the inventory. Sales of livestock held for draft, breeding, or dairy purposes are generally reported on Form 4797.

Other Methods. Two other inventory methods are available to farmers—the farm-price method and the unit-livestock-price method (¶ 1569).

Income Averaging. An individual engaged in a farming business or fishing business may elect to average farm income over three years (Code Sec. 1301; Reg. § 1.1301-1). The tax imposed in any tax year equals the sum of the tax computed on taxable income reduced by the amount of farm income elected for averaging plus the increase in tax that would result if taxable income for each of the three prior tax years were increased by an amount equal to one-third of the elected farm income. Schedule J (Form 1040) is used to report the income averaging.

Other Matters. See ¶ 1701 for income from the sale of farm property other than inventory, ¶ 1521 for tax shelter farming operations, ¶ 982 for farming expenses, and ¶ 1330 for application of the uniform capitalization rules to a farming business.

768. Income from Cooperatives (Patronage Dividends). An individual such as a farmer who buys goods and services through a cooperative may receive refunds in the form of patronage dividends that must be included in gross income. Similarly, an individual who sells products through a cooperative may receive either patronage dividends or a per-unit retain certificate from the cooperative that also must be included in gross income (Code Sec. 1385; Reg. § 1.1385-1). The income is reported to the individual on Form 1099-PATR. See ¶ 698 for the taxation of exempt and tax-exempt cooperatives.

Patronage dividends are usually reported in the year of receipt and include any money paid as a patronage dividend, the stated value of any qualified written notice of allocation, and the fair market value of other property received from a cooperative. Amounts received as patronage dividends or resulting from the redemption, sale or disposition of nonqualified written notices of allocation are excludable from gross income if taken into account as an adjustment to basis of property. Patronage dividends paid with respect to purchases of personal, living, or family items are also not includible in the patron's gross income.

If a nonqualified allocation or certificate is redeemed, sold or otherwise disposed of, and the gain exceeds its basis, that gain is treated as ordinary income. Any gain from a nonqualified per-unit retain certificate that is paid as a per-unit retain allocation must be included in gross income. The same rule applies to any gain from a nonqualified written notice of allocation that is paid as a patronage dividend or paid on a patronage basis from earnings derived from the United States or its agencies or from sources other than patronage.

769. Commodity Credit Corporation Loan. A taxpayer generally does not report loan proceeds as income. However, a farmer who pledges all or part of the crop production to secure a Commodity Credit Corporation (CCC) loan may elect to report the loan proceeds as income in the year received rather than income in the year the crops are sold (Code Sec. 77; Reg. § § 1.77-1 and 1.77-2). The taxpayer does not need IRS permission to adopt this method of reporting CCC loans.

7

INCOME

The farmer makes the election by including the loan proceeds as income on Schedule F (Form 1040) and attaching a statement showing the details of the loan. The amount reported as income becomes the farmer's basis in the commodity and is used to determine gain or loss upon its ultimate disposition. Once the CCC loan is reported as income in the year received, all succeeding CCC loans must be reported in the same way. The IRS has provided procedures for obtaining an automatic consent to change the method of accounting for CCC loans (Rev. Proc. 2015-13; Rev. Proc. 2019-43).

Market Gains. The repayment amount for a loan secured by an eligible commodity is generally based on the lower of the original loan rate or the alternative repayment rate for the commodity as of the repayment date. Thus, the farmer may realize a market gain if the loan is repaid when the alternative rate is lower than the original loan rate (Notice 2007-63). When a CCC loan is repaid, regardless of the manner of repayment, the CCC is required to file Form 1099-G to report market gain associated with the repayment (Code Sec. 6039J(a)).

Alimony Payments

See CCH® AnswerConnect: *Tax Consequences of Divorce* for more information on this topic.

771. Alimony Payments Included in Gross Income. An individual must generally include in gross income alimony or separate maintenance payments (¶ 772) received under a divorce or separation agreement executed before 2019 (Code Secs. 61(a)(8) and 71, prior to being stricken by the Tax Cuts and Jobs Act (P.L. 115-97); Reg. § 1.71-1). Alimony payments are also deductible by the payor-spouse (¶ 1008). A recapture rule prevents the front-loading of alimony payments (¶ 774). Alimony payments are not includible in gross income if made under a divorce or separation agreement (1) executed after 2018, or (2) executed before 2019 but modified after 2018 if the modification expressly provides for the repeal of the alimony rules.

772. Requirements for Alimony and Separate Maintenance Payments. Payments made under a divorce or separation instrument are generally includible in the gross income of the recipient (¶ 771) and deductible by the payor (¶ 1008) as alimony or separate maintenance payments if the following requirements are met:

• the payment is in cash, including checks and money orders payable on demand;

• the payment is received by or on behalf of a spouse under a divorce or separation instrument executed before 2019;

• the instrument does not designate the payment as being not includible in the recipient/payee's gross income and not deductible by the payor;

• spouses who are legally separated under a decree of divorce or separate maintenance are not members of the same household at the time the payment is made;

• there is no liability to make any payment for any period after the death of the payee spouse, or to make any payment, either in cash or property, as a substitute for such payments after the death of the payee spouse;

• the spouses do not file joint returns with each other; and

• the payment is not fixed by the instrument as child support (¶ 776) (Code Sec. 71(b), (c), and (e), prior to being stricken by the Tax Cuts and Jobs Act (P.L. 115-97); Temp. Reg. § 1.71-1T).

The deduction of alimony payments by the payor, as well as the inclusion of the payments in gross income by the payee, does not apply to any payment made under a divorce or separation agreement (1) executed after 2018, or (2) executed before 2019 but modified after 2018 if the modification expressly provides for the repeal of the alimony rules.

774. Three-Year Recapture of Excess Alimony Payments. A special recapture rule may apply to *excess* alimony and separate maintenance payments (¶ 771 and ¶ 772) if payments decrease or end during the first three calendar years after the spouses divorce or separate (Code Sec. 71(f), prior to being stricken by the Tax Cuts and Jobs Act (P.L. 115-97)). Its purpose is to prevent front-loading of payments and property settlement payments from qualifying for alimony treatment.

The rule requires the recapture of excess amounts that have been treated as alimony or separate maintenance either during the calendar year in which payments began (the first post-separation year) or in the next succeeding calendar year (the second post-separation year). The payor-spouse must include excess alimony payments in gross income in his or her tax year beginning in the third post-separation year. The payee, who previously included the payments in gross income, is entitled to deduct the amount recaptured from gross income in his or her tax year beginning in the third post-separation year.

Excess alimony payments are equal to the sum of the excess payments made in the first post-separation year, plus the excess payments made in the second post-separation year. For the first post-separation year, the excess payment amount is the excess, if any, of the total alimony paid in the first post-separation year minus the sum of: $15,000, plus the average of the amount of alimony paid in the second post-separation year less excess payments for that year, plus the amount of alimony paid in the third post-separation year. Thus, for the first post-separation year, the following formula is used:

$$
\begin{array}{c}
\text{1st year} \\
\text{excess} \\
\text{payments}
\end{array} =
\begin{array}{c}
\text{alimony} \\
\text{paid in} \\
\text{1st year}
\end{array} -
\left(\$15,000 + \cfrac{\left[\left(\begin{array}{c}\text{alimony}\\\text{paid in}\\\text{2nd}\\\text{year}\end{array} - \begin{array}{c}\text{excess}\\\text{payments}\\\text{in 2nd}\\\text{year}\end{array}\right) + \begin{array}{c}\text{alimony}\\\text{paid in}\\\text{3rd}\\\text{year}\end{array}\right]}{2} \right)
$$

To calculate the excess payments for the first year, it is necessary to determine the excess payments for the second post-separation year. The amount of excess payments for the second year is the excess, if any, of the amount of alimony paid during the second year minus the sum of: $15,000 plus the amount of alimony paid in the third year. Thus, for the second post-separation year, the following formula is used:

$$
\begin{array}{c}\text{2nd year}\\\text{excess payments}\end{array} = \begin{array}{c}\text{alimony paid}\\\text{in 2nd year}\end{array} - \left(\begin{array}{c}\text{alimony paid}\\\text{in 3rd year}\end{array} + \$15,000\right)
$$

Example 1: In 2017, Mr. Black makes payments totalling $50,000 to his ex-wife. He makes no payments in either 2018 or 2019. Assuming none of the exceptions set forth below apply, he must recapture $35,000 in 2019. Thus, he must report an additional $35,000 in income, while his ex-wife is entitled to a $35,000 reduction in income.

Example 2: In 2017, Ms. Gold makes payments totalling $50,000 to her ex-husband. In 2018, she makes $20,000 in payments, but in 2019 she makes no payments. Assuming that none of the exceptions set forth below apply, the total amount she must recapture in 2019 (year three) is $32,500. This represents $5,000 from 2018 (year two) ($20,000 minus $15,000) and $27,500 from 2017 (year one). The amount recaptured from year one equals the excess of $50,000 over the sum of $15,000 plus $7,500. The $7,500 is the average of the payments for years two and three after reducing the payments by the $5,000 recaptured for year two ($20,000 payment in year two plus $0 payment in year three minus the $5,000 that was required to be recaptured equals $15,000; divided by two equals $7,500).

IRS Pub. 504 contains a worksheet for computing alimony recapture.

Exceptions to Recapture Rule. There are several exceptions to the recapture rule. Recapture is not required if, before the end of the third post-separation year, the alimony or separate maintenance payments terminate because either party dies or the payee-spouse remarries. The recapture rule also does not apply to payments made under temporary support orders, such as payments made under an interlocutory decree of divorce or payments made pendente lite. Recapture is not required if the alimony or separate maintenance payments fluctuate because of a continuing liability—over at least a three-year period—to pay a fixed portion of income from the earnings of a business or property or from compensation from employment or self-employment. Additionally, the recapture rule does not apply if alimony or separate maintenance payments decline by $15,000 or less over the three-year period.

775. Income from Alimony Trust. If an individual is entitled under a divorce or separation agreement executed before 2019 to a beneficiary interest in a trust, then he or she is treated as the beneficiary of a regular trust and not a grantor trust. In such a case, trust income attributable to the agreement is includible in the gross income of the beneficiary spouse as if it meets the requirements for alimony or separate maintenance payments (¶ 772) (Code Sec. 682, prior to being stricken by the Tax Cuts and Jobs Act (P.L. 115-97); Reg. §§ 1.682(a)-1, 1.682(b)-1; Notice 2018-37).

The payor-spouse may claim a deduction for alimony (¶ 1008) for a trust distribution but only if it is includible in the payee-spouse's gross income. The deduction of alimony payments by the payor, as well as the inclusion of the payments in gross income by the payee, does not apply to any payment made under a divorce or separation agreement (1) executed after 2018, or (2) executed before 2019 but modified after 2018 if the modification expressly provides for the repeal of the alimony rules (Code Sec. 215(d), prior to being stricken by P.L. 115-97).

776. Child Support. Payments under a divorce or separation agreement executed before 2019 that are fixed as child support are not generally considered qualified alimony or separation maintenance payments (¶ 772). Thus, the payments are not deductible by the payor-spouse (¶ 1008) or includible in gross income by payee-spouse (¶ 771) (Code Sec. 71(c), prior to being stricken by the Tax Cuts and Jobs Act (P.L. 115-97); Reg. § 1.71-1(e); Temp. Reg. § 1.71-1T(c)).

If any amount specified in the instrument is to be reduced based on a contingency set out in the instrument relating to a child—such as attaining a specified age, dying, leaving school, or marrying—the amount of the specified reduction is treated as child support from the outset. The same rule applies if the reduction is to occur at a time that can clearly be associated with such contingency. Thus, payments that vary with the status of a child are not deductible. The deduction of alimony payments by the payor, as well as the inclusion of the payments in gross income by the payee, does not apply to any payment made under a divorce or separation agreement (1) executed after 2018, or (2) executed before 2019 but modified after 2018 if the modification expressly provides for the repeal of the alimony rules.

778. Property Transfers Between Spouses Incident to Divorce. No gain or loss is recognized on a transfer of property, either outright or in trust, between spouses or between former spouses incident to divorce (Code Sec. 1041; Temp. Reg. § 1.1041-1T). The transfer is treated as a gift to the transferee, and thus the property's value is not includible in the transferee's gross income. The transferee's basis in the property is equal to the transferor's adjusted basis. A transfer between former spouses is incident to divorce if it occurs within one year after the marriage ceases or is related to the cessation of the marriage.

Nonrecognition of gain or loss is not available if the transferee is a nonresident alien, or if there is a transfer in trust to the extent that liabilities assumed by the transferee, including liabilities to which the property is subject, exceed the transferor's adjusted basis in the property. The transferee's basis is increased for any such gain recognized by the transferor.

Other Income

See CCH® AnswerConnect: *Gross Income: Awards, Damages, Recoveries, Illegal Activities and Other* for more information on this topic.

785. Taxation of Miscellaneous or Other Income. Several income items are considered miscellaneous or other income (IRS Pub. 525; Instructions for Form 1040).

Prizes and Awards. Amounts received as prizes and awards are generally includible in the recipient's gross income, subject to several exceptions (Code Sec. 74). An individual may exclude qualified scholarships and fellowships from gross income (¶ 865), as well as employee achievement awards to the extent that the cost of the award is deductible by the employer (¶ 919).

Awards received by an individual for religious, charitable, scientific, educational, artistic, literary, or civic achievement (for example, Nobel and Pulitzer Prize) are excludable from gross income, but only if:

- the taxpayer is selected without any action on his or her part to enter the contest or proceeding;

- the taxpayer is not required to render substantial future services as a condition to receiving the award; and

- the award is transferred unused by the payor to a charitable organization or governmental unit designated by the recipient.

Prize money awarded to a U.S. athlete by the United States Olympic Committee (USOC), as well as the fair market value of any medal received on account of competition in the Olympic or Paralympic Games, are excluded from the athlete's gross income if the individual's adjusted gross income (AGI) does not otherwise exceed $1 million ($500,000 if married filing separately).

Gambling Income and Illegal Gains. Gain arising from gambling, betting and lotteries is includible in gross income. A gain from an illegal transaction, such as bootlegging, extortion, embezzlement or fraud, is also includible (IRS Pub 525). See ¶ 1113 for a discussion of gambling losses.

Bartering. The value of bartered services is includible in gross income, and is generally reported on Schedule C (Form 1040). If the barter involves an exchange of property, a different form may be required for reporting purposes. For example, if the owner of an apartment building permits an artist to use an apartment in exchange for works of art created by the artist, the building owner reports the fair market value of the art as rental income on Schedule E (Form 1040), and the artist reports the fair rental value of the apartment as income on Schedule C (IRS Pub 525).

If two individuals are members of a barter club and each agrees to exchange services, the value of the services received by each is includible in gross income. Barter clubs must report exchanges on Form 1099-B (¶ 2565). Trade or credit units used by a barter club to account for transactions are also includible in gross income when credited to the taxpayer's account.

Cancelled Debt. If a debt is cancelled or forgiven, other than as a gift or bequest, the cancelled amount generally must be included in gross income. Cancelled debt is not income if the debtor's payment of the debt would have been a deductible expense. Also a taxpayer can exclude discharge of debt income from gross income for insolvency, bankruptcy, qualified farm debt, qualified real property business debt, qualified principal residence debt, forgiveness of student loans in exchange for services or due to death of total and permanent disability, and forgiveness of Paycheck Protection Program (PPP) loans made by the Small Business Administration (SBA) under section 7(a) of the Small Business Act (¶ 855).

Insurance. Life insurance proceeds are generally excludable (¶ 803). However, dividends received that exceed the total net premiums paid for the contract are reportable income.

Recoveries. The recovery of an amount for which the taxpayer claimed a deduction or credit in an earlier tax year is generally reported as other income on the taxpayer's return in the tax year of the recovery (¶ 799).

Jury Duty Pay. Jury pay is includible in gross income of an individual, but an employee may be able to claim a deduction if he or she is required to surrender the pay to an employer (¶ 1010) (Reg. § 1.61-2(a)(1)).

Certain Taxable Distributions. Distributions from a Coverdell education savings account (Coverdell ESA) (¶ 867) or qualified tuition program (QTP or 529 plan) (¶ 869) that exceed qualified education expenses and are not part of a qualified rollover are includible in income. A similar rule applies to distributions from health savings accounts (HSAs) (¶ 2035), Archer medical savings accounts (Archer MSAs) (¶ 2037), and qualified ABLE accounts (¶ 870). An individual who fails to remain eligible for an HSA may

7

INCOME

¶785

have to include a portion of amounts contributed to the account in gross income (¶ 2035).

Below-Market Loans. If a below-market gift or demand loan is made, the forgone interest (at the federal rate) is interest income (¶ 795).

Income From the Rental of Personal Property. If an individual rents personal property, any rental income is includible in gross income. An individual lessor generally reports income and expenses from the rental of personal property on Schedule C (Form 1040) if the taxpayer is in the business of renting personal property. If the taxpayer is not in the business of renting personal property, the income is reported as other income on Form 1040 and any expenses are reported as an adjustment to AGI (¶ 1006A), but only up to the amount of income (¶ 1195).

Hobbies. Income from an activity not engaged for profit is considered other income. Deductions for expenses related to the activity may be limited (¶ 1195).

Recapture of Charitable Tax Benefits. The recapture of a charitable contribution deduction for property disposed of within three years of contribution (¶ 1062) or the recapture of a charitable contribution deduction relating to the contribution of a partial interest (¶ 1063) is considered other income.

Treasure Trove. Treasure trove or other found property is gross income for the tax year in which it is reduced to undisputed possession, to the extent of its value in U.S. currency (Reg. § 1.61-14).

Virtual Currency. Virtual currency is a digital representation of value that functions as a medium of exchange, a unit of account, or a store of value. Convertible virtual currency (e.g., Bitcoin), which has an equivalent value in or acts as a substitute for real currency, is treated as property for federal tax purposes. Transactions using convertible virtual currency are subject to the general tax principles that apply to property transactions. A taxpayer who receives convertible virtual currency as payment for goods or services must include in gross income the currency's fair market value, measured in U.S. dollars, as of the date it was received. If a taxpayer successfully "mines" convertible virtual currency (e.g., uses computer resources to validate Bitcoin transactions and maintain the public Bitcoin transaction ledger), the currency's fair market value is includible in gross income as of the date of receipt (Notice 2014-21; Rev. Rul. 2019-24).

Sharing Economy. The sharing economy allows individuals and groups to arrange transactions that generate revenue from their assets, such as cars and homes, or from services they provide, such as household chores or technology services. The internet is generally used to connect suppliers to consumers. The sharing economy is also used to connect workers and businesses for short-term work. Income received is generally taxable, even if the recipient does not receive a Form 1099, Form W-2, or some other income statement. Depending upon the circumstances, some or all business expenses may be deductible. Participants in the sharing economy who are employees at another job can often avoid the need to make estimated tax payments by having more tax withheld from their paychecks. The IRS has a website at https://www.irs.gov/businesses/small-businesses-self-employed/sharing-economy-tax-center to help taxpayers involved in the sharing economy quickly locate the resources they need to help them meet their tax obligations (IRS News Release IR-2016-110).

789. Shareholder's or Employee's Bargain Purchase. If an employer transfers property to an employee or an independent contractor at less than its fair market value (FMV), whether or not the transfer is in the form of a sale or exchange, the difference between the amount paid for the property and its FMV at the time of the transfer is income to the purchaser as compensation for personal services (Reg. § 1.61-2(d)(2)). However, qualified employee discounts are excludable from income (¶ 2088). See ¶ 713 for the rules on restricted property transferred in connection with the performance of services.

If a corporation transfers property to a shareholder at less than the property's FMV, the shareholder is treated as having received a distribution from the transferor-corporation and is subject to the general tax rules for including it in income (¶ 733, ¶ 735) (Reg. § 1.301-1(j)). See ¶ 1901 for treatment of securities transactions as potential income.

In computing the gain or loss on a later sale of the property, its basis is the amount paid for the property, increased by the amount previously included in income in the case of the employee or independent contractor, or by the amount of the distribution in the case of the shareholder.

793. Creditor's Financial Income. A cash-basis creditor reports interest on loans or obligations as it is received. An accrual-basis creditor reports this type of interest as it is earned (i.e., over the term of the loan, as installment payments are due, etc.), or when it is received if payment is received earlier than when due (¶ 724).

Rule of 78s. The IRS will *not* give any tax effect to a provision in a loan agreement that provides interest must be allocated in accordance with the Rule of 78s, because that method of allocating interest does not accurately reflect the true cost of borrowing. Under the Rule of 78s, the interest payable for a payment period is determined by multiplying the total interest for the loan by the following fraction: number of payment periods remaining (including the period for which the interest is being determined)/the sum of the digits of the payment periods (Rev. Rul. 87-140).

Loan Commission. A loan commission is taxed to an accrual-basis lender in the year the loan is made. A commission deducted from the face amount of the loan is taxed to a cash-basis lender only when received upon payment of the loan or sale of the obligation (*Charles Schwab Corp.*, CA-9, 99-1 ustc ¶ 50,109).

795. Imputed Interest on Below-Market Interest Loans. Loans that carry little or no interest are generally recharacterized as arm's-length transactions in which the lender is treated as having made to the borrower a demand loan bearing an interest rate that is less than the statutory federal rate of interest, or a term loan in which the loan amount is more than the present value of all payments due under the loan (Code Sec. 7872). Concurrently, there is deemed to be a transfer in the form of gift, dividend, contribution to capital, compensation, or other manner of payment, depending upon the nature of the loan, from the lender to the borrower which, in turn, is retransferred by the borrower to the lender to satisfy the accruing interest. These rules apply to:

- gift loans,
- corporation-shareholder loans,
- compensation loans between employer and employee or between independent contractor and client,
- tax-avoidance loans,
- any below-market interest loans in which the interest arrangement has a significant effect on either the lender's or borrower's tax liability, and
- loans to certain continuing care facilities that are not exempt from the rules.

In the case of a demand loan or a gift loan, the imputed interest amount is deemed to be transferred from the lender to the borrower on the last day of the calendar year of the loan. As for a term loan, other than a gift loan, the imputed amount is deemed to have been transferred on the date the loan was made.

Exceptions. A *de minimis* exception applies to gift loans totalling $10,000 or less between individuals if the loan is not directly attributable to the purchase or carrying of income-producing assets. There is also a $10,000 *de minimis* exception for compensation-related or corporation-shareholder loans that do not have tax avoidance as a principal purpose.

In the case of gift loans between individuals where the total amount outstanding does not exceed $100,000, the amount deemed transferred from the borrower to the lender at the end of the year will be imputed to the lender only to the extent of the borrower's annual net investment income. For this purpose, net investment income is the excess of investment income minus investment expenses, as under the noncorporate deduction for interest paid on investment debt (¶ 1057). If such income does not exceed $1,000, no imputed interest is deemed transferred to the lender.

The below-market interest rate rules also do not apply to below-market loans owed by a facility which, on the last day of the year in which the loan is made, is a qualified

7 INCOME

¶795

continuing care facility, if the loan was made under a continuing care contract, and if the lender or his or her spouse reaches age 62 before the close of the tax year (Code Sec. 7872(h)).

Employee Relocation Loans. In the case of an employer loan to an employee made in connection with the purchase of a principal residence at a new place of work, the applicable federal rate (AFR) for testing the loan is the rate as of the date the written contract to purchase the residence was entered into (Code Sec. 7872(f)(11); Temp. Reg. § 1.7872-5T(c)(1)). Additionally, employee relocation loans meeting certain requirements are exempt from the below-market interest loan rules. The special treatment for employee relocation loans applies only under circumstances in which the moving expense deduction would be allowed (¶ 1073 and ¶ 1075).

799.   Tax Benefit Rule–Recoveries, Refunds, and Reimbursements. The receipt of an amount that was part of a deduction or credit taken in an earlier tax year is considered a recovery and generally must be included, partially or totally, in gross income in the year of receipt (Code Sec. 111; Reg. § 1.111-1). Common types of recoveries are refunds, reimbursements, and rebates. Refunds of federal income taxes are not included in income because the taxes are not allowed as a deduction from income. Interest on amounts recovered is income in the year of the recovery. If the refund or other recovery is for amounts that were paid in separate years, the recovery is allocated between these years.

> **Example 1:** Marcia paid her 2019 estimated state income tax liability of $4,000 in four equal installments in April, June, and September of 2019 and in January of 2020. In May of 2020, she received a $400 refund based on her 2019 state income tax return. Because the tax liability was paid in two years, the amount recovered must be allocated pro rata between the years in which the liability was paid. Since 75 percent of the liability was paid in 2019, 75 percent of the $400 refund ($300) is for amounts paid in 2019 and is a recovery item in 2020 when received. The remaining $100 is offset against the otherwise deductible state tax payments made in 2020.

Itemized Deduction Recoveries. Recoveries of amounts that may be claimed only as itemized deductions (¶ 1014) are not includible in gross income if the taxpayer did not itemize in the prior tax year for which the recovery was received. If a deduction was taken, the includible amount is limited to the amount of the deduction. Thus, the amount of the recovery included in income is the lesser of the amount deducted or the amount recovered.

> **Example 2:** Brent receives a $1,500 medical expense reimbursement in 2019 for expenses incurred in 2018. However, due to the threshold on medical expenses, he claimed only a $450 deduction in 2018. The amount that he must include in income in 2019 is $450.

If an individual's itemized deductions for the prior tax year were reduced or phased-out for tax years beginning before 2018 because adjusted gross income (AGI) exceeded a threshold amount, and the taxpayer recovers all or a portion of the previously deducted amount in a later tax year, the amount includible in income in the year of receipt is the difference between (1) the amount of the prior year's itemized deductions (after the overall limitation has been applied), less (2) the deductions that would have been claimed (i.e., the greater of itemized deductions after the overall limitation or the standard deduction) had the individual paid the proper amount in the prior year and not received a recovery or refund in the later year (Rev. Rul. 93-75).

A taxpayer who recovers an itemized deduction claimed in a prior tax year must generally include in gross income the entire recovered amount in the tax year it is received if, in the prior tax year:

> • itemized deductions exceeded the standard deduction by at least the recovered amount, and were not subject to the phaseout;

> • the deduction for the recovered item equals or exceeds the recovered amount; and

> • the taxpayer had taxable income, had no unused tax credits, and was not subject to the alternative minimum tax.

¶799

If a taxpayer receives a refund of state or local income tax or state or local general sales tax, the entire refund amount must be recovered if, in addition to the three requirements listed above, the excess of the state or local tax that the taxpayer elected to deduct minus the state or local tax that the taxpayer elected not to deduct is more than the refund amount of the tax deducted.

IRS Pub 525 contains a worksheet for computing the amount of a taxable itemized deduction recovery.

Refund of State and Local Taxes. A taxpayer may elect to claim an itemized deduction for state and local sales taxes instead of state and local income taxes (¶ 1021). The maximum state and local tax (SALT) refund amount that may have to be included in gross income in the year the refund is received is limited to the excess of the tax that the taxpayer chose to deduct for the prior tax year minus the tax he or she did not choose to deduct for the prior year (IRS Pub 525). If the taxpayer pays state income taxes in Year 1, and then in Year 2 receives a refund of the state income taxes that were paid in Year 1, the refund is not taxable if, in Year 1, the taxpayer (a) did not itemize deductions, or (b) elected to deduct state and local general sales taxes instead of state and local income taxes (Instructions to Form 1040).

For tax years 2018 to 2025, an individual's SALT deduction on is limited to $10,000 ($5,000 if married filing separately) (¶ 1026). Thus, for refunds from these tax years, a taxpayer must take the limitation into account in determining their tax benefit (Rev. Rul. 2019-11).

Nonitemized Deduction Recoveries. A taxpayer that receives a recovery of a prior year deduction amount that was not required to be itemized must include the recovery amount in income in the year of receipt, but only up to the amount of the deduction that reduced the taxpayer's income tax in the prior year. If the taxpayer has both itemized and nonitemized recoveries, the amount includible in income is determined by first figuring the amount of the nonitemized recovery to include in income, adding that amount to AGI, then determining the amount of the itemized recovery to include in income (IRS Pub 525).

Amounts Recovered for Credits. If a taxpayer claims a tax credit in a prior tax year, other than the foreign tax credit (¶ 2475) or investment tax credit (¶ 1465A), and during the current tax year there is a downward price adjustment or a similar adjustment on the item for which the credit was claimed, the taxpayer's income tax for the current year is increased by the amount of the credit that is attributable to the adjustment (Code Sec. 111(b)). There is no tax increase if the credit did not reduce income tax in the prior year.

Chapter 8
EXCLUSIONS FROM GROSS INCOME

Exclusions from Gross Income

See CCH® AnswerConnect: *Gross Income: Exclusions* for more information on this topic.

801. Exclusions from Gross Income. Gross income includes all income that is not specifically excludable by statute or administrative and judicial decisions. In addition to the items listed in Code Secs. 101—140, the following are excludable from gross income:

- items of income that, under the U.S. Constitution, are not taxable by the federal government;

- items of income that are exempt from tax under the provisions of any act of Congress not inconsistent with, or repealed by, the revenue acts; and

- items that are nontaxable under the provisions of foreign tax treaties designed to prevent double taxation.

These exclusions and exemptions should not be confused with deductions from gross income (i.e., losses, expenses, bad debts, etc.) which must be shown on a tax return. An exclusion generally does *not* have to be shown on a return.

Life Insurance and Death Benefits

See CCH® AnswerConnect: *Gross Income: Life Insurance Proceeds* for more information on this topic.

803. Life Insurance Proceeds Excluded from Gross Income. A taxpayer generally may exclude from gross income the proceeds of a life insurance contract paid by reason of the death of the insured. This is the case regardless of whether they represent the return of premiums paid, the increased value of the policy due to investment, or the death benefit feature—the policy proceeds exceeding the value of the contract immediately prior to the death of the insured (Code Sec. 101); Reg. § § 1.101-1(a) and 1.101-3). It is immaterial whether the proceeds are received in a single sum or otherwise, but if the proceeds are left with the insurer under an agreement to pay interest, any interest earned and paid is income to the recipient. For example, if the beneficiary receives the proceeds in installments, any interest accruing on the proceeds after the date of the insured's death is included in the beneficiary's gross income (Code Sec. 101(d); Reg. § 1.101-4).

There is also a limit on the amount of proceeds of a company-owned life insurance (COLI) contract that may be excluded from gross income (¶ 804). If a life insurance policy is transferred for value in a taxable exchange, the amount excludable from gross income is limited to the consideration, premiums, or other amounts paid by the transferee (¶ 807).

A contract must qualify as a life insurance contract under applicable state or foreign law and meet either a cash value accumulation test or a guideline premium/cash value corridor test (Code Sec. 7702). If a contract does not satisfy at least one of these tests, it will be treated as a combination of term insurance and a currently taxable deposit fund, and the policyholder must treat income on the contract as ordinary income in any year paid or accrued.

Amounts received before the insured's death under a life insurance contract on the life of a terminally or chronically ill individual are excludable from gross income (Code Sec. 101(g)). For chronically, but not terminally, ill individuals, the exclusion is subject to a maximum amount per day, adjusted annually for inflation ($370 for 2019 and $380 for 2020), under policies that pay a set amount each day known as per diem policies (Rev. Proc. 2018-57; Rev. Proc. 2019-44). If a portion of a life insurance contract benefit is assigned or sold to a viatical settlement provider, any amount received from the sale or assignment is generally excludable. A viatical settlement provider is a person who meets certain requirements and is regularly engaged in the business of purchasing or accepting assignment of life insurance contracts on the lives of terminally or chronically ill.

804. Company-Owned Life Insurance (COLI). The exclusion of life insurance proceeds from gross income (¶ 803) is limited for proceeds paid due to an employee's death from company-owned life insurance (COLI) contracts issued after August 17, 2006 (Code Sec. 101(j); Notice 2009-48). The applicable policyholder, the employer, or a related person generally may not exclude more than the total premiums and other amounts paid by the policyholder, and must include any excess death benefits in gross income.

The income inclusion rule does not apply to an amount received by reason of the death of the following insured individuals who are U.S. citizens or resident aliens if notice and consent requirements are satisfied: (1) an employee of the applicable policyholder at any time during the 12-month period before the insured's death; or (2) an individual who at the time the contract was issued was a director, highly compensated employee (¶ 2114) determined without regard to the election regarding the top-paid 20 percent of employees, or a highly compensated individual (¶ 2017) who is in the group of the highest paid 35 percent of employees. An officer, director, or highly compensated employee is an employee for these purposes.

The inclusion rule also does not apply if notice and consent requirements are satisfied with respect to proceeds paid to:

- a member of the insured's family (¶ 1717),

- any designated beneficiary of the insured other than the applicable policyholder,

- a trust established for the benefit of the insured's family or a designated beneficiary, or

- the estate of the insured.

The rule also does not apply to proceeds that are used to buy an equity interest, or capital or profits interest, in the policyholder from the insured's heir.

Notice and Consent. To keep excess benefits from being included in income, the policyholder must satisfy the following notice and consent requirements before the issuance of the insurance contract:

- the employee must be notified in writing that the policyholder intends to insure the life of the employee and of the maximum face amount for which the employee can be insured;

- the employee must provide written consent to being insured under the contract and acknowledge that such coverage may continue after the insured terminates employment; and

- the employee must be informed in writing that an applicable policyholder will be a beneficiary of any proceeds payable upon death of the employee.

Annual Reporting. The policyholder must also satisfy annual reporting and record retention requirements (Code Sec. 6039I; Reg. § 1.6039I-1; Notice 2009-48). A policyholder satisfies the reporting requirements by attaching Form 8925 to it's tax return.

¶804

807. Transfers of Life Insurance Policies. If a life insurance policy is transferred for value (¶ 845), payments on account of the death of the insured are not excluded from gross income and must be included in income of the transferee to the extent that they exceed the consideration, premiums, and other amounts paid (Code Sec. 101(a)(2); Reg. § 1.101-1(b)). If the policy is transferred as a tax-free exchange or gift, the donor's investment basis in the contract is carried over to the donee, and the death benefits are excludable from gross income. The benefits are also excludable if the contract is transferred to the insured, a partner of the insured, a partnership including the insured, or a corporation in which the insured is a shareholder or officer.

For transfers after December 31, 2017, the above exceptions do not apply if the transfer is a reportable policy sale and some portion of the death benefit under such contracts may be includible in gross income (Code Sec. 101(a)(3); Reg. § 1.101-1(c); Reg. § 1.101-6(b)). A reportable policy sale is the acquisition of an interest in a life insurance contract, directly or indirectly, if the acquirer has no substantial family, business, or financial relationship with the insured apart from the acquirer's interest in such life insurance contract. Acquisitions of life insurance contracts in reportable policy sales and payments of reportable death benefits under the contracts are reported on Form 1099-LS and Form 1099-SB, respectively (Code Sec. 6050Y).

809. Life Insurance Dividends. Amounts received from an annuity policy prior to the annuity starting date in the nature of dividends, or return of premiums or other consideration, are not includible in gross income until the amounts received exceed the aggregate of premiums or other consideration paid or deemed to have been paid for the annuity. Amounts received in the nature of dividends after the start date of the annuity may be included in gross income (¶ 823) (Code Sec. 72(e); Reg. § 1.72-11(b)).

813. Death Benefits of Public Safety Officers. A survivor annuity paid to the spouse, former spouse, or child of a public safety officer killed in the line of duty is excludable from the recipient's gross income if the annuity is provided under a governmental plan (Code Sec. 101(h)). See ¶ 851 for a discussion of death benefits of public safety officers not paid as an annuity. Gross income also does not include amounts paid by an employer by reason of the death of an employee who is a specified terrorist victim or an astronaut killed in the line of duty. The exclusion applies to death benefits from a qualified plan that satisfy the incidental death benefit rule (Code Sec. 101(i)).

Annuities

See CCH® AnswerConnect: *Annuities* for more information on this topic.

817. Annuity Payments Excluded from Gross Income. Amounts received as an annuity under any annuity, endowment, or life insurance contract, and paid out for reasons other than death of the insured, are excludable from gross income to the extent of the taxpayer's basis in the contract (Code Sec. 72; Reg. § 1.72-1). The tax-free portion of the income is spread evenly over the annuitant's life expectancy. However, for contracts with an annuity starting date before 1987 the exclusion remains the same no matter how long the annuitant lives. The annuity rules also apply to contracts whose payments are made over a prescribed number of years. See ¶ 891 for a discussion of annuities of Armed Forces members.

A contract, with certain exceptions, will not be treated as an annuity contract unless it provides that: (1) if the contract holder dies on or after the annuity starting date, but before the entire interest in the contract is distributed, the remainder must be distributed at least as rapidly as under the method used as of the day the holder died, and (2) the entire interest in the contract must be distributed within five years of the holder's death (Code Sec. 72(s)).

To determine the portion of the annuity that is excludable from the recipient's gross income, an exclusion ratio is to be determined for each contract (¶ 819). This ratio is usually determined by dividing the investment in the contract by the expected return (Code Sec. 72(b); Reg. §§ 1.72-2 and 1.72-4). The exclusion ratio is then applied to the total amount received as an annuity during the tax year. Any excess amount over the portion determined by the application of the exclusion ratio is includible in the recipient's gross income. In the case of distributions from an individual retirement account (IRA), the exclusion ratio is determined by dividing the individual's total nondeductible contributions by the balance of the account. For this purpose, all of an individual's IRAs and distributions during a year are aggregated (¶ 2165). A nontaxable distribution of IRA assets is reported on Form 8606 (Instructions to Form 8606; IRS Pub 590-B).

For annuities with a starting date *after* 1986, the exclusion of a portion of each annuity payment cannot be continued indefinitely. Once the total of all exclusions taken for payments under the annuity contract equals the investment in the contract, all subsequent payments are included in gross income in full. If the annuitant dies before the investment in the contract is fully recovered tax free through the annuity exclusion, a deduction is provided for the annuitant's last year in an amount equal to the unrecovered portion of the investment.

Partial Annuitization of Annuity Contracts. If any amount is received as an annuity for a period of 10 years or more or for the lives of one or more individuals under any portion of an annuity, endowment, or life insurance contract, then that portion of the contract is treated as a separate contract (Code Sec. 72(a)(2)). Thus, a portion of the contract may be annuitized, while the balance is not annuitized. In these cases, the investment in the contract is allocated on a pro rata basis between each portion of the contract from which amounts are received as an annuity and the portion of the contract from which amounts are not received as an annuity. The allocation is made for purposes of applying:

- the rules relating to the exclusion ratio (¶ 819);
- the definitions of the investment in the contract (¶ 821), the expected return (¶ 825), and the annuity starting date (¶ 823); and
- the rules for amounts not received as an annuity.

In addition, a separate annuity starting date is determined with respect to each portion of the contract from which amounts are received as an annuity.

819. Exclusion Ratio Formula for Annuity Contracts. The excludable portion of an annuity payment is the annuity payment multiplied by the exclusion ratio (¶ 817) (Code Sec. 72(b); Reg. §§ 1.72-2 and 1.72-4). The remainder is taxable to the recipients, whether they are the primary annuitant or a secondary annuitant under a joint annuity or joint and survivor annuity. The exclusion ratio is the investment in the contract (¶ 821) divided by the expected return (¶ 825) under the contract as of the annuity starting date (¶ 823). For example, if as of the annuity starting date a taxpayer's investment in an annuity contract is $6,000 and the expected return is $10,000, then the exclusion ratio is $6,000/$10,000 or 60 percent. If the taxpayer receives a monthly annuity payment of $200, then the monthly exclusion is $120 ($200 × 60 percent). If the first payment an annuitant receives from an annuity is for a fractional part of a year, the annuitant need only determine the exclusion ratio as a percentage and apply it to the payment received for the fractional part of the payment period, resulting in the amount of the annuitant's exclusion for the tax year.

821. Investment in Annuity Contracts. In determining the exclusion ratio for an annuity (¶ 819), the investment in the contract generally is the total amount of premiums or other consideration paid for the contract, less amounts, if any, received before the annuity starting date and not included in gross income (Code Sec. 72(c)(1); Reg. § 1.72-6). However, a self-employed individual may not include the deductible costs of purchasing insurance as part of his or her investment in the contract (Code Sec. 72(m)(2); Reg. § 1.72-17A(c)). A special adjustment is also provided for a refund annuity (¶ 837). Special rules apply for computing an employee's investment in an annuity received through an employer (¶ 2143).

Nonresident Aliens. Certain employer or employee contributions made by or on behalf of a nonresident alien are not considered part of the individual's investment in the contract. The excluded contributions are those:

- made with respect to compensation for labor or services by an employee who was a nonresident alien at the time the labor or services were performed and treated as from sources outside the United States; and
- that were not subject to tax by the United States or a foreign country but would have been subject to tax if paid in cash.

Contributions to a foreign pension plan are included in the calculation of the participant's basis only if the participant has been subject to tax on the contribution by the United States or a foreign country (Code Sec. 72(w)).

823. Annuity Starting Date. In determining the exclusion ratio for an annuity (¶ 819), the annuity starting date is the first day of the first period for which an amount is received as an annuity under the contract. This is the later of:

- the date upon which the obligations of the contract become fixed; or

- the first day of the period (year, half-year, quarter, or month, depending on whether the payments are made annually, semi-annually, quarterly, or monthly) that ends on the date of the first annuity payment (Code Sec. 72(c)(4); Reg. § 1.72-4(b)).

825. Expected Return for Annuity Contracts. In determining the exclusion ratio for an annuity (¶ 819), the expected return under the contract is limited to amounts receivable as an annuity or as annuities. If no life expectancy is involved, as in the case of installment payments for a fixed number of years, the expected return is found by totaling the amounts to be received (Code Sec. 72(c)(3); Reg. § 1.72-5(a) and (c)). To determine the expected return under contracts involving life expectancy, actuarial tables prescribed by the IRS must be used. The tables provide a multiplier, based on life expectancy, that is applied to the annual payment to obtain the expected return under the contract (Reg. § 1.72-9).

The expected return will vary depending on when contributions were made and when amounts were received as an annuity. Gender-neutral tables must be used if the total investment in the contract is made after June 30, 1986. If there was an investment in the contract as of June 30, 1986, and there has been a further investment in the contract after that date, an individual may elect to calculate the exclusion under a special rule. Under this rule, an exclusion amount is calculated using the gender-based tables—as if the investment in the contract as of June 30, 1986, were the only investment in the contract. Then a second exclusion is calculated, using the gender-neutral tables, as if the post-June 30, 1986, investment were the only investment. The two exclusion amounts are then added together to produce the final exclusion. Although the gender-based annuity tables formerly in effect must generally still be used if all contributions were made prior to June 30, 1986, an election may be made to use the updated tables if the annuity payments are received after June 30, 1986 (Reg. §§ 1.72-5 and 1.72-6).

Example 1: Aaron purchases for $8,000 an annuity that provides him payments of $50 per month for life. At the annuity starting date, his age at his nearest birthday is 64 years. Table V (gender-neutral) in Reg. § 1.72-9 must be used since all investment in the contract is post-June 1986. The table shows that for an individual of Aaron's age, the multiple to be used in computing the expected return is 20.8. Aaron's expected return and annual exclusion are computed as follows. The annual payment is $600 ($50 per month x 12 months). The Table V multiple is 20.8. The expected return is $12,480 ($600 x 20.8). The exclusion ratio is 8,000/12,480 or 64.10%. The annual exclusion is $384.60 (64.10% of $600).

If payments under the contract are made quarterly, semiannually, or annually, or if the interval between the annuity starting date and the date of the first payment is less than the interval between future payments, an adjustment of the multiple found in the actuarial tables may be required (Reg. § 1.72-5).

Example 2: Assume the same facts as in Example 1 above, except that Aaron receives $300 payments semiannually. He receives the first payment six full months from the annuity starting date. The actuarial table in Reg. § 1.72-5 shows the adjustment to be "-.2". Therefore, Aaron's multiple from Table V, 20.8, is adjusted by subtracting 0.2. His adjusted multiple then is 20.6, and his expected return and semiannual exclusion are computed as follows. The annual payment is $600 ($300 x 2). The Table V multiple is 20.6. The expected return is $12,360 ($600 x 20.6). The exclusion ratio is 8,000/12,360 or 64.72%. The semiannual exclusion is $194.16 (64.72% of $300).

A simpler computation may be used, but only if the annuity amount does not vary from year to year. This computation determines the annual exclusion by dividing the taxpayer's investment in the contract by the appropriate multiple from the actuarial tables.

>   **Example 3:** Assume the same facts as in Example 1 above. Aaron's annual exclusion is computed as follows. The cost of the annuity is $8,000. The annual payment is $600 ($50 per month x 12 months. The Table V multiple is 20.8. The annual exclusion is $385 (8,000/20.8). Annual taxable income is $215 ($600 – $385).

827. Joint and Survivor Annuities and Joint Annuities. In the case of a joint and survivor annuity contract that provides the first annuitant with a fixed monthly income for life, and after his or her death provides an identical monthly income for life to the second annuitant, the multiple used in computing expected return is found in Table II (gender-based) or Table VI (gender-neutral) under the ages of the living annuitants as of the annuity starting date (Reg. § 1.72-5(b)).

>   **Example:** Bryce purchases a joint and survivor annuity providing for payments of $200 a month to be made to Bryce for life and upon his death, to his wife Celina during her lifetime. At the annuity starting date Bryce's age at his nearest birthday is 68 and Celina's is 66. The annuity cost is $44,710. Using Table VI (gender-neutral) from Reg. § 1.72-5(b), the expected return is as follows. The annual payment is $2,400 ($200 per month x 12 months). The Table VI multiple (age 68, age 66) is 23.3. The expected return is $55,920 ($2,400 x 23.3). The annual exclusion ratio is 79.95% (44,710/55,920). The annual exclusion is $1,918.80 (79.95% of $2,400).

If a joint and survivor annuity provides for a different monthly income, rather than an identical monthly income, payable to the second annuitant, there is a special computation of expected return that involves the use of both Table I and Table II, or Table V and Table VI, whichever are applicable. If a contract involving two annuitants provides for fixed monthly payments to be made as a joint life annuity until the death of the first annuitant—in other words, only as long as both remain alive—the expected return for the contract is determined under either Table IIA or Table VIA, whichever is applicable. Adjustment of the multiple obtained from the annuity tables, as explained at ¶ 825 for single life annuities, may also be necessary for joint and survivor annuities and joint annuities if payments are made less often than monthly or if the first payment is accelerated.

829. Multiple, Variable, and Temporary Life Annuities. To compute the exclusion ratio (¶ 819) for a contract that is acquired for a single consideration and that provides for the payment of two or more annuity obligations or elements, the investment in the contract is divided by the aggregate of the expected returns under all the annuity elements (Reg. § § 1.72-4(e), 1.72-5(e), and 1.72-6(b)). In the case of variable annuities, a special rule is provided for determining the portion of each payment to be an amount received as an annuity and excludable from gross income each year (Reg. § 1.72-2(b)(3)). The computation of the expected return for temporary life annuities is determined by multiplying the total of the annuity payments to be received annually by the multiple shown in Table IV or Table VIII of Reg. § 1.72-9, whichever is applicable. The computation uses the annuitant's age as of the annuity starting date, and if applicable, the annuitant's gender and the nearest whole number of years in the specified period (Reg. § 1.72-5(a)(3), (4), and (5)).

837. Adjustment in Annuity Contracts for Refund Features. If an annuity contract has a refund feature, including a contract for a life annuity with a minimum period of payments, an adjustment must be made to the original investment in the contract when determining the exclusion ratio (¶ 819). The original investment in the contract must be reduced by the value of the refund payment or minimum payments as of the annuity starting date (Code Sec. 72(b)(4) and (c); Reg. § 1.72-7). The computation of the adjustment is detailed and involves the use of Table III (gender-based) or Table VII (gender-neutral) of Reg. § 1.72-9. An annuity contract generally contains a refund feature if:

8

EXCLUSIONS

- the annuity payments depend, in whole or in part, upon the continuing life of one or more persons;

- there are payments on or after the death of the annuitant if a specified amount or a stated number of payments has not been made prior to death; and

- the payments are in the nature of a refund of the consideration paid.

839. Annuity Distributions from Qualified Retirement Plans. Amounts received as an annuity from qualified retirement plans for employees under Code Sec. 401(a), employee annuities under Code Sec. 403(a), and annuity contracts under Code Sec. 403(b) are subject to a simplified method for computing the taxable and tax-free portion of the distributions (Code Sec. 72(d); Notice 98-2). The investment in the contract (¶ 821) for this purpose is determined without regard to the adjustment made for a refund feature (¶ 837). Adjustments take into account the basis on which the payments are made if not made on a monthly basis. Employee contributions under a defined contribution plan may be treated as a separate contract. Railroad Retirement Act Tier 2 benefits received by retired railroad workers and their survivors are treated in the same manner as pension plan benefits paid by private employers (Code Sec. 72(r)).

For annuity starting dates after December 31, 1997, if the annuity is payable over the lives of more than one individual, the number of anticipated payments is listed in the table below:

Combined Age of Annuitants	Number of Anticipated Payments
110 and under	410
More than 110 but not more than 120	360
More than 120 but not more than 130	310
More than 130 but not more than 140	260
More than 140	210

The number of anticipated payments listed in the table above is based on the employee's age on the annuity starting date. If the number of payments is fixed under the terms of the annuity, that number is to be used rather than the number of anticipated payments listed in the table.

Example 1: At retirement, Jeff, age 65, begins receiving retirement benefits in the form of a joint and 50-percent survivor annuity to be paid for the joint lives of Jeff and his wife, Jan, age 59. Jeff's annuity starting date is January 1, 2019. Jeff contributed $24,000 to the plan and has received no distributions prior to the annuity starting date. He will receive a monthly retirement benefit of $1,000, and his wife Jan will receive a monthly survivor benefit of $500 upon his death. Jeff's investment in the contract is $24,000 (the after-tax contributions to the plan). The set number of monthly payments will be 310 (Jeff's age plus Jan's age at the starting date of the annuity equals 124). The tax-free portion of each $1,000 monthly annuity payment to Jeff is $77.42, determined by dividing Jeff's investment ($24,000) by the number of monthly payments (310). If Jeff has not recovered the full $24,000 investment at his death, Jan will exclude $77.42 from each $500 monthly annuity payment. Any annuity payments received after 310 payments have been made will be includible in gross income. If Jeff and Jan die before 310 payments have been made, a deduction is allowed on the survivor's last income tax return in the amount of the unrecovered investment.

The simplified method does not apply if the primary annuitant has attained age 75 on the annuity starting date unless there are fewer than five years of guaranteed payments under the annuity. Also, if in connection with commencement of annuity payments, the recipient receives a lump-sum payment that is not part of the annuity stream, then the payment is taxed under the annuity rules of Code Sec. 72(e) as if received before the annuity starting date and the investment in the contract used to calculate the simplified exclusion ratio for the annuity payments is reduced by the amount of the payment.

Pre-November 19, 1996, Annuities. The IRS provides an elective alternative to application of the usual annuity rules for distributions from qualified plans if the annuity starting date is before November 19, 1996 (Notice 88-118). Distributees who elected to use this method are considered to have complied with Code Sec. 72(b). Payors may also use this method to report the taxable portion of the annuity payments on Form 1099-R. The safe-harbor method may be used *only* if the following three conditions are met:

• the annuity payments depend upon the life of the distributee or the joint lives of the distributee and beneficiary;

• the annuity payments are made from an employee plan qualified under Code Sec. 401(a), an employee annuity under Code Sec. 403(a), or an annuity contract under Code Sec. 403(b); and

• the distributee is less than age 75 when annuity payments commence or, if the distributee is age 75 or older, there are fewer than five years of guaranteed payments.

Under the safe-harbor method, the total number of monthly annuity payments expected to be received is based on the distributee's age at the annuity starting date rather than on the life expectancy tables in Reg. § 1.72-9. The same expected number of payments applies to a distributee whether the individual is receiving a single life annuity or a joint and survivor annuity. These payments are set forth in the following table:

Age of Distributee	Number of Payments
55 and under	300
56-60	260
61-65	240
66-70	170
71 and over	120

Under the safe-harbor method, the distributee recovers the investment in the contract in level amounts over the number of monthly payments determined from the above table. The portion of each monthly annuity payment that is excluded from gross income by a distributee who uses the safe-harbor method for income tax purposes is a level dollar amount determined by dividing the investment in the contract, including any applicable death benefit exclusion, by the set number of annuity payments from the above table as follows:

$$\frac{\text{Investment}}{\text{Number of monthly payments}} = \frac{\text{Tax-free}}{\text{portion of}} \atop \text{monthly annuity}$$

For distributees with annuity starting dates after 1986, annuity payments received after the investment is recovered, usually after the set number of payments has been received, are fully includible in gross income.

> **Example 2:** Assume the same facts as in Example 1 above, except Jeff's annuity start date was January 1, 1996. Under the safe-harbor method, Jeff's investment in the contract is $24,000 (the after-tax contributions to the plan). The set number of monthly payments for a distributee who is age 65 is 240. The tax-free portion of each $1,000 monthly annuity payment to Jeff is $100, determined by dividing Jeff's investment ($24,000) by the number of monthly payments (240). If Jeff has not recovered the full $24,000 investment at his death, Jan will also exclude $100 from each $500 monthly annuity payment. Any annuity payments received after 240 payments have been made will be fully includible in gross income. If Jeff and Jan die before 240 payments have been made, a deduction is allowed on the survivor's last income tax return in the amount of the unrecovered investment.

The dollar amount is excluded from each monthly payment even if the annuity payment amount changes. If the amount excluded is greater than the amount of the monthly annuity, because of decreased survivor payments, each monthly annuity payment is excluded completely until the entire investment is recovered. If annuity payments cease before the set number of payments has been made, a deduction for the unrecovered investment is allowed on the distributee's last tax return. If payments are made to multiple beneficiaries, the excludable amount is based on the oldest beneficiary's age. A pro rata portion is excluded by each beneficiary.

841. Distributions in Full Discharge of Annuity Contracts. Any amount received, whether in a single sum or otherwise, under an annuity, endowment, or life insurance contract in full discharge of the obligation under the contract as a refund of the consideration paid for the contract or any amount received under such contract on its complete surrender, redemption, or maturity is includible in gross income to the extent the amounts exceed the investment in the contract (Code Sec. 72(e); Reg. § 1.72-11). The remainder is taxable to the recipient, whether the recipient is the primary annuitant or a secondary annuitant under a joint annuity or joint and survivor annuity. A penalty is imposed on a policyholder who receives a premature distribution (for example, before age 59½ unless one of a number of exceptions such as death or disability applies) (Code Sec. 72(q)).

843. Installment Options for Annuity Contracts. If an insured elects under an option in an insurance contract to receive the proceeds as an annuity instead of a lump sum, and the election is made within 60 days after the day on which the lump sum first became payable, no part of it is includible in gross income under the doctrine of constructive receipt (Code Sec. 72(h); Reg. § 1.72-12). The installment payments are taxed in accordance with the annuity rules (¶ 817).

845. Transfer of Annuity Contracts. If a life insurance, endowment, or annuity contract is transferred for a valuable consideration, and the proceeds of the contract are paid to the transferee for reasons other than the death of the insured (for example, on surrender, redemption, or maturity of the contract), the transferee, including a beneficiary of, or the estate of, a transferee, is treated as follows:

- if the proceeds are received as an annuity or in installments for a fixed period, the transferee computes the amount excludable from gross income under the exclusion ratio formula (¶ 819); or

- if the proceeds are received in a lump sum, the transferee includes in gross income only that portion of the proceeds in excess of the consideration paid.

Regardless of how the proceeds are received and included in gross income, the transferee's consideration paid consists of the actual value of the consideration paid for the transfer, plus the amount of premiums or other consideration paid after the transfer. This transferee rule, however, does not apply if the transferred contract has a basis for gain or loss in the hands of the transferee determined by reference to the transferor's basis, as in the case of a gift or tax-free exchange (Code Sec. 72(g); Reg. § 1.72-10).

A loss realized upon the surrender or forfeiture of an annuity contract by the original purchaser is deductible as an ordinary loss under Code Sec. 165, the basis of the contract being its cost less the amounts previously excluded from gross income (Rev. Rul. 61-201). For tax years beginning before 2018 and after 2025, the loss is deducted as a miscellaneous itemized deduction subject to the two-percent-of-adjusted-gross-income limitation (¶ 1079) (IRS Pub. 575). No miscellaneous itemized deductions subject to the two-percent-AGI limit may be claimed in tax years 2018 through 2025.

Bequests and Gifts

847. Bequests Excluded from Gross Income. The value of property acquired by bequest, devise, or inheritance is excludable from gross income (Code Sec. 102; Reg. § 1.102-1). The exclusion does not apply to income flowing from the property. For example, amounts received as investment income from the property or as profit from the sale of the property are not excludable. The exclusion also does not apply if the bequest consists of income from property. Thus, a bequest of annual rent from the testator's property for 10 years is taxable income to the beneficiary. The beneficiary is required to include in gross income each year the amount of the annual rent. The basis of any real or personal property acquired from a decedent is generally its fair market value on the date of the decedent's death (¶ 1633).

A bequest of a specific sum of money or specific property from an estate or trust may be excluded from the beneficiary's gross income if it is paid or credited all at once or in not more than three installments (Code Sec. 663(a)(1); Reg. § 1.663(a)-1). An amount which is paid from the estate or trust income may qualify as a bequest for this purpose if the amount could have been paid from either income or principal. However, an amount that can only be paid from the estate or trust income is not treated as a bequest and thus *not* excludable from gross income even when paid in less than four installments.

849. Gifts Excluded from Gross Income. The value of a gift is excludable from gross income, but *any income* from the gift, including profit upon sale, is includible in gross income (Code Sec. 102). A gift of income from the property of an estate or trust is not excluded from gross income except in the case of a gift of a specific sum or specific property paid or credited all at once or in not more than three installments (¶ 847). The basis of any property acquired by gift is generally the same as it would be in the hands of the donor (¶ 1630).

Tips are not gifts and are therefore includible in gross income (¶ 717). Food, clothing, and rent payments furnished as strike benefits by a labor union to a needy worker participating in a strike may be considered gifts. In determining whether a gift was made, the fact that benefits were paid only to union members is not controlling (*A. Kaiser*, SCt, 60-2 ustc ¶ 9517).

The exclusion from gross income applicable to the value of property acquired by gift does not apply to any amount transferred by or for an employer to, or for the benefit of, an employee (Code Sec. 102(c)). However, certain employee achievement awards (¶ 2069) and certain fringe benefits provided by employers are excludable (¶ 2085).

Personal Injury and Disability Proceeds

See CCH® AnswerConnect: *Gross Income: Awards, Damages, Recoveries, Illegal Activities and Other* for more information on this topic.

851. Workers' Compensation and Occupational Disability Benefits. Compensation received under a workers' compensation act for personal injuries or sickness, and amounts received by a taxpayer under a policy of accident and health insurance, are excludable from gross income (Code Sec. 104(a)(1); Reg. § 1.104-1). The exclusion also applies to benefits having the characteristics of life insurance proceeds paid under a workers' compensation act to the survivors of a deceased employee (Reg. § 1.101-1(a)). See ¶ 2025 for a discussion of disability income plans.

Amounts received as a pension, annuity, or similar allowance for personal injuries or sickness resulting from active service in the armed forces of any country, the National Oceanic and Atmospheric Administration (formerly the Coast and Geodetic Survey) or the Public Health Service, or as a disability annuity payable under section 808 of the Foreign Service Act of 1980, are also excludable from gross income (Code Sec. 104(a)(4) and (b); Reg. § 1.104-1). The exclusion generally is limited to amounts received for combat-related injury or illness. However, it will not be less than the maximum amount of disability compensation from the Department of Veterans Affairs to which the individual is, or would be, entitled upon application.

Benefits that are payable under state law for occupational injury or illness arising out of employment are excludable if the benefits are in the nature of workers' compensation payments (Reg. § 1.104-1(b)). No fault insurance disability benefits received by a passenger injured in an automobile accident under the automobile owner's policy as compensation for loss of income or earning capacity are also excludable from gross income (Rev. Rul. 73-155).

If an otherwise excludable amount is for reimbursement of medical expenses previously deducted for tax purposes, the amount must be included in gross income to the extent of the prior deduction. The IRS has ruled that if a portion of an award is specifically allocated to future injury-related medical expenses, the future expenses must be offset by the awarded portion (Rev. Rul. 79-427). However, the Ninth Circuit Court of Appeals ruled that where there is no express allocation of a lump-sum personal injury award to future medical expenses, no offset is required (*K.R. Niles*, CA-9, 83-2 ustc ¶ 9477).

Terrorist Attacks. Disability income received by an individual for injuries received in a terrorist attack while the individual was performing services as a U.S. employee outside the United States is also excludable from gross income (Code Sec. 104(a)(5)).

Death Benefits Received by Beneficiaries of Public Safety Officers. Death benefits or other amounts received by qualified beneficiaries or surviving dependents of a public safety officer who died as the direct and proximate result of a personal injury sustained in the line of duty are excludable from gross income (Code Sec. 104(a)(6)). There is no

8

EXCLUSIONS

requirement that the amounts be received under a workers' compensation statute. See ¶ 813 for a discussion of death benefits received as an annuity by beneficiaries of public safety officers.

852. Damages for Personal Injuries or Sickness. Amounts received as damages, other than punitive damages, on account of *personal physical injuries or sickness* are excludable from gross income (Code Sec. 104(a)(2)). Damages for emotional distress, including the physical symptoms of emotional distress, may not be treated as damages on account of a personal physical injury or sickness, except to the extent of amounts paid for medical care attributable to emotional distress. For example, back pay received in satisfaction of a claim for denial of a promotion due to employment discrimination is not excludable because it is completely independent of, and *not* damages received on account of, personal physical injuries or sickness (Rev. Rul. 96-65).

Interest and Punitive Damage Awards. Interest included in an award of damages for personal injury is includible in gross income (*M. Brabson*, CA-10, 96-1 ustc ¶ 50,038). Also, punitive damages arising out of personal physical injury action are generally includible in gross income (Code Sec. 104(a)(2) and (c)). Punitive damages may be excludable from income if received in a civil action for wrongful death and the applicable state law provides that *only* punitive damages may be awarded.

Attorney's Fees. The full amount of a litigant's award, including the attorney's contingent fee, regardless of whether paid directly to the attorney or to the individual, is includible in the litigant's gross income under the anticipatory assignment of income theory (*J.W. Banks II*, SCt, 2005-1 ustc ¶ 50,155). See ¶ 973 and ¶ 1093 for a discussion of the deduction of business legal expenses and nonbusiness legal expenses, respectively.

Discharge of Debt

See CCH® AnswerConnect: *Discharge of Debt* for more information on this topic.

855. Cancellation or Discharge of Debt Income. A taxpayer generally realizes income equal to the portion of a debt that is cancelled or discharged other than as a gift or bequest (Code Sec. 61(a)(11); Reg. § 1.61-12). However, income from the discharge of a debt may be excluded from gross income for:

- a debt discharge in a bankruptcy action under Title 11 of the U.S. Code in which the taxpayer is under the jurisdiction of the court and the discharge is either granted by, or is under a plan approved by, the court;

- a discharge when the taxpayer is insolvent outside bankruptcy;

- a discharge of qualified farm indebtedness;

- a discharge of qualified real property business indebtedness;

- a discharge of qualified principal residence indebtedness occurring before January 1, 2021;

- a discharge of a student loan provided the student works for a certain period of time in certain professions for any of a broad class of employers; eligible student loan discharges for students of certain closed schools (Rev. Proc. 2020-11); or for discharges of eligible student loans in 2018 through 2025, due to the student's death or total and permanent disability (Code Sec. 108, as amended by the Taxpayer Certainty and Disaster Tax Relief Act of 2019 (P.L. 116-94)); and

- Paycheck Protection Program loans made through the Small Business Administration that are forgiven (Act Sec. 1106(i) of the Coronavirus Aid, Relief, and Economic Security (CARES) Act (P.L. 116-136)).

Form 982 is filed with a debtor's income tax return to report excludable income from the discharge of a debt.

A corporation that satisfies a debt by transferring corporate stock to its creditor, or a partnership that transfers a capital or profits interest in the partnership to a creditor, is treated as if it has paid the creditor with money equal to the fair market value of the stock or interest. The corporation or partnership has income from discharge of debt to the extent that the principal of the debt exceeds the value of the stock or partnership interest and any other property transferred (Code Sec. 108(e)(8) and (e)(10)). A similar rule applies to corporate or noncorporate debtors issuing debt instruments in satisfaction of debt.

Discharge of debt income can result even if the cancelled debt is nonrecourse (no individual is personally liable for repayment of the debt). If property securing a nonrecourse debt is transferred in exchange for cancellation of the debt, such as a foreclosure sale, the amount realized from the sale or exchange includes the principal amount of the debt discharged. The IRS has ruled that the reduction of the principal amount of a nonrecourse note by a holder who was not the seller of the property results in the realization of discharge of debt income, even if there is no disposition of the property (Rev. Rul. 91-31).

Effect of Exclusion on Tax Attributes. When an amount is excluded from gross income as the result of a discharge of debt in a Title 11 bankruptcy case, insolvency, or qualified farm indebtedness, a taxpayer is required to reduce its tax attributes. The reduction in the foreign tax credit, minimum tax credit, passive activity credit, and general business credit carryovers are made at a rate of 33⅓ cents per dollar of excluded income (Code Sec. 108(b)(3)(B)).

Insolvency. A taxpayer's insolvency for this purpose refers to an excess of liabilities over the fair market value of assets immediately prior to discharge. This exclusion is limited to the amount by which the taxpayer is insolvent. The insolvent amount includes the amount by which a nonrecourse debt exceeds the fair market value of the property securing the debt, but only to the extent that the excess nonrecourse debt is discharged (IRS Pub. 4681).

Nonrecourse debt in excess of the property's fair market value is separated into two components: (1) the excess nonrecourse debt that is forgiven is treated as a liability; and (2) the excess of nonrecourse debt that is not forgiven is not treated as a liability. Thus, the nondischarged debt does not directly impede the taxpayer's ability to pay tax on discharge of recourse or nonrecourse debt and it is not relevant in determining the extent of insolvency. The IRS has extended these principles to determine the extent a partner may be insolvent due to the partnership's discharged nonrecourse debt, as determined for each partner (Rev. Rul. 2012-14, amplifying Rev. Rul. 92-53).

Qualified Farm Debt. Income arising from the discharge of qualified farm indebtedness owed to an unrelated lender, including a federal, state, or local government or agency, or instrumentality of such an agency, may be excluded from a taxpayer's gross income if certain requirements are met. The debt must be incurred directly in connection with the operation by the taxpayer of the trade or business of farming. Also, at least 50 percent of the taxpayer's aggregate gross receipts for the three tax years preceding the tax year in which the discharge occurs must be attributable to the trade or business of farming.

The discharge of debt income is excludable only to the extent absorbed by tax attributes (credits are reduced at a rate of 33⅓ cents per dollar of excluded income) and the adjusted bases of qualified property (i.e., any property held or used in a trade or business or for the production of income). Basis reduction occurs first with respect to depreciable property, then with respect to land used in the business of farming, and finally with respect to other qualified property (Code Secs. 108(g) and 1017(b)(4)).

Qualified Real Property Business Debt. A taxpayer other than a C corporation may elect on Form 982 to exclude from gross income amounts realized from the discharge of debt incurred or assumed in connection with real property used in a trade or business and secured by that property (Code Sec. 108(a)(1)(D) and (c)). If the debt is incurred or assumed after 1992, it must be incurred or assumed to acquire, construct, reconstruct, or substantially improve the real property.

The excludable amount is limited to the excess of the outstanding principal amount of the debt over the fair market value of the business real property reduced by the outstanding principal amount of any other qualified business debt secured by the property. Also, the exclusion may not exceed the aggregate adjusted bases of depreciable real property held by the taxpayer immediately before discharge. The excluded amount reduces the basis of depreciable real property. The election to exclude income from the discharge of qualified real property business debt must be filed with the taxpayer's timely income tax return, including extensions, for the tax year in which the discharge occurs (Reg. § 1.108-5(b)). The election is only revocable with the consent of the IRS.

Qualified Principal Residence Debt. An individual may exclude from gross income a limited amount of qualified principal residence debt discharged before January 1, 2021, or subject to an arrangement that is entered into and evidenced in writing before January 1, 2021. The exclusion had expired for discharges made after December 31 2017, but was extended through 2020. A taxpayer eligible for the exclusion for discharge of qualified principal residence debt for tax year 2018 must file an amended return on Form 1040-X to claim the exclusion (Code Sec. 108(a)(1)(E), as amended by P.L. 116-94 and 108(h))).

To be qualified principal residence debt, the debt must be incurred in the acquisition, construction, or substantial improvement of the individual's principle residence and secured by that residence (¶ 1048). Qualified principal residence debt also includes refinancing of such debt, to the extent new debt does not exceed the amount of the old debt. The amount excludable is limited to $2 million ($1 million for married taxpayers filing separately). Principal residence has the same meaning for purposes of the exclusion as it does for purposes of exclusion of gain from the sale of a principal residence (¶ 1705).

Several rules are included to prevent the abuse of the exclusion of income from the discharge of qualified principal residence debt. The discharge of a loan will not be excludable from gross income if it is as a result of services performed for the lender or other factors unrelated to either the financial condition of the taxpayer or a decline in value of the residence. If only a portion of discharged debt is qualified principal residence debt, the exclusion applies only to the amount of discharged debt that exceeds the portion of the debt that is not qualified principal residence debt. The basis of the taxpayer's principal residence is reduced, but not below zero, by the amount of qualified principal residence interest that is excluded from income.

Student Loans. An exclusion from gross income applies to the discharge of all or part of a student loan if, pursuant to the loan agreement, the discharge is made because the individual works for a specified period of time in certain professions for any of a broad class of employers (for example, as a doctor or nurse in an underserved rural area) (Code Sec. 108(f)). The loan generally must be made by:

(1) a federal, state, or local government or instrumentality, agency, or subdivision of that government;

(2) a tax-exempt public benefit corporation that has assumed control of a public hospital with public employees; or

(3) an educational institution if it received funds to loan from an entity described in (1) or (2) above, or the student serves, pursuant to a program of the institution, in an occupation or area with unmet needs under the direction of a governmental unit or a tax-exempt Code Sec. 501(c)(3) organization.

The exclusion also applies to discharges of eligible loans in 2018 through 2025 due to the student's death or total and permanent disability. For this purpose, an eligible loan may also include a private education loan. Loans refinanced through such a program by the institution or certain tax-exempt organizations also qualify for the exclusion.

Under a safe harbor, an individual may exclude from gross income any (1) federal or private student loan discharged based on the Department of Education's Closed School or Defense Repayment discharge process, or (2) private loans discharged based on a settlement of certain legal causes of action (Rev. Proc. 2020-11). The taxpayer does not have to increase gross income by the amount of tax credits or deductions related to the discharged loans. A creditor does not have to file information returns or furnish payee statements as a result of discharging the loans. Prior relief was provided to a taxpayer who took out private student loans to finance attendance at a school owned by Corinthian College, Inc. (CCI) or American Career Institutes, Inc. (ACI) if the private loans were discharged based on a settlement of a legal cause of action against CCI, ACI, and certain private lenders (Rev. Proc. 2018-39).

¶855

Deferral of Discharge of Debt Income Resulting from Reacquisition of Debt. A limited deferral was allowed for the discharge or debt income in connection with the reacquisition in 2009 or 2010 of an applicable business debt (Code Sec. 108(i)). At the election of the taxpayer, income from the discharge of the applicable business debt is includible in gross income ratably over a five-year period beginning in 2014. If the taxpayer issued a new debt instrument for the debt instrument being reacquired, and there is original issue discount (OID) with respect to the original instrument, the taxpayer can deduct the OID ratably over the same period as that for which the discharge of debt income is deferred. If a debt instrument was issued by the taxpayer and the proceeds were used to reacquire a debt instrument also issued by the taxpayer, the new instrument is treated as being issued for the instrument being reacquired. The election to defer OID income is made on an instrument-by-instrument basis, and is irrevocable once made. Special rules address the application of this rule to C corporations, S corporations, and partnerships, including, under certain circumstances, a required acceleration of any remaining items of a C corporation's deferred discharge of debt income (Reg. § 1.108(i)-2)

Forgiveness of Paycheck Protection Program (PPP) Loans. The Small Business Administration (SBA) section 7(a) loan program is expanded to include PPP loans made available from February 15, 2020, through June 30, 2020, to cover expenses of a small business in response to the COVID-19 (coronavirus) emergency. An eligible recipient of a PPP loan may apply for forgiveness of the loan and have the cancelled debt excluded from gross income for federal income tax purposes. The amount eligible for forgiveness is the sum of payroll costs, mortgage interest, rent, and utility expenses during the 8-week period beginning on date the PPP loan originates. The amount forgiven is reduced if the recipient reduces its workforce or its employees' salaries and wages (Act Secs. 1102 and 1106 of P.L. 116-136)

Education and Disability Benefits

See CCH® AnswerConnect: *Interest Income: Special Rules for U.S. Savings Bonds* and *Education Expenses, Tax Credits and 529 Plans* for more information on this topic.

863. Exclusion of U.S. Savings Bond Interest for Education Expenses. An individual who redeems a qualified U.S. savings bond to pay qualified higher education expenses may exclude interest on the bond from gross income if certain requirements are met (Code Sec. 135). The exclusion is subject to a phaseout depending on the taxpayer's modified adjusted gross income (AGI) in the year that the bonds are cashed, and the qualified higher education expenses are paid. For 2019, the exclusion is reduced when modified AGI exceeds $81,100 ($121,600 if married filing jointly) and is eliminated when modified AGI reaches $96,100 ($151,600 if married filing jointly) (Rev. Proc. 2018-57). For 2020, the exclusion is reduced when modified AGI exceeds $82,350 ($123,550 if married filing jointly) and is eliminated when modified AGI reaches $97,350 ($153,500 if married filing jointly) (Rev. Proc. 2019-44).

A qualified U.S. savings bond is any Series I or EE bond issued after 1989 to an individual who has reached age 24 before the date of issuance. Qualified higher education expenses include tuition and fees required for enrollment or attendance at an eligible educational institution of the taxpayer, the taxpayer's spouse, or the taxpayer's dependent (¶ 137). Also, a taxpayer is entitled to the exclusion if the redemption proceeds are contributed to a qualified tuition program (QTP or 529 plan) (¶ 869).

A taxpayer should keep records to verify the amount of excluded interest, including:

- a written record of each post-1989 Series EE or I U.S. savings bond that is cashed in including the serial number, issue date, face value, and total redemption proceeds including principal and interest (Form 8818 may be used for this purpose);

- documentation to show that qualified higher education expenses were paid during the tax year (i.e., canceled checks, credit card receipts, or bills from the educational institution).

The amount that may be excludable is limited when the aggregate proceeds of qualified U.S. savings bonds redeemed by a taxpayer during a tax year exceed the qualified higher education expenses paid during that year. Qualified higher education expenses must be *reduced* by the sum of any:

- qualified scholarship that is not includible in gross income (¶ 865);
- educational assistance allowance under certain chapters of title 38 of the United States Code;
- payment other than a gift or inheritance that is exempt from tax including employer-provided educational assistance (¶ 2067); or
- payment, waiver, or reimbursement under a 529 plan (¶ 869).

The amount must be further reduced by expenses taken into account for the American opportunity credit or lifetime learning credit (¶ 1403), as well as amounts taken into account in determining the exclusion for distributions from a 529 plan or Coverdell education savings account (¶ 867).

Modified AGI. For purposes of the exclusion, modified AGI is the taxpayer's AGI *after* applying the partial exclusion for Social Security and tier 1 railroad retirement benefits (¶ 716), the deduction for contributions to a traditional IRA (¶ 2157), and adjustments for limitations on passive activity losses and credits (¶ 1169). In addition, modified AGI is calculated *before* the exclusion of interest from U.S. Savings bonds, the exclusion for qualified adoption expenses (¶ 2063), the domestic production activities deduction for tax years beginning before 2018 (¶ 980A), the deduction for interest paid on qualified student loans (¶ 1011), the deduction for qualified tuition and related expenses before 2021 (¶ 1011A), the exclusion of foreign earned income (¶ 2402), and the exclusion for income from Puerto Rico and U.S. possessions (¶ 2414 and ¶ 2415). The exclusion is not available to married individuals who file separate returns. The excludable savings bond interest is calculated on Form 8815 and reported on Schedule B (Form 1040).

865. Scholarships, Fellowship Grants, and Tuition Reductions. Any amount received as a qualified scholarship by an individual is excluded from gross income if the individual is a candidate for a degree at a qualified educational organization, which normally maintains a regular faculty and curriculum and has a regularly enrolled body of students in attendance where its educational activities are regularly carried on (Code Sec. 117; Reg. § 1.117-1). A qualified scholarship includes any amount received by an individual as a scholarship or fellowship grant so long as the amount was used for qualified tuition and related expenses, including:

- tuition and fees required for enrollment or attendance at a qualified educational organization, and
- fees, books, supplies, and equipment required for courses of instruction at the organization.

A qualified scholarship does not include amounts used for incidental expenses such as room and board, travel, research, clerical help, equipment, and other expenses that are *not* required for either enrollment or attendance, or in a course of instruction at an educational organization (Prop. Reg. § 1.117-6(c)(2)).

Tuition Reduction. The amount of any qualified tuition reduction to employees of educational institutions is similarly excludable from gross income (Code Sec. 117(d)). The tuition reduction must be provided to an employee of a qualified educational organization. The reduction can be for education provided by the employer or by another qualified educational organization. Moreover, it can be for education provided to the employee, the employee's spouse, dependent child, or other person treated as an employee (¶ 2085). However, it can only be used for education below the graduate level unless it is for the education of an employee who is a graduate student and who is engaged in teaching or research activities for the employer. Benefits under a qualified tuition reduction program may be excludable only if the program does not discriminate in favor of highly compensated employees.

Employer-Related Scholarships or Grants. Employer-related grants are *not* excludable from gross income if they are considered to be compensation or an incentive to employees (Rev. Proc. 76-47). If educational scholarships are made available to or for the benefit of employees on a preferential basis, such preferential grants suggest an intent to provide additional compensation or an employment incentive and are included in gross income unless they are shown to fall outside the pattern of employment. This is true even if the grants are made by an independent third party, such as a private foundation or a voluntary employees' beneficiary association (VEBA). The IRS has provided guidelines for determining whether grants made by private foundations under employer-related scholarship programs to employees and/or the children of employees are treated as scholarships or fellowship grants that are excludable from gross income.

Compensation for Teaching, Research, or Other Services Performed. The exclusions for qualified scholarships and qualified tuition reductions do not apply to amounts representing payments for teaching, research, or other services performed by the student that are required as a condition for receiving the qualified scholarship or qualified tuition reduction (Code Sec. 117(c)). Athletic scholarships awarded to students who are expected, but not required, to participate in sports qualify for exclusion (Rev. Rul. 77-263). The IRS will follow these rules regardless of any decision of the National Labor Relation Board (NLRB) in respect to employment status of student athletes (INFO 2014-0016).

Under an exception, amounts received by degree candidates from the National Health Service Corps (NHSC) Scholarship Program, the Armed Forces Health Professions Scholarship and Financial Assistance Program, or a comprehensive student work-learning-service program operated by a work college for tuition, fees, books, supplies, and required equipment are excluded from the recipient's gross income even though there is a future service obligation connected to these qualified scholarships. Amounts received by health care professionals under the NHSC Loan Repayment Program are excludable from gross income and employment taxes (Code Sec. 108(f)(4)). This also extends to loan repayments received under similar state programs qualified for funding under the Public Health Service Act and repayments under other state loan repayment or forgiveness programs that are intended to provide for increased availability of health care services in underserved or health professional shortage areas.

867. Coverdell Education Savings Accounts. An individual may open a Coverdell education savings account (Coverdell ESA) created exclusively to help pay for the qualified education expenses of a designated beneficiary (Code Sec. 530). A Coverdell ESA is a tax-exempt trust or custodial account organized in the United States. At the time it is organized the trust must be designated as a Coverdell ESA and the designated beneficiary must be under age 18 or a special needs individual.

Contributions. Any individual or entity may make nondeductible contributions to a Coverdell ESA, including the designated beneficiary, a corporation, trust, or tax-exempt organization. There are two annual limits on contributions:

- the total amount that can be contributed for each designated beneficiary in any year is limited in the aggregate to $2,000;

- any one contributor can contribute up to $2,000 to a Coverdell ESA for any designated beneficiary, except the limit is phased out for individual contributors with modified adjusted gross income (AGI) over certain thresholds (between $190,000—$220,000 if married filing jointly, and between $95,000—$110,000 for other filers).

Contributions must be made in cash and before the beneficiary reaches age 18, unless made for a special needs beneficiary. They generally must be made by the due date of the contributor's tax return, not including extensions. However, the due date for filing any federal income tax return, as well as making Coverdell contributions, otherwise due on or after April 1, 2020, and before July 15, 2020, is automatically extended to July 15, 2020, in response to the COVID-19 (coronavirus) crisis (¶ 2505). If a Coverdell ESA receives excess contributions for the tax year, then the designated beneficiary is subject to an excise tax of six percent of the amount of the excess that remains in the account at the end of the tax year (Code Sec. 4973). Amounts remaining in the account must be distributed within 30 days after the designated beneficiary reaches age 30 or after his or her death. A taxpayer can contribute to both a Coverdell ESA and a qualified tuition (529) plan (¶ 869) in the same year for the same designated beneficiary.

8

EXCLUSIONS

Distributions. Distributions from a Coverdell account are excludable from gross income to the extent that the distribution does not exceed the qualified education expenses incurred by the designated beneficiary during the year in which the distribution is made (Code Sec. 530(d)). Distributions are deemed paid from both contributions and earnings. The amount of contributions distributed is determined by multiplying the distribution by the ratio that the aggregate amount of contributions bears to the total balance of the account at the time the distribution is made. If aggregate distributions exceed qualified education expenses during the tax year, then they are deemed to be paid from a pro rata share of both principal and interest. Thus, the portion of earnings excludable from gross income is based on the ratio that the qualified education expenses bear to the total amount of the distribution. The remaining portion of earnings are included in the distributee's gross income.

Distributions Not Used for Education. Distributions from a Coverdell account that exceed the designated beneficiary's qualified education expenses are includible in gross income and subject to a 10-percent addition to tax or penalty. The 10-percent addition to tax does not apply to distributions:

- made to a designated beneficiary or the estate of a designated beneficiary after the designated beneficiary's death;

- attributable to the designated beneficiary being disabled;

- made on account of a scholarship or allowance, received by the account holder to the extent the amount of the distribution does not exceed the amount of the scholarship or allowance; or

- that constitute the return of excess contributions and earnings, although earnings are includible in income.

Military Academy Attendance. Since recipients of appointments to military academies are required to fulfill service obligations, the appointments are generally not considered scholarships and the 10-percent penalty applies. Withdrawals from a Coverdell ESA made on account of the beneficiary's attendance at a service academy are not subject to the penalty to the extent the distribution is used for the costs of advanced education. The penalty waiver covers appointments to the United States Military, Navy, Air Force, Coast Guard, and Merchant Marine Academies.

Rollovers and Transfers. A distribution from a Coverdell ESA may be excluded from gross income if rolled over into a Coverdell ESA of a member of the beneficiary's family or another Coverdell ESA of the beneficiary. If the rollover is made to another Coverdell ESA of the same beneficiary, then only one such transfer is generally permitted within a 12-month period. These distributions will not be included in the distributee's gross income provided the rollover occurs within 60 days of the distribution. However, the due date for performing certain time-sensitive actions, including the 60-day rollover requirement, otherwise due on or after April 1, 2020, and before July 15, 2020, is automatically extended to July 15, 2020, in response to the COVID-19 (coronavirus) crisis (Notice 2020-23; Rev. Proc. 2018-58). Any change in the beneficiary of a Coverdell ESA does not constitute a distribution for gross income purposes if the new beneficiary is a member of the family of the original beneficiary and of the same or higher generation.

Death or divorce of the designated beneficiary does not cause a taxable distribution to the spouse or ex-spouse. The transfer of a beneficiary's interest in a Coverdell ESA to a spouse or ex-spouse under a divorce or separation agreement is not a taxable transfer, and after the transfer the interest in the account is treated as belonging to the spouse or ex-spouse (Code Sec. 530(d)(7)).

Qualified Education Expenses. Qualified education expenses of a Coverdell ESA include expenses for elementary, secondary, undergraduate, and graduate level education. Tuition, fees, books, supplies, equipment, and special needs services if required are qualified education expenses for the designated beneficiary to attend undergraduate or graduate level courses at an eligible education institution. The term also includes room and board provided that the student incurring the expense is enrolled at an eligible education institution on at least a half-time basis.

Qualified elementary and secondary expenses also include expenses for academic tutoring, computer software, technology or equipment, internet access or related services, room and board, uniforms, transportation, and supplementary items and services such as extended day programs as required or provided by the school (Code Secs. 529(e)(3), 530(b)(2), and (b)(3)). Computer expenses do *not* include software designed for sports, games, or hobbies unless the nature of the software is predominately educational.

Qualified education expenses are reduced for tax-exempt scholarships or fellowship grants (¶ 865) and any other tax-free educational benefits. Expenses will then be reduced for amounts taken into account in determining the American Opportunity and lifetime learning credits (¶ 1403). If a student receives distributions from both a Coverdell ESA and a 529 plan (¶ 869) that exceed any remaining expenses, the expenses must be allocated between the distributions (Code Sec. 530(d)(2)(C) and (D)).

Eligible Educational Institution. An eligible educational institution is generally an accredited post-secondary educational institution offering credit toward a bachelor's degree, an associate's degree, a graduate-level or professional degree, or other recognized post-secondary credential. Generally, proprietary and post-secondary vocational institutions are eligible educational institutions. Elementary and secondary schools (i.e., kindergarten through grade 12) are also eligible institutions. Schools may be public, private, or religious (Code Sec. 530(b)(2) and (b)(3)).

Prohibited Uses of Accounts. A Coverdell ESA will lose its tax-exempt status if it engages in a prohibited transaction or is pledged as security for a loan. Prohibited transactions include loans and use of account assets by the beneficiary or a fiduciary (Code Sec. 4975(c)).

Estate and Gift Tax Treatment. Any contribution to a Coverdell ESA is treated as a completed gift of a present interest from the contributor to the beneficiary at the time of the contribution. Contributions are eligible for the annual gift tax exclusion (¶ 2905) and are excludable for purposes of the generation-skipping transfer (GST) tax (Code Sec. 530(d)(3)).

Military Death Benefits as Contributions. An individual who receives a military death gratuity or Servicemembers' Group Life Insurance payment may contribute up to the full amount into a Coverdell ESA without regard to the annual contribution and income phaseout limits. A military death benefit contribution to a Coverdell ESA will be considered a tax-free rollover contribution if it is made within one year of the date on which the amount is received, and does not exceed the total amount of gratuity and life insurance payments received, less the amount of such payments contributed to a Roth IRA or to another Coverdell ESA. Such rollovers will be disregarded for purposes of the limit on the number of tax-free rollovers per year (Code Sec. 530(d)(9)).

869. Qualified Tuition Programs (QTPs or 529 Plans). A qualified tuition program (QTP or 529 plan) is a tax-favored program that allows individuals to prepay tuition or contribute to an account for the qualified education expenses of a designated beneficiary (Code Sec. 529). A 529 plan can be established and maintained by a state, state agency, or by an eligible educational institution (i.e., virtually any accredited public, nonprofit, or private college or university). A 529 plan itself is exempt from federal income taxation other than the tax imposed on unrelated business income (¶ 655).

Contributions. Contributions to a 529 plan on behalf of a designated beneficiary must be made in cash and are limited to the necessary amount of qualified education expenses for the beneficiary as determined under the program. The contributions are not deductible but are not subject to any modified adjusted gross income phaseout limits. In addition, a taxpayer can contribute to both a 529 plan and a Coverdell ESA (¶ 867) in the same year for the same designated beneficiary.

A contribution to a 529 is treated as a completed gift of a present interest and qualifies for the annual gift tax exclusion (¶ 2905) (Code Sec. 529(c)(2)). If a donor's contribution exceeds the annual exclusion amount, then he or she may elect to take the excess into account ratably over five years. A 529 plan contribution does not qualify for the unlimited gift tax exclusion for money used to pay educational expenses (¶ 2907). No portion of a contribution is generally includible in the estate of a donor unless the donor dies during the five-year period in which excess contributions to a 529 plan are being ratably taken into account.

8

EXCLUSIONS

¶869

Distributions. Distributions from a 529 plan are excludable from gross income to the extent that they are used to pay the designated beneficiary's qualified education expenses (Code Sec. 529(c)(3)). Distributions that exceed the beneficiary's qualified expenses are generally taxed under the Code Sec. 72 annuity rules (¶ 817) with the part of any distribution that represents amounts paid or contributed to the account representing a return of the investment. Any distribution from a 529 plan used to pay qualified education expenses that are later refunded to the designated beneficiary is not taxed if the beneficiary recontributes the refunded amount to the plan within 60 days. However, the due date for performing certain time-sensitive action, including the 60-day rollover requirement, otherwise due on or after April 1, 2020, and before July 15, 2020, is automatically extended to July 15, 2020, in response to the COVID-19 (coronavirus) crisis (Notice 2020-23; Rev. Proc. 2018-58). Distributions that are includable in the designated beneficiary's gross income are subject to a 10-percent addition to tax or penalty (Code Sec. 529(c)(6)).

Rollovers and Transfers. A distribution from a 529 plan may be excluded from gross income if rolled over into a 529 account of a member of the beneficiary's family or another 529 account of the beneficiary. If the rollover is made to another 529 account of the same beneficiary, then only one such transfer is generally permitted within a 12-month period. Effective for tax years beginning after December 22, 2017, and before January 1, 2026, amounts from a 529 account can be rolled over to an ABLE account (¶ 870) without penalty if the ABLE account is owned by the designated beneficiary of that 529 account or a member of the designated beneficiary's family (Code Sec. 529(c)(3)(C); Notice 2018-58). Distributions will not be included in the distributee's gross income provided the rollover occurs within 60 days of the distribution. However, the due date for performing certain time-sensitive action, including the 60-day rollover requirement, otherwise due on or after April 1, 2020, and before July 15, 2020, is automatically extended to July 15, 2020, in response to the COVID-19 (coronavirus) crisis (Notice 2020-23; Rev. Proc. 2018-58). A change of the designated beneficiary of a 529 account during the tax year is not considered a distribution required to be included in gross income if the new beneficiary is an eligible individual for the tax year and a member of the family of the former designated beneficiary.

Qualified Education Expenses. Qualified education expenses of 529 plans include qualified higher education expenses (QHEEs) required for enrollment or attendance of the designated beneficiary at an eligible educational institution, as well as up to $10,000 of qualified elementary or secondary education expenses after 2017, up to $10,000 of principal or interest for student loan payments after 2018, and expenses associated with registered apprenticeship programs after 2018.

QHEEs consist of tuition, fees, books, equipment, and expenses incurred for services for a special needs beneficiary (Code Sec. 529(e)(3)). They also include expenses for the purchase of computer or peripheral equipment, computer software, or Internet access and related services if used primarily by the beneficiary during any of the years the beneficiary is enrolled at an eligible educational institution. Room and board expenses qualify as QHEEs if incurred by an eligible student who is attending an eligible educational institution at least half time. An eligible educational institution is generally an accredited post-secondary educational institution offering credit toward a bachelor's degree, an associate's degree, a graduate-level or professional degree, or other recognized post-secondary credential.

QHEEs are reduced by any scholarships, fellowships, or other educational assistance excluded from gross income (¶ 865), as well as any expenses used claiming the American Opportunity and lifetime learning credits (¶ 1403). If a student receives distributions from both a 529 plan and a Coverdell ESA that together exceed any remaining expenses, the expenses must be allocated between the distributions.

For any distribution made after 2017, qualified education expenses of 529 plans include up to $10,000 per year of expenses for tuition in connection with the designated beneficiary's enrollment or attendance at an elementary or secondary school during the tax year, whether public, private, or religious school (Code Sec. 529(c)(7); Notice 2018-58). An elementary or secondary school for this purpose means kindergarten through grade as determined under State law.

¶869

For any distribution made after 2018, qualified education expenses of 529 plans include up to $10,000 of principal or interest on any qualified student loan of the designated beneficiary or a sibling (brother, sister, stepbrother, or stepsister) (Code Sec. 529(c)(9), as added by the Setting Every Community Up for Retirement Enhancement Act of 2019 (SECURE Act) (P.L. 116-94)). The $10,000 limit applies in the aggregate, over the course of the individual's lifetime. Separate accounting is made for student loan distributions made for the designated beneficiary and a sibling. The deduction for student loan interest is reduced by any distribution from a 529 plan excluded from gross income used to pay student loan interest (¶ 1011).

For any distribution made after 2018, qualified education expenses of 529 plans include certain expenses associated with registered apprenticeship programs (Code Sec. 529(c)(8), as added by P.L. 116-94). This includes expenses for fees, books, supplies, and equipment required for the participation of the designated beneficiary in an apprenticeship program registered and certified with the Department of Labor under section 1 of the National Apprenticeship Act.

870. ABLE Accounts. An eligible individual may open an account in an Achieve a Better Living Experience (ABLE) program to help pay for qualified disability expenses (Code Sec. 529A; Prop. Reg. § 1.529A-2). A qualified ABLE program can be established by a state, or agency or instrumentality of a state. The program itself is exempt from federal taxation other than the tax imposed on unrelated business income (¶ 655). A designated beneficiary is generally limited to only one ABLE account unless a second account is established to facilitate a rollover or transfer.

The designated beneficiary of an ABLE account is the eligible individual who established the account and is the owner of the account. An eligible individual is an individual who is disabled or blind, with the onset of the disability or blindness occurring before the individual attains age 26. The person must either be entitled to benefits based on blindness or disability under title II of the Social Security Act, or must have a disability certificate on file with the IRS for the tax year.

Contributions. Any person may make nondeductible contributions to an ABLE account for the benefit of the designated beneficiary (Code Sec. 529A(b); Prop. Reg. § 1.529A-2). Contributions must be made in cash and are treated as a completed gift of a present interest. The aggregate amount of contributions from all contributors for the tax year cannot exceed the annual gift tax exclusion amount for the year ($15,000 for 2019 and 2020).

For tax years beginning after December 22, 2017, and before January 1, 2026, a designated beneficiary may make additional contributions to the account up to the lesser of his or her compensation includible in gross income for the tax year, or the federal poverty line for a one-person household for the year (Prop. Reg. § 1.529A-8). The additional contributions may be made to an ABLE account provided no contributions are made to a qualified employer-provided retirement plan for the designated beneficiary. For tax years beginning after December 22, 2017, and before January 1, 2026, the retirement savings contribution credit (¶ 1404) can be claimed by a designated beneficiary for contributions made to ABLE account.

The annual limit on contributions does not apply to rollover contributions or transfers between ABLE accounts, but does apply to rollovers from a qualified tuition program (section 529 account). A six-percent excise tax applies to excess annual contributions to an ABLE account during the tax year unless a corrective distribution is made (Code Sec. 4973). In addition, the cumulative balance in an ABLE account may not exceed the limits established by the state under its qualified ABLE program and equal to the limits for its qualified tuition program. However, the cumulative balance in an ABLE account is disregarded for purposes of determining the designated beneficiary's eligibility for benefits under Supplemental Security Income (SSI) and certain other means-tested federal programs.

Distributions. Distributions from an ABLE account for a tax year are excluded from gross income to the extent they do not exceed the qualified disability expenses of the designated beneficiary (Code Sec. 529A(c); Prop. Reg. § 1.529A-3). Any distributions that exceed the beneficiary's qualified expenses are includible in gross income under rules

¶870

similar to annuities under Code Sec. 72 (¶ 817) with the part of any distribution that represents amounts paid or contributed to the account representing a return of the investment. Distributions that are includable in the designated beneficiary's gross income are subject to a 10-percent addition to tax or penalty unless made on or after the beneficiary's death.

Qualified disability expenses include any expense related to the eligible individual's blindness or disability that is expended for the benefit of an eligible individual who is the designated beneficiary of an ABLE account. These include expenses for: education, housing, transportation, employment training and support, assistive technology and personal support services, health, prevention and wellness, financial management and administrative services, legal fees, oversight and monitoring, and funeral and burial expenses. Under proposed regulations, qualified expenses include basic living expenses and are not limited to items for which there is a medical necessity or that solely benefit a disabled individual.

Rollovers and Transfers. A distribution from an ABLE account may be excluded from gross income if rolled over into a ABLE account of a member of the beneficiary's family or another ABLE account of the beneficiary. If the rollover is made to another ABLE account of the same beneficiary, then only one such transfer is generally permitted within a 12-month period. Effective for tax years beginning after December 22, 2017, and before January 1, 2026, amounts from a 529 tuition account can be rolled over to an ABLE account without penalty if the ABLE account is owned by the designated beneficiary of that 529 account or a member of the designated beneficiary's family (¶ 869). These distributions will not be included in the distributee's gross income provided the rollover occurs within 60 days of the distribution. However, the due date for performing certain time-sensitive action, including the 60-day rollover requirement, otherwise due on or after April 1, 2020, and before July 15, 2020, is automatically extended to July 15, 2020, in response to the COVID-19 (coronavirus) crisis (Notice 2020-23; Rev. Proc. 2018-58). A change of designated beneficiary of an ABLE account during the tax year is not considered a distribution required to be included in gross income if the new beneficiary is an eligible individual for the tax year and a member of the family of the former designated beneficiary.

Transfer to State. Upon the death of a designated beneficiary, any balance remaining in the ABLE account is distributed to the state when the state files a claim for payment, subject to any outstanding payments due (Code Sec. 529A(f)). The state is to be treated as a creditor, rather than a beneficiary, and distribution of any excess funds is not subject to taxation.

Bankruptcy Treatment. A debtor must declare any interest he or she holds in an ABLE account upon filing of a bankruptcy petition (11 U.S.C. § 521(c)). In addition, any amounts in an ABLE account are excludable from the property of a bankruptcy estate with respect to a debtor under 11 U.S.C. § 541(b) if the debtor's contributions were made not later than 365 days prior to the date of filing of the bankruptcy petition.

Other Exclusions from Gross Income

See CCH® AnswerConnect: *Gross Income: Exclusions* and *Gross Income: Awards, Damages, Recoveries, Illegal Activities and Other* for more information on this topic.

871. Exclusion or Rollover of Certain Stock Gains. Noncorporate taxpayers may exclude from gross income a certain percentage of capital gain from the sale or exchange of qualified small business stock held for more than five years and issued after August 10, 1993 (¶ 1905). Noncorporate taxpayers may also elect to roll over capital gain from the sale of qualified business stock held for more than six months if other qualified small business stock is purchased during the 60-day period beginning on the date of sale (¶ 1907). Individuals and C corporations may elect to defer recognition of capital gain realized upon the sale of publicly traded securities before 2018 if the sale proceeds are used within 60 days to purchase common stock or a partnership interest in a specialized small business investment company (SSBIC) (¶ 1909).

873. Employee Benefits Excluded From Gross Income. Compensation for personal services includes any benefits an employer provides to an employee that are not otherwise excludable from gross income (Reg. § 1.61-2(a)). Excludable employee benefits include:

- amounts received under employer-financed accident and health plans (¶ 2015);

- employer contributions to provide the accident and health benefits (¶ 2013);

- employer contributions to a health savings account (HSA) (¶ 2035), Archer medical savings account (MSA) (¶ 2037), health reimbursement arrangement (HRA) (¶ 2039), or flexible spending arrangement (FSA) (¶ 2041);

- premiums for group-term life insurance to the extent coverage does not exceed $50,000 (¶ 2055);

- qualified adoption expenses reimbursed under an employer adoption assistance program (¶ 2063);

- child and dependent care assistance benefits (¶ 2065);

- educational assistance benefits (¶ 2067);

- employee achievement awards to the extent deductible by the employer (¶ 2069); and

- certain other fringe benefits (¶ 2085).

Some excludable employee benefits may be provided to an employee through the employer's cafeteria plan (¶ 2045).

875. Minister's Housing (Parsonage) Allowance. Ministers of the gospel may exclude from gross income the rental value of homes furnished by churches as part of their compensation (Code Sec. 107; Reg. § 1.107-1). This includes the portion of a retired minister's pension designated as a rental allowance by the national governing body of a religious denomination having complete control over the retirement fund. The exclusion also applies to the rental value of a residence furnished to a retired minister but not a widow (IRS Pub. 517).

A minister is entitled to deduct mortgage interest and real property taxes paid on a personal residence even if the amounts expended are derived from a rental allowance that is excludable from the minister's gross income (Code Sec. 265(a)(6)).

877. Reimbursed Living Expenses. A taxpayer whose principal residence is damaged or destroyed by fire, storm, or other casualty and who must temporarily occupy another residence during the repair can exclude from gross income any insurance payments received as reimbursement for *increased* living expenses during such period (Code Sec. 123; Reg. § 1.123-1). The exclusion also applies to a person who is denied access to his principal residence by governmental authorities because of the occurrence or threat of occurrence of a casualty.

The exclusion is limited to the excess of actual living expenses incurred by the taxpayer and members of the household over the normal living expenses they would have incurred during the period. The exclusion covers additional costs incurred in renting suitable housing and any extraordinary expenses for transportation, food, utilities, and miscellaneous items.

881. Government Cost-Sharing Conservation Payments. Agricultural and forestry cost-sharing payments made by state or federal governments may be excluded from gross income if:

- the Secretary of Agriculture determines that the payments were made primarily for soil and water conservation, environmental protection or restoration, wildlife habitat development, or forest improvement, and

- the Secretary of Treasury determines that the payments do not result in a substantial increase in the annual income derived from the property with respect to which the payments were made (Code Sec. 126).

No adjustment to the basis of the property involved is made for the payments and no income tax deduction or credit may be taken with respect to them. Further, if the property or improvement purchased with the payments is disposed of within 20 years, the payments are recaptured as ordinary income. A 100-percent recapture rate applies if disposition occurs within the first 10 years, with an annual decrease of 10 percent thereafter (Code Sec. 1255; Temp. Reg. § § 16A.1255-1 and 16A.1255-2).

883. Foster Care Payments. Amounts received by a foster care provider from a state or qualified foster care placement agency are excludable from gross income if received for providing care for a qualified foster individual placed in the taxpayer's home or received as a difficulty of care payment (Code Sec. 131). A qualified foster care placement agency is a placement agency that is licensed or certified by a state or local government, or an entity designated by such a government, to make foster care payments to foster care providers.

A difficulty of care payment is a payment for the additional care required because the qualified foster individual placed in the taxpayer's home has a physical, mental, or emotional handicap. Qualified Medicaid waiver payments are treated as difficulty of care payments excludable from gross income, regardless of whether the care provider is related or unrelated to the eligible individual (Notice 2014-7).

Regular foster care payments are *not* excludable to the extent they are made for more than five individuals in the home who have attained age 19. Difficulty of care payments are *not* excludable to the extent they are made for more than 10 individuals under age 19 and more than five individuals who have attained 19 years of age.

887. Disaster Relief Payments. An individual who is the victim of a disaster may exclude from gross income qualified disaster relief payments received (Code Sec. 139). The exclusion also applies for self-employment and employment tax purposes. The exclusion does not apply to any individual, or a representative, identified by the Attorney General to have been a participant or conspirator in a terrorist action.

Disaster Relief Payments Defined. Qualified disaster relief payments include payments, from any source, made to or for the benefit of an individual:

- to reimburse or pay reasonable and necessary personal, family, living, or funeral expenses incurred as a result of a qualified disaster;

- to reimburse or pay reasonable and necessary expenses incurred for the repair or rehabilitation of a personal residence or for the repair, rehabilitation, or replacement of its contents to the extent attributable to a qualified disaster;

- by a common carrier that sells or furnishes transportation (e.g., commercial airlines) for death or personal physical injuries as a result of a qualified disaster; or

- if such amount is paid by a federal, state, or local government in connection with a qualified disaster to promote the general welfare.

A taxpayer in a federally declared disaster area who receives grants from state programs, charitable organizations, or employers to cover medical, transportation, or temporary housing expenses may exclude these grants from gross income (Rev. Rul. 2003-12). However, qualified disaster relief payments do not include payments for any expense compensated for by insurance or otherwise, or payments in the nature of income replacement, such as payments to an individual for lost wages, unemployment compensation, or payments in the nature of business income replacement.

A qualified disaster is:

- a disaster that results from a terroristic or military action as defined under Code Sec. 692(c)(2);

- a federally declared disaster as defined under Code Sec. 165(i)(5)(A);

- a disaster that results from an accident involving a common carrier, or from any other event, which is determined by the IRS to be of a catastrophic nature; or

- a disaster determined by an applicable federal, state or local authority, as determined by the IRS, to warrant assistance.

Air Transportation Safety Act. A taxpayer who is eligible to receive payments under Section 406 of the Air Transportation Safety and System Stabilization Act as a result of physical harm or death incurred from the terrorist-related aircraft crashes can exclude the payments from gross income (Code Sec. 139(f)).

889. Miscellaneous Income Excluded from Gross Income. Several miscellaneous items of income are excluded from gross income.

Firefighters and Emergency Medical Responders. For tax years beginning in 2020, a volunteer firefighter or emergency medical responder may exclude from gross income any state and local tax benefit (i.e., rebate or reduction), or qualified payment received in exchanged for their volunteer services (Code Sec. 139B, as amended by the Setting Every Community Up for Retirement Enhancement Act of 2019 (SECURE Act) (P.L. 116-94)). A qualified payment is any payment or reimbursement provided by a state or political subdivision of a state due to the performance of services as a member of a qualified volunteer emergency response organization. The excludible amount of qualified payments cannot exceed $50 multiplied by the number of months during the year the taxpayer performs the services.

Native American Health Care Benefits. The amount of qualified health care benefits provided by Indian tribal governments to a member of an Indian tribe or a member's spouse or dependents are excludable from the beneficiary's gross income (¶ 2027).

Alaska Native Corporations. For tax years beginning after December 31, 2016, Alaska Native Corporations may generally exclude from gross income certain payments assigned to Alaska Native Settlement Trusts (¶ 2396).

Interest to Recover Property. Effective July 1, 2019, any interest received from the federal government in connection with an action to recover property seized by the IRS in a civil forfeiture due to a claimed violation of the anti-structuring rules of the Bank Secrecy Act (31 USC § 5317(c)(2)) is excludable from the recipient's gross income (Code Sec. 139H, as added by the Taxpayer First Act (P.L. 116-25)).

Wrongfully Incarcerated Individuals. Amounts paid to a wrongfully incarcerated individual for civil damages, restitution, or other monetary awards—including compensatory or statutory damages and restitution imposed in a criminal matter—that relate to the individual's incarceration for the federal or state criminal offense for which he or she was convicted are excluded from gross income (Code Sec. 139F).

Energy Conservation Subsidies. The value of any subsidy provided, directly or indirectly, by a public utility to a customer for the purchase or installation of energy conservation measures for a dwelling unit is excludable from the customer's gross income (Code Sec. 136). Energy conservation measures are any installations or modifications designed to reduce the consumption of electricity or natural gas or to improve management of energy demand.

Clean Coal Power Grants. An eligible noncorporate recipient can exclude from gross income certain grants, awards, or allowances received under the Clean Coal Power Initiative (Act Sec. 402 of the Energy Policy Act of 2005 (P.L. 109-58); Act Sec. 343 of P.L. 114-113).

Holocaust Reparation Payments. Restitution or reparation payments received by persons who suffered Nazi persecution and survived the Holocaust are excludable from gross income (Act Sec. 2 of the Holocaust Restitution Tax Fairness Act of 2002 (P.L. 107-358)). The exclusion extends to any interest earned on the payments. The payments are also *not* included when applying any tax provision that takes into account excluded income in computing modified adjusted gross income (AGI), such as the taxation of Social Security benefits.

Other Exclusions. Exclusions from gross income are also available to human trafficking victims (Notice 2012-12) and certain settlements received by Native Americans (Notice 2013-1, modified and superseded in part by Notice 2019-23). The IRS has provided guidance on whether a medical loss ratio (MLR) rebate paid to a health insurance policyholder is excludable from the policyholder's gross income as a returned premium (¶ 2031).

Military Benefits

See CCH® AnswerConnect: *Gross Income: Exclusions* for more information on this topic.

891. Military and Government Injury, Sickness, and Disability Benefits. Amounts received by an individual from a pension, annuity, or similar payment for *personal* *injuries* or *sickness* that resulted from combat-related service in the armed forces of *any* country, the National Oceanic and Atmospheric Administration, or the Public Health Service, or from a disability annuity under the provisions of section 808 of the Foreign Service Act of 1980, are excludable from gross income (¶ 851) (Code Sec. 104(a)(4); Reg. § 1.104-1(e)).

Retirement pay received from the government by Armed Service members is *not* excludable from gross income (Code Sec. 61(a)(10); *L.G. Mitchell*, Dec. 57,611, 131 TC 215.). Disability retirement pay that is computed on the basis of the percentage of disability is fully excludable from gross income, but disability retirement pay that is computed by reference to years of service is excludable only to the extent allowed under the percentage-of-disability method (Reg. § 1.104-1(e)).

Dividends and proceeds from maturing government endowment insurance contracts under the National Service Life Insurance Act of 1940 and all other acts relating to veterans are excludable from gross income. Interest on dividends left on deposit with the Department of Veterans Affairs is also excludable. If an individual uses accumulated dividends to buy additional paid-up National Service Life Insurance, neither the dividends nor the paid-up insurance is taxable (Rev. Rul. 91-14).

Veterans' benefits under any law administered by the Department of Veterans Affairs are excludable from gross income (Code Sec. 140(a)(2)). This includes: educational, training, or subsistence allowances; disability compensation and pension payments for disabilities; compensation for participation in a work therapy program; and grants for homes designed for wheelchair living; grants for motor vehicles for veterans who lost their sight or the use of their limbs; and veterans' pensions (38 USC § 5301 and following).

893. Armed Forces and Government Allowances. Allowances for subsistence, uniforms, quarters, travel, and moving furnished to a commissioned officer, chief warrant officer, warrant officer, or enlisted personnel of the Armed Forces, National Oceanic and Atmospheric Administration, or Public Health Service are excludable from gross income (Reg. § 1.61-2(b)). Housing and cost-of-living allowances received by Armed Forces members to cover the excess cost of quarters and subsistence while on permanent duty at a post outside the United States are also excludable from gross income (Rev. Rul. 61-5). The same rule applies to family separation allowances received on account of overseas assignment. The fact that a member of the military service, National Oceanic and Atmospheric Administration, or Public Health Service receives a tax-free housing allowance does not bar a deduction for mortgage interest or real property taxes on the member's home (Code Sec. 265(a)(6)).

895. Combat Zone Compensation. Enlisted members of the Armed Forces and warrant officers, both commissioned and noncommissioned, may exclude from gross income all pay received for any month during any part of which they served in a combat zone or were hospitalized as a result of wounds, disease, or injury incurred while serving in a combat zone. The exclusion for months of hospitalization does not apply for any month beginning more than two years after the termination of combatant activities in the zone. The same exclusion applies to commissioned officers, but it is limited to the maximum enlisted amount. This amount is the highest rate of basic pay at the highest pay grade that enlisted personnel may receive, plus the amount of hostile fire/imminent danger pay that the officer receives (Code Sec. 112; Reg. § 1.112-1).

The following areas, among others, have been designated combat zones qualifying American military personnel serving in these areas for special tax benefits:

  • Afghanistan and its airspace, including Jordan, Kyrgyzstan, Pakistan, Tajikistan, and Uzbekistan effective on September 19, 2001; Djibouti effective on July 1, 2002; Yemen effective April 10, 2002, and Somalia and Syria effective on January 1, 2004 (Executive Order No. 13239);

  • the Federal Republic of Yugoslavia (Serbia/Montenegro), Albania, Kosovo, the Adriatic Sea, and the Ionian Sea above the 39th parallel effective on March 24, 1999 (Executive Order No. 13119);

  • the Persian Gulf, the Red Sea, the Gulf of Oman, part of the Arabian Sea that is north of 10 degrees north latitude and west of 68 degrees east longitude, the

Gulf of Aden and the total land areas of Iraq, Kuwait, Saudi Arabia, Oman, Bahrain, Qatar, and the United Arab Emirates, including Jordan effective on March 19, 2003, and Lebanon effective on February 12, 2015, due to their direct air support of military operations (Executive Order No. 12744);

- Sinai Peninsula of Egypt effective beginning June 9, 2015, and applicable through December 31, 2025 (Act Sec. 11026 of the Tax Cuts and Jobs Act (P.L. 115-97)).

For a complete list of designated combat zones, see IRS Pub. 3.

Combat pay excludable from gross income may nevertheless be included in earned income for purposes of the earned income tax credit (¶ 1422) and calculating the refundable portion of the child tax credit (¶ 1405). Similarly, combat pay may be treated as compensation in determining the amount military personnel can contribute to their individual retirement accounts (IRAs) (¶ 2155).

896. Qualified Military Benefits. A variety of benefits for military personnel were excludable from gross income under various statutes, regulations, and long-standing administrative practices prior to enactment of the Tax Reform Act of 1986 (P.L. 99-514). In the 1986 Act, it was determined that, in the future, no such exclusions would be permitted except under some provision of the Internal Revenue Code. However, the Act added to the Code a provision that, in effect, grandfathered all of the previous non-Code exclusions (Code Sec. 134). Under this provision, all such exclusions that were in effect on September 9, 1986, continue to be in effect. If a benefit in effect on September 9, 1986, is thereafter modified or adjusted for increases in the cost of living under authority existing on that date, the adjustments are also excludable. Benefits not otherwise categorized as qualified military benefits but provided in connection with an individual's status or service as a member of the uniformed services may be excluded from gross income under other Code sections if their requirements for exclusion are met.

Death Gratuity Payments. Section 1478, Title 10, of the U.S. Code provides that upon notification of the death of military personnel on active duty or combat-related activities (i.e., duty training) a death gratuity will be paid to or for the survivor of the service member. The death gratuity payment amount is $100,000 (National Defense Authorization Act for Fiscal Year 2006, (P.L. 109-163)).The exclusion from gross income is also allowed for any adjustment in the amount of the death gratuity payments. The limitation on post-September 9, 1986, modifications does not apply to this benefit. Thus, cost-of-living adjustments or other increases in the gratuity amount will not be subject to tax.

Dependent Care Assistance Program. Qualified military benefits include dependent care assistance provided under a dependent care assistance program (¶ 2065) for a current or former uniformed forces service member or for a dependent.

Veterans' Bonuses and Payments. The definition of qualified military benefit includes bonus payments by a state or local government entity to a member or former member of the military, or to any dependents of such a member. The payment must be made only by reason of the member's service in a combat zone. Thus, the state or local program under which the bonus is paid must specify that the bonus is *only* available with respect to members who served in a combat zone.

Chapter 9
BUSINESS EXPENSES

Trade or Business Expenses

See CCH® AnswerConnect: *Business Expenses* and *Deduction for Start-Up and Organizational Expenditures* for more information on this topic.

901. Deductibility of Business Expenses—Generally. An individual, corporation, partnership, trust, or estate generally may deduct from gross income the ordinary and necessary expenses of carrying on a trade or business that are paid or incurred during the tax year (Code Sec. 162; Reg. § 1.162-1). Business expenses incurred by a cash-basis taxpayer while conducting a business but paid in a year after terminating the business are deductible as business expenses in the year paid (Rev. Rul. 67-12). However, a deduction is not permitted for any expenditure that is a capital expense (¶ 1305). Expenses for property used for both business and personal activities must be allocated between the different activities. The origin and character of a claim control if an expense is a deductible business expense or a nondeductible personal expense.

Ordinary and Necessary. Whether a business expense is ordinary and necessary is based on the facts surrounding the expense. An expense is necessary if it is appropriate and helpful to the taxpayer's business. An expense is ordinary if it is one that is common and accepted in the particular business activity (*S.B. Heininger*, SCt, 44-1 USTC ¶ 9109).

Trade or Business. The term "trade or business" is not defined in the Internal Revenue Code, but is characterized as an activity carried on for a livelihood or for profit. A profit motive must be present and some type of economic activity must be conducted. In determining whether an activity is engaged in for profit, all facts and circumstances with respect to the activity are taken into account (Reg. § 1.183-2(b)). Among the factors that should normally be considered are: the manner in which the taxpayer carries on the activity; the expertise of the taxpayer or his or her advisors; the time and effort expended by the taxpayer in carrying on the activity; the expectation that assets used in the activity may appreciate in value; the success of the taxpayer in carrying on other similar or dissimilar activities; the taxpayer's history of income or losses with respect to the activity; the amount of occasional profits, if any, that are earned; the financial status of the taxpayer; and elements of personal pleasure or recreation.

No one factor is conclusive in making this determination. Also, it is not intended that only these factors are to be taken into account in making the determination, or that a determination is to be made on the basis that the number of factors, whether or not listed in the regulations, indicating a lack of profit objective exceeds the number of factors indicating a profit objective, or vice versa.

904. Business Start-Up Expenses. A taxpayer who enters a trade or business can elect to expense up to $5,000 of its start-up costs. The maximum deduction is reduced dollar for dollar if the start-up expenses exceed $50,000. The balance of any remaining start-up expenses is amortized over a 180-month period starting with the month in which the business begins (Code Sec. 195; Reg. § 1.195-1). The election is made on Part VI of Form 4562 and must be made no later than the due date for filing the return (including extensions) for the tax years the business begins or is acquired. The due date for filing any federal income tax return otherwise due on or after April 1, 2020, and before July 15, 2020, is automatically extended to July 15, 2020 (¶ 2505). A taxpayer who does not make the election must capitalize the start-up expenses (¶ 1305).

A taxpayer is deemed to elect to deduct and amortize start-up expenses for the tax year in which the active trade or business begins. A taxpayer may forego the deemed election by affirmatively electing to capitalize its start-up expenses. The election either to deduct and amortize start-up costs or capitalize them applies to all start-up expenses that are related to the active trade or business (Reg. § 1.195-1(b)). Start-up expenses are those paid or incurred in connection with:

- investigating the creation or acquisition of an active trade or business;

- creating an active trade or business; or

- any activity engaged in for profit or for the production of income before the day the active trade or business begins, in anticipation of that activity becoming an active trade or business.

The start-up expense must also be a cost that would be allowable as a deduction if it were paid or incurred in connection with an existing active business in the same field (Code Sec. 195(c)(1).

Start-up costs do not include any amount with respect to which a deduction is allowed for interest on debt (¶ 1043), taxes (¶ 1021), or research and experimental expenses (¶ 979). If the trade or business is disposed of completely by the taxpayer before the end of the 180-month period, any remaining deferred expenses may be deductible as a loss (¶ 1101).

The organizational costs of business entities are a separate class of expense from start-up expenses, though subject to similar rules. Corporate organization fees are discussed at ¶ 237. Costs of organizing a partnership are discussed at ¶ 477 and ¶ 481.

905. Business Expenses, Interest Deductions, and Losses for Related Taxpayers. No deduction is allowed for any trade or business expense or interest payable to the payee until the payee includes the payment in income if the payor and payee are related taxpayers (¶ 1717), and the payor is on the accrual method of accounting and the payee is on the cash method, (Code Sec. 267(a)(2)). A similar rule denies a deduction for a loss (except for a loss from a distribution in corporate liquidation) for property sold or exchanged between related taxpayers. However, the transferee's gain on a later sale or exchange of the property is recognized only to the extent that it exceeds the previously disallowed loss.

Compensation Paid

See CCH® AnswerConnect: *Business Expenses: Compensation and Employee Expenses* and *Compensation and Benefits* for more information on this topic.

906. Business Deduction for Compensation for Personal Services. A taxpayer carrying on a trade or business is entitled to deduct reasonable salaries or other compensation for personal services. The deduction is allowable for the year in which the salary is paid or incurred (Code Sec. 162(a)(1); Reg. § 1.162-7).

Reasonable compensation is the amount that would ordinarily be paid for like services by like enterprises in like circumstances. Thus, whether compensation is reasonable in a given situation depends on the relevant facts and circumstances, including personal ability, responsibility of the position, and local economic conditions. The U.S. Court of Appeals for the Seventh Circuit has used an independent-investor test that presumes that compensation is reasonable if the company's investors earn their expected rate of return (*Exacto Spring Corporation*, CA-7, 99-2 USTC ¶ 50,964). A bonus is deductible if it is paid for services performed, and when added to other salaries, it does not exceed reasonable compensation (Reg. § 1.162-9).

Compensation paid to a relative is deductible if the relative performs needed services that would otherwise be performed by an unrelated party. Likewise, the deduction is limited to the amount that would have been paid to a third party (*Transport Mfg. & Equip. Co.*, CA-8, 70-2 USTC ¶ 9627).

The IRS does not rule in advance on whether compensation is reasonable in amount (Rev. Proc. 2020-3).

Officer-Stockholders of Closely Held Corporations. An officer-shareholder of a closely-held corporation may deduct repayments of salary to the corporation that are made under an agreement requiring such repayments if the IRS determines the salaries are excessive (Rev. Rul. 69-115). The agreement must be legally enforceable and in existence *before* the excess salary is paid.

Excessive Employee Compensation. Publicly held corporations generally cannot deduct compensation paid to certain covered employees that exceeds $1 million per tax year (Code Sec. 162(m); Reg. § 1.162-27; Prop. Reg. § 1.162-33; Notice 2007-49; Notice 2018-68).

Effective for tax years beginning after 2017, publicly held corporations include all domestic publicly traded corporations and all foreign companies publicly traded through American depository receipts (ADRs). A covered employee is any employee of the taxpayer employed at any time during the tax year who:

- is the principal executive officer (PEO) or principal financial officer (PFO) of the taxpayer at any time during the tax year, including an individual acting in that capacity;
- is one of the three highest compensated officers for the tax year (other than the PEO or PFO); or
- was a covered employee of the taxpayer (or any predecessor) for any prior tax year beginning after December 31, 2016.

For tax years beginning after 2017, compensation includes any cash and noncash benefits paid for services, including commissions and performance-based compensation. It also includes any amount includible in the income of, or paid to, a person other than the covered employee, including after the death of the covered employee. Compensation does not include: (1) income from specified employee trusts, (2) annuity plans, pensions, or any benefit that is reasonably anticipated to be tax free; (3) income payable under a written binding contract which was in effect on February 17, 1993; and (4) compensation paid before a corporation became publicly held. Compensation paid after 2017 is not subject to these rules if it is paid in accordance with a written binding contract in effect on November 2, 2017 (Code Sec. 162(m); Proposed Reg. § 1.162-33(g)).

Performance-Based Compensation. For tax years beginning before January 1, 2018, the $1 million limit generally does not apply to certain performance-based compensation payable solely on account of attaining one or more performance goals (Code Sec. 162(m)(4)(C), prior to being stricken by the Tax Cuts and Jobs Act (P.L. 115-97); Reg. § 1.162-27(e)). Performance-based compensation can include compensation issued in the form of stock rights and options exercised when the plan specifies the maximum number of shares that may be granted to all employees in the aggregate. Performance-based compensation attributable to stock rights or stock options must include a specific per-employee limitation on the amount granted.

Awards paid under a corporate bonus plan are not qualified performance-based compensation if the plan allows payments to be made, even if the specified performance goals have not been met, upon the employee's retirement, termination without cause, or voluntary termination of employment for good reason (Rev. Rul. 2008-13). If the bonus was paid solely for attaining a performance goal, the goal must be determined by a compensation committee consisting solely of two or more outside directors. An outside director cannot be a current employee, a former employee who receives compensation during the year, or a current or former officer (Rev. Rul. 2008-32).

Deferred Compensation Plans. For unfunded deferred compensation plans, the employer deducts compensation when the compensation, or amount attributable to it, is included in the gross income of the recipient (¶ 723) (Code Sec. 404(a)(5) and (b)(1)). Other benefits that are excluded from the recipient's gross income are deductible when they otherwise would have been includible but for the exclusion (Code Sec. 404(b)(2)). This rule also applies to compensation paid to independent contractors (Code Sec. 404(d)).

A plan is unfunded if it consists of an unsecured promise to pay compensation at some time in the future. If the employer sets aside a reserve for the future obligation, the plan is unfunded if the employee has no rights in the reserve or its earnings, and if the reserve remains solely the property of the employer or other payor, subject to the claims of creditors (Rev. Rul. 55-525).

A plan is presumed to defer compensation if the compensation is received after the 15th day of the third calendar month after the end of the employer's tax year in which the related services are rendered. This presumption may be overcome if the employer establishes that it was administratively or economically impractical to avoid the deferral of compensation beyond the 2½-month period. Payments within the 2½-month period are not deferred compensation and may be accrued by an accrual-method employer in the year earned by the employee (Temp. Reg. § 1.404(b)-1T, Q&A-2).

See ¶ 2117 and ¶ 2199 for rules governing the employer's deduction for compensation for deferred compensation plans.

Health Insurance Providers. The deduction for compensation or remuneration paid to officers, directors, and employees of covered health insurance providers, including those that provide services for or on behalf of covered health insurance providers, is limited to $500,000 for disqualified tax years (Code Sec. 162(m)(6); Reg. § 1.162-31). A disqualified tax year is any tax year in which the employer is a covered health insurance provider. A covered health insurance provider is a health insurance issuer for any tax year during which at least 25 percent of the gross premiums it receives from providing health insurance coverage is from providing minimum essential coverage (¶ 119). A *de minimis* exception applies if health insurance premiums are less than two percent of gross revenues.

907. Golden Parachute Payments. A corporation that enters into a contract agreeing to pay an employee additional compensation if control or ownership of the corporation changes cannot take a deduction for an "excess parachute payment" made to a disqualified individual (Code Secs. 280G and 4999(a)). A disqualified individual is an officer, shareholder, or highly compensated person who performs personal services for the corporation as an employee or independent contractor. A personal service corporation is treated as an individual. The disqualified individual is subject to an excise tax of 20 percent of the excess parachute payment in addition to the income tax due.

Parachute Payment Defined. A parachute payment is any payment in the nature of compensation to a disqualified individual if:

- the payment is contingent on a change in the ownership or effective control of the corporation or a substantial portion of the assets of the corporation; and

- the aggregate present value of the contingent payments equals or exceeds three times the individual's base amount.

A payment in the nature of compensation to a disqualified individual made under an agreement that violates any securities law or regulations is also a parachute payment. Parachute payments do not include reasonable compensation for personal services to be rendered on or after the date of change or for personal services actually rendered before the date of change, or payments to or from certain qualified plans.

Base Amount. The base amount is the individual's annualized includible compensation for the base period. This is the most recent five tax years ending before the date on which the ownership or control changed, or the portion of that period during which the disqualified individual performed personal services for the corporations.

Exceptions. A parachute payment generally does not include any payment made to a disqualified individual by a small business corporation. It also does not include a payment from a corporation if, immediately before the change in ownership or control, none of the corporation's stock was readily tradable on an established securities market and the payment met shareholder approval requirements.

¶907

Excess Parachute Payment. An excess parachute payment is the portion of any parachute payment that exceeds the base amount, reduced, in the case of a change-in-control parachute payment, by the excess of the amount of the payment determined to be reasonable compensation for services performed before the date of the change, over average compensation.

908. Business Deductions for Contributions for Funded Health Benefits. An employer's deduction for contributions to a funded welfare benefit plan for sickness, accident, hospitalization, or medical benefits is governed by Code Sec. 419 (¶ 2011) (Temp. Reg. § 1.162-10T). Although amounts that are added to a self-insurance reserve account are not currently deductible, actual claims charged to the account are deductible (*General Dynamics Corp.*, SCt, 87-1 USTC ¶ 9280). Group health plans that fail to provide COBRA continuing coverage to qualified beneficiaries may subject employers to an excise tax (Code Sec. 4980B).

Self-Employed Persons. A self-employed individual may deduct 100 percent of amounts paid during the year for health insurance for himself or herself, as well as his or her spouse and dependents (Code Sec. 162(l)). The deduction cannot exceed the taxpayer's net earned income derived from the trade or business for which the insurance plan was established, minus the deduction for 50 percent of the self-employment tax and/or the deduction for contributions to qualified retirement plans, self-employed pensions (SEPs), or SIMPLE plans. The deduction is not available for amounts paid during any month, or part of a month, that the self-employed individual was able to participate in a subsidized health plan maintained by his or her employer or spouse's employer. The IRS has issued guidance providing optional calculation methods to claim the health insurance premium assistance credit (¶ 1431) and the self-employed health insurance deduction (Rev. Proc. 2014-41).

Children Under the Age of 27. Children under the age of 27 are considered dependents of a taxpayer for purposes of the deduction for the health insurance costs of a self-employed person, spouse, and dependents. See ¶ 137A for the definition of a dependent.

908A. Business Deduction for Overhead Disability Insurance. A taxpayer may deduct as a trade or business expense premiums paid on a disability insurance policy that pays overhead expenses should the taxpayer become disabled. The portion of the premiums attributable to overhead expenses that are actually incurred in the operation of the business are deductible (i.e., rent, utilities, depreciation, and employee's salaries), but the portion of the premiums paid to provide the taxpayer's salary, fees, or drawing account are not (Rev. Rul. 55-264). The proceeds of the policy are includible in gross income. If an insurance premium is paid in advance for more than one year, only a pro rata portion of the premium is deductible for each year, regardless of the taxpayer's method of accounting (Reg. § 1.461-1; Rev. Rul. 70-413).

908B. Business Deduction for Employer-Provided Day Care. An employer's payments to a day care center are a deductible business expense if the purpose of providing the day care is:

- to provide employees with a place to send their children while at work, so that the employees can be reassured that the children are receiving proper care;

- to reduce absenteeism, increase productivity, and reduce company training costs; and

- to reduce employee turnover (Rev. Rul. 73-348).

An S corporation, however, could not deduct amounts it paid for day care for its sole shareholder's preschool children if there was no direct relationship to the corporation's business, and it did not pay day care expenses for any of its other employees (*F.M. Settimo,* Dec. 56,694(M), 92 TCM 473).

Up to $5,000 of employer-provided child or dependent care assistance services is excludable from the employee's gross income (¶ 2065).

909. Business Deduction for Life Insurance Premiums. Premiums paid by an employer for insurance on the life of an employee or officer are deductible only if it can be shown that: (1) the premium payments are in the nature of additional compensation; (2) total compensation, including premiums, is not unreasonable; and (3) the employer is not directly or indirectly a beneficiary under the policy (*L. Hyman & Co.*, Dec. 6447, 21

¶908

BTA 159; *Brown Agency, Inc.*, Dec. 6615, 21 BTA 1111). However, an employer cannot deduct premiums paid under a split dollar arrangement (¶ 2057).

An employer can deduct premiums on group-term life insurance covering the lives of employees only if the employer is not a direct or indirect beneficiary (Code Sec. 264(a)(1); Reg. § 1.264-1). The premiums generally represent income to the employee to the extent that the coverage exceeds $50,000 (¶ 2055).

No deduction is generally allowed for interest paid or accrued on a debt incurred or continued to purchase or carry any single premium life insurance, endowment or annuity contract. If substantially all the premiums on a life insurance or endowment contract are paid within four years from the date of purchase, or if an amount is deposited with the insurer for payment of a substantial number of future premiums, it is regarded as a single premium contract (Code Sec. 264(a)(2) and (c)).

Interest on a debt incurred to purchase or continue a life insurance, endowment, or annuity contract under a purchase plan that contemplates the systematic borrowing of part or all of the increases in cash value is not deductible (Code Sec. 264(a)(3)). However, an interest deduction is allowed in limited situations (Code Sec. 264(d)). Special rules may permit the deduction of interest incurred for key person policies owned by corporations (Code Sec. 264(e)).

Meal, Entertainment, and Gift Expenses

See CCH® AnswerConnect: *Travel, Meals, and Entertainment Expenses for Business* for more information on this topic.

910. Business Deduction for Entertainment Expenses. Special limits are imposed on the deduction of business-related entertainment, meals, and gift expenses in addition to those imposed by other Code sections (Code Sec. 274(a)(1); Reg. § 1.274-2).

- Entertainment expenses paid or incurred after December 31, 2017, are generally not deductible as trade or business expenses including those for a facility used in connection with entertainment.

- Entertainment expenses paid or incurred before January 1, 2018, are generally not deductible as trade or business expenses unless they are (1) *directly related* to the active conduct of the trade or business (¶ 911), or (2) for entertainment directly before or after a substantial and bona fide business discussion *associated with* the conduct of the trade or business (¶ 912).

Certain entertainment expenses are not subject to these limits (¶ 915). Also, note that entertainment expenses paid or incurred before January 1, 2018, and meal expenses are subject to a 50-percent limit (¶ 916), but there are numerous exceptions to this limit (¶ 917).

For purposes of Code Sec. 274(a)(1), entertainment is generally any activity considered to constitute amusement, or recreation such as entertaining guests at nightclubs, sporting events, theaters, etc. A taxpayer's trade or business is considered in applying an objective test as to what constitutes entertainment. For example, a ticket to a play is generally an entertainment expense, but it might be a business expense if the taxpayer is a professional theater critic.

In cases where food and beverages are provided at an entertainment activity, the activity is considered entertainment, and is not deductible after December 31, 2017. However, 50 percent of the food and beverage expenses may still be deducted, so long as they are purchased separately (Notice 2018-76; Proposed Reg. § 1.274-11).

911. Directly-Related to Business Test for Entertainment Expenses Incurred Before 2018. In order for an entertainment expense paid or incurred before January 1, 2018, to meet the directly related test for a deductible business expense (¶ 910), the taxpayer must have had more than a general expectation of deriving income, or some other specific business benefit, from the entertainment at some indefinite future time. The taxpayer must engage in the active conduct of business with the person being entertained, and the active conduct of business must be the principal aspect of the combined business and entertainment (Reg. § 1.274-2(c)). Entertainment expenses paid or incurred after December 31, 2017, are generally not deductible.

912. Entertainment Associated with Trade or Business Before 2018. Entertainment expenses paid or incurred before January 1, 2018, and associated with the active conduct of the taxpayer's business are deductible if they directly precede or follow a bona fide and substantial business discussion (¶ 910). This includes goodwill expenditures to obtain new business or encourage continuation of existing business relationships. The business discussion must be the principal aspect of the combined entertainment and business discussion and must represent an active effort by the taxpayer to obtain income or other specific business benefit (Reg. § 1.274-2(d)). Entertainment expenses paid or incurred after December 31, 2017, are generally not deductible.

913. Business-Related Entertainment Facility. No business deduction is allowed for any expense for entertainment facilities, such as yachts, hunting lodges, swimming pools, tennis courts, or bowling alleys (¶ 910) (Code Sec. 274(a)(1)(B)). However, expenses for recreational facilities primarily for the benefit of non highly compensated employees generally are deductible (Reg. § 1.274-2(f)(2)(v)).

913A. Business-Related Club Dues. Club dues generally are not a business expense deduction. This rule extends to business, social, athletic, luncheon, sporting, airline, and hotel clubs (Code Sec. 274(a)(3))). Dues paid to professional or public service organizations (e.g., accounting associations, or Kiwanis and Rotary clubs) are deductible if they are paid for business reasons and the organization's principal purpose is *not* to conduct entertainment activities for members or their guests or to provide those parties with access to entertainment facilities (Reg. § 1.274-2(a)(2)(iii)).

914. Business Deduction for Meals Expenses. Entertainment expenses paid or incurred after December 31, 2017, are generally not deductible as trade or business expenses (¶ 910). However, meal expenses that are not entertainment expenses may be deducted as business expenses even after 2017 if they are ordinary and necessary expenses paid or incurred during the tax year in carrying on a trade or business. (¶ 953) (Code Sec. 274(k) and (n); Proposed Reg. § 1.274-12).

Additional restrictions placed on the deduction of meal expenses include:

- the taxpayer or the taxpayer's employee are present at the meal;
- the food or beverage is not lavish or extravagant under the circumstances;
- the food or beverage is provided to current or potential clients or business contacts; and
- in cases where food and beverages provided during entertainment, the food and beverages is purchased or invoiced separately.

These restrictions do not apply to the expenses described in exceptions (2), (3), (4), (7), (8), and (9) at ¶ 915.

Employer-Provided Meals. No deduction is allowed for amounts that an employer pays or incurs *after December 31, 2025,* for: (1) meals excludable from an employee's income because they are provided to employees and their spouses and dependents for the employer's convenience and on the employer's business premises, or (2) food, beverage, and facility expenses for meals that are a *de minimis* fringe benefit (¶ 2089) (Code Sec. 274(o)).

915. Exceptions to Entertainment Rules. The following entertainment expenses are not subject to the special rules for the deduction of entertainment expenses (¶ 912, ¶ 913, and ¶ 914). In addition, they are not subject to the elimination of the entertainment expense deduction. These expenses are deductible as long as they meet the ordinary and necessary requirements and are properly substantiated (Code Sec. 274(e)). However, they may be subject to the 50-percent limit on meals and entertainment expenses (¶ 916 and ¶ 917). The exceptions are:

(1) food and beverages for employees furnished on the business premises (Reg. § 1.274-2(f)(2)(ii));

(2) expenses for services, goods, and facilities that are treated as compensation and as wages for withholding tax purposes, but if the recipient is a specified individual such as an officer, director, or 10-percent shareholder or related person, the employer's deduction is limited to the compensation reported (Reg. § 1.274-2(f)(2)(iii));

(3) reimbursed expenses, but only:

(a) if the services relating to the expenses are performed for an employer that has not treated the expenses as wages subject to withholding, or

(b) if the services are performed for a person other than an employer and the taxpayer incurring the reimbursed expenses accounts to that person (Reg. § 1.274-2(f)(2)(iv));

(4) recreational expenses primarily for employees who are not highly compensated (¶ 2114) (e.g., a company picnic) (Reg. § 1.274-2(f)(2)(v));

(5) expenses of employees', stockholders', agents', or directors' business meetings (Reg. § 1.274-2(f)(2)(vi));

(6) expenses directly related and necessary to attendance at a business meeting of a tax-exempt business league, including a real estate board, chamber of commerce or board of trade (Reg. § 1.274-2(f)(2)(vii));

(7) expenses for goods, services, and facilities made available to the public (Reg. § 1.274-2(f)(2)(vii));

(8) expenses for entertainment sold to customers in a bona fide transaction for adequate consideration ((Reg. § 1.274-2(f)(2)(ix)); and

(9) expenses for goods, services, and facilities that are furnished to a nonemployee as entertainment, amusement or recreation and are includible in the recipient's income as compensation for services (¶ 713) or as a taxable prize or award (¶ 785).

916. 50-Percent Limit for Meal and Entertainment Expenses. The business deduction for meal expenses—and for entertainment expenses paid or incurred before January 1, 2018—is generally limited to 50 percent of such expenses (Code Sec. 274(n)). Food and beverage costs incurred in the course of travel away from home fall within the scope of this rule.

The 50-percent limit applies to all meal expenses, and entertainment expenses (paid or incurred before January 1, 2018), unless an exception applies (¶ 917). The limit is applied only after determining the amount of the otherwise allowable deductions. For instance, the portion of a travel meal that is lavish and extravagant must first be subtracted from the meal cost before the 50-percent limit is applied. Related expenses, such as taxes, tips, room rental and parking fees, must be included in the total expense before applying the 50-percent limit. Allowable deductions for transportation costs to and from a business meal are not reduced.

Transportation Workers. The deductible percentage of the cost of meals consumed while away from home by individuals subject to Department of Transportation hours of service rules (e.g., interstate truck and bus drivers and certain railroad, airline, and merchant marine employees) is 80 percent (Code Sec. 274(n)(3)).

Leased Employees. If an employee or independent contractor incurs unreimbursed meal and incidental expenses (M&IE) in connection with the performance of services for a third party, the 50-percent limit applies to any deduction claimed by the employee or independent contractor (Reg. § 1.274-2(f)(2)(iv)). However, if an employee or independent contractor accounts for the expenses to a leasing company and is reimbursed under an allowance arrangement with a payment that is treated as compensation, the leasing company, rather than the employee or independent contractor, bears the expense and is subject to the 50-percent limit. Similarly, if the leased company accounts for the expenses to the third party and is reimbursed under an allowance arrangement, the third party bears the expenses and is subject to the 50-percent limit on its deduction.

917. Exceptions to 50-Percent Limit for Meal and Entertainment Expenses. The following expenses are *not* subject to the 50-percent limit (80-percent limit for certain transportations workers (¶ 916)):

- expenses described in categories (2), (3), (4), (7), (8), and (9) at ¶ 915;

- food and beverage expenses paid or incurred before January 1, 2026, and associated with benefits that are excludable from the recipient's gross income as a *de minimis* fringe benefit (¶ 2089);

- the cost of a ticket package to a sporting event and related expenses paid or incurred before January 1, 2018, if the event is organized to benefit a tax-exempt organization, all net proceeds are contributed to the organization, and volunteers perform substantially all of the work in carrying out the event (in other situations, a deduction for a ticket is limited to the ticket's face value) (Code Sec. 274(l)(1), prior to being stricken by the Tax Cuts and Jobs Act (P.L. 115-97)). ;

- an employee's meal expenses incurred while moving that are reimbursed by the employer and includible in the employee's gross income (¶ 1073); and

- expenses for food and beverages provided to employees on certain vessels, and oil or gas platforms and drilling rigs and their support camps (Code Sec. 274(n)).

Entertainment expenses paid or incurred after December 31, 2017, are generally not deductible (¶ 910).

Skyboxes. If a skybox is rented for more than one event, the deduction for amounts paid or incurred before January 1, 2018, may not exceed the price of non-luxury box seats (subject to the usual 50-percent limit) (Code Sec. 274(l)(2), prior to being stricken by the Tax Cuts and Jobs Act (P.L. 115-97)).

Tickets to College Sporting Events. For tax years beginning before 2018, for any payment to or for an institution of higher education that would be allowable as a charitable deduction but for the fact that the taxpayer receives (directly or indirectly) the right to purchase tickets for seating at an athletic event in an athletic stadium of the institution, 80 percent of that payment is treated as a charitable contribution (¶ 1061). For tax years beginning after 2017, no charitable deduction is allowed for such a payment (Code Sec. 170(l)).

918. Business Gifts. Deductions for business gifts, whether made directly or indirectly, are limited to $25 per recipient per year (Code Sec. 274(b)(1); Reg. § 1.274-3). Items clearly of an advertising nature that cost $4 or less and signs, display racks, or other promotional materials given for use on business premises are not gifts.

919. Business Deduction for Employee Achievement Awards. An employer may deduct up to $400 of the cost of an employee achievement award for all nonqualified plan awards to each employee (Code Sec. 274(j)). The deduction for the cost of a qualified plan award made to a particular employee is limited to $1,600 per year, taking into account all other qualified and nonqualified awards made to that employee during the tax year.

An employee achievement award is an item of tangible personal property awarded to an employee as part of a meaningful presentation for length-of-service or safety achievements, and under circumstances that do not create a significant likelihood of disguised compensation (¶ 2069). Tangible personal property does not include cash, cash equivalents, gift certificates, or other intangible property such as vacations, meals, lodging, tickets to events, stocks, bonds, or other securities. For amounts paid or incurred after December 31, 2017, tangible personal property also does not include gift cards, gift coupons, or gift certificates (other than arrangements granting only the right to select and receive tangible personal property from a limited assortment of items preselected or preapproved by the employer), as well as other similar items (Code Sec. 274(j)(3)(ii)).

A qualified plan award is an employee achievement award provided under an established written plan or program that does not discriminate in favor of highly compensated employees (¶ 2114) as to eligibility or benefits (Code Sec. 274(j)(3)(B)). An employee achievement award is not a qualified plan award if the average cost of all employee achievement awards under the plan exceeds $400. This average cost calculation includes the entire cost of all qualified plan awards other than awards of nominal value (Code Sec. 274(j)(2)(A)).

A length of service award does not qualify if it is received during the employee's first five years of service or if the employee has received another length of service award (other than a *de minimis* fringe benefit (¶ 2089)) during the year or within the last four years. An award is not a safety achievement award if it is made to a manager, administrator, clerical employee, or other professional employee, or if, during the tax year, awards for safety achievement previously have been made to more than 10 percent of the employees, excluding managers, administrators, clerical employees, or other professional employees (Code Sec. 274(j)(4)).

Taxes

See CCH® AnswerConnect: *Business Expenses: Taxes and Licenses Expenses* for more information on this topic.

920. Business Deduction for Taxes. All state, local, and foreign taxes (¶ 1021) directly attributable to a taxpayer's trade or business or activities for the production of income are generally deductible in the year in which the taxes are paid or accrued (Code Sec. 164(a)). If taxes other than those specified as deductible are paid or accrued by the taxpayer in connection with the acquisition of property, then they are treated as part of the cost of the acquired property or, if in connection with the disposition of property, as a reduction in the amount realized. The uniform capitalization rules also require some taxpayers to capitalize certain taxes that would otherwise be deductible (¶ 1330).

921. Business Deduction for FUTA Taxes. The Federal Unemployment Tax Act (FUTA) tax (¶ 2649) is an *excise* tax, so an employer may deduct it as a business expense if it represents an ordinary and necessary expense paid or incurred during the tax year in the conduct of a trade or business, or the production of income (Reg. § 1.164-2(f)). The FUTA tax is deductible as a business expense after application of credits for the employer's contributions to the state unemployment fund (Code Sec. 3302(a)(1)). The tax is deductible when paid for a taxpayer on the cash-method of accounting (¶ 1515). The deduction may be accrued by a taxpayer on the accural-method of accounting (¶ 1540) for the calendar year that the wages were paid even though the tax is not due until the following year.

922. Business Deduction for State Unemployment Insurance and Disability Fund Contributions. An employer's contributions to a state unemployment insurance fund are deductible as taxes only if they are classified as taxes under state law and are incurred in carrying on a trade or business or for the production of income (IRS Pub. 535). If the state does not classify the contributions as taxes, the employer may be able to deduct them as a business expense. Similar treatment applies to employer contributions to state disability funds. An employee who is required to contribute to a state unemployment compensation fund may claim an itemized deduction for the contribution as a state income tax (¶ 1023). Also, compulsory employee contributions to state disability funds are deductible as itemized deductions by individuals as state income taxes. However, employees cannot deduct their contributions to private disability benefit plans (Rev. Rul. 81-192).

923. Business Deduction for FICA Taxes. An employer's share of the Federal Insurance Contributions Act (FICA) tax for Social Security and Medicare (¶ 2648) is an *excise* tax, so the employer may deduct it as a business expense if it represents an ordinary and necessary expense paid or incurred during the tax year in the conduct of a trade or business or for the production of income (Reg. § 1.164-2(f)). The employer contribution on wages paid to a domestic worker is not deductible unless it qualifies as a business expense (*R.A. Biggs*, CA-6, 71-1 USTC ¶ 9306).

An employee's portion of FICA taxes is not deductible (¶ 1025). However, if the employer pays the employee's portion of the tax without deduction from the employee's wages under an agreement with the employee, the amount is deductible by the employer as a business expense. It is also includes wage income to the employee (Rev. Rul. 86-14).

A self-employed individual may deduct from gross income 50 percent of the self-employment tax imposed for the tax year, other than the additional 0.9-percent Medicare tax on income over a certain threshold (¶ 2664).

924. Deduction for Federal and State Income Tax. Federal income taxes are not deductible in determining taxable income of any taxpayer (Code Sec. 275). However, they are deductible in determining the amount of a corporation's income subject to the accumulated earnings tax (¶ 251) and the personal holding company tax (¶ 275) (Reg. §§ 1.535-2 and 1.545-2). A corporation or partnership may deduct its state income taxes as a business expense. State income taxes that are based on net business income may be deducted only by self-employed individuals as an itemized deduction on Schedule A (Form 1040). If the state income tax is based on gross business income, the tax may be deducted as a business expense (Temp. Reg. § 1.62-1T(d)).

Charitable Contributions

See CCH® AnswerConnect: *Charitable Contribution Deduction for Corporations* for more information on this topic.

927. Charitable Deduction Limits for Corporations. A corporation's deduction for charitable contributions is limited to 10 percent of its taxable income for the year (25 percent for qualified contributions in 2020), computed without regard to:

- the deduction for charitable contributions;

- the corporate deductions for dividends received and for dividends paid on certain preferred stock of public utilities;

- the limitation on the deduction for bond premium;

- any net operating loss or capital loss carryback to the tax year;

- the deduction for domestic production activities for tax years beginning before January 1, 2018; and

- the deduction allowed to specified agricultural or horticultural cooperatives for qualified business income (QBI) for tax years beginning after December 31, 2017 (Code Sec. 170(b)(2); Reg. § 1.170A-11).

Corporate donors that qualify as farmers or ranchers may deduct certain qualified conservation contributions of real property interests (¶ 1063), up to the excess of the donor's taxable income over all other allowable charitable contributions. Similar treatment applies to Native Corporation donors for qualified conservation contributions of land that was conveyed under the Alaska Native Claims Settlement Act (Code Sec. 170(b)(2)(C)). A corporate and noncorporate taxpayer may claim an enhanced deduction of 15 percent of income (25 percent for 2020) for donations of food inventory (¶ 930A).

Charitable contributions that exceed the 10-percent limit may be carried over to the corporation's five succeeding tax years, but deductions in those years are also subject to the maximum limitation (Code Sec. 170(d)(2)). Excess qualified conservation contributions by qualified corporate farmers and ranchers, as well as by Native Corporations, are carried over to the 15 succeeding tax years (Code Sec. 170(b)(2)(B)).

Except for the carryover rule, a deduction is allowed only for a charitable contribution paid during the tax year. An accrual-basis corporation may elect to treat as paid during the tax year all or a portion of a contribution that is actually paid within three-and-one-half months after the close of the tax year if it was authorized by the board of directors during the year (Code Sec. 170(a)(2)). For tax years beginning before January 1, 2016 (or before January 1, 2026, for C corporations whose tax year ends on June 30), the contribution must be made within two-and-one-half months after the close of the tax year (Act Sec. 2006(a)(3)(B) of the Surface Transportation and Veterans Health Care Choice Improvement Act of 2015 (P.L. 114-41)).

COVID-19 (Coronavirus). The percentage limitation on charitable contributions deductions for corporations is temporarily increased from 10 percent to 25 percent for qualified charitable contributions made during the 2020 calendar year (Sec. 2205(a) of the Coronavirus Aid, Relief, and Economic Security (CARES) Act (P.L. 116-136)). A corporation may carry forward for five years any qualifying contribution that exceeds the 25-percent ceiling for the tax year of the contribution. A qualified contribution for this purpose is a charitable contribution made in cash during the 2020 calendar year to an organization described in Code Sec. 170(b)(1)(A). It cannot be made to a Code Sec. 509(a)(3) supporting organization under or a new or existing donor advised fund. It also does not apply to cash contributions carried over from previous tax years. If the taxpayer is a partner in a partnership or a shareholder in an S corporation, the election to claim the deduction with respect to qualified contributions is made by the partner or shareholder.

Disaster relief. The percentage limit for charitable contributions was temporarily waived for qualified contributions made for relief efforts in qualified disaster areas. The deduction for qualified contributions was limited to 100 percent of the corporation's taxable income, less the amount of all other charitable deductions allowed during the tax year. Excess contributions may be carried over to the succeeding five tax years. Qualified contributions are cash contributions:

- paid after December 31, 2017, and before February 19, 2020, for relief efforts in qualified disaster areas (Act Secs. 201 and 204(a) of the Taxpayer Certainty and Disaster Tax Relief Act of 2019 (P.L. 116-94));

- paid after October 7, 2017, and before January 1, 2018 for relief efforts in the California wildfire disaster area (Act Secs. 20101 and 20104(a) of the Bipartisan Budget Act of 2018 (P.L. 115-123)); and

- paid after August 22, 2017, and before January 1, 2018, for relief efforts in the Hurricanes Harvey, Irma, or Maria disaster areas (Act Secs. 501 and 504(a) of the Disaster Tax Relief and Airport and Airway Extension Act of 2017 (P.L. 115-63), amended by Act Sec. 20201 of P.L. 115-123).

The contributions must be paid to a 50-percent charitable organization (i.e., public charity), other than a supporting private foundation under Code Sec. 509(a)(3) (¶ 607) or donor advised fund (¶ 610). The taxpayer must obtain a contemporaneous written acknowledgment from the charity (¶ 1070A) that the contribution is used for relief efforts in the designated disaster area. The taxpayer also must elect to treat the charitable contribution as a qualified contribution. In the case of a partnership or S corporation, the election is made by each partner or shareholder.

930. Charitable Contributions of Inventory or Scientific Property. The deduction for a charitable contribution of ordinary income property is generally the fair market value of that property less the amount that would have been ordinary income if the property had been sold at its fair market value on the date of the contribution (¶ 1062). There are exceptions to this rule in the case of certain contributions by corporations.

Inventory-Type Property. If a corporation, other than an S corporation, makes a gift of inventory, property held for sale to customers in the ordinary course of business, or depreciable or real property used in the trade or business, it may deduct its basis for the property, plus one-half of the property's unrealized appreciation. However, the claimed deduction may not exceed twice the basis of the property (Code Sec. 170(e)(3)(B)). Moreover, no deduction is allowed for any part of the appreciation that would be ordinary income resulting from recapture. To qualify, the gift must be made to a qualified public charity or private operating foundation, and the donee's use of the property must be for the care of the ill, the needy, or infants.

Scientific Research Property. A corporation, other than an S corporation, personal holding company, or service organization, is entitled to the same deduction for a contribution of certain ordinary income property to an institution of higher education or to an exempt scientific research organization for research purposes as that for inventory-type property (Code Sec. 170(e)(4)). To qualify as a research contribution:

- the contributed property must be tangible personal property that is inventory or held for the sale to customers;

- the contributed property must be scientific equipment or apparatus that was constructed or assembled by the donor;

- the contribution must be made within two years of construction or assembly;

- the original use of the property must be by the donee;

- substantially all of the donee's use of the property must be in the United States, for research or experimentation, or for research training, in physical or biological sciences;

- the donee may not transfer the property for money, other property, or services; and

- the donor must receive a written statement from the donee that the organization will comply with the use and transfer requirements.

930A. Charitable Contributions of Food. Corporate and noncorporate taxpayers are entitled to an enhanced deduction for charitable donations of food inventory from any trade or business (Code Sec. 170(e)(3)(C)). The deduction is generally the fair market value of the property less the amount that would have been ordinary income if the property had been sold at its fair market value on the date of the contribution, subject to certain exceptions in the case of certain contributions by corporations (¶ 930). The food inventory must consist of items fit for human consumption and be contributed to a qualified charity or private operating foundation for use in the care of the ill, the needy, or infants.

A noncorporate taxpayer's total deduction for food inventory donations during the tax year is limited to a maximum of 15 percent of the taxpayer's net income from all trades and businesses from which the donations are made during the tax year. In the case of a C corporation, the deduction is limited to 15 percent of the corporation's taxable income. However, the deduction limitation from any trade or business is temporarily increased from 15 percent to 25 percent for percent contribution base limit applies to contributions of food inventory made during 2020 by any corporate or noncorporate taxpayer (¶ 927) (Sec. 2205(b) of the Coronavirus Aid, Relief, and Economic Security (CARES) Act (P.L. 116-136)). Excess contributions are carried forward to the five succeeding tax years. Other special rules: (1) coordinate the overall corporate deduction limitation with the food inventory contribution rules; (2) include a presumption concerning the basis of food inventory donated by certain businesses; and (3) include presumptions that may be used when valuing certain donated food inventory (Code Sec. 170(e)(3)(C)(ii) and (iii)).

931. Charitable Contribution Rules for Corporations. The rules concerning a deduction for the following charitable contributions are the same regardless of whether the contribution is made by a corporate or noncorporate taxpayer:

- gifts of appreciated property (¶ 1062);
- use of property—partial interests (¶ 1063);
- reduction for interest (¶ 1065);
- gift of future interest in tangible personal property (¶ 1069);
- transfers in trust (¶ 1070);
- appraisals (¶ 1071); and
- denial of deduction (¶ 1061).

See ¶ 1070A for the reporting, recordkeeping, and substantiation rules for charitable contributions.

Business Interest

See CCH® AnswerConnect: *Business Interest Deduction* for more information on this topic.

937. Deduction of Business Interest. Interest expenses or other borrowing costs incurred in a trade or business, or in the production of rental or royalty income, are generally deductible from gross income in the year paid or accrued depending on the taxpayer's method of accounting (Code Sec. 163). There are several limitations on the deduction of interest for prepaid interest (¶ 1055), investment interest paid by noncorporate taxpayers (¶ 1057), interest paid on debt with original issue discount (¶ 1952), and interest paid on debt not in registered form (¶ 1963). Interest may also be required to be capitalized if allocable to the production of certain property (¶ 1340).

Business Interest Deduction Limit. A taxpayer's deduction of business interest expenses paid or incurred for the tax year is generally limited to the sum of:

- the taxpayer's business interest income for the tax year for which the taxpayer is claiming the deduction (not including investment income);
- 30 percent of the taxpayer's adjusted taxable income (ATI), but not less than zero;
- the taxpayer's floor plan financing interest (Code Sec. 163(j); Prop. Reg. § 1.163(j)-2).

The limit is increased to 50 percent of ATI for the 2019 or 2020 tax year for any taxpayer other than a partnership in response to the COVID-19 (coronavirus) crisis. In the case of a partnership, the limit is increased to 50 percent of the taxpayer's ATI for the tax year beginning in 2020 only. It remains 30 percent of ATI for any tax year of the partnership beginning in 2019. However, a special allocation of excess business interest expense (EBIE) to a partner applies for the 2019 tax year unless the partner elects otherwise. A taxpayer may elect not to use the 50 percent ATI limit in 2019 or 2020 but continue to use the 30 percent limit. In addition, a taxpayer other than a partnership may elect for any tax year beginning in 2020 to use its ATI from the 2019 tax year to calculate its limitation (Code Sec. 163(j)(10), added by the Coronavirus Aid, Relief, and Economic Security (CARES) Act (P.L. 116-136); Rev. Proc. 2020-22).

Any business interest not allowed as a deduction for the tax year generally may be carried forward and treated as business interest paid or accrued in the succeeding tax year. However, any disallowed business interest of a partnership is not carried forward but instead is treated as EBIE that is allocated to each partner in the same manner as any non-separately stated taxable income or loss. Also, disallowed business interest of a C corporation is carried forward to the succeeding tax year but current-year business interest expense is deducted before any disallowed business interest carryforward from a prior tax year is deducted. Carryforwards of a C corporation are generally deducted in the order of the tax year that they arose, beginning with the earliest tax year (Prop. Reg. § 1.163(j)-5).

Small and Excepted Businesses. The § 163(j) limit applies to all taxpayers except for small businesses that meet the gross receipts test to use the cash method of accounting (¶ 1515). A taxpayer meets the small business test for the tax year if its average annual gross receipts for the three prior tax years do not exceed a threshold amount ($26 million for 2019 and 2020). The § 163(j) limit also does not apply to certain excepted businesses including a trade or business of providing services as an employee, an electing real property trade or business, an electing farming business, and certain regulated utility businesses (Prop. Reg. § 1.163(j)-9).

No election out of the § 163(j) limit is required for an excepted trade or business of providing services as an employee or utility trade or business. The election out of the § 163(j) limit by a real property trade or business and farming business is made by attaching a statement to the taxpayer's timely filed original tax return (including extensions). The due date for filing any federal income tax return otherwise due on or after April 1, 2020, and before July 15, 2020, is automatically extended to July 15, 2020 (¶ 2505). A taxpayer must make an election for a real property trade or business, or farming business, with respect to each eligible trade or business, but a taxpayer may make elections for multiple trades or businesses on a single election statement. In the case of a partnership, the election is made on the partnership return. The election applies to the current tax year and all subsequent tax years. Once made, the election is irrevocable but may automatically terminate in certain circumstances. A safe harbor is provided that allows a taxpayer to treat certain infrastructure trades or businesses as electing real property trades or businesses for this purpose (Rev. Proc. 2018-59). A taxpayer is provided an extension to file an election, or the opportunity to revoke an election, to be an electing real property trade or business or electing farming business for the 2018, 2019, or 2020 tax year by October 15, 2021 (Rev. Proc. 2020-22). The is made by filing an election statement or withdrawal statement with the taxpayer's amended return, and any collateral adjustments to taxable income for the tax year.

A real property trade or business, or farming business, that elects out of the business interest deduction limitation must depreciate certain property using alternative depreciation system (ADS) (¶ 1247). A change in the taxpayer's accounting method for this purpose is generally made under the automatic consent procedures (Code Sec. 163(j)(11); Rev. Proc. 2019-43; Rev. Proc. 2018-31, amended by Rev. Proc. 2019-8).

Business Interest Limit for Partnerships. In the case of any partnership, the § 163(j) limit is applied at the entity level and any deduction for business interest expense is taken into account in determining the non-separately stated taxable income or loss of the partnership. Any disallowed interest of a partnership is not carried forward but treated as excess business interest expense (EBIE) that is allocated to each partner in the same manner as any non-separately stated taxable income or loss (Reg. § 1.163(j)-6). The allocated EBIE for the current tax year is generally treated by the partner as business interest paid or accrued by the partner in the next succeeding year. However, a partner treats 50 percent of its allocable share of a partnership's EBIE for 2019 as an interest deduction in the partner's 2020 tax year without limitation. The remaining 50 percent of EBIE for 2019 remains subject to the § 163(j) limit applicable to EBIE carried forward at the partner level. A partner may elect out of the 50 percent EBIE rule for the 2019 tax year (Code Sec. 163(j)(10)(A)(ii)(II), added by P.L. 116-136; Rev. Proc. 2020-22).

Adjusted Taxable Income (ATI). A taxpayer uses Form 8990 to calculate its business interest deduction limitation under Code Sec. 163(j). Adjusted taxable income (ATI) for purposes of the limit is the taxpayer's regular taxable income computed without regard to:

- income, gain, deduction, or loss that is not properly allocable to a trade or business;

- business interest income or business interest expense (including floor plan financing interest expense);

- net operating loss (NOL) deduction (including NOLs arising in tax years before 2018 and carried forward to the current tax year) (¶ 1145);

- qualified business income (QBI) deduction allowed under Code Sec. 199A (¶ 980P);

- for tax years beginning before January 1, 2022, deductions for depreciations, amortization, or depletion attributable to a trade or business (including bonus depreciation);

- capital loss carryback or carryover deductions; and

- deductions or losses allocable to a nonexcepted trade or business.

Business Interest Defined. Business interest for purposes of the Code Sec. 163(j) limit is any interest that is properly allocable to a trade or business of the taxpayer or that is floor plan financing interest (Prop. Reg. § 1.163(j)-1(b)(2) and (b)(3)). It does not include interest allocable to certain excepted businesses including a trade or business of providing services as an employee, an electing real property business, an electing farming business, and certain regulated utility businesses. Rules are provided for allocating interest expense, interest income, and other items between excepted and nonexcepted trades or businesses of a taxpayer. Business interest expense and income of a noncorporate taxpayer also does not include any investment interest.

Floor plan financing interest is interest paid or accrued on debt used to finance the acquisition of motor vehicles held for sale or lease to retail customers and secured by the inventory. In the case of a partnership or S corporation, the deduction limit applies at the entity level (Prop. Reg. § 1.163(j)-6).

Tracing Rules. An individual is not allowed to claim any deduction for personal interest paid or accrued during the tax year (¶ 1043). If a taxpayer uses the proceeds of a loan for more than one purpose (for example, business and personal), interest on the loan must be allocated to each use. Interest expenses are allocated in the same manner in which the debt that gave rise to the payment or accrual of interest is allocated. Debt is allocated by tracing the proceeds to the types of expenses they are used for (Temp. Reg. § 1.163-8T).

Earnings Stripping. For tax years beginning before 2018, a corporation cannot deduct excessive interest paid if the interest will not be taxed as income to the recipient (Code Sec. 163(j), prior to amendment by the Tax Cuts and Jobs Act (P.L. 115-97); Notice 2018-28). A corporate partner's share of interest paid or accrued to or by the partnership is treated as paid or accrued by or to the corporation directly. A corporation with disqualified interest under the earnings stripping rules prior to 2018 may carryover the interest to post-2017 tax years, but subject to the limitations under the post-2017 rules.

Corporate Debt Incurred to Acquire Another Corporation's Stock. A corporation's annual deduction for interest on a debt incurred to acquire stock or two-thirds of the operating assets of another corporation is generally limited to $5 million (Code Sec. 279).

937A. Interest on Income Tax Liability. Interest paid or accrued on income tax assessed on an individual's federal, state, or local income tax liability is *not* a business deduction even though the tax due is related to income from a trade or business (Temp. Reg. § 1.163-9T(b)(2)(i)(A)). This rule also applies to an individual's partnership and S corporation activities. See ¶ 2723 and ¶ 2724 for interest allocations pursuant to compromise and partial payments. Penalties on deficiencies and underestimated tax cannot be deducted.

¶937A

Employee Business Expenses

See CCH® AnswerConnect: *Business Expenses: Substantiation Rules* for more information on this topic.

941. Employee Business Expenses. An individual is generally permitted a deduction for trade and business expenses paid or incurred in connection with the performance of services as an employee (Code Sec. 62(a)(2)). However, employee business expenses may only be deducted for tax years beginning in 2018 through 2025 by a qualified performing artist (¶ 941A), statutory employee (¶ 941B), schoolteacher (¶ 941C), fee-based government employee (¶ 941D), or employee with impairment-related work expenses (¶ 1095). An employee who does not fit into one of these categories may not deduct employee business expenses in 2018 through 2025.

The tax treatment of an employee's reimbursed business expenses depends on whether the employer's reimbursement or expense allowance arrangement is an accountable or nonaccountable plan (¶ 952A) (Code Sec. 62; Reg. § 1.62-2). If the employee expenses are reimbursed under an accountable plan of an employer, then they are excluded from the employee's gross income and no deduction may be claimed.

Unreimbursed employee business expenses, as well as expenses treated as paid under a nonaccountable plan, are deductible only as miscellaneous itemized deductions, subject to the two-percent-of-adjusted gross income (AGI) limit for tax years beginning before 2018 and after 2025. The deductible expenses must be adequately substantiated and the deduction is subject to the 50-percent limit for meals and entertainment (¶ 916). The employee reports the expenses on Form 2106. No miscellaneous itemized deductions subject to the two-percent-AGI limit may be claimed in tax years 2018 through 2025 (¶ 1079).

941A. Performing Artist Expenses. A qualified performing artist may claim an above-the-line deduction in calculating adjusted gross income (AGI) for employee business expenses. The deduction is calculated on Form 2106. An individual generally qualifies for the deduction if he or she:

- renders services in the performing arts during the tax year for at least two employers;

- has total business deductions attributable to the performance of such services that exceed 10 percent of the income received from such services; and

- has adjusted gross income of $16,000 or less (Code Sec. 62(a)(2)(B) and (b)).

941B. Expenses of Statutory Employee. A statutory employee may deduct his or her allowable employee business expenses from gross income (Code Sec. 3121(d); Rev. Rul. 90-93). A statutory employee includes:

- a full-time traveling or city salesperson who solicits orders from wholesalers, restaurants, or similar establishments on behalf of a principal where the merchandise sold is for resale (e.g., food sold to a restaurant) or for supplies used in the buyer's business;

- a full-time life insurance agent whose principal business activity is selling life insurance and/or annuity contracts for one life insurance company;

- an agent-driver or commission-driver engaged in distributing meat, vegetables, bakery goods, beverages (other than milk), or laundry or dry cleaning services; and

- a home worker performing work on material or goods furnished by the employer.

An employer should indicate on the individual's Form W-2 if he or she is classified as a statutory employee. A statutory employee reports his or her wages, income, and allowable expenses on Schedule C (Form 1040). The statutory employee is not liable for self-employment tax because his or her employer(s) must treat the individual as an employee for FICA and FUTA purposes (except for a full-time life insurance agent and home worker, who is not considered an employee for FUTA purposes).

941C. Teacher Classroom Expense Deduction. An eligible educator may claim an above-the-line deduction in calculating adjusted gross income (AGI) of up to $250 for

¶941C

2019 and 2020 for unreimbursed expenses incurred in connection with books, supplies (other than nonathletic supplies for courses in health or physical education), computer equipment, and supplementary materials used in the classroom (Code Sec. 62(a)(2)(D) and (d); Rev. Proc. 2018-57; Rev. Proc. 2019-44). An eligible educator is an individual who, for at least 900 hours during a school year, is a kindergarten through grade 12 teacher, instructor, counselor, principal, or aide in a school that provides elementary or secondary education as determined under state law.

941D. Expenses of Fee-Based Government Official. Trade or business expenses paid or incurred with respect to services performed by an official as an employee of a state or local government may be claimed as an above-the-line deduction in calculating adjusted gross income (AGI) (Code Sec. 62(a)(2)(C)). The employee must be compensated in whole or in part on a fee basis. The deduction is calculated on Form 2106.

941E. Expenses of National Guard and Reserve Members. A member of the National Guard and the U.S. Armed Forces Reserves may claim an above-the-line deduction in calculating adjusted gross income (AGI) for travel expenses paid or incurred in connection with service more than 100 miles away from home (Code Secs. 62(a)(2)(E) and 162(p)). This type of travel is travel away from home in the pursuit of a trade or business, so it is subject to the normal business deduction rules (such as the 50-percent reduction in deductible meal costs), but it is available even if the taxpayer is not considered to be acting as an employee. The amount of deductible expenses is limited to the federal per diem rate for the locality of the meeting or training session. The deduction is calculated on Form 2106.

943. Substantiation of Employee Business Expenses. Business expenses of an employee may be deducted if they exceed the reimbursements received under an employer's accountable plan (¶ 952A), are reimbursed under a nonaccountable plan, or are not reimbursed at all (¶ 941). As with any other deductible expense, the employee must adequately substantiate business expenses in order to deduct them.

More specific substantiation requirements apply with respect to the following expenses: expenses with respect to travel away from home (including meals and lodging), entertainment expenses paid or incurred before January 1, 2018 (¶ 910), business gifts, and expenses in connection with the use of listed property (¶ 1211). These expenses must generally be substantiated by adequate records or other sufficient evidence corroborating the taxpayer's own statement (Code Sec. 274(d); Temp. Reg. § 1.274-5T). The expenses must be substantiated as to amount, time, place, and business purpose. Expenses paid or incurred after December 31, 2017, must also be substantiated as to the business relationship of the person receiving the benefit. For entertainment expenses paid or incurred before January 1, 2018, and for gift expenses, the business relationship of the person being entertained or receiving the gift must also be substantiated.

Substantiation by Adequate Records. A contemporaneous log is not required, but a record of the elements of the expense or the business use of the listed property made at or near the time of the expenditure or use, supported by sufficient documentary evidence, has a high degree of credibility. Adequate accounting generally requires the submission of an account book, expense diary or log, or similar record maintained by the employee that records expenses at or near the time they are incurred. Documentary evidence, such as receipts or paid bills, is not generally required for expenses that are less than $75. However, documentary evidence is required for all lodging expenses (Reg. § 1.274-5(c)(2)(iii)). The employee should also maintain a record of any amounts charged to the employer.

Substantiation of Meal and Incidental Expenses. An employee may substantiate deductible meal and/or incidental expenses (M&IE) either by retaining evidence of the actual expenses or by use of the standard meal allowance (¶ 954B). The amount of the standard meal allowance varies by location, and for some locations, by the time of year. An individual using the standard meal allowance must still keep records, such as a daily planner or log, to prove the time, place, and business purpose of the expenses. There is no standard lodging amount similar to the standard meal allowance. Employees must be able to substantiate the actual cost of their lodging in order to deduct it.

Transportation and Car Expenses

See CCH® AnswerConnect: *Business Expenses: Automobile Expenses* for more information on this topic.

945. Business Deduction for Local Transportation Expenses. A taxpayer's local transportation costs (including self-employed persons and statutory employees) for travel between two specific business locations, whether in the same or different businesses, are deductible from gross income as an ordinary and necessary business expense (Reg. § 1.162-1(a)). The manner of the deduction generally depends on whether the employee is reimbursed under an accountable plan (¶ 952A). Local transportation expenses are generally those incurred for the business use of a car. They also include the cost of travel by rail, bus, or taxi.

Commuting Expenses. Commuting expenses between a taxpayer's residence and a business location within the area of the taxpayer's tax home generally are not deductible (Reg. § § 1.162-2(e) and 1.262-1(b)(5)). However, a deduction is allowed for expenses incurred in excess of ordinary commuting expenses for transporting job-related tools and materials (*D. Fausner*, SCt, 73-2 USTC ¶ 9515). An individual who works at two or more different places in a day may deduct the costs of getting from one place to the other (Rev. Rul. 99-7).

There is another exception for taxpayers working at a temporary work location. If a taxpayer has at least one regular place of business away from home, then daily transportation expenses for commuting between the taxpayer's residence and a temporary work location in the same trade or business can be deducted (¶ 951) (Rev. Rul. 99-7). A temporary work location is defined for this purpose using a one-year standard.

If employment at a work location is realistically expected to last (and does in fact last) for one year or less, the employment is temporary, absent facts and circumstances to the contrary. Employment at a work location is not temporary if it is realistically expected to last for more than one year, or if there is no realistic expectation that it will last for one year or less, regardless of whether it in fact lasts for more than one year. A taxpayer may at first realistically expect that employment at a work location will last one year or less, but later realistically expect that the work will last for more than one year. In this situation, the employment is treated as temporary, unless facts and circumstances indicate otherwise, until the date that the taxpayer's realistic expectation changes. After that date, the employment is treated as not temporary.

Employer Deduction for Transportation and Commuting Benefits. An employer cannot deduct expenses paid or incurred after December 31, 2017, for any qualified transportation fringe benefit, such as van pools, transit passes, qualified parking, and bicycle commuting (¶ 2091) (Code Sec. 274(a)(4)). The IRS has provided guidance to determine the nondeductible amount of parking expenses for its employees depending on whether the taxpayer pays owns, or leases, a parking facility, or pays a third party to provide parking (Notice 2018-99). An employer also cannot deduct expenses paid or incurred after 2017 for providing transportation, or any payment or reimbursement, to an employee in connection with travel between the employee's residence and place of employment, except as necessary to ensure the employee's safety. This prohibition does not apply to a qualified bicycle commuting reimbursement (¶ 2091) that is paid or incurred after December 31, 2017, and before January 1, 2026 (Code Sec. 274(l)).

Travel from a Home Office. An individual who uses his or her home as a principal place of business (¶ 961) may deduct transportation expenses between the home and another work location in the same trade or business (Rev. Rul. 99-7). This rule applies regardless of whether the work location is temporary or regular, and regardless of the distance.

946. Business-Related Car Expenses. Expenses for gasoline, oil, tires, repairs, insurance, depreciation, parking fees and tolls, licenses, and garage rent incurred for automobiles (cars and trucks) used in a trade or business are deductible (¶ 947) to the extent the expenses are attributable to business (Code Sec. 162; Reg. § 1.162-1). An employee's unreimbursed expenses generally can be deducted only as a miscellaneous itemized deduction subject to the two-percent-of-adjusted-gross-income (AGI) floor for tax years beginning before 2018 (and after 2025) (¶ 941). See ¶ 1208 and ¶ 1214 for the expensing election and depreciation of automobiles.

947. Substantiation of Business-Related Car Expenses. A taxpayer can substantiate automobile (car and truck) expenses (¶ 946) by keeping an exact record of the amount paid for gasoline, insurance, and other costs. In lieu of calculating the operating and fixed costs allocable to business purposes, a taxpayer may use the standard mileage rate method as a simplified way to compute deductions for automobile expenses (Code Sec. 274(d); Temp. Reg. § 1.274-5T; Rev. Proc. 2019-46; Rev. Proc. 2010-51).

Standard Mileage Rate. Under the standard mileage method, the taxpayer determines the allowable deduction by multiplying all the business miles driven during the year by the standard mileage rate. The business portion of parking fees and tolls may be deducted in addition to the standard mileage rate. The standard mileage rate is 58 cents per mile in 2019 and 57.5 cents per mile in 2020 (Notice 2019-2; Notice 2020-5). However, the business standard mileage rate cannot be used to claim a deduction for unreimbursed employee travel expenses for tax years beginning in 2018 through 2025 (¶ 941).

The standard mileage rate may be used by businesses, self-employed individuals, or employees in computing the deductible costs of operating automobiles they own or lease for business purposes. It may not be used to compute the deductible expenses of five or more automobiles owned or leased by a taxpayer and used simultaneously (i.e., a fleet operation). Using the standard mileage rate in the first year of business use is considered an election to exclude the car from depreciation (¶ 1236). In determining the owner's adjusted basis in the vehicle, depreciation is considered to have been allowed at the rate of 26 cents per mile in 2019 and 27 cents per mile in 2020 (Notice 2019-2; Notice 2020-5).

Fixed and Variable Rate (FAVR) Method. The fixed and variable rate allowance (FAVR) also can be used to substantiate automobile expenses. An employer's FAVR allowance includes a combination of payments such as a cents-per-mile rate to cover the employee's variable operating costs (gas, oil, tires, etc.), plus a flat amount to cover the employee's fixed costs (depreciation or lease payments, insurance, etc.). The maximum standard automobile cost for purposes of the FAVR allowance is $50,400 for passenger automobiles including trucks and vans for 2019 and 2020 (Notice 2019-2; Notice 2020-5). At least five employees must be covered by a FAVR arrangement at all times during the calendar year, and at no time can the majority of covered employees be management employees. Additional requirements must also be met.

Postal Workers. Rural mail carriers receive a qualified reimbursement for expenses incurred for the use of their vehicles for collecting and delivering mail in a rural route. They are allowed a miscellaneous itemized deduction subject to the two-percent-of-adjusted-gross-income limitation for tax years beginning before 2018 and after 2025 (¶ 1079) for their automobile expenses that exceed their qualified reimbursement (Code Sec. 162(o)). Qualified reimbursements in excess of actual automobile expenses continue to be excluded from gross income (H.R. Conf. Rep. No. 108-755).

948. Interest on Car Loans. Interest paid by an employee on a car loan is nondeductible personal interest (¶ 1043). A self-employed taxpayer may claim the interest paid on the business portion of a car as a business expense. The nonbusiness portion is nondeductible personal interest (Code Sec. 163(a)).

Traveling Expenses Away from Home

See CCH® AnswerConnect: *Travel, Meals, and Entertainment Expenses for Business* for more information on this topic.

949. Business Deduction of Travel Expenses. A taxpayer may deduct ordinary and necessary traveling expenses incurred while away from home in the conduct of a trade or business (Code Sec. 162(a)(2); Reg. § 1.162-2). An individual is away from home if it is reasonable to need sleep or rest while his or her duties require the individual to be away from his or her tax home for a period substantially longer than an ordinary workday. In some cases, travel expenses may be deductible even though the taxpayer is away from home for less than 24 hours (¶ 951).

Local Lodging. Expenses paid or incurred for lodging when not traveling away from home (i.e. local lodging) are generally nondeductible personal expenses (¶ 1001). However, local lodging expenses may be deductible as ordinary and necessary expenses of a taxpayer's trade or business, including the trade or business of being an employee, depending on the facts and circumstances (Reg. §1.162-32). Under a safe harbor for certain local lodging at business meetings and conferences, an individual's local lodging expenses are ordinary and necessary business expenses if:

- the lodging is necessary for the individual to participate fully in or be available for a bona fide business meeting, conference, training activity, or other business function;

- the lodging is for a period that does not exceed five calendar days and does not recur more than once per calendar quarter;

- if the individual is an employee, the employer requires the employee to remain at the meeting or function overnight; and

- the lodging is not lavish or extravagant under the circumstances and does not provide any significant element of personal pleasure, recreation, or benefit.

950. Tax Home Defined. A individual's tax home for purposes of deducting travel expenses (¶ 949) is: (1) the taxpayer's regular or principal (if there is more than one regular) place of business, or (2) if there is no regular or principal place of business because of the nature of the work, the taxpayer's regular place of abode in a real and substantial sense (Rev. Rul. 75-432). A taxpayer who does not fall within either category is an itinerant or someone who has a home wherever he or she happens to be working. Thus, the taxpayer is never away from home for purposes of deducting traveling expenses.

For a taxpayer with multiple areas of business activity or places of regular employment, the principal place of business is the tax home. In determining the principal place of an individual's business, the following factors are considered: (1) the time spent on business activity in each area; (2) the amount of business activity in each area; and (3) the amount of the resulting financial return in each area (Rev. Rul. 54-147; *F. Markey*, CA-6, 74-1 USTC ¶ 9192). Business travel expenses incurred while away from the principal place of business are deductible.

The tax home of a member of the U.S. Congress is the member's residence in the state or district that the member represents. For tax years beginning before December 23, 2017, the deduction for meals and lodging while in Washington, D.C., is limited to $3,000 per year, after applying the two-percent-of-adjusted-gross-income (AGI) floor for miscellaneous itemized deductions. For tax years beginning after December 22, 2017, members of Congress cannot deduct living expenses incurred while in the District of Columbia (Code Sec. 162(a)).

A member of the U.S. Armed Forces is not away from home while at the individual's permanent duty station (*H.A. Stidger*, SCt, 67-1 USTC ¶ 9309). However, members of the National Guard and Reserves can deduct qualifying travel expenses as an above-the-line deduction when attending meetings or training sessions (¶ 941E).

951. Travel Expenses for Temporary or Indefinite Employment. In determining when an individual is away from home for purposes of deducting travel expenses (¶ 949), the nature of the stay and the length of time away from the individual's principal place of business are of prime importance. If the assignment is temporary in nature, the taxpayer is considered away from home and a travel expense deduction is allowed. If the assignment is for an indefinite period of time, the location of the assignment becomes the individual's new tax home, and the individual may not deduct traveling expenses while there. If an individual works away from home at a single location for more than one year, the employment is indefinite and related travel expenses are not deductible (Code Sec. 162(a); Rev. Rul. 93-86; Rev. Rul. 99-7).

Employment expected to last more than one year is classified as indefinite, regardless of whether the work actually exceeds a year. Employment that is expected to, and does in fact, last for one year or less is temporary. The one-year rule does not apply to federal employees certified by the Attorney General as traveling on behalf of the United States in temporary duty status to investigate or prosecute, or to provide support services for the investigation or prosecution of, a federal crime. Such employees may deduct their travel expenses even if their assignment is expected to last for more than one year.

952. Travel Expenses of Taxpayer. The costs of the following items are ordinarily deductible, if paid or incurred while a business owner or employee is traveling away from home on business (¶ 949): meals and lodging; transportation, including a reasonable amount for baggage; necessary samples and display materials; hotel rooms, sample rooms, telephone and fax services, and public stenographers; and the costs, including depreciation (¶ 1211), of maintaining and operating a car for business purposes (Reg. § 1.162-2).

No deduction is allowed for the travel expenses of a spouse, dependent, or other individual who accompanies the taxpayer or employee on a business trip unless the companion is an employee of the person who is paying or reimbursing the expenses, the companion's travel serves a bona fide business purpose, and the companion's expenses are otherwise deductible (Code Sec. 274(m)(3)).

A taxpayer may deduct traveling expenses between the principal place of business and place of business at a temporary or minor post of duty. If the taxpayer's family lives at the temporary or minor post, however, the taxpayer's deduction for meals and lodging is limited to the portion of those expenses that is allocable to the taxpayer's presence there in the actual performance of the taxpayer's duties (Rev. Rul. 55-604).

The deduction for the cost of meals and lodging while away from home on business is limited to amounts that are not lavish or extravagant under the circumstances (Code Sec. 162(a)(2)). The deduction for meals is limited to 50 percent of the total expenses (¶ 916).

Travel expenses are not deductible as a trade or business expense if the expense would be deductible only on the basis that the travel itself constitutes a form of education (¶ 1082).

952A. Accountable Plan for Reimbursement of Employee Expenses. The arrangement under which an employer reimburses business expenses incurred by employees or provides advances to cover such expenses is either an accountable plan or nonaccountable plan (¶ 941). Amounts paid under an accountable plan are deductible by the employer and not reported as income to the employee. Amounts paid under a nonaccountable plan are deductible by the employer as compensation reportable on the employee's Form W-2 and subject to withholding requirements (¶ 2607 and ¶ 2608).

An accountable plan must satisfy the following three conditions:

- the expenses covered under the plan must have a business connection;
- the plan must require employees to substantiate the covered expenses; and
- the plan must require employees who receive advances to return any amounts in excess of their substantiated expenses (Reg. § 1.62-2(c)).

If a plan satisfies these requirements, but an employee fails to return an excess advance to the employer within a reasonable period, only the amount of the substantiated expenses is treated as paid under an accountable plan. The retained excess is treated as paid under a nonaccountable plan. If a plan does not satisfy these requirements, an employee cannot force the employer to treat it as an accountable plan by substantiating the expenses and returning the excess.

Business Connection. The business connection requirement is satisfied if the expenses are deductible business expenses of the employer, paid or incurred in connection with the performance of services as an employee. If a plan also covers bona fide expenses that are related to the employer's business but not deductible, such as travel that is not away from home, the plan is treated as two separate arrangements—one accountable, the other nonaccountable (Reg. § 1.62-2(d)).

Substantiation. The substantiation required by an accountable plan must be sufficient to substantiate the expense under the general rules for substantiating business expense deductions, which vary depending on the type of expense (Reg. § 1.62-2(e)). If the expense is for travel, meals, lodging, entertainment, gifts, or attributable to the use of listed property (¶ 1211), the substantiation requirement is satisfied if enough information is submitted to the employer to satisfy substantiation requirements (¶ 953), including travel and car expenses deemed substantiated.

Other expenses, such as expenses for printing a report, are substantiated if enough information is submitted to the employer to enable the employer to identify the specific nature of each expense and to conclude that the expense was attributable to the employer's business activities. The elements of each expense should be substantiated, including the amount, place, time or date, and business purpose.

An employee's expenses are deemed to be substantiated if the employee provides an adequate accounting of the expenses to the employer in the form of adequate records (Reg. § 1.274-5(f)(4)). The adequate accounting requirement can be satisfied as to the amount of car expenses and lodging and/or meals and incidental expenses by using the per diem allowances (¶ 947 and ¶ 954). An employee or self-employed worker who deducts unreimbursed lodging expenses on his or her own return must have evidence of the actual costs.

Return of Excess Advances. The return-of-excess-advances requirement is satisfied if an employee is required to return amounts received in excess of the expenses that are substantiated or deemed substantiated within a reasonable period of time (Reg. § 1.62-2(f)). Advances must be provided within a reasonable period before the covered expenses are expected to be paid or incurred and must be reasonably calculated not to exceed the anticipated expenses. If an employee fails to return the excess within a reasonable period of time, only amounts paid that are not in excess of the amounts substantiated are treated as paid under an accountable plan. Excess amounts retained are treated as paid under a nonaccountable plan and must be included in the employee's income. An accountable plan that reimburses expenses under an IRS-approved mileage (¶ 947) or per diem allowance (¶ 954) must require the return of the portion that relates to days or miles of travel not substantiated.

Reasonable Period of Time. Advances, the substantiation of expenses, and the return of excess advances must each take place within a reasonable period of time. A reasonable period depends on facts and circumstances, but there are two safe harbor methods: the fixed date method and the periodic statement method (Reg. § 1.62-2(g)).

Under the fixed date method, the following are treated as occurring within a reasonable period of time:

- advance payments made within 30 days of when an expense is paid or incurred;

- substantiation provided within 60 days after expenses are paid or incurred; or

- return of excess amounts within 120 days after expenses are paid or incurred.

Under the periodic statement method, the employer must:

- give each employee periodic statements (no less than quarterly) that set forth the amounts paid under the reimbursement arrangement in excess of the substantiated amount; and

- request that the employee either substantiate or return the excess amounts within 120 days of the statement date. An expense substantiated or amount returned within that period satisfies the reasonable period requirement.

953. Substantiation Requirements for Business Expenses. A taxpayer must be able to prove that any deducted business expense was actually paid or incurred. Small expenses and those that are clearly related to the business may be substantiated by the taxpayer's statement or by keeping receipts, sales slips, invoices, cancelled checks, or other evidence of payments. The following expenses, which are particularly susceptible to abuse, must generally be substantiated by adequate records or sufficient evidence corroborating the taxpayer's own statement:

- expenses with respect to travel away from home (including meals and lodging),

- entertainment expenses paid or incurred before January 1, 2018 (¶ 910),

- business gifts, and

- expenses in connection with the use of listed property (¶ 1211) (Code Sec. 274(d); Temp. Reg. § 1.274-5T).

The expenses must be substantiated as to amount, time, place, and business purpose. Expenses paid or incurred after December 31, 2017, must also be substantiated as to the business relationship of the person receiving the benefit. For entertainment expenses paid or incurred before January 1, 2018, and for gift expenses, the business relationship of the person being entertained or receiving the gift must also be substantiated. An employer's reimbursement arrangement must require employees to satisfy these substantiation requirements in order to be an accountable plan (¶ 952A).

Substantiation by Adequate Records. A contemporaneous log is not required, but a record of the elements of the expense or the business use of the listed property made at or near the time of the expenditure or use, supported by sufficient documentary evidence, has a high degree of credibility. Adequate accounting generally requires records such as an account book, expense diary or log, or similar record maintained by the employee and recorded at or near the time the expense is incurred. Documentary evidence, such as receipts or paid bills, is not generally required for expenses that are less than $75. However, documentary evidence is required for all lodging expenses (Reg. § 1.274-5(c)(2)(iii)). The employee should also maintain a record of any amounts charged to the employer.

The *Cohan* rule, which allows the courts to estimate the amount of a taxpayer's business expenses if adequate records do not exist, does not apply to expenses covered by the substantiation rules of Code Sec. 274(d) (Temp. Reg. § 1.274-5T(a)(1)). If a taxpayer establishes that the records were lost due to circumstances beyond the taxpayer's control, such as destruction by fire or flood, then the taxpayer has a right to substantiate claimed deductions by a reasonable construction of the expenditures or use (Temp. Reg. § 1.274-5T(c)(5)).

Employees of the executive and judicial branches and certain employees of the legislative branch of the federal government may substantiate their requests for reimbursement of ordinary and necessary business expenses with an account book or expense log instead of submitting documentary evidence (e.g., receipts or bills) (Rev. Proc. 97-45).

954. Per Diem Methods for Substantiating Meals and Lodging Expenses. A taxpayer must substantiate the amount, time, place, and business purpose of expenses paid or incurred in traveling away from home (¶ 953). Although the taxpayer has the option of keeping the actual records of travel expenses, the IRS has provided per diem allowances under which the amount of meals and incidental expenses (M&IE) may be deemed to be substantiated. The per diem allowances eliminate the need for substantiating actual costs (Rev. Proc. 2019-48; Rev. Proc. 2011-47). A taxpayer who uses per diem allowances to calculate the deductible amount must still substantiate the time, place, and business purpose of the travel by adequate records or other evidence.

Although most frequently used in the employer-employee relationship, per diem allowances may be used in arrangements between any payor and payee, such as between independent contractors and those contracting with them. However, employees related to the payor under the related party rules of Code Sec. 267(b) (using a 10-percent common ownership standard (¶ 1717)) cannot use per diem substantiation methods.

Employees. The per diem method can be used to substantiate an employee's reimbursed expenses (for purposes of the employer's return) only if the reimbursement arrangement is an accountable plan (¶ 952A) and the allowance:

• is paid with respect to ordinary and necessary expenses incurred or that the employer reasonably expects to be incurred by an employee for lodging and/or M&IE while traveling away from home in connection with the performance of services as an employee;

• is reasonably calculated not to exceed the amount of the expense or the anticipated expenses; and

• is paid at the applicable federal per diem rate, a flat rate, or stated schedule.

Types of Per Diem Allowances. There are three types of per diem allowances:

• lodging plus M&IE, which provides a per diem allowance to cover lodging as well as meals and incidental expenses (¶ 954A);

- M&IE only, which provides a per diem allowance for meals and incidental expenses only (¶ 954B); and

- incidental expenses only, to be used when no meal or lodging expenses are incurred.

Incidental expenses has the same meaning as in the Federal Travel Regulations (41 C.F.R. 300-3.1). Under those regulations, incidental expenses include *only* fees and tips given to porters, baggage carriers, hotel staff, and staff on ships. Transportation between places of lodging or business and places where meals are taken, and the mailing cost of filing travel vouchers and paying employer-sponsored charge card billings, are not incidental expenses. Taxpayers using per diem rates may separately deduct or be reimbursed for such transportation and mailing expenses (Notice 2019-55; Notice 2018-77).

Expenses of laundry, lodging taxes, and telephone calls are not incidental expenses (IRS Pub. 463). Lodging taxes for travel within the continental United States and for nonforeign travel outside the continental United States are reimbursable miscellaneous expenses. However, lodging taxes have not been removed from the foreign per diem rates set by the U.S. State Department (41 C.F.R. 301-11.27).

Allowances Exceeding Federal Rates. If expenses are substantiated using a per diem amount, regardless of whether it covers lodging plus M&IE or only M&IE, any reimbursement that exceeds the relevant federal per diem rates for that type of allowance must be included in the employee's (or independent contractor's) gross income. The excess portion is treated as paid under a nonaccountable plan; thus, it must be reported on the employee's Form W-2 and is subject to withholding (Reg. § 1.62-2(h)(2)(i)(B)(1)).

954A. Per Diem Allowance for Lodging Plus Meals and Incidental Expenses (M&IE). Under the lodging plus meals and incidental expenses (M&IE) per diem method (¶ 954), the amount of an employee's or other payee's reimbursed expenses that is deemed substantiated (for purposes of the employer's return) is equal to the lesser of the employer's per diem allowance or the federal per diem amount for the locality of travel for the period in which the employee is away from home (Rev. Proc. 2019-48; Rev. Proc. 2011-47). The employee is not required to produce lodging receipts if per diem allowances are used to substantiate such expenses. The locality of travel is the place where the employee stops for sleep or rest. An employee or self-employed individual may determine his or her allowable deductions for unreimbursed M&IE while away from home by using the applicable federal M&IE rate (¶ 954B). However, unreimbursed lodging costs must be substantiated by required records.

Per Diem Rates. The federal per diem rate for lodging plus M&IE depends upon the locality of travel. For various geographic areas within the continental United States (the 48 contiguous states plus the District of Columbia) (CONUS), the federal per diem rate for a given locality is equal to the sum of a maximum lodging amount and the M&IE rate for that locality. There are also federal per diem rates for nonforeign localities outside of the continental United States (OCONUS), such as Alaska, Hawaii, Puerto Rico, and U.S. possessions. Rates are also established for foreign travel (foreign OCONUS).

Rates for CONUS, OCONUS, and foreign travel are published under the Federal Travel Regulations for government travel and are updated periodically. The travel rates are issued to coincide with the government's fiscal year of October to September.

High-Low Method. Instead of using the maximum per diem rates from the CONUS table, taxpayers can compute per diem allowances for travel within the continental United States under the high-low method, which is a simplified method for determining a lodging plus M&IE per diem. This method divides all CONUS localities into two categories: low-cost or high-cost localities.

For travel on or after October 1, 2019, through September 30, 2020, the following per diem rates for lodging expenses and M&IE are used for high-cost and low-cost localities (Notice 2019-55):

	Lodging expense rate	M&IE rate	Maximum per diem rate
High-cost locality	$226	$71	$297
Low-cost locality	$140	$60	$200

¶954A

For travel on or after October 1, 2018, through September 30, 2019, the following per diem rates for lodging expenses and M&IE are used for high-cost and low-cost localities (Notice 2018-77):

	Lodging expense rate	M&IE rate	Maximum per diem rate
High-cost locality	$216	$71	$287
Low-cost locality	$135	$60	$195

Some areas are treated as high-cost during certain periods of the year (e.g., peak tourist season) and as low-cost during other periods. Thus, employers who use the high-low method must determine whether the employee traveled in a high-cost area and if the area was classified as high-cost during the actual period of travel.

If the high-low method is used for an employee, then the payor may not use the actual federal maximum per diem rates for that employee during the calendar year for travel within CONUS. For travel outside CONUS, the employer may use the applicable federal OCONUS rates, the M&IE-only rate, or reimbursement of actual expenses.

Proration of M&IE Allowance. If an individual is traveling away from home for only a portion of the day, there are two alternative methods that may be used to prorate the per diem rate or the M&IE rate. Under the first method, 75 percent of the M&IE rate (or the M&IE portion of the per diem rate) is allowed for each partial day during which an employee or self-employed individual is traveling on business. Under the second method, referred to as the reasonable business practice method, the M&IE rate may be prorated using any method that is consistently applied and in accordance with reasonable business practice. For example, if an employee travels from 9 a.m. one day until 5 p.m. the next day, a proration method that gives an amount equal to two times the M&IE rate is treated as in accordance with reasonable business practice (Rev. Proc. 2019-48; Rev. Proc. 2011-47).

Transition Rules. Taxpayers may continue to use the per diem rates effective prior to October 1, 2019, for the remainder of 2019, or they may begin to use the new per diem rates for reimbursement for travel, as long as they use either the pre-October 1 rates or the updated rates for the October 1 through December 31 period consistently. Taxpayers who used the per diem method or the high-low substantiation method to reimburse travel expenses during the first nine months of calendar-year 2019 must continue to use that method for the remainder of calendar-year 2019. Taxpayers who use the high-low method during the first nine months of calendar-year 2019 may either continue to use the rates and localities in effect before October 1, 2019, or use the updated rates and localities in effect for travel on and after October 1, 2019, as long as they use the same rates and localities consistently for all employees reimbursed under the high-low method.

954B. Per Diem Allowance for Meals and Incidental Expenses (M&IE) Only. A per diem allowance for meal and incidental expenses (M&IEs) only may be used to substantiate an employee's or other payee's M&IEs for purposes of the employer's return (Rev. Proc. 2019-48; Rev. Proc. 2011-47). The amount that is deemed substantiated is equal to the lesser of the per diem allowance or the amount computed at the federal M&IE rate for the locality of travel for the period that the employee is away from home. If M&IEs are substantiated using a per diem allowance, the entire amount is treated as a food and beverage expense subject to the 50-percent limitation on meal and entertainment expenses (¶ 916).

The M&IE rate must be prorated for partial days of travel away from home (¶ 954A). If an employee's meals are provided by the employer, even though the employee may be working from home, the employee is entitled to deduct only the incidental expense portion of the applicable federal per diem M&IE rates (*R.J. Zbylut*, Dec. 57,348(M), 95 TCM 1172).

Employees and Self-Employed Persons. An employee or self-employed individual whose expenses are not reimbursed may also use the M&IE-only rate to substantiate M&IEs while traveling away from home. The taxpayer must actually prove through adequate records or sufficient corroborative evidence (¶ 953) the time, place, and business purpose of the travel, and lodging costs.

¶954B

Optional Method for Incidental-Expenses-Only Deduction. A taxpayer may use an optional method to deduct only incidental expenses in lieu of using actual expenses. A taxpayer who does not incur any meal expenses may deduct $5 per calendar day (or partial day) as ordinary and necessary incidental expenses, paid or incurred, while traveling to any localities within the continental United States (CONUS) or outside the continental United States (OCONUS) (Notice 2019-55; Notice 2018-77). The optional method is subject to the proration rules for partial days and substantiation requirements for taxpayers who use the per diem method for substantiation (Rev. Proc. 2019-48; Rev. Proc. 2011-47). The optional method for incidental-expenses-only deduction also cannot be used by taxpayers who use the lodging plus M&IE per diem method, the M&IE-only method, or the high-low method and the optional M&IE-only method (¶ 954A).

Transportation Workers. The M&IE rates for travel away from home on or after October 1, 2019, for both self-employed persons and employees in the transportation industry are $66 for CONUS localities, and $71 for OCONUS localities. The M&IE rates for travel away from home on or after October 1, 2018, for both self-employed persons and employees in the transportation industry are $66 for CONUS localities, and $71 for OCONUS localities (Notice 2019-55; Notice 2018-77). An individual is in the transportation industry only if the individual's work: (1) directly involves moving people or goods by airplane, barge, bus, ship, train, or truck; and (2) regularly requires travel away from home that involves travel to localities with differing federal M&IE rates during a single trip.

Under a calendar-year convention for the transportation industry, a taxpayer who used the federal M&IE rates during the first nine months of calendar year 2019 to substantiate an individual's travel expenses may not use the special transportation industry rates for that individual until January 1, 2020 (Rev. Proc. 2019-48; Rev. Proc. 2011-47). Likewise, a taxpayer who used the special transportation industry rates for the first nine months of calendar year 2019 to substantiate an individual's travel expenses may not use the federal M&IE rates for that individual until January 1, 2020.

955. Foreign Travel Expenses. Traveling expenses (including meals and lodging) for travel outside of the United States generally must be allocated between time spent on the trip for business and for pleasure (¶ 949) (Code Sec. 274(c); Reg. § 1.274-4). Travel is outside the United States if it is not from one point in the United States to another point in the United States. Travel outside the United States does not include any travel within the United States.

If the trip is for one week or less, or if the time spent on personal activities is less than 25 percent of the total time away from home, no allocation is required and all expenses are deductible (Code Sec. 274(c)(2)). If the foreign trip is longer than a week (seven consecutive days counting the day of return but not the day of departure) or 25 percent or more of the time away from home is spent for personal reasons, deductible travel expenses are limited to those that are allocable to the taxpayer's business or management of income-producing property.

No allocation is required on a foreign trip if (1) the individual traveling had no substantial control over the arranging of the business trip, or (2) a personal vacation was not a major consideration in making the trip (Reg. § 1.274-4(f)(5)). An employee traveling under a reimbursement or expense account allowance arrangement does not have substantial control over the arranging of a business trip unless the employee owns at least 10 percent of the employer, or the employee is a managing executive of the employer who can, without being vetoed, decide on whether and when to make the trip.

See ¶ 959 and ¶ 960 for special rules governing expenses of attending foreign conventions, seminars, and other similar meetings.

956. Travel Expenses of State Legislators. A state legislator whose residence is more than 50 miles from the state capitol building may elect to be deemed to be away from home in the pursuit of a trade or business (1) on any day that the legislature is in session (including periods of up to four consecutive days when the legislature is not in session), or (2) on any day when the legislature is not in session but the legislator's presence is formally recorded at a committee meeting (Code Sec. 162(h)).

957. Luxury Water Travel. A deduction for transportation by ocean liner, cruise ship, or other form of water transportation is limited to a daily amount equal to twice the highest per diem travel amount allowable to employees of the federal government while on official business away from home within the United States. The limitation does not apply to any expense allocable to a convention, seminar, or other meeting that is held on a cruise ship (¶ 959). Separately stated meal expenses, and entertainment expenses incurred before January 1, 2018, are subject to the 50-percent limitation rule (¶ 916), prior to the application of the per diem limitation. Statutory exceptions to the 50-percent limit apply (¶ 917) (Code Sec. 274(m)(1)). Entertainment expenses paid or incurred after December 31, 2017, are generally not deductible (¶ 910).

959. Business Convention and Seminar Expenses. Deductible travel expenses include those incurred in attending a convention related to the taxpayer's business, even if the taxpayer is an employee (Code Sec. 274(h))). The fact that an employee uses vacation or leave time or that attendance at the convention is voluntary does not necessarily negate the deduction (Reg. § 1.162-2(d)). See ¶ 960 for rules applicable to foreign conventions. Expenses for a convention or meeting in connection with investments, financial planning, or other income-producing property are not deductible.

Cruise Ships. A maximum $2,000 annual deduction is available for expenses incurred for conventions on U.S. cruise ships (Code Sec. 274(h)(2)). The deduction applies only if: (1) all ports of such cruise ship are located in the United States or a U.S. possession; (2) the taxpayer establishes that the convention is directly related to the active conduct of his or her trade or business; and (3) the taxpayer includes certain specified information in the return on which the deduction is claimed.

960. Foreign Conventions and Seminar Expenses. No deduction is allowed for expenses allocable to a convention, seminar, or meeting held outside the North American area unless the taxpayer establishes that the meeting is directly related to the active conduct of his or her trade or business and that it is reasonable for the meeting to be held outside the North American area (Code Sec. 274(h)). The factors taken into account include: (1) the purpose of the meeting and the activities taking place there; (2) the purposes and activities of the sponsoring organization or group; (3) the places where the sponsoring organization's or group's active members reside and where its other meetings have been or will be held; and (4) other relevant factors that the taxpayer may present. Expenses for foreign conventions on cruise ships are never deductible.

The North American area is the 50 states of the United States and the District of Columbia, U.S. possessions, Canada, Mexico, the Republic of the Marshall Islands, the Federated States of Micronesia, and the Republic of Palau. Costs incurred in attending conventions held in the Caribbean or on certain Pacific Islands may also be deductible if the host country is a designated beneficiary country, there is a bilateral or multilateral agreement in effect providing for the exchange of tax information with the United States, and the country has not been found to discriminate in its tax laws against conventions held in the United States. A list of qualifying countries is provided in Rev. Rul. 2016-16, effective June 27, 2016. See Rev. Rul. 2011-26 for conventions prior to that date.

Home Office and Vacation Home Expenses

See CCH® AnswerConnect: *Home Office Deduction* for more information on this topic.

961. Home Office Deduction. Expenses for the business use of the taxpayer's home are deductible only if they are attributable to a portion of the home used exclusively on a regular basis:

- as the principal place of any business carried on by the taxpayer;
- as a place of business that is used by patients, clients, or customers in meeting or dealing with the taxpayer in the normal course of business; or
- in connection with the taxpayer's business, if the taxpayer is using a separate structure that is appurtenant to, but not attached to, the home (Code Sec. 280A(c)).

If the taxpayer is an employee, the business use of the home must be for the convenience of the employer (¶ 965). The allowable deduction is computed on Form 8829. The amount deductible is limited to either the taxpayer's actual expenses related to the office or an amount determined under a safe harbor method (¶ 963).

¶959

To satisfy the exclusive use test, a specific portion of the taxpayer's home generally must be used solely for the purpose of carrying on a trade or business. This requirement is not met if the portion is used for both business and personal purposes. However, a wholesale or retail seller, or an auction or consignment seller, whose dwelling unit is the sole fixed location of the trade or business may deduct the ordinary and necessary expenses allocable to space within the dwelling unit that is used to store inventory or product samples, provided that the space is used on a regular basis and is a separately identifiable space suitable for storage (Code Sec. 280A(c)(2); IRS Fact Sheet FS-2007-23). Another exception applies to licensed day care operators (¶ 964).

A home office is the taxpayer's principal place of business if the taxpayer uses it exclusively and regularly to administer or manage the trade or business and does not conduct substantial administrative or management activities at any other fixed location. This test can be satisfied by a taxpayer who:

- has others conduct administrative or management activities at locations other than the taxpayer's home office (e.g., billing activities);

- carries out administrative and management activities at sites that are not fixed locations of the business (e.g., cars or hotel rooms) in addition to performing the activities at the home office;

- conducts an insubstantial amount of administrative and management activities at a fixed location other than the home office (e.g., occasionally doing minimal paperwork at another fixed location);

- has suitable space to conduct administrative or management activities outside the home, but chooses to use the home office for those activities instead; and

- conducts substantial nonadministrative and nonmanagement business activities at a fixed location other than the home office (e.g., meeting with or providing services to customers, clients, or patients at another fixed location) (Instructions to Form 8829; IRS Pub. 587).

Residential Telephone. Basic local telephone service charges on the first line in a residence are not deductible as business expenses. Additional charges for long-distance calls, equipment, optional services (e.g., call waiting), or additional telephone lines may be deductible (Code Sec. 262(b)).

963. Limitation on Home Office Deductions. The home office deduction (¶ 961) cannot exceed the gross income from the activity, reduced by the home expenses that would be deductible in the absence of any business use (e.g., mortgage interest, property taxes, etc.) and the business expenses not related to the use of the home (Code Sec. 280A(c)(5)). Business expenses related to the home office expenses are deducted in the following order:

- business expenses that are not allocable to the use of the home (e.g., office supplies);

- home expenses that would be deductible even if the home was not used as a place of business (e.g., mortgage interest);

- household expenses that are allocable to the business use (e.g., utilities and insurance); and

- allocable depreciation (IRS Pub. 587).

The deduction of household expenses and depreciation cannot create a loss. Unused expenses for household expenses and depreciation are carried over to the next year but are still subject to the same limitation rules.

Optional Safe Harbor. A taxpayer may elect a simplified safe harbor method to compute the home office deduction without having to substantiate, calculate, and allocate deductible home office expenses (Rev. Proc. 2013-13). Under the safe harbor, the deduction is equal to $5 times the number of square feet of the home office, up to a maximum of 300 square feet (maximum deduction of $1,500). The deduction also cannot exceed the taxpayer's gross income from the business. If the safe harbor deduction exceeds the income limit, the excess cannot be carried forward to the next year. A taxpayer whose home office expenses are reimbursed by an employer cannot use the safe harbor. A taxpayer who uses the safe harbor cannot deduct actual home office expenses, though business expenses unrelated to the business use of the home may still be deducted.

964. Home Office Deduction for Day Care Services. A taxpayer who uses his or her personal residence on a regular basis in the trade or business of providing qualifying day care services (for the care of children, handicapped persons, or the elderly) does not have to meet the exclusive use test under the home office deduction rules (¶ 961) in order to deduct business-related expenses (Code Sec. 280A(c)(4)). However, the deduction is available only if the taxpayer has applied for, has been granted, or is exempt from having a license, certification, or approval as a day care center or as a family or group day care home under applicable state law. The deduction of expenses allocable to day care use is limited (¶ 963). Additionally, if the portion of the home used for day care purposes is not used exclusively for those purposes, the taxpayer must also allocate expenses based on the number of hours the space is used for day care, compared to the total hours it is available for any use. The taxpayer must file Form 8829 for this purpose.

965. Home Office Deduction by Employees. In order for an employee to qualify for the home office deduction (¶ 961), he or she must not only meet the exclusive use requirement, but the exclusive use of the home office must be for the convenience of his or her employer (Code Sec. 280A(c)(1) and (6)). However, an employee cannot claim a home office deduction for any portion of the home rented to the employer, except for expenses such as home mortgage interest and real property taxes that are deductible absent business use. An employee's home office expenses generally must be taken as a miscellaneous itemized deduction, subject to the two-percent-of-adjusted-gross-income (AGI) floor on Schedule A (Form 1040) for tax years beginning before 2018 and after 2025 (¶ 1079). Unreimbursed employee business expenses subject to the two-percent-of-AGI limit are not deductible in tax years 2018 through 2025 (¶ 941). A statutory employee (¶ 941B) claims home office deductions on Schedule C (Form 1040).

966. Deductions on Rental Residence or Vacation Home. Special rules limit the deductions that may be taken by taxpayer in connection with the rental of a residence or vacation home, or a portion thereof, that is also used as the taxpayer's residence (Code Sec. 280A). A vacation home is a dwelling unit, including a house, apartment, condominium, house trailer, boat, or similar property. Deductions that may be claimed without regard to whether or not the home is used for trade or business or for the production of income (e.g., mortgage interest, property taxes, or a casualty loss) are not limited.

Personal Usage Defined. A vacation home is used by the taxpayer for personal purposes for a day if it is used for any part of the day:

- for personal purposes by the taxpayer, any other person who owns an interest in the home, or the relatives of either (spouses, brothers, sisters, ancestors, and lineal descendants);

- by any individual who uses the home under a reciprocal arrangement, whether or not rent is charged; and

- by any other individual who uses the home unless a fair rental is charged.

If the taxpayer rents the home at a fair rental value to any person as a principal residence, including a relative, the renter's use is not personal use by the taxpayer. This exception applies to a renter who owns an interest in the home only if the rental is under a shared equity financing agreement.

Rental Use of Fewer Than 15 Days. If the property is rented for fewer than 15 days during the year, rental expenses are not deductible and the rental income is excluded from the taxpayer's gross income (Code Sec. 280A(g)).

Rental Use Exceeding 14 Days. If the property is rented for more than 14 days during the year, rental expenses are deductible. If the home is used as a personal residence for more than the greater of 14 days or 10 percent of the number of days the home is rented at a fair market rental during the year, rental deductions are limited to the gross rental income. If the taxpayer does not use the home as a personal residence, the rental deductions are not limited to the rental income. The deduction may also be reduced or eliminated under the passive activity loss rules (¶ 1169) or the hobby loss rules if the rental activity is not engaged in for profit (¶ 1195).

¶964

Ordering of Deduction. Rental expenses are deducted from gross rental income in the following order: (1) mortgage interest, real property taxes, and casualty losses attributable to the rental use; (2) operating expenses other than depreciation attributable to the rental use; and (3) depreciation and other basis adjustments attributable to rental income (Prop. Reg. §1.280A-3(d)(3)). These expenses are allocated to rental use based on the ratio that the total number of rental days bears to the total days used for all purposes during the year.

If the taxpayer's personal use exceeds the greater of either 14 days or 10 percent of the rental days, the IRS limits the deductible rental expenses in the same manner as that prescribed under the hobby loss rules (¶ 1195). Thus, the total deductions may not exceed the gross rental income, and expenses are allocated to rental use based on the total days rented divided by the total days used. However, the Tax Court has held that mortgage interest and real estate taxes should be allocated based on the ratio of the total days rented to the total days in the year because those expenses are assessed on an annual basis regardless of the days the property is used (*D.D. Bolton*, Dec. 38,075, 77 TC 104; *E.G. McKinney*, Dec. 38,077(M), 42 TCM 467). This approach can effectively reduce the amount of mortgage interest and real estate taxes that is allocated to the rental use and, thus, leave more gross rental income available to offset allocated rental expenses.

Example: Sam rents out his vacation home for 91 days and uses the home for personal purposes for 30 days during the year. He has $2,700 in gross rental income, and he pays $621 of real property taxes and $2,854 of mortgage interest. He has $2,693 in additional expenses for maintenance, repair, and utilities.

The IRS allocation of all expenses would be based on 75 percent (91 days rented ÷ 121 days used). In contrast, the Tax Court would allocate taxes and interest based on 25 percent (91 days rented ÷ 365 days) and use the 75-percent limitation for the additional expenses for maintenance, repair, etc.

	IRS	Tax Court
1. Gross rental income	$2,700	$2,700
2. Less: Interest ($2,854)	– 2,141	– 714
Property tax ($621)	– 466	– 155
3. Remaining available income	$93	$1,831
4. Utilities, maintenance, etc.	– 93	– 1,831
5. Net income	$0	$0
6. Unused expense allowable as itemized deductions:		
Interest	$713	$2,140
Property tax	155	466
7. Total allowable deductions	$3,568	$5,306

Bed and Breakfast Inns. The special restrictions on deductions related to a residence used for business and personal purposes do not apply to the portion of the residence used exclusively as a bed and breakfast inn. Expenses related to that portion of a residence may be limited under the hobby loss rules (¶ 1195) (Code Sec. 280A(f)).

967. Conversion of Personal Residence to Rental Property. An individual who converts his or her principal residence into a rental unit (or vice versa) is not considered to have used the unit for personal purposes for any day during the tax year that occurs before (or after) a qualified rental period for purposes of applying the limitation on home office deductions (¶ 966) allocable to the qualified rental period (Code Sec. 280A(d)(4)). The expenses, however, must be allocated between the periods of rental and personal use. A qualified rental period is a consecutive period of 12 or more months beginning or ending during the tax year that the unit is rented or held for rental at its fair market value. The 12-month rental requirement does not apply if the residence is sold or exchanged before it has been rented or held for rental for the full 12 months.

Example: Sue moved out of her principal residence on February 28, 2019, to accept employment in another town. The house was rented at its fair market value from March 15, 2019, through May 14, 2020. The use of the house as a principal residence from January 1 through February 28, 2019, is not counted as personal use. If Sue moved back and reoccupied the home on June 1, 2020, the use of the house as a principal residence from June 1 through December 31, 2020, is not counted as personal use.

Other Business Expenses

See CCH® AnswerConnect: *Business Expenses* for more information on this topic.

968. Business Deduction of Fire and Casualty Insurance Premiums. A premium paid for insurance against losses from fire, accident, storm, theft, or other casualty is deductible if it is an ordinary and necessary expense of a business (Reg. § 1.162-1). However, the uniform capitalization rules may require that insurance costs on real or tangible personal property acquired or produced for resale be included in inventory or capitalized, rather than being deducted (¶ 1330). An insurance company's agreement to reimburse future remediation costs that a business is certain to incur is not an insurance contract because it does not involve the requisite risk shifting. Thus, the business's payments to the insurer are not deductible insurance premiums (Rev. Rul. 2007-47, amplifying Rev. Rul. 89-96).

969. Business Deduction of Advertising Expenses. Advertising expenses are deductible as a trade or business expense if they are reasonable in amount and bear a reasonable relation to the business. Deductible expenses may be intended to develop goodwill as well as gain immediate sales. The cost of advertising is deductible when paid or incurred, even though the advertising program extends over several years or is expected to result in benefits extending over a period of years (Rev. Rul. 92-80). When a catalog is not replaced annually, the Tax Court and the IRS require the printing costs to be amortized over the expected life of the catalog. However, some courts have held to the contrary, treating catalog costs as regular advertising expenses (*Sheldon & Co.*, CA-6, 54-2 USTC ¶ 9526).

The costs of public service or other impartial advertising, such as advertising designed to encourage the public to register and to vote, are deductible (Rev. Rul. 62-156). Expenses for advertising in political programs or for admission to political fundraising or inaugural functions and similar events are not deductible (Code Sec. 276). This rule also applies to admission to any dinner or program if any part of the proceeds of the event directly or indirectly inures to or for the use of a political party or a political candidate.

Package Design Costs. Package design costs include the graphic arrangement or design of shapes, colors, words, pictures, lettering, and other elements on a given product package, or the design of a container with respect to its shape or function (Reg. § 1.263(a)-4(b)(3)(v)). The Tax Court has held that packaging design costs are a deductible advertising expense even though the design provided the company with significant future benefits (*RJR Nabisco*, Dec. 52,786(M), 76 TCM 71 (Nonacq.)).

970. Business Deduction of Expenses for Earning Tax-Exempt Income. No deduction is allowed for any expense allocable to the earning of tax-exempt income (Code Sec. 265; Reg. § 1.265-1). Also, no deduction is allowed for interest paid on a debt incurred or continued in order to purchase or carry tax-exempt bonds or other obligations, regardless of whether the interest expense was incurred in business, in a profit-inspired transaction, or in any other connection.

Banks, thrift institutions, and other financial institutions generally may not deduct any portion of their interest expenses allocable to tax-exempt interest on obligations acquired after August 7, 1986. This includes amounts paid in respect of deposits, investment certificates, or withdrawable or repurchasable shares. There is a *de minimis* safe harbor exception to the 100-percent disallowance rule for bonds issued in 2009 and 2010.

Qualified tax-exempt obligations that are issued by a qualified small issuer are not taken into account as investments in tax-exempt bonds. Thus, they are not subject to the 100-percent disallowance rule. Instead, only 20 percent of the interest expense allocable to qualified tax-exempt obligations is disallowed. A qualified small issuer is an issuer that reasonably anticipates that the amount of its tax-exempt obligations, other than certain private activity bonds, will not exceed $10 million during the calendar year. A qualified tax-exempt obligation is a tax-exempt obligation that (1) is issued after August 7, 1986, by a qualified small issuer; (2) is not a private activity bond; and (3) is designated by the issuer as qualifying for the exception from the general rule.

971. Business Deduction of Circulation Expenses. Any expenditure to establish, maintain, or increase the circulation of a newspaper, magazine, or other periodical may be deducted in the year paid or incurred even if the taxpayer reports only an allocable portion of the subscription income for each year of the subscription period (Code Sec. 173; Reg. § 1.173-1). Certain taxpayers may also elect to capitalize circulation expenses and amortize them over a three-year period to avoid treatment as a tax preference item for alternative minimum tax (AMT) purposes (¶ 196).

972. Business Deduction of Fines, Penalties, Kickbacks, Drug Trafficking. Any amount paid or incurred after December 21, 2017, by suit, agreement, or otherwise, is not deductible if paid or incurred to, or at the direction of, any government or governmental entity for the violation of a law, or the investigation or inquiry into the potential violation of a law (Code Sec. 162(f)). A fine or penalty paid to a government before December 22, 2017, for the violation of any law also is not a deductible business expense.

For affected amounts paid or incurred after December 21, 2017, the appropriate official of the government (or the nongovernmental entity treated as governmental entity for these purposes) must report to the IRS on Form 1098-F the amount of each settlement agreement or order entered into, if the aggregate amount required to be paid is at least $600. The official must also furnish similar information to individuals involved in the settlement. The IRS may adjust the $600 amount (Code Sec. 6050X; Notice 2018-23).

Prior to December 22, 2017, amounts paid or incurred under a binding order or agreement that was entered into and approved by a court are exempt from the amended rules. Certain amounts originating after December 21, 2017, may be deductible if they are paid or incurred (1) as restitution (including the remediation of property) for damages or harm that was or may be due to the violation or potential violation of a law; (2) to comply with a law that was violated or involved in the investigation or inquiry into the violation or potential violation of a law; (3) to satisfy a court order in a suit in which a government or governmental entity is not a party; or (4) for taxes due.

Bribes or Kickbacks. Any illegal bribe or kickback paid directly or indirectly to a domestic government official or employee is not deductible. Bribes and kickbacks paid directly or indirectly to an employee or official of a foreign government are not deductible if they are unlawful under the federal Foreign Corrupt Practices Act of 1977. No deduction is allowed for any payment made directly or indirectly to any person if the payment is a bribe, kickback, or other illegal payment under any U.S. law or under any generally enforced state law that subjects the payor to a criminal penalty or to the loss of license or privilege to engage in a trade or business (Code Sec. 162(c)(2) and (3); Reg. § 1.162-18). A deduction is also denied for any kickback, rebate, or bribe made by any provider of services, supplier, physician, or other person in connection with furnishing items or services or making or receiving payments under Medicare, Medicaid, or a federally funded state plan approved under Medicare or Medicaid. For all the above purposes, a kickback includes a payment in consideration of the referral of a client, patient, or customer.

Antitrust Violations. If a taxpayer is convicted of, or pleads guilty or no contest to, a criminal violation of an antitrust law that contains a treble damage provision, no deduction is allowed for two-thirds of the amount paid to satisfy the judgment or in settlement of a suit brought under section 4 of the Clayton Act (Code Sec. 162(g); Reg. § 1.162-22).

Other Penalties. No deduction is allowed for a federal tax penalty (Reg. § 1.162-21(b)(1)(ii)). Also, no deduction or credit is allowed for amounts paid or incurred in the illegal trafficking in drugs listed in the federal Controlled Substances Act, including rent and employee compensation. This is the case even if the substance is legal under applicable state law. However, an adjustment to gross receipts for the cost of goods sold is permitted (Code Sec. 280E; *M. Olive*, CA-9, 2015-2 USTC ¶ 50,377; *J.M. Loughman*, Dec. 61,195(M), 115 TCM 1472). Damage awards paid in connection with the violation of a federal civil statute and similar penalties may be deductible if they are compensatory, rather than punitive, in nature (Reg. § 1.162-21(b)(2)).

973. Business Legal Expenses. Legal expenses paid or incurred in connection with a business transaction or primarily for the purpose of preserving existing business reputation and goodwill are ordinarily deductible (*F. W. Staudt*, Dec. 20,040(M), 12 TCM 1417). Legal fees may be deductible even if no litigation is involved. Legal expenses include attorneys' fees, fees or expenses of accountants and expert witnesses, and court stenographic and printing charges.

The deductibility tests are substantially the same as those for other business expenses and preclude a current deduction for a legal expense incurred in the acquisition of capital assets (Reg. § 1.263(a)-2). Litigation costs must also be capitalized if under the origin of the claim test (or the nature of the claim leading to the payments) they are incurred to acquire a capital asset.

A deduction is not allowed for any settlement or payment paid or incurred after December 22, 2017, related to sexual harassment or sexual abuse if the settlement or payment is subject to a nondisclosure agreement. Attorney's fees related to such payments or agreements are also not deductible (Code Sec. 162(q)).

Deductible business expenses include the cost of tax return preparation that is properly allocable to the business, as well as expenses incurred in resolving asserted tax deficiencies relating to the business (*D. Pistoresi*, Dec. 53,243(M), 77 TCM 1368; *C. Wood*, Dec. 25,086, 37 TC 70 (Acq.)).

See ¶ 1085 and ¶ 1093 for the deductibility of legal expenses arising from the determination of nonbusiness taxes or income-producing property.

974. Business Deduction for Lobbying and Political Expenses. No deduction is allowed for any amount paid or incurred in connection with: (1) influencing federal or state legislation; (2) participation in, or intervention in, any political campaign on behalf of (or in opposition to) any candidate for public office; (3) any attempt to influence the general public, or segments thereof, with respect to elections, legislative matters, or referendums; or (4) any direct communication with a covered executive branch official in an attempt to influence his official actions or positions (Code Sec. 162(e); Reg. § 1.162-20(c)). Under a *de minimis* exception, the prohibition does not apply to any in-house lobbying expenditures if the expenditures do not exceed $2,000 during the tax year.

Lobbying expenses pertaining to local legislation paid or incurred before December 22, 2017, are deductible.

975. Federal National Mortgage Association Stock. Initial holders of stock issued by the Federal National Mortgage Association may deduct, as a business expense, the excess of the price paid over the market price of the stock on the date of issuance (Code Sec. 162(d); Reg. § 1.162-19(a)). The basis in the stock is reduced to reflect the deduction.

978. Expenses of Mercantile and Manufacturing Businesses. Merchants and manufacturers generally are subject to the uniform capitalization rules (¶ 1330). However, ordinary and necessary business expenses not covered by such rules may be currently deducted (Reg. § 1.162-1).

979. Research and Experimental Expenses. A taxpayer may elect to deduct certain research and experimental expenses before 2022 by claiming the deduction on the income tax return for the first tax year in which the costs are paid or incurred in connection with its business (Code Sec. 174, prior to amendment by the Tax Cuts and Jobs Act (P.L. 115-97); Reg. § 1.174-2). Only costs of research in the laboratory or for experimental purposes, whether carried on by the taxpayer or on behalf of the taxpayer by a third party, are deductible. Market research and normal product testing costs are not research expenditures. Once made, the election is applicable to all research costs incurred in the project for the current and all subsequent years. A credit is also allowed for increased research and experimental expenses (¶ 1465J), but the taxpayer's deduction is reduced by the amount of the credit.

The costs of obtaining a patent, including attorneys' fees paid or incurred in making and perfecting a patent application, qualify as research or experimental expenditures, but the costs of acquiring another's patent, model, production, or process do not qualify. If the taxpayer elects to defer the expenses, the right to amortize ceases when the patent issues. Unrecovered expenditures are recovered through depreciation over the life of the patent (Reg. § 1.174-4(a)(4)). A purchased patent may qualify as a section 197 intangible to be amortized over 15 years (¶ 1362).

Amortization Required After 2021. Research and experimental expenditures paid or incurred in tax years beginning after December 31, 2021, generally must be amortized ratably over five years (15 years for expenditures attributable to foreign research) (Code Sec. 174). The amortization period will begin at the mid-point of the tax year when the expenditures are paid or incurred. Any amount paid or incurred in connection with the development of software will be treated as a research or experimental expenditure for this purpose. Amortization must continue even if the underlying property is disposed, retired, or abandoned during the amortization period. The amount capitalized and otherwise eligible for amortization is reduced by the excess (if any) of the research credit allowed for the tax year (¶ 1465J) minus the amount allowable as a deduction for the tax year as qualified research expenses or basic research expenses (Code Sec. 280C(c)).

980. Business Deduction for Computer Software Expenses. The tax treatment of computer software used in a trade or business depends on whether the taxpayer has leased the software, developed it internally, or purchased it (Code Sec. 162; Reg. § 1.162-11; Rev. Proc. 2000-50, as modified by Rev. Proc. 2007-16).

Rental payments for leased software are generally deductible as business expenses over the term of the lease in the same manner as any other rental payments. Computer software that is purchased is amortizable over 15 years if it is a section 197 intangible (¶ 1362). Software that is not a section 197 intangible is amortized using the straight-line method over a period of 36 months beginning on the first day of the month that the software is placed in service.

Costs incurred by a taxpayer to develop software for sale to others or for internal use may be treated like research and experimental expenses (¶ 979) and may be deducted currently, amortized as research expenses over a 60-month period (or shorter if established as appropriate), or amortized as software expenses over a 36-month period, so long as the costs are treated consistently. However, in tax years beginning after 2021, no portion of software development costs paid or incurred will be currently deductible and all such expenses must be amortized as research expenditures over five years (15-years for foreign research).

Computer software is any program designed to cause a computer to perform a desired function (Code Secs. 167(f)(1)(B) and 197(e)(3)(B); Rev. Proc. 2000-50, as modified by Rev. Proc. 2007-16). It does not include any database or similar item unless the database or item is in the public domain and is incidental to the operation of otherwise qualifying computer software.

Software Bundled with Hardware. Software costs that are included, but not separately stated, in the cost of computer hardware are capitalized and depreciated as part of the hardware (Reg. § 1.167(a)-14(b)(2)). Thus, the entire amount is treated as the cost of hardware (tangible property) and is depreciable over a five-year recovery period.

Web Site Development Costs. The IRS has yet to issue formal guidance on the treatment of web site development costs.

Domestic Production Activities Deduction

See CCH® AnswerConnect: *Pre-2018 Domestic Production Activities Deduction* for more information on this topic.

980A. Domestic Production Activities Deduction. For tax years beginning before 2018, a taxpayer may claim a deduction against gross income equal to nine percent of (i) its qualified production activities income (QPAI) (¶ 980B) or (ii) adjusted gross income for an individual, estate, or trust, determined without regard to the domestic production activities. In the case of a C corporation, the deduction for AMT purposes is equal to nine percent of the lesser of QPAI or alternative minimum taxable income (AMTI) (Code Sec. 199, prior to repeal by the Tax Cuts and Jobs Act (P.L. 115-97)).Form 8903 is used to calculate the deduction. The amount of the domestic production activities deduction (DPAD) for any tax year may not exceed 50 percent of the W-2 wages paid by the taxpayer (¶ 980C) that are allocable to the taxpayer's domestic production gross receipts (¶ 980D). The DPAD is repealed for tax years beginning after 2017.

980B. Qualified Production Activities Income. For tax years beginning before 2018, a taxpayer's qualified production activities income (QPAI) for purposes of the domestic production activities deduction (¶ 980A) is its domestic production gross receipts (DPGR) attributable to the actual conduct of a trade or business during the tax year (¶ 980D), reduced by the cost of goods sold and other deductions, expenses, and losses that are properly allocable to DPGR (Code Sec. 199(c)(1), prior to repeal by the Tax Cuts and Jobs Act (P.L. 115-97); Reg. §§ 1.199-1(c) and 1.199-4).

980C. W-2 Wage Limitation for Code Sec. 199 Deduction. For tax years beginning before 2018, the deduction for domestic production activities (¶ 980A) may not exceed 50 percent of the W-2 wages paid by the taxpayer to its employees for the calendar year ending during the tax year that are properly allocable to the taxpayer's domestic gross production receipts (the wages that the taxpayer deducts in calculating its qualified production activities income (¶ 980B)) (Code Sec. 199(b)(2), prior to repeal by the Tax Cuts and Jobs Act (P.L. 115-97); Reg. § 1.199-2).

W-2 wages are amounts required to be reported for wages and compensation on Form W-2, plus compensation deferred under Code Sec. 457 plans and elective deferrals under other employer plans (i.e., 401(k)s, 403(b)s, SIMPLEs, and SEPs, as well as designated Roth contributions). Taxpayers may use one of three methods for computing W-2 wages: the unmodified box method, modified Box 1 method, or tracking wages method.

Amounts that a taxpayer treats as W-2 wages in one tax year (e.g., nonqualified deferred compensation) may not be treated as W-2 wages in another tax year or as W-2 wages of another taxpayer. If an acquisition or disposition of a trade or business causes more than one taxpayer to be an employer of the acquired or disposed of business's employees during the calendar year, the taxpayer's W-2 wages for that year are allocated between each taxpayer based on the period when the business's employees were employed by the taxpayer (Temp. Reg. §§ 1.199-2T(c)(1), 1.199-8T(i)(10)).

980D. Domestic Production Gross Receipts (DPGR). For tax years beginning before 2018, domestic production gross receipts (DPGR) for purposes of the domestic production activities (DPAD) deduction (¶ 980A) are the gross receipts of the taxpayer that are derived from:

- the lease, rental, license, sale, exchange, or other disposition of:

  — qualifying production property (generally, tangible personal property, computer software, and sound recordings) manufactured, produced, grown, or extracted by the taxpayer in whole or in significant part within the United States;

  — any qualified film produced by the taxpayer in the United States; or

  — electricity, natural gas, or potable water produced by the taxpayer in the United States;

- construction performed within the United States; and

- engineering or architectural services performed in the United States for construction projects located in the United States (Code Sec. 199(c)(4), prior to repeal by the Tax Cuts and Jobs Act (P.L. 115-97).

DPGR does not include gross receipts from:

- the sale of food and beverages prepared by the taxpayer at a retail establishment;

- transmission or distribution of electricity, natural gas, or potable water; or

- the lease, rental, license, sale, exchange, or other disposition of land.

A taxpayer generally may use any reasonable method to allocate its gross receipts between DPGR and non-DPGR. However, the taxpayer must use a specific identification method if the information is readily available and can be used without undue burden or expense (Reg. § 1.199-1(d)). Under several *de minimis* safe harbors, allocation is not required when less than five percent of gross receipts are DPGR (or non-DPGR).

¶ 980B

DPGR must be determined on an item-by-item basis (Reg. § 1.199-3(d)). An "item" is property, or any portion of property, that is offered to sale to customers and that meets all of the requirements of the DPAD deduction.

Gross receipts derived from the performance of a service other than construction, engineering, and architectural activities generally do not qualify as DPGR (Reg. § 1.199-3(i)). However, there are several exceptions to this rule.

980E. Qualified Production Property (QPP) for Code Sec. 199 Deduction. For tax years beginning before 2018, one taxpayer may claim the domestic production activities deduction (¶ 980A) with respect to the manufacture, production, growth, or extraction (MPGE) of qualifying production property (QPP) (tangible personal property, computer software, and sound recordings), as well as the disposition of electricity, natural gas, potable water, or a qualified film (Code Sec. 199(c)(5), prior to repeal by the Tax Cuts and Jobs Act (P.L. 115-97); Reg. § 1.199-3(f)(1)).

The QPP must be MPGE by the taxpayer in whole or in significant part within the United States. QPP is MPGE in significant part in the United States if the MPGE activity performed within the United States is substantial in nature. This is determined on a facts-and-circumstances basis taking into account the nature and relative value added by the taxpayer's U.S. activity (Reg. § 1.199-3(e) and (g)). Under a safe harbor, the significant-part requirement is satisfied if the taxpayer's conversion costs (i.e., direct labor and related factory expenses) to MPGE the property within the United States account for 20 percent or more of the total cost of goods sold of the property (Reg. § 1.199-3(g)(3)).

980F. Construction, Engineering, or Architectural Activities for Code Sec. 199 Deduction. For tax years beginning before 2018, the domestic production gross receipts (DPGR) (¶ 980D) of taxpayers actively engaged in construction, engineering and architectural businesses includes the proceeds from the sale, exchange, or other disposition of real property constructed by the taxpayer in the United States (whether or not sold or completed), including compensation for the performance of construction services by the taxpayer and any qualified construction warranty (Reg. § 1.199-3(m)). It also includes proceeds derived from engineering or architectural services performed in the United States for real property construction projects.

980G. Allocation of Costs and Deductions for Code Sec. 199. For tax years beginning before 2018, a taxpayer must allocate cost of goods sold (CGS) between domestic production gross receipts (DPGR) and non-DPGR (¶ 980D) using any reasonable method that is satisfactory to the IRS based on all facts and circumstances (Reg. § 1.199-4(b)). Reasonable methods may be based on gross receipts, number of units sold, number of units produced, or total production costs.

Three methods are provided for apportioning deductions properly allocable to DPGR. Most taxpayers must use the 861 method, which is based on the rules for allocating income between U.S. and foreign sources. However, some smaller taxpayers may use the simplified modified deduction method, or the small business simplified overall method (Reg. §§ 1.199-4(c) and 1.199-8(c)):

Wage Expense Safe Harbor. A taxpayer using either the Section 861 method of cost allocation or the simplified deduction method may allocate W-2 wages to DPGR by multiplying W-2 wages by the ratio of the wage expense included in calculating qualified production activities income (QPAI) to the total wage expense used in calculating taxable income (or adjusted gross income, if applicable), without regard to any wage expense disallowed by Code Secs. 465, 469, 704(d), or 1366(d) (Reg. § 1.199-2(e)(2)). A taxpayer that uses the small business simplified overall method may use a safe harbor to allocate W-2 wages to DPGR according to the ratio of DPGR to total gross receipts.

980H. Application of Code Sec. 199 to Pass-Through Entities. For tax years beginning before 2018, the deduction for domestic production activities (¶ 980A) is generally applied at the shareholder, partner, or similar level of a pass-through entity (Code Sec. 199(d)(1), prior to repeal by the Tax Cuts and Jobs Act (P.L. 115-97); Reg. § 1.199-5). The entity allocates to each partner or shareholder its share of the entity's qualified production activities income (QPAI) and W-2 wages. However, certain eligible entities may calculate QPAI and W-2 wages at the entity level (Rev. Proc. 2007-34).

The owner of a pass-through entity generally is not treated as directly conducting the qualified production activities of the entity, and vice versa, with respect to property transferred between the entity and the owner. Domestic production gross receipts (DPGR) generally do not include gain or loss recognized on the sale, exchange, or other disposition of an interest in a pass-through entity.

Special rules permit patrons of agricultural or horticultural cooperatives to claim the deduction for their portion of any patronage dividend or per-unit allocation received that is allocable to the QPAI of the cooperative (Code Sec. 199(d)(3), prior to repeal by P.L. 115-97); Reg. § 1.199-6). The repeal of the deduction does not apply to a qualified payment received by a patron from a specified cooperative in a tax year of the patron beginning after December 31, 2017, that is attributable to QPAI for which the cooperative is allowed the deduction for a tax year of the cooperative beginning before January 1, 2018. The qualified business income deduction (¶ 980P) is not allowed for the qualified payment (Act Sec. 101 of the Consolidated Appropriations Act, 2018 (Division T of P.L. 115-141)).

See ¶ 312 for application to S corporations, ¶ 431A for application to partnerships, and ¶ 536 for application to nongrantor trusts and estates.

Qualified Business Income Deduction

See CCH® AnswerConnect: *Section 199A Qualified Business Income Deduction (Pass-Through Income Deduction)* for more information on this topic.

980P. Qualified Business Income (QBI) Deduction. An individual, trust, and estate may deduct up to 20 percent of certain domestic qualified business income (QBI) from a sole proprietorship, partnership, and S corporation for tax years beginning after December 31, 2017, and before January 1, 2026 (Code Sec. 199A). The QBI deduction, also known as the "pass-through deduction," is generally the lesser of combined QBI or 20 percent of the excess (if any) of taxable income over net capital gain.

A taxpayer's combined QBI amount is the sum of the deductible amount of QBI from all qualified businesses of the taxpayer, plus 20 percent of the taxpayer's aggregate qualified REIT dividends and qualified income from a publicly traded partnership (PTP) (Code Sec. 199A(b)). If QBI from all qualified business is less than zero, the loss is carried over and reduces the QBI deduction for the next tax year by 20 percent of the carried-over loss. Similarly, a loss in combined REIT dividends and PTP income carries over to offset combined REIT dividends and PTP income in the next year (Code Sec. 199A(c)(2); Reg. § 1.199A-1(c)(2)). An individual uses the worksheet in the Instructions to Form 1040 or IRS Pub. 535 to calculate the deduction.

Wage/Capital Limit. The deductible amount of QBI for each trade or business of the taxpayer is generally limited to the *lesser* of:

- 20 percent of the taxpayer's share of the business's QBI; or

- a W-2 wage/capital limit, that is the *greater* of:

  — 50 percent of the taxpayer's share of the business's W-2 wages; or

  — 25 percent of the taxpayer's share of the business's W-2 wages, plus 2.5 percent of the taxpayer's share of the business's unadjusted basis in qualified property immediately after acquisition (UBIA) (Code Sec. 199A(b)(2)).

The W-2 wages/capital limit does not apply if the taxpayer's taxable income is less than a threshold amount, adjusted annually for inflation (Code Sec. 199A(b)(3) and (e)(2); Rev. Proc. 2018-57; Rev. Proc. 2019-44). For 2019, the threshold is $321,400 if married filing jointly, $160,725 if married filing separately, and $160,700 if single or head of household. For 2020, the threshold is $326,600 if married filing jointly and $163,300 if married filing separately, single, and head of household. The wages/capital limit is phased-in if the taxpayer's taxable income exceeds the threshold by $100,000 if married filing jointly and $50,000 for married filing separately, single, and head of household. For 2019, the limit applies in full when taxable income exceeds $421,400 if married filing jointly, $210,725 if married filing separately, and $210,700 for all other taxpayers. For 2020, the limit applies in full when taxable income exceeds $426,600 if married filing jointly and $213,300 if married filing separately, single, and head of household.

¶980P

If the taxpayer is a patron of a specified agricultural or horticultural cooperative, the deductible amount for the cooperative's trade or business is reduced by the *lesser* of: (1) nine percent of the QBI that is properly allocable to qualified payments received from the cooperative; or (2) 50 percent of the W-2 wages properly allocable to the qualified payments (Code Sec. 199A(b)(7)).

W-2 wages for this purpose are wages, plus the employees' elective deferrals and deferred compensation under 401(k) plans, simplified employee pensions, 403(b) annuities, section 457 plans, and designated Roth contributions. The wages must be properly allocable to QBI, paid during the calendar year that ends in the business's tax year, and included on Form W-2 (Code Sec. 199A(b)(4); Reg. § 1.199A-2). The IRS has provided three methods for calculating a qualified business's W-2 wages: the unmodified box method, the modified box 1 method, and the tracking wages method (Rev. Proc. 2019-11).

Qualified property of a qualified business is depreciable tangible property used during the tax year to produce QBI (Code Sec. 199A(b)(6); Reg. § 1.199A-2). The property must be held by the business and available for use at the close of the tax year. Its depreciable period also must not end before the close of the tax year. The depreciable period begins when the business first places the property into service. The depreciable period must end 10 years after the placed-in service date or, if later, the last day of the last full year in the applicable recovery period under Modified Accelerated Cost Recovery System (MACRS) without regard to the alternative depreciation system (ADS).

UBIA is the business's unadjusted basis in the property on the date it is placed in service. UBIA is not affected by depreciation deductions, tax credits, or expense elections. However, it is reduced to reflect nonbusiness use of the property. Property generally is not qualified property if it is acquired within 60 days of the end of the tax year, and disposed of within 120 days without using it in the business for at least 45 days (Reg. § 1.199A-2(c)).

Qualified Business Income. QBI is net amount of qualified items of income, gain, deduction, and loss from a qualified trade or business. Items are qualified to the extent they are effectively connected with the conduct of a trade or business within the United States, and are included or allowed in determining taxable income for the tax year. If the net amount of qualified income, gain, deduction, and loss is less than zero, the loss is carried over to the next tax year. Thus, any QBI deduction allowed in the next tax year is reduced (but not below zero) by 20 percent of the carried-over loss (Code Sec. 199A(c); Reg. § 1.199A-3(b)).

QBI does not include reasonable compensation that the business pays to the taxpayer for services, a partnership's guaranteed payments to a partner for services, or a partnership's payments to a partner for services that are treated as made to a nonpartner. Qualified items of income, gain, deduction, or loss do not include capital gains or losses, dividends (other than from a cooperative), interest, and other amounts not properly allocable to the trade or business, as well as deductions or losses allocable to these amounts (Reg. § 1.199A-3(b)(2)(ii)).

If items of QBI that are properly attributable to more than one trade or business of the taxpayer, they must be allocated to each business using any reasonable method based on all the facts and circumstances. The taxpayer may also use different allocation methods for different items of income, gain, deduction, and loss so long as they are consistently applied. An individual may aggregate qualified trade and businesses if certain requirements are met (Reg. § 1.199A-4).

Qualified Trade or Business. A qualified trade or business is generally any trade or business that may deduct business expenses under Code Sec. 162 (¶ 901), other than a trade or business of performing services as an employee or a specified service trade or business (SSTB). However, a rental activity that is not a Code Sec. 162 business is treated as a trade or business if it rents or licenses tangible or intangible property to a commonly owned trade or business (Code Sec. 199A(d)(1); Reg. § 1.199A-1(b)(14)). A business and a rental activity are commonly owned if the same person or group of persons directly or indirectly owns at least 50 percent of each of them (Reg. § 1.199A-4(b)(1)(i)).

Under a safe harbor, a rental real estate enterprise is treated as a trade or business for purposes of Code Sec. 199A if: (1) separate books and records are maintained to reflect income and expenses for each rental real estate enterprise; (2) at least 250 hours of rental services are performed per year; and (3) for tax years beginning after 2019, the taxpayer maintains sufficient contemporaneous records. Both individuals and pass-through entities can use the safe harbor if they hold the real property interest directly or through a disregarded entity. The owner must also treat each property as a separate enterprise or treat all similar properties as a single enterprise (Rev. Proc. 2019-38; Notice 2019-7).

The QBI deduction is not allowed for any SSTB that is a trade or business that involves the performance of:

- services in the fields of health, law, accounting, actuarial science, performing arts, consulting, athletics, financial services, brokerage services, or any trade or business whose principal asset is the reputation or skill of one or more of its employee/owners; or

- services consisting of investing and investment management, trading, or dealing in securities, partnership interests, or commodities (Code Sec. 199A(d)(2); Reg. § 1.199A-5).

The deduction is allowed for a trade or business providing services in architecture or engineering if it otherwise qualifies for the deduction (Reg. § 1.199A-5(b)(2)(vii)). A direct or indirect owner of a trade or business that performs a specified service is generally engaged in the performance of that service, regardless of whether the owner is passive or participated in the specified service activity (Reg. § 1.199A-5(a)(2)).

Under a *de minimis* safe harbor, a service business is not a SSTB if (1) the business has no more than $25 million in gross receipts for the tax year, and less than 10 percent of those receipts are attributable to the performance of services in a field listed above; or (2) the business has more than $25 million in gross receipts, and less than five percent are attributable to services in a field listed above (Reg. § 1.199A-5(c)(1)).

A taxpayer carrying on a SSTB may claim a modified QBI deduction if his or her taxable income is less than the W-2/capital threshold, plus $100,000 if married filing jointly and $50,000 for all other taxpayers (Code Sec. 199A(d)(3); Reg. § 1.199A-1(d)). Thus, the SSTB exclusion is fully phased in for 2019 if taxable income exceeds $421,400 if married filing jointly, $210,725 if married filing separately, and $210,700 if single or head of household. The exclusion is fully phased in for 2020 if taxable income exceeds $426,600 if married filing jointly and $213,300 if married filing separately, single, or head of household (Rev. Proc. 2018-57; Rev. Proc. 2019-44).

Partnerships and S Corporations. The QBI deduction is applied at the partner and shareholder level of a partnership and S corporation. Each partner and shareholder takes into account his or her allocable share or pro rata share of each qualified item of income, gain, deduction, and loss. A partner's and shareholder's share of the entity's W-2 wages and UBIA for the tax years is based on his or her share of the entity's W-2 wages and UBIA determined for depreciation (Code Sec. 199A(f)(1)(A); Reg. § 1.199A-6). Special rules are provided for determining QBI, REIT dividends, and publicly traded partnership (PTP) income of a partnership (Reg. § 1.199A-3; Prop. Reg. § 1.199A-3).

Trusts and Estates. A trust or estate may claim the QBI deduction (Code Sec. 199A(f)(1)(B); Reg. § 1.199A-6(d); Prop. Reg. § 1.199A-6(d)). The grantor of a grantor trust computes the deduction as if that person directly conducted the activities of the trust with respect to the owned portion of the trust. A nongrantor trust or estate calculates QBI, W-2 wages, UBIA qualified REIT dividends, and qualified PTP income at the entity level. The items are then allocated to each beneficiary and the trust or estate itself based on the relative proportion of DNI for the tax year.

Agricultural or Horticultural Cooperatives. A specified agricultural or horticultural cooperative may claim a deduction equal to nine percent of the *lesser* of the cooperative's qualified production activities income (QPAI) or its taxable income (determined without regard to allowable deductions for patronage dividends, per-unit retain allocations, or nonpatronage distributions) (Code Sec. 199A(g); Prop. Reg. § 1.199A-7; Notice 2019-27). The deduction cannot be more than 50 percent of the cooperative's W-2 wages for the tax year. A cooperative's QPAI is the excess of (1) the cooperative's domestic production gross receipts for the tax year, over (2) the sum of the cost of goods sold allocable to the receipts, plus other expenses, losses, or deductions (other than the QPAI deduction) properly allocable to the receipts. The QPAI deduction is reduced if the cooperative has oil-related QPAI. A noncorporate patron, or another specified agricultural or horticultural cooperative, that receives a qualified payment from the cooperative can claim a deduction for a portion of the amount of the cooperative's deduction.

Penalty. A taxpayer who claims the QBI deduction or the QPAI deduction may be subject to the 20-percent accuracy-related penalty for a substantial understatement of income tax if the understatement is more than the greater of $5,000 or five percent of the tax required to be shown on the return for the tax year (¶ 2858) (Code Sec. 6662(d)(1)(C)).

Professional Expenses

See CCH® AnswerConnect: *Who Must File an Individual Income Tax Return* for more information on this topic.

981. Professional Expenses. The practice of a profession is considered a trade or business, so a professional may deduct expenses incurred in the course of pursuing his or her profession. This may include expenses incurred for using a car to make professional calls, dues to professional organizations, rent paid for office space, and other ordinary and necessary business expenses. Amounts for books and equipment may be deducted if the useful life of the item is not more than one year (Reg. § 1.162-6).

No deduction is allowed for dues paid to any club organized for business, pleasure, recreation, or other social purposes (Code Sec. 274(a)(3); Reg. § 1.274-2(a)(2)(iii)). This prohibition does not extend to dues paid to professional organizations (e.g., bar and accounting associations) or public service organizations (e.g., Kiwanis and Rotary clubs) (¶ 913A). A professional who incurs unreimbursed expenses in performing services as an employee may deduct them only as miscellaneous itemized deductions subject to the two-percent-of-adjusted-gross-income (AGI) floor for tax years beginning before 2018 and after 2025. Expenses subject to the two-percent-of-AGI limit are not deductible in tax years 2018 through 2025 (¶ 941 and ¶ 1079).

Information Services. Amounts paid for subscriptions to professional journals and information services that have a useful life of one year or less, are deductible by a lawyer, accountant or other taxpayer who buys a service in connection with the performance of his or her duties (*J.I. Peyser*, Dec. 13,076(M), 1 TCM 807; *G. Nehus*, Dec. 50,308(M), 68 TCM 1503).

Other Expenses. A deduction is allowed to members of the clergy, lawyers, merchants, professors, and physicians for expenses incurred in attending business conventions (¶ 959 and ¶ 960) (Reg. § 1.162-2). A member of the medical profession is allowed a deduction for business entertainment expenses paid or incurred before January 1, 2018, subject to the limits on entertainment expenses (¶ 910), so long as there is a direct relationship between the expense and the development or expansion of a medical practice (*R.A. Sutter*, Dec. 19,966, 21 TC 170 (Acq.)). A doctor's staff privilege fee paid to a hospital is a capital expenditure (*G.L. Heigerick*, Dec. 27,846, 45 TC 475).

Farmer's Expenses

982. Farming Expenses. Deductions are permitted for expenses incurred in carrying on the business of farming, including a horticultural nursery business (Reg. § 1.162-12). Allowable deductions include costs for: small tools expected to last one year or less; feeding and raising livestock (excluding produce grown on the farm and labor of the taxpayer); and gasoline, repairs, and upkeep of a car or truck used wholly in the business of farming, or a portion of the cost if the vehicle is used for both farming and personal use. Special rules apply to certain property produced in a farming business (¶ 1342) and to farm tax shelters (¶ 1521). See also ¶ 767 for income averaging rules for farmers. Expenses for the purchase of farm machinery or equipment, breeding, dairy or work animals, a car, and drilling water wells for irrigation are capital items subject to depreciation.

Conservation Expenses. A farmer may generally elect to deduct soil and water conservation expenditures that are not depreciable or otherwise deductible if they would increase the basis of the property absent the election to deduct them (Code Sec. 175;

Reg. §§ 1.175-1—1.175-6). However, current deductions for soil and water conservation expenses are limited to those that are consistent with a conservation plan approved by the Soil Conservation Service of the U.S.D.A. or, in the absence of a federally approved plan, a soil conservation plan of a comparable state agency. The election does not apply to expenses related to the draining or filling of wetlands or to land preparation for the installation or operation of center pivot irrigation systems. The deduction is limited annually to 25 percent of the taxpayer's gross income from farming. Excess expenses can be carried over to succeeding tax years, but in each year the total deduction is limited to 25 percent of that year's gross income from farming.

Deductible soil and water conservation expenses include such costs as: leveling; grading; construction, control, and protection of diversion channels, drainage ditches, outlets, and ponds; planting of windbreaks; and other treatment or moving of earth. Also deductible are endangered species recovery expenditures paid or incurred by a taxpayer engaged in the business of farming for the purpose of achieving site-specific management actions recommended in recovery plans approved pursuant to the Endangered Species Act of 1973 (P.L. 93-205). No current deduction is allowed for the purchase, construction, installation, or improvement of depreciable masonry, tile, metal, or wood structures, appliances, and facilities, such as tanks, reservoirs, pipes, canals, and pumps. Assessments levied by a soil or water conservation or drainage district to defray district expenses may also be deductible (Code Sec. 175; IRS Pub. 225).

Schedule F Loss Limitation. For tax years beginning before 2018 and after 2025, the amount of net farm losses that can be claimed for any tax year in which a taxpayer, other than a C corporation, has received applicable subsidies is limited to the greater of $300,000 ($150,000 for a married individual filing separately) or the taxpayer's aggregate net farm income for the five preceding tax years (Code Sec. 461(j) and 461(l), as amended by the Coronavirus Aid, Relief, and Economic Security (CARES) Act (P.L. 116-136)). Any farm loss that exceeds this limitation is excess farm loss that is carried forward to the next tax year as a farming deduction. The limit on excess farm losses does not apply for tax years beginning in 2018 through 2025. For tax years beginning in 2021 through 2025, a noncorporate taxpayer is not allowed to claim a deduction for any excess business losses (¶ 1190).

983. Land Clearing Expenses. Land clearing expenditures must be capitalized and added to the farmer's basis in the land (*AMFAC, Inc.*, CA-9, 80-2 USTC ¶ 9630). However, business expenses for ordinary maintenance activities related to property already used in farming (e.g., brush clearing) are currently deductible (*E.G. Barham*, DC Ga., 69-1 USTC ¶ 9356).

985. Expensing Fertilizer Costs. A farmer, other than a farm syndicate, may elect to deduct current expenses otherwise chargeable to capital accounts for fertilizer, lime, ground limestone, marl, or other materials for enriching, neutralizing, or conditioning land used in farming. If no election is made, expenditures producing benefits extending over more than one year are capitalized and recovered by amortization (Code Sec. 180; Reg. § 1.180-1 and 1.180-2). The election, which is effective only for the tax year claimed, is made by claiming the deduction on the return. For farm syndicates and prepayments by cash-basis farmers, see ¶ 1519, ¶ 1521, and ¶ 1539.

Rents and Leasehold Payments

See CCH® AnswerConnect: *Business Expenses: Deducting Rent* for more information on this topic.

986. Business Deduction for Rents and Leasehold Payments. A tenant may deduct as a trade or business expense rent paid for business property, as well as any amounts such as property taxes and interest that the lease requires the tenant to pay on behalf of the landlord (Code Sec. 162(a)(3); Reg. § 1.162-11). An amount paid by a *lessee* for cancellation of a lease on business property is also generally deductible (*A.J. Cassatt*, CA-3, 43-2 USTC ¶ 9579). However, payments by the *lessor* for the cancellation of a lease are generally capital expenditures, amortizable over the unexpired term of the canceled lease (*Peerless Weighing & Vending Machine Corp*, Dec. 29,713, 52 TC 850).

Under the one-year rule, a cash-basis taxpayer can deduct otherwise allowable rent attributable to the current or a previous year in the year in which the taxpayer actually pays the rent (Reg. § 1.461-1(a)). This is true even though most of the lease term is in the following year if the lease expires within a year of payment. Prepaid rent for a lease extending more than one year from the date of payment must be capitalized and amortized over the term of the lease. Some rental payments are subject to the uniform capitalization rules (¶ 1330). See ¶ 1234 for an improvement made by the lessee on leased premises. If an owner of property occupies part of the property as a personal residence and rents part of it, expenses and depreciation allocable to the rented space may be deductible (¶ 966).

Payments made under a conditional sales contract are not deductible as rent. A conditional sales contract generally exists if at least a portion of the rental payments is applied to the purchase of the property under advantageous terms (IRS Fact Sheet FS-2007-14).

Under certain conditions, a taxpayer who is in the business of producing real property or tangible personal property for resale, or who purchases property for resale, may not claim rental or lease expenses as a current deduction. Instead, the taxpayer must include some or all of these costs in the basis of the property produced or acquired for resale under the uniform capitalization rules. These costs are recovered when the property is sold (IRS Fact Sheet FS-2007-14).

Mining Company's Expenses

987. Mine Exploration Expenses. A mining company may elect to deduct domestic exploration expenses (except for oil or gas), but the amount deducted must be recaptured once the mine reaches production stage or is sold (Code Sec. 617). The company recaptures the deduction by electing to either: (1) include in income for that year the previously deducted exploration expenditures chargeable to the mine, increase the basis of the property by the amount included in income, and subsequently recover this amount through depletion; or (2) forgo depletion from the property that includes or comprises the mine until the forgone deductions equal the exploration expenditures previously deducted. Expenses not recaptured by one of these methods are recaptured on the sale or other disposition of the mining property, with the amount recaptured treated as ordinary income. Certain transfers are not subject to these recapture rules.

Deductions allowed a corporation, other than an S corporation, for mineral exploration and development costs (¶ 988) must be reduced by 30 percent (Code Sec. 291(b)). The 30 percent of expenses that cannot be deducted must be capitalized and amortized over a 60-month period on Form 4562. Taxpayers may also elect to capitalize mine exploration expenses and amortize them over a 10-year period to avoid treatment as a tax preference item for alternative minimum tax (AMT) purposes (¶ 194).

Geological and geophysical (G&G) expenditures paid or incurred in connection with oil and gas exploration or development in the United States must be amortized ratably over a 24-month period beginning on the mid-point of the tax year that the expenses were paid or incurred. If a property or project is abandoned or retired during the 24-month amortization period, any remaining basis must continue to be amortized (Code Sec. 167(h)). Major integrated oil companies must ratably amortize any G&G costs over seven years.

988. Mine Development Expenses. Expenses paid or incurred with respect to a domestic mine or other natural deposit, other than oil or gas, after the existence of ores or minerals in commercially marketable quantities has been discovered can be deducted currently, unless the taxpayer elects to treat them as deferred expenses and deduct them ratably as the ore or mineral is sold (Code Sec. 616; Reg. §1.616-1). These expenses do not include those made for the acquisition or improvement of depreciable property. However, depreciation allowances are considered development costs. The 30-percent reduction in the allowable deduction and the election to amortize over a 10-year period (¶ 987) applies also to mine development expenses (Code Sec. 291(b)).

988A. Foreign Mine Exploration and Development Expenses. Foreign mining exploration and development expenses (other than oil, gas, or geothermal wells) are recovered over a 10-year, straight-line amortization schedule beginning with the tax year in which they were paid or incurred (Code Secs. 616(d) and 617(h)). However, the taxpayer may elect to add such expenses to the adjusted basis of the property for purposes of computing cost depletion.

989. Oil, Gas, or Geothermal Well Drilling Expense. An operator of a domestic oil, gas, or geothermal well may elect to currently deduct intangible drilling and development costs (IDCs) rather than charging them to capital and recovering them through depletion or depreciation (Code Sec. 263(c); Reg. §1.612-4). The election is binding upon future years. IDCs generally include all expenses made by the operator incident to and necessary for the drilling of wells and the preparation of wells for the production of oil, gas, or geothermal energy that are neither for the purchase of tangible property nor part of the acquisition price of an interest in the property. IDCs include labor, fuel, materials and supplies, truck rent, repairs to drilling equipment, and depreciation for drilling equipment.

An integrated oil company (i.e., a producer that is not an independent producer) must reduce the deduction for IDCs otherwise allowable by 30 percent (Code Sec. 291(b)). The amount disallowed as a current expense deduction must be amortized over a 60-month period. A taxpayer may elect to capitalize, rather than currently deduct, IDCs and amortize these expenditures over a 60-month period to avoid treatment as a tax preference item for alternative minimum tax (AMT) purposes (¶ 194).

If the operator elects to capitalize IDCs, and the well proves to be nonproductive (i.e., a dry hole), the operator may elect to deduct those costs as an ordinary loss (Reg. §1.612-4(b)(4)). Once made, the election is binding for all years.

Foreign Wells. An operator may not opt to currently deduct IDCs for wells located outside the United States (Code Sec. 263(i)). Such costs must be recovered over a 10-year straight-line amortization schedule or, at the operator's election, added to the adjusted basis of the property for cost depletion. Dry hole expenses incurred outside the United States are currently deductible.

989A. Advanced Mine Safety Equipment Expensing. A taxpayer may elect to expense 50 percent of the cost of advanced mine safety equipment placed in service before January 1, 2018 (Code Sec. 179E). The cost of any eligible equipment that is expensed under Code Sec. 179 (¶ 1208) cannot be taken into account in calculating the deduction. The deduction is subject to recapture as ordinary income under the Code Sec. 1245 depreciation recapture rules (¶ 1779).

Chapter 10
NONBUSINESS EXPENSES

Deductions of Individuals

1001. Deductions of Individuals. Tax deductions for individuals fall into two basic categories:

- deductions from gross income to arrive at adjusted gross income (AGI) referred to as adjustments to gross income (¶ 1005); and

- deductions from AGI, including a standard deduction based on filing status (¶ 131) or itemized deductions (¶ 1014), as well any deduction for qualified business income (QBI) for tax years beginning after 2017 (¶ 980P).

All the deductions claimed, along with the taxpayer's personal and dependency exemptions claimed for tax years beginning before 2018 (¶ 133), reduces an individual's gross income to determine taxable income (¶ 111).

Personal Expenses. Personal, living, or family expenses are *not* deductible in computing taxable income (Code Sec. 262; Reg. § 1.262-1). Only expenses that are expressly provided for by the Code are deductible from gross income. Nondeductible personal expenses include, but are not limited to, rent and insurance premiums paid for the taxpayer's own dwelling, life insurance premiums paid by the insured, and payments for food, clothing, domestic help, and upkeep of an automobile.

Adjusted Gross Income (AGI)

See CCH® AnswerConnect: *Individual and Nonbusiness Deductions and Credits* and *Education Expenses, Tax Credits and 529 Plans* for more information on this topic.

1005. Adjusted Gross Income (AGI) of Individuals. Adjusted gross income (AGI) of an individual is an intermediate figure between gross income and taxable income. It is the starting point for computing certain deductions, credits, and other tax benefits that are limited by income (Code Sec. 62, as amended by the Coronavirus Aid, Relief, and Economic Security (CARES) Act (P.L. 116-136); Temp. Reg. § 1.62-1T). See ¶ 4 for a table of the 2019 AGI phaseout thresholds. AGI is gross income of an individual, minus the following deductions (referred to as above-the-line deductions):

- expenses of a trade or business carried on by the taxpayer, generally other than as an employee (¶ 1006);

- trade or business expenses paid or incurred in connection with the taxpayer's performance of services as an employee to the extent made under an employer's reimbursement or expense allowance arrangement (¶ 941);

- certain expenses of a qualified performing artist (¶ 941A), school teacher (¶ 941C), fee-based government employee (¶ 941D), and member of the National Guard or Armed Forces Reserves (¶ 941E);

- expenses attributable to rental or royalty property (¶ 1006A);
- losses from the sale or exchange of property (¶ 1007);
- alimony or separate maintenance payments generally made under a divorce or separation agreement executed before 2019 (¶ 1008);
- certain repayments of supplemental unemployment compensation benefits (¶ 1009);
- jury duty pay remitted to employer (¶ 1010);
- interest on student loans (¶ 1011);
- tuition and fees paid before 2021 for post-secondary education (¶ 1011A);
- 50 percent of the self-employment taxes imposed on the taxpayer for the year (¶ 1027 and ¶ 2664);
- expenses of a self-employed individual for health insurance of the taxpayer, spouse, and dependents (¶ 908);
- contributions to traditional individual retirement accounts (IRAs) (¶ 2157);
- contributions by a self-employed person to pension, profit-sharing, and annuity plans (¶ 2107);
- contributions to health savings account (HSA) (¶ 2035) and Archer medical savings account (MSA) (¶ 2037);
- depreciation or depletion allowed to a life tenant of property, an income beneficiary of property held in trust, or an heir, legatee, or devisee of an estate (¶ 1085);
- interest forfeited to a bank, savings association, etc., on premature withdrawals from time savings accounts or deposits (¶ 1111);
- amortization of reforestation expenses (¶ 1360);
- moving expenses of members of Armed Forces (moving expenses of other individuals only allowed before 2018) (¶ 1073 and ¶ 1075);
- attorney fees and court costs paid in connection with an unlawful federal discrimination claim and certain whistleblower awards (¶ 1093);
- for tax years beginning in 2020, charitable contributions of up to $300 so long as the individual does not otherwise itemize deductions (¶ 1058); and
- domestic production activities in tax years beginning before 2018 (¶ 980A).

Any deduction for qualified business income (QBI) under Code Sec. 199A (¶ 980P) is not allowed in determining AGI, but may be claimed by an individual in determining taxable income regardless of whether the standard deduction or itemized deductions are claimed.

1006. Trade or Business Deductions of Individuals. Expenses directly attributable to a trade or business carried on by an individual are generally deductible in computing adjusted gross income (AGI). All deductible business expenses are subtracted from the gross receipts of the trade or business to arrive at the net profit or loss calculated on Schedule C (Form 1040) or Schedule F (Form 1040). The performance of personal services as an employee is not considered carrying on of a trade or business. The practice of a profession as a sole proprietor and not as an employee is considered the conduct of a trade or business (Code Sec. 62(a)(1); Temp. Reg. § 1.62-1T(c)(1) and (d)). See ¶ 901 for discussion of trade and business expenses generally and ¶ 941 for discussion of employee business expenses.

1006A. Deductible Rental or Royalty Expenses of Individuals. Ordinary and necessary expenses of an individual attributable to tangible or intangible property held for the production of rents or royalties may be deducted in calculating adjusted gross income (AGI), even if the property is not actually producing income (Code Sec. 62(a)(4); Temp. Reg. § 1.62-1T(c)(5)). These deductions include interest, taxes, depreciation, depletion, amortization, losses, etc. (Reg. § 1.212-1).

Income and expenses from rental real property, personal property leased with real estate, and royalties are reported on Schedule E (Form 1040). Income and expenses from the rental of personal property such as equipment or vehicles are reported on

Schedule C (Form 1040) if the taxpayer is in the business of renting personal property. If the taxpayer is not in the business of renting personal property, the income is reported as "Other Income" and the expenses are reported as an adjustment to AGI on Schedule 1 (Form 1040) (Instructions to Form 1040).

Expenses must be prorated if property is devoted to rental purposes for part of a year and to personal use for the other part. See ¶ 966 for special rules governing the deduction of expenses of rental vacation homes. See ¶ 1155 and ¶ 1165 for at-risk and passive activity rules applicable to an individual.

1007. Losses of Individuals from Sales or Exchanges. Losses from the sale or exchange of business or investment property may be claimed as a deduction by an individual in calculating adjusted gross income (AGI) (Code Sec. 62(a)(3); Temp. Reg. § 1.62-1T(c)(4)). This includes losses from sales or exchanges of capital assets (¶ 1735), losses from worthless securities or nonbusiness bad debts that are treated as from the sale or exchange of a capital asset, and any losses from sales or exchanges of noncapital assets (¶ 1701).

A loss from an involuntary conversion is deductible in computing AGI only if it is attributable to property used in a trade or business, or property held for the production of rents or royalties (¶ 1101 and ¶ 1713). However, a taxpayer may be entitled to an itemized deduction for the involuntary conversion of property used for personal purposes if the loss arises from a casualty (¶ 1121 and ¶ 1123).

Capital losses of an individual are deductible only to the extent of capital gains, plus $3,000 of ordinary income (¶ 1752). Form 8949 and Schedule D (Form 1040) are used to calculate capital gains and losses. Losses of a taxpayer from the sale or exchange of noncapital assets other than inventory used in a trade or business, or for the production of income, are calculated on Form 4797.

1008. Alimony Deduction. An individual generally may claim a deduction for alimony or separate maintenance payments under a divorce or separation agreement executed before 2019 (Code Secs. 62(a)(10) and 215, prior to being stricken by the Tax Cuts and Jobs Act (P.L. 115-97); Reg. § 1.215-1). The payments must meet certain requirements to qualify as alimony or separate maintenance payments (¶ 772). If the requirements are met, alimony is generally deductible in the year paid, regardless of the taxpayer's method of accounting.

The deduction is claimed as an adjustment to gross income on Schedule 1 (Form 1040). A recapture rule prevents the front-loading of alimony payments (¶ 774). No deduction is allowed for alimony or separate maintenance payments if made under a divorce or separation agreement (1) executed after 2018, or (2) executed before 2019 but modified after 2018 if the modification expressly provides for the repeal of the alimony rules. The spouse who receives qualified alimony payments generally must include them in gross income (¶ 771).

1009. Repayment of Unemployment Compensation Benefits. Repayments of supplemental unemployment compensation benefits to trusts or voluntary employees' beneficiary associations (VEBAs) required to qualify for trade readjustment allowances under the Trade Act of 1974 are deductible from gross income in calculating adjusted gross income (AGI) (Code Sec. 62(a)(12)). The deduction is claimed as an adjustment to gross income on Schedule 1 (Form 1040) (Instructions to Form 1040). Repayment of most other unemployment compensation benefits in a year following the year of receipt are deductible as an itemized deduction on Schedule A (Form 1040) (IRS Pub. 525). If the repayment of either type of unemployment compensation exceeds $3,000, the taxpayer may compute the tax for the tax year of the repayment under the claim-of-right doctrine (¶ 1543).

1010. Jury Duty Pay. An employee can deduct jury duty pay surrendered to an employer who continued to pay the employee's normal salary while the employee was on jury duty (Code Sec. 62(a)(13)). The deduction is claimed as an adjustment to gross income on Schedule 1 (Form 1040) (Instructions to Form 1040).

1011. Student Loan Interest Deduction. An individual may claim a deduction in calculating adjusted gross income (AGI) Schedule 1 (Form 1040) for interest paid on a qualified student loan during the tax year (Code Secs. 62(a)(17) and 221, as amended by the Coronavirus Aid, Relief, and Economic Security (CARES) Act (P.L. 116-136); Reg. § 1.221-1). The maximum student loan interest deduction is $2,500, but is phased out or reduced out if the taxpayer's modified AGI (MAGI) is between:

- $70,000 and $85,000 ($140,000 and $170,000 if married filing jointly) for 2019 (Rev. Proc. 2018-57), and

- $70,000 and $85,000 ($140,000 and $170,000 if married filing jointly) for 2020 (Rev. Proc. 2019-44).

The deduction is calculated using a worksheet in the Instructions to Form 1040 or IRS Pub. 970. An individual who pays more than $600 in student loan interest in a calendar year should receive from the payor a statement on Form 1098-E reporting the amount of interest. The student loan interest deduction may be claimed only if the taxpayer has a legal obligation to make the interest payments under the terms of the qualified student loan. If a third party makes an interest payment, the taxpayer is treated as receiving the payment from the third party and then paying the interest. The deduction may not be claimed by an individual who is married filing separately or an individual who may be claimed as a dependent on another person's tax return. In addition, no deduction can be claimed for any interest that is deductible under any other provision of the Code (for example, home mortgage interest). This includes payments made by an employer on a qualified student loan of an employee after March 27, 2020, and before January 1, 2021, that are excluded from the employee's gross income (¶ 2067). The deduction must also be reduced for any distributions from a qualified tuition program (529 plan) treated as qualified education expenses after 2018 (¶ 869).

A qualified student loan is a loan incurred solely to pay qualified education expenses that are: (1) incurred on behalf of the taxpayer, the taxpayer's spouse, or a dependent of the taxpayer as of the time of the loans; (2) paid or incurred within a reasonable period of time before or after the loans are incurred; and (3) attributable to education furnished during a period when the recipient was an eligible student. Qualified education expenses are the costs of attendance at an eligible educational institution, including tuition and fees, room and board, books, supplies, and equipment, and other necessary expenses such as transportation. However, qualified expenses are reduced by amounts that are used to pay for such expenses and are excludable from the taxpayer's gross income (for example, scholarships, employer-provided educational assistance, education tax credits, and tax-free distributions from qualified tuition programs (529 plans) and Coverdell accounts).

1011A. Tuition and Fees Deduction. For tax years beginning before January 1, 2021, an individual may claim a deduction in calculating adjusted gross income (AGI) on Schedule 1 (Form 1040) for qualifying tuition and related expenses paid for enrollment or attendance of the taxpayer, the taxpayer's spouse, or the taxpayer's dependent at an accredited post-secondary education institution (Code Secs. 62(a)(18) and 222, as amended by the Taxpayer Certainty and Disaster Tax Relief Act of 2019 (P.L. 116-94)). Qualified tuition and expenses for this purpose are defined the same as for the education credits and must be reduced by other tax benefits for education (¶ 1403). The tuition and fee deduction may not be claimed for any expenses that the taxpayer takes as part of other deductions on his or her return. In addition, the deduction may not be claimed if the taxpayer or any other person claims the education credits with respect to the student.

The amount of the tuition and fees deduction is based on the taxpayer's AGI and calculated on Form 8917. The deduction is $4,000 for a taxpayer with AGI of $65,000 or less ($130,000 if married filing jointly). The deduction is $2,000 for a taxpayer whose AGI exceeds that limit but is $80,000 or less ($160,000 if married filing jointly). No deduction may be claimed if the taxpayer's AGI exceeds $80,000 ($160,000 if married filing jointly). The deduction may not be claimed by a married individual filing separately or if another person can claim the taxpayer as a dependent on his or her return. The taxpayer or dependent must have received Form 1098-T from an eligible educational institution if more than $600 of qualified tuition expenses were paid in the calendar year.

¶1011A

Itemized Deductions

See CCH® AnswerConnect: *Itemized Deductions* for more information on this topic.

1014. Itemized Deductions. An individual may elect to claim certain itemized deductions of personal expenses in lieu of claiming a standard deduction (¶ 131) in determining taxable income (¶ 111) (Code Sec. 63(e)). A taxpayer makes the election by completing Schedule A (Form 1040) with his or her return and include deductions for:

- medical and dental expenses (¶ 1015),
- state, local, and foreign taxes (¶ 1021 and ¶ 1028),
- home mortgage interest (¶ 1047),
- investment interest (¶ 1057),
- charitable contributions (¶ 1058),
- casualty and theft losses (¶ 1121 and ¶ 1123), and
- certain miscellaneous expenses (¶ 1079 and ¶ 1095).

A taxpayer may elect to itemize deductions on his or her federal return even if less than the standard deduction (e.g., if the benefit of claiming itemized deductions on state return is greater than the benefit of claiming the standard deduction on the federal return). An amended return may be filed to change the election to claim itemized deductions or the standard deduction. In the case of married individuals filing separately, the amended return may only be filed if both spouses consent.

Phaseout of Itemized Deductions. For tax years beginning before 2018 and after 2025, an individual's allowable itemized deductions are phased out or reduced if his or her adjusted gross income (AGI) exceeds an applicable threshold amount based on filing status and adjusted annually for inflation (Code Sec. 68). The phaseout does not affect the itemized deductions for medical expenses, investment interest expenses, casualty or theft losses of personal-use or nonbusiness income-producing property, or allowable gambling losses. The reduction is applied after all other limitations on itemized deductions are applied, including the charitable contribution limit (¶ 1059), the limit on certain meal expenses, as well as entertainment expenses before 2018 (¶ 916), and the two-percent-of-AGI limitation on miscellaneous itemized deductions for tax years beginning before 2018 and after 2025 (¶ 1079).

Disaster Relief. Qualified charitable contributions made before January 1, 2018, for relief efforts in the designated disaster areas for the California wildfires, as well as Hurricanes Harvey, Irma, or Maria, are not subject the phaseout of itemized deductions (¶ 1059).

Medical Expenses

See CCH® AnswerConnect: *Medical Deductions* for more information on this topic.

1015. Itemized Deduction of Medical and Dental Expenses. An itemized deduction (¶ 1014) is allowed to an individual on Schedule A (Form 1040) for expenses paid during the tax year for the medical and dental care of the taxpayer, the taxpayer's spouse, or the taxpayer's dependent (Code Sec. 213, as amended by the Taxpayer Certainty and Disaster Tax Relief Act of 2019 (P.L. 116-94); Reg. §1.213-1). The deduction may be claimed to the extent that the expenses exceed 7.5 percent of the taxpayer's adjusted gross income (AGI) (10 percent of AGI after 2020). The percentage limitation for married individuals filing jointly is based on the total AGI of both spouses.

The deduction may be taken for any person who was the taxpayer's spouse or dependent when the medical or dental services were rendered or the expenses were paid. A dependent's status (¶ 137) for this purpose is determined without regard to whether he or she claims a dependent, files a joint return, or has gross income in excess of a threshold amount for the year. In addition, a child of divorced parents is treated as a dependent of both parents for this purpose, even without a declaration by the custodial parent releasing the claim to the dependent (¶ 139A) (Code Sec. 213(d)(5); Rev. Proc. 2008-48).

The itemized deduction for medical expenses is limited to unreimbursed medical expenses. Individuals cannot deduct medical expenses to the extent that they received an insurance payment or other reimbursement of the expenses, including amounts reimbursed by Medicare. Reimbursements received for expenses deducted in a previous tax year are includible in gross income in the year received to the extent the expenses were previously deducted. Reimbursements for an earlier tax year in which no deduction was claimed are excludable from gross income.

Medical expenses are generally deductible only in the year paid by the taxpayer, regardless of when the services were provided (Reg. § 1.213-1(a); IRS Pub. 502). However, credit card charges for medical expenses are deductible in the year the expenses are charged, regardless of when paid. Also, while advance payments are generally not deductible, prepayments for lifetime care in a retirement home, nursing center, or similar institution are deductible in the year paid if the obligation to pay was incurred at the time the payment was made and the promise to provide lifetime care was conditioned on the payment.

A decedent's medical expenses that are paid by his or her estate within one year of the day of death are treated as paid when the medical services were rendered and may be claimed as an itemized deduction on the decedent's return for the year incurred (Reg. § 1.213-1(d); Rev. Rul. 77-357). Alternatively, the estate may deduct the medical expenses as a claim against the estate for federal estate tax purposes (¶ 2925). Medical expenses disallowed for income tax purposes because of the AGI limitation may *not* be claimed on the estate tax return when the estate allocates medical expenses between a decedent's final income tax and estate tax return.

See ¶ 1016 for the definition of medical expenses and ¶ 1019 for the deduction of health insurance premiums. See ¶ 2035 for deductible contributions to health savings accounts (HSAs) and ¶ 2037 for deductible contributions to Archer medical savings accounts (MSAs).

1016. Medical Expenses Defined. Medical expenses eligible to be claimed as an itemized deduction (¶ 1015) include amounts paid for the diagnosis, cure, mitigation, treatment, or prevention of disease, and the costs for treatments affecting any part or function of the body (Code Sec. 213; Rev. Rul. 2003-58; IRS Pub. 502). This includes the costs of equipment, supplies, and diagnostic devices needed for these purposes, as well as payments for legal medical services rendered by physicians, surgeons, dentists, and other medical practitioners. Medical expenses also include the cost of medicine or drugs only if a prescribed drug or insulin. Over-the-counter medicines and drugs may not be claimed as an itemized deduction, but amounts paid or incurred after 2019 may be reimbursed through health savings accounts (HSAs) (¶ 2035), Archer medical savings accounts (MSAs) (¶ 2037), health reimbursement arrangements (HRAs) (¶ 2039), and health flexible spending accounts (FSAs) (¶ 2041). Medical expenses must be primarily to alleviate or prevent a physical or mental defect or illness to be deductible, and not merely beneficial to general health (e.g. vitamins or vacation).

Deductible medical expenses include premiums paid for insurance that covers medical care expenses (¶ 1019). This includes premiums for supplemental insurance such as Medicare Part B and Part D, and for qualified long-term care insurance contracts that do not exceed certain limits. Medical expenses that are deductible also include qualified long-term care services, as well as transportation and lodging costs (but not meals) incurred on trips primarily for, and essential to, medical care. The lodging deduction is limited to amounts that are not lavish or extravagant and cannot exceed $50 per night for each individual. The lodging deduction may be claimed for a person who must accompany the individual seeking medical care. If transportation expenses are deductible as a medical expense, the cost of operating a car may be calculated at a standard rate of 20 cents per mile for 2019 (17 cents per mile for 2020), plus parking fees and tolls (Rev. Proc. 2019-46; Rev. Proc. 2010-51; Notice 2019-2; Notice 2020-5). Medical expenses do not include any amount taken into account for the dependent care credit (¶ 1401) or funeral expenses (Code Sec. 213(e)).

The medical expenses deduction is not limited to amounts paid for the least expensive form of medical care applicable. A physician's recommendation is also not necessary if the expenditures are for items that are wholly medical in nature and serve no other function. Thus, amounts paid by a healthy individual for self-initiated diagnostic tests and similar procedures, such as an annual physical, a full body scan, or a self-administered pregnancy test kit, are deductible (Rev. Rul. 2007-72).

Most expenses to prevent conception and birth are deductible, as well as fertility enhancement expenses (IRS Pub. 502). Expenses for elective cosmetic surgery are *not* deductible unless the surgery or procedure is necessary to ameliorate a deformity arising from, or directly related to, a congenital abnormality, a personal injury resulting from accident or trauma, or a disfiguring disease. Cosmetic surgery includes any procedure directed at improving the patient's appearance that does not meaningfully promote the proper function of the body or prevent or treat illness or disease (Code Sec. 213(d)(9)); Rev. Rul. 2003-57). A weight-loss program is a medical expense if undertaken to relieve a disease or defect, such as obesity or hypertension (Rev. Rul. 2002-19). Smoking-cessation programs, whether or not prescribed, and prescription drugs to alleviate symptoms of nicotine withdrawal are also medical expenses, but over-the-counter gums or patches are not (Rev. Rul. 99-28).

Special schooling for a physically or mentally handicapped child or one needing psychiatric treatment is deductible (Rev. Rul. 78-340). Amounts paid for inpatient treatment of alcoholism or drug addiction at a therapeutic center and for meals and lodging furnished as a necessity incident to the treatment are deductible (Rev. Rul. 73-325). Amounts paid to acquire, train, and maintain a dog or other service animal for assisting a blind, deaf, or physically disabled individual are deductible (IRS Pub. 502).

The entire cost of maintenance in a nursing home or home for the aged, including meals and lodging, is a medical expense if an individual is there because of a physical condition and the availability of medical care is a principal reason for the individual's residence. If an individual is in a facility primarily for personal or family reasons, then only that portion of the cost attributable to medical or nursing care, excluding meals and lodging, is deductible. Payments to perform both nursing care and housework may be deducted only to the extent of the nursing cost (IRS Pub. 502).

Capital expenditures for home improvements and additions that are primarily for medical care qualify as a deductible medical expense only to the extent that the cost of the improvement exceeds any increase in the value of the affected property (Reg. § 1.213-1(e)(1)). The entire cost of any improvement that does not increase the value of the property is deductible. Deductions have been allowed for the installation of an elevator, a swimming pool, and a central air-conditioning system. Expenditures incurred to remove structural barriers to accommodate the condition of a physically handicapped person generally do not improve the value of the residence and are fully deductible (Rev. Rul. 87-106). The entire cost of special equipment used to mitigate the effects of a physical impairment is also deductible.

1019. Itemized Deduction of Medical Insurance Premiums. Medical expenses eligible to be claimed as an itemized deduction (¶ 1016) include premiums paid for medical care insurance that provides payment for hospitalization, surgical services, x-rays, prescription drugs and insulin, dental care, replacement of contact lenses, and long-term care (Code Sec. 213(d)(1)(D); Reg. § 1.213-1(e)(4)). If the insurance contract provides payments for more than medical care, such as an indemnity for loss of income or life, limb or sight, premiums are deductible only to the extent a reasonable charge for the medical care is stated separately in the contract or in a separate statement from the insurer.

Premiums paid by a taxpayer under age 65 for insurance covering medical care expenses of the taxpayer, the taxpayer's spouse, or the taxpayer's dependent after the taxpayer turns 65 are considered to be medical expenses in the year paid if the premiums are payable on a level payment basis under the contract: (1) for a period of 10 years or more, or (2) until the year the taxpayer reaches age 65, but in no case for a period of less than five years.

Premiums voluntarily paid for supplemental Medicare medical insurance (Medicare Part B) and Medicare prescription drug insurance (Medicare Part D) are deductible, but amounts paid as employment taxes (¶ 2648) for Medicare hospital insurance (Medicare Part A) are *not* medical expenses. Thus, premiums for Medicare Part A are not deductible unless the individual is not covered by Social Security and voluntarily paid

10

NONBUSINESS

them to be covered (IRS Pub. 502). Self-employed individuals can deduct from gross income 100 percent of amounts paid for health insurance coverage (¶ 908), including premiums for all Medicare parts (CCA 201228037).

Long-Term Care Insurance. Premiums paid for a qualified long-term care insurance contract are a medical expense, but the deductible amount is limited by the age of the individual at the close of the tax year (Code Sec. 213(d)(10); Rev. Proc. 2018-57; Rev. Proc. 2019-44). The maximum deductible amount is adjusted annually for inflation and is:

Age at close of tax year	2019	2020
40 or less	$420	$430
Over 40 but not over 50	$790	$810
Over 50 but not over 60	$1,580	$1,630
Over 60 but not over 70	$4,220	$4,350
Over 70	$5,270	$5,430

Taxes

See CCH® AnswerConnect: *Deductible Taxes* for more information on this topic.

1021. Itemized Deduction of Taxes. A deduction is generally permitted for certain taxes paid or accrued (¶ 1022) during the tax year (Code Sec. 164). This includes:

- state, local, and foreign income taxes (¶ 1023);

- state and local sales taxes in lieu of deducting state and local income taxes (¶ 1023);

- state, local, and foreign real property taxes (¶ 1028);

- state and local personal property taxes (¶ 1028); and

- generation-skipping transfer (GST) tax imposed on income distributions (¶ 2942).

Taxes paid or accrued by an individual during the tax year that are not directly connected with a trade or business, or with property held for the production of income, may be deducted only as an itemized deduction (¶ 1014) on Schedule A (Form 1040) for federal income tax purposes. The itemized deduction of state taxes by an individual is limited for tax years beginning in 2018 through 2025 (¶ 1026). A self-employed individual may deduct 50 percent of his or her federal self-employment taxes as an above-the-line deduction in computing adjusted gross income (AGI) (¶ 1027).

State, local, and foreign taxes directly attributable to a trade or business, or imposed on property held for the production of income, are deductible either as ordinary and necessary business expenses or investment expenses (¶ 920). Taxes that are otherwise deductible as business or income-producing expenses cannot be deducted but must be capitalized if paid or accrued in connection with the acquisition or disposition of property. Various taxes are not deductible, regardless of whether they are incurred in a trade or business (¶ 1025). In addition, taxes assessed for local benefits that tend to increase the value of the property, such as levies paid for paving, sewers, sidewalks, drainage, and other improvements, are capital investments and are deductible (¶ 1036).

Taxes are generally deductible only by the person on whom they are imposed. Thus, the payment of a tax that is otherwise deductible does not necessarily entitle the payer to a deduction. A taxpayer must show both that he or she paid the taxes and that the taxes were imposed on him or her. For example, a taxpayer can deduct property taxes only if he or she is the owner of the property (Reg. § 1.164-1(a); IRS Pub. 17). If real property is sold, any real property taxes must be apportioned between the buyer and seller (¶ 1032).

Tax on Gifts from Expatriates. A U.S. citizen or resident alien who is a beneficiary of a foreign trust may be subject to tax for any portion of a distribution from the trust attributable to a gift or bequest from a covered expatriate. The recipient may claim an income tax deduction for the tax paid or accrued to the extent the distribution is included in the recipient's gross income (¶ 2948).

1022. Taxes Deductible When Paid or Accrued. A deduction for taxes (¶ 1021) is generally allowed only for the year in which the taxes are paid or accrued (Code Sec.

164). The failure to deduct taxes in the proper year does not allow the taxpayer to deduct the taxes in a later year. Instead, the taxpayer must file an amended return for the year the taxes were paid or accrued.

Cash-basis taxpayers deduct taxes in the year paid, including amounts withheld from wages, payments of estimated tax, and payments applicable to other tax years (¶ 1515). However, advance payments of estimated taxes made by a cash-basis taxpayer may not be deducted when paid if the taxpayer cannot reasonably determine that there is an additional amount owed (Rev. Rul. 82-208).

Accrual-basis taxpayers may generally deduct taxes in the year in which all events occur fixing the fact of the liability, the amount can then be determined with reasonable accuracy, and economic performance has occurred (¶ 1515). Economic performance generally occurs only when the tax is paid. Thus, the date when a tax becomes due and payable is not necessarily its accrual date. An accrual method taxpayer can elect to accrue any real property tax to a definite period ratably (¶ 1031 and ¶ 1034). A contested tax accrues when the taxpayer transfers cash or property to satisfy the tax if the contest exists after the transfer and a deduction would have otherwise been allowed for the year of transfer. This rule does not apply to taxes imposed by a foreign country or U.S. possession (Code Sec. 461(f)).

State and Local Benefits. If a taxpayer makes a charitable contribution and receives or expects to receive a state and local tax (SALT) credit in return, the taxpayer may have to reduce any federal charitable contribution deduction claimed (¶ 1061). Under a safe harbor, an individual is allowed to treat the disallowed portion of the charitable deduction as a payment of SALT taxes in the tax year the credit is applied to the taxpayer's state and local tax liability (¶ 1026).

1023. Itemized Deduction of Income or Sales Taxes. An individual may claim an itemized deduction (¶ 1014) on Schedule A (Form 1040) for state, local, and foreign income taxes paid during the year, even if those taxes are not incurred in connection with a trade or business or for the production of income (Code Sec. 164(a)(3) and (b)(5)). The taxpayer may elect to claim state and local general sales taxes as an itemized deduction in lieu of state and local income taxes. However, the itemized deduction of state and local income taxes, as well as general sales taxes and property taxes, is limited to $10,000 ($5,000 if married filing separately) for tax years beginning in 2018 through 2025 (¶ 1026).

Income Tax. A state or local income tax is an income tax imposed by a state, a U.S. possession, a political subdivision thereof, or the District of Columbia. It also includes mandatory contributions from wages to benefit funds in certain states for unemployment, disability, and family leave (Code Sec. 164(b)(2); IRS Pub. 17). An individual cannot deduct state and local income taxes paid on income that is exempt from federal income tax, other than taxes on exempt interest income.

Foreign Income Tax. A deductible foreign income tax is a tax imposed on the taxpayer by a foreign country or U.S. possession. The predominant character of the levy must be that of an income tax according to U.S. tax principles. A foreign income tax is deductible only if no foreign tax credit is claimed on the tax on the taxpayer's U.S. income tax return (¶ 2475 and ¶ 2476).

State and Local Sales Tax. A deductible general sales tax is a tax imposed at one rate on all retail sales, plus any sales tax on food, clothing, medical supplies, and motor vehicles even if the tax rate is less than the general sales tax rate. The deductible amount of sales tax may be determined either by (1) substantiation of the amount paid with receipts, or (2) optional sales tax tables and worksheets in the Instructions to Schedule A (Form 1040). If the taxpayer uses the optional tables, he or she may also deduct state and local general sales taxes paid on the purchase of a motor vehicle, boat, aircraft, homes, and materials to build a home.

1025. Nondeductible Taxes. Taxes that cannot be deducted either as an itemized deduction by an individual, or as incurred in a trade or business or activity engaged in for profit, include (Code Sec. 275):

- federal income taxes, including Social Security and railroad retirement taxes paid by employees and 50 percent of the self-employment taxes (¶ 1027);
- federal war profits and excess profits taxes;
- estate, inheritance, legacy, succession, and gift taxes (¶ 2901);
- income, war profits, and excess profits taxes imposed by a foreign country or U.S. possession if the taxpayer chooses to take a foreign tax credit for these taxes (¶ 2475 and ¶ 2476);
- taxes on real property that must be treated as imposed on another taxpayer because of apportionment between buyer and seller (¶ 1032);
- certain additions to taxes imposed on public charities, private foundations, qualified pension plans, real estate investment trusts, stock compensation of insiders in expatriated corporations, golden parachute payments, and greenmail; and
- the annual fee imposed on drug manufacturers and importers for U.S. branded prescription drug sales.

1026. Limit on State and Local Tax Deduction After 2017. For tax years 2018 through 2025, the deduction of taxes paid or accrued by an individual for the year is limited to $10,000 ($5,000 if married filing separately) for:

- state and local real property taxes;
- state and local personal property taxes;
- state and local income taxes; and
- state and local general sales taxes deducted in lieu of state and local income taxes (Code Sec. 164(b)(6)).

The dollar limit applies to the combined total deduction claimed as an itemized deduction on Schedule A (Form 1040). It does not apply to *state and local property taxes* paid or accrued in carrying on a trade or business, or on property held for the production of income. Thus, state and local property taxes may be deducted on the individual's Schedule C (Form 1040), Schedule E (Form 1040), or Schedule F (Form 1040) without regard to the limit. The limit also does not apply foreign income taxes, but no deduction may be claimed for *foreign real property taxes* for tax years 2018 through 2025.

The deduction for federal and state generation-skipping transfer (GST) taxes imposed on income distributions is not affected by the $10,000/$5,000 limit. An individual who received an income distribution from a GST trust and paid GST taxes on the distribution may continue to claim an itemized deduction for the taxes without regard to the dollar limit.

A taxpayer who is impacted by the SALT limit may be required to include a portion of any SALT refund in gross income under the tax benefit rule (¶ 799). The amount included in gross income depends on whether the taxpayer paid the actual amount of SALT liability (Rev. Rul. 2019-11).

Prepayment of Taxes. If an individual prepays before 2018 a state or local income tax imposed for a tax year beginning after 2017, the payment is treated as paid on the last day of the tax year for which the tax is imposed for purposes of applying the $10,000/$5,000 limit, Thus, an individual cannot claim an itemized deduction in 2017 on a prepayment of income tax for a future tax year in order to avoid the dollar limit.

The prepayment restriction applies only to state or local income taxes. In the case of state and local property taxes, the IRS has issued guidance that a deduction for the prepayment of state and local real property taxes in 2017 depends on whether the taxes are assessed under state and local law prior to 2018. If the taxes are assessed and prepaid in 2017, then the taxpayer may deduct the prepayments in 2017. The prepayments of property taxes in 2017 that are not assessed until 2018, may not be deducted in 2017 (IRS News Release, IR-2017-210).

State and Local Benefits. A taxpayer may not overcome the SALT deduction limit by making a charitable contribution in return for a SALT credit. Effective for contributions made after August 27, 2018, a taxpayer must reduce any charitable deduction by any SALT credit received or expected to be received unless the credit is 15 percent or less of the contribution (¶ 1061). There is no reduction in a charitable contribution deduction if the taxpayer receives or expects to receive a SALT deduction that does not exceed the contribution (Reg. § 1.170A-1(h)(3); Prop. Reg. § 1.170A-1(h)(3)).

Under a safe harbor, an individual may treat the disallowed portion the charitable deduction as the payment of SALT taxes (Prop. Reg. § 1.164-3(j); Notice 2019-12). As a result, the SALT credit is deductible under Code Sec. 164 in the tax year it is applied to offset the taxpayer's SALT liability. Any excess not applied for the current tax year may be carried forward consistent with state or local law. The safe harbor does not apply to the transfer of property. It also does not allow the taxpayer to avoid the SALT deduction limit.

The reduction in a charitable contribution deduction generally does not apply to business-related payments or transfers (¶ 1061).

1027. Deduction of Self-Employment Tax. A self-employed individual can deduct 50 percent of the self-employment tax imposed on him or her for the tax year in calculating adjusted gross income (AGI) for that year (Code Sec. 164(f)). The deduction does not include the additional 0.9 percent Medicare tax imposed on self-employment income (¶ 2664). The 50-percent deduction is attributable to a trade or business carried on by the taxpayer that does not consist of the performance of services by the taxpayer as an employee. The taxpayer's self-employment tax and deduction for self-employment tax are both figured on Schedule SE (Form 1040). The taxpayer does not need to itemize deductions to claim the deduction.

Real Property Taxes

See CCH® AnswerConnect: *Itemized Deduction of Real and Personal Property Taxes* and *Real Estate Taxes Apportioned Between the Buyer and Seller* for more information on this topic.

1028. Deduction of Real and Personal Property Taxes. State, local, and foreign real property taxes are generally deductible by the taxpayer upon whom they are imposed in the year they are paid or accrued (Code Sec. 164(a)(1); Reg. § 1.164-1(a) and 1.164-3). Real property taxes are taxes imposed on interests in real property and levied for the general public welfare. This includes taxes assessed for local benefits (¶ 1036). State or local taxes include taxes imposed by a state, the District of Columbia, U.S. possession, or a political subdivision thereof. Foreign taxes include taxes imposed by the authority of a foreign country or its political subdivisions. If real property is sold, any real property taxes must be apportioned between the buyer and seller (¶ 1032). A buyer or seller of real property using the accrual method of accounting may elect to accrue real estate taxes ratably (¶ 1031).

State, local, and foreign real property taxes, as well as state and local personal property taxes, paid or accrued by an individual that are not directly connected with a trade or business, or investment property, may be deducted only as an itemized deduction (¶ 1014) on Schedule A (Form 1040). The itemized deduction of state and local property taxes is limited to $10,000 ($5,000 if married filing separately) for tax years beginning in 2018 through 2025 (¶ 1026). No itemized deduction may be claimed for foreign real property taxes for tax years beginning in 2018 through 2025. If married individuals hold property as tenants by the entirety but file separate returns, then each spouse can only deduct taxes each paid on the property. If a divorce or separation agreement provides that one spouse must pay real property taxes on a home owned jointly, then part of payment is deductible as real estate taxes and part may be deductible as alimony (IRS Pub. 17).

A stockholder-owner in a cooperative housing corporation may deduct his or her proportionate share of the real property taxes paid by the corporation (¶ 1040). A condominium unit owner may also deduct real property taxes paid on his or her personal interests in the property (Rev. Rul. 64-31). Homeowner association assessments are not deductible as real property taxes because the assessments are not paid to the state or a political subdivision (Rev. Rul. 76-495).

A minister and member of the military is allowed to deduct real property taxes paid on his or her home, even if the individual receives a parsonage or military allowance excludable from gross income (¶ 1050). A cash-basis mortgagor that pays taxes directly to the mortgagee is entitled to deduct the taxes in the year when the mortgagee pays the taxing authority.

State Assistance. An individual who receives assistance from a state housing finance agency (HFA) funded through allocations from the Treasury Department's Housing Finance Agency Innovative Fund for the Hardest-Hit Housing Markets may use a safe harbor to deduct real property taxes, mortgage interest, and mortgage insurance premiums through 2021. The homeowner may deduct the lesser of the sum of all payments actually made to the mortgage servicer or state HFA, or the sum of the three amounts shown on Form 1098 (Notice 2018-63, amplifying and modifying Notice 2017-40).

Real Property Construction and Carrying Charges. Interest and taxes on real property paid or incurred during the construction period generally must be capitalized (¶ 1332 and ¶ 1340). If a taxpayer elects to capitalize taxes on unimproved and unproductive real property, no deduction is allowed for those taxes (¶ 1614).

Personal Property Taxes. State and local taxes imposed on personal property are deductible if the tax is an ad valorem tax imposed annually with respect to the property (Code Sec. 164(a)(2); Reg. § 1.164-3(c)). An ad valorem tax is one substantially in proportion to the value of the property. Any tax imposed on other criteria is not ad valorem. For example, a motor vehicle tax based on the weight, model, year, or horsepower of a vehicle is not an ad valorem tax. A tax based in part on value and in part on other criteria may partially qualify as ad valorem.

1031. Real Property Taxes for Accrual Method Taxpayers. The economic performance rule generally delays an accrual-method taxpayer's deduction for real property taxes until they are paid (¶ 1540). However, an accrual basis seller or buyer may elect to accrue real property taxes that are related to a definite period of time ratably over that period (Code Sec. 461(c); Reg. § 1.461-1(c)). Alternatively, if the real estate taxes are a recurring item, a taxpayer may elect to accrue the taxes and claim the deduction on the date the tax is assessed or becomes a lien against the property. Whether a taxpayer should make the election to ratably accrue property taxes or adopt the recurring item exception to the economic performance rule depends on the taxpayer's tax year and lien date of the jurisdiction in which the real property is located. Except where taxes are prepaid, either option is more favorable than the payment rule.

Time and Method of Election. An accrual-method taxpayer can make the election to accrue real property taxes without the IRS's consent for the first tax year in which the taxes are incurred (Reg. § 1.461-1(c)(3)). The election must be made by the time for filing the tax return for that year, including extensions. The due date for filing any federal income tax return otherwise due on or after April 1, 2020, and before July 15, 2020, is automatically extended to July 15, 2020 (¶ 2505). The election is made by attaching a statement to the return for that year that shows:

- the trade or business, or nonbusiness activity, to which the election is to apply,

- the method of accounting used,

- the period of time to which the taxes are related, and

- the computation of the deduction for the first year of the election or a summary of the computation.

Separate elections can be made for each trade or business or nonbusiness activity. Each election will apply to all real property taxes of the trade or business or nonbusiness activity.

The IRS must consent to an election that is made after the first tax year in which the real property taxes are incurred. The election must be made within 180 days after the beginning of the affected tax year. The election is a change in accounting method that can be made using the IRS automatic consent procedures (¶ 1529) (Rev. Proc. 2019-43). The change applies only to real property taxes accrued on or after the beginning of the year of change. Real property taxes accrued prior to the year of change are accounted for under the taxpayer's former method of accounting. Since the change is made on a cut-off basis, no section 481(a) adjustment is allowed or required.

Revoking the Election. The election to accrue real property taxes is binding and cannot be revoked without IRS consent. A revocation is treated as a change in accounting method.

1032. Apportionment of Real Property Taxes Upon Sale. If real property is sold, then any real property taxes imposed on the property must be apportioned between the buyer and the seller for purposes of deducting the taxes (¶ 1028). The taxes are allocated based on the number of days each party held the property during the real property tax year. Taxes imposed on the property up to, but not including the date of sale, are allocated to the seller. Taxes imposed on the property beginning with the date of sale are allocated to the buyer. Proration is required whether or not the buyer and seller actually agree to apportion the tax and regardless of the lien dates under local law (Code Sec. 164(d); Reg. § 1.164-6).

> **Example:** Able sells his farm to Baker on August 1, 2019. Both use the cash-method of accounting on a calendar-year basis. Taxes for the real property year, April 1, 2019, to March 31, 2020, become due and payable on May 15, 2020. Baker pays the real estate taxes when they fall due. Regardless of any agreement between the parties, $122/366$ of the real estate taxes are allocated to Able and $244/366$ of the taxes are allocated to Baker.

See ¶ 1034 for the impact of the buyer's and seller's method of accounting on the timing of the deduction for allocated real estate taxes.

Real Property Tax Year. The real property tax year is the period to which the tax relates under state law or local law. If a state and one or more local governmental units each imposes a tax, the real property tax year for each tax must be determined.

If real property is sold after the property tax becomes a personal liability or lien but before the beginning of the related real property tax year, the seller may not deduct any amount for property taxes for the related real property tax year. To the extent that the buyer holds the property for that real property tax year, the buyer may deduct the amount of the taxes for the tax year in which they are paid or accrued. Conversely, if the property is sold before the tax becomes a personal liability or lien but after the end of the related real property tax year, the buyer cannot deduct any amount for taxes for the related real property tax year. To the extent that the seller holds the property for that real property tax year, the seller may deduct the amount of the taxes for the tax year they are paid or accrued.

Only real estate taxes arising during the real property tax year in which the sale takes place are allocated between the buyer and seller. Delinquent taxes from any prior year cannot be allocated to the buyer. Also, if a taxpayer pays and deducts real estate taxes in a year prior to the sale in excess of the portion allocated to him or her for the real property tax year, then the excess is required to be included in his or her gross income in the year of sale, subject to the tax benefit rule (¶ 799).

> **Example:** Charlie is a cash-basis taxpayer whose real property tax is due and payable on November 30 for the next calendar year, which is also the real property tax year. He paid the 2019 real property taxes on November 30, 2018, and deducted them on his 2018 income tax return. On June 30, 2019, Charlie sold the real property. Only the taxes from January 1 through June 29, 2019, or $179/365$ of those paid, are treated as imposed on Charlie. The excess amount deducted on his 2018 income tax return is includible in his gross income in 2019.

1034. Accounting for Allocated Real Property Taxes. The tax year in which a taxpayer deducts real property taxes allocated to him or her (¶ 1032) is affected by the taxpayer's method of accounting and date of the tax lien or liability (Reg. § 1.164-6(d)). If the *seller* uses the cash method of accounting, the taxes apportioned to him or her may be deducted in the tax year of the sale, whether or not actually paid in that tax year, if: (1) the buyer is liable for the taxes for the real property tax year; or (2) the seller is liable for the taxes for the real property tax year and the taxes are not payable until after the date of sale. If the taxes are not a liability of any person, the person who holds the property at the time the taxes become a lien on the property is considered liable for the taxes.

If the *buyer* uses the cash method of accounting, the portion of real property taxes apportioned to him or her may be deducted in the tax year of the sale, whether or not the taxes are actually paid by the buyer in the tax year of the sale, if the seller is liable for the taxes. If the taxes are not a liability of any person, the person who holds the property at the time the taxes become a lien on the property is considered liable for the taxes.

If either the buyer or seller uses the accrual method of accounting and has not elected to accrue real property taxes ratably (¶ 1031), the portion of their tax liability that may not be deducted for any tax year is treated as if accrued on the date of sale.

> **Example:** In Polk county the real property tax year is the calendar year and the real property taxes become a lien on November 30 of the year. There is no personal liability for the tax. Able is an accrual-method seller who sells real property to Baker on June 30, 2019. Neither party has elected to accrue real property taxes. Able's share is $180/365$ of the taxes and accrues on June 30, the date of the sale. She may deduct her share for her tax year within which June 30 falls. Baker's share of the taxes is $185/365$ and accrues on November 30, the lien date. He may deduct his share for his tax year within which November 30 falls.

1036. Deduction of Assessments and Taxes for Local Benefits. Any tax that is in reality an assessment for local benefits such as streets, sidewalks, water mains, sewer lines, parking facilities, and similar improvements is *not* deductible as a tax by a property owner, except where it is levied for the purpose of maintenance and repair, or meeting interest charges on local benefits. It is the taxpayer's burden to show the allocation of amounts assessed to the different purposes (Code Sec. 164(c)(1); Reg. § 1.164-4). Assessments for improvements or other items that increase the value of property are added to the basis of the property (¶ 1611).

1040. Deductions by Tenant-Shareholders of Cooperative Housing Corporation. A tenant-stockholder may deduct amounts paid or accrued to a cooperative housing corporation (CHC) to the extent that they represent the tenant's proportionate share of: (1) real estate taxes on the apartment building or houses, and the land on which they are situated; or (2) interest on debt contracted in the acquisition, construction, alteration, rehabilitation, or maintenance of such building, houses, or land (Code Sec. 216; Reg. § 1.216-1). The limitations on deductible home mortgage interest apply (¶ 1047).

For purposes of the deduction, a corporation is a CHC if:

- the corporation has only one class of outstanding stock;

- solely by reason of owning the stock, each stockholder is entitled to occupy a house or apartment in a building owned or leased by the corporation;

- no stockholder is entitled to receive any distribution which is not out of the corporation's earnings and profits, except on a partial or complete liquidation; and

- 80 percent or more of the corporation's gross income is derived from tenant-stockholders, 80 percent or more of the total square footage of its property is at all times used or available for use by the tenant-stockholders for residential purposes or purposes ancillary to residential use, or 90 percent or more of the corporation's expenses paid or incurred are for the acquisition, construction, management, maintenance, or care of the property for the tenant-stockholders' benefit.

Under the 80-percent-of-gross-income test, amounts received from tenant-stockholders to defray expenses for items like secretarial services, parking, utilities, recreation facilities, cleaning and related services are included in gross income derived from tenants, while amounts received from commercial leases and the operation of a business other than housing are excluded (Rev. Rul. 55-556). Income attributable to a unit that a governmental entity is entitled to occupy under a lease or stock ownership is also excluded.

Interest

See CCH® AnswerConnect: *Interest Deduction* for more information on this topic.

1043. Interest Deduction for Individuals. An individual may generally deduct interest paid or accrued during the tax year, subject to certain exceptions and limitations (Code Sec. 163; *P.E. Deputy v. P.S. du Pont*, SCt, 40-1 USTC ¶ 9161). Deductible interest must pertain to a debt of the taxpayer and result from a debtor-creditor relationship based upon a valid and enforceable obligation to pay a fixed or determinable sum of money.

Personal Interest. An individual is not allowed to claim any deduction for personal interest paid or accrued during the tax year (Code Sec. 163(h); Temp. Reg. § 1.163-9T). Personal interest is any interest incurred by an individual *other than*:

- interest paid or accrued on debt properly allocable to a trade or business, other than services as an employee (¶ 937);

- investment interest, but limited to net investment income (¶ 1057);

- home mortgage interest (qualified residence interest) paid or accrued on acquisition debt secured by any qualified residence of the taxpayer (¶ 1047);

- student loan interest (¶ 1011);

- interest taken into account in computing income or loss from a passive activity of the taxpayer (¶ 1165); and

- underpayment interest on estate tax payments that are deferred because of a reversionary or remainder interest in property (¶ 2939).

Any interest paid or accrued by an individual that does not fall into one of these categories is not deductible. This includes: interest on a car loan if the car is used for personal use; interest on credit cards, retail installment contracts, and revolving charge accounts incurred for personal expenses; and late payment charges by a public utility (IRS Pub. 17). Expenses that are similar to interest also are not deductible, including service charges, annual fees on credit cards, loan fees, credit investigation fees, interest to purchase or carry tax-exempt bonds (¶ 970), and interest on debt to pay premiums on certain insurance contracts (¶ 909).

Nondeductible personal interest includes interest paid on underpayments of individual federal, state, or local income taxes and debt used to pay the taxes, regardless of whether any portion of the additional tax due is attributable to trade or business income. This includes interest paid by trusts, S corporations, and other pass-through entities on underpayments of state or local income taxes. Nondeductible personal interest also includes interest incurred if a taxpayer buys property on the installment plan, unless the property is purchased for the taxpayer's trade or business.

Tracing Rules. An individual is not allowed to claim any deduction for personal interest paid or accrued during the tax year (¶ 1043). If a taxpayer uses the proceeds of a loan for more than one purpose (for example, business, investment, and personal), interest on the loan must be allocated to each use. Interest expenses are allocated in the same manner that the debt that gave rise to the payment or accrual of interest is allocated. Debt is allocated by tracing the proceeds to the types of expenses they are used for (Temp. Reg. § 1.163-8T).

Time for Deducting Interest. If a taxpayer is allowed an interest deduction, his or her method of accounting determines when it may be claimed (¶ 1515). A cash-basis taxpayer deducts interest in the year paid. In the case of prepaid interest, interest must be capitalized and deducted as if on the accrual basis unless it meets the exception for home mortgage interest (¶ 1055). An accrual-basis taxpayer deducts interest in the year in which it accrues, but the taxpayer must use the cash-basis for interest owed to a related taxpayer (¶ 1540B).

1047. Home Mortgage Interest Deduction. Interest paid on a home mortgage (i.e., qualified residence interest) may be claimed by an individual as an itemized deduction (¶ 1014) on Schedule A (Form 1040) (Code Sec. 163(h)(3); IRS Pub. 936). Home mortgage interest is deductible if paid or accrued during the tax year on acquisition or home equity indebtedness secured by the taxpayer's qualified residence (¶ 1048). A home is secured by a mortgage, deed of trust, or land contract, but not solely because of a mechanic's lien or judgment lien. The deduction is limited to debt that does not exceed $750,000 ($375,000 if married filing separately) if secured after December 15, 2017, and before January 1, 2026 ($1 million/$500,000 if secured before December 16, 2017). For tax years beginning before 2018 and after 2026, the deduction may also include interest on home equity debt of up to $100,000 ($50,000 if married filing separately).

Qualified Residence. A qualified residence is the taxpayer's principal residence and one other residence used as a residence by the taxpayer such as a vacation home. If the second home is rented out at any time during the tax year, then the taxpayer must use the home for the greater of 14 days or 10 percent of the number of days that it is rented out at a fair rental value (Code Sec. 163(h)(4); IRS Pub. 936). A taxpayer who uses part of a home other than as a residence (i.e., home office) must allocate use of the home, as well as cost and fair market value for purposes of deducting home mortgage interest (¶ 961).

A home under construction may be a qualified residence for up to 24 months, but only if it becomes the taxpayer's qualified residence at the time it is ready for occupancy. A taxpayer can continue treating a destroyed home as a qualified residence if, within a reasonable period of time after the home is destroyed the taxpayer rebuilds the home and moves into it, or sells the land on which the home was located. A residence may include stock in a cooperative housing corporation owned by a tenant-stockholder if the house or apartment that the taxpayer is entitled to occupy by virtue of owning the stock is a residence. A taxpayer can treat a home owned under a time-sharing plan as a qualified residence if it otherwise meets all the requirements.

Married taxpayers who file separate returns and own more than one home may each to take into account one residence unless both consent in writing to having only one spouse take into account both residences. If married taxpayers file jointly, then the qualified residence can be owned jointly or by only one spouse. Interest paid or accrued by a trust or estate is deductible if the debt is secured by a beneficiary's qualified residence.

Prepaid Interest and Points. Prepaid interest generally must be capitalized and deducted over the life of a loan. However, points paid by a borrower to obtain a home mortgage can be deducted as qualified residence interest in the year paid under certain circumstances (¶ 1055).

Mortgage Insurance Premiums. Premiums paid or accrued before January 1, 2021, for qualified mortgage insurance in connection with an acquisition debt for a qualified residence may be deducted as qualified residence interest (¶ 1048A). Annual or periodic redeemable ground rent payments are also deductible as qualified residence interest (¶ 1049).

Mortgage Interest Credit. If a taxpayer holds a mortgage credit certificate (¶ 1406), any home mortgage interest deduction must be reduced by the amount of any credit allowable (Code Sec. 163(g)).

Seller-Provided Financing. For seller-provided financing, a taxpayer deducting home mortgage interest must include on Schedule A (Form 1040) the name, address, and taxpayer identification number (TIN) of the person to whom interest is paid or accrued (Code Sec. 6109(h); Instructions to Schedule A).

State Assistance. An individual who receives assistance from a state housing finance agency (HFA) funded through allocations from the Treasury Department's Housing Finance Agency Innovative Fund for the Hardest-Hit Housing Markets may use a safe harbor to deduct mortgage interest, mortgage insurance premiums, and real property taxes through 2021. The homeowner may deduct the lesser of the sum of all payments actually made to the mortgage servicer or state HFA, or the sum of the three amounts shown on Form 1098 (Notice 2018-63, amplifying and modifying Notice 2017-40).

1048. Acquisition and Home Equity Indebtedness Defined. Home mortgage interest (i.e., qualified residence interest) may be claimed by an individual as an itemized deduction on Schedule A (Form 1040) (¶ 1047) if it is paid or accrued on:

- home acquisition debt used to buy, build, or substantially improve a qualified residence of the taxpayer that is secured by the residence after December 15, 2017, provided that the debt does not exceed $750,000 ($375,000 if married filing separately);

- home acquisition debt used to buy, build, or substantially improve a qualified residence of the taxpayer that is secured by the residence before December 16, 2017, provided that the debt does not exceed $1 million ($500,000 if married filing separately); and

- home equity debt secured by the residence before December 16, 2017, provided that the debt does not exceed $100,000 or the fair market value of the residence reduced by any acquisition debt (Code Sec. 163(h)(3); Notice 88-74; IRS Pub. 936).

Any secured debt used to refinance home acquisition debt is treated as acquisition debt to the extent it does not exceed the principal of the original loan amount. Any additional debt not used to buy, build, or substantially improve a qualified residence is not acquisition debt or home equity debt for tax years beginning in 2018 through 2025. Any additional debt that is not acquisition debt may qualify as home equity debt for tax years beginning before 2018 and after 2025.

Limitations in 2018 through 2025. The total amount of debt used for the home mortgage interest deduction may not exceed $750,000 ($375,000 if married filing separately) for debt secured after December 15, 2017 and before January 1, 2026. The limit applies to the combined amount of debt used to buy, build, or substantially improve a qualified residence. Thus, it applies regardless of whether the debt is labeled acquisition debt, home equity loan, home equity line of credit (HELOC) or second mortgage. Interest is not deductible for any portion of a debt that is used to pay personal expenses (e.g., credit card debt, etc.) (IRS News Release, IR-2018-32).

The $750,000/$375,000 limit generally applies to debt secured after December 15, 2017. Exceptions are provided if the taxpayer: (1) had a binding written contract before December 15, 2017, to purchase a qualifying residence before 2018; or (2) refinances an existing acquisition debt to the extent of the original loan amount. The refinancing exception expires after the expiration of the original loan, or the earlier of the expiration of the loan or the first refinanced debt or 30 years.

Limitations Before 2018 and After 2025. The total amount of acquisition debt used for the home mortgage interest deduction may not exceed $1 million ($500,000 if married filing separately) for debt secured before December 16, 2017, and after December 31, 2025. For tax years beginning before 2018 and after 2025, the total amount of home equity debt may not exceed $100,000 ($50,000 if married filing separately) or the fair market value of the residence less the total amount of any acquisition debt. Acquisition debt may constitute home equity debt to the extent the debt exceeds the $1 million/$500,000 limit, but subject to the $100,000/$50,000 and fair market value limits (Rev. Rul. 2010-25). Thus, an individual can deduct interest paid on up to $1.1 million of such debt ($550,000 if married filing separately) as qualified residence interest. Interest attributable to debt over these limits is nondeductible personal interest (¶ 1043).

Co-Owners. The dollar limits on acquisition and home equity debt apply to unmarried co-owners on a per-taxpayer basis, and not a per-residence basis (*B.H. Voss*, CA-9, 2015-2 USTC ¶ 50,427 (Acq)).

Grandfathered Debt. Interest on certain acquisition debt incurred on or before October 13, 1987, is fully deductible and not subject to the dollar limits. The amount of grandfathered debt reduces the amount of the limitation available for new acquisition debt (e.g., for improvements) (Code Sec. 163(h)(3)(D)).

1048A. Mortgage Insurance Premium Deduction. Premiums paid or accrued before January 1, 2021, for qualified mortgage insurance in connection with acquisition indebtedness (¶ 1048) are deductible as home mortgage interest (qualified residence interest) (¶ 1047) (Code Sec. 163(h)(3)(E), as amended by the Taxpayer Certainty and Disaster Tax Relief Act of 2019 (P.L. 116-94) and (h)(4)(E)). The deduction is reduced (but not below zero) by 10 percent for every $1,000 by which the taxpayer's adjusted gross income (AGI) exceeds $100,000. For married individuals filing separately, the deduction is reduced by 10 percent for every $500 that AGI exceeds $50,000.

Qualified mortgage insurance for this purpose is mortgage insurance provided by the Department of Veterans Affairs (VA), the Federal Housing Administration (FHA), the Rural Housing Service, and private insurance. The deduction does not apply with

¶1048A

respect to mortgage insurance contracts issued before 2007 or to premiums paid, accrued, or properly allocable to any period after 2020.

In the case of prepaid mortgage insurance, amounts that are allocable to periods after the payment year are capitalized and treated as paid in the allocable periods, except VA or Rural Housing Service contracts. Prepaid premiums must be allocated ratably over the shorter of the stated term of the mortgage or 84 months, beginning with the month in which the insurance was obtained. If the mortgage is satisfied before the end of its term, no deduction is allowed for any premium allocable to periods after the mortgage is satisfied (Code Sec. 163(h)(4)(F); Reg. § 1.163-11).

State Assistance. An individual who receives assistance from a state housing finance agency (HFA) funded through allocations from the Treasury Department's Housing Finance Agency Innovative Fund for the Hardest-Hit Housing Markets may use a safe harbor to deduct mortgage insurance premiums, mortgage interest, and real property taxes through 2021. The homeowner may deduct the lesser of the sum of all payments actually made to the mortgage servicer or state HFA, or the sum of the three amounts shown on Form 1098 (Notice 2018-63, amplifying and modifying Notice 2017-40).

1049. Redeemable Ground Rents. Annual or periodic payments of redeemable ground rent are treated as interest paid on a mortgage, unless paid in redemption (Code Secs. 163(c) and 1055(c)(1); Reg. § 1.1055-1). Ground rents are subject to the rules pertaining to home mortgage interest (¶ 1047). A redeemable ground rent is a ground rent payable under a freely assignable lease that is for a term in excess of 15 years, including possible renewal periods. The lessee has a right to terminate the lease and buy the lessor's interest in the land by paying a set amount, and the lessor's interest is primarily a security interest to protect the rental payments.

1050. Mortgage Interest Deduction of Ministers and Military Personnel. Ministers and military personnel are allowed to deduct home mortgage interest on their qualified residences (¶ 1047) even though they receive a parsonage or military housing allowance that is excludable from gross income (Code Sec. 265(a)(6)). Military personnel include members of the Army, Navy, Air Force, Marine Corps, Coast Guard, National Oceanic and Atmospheric Administration, and Public Health Service (Rev. Rul. 87-32).

1055. Deduction of Prepaid Interest or Points. A cash-basis taxpayer generally cannot claim a current deduction for prepaid interest, other than for points on certain home mortgage loans. Instead, the taxpayer must deduct prepaid interest over the period of the loan to the extent that the interest represents the cost of using the borrowed funds during each tax year in the period (Code Sec. 461(g)). This rule does not contemplate that interest will be treated as paid in equal payments over the term of the loan. Thus, interest paid on an amortizing loan as part of an equal constant payment, including principal and interest, is not subject to the prepaid interest rule merely because the payments consist of a larger interest portion in the earlier years of the loan than in later years.

Points paid by a cash-basis taxpayer on a home mortgage are deductible in the year paid if:

- the loan is used to purchase or improve the taxpayer's principal residence and the loan is secured by the home;

- the payment of points is an established practice in the area where the loan is made; and

- the amount paid does not exceed the points generally charged in the area for a home loan.

Points for this purpose are charges paid by the taxpayer to obtain a home mortgage and may also be referred to as loan origination fees, loan discounts, discount points, and maximum loan charges. A taxpayer may choose to amortize points over the life of the loan in certain circumstances (Rev. Proc. 87-15; IRS Pub. 936).

The IRS has provided a safe harbor under which it automatically treats points as currently deductible if:

- the HUD-1 or other settlement statement clearly designates the amounts as points, loan discount, discount points, or loan origination fees, including amounts on VA and FHA loans;

- the amount is calculated as a percentage of the principal loan amount;

- the loan is paid to acquire the taxpayer's principal residence in connection with a loan secured by that residence;

- the points are paid directly by the taxpayer, which may include earnest money, an escrow deposit, or down payment applied at closing, and not derived from loan proceeds; points paid by a seller, including points charged to the seller, are considered directly paid by the taxpayer from funds not derived from loan proceeds if they are subtracted by the taxpayer from the purchase price of the residence in computing its basis; and

- there is an established business practice in the local area to charge points on residential mortgages and the amount charged does not exceed the amount generally charged (Rev. Proc. 94-27).

No part of the points may be in lieu of appraisal, inspection, title, and attorney fees, property taxes, or other amounts that are ordinarily stated separately on the settlement statement. In addition, the safe harbor does not apply to points paid for a loan to acquire a principal residence to the extent the principal amount exceeds the limit on acquisition debt (¶ 1048). Nor does it apply to points paid on home improvement loans, second or vacation home loans, refinancing or home equity loans, or lines of credit. The fact that a taxpayer cannot satisfy the requirements of the safe harbor does not necessarily mean that points are not currently deductible. It does mean that the IRS will not automatically consider them to be currently deductible.

Refinancing. Points paid to refinance a home mortgage are not deductible in full in the year paid, but must be deducted ratably over the period of the loan because they are incurred for the repayment of the taxpayer's existing debt. However, the U.S. Court of Appeals for the Eighth Circuit allows a full deduction in the year paid for points on a long-term home mortgage loan refinancing a short-term balloon loan used to acquire the home (*J.R. Huntsman*, CA-8, 90-2 USTC ¶ 50,340, nonacq. except in the Eighth Circuit). Also, the portion of the points allocable to the proceeds of a refinancing that are used for improvements may be deducted in the year paid. The portion allocable to the repayment of existing debt or other purposes is deducted ratably over the period of the loan (Rev. Rul. 87-22).

1057. Investment Interest Deduction. A noncorporate taxpayer (individual, estate, and trust) may claim a deduction for interest paid or accrued on investment debt to the extent of the taxpayer's net investment income (Code Sec. 163(d); IRS Pub. 550; Rev. Rul. 95-16). The deduction is calculated on Form 4952 and any disallowed investment interest can be carried over to a succeeding tax year. The deduction is reported by an individual as an itemized deduction on Schedule A (Form 1040) unless the interest is attributable to a royalty in which case it is reported on Schedule E (Form 1040).

Investment interest for this purpose is interest paid or accrued by the taxpayer on debt allocable to property held for investment, including:

- property that produces interest, dividends, annuities, or royalties that are not derived in the ordinary course of a trade or business;

- property that produces gain or loss not derived in the ordinary course of a trade or business from the sale or exchange of property that produces these types of income or held for investment (other than an interest in a passive activity); and

- an interest in a trade or business activity that is not a passive activity and in which the taxpayer did not materially participate (¶ 1165).

Investment interest also includes the taxpayer's share of investment interest from a partnership, S corporation, estate, or trust. It does not include home mortgage interest (¶ 1047), interest properly allocable to a rental real estate activity in which the taxpayer actively participates (¶ 1181), or interest that is taken into account in computing income or loss from a passive activity (¶ 1167).

Net Investment Income. Net investment income equals the excess of the taxpayer's investment income over investment expenses. Investment income is gross income derived from the investment or sale of the property. This includes interest, dividends, annuities, royalties, and short-term gain of the taxpayer, as well as such income of a child that a parent elects to report on his or her return (¶ 115).

Investment income does not include any income derived from the conduct of a trade or business. Also, it generally does not include any net capital gain from the sale or disposition of investment property, or any qualified dividends subject to capital gains rates. However, the taxpayer may elect to treat all or any portion of net capital gains and qualified dividends from investment property as investment income for this purpose. Thus, the elected portion of net capital gains and qualified dividends are subject to ordinary income tax rate and not eligible for capital gain tax rates. The election is made on Form 4952 and must be on or before the due date of the return (including extensions) for the tax year in which the net capital gain or the qualified dividend income is recognized. The due date for filing any federal income tax return otherwise due on or after April 1, 2020, and before July 15, 2020, is automatically extended to July 15, 2020 (¶ 2505). The election is revocable only with the consent of the IRS.

Charitable Contributions

See CCH® AnswerConnect: *Charitable Deductions* for more information on this topic.

1058. Charitable Contributions by Individuals. An individual may claim an itemized deduction (¶ 1014) for contributions to a qualified charitable organization on Schedule A (Form 1040) (Code Sec. 170). The charitable deduction for any tax year is limited to a percentage of the taxpayer's contribution base determined by the type of organization receiving the donation and the type of property donated (¶ 1059). Any excess for the tax year may be carried forward for five years (¶ 1060). If married individuals file a joint return, the percentage limitation depends on the aggregate contribution base of the spouses. A limit also applies to the amount of a charitable deduction allowed for gifts of appreciated property and is imposed before applying the percentage limitation (¶ 1062).

Above-the-Line $300 Deduction. For tax years beginning in 2020 only, an eligible individual may claim an above-the-line deduction in computing adjusted gross income (AGI) (¶ 1011) of up to $300 for any qualified charitable contribution in response to the COVID-19 (coronavirus) crisis (Code Sec. 62(a)(22) and (f)(1), as added by the Coronavirus Aid, Relief, and Economic Security (CARES) Act (P.L. 116-136)). An individual is eligible so long as he or she does not otherwise claim any itemized deduction. A qualified charitable contribution for this purpose is a charitable contribution made in cash that would otherwise be allowed as an itemized deduction and contributed to an organization described in Code Sec. 170(b)(1)(A). It cannot be made to a Code Sec. 509(a)(3) supporting organization under or a new or existing donor advised fund. It also does not apply to cash contributions carried over from previous tax years.

Charitable Deduction Defined. A charitable contribution is a contribution or gift to a qualifying charitable organization (¶ 1061). The taxpayer generally may deduct the fair market value of property contributed subject to the percentage limitation, only in the year of payment, regardless of when the contribution was pledged (Reg. § 1.170A-1(a)). The taxpayer must reduce the deduction for the value of any goods, services, or other benefits received in consideration of the gift. Contributions charged to a bank credit card are deductible in the year charged even though paid in a later year. A contribution made by text message is deductible in the year the donor sends the text message if the contribution is charged to the donor's telephone or wireless account (IRS Pub. 526). Special rules apply to a taxpayer recognized by the Alaska Eskimo Whaling Commission as whaling captains (Code Sec. 170(n)).

IRA Distributions. An individual age 70½ or older may distribute up to $100,000 tax-free from his or her individual retirement accounts (IRAs) to certain charitable organizations without including the distribution in gross income (¶ 2165). A qualified charitable distribution must be made directly by the trustee to a 50-percent organization (¶ 1059), but *not* to a supporting organization or a donor advised fund (¶ 1061). The entire distribution must otherwise be deductible as a charitable donation, disregarding the percentage limitations, even though the individual cannot claim a charitable deduction for the donation.

Partnerships and S Corporations. A partnership cannot claim a charitable contribution deduction in determining its taxable income. Each partner is allowed a deduction for his or her distributive share of the partnership's charitable contributions (¶ 417). An S corporation also cannot claim a charitable contribution deduction in determining its taxable income. A shareholder reduces his or her basis in S corporation stock for his or her pro rata share of the corporation's charitable contribution (¶ 317).

1059. Percentage Limits on Individuals' Charitable Contributions. An individual's charitable contribution deduction for any tax year (¶ 1058) is limited to a percentage of the individual's contribution base for the year (Code Sec. 170(b)(1); Reg. § 1.170A-8). An individual's contribution base is his or her adjusted gross income (AGI), computed without regard to the charitable deduction and any net operating loss (NOL) carrybacks (¶ 1149). If married individuals file jointly, the percentage limit depends on the aggregate contributions of the spouses. Charitable contributions that exceed the percentage limit may be carried forward five years (¶ 1060).

The percentage limit depends on the type of organization receiving the donation, the type of property donated, and whether the property is simply donated to a charitable organization or for the use of the organization (¶ 1063). A donation of an income interest in property is made for the use of the charity, whether or not it is transferred in trust. A donation of a remainder interest in property is made for the use of the organization if it is transferred in trust to be held and administered for the organization.

The percentage limits for an individual generally are:

• 60 percent of the taxpayer's contribution base for contributions of cash for tax years beginning in 2018 through 2025 to public charities (cash contributions that qualify for the 60-percent limit are not taken into account in determining contributions that are allowed under the 50-percent limit);

• 50 percent of the taxpayer's contribution base for contributions of cash before 2018 and ordinary income property (¶ 1062) to tax-exempt organizations (i.e., public charities described below);

• 30 percent of the taxpayer's contribution base for contributions of capital gain property to public charities;

• for contributions of ordinary income property to qualified charitable organizations other than public charities, and gifts for the use of public charities, the lesser of: (1) 30 percent of the taxpayer's contribution base, or (2) the excess of 50 percent of the taxpayer's contribution base for the tax year over the amount of charitable contributions qualifying for the 50-percent deduction ceiling, including carryovers;

• 20 percent of the taxpayer's contribution base for contributions of capital gain property to qualified charitable organizations that are not public charities (i.e., veterans' organizations, fraternal societies, nonprofit cemeteries, and certain private nonoperating foundations).

Charitable contributions made by bona fide residents of U.S. possessions (¶ 2414) or Puerto Rico (¶ 2415) are deductible only to the extent allocable to income that is *not* excluded possession-source or Puerto Rico-source income (Reg. § 1.170A-1(j)(9)). See ¶ 927 for deduction limitations on charitable contributions by corporations.

COVID-19 (Coronavirus). The 60-percent limitation on the deduction of charitable contributions of cash by individuals is suspended for qualified charitable contributions made in 2020 in response to the COVID-19 (coronavirus) crisis (Act Sec. 2205(a) of the Coronavirus Aid, Relief, and Economic Security (CARES) Act (P.L. 116-136)). An individual may deduct any qualified cash contribution as long as the contribution does not exceed the individual's contribution base (100 percent) and any excess may be carried forward five years. A qualified contribution for this purpose is a charitable contribution made in cash during the 2020 calendar year to an organization described in Code Sec. 170(b)(1)(A). It cannot be made to a Code Sec. 509(a)(3) supporting organization under or a new or existing donor advised fund. It also does not apply to cash contributions carried over from previous tax years. If the taxpayer is a partner in a partnership or a shareholder in an S corporation, the election to claim the deduction with respect to qualified contributions is made by the partner or shareholder.

Disaster Relief. The percentage limits are temporarily waived for qualified contributions made for relief efforts in qualified disaster areas. The deduction is allowed up to the excess of the individual's contribution base, less all other charitable deductions allowed during the tax year. Any excess contributions are added to the carryover of contributions subject to the 60 percent contribution limit. Qualified contributions are cash contributions:

- paid after December 31, 2017, and before February 19, 2020, for relief efforts in qualified disaster areas (Act Secs. 201 and 204(a) of the Taxpayer Certainty and Disaster Tax Relief Act of 2019 (P.L. 116-94));

- paid after October 7, 2017, and before January 1, 2018 for relief efforts in the California wildfire disaster area (Act Sec. 20101 and 20104(a) of the Bipartisan Budget Act of 2018 (P.L. 115-123); and

- paid after August 22, 2017, and before January 1, 2018, for relief efforts in the Hurricane Harvey, Irma, or Maria disaster area (Act Secs. 501 and 504(a) of the Disaster Tax Relief and Airport and Airway Extension Act of 2017 (P.L. 115-63).

The contributions must be paid to a 50-percent charitable organization (i.e., public charity), other than a supporting private foundation under Code Sec. 509(a)(3) (¶ 607) or donor advised fund (¶ 610). The taxpayer must obtain a contemporaneous written acknowledgment from the charity (¶ 1070A) that the contribution is used for relief efforts in the designated disaster area. The taxpayer also must elect to treat the charitable contribution as a qualified contribution. In the case of a partnership or S corporation, the election is made by each partner or shareholder.

Qualified Conservation Contributions. An individual who makes a qualified conservation contribution (QCC) of real property (¶ 1063) is allowed to claim the QCC deduction against the 50-percent contribution base minus the taxpayer's deduction for all other charitable contributions. Any excess can be carried forward for 15 years. These rules are applied separately from the rules that apply to other donations (Code Sec. 170(b)(1)(E)).

Qualified Farmers and Ranchers. An individual who is a qualified farmer or rancher is allowed to make a qualified conservation contribution up to the excess of 100 percent of the taxpayer's contribution base over the amount of all other allowable charitable contributions. The 100-percent limit only applies if the contribution includes a restriction that the property must remain generally available for agriculture or livestock production (Code Sec. 170(b)(1)(E)). For this purpose, a qualified farmer or rancher is an individual if more than 50 percent of gross income for the tax year is gross income from farming or ranching. An enhanced charitable deduction for a QCC of real property by certain corporate farmers and ranchers is limited to the excess of the corporation's taxable income over the amount of other allowable charitable contributions (¶ 927).

Public Charity. The following types of organizations are public charities for purposes of the percentage limits (i.e., Code Sec. 170(b)(1)(A) or 50-percent limit organizations) (Code Sec. 170(b)(1)(A); Reg. § 1.170A-9).

(1) churches or conventions or associations of churches (¶ 604);

(2) educational institutions;

(3) hospitals or medical research organizations, not including home health care organizations, convalescent homes, homes for children or the aged, or vocational institutions that train handicapped individuals;

(4) endowment foundations in connection with a state college or university;

(5) state, federal or local government units, if the contribution is made for exclusively public purposes;

(6) certain domestic corporations, trusts, or foundations organized and operated exclusively for religious, charitable, scientific, literary, or educational purposes (¶ 1061), and normally receiving a substantial part of their support from the public or a governmental unit;

(7) private operating foundations (¶ 631 and ¶ 633);

(8) private nonoperating foundations that distribute all contributions received to public charities and private operating foundations, or make certain other qualifying distributions, within 2½ months after the end of the tax year;

(9) private foundations that pool all contributions into a common fund and allow a substantial contributor to designate a recipient charity, where income from the pool is distributed within 2½ months after the tax year in which it was realized and corpus attributable to any donor's contribution is distributed to a charity not later than one year after the death of the donor or surviving spouse with the right to designate the recipients of the corpus;

(10) publicly supported organizations normally receiving

(a) more than ⅓ of their support in each tax year from the public and organizations listed in items (1)–(6) above in the form of grants, gifts, contributions, or membership fees, and gross receipts from an activity that is not an unrelated trade or business (less certain receipts), and

(b) not more than ⅓ of their support from gross investment income and unrelated business taxable income (less taxes);

(11) certain supporting organizations (¶ 607); and

(12) certain agricultural research organizations.

1060. Carryover of Excess Charitable Contributions by Individuals. If an individual's charitable contributions exceed the applicable percentage limits (¶ 1059), any excess contributions may generally be carried forward and deducted over the following five tax years (Code Sec. 170(b)(1)(D)(ii) and (d); Reg. §1.170A-10). However, all current year contributions must be deducted first. After the current year deductions have been used, the taxpayer can deduct the carryovers subject to the same ordering and percentage limitations that apply to current year contributions.

The amount of the excess that may be deducted in any carryover year is limited to the lesser of:

• the remaining portion of any excess contribution not already deducted; or

• 50 percent (or 30 percent for capital gain carryover) of the taxpayer's contribution base after first deducting the sum of the charitable contributions (to which the 50-percent or 30-percent limitation applies) paid in the carryover year and any excess contributions that have precedence in order of time over the present carryover.

The excess must be reduced to the extent that it reduces taxable income as computed for net operating loss (NOL) carrybacks and carryovers (¶ 1149) and increases the NOL deduction for a tax year succeeding the contribution year. For each tax year beginning in 2018 through 2025, and for each tax year to which any 60-percent cash contribution is carried over, the aggregate contribution limitation allowed must be reduced (but not below zero) by the total contributions allowed under the 60-percent limit (Code Sec. 170(b)(1)(G)).

Qualified Conservation Contribution Carryover. If the taxpayer's qualified conservation contributions (QCCs) (¶ 1059) exceed the applicable limit for such donations, the excess can be carried forward for 15 years (Code Sec. 170(b)(1)(E)(ii)).

1061. Charitable Contributions That Are Deductible. A charitable contribution is deductible only if it is a contribution or gift to, or for the use of, the following qualified organizations:

• the United States, a state, a local government, the District of Columbia, or a U.S. possession, for exclusively public purposes;

• a corporation, trust or community chest, fund, or foundation, created or organized in the United States or a U.S. possession, or under the law of the United States, a possession, a state, or the District of Columbia, organized and operated exclusively for religious, charitable, scientific, literary, or educational purposes, or to foster national or international amateur sports competition, or for the prevention of cruelty to children or animals; no part of the charity's net earnings may inure to the benefit of any private shareholder or individual; also the organization must not be disqualified for tax exemption under Code Sec. 501(c)(3) by attempting to influence legislation;

- a cemetery company owned and operated exclusively for the benefit of its members or any corporation chartered solely for burial purposes as a cemetery corporation and not operated for profit or for the benefit of any private shareholder or individual;

- a post or organization of war veterans, or its auxiliary society or unit, organized in the United States or a U.S. possession, if no part of the net earnings inures to the benefit of any private shareholder or individual; or

- a domestic fraternal society, order, or association, operating under the lodge system, but only if the contributions are used exclusively for religious, charitable, scientific, literary or educational purposes, or for the prevention of cruelty to children or animals (Code Sec. 170(c)).

A contribution is not deductible unless it is made to, or for the use of, qualified organizations listed above. The donee must be a qualified organization at the time that the contribution is made. The IRS provides and maintains an online search tool—Tax Exempt Organization Search (TEOS) (formerly EO Select Check)—that allows users to determine whether an organization is eligible to receive deductible charitable contributions. Guidance is also provided on the extent taxpayers may rely on the listing of an organization in the IRS databases, if contributions or grants to such organizations may be deductible, and for certain other purposes (Rev. Proc. 2018-32).

Contributions made to individuals or nonqualified organizations are not deductible (IRS Pub. 526). If specific requirements are met, a charitable deduction is allowed for the cost of maintaining a student in the taxpayer's home (¶ 1064). The fact that an organization is tax-exempt under Code Sec. 501 does not guarantee that contributions to the organization will be deductible. Moreover, organizations that otherwise qualify to receive deductible donations can be disqualified for activities that violate public policy or for influencing or participating in legislation or political campaigns. Special rules apply for contributions to private foundations and certain trusts (¶ 538).

Contributions of Services. The value of service rendered to a charitable organization is *not* deductible as a charitable contribution (Reg. § 1.170A-1(g)). However, out-of-pocket unreimbursed expense (e.g., expenses for uniform, telephone, or equipment) is a deductible contribution (Rev. Rul. 84-61). No deduction is allowed for out-of-pocket expenses made by any person on behalf of a charitable organization other than an certain churches if the expenditure is made for the purpose of influencing legislation (Code Sec. 170(f)(6)). No charitable or business deduction is allowed for contributions made to organizations that conduct lobbying activities relating to matters of direct financial interest to the donor, unless the donor's direct conduct of the activities would have given rise to a business expense deduction (¶ 974) (Code Sec. 170(f)(9)). See ¶ 2073 for payments under leave-based donation programs.

Travel Expenses. Charitable deductions are allowed for transportation or other travel expenses, including meals and lodging, incurred in the performance of services away from home on behalf of a charitable organization if there is no significant element of personal pleasure, recreation, or vacation. If there is a personal element, deductions are denied even though the expenses are paid directly by the individual, indirectly through a contribution to the organization, or by reimbursement by the organization. This rule does not apply to the extent that an individual pays for travel for third parties who are participants in the charitable activity. However, deductions are disallowed where two unrelated taxpayers pay each other's travel expenses or members of a group contribute to a fund that pays for all travel expenses (Code Sec. 170(j)).

Individuals who qualify for a deduction for the use of an automobile during the year may use the statutory standard mileage rate of 14 cents per mile, plus parking fees and tolls, in lieu of a deduction based on the actual expenses incurred. Depreciation and insurance are not includible in the deductible contribution (Code Sec. 170(i)).

Clothing and Household Items. A deduction for a donation of clothing and household items is allowed only if the donated property is in good used condition or better.

¶1061

Household items do not include food, paintings, antiques, other objects of art, jewelry, gems, or collections. The IRS can deny a deduction for donated property that is of minimal value. These restrictions do not apply if: (1) a deduction of more than $500 is claimed for the single clothing or household item, and (2) a qualified appraisal for that item is attached to the return (¶ 1071). For partnerships and S corporations, the restrictions are applied at the entity level, and denial of the deduction is at the partner or shareholder level (Code Sec. 170(f)(16)).

Benefits to Donor. A taxpayer generally must reduce the charitable deduction for the value of any goods, services, or other benefits received in consideration of the contribution (Reg. § 1.170A-1(h); Prop. Reg. § 1.170A-1(h)). This includes any state or local tax (SALT) credit the taxpayer receives or expects to receive. No reduction is required if the SALT credit is 15 percent or less of the contribution. Also, there is no reduction if the taxpayer receives or expects to receive a SALT deduction that does not exceed the contribution. Under a safe harbor, certain individuals may treat the disallowed portion the charitable deduction as the payment of SALT taxes (¶ 1026).

The reduction in a charitable contribution deduction for any goods or services the taxpayer receives or expects to receive does not apply to a business-related payment or transfer. A payment or transfer to or for the use of a Code Sec. 170(c) entity by a business may be deducted as an ordinary and necessary business expense if it bears a direct relationship to the taxpayer's business and is made with a reasonable expectation of financial return (Proposed Reg. § 1.162-15(a); Rev. Proc. 2019-12). The financial return, however, must commensurate with the amount of the payment or transfer to be deductible as a trade or business expenses.

Fund-Raising Activities. An amount paid for a ticket to a charity event such as a ball, bazaar, show, or athletic event is presumed to represent the purchase price for an item of value. The burden is on the taxpayer to show either that the payment is not a purchase or that the payment exceeds the fair market value of the admission or other privileges associated with the event. The purchase price of a raffle ticket is not deductible (Rev. Rul. 83-130; Rev. Proc. 90-12).

> **Example:** Able pays $20 to see a special showing of a motion picture, the net proceeds of which go to a qualified charitable organization. Printed on the ticket is "Contribution—$20." If the regular price for the movie is $9, Able made a contribution of $11 to a qualified charitable organization.

A fund-raising organization that provides token benefits to contributors can advise them that their donations are fully deductible only if the token benefits have an insignificant or insubstantial value. For this purpose

- the fair market value of all benefits received may not exceed the lesser of two percent of the payment or $111 for 2019 ($112 for 2020), or
- the payment is at least $55.50 for 2019 ($56.00 for 2020), the items provided have the organization's name or logo (e.g., calendars, mugs), and the cost of the items is within the limit for low-cost articles $11.10 for 2019 ($11.20 for 2020) (Rev. Proc. 2018-57; Rev. Proc. 2019-44).

If items are mailed to potential donors, the organization can advise that a contribution is fully deductible only if the items are low cost, provided for free, and not distributed at the donor's request or consent. A charity that receives a *quid pro quo contribution* in excess of $75 must provide a statement to the donor describing what portion of the donation represents consideration for goods or services (¶ 627).

For tax years beginning before 2018, 80 percent of a payment to a higher-education institution that would be allowable as a charitable deduction but for the fact that the taxpayer receives the right to purchase tickets for seating at an athletic event in an athletic stadium of the institution is deductible as a charitable contribution. For tax years beginning after 2017, no charitable deduction is allowed for such payments (Code Sec. 170(l)).

Transfers of property to a charitable organization that are directly related to the donor's business and made with a reasonable expectation of financial return equivalent to the value transferred does not qualify for a charitable deduction but may qualify as a trade or business expense (Reg. § 1.170A-1(c)(5)).

10

NONBUSINESS

Donor Advised Funds. The deduction for a contribution made to a donor advised fund (¶ 610) is allowed only if: (1) the fund's sponsoring organization is not a cemetery, war veterans' organization, lodge, or Type III supporting organization that is not a "functionally integrated Type III supporting organization" (¶ 607), and (2) the donor obtains a contemporaneous written acknowledgment from the sponsoring organization that the organization has exclusive legal control over the assets contributed (Code Sec. 170(f)(18)). Distributions from donor advised funds that are for noncharitable purposes are taxable, as are certain transactions between a donor advised fund and its donors, advisors, or related persons.

1062. Charitable Contributions of Appreciated Property. The deduction for the charitable contribution of property is generally equal to the property's fair market value at the time of the contribution, reduced by the amount of gain that would have resulted if the donor had sold the property for its fair market value at the time of the contribution (Code Sec. 170(e); Reg. § § 1.170A-1(c) and 1.170A-4; IRS Pub. 526). The reduction depends on whether the property is ordinary income property, capital gain property, or a combination of both. The charitable contribution does not have to be reduced if, due to the transfer of the contributed property, the donor recognizes income or gain in the same tax year in which the contribution is made. If the taxpayer contributes property with a fair market value that is less than his or her basis, then the deduction is limited to its fair market value.

Ordinary Income Property. Ordinary income property is property that, if sold at its fair market value on the date of contribution, would give rise to ordinary income or short-term capital gain. It includes inventory and stock in trade, artworks and manuscripts created by the donor, letters and memoranda, capital assets held one year or less, and section 306 stock (¶ 739 and ¶ 740). A charitable contribution deduction for ordinary income property is limited to the fair market value of the property less the amount that would be ordinary income.

Capital Gain Property. Capital gain property includes any asset on which long-term capital gain would be realized if the taxpayer sold the asset for fair market value on the date of contribution. A charitable contribution of capital gain property is generally limited to the fair market value of the property on the date of contribution, reduced by the potential long-term gain if:

- the property is contributed to certain private nonoperating foundations (¶ 633), other than qualified appreciated stock (publicly traded stock that would produce long-term capital gain if sold);

- the gift is tangible personal property put to a use that is unrelated to the purpose or function upon which the charitable organization's exemption is based;

- the gift is tangible personal property that has a claimed value of more than $5,000 and is sold, traded, or otherwise disposed of by the qualified organization during the year the contribution was made, and the qualified organization has not made the required certification of exempt use (such as on Form 8282);

- the donation consists of patents, certain copyrights, trademarks, trade names, trade secrets, know-how, certain software, or similar intellectual property or applications or registrations of such property;

- the donation consists of taxidermy property contributed by the individual who prepared, stuffed or mounted the property, or who paid or incurred the cost of preparation, stuffing or mounting; or

- the taxpayer elects to disregard the special 30-percent capital gains limitation in favor of the 50-percent limitation.

A taxpayer who contributes qualified intellectual property to a charitable organization is allowed an additional charitable deduction based on a sliding-scale percentage of net income received (¶ 1062A).

Combination Property. If the donor's sale of the contributed property at fair market value would have produced both ordinary income and capital gain, the charitable contribution is the fair market value reduced by the ordinary income that would have resulted from the sale. The remainder of the fair market value is treated as capital gain property. The types of property to which this computation applies include property subject to depreciation recapture (¶ 1779 and ¶ 1788), farmland expenditures subject to recapture (¶ 1797), and interests in oil, gas, or geothermal property.

Recapture of Charitable Tax Benefits. If a donee organization disposes of "applicable property" within three years of the contribution and does not provide certification regarding the property, the donor is required to recapture as ordinary income for the year of the disposition the difference between the amount of the charitable deduction allowed for the donated property and the donor's basis. Applicable property is appreciated tangible personal property with a claimed value over $5,000, the use of which the donee certifies as related to its exempt function or purpose, and that a deduction greater than the donor's basis is allowed. The certification is a written statement, signed under penalty of perjury by an officer of the donee, that:

- certifies that the property's use was *substantial and related* to the donee's exempt purpose, and describes how the property was used and how such use furthered the exempt purpose, or

- states the donee's intended use of the property at the time of the contribution and certifies that such use became impossible or infeasible to implement.

Food Inventories. Noncorporate and corporate taxpayers are allowed to claim an enhanced deduction for certain donations of food inventories from a trade or business subject to certain limits (¶ 930A).

1062A. Charitable Contributions of Intellectual Property. A taxpayer who contributes qualified intellectual property to a charitable organization is allowed an additional charitable deduction based on a sliding-scale percentage of net income received or accrued by the donee that is allocable to the donated property over a 10-year period (Code Secs. 170(m)). The additional deduction is allowed only to the extent that the total amount calculated using the sliding scale exceeds the deduction amount claimed on the property contribution without regard to the additional amount.

Qualified intellectual property includes patents and other intellectual property (¶ 1062), but does not include property donated to certain private nonoperating foundations (¶ 633). The donor must inform the donee at the time of the contribution of its intent to treat the donation as a qualified intellectual property contribution. A donee that receives or accrues net income from a qualified intellectual property contribution must file Form 8899 and provide a copy to the donor (Code Sec. 6050L(b); Notice 2005-41).

1063. Charitable Contributions of Partial Interests. No charitable deduction is allowed for contributions to charitable organizations of less than the taxpayer's entire interest in the property except for:

- a contribution of an undivided portion of a taxpayer's entire interest in property (e.g., a one-fourth interest in property);

- a contribution of a remainder interest in a personal residence or farm;

- a qualified conservation contribution; or

- a charitable deduction that would have been allowed had the interest been transferred in trust (¶ 538 and ¶ 1070) (Code Sec. 170(f)(3); Reg. § 1.170A-7).

Fractional Interest in Tangible Personal Property. No deduction is allowed for a contribution of an undivided portion of a taxpayer's entire interest in tangible personal property unless the interest in the property is held immediately before the contribution by the taxpayer, or the taxpayer and the donee. If the taxpayer makes an additional contribution later, then the charitable deduction is equal to the lesser of the fair market value of the property used to determine the deduction for the initial fractional contribution or the fair market value of the property at the time of the additional contribution.

The deduction is recaptured if, on or before the earlier of the 10th anniversary of the initial fractional contribution or the donor's date of death, either: (1) the donor fails to contribute the remaining interests to the donee, or (2) the donee fails to take substantial physical possession of the property and use it in a manner related to its exempt purpose. The recaptured amount will be subject to interest and a 10-percent additional tax (Code Sec. 170(o)). See ¶ 1069 for charitable contributions of future interests in tangible personal property.

Qualified Conservation Contributions (QCC). A QCC is a contribution of a qualified real property interest to a qualified organization exclusively for conservation purposes that are protected in perpetuity. Qualified real property includes a donor's entire interest in real property other than an interest in subsurface oil, gas, or other minerals, and the right to access to such minerals, a remainder interest, and a restriction granted in perpetuity on the property's use (i.e., an easement).

A qualified organization includes certain governmental units, public charities that meet certain public support tests, and certain supporting organizations. A qualified conservation purpose includes:

- preserving land for public outdoor recreation or education;

- protecting a relatively natural habitat of fish, wildlife, or plants;

- preserving open space for the public's scenic enjoyment or under a governmental conservation policy that will yield significant public benefit; and

- preserving an historically important land area or certified historic structure (Code Sec. 170(h); Reg. § 1.170A-14).

The deduction for a QCC is reduced by an amount equal to the contribution's fair market value multiplied by a fraction: the sum of the rehabilitation credits (¶ 1465B) allowed to the taxpayer for the five preceding tax years on any building that is part of the donation, over the building's fair market value on the contribution date (Code Sec. 170(f)(14)).

Facade Easements. A facade easement may qualify as a QCC. There are several requirements for contributions of facade easements regarding buildings located in registered historic districts and certified as being of historic significance. The easement must preserve the building's entire exterior and prohibit any change that is inconsistent with the exterior's historical character. Both the donor and donee must certify in writing that the donee: (1) is a qualified organization whose purpose is environmental protection, land conservation, or open space or historic preservation, and (2) has the resources and a commitment to manage and enforce the restriction. The donor's return must include a qualified appraisal of the property interest (¶ 1071), photographs of the building's entire exterior, and a description of all restrictions on the building's development (Code Sec. 170(h)(4)(B)). Taxpayers who seek deductions over $10,000 for such contributions must submit a statutory $500 filing fee with their return (Code Sec. 170(f)(13)).

1064. Charitable Contribution for Care of Unrelated Student. A charitable contribution deduction may be claimed for unreimbursed amounts spent to maintain a full-time elementary or high school student who is *not* a dependent or relative in the taxpayer's home (Code Sec. 170(g); Reg. § 1.170A-2). The student must be a member of the taxpayer's household under a written agreement with a program sponsored by a charitable organization providing educational opportunities. The deduction is limited to actual expenditures, up to $50 per month, while the student is a member of the taxpayer's household. A dependent's status (¶ 137) for this purpose is determined without regard to whether he or she claims a dependent, files a joint return, or has gross income in excess of a threshold amount for the year.

1065. Reduction of Charitable Contribution for Interest. The amount of a taxpayer's charitable contribution (¶ 1058) must be reduced by the amount of interest the taxpayer has paid or will pay attributable to a donated liability-encumbering property that the donee or any other person assumes and that is attributable to a period after the contribution is made (Code Sec. 170(f)(5); Reg. § 1.170A-3). If the gift is a bond, note, or other evidence of debt, the amount of the contribution is further reduced by the interest that is paid or to be paid by the taxpayer-donor on debt incurred or continued to purchase or carry such bond that is attributable to any period prior to the contribution.

1069. Charitable Contribution of Future Interests in Tangible Personal Property. A charitable contribution of a future interest in tangible personal property may be deducted only after all intervening interests and rights to actual possession of the property have expired or are held by persons other than a taxpayer, related persons, or related organizations (Code Sec. 170(a)(3); Reg. § 1.170A-5). This rule applies whether the property is contributed in trust or outright. The amount deductible is the value of the property at the time the contribution is considered made, but reduced by limitations that apply to appreciated property (¶ 1062). See also ¶ 1063 for charitable contributions of fractional interests in tangible personal property. Future interests include reversions, remainders, and other interests or estates, whether vested or contingent, that commence in use, possession or enjoyment at some future date or time.

1070. Charitable Contributions in Trust. No charitable deduction is allowed for the value of a contribution in trust of any interest in property that is less than the taxpayer's entire interest in the property (¶ 1063) unless the trust is a pooled income fund (¶ 593), charitable remainder annuity trust, or charitable remainder unitrust (¶ 590) (Code Sec. 170(f)(2); Reg. § 1.170A-6). If the donor gives *all* the interests in a trust to charity, a deduction is allowable.

1070A. Recordkeeping and Substantiation for Charitable Contributions. A taxpayer who claims a charitable contribution deduction (¶ 927 and ¶ 1058) must maintain records to substantiate that the contributions were actually made in the amounts claimed on the tax return.

Cash Donations. No deduction is allowed for contributions of cash, checks, or other monetary gifts, *regardless of the amount*, unless the donor maintains either: (1) a bank record, including a cancelled check, a bank or credit union statement, or a credit card statement; or (2) written communication (including email) from the donee, indicating the donee's name, the contribution date, and amount of the contribution (Code Sec. 170(f)(17); Reg. §§ 1.170A-13(a) and 1.170A-15; IRS Pub. 526).

Payroll Deductions. If a charitable contribution is made by payroll deduction, the donation must be substantiated by a pay stub, Form W-2, or other employer-furnished document that shows the date and amount of the contribution. The donor must also have a pledge card or other document prepared by or for the donee organization that shows the donee's name. For contributions of $250 or more from a single paycheck, the pledge card or other document must also include a statement that the donee does not provide goods or services in consideration for any contributions made to it by payroll deduction. The deduction from each paycheck is a separate charitable contribution for substantiation purposes.

Distributing Organizations. If a charitable contribution of cash is made to an organization that distributes the amount received to a public charity, the distributing organization is treated as the donee for purposes of the substantiation purposes if the distributing organization is itself a charitable organization. Similarly, for contributions through the Combined Federal Campaign (CFC) (e.g., the United Way Campaign), the CFC is treated as the donee.

Noncash Donations of Less than $250. If a taxpayer claims a charitable deduction of less than $250 for a noncash donation, he or she generally must maintain a receipt from the donee indicating the donee's name and address, the date and location of the donation, and a detailed description of the property in reasonably sufficient detail to identify the particular property contributed (Reg. §§ 1.170A-13(b) and Reg. § 1.170A-16(a)). The value of the property is not required, but the fair market value is a factor taken into account in determining the amount of detail to be included on the receipt. For contributions of securities, the receipt must also include the name of the issuer, the type of security, and whether the securities are publicly traded. If it would be impracticable to obtain a receipt, the donor must maintain reliable written records regarding each item contributed.

Contributions of $250 or More. Charitable contributions of $250 or more of cash or property must be substantiated by a taxpayer with a contemporaneous written acknowledgment received from the donee organization (Code Sec. 170(f)(8); Reg. §§ 1.170A-13(f), 1.170A-15(a)(2), and 1.170A-16(b)). The acknowledgment must include:

- the amount of cash and a description of any property contributed;

- a description and good-faith estimate of the value of any goods or services with more than insubstantial value received in exchange for the contributions; and

- if a donee provides intangible religious benefits, a statement that it provides such benefits.

A taxpayer who makes more than one contribution of $250 or more to a donee organization in a tax year may substantiate the contributions with one or more contemporaneous written acknowledgments. The requirement does not apply to payments if the value of the actual donation is less than $250. Separate contributions of less than $250 each are not aggregated to determine whether a donor has reached the $250 threshold in a tax year. A donee organization that receives more than one $250 contribution from a donor in a tax year may use a single written acknowledgment to substantiate the multiple contributions.

Noncash Donations of More than $500. If a taxpayer claims a charitable deduction of more than $500 for a noncash donation, the taxpayer must satisfy the general contemporaneous written acknowledgment requirement for contributions of $250 or more described above. In addition, the taxpayer must include with his or her return for the tax year of the contribution a written description of the donated property in Section A of Form 8283 (Code Sec. 170(f)(11); Reg. §§ 1.170A-13(b) and 1.170A-16(c)). This requirement does not apply to a personal service corporation or closely-held C corporation. All noncash charitable contributions of more than $5,000 also must meet the appraisal requirements (¶ 1071).

If either of these additional documentation requirements are not met, the charitable contribution deduction will be denied unless the failure is due to reasonable cause and not willful neglect. The taxpayer must also maintain written records that include:

- how the taxpayer acquired by the property (for example, by purchase, gift, bequest, inheritance, or exchange);

- the approximate date the taxpayer received the property, or if created, produced, or manufactured by or for the taxpayer, the approximate date the property was substantially completed; and

- the taxpayer's adjusted basis of the donated property, other than publicly traded securities (Reg. § 1.170A-13(b)(3); IRS Pub. 526).

Donations of Clothing or Household Items. Donations of clothing or household items that are *not* in good used condition or better are allowed only if a deduction of more than $500 is claimed for a single item and a qualified appraisal (¶ 1071) for that item is attached to the taxpayer's return (IRS Pub. 526).

Vehicle Donations. A taxpayer donating a car, truck, boat, or aircraft with a claimed fair market value of more than $500 must obtain from the charity and attach to his or her return either a Form 1098-C or a similar contemporaneous written acknowledgment of the contribution (Code Sec. 170(f)(12); Notice 2005-44; Notice 2006-1; IRS Pub. 4303). The acknowledgment must identify the donor taxpayer, list the taxpayer's and the qualified vehicle's identification number, and include a description and good faith estimate of the value of any goods or services provided by the charity in exchange for the vehicle. If the goods or services consist solely of intangible religious benefits, the acknowledgment must say so.

If the charity sells the vehicle without significant intervening use or material improvement, the acknowledgment must also certify that the vehicle was sold in an arm's-length transaction between unrelated parties, list the gross proceeds, and state that the deduction may not exceed the gross proceeds. If the charity retains the vehicle for its significant use or makes a material improvement, the acknowledgment must certify the use or improvement, the time frame the charity will use the vehicle, and that the vehicle will not be transferred before the use or improvement is completed. The taxpayer is then allowed to claim the fair market value of the vehicle as a charitable donation.

If the charity sells the vehicle to a needy individual at a price significantly below fair market value, or gratuitously transfers the vehicle, the taxpayer can claim the donated vehicle's fair market value only if the sale or transfer directly furthers the charity's purpose. However, if a charity sells the vehicle at auction, the IRS will not accept as substantiation an acknowledgment stating that the vehicle is to be transferred to a needy individual for significantly below fair market value. In that case, the donor taxpayer may claim a deduction greater than $500, but only to the extent that the gross sale proceeds

¶ 1070A

exceed that amount and the donor substantiates the contribution with an acknowledgment listing the gross proceeds (Notice 2007-70).

Qualified Conservation Contributions (QCCs). Documentation and certification requirements must be met for certain QCCs of facade easements (¶ 1063).

1071. Appraisals for Charitable Contributions. A taxpayer may not claim a charitable deduction for a noncash contribution of over $5,000 unless the taxpayer obtains a qualified written appraisal of the donated property. An exception exists if the failure is due to reasonable cause and not willful neglect (Code Sec. 170(f)(11); Reg. §§ 1.170A-13(c) and Reg. § 1.170A-17). The taxpayer generally must attach an appraisal summary made in Section B of Form 8283, not the appraisal itself, to the income tax return on which the deduction is first claimed or reported. The appraisal summary must be signed and dated by the donee and the qualified appraiser who prepared it. The taxpayer must maintain records regarding the cost basis and acquisition date of the contributed property. If the contribution is more than $500,000, then the qualified appraisal must be attached to the return when filed.

A separate appraisal and Form 8283 is required for each item of contributed property. However, if the taxpayer contributes similar items of property (e.g., coins, stamps, books, lithographs, or photographs) during the year to the same donee that total more than $5,000, then only one Form 8283 need be filed. If the donor is a partnership or S corporation, it must obtain the qualified appraisal and provide a copy of the appraisal summary to each partner or shareholder who receives an allocation of the charitable contribution deduction with respect to the property described in the summary. The partner or shareholder must attach a copy of the appraisal summary to the tax return on which the charitable contribution is first claimed.

The appraisal rules apply in addition to the substantiation and disclosure requirements of any contribution exceeding $250 (¶ 1070A). They do not apply to donations of cash, publicly traded securities, patents and other intellectual property (¶ 1062), inventory or stock in trade (¶ 1741), or a qualified vehicle sold by the donee organization without any significant intervening use or material improvement. In the case of nonpublicly traded stock with a claimed value between $5,000 and $10,000, only the appraisal summary on Form 8283 is required.

Qualified Appraisal. A qualified appraisal is an appraisal conducted by a qualified appraiser under generally-accepted appraisal standards. It must relate to an appraisal made no earlier than 60 days before the contribution of the appraised property. The qualified appraisal must be prepared, signed, and dated by the qualified appraiser, and it may not involve fees based on the assessed value of the property. The appraisal fees incurred by an individual in determining the fair market value of donated property are not treated as part of the charitable contribution. For tax years beginning before 2018 and after 2025, appraisal fees may be claimed by an individual as a miscellaneous itemized deduction subject to the two-percent-of-adjusted-gross-income (AGI) limitation (¶ 1079).

Qualified Appraiser. A qualified appraiser is an individual who has earned an appraisal designation from a recognized professional appraiser organization or has otherwise met minimum education and experience requirements, regularly performs appraisals for compensation, and meets certain other requirements. The qualified appraiser must have verifiable education and experience in valuing the type of property for which the appraisal is performed and must either hold himself or herself out to the public as an appraiser or perform appraisals on a regular basis.

Accuracy-Related Penalties. Appraisers are subject to civil penalties for certain appraisals that result in substantial or gross valuation misstatements (Code Sec. 6695A).

Moving Expenses

See CCH® AnswerConnect: *Moving Expenses* for more information on this topic.

1073. Moving Expense Deduction. For tax years beginning before 2018 and after 2025, an employee or self-employed individual may claim a deduction for moving expenses if related to starting work at a new location (Code Secs. 62(a)(15) and 217). The taxpayer generally must meet requirements for distance and time. The deduction is computed on Form 3903. For tax years beginning before 2018 and after 2025, an employee may also exclude any qualified moving expense reimbursement from gross income and wages as a fringe benefit (¶ 2092). Special rules apply to an Armed Forces member for all tax years (¶ 1075).

Moving Expenses. Deductible moving expenses are the reasonable cost of transportation and temporary storage of household goods and personal effects, as well as travel to the new residence including lodging but not meals. If an automobile is used, the taxpayer may deduct actual out-of-pocket expenses incurred or a standard mileage allowance, plus parking fees and tolls. The standard mileage rate for moving expenses of Armed Forces members is 20 cents per mile for 2019 and 17 cents per miles for 2020 (Rev. Proc. 2019-46; Rev. Proc. 2010-51; Notice 2019-2; Notice 2020-5).

The deduction may also be claimed for moving and storage expenses for the commencement of work outside the United States. An individual who retires from an overseas job may deduct moving expenses incurred in returning to the United States. A surviving spouse or dependent who shared the residence of a decedent who worked outside the United States at the time of death may also deduct moving expenses incurred in returning to the United States within six months after the death.

Distance Test. The taxpayer's new principal place of work must be at least 50 miles farther from his or her old residence than the old residence was from the taxpayer's old place of work. If there was no old place of work, the new place of work must be at least 50 miles from the old residence.

Time Test. During the 12-month period immediately following the move, the taxpayer must work full time for at least 39 weeks. A self-employed taxpayer must work full time for at least 78 weeks of the 24-month period immediately following the move and at least 39 weeks during the first 12 months. The work requirement is waived due to death, disability, involuntary separation other than for willful misconduct, or transfer to another location for the benefit of the employer. A taxpayer may deduct moving expenses even if the work requirement has not been satisfied by the due date for the return including extensions for the tax year in which the moving expenses were incurred and paid. If the taxpayer fails the work requirement, then he or she must file an amended return or include the amount previously deducted as gross income on the following year's return.

Commencement of Work. The move generally must be in connection with the commencement of work at the new location and the moving expenses must be incurred within one year from when the taxpayer reports to the new job or business. If the move is not made within one year, the expenses are not deductible unless circumstances prevented the taxpayer from incurring them within one year.

1075. Moving Expenses of Members of Armed Forces. A member of the Armed Forces on active duty may claim a deduction in any tax year for unreimbursed moving and storage expenses (¶ 1073) incurred due to a military order and a permanent change of station (Code Sec. 217(g); Reg. § 1.217-2(g); IRS Pub. 521). A permanent change of station includes a move within one year of retirement or other termination of active duty. The deduction is computed on Form 3903 and reported on Form 1040 as an adjustment to gross income (AGI).

Any reimbursement or in-kind benefit provided by the government is excluded from gross income to the extent of the taxpayer's actual moving expenses. If the Armed Forces member and family move to or from separate locations, the moves are treated as a single move. If any reimbursement exceeds actual expenses, the excess is included in the taxpayer's wages on Form W-2 except for certain dislocation and temporary lodging allowances. If any reimbursement is less than the actual expenses, then the unreimbursed expenses may be claimed as a deduction. A member of the Armed Forces is not subject to the time and distance requirements applicable for tax years beginning before 2018 and after 2025.

Spouse and Dependents. If the Armed Forces member dies, deserts, or is imprisoned, a permanent change of station for a spouse and dependents includes a move to the place of enlistment, to the member's home, to the spouse's home, to the dependent's home, or to any closer point in the United States.

Miscellaneous Deductions

See CCH® AnswerConnect: *Itemized Deductions* for more information on this topic.

1079. Miscellaneous Itemized Deductions Subject to 2% AGI Limit. For tax years beginning before 2018 and after 2025, an individual, estate, or trust may claim certain miscellaneous itemized deductions only to the extent that the aggregate amount exceeds two percent of the taxpayer's adjusted gross income (AGI) (Code Sec. 67; Reg. § 1.67-1T). None of the miscellaneous itemized deductions subject to the two-percent-AGI limit may be claimed in tax years 2018 through 2025. A few miscellaneous itemized deductions are not subject to the two-percent-AGI-limit and may be claimed in all tax years (¶ 1095). An individual claims miscellaneous itemized deductions on Schedule A (Form 1040).

The two-percent-of-AGI limit is applied after other deduction limits such as the limit on meals and entertainment expenses (¶ 916). It is also applied to deductions passed through to the taxpayer by a partnership, S corporation, or other pass-through entity other than an estate or trust (¶ 528) (Code Sec. 67(c); Temp. Reg. § 1.67-2T). Miscellaneous itemized deductions subject to the two-percent-of-AGI limit are generally: (1) unreimbursed employee business expenses reported on Form 2106 (¶ 941), and (2) other expenses incurred for the production or collection of income, or the preparation of taxes (¶ 1085). They include the following expenses (IRS Pub. 529 (2017)).

Job Search Expenses. An individual may deduct expenses before 2018 and after 2025 looking for a new job in his or her present occupation, even if the search is unsuccessful. Deductible expenses include (1) typing, printing, and mailing of resumes, (2) employment or outplacement agency fees, and (3) travel and transportation expenses if primarily related to seeking new employment. Job-hunting expenses are not deductible if the individual is seeking his or her first job, a job in a new occupation, or there is a substantial break since the end of his or her last job.

Uniforms and Work-Clothes. An individual may deduct the unreimbursed cost and upkeep of a uniform or work clothes if they are required as a condition of employment and they are not adaptable to general wear (e.g., protective clothing, special work shoes and gloves, and shop caps) (IRS Pub. 529 (2017)). An Armed Forces member on full-time active duty may not deduct the cost of uniforms, but Armed Forces reservists may deduct the unreimbursed cost, less nontaxable uniform allowance, of a uniform required at drills or other functions if they are prohibited from wearing it for regular use (Reg. § 1.262-1(b)(8)).

Union Dues and Expenses. Dues, initiation fees, and out-of-work-benefit assessments for a union member are deductible. Any payment, assessment, or contribution that provides funds for payment of sickness, accident, or death benefits, or contributions to a pension plan, are not deductible even if the union requires the taxpayer to contribute (Reg. § 1.162-15(c)). A self-employed individual may deduct union dues as a business expense (¶ 1006).

Work-Related Education. An employee may deduct education expenses as an unreimbursed business expense if it (1) maintains or improves skills required in the taxpayer's trade or business, or (2) is required by an employer or the law to keep his or her current job (¶ 1082).

Other Expenses. Unreimbursed employee expenses may also include: dues for professional memberships or societies; home office expenses (¶ 961); legal fees related to employment; liability or malpractice insurance; licenses or regulatory fees; occupational taxes; travel expenses; subscriptions to professional journals or trade magazines; and tools and supplies.

1082. Work-Related Education Expenses. A self-employed individual, as well as an employee for tax years beginning before 2018 and after 2025, may deduct his or her education expenses as a business expense, even if the education leads to a degree, if the education either:

> • maintains or improves skills *required* in the taxpayer's employment or other trade or business, including refresher courses, current developments courses, or academic or vocational courses; or

¶1082

- meets the express *requirements* of the taxpayer's employer, or laws or regulations, *imposed* for a bona fide business purpose of the employer and as a condition to the taxpayer's retention of an established employment relationship, status, or rate of compensation (Reg. § 1.162-5; IRS Pub. 970).

Education in excess of the minimum requirement may qualify as education undertaken to maintain or improve the required skills.

Educational expenses that are personal or constitute an inseparable aggregate of personal and capital expenditures are not deductible, even though they may maintain or improve a skill or meet the express requirements of the employer or under law. Nondeductible capital or personal education expenses are those that: (1) are required of the taxpayer in order to meet the minimum educational requirements for qualification in the taxpayer's present employment, trade, or business, or (2) qualify the taxpayer for a new trade or business.

The minimum education necessary to qualify for a position or other trade or business is determined from a consideration of such factors as requirements of the employer, laws or regulations, and the standards of the profession, trade, or business involved. The fact that an individual is already performing service in an employment status does not mean he or she has met the minimum educational requirements. However, once an individual has met the minimum requirements in effect when he or she enters the employment, profession, or trade or business, the individual is treated as continuing to meet those requirements even though they have changed. For these individuals, expenses for meeting the new requirements would be deductible.

A change of duties is not a new trade or business if the new duties and the taxpayer's present employment involve the same general work. For example, there is no new trade or business if a teacher moves from an elementary to a secondary school, from one subject to another, or from a teaching position to a principal's position.

Reporting Requirements. A self-employed individual deducts work-related education expenses from total business income on his or her Schedule C (Form 1040). For tax years beginning before 2018 and after 2025, an employee can deduct work-related education expenses as a miscellaneous itemized deduction on Schedule A (Form 1040) subject to the two-percent of adjusted gross income (AGI) limitation (¶ 1079). The deduction may be claimed only for unreimbursed expenses calculated on Form 2106 (¶ 942). The amount reported on Schedule A must be reduced by the amount of any tuition or fees deduction claimed (¶ 1011A). No work-related education expenses may be claimed as a miscellaneous deduction by an employee in tax years 2018 through 2025.

Travel as a Form of Education. No deduction is allowed for travel as a form of education (Code Sec. 274(m)(2)). Travel in pursuit of an education may be deductible if the educational expense itself is deductible as a business expense.

1085. Expenses for the Production of Income. For tax years beginning before 2018 and after 2025, an individual, estate, or trust may claim a miscellaneous itemized deduction for ordinary and necessary expenses paid or incurred for: (1) the production or collection of income; (2) the management, conservation, or maintenance of property held for the production of income; or (3) the determination, collection, or refund of any tax (Code Sec. 212; Reg. § 1.212-1; IRS Pub. 529 (2017)). The deduction is subject to the two-percent-of-adjusted-gross-income (AGI) limit (¶ 1079), but a taxpayer may not claim the deduction for tax years beginning in 2018 through 2025. Expenses attributable to property held for rents or royalties are deductible as an adjustment to gross income in any tax year (¶ 1006A).

Expenses are deductible only if they are related to the production of income, management of investments, and tax preparation and reasonable in amount. Examples include appraisal fees, casualty and theft losses incurred as an employee, clerical help and office rent, custodial or trust fees, repayments of income, hobby expenses (¶ 1195), legal fees (¶ 1093), investment fees and expenses, loss on deposits or IRAs, repayments of income, safe deposit box rental, and tax advice. No deduction is allowed for any expense allocable to tax-exempt income (¶ 970). If the taxpayer holds an interest in a partnership, S corporation, or nonpublicly offered mutual fund, then he or she can deduct their share of the entity's pass-through deduction of investment expenses.

Expenditures incurred for the acquisition or disposition of investment property generally must be capitalized but a taxpayer may elect a *de minimis* safe harbor not to capitalize the expenses (¶ 1305). Investment interest is deductible only to the extent of amount of net investment income (¶ 1057). A dealer or trader in securities is *not* an investor and may deduct investment expenses as business expenses, subject to the uniform capitalization (UNICAP) rules (¶ 1330) (*F.R. Mayer*, FedCl, 94-2 USTC ¶ 50,509). In addition, expenses attributable to property held for rents or royalties are deductible as an adjustment to gross income and are not subject to the two-percent of AGI floor (¶ 1006A).

Tax Preparation Fees. All ordinary and necessary expenses paid or incurred in connection with the determination, collection, or refund of any tax may be claimed as a miscellaneous itemized deduction before 2018 and after 2025. This includes any fees for tax prep software or electronic filing of returns, as well as legal or appraisal expenses (Code Sec. 212(3); Reg. § 1.212-1(l)). This applies to any income, estate, gift, property, or other tax imposed at the federal, state, or local level. Tax prep expenses attributable to a trade or business, rentals or royalties, or farm income and expenses may be deducted in any tax year on the appropriate schedule regardless of the taxpayer's AGI.

Life Tenant or Income Beneficiary. In the case of business or investment property held by a life tenant, the deduction for depreciation or depletion is allowed to the life tenant and is computed as if the life tenant were the absolute owner of the property (Reg. § § 1.167(h)-1 and 1.611-1(c)). In the case of investment property held by a life tenant, the deduction is claimed in tax years beginning before 2018 and after 2025 as a miscellaneous itemized deduction. After the life tenant's death, the deduction, if any, is allowed to the remainderman. The deduction is apportioned for property held in trust or by an estate (¶ 530).

Guardian Expenses. A deduction is permitted for a reasonable amount paid or incurred for the services of a guardian or committee for a ward or minor and for other ordinary and necessary expenses incurred in connection with the production or collection of income inuring to the ward or minor, or in connection with the management, conservation, or maintenance of income-producing property belonging to the ward or minor (Reg. § 1.212-1(j)). Expenses of a competency proceeding are deductible if the purpose of the proceeding is the management and conservation of income-producing property owned by the taxpayer.

1093. Nonbusiness Legal Expenses. For tax years beginning before 2018 and after 2025, an individual, estate, or trust may claim a miscellaneous itemized deduction for nonbusiness legal expenses (Code Sec. 212; Reg. § 1.212-1; IRS Pub. 529 (2017)). The deduction is subject to the two-percent-of-adjusted-gross-income (AGI) limit (¶ 1079), but a taxpayer may not claim the deduction for tax years beginning in 2018 through 2025 except that legal expenses related to certain discrimination, credit, and whistleblower claims, are deductible as an adjustment to gross income in any tax year.

Discrimination and Credit Claims. An individual can claim as a deduction in calculating adjusted gross income (AGI) for attorney's fees and court costs incurred in connection with an action involving: (1) a claim of unlawful discrimination; (2) certain claims against the federal government; or (3) a private cause of action under the Medicare Secondary Payer statute (Code Sec. 62(a)(20)). The deduction is limited to the amount includible in gross income on account of a judgment or settlement, whether as a lump sum or in periodic payments. The deduction is claimed as an adjustment to gross income on Schedule 1 (Form 1040) (Instructions to Form 1040).

Whistleblower Awards. An above-the-line deduction is also allowed for attorney's fees and court costs paid by or on behalf of the taxpayer in connection with any whistleblower award under Code Sec. 7623(b) for providing information regarding tax law violations, as well as under the SEC whistleblower program, Commodity Futures Trading Commission whistleblower program, and state false claims acts (Code Sec. 62(a)(21)). The deduction cannot exceed the amount includible in gross income as a result of the award. The deduction is claimed as an adjustment to gross income on Schedule 1 (Form 1040) (Instruction to Form 1040).

Expenses Paid Before 2018 and After 2025. Nonlegal business expenses may be claimed as a miscellaneous itemized deduction for tax years beginning before 2018 and after 2025 if paid or incurred for the production of income or for the management, conservation, or maintenance of income-producing property (¶ 1185). Legal expenses incurred in defending or perfecting title to property, in the acquisition or disposition of property, or in developing or improving property are *not* deductible and must be capitalized. Legal expenses paid or incurred in recovering investment property and amounts of income includible in gross income are generally deductible, but legal expenses incurred in recovering stock may be deductible only to the extent that they were allocable to the recovery of interest and dividends (*J.K. Nickell*, CA-6, 87-2 USTC ¶ 9585).

Legal expenses paid by one spouse in resisting the other's monetary demands in connection with a divorce, separation, or support decree are generally nondeductible personal expenses (¶ 1001). Legal expenses properly attributable to producing or collecting alimony under a divorce decree, separation agreement, or support decree may be deductible as a miscellaneous itemized deduction (Reg. § 1.262-1(b)(7)).

1095. Miscellaneous Deductions Not Subject to 2% AGI Limit. An individual, estate, or trust may claim certain miscellaneous itemized deductions without regard to the two-percent-of-adjusted-gross-income (AGI) limit (Code Sec. 67(b); Reg. § 1.67-1T; Notice 2018-61). An estate or trust may also claim certain deductions for administration expenses, personal exemption amount, and any beneficiary distribution in calculating AGI (¶ 528). No other miscellaneous itemized deductions may be claimed in 2018 through 2025. For tax years beginning before 2018 and after 2026, certain miscellaneous itemized deductions may only be claimed to the extent of they exceed two percent of the taxpayer's AGI (¶ 1079).

Itemized deductions *not* subject to the two-percent-of-AGI limitation include those which are permitted by other Code provisions, including the deductions for medical and dental expenses (¶ 1015), taxes (¶ 1021), interest (¶ 1043), charitable contributions (¶ 1058), and casualty and theft losses (¶ 1121 and ¶ 1123). Other miscellaneous itemized deductions *not* subject to the two-percent-of-AGI limit include:

- amortizable bond premiums (¶ 1967);

- deductions by tenant-stockholder of cooperative housing corporation (¶ 1040);

- deductions allowable in connection with personal property used in a short sale (¶ 1944);

- federal estate tax on income in respect of a decedent (¶ 186);

- gambling losses to the extent of gambling winnings (¶ 1113);

- impairment-related work expenses;

- losses from Ponzi-type investment schemes;

- repayments of more than $3,000 held under claim of right (¶ 1543); and

- unrecovered investment in an annuity (¶ 817).

Impairment-related work expenses are ordinary and necessary business expenses incurred by a handicapped worker for attendant care services at the worker's place of employment, or for other expenses in connection with the worker's place of employment that are necessary for the individual to be able to work. Handicapped persons include individuals who have a physical or mental disability, including blindness or deafness that limits employment, or a physical or mental impairment, including sight or hearing impairment, that substantially limits one or more major life activities (Code Sec. 67(d); IRS Pub. 529). A taxpayer who claims the deduction for impairment-related work expenses must file Form 2106 with his or her tax return. A self-employed individual claims the deduction on Schedule C (Form 1040).

¶1095

Chapter 11
LOSSES □ PASSIVE ACTIVITY LOSSES

Deduction of Losses

See CCH® AnswerConnect: *What is a Loss* and *Nonbusiness Casualty and Theft Losses* for more information on this topic.

1101. Deductible Losses. A taxpayer may generally deduct losses that have not been compensated for by insurance or otherwise (Code Sec. 165(a); Reg. § 1.165-1). In order to be deductible, a loss generally must be evidenced by a closed and completed transaction and fixed by an identifiable event during the tax year, such as a sale, foreclosure, or condemnation. However, any loss arising from theft is treated as sustained during the tax year in which the taxpayer discovers the loss (¶ 1123). In addition, a special election exists for determining the year to deduct a loss attributable to a federally declared disaster (¶ 1133). Only a bona fide loss sustained by the taxpayer may be deducted, and the substance of a transaction, not its form, governs whether there is a deductible loss. Thus, a loss deduction may be disallowed for a transaction that lacks economic substance and is entered into solely for tax benefits.

No portion of a loss may be deducted if there is a reasonable prospect of recovery or reimbursement. Similarly, no deduction is generally allowed for a partial loss resulting from the decline in the value of property, except as reflected in inventory. An exception is provided for the deduction of an addition to a bad debt reserve and a charge-off of part of a debt that is worthless (¶ 1137). A taxpayer may also claim a deduction for losses sustained from the abandonment of property (¶ 1109).

Losses realized by an individual may be deducted only if they are: (1) losses incurred in a trade or business; (2) losses incurred in a transaction entered into for profit; or (3) casualty and theft losses (limited in tax years 2018 through 2025 to losses attributable to federally declared disasters) (Code Sec. 165; Reg. § 1.165-1(e)). Thus, an individual's personal losses that are not related to a business or profit-making activity may not be deducted unless they are the result of a casualty (¶ 1121) or theft (¶ 1123). In addition, an individual's loss deductions are limited by the at-risk rules (¶ 1155), passive activity loss rules (¶ 1165), and related-party rules (¶ 1717). Losses from gambling or other wagering transactions are also allowed only to the extent of gains from those transactions (¶ 1113). An individual, estate, trust, S corporation, and partnership may deduct expenses attributable to activities not engaged in for profit only to the extent of the amount of gross income from the activity under the hobby loss rules (¶ 1195). Excess business losses of a noncorporate taxpayer are not allowed for tax years beginning in 2021 through 2025 (¶ 1190).

Amount of Loss. The amount deducted for a loss cannot exceed the taxpayer's adjusted basis in the property (Code Sec. 165(b); Reg. § 1.165-1(c)). The basis of the property must be adjusted for expenses, receipts, or losses properly chargeable to a capital account, and for depreciation, obsolescence, amortization, and depletion to determine the amount of loss allowable as a deduction (¶ 1604). Adjustments must also

¶1101

be made for any salvage value, as well as any insurance or other compensation received by the taxpayer.

The amount or character of a loss may be limited by a number of other rules. For example, a taxpayer may deduct capital losses only to the extent allowed under the capital loss limitation rules (¶ 1752) (Code Sec. 165(f); Reg. § 1.165-1(c)(3)). A worthless nonbusiness bad debt is only deductible as a short-term capital loss (¶ 1143). Special rules also apply for losses on small business stock (¶ 1911), losses on worthless securities (¶ 1916), losses on wash sales of securities (¶ 1935), and losses on debt obligations required to be in registered form (¶ 1963).

1103. Loss on Sale of Residential Property. An individual may not deduct a loss realized from a sale or exchange of the taxpayer's personal residence. However, a loss on the sale or exchange of residential property realized at the time it is being rented or otherwise used for income-producing purposes is deductible (Reg. § 1.165-9). If the property is used as the taxpayer's personal residence after having been acquired as income-producing property, then a loss realized on its sale or exchange at the time it is being used as a residence is not deductible. See ¶ 1626 for a discussion of the basis of residential or converted property.

1105. Demolition Losses. A taxpayer may not deduct losses sustained in the demolition of buildings and their structural components, including certified historic structures. Any amount expended or loss sustained by an owner or lessee on account of the demolition of any structure must be capitalized as part of the basis of the land on which the structure was located (Code Sec. 280B; Rev. Proc. 95-27). The IRS has provided a safe harbor for certain structural modifications to a building that are not treated as a demolition and thus, not properly chargeable to the capital account with respect to the land on which the building is located. While demolition costs are nondeductible, a taxpayer may claim a loss deduction when depreciable business property is retired from use in a trade or business or from use in production of income (¶ 1109).

1107. Loss on Foreclosure or Tax Sale of Real Property. The foreclosure of a mortgage by a judicial sale and disposition of the encumbered real property is a sale of an asset. If the owner of an equity interest receives less than his or her basis in the property when it is sold upon foreclosure, his or her investment may represent a deductible loss only if the property was used in a trade or business or a transaction entered into for profit (IRS Pub. 4681). The character of the loss—capital loss or ordinary loss—depends on the nature of the property foreclosed upon and whether or not it was a capital asset (¶ 1741) or section 1231 property (¶ 1747).

The loss occurs when the redemption period expires or in the year the property becomes worthless. If there is no equity of redemption, the loss is fixed by the foreclosure sale and not by the decree of foreclosure that ordered the sale (*G. Hammel*, SCt, 41-1 USTC ¶ 9169). These principles also apply to a sale for delinquent taxes (*R.H. McNeill*, CA-4, 58-1 USTC ¶ 9229).

If real property is disposed of by reason of foreclosure or similar proceedings, the amount of depreciation subject to recapture (¶ 1779) is determined as if the taxpayer ceased to hold the property on the date the proceedings began (Code Sec. 1250(d)(7)).

1109. Abandonment and Obsolescence Losses. A taxpayer is allowed a deduction for a loss sustained upon the abandonment of property used in a trade or business, or a transaction entered into for profit. In the case of property depreciated under the Modified Accelerated Cost Recovery System (MACRS) an asset is abandoned if the taxpayer discards it irrevocably so that the taxpayer will neither use the asset again nor retrieve it for sale, exchange, or other disposition. If a MACRS asset that is not subject to nonrecourse indebtedness is disposed of by physical abandonment, loss is recognized in the amount of the adjusted depreciable basis of the asset at the time of the abandonment, taking into account the applicable convention (Reg. § 1.168(i)-8(e)(2)). If only a portion of an MACRS asset is abandoned, a taxpayer generally must make a partial disposition election in order to claim a loss (¶ 1239) (Reg. § 1.168(i)-8(d)). An abandonment of property is not treated as a sale or exchange. Thus, an abandonment loss is an ordinary loss—regardless of whether or not the abandoned asset is a capital asset—and is reported on Form 4797 (IRS Pub. 544).

If nondepreciable property is abandoned following a sudden termination of its usefulness, an obsolescence loss is allowed in an amount equal to its adjusted basis. The obsolescence loss is deductible in the tax year in which it is sustained, even though the overt act of abandonment or the loss of title to the property may not occur in that year (Reg. § 1.165-2).

A taxpayer cannot deduct the costs of acquiring and developing creative property (i.e., screenplays, scripts, story outlines, and similar property for film development or production) as an abandonment loss unless the taxpayer establishes either: (1) an intent to abandon the property and an affirmative act of abandonment, or (2) identifiable event(s) which show a closed and completed transaction establishing the property's worthlessness (Rev. Rul. 2004-58). Mere nonuse of an asset does not constitute abandonment, and the treatment of abandonment losses for financial reporting purposes does not control the federal tax treatment. To minimize accounting disputes, the IRS has provided a safe harbor allowing taxpayers to amortize ratably over a 15-year period any creative property costs that the taxpayer has properly written off under the generally accepted accounting principles (GAAP) for financial reporting purposes (¶ 1229).

1111. Interest Forfeited on Premature Withdrawals. Interest that was previously earned on a time savings account or deposit with a savings institution and that is later forfeited because of premature withdrawals is deductible by an individual in computing adjusted gross income (AGI) in the year when the interest is forfeited (Code Sec. 62(a)(9)). The necessary information is provided on Form 1099-INT. The deduction must be claimed on Form 1040.

1113. Gambling Losses. An individual can deduct gambling losses only to the extent of his or her gambling winnings included in gross income (Code Sec. 165(d); Reg. § 1.165-10). For tax years beginning in 2018 through 2025, gambling losses for this purpose include any deduction otherwise allowed to the taxpayer in carrying on a wagering transaction (e.g., travel expenses). Deductible gambling losses are generally reported by the individual as a miscellaneous itemized deduction *not* subject to the two-percent-of-adjusted-gross-income floor (¶ 1095). A professional gambler reports gambling income and losses on Schedule C (Form 1040). Married individuals who file a joint return can combine their gambling winnings and losses.

Casualty and Theft Losses

See CCH® AnswerConnect: *Business Casualty Losses* and *Nonbusiness Casualty and Theft Losses* for more information on this topic.

1121. Casualty Losses. A taxpayer may deduct losses resulting from damage to or destruction of property (Code Sec. 165(c)(3) and (h)(5)). In the case of nonbusiness property, the deduction is limited to losses arising from fire, storm, shipwreck, or other casualty, or from theft. However, for tax years beginning in 2018 through 2025, the deduction for personal casualty and theft losses is limited only to losses attributable to federally declared disasters. A taxpayer may still claim personal casualty and theft losses not attributable federally declared disasters to the extent of any personal casualty and theft gains during 2018 through 2025.

Each casualty loss is generally subject to a $100 floor (¶ 1129), and net losses from combined personal casualty and theft losses for the tax year generally are deductible only to the extent they exceed 10 percent of the taxpayer's adjusted gross income (AGI) (¶ 1131). An individual cannot claim a personal casualty loss deduction for damage to insured property unless a timely insurance claim is filed (Code Sec. 165(h)(4)(E)). See ¶ 1127 for a discussion of how to determine the amount of the deduction for a casualty loss. Casualty and theft losses are reported on Form 4684. Theft losses are discussed at ¶ 1123.

A casualty loss is generally deductible only for the tax year in which the loss is sustained (¶ 1101) (Reg. § 1.165-7(a)(1)). If the extent of the damage cannot reasonably be ascertained in the year of occurrence, the deduction can be taken in a later year when the extent of the damage is known. A special election also exists for determining the year to deduct a loss attributable to a federally declared disaster (¶ 1133).

Casualty Defined. A casualty is the damage, destruction, or loss of property resulting from an identifiable event due to some sudden, unexpected, or unusual cause (IRS Pub. 547). Examples of casualties include earthquakes, fires (not willfully set), floods, storms, hurricanes, tornadoes, volcanic eruptions, government-ordered demolition or relocation, mine cave-ins, shipwrecks, sonic booms, terrorist attacks, and vandalism. A casualty also includes damage that is a result of any ordinary automobile accident whether the taxpayer, or someone else driving his or her car, is at fault in a collision, or whether the other driver is at fault (Reg. § 1.165-7(a)(3)). If a car accident was caused by the willful act or willful negligence of the taxpayer, or his or her agent, the casualty loss deduction is not allowed.

The damage or loss of property due to progressive deterioration is not considered a casualty and is not deductible (IRS Pub. 547). Examples include the weakening of property due to normal weather conditions, losses caused by drought to property not used in a trade or business or for the production of income unless the drought can be characterized as sudden or unusual, the deterioration and damage to a water heater, and damage to trees or other plants by normal infestations of fungi, disease, worms, or similar pests. The IRS takes the position that a casualty loss deduction for termite damage is not permitted because the suddenness requirement is not met, but some courts have allowed the deduction (IRS Pub. 547; *see M.A. Rosenberg*, CA-8, 52-2 USTC ¶ 9377).

A casualty loss is deductible only to the extent it is not compensated for by insurance or otherwise (¶ 1101). If there is no limitation on the manner in which money or property received as compensation for damaged property must be used, the amount received is a gift and does not reduce the amount of the taxpayer's casualty loss (IRS Pub. 547). If, as the result of insurance or other reimbursement, a taxpayer realizes a gain from a casualty or theft loss, the taxpayer can defer recognition of the gain under the involuntary conversion rules by making an election and purchasing qualifying replacement property within the applicable replacement period (¶ 1715).

A casualty loss incurred with respect to either business or nonbusiness property can result in a net operating loss (NOL) (¶ 1147). The $100 floor and the 10-percent-of-AGI limitation are applied in the nonbusiness situation in determining an NOL.

Concrete Foundations. The IRS has provided a safe harbor for individuals to claim a casualty loss for damages to their personal residence by a deteriorating concrete foundation that contains the mineral pyrrhotite. Taxpayers who have a pending claim for reimbursement, or who intend to pursue reimbursement, may claim a loss for 75 percent of the unreimbursed amounts paid during the tax year to repair the damage. The safe harbor is effective for returns filed after November 21, 2017 (Rev. Proc. 2018-14; Rev. Proc. 2017-60).

1123. Theft Losses. A taxpayer may deduct a loss from the theft of property that is not compensated for by insurance or otherwise. A theft loss is generally deductible for the tax years in which the taxpayer discovers the loss, but no deduction may be claimed if a reimbursement claim exists with respect to which there is a reasonable prospect of recovery (Code Sec. 165(e) and (h)(5); Reg. § 1.165-8(a)). For tax years beginning in 2018 through 2025, the deduction for personal casualty and theft losses is limited only to losses attributable to federally declared disasters. A taxpayer may still claim personal casualty and theft losses not attributable to federally declared disasters to the extent of any personal casualty and theft gains during 2018 through 2025.

Each theft loss is generally subject to a $100 floor (¶ 1129), and net losses from combined personal casualty and theft losses for the tax year generally are deductible only to the extent they exceed 10 percent of the taxpayer's adjusted gross income (AGI) (¶ 1131). An individual cannot claim a personal theft loss deduction for insured property unless a timely insurance claim is filed (Code Sec. 165(h)(4)(E)). See ¶ 1127 for a discussion of how to determine the amount of the deduction for personal theft loss. Casualty and theft losses are reported on Form 4684. Casualty losses are discussed at ¶ 1121.

¶1123

A theft includes the taking of money or property by robbery, larceny, burglary, blackmail, embezzlement, extortion, or kidnapping for ransom. Theft does not include property that was lost or misplaced. It also does not include the decline in value of stock acquired in the open market caused by the disclosure of accounting fraud by officers or directors of the corporation (IRS Pub. 547). The deduction for theft losses is determined in the same way as for other casualty losses (¶ 1127).

Losses from Ponzi-Type Schemes. Investors who incur losses from criminally fraudulent investment arrangements such as "Ponzi" schemes are entitled to claim a theft loss, rather than a capital loss (Rev. Rul. 2009-9). The loss is deductible as a loss on a transaction entered into for profit, and it is not subject to the $100 floor or the 10-percent-of-AGI limitation for personal theft losses, or the limitations on itemized deductions before 2018 (¶ 1014). The theft loss is deductible in the year it is discovered, and the amount of the deduction includes the amount invested in the scheme, less any amounts withdrawn, reimbursements, and claims as to which there is a reasonable prospect of recovery. If the theft loss deduction creates or increases a net operating loss (NOL) in the year the loss is deducted, the taxpayer may carry forward the portion of the NOL attributable to the theft loss (¶ 1149).

The IRS has also provided an optional safe harbor under which a qualified investor may deduct as a theft loss up to 95 percent of a qualified investment if the investor does not pursue any potential third-party recovery, or 75 percent of a qualified investment if the investor is pursuing or intends to pursue any potential third-party recovery. The deduction is reduced by the amount of any actual recovery and any recovery from insurance or the Securities Investor Protection Corporation (Rev. Proc. 2011-58).

1125. Loss on Bank Deposits. An individual may elect to treat the loss on a nonbusiness account in an insolvent or bankrupt financial institution as a personal casualty loss in the year in which the loss can reasonably be estimated (Code Sec. 165(l) and (h)(5)). The election is made on Form 4684, but for tax years beginning in 2018 through 2025, the deduction for personal casualty and theft losses is limited to losses attributable to federally declared disasters (¶ 1121). A taxpayer may still claim personal casualty losses not attributable to federally declared disasters to offset any personal casualty gains during 2018 through 2025.

For tax years beginning before 2018 and after 2025, an individual can elect to treat the loss as an ordinary loss in the year the loss can be reasonably estimated, provided that no portion of the deposit is federally insured. The maximum amount that a taxpayer may claim as ordinary loss in any tax year is limited to $20,000 ($10,000 in the case of a married individual filing separately) for each financial institution, reduced by the amount of insurance proceeds that the taxpayer can reasonably expect to receive under state law. The loss is deducted on Schedule A (Form 1040) as a miscellaneous itemized deduction subject to the two-percent-of-adjusted-gross income limit applicable for tax years beginning before 2018 and after 2025 (¶ 1079). The calculation of the deducted loss should be included with the return (IRS Pub. 529).

Once made, either election applies to all losses on deposits in the financial institution during the tax year and it is revocable only with IRS consent. A taxpayer making either election is prohibited from deducting the loss as a bad debt deduction. Neither election can be made by an individual who is an owner of one percent or more of the value of the institution's stock, an officer of the institution, or a relative of an owner or officer. If neither election is made, then the loss is treated as a nonbusiness bad debt in the year of final determination of the actual loss and is reported as a short-term capital loss on Form 8949 (¶ 1143 and ¶ 1752).

1127. Amount of Casualty or Theft Loss. The amount of a casualty loss (¶ 1121) that is deductible for business and income-producing property or nonbusiness property is the *lesser* of:

- the fair market value (FMV) of the property immediately before the casualty reduced by its FMV immediately after the casualty, or

- the adjusted basis of the property immediately before the casualty (Reg. § 1.165-7(b)).

If business or income-producing property is totally destroyed and the property's FMV immediately before the casualty is less than its adjusted basis, then the casualty loss is the adjusted basis of the property.

The amount of a theft loss (¶ 1123) that is deductible is the fair market value or the adjusted basis of the property stolen (Reg. § 1.165-8(c)). If money is stolen, the theft loss is the amount stolen. The amount of a theft loss in the case of nonbusiness property other than money is the lesser of the value of the property or its adjusted basis. In the case of stolen business or income-producing property, the theft loss is the adjusted basis of the property stolen.

For tax years beginning in 2018 through 2025, the deduction for personal casualty and theft losses is limited to losses attributable to federally declared disasters. A taxpayer may still claim personal casualty and theft losses not attributable to federally declared disasters to offset any personal casualty and theft gains during 2018 through 2025 (Code Sec. 165(h)(5)). Any personal casualty or theft loss deduction claimed is subject to a $100 floor (¶ 1129) and a 10-percent-of-adjusted-gross-income (AGI) limit (¶ 1131). The $100 floor and AGI limit do not apply to a business or income-producing property casualty or theft loss.

A casualty or theft loss is reduced by any insurance or other compensation received by the taxpayer. In the case of a casualty loss, it is also reduced by any salvage value (¶ 1101). An individual cannot claim a personal casualty or theft loss to the extent the loss is covered by insurance, unless a timely insurance claim is filed with respect to the loss (¶ 1121 and ¶ 1123).

If there is damage to different kinds of business property, losses must be computed separately for each single, identifiable property damaged or destroyed. This rule does not apply to nonbusiness property. For example, if a tree is blown down in the front yard of a taxpayer's residence, the loss is the difference in the FMV of the taxpayer's whole property before and after damage to the tree (Reg. § 1.165-7(b)).

The taxpayer's basis for property damaged or destroyed by casualty or theft is reduced by the amount allowable as a casualty or theft loss deduction, as well as by the amount of any insurance or other recovery for the loss (Rev. Rul. 71-161).

Safe Harbor for Natural Disasters. The IRS has issued safe harbor methods for an individual to calculate casualty losses to his or her residence and personal belongings due to natural disaster, including losses due to Hurricanes Harvey, Irma, and Maria. An individual using any of the safe harbor methods must reduce loss by the value of any no-cost repairs and any insurance amounts received. If an individual owns more than one parcel of personal use residential property, use of one of the safe harbors for one parcel of property does not require the individual to use the same safe harbor, or any safe harbor method, for any other parcel. The safe harbors are generally effective December 13, 2017, except that the safe harbors are effective after August 22, 2017, for losses that are attributable to the 2017 Hurricanes and that arose in a 2017 disaster area after August 22, 2017 (Rev. Proc. 2018-8; Rev. Proc. 2018-9).

1129. $100 Floor for Personal Casualty or Theft Losses. For tax years beginning in 2018 through 2025, the deduction for personal casualty and theft losses is limited to losses attributable to federally declared disasters. A taxpayer may still claim personal casualty and theft losses not attributable federally declared disasters to the extent of any personal casualty and theft gains during 2018 through 2025. Any losses that are deductible are further limited by applying a $100 floor to each personal casualty (¶ 1121) or theft (¶ 1123) (Code Sec. 165(h)(1) and (h)(5); Reg. § 1.165-7(b)(4)).

The floor is increased to $500 for casualty losses if the taxpayer has a net disaster loss from: a qualified federal disaster declared between January 1, 2018, and February 18, 2020; the California wildfires of 2017; Hurricanes Harvey, Irma, or Maria in 2017; or a federally declared disaster in 2016. A net disaster loss is the excess of personal casualty losses over personal casualty gains in the designated disaster area (Act Secs. 201 and 204(b) of the Taxpayer Certainty and Disaster Tax Relief Act of 2019 (P.L. 116-94); Act Sec. 20104(b) of the Bipartisan Budget Act of 2018 (P.L. 115-123); Act Sec. 11028(c) of the Tax Cuts and Jobs Act (P.L. 115-97); Act Secs. 501 and 504(b) of the Disaster Tax

Relief and Airport and Airway Extension Act of 2017 (P.L. 115-63), as amended by P.L. 115-123).

The dollar floor applies separately to the loss from each single casualty or theft, regardless of how many pieces of property are involved in the event. Thus, if several items of nonbusiness property are damaged or stolen in the course of a single casualty or theft, the floor is applied only once against the sum of the allowable losses. In the case of married taxpayers filing a joint return, *only one* $100 floor ($500 in case of a net disaster loss) applies to each casualty or theft loss; it does not matter if the property is owned jointly or separately. If married taxpayers file separate returns, each spouse is subject to the $100 floor for each casualty or theft loss.

If property is used for both business and personal purposes, the $100 floor applies only to the net loss attributable to that portion of the property used for personal purposes. After the first $100 is subtracted from each personal casualty and theft loss, all personal casualty and theft losses for the tax year are netted against any personal casualty and theft gains. If personal casualty losses and theft losses exceed personal casualty and theft gains, a loss deduction is allowed to the extent that the excess is greater than 10 percent of the taxpayer's adjusted-gross-income (AGI) (¶ 1131).

1131. 10 Percent of AGI Floor for Personal Casualty or Theft Losses. For tax years beginning in 2018 through 2025, the deduction for personal casualty and theft losses is limited to losses attributable to federally declared disasters. A taxpayer may still claim personal casualty and theft losses not attributable to federally declared disasters to the extent of any personal casualty and theft gains during 2018 through 2025. Any losses that are deductible are further limited if the taxpayer's personal casualty (¶ 1121) or theft losses (¶ 1123) exceed his or her personal casualty or theft gains for the tax year. The excess generally is deductible only to the extent that it exceeds 10 percent of his or her adjusted gross income (AGI) for the year (Code Sec. 165(h)(2) and (h)(5)).

Gains and losses from personal casualties and thefts calculated on Form 4684 are netted for this purpose without regard to holding periods for the initial determination of whether there was a gain or loss. The $100 floor (¶ 1129) is applied to each personal casualty or theft before this netting occurs. If the recognized gains exceed the recognized losses, the net gain is reported as a capital gain on Schedule D (Form 1040). If the recognized losses exceed the recognized gains after netting, the net loss is deductible as an itemized deduction on Schedule A (Form 1040) but only to the extent it exceeds 10 percent of the taxpayer's AGI.

Limitation for Estates and Trusts. The 10-percent-of-AGI limitation on personal casualty and theft losses applies to an estate or trust. AGI is computed in the same manner as it is for an individual, except that an estate or trust is allowed to deduct its administration expenses in arriving at AGI (Code Sec. 165(h)(4)(C)). No deduction for a personal casualty or theft loss may be taken if, at the time of filing a decedent's return, the loss has been claimed for estate tax purposes (¶ 531).

Net Disaster Losses. The 10-percent AGI limit is waived for personal casualty losses if the taxpayer has a net disaster loss from: a qualified federal disaster declared between January 1, 2018, and February 18, 2020; the California wildfires of 2017; Hurricanes Harvey, Irma, or Maria in 2017; or a federally declared disaster in 2016. A net disaster loss is the excess of personal casualty losses over personal casualty gains in the designated disaster area. The 10-percent AGI limit continues to apply to casualty and theft losses, but without regard to net disaster losses. An individual who does not itemize deductions may claim an additional standard deduction amount (¶ 131) for net qualified disaster losses in computing regular taxable income and alternative minimum tax (AMT) liability (Act Secs. 201 and 204(b) of the Taxpayer Certainty and Disaster Tax Relief Act of 2019 (P.L. 116-94); Act Sec. 20104(b) of the Bipartisan Budget Act of 2018 (P.L. 115-123); Act Sec. 11028(c) of the Tax Cuts and Jobs Act (P.L. 115-97); Act Secs. 501 and 504(b) of the Disaster Tax Relief and Airport and Airway Extension Act of 2017 (P.L. 115-63), as amended by P.L. 115-123).

1133. Disaster Area Loss. For tax years beginning in 2018 through 2025, the deduction for personal casualty and theft losses is limited to losses attributable to federally declared disasters. A taxpayer may still claim personal casualty and theft losses not attributable to federally declared disasters to the extent of any personal casualty and theft gains during 2018 through 2025. A taxpayer that sustains a loss occurring in a disaster area and attributable to a federally declared disaster can either (1) deduct the loss on the tax return for the year in which the loss occurred, or (2) elect to deduct the loss on the return for the preceding tax year (Code Sec. 165(h)(5) and (i); Reg. § 1.165-11).

The disaster area loss deduction is calculated using the same rules as those for any other personal casualty losses (¶ 1127). If, however, the taxpayer elects to claim a disaster area loss on the return for the year immediately preceding the loss year, the 10-percent-of-adjusted-gross-income (AGI) limit (¶ 1131) is determined with respect to the preceding year's AGI. In addition, the IRS is authorized to issue guidance allowing the use of an appraisal used to secure a federal loan or loan guarantee as a result of federally declared disaster to establish the disaster loss amount. The $100 floor for each casualty related to the disaster is increased to $500 (¶ 1129) and the 10 percent AGI limitation is waived (¶ 1131) if the taxpayer has a net disaster loss from: a qualified federal disaster declared between January 1, 2018, and February 18, 2020; the California wildfires of 2017; Hurricanes Harvey, Irma, or Maria in 2017; or a federally declared disaster in 2016.

The election to deduct a disaster area loss in the tax year prior to the loss year is made by filing a return, an amended return, or a refund claim that clearly shows that the election is being made. The election applies to the entire loss sustained by the taxpayer in the disaster area during the disaster period. The election generally must be made by the date that is six months after the due date of the tax return for the year of the loss without regard to extensions. For example, the election to deduct a 2019 disaster area loss in 2018 must be made on or before October 15, 2020, for a calendar-year individual. A taxpayer may revoke the election within 90 days after the required due date.

Although a taxpayer may not deduct a loss incurred on the sale of his or her personal residence, the loss is treated as a disaster area loss if the personal residence is rendered unsafe by a disaster in an area determined by the President of the United States to warrant federal government assistance. In addition, the individual must have been ordered by the state or local government within 120 days after the area is declared a disaster area to demolish or relocate the residence (Code Sec. 165(k)). The amount of the deduction is reduced by any partial payments received from the state in the form of disaster aid.

Bad Debts

See CCH® AnswerConnect: *Business Bad Debt* and *Nonbusiness Bad Debt* for more information on this topic.

1135. Business Bad Debts. Business bad debts can generally be deducted from gross income as an ordinary loss when and to the extent that they become totally worthless (Code Sec. 166; Reg. § 1.166-5(b)). If a business bad debt is only partially worthless and is recoverable in part, then the worthless portion is deductible to the extent it is charged off during the tax year (¶ 1137). A business debt is a debt: (1) created or acquired in connection with the trade or business of the taxpayer who is claiming the deduction, or (2) the worthlessness of which has been incurred in the taxpayer's trade or business. If the taxpayer's primary motive for incurring the debt is not business related, then it is a nonbusiness debt and deductible only as a short-term capital loss when the debt becomes totally worthless (¶ 1143).

Only a bona fide debt qualifies for purposes of deducting a bad debt (Reg. § 1.166-1(c)). A debt is considered bona fide if it arises from a true debtor-creditor relationship based on a valid and enforceable obligation to pay a fixed or determinable amount of money. For example, a business bad debt deduction is not available to shareholders who have advanced money to a corporation as a contribution to capital (IRS Pub. 535). In addition, the bad debt deduction rules do not apply to a debt that is evidenced by a security (Code Sec. 166(e)). If a security held by a taxpayer other than a bank becomes worthless during the tax year, it is treated as sold or exchanged at a loss on the last day of the tax year (¶ 1916). A bank may treat a loss from a worthless security as a bad debt loss (¶ 2383).

Whether a debt is wholly or partially worthless is a question of fact, requiring consideration of all pertinent evidence, including the debtor's financial condition and the value of any collateral secured by the debt (Reg. § 1.166-2). A debt becomes worthless when there is no longer any chance the amount owed will be paid. This can be evidenced (1) by the fact that legal action to enforce payment would result in an uncollectible judgment, or (2) upon a settlement in bankruptcy (although worthlessness may sometimes be determined after bankruptcy and before settlement). It is not necessary for the taxpayer to go to court to demonstrate worthlessness. The taxpayer only has to show that reasonable steps were taken to collect the debt, but he or she was unable to do so (IRS Pub. 535).

Guarantors. A taxpayer is eligible for a business bad debt deduction if in the course of a trade or business, the taxpayer pays an obligation as a guarantor, endorser, or indemnitor (Reg. § 1.166-9). A noncorporate taxpayer is eligible for a nonbusiness bad debt deduction if the taxpayer pays an obligation as a guarantor, endorser, or indemnitor as part of a transaction entered into for profit. In the case of a business bad debt, no deduction is available if the agreement to act as guarantor, endorser, or indemnitor was not made in the course of the taxpayer's trade or business or a transaction for profit, if there is no legal obligation on the taxpayer to make the guaranty payment, or if the agreement was entered into after the debt became worthless.

Employee Loans. An employee's rendering of services for pay is a trade or business for purposes of the bad debt provisions. Therefore, a loan to an employer to protect a job can give rise to a business bad debt deduction if the employer defaults. If a loan by a shareholder-employee is intended to protect the shareholder's job rather than to protect the shareholder's investment in the company, then the failure to repay the loan results in a business bad debt deduction. The larger the shareholder's investment, the smaller his or her salary, and the larger his or her other sources of income, the more likely that a dominant nonbusiness motive exists for making the loan (IRS Pub. 535).

1137. Accounting for Bad Debt Deduction. Bad debts are generally deductible in the tax year in which they become worthless (Code Sec. 166(a); Reg. § 1.166-3). For a nonbusiness debt (¶ 1143), the deduction is available when the debt becomes wholly worthless. A deduction is allowed for a business debt (¶ 1135) that becomes wholly or partially worthless, but only to the extent the debt is charged off of the taxpayer's books during the tax year. The bad debt deduction is not available for nonbusiness debts that are only partially worthless. A worthless debt arising from unpaid wages, rent, interest, or a similar item is not deductible unless the income that these items represent has been reported as income by the taxpayer (Reg. §§ 1.166-1(e) and 1.166-6(a)(2)).

A taxpayer generally must use the specific charge-off method to claim a deduction for a business bad debt. If a business debt becomes totally worthless during the year, the taxpayer can deduct the entire amount in that year. If a business debt becomes partially worthless during the year, the taxpayer can deduct that amount of the debt charged off his or her books for the year. An exception to the charge-off rule exists for debt which has been significantly modified. Some accrual taxpayers may use the nonaccrual experience method of accounting for bad debts with respect to income to be received from the performance of services (¶ 1538). Small banks and thrift institutions can use the experience method of accounting to deduct bad debts (¶ 2383).

1139. Secured Bad Debt. If secured or mortgaged property is sold either to the secured party or to a third party for less than the amount of the debt, then the creditor is entitled to a bad debt deduction (¶ 1135 and ¶ 1143) in an amount equal to the difference between the sale price and the amount of the debt to the extent that the creditor can show that such difference is wholly or partially uncollectible (Reg. § 1.166-6). No bad debt deduction is allowed if a mortgage is foreclosed and the creditor buys the mortgaged property at a price equal to the unpaid debt. However, gain or loss is realized on the transaction. This is the difference between the obligations of the debtor that are applied to the purchase or bid price of the property and the fair market value of the property, to the extent that the obligations are capital or represent income returned by the creditor. See ¶ 1838 and ¶ 1841 for a discussion on repossession of property sold on the installment plan.

1141. Debts Owed by Political Parties. No deduction is generally allowable for a worthless debt owed by a political party. However, banks and accrual-basis taxpayers (¶ 1515) who are in the business of providing goods and services (e.g., polling, media, or organizational services) to political campaigns and candidates may deduct such bad debts (Code Sec. 271).

1143. Nonbusiness Bad Debts. If a nonbusiness bad debt held by a taxpayer other than a corporation becomes *totally* worthless during the tax year, then the loss may be deducted as a short-term capital loss regardless of how long the taxpayer held the debt (Code Sec. 166(d); Reg. § 1.166-5). Unlike business bad debts (¶ 1135), no deduction is permitted unless and until the debt becomes totally worthless. A nonbusiness bad debt is any debt *other than* one created or acquired in connection with the taxpayer's trade or business, or one that, when worthless, creates a loss that is incurred in the taxpayer's trade or business. See ¶ 1752 or limitations on deduction of a capital loss. See ¶ 1916 for worthlessness of a debt evidenced by a bond or other security of a corporation or a government.

Net Operating Losses (NOLs)

See CCH® AnswerConnect: *Net Operating Losses* for more information on this topic.

1145. Net Operating Loss (NOL). A taxpayer may claim a deduction in the current tax year for the aggregate amount of net operating losses (NOLs) carried back or carried forward from other tax years (Code Sec. 172(a), as amended by the Coronavirus Aid, Relief, and Economic Security (CARES) Act (P.L. 116-136); Reg. § 1.172-1). An NOL arises in any tax year when the taxpayer's deductible expenses for the year exceed its gross income subject to certain adjustments (¶ 1147).

A 2-year carryback and 20-year carryforward generally apply to NOLs arising in tax years beginning before 2018. A 5-year carryback and unlimited carryforward apply to NOLs arising in tax years beginning in 2018, 2019, and 2020. No carryback and an unlimited carryforward period apply to NOLs arising in tax years beginning after 2020. See ¶ 1149 for discussion of carryback and carryforward periods.

For tax years beginning before 2021, the NOL deduction may offset the taxpayer's entire taxable income for the carryback or carryforward year. For tax years beginning after 2020, NOLs arising in tax years beginning after 2017 may offset no more than 80 percent of the taxpayer's taxable income in the carryback or carryforward year (Code Sec. 172(a)(2), as amended by P.L. 116-136). Taxable income for this purpose is computed without regard to the deduction for qualified business income (QBI) (¶ 980P), as well as for foreign-derived intangible income (FDII) global intangible low-taxed income (GILTI) (¶ 2488B). Taxable income is reduced by any pre-2018 NOLs that are carried to the tax year before applying the 80 percent limitation. NOL carrybacks and carryforwards attributable to losses that arose in tax years beginning before 2018 are not subject to the 80 percent taxable income limit.

The NOL deduction is available to most taxpayers, including corporations, individuals, estates and trusts, and participants in common trust funds. The deduction may not be claimed by partnerships or S corporations, but partners and S corporation shareholders use their distributive shares of partnership or S corporation income to calculate their own NOLs (¶ 319 and ¶ 417). The NOL deduction may also not be claimed by regulated investment companies (¶ 2303). Life insurance companies can claim NOLs that arise in tax years beginning after 2017 (¶ 2370).

Quick Refunds for Noncorporate Taxpayers. Individuals, estates, and trusts may use Form 1045 to claim a quick refund resulting from the *carryback* of an NOL (Code Sec. 6411; Reg. § 1.6411-1). Form 1045 also contains schedules that can be used to determine the amount of NOL available for carryback or carryover, the NOL deduction for each carryback year, and the amount to be carried over. Form 1045 generally must be filed on or after the date for filing a tax return for the NOL year, but no later than one year after the end of the NOL year. The due date for performing certain time-sensitive actions, including the due date for filing Form 1045, otherwise due on or after April 1, 2020, and before July 15, 2020, is automatically extended to July 15, 2020, in response to the COVID-19 (coronavirus) crisis (Notice 2020-23; Rev. Proc. 2018-58). Taxpayers are also granted a six-month extension to file Form 1045 with respect to the carryback of NOLs arising in a tax year beginning in 2018 and ending on or before June 30, 2019 (Notice 2020-26).

As an alternative to Form 1045, individuals may file an amended return on Form 1040-X for each carryback year to claim a refund from the *carryback* of an NOL. Form 1040-X must generally be filed within three years after the due date of the return for the NOL year. Estates and trusts file an amended Form 1041 for each carryback year and check the "amended return" box. If an amended return is filed, the taxpayer must still attach the NOL computations using the Form 1045 computation schedules.

No special form is used to *carryforward* an NOL deduction. However, if the taxpayer elects to waive the carryback of an NOL (¶ 1149), a statement making the election must be attached to the return or amended return for the tax year. Individuals list an NOL carryover deduction as a negative figure on the "Other Income" line of Form 1040 or Form 1040-NR. Estates and trusts include an NOL carryover deduction on Form 1041 with other deductions not subject to the two-percent-of-adjusted-gross-income limit.

Quick Refunds for Corporations. Corporations may use Form 1139 to claim a quick refund resulting from the carryback of an NOL. Form 1139 generally must be filed or after the date for filing a tax return for the NOL year, but no later than one year after the end of the NOL year. The due date for performing certain time-sensitive actions, including the due date for filing Form 1139, otherwise due on or after April 1, 2020, and before July 15, 2020, is automatically extended to July 15, 2020, in response to the COVID-19 (coronavirus) crisis (Notice 2020-23; Rev. Proc. 2018-58). Taxpayers are also granted a six-month extension to file Form 1139 with respect to the carryback of NOLs arising in a tax year beginning in 2018 and ending on or before June 30, 2019 (Notice 2020-26). As an alternative to Form 1139, corporations may file an amended return on Form 1120-X for each carryback year to claim a refund from the carryback of an NOL. Form 1120-X must generally be filed within three years after the due date of the return for the NOL year. Corporations must file Form 1120-X rather than Form 1139 to carryback a prior year foreign tax credit, minimum tax credit, or general business credit released due to an NOL.

A corporation that expects an NOL in the current tax year may file Form 1138 to extend the time for payment of the tax for the immediately preceding tax year (Code Sec. 6164; Reg. § 1.6164-1). The extension applies only to payments of tax that are required to be paid after Form 1138 is filed. The extension expires at the end of the month in which the return for the tax year of the expected NOL is required to be filed including extensions. If the corporation files Form 1139 before the extension period ends, the time for payments is further extended until the date that the IRS mails notice that it has allowed or disallowed the application (Reg. § 1.6164-5).

NOLs Arising in 2017/2018 Fiscal Year. A technical correction clarifies that an NOL arising in a fiscal year beginning in 2017 and ending in 2018 has a two-year carryback period and twenty-year carryforward period (Section 13302(e)(2) of the Tax Cuts and Jobs Act (P.L. 115-97), as amended by P.L. 116-136). A 2017/2018 fiscal-year taxpayer may file an application for a tentative refund by July 27, 2020. An election to waive the carryback period or revoke a waiver of the carryback period may also be made by July 27, 2020 (Act Sec. 2303(d)(4) of P.L. 116-136; Rev. Proc. 2020-24).

1147. Net Operating Loss (NOL) Defined. A net operating loss (NOL) for the tax year is the excess of allowable deductions over gross income, with certain modifications (Code Sec. 172(c); Reg. § 1.172-1). For calculating the NOL, income and deductions from separate businesses are aggregated, and items that are excludable from gross income are generally excluded. The NOL for any tax year is determined under the law applicable to that tax year, without regard to the law applicable to the tax year to which the NOL is carried (¶ 1149). A taxpayer with a short tax year cannot annualize an NOL.

Noncorporate Taxpayers. The following adjustments are made in computing the NOL of a noncorporate taxpayer (Code Sec. 172(d)); Reg. § 1.172-3):

- no deduction is allowed for NOL carryovers or carrybacks from other years;

- no deduction is allowed for personal or dependency exemptions that are available in tax years before 2018 and after 2025 (¶ 133);

¶1147

- nonbusiness capital losses are deductible only to the extent of nonbusiness capital gains determined without regard to the exclusion for gain from qualified small business stock (¶ 1905);

- business capital losses are deductible only to the extent of the sum of (1) business capital gains determined without regard to the exclusion for gain from qualified small business stock, and (2) any nonbusiness capital gains that remain after deducting nonbusiness capital losses and excess nonbusiness deductions;

- nonbusiness deductions are allowed only to the extent of nonbusiness income including net nonbusiness capital gains (examples of nonbusiness deductions include standard deduction, itemized deductions, contributions to health savings accounts (HSAs); examples of nonbusiness income include income from passive investments, such as dividends, interest, annuities, nonbusiness income from a partnership or S corporation; wages and salary are considered attributable to the taxpayer's trade or business); and

- no deduction is allowed for domestic production activities for tax years beginning before 2018 (¶ 980A) and qualified business income (QBI) for tax years beginning after 2017 (¶ 980P).

Corporations. The following adjustments are made in computing the NOL of a corporation (Code Sec. 172(d); Reg. § 1.172-2):

- no deduction is allowed for NOL carryovers or carrybacks from other years;

- the deductions for dividends received from a domestic corporation, received on certain preferred stock of public utilities, received from certain foreign corporations, and paid on certain preferred stock of public utilities, are allowed without regard to the limitations imposed on such deductions in computing taxable income (¶ 223 and ¶ 231); and

- no deduction is allowed for domestic production activities for tax years beginning before 2018 (¶ 980A) and foreign-derived intangible income (FDII) and global intangible low-taxed income (GILTI) for tax years beginning after 2017 (¶ 2488B).

1149. Carryback and Carryforward of Net Operating Losses (NOLs). If a taxpayer has a net operating loss (NOL) for the current tax year (¶ 1147), it is not deducted in the tax year it occurs (the loss year) but instead is deducted during the following carryback and carryforward periods (¶ 1145):

- NOLs arising in tax years *beginning before 2018* may be carried back 2 years and then carried forward 20 years following the loss year;

- NOLs arising in tax years *beginning in 2018, 2019, and 2020* may be carried back 5 years and then carried forward indefinitely following the loss year;

- NOLs arising in tax years *beginning after 2020* generally may not be carried back, but may be carried forward indefinitely after the loss year; and

- NOLs from farming losses arising in tax years *beginning after 2020* may be carried back two years and have an indefinite carryforward period after the loss year (Code Sec. 172(b)(1), as amended by the Coronavirus Aid, Relief, and Economic Security (CARES) Act (P.L. 116-136)).

Special carryback periods are available for NOLs arising in tax years that began before 2018 and that are attributable to casualties, disasters, farming losses, and certain other activities (¶ 1151). In determining the amount of an NOL carryback or carryover, the law in effect during the year to which the NOL is carried back or carried over is applied (Code Sec. 172(e)).

If an NOL has a carryback period, then the entire NOL is first carried back to the earliest tax year in the carryback period before the loss year, then the next carryback year. If the taxpayer elects to waive the carryback period, the entire NOL is carried to the first tax year after the loss year. If an NOL carryover is not fully absorbed in a carryback or carryover year, then certain adjustments are made to taxable income in the carryback or carryover year (but not less than zero) to determine the portion of the NOL still available to be carried to the next year in the carryback or carryover period (Code Sec. 172(b)(2), as amended by P.L. 116-136; Reg. § 1.172-5).

In a year in which an NOL is carried back, any income, deductions, or credits that are based on or limited to a percentage of adjusted gross income (AGI) must be recomputed based on AGI after applying the NOL deduction for the carryback year, but any charitable contribution deduction is *not* recomputed. Taxable income is recomputed taking into account the NOL and the preceding adjustments. Income tax, alternative minimum tax, and any credits that are based on or limited to the amount of tax are then recomputed.

Married Taxpayers. Married individuals who file a joint return for each year considered in figuring NOL carrybacks and carryforwrds calculate their NOL as though all the income and deductions on the return are those of one taxpayer (Reg. § 1.172-7). If married individuals file separate returns for each year considered in figuring NOL carrybacks and carryovers, then each spouse is entitled to their own NOLs without regard to the income or deductions of the other spouse. Special rules apply for figuring the NOL carrybacks and carryforwards of married individuals whose filing status changes for any tax year considered in figuring an NOL carryback or carryforward.

Election to Waive Carryback Period. A taxpayer can make an irrevocable election to waive the entire carryback period for an NOL and carry it forward to years following the loss year (Code Sec. 172(b)(3)). The election generally must be made by the return due date for the tax year of the NOL (including extensions). The election may also be made on an amended return filed within six months of an originally filed return (excluding extensions). For NOLs arising in tax years beginning in 2018 and 2019, the election to waive the 5-year carryback period is extended to the return due date (including extensions) for the tax year *ending after* March 27, 2020 (Code Sec. 172(b)(1)(D)(v)(II), added by P.L. 116-136; Rev. Proc. 2020-24). The election to waive the carryback period is made by attaching a statement to the return indicating that the taxpayer is waiving the entire carryback period. The Instructions to Form 1045 and Instructions to Form 1139 provide the specific statement requirements.

Election to Exclude Code Sec. 965 Tax Years. A taxpayer with an NOL arising in tax years beginning in 2018, 2019, or 2020 may elect to either (1) waive the carryback period for those losses entirely or (2) to exclude from the carryback period for those losses any years in which the taxpayer has any Code Sec. 965 transition tax liability (¶ 2488B). The election to exclude a year from the carryback period generally must be made by the due date of the taxpayer's return (including extensions) of the tax year that the NOL arises. However, the election for an NOL arising in a tax year beginning in 2018 or 2019 must be made by the due date (including extensions) for filing the taxpayers return for the first tax year *ending after* March 27, 2020 (Code Sec. 172(b)(1)(D)(iv) and (v)(I), as added by P.L. 116-136; Rev. Proc. 2020-24).

1151. Special NOL Carryforward and Carryback Periods. A net operating loss (NOL) arising in tax years beginning before 2018 generally may be carried back to the two years preceding the loss year and then carried forward 20 years following the loss year. A five year carryback and indefinite carryforward period generally apply to NOLs arising in tax years beginning in 2018, 2019, and 2020 (Code Sec. 172(b)(1)(D), as added by the Coronavirus Aid, Relief, and Economic Security (CARES) Act (P.L. 116-136)). An NOL arising in tax years beginning after 2020 generally has no carryback period but may be carried forward indefinitely (¶ 1149). However, special carryback periods are available for certain types of NOLs as discussed below.

Casualties and Disasters. For an NOL arising in tax years beginning before 2018, a three-year carryback period is available if: (1) it is an NOL of an individual arising from a fire, storm, shipwreck, other casualty, or theft, and (2) an NOL of a small business or taxpayer engaged in farming if the loss is attributable to a federally declared disaster (Code Sec. 172(b)(1)(E), prior to being stricken by the Tax Cuts and Jobs Act (P.L. 115-97)). A small business is one with an average annual gross receipts of $5 million or less for the three-year period ending with the prior tax year. An eligible loss does not include a farming loss described below.

Farming Loss. A farming loss arising in tax years beginning before 2018 is carried back for five years (Code Sec. 172(b)(1)(F) and (h), prior to being stricken by P.L. 115-97). The carryback period for a farming loss arising in tax years beginning in 2018, 2019, and 2020 is also five years. A farming loss arising in a tax year beginning after 2020 is carried back two years (Code Sec. 172(b)(1)(B)). A farming loss is the *smaller* of (1) the amount that would be the NOL for the tax year if only income and deductions attributable to farming businesses (¶ 982) were taken into account, or (2) the NOL for the tax year.

A taxpayer may elect to waive the five-year carryback for a farming loss arising in tax years beginning before 2018 (¶ 1149). In this case, a two-year carryback period applies unless the two-year period is also waived. For farming NOLs arising in tax years beginning in 2018, 2019, or 2020 the five-year carryback may be waived. For farming NOLs arising in tax years beginning after 2020 the two-year carryback may be waived. For ordering purposes, the farming loss is treated as a separate NOL to be taken into account *after* the remaining portion of the NOL for the tax year.

Short Tax Years. If the IRS approves a request for a change in accounting period when the short period required to effect the change is a tax year in which the taxpayer has an NOL, the taxpayer can carry back a short-period NOL only if it is either $50,000 or less, or less than the full 12-month period NOL beginning with the first day of the short period as determined when the 12-month period has expired (Rev. Proc. 2003-34).

Specified Liability Losses. A 10-year carryback period applies to specified liability losses arising in tax years beginning before 2018 (Code Sec. 172(b)(1)(C) and (f), prior to being stricken by P.L. 115-97; Notice 2005-20). A specified liability loss is the portion of an NOL that (1) is attributable to product liability or (2) arises out of satisfaction of a liability under federal or state law requiring land reclamation, nuclear power plant decommissioning, drilling platform dismantling, environmental remediation, or a payment under any workers' compensation act. For ordering purposes, the specified liability loss is treated as a separate NOL to be taken into account *after* the remaining portion of the NOL for the tax year.

Real Estate Investment Trusts (REITs). An NOL arising from a REIT year beginning before 2018—a tax year in which an entity operated as a REIT (¶ 2326)—cannot be carried back to any preceding tax year but only carried forward 20 years. An NOL arising from a non-REIT year ending before 2018 cannot be carried back to a REIT year (Code Sec. 172(b)(1)(B), prior to being stricken by P.L. 115-97; Reg. § 1.172-10). The 5-year carryback for NOLs arising in tax years beginning in 2018, 2019, or 2020 does not apply to an NOL for a REIT year. Furthermore, an NOL for a tax year beginning in 2018, 2019, or 2020 is not carried to any preceding tax year in the five-year carryback period that is a REIT year (Code Sec. 172(b)(1)(D)(ii), as added by P.L. 116-136).

Insurance Companies. The carryback period for a non-life insurance company (i.e., property and casualty insurance company) for a tax year beginning in 2018, 2019, and 2020 is five years. The NOL of an insurance company other than a life insurance company arising in tax years beginning before 2018 or after 2020 is carried back two years and forward twenty years (Code Sec. 172(b)(1)(C) and (f)). In addition, the 80 percent taxable income limitation, which is effective for tax years beginning after 2020, does not apply to a non-life insurance company. The carryforward period for a non-life insurance company is twenty years. If an NOL of a life insurance company that arises in a tax year beginning in 2018, 2019, or 2020 is carried back during the five year carryback period to a tax year beginning before 2018, the NOL is treated like an operations loss carryback under Code Sec. 810 prior to its repeal (Code Sec. 172(b)(1)(D)(iii), as added by P.L. 116-136).

Corporate Equity Reduction Transactions (CERTs). A C corporation may not carry back a portion of its NOL arising in tax years beginning before 2018 if $1 million or more of interest expense is incurred in a major stock acquisition of another corporation or in an excess distribution by the corporation (Code Sec. 172(b)(1)(D) and (g), prior to being stricken by P.L. 115-97). The amount subject to the limitation is the lesser of: (1) the corporation's deductible interest expense allocable to the CERT, or (2) the amount by which the corporation's interest expense for the current tax year exceeds the average

¶1151

interest expense for the three tax years preceding the tax year in which the CERT occurs.

1153. NOL Carryovers Between Predecessors and Successors. A net operating loss (NOL) may generally be carried back or carried forward only by the taxpayer who sustained the loss (¶ 1145). A beneficiary of an estate or trust, is entitled to any carryover amount remaining unused after the last tax year of the estate or trust. Similarly, a bankruptcy estate succeeds to an individual debtor's NOLs (¶ 535). A successor corporation also is allowed to carry over the NOL and certain other items of its predecessor under specified conditions (¶ 2277).

At-Risk Limitations

See CCH® AnswerConnect: *At-Risk Limitations on Loss Deductions* for more information on this topic.

1155. At-Risk Limitations on Losses. A deductible loss with respect to an activity is generally limited to the amount that the taxpayer has at risk with respect to the activity (Code Sec. 465). The at-risk rules are designed to prevent certain taxpayers (¶ 1157) from offsetting trade, business, or professional income with losses from investments in activities (¶ 1159) that are largely financed by nonrecourse loans for which they are not personally liable. Even if it has been determined that the loss is deductible under the at-risk rules, the loss may still be limited by the passive activity loss rules (¶ 1165) and the limit on excess business losses for tax years beginning in 2021 through 2025 (¶ 1190).

Under the at-risk rules, loss deductions are limited to the amount the taxpayer has at risk in the activity. This is the money and the adjusted basis of other property the taxpayer contributes to the activity. It also includes any amounts borrowed for use in the activity if the taxpayer has personal liability for repayment of the loan (recourse) or has pledged assets not used in the activity as security for the loan (Code Sec. 465(b)).

Amounts are not at risk if they are borrowed from (1) a person who has an interest in the activity other than as a creditor, or (2) a person related to someone other than the taxpayer who has an interest in the activity. Exceptions are available for corporations that borrow from shareholders and qualified nonrecourse financing secured by real property used in an activity. Personal liability of the taxpayer for borrowed amounts generally hinges on whether the taxpayer is the ultimate obligor of the liability with no recourse against any other party (*S.H. Bennion*, Dec. 43,801, 88 TC 684). The taxpayer is not considered at risk with respect to amounts protected against loss through nonrecourse financing, guarantees, stop-loss agreements, or similar arrangements.

Any loss not allowed because of the at-risk limitation is carried over to the following tax year, to be deducted subject to the same limitation. The amount allowed as a loss for any year reduces the amount at risk for later years. Conversely, if a taxpayer's amount at risk at the end of any tax year is less than zero, the loss equal to the difference is recaptured (Code Sec. 465(e)). Unused amounts generally are allowed when the activity is transferred or otherwise disposed (¶ 1161).

Form 6198 is used to compute the deductible loss under the at-risk rules. An activity subject to the passive loss rules must file Form 8582. If the activity is subject to both limitations, Form 6198 is completed first, and any allowable loss must be carried over to Form 8582. See also ¶ 1465A for investment tax credit at-risk rules.

1157. Taxpayers Affected by At-Risk Rules. The at-risk rules (¶ 1155) apply to individuals, estates, and trusts (Code Sec. 465(a)(1)). They also apply to partners and S corporation shareholders at the partner or shareholder level, not at the entity level. Closely held corporations are generally subject to the at-risk rules if they meet the personal holding company stock ownership requirements (¶ 277). However, certain closely held corporations are not subject to the at-risk limits for any qualifying active business carried on; instead, each qualifying business of a corporation is treated as a separate activity (Code Sec. 465(c)(7)). In addition, if a closely held corporation is actively engaged in equipment leasing, the equipment leasing is treated as a separate activity not covered by the at-risk rules (Code Sec. 465(c)(4)).

11

LOSSES

1159. Activities Covered by At-Risk Rules. The at-risk limit on losses (¶ 1155) generally applies to all activities of a taxpayer engaged in as a trade or business or for the production of income (Code Sec. 465(c)). It also specifically applies to any taxpayer engaged in: the activity of holding, producing, or distributing motion picture films or video tapes; farming; leasing of section 1245 property; or exploring for or exploiting oil and gas resources or geothermal deposits. The at-risk rules do not apply to:

- the leasing of equipment by closely held corporations (¶ 1157);

- a qualifying active business carried on by certain closely held corporations; or

- the holding of real property other than mineral property acquired before 1987 as an interest in a pass-through entity engaged in holding real property placed in service before 1987.

In the case of the specifically identified activities listed previously, each film or tape, each piece of section 1245 property, each farm, and each oil, gas, or geothermal property is treated as a separate activity. For a partnership or an S corporation, all leased section 1245 properties that are placed in service in the same tax year are treated as a single activity. Trade or business activities subject to the at-risk rules are aggregated and treated as a single activity if the taxpayer actively participates in the management of the trade or business. They are also aggregated where the trade or business is carried on by a partnership or S corporation, and 65 percent or more of the losses for the tax year are allocable to persons who actively participate in the management of the trade or business.

1161. Application of At-Risk Rules on Disposition of Activity. Under proposed regulations, if a taxpayer transfers or otherwise disposes of an activity, any gain realized on the transfer or disposition of the activity is treated as gain from the activity, which generally permits the taxpayer to recognize any losses suspended under the at-risk rules (¶ 1155) (Prop. Reg. § 1.465-66). The same rules apply if a partnership liquidates a partner's interest or an S corporation completely redeems a shareholder's interest.

Passive Activity Losses and Credits

See CCH® AnswerConnect: *Passive Activity Losses* for more information on this topic.

1165. Passive Activity Defined. A passive activity for purposes of the passive activity limit on losses (¶ 1169) is an activity that involves the conduct of any trade or business in which the taxpayer does not materially participate (Code Sec. 469(c); Temp. Reg. § 1.469-1T(e)). Any rental activity is a passive activity whether or not the taxpayer materially participates (¶ 1181). However, there are special rules for real estate rental activities (¶ 1183) and real estate professionals (¶ 1185). Trading personal property that is actively traded, such as stocks and bonds, for the account of owners of interests in the activity is not a passive activity. For example, the activity of a partnership that trades stock using money contributed by the partners is not a passive activity.

Material participation in an activity requires that a taxpayer is involved in the operations of the activity on a regular, continuous, and substantial basis (Code Sec. 469(h); Temp. Reg. § 1.469-5T). An individual is generally considered as materially participating in an activity during a tax year if he or she satisfies one of the following tests:

(1) the individual participates more than 500 hours;

(2) the individual's participation constitutes substantially all of the participation in the activity;

(3) the individual participates for more than 100 hours and this participation is not less than the participation of any other individual;

(4) the activity is a "significant participation activity" and the individual's participation in all significant participation activities exceeds 500 hours;

(5) the individual materially participated in the activity for any five years of the 10 years that preceded the year in question;

(6) the activity is a "personal service activity" and the individual materially participated in the activity for any three years preceding the tax year in question; or

(7) the individual satisfies a facts and circumstances test that requires the individual to show participation on a regular, continuous, and substantial basis for more than 100 hours during the tax year.

With respect to test (7), an individual's participation in managing the activity does not count toward the 100-hour requirement if any other person received compensation for managing the activity or any other person spent more time managing the activity.

Special rules are provided for determining the material participation of certain retired or disabled farmers and participation in the activity of a personal service or closely held corporation (Temp. Reg. § 1.469-5T(h)).

Limited Partners. A limited partner's share of income, losses, and credits from a partnership are treated as arising from a passive activity unless the limited partner participated in the activity for more than 500 hours, the limited partner materially participated in the activity five of the 10 preceding tax years, or the activity is a personal service activity in which the limited partner materially participated for any three preceding tax years. A general partner who also holds a limited partnership interest is not treated as a limited partner (Code Sec. 469(h)(2); Temp. Reg. § 1.469-5T(e)).

Significant Participation Activity. A significant participation activity is one in which the taxpayer participates more than 100 hours during the tax year but does not materially participate under any of the other six tests set forth above (Temp. Reg. § 1.469-5T(c)).

Personal Service Activity. A personal service activity involves the performance of personal service in the fields of health (including veterinary services), law, engineering, architecture, accounting, actuarial science, the performing arts, consulting, or any other trade or business in which capital is not a material income-producing factor (Temp. Reg. § 1.469-5T(d)).

Definition of Participation. Any work done by an individual with respect to an activity in which the individual owns an interest is generally treated as participation (Reg. § 1.469-5(f)(1); Temp. Reg. § 1.469-5T(f)). Participation does not include work that is not customarily done by an owner if one of the principal purposes for performing the work is to avoid the passive activity limitations. Furthermore, work done in an individual's capacity as an investor in an activity, such as studying and reviewing the activity's financial statements and operational reports, preparing summaries or analyses of the activity's finances or operations for personal use, and monitoring the finances or operations of the activity in a nonmanagerial capacity, is not counted as participation.

A married individual's participation does include the participation of his or her spouse even if the spouse does not own an interest in the activity and separate returns are filed. Participation may be established by any reasonable means. It is not necessary to maintain contemporaneous daily records of participation. An approximate number of hours of participation may be based on appointment books, calendars, or narrative summaries.

1167. Passive Activity Income and Deductions. Passive income or loss for purposes of the passive activity limit on losses (¶ 1169) generally is determined by aggregating gross income and deductions from all passive activities during the year (Temp. Reg. § 1.469-2T). Certain types of income and deductions from a passive activity are subject to special rules and must be excluded and reported separately as nonpassive income or deductions.

Portfolio income is excluded from passive activity income and expenses directly allocable to such income are not deductible in computing passive activity losses (Code Sec. 469(e)(1)). Portfolio income includes interest, dividends, annuities, royalties, and gain or loss from the disposition of investment property not derived in the ordinary course of a trade or business. No exception is provided for the treatment of portfolio income arising from working capital (i.e., amounts set aside for the reasonable needs of the business).

Passive activity income also does not include: personal service income; income or gain from investments of working capital; income from intangible property if the taxpayer's personal efforts significantly contributed to its creation; refunds of state and local taxes; reimbursements of casualty and theft losses; and cancellation of debt

11

LOSSES

income. Passive activity deductions do not include: qualified home mortgage interest expense, capitalization interest expense, and most other interest expenses properly allocable to a passive activity; state and local taxes; charitable contributions; disallowed miscellaneous itemized deductions; net operating losses (NOLs); and capital loss carrybacks and carryforwards.

Certain self-charged interest income or deductions may be treated as passive activity income or deductions if the loan proceeds are used in a passive activity. Self-charged interest and expenses are items from a lending transaction between a taxpayer and a pass-through entity in which the taxpayer owns a direct or indirect interest (Reg. § 1.469-7). These rules also apply to lending transactions between pass-through entities with identical ownership.

1169. Passive Activity Loss Limitations. Under the passive activity rules, losses and expenses attributable to passive activities of certain taxpayers (¶ 1173) may only be deducted from income attributable to passive activities (Code Sec. 469). Similarly, tax credits attributable to passive activities may only be used to offset taxes attributable to income from passive activities. A passive activity for this purpose is any activity that involves the conduct of a trade or business in which the taxpayer does not materially participate (¶ 1165). Any rental activity is a passive activity whether or not the taxpayer materially participates (¶ 1181). However, there are special rules for real estate rental activities (¶ 1183) and real estate professionals (¶ 1185).

To the extent that the total deductions from passive activities exceed the total income from passive activities for the tax year, the excess (the passive activity loss) is not allowed as a deduction for that year. Instead, the disallowed loss is suspended and carried forward as a deduction against income from the passive activity in the next succeeding tax year (Code Sec. 469(b)). Any unused suspended losses are allowed in full when the taxpayer disposes of his or her entire interest in the activity in a fully taxable transaction (¶ 1177). In determining a taxpayer's allowable loss, the at-risk rules (¶ 1155) are applied before the passive activity loss rules and the passive activity loss rules are applied before the limit on excess business losses for tax years beginning in 2021 through 2025 (¶ 1190).

Passive Activity Credit. Tax credits arising with respect to passive activities are generally treated in the same manner as losses, except that suspended credits are not allowed on disposition of the activity (Code Sec. 469(a)(1)(B) and (d)(2)). Thus, credits may be used to offset the tax attributable to net passive income—the difference between the tax on all income, and the tax on taxable income other than net passive income. In both cases, the effect of credits is disregarded.

Unused credits can generally be carried forward indefinitely. However, the character of a credit relating to a passive activity changes if the credit becomes allowable under the passive loss rules either because there is sufficient passive income to allow its use or it is within the scope of the $25,000 benefit for real estate activities (¶ 1183). At this time, the credit is aggregated with credits relating to nonpassive activities of the taxpayer to determine whether all such credits are allowable considering the other limitations that apply to the use of credits (¶ 1465).

Reporting Requirements. An individual, estate, and trust uses Form 8582 or Form 8582-CR to calculate their allowable passive losses and credits. Form 8582 generally must also be filed by a taxpayer that has an overall gain from business or rental passive activities for the year (even after including suspended passive losses from earlier tax years). Form 8582 does not need to be filed if the taxpayer actively participated in rental real estate activities. Form 8810 is used by a personal service corporation and closely held C corporation to calculate passive activity losses and credits. Form 8825 is used by a partnership and S corporation to report income and deductible expenses from rental real estate activities.

1171. Passive Activity Losses of Publicly Traded Partnerships. Special rules apply to passive activity losses from a publicly traded partnership (PTP) (Code Sec. 469(k)). A PTP is a partnership whose interests are traded on an established securities market or are readily tradable on a secondary market or its substantial equivalent. A taxpayer's net income from a PTP may not be used to offset net losses from other PTPs or net losses from other passive activities. A disallowed loss from a PTP is carried forward and allowed as a deduction in a tax year when the PTP has net income or when the taxpayer disposes of his or her entire interest in the PTP. These rules apply to a regulated investment company (¶ 2301) holding an interest in a PTP, with respect to items attributable to the interest in the partnership.

1173. Taxpayers Covered by Passive Activity Rules. The passive activity rules (¶ 1169) apply to individuals, estates, trusts other than grantor trusts, and personal service corporations (Code Sec. 469(a)(2)). The passive activity rules do not apply to partnerships, S corporations, and grantor trusts directly, but are applied at the partner, shareholder, beneficiary, or grantor level. See ¶ 1171 for discussion of special rules applicable to publicly traded partnerships.

Closely Held C Corporations. A C corporation is generally not subject to the passive activity rules. However, the passive activity rules do apply to a closely held C corporation (other than a personal service corporation) to the extent of its net active income. The corporation cannot use passive losses to offset portfolio income (¶ 1167). A closely held C corporation's net active income is equal to its taxable income, figured without any income or loss from a passive activity or any portfolio income or loss (Code Sec. 469(e)(2)).

1175. Grouping Activities Under the Passive Activity Rules. In applying the passive activity rules (¶ 1169), one or more trade or business activities, or rental activities, may be treated as a single activity if the activities constitute an appropriate economic unit (Reg. § 1.469-4). Whether activities constitute an appropriate economic unit depends upon all the relevant facts and circumstances. The following factors are given greatest weight in determining whether several activities can be combined:

- similarities or differences in types of business,
- extent of common control,
- extent of common ownership,
- geographical location, and
- business interdependencies among the activities.

Once activities are grouped together or kept separate, the taxpayer must be consistent in the treatment of these activities in subsequent tax years. A taxpayer generally may not regroup activities unless the original grouping was clearly inappropriate or became inappropriate due to a material change in facts and circumstances (Reg. § 1.469-4(e); Rev. Proc. 2010-13). A taxpayer is required to disclose his or her grouping and regrouping of activities in a written statement with the taxpayer's income tax return. The statement must be filed for:

- the first tax year in which two or more trade or business activities or rental activities are originally grouped as a single activity;
- a tax year in which a taxpayer adds a new trade or business activity or a rental activity to an existing grouping; or
- a tax year in which a taxpayer regroups activities.

The IRS may disallow and regroup a taxpayer's grouping of activities if the grouping does not reflect an appropriate economic unit and has circumvention of the passive activity loss rules as a primary purpose (Reg. § 1.469-4(f)).

Regrouping and Net Investment Income Tax. A one-time regrouping of activities can be made by an individual, trust, or estate in the first tax year beginning after December 31, 2012, in which it satisfies the eligibility criteria for the net investment income (NII) tax (¶ 117) (Reg. § 1.469-11(b)(3)(iv)). The determination of whether a taxpayer meets the eligibility criteria for the NII tax is made without regard to the effect of the regrouping and any regrouping applies to the tax year in which the regrouping is done and all subsequent tax years.

The one-time regrouping generally must be made on an original return, but may be made on an amended return if a change reported on the amended return causes the taxpayer to meet the eligibility criteria for the first time. If it is later determined that the taxpayer did not satisfy the eligibility criteria in a tax year in which a regrouping was

11 LOSSES

made, the regrouping is void for the tax year it was made and all future years, unless the taxpayer's failure to satisfy the eligibility criteria is due to the carryback of a net operating loss arising in the tax years ending before 2018.

Activities Conducted Through Entities. Activities conducted through a partnership, S corporation, personal service corporation, or closely-held corporation are first grouped at the entity level (Reg. § 1.469-4(d)(5)). Once the entity groups its activities, a partner or shareholder may group those activities with each other, with activities conducted directly by the partner or shareholder, and with activities conducted through other entities. An activity that a taxpayer conducts through a C corporation may be grouped with another activity of the taxpayer only for purposes of determining whether the taxpayer materially or significantly participates in the other activity.

Rental Activities. A taxpayer generally may not treat an activity involving the rental of real property and an activity involving the rental of personal property as a single activity (Reg. § 1.469-4(d)). These two activities can be treated as a single activity only if the taxpayer provides the personal property in connection with the real property or the real property in connection with the personal property.

A rental activity may not be grouped with a trade or business activity unless either: (1) the rental activity is insubstantial in relation to the trade or business activity; or (2) the trade or business activity is insubstantial in relation to the rental activity. There is a third alternative when each owner of the trade or business has the same proportionate ownership interest in the rental activity, in which case the portion of the rental activity that involves the rental of items of property to a trade or business activity may be grouped with the trade or business activity.

> **Example:** The Getaway Partnership owns a 10-story building in which it operates a travel agency on three floors and rents seven floors to tenants. The partnership is divided into two activities: a travel agency activity and rental real estate activity. Deductions and credits attributable to the building are allocable to the travel agency activity only to the extent that they relate to the space occupied by the travel agency during the tax year.

Partial Disposition of Activity. If the taxpayer disposes of *substantially all* of an activity, he or she may treat the interest disposed of as a separate activity, provided that the taxpayer can establish the amount of gross income, deductions, and credits allocable to that part of the activity for the tax year (Reg. § 1.469-4(g)). Without this rule, taxpayers generally cannot claim suspended passive losses until they have disposed of their entire interest in an activity (¶ 1177).

1177. Disposition of Interest in Passive Activity. If a taxpayer disposes of his or her entire interest in a passive activity (¶ 1165) in a fully taxable transaction, then any suspended passive activity losses (¶ 1169) may be applied against his or her nonpassive income (Code Sec. 469(g)). Specifically, any net passive losses must first be applied against the taxpayer's net income or gain from passive activities. Any remaining loss from the activity is then classified as nonpassive and may be used to offset income from nonpassive activities (e.g., wages). Suspended credits are not allowed on the disposition of a passive activity.

Entire Interest. A disposition of a taxpayer's entire interest involves a disposition of the interest in all entities that are engaged in the activity. To the extent the activity is held in the form of a sole proprietorship, disposition of a taxpayer's entire interest includes disposition of all of the assets used or created in the activity. If a partnership, S corporation, or grantor trust conducts two or more separate activities and the entity disposes of all the assets used or created in one activity, the disposition constitutes a disposition of the entire interest (IRS Pub. 925). In some instances, a taxpayer may claim a deduction for suspended losses even though he or she disposes of less than his or her entire interest (¶ 1175).

Taxable Transactions. To qualify as a fully taxable disposition, the disposition generally must be a sale of the interest to a third party in an arm's-length transaction and must not be a sham, a wash sale, or a transfer of repurchase rights. If a taxpayer disposes of an interest in a passive activity in a taxable transaction with a related party as defined by Code Sec. 267(b) (¶ 1717) or with a controlled partnership as defined by

Code Sec. 707(b)(1) (¶ 432) the suspended losses are not triggered. In these circumstances, the taxpayer is able to claim the loss only when the related person or controlled partnership disposes of the activity in a taxable transaction with an unrelated person. Abandonment is a fully taxable disposition.

Installment Sales. If a taxpayer sells his or her entire interest in a passive activity and reports the gain under the installment sale method (¶ 1801), only a portion of the suspended loss may be deducted in the year of the sale. Suspended losses are allowed in the year of sale and thereafter in the ratio that the gain recognized in a tax year bears to the total gross profit from the sale to be realized when payment is completed.

Death. A transfer of an individual's entire interest in a passive activity by reason of his or her death causes suspended losses to be allowed in the year of death to the extent that they exceed the amount by which the basis of the interest is stepped up at death (¶ 1633).

Gifts. Disposition of an interest in a passive activity by gift does *not* trigger suspended losses. Instead, the basis of the transferred interest is increased by the amount of such losses (Code Sec. 469(j)(6)).

Nontaxable Exchanges. An exchange of a taxpayer's interest in a passive activity in a nonrecognition transaction such as a like-kind exchange (¶ 1721) does not trigger suspended losses. However, to the extent that the taxpayer recognizes gain on the transaction (i.e., boot), the gain is treated as passive activity income against which passive losses may be deducted (Code Sec. 469(g)).

Casualty or Theft. A casualty (¶ 1121) or theft (¶ 1123) loss involving property used in a passive activity does not constitute a complete disposition of the taxpayer's interest in the activity unless the casualty or theft results in a loss of all property used or created in the activity (Senate Committee Report to P.L. 99-514 (1986), S. Rep. 99-313).

Former Passive Activity. In the tax year that an activity ceases to be a passive activity, previously suspended losses from that activity are permitted to be claimed as deductions against the activity's net income (Code Sec. 469(f)(1)). Similarly, prior year suspended passive activity credits may offset the current year's tax liability that is allocable to the current year's net income from the former passive activity. Tax liability for this purpose is figured on the net income as reduced by the prior year suspended losses.

Cessation of Closely Held C Corporation or PSC Status. If a closely held C corporation or a personal service corporation (PSC) changes its status, suspended losses from prior years continue to be subject to the limitations that were imposed before the status changed (¶ 1173). Losses arising in years after the year in which the corporation's status changes are not subject to the passive activity rules (Code Sec. 469(f)(2)).

Rental Activities Subject to Passive Activity Rules

See CCH® AnswerConnect: *Passive Activity Losses* for more information on this topic.

1181. Rental Activities Subject to Passive Activity Rules. A rental activity is generally treated as a passive activity regardless of whether the taxpayer materially participates in the activity (¶ 1165) (Code Sec. 469(c)(2); Temp. Reg. § 1.469-1T(e)(3)). An activity is a "rental activity" if (1) during the tax year, tangible property held in connection with the activity is used by customers or is held for use by customers, and (2) the gross income of the activity represents amounts paid mainly for the use of the tangible property.

A taxpayer's rental real estate activity is not a passive activity if the taxpayer materially participates in the activity and is a real estate professional (¶ 1185). In addition, if any one of the following tests is met, the activity is not considered to be a rental activity for purposes of the passive loss rules (¶ 1169):

- the average period of customer use of the property is seven days or less;

- the average period of customer use is 30 days or less and significant personal services are provided by or on behalf of the owner;

11

LOSSES

- without regard to the period of customer use, extraordinary personal services are provided by or on behalf of the owner;

- the rental of the property is incidental to a nonrental activity;

- the property is customarily made available during defined business hours for the nonexclusive use of customers; or

- the taxpayer provides property for use in an activity that is conducted by a partnership, S corporation, or joint venture in which the taxpayer owns an interest and the activity is not a rental activity.

If a taxpayer does not meet the requirements to be a real estate professional, but owns and actively participates in a rental real estate activity, then the taxpayer may deduct up to $25,000 of losses from a passive rental real estate activity from nonpassive income (¶ 1183).

1183. $25,000 Offset for Active Participation in Rental Real Estate Activity. An individual who owns and actively participates in a rental real estate activity may offset up to $25,000 of passive activity losses and credits ($12,500 for married filing separately) from the activity against nonpassive income (Code Sec. 469(i)). To be eligible, the individual must own at least 10-percent by value of all interests in the activity throughout the year. The interest of an individual's spouse is taken into account in determining 10-percent ownership whether or not a joint return is filed.

While the offset is available only to an individual who actively participates in rental real estate activities, a decedent's estate also qualifies for tax years ending less than two years after the date of the decedent's death if it has an interest in a rental real estate activity in which the decedent actively participated in the year of death. A decedent's qualified revocable trust can also be treated as actively participating if both the trustee and the executor of the estate (if any) choose to treat the trust as part of the estate.

The active participation standard is less stringent than the material participation standard (¶ 1165). An individual may meet the active participation requirement if he or she participates in the making of management decisions (for example, approving new tenants, deciding on rental terms, approving expenditures) or arranges for others to provide services (for example, repairs) in a significant and bona fide sense. The active participation requirement applies in the year in which the loss arose as well as the year in which the loss is allowed. However, a real estate professional may be able to treat rental property activities as nonpassive activities (¶ 1185).

The $25,000 maximum offset amount is reduced, but not less than zero, by 50 percent of the amount by which the taxpayer's adjusted gross income (AGI) exceeds $100,000. It is completely phased out when AGI reaches $150,000. AGI is computed for the purpose without regard to: taxable Social Security and railroad retirement benefits (¶ 716); the exclusion for qualified U.S. savings bonds used to pay higher education expenses (¶ 863); the exclusion for employer adoption assistance payments (¶ 2063); passive activity income or loss included on Form 8582; any overall loss from a publicly traded partnership (¶ 1171); rental real estate losses allowed to real estate professionals; and deductions for contributions to IRAs and pension plans (¶ 2107), for one-half of self-employment tax (¶ 1027), interest on student loans (¶ 1011), tuition and fees for tax years beginning before 2021 (¶ 1011A), domestic production activities for tax years beginning before 2018 (¶ 980A), and foreign-derived intangible income (FDII) for tax years beginning after 2017 (¶ 2488B).

Separate Returns. For married individuals who file separate returns and live apart, up to $12,500 of passive losses may be used to offset nonpassive income. This amount is reduced by 50 percent of the amount by which the taxpayer's modified AGI exceeds $50,000. The special allowance is completely phased out when modified AGI reaches $75,000. Married individuals who file separately and live together at any time during the tax year are not eligible for the special allowance.

Offset of Credits. Passive activity credits attributable to rental real estate activities in which the taxpayer actively participates may be claimed under the $25,000 offset provision, but only after all eligible losses have been used. Special rules apply for the phaseout of the rehabilitation credit (¶ 1465B) and low-income housing credit (¶ 1465K).

1185. Real Estate Professionals. A real estate professional may treat rental real estate activities as nonpassive and thus not subject to the passive activity rules (¶ 1165) (Code Sec. 469(c)(7); Reg. § 1.469-9(g)). To qualify:

- more than one-half of the personal services performed in trades or businesses by the taxpayer during the tax year must involve real property trades or businesses in which the taxpayer or the taxpayer's spouse materially participates; and

- the taxpayer must perform more than 750 hours of service during the tax year in real property trades or businesses in which the taxpayer or the taxpayer's spouse materially participates.

These two requirements must be satisfied by one spouse if married individuals file a joint return. Personal services performed as an employee are not taken into account under either requirement unless the employee owns more than a five-percent interest in the employer. A real property trade or business is a business with respect to which real property is developed or redeveloped, constructed or reconstructed, acquired, converted, rented or leased, operated or managed, or brokered.

The exception for real estate professionals is applied as if each interest of the taxpayer in rental real estate is a separate activity. However, a taxpayer may elect to treat all interests in rental real estate as a single activity for purposes of satisfying the material participation requirements. A taxpayer makes the election by filing a statement with his or her original income tax return for the tax year declaring that he or she is a qualified taxpayer for the tax year and is making the election. The due date for filing any federal income tax return otherwise due on or after April 1, 2020, and before July 15, 2020, is automatically extended to July 15, 2020 (¶ 2505). Certain taxpayers may be permitted to make late elections (Rev. Proc. 2011-34).

A closely held corporation qualifies as a real estate professional if more than 50 percent of its annual gross receipts for the tax year are from real property trades or businesses in which it materially participates.

Excess Business Loss and Tax-Exempt Use Property

1190. Excess Business Losses of Noncorporate Taxpayers. A noncorporate taxpayer is not allowed to claim a deduction for any excess business losses in tax years beginning in 2021 through 2025 (Code Sec. 461(l), as amended by the Coronavirus Aid, Relief, and Economic Security (CARES) Act (P.L. 116-136)). Any disallowed excess business losses are treated as a net operating loss (NOL) for the current year for purposes of determining any NOL carryover to subsequent tax years (¶ 1149). The taxpayer applies the passive activity loss rules (¶ 1169) before application of the rules for excess business losses.

An "excess business loss" is the excess, if any, of:

- the taxpayer's aggregate deductions for the tax year from the taxpayer's trades or businesses, determined without regard to whether or not such deductions are disallowed for such tax year under the excess business loss limitation and any deduction allowable for NOLs or qualified business income (¶ 980P); over

- the sum of (1) the taxpayer's aggregate gross income or gain for the tax year from such trades or businesses (determined without regard to any deductions, gross income, or gains attributable to any trade or business of performing services as an employee), plus (2) $250,000, adjusted annually for inflation after 2018 (200 percent of the $250,000 amount for a joint returns).

The amount of gains from sales or exchanges of capital assets taken into account in determining aggregate gross income or gain may not exceed the lesser of (1) the capital gain net income determined by taking into account only gains and losses attributable to a trade or business, or (2) the capital gain net income. Deductions for losses from sales or exchanges of capital assets are not taken into account as aggregate deductions in determining the loss.

For a partnership and S corporation, the limit is applied at the partner or shareholder level. Each partner's distributive share or each S corporation shareholder's pro rata share of items of income, gain, deduction, or loss of the partnership or S corporation is taken into account by the partner or shareholder in applying the excess business loss limit to the partner's or shareholder's tax year with or within which the partnership's or S corporation's tax year ends.

1191. Limits on Tax-Exempt Use Losses. A taxpayer leasing property to a government or other tax-exempt entity (i.e., sale-in, lease-out (SILO) arrangement) is not allowed to claim deductions that are related to the property (known as tax-exempt use property) to the extent that they exceed the taxpayer's income from the lease payments (a tax-exempt use loss), subject to certain exceptions (Code Sec. 470). Tax-exempt use property includes property owned by a partnership or other pass-through entity that has at least one tax-exempt partner and the allocations of partnership items attempt to inappropriately transfer the deductions from the tax-exempt partner to the taxable partners (Code Sec. 168(h)).

Tax-exempt losses disallowed may be carried over to the next tax year and can be deducted to the extent of the taxpayer's net income from the property for that year. If property ceases to be tax-exempt use property during the lease term, the carried-over loss cannot be used to offset income from other property. If the property is disposed of, any disallowed loss is available under rules similar to passive activity losses (¶ 1177), but the limitation on tax-exempt use property losses is applied before the passive activity rules (¶ 1169).

Hobby Losses

See CCH® AnswerConnect: *Hobby Losses* for more information on this topic.

1195. Hobby Expenses and Losses. Expenses incurred by an individual, estate, trust, partnership, and S corporation that are attributable to an activity not engaged in for profit (i.e., a hobby), are generally deductible only to the extent of income produced by the activity (Code Sec. 183; Reg. § 1.183-1). Specifically, if any activity is not engaged in for profit, deductions are allowed as follows:

> (1) deductions a taxpayer can claim whether or not they are incurred with a hobby (e.g., taxes, interest, and casualty losses) are allowed even if they exceed hobby income;

> (2) deductions that do not result in an adjustment to the basis of property (e.g., operating expenses, supplies, etc.) are allowed, but only to the extent that gross income from the hobby exceeds the deductions under category (1); and

> (3) deductions that result in an adjustment to the basis of property (e.g., depreciation and amortization) are allowed, but only to the extent that gross income from the hobby that exceeds the deductions under category (1) and (2).

For tax years beginning before 2018 and after 2025, an individual, estate, and trust may claim the deductions in categories (2) and (3) above only as a miscellaneous itemized deductions subject to the two-percent-of-adjusted-gross-income limitation (¶ 1079). The deductions may not be claimed in tax years beginning in 2018 through 2025. If a partnership or S corporation carries on a hobby, the deduction limits apply at the entity level and are reflected in the distributive share of the partner or shareholder.

Whether an activity is engaged in for profit is generally determined based on the facts and circumstances. An activity is presumed not to be a hobby if it produced a profit (gross income exceeded deductions) in any three of five consecutive tax years ending with the tax year in question, unless the IRS proves otherwise. An activity involving the breeding, training, showing, or racing of horses is presumed not to be a hobby if it produced a profit in two out of seven consecutive tax years.

A special election on Form 5213 permits suspension of the presumption until after the fourth tax year (or sixth tax year for horse breeding, training, showing, or racing) after which the taxpayer first engages in the activity. Filing the form automatically extends the statute of limitations for the IRS to assess a deficiency for any deductions of the activity in any year in the five-year or seven-year period to two years after the due date of the return for the last year of the period.

Chapter 12
DEPRECIATION

Allowance for Depreciation

See CCH® AnswerConnect: *General Depreciation Rules* for more information on this topic.

1201. Property Subject to Depreciation. Taxpayers may deduct a reasonable allowance for the exhaustion, wear and tear of property used in a trade or business, or property held for the production of income (Reg. § 1.167(a)-1). Depreciation is not allowable for property used solely for personal purposes, such as a residence.

Depreciation begins in the tax year that an asset is placed in service and ends in the tax year that it is retired from service or is fully depreciated (Reg. § 1.167(a)-10). An asset is generally considered placed in service when it is in a condition or state of readiness and available for a specifically assigned function (Prop. Reg. § 1.168-2(l)(2)).

Methods of Depreciation. The Modified Accelerated Cost Recovery System (MACRS) (¶ 1236) applies to tangible property generally placed in service after 1986 and the Accelerated Cost Recovery System (ACRS) applies to property placed in service after 1980 and before 1987 (¶ 1252). Under MACRS and ACRS, the cost or other basis of an asset is generally recovered over a specific recovery period.

Post-1980 depreciation on tangible assets first placed in service before 1981 is computed under the method elected for the years they were placed in service. For assets placed in service after 1970 and before 1981, the taxpayer had a choice of the Asset Depreciation Range (ADR) System (¶ 1282) or the general depreciation rules (¶ 1216). For tangible assets first placed in service before 1971, the taxpayer could have elected the Class Life System (CLS) for pre-1971 assets or the general depreciation rules. An asset that is not subject to MACRS or ACRS cannot be depreciated below a reasonable salvage value (Reg. § 1.167(a)-1(a)). Depreciation based on a useful life under the pre-ACRS/MACRS rules is calculated over the estimated useful life of the asset while it is actually used by the taxpayer, not over the longer period of the asset's physical life (Reg. § 1.167(a)-1(b)).

UNICAP Rules. The uniform capitalization rules of Code Sec. 263A require the capitalization of depreciation on equipment and facilities to the extent allocable to property produced or acquired for resale (¶ 1330).

Converted Residence. Depreciation may be taken on a personal residence that has been converted to an income-producing use if the taxpayer proves that (1) the house has in fact been abandoned as a personal residence, and (2) that the property is being held for the production of income. For example, a vacated principle residence offered for sale may be depreciable for the period before the sale if the individual is seeking a profit based on post-conversion appreciation in value (*F.A. Newcombe*, Dec. 30,178, 54 TC 1298). Placing a property for sale immediately or shortly after the time of its abandonment as a residence is strong evidence that the property is not held for post-conversion appreciation in value. MACRS must be used to depreciate a residence converted to business use after 1986. See ¶ 961 for computation of depreciation when a home is used partly for business or rental purposes. See ¶ 1203 for basis for depreciation.

Estates and Trusts. See ¶ 530 for depreciation by an estate or trust.

Inventory and Land. Depreciation is allowed for tangible property, but not for inventories, stock in trade, land apart from its improvements, or a depletable natural resource (Reg. § 1.167(a)-2).

Farmers. Farm buildings and other physical farm property (except land) are depreciable. Livestock acquired for work, breeding, or dairy purposes may be depreciated unless included in inventory (Reg. § 1.167(a)-6(b)).

Intangibles. An intangible business asset that is not amortizable over 15 years under Code Sec. 197 (¶ 1362) may be amortized under Code Sec. 167, generally using the straight-line method, provided that it has an ascertainable value and useful life that can be measured with reasonable accuracy (Reg. § 1.167(a)-3). Certain intangibles with no ascertainable useful life that are created by a taxpayer may be amortized over 15 years (¶ 1364).

Software. Computer software that is not an amortizable Code Sec. 197 intangible (¶ 1362) may be depreciated using the straight-line method over 36 months beginning on the first day of the month the software is placed in service (¶ 980) (Code Sec. 167(f)(1); Reg. § 1.167(a)-14(b); Rev. Proc. 2000-50). However, the cost of software developed for internal use or sale may be currently deducted as a research and development expense, amortized using the straight-line method over 60 months beginning on the date its development is complete, or amortized over 36 months from the date it is placed in service. Expenditures paid or incurred in tax years beginning after 2021 for developing software must be amortized over 60 months as research and development expenditures (¶ 979). Off-the-shelf computer software may be expensed under Code Sec. 179 (¶ 1208). Software included as part of the purchase price of a computer that has no separately stated cost is depreciated as part of the cost of the computer over a five-year recovery period.

Web Site Development Costs. The IRS has not issued formal guidance on the treatment of web site development costs, but informal internal IRS guidance suggests that one appropriate approach is to treat these costs like an item of software and depreciate them over three years. It is clear, however, that taxpayers who pay large amounts to develop sophisticated sites have been allocating their costs to items such as software development (currently deductible like research and development costs under Code Sec. 174) and currently deductible advertising expense (Code Sec. 167(f); Spring 2000, ISP Digest Data Processing).

Residential Mortgage-Servicing Rights. Depreciable residential mortgage-servicing rights that are not Code Sec. 197 intangibles may be depreciated under the straight-line method over 108 months (Code Sec. 167(f)(3)).

Term Interests. The purchaser of a term interest in property held for business or investment is generally entitled to recover its cost over its expected life. However, no depreciation or amortization deduction is allowed for certain term interests in property for any period during which the remainder interest is held directly (or indirectly) by a related person (Code Sec. 167(e)).

Form 4562. Form 4562 is generally used to claim the depreciation or amortization deduction. Individuals and other noncorporate taxpayers (including S corporations) need not complete Form 4562 if their only depreciation or amortization deduction is for property (other than listed property (¶ 1211) placed in service before the current tax year. Form 4562 must be filed if a section 179 deduction (including a carryover) is claimed in the current tax year.

Basis for Depreciation

See CCH® AnswerConnect: *General Depreciation Rules* for more information on this topic.

1203. Cost or Other Basis Recoverable Through Depreciation. The cost of a depreciable asset is recovered through depreciation, after being reduced by any amount claimed as an expense deduction under Code Sec. 179 (¶ 1208) or as first-year bonus depreciation (¶ 1237). Other downward adjustments to cost prior to depreciation may also be necessary to prevent a duplication of benefits from credits and deductions claimed with respect to the property in the tax year of purchase. See ¶ 1465A for the effect of the investment credit on depreciable basis.

If property held for personal use, such as a residence, is converted to business or income-producing use, the basis for depreciation is the lesser of the property's fair market value or adjusted basis on the date of conversion (Reg. § 1.167(g)-1; Reg. § 1.168(i)-4(b)). In the case of a residence converted to business use after 1986, the Modified Accelerated Cost Recovery System (MACRS) must be used (¶ 1236).

If a building and land are acquired for a lump sum, only the building is depreciated. The basis must be allocated between the land and the building in proportion to their relative fair market values at the time of acquisition (Reg. § 1.167(a)-5). If property is subject to both depreciation and amortization, depreciation is allowable only for the portion that is not subject to amortization and may be taken concurrently with amortization.

Section 179 Expense Election

See CCH® AnswerConnect: *Section 179 Deduction* for more information on this topic.

1208. Code Sec. 179 Expense Election. A taxpayer other than an estate, trust, and specified noncorporate lessor may elect to expense the cost of qualifying section 179 property placed in service during the tax year rather than treating the cost as a capital expenditure (Code Sec. 179). The election is made on Form 4562 and must be made with the original return of the tax year the property is placed in service (whether or not filed on time). A taxpayer may also make, revoke, or change an election without IRS consent on an amended return filed during the period prescribed for filing an amended return (Code Sec. 179(c)(2); Reg. § 1.179-5(c)).

De Minimis Expensing Rule. A separate rule allows a taxpayer to elect to deduct amounts paid or incurred to acquire materials and supplies, and amounts paid or incurred to acquire or produce units of property costing less than a prescribed amount, if specific requirements are met (¶ 1311).

Dollar Limitation. The maximum amount that a taxpayer may elect to expense under Code Sec. 179 is $1.02 million for tax years beginning in 2019 ($1.04 million for tax years beginning in 2020) (Code Sec. 179(b)(1) and (b)(6); Rev. Proc. 2018-57; Rev. Proc. 2019-44). The dollar limit is $1 million for tax years beginning in 2018, $510,000 for tax years beginning in 2017, and $500,000 for tax years beginning in 2010 through 2016. See ¶ 1214 for a discussion of the $25,000 section 179 deduction limit for sport utility vehicles, short-bed trucks, and certain vans that are exempt from the luxury car depreciation caps.

Investment Limitation. The maximum dollar limitation is reduced by the cost of section 179 property placed in service during the tax year that exceeds an investment limitation. The investment limitation is $2.55 million for tax years beginning in 2019 ($2.59 million for tax years beginning in 2020). The investment limitation is $2.5 million for tax years beginning in 2018, $2.03 million for tax years beginning in 2017, $2.01 million for tax years beginning in 2016, and $2 million for tax years beginning 2010 through 2015. Any reduction in the dollar limitation attributable to the investment limitation is not carried over (Code Sec. 179(b)(2) and (b)(6); Reg. § 1.179-2(b)(2)).

> **Example 1:** ZYX Corp. is a calendar year corporation that places in service section 179 property in 2019. ZYX may not claim a deduction under Code Sec. 179 if the amount placed in service is more than $3.57 million for the year ($3.57 million – $2.55 million = $1.02 million).

Taxable Income Limitation. The total cost of section 179 property for which an election to expense is made that may be deducted cannot exceed the total amount of taxable income derived from the active conduct of the taxpayer's trades or businesses during the tax year, including salary and wages received as an employee (Code Sec. 179(b)(3); Reg. § 1.179-2(c)).

Carryforwards. The amount elected to be expensed after any reduction on account of the investment limitation and that is disallowed as a deduction as a result of the taxable income limitation is carried forward for an unlimited number of years (Code Sec. 179(b)(3); Reg. § 1.179-3).

12 DEPRECIATION

Example 2: ABC Corp., a calendar-year taxpayer, places $3.1 million of section 179 property in service in 2018. The $1 million expensing limit for 2018 is reduced under the investment limit by $600,000 ($3.1 million – $2.5 million). ABC may elect to expense up to $400,000 ($1 million – $600,000) of the cost of the section 179 property placed in service in 2018. The $600,000 reduction in the expensing limit is not carried forward to 2019. If ABC elects to expense the full $400,000 and it's 2018 taxable income from the active conduct of its trade or business during the year is $300,000, then ABC's section 179 deduction for 2018 is limited to $300,000. The $100,000 disallowed deduction is carried forward to 2019.

The amount allowable as a section 179 deduction in a carryforward year is increased by the lesser of (1) the aggregate amount of unused carryforwards for all prior tax years, or (2) the amount of any unused section 179 expense allowance for the carryforward year. The amount of the unused section 179 expense allowance for the carryforward year equals the excess (if any) of (1) the maximum cost of section 179 property that the taxpayer may deduct for the carryforward year after applying the investment limitation and taxable income limitation, over (2) the amount of section 179 property that the taxpayer actually elects to expense in the carryforward year.

Example 3: Assume the same facts as in Example 2 above, except that in 2019 ABC places $1.01 million of section 179 property in service. No reduction in the $1.02 million expensing limit for 2019 is required under the investment limit because ABC did not place more than $2.55 million of section 179 property in service. ABC may only elect to expense up to $1.01 million in 2019 since the $1.01 million cost of the section 179 property placed in service is less than the $1.02 million expensing limit after application of the investment limit.

If ABC's 2019 taxable income is $1.5 million, it may claim a $1.01 expense deduction for the section 179 property placed in service in 2019 since its taxable income exceeds the $1.01 cost of the property placed in service during the year. ABC's unused section 179 allowance is $10,000 ($1.02 million - $1.01 million). Therefore, ABC may deduct $10,000 of the $100,000 2018 carryforward in 2019. The remaining $90,000 carryforward from 2018 is carried to 2020. None of the carryforward would have been deductible in 2019 if ABC's taxable income had been $1.01 million and ABC elected to expense $1.01 million.

Carryforwards are considered used from the earliest year in which a carryforward arose. To the extent a carryforward is attributable to multiple properties placed in service in the same tax year, a taxpayer may select the properties and apportionment of cost for purposes of determining the source of the carryforward. This selection, however, must be recorded on the taxpayer's books and records in the tax year the property was placed in service and followed consistently in subsequent tax years. If no selection is made the carryover is apportioned equally among the items of section 179 property that were expensed in the tax year that the carryforward arose. For this purpose, allocations of a section 179 expense from a partnership or S corporation are treated as a single item of section 179 property (Reg. § 1.179-3(e)).

Basis Reduction. The basis of an expensed property for purposes of computing depreciation is reduced by the full amount elected to be expensed (after application of the investment limitation) even if a portion of the elected amount is disallowed as a deduction under the taxable income limitation and carried forward. If the property is sold, disposed of, or transferred in a nonrecognition transaction (including transfers at death) before the carryforward is deducted, the basis of the property is increased immediately before the transfer by the carryforward attributable to the property that was not deducted. The unused carryforward that increases the basis of the property is not deducted by the transferor or transferee (Reg. § 1.179-3(f)(1)).

Short Tax Year. The computation of the section 179 deduction is not affected by a short tax year (Reg. § 1.179-1(c)(1)).

Married Taxpayers. Married individuals filing jointly are treated as one taxpayer for purposes of applying the dollar, investment, and taxable income limitations regardless of which spouse placed the qualifying property in service (Reg. § 1.179-2(b)(5)(i) and (c)(7)(i)). Married individuals filing separately may allocate the dollar limitation after any reduction by the investment limitation between themselves or, in the absence of an allocation agreement, divide it equally. Separate filers aggregate section 179 property for purposes of applying the investment limitation (Code Sec. 179(b)(4); Reg.

§ 1.179-2(b)(6)). The taxable income limitation is applied individually to separate filers (Reg. § 1.179-2(c)(8)).

Partnerships and S Corporations. The dollar limitation, investment limitation, and taxable income limitation are applied separately at the partnership and partner levels (Code Sec. 179(d)(8); Reg. § 1.179-2(b)(3), (b)(4), (c)(2), and (c)(3)). In applying the investment limitation, the cost of section 179 property placed in service by the partnership is not attributed to any partner. A similar rule applies to an S corporation and its shareholders.

For purposes of applying the taxable income limitation at the partnership or S corporation level, taxable income (or loss) derived by the partnership or S corporation from the active conduct of a trade or business is computed by aggregating the net income (or loss) from all the trades or businesses actively conducted by the entity during the tax year.

A partner's or S corporation shareholder's taxable income includes net distributable profit or loss from the pass-through entity in which the taxpayer is an active participant. A partner and S corporation shareholder is required to reduce the basis of their partnership or S corporation interest by the full amount of an expense deduction allocated to them even though part of the deduction must be carried over because of the partner's or S corporation shareholder's taxable income limitation or disallowed because of the dollar limitation (Reg. § 1.179-3(h)(1); Rev. Rul. 89-7).

Controlled Groups. Members of a controlled group on December 31 are treated as a single taxpayer for purposes of the dollar, investment, and taxable income limitation even if a consolidated return is not filed (Code Sec. 179(d)(6)). The allowable expense deduction may be allocated among members in any manner, but the amount allocated to any member may not exceed the cost of section 179 property actually purchased and placed in service during the tax year by the member (Reg.§ 1.179-2(b)(7)).

Noncorporate Lessors. A lessor, other than a corporation, may not claim the section 179 deduction on leased property unless the property was manufactured or produced by the lessor, or the term of the lease is less than one-half of the property's class life (i.e. MACRS alternative depreciation system (ADS) period). In addition, for the 12-month period following the date that the leased property is transferred to the lessee, the total ordinary and necessary business deductions allowed to the lessor for the property must exceed 15 percent of the rental income produced by the property (Code Sec. 179(d)(5); Reg. § 1.179-1(i)(2)).

Exemption from UNICAP and Section 263 Capitalization. The section 179 deduction is an indirect cost that is not required to be capitalized under the uniform capitalization (UNICAP) rules (Reg. §§ 1.179-1(j) and 1.263A-1(e)(3)(iii)). Amounts expensed under Code Sec. 179 are also not required to be capitalized under Code Sec. 263 (Code Sec. 263(a)(1)(G); Reg. § 1.179-1(j)).

Section 179 Property Defined. Section 179 property is tangible section 1245 property (new or used) depreciable under the Modified Accelerated Cost Recovery System (MACRS) and acquired by purchase for use in the active conduct of a trade or business (Code Sec. 179(d)). Property used predominantly outside of the United States and property used by tax-exempt organizations (unless the property is used predominantly in connection with an unrelated business income activity) do not qualify as section 179 property (Code Sec. 50(b)).

In tax years beginning before 2018, property used with respect to lodging, such as apartment buildings but not hotels and motels, does not qualify for expensing (Code Sec. 179(d)(1), prior to amendment by the Tax Cuts and Jobs Act (P.L. 115-97)).

Depreciable off-the-shelf computer software may be expensed under Code Sec. 179 (Code Sec. 179(d)(1)(A)). This is software described in Code Sec. 197(e)(3)(A)(i) that is readily available for purchase by the general public, is subject to a nonexclusive license, has not been substantially modified, and is depreciable over three years.

Portable air conditioning and heating units placed in service in tax years beginning after 2015 may also qualify as section 179 property (Rev. Proc. 2017-33).

Qualified Real Property. A taxpayer may elect to treat the cost of qualified real property placed in service during the tax year as section 179 property (Code Sec. 179(d)(1)(B)(ii) and (e); Notice 2013-59).

Example 4: A calendar-year taxpayer places $1.6 million of qualified real property in service in 2019 and elects to treat it as section 179 property. The taxpayer also places $420,000 of other section 179 property in service in 2019. The $1.02 million expensing limit for 2019 is not subject to reduction under the investment limit because the taxpayer did not place more than $2.55 million of section 179 property in service in 2019. The taxpayer may elect to expense up to $1.02 million of the cost of its qualified real property. If it elects to expense $1.02 million of the qualified real property, then it may not elect to expense any other section 179 property in 2019 since the full $1.02 million expensing limit has been used. If the taxpayer elected to expense only $600,000 of qualified real property, it could elect to expense up to $420,000 of its other section 179 property.

In tax years beginning after 2017, qualified real property is defined as:

- qualified improvement property (Code Sec. 168(e)(6)) (¶ 1240); and

- any of the following improvements to nonresidential real property placed in service after the date such property was first placed in service: roofs; heating, ventilation, and air-conditioning property; fire protection and alarm systems; and security systems (Code Sec. 179(e)).

In tax years beginning before 2018, qualified real property is defined as: qualified leasehold improvement property (¶ 1234 and ¶ 1237); qualified restaurant property (¶ 1240); and qualified retail improvement property (¶ 1240) (Code Sec. 179(f), prior to amendment by P.L. 115-97). These three types of property have a 15-year recovery period under MACRS if placed in service before 2018.

The amount of qualified real property that is expensed under Code Sec. 179 is subject to the section 1245 ordinary income recapture rules (¶ 1785) (Code Sec. 1245(a)(3)(C)). If only a portion of the cost of a qualified real property is expensed, a taxpayer may use any reasonable method to determine the amount of gain on the disposition of the property that is attributable to section 1245 property and section 1250 property, including a pro rata allocation and gain allocation methodology (Notice 2013-59). The section 1245 recapture amount is limited to the gain allocated to the section 1245 property.

Purchase Defined. Section 179 property is acquired by purchase unless it: (1) is acquired from a related person (¶ 432 and ¶ 717); (2) is acquired by one member of a controlled group of corporations from another member (substituting 50 percent for the 80 percent that would otherwise apply with respect to stock ownership requirements); (3) has a basis in the hands of the acquiring taxpayer determined in whole or in part by reference to the adjusted basis of the person from who the property was acquired (e.g., a gift); (4) has a basis determined under Code Sec. 1014(a) relating to inherited or bequested property; (5) is acquired by a corporation in a transaction to which Code Sec. 351 applies; (6) is acquired by a partnership through a Code Sec. 723 contribution or is acquired from a partnership in a distribution that has a carryover basis; or (7) is by a new target corporation as the result of a Code Sec. 338 deemed asset election or a Code Sec. 336(e) election (relating to certain stock dispositions treated as asset transfers) made for a disposition described in Reg. § 1.336-2(b)(1) (Code Sec. 179(d)(2); Reg. § 1.179-4(c)).

Carryover Basis in Trade-Ins and Involuntary Conversions. The portion of the basis of property that is attributable to the basis of property that was previously held by the taxpayer (e.g., carryover basis under Code Sec. 1031 and 1033) does not qualify for the expense deduction (Code Sec. 179(d)(3); Reg. § 1.179-4(d)).

Recapture Upon Sale or Disposition. The Code Sec. 179 expense deduction is treated as depreciation for recapture purposes (¶ 1779) (Code Sec. 1245(a)(2)(C)). Thus, gain on a disposition of section 179 property that is section 1245 property is treated as ordinary income to the extent of the section 179 expense allowance claimed plus any depreciation claimed. Qualified real property and certain land improvements are section 1250 property. Nevertheless, a section 179 expense deduction for qualified real property and section 1250 land improvements is also subject to recapture as ordinary income under the rules that apply to section 1245 property (¶ 1785) (Code Sec. 1245(a)(3)(C)).

Recapture Upon Decline in Business Use. If business use of section 179 property does not exceed 50 percent during any year of the property's depreciation period, a portion of the amount expensed is recaptured as ordinary income (Code Sec. 179(d)(10); Reg.

§ 1.179-1(e)). The recapture amount is the difference between the expense claimed and the depreciation that would have been allowed on the expensed amount for prior tax years and the tax year of recapture. However, the recapture rules that apply to listed property such as passenger automobiles used less than 50 percent for business (¶ 1211) take precedence over this section 179 recapture rule. Recapture is reported on Form 4797.

Alternative Minimum Tax. The Code Sec. 179 expense deduction is allowed in full for alternative minimum tax (AMT) purposes (Instructions to Form 6251).

Empowerment Zones. The section 179 annual dollar limitation is increased an additional $35,000 for section 179 property placed in service in designated empowerment zones by an enterprise zone business (Code Sec. 1397A). The $35,000 increase is subject to recapture if the property is removed from the empowerment zone. In general, the qualifying property must be placed in service in the empowerment zone before January 1, 2021 (¶ 1799B).

Limitations on Automobiles and Other Listed Property

See CCH® AnswerConnect: *Depreciation Limitations, Recapture, and Lease Inclusion Amounts for Passenger Automobiles and Other Listed Property* for more information on this topic.

1211. Business Usage Requirement for Listed Property. Depreciation deductions for "listed property" are subject to special rules (Code Sec. 280F). Listed property includes: passenger automobiles (¶ 1214); other forms of transportation, if the property's nature lends itself to personal use (e.g., airplanes, boats, vehicles excluded from the definition of a passenger automobile); entertainment, recreational and amusement property; computers and peripheral equipment if placed in service before 2018; and any other property specified by regulation. Computers and related peripheral equipment are not listed property if placed in service after 2017.

If an item of listed property is not used more than 50 percent for business, depreciation under the Modified Accelerated Cost Recovery System (MACRS) on the property must be determined under the alternative depreciation system (ADS) (¶ 1247). In addition, if the more-than-50-percent business use test is not satisfied in the tax year the property is placed in service, the property does not qualify for the Code Sec. 179 expensing election (¶ 1208) or the bonus depreciation deduction (¶ 1237).

If the listed property satisfies the more-than-50-percent business use requirement in the tax year it is placed in service but fails to meet that test in a later tax year that occurs during any year of the property's ADS recovery period, depreciation deductions (including any section 179 deduction and bonus depreciation) previously taken are subject to recapture (Code Secs. 168(k)(2)(F)(ii), 280F(b)(2), and (d)(1)). MACRS depreciation for years preceding the year in which the business use falls to 50 percent or less is recaptured to the extent that the MACRS depreciation (including the section 179 deduction and bonus depreciation) for such years exceeds the depreciation that would have been allowed under ADS computed as if the section 179 allowance and bonus depreciation had not been claimed. Depreciation thereafter must be computed using ADS. For example, if a taxpayer expenses the entire cost of a listed property, the difference between the amount expensed and the ADS deductions that would have been allowed on that amount prior to the recapture year is recaptured as ordinary income. Part IV of Form 4797 is used to calculate any recapture amount.

See ¶ 1214 for additional limits on passenger automobiles.

1214. Depreciation Limits on Automobiles, Trucks, SUVs, and Vans. The maximum depreciation deductions under the Modified Accelerated Cost Recovery System (MACRS) (including the Section 179 expensing deduction (¶ 1208) and bonus depreciation deduction (¶ 1237) that may be claimed for a passenger automobile, including vans, trucks, and SUVs, placed in service in calendar year 2018 or 2019 are shown in the first table below. For earlier calendar years the limitations for passenger cars are different than the limits that apply to trucks, vans, and SUVs. The second table shows the limitations that apply to cars and the third table shows the limitations that apply to trucks, vans, and SUVs (Code Sec. 280F). See IRS Pub. 463 for limitations that apply to vehicles placed in service in calendar years beginning before 2011.

12

DEPRECIATION

For Vehicles Placed in Service		*Depreciation Allowable in—*				
After	Before	Year 1	Year 2	Year 3	Year 4, etc.	Authority
12/31/17	1/01/19	18,000 * 10,000	16,000	9,600	5,760	Rev. Proc. 2018-25
12/31/18	1/01/20	18,100 * 10,100	16,100	9,700	5,760	Rev. Proc. 2019-26

* The higher first-year limit applies if the vehicle qualifies for bonus depreciation (¶ 1237) and no election out is made.

For Cars Placed in Service		*Depreciation Allowable in—*				
After	Before	Year 1	Year 2	Year 3	Year 4, etc.	Authority
12/31/10	1/01/12	11,060 * 3,060	4,900	2,950	1,775	Rev. Proc. 2011-21
12/31/11	1/01/13	11,160 * 3,160	5,100	3,050	1,875	Rev. Proc. 2012-23
12/31/12	1/01/14	11,160 * 3,160	5,100	3,050	1,875	Rev. Proc. 2013-21
12/31/13	1/01/15	11,160 * 3,160	5,100	3,050	1,875	Rev. Proc. 2014-21, modified by Rev. Proc. 2015-19
12/31/14	1/01/16	11,160 * 3,160	5,100	3,050	1,875	Rev. Proc. 2015-19, modified by Rev. Proc. 2016-23
12/31/15	1/01/17	11,160 * 3,160	5,100	3,050	1,875	Rev. Proc. 2016-23
12/31/16	1/01/18	11,160 * 3,160	5,100	3,050	1,875	Rev. Proc. 2017-29

* The higher first-year limit applies if the vehicle qualifies for bonus depreciation (¶ 1237) and no election out is made.

Assuming that the 200-percent declining balance method and half-year convention apply, a vehicle placed in service in 2019 on which bonus depreciation is not claimed is subject to the first-year cap if the cost of the vehicle exceeds $50,500 ($50,500 × 20 percent = $10,100).

Special rules for vehicles acquired before September 28, 2017 and placed in service in 2018 or 2019. The first-year cap for a passenger car acquired before September 28, 2017, and placed in service in 2018 is $16,400 ($10,000 + $6,400) if bonus depreciation is claimed (Rev. Proc. 2018-25). The first-year cap for a passenger car acquired before September 28, 2017, and placed in service in 2019 is $14,900 if bonus depreciation is claimed (Rev. Proc. 2019-26).

Trucks (including SUVs) and vans are subject to their own set of depreciation caps if placed in service after 2002 and before 2018. These caps (reproduced in the table below) reflect the higher costs associated with such vehicles. However, trucks and vans that have a gross vehicle weight rating greater than 6,000 pounds are not subject to any caps (discussed below). Also, certain trucks and vans are not subject to the caps if, because of their design, they are not likely to be used for personal purposes (discussed below).

For Trucks and Vans Placed in Service After	Before	*Depreciation Allowable in—* Year 1	Year 2	Year 3	Year 4, etc.	Authority
12/31/10	1/01/12	11,260 * 3,260	5,200	3,150	1,875	Rev. Proc. 2011-21
12/31/11	1/01/13	11,360 * 3,360	5,300	3,150	1,875	Rev. Proc. 2012-23
12/31/12	1/01/14	11,360 * 3,360	5,400	3,250	1,975	Rev. Proc. 2013-21
12/31/13	1/01/15	11,460 * 3,460	5,500	3,350	1,975	Rev. Proc. 2014-21, modified by Rev. Proc. 2015-19
12/31/14	1/01/16	11,460 * 3,460	5,600	3,350	1,975	Rev. Proc. 2015-19 modified by Rev. Proc. 2016-23
12/31/15	1/01/17	11,560 * 3,560	5,700	3,350	2,075	Rev. Proc. 2016-23
12/31/16	1/01/18	11,560 * 3,560	5,700	3,450	2,075	Rev. Proc. 2017-29

* The higher first-year limit applies if the vehicle qualifies for bonus depreciation and no election out is made (¶ 1237).

Reduction for personal use. The above maximum annual limits (often referred to as the luxury car limits) are based on 100-percent business/investment use. If business/investment use is less than 100 percent, the limits must be reduced to reflect the actual business/investment use percentage.

Passenger Automobile Defined. For purposes of the depreciation caps, a passenger automobile includes any four-wheeled vehicle manufactured primarily for use on public streets, roads, and highways that has an *unloaded* gross vehicle weight rating (GVWR) (i.e., curb weight fully equipped for service but without passengers or cargo) of 6,000 pounds or less (Code Sec. 280F(d)(5)). A truck or van is treated as a passenger automobile subject to the caps only if it has a GVWR (i.e., maximum total weight of a loaded vehicle as specified by the manufacturer) of 6,000 pounds or less. A truck or van, therefore, is not subject to the depreciation caps if its GVWR exceeds 6,000 pounds. A sport utility vehicle (SUV) is generally treated as a truck (even if built on a unibody or car chassis) and if its GVWR is in excess of 6,000 pounds and as such it is also exempt from the caps. Ambulances or hearses and vehicles used directly in the trade or business of transporting persons or property for hire (e.g., taxis and limousines) are not considered passenger automobiles subject to the caps regardless of their weight.

Luxury Car Depreciation Examples. The depreciation deduction that is claimed on the return for any tax year during a vehicle's recovery (depreciation) period is the lesser of the depreciation deduction for the tax year (computed as if there were no depreciation caps) or the cap that applies for the tax year.

If, after the recovery period for a passenger automobile ends, the taxpayer continues to use the car in its trade or business, the unrecovered basis (referred to as "section 280F unrecovered basis") may be deducted at the maximum annual rate provided in the chart above for the fourth and succeeding years. This rule permits depreciation deductions beyond the recovery period. Unrecovered basis is the difference between the cost of the vehicle and the amount of depreciation claimed on the return during the recovery period (or that would have been claimed on the return if business use had been 100 percent). The MACRS recovery period for a passenger automobile is five full years from the date the vehicle is deemed placed in service under the applicable half-year or mid-quarter convention (¶ 1245). Due to operation of the applicable convention, depreciation deductions are claimed over the six tax years that the five-year recovery period falls within.

The following example illustrates how depreciation is computed if the bonus depreciation allowance is not claimed.

12 | DEPRECIATION

¶1214

Example 1: On April 5, 2019, a calendar-year taxpayer purchased a car for $70,000. Business use of the car each year is 100 percent. Depreciation is computed under the general MACRS 200-percent declining-balance method over a five-year recovery period using a half-year convention subject to the luxury car limitations. An election out of bonus depreciation is made. Allowable depreciation during the regular recovery period (2019 through 2024) is computed as follows:

Year	100% Business-Use MACRS Depreciation	Luxury Car Limit	Deduction: Lesser of Col. 2 or 3	Sec. 280F Unrecovered Basis
2019.......	$14,000	$10,100	$10,100	$59,900
2020.......	22,400	16,100	16,100	43,800
2021.......	13,440	9,700	9,700	34,100
2022.......	8,064	5,760	5,760	28,340
2023.......	8,064	5,760	5,760	22,580
2024.......	4,032	5,760	4,032	18,548

100% business use MACRS depreciation (column 2) is computed by applying the applicable table percentage to the $70,000 cost.

The unrecovered basis is computed by subtracting the depreciation that would have been allowed (taking the applicable cap into consideration) if business use was 100 percent, even if business use is less than 100 percent. The unrecovered basis at the close of 2019 is $59,900 ($70,000 – $10,100). The $18,548 unrecovered basis at the close of the regular recovery period is deducted in the post recovery period years at the rate of $5,760 per year assuming 100-percent business use continues. The unrecovered basis is reduced by $5,760 each year regardless of the percentage of business use.

The following example shows how luxury car depreciation is computed if the 50-percent bonus deduction is claimed.

Example 2: On April 5, 2017, a calendar-year taxpayer purchased a new car for $30,000. Business use of the car each year is 100 percent. Depreciation is computed under the general MACRS 200-percent declining-balance method over a five-year recovery period using a half-year convention subject to the luxury car limitations. Allowable depreciation during the regular recovery period (2017 through 2022) is computed as follows:

Year	100% Business-Use MACRS Depreciation	Luxury Car Limit	Deduction: Lesser of Col. 2 or 3	Sec. 280F Unrecovered Basis
2017.......	$18,000	$11,160	$11,160	$18,840
2018.......	4,800	5,100	4,800	14,040
2019.......	2,880	3,050	2,880	11,160
2020.......	1,728	1,875	1,728	9,432
2021.......	1,728	1,875	1,728	7,704
2022.......	864	1,875	864	6,840

Beginning in 2023, the unrecovered basis is the $6,840 difference between the $30,000 cost and the sum of the return deductions claimed in 2017 through 2022. The unrecovered basis is deducted at the rate of $1,875 per year assuming that 100-percent business use continues. The unrecovered basis is reduced by $1,875 each year regardless of the percentage of business use.

Safe-harbor for 100 percent bonus depreciation. The IRS has provided a safe harbor for computing depreciation on a vehicle acquired after September 27, 2017, and placed in service before January 1, 2023, on which 100 percent bonus depreciation is claimed (Rev. Proc. 2019-13). Without the safe harbor, a taxpayer claiming the 100-percent bonus deduction may not claim any depreciation deductions on the unrecovered basis (cost less first-year cap ($18,100 in 2019)) until after the end of the vehicle's regular recovery period. This is because the vehicle is considered to have a basis of zero (cost less the 100 percent bonus allowance) for purposes of computing depreciation in the remaining years of the regular recovery period even though the 100 percent bonus is limited to the first-year cap (Code Sec. 280F(a)(1)(B)).

The election is made by computing depreciation in accordance with the safe harbor. The first-year deduction is equal to the first-year cap ($18,100 for a vehicle placed in service in 2019). The depreciation deduction for each remaining tax year in the recovery period is equal to the lesser of (1) the applicable depreciation cap for the recovery year or (2) the depreciation deduction computed by applying the applicable table percentage for the tax year to the cost of the vehicle as reduced by the first year cap. The disallowed depreciation (i.e., the unrecovered basis) is recovered beginning with the first tax year after the end of the recovery period at the regularly prescribed rate ($5,760 per year for a vehicle placed in service in 2019).

The safe harbor may not be elected if the vehicle cost less then the first-year cap or the section 179 allowance is claimed. A taxpayer electing the safe harbor must compute depreciation using the table percentages.

The following example shows how depreciation is computed if the safe harbor is elected.

Example 3: On April 5, 2019, a calendar-year taxpayer purchased a car for $70,000. Business use of the car each year is 100 percent. Depreciation is computed under the general MACRS 200-percent declining-balance method over a five-year recovery period using a half-year convention subject to the luxury car limitations. Bonus depreciation is claimed. Allowable depreciation during the regular recovery period (2019 through 2024) is computed as follows:

Year	100% Business-Use MACRS Depreciation	Luxury Car Limit	Deduction: Lesser of Col. 2 or 3	Sec. 280F Unrecovered Basis
2019	$70,000	$18,100	$18,100	$51,900
2020	16,608	16,100	16,100	35,800
2021	9,965	9,700	9,700	26,100
2022	5,979	5,760	5,760	20,340
2023	5,979	5,760	5,760	14,580
2024	2,989	5,760	2,989	11,591

Under the safe harbor, the first-year 100 percent business use MACRS deduction without regard to the first-year cap is $70,000 since 100 percent bonus applies. The deduction, however, is limited to the $18,100 first-year cap. In each subsequent year the table percentages are applied to $51,900 ($70,000 cost - $18,100 first-year cap) to determine the 100% business use MACRS deduction. The lesser of the deduction or the cap is claimed. The unrecovered basis of $11,591 is claimed at the rate of $5,760 in each post-recovery year.

$25,000 Section 179 Expensing Cap on SUVs, Trucks, and Vans Exempt from Luxury Car Depreciation Caps. The maximum amount of the cost of an SUV that may be expensed under Code Sec. 179 if the SUV is exempt from the luxury car caps (e.g., has a GVWR in excess of 6,000 pounds) is limited to $25,500 for 2019 ($25,900 for 2020). The limit is $25,000 for 2018 and earlier (Code Sec. 179(b)(5) and (b)(6); Rev. Proc. 2018-57; Rev. Proc. 2019-44). The limitation also applies to exempt trucks with an interior cargo bed length of less than six feet and exempt passenger vans that seat fewer than ten persons behind the driver's seat. Exempt cargo vans are generally not subject to the limitation.

Exclusion from Depreciation Caps for Trucks and Vans Used for Nonpersonal Purposes. A truck or van that is a qualified nonpersonal use vehicle as defined in Reg. §1.274-5(k) is excluded from the definition of a passenger automobile and is not subject to the annual depreciation limits (Reg. §1.280F-6(c)(3)(iii)). A qualified nonpersonal use vehicle generally is one that has been specially modified in such a way that it is not likely to be used more than a *de minimis* amount for personal purposes.

Reporting. The allowable depreciation deduction for any listed property, including automobiles, is reported on Form 4562 (Part V).

1215. Leased Listed Property Inclusion Amounts. The lessee of a passenger automobile (¶ 1214) used for business must include an additional amount in income to offset rental deductions for each tax year during which the vehicle is leased (Code Sec. 280F(c)(2); Reg. §1.280F-7). The inclusion amount is based on the cost of the vehicle and generally applies to a vehicle with a fair market value exceeding an inflation-adjusted dollar amount. The inclusion amount is not required on trucks, vans, and sport utility vehicles (SUVs) that would be exempt from the depreciation caps if owned by the lessee (e.g., an SUV treated as a truck with a gross vehicle weight rating (GVWR) in excess of 6,000 pounds).

12

DEPRECIATION

Lease inclusion tables are issued annually by the IRS. The appropriate table is based on the calendar year that the vehicle was first leased. The same table is used for each year of the lease term. The inclusion tables are issued annually in the same revenue procedure that provides the annual depreciation caps. The 2019 lease inclusion table is provided in Rev. Proc. 2019-26. The 2018 lease inclusion table is provided in Rev. Proc. 2018-25. For leases entered into prior to 2018, separate lease inclusion tables are provided for trucks and vans and cars.

A lessee's inclusion amount for each tax year that the vehicle is leased is computed as follows: (1) use the fair market value of the vehicle on the first day of the lease term to find the appropriate dollar (inclusion) amounts on the IRS table; (2) prorate the dollar amount from the table for the number of days of the lease term included in the tax year; and (3) multiply the prorated amount by the percentage of business and investment use for the tax year. For the last tax year during any lease that does not begin and end in the same tax year, the dollar amount for the preceding tax year should be used.

Example: A car costing $61,000 is leased for four years by a calendar-year taxpayer beginning on April 1, 2019, and is used 100 percent for business. The annual dollar amounts from the table contained in Rev. Proc. 2019-26 for leases beginning in 2019 are: $46 for the first tax year during the lease, $102 for the second tax year, $151 for the third tax year, $181 for the fourth tax year, and $211 for the fifth and following tax years. In 2019, the inclusion amount is $34.66 (275/365 × $46). The inclusion amounts for 2020, 2021, and 2022 are $102, $151, and $181, respectively, since the vehicle is leased for the entire year during these tax years. In 2023, the inclusion amount is $44.63 (90/365 × $181 (the dollar amount for 2022, the preceding tax year, is used in the last year of the lease).

Listed Property Other Than Passenger Automobiles. Lessees of listed property other than passenger automobiles (¶ 1211) are required to include in income a usage-based inclusion amount in the first tax year that the business use percentage of such property is 50 percent or less (Code Sec. 280F(c); Reg. § 1.280F-7(b)).

Reporting. The inclusion amount is reported on Form 2106 by employees, Schedule C (Form 1040) by the self-employed, and Schedule F (Form 1040) by farmers.

Depreciation Methods

See CCH® AnswerConnect: *General Depreciation Rules* for more information on this topic.

1216. Methods of Computing Depreciation. Most tangible property placed in service after 1986 must be depreciated using the Modified Accelerated Cost Recovery System (MACRS) (¶ 1243). Depreciation for tangible property placed in service after 1980 and before 1987 is computed under ACRS (¶ 1252).

For tangible property placed in service before 1981, depreciation may be computed under the straight-line method (¶ 1224), the double declining-balance method (¶ 1226), the sum-of-the-years-digits method (¶ 1228), and other consistent methods (¶ 1231), depending on the taxpayer's election in the year the property was placed in service (former Code Sec. 167(b)). However, accelerated depreciation for pre-1981 realty is limited (former Code Sec. 167(j)).

For an asset purchased before 1981, only a part of a full year's depreciation was allowed in the year it was placed in service. The allowable deduction was computed by multiplying the first full year's depreciation allowance by the months the property was owned and dividing by 12. The same rule applies in the year of sale.

1218. Methods for Depreciating Real Estate. Real property placed in service after 1986 is depreciated under the Modified Accelerated Cost Recovery System (MACRS) (¶ 1236). Real property placed in service after 1980 and before 1987 is depreciated under the Accelerated Cost Recovery System (ACRS) (¶ 1252). Additions and improvements to a building, including structural components of a building, placed in service after 1986 are depreciated under MACRS (¶ 1240). Post-1986 rehabilitation expenditures are also depreciated using MACRS. Elements of a building that qualify as personal property may be separately depreciated under the cost segregation rules using shortened MACRS recovery periods. Real property that is converted from personal use to residential rental property or nonresidential real property is depreciated as MACRS 27.5-year residential rental property or MACRS 39-year nonresidential real property respectively even if the property was acquired for personal use prior to 1987.

1221. Change in Depreciation Method—Accounting Method Changes. A change in the method of computing depreciation is generally a change in accounting method that requires the consent of the IRS and the filing of Form 3115 (Reg. § 1.167(e)-1). If the change from an impermissible accounting method to a permissible accounting method results in a negative section 481(a) adjustment, the adjustment is taken into account in a single tax year (¶ 1531). A positive section 481(a) adjustment is taken into account over four tax years—one-year if the positive adjustment is less than $50,000 and the taxpayer makes an election to include it in income in one year. No section 481(a) adjustment is allowed when a taxpayer changes from one permissible method to another permissible method. These changes are applied on a "cut-off" basis (Rev. Proc. 2015-13). Reg. § 1.446-1(e)(2)(ii)(d)(2) and (3) list changes in depreciation or amortization that are or are not considered a change in accounting method.

Although a taxpayer has not adopted an accounting method unless two or more returns have been filed, the IRS allows a taxpayer who has only filed one return that claimed incorrect depreciation to either file Form 3115 and claim a section 481(a) adjustment on the current-year return or file an amended return. The asset must have been placed in service in the tax year immediately preceding the tax year of the change (Rev. Proc. 2007-16).

For changes that are not a change in accounting method, such as mathematical or posting errors, a taxpayer may only file amended returns for open years. Changes in accounting method are generally made by filing Form 3115. Procedures for changing from an impermissible method (e.g., where incorrect or no depreciation was claimed, including bonus depreciation) to a permissible method are generally governed by the automatic consent procedures of Section 6.01 of Rev. Proc. 2019-43, effective for Form 3115 filed on or after November 8, 2019, for a year change ending on or after March 31, 2019. The automatic consent procedures of Section 6.01 of Rev. Proc. 2018-31, are effective for Forms 3115 filed on or after May 9, 2018, for a year of change ending on or after September 30, 2017. Numerous additional types of automatic accounting method changes for depreciation are provided in Section 6. For changes not listed in Section 6, the advance consent procedures of Rev. Proc. 2015-13 are followed.

A taxpayer who has sold depreciable property without claiming any depreciation or all of the depreciation allowable may claim the depreciation by filing Form 3115 during the limitations period for filing an amended return for the year of the sale. The Form 3115 may be filed with the original federal tax return for the tax year in which the depreciable property is disposed (Rev. Proc. 2007-16; Rev. Proc. 2019-43, Section 6.07).

For depreciable property placed in service in a tax year ending before December 30, 2003, the IRS will not assert that a change in computing depreciation is a change in accounting method (Chief Counsel Notice 2004-007, January 28, 2004, as clarified by Chief Counsel Notice 2004-24, July 14, 2004).

1224. Straight-Line or Fixed-Percentage Method of Depreciation. The "straight-line" method of computing the depreciation deduction assumes that the depreciation sustained is uniform during the useful life of the property. The cost or other basis, less estimated salvage value, is deductible in equal annual amounts over the estimated useful life (Reg. § 1.167(b)-1). An asset may not be depreciated below its salvage value. Straight-line depreciation under the Modified Accelerated Cost Recovery System (MACRS) (¶ 1243) and the Accelerated Cost Recovery System (ACRS) (¶ 1252) is generally computed in this manner, except that a recovery period is used instead of the useful life and salvage value is not considered (Code Sec. 168(b)(4)).

1226. Declining-Balance Method of Depreciation. Under the declining-balance depreciation method, depreciation is greatest in the first year and smaller in each succeeding year (Reg. § 1.167(b)-2). The depreciable basis (e.g., cost) is reduced each year by the amount of the depreciation deduction, and a uniform rate of 200 percent of the straight-line rate (double-declining balance or 200-percent declining balance method) or 150 percent of the straight-line rate (150-percent declining balance method) is applied to the resulting balances (Reg. § 1.167(b)-2). Under the Modified Accelerated Cost Recovery System (MACRS), the 200-percent declining balance method is used to depreciate 3-, 5-, 7-, and 10-year property and the 150-percent declining balance method is used to depreciate 15- and 20-year property (¶ 1243).

1228. Sum-of-the-Years-Digits Method of Depreciation. Under the sum-of-the-years-digits method of depreciation, changing fractions are applied each year to the original cost or other basis, less salvage value. The numerator of the fraction each year represents the remaining useful life of the asset and the denominator, which remains constant, is the sum of the numerals representing each of the years of the estimated useful life (the sum-of-the-years digits). The taxpayer may elect this method for group, classified, or composite accounts (Reg. § 1.167(b)-3).

1229. Income Forecast Method of Depreciation. The income forecast method of depreciation may be used only for film, videotape, sound recordings, copyrights, books, patents, and other property identified by IRS regulations. The income forecast method may not be used to depreciate intangible property that is amortizable under Code Sec. 197 (¶ 1362) or consumer durables subject to rent-to-own contracts (¶ 1240) (Code Sec. 167(g)(6); Rev. Rul. 60-358).

Under the income forecast method, the cost of an asset (less any salvage value) is multiplied by a fraction, the numerator of which is the net income from the asset for the tax year and the denominator of which is the total net income forecast to be derived from the asset before the close of the 10th tax year following the tax year in which the asset is placed in service. The unrecovered adjusted basis of the property as of the beginning of the 10th tax year is claimed as a depreciation deduction in the 10th tax year following the tax year in which the asset was placed in service.

If the income forecast changes during the 10-year period, the unrecovered depreciable cost of the asset at the beginning of the tax year of revision is multiplied by a fraction. The numerator is the net income from the asset for the tax year of revision. The denominator is the revised forecasted total net income from the asset for the year of revision and the remaining years before the close of the 10th tax year following the tax year in which the asset was placed in service.

During the 3rd and 10th tax years after the asset is placed in service, a taxpayer is generally required to pay or may receive interest based on the recalculation of depreciation using actual income figures. This look-back rule does not apply to property that has a cost basis of $100,000 or less, or if the taxpayer's income projections were within 10 percent of the income actually earned.

Residuals and participations may be included in the adjusted basis of a property in the tax year that it is placed in service or excluded from adjusted basis and deducted in the year of payment (Code Sec. 167(g)(7); Notice 2006-47).

Reporting. Form 8866 is used to compute the look-back interest due or owed.

Creative Property Costs of Film Makers. A taxpayer may choose to amortize creative property costs ratably over 15 years beginning on the first day of the second half of the tax year in which the cost is written off for financial accounting purposes in accordance with Statement of Position 00-2 (SOP 00-2), as issued by the American Institute of Certified Public Accountants (AICPA) on June 12, 2000 (Rev. Proc. 2004-36). Creative property costs are costs to acquire and develop for purposes of potential future film development, production, and exploitation. If the election is not made, these costs are generally recovered under the income forecast method only if a film is actually produced. If a film is not made, the costs generally are not deductible as a loss (Rev. Rul. 2004-58).

Election to Expense Film, Television, Live Theatre Costs. A taxpayer may elect to deduct the cost of any qualified film or television production, and any qualified live theatrical production, commenced before January 1, 2021 (Code Sec. 181, as amended by the Taxpayer Certainty and Disaster Tax Relief Act of 2019 (P.L. 116-94); Reg. § 1.181-2). The maximum deduction is $15 million ($20 million for films produced in certain low-income or distressed communities).

1231. Other Consistent Depreciation Methods. In addition to the general depreciation methods (¶ 1216), a taxpayer may use any other consistent method, such as the sinking fund method, if the total deductions during the first two-thirds of the useful life are not more than the total allowable under the declining-balance method (Reg. § 1.167(b)-4).

Leased Property

See CCH® AnswerConnect: *Leasehold Improvements* for more information on this topic.

1234. Lessee/Lessor Improvements, Lease Acquisition Costs. The cost of an addition or improvement made by a lessee or lessor to real property is generally depreciated under the Modified Accelerated Cost Recovery System (MACRS) in the same manner as real property (Code Sec. 168(i)(6) and (8)(A); Reg. § 1.167(a)-4). Exceptions exist if the improvement is placed in service after 2017 and is eligible for a 15-year recovery period as qualified improvement property (¶ 1240), as well as improvements placed in service before 2018 and eligible for a 15-year recovery period as qualified leasehold improvement property (discussed below), qualified retail improvement property (¶ 1240), or qualified restaurant property (¶ 1240). For example, windows installed on a residential rental building (structural components) are separately depreciated as 27.5-year residential rental property beginning in the month that the windows are placed in service using the mid-month convention, assuming the replacement is not considered a repair expense.

Leasehold additions and improvements that are section 1245 property (i.e., personal as opposed to real property) are generally depreciated over a shortened MACRS recovery period under cost segregation principles. If, upon termination of the lease, a lessee does not retain an improvement (paid for by the lessee), the lessee's loss is computed by reference to the improvement's adjusted basis at the time of the lease termination. A lessor that disposes of or abandons a leasehold improvement (paid for by the lessor) upon termination of the lease may use the adjusted basis of the improvement at such time to determine gain or loss (Code Sec. 168(i)(8)(B); Reg. § 1.168(i)-8(c)(3)).

15-Year Qualified Leasehold Improvement Property. Qualified leasehold improvement property placed in service after October 22, 2004, and before January 1, 2018, is depreciated under MACRS over 15 years using the straight-line method and the half-year or mid-quarter convention, as applicable (Code Sec. 168(b)(3)(G) and (e)(3)(E)(iv), prior to repeal by the Tax Cuts and Jobs Act (P.L. 115-97)). The alternative depreciation system (ADS) recovery period is 39 years. Qualified leasehold improvement property is generally an improvement made to the interior portion of nonresidential real property that is more than three years old by the lessor or lessee under or pursuant to the terms of a lease. Elevators and escalators, internal structural framework of the building, structural components that benefit a common area, and improvements relating to the enlargement of a building do not qualify. A lease between related persons is not considered a lease (Code Sec. 168(e)(6), prior to amendment by P.L. 115-97).

Lease Acquisition Costs. The cost of acquiring a lease is amortized over the lease term. A renewal period is counted as part of the lease term if less than 75 percent of the acquisition cost is attributable to the unexpired lease period (not counting the renewal period) (Code Sec. 178).

If property subject to a lease is acquired, the value of the lease is not separately amortized. Instead it is depreciated as part of the cost of the property (Code Sec. 167(c)).

Construction Allowances. A lessor must depreciate improvements made by the lessee with a qualified construction allowance as nonresidential real property (Code Sec. 110) (¶ 764).

1235. Sale v. Lease of Depreciable Property. Whether a transaction is treated as a lease or as a purchase is important in determining who is entitled to claim depreciation and other deductions for related business expenses. In most situations, the rules for determining whether a transaction is a lease or a purchase evolved from court decisions and IRS rulings. The rules generally look to the economic substance of a transaction, not its form, to determine who owns property that the parties characterize as leased (Rev. Proc. 2001-28, Rev. Proc. 2001-29).

12 DEPRECIATION

Modified Accelerated Cost Recovery System (MACRS)

See CCH® AnswerConnect: *Bonus Depreciation or First-Year Additional Depreciation Allowance* and *Depreciation: Asset Class Lives and Recovery Periods* for more information on this topic.

1236. MACRS in General. The Modified Accelerated Cost Recovery System (MACRS) is mandatory for most tangible depreciable property placed in service after December 31, 1986, unless transitional rules apply (Code Sec. 168). Under MACRS, the cost of eligible property is recovered over a 3-, 5-, 7-, 10-, 15-, 20-, 27.5-, 31.5-, or 39-year period, depending upon the type of property (¶ 1240) by using statutory recovery methods (¶ 1243) and conventions (¶ 1245). Special transferee rules apply to property received in specified nonrecognition transactions (¶ 1248).

1237. MACRS Bonus Depreciation. Under the Modified Accelerated Cost Recovery System (MACRS), a bonus depreciation deduction is allowed for qualifying MACRS property placed in service before January 1, 2027 (Code Sec. 168(k)). The original use of the qualifying property must begin with the taxpayer. However, used property acquired by purchase (as defined in Code Sec. 179(d)(2)) will also qualify for bonus depreciation, effective for property acquired and placed in service after September 27, 2017 (discussed below).

Bonus Rate. The bonus rate for property acquired and placed in service after September 27, 2017, is:

- 100 percent for property placed in service in 2017 through 2022,
- 80 percent for property place in service in 2023,
- 60 percent for property place in service in 2024,
- 40 percent for property place in service in 2025, and
- 20 percent for property place in service in 2026.

The bonus rate for property acquired before September 28, 2017, is 50 percent if placed in service before 2018, 40 percent if placed in service in 2018, and 30 percent if placed in service in 2019 (Code Sec. 168(k)(8)).

A taxpayer may elect to apply the 50-percent rate instead of the 100-percent rate for all qualified property placed in service during the taxpayer's first tax year that includes September 28, 2017 (Code Sec. 168(k)(10); Instructions to Form 4562; Reg. § 1.168(k)-2(f)(3)). The election applies to all qualified bonus depreciation property placed in service during the tax year and is not made separately for each property class. A taxpayer may make a late election or revoke a prior election to apply the 50-perent rate the same as making or revoking an election out of bonus depreciation discussed below (Rev. Proc. 2020-25; Rev. Proc. 2019-33).

Written binding contracts. The acquisition date of property acquired pursuant to a written binding contract is the later of (1) the date the contract is entered into; (2) the date the contract is enforceable under State law; (3) if the contract has one or more cancellation periods, the date on which all of the cancellation periods end; or (4) if the contract has one or more contingency clauses, the date on which all conditions subject to the clauses are satisfied (Reg. § 1.168(k)-2(b)(5)(ii)(B)).

The definition of a written binding contract is provided in the regulations (Reg. § 1.168(k)-2(b)(5)(iii)). If property is acquired after September 27, 2017 pursuant to a contract that is not a written binding contract, the acquisition date is the date that more than 10 percent of the total cost of the property, excluding the cost of land preliminary activities, is paid or incurred (Proposed Reg. § 1.168(k)-(b)(5)(v)).

Computation. The bonus depreciation deduction is claimed on the cost of the property after reduction by any portion of the basis for which an election to expense under Code Sec. 179 is made (¶ 1208). Regular MACRS deductions are computed on the cost as reduced by the amount of the expense election and bonus depreciation.

> **Example 1:** Amanda purchases qualifying five-year MACRS property subject to the half-year convention for $1,500 and elects to expense $600 under Code Sec. 179. Using the 50-percent rate, bonus depreciation is $450 (($1,500 – $600) × 50 percent). Regular MACRS depreciation deductions are computed on a depreciable basis of $450 ($1,500 – $600 – $450). The regular first-year MACRS allowance is $90 ($450 × 20 percent (first-year table percentage)).

Unlike the section 179 expensing allowance, there is no taxable income or investment limitation on the bonus depreciation allowance. There is also no limit on the overall amount of bonus depreciation that may be claimed on qualifying property. The length of the tax year or date during the tax year that the qualifying property is placed in service does not affect the amount of the otherwise allowable bonus depreciation deduction.

Recapture. Bonus depreciation is subject to the section 1245 and section 1250 recapture rules (¶ 1779) (Reg. § 1.168(k)-1(f)(3); Reg. § 1.168(k)-2(g)(3)). If bonus depreciation is claimed on section 1250 property (e.g., a section 1250 land improvement), the bonus deduction is treated as an accelerated depreciation deduction for recapture purposes and the difference between the bonus deduction and the amount of straight-line depreciation that could have been claimed on the bonus deduction prior to the recapture year is subject to recapture.

Long Production Property. The placed-in-service-deadline is extended one year (before January 1, 2028) for long production property that is acquired and placed in service after September 27, 2017 (Code Sec. 168(k)(2)(B)). Long production property is MACRS property that:

- is subject to the uniform capitalization rules;
- has a production period greater than one year and a cost exceeding $1 million;
- has a MACRS recovery period of at least 10 years or is transportation property (i.e., property used in the trade or business of transporting persons or property for hire, such as commercial aircraft); and
- is acquired by the taxpayer (or acquired pursuant to a binding written contract entered into) after September 27, 2017, and before January 1, 2027.

Only pre-January 1, 2027, progress expenditures are taken into account in computing the bonus deduction if the extended placed-in-service deadline applies. The extended placed-in-service deadline also applies to certain noncommercial aircraft acquired by purchase (Code Sec. 168(k)(2)(C)). Unlike long production property, however, progress expenditures made in 2027 on qualifying noncommercial aircraft placed in service before January 1, 2028, are eligible for bonus depreciation.

The bonus rate for long production property acquired after September 27, 2017, is 100 percent if placed in service in 2017 through 2023, 80 percent in 2024, 60 percent in 2025, 40 percent in 2026, and 20 percent in 2027 (Code Sec. 168(k)(6)(B)).

Long production property and noncommercial aircraft acquired before September 28, 2017, and placed in service before 2021 are eligible for a 50 percent rate if placed in service in 2017 or 2018, 40 percent in 2019, and 30 percent in 2020 (Code Sec. 168(k)(8)). Progress expenditures made in 2020 for long production property acquired before September 28, 2017 are not eligible for bonus depreciation.

Constructed, Manufactured, Produced Property. Property constructed, manufactured, or produced by a taxpayer is deemed acquired when work of a significant physical nature begins. Under an elective safe-harbor, work of a significant physical nature begins when more than 10 percent of the total cost of a project has been paid for by a cash basis taxpayer or incurred by an accrual basis taxpayer (Reg. § 1.168(k)-1(b)(4)(iii); Reg. § 1.168(k)-2(b)(5)(iv)).

If a taxpayer enters into a written binding contract for the construction of the property before construction begins, the property is considered self-constructed and acquired when work of a significant physical nature begins or the taxpayer pays or incurs more than 10 percent of the project's total cost (Reg. § 1.168(k)-2(b)(5)(iv)).

Qualifying Property. The bonus depreciation allowance is available only for the following types of property:

- property which is depreciable under MACRS and has a recovery period of 20 years or less;
- qualified improvement property (discussed below) placed in service after 2015;
- qualified leasehold improvement property (discussed below) placed in service after 2015;
- MACRS water utility property;

12

DEPRECIATION

- computer software depreciable over three years under Code Sec. 167(f) (¶ 980); and

- a qualified film, television show, or theatrical production acquired and placed in service after September 27, 2017, if it qualifies for the Code Sec. 181 expense election without regard to the $15 million expensing limit or the December 31, 2020, expiration date (Code Sec. 168(k)(2)(A)).

The original use of qualifying property must begin with the taxpayer or, in the case of used property, the property must be acquired by purchase after September 27, 2017. Intangible property does not qualify for bonus depreciation, except for computer software and film, television, and theatrical productions as described above.

Property used primarily in the trade or business of a rate-regulated utility is ineligible for bonus depreciation, effective for property placed in service in tax years beginning after 2017 (Code Sec. 168(k)(9) and (j)(7)(A)(iv); Reg. § 1.168(k)-2(b)(2)(ii)(F); Proposed Reg. § 1.168(k)-2(b)(2)(ii)(F)).

Property used in a trade or business that has floor plan financing indebtedness does not qualify for bonus depreciation if the floor plan financing interest on the indebtedness was taken into account under the rules that limit the business interest deduction, effective for property placed in service in tax years beginning after 2017 (¶ 937) (Code Sec. 168(k)(9) and (j)(9); Reg. § 1.168(k)-2(b)(2)(ii)(G)). Proposed regulations provide that only property that is placed in service during a tax year in which a taxpayer benefits from an interest deduction on the floor plan financing indebtedness is ineligible for bonus depreciation (Proposed Reg. § 1.168(k)-2(b)(2)(ii)(G)). Floor plan financing indebtedness is debt used to finance the acquisition of motor vehicles held for sale or lease and secured by the inventory acquired. A motor vehicle is any self-propelled vehicle designed for transporting persons or property on a public street, highway, or road; a boat; or farm machinery or equipment.

Property that must be depreciated using the MACRS alternative depreciation system (ADS) (¶ 1247) also does not qualify. However, if ADS is elected, then the property remains eligible for bonus depreciation (Code Sec. 168(k)(2)(D)(i)).

Listed property (¶ 1211), such as a passenger automobile (¶ 1214), that is used 50 percent or less for business, does not qualify for bonus depreciation because such property must be depreciated using ADS (Code Sec. 168(k)(2)(D)(ii)). If business use of a listed property falls to 50 percent or less, bonus depreciation and any amount deducted under Code Sec. 179 (¶ 1208) must be recaptured under the listed property recapture rules (Code Sec. 168(k)(2)(F)(ii)).

Used Property. Effective for property acquired and placed in service after September 27, 2017, property previously used by an unrelated person may qualify for bonus depreciation (Code Sec. 168(k)(2)(A)(ii) and (E)(ii); Reg. § 1.168(k)-2(b)(3)(iii)). The taxpayer or predecessor must not have used the property during five calendar years immediately preceding the current placed in service year and the taxpayer must acquire the property by "purchase" within the meaning of Code Sec. 179(d)(2) (¶ 1208). Property is considered previously used by a taxpayer or predecessor if the taxpayer or predecessor previously had a depreciable interest in the property during the placed in service year and the five-year look back period. A depreciable interest in a property that was disposed of within 90 days after placing it in service is not taken into account (Proposed Reg. § 1.168(k)-2(b)(3)(iii)(B)(4)).

The basis of used property determined by reference to the basis of other property held at any time by the taxpayer does not qualify for bonus depreciation.

Qualified Improvement Property. For property placed in service in 2016 and 2017, qualified improvement property is a separate category of bonus depreciation property and qualifies for bonus depreciation regardless of the length of the recovery period that applies to the property (Code Sec. 168(k)(3), prior to repeal by the Tax Cuts and Jobs Act (P.L. 115-97)). As the result of a drafting error qualified improvement property placed in service after 2017 was removed as a separate category of bonus depreciation property and it was not assigned a 15-year recovery period.

A technical correction retroactively provides that qualified improvement property placed in service after 2017 is assigned a 15-year recovery period and qualifies for bonus depreciation under the general rule that bonus depreciation applies to MACRS property with a recovery period of 20 years or less (Code Sec. 168(e)(3)(E)(vii), as added by the Coronavirus, Aid, Relief, and Economic Security (CARES) Act P.L. 116-136)).

The IRS has modified the automatic consent procedures for a taxpayer to change accounting methods in tax years ending in 2018, 2019, and 2020 for this purpose. A taxpayer who previously filed two or more returns using the "incorrect" depreciation period (usually 39 years) must file Form 3115 for an accounting method change to claim bonus depreciation and/or depreciation based on the 15-year recovery period. If only one return has been filed, then the taxpayer may either file Form 3115 or an amended return for the year the property was placed in service. An amended return (administrative adjustment request (AAR) by a partnership subject to the centralized partnership audit regime) is due on or before October 15, 2021 (or expiration of limitations period if earlier) (Rev. Proc. 2020-25, amending Rev. Proc. 2019-43).

Qualified improvement property is any improvement *made by the taxpayer* to an interior portion of a building which is nonresidential real property (whether or not the building is depreciated under MACRS) if the improvement is placed in service after the date the building was first placed in service. Expenditures which are attributable to the enlargement of a building, any elevator or escalator, or the internal structural framework of the building are excluded from the definition of qualified improvement property, but structural components that benefit a common area are not (Code Sec. 168(e)(6), as amended by P.L. 116-136).

Any 15-year qualified leasehold improvement property (¶ 1234) and 15-year qualified retail improvement property placed in service in 2016 and 2017 (¶ 1240) meets the definition of qualified improvement property for bonus depreciation purposes. This property qualifies for bonus depreciation for two reasons. First it has a recovery period of 20 years or less. Second it meets the definition of qualified improvement property. However, any 15-year qualified restaurant property placed in service in 2016 and 2017 may only qualify for bonus depreciation if it meets the definition of qualified improvement property (Code Sec. 168(e)(7)(B), prior to repeal by P.L. 115-97).

The categories of 15-year qualified leasehold improvement property, 15-year qualified retail improvement property and 15-year qualified restaurant property are eliminated effective for property placed in service after 2017. Qualification for bonus depreciation after 2017 is based on satisfying the definition of qualified improvement property.

Qualified Leasehold Improvement Property. In the case of property placed in service before January 1, 2016, qualified leasehold improvement property is a separate category of bonus depreciation property (Code Sec. 168(k)(3), prior to repeal by P.L. 114-113). Qualified leasehold improvement property is defined as an improvement to an interior portion of nonresidential real property (whether or not depreciated under MACRS) by a lessor or lessee under or pursuant to a lease. The improvement must be placed in service more than three years after the building was first placed in service. The lessor and lessee may not be related persons. Expenditures for (1) the enlargement of a building, (2) any elevator or escalator, (3) any structural component that benefits a common area, or (4) the internal structural framework of the building do not qualify. Any 15-year qualified retail improvement property and 15-year qualified restaurant improvements placed in service before January 1, 2016, must satisfy the definition of qualified leasehold improvement property in order to qualify for bonus depreciation even though the recovery period is 20 years or less (Code Sec. 168(e)(7)(B), prior to amendment by the Consolidated Appropriations Act, 2016 (P.L. 114-113); Code Sec. 168(e)(8)(D), prior to repeal by P.L. 114-113).

Luxury Car Depreciation Caps. If the taxpayer does not elect out of bonus depreciation, the first-year Code Sec. 280F depreciation cap (¶ 1214) for a vehicle that qualifies for bonus depreciation is increased by $8,000. However, if the vehicle is acquired before September 28, 2017, and placed in service in 2018, the increase is limited to $6,400 and if the vehicle is acquired before September 28, 2017, and placed in service in 2019, the increase is limited to $4,800 (Code Sec. 168(k)(2)(F)).

Alternative Minimum Tax. Bonus depreciation is allowed in full for alternative minimum tax (AMT) purposes. Effective for property placed in service after 2015, if property qualifies for bonus depreciation, then no AMT adjustment is required on the regular MACRS deductions (i.e., the deductions are allowed in full for AMT purposes) even if the election out of bonus depreciation is made (Code Sec. 168(k)(2)(G) and (k)(7)). For property placed in service before 2016, no AMT adjustment is required on regular depreciation deductions if bonus depreciation was claimed on the property (Code Sec. 168(k)(2)(G), prior to amendment by P.L. 114-113; Code Sec. 168(k)(2)(D)(iii), prior to repeal by P.L. 114-113; Reg. §1.168(k)-1(d)(iii); Rev. Proc. 2017-33).

Accelerated Bonus Depreciation Allowance for Specified Plants. Effective for specified plants that are planted or grafted onto a planted plant after 2015 and before 2027, a taxpayer may make an annual election to claim bonus depreciation on the adjusted basis of the specified plant in the tax year in which it is planted or grafted in the ordinary course of the taxpayer's farming business as defined in Code Sec. 263A(e)(4) (Code Sec. 168(k)(5)). This accelerates the regular bonus depreciation deduction from the tax year that the specified plant was placed in service (i.e., became productive) to the earlier tax year of planting or grafting.

The bonus rate is 50 percent for plantings and graftings after 2015 and prior to September 28, 2017. In the case of a plant which is planted or grafted after September 27, 2017, and before January 1, 2023, the bonus rate is 100 percent. The bonus rate is 80 percent for plantings and graftings in 2023, 60 percent for 2024, 40 percent for 2025 and 20 percent for 2026 (Code Sec. 168(k)(6)(C)). The accelerated bonus deduction reduces the adjusted basis of the specified plant. If the accelerated bonus deduction is claimed, the regular bonus depreciation deduction under Code Sec. 168(k) may not be claimed in the tax year that the specified plant is placed in service.

A taxpayer may elect the 50 percent rate in place of the 100 percent rate in a tax year that includes September 28, 2017 for all plants for which the election to claim bonus depreciation in the year of planting or grafting is made (Code Sec. 168(k)(10)). A taxpayer may make a late election or revoke a prior election to claim bonus depreciation for specified plants the same as making or revoking an election out of bonus depreciation discussed below (Rev. Proc. 2020-25; Rev. Proc. 2019-33).

A specified plant is (1) any tree or vine which bears fruits or nuts, and (2) any other plant which will have more than one yield of crops or fruits or nuts and which generally has a pre-productive period of more than two years from the time of planting or grafting to the time at which the plant begins bearing a marketable crop or yield of fruits or nuts (Code Sec. 168(k)(5)(B)).

If the accelerated bonus deduction is claimed, neither the accelerated bonus deduction nor any regular depreciation deductions on the specified plant are subject to AMT adjustments (i.e., the deductions are claimed in full for AMT purposes) (Code Sec. 168(k)(5)(E)). The accelerated bonus deduction is not subject to capitalization under the uniform capitalization rules (Code Sec. 263A(c)(7)).

Election Out of Bonus Depreciation. A taxpayer may elect out of bonus depreciation with respect to any class of MACRS property placed in service during the tax year (Code Sec. 168(k)(7)). A taxpayer may make a late election or revoke a prior election out of bonus depreciation in certain circumstances. Similar rules apply with respect to the election to apply the 50-percent rate instead of the 100-percent rate and the election to claim bonus depreciation in the year of planting or grafting a specified plant.

A late election or revocation of a previous election may be made for depreciable property placed in service in a tax year ending in 2018, 2019, or 2020. If the taxpayer is revoking a prior election, then it must have been made on a return timely filed before April 17, 2020. A late election or revocation is made by filing an amended return (administrative adjustment request (AAR) by a partnership subject to the centralized partnership audit regime) for the placed-in-service year of the property by October 15, 2021 (or expiration of limitations period if earlier). If a taxpayer chooses not to file an amended return, a Form 3115 must be filed with a timely filed original return for the first and second tax year after the year the property was placed in service. Form 3115 may also be included with a timely filed original return filed on or after April 17, 2020, and on or before October 15, 2021 (Rev. Proc. 2020-25).

A late election or revocation of a previous election also may be made for property acquired and placed in service after September 27, 2017, that included September 28, 2017. A late election out of bonus depreciation only applies to property within a class that is eligible for the 100 percent rate. A late election or revocation is made by filing an automatic accounting method change for the first, second, or third tax year that follows the tax year that includes September 28, 2017. An amended return (administrative adjustment request by a partnership subject to the centralized partnership audit regime) may also be filed to make or revoke these elections if the taxpayer has not filed the tax return for the tax year immediately following the tax year that includes September 28, 2017 (Rev. Proc. 2019-33).

Corporation's Election to Forgo Bonus Depreciation and Claim AMT Credit Carryforward. For tax years beginning before 2018, a corporation may make an election on an annual basis to forgo bonus depreciation on property placed in service during its tax year and claim unused AMT credits based on the amount of bonus depreciation that is forgone (Code Sec. 168(k)(4), prior to repeal by P.L. 115-97). The computation of the refundable AMT credit is made on a worksheet provided with Form 8827. The AMT is repealed for corporations in tax years beginning after 2017 and corporations will be able to recover their unused AMT credits in tax years 2018 through 2021 (¶ 1409). If a regular election out of bonus depreciation is made for a class of property, then an election to forgo bonus depreciation in favor of an AMT credit does not apply to the class of property for which the regular election out was made (Act Sec. 101(d)(4) of the Consolidated Appropriations Act, 2018 (P.L. 115-141)).

50-Percent Bonus Depreciation Allowance for Mine Safety Equipment. A taxpayer may elect to deduct 50 percent of the cost of qualified advanced mine safety equipment that is placed in service before January 1, 2018 (Code Sec. 179E).

50-Percent Bonus Depreciation Allowance for Qualified Reuse and Recycling Property. A 50-percent additional depreciation allowance may be claimed on the adjusted basis of qualified reuse and recycling property acquired and placed in service during the tax year. The property must be acquired by purchase, its original use must begin with the taxpayer, it must have a useful life of a least five years, and no pre-September 1, 2008, binding acquisition contract may be in effect. Reuse and recycling property is machinery and equipment (not including buildings, real estate, rolling stock or equipment used to transport reuse and recyclable materials) that is used exclusively to collect, distribute, or recycle qualified reuse and recyclable materials. Machinery and equipment include appurtenances such as software necessary to operate the equipment. Qualified reuse and recyclable materials are scrap plastic, glass, textiles, rubber, packaging, and metal, as well as recovered fiber and electronic scrap. A taxpayer may elect out for any class of property (Code Sec. 168(m)).

50-Percent Bonus Depreciation Allowance for Second Generation Biofuel Plant Property. A 50-percent additional depreciation allowance may be claimed on the adjusted basis of certain plant property placed in service before January 1, 2021, that is used to produce certain qualified biofuels (Code Sec. 168(l), as amended by the Taxpayer Certainty and Disaster Tax Relief Act of 2019 (P.L. 116-94)). For property placed in service after January 2, 2013, and before January 1, 2021, this bonus depreciation allowance may be claimed only on the adjusted basis of second generation biofuel plant property used to produce second generation biofuel. Second generation biofuel is defined under Code Sec. 40(b)(6)(E) and includes algae treated as qualified feedstock.

1238. Property Subject to MACRS. Most tangible depreciable property placed in service after 1986 is depreciated using the Modified Accelerated Cost Recovery System (MACRS). MACRS property is depreciable if it wears out, has a useful life that exceeds one year, and is used in a trade or business or for the production of income. MACRS property *does not* include:

- property covered by the taxpayer's election to use a depreciation method not expressed in terms of years, such as the unit of production or income forecast method;

- public utility property (unless a normalization method of accounting is used);

- motion picture films and videotapes;

- sound recordings;

- intangible property; and

- property placed in service before 1987 that is excluded from MACRS under the anti-churning rules (Code Sec. 168(f)).

Public utility property that does not qualify under MACRS is depreciated under Code Sec. 167(a) using the same depreciation method and useful life as is used to compute the rate-making depreciation allowance for the property (Code Sec. 168(f)(2)).

1239. Accounting for MACRS Property in Item, Multiple Asset, and General Asset Accounts. Under the Modified Accelerated Cost Recovery System (MACRS), property may be accounted for individually in an item account or by placing a group of identically depreciated assets (i.e., assets with the same recovery period, depreciation method, convention, and placed-in-service tax year) in a multiple asset (pool) account (Reg. § 1.168(i)-7). Alternatively, a taxpayer may elect to include a single asset or a group of identically depreciated assets in a general asset account (GAA) (Reg. § 1.168(i)-1).

Depreciation (including bonus depreciation) on a multiple asset account is computed on the combined bases of the assets in the multiple asset account (after reduction by any amounts expensed under Code Sec. 179) as if the multiple asset account is a single asset. Depreciation allowances determined for each multiple asset account must be recorded in a depreciation reserve account for each account (Reg. § 1.168(i)-7). Similar rules apply to a GAA (Reg. § 1.168(i)-1(d)(1)).

If a taxpayer disposes of an asset in a multiple asset account, the asset is placed into a single asset account as of the first day of the tax year of disposition, and gain or loss is generally computed on the disposition. In computing the asset's adjusted depreciable basis, the depreciation allowed or allowable is computed by using the depreciation method, recovery period, and convention applicable to the multiple asset account or pool that included the asset. The unadjusted depreciable basis of the multiple asset account is reduced by the unadjusted depreciable basis of the asset as of the first day of the tax year of disposition. The depreciation reserve of the multiple asset account is reduced by the depreciation allowed or allowable for the asset in the tax years prior to the tax year of disposition (Reg. § 1.168(i)-8(h)(2)).

A disposition that is not the disposition of all of the assets or the last asset in a GAA generally does not reduce the unadjusted depreciable basis of the GAA. The asset is treated as having an adjusted depreciable basis of $0 immediately before the disposition and no loss is realized. The amount realized is recognized as ordinary income up to (1) the sum of the unadjusted depreciable basis of the account and the amount expensed under Code Sec. 179 for all assets in the account, and (2) reduced by amounts previously recognized as ordinary income (Reg. § 1.168(i)-1(e)(2)).

If all of the assets or the last asset in the GAA account is disposed, a taxpayer may apply the preceding rule or elect to terminate the account and recognize gain or loss by reference to the adjusted basis of the GAA (i.e., unadjusted depreciable basis of the GAA less prior depreciation on assets in account) (Reg. § 1.168(i)-1(e)(3)(ii)).

In a qualifying disposition, a taxpayer may also elect to recognize gain or loss by reference to the adjusted basis of the disposed asset in the GAA. However, a qualifying disposition cannot involve all of the assets or the last asset in the account, and it must be:

- the direct result of a casualty or theft;
- a deductible charitable contribution;
- a direct result of a cessation, termination, or disposition of a business, manufacturing, or other income-producing process; or
- a certain type of nonrecognition transaction (Reg. § 1.168(i)-1(e)(3)(iii)).

Disposition Defined. A disposition from an MACRS item, multiple asset account, or GAA occurs when ownership of an asset is transferred or when the asset is permanently withdrawn from use either in the taxpayer's trade or business or in the production of income. A disposition includes the sale, exchange, retirement, physical abandonment, or destruction of an asset. A disposition also occurs when an asset is transferred to a supplies, scrap, or similar account (Reg. § 1.168(i)-1(e)(1) and 8(b)(2)).

The following dispositions of a portion of an asset in a item, multiple asset, or general asset account are also treated as dispositions (Reg. § 1.168(i)-1(e)(1)(ii) and 8(d)(1)):

- a sale of a portion of an asset;
- a disposition of a portion of an asset as the result of a casualty event described in Code Sec. 165;

- a disposition of a portion of an asset for which gain (determined without regard to recapture under Code Sec. 1245 or Code Sec. 1250) is not recognized in a like kind exchange or involuntary conversion; or

- a transfer of a portion of an asset in a step-in-the-shoes nonrecognition transaction described in Code Sec. 168(i)(7)(B) (¶ 1248).

Partial Disposition Election. The disposition of a portion of an asset in an MACRS item or multiple asset account that is not described above may be treated as a disposition on which gain or loss is recognized by making a partial disposition election (Reg. § 1.168(i)-8(d)). This election does not apply to the disposition of a portion of an asset in a general asset account.

A building, including its original structural components, which is depreciated under MACRS, is treated as a single asset and a taxpayer may claim a loss upon the retirement of an original structural component of the building by making a partial disposition election (Reg. § 1.168(i)-8(d)). Without a partial disposition election, depreciation continues on the retired structural component and the basis of the building is not adjusted to account for a retirement loss. The partial disposition election may also be made for retired components of assets that are section 1245 property, such as machinery and equipment.

A replacement component which is separately depreciated because it is placed in service after the building (or section 1245 asset) is placed in service is a separate asset. If a separately depreciated component is retired then a retirement loss is claimed without regard to the partial disposition election because an entire asset has been disposed. For example, a replacement roof depreciated under MACRS is a separately depreciated asset and a retirement loss must be claimed if the entire replacement roof is again replaced. However, if the shingles on the replacement roof are replaced, a partial disposition of an MACRS asset has occurred and a loss on the remaining basis of the shingles may be claimed if the partial disposition election is made.

If a taxpayer makes a partial disposition election, the costs of related expenditures that would otherwise be deductible as repairs must be capitalized as a restoration (¶ 1313). For example, if a taxpayer makes a partial disposition election to deduct the remaining basis of shingles on an original or replacement roof, the cost of replacing the shingles is capitalized as a restoration even though without the election the cost would be deductible as a repair. If the replacement expenditures must be capitalized without regard to the partial disposition election (e.g., an entire original roof is replaced), the partial disposition election carries no adverse consequence.

The partial disposition election must be made by the due date (including extensions) of the original federal tax return for the tax year in which the portion of the asset is disposed. The due date for filing any federal income tax return otherwise due on or after April 1, 2020, and before July 15, 2020, is automatically extended to July 15, 2020 (¶ 2505). No formal election statement is required. The taxpayer simply reports the loss on the disposed portion of the asset on the appropriate form (i.e., Form 4797). The election may be revoked only with IRS consent (Reg. § 1.168(i)-8(d)(2)).

1240. MACRS Depreciation Periods. The Modified Accelerated Cost Recovery System (MACRS) depreciation (recovery) period for an asset is based on its class life as of January 1, 1986, or is specifically prescribed by Code Sec. 168. The recovery periods for MACRS assets can be found in a table that appears in IRS Pub. 946. This table is an updated version of the table that appears in Rev. Proc. 87-56. Under MACRS, an asset is classified according to its class life as follows.

Three-Year Property. Three-year property includes property with a class life of four years or less. Any race horse placed in service before January 1, 2021, or any other horse over 12 years old at the time it is placed in service is classified as three-year property (Code Sec. 168(e)(1) and (e)(3)(A), as amended by the Taxpayer Certainty and Disaster Tax Relief Act of 2019 (P.L. 116-94)). A race horse that is more than two years old when it is placed in service is three-year property (seven-year property if two years old or less when placed in service) if placed in service after December 31, 2020. Certain "rent-to-own" consumer durable property (e.g., televisions and furniture) is three-year property. Breeding hogs (Asset Class 01.236) and tractor units for use over the road (Asset Class 00.26) are three-year property. A tractor unit is a highway truck designed to tow a trailer or semitrailer and that does not carry cargo on the same chassis as the engine (Reg. § 145.4051-1(e)(1)).

Five-Year Property. Five-year property generally includes property with a class life of more than four years and less than 10 years. This property includes: cars; light and heavy general-purpose trucks; qualified technological equipment; computer-based telephone central office switching equipment; research and experimentation property that is section 1245 property; semi-conductor manufacturing equipment; geothermal, solar and wind energy properties; certain biomass properties that are small power production facilities; computers and peripheral equipment; and office machinery (typewriters, calculators, etc.) (Code Sec. 168(e)(1) and (e)(3)(B)).

Furniture, appliances, window treatments, and carpeting used in residential rental property are five-year property (Announcement 99-82). Personal property used in wholesale or retail trade or in the provision of personal and professional services is five-year property if a specific recovery period is not otherwise provided (Asset Class 57.0). For example, a professional library used by an accountant or attorney is five-year property. Examples of *personal* service businesses include hotels and motels, laundry and dry cleaning establishments, beauty and barber shops, photographic studios and mortuaries. Examples of *professional* service businesses include services offered by doctors, dentists, lawyers, accountants, architects, engineers, and veterinarians (Rev. Proc. 77-10).

Five-year property also includes taxis (Asset Class 00.22), buses (Asset Class 00.23), airplanes not used in commercial or contract carrying of passengers or freight, and all helicopters (Asset Class 00.21), trailers and trailer-mounted containers (Asset Class 00.27), breeding cattle and dairy cattle (Asset Class 01.21), breeding sheep and breeding goats (Asset Class 01.21), and assets used in construction by certain contractors, builders, and real estate subdividers and developers (Asset Class 15.0).

Seven-Year Property. Seven-year property includes property with a class life of 10 years or more, but less than 16 years (Code Sec. 168(e)(1) and (e)(3)(C)). This property includes office furniture, equipment and fixtures that are not structural components (Asset Class 00.11). Desks, files, safes, overhead projectors, cell phones, fax machines and other communication equipment not included in any other class fall within this category. Seven-year property also includes: assets (except helicopters) used in commercial and contract carrying of passengers and freight by air (Asset Class 45.0); certain livestock (Asset Class 01.1); breeding or work horses 12 years old or less when placed in service (Asset Class 01.221); other horses that are not three-year property (Asset Class 01.225); assets used in recreation businesses (Asset Class 80.0); and assets used in theme and amusement parks (Asset Class 80.0). Any railroad track, motorsports entertainment complex placed in service before January 1, 2021, and any property that does not have a class life (such as a fishing vessel) and is not otherwise classified is seven-year property.

10-Year Property. Ten-year property is property with a class life of 16 years or more and less than 20 years (Code Sec. 168(e)(1) and (e)(3)(D)). This property class includes vessels, barges, tugs, and similar means of water transportation not used in marine construction or as a fishing vessel (Asset Class 00.28). Ten-year property also includes smart electric meters and qualified smart electric grid systems. MACRS deductions for trees or vines bearing fruit or nuts that are placed in service after 1988 are determined under the straight-line method over a 10-year recovery period (Code Sec. 168(b)(1)). Single purpose agricultural or horticultural structures placed in service after 1988 are 10-year property.

15-Year Property. Property with a class life of 20 years or more but less than 25 years is generally considered 15-year property (Code Sec. 168(e)(1) and (e)(3)(E)). This property class includes municipal wastewater treatment plants, telephone distribution plants and other comparable equipment used for the two-way exchange of voice and data communications, retail motor fuels outlets, and initial gas utility clearing and grading improvements to place pipelines into service.

A property qualifies as a retail motor fuels outlet (as opposed, for example, to a convenience store, which is 39-year real property) if: (1) 50 percent or more of gross revenues are derived from petroleum sales; (2) 50 percent or more of the floor space is devoted to petroleum marketing sales; or (3) the property is 1,400 square feet or less (Rev. Proc. 97-10). Fifteen-year property includes car wash buildings and related land improvements, billboards, and section 1250 real property (including service station buildings) and depreciable land improvements used in marketing petroleum and petroleum products (Asset Class 57.1). Water transportation assets (other than vessels) used in the commercial and contract carrying of freight and passengers by water are 15-year property (Asset Class 44.0).

Otherwise depreciable land improvements that are not specifically included in any other asset class are 15-year property (Asset Class 00.3). Examples include sidewalks, driveways, curbs, roads, parking lots, canals, waterways, drainage facilities, sewers (but not municipal sewers), wharves and docks, bridges, and nonagricultural fences. Landscaping and shrubbery is a depreciable land improvement if it is located near a building and would be destroyed if the building were replaced (Rev. Rul. 74-265; IRS Pub. 946). Playground equipment attached to the ground is a land improvement (LTR 8848039).

15-Year Leasehold Improvement Property. See ¶ 1234 and ¶ 1237.

15-Year Restaurant Improvements and Buildings. Qualified restaurant property placed in service after October 22, 2004, and before January 1, 2018, is a category of 15-year MACRS property, depreciable using the straight-line method and the half-year or mid-quarter convention, as applicable (Code Sec. 168(e)(3)(E)(v) and (e)(7), prior to repeal by the Tax Cuts and Jobs Act (P.L. 115-97)). The ADS recovery period is 39 years. Qualified restaurant property is removed as a category of 15-year property effective for property placed in service after 2017. 15-year qualified improvement property replaces the 15-year qualified restaurant category, effective for property placed in service after 2017. See below, "*Qualified Improvement Property*".

Qualified restaurant property is section 1250 property that is an improvement to a building. More than 50 percent of the building's square footage must be devoted to preparation of and seating for on-premises consumption of prepared meals. For restaurant improvements placed in service before 2009, the building must also be more than three years old. A restaurant building placed in service after 2008 and before 2018 is included in the definition of qualified restaurant property and is depreciated as 15-year property using the straight-line method and half-year or mid-quarter convention if more than 50 percent of the building's square footage is devoted to preparation of and seating for the on-premises consumption of prepared meals.

The bonus depreciation deduction may not be claimed on qualified restaurant property placed in service after 2008 and before 2016 unless it meets the definition of qualified *leasehold* improvement property (¶ 1234 and ¶ 1237) (Code Sec. 168(e)(7)(B), prior to amendment by the Consolidated Appropriations Act, 2016 (P.L. 114-113); Rev. Proc. 2011-26). Qualified restaurant property placed in service in 2016 and 2017 qualifies for bonus depreciation if it meets the definitional requirements of qualified improvement property (Code Sec. 168(e)(7)(B), prior to repeal by P.L. 115-97). Qualified restaurant property is a type of qualified real property that qualifies for expensing under Code Sec. 179 if placed in service in a tax year beginning before 2018 (¶ 1208).

15-Year Qualified Retail Improvement Property. Qualified retail improvement property placed in service after 2008 and before 2018 is a separate category of MACRS 15-year property which is depreciated under MACRS using a 15-year recovery period, the straight-line method, and the half-year or mid-quarter convention (Code Secs. 168(b)(3)(I) and (e)(3)(E)(ix), prior to repeal by P.L. 115-97). The ADS recovery period is 39 years.

Qualified retail improvement property means any improvement to an interior portion of a building which is nonresidential real property if the improved portion is (1) open to the general public, (2) used in the retail trade or business of selling tangible personal property to the general public, and (3) placed in service more than three years after the date the building was first placed in service by any taxpayer. Elevators and escalators, internal structural framework of the building, structural components that benefit a common area, and improvements relating to the enlargement of a building do not qualify.

Qualified retail improvement property placed in service before 2016 is ineligible for bonus depreciation unless it also meets the definition of qualified leasehold improvement property (¶ 1234 and ¶ 1237) (Code Sec. 168(e)(8)(D), prior to amendment by P.L. 114-113; Rev. Proc. 2011-26). Qualified retail improvement property placed in service in 2016 and 2017 qualifies for bonus depreciation because it meets the definition of qualified improvement property. Qualified retail improvement property is a type of qualified real property that qualifies for expensing under Code Sec. 179 when placed in service in a tax year beginning before 2018 (¶ 1208).

Qualified Improvement Property. Qualified improvement property placed in service after December 31, 2017, is a separate category of MACRS 15-year property (Code Sec. 168(e)(3)(E)(vii), as added by the Coronavirus Aid, Relief, and Economic Security (CARES) Act (P.L. 116-136)). The straight-line method and half-year or mid-quarter convention apply (Code Sec. 168(b)(3)(G)). Qualified improvement property replaces the categories of 15-year qualified leasehold improvement property, 15-year qualified retail improvement property, and 15-year restaurant property effective for property placed in service after 2017.

As the result of a drafting error by the Tax Cuts and Jobs Act (P.L. 115-97) the intended 15-year recovery period for qualified improvement property placed in service after 2017 was not assigned. Thus, qualified improvement property placed in service after 2017 was depreciated as MACRS 39-year nonresidential real property. A technical correction made by the CARES retroactively assigns the 15-year recovery period. As a result, qualified improvement property placed in service after 2017 may also qualify for bonus depreciation under the general rule that bonus depreciation applies to MACRS property with a recovery period of 20 years or less.

Qualified improvement property is any improvement *made by the taxpayer* to an interior portion of a building which is nonresidential real property (whether or not the building is depreciated under MACRS) if the improvement is placed in service after the date the building was first placed in service. Expenditures which are attributable to the enlargement of a building, any elevator or escalator, or the internal structural framework of the building are excluded from the definition of qualified improvement property, but structural components that benefit a common area are not (Code Sec. 168(e)(6), as amended by P.L. 116-136).

20-Year Property. Twenty-year property includes property with a class life of 25 years or more, other than Code Sec. 1250 real property with a class life of 27.5 years or more. Water utility property and municipal sewers placed in service before June 13, 1996, and farm buildings (e.g., barns and machine sheds) are included within this class (Code Sec. 168(e)(1) and (e)(3)(F)). Depreciable electric utility clearing and grading costs to place transmission and distribution lines into service are 20-year property.

25-Year Property. Water utility property and municipal sewers have a 25-year recovery period (Code Sec. 168(c) and (e)(5)). The straight-line depreciation method is mandatory for 25-year property (Code Sec. 168(b)(3)(F)).

27.5-Year Residential Rental Property. Residential rental property has a recovery period of 27.5 years. Residential rental property includes buildings or structures with respect to which 80 percent or more of the gross rental income is from dwelling units (Code Sec. 168(e)(2)(A)). It also includes manufactured homes that are residential rental property and elevators and escalators.

Nonresidential Real Property. Nonresidential real property is Code Sec. 1250 real property (¶ 1786) that is not residential rental property or property with a class life of less than 27.5 years (Code Sec. 168(e)(2)(B); Rev. Proc. 87-56). The cost of nonresidential real property placed in service after May 12, 1993, is recovered over 39 years. For property placed in service after 1986 and before May 13, 1993, cost is recovered over 31.5 years.

Farm Machinery and Equipment. Machinery and equipment, grain bins, and fences (but no other land improvements) used in specified agricultural activities are MACRS 7-year property and have a 10-year ADS recovery period (Asset Class 01.1). However, any machinery or equipment (other than any grain bin, cotton ginning asset, fence, or other land improvement) that is used in a farming business (as defined in Code Sec. 263A(e)(4)), the original use of which commences with the taxpayer after December 31, 2017, and which is placed in service after December 31, 2017, is classified as MACRS 5-year property and has a 10-year ADS recovery period (Code Sec. 168(e)(3)(B)). The same rule applied to new machinery and equipment placed in service in 2009 (Code Sec. 168(e)(3)(B)(vii), prior to amendment by P.L. 115-97).

Indian Reservation Property. For qualified Indian reservation property placed in service after December 31, 1993, and before January 1, 2021, special MACRS recovery periods are provided for both regular tax and alternative minimum tax (AMT) purposes. No AMT adjustment is required even if an election out of the shortened recovery period is made (Code Sec. 168(j), as amended by P.L. 116-94). Effective for tax years beginning after 2015, a taxpayer may make an irrevocable election to use the regular recovery periods for any class of MACRS Indian reservation property placed in service during the tax year.

Additions and Improvements. Additions and improvements, including the cost of capitalized structural components, are depreciated under MACRS in the same way that the improved property would be depreciated if it were placed in service at the same time as the addition or improvement (Code Sec. 168(i)(6)). For example, a replacement roof or other structural component added to a commercial building in 2019 is treated as 39-year MACRS nonresidential real property even if the building is depreciated under a pre-MACRS method. Any elements of an addition or improvement to a building that qualify as personal property may be depreciated over a shorter recovery period as personal rather than real property under the cost segregation rules (discussed below).

Effective for property placed in service after 2017, most improvements to the interior of nonresidential real property are depreciated over a 15-year recovery period as qualified improvement property (Code Sec. 168(e)(6); Code Sec. 168(e)(3)(E)(vii), as added by the CARES Act (P.L. 116-136)). See above, *"Qualified Improvement Property."*

Interior improvements placed in service before 2018 may qualify for a 15-year recovery period as qualified leasehold improvement property (¶ 1234) or qualified retail improvement property (discussed above). A 15-year recovery period may also apply to qualified restaurant property (discussed above), which includes most interior and exterior improvements and restaurant buildings, placed in service before 2018.

Roofs. The replacement of an entire roof (including the sheathing and rafters) or a significant portion of a roof that has deteriorated over time is a restoration that is capitalized as an improvement (Reg. § 1.263(a)-3(k)(6)(ii)(A) and (k)(7), Example 14). The replacement of a worn and leaking waterproof membrane on a roof comprised of structural elements, insulation, and a waterproof membrane with a similar but new membrane is not required to be capitalized if the membrane was not leaking when the taxpayer placed the building in service (Reg. § 1.263(a)-3(j)(3), Example 13, and (k)(7), Example 15). Another IRS example dealing with removal costs (¶ 1313) assumes that the cost of replacement shingles that are similar to shingles that became leaky while the taxpayer owned the building is not capitalized (Reg. § 1.263(a)-3(g)(2)(ii), Example 3). In tax years beginning after 2017, a replacement roof on nonresidential real property is a type of qualified real property which may qualify for section 179 expensing (¶ 1208).

Cost Segregation. The Tax Court has ruled that elements of a building that are treated as personal property under the former investment tax credit rules (Reg. § 1.48-1(c)) may be separately depreciated under MACRS and ACRS as personal property (*Hospital Corp. of America*, 109 TC 21, Dec. 52,163). The IRS has acquiesced to the court's holding that the former investment tax credit rules apply in determining whether an item is a structural component (i.e., real property) or personal property (Notice of Acquiescence, 1999-35 I.R.B. 314). The separate depreciation of personal property elements of a building is referred to as cost segregation.

The determination of whether an item is personal property or a structural component often depends on the specific facts. One important factor is whether the item is permanently attached to the building (*Whiteco Industries*, 65 TC 664, Dec. 33,596). However, items relating to the operation and maintenance of the building are structural components even if not permanently attached. The following items are examples of structural components: bathtubs, boilers, ceilings (including acoustical ceilings), central air conditioning and heating systems, chimneys, doors, electric wiring, fire escapes, floors, hot water heaters, HVAC units, lighting fixtures, paneling, partitions (if not readily removable), plumbing, roofs, sinks, sprinkler systems, stairs, tiling, walls, and windows (Reg. § 1.48-1(e)(2)).

12

DEPRECIATION

¶1240

1243. MACRS Recovery Methods. Under the Modified Accelerated Cost Recovery System (MACRS), the cost of depreciable property is recovered using the applicable depreciation method, the applicable recovery period, and the applicable convention (Code Sec. 168(a)).

The cost of property in the 3-, 5-, 7-, and 10-year classes is recovered using the 200-percent declining-balance method over three, five, seven, and ten years, respectively (i.e., the applicable recovery period), and the half-year convention (unless the mid-quarter convention applies), with a switch to the straight-line method in the year when that maximizes the deduction (Code Sec. 168(b)(1)). The cost of 15- and 20-year property is recovered using the 150-percent declining-balance method over 15 and 20 years, respectively, and the half-year convention (unless the mid-quarter convention applies), with a switch to the straight-line method to maximize the deduction (Code Sec. 168(b)(2)). The cost of residential rental and nonresidential real property is recovered using the straight-line method and the mid-month convention over 27.5- and 39-year recovery periods, respectively (Code Sec. 168(b)(3)).

A taxpayer may irrevocably elect to claim straight-line MACRS deductions over the regular recovery period in place of the applicable depreciation method (200-percent declining balance method for 3-, 5-, 7-, and 10-year property and 150-percent declining balance method for 10- and 15-year property). The election applies to all property in the MACRS class for which the election is made that is placed in service during the tax year. A taxpayer makes the election on the return for the year the property is first placed in service (Code Sec. 168(b)(5)). For example, if the election is made for 3-year property, it applies to all 3-year property placed in service in the tax year of the election.

A taxpayer may elect to recover the cost of 3-, 5-, 7-, and 10-year property using the 150-percent declining-balance method over the regular recovery periods (the MACRS alternative depreciation system (ADS) recovery period for property placed in service before 1999) (¶ 1247) (Code Sec. 168(b)(2)(C)). This election, like the straight-line election above, is made separately for each property class placed in service during the tax year of the election. A taxpayer may also elect the MACRS ADS with respect to any class of property.

If 3-, 5-, 7-, and 10-year property placed in service before 2018 is used in the trade or business of farming, it must be depreciated under the 150-percent declining balance method, unless the taxpayer elects the MACRS straight-line method or alternative depreciation system (ADS), or the taxpayer must use ADS because the taxpayer elected to deduct preproductive period expenditures (Code Sec. 168(b)(2)(B), prior to repeal by the Tax Cuts and Jobs Act (P.L. 115-97)). Consequently, Tables 1-8, below, may not be used for such property. 3-, 5-, 7-, and 10-year farm property is depreciated using the 200-percent declining balance method if placed in service after 2017 unless an election to use the 150-percent declining balance method, straight-line method, or ADS is made, or the taxpayer elects to deduct preproductive period expenditures.

Computation of Deduction Without Tables. The MACRS deduction on personal property is computed by first determining the rate of depreciation (dividing the number one by the recovery period) (Rev. Proc. 87-57). This basic rate is multiplied by 1.5 or 2 for the 150-percent or 200-percent declining-balance method, as applicable, to determine the declining balance rate. The adjusted basis of the property is multiplied by the declining-balance rate and the half-year or mid-quarter convention (whichever is applicable) is applied in computing depreciation for the first year. The depreciation claimed in the first year is subtracted from the adjusted basis before applying the declining-balance rate in determining the depreciation deduction for the second year.

Under the MACRS straight-line method (used, for example, on real property or if ADS applies), a new applicable depreciation rate is determined for each tax year in the applicable recovery period. For any tax year, the applicable depreciation rate (in percentage terms) is determined by dividing one by the length of the applicable recovery period remaining as of the beginning of such tax year. The rate is applied to the unrecovered basis of the property in conjunction with the appropriate convention. If as of the beginning of the tax year the remaining recovery period is less than one year, the applicable depreciation rate under the straight-line method for that year is 100 percent.

Example 1: A calendar-year taxpayer buys an item of five-year property in January ("Year 1") for $10,000. The taxpayer does not claim any Code Sec. 179

expense allowance or bonus depreciation. The 200-percent declining-balance method and half-year convention apply. Depreciation computed without the use of the IRS tables is determined as follows: the declining-balance depreciation rate is determined and compared with the straight-line rate. A switch is made to the straight-line rate in the year depreciation equals or exceeds that determined under the declining-balance method. The applicable rate is applied to the unrecovered basis.

The 200-percent declining-balance depreciation rate is 40 percent (1 divided by 5 (recovery period) times 2). The straight-line rate (which changes each year) is 1 divided by the length of the applicable recovery period remaining as of the beginning of each tax year (after considering the applicable convention in determining how much of the applicable recovery period remains as of the beginning of the year). For Year 4, the straight-line rate is .40 (1 divided by 2.5), which is the same as the declining balance rate. For Year 5, the straight-line rate is .6667 (1 divided by 1.5). For Year 6, the straight-line rate is 100 percent because the remaining recovery period is less than one year.

Year	Method	Rate	Unrecovered Basis			Depreciation	
1	DB	.40	× $ 10,000 × .5 (half-yr. conv.)	....		=	$ 2,000
2	DB	.40	× (10,000 – 2,000)	= $8,000	..	=	3,200
3	DB	.40	× (8,000 – 3,200)	= 4,800	..	=	1,920
4	DB	.40	× (4,800 – 1,920)	= 2,880	..	=	1,152
5	SL	.6667	× (2,880 – 1,152)	= 1,728	..	=	1,152
6	SL	1.000	× (1,728 – 1,152)	= 576	..	=	576
				0			
				Total	..		$10,000

Rev. Proc. 87-57 provides a detailed discussion of computing MACRS without tables.

Computation of Deduction Using Tables. Instead of using the rules above, taxpayers may compute depreciation using MACRS depreciation tables that contain the annual percentage depreciation rates to be applied to the unadjusted basis of property in each tax year (Rev. Proc. 87-57). The tables incorporate the appropriate convention and a switch from the declining-balance method to the straight-line method in the year that the latter provides a depreciation allowance equal to, or larger than, the former. The tables may be used for any item of property that qualifies for MACRS. Selected MACRS depreciation tables are reproduced below.

An MACRS depreciation table that is used to compute the annual depreciation allowance for any item of property generally must be used throughout the entire recovery period. However, a taxpayer may not continue to use a table if there are any adjustments to the basis of the property for reasons other than (1) depreciation allowances, or (2) an addition or improvement to the property that is subject to depreciation as a separate item of property. The MACRS depreciation table percentages may not be used in short tax years (¶ 1244).

Example 2: Depreciation on five-year property purchased by a calendar-year taxpayer in January of the current tax year at a cost of $10,000 is computed under the general MACRS 200-percent declining-balance method over a five-year recovery period using the half-year convention. No amount is expensed under Code Sec. 179 or claimed as a bonus depreciation deduction.

If the depreciation tables provided by the IRS are used, depreciation is computed as follows: the applicable depreciation rate in Table 1 under the column for a five-year recovery period for the applicable recovery year is applied to the cost of the property.

Year	Rate	Unadj. Basis	Depreciation	Basis			
1	.20 ×	$ 10,000 =	$ 2,000	($10,000 –	$2,000)	=	$8,000
2	.32 ×	10,000 =	3,200	(8,000 –	3,200)	=	4,800
3	.192 ×	10,000 =	1,920	(4,800 –	1,920)	=	2,880
4	.1152 ×	10,000 =	1,152	(2,880 –	1,152)	=	1,728
5	.1152 ×	10,000 =	1,152	(1,728 –	1,152)	=	576
6	.0576 ×	10,000 =	576	(576 –	576)	=	0
		Total	$10,000				

Table 1. General Depreciation System
Applicable Depreciation Method: 200 or 150 Percent
Declining Balance Switching to Straight Line
Applicable Recovery Periods: 3, 5, 7, 10, 15, 20 years
Applicable Convention: Half-year

If the Recovery Year is:	and the Recovery Period is:					
	3-year	5-year	7-year	10-year	15-year	20-year
	the Depreciation Rate is:					
1	33.33	20.00	14.29	10.00	5.00	3.750
2	44.45	32.00	24.49	18.00	9.50	7.219
3	14.81	19.20	17.49	14.40	8.55	6.677
4	7.41	11.52	12.49	11.52	7.70	6.177
5		11.52	8.93	9.22	6.93	5.713
6		5.76	8.92	7.37	6.23	5.285
7			8.93	6.55	5.90	4.888
8			4.46	6.55	5.90	4.522
9				6.56	5.91	4.462
10				6.55	5.90	4.461
11				3.28	5.91	4.462
12					5.90	4.461
13					5.91	4.462
14					5.90	4.461
15					5.91	4.462
16					2.95	4.461
17						4.462
18						4.461
19						4.462
20						4.461
21						2.231

Table 2. General Depreciation System
Applicable Depreciation Method: 200 or 150 Percent
Declining Balance Switching to Straight Line
Applicable Recovery Periods: 3, 5, 7, 10, 15, 20 years
Applicable Convention: Mid-quarter (property placed in
service in first quarter)

If the Recovery Year is:	and the Recovery Period is:					
	3-year	5-year	7-year	10-year	15-year	20-year
	the Depreciation Rate is:					
1	58.33	35.00	25.00	17.50	8.75	6.563
2	27.78	26.00	21.43	16.50	9.13	7.000
3	12.35	15.60	15.31	13.20	8.21	6.482
4	1.54	11.01	10.93	10.56	7.39	5.996
5		11.01	8.75	8.45	6.65	5.546
6		1.38	8.74	6.76	5.99	5.130
7			8.75	6.55	5.90	4.746
8			1.09	6.55	5.91	4.459
9				6.56	5.90	4.459
10				6.55	5.91	4.459
11				0.82	5.90	4.459
12					5.91	4.460
13					5.90	4.459
14					5.91	4.460
15					5.90	4.459
16					0.74	4.460
17						4.459
18						4.460
19						4.459
20						4.460
21						0.565

Table 3. General Depreciation System
Applicable Depreciation Method: 200 or 150 Percent
Declining Balance Switching to Straight Line
Applicable Recovery Periods: 3, 5, 7, 10, 15, 20 years
Applicable Convention: Mid-quarter (property placed in
service in second quarter)

If the Recovery Year is:	and the Recovery Period is:					
	3-year	5-year	7-year	10-year	15-year	20-year
	the Depreciation Rate is:					
1	41.67	25.00	17.85	12.50	6.25	4.688
2	38.89	30.00	23.47	17.50	9.38	7.148
3	14.14	18.00	16.76	14.00	8.44	6.612
4	5.30	11.37	11.97	11.20	7.59	6.116
5		11.37	8.87	8.96	6.83	5.658
6		4.26	8.87	7.17	6.15	5.233
7			8.87	6.55	5.91	4.841
8			3.33	6.55	5.90	4.478
9				6.56	5.91	4.463
10				6.55	5.90	4.463
11				2.46	5.91	4.463
12					5.90	4.463
13					5.91	4.463
14					5.90	4.463
15					5.91	4.462
16					2.21	4.463
17						4.462
18						4.463
19						4.462
20						4.463
21						1.673

Table 4. General Depreciation System
Applicable Depreciation Method: 200 or 150 Percent
Declining Balance Switching to Straight Line
Applicable Recovery Periods: 3, 5, 7, 10, 15, 20 years
Applicable Convention: Mid-quarter (property placed in
service in third quarter)

If the Recovery Year is:	and the Recovery Period is:					
	3-year	5-year	7-year	10-year	15-year	20-year
	the Depreciation Rate is:					
1	25.00	15.00	10.71	7.50	3.75	2.813
2	50.00	34.00	25.51	18.50	9.63	7.289
3	16.67	20.40	18.22	14.80	8.66	6.742
4	8.33	12.24	13.02	11.84	7.80	6.237
5		11.30	9.30	9.47	7.02	5.769
6		7.06	8.85	7.58	6.31	5.336
7			8.86	6.55	5.90	4.936
8			5.53	6.55	5.90	4.566
9				6.56	5.91	4.460
10				6.55	5.90	4.460
11				4.10	5.91	4.460
12					5.90	4.460
13					5.91	4.461
14					5.90	4.460
15					5.91	4.461
16					3.69	4.460
17						4.461
18						4.460
19						4.461
20						4.460
21						2.788

12

DEPRECIATION

Table 5. General Depreciation System
Applicable Depreciation Method: 200 or 150 Percent Declining Balance Switching to Straight Line
Applicable Recovery Periods: 3, 5, 7, 10, 15, 20 years
Applicable Convention: Mid-quarter (property placed in service in fourth quarter)

If the Recovery Year is:	3-year	5-year	7-year	10-year	15-year	20-year
			the Depreciation Rate is:			
1	8.33	5.00	3.57	2.50	1.25	0.938
2	61.11	38.00	27.55	19.50	9.88	7.430
3	20.37	22.80	19.68	15.60	8.89	6.872
4	10.19	13.68	14.06	12.48	8.00	6.357
5		10.94	10.04	9.98	7.20	5.880
6		9.58	8.73	7.99	6.48	5.439
7			8.73	6.55	5.90	5.031
8			7.64	6.55	5.90	4.654
9				6.56	5.90	4.458
10				6.55	5.91	4.458
11				5.74	5.90	4.458
12					5.91	4.458
13					5.90	4.458
14					5.91	4.458
15					5.90	4.458
16					5.17	4.458
17						4.458
18						4.459
19						4.458
20						4.459
21						3.901

Table 6. General Depreciation System
Applicable Depreciation Method: Straight Line
Applicable Recovery Period: 27.5 years
Applicable Convention: Mid-month

If the Recovery Year is:	And the Month in the First Recovery Year the Property is Placed in Service is:											
	1	2	3	4	5	6	7	8	9	10	11	12
						the Depreciation Rate is:						
1	3.485	3.182	2.879	2.576	2.273	1.970	1.667	1.364	1.061	0.758	0.455	0.152
2	3.636	3.636	3.636	3.636	3.636	3.636	3.636	3.636	3.636	3.636	3.636	3.636
3	3.636	3.636	3.636	3.636	3.636	3.636	3.636	3.636	3.636	3.636	3.636	3.636
4	3.636	3.636	3.636	3.636	3.636	3.636	3.636	3.636	3.636	3.636	3.636	3.636
5	3.636	3.636	3.636	3.636	3.636	3.636	3.636	3.636	3.636	3.636	3.636	3.636
6	3.636	3.636	3.636	3.636	3.636	3.636	3.636	3.636	3.636	3.636	3.636	3.636
7	3.636	3.636	3.636	3.636	3.636	3.636	3.636	3.636	3.636	3.636	3.636	3.636
8	3.636	3.636	3.636	3.636	3.636	3.636	3.636	3.636	3.636	3.636	3.636	3.636
9	3.636	3.636	3.636	3.636	3.636	3.636	3.636	3.636	3.636	3.636	3.636	3.636
10	3.637	3.637	3.637	3.637	3.637	3.637	3.636	3.636	3.636	3.636	3.636	3.636
11	3.636	3.636	3.636	3.636	3.636	3.636	3.637	3.637	3.637	3.637	3.637	3.637
12	3.637	3.637	3.637	3.637	3.637	3.637	3.636	3.636	3.636	3.636	3.636	3.636
13	3.636	3.636	3.636	3.636	3.636	3.636	3.637	3.637	3.637	3.637	3.637	3.637
14	3.637	3.637	3.637	3.637	3.637	3.637	3.636	3.636	3.636	3.636	3.636	3.636
15	3.636	3.636	3.636	3.636	3.636	3.636	3.637	3.637	3.637	3.637	3.637	3.637
16	3.637	3.637	3.637	3.637	3.637	3.637	3.636	3.636	3.636	3.636	3.636	3.636
17	3.636	3.636	3.636	3.636	3.636	3.636	3.637	3.637	3.637	3.637	3.637	3.637
18	3.637	3.637	3.637	3.637	3.637	3.637	3.636	3.636	3.636	3.636	3.636	3.636
19	3.636	3.636	3.636	3.636	3.636	3.636	3.637	3.637	3.637	3.637	3.637	3.637
20	3.637	3.637	3.637	3.637	3.637	3.637	3.636	3.636	3.636	3.636	3.636	3.636
21	3.636	3.636	3.636	3.636	3.636	3.636	3.637	3.637	3.637	3.637	3.637	3.637
22	3.637	3.637	3.637	3.637	3.637	3.637	3.636	3.636	3.636	3.636	3.636	3.636
23	3.636	3.636	3.636	3.636	3.636	3.636	3.637	3.637	3.637	3.637	3.637	3.637
24	3.637	3.637	3.637	3.637	3.637	3.637	3.636	3.636	3.636	3.636	3.636	3.636
25	3.636	3.636	3.636	3.636	3.636	3.636	3.637	3.637	3.637	3.637	3.637	3.637
26	3.637	3.637	3.637	3.637	3.637	3.637	3.636	3.636	3.636	3.636	3.636	3.636
27	3.636	3.636	3.636	3.636	3.636	3.636	3.637	3.637	3.637	3.637	3.637	3.637
28	1.970	2.273	2.576	2.879	3.182	3.485	3.636	3.636	3.636	3.636	3.636	3.636
29	0.000	0.000	0.000	0.000	0.000	0.000	0.152	0.455	0.758	1.061	1.364	1.667

Table 7. General Depreciation System
Applicable Depreciation Method: Straight Line
Applicable Recovery Period: 31.5 years
Applicable Convention: Mid-month

If the Recovery Year is:	And the Month in the First Recovery Year the Property is Placed in Service is:											
	1	2	3	4	5	6	7	8	9	10	11	12
	the Depreciation Rate is:											
1	3.042	2.778	2.513	2.249	1.984	1.720	1.455	1.190	0.926	0.661	0.397	0.132
2	3.175	3.175	3.175	3.175	3.175	3.175	3.175	3.175	3.175	3.175	3.175	3.175
3	3.175	3.175	3.175	3.175	3.175	3.175	3.175	3.175	3.175	3.175	3.175	3.175
4	3.175	3.175	3.175	3.175	3.175	3.175	3.175	3.175	3.175	3.175	3.175	3.175
5	3.175	3.175	3.175	3.175	3.175	3.175	3.175	3.175	3.175	3.175	3.175	3.175
6	3.175	3.175	3.175	3.175	3.175	3.175	3.175	3.175	3.175	3.175	3.175	3.175
7	3.175	3.175	3.175	3.175	3.175	3.175	3.175	3.175	3.175	3.175	3.175	3.175
8	3.175	3.174	3.175	3.174	3.175	3.174	3.175	3.175	3.175	3.175	3.175	3.175
9	3.174	3.175	3.174	3.175	3.174	3.175	3.174	3.175	3.174	3.175	3.174	3.175
10	3.175	3.174	3.175	3.174	3.175	3.174	3.175	3.174	3.175	3.174	3.175	3.174
11	3.174	3.175	3.174	3.175	3.174	3.175	3.174	3.175	3.174	3.175	3.174	3.175
12	3.175	3.174	3.175	3.174	3.175	3.174	3.175	3.174	3.175	3.174	3.175	3.174
13	3.174	3.175	3.174	3.175	3.174	3.175	3.174	3.175	3.174	3.175	3.174	3.175
14	3.175	3.174	3.175	3.174	3.175	3.174	3.175	3.174	3.175	3.174	3.175	3.174
15	3.174	3.175	3.174	3.175	3.174	3.175	3.174	3.175	3.174	3.175	3.174	3.175
16	3.175	3.174	3.175	3.174	3.175	3.174	3.175	3.174	3.175	3.174	3.175	3.174
17	3.174	3.175	3.174	3.175	3.174	3.175	3.174	3.175	3.174	3.175	3.174	3.175
18	3.175	3.174	3.175	3.174	3.175	3.174	3.175	3.174	3.175	3.174	3.175	3.174
19	3.174	3.175	3.174	3.175	3.174	3.175	3.174	3.175	3.174	3.175	3.174	3.175
20	3.175	3.174	3.175	3.174	3.175	3.174	3.175	3.174	3.175	3.174	3.175	3.174
21	3.174	3.175	3.174	3.175	3.174	3.175	3.174	3.175	3.174	3.175	3.174	3.175
22	3.175	3.174	3.175	3.174	3.175	3.174	3.175	3.174	3.175	3.174	3.175	3.174
23	3.174	3.175	3.174	3.175	3.174	3.175	3.174	3.175	3.174	3.175	3.174	3.175
24	3.175	3.174	3.175	3.174	3.175	3.174	3.175	3.174	3.175	3.174	3.175	3.174
25	3.174	3.175	3.174	3.175	3.174	3.175	3.174	3.175	3.174	3.175	3.174	3.175
26	3.175	3.174	3.175	3.174	3.175	3.174	3.175	3.174	3.175	3.174	3.175	3.174
27	3.174	3.175	3.174	3.175	3.174	3.175	3.174	3.175	3.174	3.175	3.174	3.175
28	3.175	3.174	3.175	3.174	3.175	3.174	3.175	3.174	3.175	3.174	3.175	3.174
29	3.174	3.175	3.174	3.175	3.174	3.175	3.174	3.175	3.174	3.175	3.174	3.175
30	3.175	3.174	3.175	3.174	3.175	3.174	3.175	3.174	3.175	3.174	3.175	3.174
31	3.174	3.175	3.174	3.175	3.174	3.175	3.174	3.175	3.174	3.175	3.174	3.175
32	1.720	1.984	2.249	2.513	2.778	3.042	3.175	3.174	3.175	3.174	3.175	3.174
33	0.000	0.000	0.000	0.000	0.000	0.000	0.132	0.397	0.661	0.926	1.190	1.455

Table 7A. General Depreciation System
Applicable Depreciation Method: Straight-Line
Applicable Recovery Period: 39 years
Applicable Convention: Mid-month—taken from the
IRS Pub. 946

If the Recovery Year is:	And the Month in the First Recovery Year the Property is Placed in Service is:											
	1	2	3	4	5	6	7	8	9	10	11	12
	the Depreciation Rate is:											
1	2.461	2.247	2.033	1.819	1.605	1.391	1.177	0.963	0.749	0.535	0.321	0.107
2—39	2.564	2.564	2.564	2.564	2.564	2.564	2.564	2.564	2.564	2.564	2.564	2.564
40	0.107	0.321	0.535	0.749	0.963	1.177	1.391	1.605	1.819	2.033	2.247	2.461

Table 7B. Alternative Depreciation System
Applicable Depreciation Method: Straight-Line
Applicable Recovery Period: 40 years
Applicable Convention: Mid-month

If the Recovery Year is:	and the Month in the First Recovery Year the Property is Placed in Service is:											
	1	2	3	4	5	6	7	8	9	10	11	12
	the Depreciation Rate is:											
1	2.396	2.188	1.979	1.771	1.563	1.354	1.146	0.938	0.729	0.521	0.313	0.104
2—40	2.500	2.500	2.500	2.500	2.500	2.500	2.500	2.500	2.500	2.500	2.500	2.500
41	0.104	0.312	0.521	0.729	0.937	1.146	1.354	1.562	1.771	1.979	2.187	2.396

12

DEPRECIATION

Table 8. General and Alternative Depreciation Systems
Applicable Depreciation Method: Straight Line
Applicable Recovery Periods: 2.5 — 50 years
Applicable Convention: Half-year

If the Recovery Year is: — and the Recovery Period is: — the Depreciation Rate is:

Recovery Year	2.5	3.0	3.5	4.0	4.5	5.0	5.5	6.0	6.5	7.0	7.5	8.0	8.5	9.0	9.5
1	20.00	16.67	14.29	12.50	11.11	10.00	9.09	8.33	7.69	7.14	6.67	6.25	5.88	5.56	5.26
2	40.00	33.33	28.57	25.00	22.22	20.00	18.18	16.67	15.39	14.29	13.33	12.50	11.76	11.11	10.53
3	40.00	33.33	28.57	25.00	22.22	20.00	18.18	16.67	15.38	14.29	13.33	12.50	11.76	11.11	10.53
4		16.67	28.57	25.00	22.23	20.00	18.18	16.67	15.39	14.28	13.33	12.50	11.77	11.11	10.53
5				12.50	22.22	20.00	18.19	16.66	15.38	14.29	13.34	12.50	11.76	11.11	10.52
6						10.00	18.18	16.67	15.39	14.28	13.33	12.50	11.77	11.11	10.53
7								8.33	15.38	14.29	13.34	12.50	11.76	11.11	10.52
8										7.14	13.33	12.50	11.77	11.11	10.53
9												6.25	11.76	11.11	10.52
10														5.56	10.53

If the Recovery Year is: — and the Recovery Period is: — the Depreciation Rate is:

Recovery Year	10.0	10.5	11.0	11.5	12.0	12.5	13.0	13.5	14.0	14.5	15.0	15.5	16.0	16.5	17.0
1	5.00	4.76	4.55	4.35	4.17	4.00	3.85	3.70	3.57	3.45	3.33	3.23	3.13	3.03	2.94
2	10.00	9.52	9.09	8.70	8.33	8.00	7.69	7.41	7.14	6.90	6.67	6.45	6.25	6.06	5.88
3	10.00	9.52	9.09	8.70	8.33	8.00	7.69	7.41	7.14	6.90	6.67	6.45	6.25	6.06	5.88
4	10.00	9.53	9.09	8.69	8.33	8.00	7.69	7.41	7.14	6.90	6.67	6.45	6.25	6.06	5.88
5	10.00	9.52	9.09	8.70	8.33	8.00	7.69	7.41	7.14	6.90	6.67	6.45	6.25	6.06	5.88
6	10.00	9.53	9.09	8.69	8.33	8.00	7.69	7.41	7.14	6.89	6.67	6.45	6.25	6.06	5.88
7	10.00	9.52	9.09	8.70	8.34	8.00	7.69	7.41	7.14	6.90	6.67	6.45	6.25	6.06	5.88
8	10.00	9.53	9.09	8.69	8.33	8.00	7.69	7.41	7.15	6.89	6.66	6.45	6.25	6.06	5.88
9	10.00	9.52	9.09	8.70	8.33	8.00	7.69	7.41	7.14	6.90	6.67	6.45	6.25	6.06	5.88
10	10.00	9.53	9.09	8.69	8.33	8.00	7.70	7.40	7.15	6.89	6.66	6.45	6.25	6.06	5.88
11	5.00	9.52	9.09	8.70	8.34	8.00	7.69	7.41	7.14	6.90	6.67	6.45	6.25	6.06	5.89
12			4.55	8.69	8.33	8.00	7.69	7.40	7.15	6.89	6.66	6.45	6.25	6.06	5.88
13					4.17	8.00	7.69	7.41	7.14	6.90	6.67	6.45	6.25	6.06	5.89
14							3.85	7.40	7.15	6.89	6.66	6.46	6.25	6.06	5.88
15									3.57	6.90	6.67	6.45	6.25	6.06	5.89
16											3.33	6.46	6.25	6.06	5.88
17													3.12	6.07	5.89
18															2.94

If the Recovery Year is: — and the Recovery Period is: — the Depreciation Rate is:

Recovery Year	17.5	18.0	18.5	19.0	19.5	20.0	20.5	21.0	21.5	22.0	22.5	23.0	23.5	24.0	24.5
1	2.86	2.78	2.70	2.63	2.56	2.500	2.439	2.381	2.326	2.273	2.222	2.174	2.128	2.083	2.041
2	5.71	5.56	5.41	5.26	5.13	5.000	4.878	4.762	4.651	4.545	4.444	4.348	4.255	4.167	4.082
3	5.71	5.56	5.41	5.26	5.13	5.000	4.878	4.762	4.651	4.545	4.444	4.348	4.255	4.167	4.082
4	5.71	5.55	5.41	5.26	5.13	5.000	4.878	4.762	4.651	4.545	4.445	4.348	4.255	4.167	4.082
5	5.72	5.56	5.40	5.26	5.13	5.000	4.878	4.762	4.651	4.546	4.444	4.348	4.255	4.167	4.082
6	5.71	5.55	5.41	5.26	5.13	5.000	4.878	4.762	4.651	4.545	4.445	4.348	4.255	4.167	4.082
7	5.72	5.56	5.40	5.26	5.13	5.000	4.878	4.762	4.651	4.546	4.444	4.348	4.255	4.167	4.082
8	5.71	5.55	5.41	5.26	5.13	5.000	4.878	4.762	4.651	4.545	4.445	4.318	4.255	4.167	4.082
9	5.72	5.56	5.40	5.27	5.13	5.000	4.878	4.762	4.651	4.546	4.444	4.348	4.255	4.167	4.081
10	5.71	5.55	5.41	5.26	5.13	5.000	4.878	4.762	4.651	4.545	4.445	4.348	4.255	4.167	4.082
11	5.72	5.56	5.40	5.27	5.13	5.000	4.878	4.762	4.651	4.546	4.444	4.348	4.256	4.166	4.081
12	5.71	5.55	5.41	5.26	5.13	5.000	4.878	4.762	4.651	4.545	4.445	4.348	4.255	4.167	4.082
13	5.72	5.56	5.40	5.27	5.13	5.000	4.878	4.762	4.651	4.546	4.444	4.348	4.256	4.166	4.081
14	5.71	5.55	5.41	5.26	5.13	5.000	4.878	4.762	4.651	4.545	4.445	4.348	4.255	4.167	4.082
15	5.72	5.56	5.40	5.27	5.13	5.000	4.878	4.762	4.651	4.546	4.444	4.348	4.256	4.166	4.081
16	5.71	5.55	5.41	5.26	5.12	5.000	4.878	4.762	4.651	4.545	4.445	4.348	4.255	4.167	4.082
17	5.72	5.56	5.40	5.27	5.13	5.000	4.878	4.762	4.652	4.546	4.444	4.347	4.256	4.166	4.081
18	5.71	5.55	5.41	5.26	5.12	5.000	4.878	4.762	4.651	4.545	4.445	4.348	4.255	4.167	4.082
19		2.78	5.40	5.27	5.13	5.000	4.878	4.761	4.652	4.546	4.445	4.347	4.256	4.166	4.081
20				2.63	5.12	5.000	4.879	4.762	4.651	4.545	4.445	4.348	4.255	4.167	4.082
21						2.500	4.878	4.761	4.652	4.545	4.445	4.347	4.256	4.166	4.081
22								2.381	4.651	4.545	4.445	4.348	4.255	4.167	4.082
23										2.273	4.444	4.347	4.256	4.166	4.081
24												2.174	4.255	4.167	4.082
25														2.083	4.081

If the Recovery Year is:	25.0	25.5	26.0	26.5	27.0	27.5	28.0	28.5	29.0	29.5	30.0	30.5	31.0	31.5	32.0
						the Depreciation Rate is:									
1	2.000	1.961	1.923	1.887	1.852	1.818	1.786	1.754	1.724	1.695	1.667	1.639	1.613	1.587	1.563
2	4.000	3.922	3.846	3.774	3.704	3.636	3.571	3.509	3.448	3.390	3.333	3.279	3.226	3.175	3.125
3	4.000	3.922	3.846	3.774	3.704	3.636	3.571	3.509	3.448	3.390	3.333	3.279	3.226	3.175	3.125
4	4.000	3.922	3.846	3.774	3.704	3.636	3.571	3.509	3.448	3.390	3.333	3.279	3.226	3.175	3.125
5	4.000	3.922	3.846	3.774	3.704	3.636	3.571	3.509	3.448	3.390	3.333	3.279	3.226	3.175	3.125
6	4.000	3.921	3.846	3.774	3.704	3.636	3.571	3.509	3.448	3.390	3.333	3.279	3.226	3.175	3.125
7	4.000	3.922	3.846	3.773	3.704	3.636	3.572	3.509	3.448	3.390	3.333	3.279	3.226	3.175	3.125
8	4.000	3.921	3.846	3.774	3.704	3.636	3.571	3.509	3.448	3.390	3.333	3.279	3.226	3.175	3.125
9	4.000	3.922	3.846	3.773	3.704	3.637	3.572	3.509	3.448	3.390	3.333	3.279	3.226	3.175	3.125
10	4.000	3.921	3.846	3.774	3.704	3.636	3.571	3.509	3.448	3.390	3.333	3.279	3.226	3.174	3.125
11	4.000	3.922	3.846	3.773	3.704	3.637	3.572	3.509	3.448	3.390	3.333	3.279	3.226	3.175	3.125
12	4.000	3.921	3.846	3.774	3.704	3.636	3.571	3.509	3.448	3.390	3.333	3.279	3.226	3.174	3.125
13	4.000	3.922	3.846	3.773	3.703	3.637	3.572	3.509	3.448	3.390	3.334	3.279	3.226	3.175	3.125
14	4.000	3.921	3.846	3.774	3.704	3.636	3.571	3.509	3.448	3.390	3.333	3.279	3.226	3.174	3.125
15	4.000	3.922	3.846	3.774	3.703	3.637	3.572	3.509	3.449	3.390	3.334	3.278	3.226	3.175	3.125
16	4.000	3.921	3.846	3.773	3.704	3.636	3.571	3.509	3.448	3.390	3.333	3.279	3.226	3.174	3.125
17	4.000	3.922	3.846	3.773	3.703	3.637	3.572	3.509	3.449	3.390	3.334	3.278	3.226	3.175	3.125
18	4.000	3.921	3.846	3.773	3.704	3.636	3.571	3.508	3.448	3.390	3.333	3.279	3.226	3.174	3.125
19	4.000	3.922	3.846	3.774	3.703	3.637	3.572	3.509	3.449	3.390	3.334	3.278	3.226	3.175	3.125
20	4.000	3.921	3.847	3.773	3.704	3.636	3.571	3.508	3.448	3.390	3.333	3.279	3.226	3.174	3.125
21	4.000	3.922	3.846	3.774	3.703	3.637	3.572	3.509	3.449	3.389	3.334	3.279	3.225	3.175	3.125
22	4.000	3.921	3.847	3.773	3.704	3.636	3.571	3.508	3.448	3.390	3.333	3.279	3.226	3.174	3.125
23	4.000	3.922	3.846	3.774	3.703	3.637	3.572	3.509	3.449	3.389	3.334	3.278	3.225	3.175	3.125
24	4.000	3.921	3.847	3.773	3.704	3.636	3.571	3.508	3.448	3.390	3.333	3.279	3.226	3.174	3.125
25	4.000	3.922	3.846	3.774	3.703	3.637	3.572	3.509	3.449	3.389	3.334	3.278	3.225	3.175	3.125
26	2.000	3.921	3.847	3.773	3.704	3.636	3.571	3.508	3.448	3.390	3.333	3.279	3.226	3.174	3.125
27			1.923	3.774	3.703	3.637	3.572	3.509	3.449	3.389	3.334	3.278	3.225	3.175	3.125
28					1.852	3.636	3.571	3.508	3.448	3.390	3.333	3.279	3.226	3.174	3.125
29							1.786	3.509	3.449	3.389	3.334	3.278	3.225	3.175	3.125
30									1.724	3.390	3.333	3.279	3.226	3.174	3.125
31											1.667	3.278	3.225	3.175	3.125
32													1.613	3.174	3.125
33															1.562

12 | DEPRECIATION

¶1243

If the Recovery Year is:	and the Recovery Period is:														
	32.5	33.0	33.5	34.0	34.5	35.0	35.5	36.0	36.5	37.0	37.5	38.0	38.5	39.0	39.5
	the Depreciation Rate is:														
1	1.538	1.515	1.493	1.471	1.449	1.429	1.408	1.389	1.370	1.351	1.333	1.316	1.299	1.282	1.266
2	3.077	3.030	2.985	2.941	2.899	2.857	2.817	2.778	2.740	2.703	2.667	2.632	2.597	2.564	2.532
3	3.077	3.030	2.985	2.941	2.899	2.857	2.817	2.778	2.740	2.703	2.667	2.632	2.597	2.564	2.532
4	3.077	3.030	2.985	2.941	2.899	2.857	2.817	2.778	2.740	2.703	2.667	2.632	2.597	2.564	2.532
5	3.077	3.030	2.985	2.941	2.899	2.857	2.817	2.778	2.740	2.703	2.667	2.632	2.597	2.564	2.532
6	3.077	3.030	2.985	2.941	2.899	2.857	2.817	2.778	2.740	2.703	2.667	2.632	2.597	2.564	2.532
7	3.077	3.030	2.985	2.941	2.898	2.857	2.817	2.778	2.740	2.703	2.667	2.632	2.597	2.564	2.532
8	3.077	3.030	2.985	2.941	2.899	2.857	2.817	2.778	2.740	2.703	2.667	2.631	2.597	2.564	2.532
9	3.077	3.030	2.985	2.941	2.898	2.857	2.817	2.778	2.740	2.703	2.667	2.632	2.597	2.564	2.532
10	3.077	3.030	2.985	2.941	2.899	2.857	2.817	2.778	2.740	2.703	2.667	2.631	2.598	2.564	2.532
11	3.077	3.030	2.985	2.941	2.898	2.857	2.817	2.778	2.740	2.703	2.667	2.632	2.597	2.564	2.532
12	3.077	3.030	2.985	2.941	2.899	2.857	2.817	2.778	2.740	2.703	2.667	2.631	2.598	2.564	2.532
13	3.077	3.030	2.985	2.941	2.898	2.857	2.817	2.778	2.740	2.703	2.667	2.632	2.597	2.564	2.532
14	3.077	3.030	2.985	2.941	2.899	2.857	2.817	2.778	2.740	2.703	2.667	2.631	2.598	2.564	2.531
15	3.077	3.031	2.985	2.941	2.898	2.857	2.817	2.778	2.740	2.703	2.666	2.632	2.597	2.564	2.532
16	3.077	3.030	2.985	2.941	2.899	2.857	2.817	2.778	2.740	2.703	2.667	2.631	2.598	2.564	2.531
17	3.077	3.031	2.985	2.941	2.898	2.857	2.817	2.778	2.740	2.703	2.666	2.632	2.597	2.564	2.532
18	3.077	3.030	2.985	2.841	2.899	2.857	2.817	2.778	2.740	2.702	2.667	2.631	2.598	2.564	2.531
19	3.077	3.031	2.985	2.941	2.898	2.857	2.817	2.778	2.739	2.703	2.666	2.632	2.597	2.564	2.532
20	3.077	3.030	2.985	2.941	2.898	2.857	2.817	2.778	2.740	2.702	2.667	2.631	2.598	2.564	2.531
21	3.077	3.031	2.985	2.941	2.899	2.857	2.817	2.778	2.739	2.703	2.666	2.632	2.597	2.564	2.532
22	3.077	3.030	2.985	2.941	2.898	2.857	2.817	2.777	2.740	2.702	2.667	2.631	2.598	2.564	2.531
23	3.077	3.031	2.985	2.941	2.899	2.857	2.817	2.778	2.739	2.703	2.666	2.632	2.597	2.564	2.532
24	3.077	3.030	2.985	2.941	2.898	2.857	2.817	2.777	2.740	2.702	2.667	2.631	2.598	2.564	2.531
25	3.077	3.031	2.985	2.942	2.899	2.857	2.817	2.778	2.739	2.703	2.666	2.632	2.597	2.564	2.532
26	3.077	3.030	2.985	2.941	2.898	2.857	2.817	2.777	2.740	2.702	2.667	2.631	2.598	2.564	2.531
27	3.077	3.031	2.985	2.942	2.899	2.857	2.817	2.778	2.739	2.703	2.666	2.632	2.597	2.564	2.532
28	3.077	3.030	2.985	2.941	2.898	2.858	2.817	2.777	2.740	2.702	2.667	2.631	2.598	2.564	2.531
29	3.077	3.031	2.985	2.942	2.899	2.857	2.817	2.778	2.739	2.703	2.666	2.632	2.597	2.564	2.532
30	3.077	3.030	2.985	2.941	2.898	2.858	2.817	2.777	2.740	2.702	2.667	2.631	2.598	2.564	2.531
31	3.076	3.031	2.986	2.942	2.899	2.857	2.817	2.778	2.739	2.703	2.666	2.632	2.597	2.564	2.532
32	3.077	3.030	2.985	2.941	2.898	2.858	2.816	2.777	2.740	2.702	2.667	2.631	2.598	2.564	2.531
33	3.076	3.031	2.986	2.942	2.899	2.857	2.817	2.778	2.739	2.703	2.666	2.632	2.597	2.565	2.532
34		1.515	2.985	2.941	2.898	2.858	2.816	2.777	2.740	2.702	2.667	2.631	2.598	2.564	2.531
35				1.471	2.899	2.857	2.817	2.778	2.739	2.703	2.666	2.632	2.597	2.565	2.532
36						1.429	2.816	2.777	2.740	2.702	2.667	2.631	2.598	2.564	2.531
37								1.389	2.739	2.703	2.666	2.632	2.597	2.565	2.532
38										1.351	2.667	2.631	2.598	2.564	2.531
39												1.316	2.597	2.565	2.532
40														1.282	2.531

If the Recovery Year is:

and the Recovery Period is:	40.0	40.5	41.0	41.5	42.0	42.5	43.0	43.5	44.0	44.5	45.0	45.5	46.0	46.5	47.0
the Depreciation Rate is:															
1	1.250	1.235	1.220	1.205	1.190	1.176	1.163	1.149	1.136	1.124	1.111	1.099	1.087	1.075	1.064
2	2.500	2.469	2.439	2.410	2.381	2.353	2.326	2.299	2.273	2.247	2.222	2.198	2.174	2.151	2.128
3	2.500	2.469	2.439	2.410	2.381	2.353	2.326	2.299	2.273	2.247	2.222	2.198	2.174	2.151	2.128
4	2.500	2.469	2.439	2.410	2.381	2.353	2.326	2.299	2.273	2.247	2.222	2.198	2.174	2.151	2.128
5	2.500	2.469	2.439	2.410	2.381	2.353	2.326	2.299	2.273	2.247	2.222	2.198	2.174	2.151	2.128
6	2.500	2.469	2.439	2.410	2.381	2.353	2.326	2.299	2.273	2.247	2.222	2.198	2.174	2.151	2.128
7	2.500	2.469	2.439	2.410	2.381	2.353	2.326	2.299	2.273	2.247	2.222	2.198	2.174	2.150	2.128
8	2.500	2.469	2.439	2.410	2.381	2.353	2.326	2.299	2.273	2.247	2.222	2.198	2.174	2.151	2.128
9	2.500	2.469	2.439	2.410	2.381	2.353	2.325	2.299	2.273	2.247	2.222	2.198	2.174	2.150	2.128
10	2.500	2.469	2.439	2.410	2.381	2.353	2.326	2.299	2.273	2.247	2.222	2.198	2.174	2.151	2.128
11	2.500	2.469	2.439	2.410	2.381	2.353	2.325	2.299	2.273	2.247	2.222	2.198	2.174	2.150	2.128
12	2.500	2.469	2.439	2.410	2.381	2.353	2.326	2.299	2.273	2.247	2.222	2.198	2.174	2.151	2.128
13	2.500	2.469	2.439	2.410	2.381	2.353	2.325	2.299	2.273	2.247	2.222	2.198	2.174	2.150	2.128
14	2.500	2.469	2.439	2.409	2.381	2.353	2.326	2.299	2.273	2.247	2.222	2.198	2.174	2.151	2.128
15	2.500	2.469	2.439	2.410	2.381	2.353	2.325	2.299	2.273	2.247	2.222	2.198	2.174	2.150	2.128
16	2.500	2.469	2.439	2.409	2.381	2.353	2.326	2.299	2.273	2.247	2.222	2.198	2.174	2.151	2.128
17	2.500	2.469	2.439	2.410	2.381	2.353	2.325	2.299	2.273	2.247	2.222	2.198	2.174	2.150	2.127
18	2.500	2.469	2.439	2.409	2.381	2.353	2.326	2.299	2.273	2.247	2.222	2.198	2.174	2.151	2.128
19	2.500	2.469	2.439	2.410	2.381	2.353	2.325	2.299	2.273	2.247	2.222	2.198	2.174	2.150	2.127
20	2.500	2.469	2.439	2.409	2.381	2.353	2.326	2.299	2.273	2.247	2.222	2.198	2.174	2.151	2.128
21	2.500	2.469	2.439	2.410	2.381	2.353	2.325	2.299	2.273	2.247	2.222	2.198	2.174	2.150	2.127
22	2.500	2.469	2.439	2.409	2.381	2.353	2.326	2.299	2.273	2.247	2.222	2.198	2.174	2.151	2.128
23	2.500	2.469	2.439	2.410	2.381	2.353	2.325	2.299	2.272	2.247	2.222	2.198	2.174	2.150	2.127
24	2.500	2.469	2.439	2.409	2.381	2.353	2.326	2.299	2.273	2.247	2.222	2.198	2.174	2.151	2.128
25	2.500	2.469	2.439	2.410	2.381	2.353	2.325	2.299	2.272	2.247	2.222	2.198	2.174	2.150	2.127
26	2.500	2.469	2.439	2.409	2.381	2.353	2.326	2.299	2.273	2.247	2.222	2.198	2.174	2.151	2.128
27	2.500	2.469	2.439	2.410	2.381	2.353	2.325	2.299	2.272	2.247	2.223	2.198	2.174	2.150	2.127
28	2.500	2.469	2.439	2.409	2.381	2.353	2.326	2.299	2.273	2.247	2.222	2.198	2.174	2.151	2.128
29	2.500	2.469	2.439	2.410	2.381	2.353	2.325	2.299	2.272	2.247	2.223	2.198	2.174	2.150	2.127
30	2.500	2.469	2.439	2.409	2.381	2.353	2.326	2.299	2.273	2.248	2.222	2.197	2.174	2.151	2.128
31	2.500	2.469	2.439	2.410	2.381	2.353	2.325	2.299	2.272	2.247	2.223	2.198	2.174	2.150	2.127
32	2.500	2.470	2.439	2.409	2.381	2.353	2.326	2.299	2.273	2.248	2.222	2.197	2.174	2.151	2.128
33	2.500	2.469	2.439	2.410	2.381	2.353	2.325	2.298	2.272	2.247	2.223	2.198	2.174	2.150	2.127
34	2.500	2.470	2.439	2.409	2.381	2.353	2.326	2.299	2.273	2.248	2.222	2.197	2.174	2.151	2.128
35	2.500	2.469	2.439	2.410	2.381	2.353	2.325	2.299	2.272	2.247	2.223	2.198	2.174	2.150	2.127
36	2.500	2.470	2.139	2.409	2.381	2.353	2.326	2.299	2.273	2.248	2.222	2.197	2.174	2.151	2.128
37	2.500	2.469	2.439	2.410	2.381	2.353	2.325	2.298	2.272	2.247	2.223	2.198	2.174	2.150	2.127
38	2.500	2.470	2.439	2.409	2.381	2.353	2.326	2.299	2.273	2.248	2.222	2.197	2.174	2.151	2.128
39	2.500	2.469	2.439	2.410	2.381	2.353	2.325	2.298	2.272	2.247	2.223	2.198	2.174	2.150	2.127
40	2.500	2.470	2.439	2.409	2.381	2.353	2.326	2.299	2.273	2.248	2.222	2.197	2.173	2.151	2.128
41	1.250	2.469	2.439	2.410	2.380	2.352	2.325	2.299	2.272	2.247	2.223	2.198	2.174	2.150	2.127
42			1.220	2.409	2.381	2.353	2.326	2.299	2.273	2.248	2.222	2.197	2.173	2.151	2.128
43				1.190	2.352	2.325	2.298	2.272	2.247	2.223	2.198	2.174	2.150	2.127
44					1.163	2.299	2.273	2.248	2.222	2.197	2.173	2.151	2.128
45						1.136	2.247	2.223	2.198	2.174	2.150	2.127
46							1.111	2.197	2.173	2.151	2.128
47								1.087	2.150	2.127
48									1.064

12 DEPRECIATION

¶1243

If the Recovery Year is:	and the Recovery Period is:					
	47.5	48.0	48.5	49.0	49.5	50.0
	the Depreciation Rate is:					
1	1.053	1.042	1.031	1.020	1.010	1.000
2	2.105	2.083	2.062	2.041	2.020	2.000
3	2.105	2.083	2.062	2.041	2.020	2.000
4	2.105	2.083	2.062	2.041	2.020	2.000
5	2.105	2.083	2.062	2.041	2.020	2.000
6	2.105	2.083	2.062	2.041	2.020	2.000
7	2.105	2.083	2.062	2.041	2.020	2.000
8	2.105	2.083	2.062	2.041	2.020	2.000
9	2.105	2.083	2.062	2.041	2.020	2.000
10	2.105	2.083	2.062	2.041	2.020	2.000
11	2.105	2.083	2.062	2.041	2.020	2.000
12	2.105	2.083	2.062	2.041	2.020	2.000
13	2.105	2.083	2.062	2.041	2.020	2.000
14	2.105	2.083	2.062	2.041	2.020	2.000
15	2.105	2.083	2.062	2.041	2.020	2.000
16	2.105	2.083	2.062	2.041	2.020	2.000
17	2.105	2.083	2.062	2.041	2.020	2.000
18	2.105	2.083	2.062	2.041	2.020	2.000
19	2.105	2.084	2.062	2.041	2.020	2.000
20	2.105	2.083	2.062	2.041	2.020	2.000
21	2.105	2.084	2.062	2.041	2.020	2.000
22	2.105	2.083	2.062	2.041	2.020	2.000
23	2.105	2.084	2.062	2.041	2.020	2.000
24	2.105	2.083	2.062	2.041	2.020	2.000
25	2.105	2.084	2.062	2.041	2.020	2.000
26	2.106	2.083	2.062	2.041	2.020	2.000
27	2.105	2.084	2.062	2.041	2.020	2.000
28	2.106	2.083	2.062	2.041	2.020	2.000
29	2.105	2.084	2.062	2.041	2.020	2.000
30	2.106	2.083	2.062	2.041	2.020	2.000
31	2.105	2.084	2.062	2.041	2.021	2.000
32	2.106	2.083	2.062	2.041	2.020	2.000
33	2.105	2.084	2.062	2.041	2.021	2.000
34	2.106	2.083	2.062	2.040	2.020	2.000
35	2.105	2.084	2.062	2.041	2.021	2.000
36	2.106	2.083	2.062	2.040	2.020	2.000
37	2.105	2.084	2.061	2.041	2.021	2.000
38	2.106	2.083	2.062	2.040	2.020	2.000
39	2.105	2.084	2.061	2.041	2.021	2.000
40	2.106	2.083	2.062	2.040	2.020	2.000
41	2.105	2.084	2.061	2.041	2.021	2.000
42	2.106	2.083	2.062	2.040	2.020	2.000
43	2.105	2.084	2.061	2.041	2.021	2.000
44	2.106	2.083	2.062	2.040	2.020	2.000
45	2.105	2.084	2.061	2.041	2.021	2.000
46	2.106	2.083	2.062	2.040	2.020	2.000
47	2.105	2.084	2.061	2.041	2.021	2.000
48	2.106	2.083	2.062	2.040	2.020	2.000
49		1.042	2.061	2.041	2.021	2.000
50				1.020	2.020	2.000
51						1.000

1244. MACRS Short Tax Years. Special rules are provided for determining deductions under the Modified Accelerated Cost Recovery System (MACRS) if: (1) property is placed in service in a short tax year (any tax year with less than 12 months); (2) a short tax year occurs during the recovery period; or (3) property is disposed of before the end of the recovery period. In any of these situations, refinements are made to the use of the applicable conventions and the MACRS depreciation tables at ¶ 1243 may *not* be used (Rev. Proc. 89-15).

The mid-month convention is applied without regard to the length of the tax year. For example if residential rental property is placed in service in the first month of a six-month tax year, 5½ months depreciation is claimed.

Under the half-year convention, property placed in service or disposed of in a short tax year is deemed placed in service or disposed on the midpoint of the short tax year, which always falls on either the first day or the midpoint of the month.

Under the mid-quarter convention, property is deemed placed in service or disposed of on the midpoint of the quarter, which always falls on either the first day or the midpoint of a month, in the short tax year that it is placed in service or disposed.

Depreciation for the first recovery year in the recovery period is computed by multiplying the basis in the property by the applicable depreciation rate. The depreciation allowance allocable to the first tax year that includes a portion of the first recovery year is derived by multiplying the depreciation for the first recovery year by a fraction. The numerator is the number of months (including fractions of months) the property is deemed to be in service during the tax year under the applicable convention, and the denominator is 12.

Taxpayers may use either an allocation or a simplified method to correlate a depreciation allowance between recovery years and tax years after the first tax year in the recovery period.

1245. Applicable MACRS Conventions. Specified averaging conventions apply to depreciation computations made under the Modified Accelerated Cost Recovery System (MACRS) (Code Sec. 168(d); Reg. §§1.168(d)-1(b)(3)(ii), (d), and 1.168(i)-4(c); IRS Pub. 946). The recovery period begins on the date the property is placed in service under the applicable convention. The depreciation table percentages take into account the applicable convention in the first and last year of the regular recovery period. If property is disposed of prior to the end of the regular recovery period, the result obtained by using the table percentage for the year of disposition must be adjusted to take into account the applicable convention. No depreciation deduction is allowed if MACRS property is placed in service and disposed of in the same tax year.

Half-Year Convention. Under the half-year convention, which applies to property to which the mid-quarter convention does not apply and which is not residential rental or nonresidential real property, an asset is treated as placed in service or disposed of on the midpoint of the tax year. Thus, one-half of a full year's depreciation is allowed in the tax year in which the asset is placed in service regardless of the date that the asset is placed in service.

A half-year of depreciation is allowed in the tax year in which the recovery period ends and in a tax year in which a disposition occurs, except that no depreciation may be claimed if the disposition occurs in the same tax year that the asset was placed in service. The applicable table percentage for the year of disposition does not take the half-year convention into account unless the disposition falls in the tax year in which the recovery period ends. Thus, only one-half of the depreciation as computed using the applicable table percentage is allowed in a tax year other than the tax year in which the recovery period ends.

> **Example 1:** Five-year property with a depreciable basis of $1,000 and subject to the half-year convention is placed in service in 2017 by a calendar year taxpayer. Assume that the straight-line method is elected and the half-year convention applies. An election out of bonus depreciation is made. The recovery period begins on July 1, 2017, and ends five years later on June 30, 2022. However, the recovery (depreciation) period extends over six tax years. One-half of a full year's depreciation is allowed in 2017 and in 2022 under the half-year convention. Assume the asset is sold in 2019.

Using Table 8 at ¶ 1243, 2017 depreciation is $100 ($1,000 × 10 percent (first-year table percentage which reflects half-year convention allowing depreciation from July 1 through December 31, 2017); 2018 depreciation is $200 ($1,000 × 20 percent second-year table percentage); and 2019 depreciation is $100 ($1,000 × 20 percent third-year table percentage × 50 percent to reflect half-year convention in year of disposition). If the asset was not sold in 2019, the depreciation deduction for 2022 is $100 ($1,000 × 10 percent sixth-year table percentage which already reflects the half-year convention allowing depreciation from January 1, 2022, through June 30, 2022). Another $100 of depreciation would also be allowed if the asset was sold in 2022 since, under the half-year convention, the asset is deemed sold on June 30, 2022, at the end of the recovery period.

Mid-Month Convention. A mid-month convention applies to residential rental property, including low-income housing, and nonresidential real property. Property is deemed placed in service or disposed of on the midpoint of the month. The deduction is based on the number of months the property was in service. Thus, one-half month's depreciation is allowed for the month the property is placed in service, as well as for the month of a disposition that occurs before the end of the recovery period. However, no depreciation is allowed if a building is placed in service and disposed of in the same tax year.

Example 2: A commercial building costing $100,000 is purchased by a calendar-year taxpayer in February 2018 and sold in August 2019. Using Table 7A at ¶ 1243, the 2018 depreciation is $2,247 ($100,000 × 2.247 percent (first-year percentage for property placed in service in second month of tax year)) and the 2019 depreciation is $1,603 ($100,000 × 2.564 percent (second-year percentage for property placed in service in second month) × 7.5/12 to reflect 7.5 months in service in 2019 (January through mid-August) under the mid-month convention).

Mid-Quarter Convention. Under the mid-quarter convention, all property placed in service or disposed of during any quarter of a tax year is treated as placed in service at the midpoint of the quarter (Code Sec. 168(d)(3); Reg. § 1.168(d)-1). Depreciation under the mid-quarter convention may be determined using Tables 2-5 at ¶ 1243.

The mid-quarter convention applies to all property, other than nonresidential real property and residential rental property, if more than 40 percent of the aggregate bases of the property is placed in service during the last three months of the tax year. Property placed in service and disposed of within the same tax year is disregarded for purposes of the 40-percent test since depreciation may not be claimed on such property.

The aggregate basis of property placed in service in the last three months of the tax year must be computed regardless of the length of the tax year. Thus, if a short tax year consists of three months or less, the mid-quarter convention applies regardless of when the depreciable property is placed in service during the tax year.

The bonus depreciation deduction (¶ 1237) does not reduce the aggregate basis of property taken into account for purposes of determining whether the mid-quarter convention applies. However, any amount properly expensed under Code Sec. 179 (¶ 1208) does reduce aggregate basis. Thus, a taxpayer may be able to avoid the mid-quarter convention (if desired) by allocating the Code Sec. 179 deduction to property placed in service in the last quarter. Also, the mid-quarter convention does not operate to reduce the deduction otherwise allowable under Code Sec. 179 or for bonus depreciation.

Example 3: A calendar-year taxpayer places $100 of used five-year property in service in the first quarter of 2019 and $100 of new 10-year property in service in the fourth quarter. The taxpayer claims a 100 percent bonus depreciation allowance on the 10-year property. The mid-quarter convention applies to the five-year property because 50 percent of the aggregate adjusted basis of the property placed in service in 2019 (without regard to the bonus depreciation allowance) was placed in service in the fourth quarter. If the taxpayer did not claim bonus depreciation on the 10-year property and expensed the entire basis under section 179, the half-year convention would apply to the five-year property placed in service in the first quarter.

For purposes of the 40-percent test, depreciable basis does not include adjustments resulting from transfers of property between members of the same affiliated group filing a consolidated return.

If the MACRS deduction for property subject to the mid-quarter convention is computed without tables, depreciation for the first year is determined by computing the depreciation for the full tax year and then multiplying it by the following percentages for the quarter of the tax year the property is placed in service: first quarter, 87.5 percent; second quarter, 62.5 percent; third quarter, 37.5 percent; and fourth quarter, 12.5 percent. In the year of disposition (whether or not the table percentages are used) the deduction for a full year is multiplied by the following percentages for the quarter in which the asset is disposed of: first quarter, 12.5 percent; second quarter, 37.5 percent; third quarter, 62.5 percent, and fourth quarter 87.5 percent.

1247. MACRS Alternative Depreciation System (ADS). The Modified Accelerated Cost Recovery System (MACRS) alternative depreciation system (ADS) must be used for:

- tangible property used outside the United States;

- tax-exempt use property;

- tax-exempt bond-financed property;

- property imported from a foreign country for which an Executive Order is in effect because the country maintains trade restrictions or engages in other discriminatory acts;

- property of a farmer placed in service in a tax year in which an election to deduct preproductive period expenditures is in effect (Code Sec. 263A(e)(2)) (see below for a rule allowing revocation of this election);

- residential rental property, nonresidential real property, and qualified improvement property owned by a real property trade or business that elects out of the business interest deduction limitation (Code Sec. 163(j)), effective for tax years beginning after 2017 (¶ 937);

- any property with a recovery period of 10 years or greater which is held by an electing farming business that makes an election out of the business interest deduction limitation (Code Sec. 163(j)), effective for tax years beginning after 2017; and

- property for which an ADS election has been made (Code Sec. 168(g)).

Mandatory ADS property does not qualify for bonus depreciation (¶ 1237).

A farmer exempt from the uniform capitalization rules because average annual gross receipts are $25 million or less (Code Sec. 263A(i)) (¶ 1330) may receive automatic consent to revoke an election to deduct preproductive period expenditures. If the election is revoked the farmer applies the MACRS change in use rules (Reg. § 1.168(i)-4) to switch from the ADS method of depreciating its farming property to a method under the MACRS general depreciation system (GDS). The revocation may be made retroactively to a 2018 tax year (Rev. Proc. 2020-13).

A real property trade or business or farming business that elects out of the business interest deduction limitation under Code Sec. 163(j) must switch to ADS for certain property beginning in the year of the election (¶ 937). ADS applies to affected property placed in service before, during, and after the election year. The change-in-use rules apply for purposes of switching property placed in service before the election year to ADS. Automatic consent procedures are provided for a taxpayer to change its method of accounting for this purpose if a taxpayer fails to timely apply the change in use rules and is treated as adopting an impermissible accounting method (Rev. Proc. 2019-8).

Under ADS, the deduction is computed by applying the straight-line method, the applicable convention and the applicable longer recovery period for the respective class of property. The recovery period is 12 years for personal property with no class life, 30 years for residential rental property placed in service after 2017, 40 years for residential rental property placed in service before 2018, 40 years for nonresidential real property, 50 years for railroad grading and tunnel bores, and the class life for all other property. ADS is also used to compute the earnings and profits of a foreign or domestic corporation. The allowable depreciation deductions for passenger automobiles and other types of listed property used 50 percent or less in business are also determined under this method (¶ 1211 and ¶ 1214).

12 | DEPRECIATION

Electing ADS. In lieu of the regular MACRS deduction, taxpayers may elect to apply ADS to any class of property for any tax year (Code Sec. 168(g)(7)). An ADS election applies to all property in the MACRS class placed in service during the tax year. For example, an ADS election for five-year property applies to all five-year property placed in service in the tax year of the election. For residential rental property and nonresidential real property, the election is made on a property-by-property basis. Property for which ADS is elected may qualify for bonus depreciation (¶ 1237). The election to apply ADS is generally irrevocable, but a taxpayer may make a late election or revoke a prior election the same as making or revoking an election out of bonus depreciation with respect to depreciable property placed in service during a tax year ending in 2018, 2019, or 2020 tax year (Rev. Proc. 2020-25).

1248. Special Transferee Rules for Depreciation. A transferee in certain corporate and partnership transactions is treated as the transferor and must use the latter's recovery period and method in computing the deduction under the Modified Accelerated Cost Recovery System (MACRS) for the portion of the transferee's basis that does not exceed the transferor's adjusted basis in the property (Code Sec. 168(i)(7)). This rule applies to nonrecognition transfers under Code Sec. 332 (subsidiary liquidations) (¶ 2261); transfers to a controlled corporation (¶ 1731); transfers related to certain reorganizations (¶ 2209); contributions to a partnership (¶ 443); certain partnership distributions (¶ 453); and transactions between members of the same affiliated group during any tax year for which the group files a consolidated return. It does not apply to transactions relating to the sale or exchange of 50 percent or more of the total interest in a partnership's capital and profits within a 12-month period.

1250. Depreciable Property in Like-Kind Exchanges and Involuntary Conversions. The exchanged basis (i.e., carryover basis) of property under the Modified Accelerated Cost Recovery System (MACRS) acquired in a like-kind exchange (Code Sec. 1031) or involuntary conversion (Code Sec. 1033) for other MACRS property is depreciated by applying the following rules (Reg. § 1.168(i)-6).

- If the replacement MACRS property has the same or a shorter recovery period and the same or a more accelerated depreciation method than the relinquished MACRS property, the exchanged (carryover) basis is depreciated over the remaining recovery period of, and using the depreciation method and convention of, the relinquished MACRS property.

- If the recovery period of the replacement MACRS property is longer than that of the relinquished MACRS property, the exchanged basis is depreciated over the remainder of the recovery period that would have applied to the replacement MACRS property if the replacement MACRS property had originally been placed in service when the relinquished MACRS property was placed in service by the acquiring taxpayer.

- If the depreciation method of the replacement MACRS property is less accelerated than that of the relinquished MACRS property, the exchanged basis is depreciated beginning in the year of replacement using the less accelerated depreciation method of the replacement MACRS property that would have applied to the replacement MACRS property if the replacement MACRS property had originally been placed in service when the relinquished MACRS property was placed in service by the acquiring taxpayer.

The excess basis of the replacement property (i.e., the non-carryover basis usually attributable to additional cash paid for the replacement property) is separately depreciated as if originally acquired in the year of replacement.

In lieu of the preceding rules, a taxpayer may elect to depreciate the entire basis of the acquired property as a single depreciable asset beginning in the tax year of replacement (Reg. § 1.168(i)-6(i) and (j); Instructions to Form 4562).

Bonus depreciation may be claimed on the entire basis of qualifying acquired property (¶ 1237) (Reg. § 1.168(k)-1(f)(5)). If used property is acquired in a like-kind exchange or involuntary conversion, the carryover basis does not qualify for bonus depreciation (Reg. § 1.168(k)-2(g)(5)). Only the excess basis (non-carryover basis) may qualify for expensing under Code Sec. 179 even if the taxpayer elects to depreciate the entire basis of the acquired property as a single asset (Reg. § 1.168(i)-6(g) and (i)).

Code Sec. 1031 like-kind exchange treatment only applies to real property, generally effective for exchanges completed after 2017 (¶ 1721).

Accelerated Cost Recovery System (ACRS)

1252. Pre-1987 ACRS in General. The Accelerated Cost Recovery System (ACRS) must be used to compute the depreciation deduction for most tangible depreciable property placed in service after 1980 and before 1987 (Code Sec. 168, prior to P.L. 99-514). Cost recovery methods and periods are the same for both new and used property, and salvage value is disregarded in computing ACRS allowances. Post-1980 depreciation on tangible assets first placed in service before 1981 is computed using the method elected by the taxpayer when the property was placed in service (including the Class Life ADR depreciation system (¶ 1284) and other methods of depreciation discussed at ¶ 1216).

Under ACRS, the cost of eligible property is recovered over a 3-, 5-, 10-, 15-, 18-, or 19-year period, depending on the type of property. ACRS applies to recovery property (¶ 1255). The deduction is determined by applying the statutory table percentage for the appropriate class of property to its unadjusted basis. The unadjusted basis of property under ACRS is the basis of the property as determined for purposes of computing gain or loss, unadjusted for depreciation, amortization or depletion. It does not include that portion of the basis that is covered by an election to amortize or to expense the cost of section 179 property (¶ 1208) (Code Sec. 168(d)(1), prior to P.L. 99-514).

For personal ACRS recovery property placed in service after 1980 and before 1987, one-half year's depreciation is allowed in the year that it is placed in service, regardless of how long it is held. No deduction is allowed in the year personal recovery property is disposed of. Special prorations by month (using a mid-month convention) are provided for real recovery property (¶ 1261).

Straight-Line Election. An election to recover costs by using a straight-line method over the regular recovery period or a longer recovery period was also available under ACRS and was made on the taxpayer's return for the year in which the property was placed in service (Code Sec. 168(f)(4), prior to P.L. 99-514).

1255. ACRS Recovery Property. For purposes of the Accelerated Cost Recovery System (ACRS) (¶ 1252), recovery property is tangible depreciable property that is placed in service after 1980 and before 1987. It does not include property that is covered by an election to compute depreciation on a method not based on a depreciation period (unit-of-production method, income forecast method, etc.), public utility property for which the normalization method of accounting is not used, intangible assets such as patents and copyrights (¶ 1201), property covered by an election to amortize, or motion picture films and videotapes (Code Sec. 168(c) and (e), prior to P.L. 99-514).

For purposes of determining an asset's recovery property class, recovery property is defined as either Code Sec. 1245 class property or Code Sec. 1250 class property. Code Sec. 1245 class property includes tangible section 1245 property (¶ 1785), other than elevators and escalators, and certain rapidly amortized realty. Code Sec. 1250 class property includes tangible section 1250 property (¶ 1786), and elevators and escalators.

1258. ACRS Personal Property. Under the Accelerated Cost Recovery System (ACRS) (¶ 1252), the statutory percentage for personal property placed in service after 1980 and before 1987 is determined using prescribed percentage tables based on the type of property (3-, 5-, 10-, or 15-years). These table percentages are not reproduced because ACRS personal property should generally be fully depreciated at this time, but they appear in Prop. Reg. § 1.168-2. No recovery deduction is generally allowed in the year of disposition of ACRS personal property.

1261. ACRS Real Property. Under the Accelerated Cost Recovery System (ACRS) (¶ 1252), unadjusted basis is recovered over a period of 19 years for real property placed in service after May 8, 1985, and before January 1, 1987. For real property placed in service after March 15, 1984, and before May 9, 1985, unadjusted basis is recovered over a period of 18 years. A 15-year recovery period applies to real property placed in service after 1980 and before March 16, 1984, and to low-income housing (Code Sec. 168, prior to P.L. 99-514).

In computing the ACRS deduction, a full-month convention is used for low-income housing and real recovery property placed in service before March 16, 1984, and a mid-month convention is used for real recovery property (other than low-income housing) placed in service after March 15, 1984. Under the full-month convention, real property placed in service at any time during a particular month is treated as placed in service on the first day of such month, thereby permitting a full month's cost recovery for the month the property is placed in service. No cost recovery is permitted for the month of disposition. Under the mid-month convention, real property placed in service at any time during a particular month is treated as placed in service in the middle of such month, thereby permitting one-half month's cost recovery for the month the property is placed in service. For a disposition of real property during a month before the end of a recovery period, one-half month's cost recovery is allowed for the month of disposition.

In using the following tables, there are separate rate schedules depending upon the month in the first tax year that the property is placed in service. Further, if real property is sold before the end of the recovery period, the ACRS deduction for the year of disposition should reflect only the months of the year during which the property was in service. For a short tax year, appropriate adjustments must also be made to the table amounts (¶ 1270). A complete set of ACRS depreciation tables is provided in IRS Pub. 534.

Table I *18-Year Real Property*
(placed in service after June 22, 1984) for Which Alternate ACRS Method
Over a 35-Year Period Is Elected

Year	Month Placed in Service				
	1-2	3-6	7-10	11	12
1st	3%	2%	1%	0.4%	0.1%
2-30th	3%	3%	3%	3%	3%
31st	2%	2%	2%	2.6%	2.9%
32-35th	2%	2%	2%	2%	2%
36th		1%	2%	2%	2%

Table II *18-Year Real Property*
(placed in service after March 15 and before June 23, 1984)
15-Year Real Property and Low-Income Housing
(placed in service before May 9, 1985) for Which Alternate
ACRS Method Over a 35-Year Period Is Elected

Year	Month Placed in Service		
	1-2	3-6	7-12
1st	3%	2%	1%
2-30th	3%	3%	3%
31-35th	2%	2%	2%
36th		1%	2%

Table III *Low-Income Housing (placed in service after May 8, 1985)*
for Which Alternate ACRS Method Over a 35-Year Period Is Elected

Year	Month Placed in Service											
	1	2	3	4	5	6	7	8	9	10	11	12
1st	2.9%	2.6%	2.4%	2.1%	1.9%	1.7%	1.4%	1.2%	1.0%	0.7%	0.5%	0.2%
2-20th	2.9%	2.9%	2.9%	2.9%	2.9%	2.9%	2.9%	2.9%	2.9%	2.9%	2.9%	2.9%
21-35th	2.8%	2.8%	2.8%	2.8%	2.8%	2.8%	2.8%	2.8%	2.8%	2.8%	2.8%	2.8%
36th		0.3%	0.5%	0.8%	1.0%	1.2%	1.5%	1.7%	1.9%	2.2%	2.4%	2.7%

Table IV *19-Year Real Property*
for Which Alternate ACRS Method Over a 35-Year Period Is Elected

Year	Month Placed in Service											
	1	2	3	4	5	6	7	8	9	10	11	12
1st	2.7%	2.5%	2.3%	2.0%	1.8%	1.5%	1.3%	1.1%	0.8%	0.6%	0.4%	0.1%
2-20th	2.9%	2.9%	2.9%	2.9%	2.9%	2.9%	2.9%	2.9%	2.9%	2.9%	2.9%	2.9%
21-35th	2.8%	2.8%	2.8%	2.8%	2.8%	2.8%	2.8%	2.8%	2.8%	2.8%	2.8%	2.8%
36th	0.2%	0.4%	0.6%	0.9%	1.1%	1.4%	1.6%	1.8%	2.1%	2.3%	2.5%	2.8%

Table V *18-Year Real Property*
(placed in service after June 22, 1984) 19-Year Real Property for Which
Alternate ACRS Method Over a 45-Year Period Is Elected

Year	Month Placed in Service											
	1	2	3	4	5	6	7	8	9	10	11	12
1st	2.1%	1.9%	1.8%	1.6%	1.4%	1.2%	1%	0.8%	0.6%	0.5%	0.3%	0.1%
2-11th	2.3%	2.3%	2.3%	2.3%	2.3%	2.3%	2.3%	2.3%	2.3%	2.3%	2.3%	2.3%
12-45th	2.2%	2.2%	2.2%	2.2%	2.2%	2.2%	2.2%	2.2%	2.2%	2.2%	2.2%	2.2%
46th	0.1%	0.3%	0.4%	0.6%	0.8%	1%	1.2%	1.4%	1.6%	1.7%	1.9%	2.1%

Table VI *18-Year Real Property*
(placed in service after March 15 and before June 23, 1984) 15-Year Real Property
and Low-Income Housing (placed in service after December 31, 1980) for Which
Alternate ACRS Method Over a 45-Year Period Is Elected

Year	Month Placed in Service											
	1	2	3	4	5	6	7	8	9	10	11	12
1st	2.3%	2%	1.9%	1.7%	1.5%	1.3%	1.2%	0.9%	0.7%	0.6%	0.4%	0.2%
2-10th	2.3%	2.3%	2.3%	2.3%	2.3%	2.3%	2.3%	2.3%	2.3%	2.3%	2.3%	2.3%
11-45th	2.2%	2.2%	2.2%	2.2%	2.2%	2.2%	2.2%	2.2%	2.2%	2.2%	2.2%	2.2%
46th		0.3%	0.4%	0.6%	0.8%	1%	1.1%	1.4%	1.6%	1.7%	1.9%	2.1%

1264. ACRS: Predominant Use Outside the United States. Under the Accelerated Cost Recovery System (ACRS) (¶ 1252), the unadjusted basis of personal property used outside the United States is recovered over a period equal to the Asset Depreciation Range (ADR) class life for that property as of January 1, 1981 (¶ 1284) (Code Sec. 168, prior to P.L. 99-514). No recovery deduction is generally allowed in the year of disposition of personal recovery property used predominantly outside the United States. The unadjusted basis of real property and low income housing used predominantly outside the United States is recovered over a period of 35 years. For real recovery property (other than low-income housing) placed in service after March 15, 1984, a mid-month convention is used. There are separate rate schedules depending on the month in the first tax year that the property is placed in service.

1267. ACRS: Components of Sec. 1250 Class Property. Under the Accelerated Cost Recovery System (ACRS), structural components of section 1250 class property may not be depreciated separately. Composite depreciation is required on the entire building, unless the components qualify for amortization elections (Code Sec. 168(f)(1), prior to P.L. 99-514). Components that are considered personal property can be separately depreciated under the cost segregation rules (¶ 1240).

Substantial Improvements. A substantial improvement to a building was treated as a separate building rather than as one or more components. The taxpayer could use the regular ACRS deduction or elect the straight-line ACRS deduction for the improvement over the regular or a longer recovery period regardless of the ACRS method that is used for the rest of the building.

Components and improvements placed in service after 1986 are depreciated using the Modified Accelerated Cost Recovery System (MACRS) even if the building is not MACRS property (¶ 1240).

1270. ACRS: Short Tax Years. Under the Accelerated Cost Recovery System (ACRS) (¶ 1252), the depreciation deduction for a tax year that is less than 12 months is the amount that bears the same relationship to the amount of the deduction that would have been allowable if the recovery year were not a short tax year as the number of months and partial months in the short year bears to 12 (Code Sec. 168(f)(5), prior to P.L. 99-514). For real property and low-income housing placed in service or disposed of in a short tax year, this rule generally does not apply. Instead, the deduction is based on the number of months the property is in service during the year, regardless of the length of the tax year and regardless of the recovery period and method used.

Any unrecovered allowance (the difference between the recovery allowance properly allowable for the short tax year and the recovery allowance that would have been allowable if it were not a short tax year) is claimed in the tax year following the last year in the recovery period (Prop. Reg. § 1.168-2(f)(3)). However, the unrecovered allowance claimed as a recovery allowance in the tax year following the last year of the recovery period may not exceed the amount of the recovery allowance permitted for the last year of the recovery period, assuming that such year consists of 12 months. Any remainder is carried forward until exhausted.

Class Life ADR System

1282. Post-1980 Depreciation Under ADR. If the Asset Depreciation Range (ADR) System was elected for tangible assets first placed in service after 1970 and before 1981, post-1980 depreciation on such assets must be computed under the ADR System (Reg. § 1.167(a)-11).

1284. ADR in General. Under the Asset Depreciation Range (ADR) System, all tangible assets were placed in specific classes. A class life or "asset guideline period" was given for each class of assets in Reg. § 1.167(a)-11. Each class of assets other than land improvements and buildings was also given a range of years or "asset depreciation range" that was about 20 percent above and below the class life.

Energy Efficient Commercial Buildings Deduction

1286. Energy Efficient Commercial Buildings Deduction. A taxpayer may deduct the cost of certain energy efficiency improvements installed on or in a depreciable building located in the United States, and placed in service before January 1, 2021 (Code Sec. 179D, as amended by the Taxpayer Certainty and Disaster Tax Relief Act of 2019 (P.L. 116-94); Notice 2006-52, as clarified by Notice 2008-40, modified by Notice 2012-26). The deduction applies to energy efficient commercial building property, which is depreciable property installed as part of a building's (1) interior lighting systems, (2) heating, cooling, ventilation, and hot water systems, or (3) envelope as part of a certified plan to reduce the total annual energy and power costs of these systems by at least 50 percent in comparison to a reference building that meets specified minimum standards.

The deduction is limited to the lesser of the cost of the qualifying property reduced by the aggregate amount deducted in any prior tax year, or the product of $1.80 and the total square footage of the building reduced by the aggregate amount deducted in any prior tax year. A taxpayer may also claim a partial deduction for the costs of property that meets certain energy savings targets set by the IRS (Notice 2006-52, modified by Notice 2012-26). The deduction is determined by substituting $.60 for $1.80.

A taxpayer may use the following energy savings percentages to determine if a partial deduction is available: (1) building envelope—10 percent; heating, cooling, ventilation, and hot water systems—15 percent; and interior lighting systems—25 percent; or (2) building envelope—10 percent; heating, cooling, ventilation, and hot water systems—20 percent; and interior lighting systems—20 percent.

The deduction is generally claimed by the building's owner. However, the person who is primarily responsible for designing a public building may claim the deduction. The deduction reduces the depreciable basis of the building and is treated as a depreciation deduction for section 1245 recapture purposes (Code Sec. 1245(a)(3)(C)).

The Department of Energy maintains a list of the software that must be used to calculate power consumption and energy costs for purposes of certifying the required energy savings necessary to claim the deduction (Notice 2008-40). The certification is not attached to the taxpayer's return but must be retained as part of the taxpayer's books and records. The deduction is claimed on the "Other deductions" line of the taxpayer's return. There is no special form for computing the deduction.

Chapter 13

CAPITALIZATION, AMORTIZATION, AND DEPLETION

Capital Expenditures

See CCH® AnswerConnect: *Tangible Property Regulations (Repair Regulations)* for more information on this topic.

1305. Capital Expenditures. A taxpayer may not currently deduct a capital expenditure. A capital expenditure is: (1) any amount paid out for new buildings, permanent improvements, or betterments made to increase the value of any property or estate; or (2) any amount expended in restoring property or in making good the exhaustion thereof for which an allowance has been made (Code Sec. 263; Reg. § 1.263(a)-1). Capital expenditures are included in basis (¶ 1611) and generally recovered through depreciation, amortization, or depletion (¶ 1201). Amounts paid or incurred for incidental repairs and maintenance of property are not capital expenditures.

Capital expenses include amounts paid to produce or acquire tangible or intangible property, to improve tangible property, to facilitate the acquisition of a trade or business or a change in a business entity's capital structure, or to acquire or create an interest in land. They also include amounts paid in a corporate financing or restructuring, such as amounts paid by bondholders and shareholders to be used in a corporate reorganization, voluntary contributions by shareholders to a corporation, and amounts paid by a holding company to carry out a guaranty of dividends on the stock of a subsidiary corporation in certain circumstances.

A taxpayer may elect to treat certain capital expenditures as deductible or deferred expenses, or treat certain deductible expenses as capital expenditures (Reg. § 1.263(a)-6). These include:

- expenses related to newspaper or magazine circulation (¶ 971);
- research and experiments (¶ 979);
- soil and water conservation (¶ 982);
- Code Sec. 179 property (¶ 1208);
- energy efficient commercial buildings (¶ 1286);
- advanced mine safety equipment (¶ 989A);
- fertilizer (¶ 985);
- film, television production, and live theatrical production (¶ 1229);
- removal of barriers to the handicapped and elderly (¶ 1360);
- tertiary injectants (Code Sec. 193);
- reforestation (¶ 1360);
- business start-up (¶ 904);
- corporate organization (¶ 237);
- carrying charges (¶ 1614);

13 CAPITALIZATION

- mine development (¶ 988); and

- partnership organization and syndication (¶ 477).

Intangible Property. Amounts must be capitalized if they are paid or incurred for: (1) specific categories of expenditures that are incurred in acquiring, creating, or enhancing, or that facilitate the acquisition or creation of intangible property that is acquired from another person in a purchase or similar transaction; (2) certain rights, privileges, or benefits that are created or originated by the taxpayer; (3) a separate and distinct intangible asset; or (4) a future benefit that the IRS identifies in published guidance (Reg. § 1.263(a)-4).

1307. Accounting Method Change for Tangible Property Regulations (Repair Regulations). A taxpayer generally must capitalize amounts paid or incurred to acquire or produce a unit of real or personal property under Reg. § 1.263(a)-2 (¶ 1309). The capitalization rules are part of a group of regulations known as the "repair regulations" and generally apply to tax years beginning on or after January 1, 2014. A change in the way a taxpayer accounts for amounts paid or incurred to acquire or produce a unit of tangible property to comply with the repair regulations is a change in method of accounting (Reg. § 1.263(a)-2(i)).

Guidance for obtaining automatic consent to make an accounting method change to comply with the repair regulations is available in Sec. 11.08 of Rev. Proc. 2019-43, effective for a Form 3115 filed on or after November 8, 2019, for a year of change ending on or after March 31, 2019, and Rev. Proc. 2018-31, effective for changes filed on or after May 9, 2018, for a year of change ending on or after September 30, 2017.

1309. Acquired or Produced Tangible Property (Tangible Property Regulations). A taxpayer is generally required to capitalize amounts paid or incurred to produce or acquire a unit of tangible real or personal property, including leasehold improvement property, land and land improvements, buildings, machinery, equipment, furniture, and fixtures (Reg. § 1.263(a)-2). A current deduction is allowed and no capitalization is required under a de minimis safe harbor (¶ 1311), for repairs and improvements (¶ 1313), and materials and supplies (¶ 1317). See ¶ 1307 for accounting method changes to comply with the tangible property regulations.

Capitalized amounts under the tangible property regulations includes the invoice price, amounts that facilitate the acquisition of a unit of property (i.e., transactions costs), and costs for work performed before the taxpayer places the property in service (e.g., repairs). See ¶ 1319 for the definition of a unit of property for this purpose. Amounts paid to acquire real or personal property for resale are also capitalized.

An amount facilitates the acquisition of property if the amount is paid in the process of investigating or otherwise pursuing the acquisition or production of the property. Inherently facilitative costs of acquiring or producing property that must be capitalized are amounts paid for: (1) transporting the property (e.g., shipping fees and moving costs); (2) appraisals and valuations; (3) negotiating the terms or structure of the acquisition; (4) tax advice on the acquisition; (5) application fees, bidding costs, or similar expenses; (6) preparing and reviewing the documents that effectuate the acquisition of the property (e.g., preparing the bid, offer, sales contract, or purchase agreement); (7) title examination and evaluation; (8) obtaining regulatory approval of the acquisition; (9) securing permits related to the acquisition, including application fees; (10) conveying property between the parties, including sales and transfer taxes, and title registration costs; (11) finders' fees or brokers' commissions, including contingency fees; (12) architectural, geological, survey, engineering, environmental, or inspection services pertaining to particular properties; and (13) services provided by a qualified intermediary or other facilitator of a like-kind exchange (Reg. § 1.263(a)-2(f)).

Activities performed in the process of determining whether to acquire real property and which real property to acquire are currently deductible. Inherently facilitative amounts are capitalized even if paid or incurred during the "whether and which" process.

Employee compensation and overhead do not facilitate the acquisition of real or personal property but may need to be capitalized under the uniform capitalization rules for property produced by the taxpayer or property acquired for resale (¶ 1330). A taxpayer may elect to capitalize employee compensation and overhead on a timely filed original federal tax return (including extensions) for the tax year during which the amounts are paid or incurred.

1311. De Minimis Expensing Safe Harbor (Tangible Property Regulations). A taxpayer may make a *de minimis* safe harbor expensing election to not capitalize amounts paid or incurred during the tax year to acquire or produce a unit of tangible property (¶ 1309) (Reg. § 1.263(a)-1(f); Notice 2015-82). The taxpayer may also not treat as a material or supply (¶ 1317) amounts paid or incurred for tangible property that costs no more than $5,000 if the taxpayer has an applicable financial statement (AFS) and $2,500 if the taxpayer does not have an AFS.

A taxpayer with an applicable financial statement (AFS) may elect the *de minimis* expensing safe harbor for a tax year if: (1) at the beginning of the tax year, the taxpayer has written accounting procedures that expense for non-tax purposes amounts paid for property that costs less than a specified dollar amount or that has an economic useful life of 12 months or less; and (2) the taxpayer treats such amounts paid or incurred during the tax year as an expense on the AFS. A taxpayer without an AFS must have similar accounting procedures in effect at the beginning of the tax year, but the procedures do not need to be written. A taxpayer without an AFS must expense the amount paid for the property on its books and records in accordance with its accounting procedures.

The *de minimis* election must be made on a timely filed income tax return (including extensions) for the year by attaching a statement to the return. Amounts that qualify for the safe harbor can be currently deducted if they are otherwise deductible business expenses. They cannot be capitalized under the general capitalization rules, though they may still be subject to UNICAP as a direct and allocable indirect cost of property produced by the taxpayer or property acquired for resale (¶ 1332).

1313. Repairs and Improvements (Tangible Property Regulations). A taxpayer generally may currently deduct repair and maintenance expenses that keep tangible property in an ordinarily efficient operating condition and do not add to its value or appreciably prolong its useful life (Reg. § 1.162-4). A taxpayer, however, may elect to capitalize certain repair expenses (discussed below).

Improvements. Expenses that improve a unit of property must be capitalized (Reg. § 1.263(a)-3). A unit of property is improved if the amounts paid for activities performed after the property is placed in service by the taxpayer either result in a betterment to the unit of property, restore the unit of property, or adapt the unit of property to a new or different use. A taxpayer generally must capitalize all the direct costs of an improvement, as well as all the indirect costs, such as otherwise deductible repair costs, that directly benefit or are incurred by reason of an improvement. Indirect costs that do not directly benefit and are not incurred by reason of an improvement generally are not capital improvements, regardless of whether they are paid or incurred at the same time as a capital improvement.

A betterment is an expenditure that:

- ameliorates a material condition or defect that existed prior to the taxpayer's acquisition of the unit of property or arose during the production of the property, whether or not the taxpayer was aware of the condition or defect at the time of acquisition;

- is for a material addition to the unit of property, such as a physical enlargement, expansion, extension, or addition of a new major component;

- is for a material increase in the capacity of the unit of property, such as additional cubic or linear space; or

- is reasonably expected to materially increase the productivity, efficiency, strength, quality, or output of the unit of property.

An amount is paid to restore a unit of property if:

- the taxpayer replaces a component of a unit of property and deducts a loss for that component, other than a casualty loss (for example, by making a partial disposition election under Reg. § 1.168(i)-8(d));

- the taxpayer replaces a component of a unit of property and realizes gain or loss by selling or exchanging the component;

- the expenditure is for the restoration of damage to a unit of property caused by a casualty and the taxpayer is required to make a basis adjustment to the unit of property on account of a casualty loss or the receipt of insurance;

- the expenditure is for a return a unit of property to its ordinary efficient operating condition after the property has deteriorated to a state of disrepair and is no longer functional for its intended use;

- the expenditure is to rebuild a unit of property to a like-new condition after the end of its class life (i.e., its MACRS alternative depreciation system recovery period); or

- the expenditure is for the replacement of a part or a combination of parts that comprise a major component or a substantial structural part of a unit of property (Reg. § 1.263(a)-3(k)(1)).

Repair expenditures paid in connection with a casualty are currently deductible if the capitalized restoration expenditures exceed the adjusted basis of the property prior to reduction by the casualty loss deduction or insurance reimbursement. If the capitalized restoration expenditures do not exceed the adjusted basis, but the sum of the capitalized restoration expenditures and repair expenditures exceed the adjusted basis, then the repair expenditures not used to offset the adjusted basis may be deducted (Reg. § 1.263(a)-3(k)(4)(i) and (k)(7), Example 5). Repair expenditures are not deductible if a basis adjustment is made to a property on account of a casualty loss or event, such as the receipt of insurance (Reg. § 1.263(a)-3(k)(1)(iii)).

An adaptation to a new or different use is a type of improvement that is capitalized. An amount is generally paid to adapt a unit of property to a new or different use if the adaptation is not consistent with the taxpayer's ordinary use of the unit of property at the time it was originally placed in service by the taxpayer (Reg. § 1.263(a)-3(l)).

Removal Costs. If a taxpayer disposes of a depreciable asset, including a partial disposition (¶ 1239), and has taken into account the adjusted basis of the asset or component of the asset in realizing gain or loss, then the costs of removing the asset or component are deductible. If a taxpayer disposes of a component of a unit of property, but the disposal is not a disposition, then the taxpayer must capitalize the removal cost if it directly benefits or is incurred by reason of an improvement to the unit of property (Reg. § 1.263(a)-3(g)(2)). For example, the cost of removing shingles on a roof is deductible if the replacement costs are a deductible repair. However, if the entire roof is replaced and the replacement costs are capitalized, then the removal costs are capitalized provided the taxpayer does not make a partial disposition election and claim a loss deduction on the replaced roof. Special rules apply to demolitions (¶ 1105).

Remodel-Refresh Safe Harbor. A qualified taxpayer engaged in the trade or business of operating a retail establishment or a restaurant may adopt a safe harbor method of accounting under which 25 percent of qualified remodel/refresh costs are capital expenditures, and 75 percent of such costs are currently deductible (Rev. Proc. 2015-56; Rev. Proc. 2018-31; Rev. Proc. 2019-43; Rev. Proc. 2020-25). A qualified taxpayer must have an AFS as defined in Reg.§ 1.263(a)-1(f). The building and improvements capitalized under the safe harbor must be placed in separate MACRS general asset accounts (GAAs). A late election to place the building in a GAA may be made in the tax year that the safe harbor is first used as part of the safe harbor accounting method change. Improvements that are depreciable under MACRS and made prior to the year that the safe harbor is first used generally must also be placed in a GAA by making a late election. A taxpayer may not make a partial disposition election (¶ 1239) to claim retirement losses on building components once this safe harbor is used.

¶1313

Routine Maintenance Safe Harbor. Under a safe harbor, routine maintenance activities on a unit of property do not improve that unit (Reg. § 1.263(a)-3(i)). The safe harbor is an accounting method and not an election. Routine maintenance activities are the recurring activities expected to be performed to keep a unit of property in ordinarily efficient operating order. The activities are routine only if at the time the unit of property is placed in service the taxpayer reasonably expects to perform the activities more than once during the class life (i.e., MACRS alternative depreciation system recovery period) of the unit of property or, in the case of a building, more than once during a ten-year period beginning on the date the taxpayer places the building in service.

Routine maintenance *does not* include amounts paid or incurred for a betterment or adaptation. The following types of restorations also *do not* qualify:

• the cost of replacing a component if a retirement loss is claimed or gain or loss is realized upon a sale of the replaced component;

• amounts paid for the restoration of damage to a unit of property for which a basis adjustment as a result of a casualty loss or casualty event is required; and

• the cost of restoring deteriorated and nonfunctional property to its ordinarily efficient operating condition.

Routine maintenance also does not include amounts paid for repairs, maintenance, or improvement of rotable and temporary spare parts if the taxpayer applies the optional method of accounting for the spare parts. Routine maintenance may include the replacement of a major component or substantial structural part of a unit of property. Routine maintenance performed on a building structure or any of its building systems qualifies for the routine maintenance safe harbor. However, repairs, maintenance, or improvement of network assets (e.g., railroad track, oil and gas pipelines, water and sewage pipelines, power transmission and distribution lines, and telephone and cable lines) does not qualify for the safe harbor.

Building Improvements Safe Harbor for Small Taxpayers. A taxpayer with $10 million or less of average annual gross receipts in the three preceding tax years may elect not to capitalize improvements on a building, condominium, or cooperative that has an unadjusted basis of $1 million or less if the total amount paid or incurred for repairs, maintenance, and improvements for the tax year of the election does not exceed the lesser of $10,000 or two percent of the unadjusted basis of the building. Amounts deducted under the *de minimis* safe harbor (¶ 1311) or the safe harbor for routine maintenance are counted toward the $10,000 limit. This election must be made by the due date of the return (including extensions) for the year of the election. The safe harbor is applied separately to each eligible building owned or leased by the taxpayer. A lessee's unadjusted basis of a leased building or leased building space is equal to the total amount of undiscounted rent paid or expected to be paid over the entire lease term, including expected renewal periods (Reg. § 1.263(a)-3(h)).

Election to Capitalize Repair and Maintenance Costs. A taxpayer may elect on a timely filed original return (including extensions) to capitalize as improvements all amounts paid during the tax year for repair and maintenance of tangible property, if the taxpayer incurs these amounts in carrying on its trade or business and treats them as capital expenditures on its books and records for the tax year covered by the election (Reg. § 1.263(a)-3(n)). An electing taxpayer cannot currently deduct the repair and maintenance amounts affected by the election. The election does not apply to amounts paid for repairs or maintenance of rotable or temporary spare parts to which the optional method of accounting is applied.

1317. Materials and Supplies (Tangible Property Regulations). Amounts paid or incurred by a taxpayer to acquire or produce non-incidental materials and supplies that do not improve a unit of property are generally deductible in the tax year in which the materials and supplies are used or consumed in the taxpayer's operations (Reg. § 1.162-3). Amounts paid to acquire or produce incidental materials and supplies that are carried on hand and for which no record of consumption is kept or of which physical inventories at the beginning and end of the tax year are not taken, are deductible in the tax year in which these amounts are paid, provided taxable income is clearly reflected.

Materials and supplies that improve tangible property are capitalized (Reg. § 1.263(a)-3(c)). In addition, the uniform capitalization rules require taxpayers to capitalize the direct and allocable indirect costs (¶ 1332), including the cost of materials and supplies, of property produced by the taxpayer and property acquired for resale. Taxpayers may also be required to include in inventory certain materials and supplies (¶ 1553). Finally, the cost of materials and supplies that meet the requirements of the *de minimis* safe harbor (¶ 1311) are deductible in the year paid or incurred if a taxpayer makes the *de minimis* safe harbor election.

Material and supplies include tangible property that is used or consumed in the taxpayer's business operations, not inventory, and:

- a component that is acquired to maintain, repair, or improve a unit of tangible property owned, leased, or serviced by the taxpayer, but is not acquired as part of any single unit of tangible property;

- fuel, lubricants, water, and similar items that are reasonably expected to be consumed in 12 months or less, beginning when used in a taxpayer's operations;

- a unit of property that has an economic useful life of 12 months or less, beginning when the property is used or consumed in the taxpayer's operations;

- a unit of property with an acquisition or production cost of $200 or less; or

- identified as a material or supply by the IRS in published guidance.

Rotable, Temporary, and Standby Emergency Parts. Rotable and temporary spare parts are materials and supplies. Their cost is deducted in the year used or consumed unless the taxpayer uses the optional method of accounting to deduct their cost in the year of installation (Reg. § 1.162-3(c)(2)). If the election is not made, rotable and temporary spare parts are treated as used or consumed in the year they are discarded (Reg. § 1.162-3(a)(3)).

Rotable spare parts are parts that are acquired for installation on a unit of property, removable from that unit of property, generally repaired or improved, and either reinstalled on the same or other property or stored for later installation. Temporary spare parts are parts that are used temporarily until a new or repaired part can be installed and then are removed and stored for later installation (Reg. § 1.162-3(c)(2)).

A taxpayer may elect to capitalize and depreciate the cost of rotable, temporary, and standby emergency spare parts. The election does not apply to rotable and temporary spare parts for which the optional method of accounting is used (Reg. § 1.162-3(d)). The *de minimis* safe harbor election does not apply to rotable, temporary, or standby emergency spare parts that a taxpayer elects to capitalize and depreciate, or to rotable and temporary spare parts that are accounted for under the optional method (Reg. § 1.162-3(f)).

1319. Unit of Property (Tangible Property Regulations). All components that are functionally interdependent comprise a single unit of property for purposes of the capitalization of costs to acquire or produce tangible property (¶ 1309). Components are functionally interdependent if the placing in service of one component is dependent on the placing in service of the other components (Reg. § 1.263(a)-3(e)). Although a building, including its structural components, is a unit of property, the improvement rules are applied separately to each building system and the building structure.

A building structure consists of a building and its structural components, *other than* those designated as building systems. Designated building systems, including their components, that are separate from the building structure are:

- heating, ventilation, and air conditioning (HVAC) systems, including motors, compressors, boilers, furnace, chillers, pipes, ducts, and radiators;

- plumbing systems, including pipes, drains, valves, sinks, bathtubs, toilets, water and sanitary sewer collection equipment, and site utility equipment;

- electrical systems, including wiring, outlets, junction boxes, lighting fixtures and associated connectors, and site utility equipment;

- all escalators and elevators;

- fire-protection and alarm systems, including sensing devices, computer controls, sprinkler heads, sprinkler mains, associated pipes or plumbing, pumps, visual and audible alarms, alarms control panels, heat and smoke detection devices, fire escapes, fire doors, emergency exit lighting and signage, and fire fighting equipment;

- security systems for the protection of the building and its occupants, including windows and door locks, security cameras, recorders, monitors, motion detectors, security lighting, alarm systems, entry and access systems, and related junction boxes, wiring and conduits;

- gas distribution systems, including associated pipes and equipment used to distribute gas to and from the property line and between buildings; and

- any other structural components designated as a building system by the IRS in published guidance.

Example: A taxpayer replaces the steps on the sole escalator in a building. The improvement rules are applied separately to the escalator because it is a building system. Since the steps are a major component of the escalator, the cost of replacing the steps is for a restoration and must be capitalized. If the improvement rules applied to the entire building, including its building systems, then the steps might not be considered a major component of the building and a repair deduction could be claimed. The larger the unit of property the more likely an expenditure is generally for a repair.

Uniform Capitalization Rules (UNICAP)

See CCH® AnswerConnect: *Uniform Capitalization Rules (UNICAP)* for more information on this topic.

1330. Uniform Capitalization Rules (UNICAP). A taxpayer subject to the uniform capitalization (UNICAP) rules must capitalize all direct costs and an allocable portion of most indirect costs that are associated with production or resale activities. The uniform capitalization rules generally apply to:

- real or tangible personal property produced by the taxpayer for use in a trade or business or in an activity engaged in for profit;

- real or tangible personal property produced by the taxpayer for sale to customers; and

- real or personal property, both tangible and intangible, acquired by the taxpayer for resale (Code Sec. 263A).

Property acquired for resale includes stock in trade of the reseller or other property which is includible in the reseller's inventory if on hand at the close of the tax year and property held primarily for sale to customers in the ordinary course of the reseller's trade or business (Code Sec. 263A(b)(2); Reg. § 1.263A-3(a)(1)).

Costs attributable to producing or acquiring property generally are capitalized by charging them to capital accounts or basis, and costs attributable to property that is inventory in the hands of the taxpayer generally are capitalized by including them in inventory.

Property Excepted from Rules. Among the classes of property excepted from the UNICAP rules are:

- property produced by the taxpayer for its own use other than in a trade or business or in an activity conducted for profit;

- research and experimental expenditures (¶ 979);

- intangible drilling and development costs (¶ 989), and mine development and exploration (¶ 987 and ¶ 988);

- any property produced by the taxpayer under a long-term contract;

- any costs incurred in raising, growing or harvesting trees (including the costs associated with the underlying real property) other than trees bearing fruit, nuts, or other crops and ornamental trees (those that are six years old or less when severed from the roots); and

- amounts allowable as a deduction relating to the optional ten-year write-off of certain tax preferences under the alternative minimum tax (AMT) rules, with respect to mining exploration and development costs, research and experimental expenditures, and intangible drilling costs (60-month write-off for IDCs), but not circulation expenditures (¶ 194).

Small Producer or Reseller Exception. A producer or reseller is exempt from the UNICAP rules if it meets the gross receipts test for using the cash method of accounting (¶ 1515) (Code Sec. 263A(i)).

A taxpayer meets the small business test for the tax year if its average annual gross receipts for the three prior tax years do not exceed $26 million for 2019 and 2020, and $25 million for 2018. For tax years beginning before 2018, the threshold was $10 million but the exception to the UNICAP rules only applied to property acquired for resale. A sole proprietorship applies the gross receipts test as if each trade or business of the taxpayer were a corporation or a partnership. A tax shelter that is not allowed to use the cash method of accounting does not qualify for the small business exception.

A taxpayer making a change in accounting method to apply this UNICAP exception should treat the change as initiated by the taxpayer and made with the IRS's consent for Code Sec. 481 adjustment purposes (¶ 1531). An automatic change in accounting method procedure allows a small business taxpayer to change to a method of accounting that no longer capitalizes costs under the UNICAP rules (Rev. Proc. 2018-40).

1332. Direct and Indirect Expenses Subject to UNICAP Rules. Direct material and labor costs and indirect costs generally must be capitalized under the uniform capitalization (UNICAP) rules (¶ 1330) with respect to property that is produced or acquired for resale (Code Sec. 263A(a)(2); Reg. § 1.263A-1(e)). Direct material costs include the costs of materials that become an integral part of the subject matter and materials that are consumed in the ordinary course of the activity. Direct labor costs include the cost of labor that can be identified or associated with a particular activity such as basic compensation, overtime pay, vacation pay, and payroll taxes.

Indirect costs include all costs other than direct material and labor costs. Indirect costs require a reasonable allocation to determine the portion of such costs that are attributable to each activity of the taxpayer. This includes: repair and maintenance of equipment or facilities; utilities; rental of equipment, facilities, or land; indirect labor and contract supervisory wages; indirect materials and supplies; depreciation, amortization and cost recovery allowance on equipment and facilities (to the extent allowable as deductions); certain administrative costs; insurance; contributions paid to or under a stock bonus, pension, profit-sharing, annuity, or other deferred compensation plan; rework labor, scrap and spoilage; and certain engineering and design expenses.

Expenses that are not required to be capitalized under the UNICAP rules with respect to property produced or acquired for resale include marketing, selling, advertising, and distribution expenses (Reg. § 1.263A-1(e)(4)(iv)). IRS procedures allow for the capitalization or amortization of package design costs (Rev. Proc. 98-39). Other costs that need not be capitalized include: bidding expenses incurred in the solicitation of contracts not awarded the taxpayer; certain general and administrative expenses; and compensation paid to officers attributable to the performance of services that do not directly benefit or are not incurred by reason of a particular production activity.

1334. Simplified Allocation Method for Resale Costs Under UNICAP. A taxpayer may elect to use one of the simplified resale methods for allocating costs to property acquired for resale under the uniform capitalization (UNICAP) rules (¶ 1330) (Reg. § 1.263A-3(d)). However, a single trade or business that consists of both production and resale activities must use the simplified production method (¶ 1336).

¶1332

Under the simplified resale methods, preliminary inventory balances are calculated without including the additional costs required to be capitalized. The amount of additional costs attributable to prior periods and the amount of additional costs determined to be capitalized for the current period are then taken into account with the inventory balances as initially calculated in order to arrive at an ending inventory balance. The following categories of costs are required to be capitalized with respect to property acquired for resale, regardless of whether a taxpayer elects one of the simplified resale methods: (1) off-site storage or warehousing; (2) purchasing; (3) handling, processing, assembly, and repackaging; and (4) certain general and administrative expenses (Reg. § 1.263A-3(c)).

1336. Simplified Allocation Method for Production Costs Under UNICAP. A taxpayer may elect to use the simplified production method to account for the additional costs required to be capitalized under the uniform capitalization (UNICAP) rules (¶ 1332) with respect to property produced by the taxpayer that is (1) stock in trade or other property properly includible in inventory, or (2) noninventory property held primarily for sale to customers in the ordinary course of business (Reg. § 1.263A-2(b)). Categories of property eligible for the simplified production method also include properties constructed by a taxpayer for use in its trade or business if the taxpayer: (1) is also producing inventory property that is substantially identical in nature and is produced in the same manner, or (2) produces such property on a routine and repetitive basis.

A modified simplified production method is also available for tax years beginning after November 19, 2018, for allocating additional costs including negative adjustments, among raw materials, work-in-process, and finished goods inventories on hand at the end of the year (Reg. § 1.263A-2(c)). A taxpayer using the modified method is not required to separately track direct material costs that are integrated into work-in-process and finished goods inventories. In addition, the types of methods permitted to allocate mixed service costs between pre-production and production additional section 263A costs are expanded. A taxpayer using the modified method may also allocate 100 percent of capitalizable mixed-service costs to pre-production or production additional costs if 90 percent or more of the costs would otherwise be allocated to that amount. The IRS has provided automatic consent procedures for a taxpayer to change its accounting method to comply with the modified simplified production method (Rev. Proc. 2019-43).

1338. Simplified UNICAP Method for Service Costs. A simplified method is available under uniform capitalization (UNICAP) rules (¶ 1330) for determining capitalization of mixed service costs for eligible property (Reg. § 1.263A-1). The election to use the simplified method must be made independently from other allowable simplified methods.

1340. Capitalization of Interest Under UNICAP Rules. Interest costs paid or incurred during the production period to finance the construction, building, installation, manufacture, development, or improvement of real or tangible personal property that is produced by the taxpayer must be capitalized under the uniform capitalization (UNICAP) rules in certain cases (Code Sec. 263A(f); Reg. § 1.263A-8). This rule applies to property that is produced by the taxpayer for use in its trade or business or in an activity for profit with:

- a long useful life (real property or any other property with a class life of 20 years or more),

- an estimated production period exceeding two years, or

- an estimated production period exceeding one year and a cost exceeding $1 million.

The production period begins on the date production of the property starts and ends on the date the property is ready to be placed in service or is ready to be held for sale. Interest capitalization is not required for property acquired for resale (e.g., inventory held by a dealer), and interest that constitutes qualified residence interest (¶ 1047).

The taxpayer is treated as producing any property that is produced for the taxpayer under a contract (Code Sec. 263A(g)(2)). Thus, the taxpayer-customer must capitalize its share of this interest expense allocable to capital costs, including progress payments, advances to the contractor, and an allocable portion of the taxpayer's general and administrative expenses.

In determining whether interest expense is allocable to the production of property, interest on a debt that financed production or construction costs of a particular asset is first allocated and capitalized as part of the cost of the item (Reg. §§1.263A-9 and 1.263A-11). Interest on other loans is also subject to capitalization under an avoided-cost rule to the extent of the production or construction costs that exceed the amount of this direct debt. An assumed interest rate based on the average interest rates on the taxpayer's outstanding debt, excluding debt specifically traceable to production or construction, may be used for this purpose. Production or construction expenditures include cumulative production costs (including previously capitalized interest) required to be capitalized.

Interest relating to property used to produce property subject to the interest capitalization rules is also subject to capitalization to the extent that interest is allocable to the produced property as determined under the above rules (Code Sec. 263A(f)(3)).

For interest costs paid or accrued in 2018, 2019, and 2020, the aging period for beer, wine, and distilled spirits (other than spirits unfit for beverage purposes) are excluded from the production period (Code Sec. 263A(f)(4), as amended by the Taxpayer Certainty and Disaster Tax Relief Act of 2019 (P.L. 116-94)).

For flow-through entities (i.e., partnerships, S corporations, estates, and trusts), the interest capitalization rules are applied first at the entity level and then at the beneficiary level (Code Sec. 263A(f)(2)(C)).

1342. Capitalization of Farming Business Expenses Under UNICAP. The uniform capitalization (UNICAP) rules (¶1330) apply to plants and animals produced by certain farming businesses (corporations, partnerships, and tax shelters) that are required to use the accrual method. For other farming businesses, the UNICAP rules apply only to plants produced in the farming business that have a preproductive period of more than two years (Code Sec. 263A(d)(1)).

The rules generally do not apply to costs that are attributable to the replanting, cultivation, maintenance, and development of any plants (of the same type of crop) bearing an edible crop for human consumption (normally eaten or drunk by humans) that were lost or damaged while in the hands of the taxpayer as the result of freezing temperatures, disease, drought, pests, or casualty (Code Sec. 263A(d)(2)). Replanting or maintenance costs may be incurred on property other than the damaged property if the acreage does not exceed the acreage of the damaged property.

A temporary exception to the UNICAP rules allows a person other than the taxpayer to deduct certain costs paid or incurred before December 23, 2027, in connection with replanting citrus plants lost to casualty. The exception applies if the taxpayer has at least a 50-percent equity interest in the replanted citrus plants at all times during the tax year when the replanting costs were paid or incurred, and the other person holds any part of the remaining interest in the replanted plants. It also applies if the other person acquired all of the taxpayer's equity interest in the land on which plants were located at the time of the casualty, and replanting is on that land. The IRS has provided procedures to obtain automatic consent to change accounting methods for this purpose (Code Sec. 263A(d)(2)(C); Rev. Proc. 2019-43).

A farming business is a trade or business involving the cultivation of land or the raising or harvesting of any agricultural or horticultural commodity (Code Sec. 263A(e)(4)). Examples include: a nursery or sod farm; the raising of ornamental trees (including evergreen trees six years old or less when severed from their roots); the raising or harvesting of trees bearing fruit, nuts, or other crops; and the raising, shearing, feeding, caring for, training, and managing of animals.

Any farmer, other than a corporation, partnership, or tax shelter required to use the accrual method, may elect not to apply the UNICAP rules to any plant produced in the farming business (i.e., may elect to deduct preproductive expenditures) (Code Sec.

263A(d)(3) and (e); Reg. § 1.263A-1(b)(3)). The election may not be made for any costs incurred within the first four years in which any almond or citrus trees were planted.

If the election is made the farmer must use the Modified Accelerated Cost Recovery System (MACRS) alternative depreciation system (ADS) to depreciate farm property placed in service in the election year and any subsequent year that the election remains in effect. Furthermore, preproductive expenditures that are not capitalized are subject to recapture under the section 1245 recapture rules (Code Sec. 263A(e)).

Unless IRS consent is obtained, a farmer may elect out of the UNICAP rules only for the first tax year in which the taxpayer is otherwise required to capitalize preproductive costs (Code Sec. 263A(d)(3); Reg. § 1.263A-4(d)(3)). Once the election is made, it is revocable only with the consent of the IRS. Farmers exempt from the uniform capitalization rules because average annual gross receipts are $25 million or less (¶ 1330) may receive automatic consent to revoke a prior election. If the election is revoked, then the MACRS change in use rules (Reg. § 1.168(i)-4) are used to switch depreciating property placed in service while the election was in effect from ADS to the MACRS general depreciation system (GDS) (Rev. Proc. 2020-13).

1344. Exception to Uniform Capitalization Rules for Production of Creative Property. The uniform capitalization (UNICAP) rules (¶ 1330) do not apply to expenses paid or incurred by a self-employed individual, including expenses of a corporation owned by a free-lancer and directly related to the activities of a qualified employee-owner, in the business of being a writer, photographer, or artist whose personal efforts create or may reasonably be expected to create the product (Code Sec. 263A(h)). Expenses for producing jewelry, silverware, pottery, furniture, and similar household items are generally not exempt.

Amortization

See CCH® AnswerConnect: *Intangible Property and IRC § 197* for more information on this topic.

1360. Property Subject to Amortization. Amortization is the recovery of certain capital expenditures, that are not ordinarily deductible, in a manner that is similar to straight-line depreciation. That portion of the basis of property that is recovered through amortization deductions may not also be depreciated.

Pollution Control Facilities. Taxpayers may elect to amortize over a 60-month period the cost of certified pollution control facilities added to or used in connection with a plant in operation before 1976. The amortization deduction is available only for the portion of the facility's basis attributable to the first 15 years of its recovery period if it has a recovery period under the Modified Accelerated Cost Recovery System (MACRS) in excess of 15 years. The remaining basis is depreciable. An air pollution control facility placed in service after April 11, 2005, in connection with a coal-fired plant placed in operation after 1975 qualifies for an 84-month amortization period. The 60-month amortization period continues to apply to an air pollution facility placed in service after April 11, 2005, in connection with a coal-fired plant placed in operation before 1976 (Code Sec. 169).

Architectural and Transportation Barriers. Business taxpayers can elect to deduct up to $15,000 of the costs of removing certain architectural and transportation barriers for handicapped or elderly persons in the year paid or incurred instead of capitalizing and depreciating such costs (Code Sec. 190).

Reforestation Expenditures. A taxpayer (other than a trust) may elect to expense up to $10,000 of qualified reforestation expenditures each tax year for each qualified timber property. Any taxpayer, including a trust or estate, may elect to amortize over 84 months amounts for which a current deduction is not elected (Code Sec. 194; Notice 2006-47).

Start-Up and Organizational Costs. A taxpayer who enters into a trade or business can elect to expense up to $5,000 of start-up costs, reduced dollar for dollar when the start-up expenses exceed $50,000. Any remaining balance is amortized over the 180-month period (Code Sec. 195) (¶ 904). See ¶ 237 for corporate organization fees. See ¶ 477 and ¶ 481 for costs of organizing a partnership.

Oil and Gas Geological and Geophysical Expenditures. Geological and geophysical (G&G) expenditures paid or incurred in connection with oil and gas exploration or development in the United States must be amortized ratably over a 24-month period beginning on the mid-point of the tax year that the expenses were paid or incurred. If a property or project is abandoned or retired during the 24-month amortization period, any remaining basis must continue to be amortized (Code Sec. 167(h)). However, major integrated oil companies must ratably amortize any G&G costs over five years.

1362. Amortization of Section 197 Intangibles. The capitalized cost of goodwill and many other intangibles acquired by a taxpayer and held in connection with a trade or business or for the production of income are ratably amortized over a 15-year period generally beginning in the month of acquisition (Code Sec. 197). Intangibles that are amortizable under this provision are referred to as amortizable section 197 intangibles.

Section 197 intangibles include:

- goodwill, going concern value, and covenants not to compete entered into in connection with the acquisition of a trade or business (¶ 1743);

- workforce in place;

- information base;

- a patent, copyright, formula, design, or similar item;

- any customer-based intangible;

- any supplier-based intangible;

- any license, permit, or other right granted by a governmental unit or agency; and

- any franchise, trademark, or trade name (Code Sec. 197(d)).

In order for a section 197 intangible to be amortizable it generally must be separately acquired for use in a trade or business or acquired as part of the acquisition of a trade or business. For example, goodwill that is created through a taxpayer's own efforts is not amortizable under section 197. Goodwill acquired in connection with the acquisition of a trade or business is amortizable under Code Sec. 197.

Self-created intangibles are generally not amortized under Code Sec. 197 unless they are created by a taxpayer in connection with the acquisition of a trade or business. Exceptions apply to government-granted licenses, permits, and rights, covenants not to compete entered into in connection with the purchase of a business, and franchises, trademarks, and trade names (Code Sec. 197(c)(2)). Certain self-created intangibles without an ascertainable useful life may be amortized over 15 years (¶ 1364).

The following intangibles are only amortizable under Code Sec. 197 if acquired as part of the acquisition of a trade or business: (1) any interest in a film, sound recording, video tape, book, or similar property; (2) any right to receive tangible property or services under a contract or granted by a governmental unit or agency or instrumentality thereof; (3) any interest in a patent or copyright; and (4) any right under a contract (or granted by a governmental unit or an agency or instrumentality thereof) if such right has a fixed duration of less than 15 years or is fixed as to amount and could be recoverable under a method similar to the unit-of-production method (Code Sec. 197(e)(4)).

The following intangibles are specifically *excluded* from the definition of a section 197 intangible:

- interests in a corporation, partnership, trust, or estate;

- interests under certain financial contracts;

- interests in land;

- computer software which is readily available for purchase by the general public, is subject to a nonexclusive license, and has not been substantially modified (i.e., off-the-shelf software), and other computer software which is not acquired in a transaction (or series of related transactions) involving the acquisition of assets constituting a trade or business or substantial portion thereof (¶ 980);

- interests under existing leases of tangible property;

- interests under existing debt;

- sports franchises acquired on or before October 22, 2004;

- residential mortgage servicing rights not acquired in connection with the acquisition of a business; and

- professional fees and transaction costs incurred in a corporate organization or reorganization (Code Sec. 197(e)).

No loss may be claimed when an amortizable section 197 intangible is disposed of if any other section 197 intangibles acquired in the same transaction are retained. The bases of the retained section 197 intangibles are increased by the amount of the unrecognized loss (Code Sec. 197(f)).

1364. 15-Year Safe-Harbor Amortization for Certain Self-Created Intangibles. A taxpayer is permitted to amortize certain self-created intangibles that do not have readily ascertainable useful lives over a 15-year period using the straight-line method and no salvage value (Reg. § 1.167(a)-3(b); Rev. Proc. 2006-12, modified by Rev. Proc. 2006-37). For example, amounts paid to acquire memberships or privileges of indefinite duration, such as a trade association membership, are covered by this safe harbor.

A taxpayer may use the 15-year amortization period on any intangible other than: (1) any intangible acquired from another person; (2) created financial interests; (3) any intangible that has a useful life that can be estimated with reasonable accuracy; or (4) an intangible asset for which an amortization period or useful life is specifically provided by the Code, regulations, or published IRS guidance. In addition, amounts paid to facilitate an acquisition of a trade or business, a change in the capital structure of a business entity, and certain other similar transactions described in Reg. § 1.263(a)-5 do not qualify.

The 15-year amortization period is extended to 25 years for an intangible benefit described in Reg. § 1.263(a)-4(d)(8). These are intangibles created by transferring ownership of real property to another person or by making a monetary contribution for the acquisition or improvement of real property owned by another person. However, see Rev. Rul. 2002-9, which requires developers to allocate the cost of impact fees to the basis of the buildings constructed.

Depletion

1380. Depletion Deduction. A deduction for depletion is allowed in determining the taxable income from natural resources. The deduction is similar to depreciation in that it allows the taxpayer to recover the cost of an asset over the resource's productive life. Depletion is the exhaustion of natural resources, such as mines, wells, and timberlands, as a result of production. The right to a depletion allowance is based upon the taxpayer's economic interest in the property (Reg. § 1.611-1(b)). An economic interest exists if the taxpayer (1) has acquired by investment any interest in minerals in place or in standing timber, and (2) looks to the income from the extraction of the minerals or severance of the timber for a return on investment.

The basic method of computing depletion is cost depletion (Code Sec. 612). The deduction is allowed on the adjusted basis of the property (Reg. § 1.612-1). The part of the cost or other adjusted basis of the property that is allocable to the depletable reserves is divided by the number of units (tons, barrels, etc.) that is estimated to be in the deposit. The quotient is the cost depletion per unit. This amount, multiplied by the number of units extracted and sold during the year, determines the cost depletion deduction for the year. Each year the cost basis of the property is reduced, but not below zero, by the amount of depletion deducted for that year, whether cost or percentage depletion was used. The remaining basis is used in computing cost depletion for the next year.

An alternative method of computing depletion, known as percentage depletion, may be used for almost all depletable property other than timber (Reg. § 1.611-1(a)(1)). Under this method, the depletion deduction is equal to a flat percentage of *gross income* from the property. The percentage depletion deduction may not exceed 50 percent (100 percent in the case of oil or gas properties) of the *taxable income* from the property, computed without regard to the depletion allowance, the deduction for domestic production activities before 2018 (¶ 980), and any qualified business income (QBI) deduction after 2017 (¶ 980P). See ¶ 1384 for special rules concerning independent producers and royalty owners. In computing taxable income, deductible mining expenses must be decreased by the amount of section 1245 gains allocable to the property (Code Sec. 613(a); Reg. § 1.613-1). The taxpayer must use cost depletion if it results in a greater deduction.

Ordinarily, the lease of a mineral property requires the lessee to make an advance payment, known as a bonus or advance royalty. In such a case, the lessor's cost depletion deduction must be allocated between the advance lump-sum payment and the royalties received during the period of extraction (Reg. § 1.612-3). Unlike bonuses or advance royalties, "shut-in" oil payments and delay rentals are not depletable (*F.I. Johnson*, CA-5, 61-1 USTC ¶ 9307).

Coal and iron ore royalties retained upon the disposition of ore that was generally held for more than one year before mining are eligible for percentage depletion for any tax year in which the maximum rate of tax imposed on net capital gain equals or exceeds the maximum rate for ordinary income (Code Sec. 631(c)).

Depletion is subject to recapture as ordinary income upon the sale or other disposition of an oil, gas, geothermal, or other mineral property at a gain (Code Sec. 1254). Recapture is limited to the amount by which the depletion deduction reduced the adjusted basis of the disposed property.

1382. Mineral Production Payments. A mineral production payment is treated as a loan by the owner of the production payment to the owner of the mineral property (Code Sec. 636). Thus, a carved-out mineral production payment—created when the owner of a mineral property sells or carves out a portion of the future production with payment secured by an interest in the minerals—is treated as a mortgage loan on the mineral property rather than as an economic interest in the property. All the income from the property is taxed to the seller (owner of the working interest) and is subject to depletion by him or her. The owner of the production payment does not get depletion.

If the owner of a mineral interest sells the working interest, a retained production payment is treated as a purchase money mortgage loan and not as an economic interest in the mineral property. Accordingly, all the income from the property is taxed to the purchaser and is subject to depletion by the purchaser. The seller who retains the production payment is not entitled to depletion.

1384. Depletion for Oil and Gas Production. A 22-percent depletion rate is allowed for oil and gas production in the case of regulated natural gas and natural gas sold under a fixed contract (but not certain casinghead gas contracts). A 10-percent rate applies to geopressurized methane gas wells (Code Sec. 613A(b)).

For independent producers and royalty owners, a 15-percent depletion rate applies to an average daily production of 1,000 barrels of oil and six million cubic feet of gas (Code Sec. 613A(c)). The percentage depletion deduction is generally limited for independent producers to the lesser of 65 percent of the *taxable income* before the depletion allowance or 100 percent of the *taxable income from the property* before the depletion allowance (¶ 1380) (Code Sec. 613A(d)(1))

For purposes of the 65-percent limit, taxable income is computed without regard to any net operating loss carryback, capital loss carryback, the deduction for domestic production activities prior to 2018 (¶ 980), and any qualified business income deduction after 2017 (¶ 980P). Any portion of a depletion allowance disallowed under the 65-percent limit may be carried over. Percentage depletion is also denied for lease bonuses, advance royalty payments, or other amounts payable without regard to actual production from an oil, gas or geothermal property (¶ 1386) (Code Secs. 613(e)(3) and 613A(d)(5)).

The 15-percent depletion rate for marginal oil or gas production properties held by independent producers or royalty owners increases by one percent (up to a maximum 25-percent rate) for each whole dollar that the reference price for crude oil for the preceding calendar year is less than $20 per barrel (Code Sec. 613A(c)(6)). The allowance for depletion is computed using the increased rate with respect to the portion of the taxpayer's average daily marginal production of domestic crude oil and natural gas that does not exceed the taxpayer's depletable quantities of those products. An election may be made to apply this rule to the pro rata portion of marginal production. The applicable percentage for marginal production for tax years beginning in 2001 through 2019 is 15 percent (Notice 2019-38).

1386. Depletion for Geothermal Deposits. Geothermal deposits (geothermal reservoirs consisting of natural heat that is stored in rocks or in an aqueous liquid or vapor, whether or not under pressure) are eligible for a 15-percent depletion allowance (Code Sec. 613(e)).

1388. Depletion for Coal or Other Minerals. Percentage depletion is allowed at the following percentages of gross income from the property (Code Sec. 613(b)):

- 22%—sulphur and uranium; and, if from deposits in the United States, anorthosite, clay, laterite, and nephelite syenite (to the extent that alumina and aluminum compounds are extracted therefrom), asbestos, bauxite, celestite, chromite, corundum, fluorspar, graphite, ilmenite, kyanite, mica, olivine, quartz crystals (radio grade), rutile, block steatite talc, and zircon, and ores of the following metals: antimony, beryllium, bismuth, cadmium, cobalt, columbium, lead lithium, manganese, mercury, molybdenum, nickel, platinum and platinum group metals, tantalum, thorium, tin, titanium, tungsten, vanadium and zinc;

- 15%—if from deposits in the United States, gold, silver, copper, iron ore, and oil shale (except shale described in the 7½% rate below);

- 14%—metal mines (other than metals from deposits in the United States to which the 22% rate applies), rock asphalt, and vermiculite; if the 22% rate above, and the 7½% and 5% rates below, do not apply, ball clay, bentonite, china clay, sagger clay, and clay used or sold for use for purposes dependent on its refractory properties;

- 10%—asbestos from deposits outside the United States, brucite, coal, lignite, perlite, sodium chloride, and wollastonite;

- 7½%—clay and shale used or sold for use in the manufacture of sewer pipe or brick, and clay, shale, and slate used or sold for use as sintered or burned lightweight aggregates;

- 5%—gravel, peat, pumice, sand, scoria, shale (except shale described in 15% and 7½% rates above) and stone (except stone falling within the general 14-percent group described below); clay used, or sold for use, in the manufacture of drainage and roofing tile, flower pots, and kindred products; also, if from brine wells, bromite, calcium chloride, and magnesium chloride; and

- 14%—all other minerals not included in any of the categories listed above. For purposes of this paragraph, the term "all other minerals" does not include: soil, sod, dirt, turf, water, or mosses; minerals from sea water, the air, or similar inexhaustible sources; or oil and gas wells.

Gross income from the property is the amount of income that comes from the extraction of the ores or minerals from the ground and the application of mining processes, including mining transportation and certain specified treatment processes (Code Sec. 613(c)). The percentage depletion allowance is generally based on the mined product after application of the treatment processes applied by ordinary miners. Hence, an integrated miner-manufacturer computes gross income from mining at the point when the nonintegrated miner disposes of the product. Gross income is computed by using the representative market or field price, or if it is impossible to determine such a field price and where the IRS does not determine that a more appropriate method should be used, the proportionate profits method (Reg. § 1.613-4(d)).

Chapter 14

TAX CREDITS

Nonrefundable Personal Credits

See CCH® AnswerConnect: *Personal Tax Credits* for more information on this topic.

1401. Child and Dependent Care Credit. A taxpayer with at least one qualifying individual may claim a nonrefundable credit for a portion of qualifying dependent care expenses paid during the year to allow the taxpayer, and the taxpayer's spouse if filing a joint return, to be gainfully employed (Code Sec. 21). The credit is computed on Form 2441.

A qualifying individual is:

- a dependent of the taxpayer who is a qualifying child under the age of 13 (¶ 137A);

- a dependent of the taxpayer (¶ 137) (determined without regard to whether the individual has any dependents, files a joint return, or has gross income in excess of a threshold amount) who is physically or mentally incapable of caring for himself or herself, and who has the same principal place of adobe as the taxpayer for more than half of the year; or

- the taxpayer's spouse if the spouse is physically or mentally incapable of caring for himself or herself, and has the same principal place of adobe as the taxpayer for more than half of the year.

Credit Amount. The credit is equal to the amount of qualified expenses multiplied by an applicable percentage determined by the taxpayer's adjusted gross income (AGI). The credit is 35 percent of qualified expenses for a taxpayer with an AGI of $15,000 or less. The credit is reduced by one percentage point for each $2,000 of AGI or fraction over $15,000. The minimum applicable percentage is 20 percent for a taxpayer with an AGI greater than $43,000. The maximum credit is $1,050 for one qualifying individual and $2,100 for two or more qualifying individuals.

The maximum amount of qualified expenses taken into account is $3,000 for one qualifying individual, or $6,000 for two or more qualifying individuals. These expense limits are reduced by any excludable employer dependent care assistance program payments (¶ 2065). Qualifying employment-related expenses may not exceed the taxpayer's earned income. Earned income includes wages, salaries, remuneration for personal services, net earnings from self-employment, and nontaxable combat pay the taxpayer elects to include.

For married taxpayers, expenses are limited to the earned income of the lower-earning spouse. If one spouse is not working, then no credit is allowed unless the nonworking spouse is physically or mentally incapable of caring for himself or herself, or is a full-time student at an educational institution for at least five calendar months during the year. In such cases, the earned income amount is assumed to be $250 per month for one qualifying individual or $500 per month for two or more qualifying individuals.

Qualifying Expenses. Qualifying expenses include expenses paid for the care of a qualifying individual or household services that allow the taxpayer (and spouse on a joint return) to be gainfully employed or search for employment. Services provided for the individual's care must be primarily intended to assure the individual's well-being and protection. Household service expenses include those that are paid for the ordinary and usual services of maintaining a household and that are attributable in part to the care of the qualifying individual. Services outside the home qualify only for the care of the taxpayer's dependent under age 13 or any other qualifying individual who regularly spends at least eight hours a day in the taxpayer's home. Payments to a relative may be qualifying expenses unless the taxpayer claims the relative as a dependent or if the relative is the taxpayer's child under age 19. No expenses incurred to send a child or other dependent to an overnight camp are qualifying expenses.

Claiming the Credit. The taxpayer must provide each qualifying individual's tax-payer identification number in order to claim the credit (generally a Social Security number (SSN)), as well as an identifying number of the dependent care service provider (either an SSN or employer identification number (EIN)). Married taxpayers must file a joint return to claim the credit. However, a married taxpayer is not considered married and may claim the credit if he or she: (1) lived apart from the spouse for the last six months of the tax year, (2) provided more than one-half of the cost of maintaining a home that was the principal place of abode of the qualifying individual for more than six months during the tax year, and (3) files a separate return. A divorced or legally separated taxpayer with custody of a child who is disabled or under age 13 may claim the credit even if he or she has released the right to claim the child as a dependent (¶ 139A).

1402. Elderly or Disabled Credit. A nonrefundable tax credit is available to individuals who are: (1) age 65 before the close of the tax year, or (2) under age 65 but retired, and permanently and totally disabled when retired (Code Sec. 22). Married individuals generally must file a joint return to claim the credit, unless the spouses lived apart for the entire tax year. The credit is computed on Schedule R (Form 1040).

The credit is 15 percent of an applicable initial amount based on an individual's filing status and reduced by certain income. The applicable initial amount for an individual age 65 or older is:

Single	$5,000
Married filing jointly, one spouse is a qualified individual	5,000
Married filing jointly, both spouses are qualified individuals	7,500
Married filing separately	3,750

The initial amount is reduced by any nontaxable pension, annuity, or disability benefits received including social security, railroad retirement, and veteran benefits, or that are otherwise excludable under a non-Code provision. No reduction is made for any pension, annuity, or disability benefits for personal injuries or sickness payable from a Department of Veterans Affairs program.

The maximum amount is further reduced by one-half of the excess of the taxpayer's adjusted gross income (AGI) over the following levels:

Single	$7,500
Married filing jointly	10,000
Married filing separately	5,000

The applicable initial amount for a permanently and totally disabled individual under age 65 may not exceed the amount of disability income for the tax year. Disability income means the total amount that is included in an individual's gross income for the tax year under the rules for annuities (¶ 817) or accident and health plans (¶ 2015) to the extent the amount constitutes wages, or payments in lieu of wages, for periods during which the individual is absent from work due to permanent and total disability. Special rules apply to married individuals filing jointly if both spouses qualify for the credit and at least one of them is under age 65.

An individual is considered permanently and totally disabled for this purpose if he or she is unable to engage in any substantial gainful activity by reason of any medically determinable physical or mental impairment that can be expected to result in death or to last for a continuous period of not less than 12 months. The impairment should be substantiated by a letter from a certified physician kept in the taxpayer's records.

14

TAX CREDITS

1403. Education Credits (American Opportunity and Lifetime Learning Credits). An individual may claim two types of educated-related tax credits, the American Opportunity tax credit (AOTC) and the lifetime learning credit, for qualified tuition and related expenses paid or incurred during the tax year (Code Sec. 25A; Reg. § 1.25A-1; Prop. Reg. § 1.25A-1). The credits are elective and generally nonrefundable except that up to 40 percent of the AOTC may be refunded.

The education credits are calculated on Form 8863. The credits cannot be claimed by a married individual filing separately or by a person who is a dependent of another taxpayer (¶ 137). Any qualified expenses paid by a student are treated as paid by the taxpayer for whom the student may be claimed as a dependent. A taxpayer's return must include the student's name and taxpayer identification number (TIN). For the AOTC, the TIN must be issued prior to filing the taxpayer's return. The taxpayer also must receive a copy of Form 1098-T from the eligible educational institution before claiming either credit.

American Opportunity Tax Credit (AOTC). The AOTC is the sum of 100 percent of the first $2,000 of qualified tuition and related expenses paid by the taxpayer for an eligible student, plus 25 percent of the next $2,000 of qualified expenses paid. The maximum credit is $2,500 per eligible student per year (Code Sec. 25A(b)(1) and (d)). The credit amount phases out ratably for taxpayers with modified adjusted gross income (MAGI) between $80,000 and $90,000 ($160,000 and $180,000 for joint filers). MAGI is AGI determined without regard to the exclusions for foreign earned income (¶ 2402), foreign housing expenses (¶ 2403), and U.S. possession income (¶ 2414 and ¶ 2415). Up to 40 percent of the credit amount is refundable if it exceeds the taxpayer's regular tax and alternative minimum tax (AMT) liability. However, if the student is subject to the kiddie tax (¶ 115), then no portion of the credit is refundable (Code Sec. 25A(i)). A student may qualify for the AOTC for only four tax years.

An eligible student for the AOTC is any individual who:

- has not completed the first four years of post-secondary education at an eligible institution before the beginning of the current tax year;

- is enrolled at least half-time in an academic program during the calendar year or the first three months of the following calendar year that leads to a degree, certificate, or other recognized educational credentials; and

- has not been convicted of any federal or state felony class offense for possession or distribution of a controlled substance as of the end of the year (Code Sec. 25A(b)(2) and (b)(3)).

Lifetime Learning Credit. The lifetime learning credit is equal to 20 percent of the qualified tuition and related expenses paid by the taxpayer during the tax year on the first $10,000 of tuition (Code Sec. 25A(c) and (d)). The credit is calculated on a per-taxpayer rather than a per-student basis. A student is eligible for the credit if he or she is enrolled in one or more courses at an eligible educational institution. The allowable credit is reduced if the taxpayer has MAGI above certain thresholds. The phaseout begins for single taxpayers in 2019 when MAGI reaches $58,000 ($59,000 for 2020) and completely phases out when MAGI reaches $68,000 ($69,000 for 2020). The phaseout begins for married individuals filing jointly in 2019 when MAGI reaches $116,000 ($118,000 for 2020) and completely phases out when MAGI reaches $136,000 ($138,000 for 2020) (Rev. Proc. 2018-57; Rev. Proc. 2019-44).

Qualified Tuition and Related Expenses. The education credits may be claimed for qualified tuition and related expenses required for the enrollment or attendance of the taxpayer, the taxpayer's spouse, or the taxpayer's dependent as an eligible student at an eligible educational institution of higher education (Code Sec. 25A(f); Reg. § 1.25A-2; Prop. Reg. § 1.25A-2). Qualified expenses generally include course materials such as books, supplies, or equipment only if required for enrollment. They do not include room and board, insurance, student health fees, transportation costs, or expenses that relate to any education that involves sports, games, or hobbies unless part of the student's degree program. Qualified expenses paid during the year for an academic period that begins in the first three months of the following year can be used in figuring the education credits during the current year. The same expenses cannot be used to qualify for more than one of the credits.

Coordination with Other Education Benefits. Qualified expenses eligible for the education credits for any student must first be reduced by any tax-free educational assistance received, including scholarships or fellowships (¶ 865), veterans' educational assistance allowances, employer-provided educational assistance (¶ 2067), or any other educational assistance excluded from gross income (e.g., Pell grants), other than gifts, bequests, devises, or inheritances (Code Sec. 25A(g)(2) and (g)(5); Reg. § 1.25A-5(c) and (d)). Tuition and related expenses that are deducted under any other Code Section do not qualify for the education credits (Reg. § 1.25A-5(d)) (¶ 1011A).

The expenses used to claim the education credits also reduce the amount of eligible expenses available for purposes of determining excludable distributions from Coverdell educational savings accounts (ESAs) (¶ 867) and qualified tuition programs (QTPs) (¶ 869). The 10-percent additional tax for excess distributions from Coverdell ESAs or QTPs is waived if the excess is caused by claiming an educational credit. After eligible expenses are reduced by an educational credit and distributions from Coverdell ESAs or QTPs, the remaining expenses may be used to determine the exclusion amount for Series EE United States Savings Bonds (¶ 730) (Code Secs. 135(d)(2), 529(c)(3)(B), and 530(d)(2)(C)).

Fraudulent, Reckless, or Improper Claims. A taxpayer who fraudulently or recklessly claims the AOTC in a tax year is temporarily prohibited from claiming the credit in subsequent tax years. A taxpayer who is denied the credit as a result of deficiency procedures under the Code cannot claim it in a subsequent tax year unless he or she demonstrates eligibility for the credit by filing Form 8862 (Code Sec. 25A(b)(4)).

Paid Preparer's Due Diligence. A paid tax return preparer is subject to a penalty for failing to comply with certain due diligence requirements for any return claiming the AOTC. This includes completing and submitting Form 8867 with the taxpayer's return or claim for refund (¶ 2807).

1404. Retirement Savings Contributions Credit. An eligible low-income taxpayer may claim a nonrefundable credit for contributions and elective deferrals to certain retirement plans and individual retirement accounts (IRAs) (Code Sec. 25B). An eligible taxpayer must be at least 18 years of age at the close of the tax year, and must not be claimed as a dependent on another taxpayer's return (¶ 137) or a full-time student (¶ 137A).

The retirement savings credit (or saver's credit) equals the eligible taxpayer's applicable percentage, determined by filing status and adjusted gross income (AGI), multiplied by the total qualified retirement savings contributions, not to exceed $2,000 for the tax year. The maximum credit amount is $1,000. The credit is in addition to the exclusion or deduction from gross income for making elective deferrals and IRA contributions. A qualified retirement savings plan contribution is the sum of:

- contributions to a traditional or Roth IRA, other than rollover contributions (Code Sec. 219(e));

- elective deferrals of compensation to a 401(k), 403(b) tax-sheltered annuity, SIMPLE, or SEP plan (Code Sec. 402(g)(3));

- elective deferrals of compensation to a Code Sec. 457(b) plan of a state or local government, or tax-exempt organization;

- voluntary employee contributions to any qualified retirement plan (Code Sec. 4974(c)); and

- contributions to the individual's own ABLE account (¶ 870) for tax years beginning in 2018 through 2025.

The amount of contributions taken into account is reduced by any distributions from such qualified retirement plans over a test period. The test period is the current tax year, the two preceding tax years, and the following tax year up to the due date of the return including extensions. Distributions that qualify as a trustee-to-trustee transfer or as a rollover distribution to another qualified retirement account are not included in the reduction calculation.

Claiming the Credit. Form 8880 is used to calculate the credit. For 2019, the credit is completely phased out when AGI exceeds $64,000 for married filing jointly, $48,000 for head of household, and $32,000 for single and married filing separately ($65,000, $48,750, and $32,500, respectively, for 2020) (Notice 2018-83; Notice 2019-59).

14

TAX CREDITS

For 2019, the applicable percentages for calculating the credit are as follows:

Adjusted Gross Income						Applicable percentage
Joint return		Head of a household		All other cases		
Over	Not over	Over	Not over	Over	Not over	
$0	$38,500	$0	$28,875	$0	$19,250	50
$38,500	$41,500	$28,875	$31,125	$19,250	$20,750	20
$41,500	$64,000	$31,125	$48,000	$20,750	$32,000	10
$64,000	—	$48,000	—	$32,000	—	0

1405. Child Tax Credit. An individual may claim a child tax credit for a qualifying child who is under the age of 17 and may be claimed as the taxpayer's dependent. An individual may also claim a partial child tax credit for tax years beginning in 2018 through 2025 for any other dependent (Code Sec. 24). A qualifying child includes the taxpayer's children and siblings (brother, sister, stepbrother, stepsister), as well as their descendants (the taxpayer's grandchildren, nieces, nephews, etc.) (Code Sec. 152(c)(2)). The qualifying child or dependent must be a U.S. citizen, national, or resident (Code Sec. 24(c)(2) and (h)(4)(B)). For the definition of a qualifying child see ¶ 137A. For the definition of a dependent see ¶ 137.

The maximum credit amount is:

- $2,000 for each qualifying child under the age of 17 ($1,000 for tax years beginning before 2018 and after 2025); and

- $500 for any other dependent.

The child tax credit is calculated on the worksheet in Instructions to Form 1040 or IRS Pub. 972. The return must include the name and taxpayer identification number (TIN) of each dependent for whom the credit is claimed. The TIN of a qualifying child must be a social security number (SSN) issued before the due date of the return for tax years beginning in 2018 through 2025. A qualifying child without a SSN may qualify for the partial credit for dependents. The credit is allowed only for tax years consisting of 12 months unless a short tax year results from the taxpayer's death.

Limit on Credit Amount. In tax years beginning in 2018 through 2025, the child tax credit is phased out or reduced if the taxpayer's modified adjusted gross income (MAGI) exceeds $400,000 for married filing jointly and $200,000 for any other filing status. In tax years beginning before 2018 and after 2025, the threshold is $110,000 for married filing jointly, $55,000 for married filing separately, and $75,000 for single. MAGI is AGI determined without regard to the exclusions for foreign earned income (¶ 2402), foreign housing expenses (¶ 2403), and U.S. possession income (¶ 2414 and ¶ 2415).

Refundable Additional Child Tax Credit. The child tax credit is generally a nonrefundable personal credit. However, a portion of the credit is refundable, referred to as the additional child tax credit (ACTC). The ACTC is disallowed for any taxpayer electing to exclude any amount of foreign earned income and housing expenses from gross income. Any claim of the ACTC will not be refunded until the 15th day of the second month of the following tax year (i.e., February 15) (Code Sec. 6402(m)).

Schedule 8812 is used to calculate the ACTC. It is generally equal to the lesser of the portion of the child tax credit the taxpayer cannot claim due to the tax liability limitation, or 15 percent of the taxpayer's earned income in excess of $2,500 ($3,000 for tax years beginning before 2018 and after 2025) (Code Sec. 24(d), (h)(5), and (h)(6)). If the taxpayer has three or more qualifying children, the threshold is the excess of the taxpayer's share of Social Security taxes, over earned income for the year (¶ 1422). The ACTC may not exceed $1,400 for 2019 and 2020 per qualifying child under the age of 17 (Rev. Proc. 2018-57; Rev. Proc. 2019-44). The $500 partial credit for any other dependent is nonrefundable.

A taxpayer who is a member of the Armed Forces may elect to treat combat pay that is otherwise excludable from gross income (¶ 895) as earned income for purposes of calculating the ACTC. In addition, a qualified individual affected by a qualified federal disaster occurring from January 1, 2018, through February 18, 2020, may elect to use earned income from the preceding tax year to calculate the ACTC and the earned income credit (EIC) for the applicable tax year (¶ 1422). Similarly, a qualified individual affected by the 2017 California wildfire or Hurricanes Harvey, Irma, or Maria may elect to use earned income from 2016 to calculate the ACTC and EIC for the 2017.

Fraudulent, Reckless, or Improper Claims. A taxpayer who fraudulently or recklessly claims the child tax credit is temporarily prohibited from claiming the credit in subsequent tax years. If the credit is denied as a result of deficiency procedures, the taxpayer cannot claim it in a subsequent tax year without filing Form 8862 to show eligibility for the credit (Code Sec. 24(g)).

Paid Preparer's Due Diligence. A paid tax return preparer is subject to a penalty for failing to comply with certain due diligence requirements for any return claiming the child tax credit. This includes completing and submitting Form 8867 with the taxpayer's return or claim for refund (¶ 2807).

1406. Mortgage Interest Credit. An individual with a qualified mortgage credit certificate (MCC) from a state or local government may claim a nonrefundable tax credit for a portion of the interest paid or incurred on a home mortgage during any tax year the certificate is in effect (Code Sec. 25; IRS Pub. 530). An MCC is generally attributable to the period beginning on the date the certificate is issued and ending when (1) it is revoked by the issuing authority, or (2) the taxpayer sells the residence or ceases to use it as a personal residence. Any mortgage interest claimed as an itemized deduction must be reduced by any credit claimed (¶ 1047).

Amount of Credit. The credit is computed on Form 8396 and is: (1) the certificate credit rate, which may not be less than 10 percent or more than 50 percent, multiplied by (2) the interest paid or accrued by the taxpayer for the year on the remaining principal of the certified indebtedness. If the credit rate exceeds 20 percent, the tax credit for any year may not exceed $2,000.

Tax Liability Limitation. The amount of the mortgage interest credit cannot exceed the limit on nonrefundable personal credits (¶ 1415), reduced by all nonrefundable credits other than the mortgage interest credit, the adoption credit (¶ 1407), and the credit for residential energy efficient property (¶ 1442). Any unclaimed credit may be carried over to the next three succeeding tax years. The carryover amount is added to the current year credit amount and subject to the same tax liability limitation.

Recapture of Tax Benefit. The tax benefit received from a MCC is recaptured if the taxpayer disposes of the home or stops using it as a principal residence during the first nine years after the testing date (Code Sec. 143(m)). The testing date is the date the taxpayer becomes liable for any portion of the federally subsidized debt on the principal residence. The recapture amount is the federally subsidized debt, multiplied by the holding period percentage and the income percentage. It is treated as an addition to tax for the disposition tax year and calculated using Form 8828.

1407. Adoption Credit. An individual may claim a nonrefundable credit for qualified adoption expenses paid or incurred for each eligible child (Code Sec. 23). The maximum credit amount is $14,080 for 2019 ($14,300 for 2020). The credit is phased out ratably for taxpayers with a modified adjusted gross income (MAGI) over $211,160 for 2019 ($214,520 for 2020), and is completely eliminated when MAGI exceeds $251,160 for 2019 ($254,520 for 2020) (Rev. Proc. 2018-57; Rev. Proc. 2019-44). MAGI is AGI determined without regard to the exclusions for foreign earned income (¶ 2402), foreign housing expenses (¶ 2403), and U.S. possession income (¶ 2414 and ¶ 2415).

Qualified Adoption Expenses. Qualified adoption expenses are reasonable and necessary adoption fees, court costs, attorney fees, traveling expenses, and other expenses directly related to the legal adoption of an eligible child. Qualified adoption expenses do not include expenses: (1) that are paid or reimbursed under any federal, state or local program; (2) that violate federal or state law; (3) for carrying out a surrogate parent arrangement; or (4) for the adoption of a child of the taxpayer's spouse.

Expenses used to claim any other deduction or credit may not be used to claim the adoption credit. This includes amounts paid or reimbursed by an employer's adoption assistance program that are excludable from an employee's income (¶ 2063). An employee may claim the adoption credit and exclusion in the same tax year, as long as they do not cover the same qualified adoption expenses. The dollar limit and income phaseouts applicable to the credit are the same for the exclusion.

14

TAX CREDITS

Eligible Child and Special Needs Child. An eligible child for the adoption credit is an individual who has not attained the age of 18 as of the time of the adoption, or who is physically or mentally incapable of caring for himself or herself. It also includes a child with special needs. A child with special needs is any child who is a citizen or resident of the United States or a U.S. possession, if a state has determined that: (1) the child cannot or should not be returned to the parental home , and (2) a specific factor or condition makes it reasonable to conclude that the child cannot be placed with adoptive parents unless assistance is provided.

Claiming the Credit. Adoption expenses incurred or paid prior to the tax year the adoption is finalized may be claimed as a credit in the tax year following the year they are incurred. Adoption expenses incurred during the year the adoption becomes final or in the following year are claimed in the year they are incurred. Adoption expenses for an eligible child who is not a U.S. citizen or resident cannot be claimed as a credit until the adoption is finalized. A taxpayer who adopts a child with special needs may claim the full amount of the credit regardless of actual expenses paid or incurred in the year the adoption becomes final. Married taxpayers must file a joint return to claim the credit. A married taxpayer may claim the credit on a separate return if he or she lived apart from the spouse for the last six months of the tax year, and paid more than one-half of the cost of maintaining a home in which the eligible child resided for more than six months during the tax year (Notice 97-9). The credit must be claimed on Form 8839 with proper documentation attached.

Tax Liability Limitation. The adoption credit may be claimed against both regular tax liability, reduced by any allowable foreign tax credit, and alternative minimum tax (AMT) liability. The credit cannot exceed the sum of the taxpayer's regular tax liability, reduced by any foreign tax credit, plus AMT liability, and reduced by the sum of all other nonrefundable credits except the adoption credit and residential energy efficient property credit (¶ 1442). Any credit that exceeds this limit may be carried forward for up to five years.

1408. First-Time Homebuyer Credit for District of Columbia. A first-time homebuyer who purchased a principal residence in the District of Columbia from an unrelated person before January 1, 2012, could claim a credit of up to $5,000 of the purchase price ($2,500 if married filing separately) (Code Sec. 1400C, prior to being stricken by the Tax Technical Corrections Act of 2018 (P.L. 115-141)). The credit was a nonrefundable personal credit limited by the taxpayer's tax liability. Any unused credit can be carried forward to succeeding tax years and is claimed on Form 8859.

1409. Alternative Minimum Tax Credit. A taxpayer is permitted a tax credit against regular income tax liability for some or all of alternative minimum tax (AMT) paid in previous years (¶ 190). The minimum tax credit is the amount of adjusted net minimum tax for all tax years reduced by the minimum tax credit for all prior tax years (Code Sec. 53). Any unused credit may be carried forward indefinitely as a credit against regular tax liability to the extent that regular tax liability reduced by all other nonrefundable credits exceeds tentative AMT liability for the tax year. The credit may not be used to offset AMT liability. The credit is claimed by individuals, trusts, and estates on Form 8801 and by corporations on Form 8827.

For noncorporate taxpayers, the adjusted net minimum tax is the taxpayer's AMT liability reduced by the amount that would have been the taxpayer's AMT liability if only certain AMT adjustments and preferences had been taken into account. The adjustments include those related to the standard deduction, personal exemptions, medical and dental expenses, miscellaneous itemized deductions, taxes, and interest expenses (¶ 196). The preference items include certain depletion deductions exceeding adjusted basis, tax-exempt interest on specified private activity bonds, and the exclusion of gain on the sale of qualified small business stock (¶ 194).

The AMT is repealed for corporations for tax years beginning after 2017 (¶ 239). A corporation's tentative minimum tax is zero and any minimum tax credit claimed by a corporation after 2017 is generally limited to regular tax liability, reduced by other nonrefundable credits. The minimum tax credit is the corporation's AMT liability from tax years prior to the repeal and carried over to tax years after 2017. Any unused minimum tax credit is refundable for tax years beginning in 2018, 2019, 2020, and 2021. The refundable credit amount is equal to 50 percent (100 percent for tax years beginning in 2021) of the excess of the minimum tax credit for the tax year, over the amount allowable for the year against regular tax liability. The refundable credit amount for a short tax year is prorated based on the number of days in the short year compared to 365 days. In tax years beginning before 2018, the credit allowed against the regular tax of an exempt small corporation is limited.

1415. Limitation on Nonrefundable Credits. An individual may claim nonrefundable personal tax credits against regular tax liability, as reduced by the foreign tax credit, plus alternative minimum tax (AMT) liability (Code Sec. 26). Any credit disallowed by the tax liability limitation generally is not refundable and may not be carried over to other tax years. However, some nonrefundable personal credits may be carried forward under the particular rules for that credit, including the mortgage interest credit (¶ 1406) and the adoption credit (¶ 1407).

Regular tax liability for this purpose is regular income tax liability, excluding the following:

- alternative minimum tax (AMT);

- base erosion and anti-abuse tax (BEAT) (Code Sec. 59A);

- additional tax on early distributions from retirement plans (Code Sec. 72(m)(5)(B), (q), (t), and (v));

- tax on recaptured federal subsidies for mortgage bonds (Code Sec. 143(m));

- the additional tax on certain distributions from Coverdell education savings accounts (Code Sec. 530(d)(4));

- accumulated earnings and personal holding company taxes (Code Secs. 531 and 541);

- tax on foreign expropriation loss recoveries (Code Sec. 1351(d));

- tax on an S corporation's built-in gains and passive investment income (Code Secs. 1374 and 1375);

- tax on nonqualified withdrawals from certain Merchant Marine capital construction funds (Code Sec. 7518(g)(6));

- 30-percent withholding tax on the fixed or determinable annual or periodical (FDAP) income of nonresident aliens and foreign corporations (Code Secs. 871(a) and 881);

- excise tax on the transfer of a residual interest in a real estate mortgage investment company (REMIC) to a disqualified organization (Code Sec. 860E(e));

- foreign corporations' branch profits taxes (Code Sec. 884);

- interest on tax liabilities deferred under the installment method (Code Secs. 453(l)(3) and 453A(c));

- the additional tax on distributions from health savings accounts (HSAs), Archer medical savings accounts (MSAs), and Medicare Advantage medical savings accounts not used for qualified medical expenses (Code Secs. 138(c)(2), 220(f)(4), and 223(f)(4));

- taxes relating to certain failures to maintain high deductible health plan coverage (Code Secs. 106(e)(3)(A)(ii), 223(b)(8)(B)(i)(II), and 408(d)(9)(D)(i)(II));

- tax relating to recapture of certain deductions for fractional gifts (Code Sec. 170(o)(3)(B));

- the additional tax on income from nonqualified deferred compensation plans (Code Sec. 409A(a)(1)(B) and (b)(5)(A));

- the recapture of the first-time homebuyer credit (Code Sec. 36(f));

- the tax (including interest and an additional tax) on certain compensation that is deferred under a nonqualified deferred compensation plan (Code Sec. 457A(c)(1)(B)); and

- the additional tax on nonqualified distributions from ABLE accounts (Code Sec. 529A(c)(3)(A)).

14

TAX CREDITS

¶1415

Refundable Personal Credits

See CCH® AnswerConnect: *Personal Tax Credits* for more information on this topic.

1420. Recovery Rebate Credits (Economic Impact Payments). An eligible individual is entitled to a refundable Recovery Rebate Credit for their first tax year beginning in 2020, payable in advance as an economic impact payment in response to the COVID-19 (coronavirus) crisis (Code Sec. 6428, as added by the Coronavirus Aid, Relief, and Economic Security (CARES) Act (P.L. 116-136)). The maximum amount of the credit is:

- $1,200 for each eligible individual (so $2,400 for two eligible individuals who file a joint return), plus
- $500 for each qualifying child.

The maximum credit amount is reduced (but not below zero) by five percent of AGI that exceeds:

- $150,000 if married filing jointly—so the $2,400 credit phases out completely at $198,000;
- $112,500 if filing as head of household—so the $1,200 credit phases out completely at $136,500; or
- $75,000 if filing as single or married filing separately—so the $1,200 credit phases out completely at $99,000.

The total credit is reduced by $5 for each $100 in AGI above the applicable threshold. Thus, once the credit for an eligible individual phases out, the $500 credit for a qualifying child phases out with another $10,000 in AGI over the threshold.

Eligible Individual. An eligible individual for purpose of the Recovery Rebate Credit and is any individual *other than*: an individual who qualifies as another taxpayer's dependent for a tax year beginning during the calendar year in which the individual's tax year begins; a nonresident alien; or an estate or trust. A qualifying child is the taxpayer's qualifying child for purposes of the child tax credit (¶ 1405). An eligible individual's tax return must include a valid identification number for each eligible individual and qualifying child (for example, social security number (SSN) or adoption taxpayer identification number (ATIN)).

Economic Impact Payments. The IRS will make advance refunds of the credit to a taxpayer via economic impact payments. The payments are based on the eligible individual's 2019 return, or 2018 return if the individual has not filed a 2019 return by the time the payments are determined. If the individual has not filed a 2018 return by the time the economic impact payments are determined, the advance refund is based on information provided by the Social Security Administration or Railroad Retirement Board (as applicable) for the calendar year on Form SSA-1099 or Form RRB-1099, including Social Security retirement, disability (SSDI), survivor benefits, or Supplemental Security Income (SSI). Recipients of compensation and pension (C&P) benefits from the Department of Veterans Affairs (VA benefits) also will automatically receive the payments. An eligible individual who is not otherwise required to file federal income tax returns for 2019 may use a new simplified return filing procedure to make sure they receive the payment (Rev. Proc. 2020-28). Alternatively, a nonfiler may use the Non-filers: Enter Payment Info Here tool on the IRS website to register for economic impact payments.

Economic impact payments are made automatically by direct deposit for taxpayers who provided direct deposit information on a 2018 or 2019 return. A taxpayers for whom direct deposit information cannot be ascertained by the IRS will receive a paper check, which the IRS may distribute throughout 2020 (IRS News Release IR-2020-61). The Get My Payment tool on the IRS website can be used to check on the status of their payments as well as enter their direct deposit information if the IRS does not already have it.

The Recover Rebate credit will be calculated on a 2020 tax return as a refundable credit against 2020 taxes, then reduced by the amount of the advance Economic Impact Payment received during 2020. However, the credit will not be reduced below zero. One half of any advance payment or refund made on a joint return is treated on having been made or allowed to each spouse. The credit is not to be reduced by any amounts owed to

¶1420

other federal agencies or by other assessed federal taxes otherwise subject to levy or collection (Act Sec. 2201(d) of P.L. 116-136).

1421. Credit for Taxes Withheld on Wages. An individual is allowed a credit against income tax liability for income taxes withheld from salary or wages (Code Sec. 31). A taxpayer is also allowed a refund of any Social Security taxes that were overwithheld from wages. Excess Social Security taxes may be withheld where an individual works for more than one employer and earns more than the Social Security wage base in total—$132,900 for 2019 ($137,700 for 2020). The maximum amount of Social Security taxes that may be withheld is 6.2 percent of the wage base (¶ 2648). The same rule applies to excess withheld railroad retirement taxes. Medicare taxes cannot be over withheld since there is no wage base for the taxes.

Overwithheld Social Security or railroad retirement taxes may be claimed as a credit on Schedule 3 (Form 1040). An individual who is not required to file an income tax return may file a refund claim on Form 843 (Reg. § 31.6413(c)-1). A nonresident alien (or foreign corporation) is allowed a credit against income tax liability for taxes withheld on U.S. source income that is not effectively connected with a U.S. trade or business (Code Sec. 33). See ¶ 2455 for the withholding of tax on payments other than wages to nonresident aliens.

1422. Earned Income Credit. The earned income credit (EIC or EITC) is a refundable tax credit based on the taxpayer's earned income (up to a threshold amount), and number of qualifying children (Code Sec. 32). An individual who does not have a qualifying child is eligible for the credit if:

- the principal residence of the individual is in the United States for more than half of the tax year;

- the individual, or the spouse if married filing jointly, is at least age 25 and under age 65 before the close of the tax year; and

- the individual is not a dependent of another taxpayer.

The EIC is not available if the taxpayer is a qualifying child of another taxpayer, claims the exclusion of foreign earned income or housing expenses (¶ 2402 and ¶ 2403), is a nonresident alien who has not elected to be a resident alien (¶ 2410), or has excessive investment income. The credit may be claimed only for a full 12-month tax year, except in the case of death of the taxpayer. The IRS will not refund the EIC until the 15th day of the second month following the close of the tax year (i.e., February 15 for a calendar year taxpayer) (Code Sec. 6402(m)). Married individuals generally must file a joint return to claim the credit. However, a married individual living apart from the spouse for the last six months of the tax year may qualify for head of household filing status and claim the credit on a separate return (¶ 173).

A taxpayer with one or more qualifying children completes Schedule EIC (Form 1040) to claim the credit. The return must include a valid Social Security number (SSN) for the taxpayer, the taxpayer's spouse, and each qualifying child. An individual taxpayer identification number (ITIN) or adoption taxpayer identification number (ATIN) may not be used for EIC purposes. The SSN must be valid for work in the United States and issued before the due date of the taxpayer's return (including extensions).

Credit Amount. The amount of the EIC is the taxpayer's earned income up to a designated level (the earned income amount) multiplied by a credit percentage that depends on whether the taxpayer has one qualifying child, two or more qualifying children, or no qualifying children. The IRS provides an EIC Worksheet and EIC Tables with the Instructions for Form 1040. A copy of the tables appear at ¶ 87. An eligible taxpayer may ask the IRS to calculate the credit amount. For 2019, the maximum earned income amount is $6,920 if the taxpayer has no qualifying child, $10,370 if the taxpayer has one qualifying child, and $14,570 if the taxpayer has two or more qualifying children (Rev. Proc. 2018-57). For 2020, the maximum earned income amounts are $7,030, $10,540, and $14,800, respectively (Rev. Proc. 2019-44).

The credit amount is reduced by multiplying the applicable phaseout percentage by the excess of the greater of the individual's adjusted gross income (AGI) or earned income over a phaseout amount, adjusted annually for inflation. For 2019, the credit is completely phased out if the taxpayer's AGI equals or exceeds: $15,570 ($21,370 if married filing jointly) if the taxpayer has no qualifying children; $41,094 ($46,884 if married filing jointly) if the taxpayer has one qualifying child; $46,703 ($52,493 if married filing jointly) if the taxpayer has two qualifying children; and $50,162 ($55,952 if married filing jointly) if the taxpayer has three or more qualifying children. For 2020, the credit completely phased out if the taxpayer's AGI equals or exceeds: $15,820 ($21,710 if married filing jointly) if the taxpayer has no qualifying children; $41,756 ($47,646 if married filing jointly) if the taxpayer has one qualifying child; $47,440 ($53,330 if married filing jointly) if the taxpayer has two qualifying children; and $50,954 ($56,844 if married filing jointly) if the taxpayer has three or more qualifying children.

The credit and phaseout percentages limit the maximum amount of credit that may be claimed. For 2019, the maximum earned income credit is $529 for a taxpayer with no qualifying children, $3,526 for a taxpayer with one qualifying child, $5,828 for a taxpayer with two qualifying children, and $6,557 for a taxpayer with three or more qualifying children. For 2020, the maximum earned credit is $538, $3,584, $5,920, and $6,660, respectively.

Earned Income. Since the EIC is based on a percentage of earned income, the taxpayer must therefore have earned income to qualify for the credit. For joint returns, at least one spouse must have earned income. Earned income generally includes all taxable compensation including, wages, salaries, tips, and other employee compensation including union strike benefits, plus the taxpayer's net earnings from self-employment. The taxpayer is allowed to deduct one-half of applicable self-employment taxes from earned income arising from self-employment (¶ 923). Earned income is determined without regard to community property laws.

Earned income generally does not include employee compensation that is excluded from gross income, such as dependent care or adoption benefits. It also does not include: pension or annuity benefits; Social Security or railroad retirement benefits (including disability benefits); unemployment or workers compensation; workfare payments subsidized under a state workfare program funded under the federal TANF program; welfare payments; interest and dividends; alimony, child support, and nontaxable foster care payments; income of a nonresident alien not connected with U.S. trade or business; and amounts earned for services provided by an individual while an inmate at a penal institution. A taxpayer who is a member of the Armed Forces may elect to treat combat pay that is otherwise excludable from gross income (¶ 895) as earned income for purposes of the EIC. The election applies to all excludable combat pay received by the taxpayer.

Disaster Relief. A qualified individual affected by a qualified federal disaster occurring from January 1, 2018, through February 18, 2020, may elect to use earned income from the preceding tax year, to calculate the EIC and the additional child tax credit (ACTC) for the applicable year (¶ 1405). The applicable year is (1) any tax year that includes any portion of the disaster incident period if the individual is in the disaster zone, and (2) any tax year that the individual is displaced by the disaster, if the individual is outside the disaster zone. The election applies to both the EIC and the ACTC, but it has no effect on any other tax provision including the calculation of taxable income. Married taxpayers who file a joint return for the applicable tax year may make the election if either of them is a qualified individual, but they must use their combined earned income for the preceding tax year (Act Secs. 201 and 204(c) of the Taxpayer Certainty and Disaster Tax Relief Act of 2019 (P.L. 116-94)).

A qualified individual affected by the California wildfires in 2017 or Hurricanes Harvey, Irma, or Maria may elect to use earned income from 2016 to calculate the EIC and additional child tax credit for 2017. Joint return filers may make the election if either spouse is a qualified individual, but they must use the sum of their earned income from 2016. The election has no effect on determination of the correct taxable income for 2017 (Act Secs. 501 and 504(c) of the Disaster Tax Relief and Airport and Airway Extension Act of 2017 (P.L. 115-63); Act Secs. 20101 and 20104(c) of the Bipartisan Budget Act of 2018 (P.L. 115-123)).

Excessive Investment Income. An individual who has disqualified investment income that exceeds an inflation-adjusted threshold amount cannot claim the EIC. The threshold for excessive investment income is $3,600 for 2019 ($3,650 for 2020) (Rev. Proc. 2018-57; Rev. Proc. 2019-44). Disqualified income includes: interest and dividends included in gross income, tax-exempt interest, net income from rents or royalties not derived in the ordinary course of a trade or business, capital gain net income, and the excess of aggregate passive income over aggregate passive losses.

Qualifying Child. A qualifying child for EIC purposes is a qualifying child who is a dependent of the taxpayer (¶ 137A) but determined without regard to the support test. In addition, the relationship and residency tests must be met with the following modifications: (1) a married child is not a qualifying child unless the taxpayer is entitled to claim the child as a dependent; and (2) the principal place of abode that the taxpayer must share with a qualifying child for more than half of the tax year must be located in the United States. The rules for determining who may claim a qualifying child among several taxpayers for purposes of the EIC are the same as for determining who may claim a qualifying child as a dependent (¶ 139).

Fraudulent, Reckless, or Improper Claims. A taxpayer who fraudulently or recklessly claims the EIC is temporarily prohibited from claiming the credit in subsequent tax years. If the credit is denied as a result of deficiency procedures, the taxpayer cannot claim it in a subsequent year unless he or she demonstrates eligibility by filing Form 8862 (Code Sec. 32(k); Reg. § 1.32-3).

Paid Preparer's Due Diligence. A paid tax return preparer is subject to a penalty for failing to comply with certain due diligence requirements for any return claiming the EIC. This includes completing and submitting Form 8867 with the taxpayer's return or claim for refund (¶ 2807).

1424. Repayment of First-Time Homebuyer Credit. A refundable tax credit was allowed to a first-time homebuyer who purchased a principal residence in the United States generally before May 1, 2010 (generally before May 1, 2011, for a taxpayer who served on qualified extended service duty outside the United States) (Code Sec. 36). For a residence purchased before 2009, the credit must be recaptured ratably over a 15-year period. For a residence purchased after 2008, no recapture is required if the taxpayer owns and maintains the home as a principal residence for at least 36 months. If the taxpayer sells or ceases to use the home as a principal residence before the end of the applicable period, then all of the recapture is accelerated to the current tax year unless due to death, divorce, or involuntary conversion. For any tax year in which the credit must be recaptured, the taxpayer must file an income tax return. The 15-year recapture of the credit for a residence purchased before 2009 is reported on Schedule 2 (Form 1040). Any accelerated recapture of the credit is reported on Form 5405.

1429. Income Tax Credit for Gasoline and Special Fuels. An income tax credit may be claimed for federal excise taxes paid on gasoline and special fuels that are used for: farming purposes; nonhighway purposes of a trade or business; operation of intercity, local, or school buses; or certain nontaxable purposes (Code Sec. 34). The credit is computed annually on Form 4136, or as a credit against fuel tax liability quarterly on Form 720. Alternatively, the taxpayer can file a refund claim on Form 8849.

1430. Credit for Undistributed Capital Gains from REITS and RICs. Undistributed capital gain of a regulated investment company (RIC) or real estate investment trust (REIT) must be included proportionately in the gross income of its shareholders (¶ 2305). The capital gain tax that the company pays on this gain is treated as having been paid by the shareholders and is allowed as a credit against the tax (Code Secs. 852(b)(3)(D) and 857(b)(3)(C)). In order to claim the credit, Copy B of Form 2439 must be attached to the taxpayer's return.

1431. Health Insurance Premium Assistance Credit. An applicable taxpayer who enrolls in, or enrolls at least one family member in a qualified health plan may claim a refundable income tax credit to help pay for individual or family health coverage obtained through a Marketplace Exchange (Code Sec. 36B). The premium assistance tax credit is determined on a sliding scale depending on the size of the family and household income, and is calculated on Form 8962. The taxpayer may elect to have all or a portion of the credit advanced in the form of lower insurance premiums throughout the year.

Eligibility. An applicable taxpayer is eligible for the credit if household income is at least 100 percent, but not more than 400 percent, of the federal poverty line (FPL) for a family of the same size. An exception exists for a resident alien who is ineligible for Medicaid and has household income below 100 percent of the FPL (Code Sec. 36B(c)(1) and (e); Reg. § 1.36B-2).

¶1431

14

TAX CREDITS

Married individuals generally must file a joint return to claim the credit. Married taxpayers who file separate returns may not claim the credit unless they are victims of domestic abuse. However, a married individual living apart from the spouse for the last six months of the tax year may qualify for head of household filing status and claim the credit (¶ 173). An individual who can be claimed as a dependent by another taxpayer (¶ 137) cannot claim the credit. Although individuals who are incarcerated (unless pending disposition of charges) or are not lawfully present in the U.S. cannot enroll in qualified health plans, they may be eligible for the credit for family members who are enrolled in qualified plans (Reg. § 1.36B-2(b)).

Family size is equal to the number of the taxpayer's personal and dependency exemptions (i.e., the taxpayer, spouse if filing jointly, and dependents) (Code Sec. 36B(d); Reg. § 1.36B-1(d) and (e); Notice 2018-84). Household income is the modified adjusted gross income (MAGI) of the taxpayer (and spouse on a joint return), and of each of the taxpayer's dependents who is required to file a return other than for a refund. MAGI is AGI increased by foreign earned income, tax-exempt interest, and Social Security benefits that are excluded from gross income.

Credit Amount. The premium assistance credit is the sum of the premium assistance amounts for all of the taxpayer's coverage months during the tax year (Code Sec. 36B(b); Reg. § 1.36B-3). An eligible individual should receive a copy of Form 1095-A from the Exchange indicating months of coverage during the year.

The premium assistance amount for any coverage month is the lesser of:

- the monthly premium for a qualified health plan offered through the Exchange covering the taxpayer, the taxpayer's spouse, or any dependent, or

- the excess of the adjusted monthly premium for the applicable second lowest cost silver plan, over $1/12$th of an applicable percentage and the taxpayer's household income for the tax year (between 2.08 percent and 9.86 percent for 2019, and between 2.06 percent and 9.78 percent for 2020 (Rev. Proc. 2018-34; Rev. Proc. 2019-29)).

A coverage month is any month in which the taxpayer, the taxpayer's spouse, or any dependent is covered by a qualified health plan through the Exchange and the premium is paid by the taxpayer or through an advance payment of the credit (Code Sec. 36B(c)(2) and (c)(4); Reg. § 1.36B-3(c)). A coverage month does not include any month that the individual is eligible for minimum essential coverage outside the individual market or provided by an employer's qualified small business health reimbursement account (QSEHRA) (¶ 2039). A month also is not a coverage month if the taxpayer's share of premiums is not paid in full by the due date for filing his or her income tax return for the tax year (without regard to extensions).

Minimum essential coverage includes coverage under government-sponsored programs such as Medicare, Medicaid, Children's Health Insurance Program (CHIP), or TRICARE programs, or through self-funded student health plans and state high risk pools (Code Sec. 36B(c)(2)(B) and (c)(2)(C); Reg. § 1.36B-2(c); Notice 2013-41). An employee is not eligible for minimum essential coverage outside of the market if the coverage is an employer-sponsored plan, including a grandfathered health plan, and either:

- the employee's required contribution is unaffordable for the employee or a related individual (i.e., self-only coverage would exceed a percentage of the employee's household income—9.86 percent for 2019, and 9.78 for 2020 (Rev. Proc. 2018-34; Rev. Proc. 2019-29)); or

- the plan provides less than 60 percent coverage for total allowed costs.

Advance Payment An applicable taxpayer may elect to advance all or a portion of the premium assistance credit in the form of lower insurance premiums throughout the year. The advance payments reduce the credit, but not below zero (Code Sec. 36B(f); Reg. § 1.36B-4). If the advance payments exceed the credit allowed, the excess is an increase to the tax imposed for the tax year. However, if household income is less than 400 percent of FPL, then the increase for 2019 is limited to between $600 and $2,650 ($300 and $1,325 for single taxpayers) (Rev. Proc. 2018-57). For 2020, the increase is limited between $650 and $2,700 ($325 and $1,350 for single taxpayers) (Rev. Proc. 2019-44).

¶1431

1432. Health Coverage Tax Credit (HCTC). An eligible individual may elect a refundable tax credit for coverage months beginning before January 1, 2021, for the cost of qualified health insurance for himself or herself, a spouse if filing jointly, and dependents. The health coverage tax credit (HCTC) is available only if the individual is either eligible to receive trade adjustment assistance (TAA) (TAA-alternative payments) or a retiree age 55 or older receiving benefits from the Pension Benefit Guaranty Corporation (PBGC) (Code Sec. 35, as amended by the Taxpayer Certainty and Disaster Tax Relief Act of 2019 (P.L. 116-94)).

The HCTC is 72.5 percent of the costs paid or incurred during all coverage months during the tax year. An eligible coverage month occurs when, on the first day of the month during the tax year, the taxpayer: (1) is an eligible individual; (2) is covered by a qualified health insurance plan for which the taxpayer paid the premiums; (3) has no other specified coverage; and (4) is not imprisoned by any federal, state, or local authority. Form 8885 is used to elect and calculate the credit. The election generally must be made no later than the due date of the taxpayer's return (including extensions). The taxpayer cannot claim the HCTC and the premium tax credit (¶ 1431) for the same coverage month.

Qualified Insurance. Qualified health insurance includes: federal COBRA continuation coverage; state-based continuation coverage and coverage under other state health plans; coverage under a group health plan through the employment of the taxpayer's spouse; coverage under an individual health insurance plan not purchased through a Marketplace Exchange; and coverage under a health plan funded by a voluntary employee's beneficiary association (VEBA) established through a bankruptcy court. Qualified health insurance does not include a flexible spending arrangement (FSA) (¶ 2041) or any insurance if the coverage is substantially for certain excepted benefits (e.g., dental or vision benefits purchased separately).

A taxpayer is not eligible for the credit for any month during which the taxpayer or a family member is covered by other specified coverage, including: (1) insurance under a health plan maintained by the employer of the taxpayer or the taxpayer's spouse, if at least 50 percent of the cost is paid or incurred by the employer; (2) insurance coverage under a cafeteria plan (¶ 2045); (3) participation in Medicare, Medicaid, or State Child Health Insurance Program (SCHIP); or (4) participation in a health benefits plan for federal employees and military personnel.

Coordination with Other Provisions. Amounts taken into account for the determination of the HCTC may not be used in computing the deduction for self-employed health insurance costs (¶ 908) or the itemized deduction for medical expenses (¶ 1015). Amounts received from health savings accounts (HSAs) (¶ 2035) or Archer medical saving accounts (¶ 2037) may not be used to compute the HCTC.

Advance Payment. Certified individuals may elect to have the HCTC paid in advance directly to the provider of qualified health insurance. The advance payments cannot equal more than the credit percentage (72.5 percent) of the taxpayer's anticipated health insurance costs. The aggregate amount of all advance payments during the tax year reduces the HCTC but not below zero. An individual who is certified to received the advance payment will receive Form 1099-H from the health plan administrator.

Nonbusiness Energy Credits

See CCH® AnswerConnect: *Personal Tax Credits* for more information on this topic.

1441. Nonbusiness Energy Property Credit. A tax credit is available to an individual for the installation of qualified energy efficiency improvements (building envelope components) or qualified residential energy property expenditures (furnaces and certain fans, central air conditioners, water heaters, certain heat pumps, biomass stoves) placed in service before January 1, 2021 (Code Sec. 25C, as amended by the Taxpayer Certainty and Disaster Tax Relief Act of 2019 (P.L. 116-94); Notice 2013-70). The qualified property must be installed on, or in connection with, a dwelling unit in the United States that is owned and used by the taxpayer as the taxpayer's principal residence. Original use of the property must commence with the taxpayer.

The credit is calculated on Form 5695. The credit is a nonrefundable personal credit and may be claimed against regular tax and alternative minimum tax (AMT) liabilities (¶ 1415). Unlike the residential energy efficient property credit (¶ 1442), any excess of the nonbusiness energy property credit may *not* be carried forward to another tax year. The basis of the residence is reduced by the allowed credit.

Credit Amount. The credit is equal to 10 percent of the amount paid or incurred for qualified energy efficiency improvements during the tax year, plus 100 percent of the amount paid or incurred for qualified energy property during the tax year. The maximum credit allowable is $500 over the lifetime of the taxpayer. The maximum credit is $200 for exterior windows and skylights, reduced by the aggregate credit allowed for exterior windows and skylights in prior years. The maximum credit for any single tax year is: $50 for any advanced main air circulating fan; $150 for any qualified furnace or boiler; and $300 for any other item. The credit cannot be claimed for amounts provided for by subsidized energy financing under a federal, state, or local program.

Qualified Energy Efficiency Improvements. Qualified energy improvements include any energy efficient building envelope component that meets certain energy conservation criteria. A building envelope component includes any insulation material or system which is designed to prevent heat loss or gain, exterior windows (including skylights), exterior doors, and any metal roof with either pigmented coating or cooling granules designed to reduce heat gain.

Residential Energy Property Expenditures. Qualified residential energy property expenditures include the purchase price of qualified energy property and any labor costs allocable to the on-site preparation, assembly, or installation of the property. Qualified energy property is energy-efficient building property, a qualified natural gas, propane, or oil furnace or hot water boiler, or an advance main air circulating fan that meet specific performance and quality standards. Qualified energy-efficient building property includes electric heat pump water heaters, qualified electric heat pumps, qualified central air conditioners, and qualified stoves that use biomass fuels.

Manufacturers Certificate. The taxpayer can rely on the manufacturers written certificate that a product qualifies for the nonbusiness energy property credit. The certification does not need to be attached to the taxpayer's return, but should be retained in his or her records (Notice 2009-53).

1442. Residential Energy Efficient Property Credit. A tax credit is available to an individual for residential energy efficient property placed in service before January 1, 2022, and installed on, or in connection with, a dwelling unit located in the United States and used as a residence by the taxpayer (Code Sec. 25D). The credit is available for qualified solar electric property, qualified solar water heating property, qualified fuel cell property, qualified small wind energy property, and geothermal heat pump property. Cooperative and condominium dwellers can claim the credit by splitting the cost of installing equipment with other unit owners.

The credit is 30 percent of the cost of eligible property placed in service in 2017, 2018, or 2019; 26 percent of the cost of eligible property placed in service in 2020; and 22 percent of the cost of eligible property placed in service in 2021. There is also a $500 credit limit with respect to each 0.5 kilowatt of capacity of qualified fuel cell property expenditures for each tax year. The credit is calculated on Form 5695. The credit is a nonrefundable personal credit and may be claimed against regular tax and alternative minimum tax (AMT) liabilities (¶ 1415). Unlike the nonbusiness energy property credit (¶ 1441), any excess of the nonbusiness energy property credit may be carried forward to another tax year. The basis of the residence is reduced by the allowed credit.

Qualifying Property. Qualifying solar water heating property is any property that receives at least half of its energy from the sun and is used to heat water for use in a dwelling unit. Costs allocated to heat a swimming pool or hot tub may not be considered. Qualifying solar electric property is any property that generates electricity from solar energy to be used in a dwelling unit. Qualified fuel cell property is any fuel cell property with a nameplate capacity of least 0.5 kilowatt hours of electricity generated by using an electrochemical process with an electricity-generating efficiency greater than 30 percent. Qualified small wind energy property is any wind turbine that generates electricity for use in the residence of the taxpayer. It does not include any wind facility for which a credit can be claimed for electricity produced from renewable resources (¶ 1465N). Qualified geothermal heat pump property is any property that uses the ground or ground water as a thermal source to heat a dwelling unit.

¶1442

Manufacturers Certificate. The taxpayer can rely on the manufacturers written certification that a product qualifies for the residential energy efficient property credit. The certification does not need to be attached to the taxpayer's return, but should be retained as part of his or her records (Notice 2009-53).

Alternative Motor Vehicle Credits

1446. Fuel Cell Motor Vehicle Credit. As part of the alternative motor vehicle credit, a taxpayer may claim a credit for a new qualified fuel cell motor vehicle purchased before January 1, 2021, and placed in service during the tax year (Code Sec. 30B(a)(1), (b), and (k)(1), as amended by the Taxpayer Certainty and Disaster Tax Relief Act of 2019 (P.L. 116-94)). A new qualified fuel cell motor vehicle must be propelled by power derived from one or more cells that convert chemical energy directly into electricity by combining oxygen with hydrogen fuel. A passenger vehicle or light truck must also be certified to meet specific environmental emission standards. A taxpayer may generally rely on the manufacturers certification that a vehicle qualifies for the credit (Notice 2008-33).

In addition, (1) the original use of the vehicle must commence with the taxpayer; (2) the taxpayer must acquire the vehicle for use or lease and not for resale; (3) the vehicle must be made by a manufacturer; and (4) the vehicle must be primarily used in the United States. A motor vehicle is any vehicle that has at least four wheels, is manufactured primarily for use on public streets, roads, and highways, and complies certain federal and state motor safety and clean air standards. The basis of any vehicle is reduced by the amount of the allowable credit (Code Sec. 30B(b)(3)).

The amount of the credit is calculated based on the vehicle's fuel efficiency relative to the 2002 model-year city, and its gross vehicle weight rating (GVWR). The credit can range from $8,000 for vehicles up to 8,500 pounds GVWR, and up to $40,000 for vehicles over 26,000 pounds GVWR. The credit may be increased from between $1,000 and $4,000 for a qualified fuel cell passenger automobile or light truck and meet certain standards for increased fuel efficiency.

The credit is calculated on Form 8910 and claimed on the taxpayer's return. Any portion of the credit attributable to personal use of the alternative motor vehicle is treated as a nonrefundable personal credit (¶ 1415). The portion attributable to use for trade, business, or investment purposes and subject to depreciation is treated as part of the general business credit (¶ 1465). A seller claiming the credit for a vehicle sold to a tax-exempt entity can only claim the credit as a part of the general business credit.

1451. Plug-In Electric Drive Motor Vehicle Credit. A taxpayer may claim a tax credit with respect to a new qualified plug-in electric drive motor vehicle placed in service during the tax year (Code Sec. 30D). The credit is $2,500, plus $417 in the case of a vehicle that draws propulsion energy from a battery with not less than five kilowatt hours of capacity, and an additional $417 for each kilowatt hour of battery capacity in excess of five kilowatt hours. The additional amount cannot exceed $5,000. Thus, the maximum credit amount per vehicle is $7,500.

The new qualified plug-in electric drive motor vehicle credit is calculated on Form 8936 and claimed on the taxpayer's return. Any portion of the credit attributable to personal use of the qualified vehicle is a nonrefundable personal credit (¶ 1415). The portion attributable to use for trade, business, or investment purposes and subject to depreciation is part of the general business credit (¶ 1465). The basis of the qualified vehicle is reduced by the amount of the credit allowed. The amount of any deduction or other credit allowable for a qualified vehicle is also reduced by the amount of the credit allowed. The credit begins to phase out for a particular manufacturer that sells 200,000 qualified vehicles for use in the United States. The credit phases out beginning January 1, 2019, for vehicles sold by Tesla, Inc. It phases out beginning April 1, 2019, for vehicles sold by General Motors, LLC (Notice 2019-22; Notice 2018-96).

Qualified Vehicles. A new qualified plug-in electric drive motor vehicle is a motor vehicle: (1) made by a manufacturer; (2) acquired for use or lease by the taxpayer and not resale; (3) the original use of which commences with the taxpayer; (4) treated as a motor vehicle for purposes of Title II of the Clean Air Act; (5) with a gross vehicle weight rating (GVWR) of not more than 14,000 pounds; and (6) that is propelled to a significant degree by an electric motor that draws electricity from a battery with a capacity of not less than four kilowatt hours and that is capable of being recharged from an external source of electricity. A motor vehicle is any vehicle that has at least four wheels and is manufactured primarily for use on public streets, roads, and highways. The vehicle must be used predominantly in the United States.

2-Wheeled Plug-in Electric Vehicles. The credit may also be claimed for certain two-wheeled plug-in electric vehicles (i.e., electric motorcycles) placed in service during the tax year and acquired before January 1, 2021 (Code Sec. 30D(g), as amended by the Taxpayer Certainty and Disaster Tax Relief Act of 2019 (P.L. 116-94)). The credit is equal to the lesser of 10 percent of the cost of the vehicle or $2,500.

A two-wheeled plug-in electric vehicle is vehicle that: (1) has only two wheels; (2) the original use of which commences with the taxpayer; (3) is acquired for use or lease by the taxpayer and not for resale; (4) is made by the manufacturer; (5) has a gross vehicle weight rating (GVWR) of less than 14,000 pounds; (6) is propelled in a significant extent by an electric motor that draws electricity from a battery with a capacity of not less than 2.5 kilowatt hours and is capable of being recharged from an external source; (7) is manufactured primarily for use on public streets, roads and highways; and (8) is capable of achieving a speed of 45 miles per hour or greater. A taxpayer may generally rely on the manufacturer's certification that a vehicle qualifies for the credit (Notice 2013-67, as modified by Notice 2016-51).

1455. Alternative Fuel Vehicle Refueling Property Credit. A taxpayer may claim a tax credit for the installation of qualified alternative fuel vehicle refueling property placed in service before January 1, 2021 (Code Sec. 30C, as amended by the Taxpayer Certainty and Disaster Tax Relief Act of 2019 (P.L. 116-94)). The credit amount is 30 percent of the cost of qualified property placed in service by the taxpayer during the tax year. The credit for any particular qualified property is limited to $30,000 for property that is subject to depreciation and $1,000 for any personal use property. The dollar limits apply at each location where qualified property is installed. The cost of each property must also be reduced by any Code Sec. 179 expense deduction taken for the property.

The alternative fuel vehicle refueling property credit is calculated on Form 8911 and claimed on the taxpayer's return. Any portion of the credit attributable to personal use of the qualified property is treated as a nonrefundable personal credit. The portion attributable to use in a trade or business, or for investment purposes, and subject to depreciation is treated as part of the general business credit (¶ 1465). The basis of the qualified property is reduced by the amount of the credit allowed.

Qualifying Property. Qualifying alternative fuel vehicle refueling property is property used for storing a clean-burning fuel or for dispensing clean-burning fuel into the fuel tank of a motor vehicle. It also includes any equipment that is used to recharge a motor vehicle that is propelled by electricity. Clean burning fuels are:

- any fuel that is at least 85 percent by volume consisting of ethanol, natural gas, compressed natural gas, liquefied natural gas, liquefied petroleum gas, or hydrogen;
- any fuel mixture that consists of a combination of at least two fuels which include biodiesel, diesel fuel, or kerosene with at least 20 percent of the volume being biodiesel without regard to any kerosene in the mixture; and
- electricity.

The refueling property must be placed in service during the tax year. Property that is not used in a business or for investment purposes must be installed on the taxpayer's principal residence. In addition, the original use of the property must commence with the taxpayer and it cannot be used predominantly outside the United States. If a person sells new refueling property to a tax-exempt organization, governmental unit, or a foreign person, the seller can claim the credit if the seller discloses in writing the amount of the tentative credit to the purchaser. If property ceases to be qualifying alternative fuel vehicle refueling property, the credit may be recaptured.

Foreign and Possession Credits

See CCH® AnswerConnect: *Foreign Tax Credit* for more information on this topic.

1461. Foreign Tax Credit for Individuals. An individual may either deduct foreign income taxes paid or accrued as an itemized deduction (¶ 1021) or claim them as a tax credit against U.S. income tax liability (¶ 2475) (Code Sec. 27). The credit is generally claimed on Form 1116, but if the total foreign taxes paid are not more than $300 for single filers ($600 for joint filers), the credit may be claimed on Schedule 3 (Form 1040) if all filing requirements are satisfied (¶ 2476).

1462. American Samoa Economic Development Credit. A U.S. domestic corporation with qualifying production activities income (QPAI) (¶ 980B) from America Samoa may claim an economic development credit for its first nine tax years beginning before January 1, 2021. Also, a qualifying corporation that is an existing claimant of the U.S. possession tax credit operating in American Samoa can claim the credit for the first 15 tax years of the corporation beginning before January 1, 2021 (Act Sec. 119(d) of the Tax Relief and Health Care Act of 2006 (P.L. 109-432), as amended by Act Sec. 119 of the Taxpayer Certainty and Disaster Tax Relief Act of 2019 (P.L. 116-94); Code Secs. 30A and 936, prior to being stricken by P.L. 115-141). Income eligible for the American Samoa economic development credit is not taxed under the alternative minimum tax rules (Code Sec. 59(b), prior to being stricken by P.L. 115-97). The credit is calculated on Form 5735.

General Business Credit

See CCH® AnswerConnect: *General Business Credit* for more information on this topic.

1465. General Business Credit. The general business credit is a nonrefundable credit comprised of a number of individual business credits. The general business credit is the sum of: (1) the business credit carried forward to the current year, (2) the amount of the current year business credit, and (3) the business credit carried back to that tax year (Code Sec. 38).

The current year general business credit is the sum of:

- the investment credit (¶ 1465A);
- the work opportunity credit (¶ 1465G);
- the biofuel producer credit (¶ 1465I);
- the research activities credit (¶ 1465J);
- the low-income housing credit (¶ 1465K);
- the enhanced oil recovery credit (¶ 1465L);
- the disabled access credit (¶ 1465M);
- the renewable electricity production credit (¶ 1465N);
- the empowerment zone employment credit (¶ 1465O);
- the Indian employment credit (¶ 1465Q);
- the employer Social Security credit (FICA tip credit) (¶ 1465R);
- the orphan drug credit (¶ 1465S);
- the new markets credit (¶ 1465T);
- the small employer pension plan start-up costs credit (¶ 1465U);
- the small employer automatic enrollment credit for tax years after 2019 (¶ 1465UA);
- the employer-provided child care facilities and services credit (¶ 1465V);
- the railroad track maintenance credit (¶ 1465W);
- the biodiesel and renewable diesel fuels credit (¶ 1465X);
- the marginal oil and gas well production credit (¶ 1465KK);
- the distilled spirits credit (¶ 1465Z);
- the advanced nuclear power facility production credit (¶ 1465AA);
- the energy efficient home credit (¶ 1465CC);
- the alternative motor vehicle credit (portion allocable to a trade or business) (¶ 1446);
- the alternative fuel vehicle refueling property credit (portion allocable to a trade or business) (¶ 1455);
- the mine rescue team training credit (¶ 1465GG);
- the differential wage payment credit (¶ 1465II);

- the carbon oxide (carbon dioxide) sequestration credit (¶ 1465JJ);
- the qualified plug-in electric drive motor vehicle credit (portion allocable to a trade or business) (¶ 1451);
- the small employer health insurance credit (¶ 1465HA);
- the family and medical leave credit (¶ 1465H);
- the employee retention credit (¶ 1465P); and
- general credits from an electing large partnership (¶ 482).

Each of these credits is computed separately on its applicable IRS form. The total credit amount is reported on Form 3800. A taxpayer must also attach a credit computation form, unless the taxpayer's only source for the credit is from a partnership, S corporation, estate, trust, or cooperative, and the taxpayer itself is not a partnership or S corporation. However, a credit computation form is still required if the taxpayer is claiming an investment credit (Form 3468) or the biodiesel and renewable diesel fuels credit (Form 8864), the taxpayer is an estate or trust and a credit is allocated to beneficiaries, or the taxpayer is a cooperative and a credit is allocated to patrons (Instructions to Form 3800).

Tax Liability Limitations. The general business credit may not exceed the excess of the taxpayer's net income tax over the greater of the taxpayer's tentative minimum tax liability or 25 percent of net regular tax liability above $25,000 (Code Sec. 38(c)). Net income tax is the sum of the taxpayer's regular tax liability and AMT liability, less all other nonrefundable credits. Net regular tax liability is the regular tax liability reduced by these credits. The AMT is repealed for corporations for tax years beginning after 2017, so a corporation has no tentative minimum tax after 2017 (¶ 239).

The tax liability limitation is determined separately for the portion of the general business credit attributable to the following specified credits: biofuel producer credit, low-income housing credit attributable to buildings placed in service after 2007, renewable electricity production credit for electricity or refined coal produced at a facility originally placed in service after October 22, 2004, during the four-year period beginning on the date the facility was originally placed in service, Indian coal production credit, FICA tip credit, railroad track maintenance credit, small employer health insurance premium credit, family and medical leave credit, energy credit component of the investment credit, rehabilitation credit component of the investment credit attributable to expenditures after 2007, and work opportunity credit. The tentative minimum tax is zero when calculating the tax liability limitation to the specified credits. Thus, the specified credits are allowed against net income tax that is in excess of 25 percent of the taxpayer's net regular tax in excess of $25,000. This limit is first reduced by the general business credits allowed for the tax year other than the specified credits.

The empowerment zone employment credit (¶ 1465O) amount may not exceed the excess of the taxpayer's net income tax over the greater of 75 percent of the taxpayer's tentative minimum tax liability or 25 percent of net regular tax liability above $25,000. This result is then reduced by the general business credit allowed for the tax year other than the empowerment zone employment credit and the specified credits listed above.

For married individuals filing separately, the $25,000 figure is limited to $12,500 for each spouse. If, however, one spouse has no current credit or unused credit, the spouse with a current credit or unused credit may use the full $25,000 figure in determining his or her credit for the year. Members of a controlled group of corporations may divide the $25,000 figure among themselves however they choose. An estate or trust must reduce the $25,000 figure to an amount that bears the same ratio to $25,000 as the portion of the estate's or trust's income that is not allocated to the beneficiaries bears to the total income of the estate or trust.

Carrybacks and Carryforwards. If the tax liability limit is exceeded for the tax year, the components of the general business credit are generally deemed used in the order listed above (Code Sec. 38(d); Instructions to Form 3800). Any excess or unused amount may be carried back one year and forward 20 years, except that the employee retention credit may not be carried back to a tax year prior to the tax year in which the credit was first available (Code Sec. 39). The order in which these credits are claimed in any carryback or carryforward year is: (1) the carryforwards to that year on a first-in, first-out

(FIFO) basis, (2) the general business credit earned in that year, and (3) the carrybacks to that year on a FIFO basis.

Eligible credits of an eligible small business determined for its first tax year beginning in 2010 may be carried back five years and forward 20 years (Code Sec. 39(a)(4), prior to being stricken by P.L. 115-141). Eligible small business credits are the current year business credit components of the general business credit. An eligible small business is a sole proprietorship, partnership, or non-publicly traded corporation with $50 million or less in average annual gross receipts during the three tax years preceding the first tax year beginning in 2010. The eligible small business credits determined for 2010 may be claimed against the eligible small business's regular tax and AMT liabilities.

The taxpayer must maintain separate carryback and carryforward records for the general business credit attributable to the empowerment zone employment credit, and to each of the other components of the general business credit. Separate recordkeeping is necessary because the empowerment zone employment credit may offset up to 25 percent of the taxpayer's AMT. Several of the credits that remain unused at the end of the carryforward period, or when the taxpayer ceases to exist, may be claimed as a deduction in the following year (Code Sec. 196).

1465A. Investment Credit. A taxpayer may claim an investment credit that is the sum of the rehabilitation credit (¶ 1465B), the energy credit (¶ 1465C), the qualifying advanced coal project credit (¶ 1465D), the qualifying gasification project credit (¶ 1465E), and the qualifying advanced energy project credit (¶ 1465F) (Code Sec. 46). The investment credit is claimed on Form 3468 and is part of the general business credit subject to its tax liability limitation and carryover rules (¶ 1465).

The investment credit for partnership property is generally apportioned among partners in the same ratio the partners divide the partnership's general profits (Reg. § 1.46-3(f)). An S corporation's credit is apportioned among the shareholders on a daily basis according to each shareholder's proportion of ownership (Reg. § 1.48-5). The credit for an estate or trust is apportioned between the estate or trust and the beneficiaries based on the income allocable to each (Code Sec. 50(d)(6); Reg. § 1.48-6).

At-Risk Limitation. No investment credit is allowed to the extent that the investment property is financed with nonqualified nonrecourse borrowing (Code Sec. 49). Thus, the credit base of investment credit property is reduced by the amount of nonqualified nonrecourse financing for the property, as determined at the close of the tax year the property is placed in service.

Nonqualified nonrecourse financing is any nonrecourse financing that is not qualified commercial financing. Financing is qualified commercial financing if: (1) the property is acquired from an unrelated person; (2) the amount of the nonrecourse financing does not exceed 80 percent of the property's credit base; and (3) the financing is borrowed from a qualified person, or it represents a loan that is from or guaranteed by a federal, state, or local government or instrumentality. The credit base is equal to the sum of the portion of the basis of a qualified rehabilitation building attributable to qualified rehabilitation expenditures, the basis of energy property, and the basis of any property that is part of a qualifying advanced coal project, a qualifying gasification project, or a qualified advanced energy project. A qualified person is one who actively and regularly engages in the business of lending money, is not related to the taxpayer, and did not transfer the property to the taxpayer or receive a fee with respect to the taxpayer's investment.

Decreases in nonqualified recourse financing on the property in years after the property was placed in service increase the credit base of the property. This rule does not apply if the decrease occurs through the surrender or other use of property financed by nonqualified nonrecourse financing. Similarly, increases in nonqualified nonrecourse financing on the property in years after the year the property was placed in service decrease the credit base of the property and trigger recapture.

The at-risk limitation applies to investment credit property placed in service by an individual and a closely held corporation engaged in business activities that are subject to the loss limitation of the at-risk rules (¶ 1155). The investment credit at-risk limitation applies at the partner or shareholder level in the case of a partnership or S corporation.

¶**1465A**

The investment credit at-risk limitation does not apply to certain energy property if (1) nonqualified nonrecourse financing does not exceed 75 percent of the basis of energy property at the close of the tax year the property is placed in service; and (2) any nonqualified nonrecourse financing for the property is a level payment loan (a loan repaid in substantially equal installments, including both principal and interest).

An increase in the amount at risk is treated as if it occurred in the year the property was first placed in service for purposes of computing the investment credit and any recapture of the credit. However, the investment credit attributable to the increase in the amount at risk is claimed by the taxpayer in the tax year the decrease in the amount of nonqualified nonrecourse financing occurs.

If at the close of a tax year there is a net increase in the amount of nonqualified nonrecourse financing for the property, thereby decreasing the taxpayer's amount at risk, the investment credit must be recomputed, and the decrease in the investment credit for previous tax years is recaptured as additional tax in the year that the net increase in nonqualified nonrecourse financing occurs.

Ineligible Property. No investment credit is allowed for: (1) property used predominantly outside the United States except in limited circumstances; (2) property used predominantly to furnish lodging (or in connection with the furnishing of lodging), except in the case of nonlodging commercial facilities, a hotel or motel furnishing accommodations predominantly to transients, energy property and the portion of the basis in certified historic structures that is attributable to qualified rehabilitation expenditures; and (3) property used by a tax-exempt organization (other than a farmers' cooperative) unless it is used predominantly in an unrelated trade or business (Code Sec. 50(b)). Property used by, or leased to, a governmental unit, foreign person, or foreign entity is generally not eligible for the investment credit. However, the portion of the property attributable to qualified rehabilitation expenditures or held under a short-term lease (generally under six months) does qualify for the credit.

Basis Reduction. The investment credit reduces basis in the investment property, except that basis in energy credit property is reduced by only 50 percent of the credit amount (¶ 1465B) (Code Sec. 50(c)). The reduced basis is used to compute depreciation and any gain or loss on the disposition of property.

If the investment credit is recaptured on property on which an investment credit downward basis adjustment was made, the basis of the property immediately before the event resulting in recapture must be increased by the recapture amount and by 50 percent of the recapture amount for an energy credit. In determining the amount of gain that is recaptured as ordinary income on a sale or disposition of depreciable personal property (Code Sec. 1245) or depreciable real property (Code Sec. 1250), the amount of the investment credit downward basis adjustment is treated as a depreciation deduction that is subject to ordinary income recapture. For section 1250 property, the recapture applies only to the excess of depreciation claimed over depreciation computed under the straight-line method, with the latter computed on the basis without reduction for the applicable investment credit downward basis adjustment.

If an investment credit for which a downward basis adjustment was made does not result in a tax benefit because it remains unused at the end of the 20-year credit carryover period, the taxpayer may deduct 50 percent of the unused energy and 100 percent of any other unused investment credit attributable to the basis reduction (Code Sec. 196).

Special Investment Credit Rules. Special limitations apply to the amount of investment credit that may be claimed by regulated investment companies (RICs), real estate investment trusts (REITs), noncorporate lessors, and certain other regulated companies (Code Sec. 50(d)).

Recapture of Credit. If investment credit property is disposed of by the taxpayer (including dispositions due to casualties or thefts), or ceases to be investment credit property before the end of its recapture period, the tax for the year of disposal or cessation is increased by the amount of the credit that is recaptured (Code Sec. 50(a)). A taxpayer subject to recapture must file Form 4255.

The amount of the recapture is a percentage of the original credit claimed, depending on how long the property is held before recapture is required. The recapture percentages are 100 percent within the first full year after placement in service, 80

¶1465A

percent within the second full year, 60 percent within the third full year, 40 percent within the fourth full year, 20 percent within the fifth full year, and zero thereafter. Advance rehabilitation or energy credits on progress expenditures are also subject to recapture. Special recapture rules apply to certain energy property.

The recapture rules do not apply to: (1) a transfer between spouses or incident to divorce (¶ 778) (but a later disposition by the transferee results in recapture to the same extent as if the disposition had been made by the transferor at that date), (2) a transfer because of death, and (3) a transfer involving carryovers after Code Sec. 381(a) corporate acquisitions. Similarly, the recapture rules do not apply where there is a mere change in the form of operating a business, provided that the business retains the property and the taxpayer retains a substantial interest in the business.

1465B. Rehabilitation Credit. A rehabilitation credit may be claimed for qualified rehabilitation expenditures (QREs) to preserve and rehabilitate qualified rehabilitated buildings (QRBs). The credit is claimed on Form 3468 as part of the investment credit (¶ 1465A). The credit amount is:

- for amounts paid or incurred after 2017, 20 percent of the taxpayer's QREs for QRBs that are certified historic structures claimed ratably over a five-year period; or

- for amounts paid or incurred before 2018, 10 percent of the taxpayer's QREs for QRBs that are not certified historic structures and are first placed in service before 1936, plus 20 percent of the taxpayer's QREs for QRBs that are certified historic structures (Code Sec. 47).

Under a transition rule, QREs paid or incurred after 2017 remain subject to the more favorable pre-2018 rules if: (1) the taxpayer owns or leases the building during the entire 24-month or 60-month period selected for determining whether it is substantially rehabilitated, and (2) the applicable measurement period begins no later than June 20, 2018. The pre-2018 rules only apply to expenditures paid or incurred by the end of the tax year in which the 24-month or 60-month period ends (Act Sec. 13402(c)(2) of the Tax Cuts and Jobs Act (P.L. 115-97)).

No energy credit (¶ 1465C) is allowed on the portion of the basis of property that is attributable to QREs. Certain restrictions also apply to property used as lodging (¶ 1465A).

Eligibility. A building and its structural components are a QRB if they are substantially rehabilitated for the tax year and placed in service by any person before the beginning of the rehabilitation. For amounts paid or incurred before 2018 on property other than a certified historic structure, the property must also satisfy the applicable wall retention test, an age requirement, and a location-of-rehabilitation requirement (Code Sec. 47(c)(1), prior to amendment by P.L. 115-97; Reg. § 1.48-12). Property is substantially rehabilitated only if the expenditures during an elected 24-month measurement period (60-month period for phased rehabilitations) ending with or within the tax year exceed the greater of the adjusted basis of the property or $5,000.

QREs do not include: (1) an enlargement or new construction; (2) the cost of acquisition; (3) noncertified rehabilitation of a certified historic structure; (4) rehabilitation of tax-exempt use property; (5) certain expenditures that are not depreciated under the MACRS straight-line method over specified recovery periods; or (6) a lessee-incurred expenditure if, on the date the rehabilitation of the building is completed, the remaining term of the lease (determined without regard to renewal periods) is less than the applicable recovery period.

The credit for expenditures subject to the pre-2018 rules is generally claimed in the tax year that the building is placed in service. The amortization period for expenditures subject to the post-2017 rules generally begins in the placed-in-service year.

Advance Credits for Progress Expenditures. The taxpayer may elect an advance rehabilitation investment credit for progress expenditures on certain rehabilitated buildings before the property is placed in service (Code Sec. 47(d)). Property qualifying for an advance credit on progress expenditures includes a building that is being rehabilitated by or for the taxpayer, if the normal rehabilitation period for the building is two or more years and it is reasonable to expect that the building will be a QRB when it is placed in service.

The amount of QREs that are qualified progress expenditures is (1) the amount of QREs properly chargeable to the capital account for self-rehabilitated buildings; and (2) for other rehabilitated buildings the lesser of the QRE paid to another person for the rehabilitation of the building during the tax year or the portion of the overall cost of the rehabilitation completed during the tax year.

1465C. Energy Credit. An energy credit may be claimed for a percentage of a taxpayer's basis in qualified energy property placed in service during the tax year (Code Sec. 48). The credit is claimed on Form 3468 as part of the investment credit (¶ 1465A). It is not subject to the general tax liability limitation for the general business credit. Instead, the tax liability limit is calculated separately with tentative minimum tax treated as zero, allowing the taxpayer to utilize the credit against both regular tax and alternative minimum tax liability.

The credit percentage is 10 percent for:

- combined heat and power system property;
- qualified microturbine property;
- equipment that uses the ground or ground water as a thermal energy source to heat a structure or as a sink to cool a structure; and
- equipment used to produce, distribute, or use energy derived from a geothermal deposit.

The credit is 30 percent for:

- qualified fuel cell property;
- qualified small wind energy property;
- equipment that uses solar energy to illuminate the inside of a structure using fiber-optic distributed sunlight; and
- equipment that uses solar energy to generate electricity, heat or cool a structure, provide hot water in a structure, or provide solar process heat (but not to heat a swimming pool).

The construction of the energy property must begin before January 1, 2022, with the exception of geothermal property.

The credit for solar energy used to generate electricity, etc., is reduced to 26 percent if construction begins during 2020, and to 22 percent if construction begins during 2021. In all cases, the credit is limited to 10 percent if construction begins before 2022 but the property is not placed in service before 2024. The credit for fiber optic solar energy property, qualified fuel cell property, and qualified small wind property, is also reduced to 26 percent if construction begins in 2020, 22 percent if construction begins during 2021, and 0 percent if the property is not placed in service before 2024. The credit for qualified fuel cell property may not exceed $1,500 for each 0.5 kilowatt of capacity.

A taxpayer establishes the beginning of construction by starting physical work of a significant nature (physical work test) or by paying or incurring five percent or more of the total cost of the energy property (five-percent safe harbor). These safe harbors do not apply unless a taxpayer makes continuous progress towards completion once construction has begun (Notice 2018-59).

The energy property must be depreciable or amortizable to qualify for the energy credit, and must meet performance and quality standards prescribed by the IRS. The taxpayer must complete the construction, reconstruction, or erection of the property or, if the property is acquired by the taxpayer, the original use must begin with the taxpayer. Energy property does not include any property that is part of a facility the production from which is allowed as a credit for electricity produced from renewable sources (¶ 1465N) for the tax year or any prior tax year. No energy credit is allowed for the portion of the basis of property for which a rehabilitation investment credit (¶ 1465B) is claimed. An advance energy investment credit may be claimed under special rules for progress expenditures (Code Sec. 48(b)).

Investment Credit Election. A taxpayer may make an irrevocable election to treat certain qualified property that is part of a qualified investment credit facility as energy property eligible for a 30-percent investment credit (Code Sec. 48(a)(5)). If the election is made, no renewable electricity production credit is allowed (¶ 1465N) for any tax year with respect to the facility. Qualified investment credit facilities are facilities that are placed in service after 2008, otherwise eligible for the renewable electricity production credit, and produce electricity using wind or solar power, closed-loop biomass, open-loop biomass, geothermal energy, landfill gas, municipal solid waste (trash), hydropower, or marine and hydrokinetic renewable energy. Construction of the facility generally must begin before 2021. For a wind facility, construction must begin before 2021, but the credit is reduced by 20 percent if construction begins in 2017, by 40 percent if construction begins in 2018, and by 60 percent if construction begins in 2019 and 2020. Qualified investment credit property must also be depreciable or amortizable tangible personal property or other tangible property (not including a building or its structural components) that is used as an integral part of the qualified investment credit facility. In addition, it must be constructed, reconstructed, erected, or acquired by the taxpayer, with the original use of the property commencing with the taxpayer.

Coordination With Section 1603 Grants. The Secretary of Treasury is authorized to provide a grant to each person who places into service specified energy property that is either: (1) an electricity production facility otherwise eligible for the renewable electricity production credit, or (2) qualifying property otherwise eligible for the energy investment credit (Act Sec. 1603(a) of the American Recovery and Reinvestment Act of 2009 (P.L. 111-5), as amended by the Tax Relief, Unemployment Insurance Reauthorization, and Job Creation Act of 2010 (P.L. 111-312)). To be eligible for the grant, (1) the specified energy property must be placed in service during 2009, 2010, or 2011, or (2) construction must begin during 2009, 2010 or 2011, and the property must be placed in service after 2011 and before the applicable credit termination date.

No energy credit or electricity production credit is allowed for the year of the grant or any subsequent year (Code Sec. 48(d)). A credit that was claimed for the facility before the grant was made is recaptured by adding the prior claimed credit amounts to the tax liability of the grant year. The taxpayer must adjust any carryovers of general business credits to reflect the amount of the recaptured credit. The energy credit and electricity production credit may not be claimed because of the reduction of a section 1603 grant under the sequestration rules (Notice 2014-39).

1465D. Qualified Advanced Coal Project Credit. A qualifying advanced coal project credit may be claimed on Form 3468 as part of the investment credit (¶ 1465A) (Code Sec. 48A). The taxpayer must have applied for and received certification that the project satisfies the relevant requirements outlined by the IRS, in consultation with the Secretary of Energy. The credit is equal to 20 percent of qualified investments in integrated combined cycle projects, 15 percent of qualified investments in other advanced coal-based projects, and 30 percent of qualified investments in advanced coal-based generation technology projects. The credit is recaptured if the project fails to maintain carbon dioxide separation and sequestration.

1465E. Qualified Gasification Project Credit. A qualifying gasification project credit may be claimed on Form 3468 as part of the investment credit (¶ 1465A) (Code Sec. 48B). The taxpayer must have applied for and received certification that the project satisfies the relevant requirements outlined by the IRS, in consultation with the Secretary of Energy. The credit is equal to 20 percent of qualified investments in qualifying gasification projects, increased to 30 percent for qualifying gasification projects that include equipment that separates and sequesters at least 75 percent of the project's total carbon dioxide emissions. A qualifying gasification facility is one that combines coal, petroleum residue, biomass, or other materials with steam under high pressure to create a synthetic gas, or "syngas." The credit is recaptured if the project fails to attain or maintain the 75-percent separation and sequestration requirement.

1465F. Advanced Energy Project Credit. A tax credit equal to 30 percent of a taxpayer's qualified investment in a qualifying advanced energy project (Code Sec. 48C). The credit is claimed on Form 3468 as part of the investment credit (¶ 1465A). The basis of any property that is part of a qualifying advanced energy project is included in the credit base for purposes of the investment credit at-risk limitation rules. If the energy credit (¶ 1465C), the qualifying advanced coal project credit (¶ 1465D), or the qualifying gasification project credit (¶ 1465E) is allowed for an investment, the advanced energy project credit cannot be claimed for the same investment.

A qualifying advanced energy project is a project that re-equips, expands, or establishes a manufacturing facility for the production of: (1) property designed to be used to produce energy from the sun, wind, or geothermal deposits or other renewable resources; (2) fuel cells, microturbines, or an energy storage system for use with electric or hybrid-electric motor vehicles; (3) electric grids to support the transmission of intermittent sources of renewable energy, including storage of such energy; (4) property designed to capture and sequester carbon dioxide emissions; (5) property designed to refine or blend renewable fuels or to produce energy conservation technologies (including energy-conserving lighting technologies and smart grid technologies); (6) new qualified plug-in electric drive motor vehicles or components which are designed specifically for use with such vehicles, including electric motors, generators, and power control units; or (7) other advanced energy property designed to reduce greenhouse gas emissions as may be determined by the Secretary of Treasury. Any portion of the qualified investment in the qualifying project must be certified by the Secretary of Treasury as eligible for the credit. A qualifying project does not include any portion of a project for the production of any property used in the refining or blending of non-renewable transportation fuel.

1465G. Work Opportunity Tax Credit. An employer may claim the work opportunity credit for wages paid to hire individuals from certain targeted hard-to-employ groups (Code Sec. 51, as amended by the Taxpayer Certainty and Disaster Tax Relief Act of 2019 (P.L. 116-94)). The credit is generally 40 percent of the first $6,000 of qualified wages (unless otherwise noted below) paid to each member of a targeted group during the first year of employment and 25 percent of the first $6,000 of wages attributable to individuals meeting only minimum employment levels. The credit is computed on Form 5884 and reduces the taxpayer's deduction for wages and salaries (Code Sec. 280C).

Wages paid or incurred to an individual who begins work for the employer after December 31, 2020, are not eligible for the credit. Also, no credit is allowed for wages paid to an individual for services rendered at the employer's plant or facility that are substantially similar to services performed by employees who are participants in a strike or are affected by a lockout. The work opportunity credit is part of the general business credit, but the tax liability limitation is calculated separately and the credit amount may be claimed against both the regular and the alternative minimum tax liabilities (¶ 1465). The credit limitation applies to any carrybacks of the credit amounts to any previous year.

Minimum Employment Period. An employee must complete a minimum of 120 hours of service for the wages to be taken into account for calculation of the credit. The hours-of-service test is the only way the minimum employment period is calculated. Once an employee satisfies the 120-hour test, the credit percentage is 40 percent if the employee performs 400 or more hours of service, or 25 percent if the employee performs less than 400 hours of service.

Target Groups. Wages paid to an individual who is a certified member of one of the following groups qualifies for the work opportunity credit (Code Sec. 51(d)):

- a qualified IV-A recipient (an individual who is a member of a family that received Temporary Assistance for Needy Families (TANF) assistance for any nine of the 18 months ending on the hire date);

- a qualified veteran (discussed below);

- a qualified ex-felon (an individual hired within one year of being released from prison);

- a designated community resident (an individual who is at least age 18 but not yet age 40 when hired and lives in an empowerment zone or rural renewal county);

- a vocational rehabilitation referral (an individual with a physical or mental disability resulting in a substantial handicap to employment who is referred to the employer upon completion of rehabilitative services);

- a qualified summer youth employee (an individual who performs services between May 1 and September 15, is age 16 or 17 on the later of the hire date or May 1, and lives in an empowerment zone), but the qualified wage limit for the individual is $3,000;

- a qualified food stamps (SNAP) recipient (an individual who is at least age 18 but not yet 40 when hired, and is a member of a family that either received SNAP benefits for the six month period ending on the hire date, or received SNAP benefits for three of the five months ending on the hire date but lost the benefits for failure to comply with the program's work requirements);

- a qualified supplemental security income (SSI) recipient (an individual receiving SSI for any month ending during the 60-day period ending on the hiring date);

- a long-term family assistance (TANF) recipient (described below), but the maximum qualified wages is $10,000 for the first and second year, and the credit percentage equals 50 percent for the second year; or

- a long-term unemployment recipient (an individual unemployed for at least 27 weeks that includes a period when he or she was receiving unemployment compensation under state or federal law).

Certifications. An employer of a member of a targeted group must have the individual certified by an authorized local agency prior to the individual's first day of work, or apply to certify the individual within 28 days of the first day of work. The employer uses Form 8850 to pre-screen employees and to make a written request that the local agency certify an employee as being a member of a targeted group (Notice 2012-13). The due date for performing certain time-sensitive actions, including submitting Form 8850, otherwise due on or after April 1, 2020, and before July 15, 2020, is automatically extended to July 15, 2020, in response to the COVID-19 (coronavirus) crisis (Notice 2020-23; Rev. Proc. 2018-58).

TANF recipients. A long-term family assistance recipient is an individual who is certified by the designated local agency as a member of a family that:

- has been receiving TANF payments for at least the 18-month period ending on the hiring date;

- receives TANF payments for at least 18 months and the worker's hiring date is not more than two years after the 18-month total is reached; or

- is no longer eligible for TANF payments because of a limitation imposed under federal or state law on the maximum duration such assistance is payable, if the worker's hiring date is not more than two years after eligibility expires.

Qualified Veterans. A qualified veteran is a veteran who is certified as (Code Sec. 51(b)(3), (d)(3), and (d)(13)(D)):

- a member of a family receiving SNAP benefits for at least a three-month period ending during the 12-month period ending on the hiring date;

- unemployed for at least four weeks (consecutive or not) but less than six months during the one-year period ending on the hiring date;

- unemployed for at least six months (consecutive or not) during the one-year period ending on the hiring date, but the qualified wage limit is $14,000;

- entitled to compensation for a service-connected disability and hired within one year of being discharged or released from active duty in the U.S. Armed Forces, but the qualified wage limit is $12,000; or

- entitled to compensation for a service-connected disability, and was unemployed for at least six months (consecutive or not) during the one-year period ending on the hiring date, but the qualified wage limit for the individual is $24,000.

Tax-Exempt Organizations and Qualified Veterans. A tax-exempt organization, other than an exempt farmers' cooperative generally cannot claim the work opportunity credit (Code Sec. 52(c)). However, a Code Sec. 501(c) exempt organization may claim a reduced credit of 26 percent of qualified wages paid to qualified veterans using Form 5884-C. The form is filed separately and is not attached to any other return filed by the exempt organization. The credit is allowed against the organization's FICA tax obligation on wages paid to the veteran within one year of hiring (Code Sec. 3111(e)). The liability on the organization's employment tax return is not reduced by the credit. Instead, the credit is processed separately and the amount properly claimed is refunded to the exempt organization. This is likely to occur after the filing of the return, so an organization is cautioned not to reduce its FICA obligations on returns in anticipation of the refund (Notice 2012-13).

14

TAX CREDITS

¶1465G

Employee Retention Credit. An eligible employer may claim a tax credit equal to 40 percent of up to $6,000 of wages paid to each employee if the employer is affected by (1) a qualified disaster occurring from January 1, 2018, through February 18, 2020, (2) the California wildfires in 2017, and (3) Hurricane Harvey, Irma, or Maria (¶ 1465P). The employee retention credit may not be claimed for an employee during any period that the employer claims the work opportunity credit with respect to the employee.

1465H. Employer Credit for Paid Family and Medical Leave. An eligible employer may claim a credit in tax years beginning in 2018, 2019, and 2020 for an applicable percentage of the wages paid to qualifying employees for family and medical leave under the Family and Medical Leave Act (FMLA) (Code Sec. 45S, as amended by the Taxpayer Certainty and Disaster Tax Relief Act of 2019 (P.L. 116-94); Notice 2018-71). The credit is part of the general business credit, subject to its tax liability limitation and carryover rules (¶ 1465). The credit reduces the employer's deduction for wages and salaries (Code Sec. 280C). An employer claims the credit on Form 8994.

The applicable percentage is 12.5 percent of wages paid during the leave period if the rate of payment is at least 50 percent of wages normally paid. The percentage is increased by .25 percentage points for each percentage point that the rate of payment exceeds 50 percent, up to a maximum applicable percentage of 25 percent. The credit with respect to any employee for any tax year is limited to the employee's normal hourly wage rate multiplied by the number of hours of family and medical leave taken. Wages for an employee who is not paid an hourly wage rate are prorated to an hourly wage rate. The credit covers a maximum of 12 weeks of family and medical leave.

Eligible Employer. An eligible employer must have a written policy that provides all qualifying employees at least two weeks of annual paid FMLA leave, prorated for part-time employees. Only the following family and medical leave qualifies for the credit: birth of an employee's child; placement of child with the employee for adoption or foster care; the employee's serious health condition, or care for the employee's spouse, child, or parent with a serious health condition; any qualifying exigency due to an employee's spouse, child, or parent being on active duty (or notified of an impending call to active duty) in the Armed Forces; and care for a service member who is the employee's spouse, child, parent, or next of kin.

The policy must provide a payment rate of at least 50 percent of an employee's normal wages. Any leave paid by a state or local government, or required by state or local law, is not taken in account for this purpose. If the employer employs any qualifying employees who are not covered by title I of the FMLA (e.g. works less than 1,250 hours), the policy must include certain noninterference language. A transitional rule for the 2018 tax year provides that a policy (or amendment to an existing policy) is treated as in place on the retroactive effective date if the policy is adopted on or before December 31, 2018. The employer may make retroactive leave payments under the policy by the end of its 2018 tax year. An employer is not required to notify employees that it has a written policy for providing paid family and medical leave, but if notice is given then all eligible employees must be notified.

Qualifying Employee. A qualifying employee is any employee who has been employed by the employer for at least one year and whose compensation for the preceding year does not exceed 60 percent of the threshold for a highly-compensated individual (¶ 2114). Thus, a qualifying employee for 2019 cannot have earned more than $72,000 in 2018 and a qualifying employee for 2020 cannot have earned more than $75,000 in 2019. An employer may use any reasonable method to determine length of employment, but it cannot require employment for 12 consecutive months, require an employee to work a minimum number of hours per year, or exclude any classification of employees from eligibility for paid family and medical leave. The employee must be a qualifying employee when the family or medical leave is taken. The credit is not available if the employee becomes a qualifying employee later during the tax year.

Wages Defined. A qualifying employee's wages for purposes of calculating the credit are the same as for federal unemployment taxes (FUTA) without regard to the $7,000 FUTA wage limitation. They generally includes all remuneration paid for employment but not any amount taken into account to determine other business-related tax credits (e.g., research credit). Wages paid by a third-party payer (e.g., insurance company, professional employer organization) to qualifying employees for services performed for

¶1465H

an eligible employer are considered paid by the eligible employer. Wages paid through an employer's short-term disability program for family and medical leave are also taken into account if the program meets the minimum paid leave requirements.

1465HA. Small Employer Health Insurance Credit. An eligible small employer with 25 or fewer full-time equivalent employees may claim a tax credit for premiums it pays toward employee health coverage (Code Sec. 45R; Reg. § 1.45R-5). The credit is only available for a two-consecutive-tax-year credit period. The credit is computed on Form 8941 and claimed as a component of the general business credit (¶ 1465). Any portion of the credit that is not claimed by the expiration of the 20-year carryforward period for the general business credit may be claimed as a deduction in the first tax year after expiration of the carryforward period (Code Sec. 196). The deduction for employer-paid premiums for qualified health plans is reduced by the amount of the credit (Code Sec. 280C(h)).

Credit Amount. The credit is generally equal to 50 percent of the lesser of:

(1) the total nonelective contributions the employer makes on behalf of its employees during the tax year under a contribution arrangement for premiums to qualified health plans offered through a state-sponsored Small Business Health Options Program (SHOP) Exchange; or

(2) the total nonelective contributions that would have been made during the tax year if each employee taken into account in item (1) had enrolled in a qualified health plan that had a premium equal to the average premium for the small group market in the rating area where the employee enrolls for coverage (Code Sec. 45R(b); Reg. § 1.45R-3).

The contribution arrangement must require an employer to make a nonelective contribution on behalf of each employee who enrolls in a qualified health plan offered by the employer in an amount equal to a uniform percentage, but not less than 50 percent, of the premium cost. An employer contribution is nonelective so long as it is not made through a salary reduction arrangement (Code Sec. 45R(e)(3)). In addition, the contribution arrangement must offer the insurance through a SHOP Exchange.

The credit percentage for a tax-exempt eligible small employer is 35 percent, but the credit may not exceed the exempt organization's payroll taxes during the calendar year in which the tax year begins (Code Sec. 45R(f)). A tax-exempt eligible small employer is a small employer that is also a Code Sec. 501(c) organization. The organization claims the credit by filing Form 990-T with Form 8941 attached.

Credit Phaseout. The credit amount is reduced, but not below zero, by the sum of:

• the credit multiplied by the number of the employer's full-time equivalent employees for the tax year in excess of 10, divided by 15; and

• the credit multiplied by the employer's average annual wages in excess of the applicable dollar amount for the tax year ($27,100 for 2019 and $27,600 for 2020), divided by the applicable dollar amount (Code Sec. 45R(c); Reg. § 1.45R-3(c); Rev. Proc. 2018-57; Rev. Proc. 2019-44).

Eligible Employer and Employees. An employer is an eligible small employer if, during the tax year:

• the employer has 25 or fewer full-time equivalent employees;

• the average annual wages of these employees is not greater than twice the applicable dollar amount for the tax year ($54,200 for 2019 and $55,200 for 2020); and

• the employer has a qualified health care arrangement in effect (Code Sec. 45R(d); Reg. § 1.45R-2).

All controlled groups, partnerships, and affiliated service groups treated as a single employer under Code Sec. 414(b), (c), (m), or (o) are treated as one employer (Code Sec. 45R(e)(5)(A)).

The number of full-time equivalent employees during a tax year is equal to the total number of hours for which the employer paid wages to the employees, divided by 2,080. A fractional result is rounded to the next lowest whole number. Only the first 2,080 hours of each employee's wages are taken into account. For purposes of determining average annual wages and the number of full-time equivalent employees, hours of

¶1465HA

service worked by, and wages paid to, a seasonal worker are not taken into account unless the worker works for the employer on more than 120 days during the tax year.

An individual is not an employee, and the hours, wages, and premiums paid for the individual are not counted when figuring the credit, if he or she is: the owner of a sole proprietorship (i.e., self-employed); partner in partnership; a shareholder who owns more than two percent of an S corporation; a shareholder who owns more than five percent of a business that is not an S corporation; or any family member, or a member of the household who is not a family member but can be claimed as a qualifying relative (¶ 137B), on the income tax return of one of the other persons listed, as well as the individual's spouse (Code Sec. 45R(e)(1); Reg. § 1.45R-1(a)(5)). Leased employees are considered employees.

Credit Period. The small employer health insurance credit may be claimed only during the employer's two-year credit period. The credit period is the two-consecutive-tax-year period beginning with the first tax year in which the employer offers one or more qualified health plans to its employees through a SHOP Exchange. The credit period does not begin until the first year the employer files a return claiming the credit (Code Sec. 45R(e)(2); Reg. § 1.45R-1(a)(3)). The IRS has provided relief to an employer to claim the credit if coverage is provided under a SHOP Exchange for all or part of the tax year but the employer is not able to provide a qualified health plan for the remainder of the credit period because the employer's principal business address is in a county where no SHOP plans are available (Notice 2018-27).

1465I. Biofuel Producer Credit. A producer may claim a credit for any sale or use of alcohol fuels or alcohol fuel mixtures unless produced outside the United States for use as a fuel outside the United States (Code Sec. 40, as amended by the Taxpayer Certainty and Disaster Tax Relief Act of 2019 (P.L. 116-94)). The credit has several components, but currently is only available for second generation biofuel producer (formerly, the cellulosic biofuel producer credit) produced before January 1, 2021. All other components of the credit expired and may not be claimed with respect to sales or uses after 2011 including: alcohol mixture credit, the alcohol credit, and the small ethanol producer credit.

The biofuel producer credit is part of the general business credit but the tax liability limitation is calculated separately and may be claimed against both regular and alternative minimum tax liability (¶ 1465). Also, the carryforward period is limited to three tax years after the relevant fuel's termination year and any carryforward that is unused at the end of the carryforward period is deductible in the following tax year (Code Sec. 196). The credit is calculated on Form 6478. A taxpayer may elect not to claim the credit.

Second Generation Biofuel Producer Credit. The second generation biofuel producer credit is equal to $1.01 per gallon of qualified second generation biofuel produced by a qualified second generation biofuel producer before January 1, 2021 (Code Sec. 40(b)(6), as amended by P.L. 116-94). Second generation biofuel is any liquid fuel derived from qualified feedstock including lignocellulosic or hemicellulosic matter available on a renewable or recurring basis, and any cultivated algae, cyanobacteria, or lemna. The fuel must meet the Environmental Protection Agency registration requirements for fuel and fuel additives established under the Clear Air Act, and must not be alcohol of less than 150 proof.

Second generation biofuel does not include any fuel if: more than four percent is any combination of water and sediment, the ash content of the fuel is more than one percent, or the fuel has an acid number greater than 25. Renewable sources of lignocellulosic and hemicellulosic matter include energy crops and trees, wood and wood residues, plants, grasses, agricultural residues, fibers, animal wastes, and other waste material, including municipal solid waste. Any second generation biofuel claimed on Form 6478 cannot also be claimed as part of the biodiesel and renewable diesel fuels credit (¶ 1465X).

The second generation biofuel must be used by the producer or sold to another person: (1) for use in a trade or business to produce a second generation biofuel mixture (other than casual off-farm production), (2) for use as a fuel in a trade or business, or (3) to sell to another person at retail and place the second generation biofuel in the retail buyer's fuel tank. Second generation biofuel production does not include purchasing alcohol and increasing the proof of the alcohol through additional distillation. A producer of second generation biofuel must register with the IRS using Form 637. The credit is recaptured on each gallon of second generation biofuel at the original credit rate if the producer does not use the fuel for the required purposes (Code Sec. 40(d)(3)). The tax must be reported on Form 720.

1465J. Research Credit. A taxpayer may claim a credit for incremental research expenses as part of the general business credit (Code Sec. 41). The credit is calculated on Form 6765 and is generally subject to the general tax liability limitation and carryover rules (¶ 1465). An eligible small business may calculate the tax liability limitation for the research credit separately, and use it against both regular and alternative minimum tax liabilities. An eligible small business is a partnership, sole proprietorship, or corporation (without publicly traded stock) if average annual gross receipts for the three preceding tax years are less than $50 million (Code Sec. 38(c)(4) and (c)(5)). Any credit that remains unused at the end of the carryforward period is deductible in the following tax year unless the taxpayer elected to reduce the credit in order to claim a larger deduction (Code Sec. 196).

Credit Amount. Unless the taxpayer elects to use the alternative simplified credit computation (discussed below), the research credit is the sum of:

- 20 percent of the excess of qualified research expenses for the current tax year over a base period amount;

- 20 percent of the basic research payments made to a qualified organization; and

- 20 percent of the amounts paid or incurred by a taxpayer in carrying on any trade or business to an energy research consortium for qualified energy research (Code Sec. 41(a)).

Special base period adjustments are required when there is an acquisition or disposition of the major portion of a business that paid or incurred research expenses.

Base Amount. The base period amount is the product of the taxpayer's fixed-base percentage and average annual gross receipts for the four tax years preceding the credit period (Code Sec. 41(c)). The base amount may not be less than 50 percent of the qualified research expenses for the credit year. The fixed-base percentage (aggregate qualified research expenses compared to aggregate gross receipts for 1984 through 1988 tax years) may not exceed 16 percent.

Start-Up Company. A start-up company's fixed-base percentage is three percent for each of the first five tax years that it has qualified research expenses. The fixed-base percentage for the sixth through tenth tax years in which qualified research expenses are incurred is a portion of the percentage that qualified research expenses bear to gross receipts for specified preceding years. For subsequent years, the fixed-base percentage is the whole percentage that qualified research expenses bear to gross receipts for any five years selected by the taxpayer from the fifth through tenth tax years. A start-up company includes a taxpayer who has both gross receipts and qualified research expenses for the first time in a tax year that begins after 1983.

Alternative Simplified Credit. A taxpayer may elect an alternative method to calculate the research credit (Code Sec. 41(c)(4)). Under the alternative simplified credit method, the credit is equal to 14 percent of the amount of qualified research expenses that exceed 50 percent of the average qualified research expenses for the three preceding tax years. If the taxpayer has no qualified research expenses for any of those years, the credit is equal to six percent of the qualified research expenses for the current tax year. An election to use the alternative simplified credit method is effective for succeeding tax years unless revoked with the consent of the IRS.

Deduction for Research and Experimental Expenditures. For expenses paid or incurred in tax years beginning before 2022, a taxpayer's deduction for research and experimental expenditures (¶ 979) is reduced by the amount of the research credit (Code Sec. 280C(c), prior to amendment by the Tax Cuts and Jobs Act (P.L. 115-97)). Capitalized expenses must also be reduced by the amount of the research credit that exceeds the amount otherwise allowable as a deduction for such expenses. The taxpayer can make an annual irrevocable election to claim a reduced research credit and thereby avoid reducing the research expense deduction or capital expenditures. An electing taxpayer must reduce the research credit by the product of the research credit computed in the regular manner and the maximum corporate income tax rate. For expendi-

¶1465J

tures paid or incurred in tax years beginning after 2021, the amount capitalized and otherwise eligible for amortization over five-years (15-years for foreign research) is reduced by the excess (if any) of the research credit allowed for the tax year and the amount allowable as a deduction for the tax year as qualified research expenses or basic research expenses.

Qualified Research Expenses. Qualified research expenses are the same as those for the business expense deduction for research expenses (¶ 979), other than expenses for foreign research, research in the social sciences, arts or humanities, or subsidized research. Research eligible for the credit is limited to research undertaken to discover information that is technological in nature and intended to be useful in the development of a new or improved business component. The research must relate to elements of a process of experimentation for a functional purpose (i.e., it must relate to a new or improved function, performance, reliability, or quality).

Qualified research expenses cover in-house expenses for the taxpayer's own research (i.e., wages, including income from employees' exercise of stock options, for substantially engaging in or directly supervising or supporting research activities, supplies, and computer use charges) and 65 percent of amounts paid or incurred for qualified research done by a person other than an employee of the taxpayer. The percentage is increased to 75 percent of amounts paid or incurred for qualified research performed by a qualified research consortium, which is a tax-exempt organization under either Code Sec. 501(c)(3) or (c)(6) that (1) operates primarily to conduct energy research, and (2) has at least five unrelated customers, with no single person accounting for more than 50 percent of the revenues of the organization.

The IRS will accept an ACS 730 Financial Statement as the amount of the taxpayer's qualified research expenses for the tax year if the taxpayer (1) has at least $10 million in assets and (2) follows U.S. GAAP to prepare certified financial statements. This audit protection applies to original returns timely filed (including extensions) on or after September 11, 2017 (IRS News Release 2017-158; Large Business and International Directive (LB&I-04-0917-005)).

Qualified Energy Research Expenditures. The credit for expenditures to an energy research consortium applies to qualified energy research only. The percent limitation placed on outside research does not apply to energy research. Amounts paid or incurred for any energy research conducted outside of the United States, Puerto Rico, or a U.S. possession cannot be taken into account in determining the 20 percent of amounts paid or incurred by a taxpayer in carrying on any trade or business during the tax year to an energy research consortium (Code Sec. 41(f)(6)(C)).

Pass-Through Entities. An individual who owns an interest in an unincorporated trade or business, or who is a partner in a partnership, a beneficiary of an estate or trust, or an S corporation shareholder, may not claim the research credit in excess of the amount of tax attributable to his or her interest in the trade, business, or entity. Any credit in excess of the amount that can be passed through in one tax year may be carried to other tax years (Code Sec. 41(g)).

Payroll Tax Credit in Lieu of Research Credit. A qualified small business may elect to apply a portion of its research credit against the 6.2 percent payroll tax imposed on the employer's wage payments to employees (Code Sec. 41(h); Notice 2017-23). A partnership or corporation (including an S corporation) is a qualified small business during a tax year if its gross receipts are less than $5 million and the entity did not have gross receipts in any tax year preceding the five-tax-year period that ends with the tax year of the election. A taxpayer other than a partnership or a corporation is also a qualified small business during a tax year if the taxpayer's gross receipts for the election year are less than $5 million (determined under Code Sec. 448(c)) and it had no gross receipts in any tax year preceding the five-tax-year period that ends with the tax year of the election. Gross receipts include all gross receipts received by the taxpayer in carrying on all of its trades or businesses.

The taxpayer may make the election for any five tax years. The election and amount of credit to be applied toward payroll tax is made on Form 6765. The election is then completed on Form 8974 and attached to Form 941 or other applicable payroll tax return each quarter that the credit is claimed. The election deadline is on or before the due date (including extensions) of the qualified small business's income tax return or information return. The election may be revoked only with IRS consent. A transition rule allows a taxpayer that did not make the election on its timely filed return for a tax year beginning after 2015 to make the election on an amended return filed before January 1, 2018.

1465K. Low-Income Housing Credit. A taxpayer may claim a credit on a per-unit basis for low-income units in qualified low-income buildings in qualified low-income housing projects (Code Sec. 42). The credit is computed on Form 8586 and is part of the general business credit, subject to its tax liability limitation and carryover rules (¶ 1465).

A qualified low-income housing project is a housing project or residential rental property that is subject to MACRS depreciation, and meets requirements for low-income tenant occupancy, gross rent restrictions, state credit authority, and IRS certification. The project must continue to meet these requirements for 15 years, or the taxpayer may have to recapture a portion of the credit on Form 8611. Unless the housing project is financed by tax-exempt bonds subject to the volume cap (¶ 729), the taxpayer's credit is limited to the amount that a state or local housing credit agency allocates on Form 8609.

The owner of a qualified low-income housing project that is constructed, rehabilitated, or acquired may claim the credit over a 10-year period in an amount equal to the applicable credit percentage appropriate to the type of project, multiplied by the qualified basis allocable to the low-income units in each qualified low-income building. The taxpayer begins to claim the credit in the tax year the project is placed in service. However, the taxpayer can elect to start claiming the credit in the next tax year if the building is a qualified low-income building at the end of the first year of the 10-year credit period). The first-year credit is reduced to reflect any time the qualified low-income unit is unoccupied, but the reduction amount is allowed as a credit in the first year after the credit period ends. The credit cannot be claimed unless the owner of the qualified building is subject to an enforceable 30-year low-income use agreement with the housing credit agency. The credit is not limited or disallowed by the hobby loss rules (¶ 1195) (Reg. § 1.42-4).

The applicable credit rates are the appropriate percentages issued by the IRS for the month in which the building is placed in service (¶ 86), which are lower for federally subsidized projects. The taxpayer may make an irrevocable election to determine the credit percentage for a building before it is placed in service.

Rehabilitation expenditures may be treated as expenditures for a separate new building if they are (1) allocable to, or substantially benefit, low-income units, (2) incurred during any 24-month period, and (3) at least equal to the greater of 20 percent of the adjusted basis of the building or $7,000 for 2019 ($7,100 for 2020) per low-income unit (Rev. Proc. 2018-57; Rev. Proc. 2019-44).

1465L. Enhanced Oil Recovery Credit. An enhanced oil recovery credit may be claimed for up to 15 percent of the taxpayer's qualified enhanced oil recovery costs attributable to a qualified domestic project for increasing the production of crude oil or for production of Alaskan natural gas (Code Sec. 43). The credit is phased out in any tax year in which the reference price for the preceding calendar year exceeds $28 per barrel, as adjusted for inflation, by $6 or more. The reference price for the 2018 calendar year ($61.41) exceeds $28 multiplied by the inflation adjustment factor for the year (1.7008) by $6 or more (Notice 2019-36). The reference price for the 2017 calendar year ($48.05) exceeds $28 multiplied by the inflation adjustment factor for the year (1.7008) by $6 or more (Notice 2018-49). Thus, the credit is phased out for 2018 and 2019. The credit is claimed as part of the general business credit and is subject to its tax liability limitation and the carryover rules (¶ 1465). Any unused credit remaining after the carryforward period expires is deductible (Code Sec. 196).

1465M. Disabled Access Credit. An eligible small business is entitled to a nonrefundable tax credit for expenditures incurred to make a business accessible to disabled individuals (Code Sec. 44). The credit is 50 percent of the eligible access expenditures for the year that exceed $250 but do not exceed $10,250. The credit is computed on Form 8826 and is part of the general business credit, subject to its tax liability limitation and carryover rules (¶ 1465). Any unused credit remaining at the end of the carryforward period is lost. No other credit or deduction is permitted for any amount for which the disabled access credit is allowed.

Eligibility. An eligible small business is any person that, for the preceding tax year, either had gross receipts (less returns and allowances) that did not exceed $1 million, or employed no more than 30 full-time employees. Eligible access expenditures include reasonable and necessary amounts paid or incurred to enable the business to comply with the Americans with Disabilities Act of 1990.

Eligible expenditures also include expenditures: (1) to remove architectural, communication, physical, or transportation barriers that prevent a business from being accessible to or usable by disabled individuals (other than amounts for new construction); (2) to provide qualified interpreters or other effective methods of making aurally delivered materials available to hearing-impaired individuals; (3) to provide qualified readers, taped texts, and other effective methods to make visually delivered materials available to visually impaired individuals; (4) to acquire or modify equipment or devices for disabled individuals; or (5) to provide other similar services, modifications, materials, or equipment.

1465N. Renewable Electricity, Refined Coal, and Indian Coal Production Credit. A credit is available for electricity produced from qualified energy resources at a qualified facility in the United States and sold to an unrelated third party (Code Sec. 45, as amended by the Taxpayer Certainty and Disaster Tax Relief Act of 2019 (P.L. 116-94)). The credit is also allowed for certain types of refined coal produced at a domestic qualified facility and sold to an unrelated person. The credit is part of the general business credit, but the tax liability limitation is calculated separately and may be claimed against both regular and the alternative minimum tax liability (¶ 1465). The credit is calculated on Form 8835.

Credit Amounts and Phaseout. The credit for electricity produced at a qualified wind, closed-loop biomass, and geothermal energy facility is 2.5 cents per kilowatt hour for 2019, and 2.4 cents for 2018. The credit for electricity produced at a qualified open-loop biomass, small irrigation power, landfill gas, trash combustion, qualified hydroelectric, and marine and hydrokinetic energy facility is 1.2 cents per kilowatt hour for 2019 and 2018. The credit for production of refined coal is $7.173 per ton for 2019 and $7.032 for 2018 (Notice 2019-41; Notice 2018-50).

The credit is reduced in the same ratio as the excess of the reference price for the calendar year of the sale over eight cents bears to three cents, both as adjusted annually for inflation. Refined coal production is subject to a separate phase-out rule if prices exceed a specified level. The phaseout does not apply to electricity or coal produced from a qualified facility and sold during the 2019 and 2018 calendar years (Notice 2019-41; Notice 2018-50).

Credit Period. The credit for electricity produced at a qualified energy facility placed in service after August 8, 2005, may be claimed for the 10-year period beginning on the date the facility was originally placed in service. The credit period for qualified facilities placed in service on or prior to August 8, 2005, was either five or ten years depending upon the type of facility.

Qualified Energy Facilities. The following facilities are qualified energy facilities:

- wind facilities if construction begins before January 1, 2021 (the credit is reduced by 20 percent if construction begins in 2017, by 40 percent if construction begins during 2018, and by 60 percent if construction begins in 2019 or 2020);

- open-loop biomass facilities if construction begins before January 1, 2021, or certain expansions are placed in service after October 3, 2008;

- closed-loop biomass facilities modified to use closed-loop biomass to co-fire with coal, other biomass, or both originally placed in service before January 1, 2021, if construction of the modification begins before January 1, 2021;

- any other closed-loop biomass facilities if construction begins before January 1, 2021, and certain expansions of such facilities placed in service after October 3, 2008;

- geothermal facilities if construction begins before January 1, 2021;

- solar energy facilities originally placed in service after October 22, 2004, and before January 1, 2006;

- small irrigation power facilities originally placed in service after October 22, 2004, and before October 3, 2008;

• landfill gas facilities originally placed in service after October 22, 2004, if construction begins before January 1, 2021;

• trash facilities originally placed in service after October 22, 2004, if construction begins before January 1, 2021, including new units placed in service in connection with a trash facility that was placed in service on or before October 22, 2004;

• refined coal production facilities placed in service after October 22, 2004, and before January 1, 2012;

• hydropower facility efficiency improvements or additions to capacity placed in service after August 8, 2005, and before January 1, 2021;

• hydropower facilities placed in service after August 8, 2005, if construction begins before January 1, 2021; and

• marine and hydrokinetic renewable energy facility placed in service on or after October 3, 2008, if construction begins before January 1, 2021 (Code Sec. 45(d), as amended by P.L. 116-94).

Construction Starting Date. Construction on a facility is deemed to begin before the deadline if a taxpayer either begins physical work of a significant nature, or pays or incurs at least five percent of the total cost of the facility before the deadline. If a single project consists of multiple facilities, a taxpayer that pays or incurs at least three percent but less than five percent of the total cost of the project before the deadline may treat the number of individual facilities with a total aggregate cost not greater than twenty times the amount paid or incurred before the deadline as eligible for the credit (Notice 2013-29, clarified and modified by Notice 2013-60, Notice 2014-46, Notice 2015-25, Notice 2016-31, Notice 2017-4, Notice 2018-59, and Notice 2019-43).

Indian Coal Credit. A credit applies to Indian coal produced and sold during the 15-year period beginning after January 1, 2006, and before January 1, 2021 (Code Sec. 45(e)(10), as amended by P.L. 116-94; Notice 2020-9). The credit for Indian coal production is $2.466 per ton sold in 2018 and $2.525 per ton sold in 2019.

1465O. Empowerment Zone Credit. An employer located in a designated empowerment zone may claim a credit of 20-percent of the first $15,000 of annual wages paid or incurred for services performed within an empowerment zone by residents of the empowerment zone (Code Sec. 1396). Empowerment zones designations are effective through December 31, 2020 (¶ 1799B). The credit is computed on wages paid during the calendar year that ends within the employer's tax year. The credit is calculated on Form 8844 and is part of the general business credit, but the tax liability limitation is calculated separately from the general business credit limitation and may offset up to 25 percent of alternative minimum tax liability. The taxpayer's deduction for wages and salaries is reduced by the amount of the credit claimed (Code Sec. 280C).

1465P. Employee Retention Credit. An eligible employer affected by a qualified disaster occurring from January 1, 2018, through February 18, 2020, may claim a tax credit equal to 40 percent of up to $6,000 of qualified wages paid or incurred with respect to each eligible employee. The credit is claimed on Form 5884-A and is part of the general business credit, subject to its tax liability limitation and carryover rules except that the employee retention credit may not be carried back to a tax year prior to the tax year in which the credit was first available (¶ 1465). The credit may not be claimed for an employee during any period that the employer claims the work opportunity credit (¶ 1465G) with respect to the employee (Act Secs. 201 and 203 of the Taxpayer Certainty and Disaster Tax Relief Act of 2019 (P.L. 116-94)).

An employer is eligible for the 2018 through 2019 qualified disaster employee retention credit if it conducted an active trade or business in a qualified disaster zone at any time during the incident period of a qualified disaster. The trade or business must have been inoperable at any time during the period beginning on the first day of the disaster's incident period and ending on December 20, 2019, because of damages sustained by reason of the disaster.

The credit applies to qualified wages paid or incurred (1) beginning on the date the business became inoperable at the principal place of employment of the employee; and (2) ending on the earlier of the date significant operations are resumed or 150 days after the last day of the incident period. Qualified wages are those paid or incurred with respect to an eligible employee during the period when the trade or business becomes inoperable because of the qualified disaster. Wages qualify for the credit even if the employee performs no services for the employer, performs services for the employer at a different place of employment, or performs services at the principal place of employment before significant operations resume. An eligible employee is an employee whose principal place of employment with the employer immediately before the disaster was in the qualified disaster zone.

Qualified Disaster. A qualified disaster for this purpose is any major disaster declared between January 1, 2018, and February 18, 2020, by the President under section 401 of the Robert T. Stafford Disaster Relief and Emergency Assistance Act if the incident period of the disaster begins on or before December 20, 2019. The incident period is the period specified by the Federal Emergency Management Agency as the period that the disaster occurred, except it is not treated as beginning before January 1, 2018, and ending after January 19, 2020. For a list of disaster declarations and incident periods, see https://www.fema.gov/disasters/year.

The California wildfire disaster area is not considered a qualified disaster area for purposes of this credit. A separate employee retention credit applies to the California wildfire disaster of 2017, as well Hurricanes Harvey, Irma, and Maria in 2017. An eligible employer affected by the California wildfires or the hurricanes may claim a tax credit equal to 40 percent of up to $6,000 of qualified wages paid or incurred with respect to an eligible employee (Act Secs. 20101 and 20103 of the Bipartisan Budget Act of 2018 (P.L. 115-123); Act Secs. 501 and 503 of the Disaster Tax Relief and Airport and Airway Extension Act (P.L. 115-63)).

1465Q. Indian Employment Credit. An employer may claim a credit for certain wages and health insurance costs paid or incurred in a tax year beginning before January 1, 2021, for qualified employees and their spouses who are enrolled members of an Indian tribe (Code Sec. 45A, as amended by the Taxpayer Certainty and Disaster Tax Relief Act of 2019 (P.L. 116-94)). The credit is calculated on Form 8845 and is part of the general business credit, subject to its tax liability limitation and carryover rules (¶ 1465). Any unused credit at the end of the carryforward period is allowed as a deduction in the year following the expiration of the period (Code Sec. 196). The taxpayer's deduction for wages and salaries is reduced by the amount of the credit claimed (Code Sec. 280C).

The credit is equal to 20 percent of the excess of eligible employee qualified wages and health insurance costs paid or incurred during a tax year over the amount of the costs paid or incurred during 1993. The credit is available only for the first $20,000 of qualified wages and health insurance costs paid for each qualified employee. Qualified wages are wages paid or incurred by an employer for services performed by a qualified employee, excluding wages for which the work opportunity credit (¶ 1465G) is allowed. Qualified health insurance costs are costs paid or incurred by an employer for a qualified employee, except for costs paid under a salary reduction agreement.

An individual who receives more than 50 percent of wages from services performed in the trade or business of the employer is a qualified employee for any period only if: (1) the individual was an enrolled member of an Indian tribe or the spouse thereof; (2) substantially all of the employee's services performed for the employer were within an Indian reservation; and (3) the employee's principal place of abode while performing the services was on or near the reservation on which the services are performed. Employees whose wages exceed $45,000 are not eligible employees.

1465R. FICA Tip Credit (for Employer-Paid FICA Taxes on Employee Cash Tips). An employer in the food and beverage industry may claim an income tax credit for a portion of the employer's Social Security and Medicare taxes (FICA taxes) paid or incurred on employee tips (Code Sec. 45B). Employee tip income is treated as employer-provided wages for purposes of FICA taxes (Code Sec. 3121(q)). The FICA tip credit is claimed on Form 8846 and is part of the general business credit, but the tax liability limitation is calculated separately and the credit may be claimed against both regular and alternative minimum tax liability (¶ 1465).

The credit is equal to the employer's FICA obligation to an employee attributable to excess tips treated as wages for purposes of satisfying the minimum wage provisions of the Fair Labor Standards Act. The credit cannot be claimed for the employer's portion of FICA taxes on tips used to meet a federal minimum wage rate of $5.15 per hour. The credit is allowed for tips received from customers in connection with providing, delivering, or serving food or beverages for consumption, if tipping by customers is customary. The credit is available whether or not the employee reported the tips and regardless of where the services were performed. The employer may not deduct any amount considered in determining the credit to claim any other tax benefit. The employer may elect not to apply this credit.

1465S. Orphan Drug Credit. A taxpayer that invests in the development of drugs to diagnose, treat, or prevent qualified rare diseases and conditions that affect fewer than 200,000 persons in the United States can claim a tax credit (orphan drug credit) equal to 25 percent of qualified clinical testing expenses incurred or paid during the development process (50 percent of qualified expenses for tax years beginning before 2018) (Code Sec. 45C). The credit is claimed on Form 8820 and is part of the general business credit, subject to its tax liability limitation and carryover rules (¶ 1465). A taxpayer's amortization or deduction of qualified expenses is generally reduced by the amount of the credit claimed, but the taxpayer may elect a reduced credit amount after 2017 in lieu of reducing the amortization or deduction of the expenses (Code Sec. 280C(b)).

1465T. New Markets Tax Credit. The new markets tax credit may be claimed for equity investments made in low-income communities through a qualified community development entity (CDE) (Code Sec. 45D, as amended by the Taxpayer Certainty and Disaster Tax Relief Act of 2019 (P.L. 116-94)). The investment must be made within five years after the CDE receives an allocation of the national credit limitation amount for the calendar year ($3.5 billion for each calendar year through 2019; $5 billion for 2020). The credit is equal to five percent of the investment for the first three allowance dates, and six percent of the investment for the next four allowance dates. The total credit available is equal to 39 percent of the investment over seven years.

The credit is calculated on Form 8874 and is part of the general business credit, subject to its tax liability limitation and carryover rules (¶ 1465). Any unused credit at the end of the carryforward period is allowed as a deduction in the following tax year (Code Sec. 196). The credit must be recaptured with interest if: the CDE redeems the investment or ceases to be a CDE; if the investment ceases to qualify for the credit; or if a transaction violates an anti-abuse rule. The recapture is treated as an addition to tax in the termination year, and carried-over amounts must be adjusted accordingly. The credit reduces the basis of the investment in the CDE.

1465U. Small Employer Pension Plan Startup Costs Credit. An eligible small business may claim a credit for 50 percent of qualified startup costs incurred in establishing and administering a new eligible employee benefit plan for its employees (Code Sec. 45E, as amended by the Setting Every Community Up for Retirement Enhancement Act of 2019 (P.L. 116-94)). For tax years beginning before 2020, the credit is limited to $500 per for tax year. For tax years beginning after 2019, the credit is limited to the greater of $500, or the lesser of $250 for each employee eligible to participate in the plan who is not highly compensated (¶ 2114) or $5,000. The credit may be claimed for a total of three years and is computed on Form 8881. It is part of the general business credit, subject to its tax liability limitation and carryover rules (¶ 1465).

Eligibility. An eligible small business is one that had no more than 100 employees in the preceding year who received at least $5,000 of compensation from the employer. A business is not eligible if during the preceding three tax years, it established or maintained a qualified employer plan to which contributions were made, or benefits were accrued, for substantially the same employees as are in the new qualified employer plan. An eligible plan includes a new qualified defined contribution or defined benefit plan (¶ 2101), savings incentive match plans for employees (SIMPLEs) (¶ 2187), or simplified employee pension plans (SEP) (¶ 2189).

Qualified startup costs are ordinary and necessary expenses incurred to establish or administer an eligible plan or to educate employees about retirement planning. Qualified costs are not deductible to the extent that they are effectively offset by the tax credit. The credit is applied to the first $1,000 of qualified costs incurred in the first year the new plan is effective and in each of the following two years. The employer may elect to take the credit in the year immediately preceding the first year the new plan is effective or elect not to claim the credit for a tax year.

1465UA. Small Employer Automatic Enrollment Credit. For tax years beginning after 2019, an eligible employer may claim a credit of $500 per year for an automatic contribution feature included in a new or existing qualified retirement plan (Code Sec. 45T, as added by Setting Every Community Up for Retirement Enhancement Act of 2019 (P.L. 116-94)). The credit is claimed each tax year in a three-consecutive tax year period beginning with the first tax year in which the employer includes an eligible automatic contribution arrangement in a qualified employer plan sponsored by the employer. It may not be claimed for any year in the credit period that fails to include the auto-enrollment feature. The credit is part of the general business credit, subject to its tax liability limitation and carryover rules (¶ 1465).

An eligible automatic contribution arrangement is a provision in a qualified employer plan that provides that contributions (i.e., elective deferrals) are made at a specified rate unless the employee affirmatively elects not to make contributions or to make contributions at a different rate A qualified employer plan is defined as any qualified defined benefit plan, defined contribution plan (including a 401(k) plan), savings incentive match plan for employees (SIMPLE) plan, or simplified employee pension (SEP) plan.

1465V. Employer-Provided Child Care Credit. An employer may claim a tax credit for qualified expenses paid for an employer-provided child care center or services related to locating qualified child care for its employees (Code Sec. 45F). The credit is 25 percent of the qualified child care expenditures, plus 10 percent of the qualified resource and referral expenditures. The maximum credit allowed in any given year is $150,000. The credit is calculated on Form 8882 and is part of the general business credit, subject to its tax liability limitation and carryover rules (¶ 1465).

No double benefit is allowed for expenditures used to claim the employer-provided child care credit, and the credit reduces the basis of the qualified child care facility. In addition, no deduction is allowed in the year following the final year of any carryforward of an unused employer-provided child care credit. The credit is recaptured if a facility ceases to operate as a qualified child care facility or there is a change in ownership. Tax liability for the recapture year must be increased by an amount equal to the applicable percentage times the aggregate decrease in the general business credit computed as if all previously allowed employer-provided child care credits with respect to the facility had been zero. Any carryforward or carryback amounts of the credit must also be adjusted.

Qualifying Facility. A qualified child care facility must meet the requirements of all applicable state and local laws and regulations where it is located, including licensing requirements. Its principal use must be to provide child care assistance, unless it is located in the principal residence of the facility operator. Also,

- enrollment must be open to the taxpayer's employees during the tax year,
- if the facility is the taxpayer's principal trade or business, at least 30 percent of the enrollees must be dependents of the taxpayer's employees (¶ 133), and
- the use of the child care facility must not discriminate in favor of highly compensated employees (¶ 2017).

Qualifying Expenditures. Qualified child care expenditures are amounts paid or incurred: (1) to acquire, construct, rehabilitate, or expand property that is to be used as a qualified child care facility of the taxpayer; (2) for the operating costs of a qualified child care facility, including costs related to training employees, scholarship programs, and increased compensation for employees with high levels of child care training; or (3) under a contract with a qualified child care facility to provide child care services to the taxpayer's employees. Costs associated with item (1) must qualify for depreciation or amortization and must not be the taxpayer's principal residence. Expenses for child care cannot exceed the fair market value of the care. Qualified child care resources and referral expenditures are expenses paid or incurred by the taxpayer under a contract to provide child care resources and referral services to the taxpayer's employees. These expenditures cannot discriminate in favor of highly compensated employees.

1465W. Railroad Track Maintenance Credit. An income tax credit is available to small-and mid-sized railroad companies for qualified railroad track maintenance expenses paid or incurred in tax years beginning before January 1, 2023 (Code Sec. 45G, as amended by the Taxpayer Certainty and Disaster Tax Relief Act of 2019 (P.L.

116-94)). The credit cannot exceed $3,500 multiplied by the number of miles of railroad track owned or leased by the eligible taxpayer as of the close of the tax year. Eligible taxpayers are Class II and Class III railroad companies and persons who operate over their rail lines or provide related rail services. The credit is claimed on Form 8900 and is a part of the general business credit, but the tax liability limitation is calculated separately and the credit may be claimed against both regular and alternative minimum tax liability (¶ 1465). Any unused credit may not be deducted at the end of the carryforward period or if the taxpayer ceases to exist.

1465X. Biodiesel and Renewable Diesel Fuels Credit. A producer of biodiesel fuels may claim an income tax credit equal to the sum of the biodiesel mixture credit, the biodiesel credit, and the small agri-biodiesel producer credit for fuels sold or used before January 1, 2023 (Code Sec. 40A, as amended by the Taxpayer Certainty and Disaster Tax Relief Act of 2019 (P.L. 116-94)). The credit is computed on Form 8864 and is part of the general business credit, subject to its tax liability limitation and carryover rules (¶ 1465). Any unused credit at the end of the carryforward period, or if the taxpayer ceases to exist, may be claimed as a deduction (Code Sec. 196). No credit is allowed for any biodiesel produced outside the United States for use as a fuel outside the United States.

The biodiesel mixture credit is $1.00 for each gallon of biodiesel used by the taxpayer in the production of a qualified biodiesel mixture. This is a mixture of biodiesel and diesel fuel, determined without regard to any use of kerosene, that the taxpayer producing the mixture uses as a fuel or sells to any person for use as a fuel. The sale or use by the taxpayer must be in the taxpayer's trade or business. Casual off-farm production is not eligible for the credit.

For biodiesel that is not in a mixture with diesel fuel, the biodiesel credit is $1.00 for each gallon that is used by the taxpayer as a fuel in a trade or business or is sold by the taxpayer at retail to a person and placed in the fuel tank of the person's vehicle. Biodiesel fuels are monoalkyl esters of long chain fatty acids derived from plant or animal matter that meet the requirements for fuels or fuel additives imposed by the Environmental Protection Agency and which meet the requirements of the American Society of Testing and Materials D6751.

The small agri-biodiesel producer credit is 10 cents for each gallon of agri-biodiesel produced by an eligible small agri-biodiesel producer. The agri-biodiesel must be used by the producer or sold to another person for the following purposes: (1) for use in a trade or business to produce a qualified biodiesel mixture (other than casual off-farm production), (2) for use as a fuel in a trade or business, or (3) to sell to another person at retail and place in the retail buyer's fuel tank. The production of agri-biodiesel by an eligible small agri-biodiesel producer cannot exceed 15 million gallons per tax year. An eligible small agri-biodiesel producer is a person with a productive capacity for agri-biodiesel not in excess of 60 million gallons per tax year. Agri-biodiesel is biodiesel derived solely from virgin oils, including esters derived from virgin vegetable oils from corn, soybeans, sunflower seeds, cottonseeds, canola, crambe, rapeseeds, safflowers, flaxseeds, rice bran, and mustard seeds, camelina, and animal fats.

If a credit was claimed on biodiesel used in the production of a qualified biodiesel fuel mixture, a tax equal to the $1 per gallon credit rate is imposed on any person who separates the biodiesel from the mixture or does not use the mixture as a fuel. A $1 per gallon tax is imposed on any person who mixes biodiesel or uses it other than as a fuel if the biodiesel credit was claimed with respect to the retail sale of the biodiesel. A 10 cent per gallon tax is imposed on a person who does not use agri-biodiesel for which a small agri-biodiesel producer credit was claimed.

Renewable diesel (i.e, liquid fuel derived from biomass that meets specified requirements) is treated like biodiesel for purposes of the biodiesel mixture credit and biodiesel credit.

1465Z. Distilled Spirits Excise Tax Carrying Credit. An income tax credit is available for wholesalers, qualified distillers, and importers that carry distilled spirits subject to excise taxes in inventory (Code Sec. 5011). The credit is generally calculated to equal the approximate interest charges that the eligible taxpayer would incur while holding the distilled spirits in inventory. The credit is claimed on Form 8906 and is part of the general business credit, subject to its tax liability limitation and carryover rules (¶ 1465).

1465AA. Advanced Nuclear Power Facilities Production Credit. A tax credit may be claimed by a taxpayer that produces electricity from an advanced nuclear power facility (Code Sec. 45J). The credit is 1.8 cents per kilowatt hour of electricity produced at the facility and sold to an unrelated person during the tax year. It may be claimed only during the eight-year period beginning on the date the facility was originally placed in service. A qualifying advanced nuclear power facility is any facility owned by the taxpayer that uses nuclear energy to produce electricity and was placed in service after August 8, 2005, and before January 1, 2021. Any nuclear facility with a reactor design (or a substantially similar design of comparable capacity) approved before 1994 by the Nuclear Regulatory Commission is not a qualifying advanced nuclear power facility. Certain limitations restrict the amount of credit that may be claimed in any tax year. The credit is part of the general business credit, subject to its tax liability limitation and carryover rules (¶ 1465).

1465CC. Energy Efficient Home Credit. An eligible contractor who builds an energy-efficient home acquired by a person for use as a residence before January 1, 2021, can claim an income tax credit of up to $2,000 (Code Sec. 45L, as amended by the Taxpayer Certainty and Disaster Tax Relief Act of 2019 (P.L. 116-94)). An eligible contractor may include a manufacturer of energy-efficient manufactured homes. A residence is an energy-efficient home if it is located in the United States and is certified to have an annual heating and/or cooling consumption at least 50 percent less than a comparable house with at least 10 percent of the 50 percent saving coming from the building envelope. A reduced credit of $1,000 is available for homes with a heating or cooling consumption at least 30 percent less than a comparable house and for homes with the Energy Star label. The credit is claimed on Form 8908 and is part of the general business credit, subject to its tax liability limitation and carryover rules (¶ 1465).

1465GG. Mine Rescue Team Training Credit. An eligible employer may claim a tax credit for mine rescue team training expenses paid or incurred in tax years beginning before January 1, 2021 (Code Sec. 45N, as amended by the Taxpayer Certainty and Disaster Tax Relief Act of 2019 (P.L. 116-94)). The credit is equal to the lesser of: (1) 20 percent of the training program costs paid or incurred during the tax year for each qualified mine rescue team employee, including wages paid while attending the training program, or (2) $10,000. An eligible employer is any taxpayer that employs individuals as miners in underground mines located in the United States. A qualified mine rescue team employee is a full-time miner employee who is eligible for more than six months of the tax year to serve as a mine rescue team member because he or she has met certain training requirements. The credit is claimed on Form 8923 and is part of the general business credit, subject to its tax liability limitation and carryover rules (¶ 1465). The employer must reduce its compensation deduction by the amount of any mine rescue team training credit claimed (Code Sec. 280C).

1465II. Employer Credit for Differential Wage Payments to Military Personnel. An employer may claim a tax credit equal to 20 percent of a differential wage payment to a qualified employee (Code Sec. 45P). The credit is claimed on Form 8932 and is part of the general business credit, subject to its tax liability and carryover rules (¶ 1465). The credit reduces the employer's business expense deduction for wages paid to the employee (¶ 906), as well as any other credit related to compensation paid to the employee (Code Sec. 280C).

An eligible differential wage payment is a payment that: (1) an employer makes to an individual with respect to any period during which the individual is performing services in the uniformed armed forces on active duty for more than 30 days, and (2) represents all or a portion of the wages the individual would have received from the employer for performing services for the employer (Code Sec. 3401) (¶ 895 and ¶ 2609). The differential wage payment is limited to $20,000 per qualified employee paid during the tax year. A qualified employee is an individual who has been employed by the employer for 91 days immediately preceding the period for which any differential wage payments are made.

1465JJ. Carbon Oxide Sequestration Credit. A tax credit is available for the capture and transport of carbon oxide (carbon dioxide for tax years beginning before

2018) from an industrial source for use in enhanced oil recovery or for permanent storage in a geologic formation (Code Sec. 45Q). The credit is claimed on Form 8933 and is part of the general business credit, subject to its tax liability limitation and carryover rules (¶ 1465). The credit is recaptured with respect to any qualified carbon oxide or carbon dioxide that ceases to be captured, disposed of, or used as a tertiary injectant in accordance with the credit requirements.

For tax years beginning after 2017, the credit is the sum of:

- an inflation-adjusted amount per metric ton ($23.40 for 2019, $22.87 for 2018) of *carbon oxide* captured using equipment placed in service at a qualified facility before February 9, 2018, and disposed of in secure geological storage not used for tertiary injectant;

- an inflation-adjusted amount per metric ton ($11.70 for 2019, $11.44 for 2018) of *carbon oxide* captured using equipment placed in service at a qualified facility before February 9, 2018, and first used as a tertiary injectant in a qualified project before secure storage or is used in a manner that meets certain utilization requirements (Notice 2019-31; Notice 2018-40; Announcement 2018-9);

- an applicable dollar amount per metric ton of *carbon oxide* captured using carbon capture equipment placed in service at a qualified facility on or after February 9, 2018, and disposed of in a secure geological facility not used for tertiary injectant during the 12-year period beginning on the date the equipment is placed into service; and

- an applicable dollar amount per metric ton of *carbon oxide* captured using carbon capture equipment placed in service at a qualified facility on or after February 9, 2018, and used as a tertiary injectant in a qualified enhanced oil or natural gas recovery project or used in a manner that meets utilization requirements

For calendar years 2017 through 2026, the applicable dollar amount is determined by linear interpolation between $22.66 and $50 for the storage portion of the credit, and $12.83 and $35 for the tertiary injectant portion of the credit. The result is that the $22.66 and $12.83 amounts increase annually by $3.04 and $2.47 (to $28.74 and $17.76 for 2019; to $25.70 and $15.29 for 2018) until reaching $50 and $35 for 2026 (Notice 2018-93). For calendar years after 2026, the inflation adjustments return to the method used in determining the phaseout of the enhanced oil recovery credit (¶ 1465L).

For tax years beginning before 2018, the credit is: (1) an inflation-adjusted amount ($22.48 for 2017) per metric ton of qualified *carbon dioxide* that is captured by the taxpayer at a qualified facility, disposed of in secure geological storage, and not used by the taxpayer as a tertiary injectant in a qualified enhanced oil or natural gas recovery project; and (2) an inflation-adjusted amount ($11.24 for 2017) per metric ton of qualified *carbon dioxide* that is captured by the taxpayer at a qualified facility, used as a tertiary injectant in a qualified enhanced oil or natural gas recovery project, and disposed of in secure geologic storage (Notice 2017-32).

Termination. For carbon recapture equipment placed in service before February 9, 2018, the credit applies to qualified carbon dioxide before the end of the calendar year in which the IRS certifies that the credit has been claimed with respect to 75 million metric tons of qualified carbon oxide. For facilities placed in service after 2018, the credit is available only if construction of the facility begins before January 1, 2024. The IRS has provided safe harbors to establish that construction of a qualified facility or carbon capture equipment has begun for purposes of the credit (Notice 2020-12).

1465KK. Credit for Producing Oil and Gas from Marginal Wells. A taxpayer owning an interest in a qualified marginal well producing crude oil or natural gas may claim a tax credit for the amount of oil and gas produced (Code Sec. 45I). The credit is equal to $3 per barrel of qualified crude oil and 50 cents per 1000 cubic feet of qualified natural gas production. The credit begins to phase out when the reference price of crude oil exceeds $15 per barrel and $1.67 per metric cubic foot (mcf) of gas production, and is completely phased out if the reference price exceeds $18 per barrel or $2.00 per mcf, respectively (both adjusted for inflation). The credit for producing oil from marginal wells is completely phased out due to continued high oil wellhead prices and, therefore, unavailable to taxpayers. The credit amount for producing natural gas for tax years beginning in calendar year 2018 is $0.64 per mcf (Notice 2019-37). The credit is claimed on Form 8904 and is part of the general business credit, subject to its tax liability limitation and carryover rules (¶ 1465).

Tax Credit Bonds

1471. Tax Credit Bonds. A taxpayer holding a qualified tax credit bond on a credit-allowance date may claim a tax credit calculated on Form 8912 (Code Sec. 54A, prior to repeal by the Tax Cuts and Jobs Act (P.L. 115-97)). A state or local government generally may issue qualified tax credit bonds before January 1, 2018, but the taxpayer holding the bond continues to receive a tax credit after that date. A state or local government also may have issued Build America bonds before 2011 that pays interest to the bondholders and also provide a tax credit.

If the qualified bond is held by a partnership or S corporation, the allocation of the credit to the partners or shareholders is treated as a distribution. If the bond is held by a regulated investment company (RIC) or real estate investment trust (REIT), the credit is allocated and any interest treated as gross income is distributed to the shareholders or beneficiaries under IRS procedures. A RIC may elect to pass through to its shareholders credits attributable to tax credit bonds held by the entity (¶ 1485).

Credit Amount. The credit amount that accrues quarterly with respect to any allowance date is 25 percent of the annual credit amount determined on that allowance date. The allowance dates are: March 15, June 15, September 15, and December 15. The annual credit amount is determined by multiplying the bond's applicable credit rate set by the Secretary of the Treasury by the face amount on the holder's bond. The taxpayer holding a tax credit bond on a quarterly credit-allowance date is entitled to the tax credit and should receive a Form 1099-INT from the issuer if the credit amount is $10 or more.

The credit in a tax year cannot be larger than the sum of the taxpayer's regular tax liability plus alternative minimum tax liability, minus the taxpayer's other nonrefundable tax credits. Unused qualified tax credit bond amounts may be carried over to succeeding tax years.

Qualified Bonds. Qualified tax credit bonds must meet certain requirements with respect to expenditures, arbitrage, maturity limitations, and conflicts of interest. There are five types of qualified tax credit bonds:

- qualified forestry conservation bonds (Code Sec. 54B, prior to repeal by P.L. 115-97);
- new clean renewable energy bonds (Code Sec. 54C, prior to repeal by P.L. 115-97);
- qualified energy conservation bonds (Code Sec. 54D, prior to repeal by the P.L. 115-97);
- qualified zone academy bonds issued before 2017 (Code Secs. 54E and 1397E, prior to repeal by P.L. 115-97); and
- qualified school construction bonds issued before 2011 (Code Sec. 54F, prior to repeal by P.L. 115-97).

Issuers of certain tax credit bonds may elect to claim a refundable credit generally equal to the amount of interest that would be payable to the holders of the bonds (Code Sec. 6431(f), prior to repeal by P.L. 115-97).

Build America Bonds. A Build America bond issued before 2011 provides the bondholder taxable interest and a tax credit (Code Sec. 54AA, prior to repeal by P.L. 115-97). The bondholder includes the interest in gross income but is allowed a credit against federal income tax liability for a portion of the interest payments received. The credit itself is treated as interest that is includible in gross income. The tax credit is equal to 35 percent of the interest payable on the interest payment date of the bond. The interest payment date is any date on which the bondholder of record is entitled to a payment of interest under the bond.

1485. Tax Credit Bond Election of Regulated Investment Companies (RICs). A regulated investment company (RIC) (¶ 2301) may elect to pass through to its share-holders credits attributable to tax credit bonds held by the entity, replacing the required pass through of the credits (Code Sec. 853A). If the election is made, the RIC is not allowed any credits attributable to the tax credit bonds and includes in gross income, as interest, the amount of income that the entity would have included if the election did not apply, increasing the amount of the dividends paid by the same amount.

To qualify for the election, a RIC must hold directly or indirectly, one or more tax credit bonds on one or more applicable dates during the tax year and must also meet the 90 percent distribution requirements of a RIC. The corporation must also have been taxed as a RIC for all tax years ending on or after November 8, 1983, or have no accumulated earnings and profits from a tax year to which the RIC provisions did not apply.

Where the election is made, shareholders of the corporation include in income the shareholder's proportionate share of the interest income attributable to the credits and are simultaneously allowed the proportionate share of credits. The corporation must report to shareholders in a written notice the shareholder's proportionate share of credits and gross income in respect of the credits. The shareholder's proportionate share of credits and gross income in respect of the credits cannot exceed the amounts designated by the RIC in the notice.

Chapter 15

TAX ACCOUNTING

Accounting Periods

See CCH® AnswerConnect: *Accounting Periods* for more information on this topic.

1501. Tax Year. Taxable income is computed on the basis of a taxpayer's tax year (Code Sec. 441). A tax year is the annual accounting period regularly used by a taxpayer in keeping books and records to compute income. This period is usually a calendar year of 12 months ending on December 31 or a fiscal year of 12 months ending on the last day of any month other than December. A taxpayer may elect to use a 52-53 week fiscal year that always ends on the same day of the week, rather than the last day of the month (¶ 1503). A taxpayer with a short tax year must file a return for a period that is less than 12 months (short-period return) under special rules (¶ 1505).

> **Example 1:** A corporation began doing business on August 15, 2019. The end of its first tax year cannot be later than July 31, 2020, because a tax year may not cover more than a 12-month period and must end on the last day of a month, unless it is a 52-53 week tax year.

A new taxpayer may adopt either a calendar or fiscal year on its first tax return, but certain taxpayers must adopt a specific tax year (Reg. § 1.441-1). An existing taxpayer must follow IRS procedures to change a tax year (¶ 1513). If a taxpayer adopts an improper tax year, such as a fiscal year (other than a 52-53 week tax year) that does not end on the last day of a calendar month, the IRS may require the taxpayer to adopt a proper tax year or to request IRS approval to change tax years (Rev. Rul. 85-22).

> **Example 2:** Assume the same facts as in Example 1 above, except that the corporation determines there is no advantage in keeping its books on the basis of any year other than the calendar year. Therefore, it adopts the calendar year as its tax year. It should close its books as of December 31, 2019, and file its first return for the short period from August 15, 2019, through December 31, 2019. This short period is its first tax year. All of its later tax years will be full calendar years until its dissolution or until it changes to a fiscal year.

A fiscal year will be recognized only if it is established as the taxpayer's annual accounting period and only if the taxpayer keeps books and records on the same basis. A taxpayer who has no annual accounting period, does not keep adequate records, or whose present tax year does not qualify as a fiscal year must compute taxable income on a calendar-year basis (Reg. § 1.441-1).

Partnerships. A partnership generally must use the same tax year as that of its owners, unless the partnership can establish a business purpose for having a different tax year (Code Sec. 706(b); Reg. § 1.706-1). The tax year of the owners is the tax year of the partner(s) owning the majority interest in the partnership—that is, the tax year of the partner(s) owning in total more than a 50-percent interest in partnership profits and capital (¶ 416). If there is no majority interest tax year, the partnership must adopt the same tax year as that of its principal partners, each of whom must have at least a five-percent interest in partnership profits or capital. If neither condition is met, the partner-

¶1501

ship must use the tax year that produces the least aggregate deferral of income to the partners.

Corporations. An S corporation or personal service corporation (PSC) (¶ 273) must use the calendar year as its tax year unless the entity can establish a business purpose for having a different tax year (Code Secs. 441(i) and 1378(b)). An S corporation has a valid business purpose if it adopts its ownership tax year—the year used by its majority shareholders. A corporation is not considered a PSC unless more than 10 percent of its stock, by value, is held by employee-owners. If a corporation is a member of an affiliated group filing a consolidated return, all members of that group are considered in determining whether the corporation is a PSC.

Section 444 Election of Nonrequired Year. A partnership, S corporation, or PSC may make a section 444 election on Form 8716 to use a tax year other than a required tax year if the deferral period of the elected year is not longer than three months (Code Sec. 444). The section 444 election generally must be made by the earlier of: (1) the 15th day of the fifth month following the month that includes the first day of the tax year that the election is first effective, or (2) the due date, without extensions, of the return that results from the election (Code Sec. 444(d); Temp. Reg. § 1.444-3T).

The due date for certain performing certain time-sensitive actions, including filing Form 8716, otherwise due on or after April 1, 2020, and before July 15, 2020, is automatically extended to July 15, 2020, in response to the COVID-19 (coronavirus) crisis (Notice 2020-23, amplifying Notice 2020-18). The election will remain in effect until the entity changes its tax year or otherwise terminates the election. An entity that is a member of a tiered structure may not make the election unless the tiered structure consists only of partnerships and S corporations, all of which have the same tax year.

To neutralize the tax benefits resulting from using a tax year other than a required tax year, an electing partnership or S corporation must compute and make any required payments of tax exceeding $500. Required payments are the amount of tax that would otherwise be due from partners and stockholders had the entity used the required tax year (Code Sec. 7519; Temp. Reg. § 1.7519-2T). A partnership or S corporation must file a Form 8752 any required payment generally must be made by May 15 of the calendar year following the calendar year in which the section 444 election begins.

The due date for performing certain time-sensitive actions, including filing Form 8752 and making the required payment, otherwise due on or after April 1, 2020, and before July 15, 2020, is automatically extended to July 15, 2020, in response to the COVID-19 (coronavirus) crisis (Notice 2020-23; Rev. Proc. 2018-58). An electing PSC must make minimum distributions to its employee-owners by the end of a calendar year falling within the tax year to avoid certain deduction deferrals for amounts paid to employee-owners (Code Sec. 280H).

Common Trust Funds. Common trust funds maintained by a bank (¶ 2389) must adopt the calendar year as their tax year (Code Sec. 584(i)).

DISCs. A domestic international sales corporation (DISC) (¶ 2498) must have the same tax year as that of the shareholder(s) with the highest percentage of voting power (Code Sec. 441(h)).

1503. 52- or 53-Week Accounting Period. A taxpayer may elect to use a fiscal tax year (¶ 1501) that varies from 52 to 53 weeks if that period always ends on the same day of the week (Monday, Tuesday, etc.) and that day is either the last such day in a calendar month or the closest such day to the last day of a calendar month (Code Sec. 441(f); Reg. § 1.441-2).

> **Example:** A new taxpayer wishes to have its accounting period end on the last Friday in August. In 2018, its tax year ends on August 31, completing a 53-week year (August 26, 2017, through August 31, 2018). In 2019, its tax year ends on August 30, completing a 52-week year (September 1, 2018, through August 30, 2019). With this type of tax year, most of the taxpayer's tax years are 52 weeks long. As an alternative, the taxpayer could select a tax year that ends on the Friday that is nearest to the end of August. The tax year would end on the same day in 2018 and 2019, but in 2017, the tax year would have ended on September 1 (the Friday nearest the end of August).

If a pass-through entity or owner of a pass-through entity uses a 52-53-week tax year and the entity's tax year and the owner's tax year end with reference to the same calendar month, then in determining the tax year in which the owner takes into account items of income, gain, loss, deductions, or credits from the entity, the owner's tax year is deemed to end on the last day of the entity's tax year. Under this rule, a pass-through entity is a partnership, S corporation, trust, estate, closely held real estate investment trust (REIT) (¶ 2326), common trust fund (¶ 2389), controlled foreign corporation (CFC) (¶ 2487), or passive foreign investment company (PFIC) (¶ 2490) (Reg. § 1.441-2(e)).

1505. Short-Period Return. A short-period return is a tax return for a period of less than 12 months. A taxpayer may need to file a short-period return if the taxpayer changes its annual accounting period (¶ 1513) or is in existence during only part of what would otherwise be the tax year (Code Sec. 443; Reg. § 1.443-1). Taxpayers who are not in existence for a full 12-month period include:

- a corporation that begins business or goes out of business at any time other than the beginning or end of its accounting period,

- an individual who dies prior to the end of the accounting period, and

- a decedent's estate that comes into existence on the date of the decedent's death and adopts an accounting period ending less than 12 months from that date.

If the taxpayer is not in existence for a full tax year, the tax is computed as if the return had actually covered a full tax year. If a short period occurs as a result of a change in accounting period, the tax is computed on an annualized basis (¶ 1507). An alternative relief method is also available for taxpayers that change their accounting period (¶ 1509). A short-period return of a decedent and dissolving corporation, and the first return of a new corporation, is not required to be annualized.

If a change to or from a 52-53 week tax year results in a short period of 359 days or more, the tax is computed as if the return had actually covered a full tax year. If the short period is less than seven days, the short period becomes part of the following tax year. If the short period is more than six days but less than 359 days, the tax is computed under the annualized method (Code Sec. 441(f)(2)). Special annualization rules apply to taxpayers that make such a change.

1507. General Method for Annualizing Income for Short Periods. If there has been a change in an accounting period that requires filing a short-period return (¶ 1505), income for the short period must be converted to an annual basis. This conversion is generally accomplished by: (1) multiplying the taxpayer's modified taxable income for the short period by 12, and (2) dividing the result by the number of months in the short period. The tax is computed on the resulting taxable income; an individual must use the tax rate schedules to compute the tax and not the tax tables. The tax computed is divided by 12 and multiplied by the number of months in the short period (Code Sec. 443). See ¶ 1509 for an alternative method for annualizing income for short periods.

The modified taxable income for the short period is the taxpayer's gross income for the period less any allowable deductions. An individual is allowed itemized deductions (¶ 1014) (Code Sec. 63(c)(6)(C)), but not the standard deduction (¶ 131). In addition, the deduction for personal exemptions for tax years beginning before 2018 (¶ 133) is only allowed in proportion to the ratio that the number of months in the short period bears to 12. No personal exemption deduction is allowed for tax years beginning after 2017 and before 2026.

Example: Tom has been filing his returns on the basis of a fiscal year ending April 30. He changes to a year ending June 30 in 2019. He must file his return for the year ending April 30, 2019, on or before August 15, 2019. On or before October 15, 2019, he must file his return for the short period of two months beginning May 1, 2019, and ending June 30, 2019. His gross income for the short period is $9,600, and his itemized deductions total $600. He is married, age 60, and has no dependents. His wife has no income or deductions. Tom's income tax liability before credits on their joint return for the short period is computed as follows:

Gross income	$9,600
Itemized deductions*	600
Net income	9,000
Less $0 personal exemptions (no personal exemption deduction is allowed in 2019)	0
Modified taxable income for short period	9,000
Annualized taxable income—$9,000 × 12/2	54,000
Tax on $54,000..........................	$6,095
Tax for short period, 2/12 of $6,095............	$1,016

* Assume that the itemized deductions are not miscellaneous itemized deductions and that amounts are rounded to the nearest dollar.

If the taxpayer files a short-period return, the taxpayer computes self-employment tax (¶ 2664) on the actual amount of self-employment income earned for the short period and not prorated for a portion of a 12-month period (IRS Pub. 538). A net operating loss deduction (¶ 1145) is applied against actual income for the short period before annualizing (Reg. § 1.443-1(b); Rev. Proc. 2002-39, modified by Rev. Proc. 2003-34, Rev. Proc. 2003-79, and Rev. Proc. 2018-17).

A taxpayer that is changing to or from a 52-53-week fiscal tax year and that must annualize income applies the same rules as other taxpayers in determining the income for the short period. The taxpayer calculates income on an annual basis by multiplying the income for the short period by 365 and dividing the result by the number of days in the short period (Code Sec. 441(f)(2)(B)(iii)). Tax is computed on the annualized income and then is multiplied by the ratio of the number of days in the short period to 365; the resulting figure is the tax for the short year.

1509. Alternative Method for Annualizing Income for Short Periods. An alternative method is provided for annualizing income when computing tax for a short-period return (¶ 1505) (Code Sec. 443(b)(2); Reg. § 1.443-1(b)(2)). Under this method, the tax for the short period is the greater of:

- a tax on the actual taxable income for the 12-month period beginning with the start of the short period (using the law in effect for that 12-month period), multiplied by the modified taxable income (¶ 1507) for the short period and divided by the modified taxable income for the 12-month period, or

- a tax on the modified taxable income for the short period.

If a taxpayer does not exist at the end of the 12-month period described above, or if a corporate taxpayer has distributed substantially all its assets before the end of that period, the tax is computed by using a 12-month period ending with the last day of the short period. In such cases, in order to claim the benefits of the alternative method, the taxpayer must attach a return covering the 12-month period ending on the last day of the short year to the return initially filed with tax computed for the short period.

If there was a change in accounting period resulting in a short period (¶ 1513), the taxpayer must first compute the tax using the general annualization method and file the return. If the alternate method would result in lower taxes, a claim for credit or refund must be filed no later than the due date by which a return would have been required to be filed if the 12-month period beginning with the short period were considered a tax year. The application for use of the alternate method is considered as a claim for credit or refund.

1511. Prorating Taxes by Fiscal-Year Taxpayers for Rate Changes. If the tax rate changes within a tax year, a fiscal year taxpayer (¶ 1501) generally must compute the tentative tax for the entire tax year by using both the old and the new rates (i.e., blended rate) (Code Sec. 15). The final tax is the sum of: (1) the tax calculated at the old rates that is proportionate to the portion of the tax year before the effective date of the new tax, and (2) the tax calculated at the new rates that is proportionate to the portion of the tax year beginning with the effective date. If the tax rate change involves the highest rate of income tax, the taxpayer must compute the tax for the year by using a weighted average of the highest rates before and after the change determined on the basis of the respective portions of the tax year before the date of change and on or after the date of change. A corporation with a fiscal year that includes January 1, 2018, calculates federal income tax using a blended tax rate and not the flat 21-percent tax rate that generally applies to tax years beginning after December 31, 2017 (¶ 219) (Notice 2018-38).

1513. Change of Accounting Period. A change from one accounting period (¶ 1501) to another generally requires prior IRS permission and filing a return for the short period (¶ 1505). To request IRS approval to change, Form 1128 must be filed by the due date of the taxpayer's return (not including extensions) for the first effective year.

The due date for certain performing certain time-sensitive actions, including filing Form 1128 for change of accounting periods, otherwise due on or after April 1, 2020, and before July 15, 2020, is automatically extended to July 15, 2020, in response to the COVID-19 (coronavirus) crisis (Notice 2020-23, amplifying Notice 2020-18). A change in the accounting period will be approved if it is established that a substantial business purpose exists for making the change. It will generally not be approved if the sole purpose of the change is to maintain or obtain a preferential tax status (Reg. § 1.442-1(b)).

The IRS will consider all the facts and circumstances relating to the change, including the tax consequences. Among the non-tax factors is the effect of the change on the taxpayer's annual cycle of business activity. The agreement between the taxpayer and the IRS under which the change is carried out will, in appropriate cases, provide terms, conditions, and adjustments necessary to prevent a substantial distortion of income that would otherwise result from the change. For example, effects that would constitute substantial distortions of income include:

- deferring a substantial portion of the taxpayer's income or shifting a substantial portion of deductions from one year to another so as to reduce substantially the taxpayer's tax liability;

- causing a similar deferral or shift in the case of any other person, such as a partner, a beneficiary, or an S corporation shareholder; or

- creating a short period in which there is either: (i) a substantial net operating loss, capital loss or credit, including a general business credit; or (ii) a substantial amount of income to offset an expiring net operating loss, capital loss, or credit (Reg. § 1.442-1(b)(3)).

Non-Individual Taxpayers. Automatic approval procedures are provided for certain corporations that have not requested a tax year change within the most recent 48-month period ending with the last month of the requested tax year (Rev. Proc. 2006-45, modified by Rev. Proc. 2007-64 and Rev. Proc. 2018-17). Automatic approval procedures are also provided for trusts and certain partnerships, S corporations, electing S corporations, and personal service corporations that have not requested a tax year change within the most recent 48-month period ending with the last month of the requested tax year and that meet certain conditions (Rev. Proc. 2006-46). If the automatic approval procedures do not apply, the IRS has provided other procedures for taxpayers to follow in order to obtain the IRS's approval of an adoption, change, or retention of an annual accounting period through application to the IRS national office with payment of a user fee (Reg. § 1.442-1(b)(3); Rev. Proc. 2002-39, modified by Rev. Proc. 2003-34, Rev. Proc. 2003-79, and Rev. Proc. 2018-17).

Individuals. A newly married individual who is adopting the annual accounting period of his or her spouse in order to file a joint return can make the change in tax year without IRS consent (Reg. § 1.442-1(d); Rev. Proc. 2003-62). In addition, the IRS has provided procedures for an individual filing a federal income tax return on a fiscal year to obtain automatic approval to change his or her annual accounting method to a calendar year.

Improper Tax Year. As an alternative to the above procedures, any taxpayer may correct a prior adoption of an improper tax year by filing Form 1128 with an amended return on a calendar year basis (Rev. Proc. 85-15).

Accounting Methods

See CCH® AnswerConnect: *Accounting Methods and Changes in Accounting Methods* for more information on this topic.

1515. Cash or Accrual Accounting Method. Taxable income must be computed not only on the basis of a fixed accounting period (¶ 1501) but also according to the method of accounting regularly employed in keeping the taxpayer's books (Code Sec. 446; Reg. § 1.446-1(a)). A method of accounting includes the overall method of accounting for income and expenses, as well as the method of accounting for special items such as depreciation. There are two common overall methods of accounting for income: the cash basis and the accrual basis.

Cash Method. The cash method (cash receipts and disbursements) is the accounting method used by most individuals. Income is generally reported in the year that it is actually or constructively received in the form of cash, or its equivalent, or other property. Income is constructively received when it is within the taxpayer's control, but has not been actually received (¶ 1533). There is no constructive receipt, however, if there are substantial limits or restrictions on the right to receive the income. Deductions or credits are generally taken for the year in which the related expenditures are actually paid, unless they should be taken in a different period to more clearly reflect income, such as depreciation allowances and prepaid expenses (¶ 1539) (Reg. § 1.446-1(c)(1)(i)).

Accrual Method. Under the accrual method, income is accounted for when all events have occurred that fix the taxpayer's right to receive the income and the amount can be determined with reasonable accuracy (Code Sec. 451(b); Reg. § 1.446-1(c)(1)(ii)). The all-events test is not met before economic performance occurs with respect to the expense or obligation that underlies the taxpayer's liability (¶ 1540). Thus, it is not the actual receipt but the right to receive that governs.

For tax years beginning after 2017, the all-events test with respect to any item of gross income cannot be treated as met any later than when the item of gross income is taken into account in revenue in the taxpayer's applicable financial statement (AFS). This rule does not apply if the taxpayer does not have an AFS or to any item of gross income in connection with a mortgage servicing contract. In addition, an accrual-method taxpayer can elect to defer including certain advance payments in income until the tax year after the tax year in which the payments were received (¶ 1536). The IRS has provided automatic consent for a taxpayer with an AFS to change its accounting method for this purpose, as well as if the taxpayer is not adopting financial accounting standards for revenue recognition for the year of change (Rev. Proc. 2019-43).

Under proposed regulations that taxpayers may generally rely on, the income inclusion rule applies only to taxpayers that have one or more AFS covering the entire tax year (Prop. Reg. § 1.451-3). If a taxpayer uses a special method of accounting, the special method of accounting determines the timing of the income inclusion. For a contract with multiple performance obligations, the allocation of the transaction price to each performance obligation equals the amount allocated to each performance obligation for purposes of including the item in revenue in the taxpayer's applicable financial statements. For specified credit card fees, taxpayer may rely on the proposed regulations for tax years beginning after 2018. Taxpayers may use automatic consent procedures to change accounting method to implement the proposed regulations (Rev. Proc. 2019-43).

Clearly Reflect Income. A taxpayer's accounting method must clearly reflect income (¶ 1525). An approved standard method of accounting (i.e., the cash basis or the accrual basis) ordinarily is regarded as clearly reflecting income. An individual may use one accounting method to keep personal books and another to keep trade or business books. A taxpayer may use different accounting methods if the taxpayer has two or more separate businesses as long as the taxpayer maintains separate and distinct sets of records. However, the taxpayer may not use multiple accounting methods if there is a creation or shifting of profits or losses between the taxpayer's various trades or businesses (Reg. § 1.446-1). Except as otherwise required, a taxpayer may use a hybrid method combining two or more methods of accounting—such as a combination of the cash method as the overall method of accounting and the accrual method for inventories—so long as the combination clearly reflects income and is consistently used (Reg. § 1.446-1(c)(1)(iv)).

Inventories. Taxpayers that are required to use inventories (¶ 1553) generally must use the accrual method to account for purchases and sales (Reg. § 1.446-1(c)(2)). Furthermore, the following taxpayers must generally use the accrual method of accounting as their overall method of accounting for tax purposes: C corporations; partnerships that have a C corporation as a partner; charitable trusts that are subject to the tax on unrelated trade or business income (¶ 655), but only for that income; and tax shelters (Code Sec. 448(a) and (d)(6)). Qualified personal service corporations (¶ 273) are treated as individuals rather than as corporations for this purpose.

Businesses Allowed to Use Cash Method. Small businesses, farmers and ranchers (¶ 1519), and qualified personal service corporations generally are not required to use the accrual method of accounting and may use the cash method (Code Sec. 448(b)). This exception does not apply to tax shelters. A small business may use the cash method for the current tax year if its average annual gross receipts for the prior three tax years do not exceed a threshold amount ($26 million for 2019 and 2020, $25 million for 2018, and $5 million for tax years beginning before 2018) (Code Sec. 448(c); Temp. Reg. § 1.448-1T(f); Rev. Proc. 2018-57; Rev. Proc. 2019-44).

For tax years beginning before 2018, exceptions to the inventory requirement are provided for taxpayers having average annual gross receipts of $1 million or less, regardless of their trade or business, and for taxpayers with eligible trades or businesses having average annual gross receipts of $10 million or less. These businesses are therefore also exempt from the requirement to use the accrual method (Rev. Proc. 2001-10 and Rev. Proc. 2002-28, obsoleted by Rev. Proc. 2018-40). For tax years beginning after 2017, most taxpayers qualifying under these exceptions are able to use the cash method under the gross receipts test for small businesses.

1519. Accrual Accounting for Farm Corporations. Corporations and partnerships having a corporation as a partner that are engaged in the business of farming are generally required to use the accrual method of accounting (¶ 1515) (Code Sec. 447). These taxpayers are also required to capitalize their preproductive period expenses (¶ 1342). A business engaged in operating a nursery or sod farm, or the raising or harvesting of trees (other than fruit and nut trees), is not required to use an accrual method.

For tax years beginning before 2018, farming corporations that are not required to use the accrual method include any S corporation, any corporation (other than a family farming corporation) with gross annual receipts not exceeding $1 million for each prior tax year beginning after 1975, and any family farming corporation with annual gross receipts not exceeding $25 million for each prior tax year beginning after 1985. If a corporation or qualified partnership (each of the partners of which is a corporation) has for a 10-year period ending with its first tax year after 1975, and for all subsequent years, used an annual accrual method of accounting with respect to its trade or business of farming, and the entity raises crops that are harvested a year or more after planting, it may continue to use this method.

For tax years beginning after December 31, 2017, a farming C corporation or a farming partnership in which a C corporation is a partner can use the cash method of accounting (¶ 1515) if it meets the gross receipts test of Code Sec. 448(c) for a small business.

1521. Expenses of Farming Syndicates. A farming syndicate is a tax shelter and must use the accrual method of accounting (¶ 1515) (Code Secs. 448(d) and 461(i)(4)). A farming syndicate is any farming partnership or enterprise, other than a corporation that is not an S corporation, if at any time: (1) interests in the enterprise or partnership have been offered for sale in an offering required to be registered with any federal or state agency having authority to regulate such offering, or (2) more than 35 percent of the losses during any period are allocable to limited partners or limited entrepreneurs (Code Sec. 461(k)). An individual is not treated as a limited partner or limited entrepreneur if the individual:

(1) has his or her principal residence on the farm on which the farming enterprise is being carried on;

(2) has an interest attributable to active participation in management of the farming enterprise for a period of not less than five years;

(3) actively participates in the management of a farming enterprise as his or her principal business activity, regardless of whether he or she actively participates in the management of the enterprise in question; or

(4) actively participates in the management of another farming enterprise involving the raising of livestock (or is so treated under either (1) or (2)) and owns an interest in an enterprise involving the further processing of the livestock raised in the enterprise.

If an individual meets any of these conditions, any member of his or her family who owns an interest in a farming enterprise that is attributable to the individual's active participation is not treated as a limited partner or limited entrepreneur.

1525. Accounting Method Prescribed by IRS. The IRS can prescribe a method of accounting (¶ 1515) that will clearly reflect income if, in its opinion, the method used by the taxpayer fails to do so (Code Sec. 446(b)). If the IRS requires a change in accounting methods, the taxpayer must compute an income adjustment due to the change, referred to as a section 481(a) adjustment (¶ 1531).

1529. Change of Accounting Method. A taxpayer generally may not change his or her method of accounting (¶ 1515) without obtaining advance permission from the IRS (Code Sec. 446(e); Reg. § 1.446-1(e)). A change of accounting method includes a change in the overall plan of accounting as well as a change in the treatment of any material item. In most cases, a method of accounting is not established for an item unless there is a pattern of consistent treatment. A change in the treatment of a material item is one involving the timing of its inclusion in income or deduction; not the traditional accounting meaning dealing with the relationship of amounts.

IRS consent is required whether the change is made from an acceptable or an unacceptable method of accounting. If the taxpayer fails to file a request to change his or her method of accounting, the absence of IRS consent to the change will not prevent the imposition of or diminish any resulting penalties (i.e., additions to tax) (Code Sec. 446(f)). A taxpayer that changes its method of accounting for a tax year generally must make certain adjustments to its income, referred to as section 481(a) adjustments (¶ 1531).

Application to request a change in the taxpayer's accounting method is made on Form 3115 and generally must be filed with the taxpayer's timely filed (including extensions) tax return for the year of change. The due date for performing certain time-sensitive actions, including filing Form 3115 for a change in overall accounting methods, otherwise due on or after April 1, 2020, and before July 15, 2020, is automatically extended to July 15, 2020, in response to the COVID-19 (coronavirus) crisis (Notice 2020-23; Rev. Proc. 2018-58).

Changes in accounting method include, but are not limited to:

- a change from the cash to the accrual basis;

- any change in the method of valuing inventories (¶ 1571);

- a change in depreciation or amortization method (¶ 1221);

- a change from the cash or accrual basis to one of the long-term contract methods (¶ 1551), from one of the long-term contract methods to the cash or accrual basis, or from one long-term contract method to another;

- a change involving the adoption, use, or discontinuance of any other specialized method (i.e., the crop method) (¶ 1569); and

- a change where the Code and regulations specifically require that IRS consent be obtained.

The IRS will automatically approve certain changes of a taxpayer's accounting method. If the taxpayer complies with the automatic change procedures in Rev. Proc. 2015-13, automatic approval is granted for the tax year for which the taxpayer requests the change. A current list of accounting method changes to which the automatic change procedures apply, as well as specific procedures for each of the listed changes is provided in Rev. Proc. 2019-43, for changes on or after November 8, 2019, for a year of change ending on or after March 31, 2019. The list is frequently updated to add, remove, or clarify changes as needed. For changes of accounting method which are not granted automatic approval by the IRS, taxpayers must comply with the advance consent procedures in Rev. Proc. 2015-13.

For changes on or after May 9, 2018, for a year of change ending on or after September 30, 2017, the list of accounting method changes to which the automatic change procedures apply is provided in Rev. Proc. 2018-31, modified by Rev. Proc. 2018-35, Rev. Proc. 2018-40, Rev. Proc. 2018-44, Rev. Proc. 2018-49, Rev. Proc. 2018-56, Rev. Proc. 2018-60, Rev. Proc. 2019-8, Rev. Proc. 2019-10, Rev. Proc. 2019-33, and Rev. Proc. 2019-37.

1531. Adjustments Required by Changes in Method of Accounting. A taxpayer who voluntarily changes its method of accounting with the IRS's permission (¶ 1529), or who is compelled by the IRS to make a change because the method used does not clearly reflect income (¶ 1525), must make certain adjustments to income in the year of the change (Code Sec. 481(a); Reg. § 1.481-1). The adjustments are those determined to be necessary to prevent duplication or omission of items.

The adjustment period for most voluntary accounting method changes initiated by the taxpayer is one tax year (the year of change) for a net negative section 481(a) adjustment and four tax years (the year of change and next three tax years) for a net positive section 481(a) adjustment. A net positive section 481(a) adjustment is taken into account ratably over the four-year adjustment period for taxpayers that agree to the IRS conditions. A taxpayer may elect to use a one-year adjustment period (the year of change) in lieu of the four-year adjustment period otherwise provided for a positive adjustment if the net adjustment is less than $50,000. Moreover, a taxpayer may request approval of an alternative method of allocating the amount of the adjustments (Reg. § 1.481-4; Rev. Proc. 2015-13).

Any section 481(a) adjustment attributable to an S corporation's revocation of its S corporation election during the two-year period beginning on December 22, 2017, is taken into account ratably over a six-year period (¶ 307 and ¶ 329) (Code Sec. 481(d)). A terminated S corporation that is required to change to the accrual method must use the six-year adjustment period, and a terminated S corporation that would be allowed to continue to use the cash method but chooses to change to the accrual method can use the six-year adjustment period (Rev. Proc. 2018-44).

For tax years beginning after 2017, a change in accounting method resulting from the limits on the use of the cash method of accounting (¶ 1515) or the required use of the accrual method of accounting by a large farming corporation or farming partnership with a corporate partner (¶ 1519) is treated as a change initiated by the taxpayer with the consent of the IRS. For tax years beginning before 2018, the related section 481(a) adjustment is includible in income over a period generally not exceeding four years (Code Sec. 447(d) and 448(d)(7)).

Limitations on Tax. Since the adjustments for the year of change might result in the bunching of income, two statutory methods of limiting the tax in the changeover year may be applied if the adjustments for the changeover year increase taxable income by more than $3,000 (Code Sec. 481(b); Reg. § 1.481-2). If both limitations apply, the one resulting in the lower tax should be used.

Under the first method, the old method of accounting must have been used in the two preceding years; if so, the tax increase in the changeover year is limited to the tax increases that would result if the adjustments were spread ratably over that year and the two preceding years. Under the second method, the taxpayer must be able to reconstruct his or her income under the new method of accounting for one or more consecutive years immediately preceding the changeover year. The increase in the changeover year's tax because of the adjustments may not be more than the net tax increases that would result if the adjustments were allocated back to those preceding years under the new method. Any amounts that cannot be allocated back must be included in the changeover year's income for purposes of computing the limitation.

Timing of Income and Expenses

See CCH® AnswerConnect: *Accounting Methods and Changes in Accounting Methods* for more information on this topic.

1533. Constructive Receipt of Income for Cash-Basis Taxpayers. It is not always necessary that a taxpayer take possession of money or property representing income before it is considered received. Income that is constructively received is taxed to a cash-basis taxpayer (¶ 1515) as though it had been actually received (Reg. § 1.451-2(a)). There is constructive receipt if income is credited without restriction and made available to the taxpayer. There must be no substantial limitation or condition on the taxpayer's right to bring the funds within his or her control. An insubstantial forfeiture provision, a notice requirement, or the loss of bonus interest for deposits or accounts in certain financial institutions is not a substantial limitation.

Common examples of constructive receipt include matured and payable interest coupons, interest credited on savings bank deposits, and dividends unqualifiedly made subject to a stockholder's demand. However, if a dividend is declared payable on December 31 and the corporation follows a practice of paying the dividend by checks mailed so that the shareholders will not receive them until January of the following year, the dividend is not considered to be constructively received by the stockholders in December (Reg. § 1.451-2(b); *S.L. Avery*, SCt, 4 ustc ¶ 1277). See ¶ 2309 for the time of receipt by shareholders of certain dividends from regulated investment companies (RICs). Accrued interest on an unwithdrawn insurance policy dividend is gross income to the taxpayer for the first tax year that the interest may be withdrawn.

Salaries credited on corporate books are taxable to an officer in the year when the officer may withdraw the compensation at will if the corporation has funds available to pay the salaries without causing financial difficulties. Bonuses that are based on yearly sales and that are otherwise not available to an officer are taxable in the year of receipt (Rev. Rul. 72-317; Rev. Rul. 75-180).

Accrued interest on a deposit that may not be withdrawn at the close of an individual's tax year because of an institution's actual or threatened bankruptcy or insolvency is not includible in the depositor's income until the year in which that interest is withdrawable (Code Sec. 451(i)).

Constructive receipt does not give rise to constructive payment. For example, a negotiable note of a responsible and solvent maker received in payment of salary, interest, rent, etc., must be reported as income by a cash-basis recipient to the extent of its fair market value when received. It does not mean that the cash-basis maker may also deduct the same amount at that time (*Unico Sales & Marketing, Inc.*, Dec. 53,468(M), 78 TCM 150). Delivery of a note is not a payment on the cash basis, and the deduction may be taken only in the year when the note is paid. Giving collateral to secure the note does not change the promise to pay into an actual payment (*Price*, SCt, 40-1 ustc ¶ 9336).

1536. Accounting for Advance Payments and Other Prepaid Income (After 2017). For tax years beginning after 2017, an accrual-method taxpayer who receives an advance payment or other prepaid income during the tax year must either include the payment in gross income for the tax year of receipt or make an election to defer the inclusion of the payment in gross income with respect to the category of advance payments to which it belongs (Code Sec. 451(c)). Under the deferral election, any portion of the advance payment that is required to be included in gross income in the taxpayer's applicable financial statement (¶ 1515) is included in gross income in the tax year actually or constructively received and any remaining portion is included in gross income in the following tax year. See ¶ 1537 for the rules on advance payments for tax years beginning before 2018.

An advance payment for this purpose is any payment if:

- the full inclusion in the taxpayer's gross income for the tax year of receipt is a permissible method of accounting,

- any portion is included in revenue by the taxpayer in a 10-K, Annual Statement to Shareholders, or audited financial statement that is used for credit purposes or other reporting for a later tax year, and

- it is for goods, services, or other items identified by the IRS.

An advance payment does not include rent, insurance premiums, payments with respect to financial instruments, payments with respect to warranty or guarantee contracts, payments of U.S. source income to a nonresident alien or foreign corporation subject to withholding, payments for property transferred in connection with the performance of services, and any other payment identified by the IRS. If advance payments are received for a combination of services, goods, or other specified items, the taxpayer must allocate the transaction price according to the allocation made in the taxpayer's applicable financial statement.

The deferral election for advance payments will not apply to advance payments received by a taxpayer during a tax year if the taxpayer ceases to exist during or with the close of such tax year.

The computation of taxable income under the deferral election is treated as a method of accounting and any qualified change of accounting method for the taxpayer's first tax year beginning after 2017 is treated as initiated by the taxpayer and made with the IRS's consent (Act Sec. 13221(d) of the Tax Cuts and Jobs Act (P.L. 115-97)). The IRS has provided automatic consent for taxpayers changing to a method permitted under Rev. Proc. 2004-34 (Notice 2018-35; Rev. Proc. 2018-31; Rev. Proc. 2019-43).

The IRS has released proposed regulations on the deferral of advance payments under the post-2017 rules (Prop. Reg. § 1.451-8). A taxpayer may rely on these proposed regulations for tax years beginning after December 31, 2017, provided that the taxpayer: (1) applies all the applicable rules contained in these proposed regulations, and (2) consistently applies these proposed regulations to all advance payments. The proposed regulations include provisions similar to those of Rev. Proc. 2004-34 for advance payments for goods and services in pre-2018 tax years (¶ 1537). Taxpayers receiving advance payments can rely on the proposed regulations or on guidance in Rev. Proc. 2004-34 (Notice 2018-35). A taxpayer may use automatic consent procedures to change accounting method to implement the proposed regulations (Rev. Proc. 2019-43).

1537. Accounting for Advance Payments and Other Prepaid Income (Before 2018). For tax years beginning before 2018, payments received in advance of future services or transfers of property are generally income to an accrual-basis or cash-basis taxpayer (¶ 1515) in the year of receipt, provided that there is no restriction on the use of the payments. This is true even though the prepayments are returnable on the happening of some specified event, but a distinction is made for prepayments that may be refunded for services or goods and deposits over which the taxpayer does not have complete dominion and control on receipt (*Indianapolis Power & Light Co.*, SCt, 90-1 USTC ¶ 50,007). For example, a utility company was not required to include deposits from uncreditworthy customers in income on receipt because it was required to return the deposit on request by a customer who established creditworthiness. See ¶ 1536 for the rules on advance payments for tax years beginning after 2017.

Prepaid Merchandise. Inclusion in the year of receipt is required for advance payments received on the sale of merchandise. However, under certain circumstances the IRS permits accrual-basis sellers to include certain advance payments in income in the tax year in which those payments are properly accruable under the method of accounting used for tax purposes if they are reported at that time or later for financial reporting purposes (Reg. § 1.451-5). If the method used for financial reporting results in an earlier accrual, then the advance payments are taxed according to the financial reporting method. If a long-term contract method of accounting (¶ 1551) is used, advances are included in income under that method without regard to how the income from these payments is accounted for in the seller's financial reports.

An advance payment for this purpose is any amount received by an accrual-basis taxpayer under an agreement:

¶1537

15

ACCOUNTING

- for the sale or other disposition in a future tax year of goods held by the taxpayer primarily for sale to customers in the ordinary course of its trade or business, or

- for the building, installation, construction, or manufacture of items by the taxpayer where the agreement is not completed within that tax year.

An exception exists where substantial advance payments for inventoriable goods have been received and goods are on hand or available to satisfy the agreement in the year of receipt. Payments for gift certificates are substantial when received, but in other cases, advance payments are not substantial until they exceed the cost of goods to be sold. In such cases, all advance payments received by the last day of the second tax year following the year in which the substantial advance payments are received and not previously included in income under the taxpayer's method of accounting must be included in income in the second tax year (Reg. § 1.451-5(c)).

Certain manufacturers, wholesalers, and retailers that receive advance payments for multi-year service warranty contracts may elect to recognize income from the payments as a series of equal payments over the life of the contracts. The election is permitted only if an eligible taxpayer purchases insurance to cover its obligations under a service warranty contract within 60 days after the sale of the contract (Rev. Proc. 97-38).

Prepaid Services and Mixed Prepayments. Taxpayers who receive advance payments for services and advance payments for the transfer of both goods and services are allowed a limited deferral beyond the tax year of receipt for certain advance payments (Rev. Proc. 2004-34, modified by Rev. Proc. 2011-18, modified by Rev. Proc. 2013-29). Excludable payments generally include: the payment for services; the sale of goods other than those for which the taxpayer uses a method of deferral allowed for advance payments of goods discussed previously; the use of intellectual property, including license or lease; the use of property ancillary to the provision of services (e.g., hotel rooms, booths at trade shows, campsites, and banquet facilities); the sale, lease, or license of computer software; guaranty or warranty contracts ancillary to any of the above; subscriptions; memberships in an organization; an eligible gift card sale; or any combination of the above. An eligible gift card sale is a sale in which the taxpayer is primarily liable to the customer and the gift card is redeemable by the taxpayer or an entity legally obligated to the taxpayer.

An advance payment does not include: rent, other than that paid for the use of intellectual property, computer software, and property ancillary to the provision of services; insurance premiums to the extent governed by the taxation of insurance companies; payments with respect to financial instruments, such as debt instruments, deposits, letters of credit, notional principal contracts, options, forward contracts, futures contracts, foreign currency contracts, credit card agreements, and financial derivatives; payments with respect to service warranty contracts; payments with respect to warranty and guaranty contracts under which a third party is the primary obligor; certain payments with respect to nonresident aliens and foreign corporations; and payments in property transferred in connection with the performance of services to which the restricted property rules of Code Sec. 83 apply (¶ 713).

Qualifying taxpayers generally may defer including advance payments in gross income to the next succeeding tax year for federal income tax purposes to the extent the advance payments are not recognized in revenues for financial statement purposes or, in certain cases, are not earned in the tax year of receipt. Except in the case of certain short tax years, the IRS does not permit deferral to a tax year later than the next succeeding tax year. These rules neither restrict a taxpayer's ability to use the methods of deferral for the advance payment of merchandise discussed above, nor limit the period of deferral available.

Certain accrual-basis membership organizations and publishers can defer prepaid dues and subscription income (Code Secs. 455 and 456).

Accrued Income. In certain situations, cash-basis taxpayers may be required to report income that has not yet been received, and accrual-basis taxpayers may compute income in a manner that differs from general accrual principles. For example, both accrual-basis and cash-basis taxpayers may be required to use present value concepts to compute and report income arising out of a section 467 rental agreement (¶ 1541), original issue discount (OID) from any debt obligation held by the taxpayer (¶ 1952), and amounts arising from debt instruments issued for property (¶ 1868 and ¶ 1954). In addition, an accrual-method publisher of magazines, paperbacks, or records may elect to exclude from gross income the income attributable to the qualified sale of magazines, paperbacks, or records that are returned before the close of the merchandise return period (Code Sec. 458).

1538. Accruing Income Doubtful of Collection. If a taxpayer is on the accrual basis of accounting (¶ 1515), income such as interest is taxable as it accrues even though it is received at a later date. However, if there is a real doubt that the interest is collectible when it becomes due, it need not be accrued (*The Corn Exchange Bank*, CA-2, 2 USTC ¶ 455). On the other hand, where the uncollectible item arises from a sale of property, the proper procedure is to report the sale and then take a bad debt deduction as appropriate (¶ 1135 and ¶ 1143).

An accrual-basis taxpayer that elects to use the nonaccrual-experience (NAE) accounting method is generally not required to accrue as income any amount to be received for the performance of services that, based on experience, will not be collected (Code Sec. 448(d)(5); Reg. § 1.448-2(a)). The NAE method is limited to amounts to be received for the performance of qualified services (health, law, engineering, architecture, accounting, actuarial science, performing arts, or consulting) and for services provided by certain small businesses.

1539. Prepaid Expenses of Cash-Basis Taxpayers. A taxpayer using the cash method of accounting (¶ 1515) may deduct certain prepaid *expenses* in the year paid under certain conditions (Code Sec. 461; Reg. § 1.461-1). A distinction is made between expenditures that are more in the nature of expenses and those that are capital in nature. If the payment creates an asset having a useful life extending substantially beyond the end of the tax year in which the payment is made, the expenditure may not be deductible, or may be deductible only in part, in that year. If payment is made for a capital asset or is capital in nature, a deferment and charge-off for depreciation, amortization, or other comparable allowance is proper (¶ 1201).

A taxpayer is generally not required to capitalize amounts paid for a right or benefit such as rent or insurance that does not extend beyond the earlier of: (1) 12 months after the first date on which the taxpayer realizes the right or benefit, or (2) the end of the tax year following the tax year in which the payment is made (Reg. § 1.263(a)-4(f)(1)). Special rules apply to certain rental agreements (¶ 1541). See ¶ 1055 for the allowance of deductions for prepaid interest payments.

> **Example:** Mathis is a calendar-year taxpayer who uses the cash basis of accounting. He signs a three-year business property lease on December 1 of the tax year and agrees to pay $18,000 up front, plus a monthly rental of $1,000 for 36 months. He can deduct only $1,500 for the tax year ($1,000 rent plus 1/36 of $18,000). The $18,000 is an amount paid for securing the lease and must be amortized over the lease term.

A cash-basis farmer and rancher can deduct prepaid feed costs in the year of payment if the advance feed expenditure is a payment and not a deposit, the payment is for a business purpose, and the deduction does not cause a material distortion of income. No deduction is generally allowed to a cash-basis farmer in the year of prepayment for advance payments for feed, seed, fertilizer, or other supplies to the extent those prepayments exceed 50 percent of total deductible farming expenses, excluding prepaid supplies (Code Sec. 464). See ¶ 1521 for rules applicable to farming syndicates. The limitation does not apply to a farm-related taxpayer if:

- the aggregate prepaid farm supplies for the preceding three tax years are less than 50 percent of the aggregate deductible farming expenses, other than prepaid farm supplies, for that period, or

- the taxpayer has excess prepaid farm supplies for the tax year by reason of any change in business operation directly attributable to extraordinary circumstances.

A farm-related taxpayer is one whose principal residence is on a farm, who has a principal occupation of farming, or who is a family member of such a taxpayer. The family of an individual includes brothers and sisters, whether by whole or half blood, spouse, ancestors, and lineal descendants (Code Sec. 461(k)(2)(E)). It may also include a corporation that is engaged full-time in farming activities.

Estimated state income taxes paid in advance are deductible by a cash-basis taxpayer in the year paid (Rev. Rul. 56-124).

1540. Expenses of Accrual-Basis Taxpayers. Under the all-events test, an accrual-basis taxpayer (¶ 1515) generally deducts the face amount of an accrued expense in the tax year in which:

- all of the events have occurred that determine the fact of liability, and

- the amount of the liability can be determined with reasonable accuracy (Code Sec. 461(h)).

The all-events test is not treated as met before economic performance occurs with respect to the particular item of expense or obligation that underlies the taxpayer's liability. For a liability of a taxpayer that requires a payment for property or services, economic performance is deemed to occur as the property or services are provided to the taxpayer. If the liability arises out of the taxpayer's use of property, economic performance occurs as the taxpayer uses the property (Reg. § 1.461-4(d)).

Example 1: Abe Corp., a calendar-year, accrual-method taxpayer, contractually obligates itself in October 2019 to pay $10,000 for research and development to be performed in 2020. No amount is deductible before performance is rendered in 2020.

A taxpayer is permitted to accrue payments before services are rendered or property is received if the taxpayer can reasonably expect the services or property to be provided within 3½ months after payment.

Example 2: Hal Corp., a calendar-year, accrual-method taxpayer, makes payment on December 1, 2019, for goods it expects to receive by March 12, 2020. It may deduct the payment or otherwise take it into account for its 2019 tax year.

If the taxpayer's liability requires the taxpayer to provide services or property, then economic performance occurs as the taxpayer incurs costs. However, economic performance with respect to the drilling of an oil or gas well is considered to have occurred within a tax year if drilling commences within 90 days after the close of the tax year.

Example 3: Zop Corp., a calendar-year, accrual-method taxpayer, sells lawn mowers under a three-year warranty that obligates it to make reasonable repairs to each mower it sells. In 2019, Zop repairs 12 mowers sold in 2018 at a cost of $2,500. Economic performance with respect to Zop's liability to perform services under the warranty occurs as Zop incurs costs in connection with the liability. The $2,500 expense incurred by Zop is a deduction for the 2019 tax year.

Certain manufacturers, wholesalers, and retailers that make advance payments to purchase insurance policies that cover their obligations under multi-year service warranty contracts must capitalize the cost of the policies and deduct that cost ratably over the life of the policies. This rule applies regardless of whether the taxpayer uses the cash or accrual method of accounting (Rev. Proc. 97-38).

Economic performance generally occurs only when payment is made to the person to whom the liability is owed. Payment is considered to be economic performance for the following:

- liabilities to another person arising out of any workers' compensation, tort, or breach of contract claims against the taxpayer or any violation of law by the taxpayer;

- rebates and refunds;

- awards, prizes, and jackpots;

- insurance, warranty, and service contracts; and

- taxes other than creditable foreign taxes (Reg. § 1.461-4(g)).

Under certain limited circumstances, an irrevocable payment to a court-ordered settlement fund that completely extinguishes specified tort liabilities will also constitute economic performance (Code Sec. 468B).

Recurring Items. Certain recurring items are treated as incurred in advance of economic performance by a taxpayer other than a tax shelter. Under this exception, an item is treated as incurred during a tax year if:

- the all-events test, without regard to economic performance, is satisfied during that year;

- the economic performance test is met within the shorter of 8½ months or a reasonable time after the close of the year;

- the item is recurring in nature and the taxpayer consistently treats similar items as incurred in the tax year in which the all-events test is met; and

- either the item is not material or accrual of the item in the year that the all-events test is met results in a better matching against the income to which it relates than accrual of the item in the tax year of economic performance (Code Sec. 461(h)(3); Reg. § 1.461-5).

In determining whether an item is material or whether a more proper matching against income results from deduction of an expense prior to economic performance, the treatment of the expense on financial statements is to be taken into account but will not necessarily govern the tax treatment of the expense.

An item is recurring if it can generally be expected to be incurred from one tax year to the next (Reg. § 1.461-5(b)(3)). However, a taxpayer may treat a liability as recurring even if it is not actually incurred in each tax year. Also, a liability that has never previously been incurred may be treated as recurring if it is reasonable to expect that it will be incurred on a recurring basis in the future.

A taxpayer may adopt the recurring item exception as part of its method of accounting for any type of expense for the first tax year in which that type of expense is incurred. Any change to or from the recurring item exception is generally treated as a change in the taxpayer's method of accounting (¶ 1529) (Reg. § 1.461-5(d)). A tax shelter is generally prohibited from using the recurring item exception (Code Sec. 461(i)).

Ratable Service Contract Safe Harbor. A taxpayer can use a safe harbor accounting method for a ratable service contract, such as a janitorial service contract, with a term of 12 months or less. Under this method, the taxpayer treats economic performance as occurring on a ratable basis over the term of the service contract (Rev. Proc. 2015-39).

1540A. Accruing Uncertain and Contingent Liabilities. Under the accrual-basis of accounting (¶ 1515), expenses are deductible in the tax year when all events have occurred that fix the amount of the item and determine the liability of the taxpayer to pay it (¶ 1540). Thus, there can be no accrual of an expense until any contingency is resolved and the liability becomes fixed and certain (Reg. § 1.461-1). Similarly, an accrual-method taxpayer generally cannot accrue a liability that the taxpayer is contesting, as the liability is not fixed and certain. However, if the taxpayer is contesting an asserted liability and transfers money or property to provide for the satisfaction of the liability, the taxpayer can take a deduction in the year of the transfer if the contest continues to exist after the transfer and the liability would otherwise be allowed as a deduction in the year of transfer or an earlier tax year (Code Sec. 461(f)). See ¶ 1547 for reserves of contingent or estimated expenses.

1540B. Accruing Interest and Expenses Owed to Related Taxpayers. If related taxpayers use different methods of accounting (¶ 1515), accrued interest and expenses owed to a related taxpayer may not be deducted until the interest or expense payment is includible in the gross income of the cash-basis payee (Code Sec. 267(a)(2)). Thus, an accrual-basis payor is placed on the cash basis for the purpose of deducting business expenses and interest owed to a related cash-basis taxpayer. The deduction is deferred until the cash-basis payee takes the item into income.

A related person for this purpose includes persons described in Code Sec. 267(b) (¶ 1717), as well as a personal service corporation (PSC) and any of its employee-owners

(¶ 273). Thus, a PSC may not deduct payments made to owner-employees before the tax year in which such persons must include the payment in gross income. A special pass-through entity rule treats a partnership or S corporation as related to a taxpayer who owns any capital or profits interest in the partnership or stock of the S corporation and persons related to that taxpayer (Code Sec. 267(e)).

1541. Deferred Payments Under Certain Rental Agreements. A lessor and lessee of certain leaseback and long-term rental agreements that involve the use of property must report income and expenses arising out of those agreements by applying statutory accrual-basis and present-value principles (Code Sec. 467; Reg. § 1.467-1). This treatment, in effect, is an extension of the principles governing the taxation of original issue discount (OID) (¶ 1952). Although the Code Sec. 467 rules apply to the use of property, the IRS is authorized to extend similar rules to agreements for services.

Section 467 rental agreements cover tangible property with respect to which either: (1) at least one payment allocable to the use of property in the calendar year is to be paid after the close of the following calendar year (deferred payments); or (2) there are increases in the amount to be paid as rent under the agreement (stepped rents). A section 467 rental agreement does not encompass a rental agreement in which the sum of the amounts to be paid is $250,000 or less.

Regardless of the accounting method used (¶ 1515), the lessor or lessee of any section 467 rental agreement must report for any tax year the sum of the accrued rental payments, and any interest for the year (calculated at the rate of 110 percent of the applicable federal rate compounded semiannually (¶ 83) on unpaid rents (i.e., amounts that were attributed to a prior tax year but are still unpaid as of the current tax year).

The accrued rental payments—except in tax-avoidance transactions and agreements that do not allocate rents—are calculated by allocating rents in accordance with the agreement, and including the present value of rents allocable to the period but paid after the close of the period. In tax-avoidance transactions and agreements that do not allocate rents, the rent that accrues during the tax year is equal to the allocable portion of the constant rental amount. This is the amount that, if paid as of the close of each lease period, would result in an aggregate present value equal to the present value of the aggregate payments required under the lease.

1543. Claim-of-Right Doctrine. Under the claim-of-right doctrine, payments must be included in gross income if the taxpayer receives them without restriction under a claim of right. This is true even though the taxpayer may discover in a later year that he or she had no right to the payments in the earlier year and is required to repay the same amount (*E.R. Lewis*, SCt, 51-1 USTC ¶ 9211). The taxpayer may deduct the repayments in the year in which they are made.

The deduction does not compensate the taxpayer adequately for the tax paid in the earlier year if the repayments exceed income for the year of repayment or the income (after subtraction of those repayments) is taxed at a lower tax rate than the income in the year of inclusion was taxed. The law eliminates this inequity if the amount repaid exceeds $3,000. In that case, the taxpayer is required to reduce his or her tax for the year of repayment by the amount of tax for the previous year that was attributable to inclusion of this amount. Any excess may be claimed as a refund. If a smaller tax liability results from simply deducting the repaid amount in the year of repayment, the taxpayer should claim the deduction instead (Code Sec. 1341; Reg. § 1.1341-1).

In either case, the adjustment is made for the year of repayment. The return for the prior year—the year in which the item was received—is not reopened; in no case will there be an allowance for interest on the tax paid for the earlier year.

Example: In 2018, Castro is unmarried and reports taxable income of $53,000 (adjusted gross income of $65,000 minus the $12,000 standard deduction), consisting entirely of sales commissions, on which he paid a tax of $7,605. In 2019, it is determined that the commissions were erroneously computed for 2018, and Castro pays back $6,000 of the commissions. His taxable income for 2019, without regard to the $6,000 repayment, is $15,000. The tax for 2019 will be computed as follows:

(1) Tax on $9,000 ($15,000 less $6,000)		$903
(2) Tax on $15,000		$1,609
Less: Difference between—		
Tax paid for 2018 on $53,000	7,605	
Tax payable in 2018 on $47,000		
($53,000 – $6,000)	6,285	1,320
		289

The tax for 2019 is the lesser of the amount computed under (1) or (2). In this case, the amount computed under (2) is less than the amount computed under (1). Thus, the tax for 2019 is $289, the amount computed under (2).

If the tax for the year of restoration under a claim of right is reduced by the amount of the tax already paid on the item in a previous year, the amount restored is not considered for any purpose. For example, a taxpayer cannot use that amount in computing a net operating loss for the year of restoration (Reg. § 1.1341-1(b)(2)). The reduction of tax in the year of repayment does not apply where the taxpayer did, in fact, have an unrestricted right to receive the amount in the prior year and the obligation to repay arose as the result of subsequent events.

1545. Dealer's Reserve for Income. A dealer who discounts customers' installment paper with financial institutions that withhold a small percentage of the price and credit it to a reserve account as security for the dealer's guaranty of payment of the installment paper must accrue those credits as income in the year when the installment paper is transferred to the financial institution (*J.R. Hansen*, SCt, 59-2 ustc ¶ 9533). This rule has been applied to an accrual-basis home seller who guaranteed a buyer's loan by requiring the home seller to accrue as income in the year of sale the proceeds pledged as loan security to the lender. For a cash-basis dealer, the pledged amounts are taxable to the dealer only as they become available for withdrawal (i.e., where the pledged amount was in a restricted savings account and could be withdrawn in specified amounts only as the buyer reduced the loan principal by certain amounts).

1547. Accrual of Reserves for Estimated Expenses. Although reserves for contingent liabilities are often set up in business practice, amounts credited to reserves are generally not deductible for income tax purposes because the fact of liability is not fixed (*Portland Copper & Tank Works, Inc.*, CA-1, 65-2 ustc ¶ 9687). For example, advance deductions have been denied for additions to a reserve for expected cash discounts on outstanding receivables, amounts credited by a manufacturer to a reserve for possible future warranty service, and additions to a reserve covering estimated liability of a carrier for tort claims. However, to the extent that the Code specifically provides for a deduction for a reserve for estimated expenses, the economic performance rules (¶ 1540) do not apply (Code Sec. 461(h)(5)).

1549. Accrual of Vacation and Sick Leave Pay. The deduction by an employer for vacation and sick leave pay is generally limited to the amount of pay earned during the year to the extent: (1) the amount is paid to employees during the year, or (2) the amount is vested as of the last day of the tax year and is paid to employees within 2½ months after the end of the year. If the vacation or sick leave pay is not paid until after the expiration of that period, the employer may deduct vacation pay when paid and sick leave pay in its tax year that includes the last day of the employee's tax year for which the employee reports the payment as income (Code Sec. 404(a)(5); Temp. Reg. § 1.404(b)-1T). Vacation and sick leave pay incurred with respect to the production of real and tangible personal property, or with respect to property acquired for resale, is considered a direct labor cost that must be capitalized by a taxpayer subject to the uniform capitalization rules (¶ 1332) (Reg. § 1.263A-1(e)(2)(i)(B)).

Regardless of whether or not vested vacation pay is considered deferred compensation, FICA and FUTA taxes may be deducted by an accrual-basis taxpayer prior to the tax year that the FICA and FUTA taxes are actually paid if:

• all events have occurred to establish the fact of the taxpayer's liability for the FICA and FUTA taxes,

• the amount of the payroll tax liability can be determined with reasonable accuracy, and

• the taxpayer properly adopts the recurring item exception (¶ 1540) as a method of accounting with respect to the payroll taxes (Rev. Rul. 2007-12).

Long-Term Contracts

See CCH® AnswerConnect: *Long-Term Contracts* for more information on this topic.

1551. Long-Term Contract Method of Accounting. Taxable income from a long-term contract generally must be accounted for under the percentage-of-completion method of accounting (Code Sec. 460). However, a taxpayer who has entered into a small construction contract or home construction contract may use an exempt contract method of accounting (¶ 1552).

A long-term contract is a building, installation, construction, or manufacturing contract that is not completed within the tax year in which it is entered into. A manufacturing contract is not considered long term unless the contract involves the manufacture of: (1) unique items not normally carried in the finished goods inventory, or (2) items normally requiring more than 12 calendar months to complete, regardless of the duration of the actual contract.

Percentage-of-Completion Method. Under the percentage-of-completion method, gross income is reported annually according to the percentage of the contract completed in that year. The completion percentage is determined by comparing costs allocated and incurred before the end of the tax year to the estimated total contract costs (cost-to-cost method or simplified cost-to-cost method). Thus, for a particular tax year, the business includes a portion of the total contract price in gross income as it incurs allocable contract costs for the year. Any contract income that has not been included in the taxpayer's gross income by the end of the tax year in which the contract is completed is included in gross income for the following tax year (Code Sec. 460(b); Reg. § 1.460-4(b)).

Modified Percentage-of-Completion Method (10-Percent Method). A taxpayer may elect to defer the recognition of income and accounting for costs until the first tax year in which at least 10 percent of the estimated total costs of the contract have been incurred (Code Sec. 460(b)(5)).

Look-Back Rule. To the extent that the percentage-of-completion method applies to a long-term contract, a business that errs in its estimate of the contract price or costs must look back and recompute its tax liability on the basis of the actual contract price and costs for the years for which that method was used. The business will either pay or receive interest at the rate for overpayment of tax (¶ 2765), compounded daily and figured on Form 8697, on the amount that the recomputed tax liability for a year exceeds or is less than the previously reported tax liability (Code Sec. 460(b); Reg. § 1.460-6).

Only one rate of interest will apply for each accrual period—the period that begins on the date after the original return due date for the tax year and ends on the original return due date for the following tax year. The applicable overpayment rate of interest is the overpayment rate in effect for the calendar quarter in which the accrual period begins. The look-back method does not have to be applied in computing taxable income with respect to home construction contracts and long-term construction contracts of small businesses and small long-term contracts. A taxpayer can also elect not to apply the look-back method if the differences between estimated and actual amounts are *de minimis*.

A pass-through entity such as a partnership, S corporation, and trust that is not closely held must use a simplified look-back method if substantially all of the income under a long-term contract is from sources in the United States (Code Sec. 460(b)(4)). An entity is a closely held entity if five or fewer persons own 50 percent or more of the value of its beneficial interests. The amount of taxes deemed overpaid or underpaid under a contract in any year is determined at the entity level and is the product of the amount of contract income overreported or underreported for the year times the top marginal tax rate applicable for the year (i.e., the top corporate tax rate, or the top individual tax rate if more than 50 percent of the beneficial interests in the entity are held by individuals).

Allocation and Capitalization of Costs. A taxpayer generally must allocate costs to long-term contracts accounted for under the percentage-of-completion method in the same manner as direct and indirect costs are capitalized to property produced by a taxpayer under the uniform capitalization rules (Code Sec. 460(c); Reg. § 1.460-5). Thus, the taxpayer must allocate to each long-term contract all direct costs and certain indirect costs properly allocable to the long-term contract. While bonus depreciation (¶ 1237) is generally taken into account when allocating contract costs, solely for purposes of determining the percentage of completion, the cost of qualified property is taken into account as if the bonus depreciation rules had not been enacted. This rule generally applies to property with a recovery period of seven years or less that is placed in service before 2027 (2028 for certain long-production property).

Under the general cost allocation method, research and experimental expenses, other than independent research and development expenses, must be allocated to the contract. Independent research and development expenses, expenses incurred in making unsuccessful bids and proposals, and marketing, selling, and advertising costs may be expensed. Production period interest generally must be allocated to the contract (¶ 1561). Contributions to a pension or annuity plan, whether related to current or past services, are subject to the long-term contract rules and are treated as costs allocable to a long-term contract.

A taxpayer can elect to use a simplified cost-to-cost method of allocation if all the taxpayer's contracts are accounted for under the percentage-of-completion method and the 10-percent method is not used (Reg. § 1.460-5(c)). Small construction and home construction contracts accounted for under an exempt contract method are not subject to the general cost allocation rules (¶ 1552). Special rules are also provided for allocating costs to cost-plus long-term contracts and to federal long-term contracts.

1552. Exempt Contract Methods of Accounting. Although taxable income from a long-term contract generally must be accounted for under the percentage-of-completion method of accounting (¶ 1551), income from a small construction contract or a home construction contract may be taken into account using the exempt-contract-percentage-of-completion method or the completed contract method. The look-back rule and the cost allocation rules, except for the allocation of production period interest, are also not required for these contracts (Code Sec. 460(e); Reg. § 1.460-4). The contractor may change its method of accounting to conform with either of these special methods only after securing permission from the IRS (¶ 1529). An eligible taxpayer is not required to use these methods of accounting and may instead elect any other permissible method, such as a cash, accrual, or hybrid method (¶ 1515).

Small Construction Contracts. A small construction contract is a construction contract expected to be completed within two years that is performed by a taxpayer who meets the $25 million gross receipts test for using the cash method of accounting (¶ 1515) ($10 million for contracts entered into before 2018). For contracts entered into after 2017, a sole proprietorship applies the gross receipts test as if each trade or business of the taxpayer were a corporation or a partnership. If a taxpayer changes its method of accounting based on the small construction contract exception, then the change is treated as initiated by the taxpayer, made with the IRS's consent, and made on a cut-off basis for all similarly classified contracts.

Home and Residential Construction Contracts. A home construction contract is any construction contract where 80 percent or more of the estimated total contract costs are reasonably expected to be attributable to dwelling units contained in buildings with four or fewer dwelling units, and to improvements to real property related to such dwelling units. A home construction contract related to buildings with more than four dwelling units is a residential construction contract, for which the availability of the exempt contract methods is limited (see below).

Exempt-Contract-Percentage-of-Completion Method. Under the exempt-contract-percentage-of-completion method, the taxpayer includes in income the portion of the total contract price that corresponds to the percentage of the entire contract that the taxpayer has completed during the tax year. The percentage is determined by using any method of cost comparison that clearly reflects income and is used consistently (Reg. § 1.460-4(c)).

Completed Contract Method. Under the completed contract method, the taxpayer does not report income until the tax year in which the contract is completed and accepted (Reg. § 1.460-4(d)). Expenses allocable to the contract are deductible in the year in which the contract is completed. Expenses not allocated to the contract (i.e., period costs) are deductible in the year in which they are paid or incurred, depending on the method of accounting used.

Percentage-of-Completion/Capitalized-Cost Method. For residential construction contracts, the taxpayer may report 70 percent of the income using the percentage-of-completion method and the remaining 30 percent using an exempt contract method (Reg. § 1.460-4(e)).

Inventories

See CCH® AnswerConnect: *Tax Accounting Rules for Inventory* for more information on this topic.

1553. Accounting Requirement to Use Inventories. A taxpayer generally must use inventories to clearly reflect income if the production, purchase, or sale of merchandise is an income-producing factor (Code Sec. 471(a); Reg. § 1.471-1). To figure taxable income, a taxpayer must value inventory at the beginning and end of each tax year. This valuation depends on the items included in inventory (¶ 1557) and the method of valuation (¶ 1559). Inventory practices must be consistent from year to year. A taxpayer who must use inventories to clearly reflect income generally must use the accrual method of accounting for purchases and sales (¶ 1515).

A business is not required to use inventories or account for them using the accrual method if it meets the gross receipts test for using the cash method of accounting by a small business (¶ 1515) (Code Sec. 471(c)). A taxpayer meets the gross receipts test for the tax year if its average annual gross receipts for the three prior tax years do not exceed a threshold amount ($26 million for 2019 and 2020, and $25 million for 2018). For tax years beginning before 2018, a business was not required to use inventories or account for them using the accrual method if its average annual gross receipts did not exceed $1 million or if it was engaged in an eligible trade or business and its average annual gross receipts did not exceed $10 million (Rev. Proc. 2002-28 and Rev. Proc. 2001-10, obsoleted by Rev. Proc. 2018-40). A sole proprietorship applies the gross receipts test as if each trade or business of the taxpayer were a corporation or a partnership. A business that meets the gross receipts test can use a method that treats inventory as non-incidental materials and supplies (¶ 1317) or conforms to the business's financial accounting treatment of inventories.

The IRS has granted its consent to changes of accounting method gross receipts exception for inventories (Rev. Proc. 2018-40).

1557. Items Included in Inventory. An inventory is an itemized list, with valuations, of goods held for sale or consumption in a manufacturing or merchandising business. A taxpayer must usually verify the amount of items in inventory by a physical count of the items as of the last day of the tax year. The taxpayer may use estimates of inventory shrinkage that are confirmed by a physical count after year-end if the taxpayer normally does a physical inventory count at each location on a regular and consistent basis and makes proper adjustments to those inventories and to its estimating methods to the extent the estimates are greater than or less than the actual shrinkage (Code Sec. 471(b)).

Inventory should include all finished or partly finished goods and only those raw materials and supplies that have been acquired for sale or will physically become a part of merchandise intended for sale (Reg. § 1.471-1). Merchandise should be included in inventory only if title to it is vested in the taxpayer. A seller should include in inventory goods under contract for sale but not yet segregated and applied to the contract, as well as goods out on consignment. The seller should not include goods sold, including containers, in inventory where title has passed to the buyer. A buyer should include goods purchased, including containers, in inventory where title has passed to the buyer, even where the goods are in transit or have not been physically received.

The particular goods in inventory must be identified so that proper costs can be applied to the items. Identification of inventories is ordinarily accomplished by the first-in, first-out (FIFO) rule (¶ 1564), unless the items are specifically identified. A taxpayer can also elect to identify inventory items by use of the last-in, first-out (LIFO) rule (¶ 1565).

Real property held for sale by a dealer may not be inventoried because each parcel of real estate is unique (*Homes By Ayres*, CA-9, 86-2 USTC ¶ 9572). Likewise, capital assets, equipment, accounts, notes, investments, cash, or similar assets may not be included in inventories. See ¶ 1569 and ¶ 1903 for inventories of farmers and dealers in securities, respectively.

1559. Valuation of Inventory. An inventory must conform to the best accounting practice in the particular trade or business and must clearly reflect income (Reg. § 1.471-2(a) and (b)). An inventory that, under the best accounting practice, can be used in a balance sheet showing the financial position of the taxpayer will generally be regarded as clearly reflecting income. In determining whether income is clearly reflected, great weight is given to consistency in inventory practice, but a legitimate accounting system will be disallowed if it distorts income.

Two methods commonly used to value inventories are the cost method (¶ 1561) and the lower of cost or market method (¶ 1563) (Reg. § 1.471-2(c) and (d)). Opening and closing inventories must be valued by the same method. If the lower of cost or market method is used, it must be consistently applied to each item in the inventory. Cost and market value are determined as to each item, and the lower amount is included in the inventory valuation. A taxpayer is not permitted to value the entire stock at cost and also at market and use the lower of the two results (Reg. § 1.471-4). Deviations are permitted for goods inventoried under the last-in, first-out (LIFO) identification method (¶ 1565) and animals inventoried under the unit-livestock-price method (¶ 1569).

The IRS will also generally accept the rolling-average inventory valuation method used to value inventories for financial accounting purposes as clearly reflecting income for federal income tax purposes (Rev. Proc. 2008-43, modified by Rev. Proc. 2008-52). However, if inventory is held for several years or costs fluctuate substantially, the rolling-average cost method may not clearly reflect income, depending on the particular facts and circumstances. Moreover, if the taxpayer does not use the rolling-average method for financial accounting purposes, then that method may not accurately determine costs or clearly reflect income for tax purposes. Special rules apply to dealers in securities (¶ 1903).

Whether the cost or the lower of cost or market method is used, inventoried goods that are unsalable, or unusable in normal transactions because of wear and tear, obsolescence, or broken lots, should be valued at bona fide selling price, less cost of selling (Reg. § 1.471-2(c)). A bona fide selling price is the actual offering of goods during a period ending not later than 30 days after inventory date. Adjustment of the valuation on a reasonable basis, not less than scrap value, is permitted in the case of unsalable or unusable raw material or partly finished goods.

1561. Inventory at Cost: Uniform Capitalization Rules. Uniform capitalization rules govern the inclusion in inventory or capital accounts of all allocable costs that are incurred with respect to real and tangible personal property that is produced by the taxpayer or acquired for resale and would otherwise be considered in computing taxable income (Code Sec. 263A(a) and (b); Reg. § 1.263A-2). For this purpose, tangible personal property includes a film, sound recording, videotape, book, or similar property. Except for the interest capitalization rules, the uniform capitalization rules also apply to costs incurred with respect to real or personal property, whether tangible or intangible, that is acquired for resale.

A producer or reseller that meets the gross receipts test for using the cash method of accounting by a small business (¶ 1515) is exempt from the UNICAP rules (Code Sec. 263A(i)). A sole proprietorship applies the gross receipts test as if each trade or business of the taxpayer were a corporation or a partnership. A taxpayer meets the gross receipts test for the tax year if its average annual gross receipts for the three prior tax years do not exceed a threshold amount ($26 million for 2019 and 2020; $25 million for 2018). For tax years beginning before 2018, a small business had to meet a $10 million gross receipts test and the exception to the UNICAP rules only applied to personal property acquired for resale.

Costs attributable to inventory must be added to costs of producing or acquiring the inventory, and costs attributable to producing other property must be capitalized. Direct material and labor costs, as well as the portion of indirect costs allocable to that property, are subject to the capitalization rules (Reg. § 1.263A-1(a)(3)).

The uniform capitalization rules replace the inventory cost rules of Code Sec. 471 (see below) in the case of property to which they apply. The uniform capitalization rules do not apply to inventories valued at market under either the market method or the lower of cost or market method (¶ 1563) if the market valuation used by the taxpayer generally equals the property's fair market value (i.e., price of sale to customers less direct disposition costs). However, the uniform capitalization rules do apply in determining the market value of any inventory for which market is determined with reference to replacement cost or reproduction cost.

The uniform capitalization rules do not apply to:

- property produced for personal use or pursuant to a long-term contract (¶ 1551);

- timber, including certain ornamental trees;

- costs deductible as Code Sec. 174 research and experimental expenditures (¶ 979);

- costs associated with certain oil, gas, and other mineral property, foreign drilling, and amortizable or developmental expenditures; and

- costs, other than circulation expenditures, subject to the 10-year amortization rule for certain alternative minimum tax preference items (¶ 194).

Certain costs incurred by an individual or personal service corporation (¶ 273) engaged in the business of being a writer, photographer, or artist (¶ 1344) that are otherwise deductible are also exempt from those rules. In addition, costs may be currently deducted for marketing and selling expenses, as well as general and administration expenses that do not directly benefit production or the acquisition of inventory (¶ 1332) (Code Sec. 263A(c) and (h)); Reg. § 1.263A-1(b) and (e)(4)).

Interest Capitalization Rules. Interest costs paid or incurred during the production period and allocable to real property or tangible personal property produced by the taxpayer must be capitalized if the property has: (1) a long useful life (real property or any other property that has a class life of 20 years or more), (2) an estimated production period exceeding two years, or (3) an estimated production period exceeding one year and a cost exceeding $1 million (¶ 1340).

Farming Businesses. See ¶ 1342 for the uniform capitalization rules pertaining to farm businesses.

Code Sec. 471 Rules. The following rules are used to value inventory at cost where the uniform capitalization rules do not apply. For merchandise on hand at the beginning of the year, cost is the amount that was included in the closing inventory of the preceding period. For merchandise *bought* after the beginning of the year, cost means the invoice price less trade or other discounts, except cash discounts approximating a fair interest rate, which may be deducted from cost, or reported as income, at the option of the taxpayer. Cost also includes transportation or other acquisition charges. For merchandise *produced* by the taxpayer, the costs attributed to inventoried goods must be determined under the uniform capitalization rules (see above).

1563. Inventory at Lower of Cost or Market. If the lower of cost or market inventory method is used, the market value of each item is compared with the cost of the item (¶ 1561), and the lower of the two values is used for that item (Reg. § 1.471-4).

Example: A lumber dealer has three grades of lumber at the end of the tax year. They are valued as follows:

Grade	Cost	Market	Lower of Two
A	$45,000	$60,000	$45,000
B	20,000	15,000	15,000
C	5,000	5,000	5,000
	$70,000	$80,000	$65,000

If the lumber dealer is using the cost method, the ending inventory is valued at $70,000. If the dealer is using the lower of cost or market method, the ending inventory is valued at $65,000.

Under normal conditions, market value is the prevailing current bid price at the inventory date in the volume that the items are usually purchased by the taxpayer. If a current bid price is unobtainable, the best available evidence of fair market value must be used. Specific purchases or sales by the taxpayer or others, or compensation paid for cancellation of contracts for purchase commitments, may be used.

The market value of goods in process and finished goods, for a manufacturer or processor, is reproduction cost. This is the total that materials, labor, and factory burden or overhead would cost at current prices to bring the article to a comparable state of completion. The market price basis does not apply to goods on hand or in the process of manufacture for delivery under firm sale contracts at fixed prices entered into before the inventory date where the taxpayer is protected against actual loss. Such goods must be inventoried at cost.

A merchant may also use the retail method to approximate the lower of cost or market of goods in inventory (Reg. § 1.471-8). The retail selling prices of goods on hand at the end of the year are multiplied by a ratio or cost complement to arrive the value of ending inventory.

If inventories are valued at cost under the lower of cost or market method, that valuation is subject to the uniform capitalization rules.

1564. First-In, First-Out (FIFO) Inventory Method. The first-in, first-out (FIFO) method of identifying inventory assumes that items purchased or produced first are the first items sold, consumed, or otherwise disposed (Code Sec. 471; Reg. § 1.471-2). Accordingly, items in inventory at the end of the year are matched with the costs of similar items that were most recently purchased or produced. The FIFO method is used for items in inventory that have been so commingled that they cannot be identified with specific invoices; thus, they are considered to be the items most recently purchased or produced. The cost is the actual cost of the items purchased and produced during the period in which the quantity of items in inventory was acquired. In the absence of an election to use the last-in, first-out (LIFO) method (¶ 1565), inventory is identified under the FIFO method.

1565. Last-In, First-Out (LIFO) Inventory Method. The last-in, first-out (LIFO) method of identifying inventory is based on cost values (Code Sec. 472). Under the LIFO method, inventory is taken at cost, but the items contained in the inventory are treated as being those contained in opening inventory to the extent of the opening inventory (whether or not they are physically on hand), and then those acquired during the tax year. The items treated as still in the opening inventory are taken in order of acquisition, except for the first year in which the method is used. For that year, the items in the opening inventory are taken at the average cost of those items. The closing inventory of the preceding year must also be adjusted and an amended return filed to reflect the changes. In the case of a retailer or certain manufacturers, items deemed to have been purchased during the year (i.e., inventory increases) may be taken at the taxpayer's election on the basis of the most recent purchases, at average cost for the year, or in order of acquisition.

A taxpayer need not obtain advance permission from the IRS to elect to use the LIFO method but must adopt it on the return for the year in which the method is first used. In addition, the taxpayer must file Form 970 with the return and accept any modifications or adjustments required by the IRS. The election applies only to the class or classes of goods specified in the application. Although the election to adopt LIFO must generally cover the entire inventory of a business, manufacturers or processors may elect to have the method apply to raw materials only, including those in finished goods and work-in-process (Reg. § 1.472-1(h)). Furthermore, if LIFO is used for tax purposes, it generally must also be used in preparing annual financial statements for credit purposes or for the purpose of reports to stockholders, partners, or proprietors. For purposes of this reporting rule, all members of the same group of financially related corporations are treated as one taxpayer.

As an alternative to the regular LIFO method, a taxpayer with numerous items in an inventory may use the dollar-value LIFO method (¶ 1567).

1567. Dollar-Value LIFO Inventory Method. Instead of determining quantity increases of each item in the inventory and then pricing them, as is required under the regular last-in, last (LIFO) method (¶ 1565), the dollar-value LIFO method may be used (Code Sec. 472(f); Reg. § 1.472-8). The increase in LIFO value is determined by comparing the total dollar value of the beginning and ending inventories at base year prices (the first LIFO year) and then converting any dollar-value increase to current prices by means of an index. Under the dollar-value LIFO method, taxpayers are allowed to determine base year dollars through the use of government indexes.

Simplified Dollar-Value LIFO Method. A small business with average gross receipts for the three preceding years of $5 million or less may elect to use a simplified dollar-value LIFO method to account for inventories (Code Sec. 474). This method requires separate inventory pools for each major category in the applicable government price index. The election applies to all succeeding years unless the taxpayer obtains IRS permission to change to another method or becomes ineligible to use that method. If elected, it must be used to value all LIFO inventories.

1569. Special Inventory Valuation Methods for Farmers. A farmer on the accrual basis of accounting has a choice of two other methods for valuing inventory in addition to the standard cost (¶ 1561) and the lower of cost or market (¶ 1563) methods. The farm-price method provides for the valuation of inventories at market price less the direct cost of disposition. If this method is used, it must be applied to the entire inventory except livestock that the taxpayer has elected to inventory under the unit-livestock-price method (Reg. § 1.471-6(d)).

The unit-livestock-price method—adoptable if the farmer raises his or her own livestock or purchases young animals and raises them to maturity—provides for the valuation *of different classes* of animals at a standard unit price for each animal within a class. This method, once elected, must be applied to all livestock raised to maturity or purchased before maturity and raised to maturity, whether held for sale or for breeding, draft, or dairy purposes. This includes unweaned calves. Unit prices assigned to classes must account for normal cost of production. For purchased livestock, the cost should be increased in accordance with unit prices only for animals acquired in the first six months of the tax year (Reg. § 1.471-6(e), (f) and (g)).

The crop basis of accounting may be used with IRS consent for crops that have not been gathered and disposed of during the tax year in which they are planted (Reg. § 1.61-4(c)). The entire cost of producing the crop must be deducted no earlier than in the year in which the crop income is realized.

1571. Change in Inventory Accounting. A change in the method used to account for an inventory can be made only when authorized by the IRS. A change from a cash method to an inventory method is, in effect, a change to the accrual method of accounting for purchases and sales (Reg. § 1.446-1(c)(2)). Permission to make the change generally must be requested within the tax year that the change is to be effective (¶ 1529), with the exception of an election to change to the last-in, first-out (LIFO method) (¶ 1565). An election to use this method may be made by a statement on Form 970 attached to the first tax return in which it is used. Adjustments are required to prevent duplications and omissions of income and expenses (Reg. §§ 1.472-3 and 1.472-4).

Allocation and Reconstruction of Income

1573. Allocation of Income and Deductions by IRS. If two or more organizations, trades, or businesses are owned or controlled by the same interests, the IRS may allocate gross income, deductions, or credits between them if it determines the action necessary to prevent evasion of taxes or to clearly reflect income (Code Sec. 482). Moreover, the IRS is specifically authorized to allocate any income, deduction, credit, exclusion, or other allowance between certain personal service corporations (¶ 273) and their employee-owners if the principal purpose of forming or using the corporation is to avoid or evade income tax (¶ 1575). Effective for transfers made in tax years beginning after 2017, the IRS is also authorized to value transfers of intangible property on an aggregate basis or based on realistic alternatives as par of intercompany pricing allocations.

1575. Corporate Acquisitions to Avoid Tax. If a taxpayer acquires control of a corporation, directly or indirectly, to evade or avoid income tax by securing the benefit of a deduction, credit, or other allowance that would not otherwise be enjoyed, then that deduction, credit or other allowance will not be permitted. The same rules of disallowance apply to a corporation that acquires property of another corporation that was not controlled by the acquiring corporation or its stockholders and that acquires a basis determined by reference to the basis in the hands of the transferor corporation (Code Sec. 269).

The IRS is authorized to deny an acquiring corporation the carryover and other tax benefits of a subsidiary corporation, acquired in a qualified stock purchase for which an election of asset acquisition treatment is not made, if the subsidiary corporation is liquidated under a plan adopted within two years of the acquisition date and the principal purpose of the liquidation is tax avoidance or evasion. See ¶ 273 for a discussion of the use or formation of a personal service corporation (PSC) by another entity to avoid or evade income tax and the IRS's authority to allocate amounts between the PSC and its employee-owners to clearly reflect income.

1577. Income Reconstruction by the IRS. If a taxpayer has kept either inadequate or no books or records, the IRS has authority to compute income to clearly reflect the taxpayer's income (Code Sec. 446(b)). The methods for reconstructing income vary depending on the facts and circumstances, and the records that are available. The IRS has developed several methods for reconstructing a taxpayer's income.

Bank Deposits and Expenditures Method. All bank deposits are assumed to represent income unless the taxpayer can establish otherwise. Although the taxpayer is given an opportunity to show that the deposits do not represent income, the IRS is not required to link the bank deposits with an identified income-producing activity (*G.G. Goe*, CA-3, 52-2 USTC ¶ 9420).

Net Worth Method. An opening net worth or total value of assets at the beginning of a given year is established. The IRS then shows increases in the taxpayer's net worth for each subsequent year and calculates the difference between the adjusted net values of the assets at the beginning and end of each year under examination. Nondeductible expenses are added to the increases. If the resulting amount is greater than reported taxable income for that year, then the excess is treated as unreported taxable income (*M.L. Holland*, SCt, 54-2 ustc ¶ 9714).

Percentage or Unit Mark-Up Method. A percentage or unit mark-up method is used where inventories are a necessary income-producing factor but have not been kept or were incorrectly taken. Net income is determined by applying certain percentages, such as gross profits to sales, net income to gross income, or net income to sales, derived from other taxpayers in similar types of businesses (*L. Bernstein*, CA-5, 59-1 ustc ¶ 9483).

Chapter 16

BASIS FOR GAIN OR LOSS

Computing Gain or Loss

See CCH® AnswerConnect: *Basis* for more information on this topic.

1601. Basis of Property. The rules on determining the basis for computing gain or loss or depreciation on property acquired in most common transactions are outlined below, with references to the paragraphs where additional details appear. Basis, after adjustments (¶ 1604), is subtracted from the amount realized to determine the amount of gain or loss from a sale or other disposition (Code Sec. 1001). Except where other rules are prescribed, the basis for gain or loss is determined under the law in effect when the property is sold or disposed.

Type of acquisition	Basis for gain or loss
Bargain purchases	
arm's-length	Cost (¶ 789)
corporation's, from nonstockholder	Cost (¶ 1660)
corporation's, from stockholder	Cost, unless saving is paid-in surplus (¶ 1660)
employee's	Cost, plus amount taxable as compensation for services (¶ 789)
relative or friend	Cost, unless saving is a gift (¶ 1630)
stockholder's	Cost, plus amount taxable as a dividend (¶ 789)
Bequests	Fair market value at the date of the decedent's death, but no more than the estate tax value or value reported to IRS (¶ 1633)
Cash purchases	Cost (¶ 1604)
mortgage also assumed, or property taken subject to the mortgage	Full price, including mortgage amount (¶ 1611)
purchase money mortgage also given	Full purchase price (¶ 1611)
purchase notes also given	Full purchase price (¶ 1611)
redeemable ground rent assumed, or property taken subject to ground rent	Full purchase price (¶ 1611)
Community property	
survivor (death of spouse)	See Bequests above
Corporate property	
acquired for stock by controlled corporation	Transferor's basis (¶ 1660)
acquired for stock in taxable exchange	Fair market value of stock at time of exchange (¶ 1648)
contributions by nonstockholders	Zero (¶ 1660)
paid-in surplus	Transferor's basis (¶ 1660)
Dividend property	
corporate, stockholder of domestic corporation	Fair market value (¶ 735)
corporate, stockholder of foreign corporation	Fair market value (¶ 735)
noncorporate, stockholder	Fair market value (¶ 735)
Divorce or separation agreement	Transferors' basis (¶ 1734)

Type of acquisition	Basis for gain or loss
Gift property	Donor's basis, increased by gift tax in some cases; basis for loss *limited* to lesser of donor's basis or fair market value at time of gift (¶ 1630)
Inventory	Last inventory value (¶ 1559)
Joint tenancy	
after death of one tenant	Basis depends on amount contributed by each joint tenant toward the original purchase price (¶ 1634, ¶ 1636)
Lessor's acquisitions of lessee's improvements	Zero, if excluded from income (¶ 764)
Life estate	Zero, if disposed of after October 9, 1969 (¶ 1633)
Livestock	
inventory	Last inventory value (¶ 767)
purchased	Cost (¶ 767)
raised by accrual-basis farmer	Cost of raising (¶ 767)
raised by cash-basis farmer	Zero, if costs were charged to expense (¶ 767)
Mortgaged property (or property subject to redeemable ground rent)	Basis includes mortgage (or ground rent) (¶ 1611)
Partners' property	
partnership interest in exchange for contribution	Partners' adjusted basis of property contributed (¶ 443)
partnership interest purchased	Cost (¶ 434)
received in distribution other than liquidation	Partnership's adjusted basis at time of distribution (limited to partner's basis of his interest) (¶ 456)
received in partnership liquidation	Adjusted basis of partnership interest less cash received (¶ 456)
Partnership property	
after transfer of partnership interest or distributions to partners	Unaffected, unless election is made to adjust values (¶ 459, ¶ 467)
capital contribution	Partner's adjusted basis (¶ 443)
Purchase for more than value	Cost (¶ 1604), but excess may be a gift
Rehabilitated buildings, other than certified historic structures	Basis is reduced by allowable investment credit and the recaptured credit is added to basis (¶ 1465B)
Repossessed property after installment sale	
personal property	Fair market value (¶ 1838)
real property reacquired in satisfaction of purchaser's debt secured by property	Adjusted basis of debt plus gain resulting from reacquisition and reacquisition costs (¶ 1843)
Spousal transfers	Transferor's basis (¶ 1734)
Stock	
acquired in wash sale	Basis of stock sold, adjusted for difference between selling price of sold stock and purchase price of acquired stock (¶ 1935)
bonus stock	Allocable portion of basis of old stock (¶ 1620, ¶ 1682)
nontaxable stock dividend	Allocable share of basis of stock on which declared (¶ 1620, ¶ 1682)
qualified small business stock rollover	Cost, reduced by gain rolled over (¶ 1907)
purchased	Cost, if adequately identified (¶ 1975)
received for services	Amount reported as income, plus cash paid (¶ 1681)
S corporation	See ¶ 315, ¶ 317
specialized small business investment company stock rollover	Cost, reduced by gain rolled over (¶ 1907)
taxable stock dividend	Fair market value when issued (¶ 733A)
Stock rights	
nontaxable	Allocable share of basis of stock unless rights value is less than 15% of stock value (¶ 733A, ¶ 1682)
taxable	Fair market value when issued (¶ 733A)
Transfer in trust	Grantor's basis, plus gain or minus loss, upon transfer (¶ 1678)

1604. Adjusted Basis of Property. Gain or loss from the sale or other disposition of property is the difference between the amount realized from the sale and the taxpayer's basis in the property (Code Sec. 1011; Reg. § 1.1011-1). Basis is generally the taxpayer's original investment in the property (cost basis), but the taxpayer may have a substitute or carryover basis in certain cases (¶ 1607) (Code Sec. 1012). If property is acquired in a fully taxable exchange, the cost of the property acquired is the fair market value of the property given up. In an arm's-length transaction, both are presumed to be equal in value.

Regardless of the manner in which the taxpayer's original basis in property is determined, certain upward or downward adjustments are made to that basis. For example, capital expenditures increase basis (¶ 1611), while depreciation decreases basis (¶ 1617). The original basis, increased or decreased by these adjustments, is the taxpayer's adjusted basis.

1607. Substituted or Carryover Basis. A substituted basis in property is one that is continued or carried over from one taxpayer to another, or from one piece of property to another (Code Sec. 7701(a)(42), (43), and (44)). The taxpayer has a substituted or carryover basis in property received as a gift (¶ 1630), in a transfer in trust (¶ 1678), in a tax-free exchange (¶ 1651), or acquired from a decedent dying in 2010 whose estate elects not to have federal estate tax apply (¶ 1636). The taxpayer also has a substituted basis in a personal residence purchased before May 7, 1997, if the recognition of gain realized on the sale of a prior residence was deferred under former Code Sec. 1034.

Property Acquired by Purchase

See CCH® AnswerConnect: *Basis* for more information on this topic.

1611. Additions to Basis of Property. In computing gain or loss on the sale of business or investment property, or gain on the sale of personal property, the cost or other basis must be *adjusted* for any expenditure, receipt, loss, or other item that is a capital expenditure other than taxes or carrying charges (¶ 1614) that the taxpayer deducts in determining taxable income (Code Sec. 1016(a)(1); Reg. § 1.1016-2).

This necessitates an addition to basis for improvements made to the property since its acquisition. For example, the cost of capital improvements such as an addition, new roof, newly installed central air conditioning, or electrical rewiring is added to the owner's basis. Other components that add to the cost basis of property include: brokers' commissions and lawyers' fees incurred in buying real estate; expenditures incurred in defending or perfecting the title to property; zoning costs; the capitalized value of a redeemable ground rent; and sales tax, freight, installation and testing costs, excise taxes, and revenue stamps (Code Sec. 1055; IRS Pub. 551).

Settlement Fees and Other Costs. The basis of real property includes settlement fees and closing costs such as abstract fees, charges for installing utility services, legal fees (including title search and preparation of the sales contract and deed), recording fees, surveys, transfer taxes, and owner's title insurance. Also included in basis are amounts owed by the seller but paid by the buyer, such as back taxes or interest, recording or mortgage fees, charges for improvements or repairs, and sales commissions (Code Sec. 1012; Reg. § 1.1012-1(b); Rev. Rul. 68-528). Amounts placed in escrow for future payments of items such as insurance and taxes do not increase basis.

The creation of a mortgage does not diminish the owner's basis in a property. If a buyer assumes an existing mortgage and pays cash or other consideration, the buyer's basis in the property includes the outstanding portion of the mortgage and the value of the other consideration. The seller realizes a benefit in the amount of the assumed mortgage and the additional consideration (*B.B. Crane*, SCt, 47-1 USTC ¶ 9217). Fees and costs related to getting a loan to purchase the property are not included in the basis of the property.

Assessments. Assessments for improvements or other items that increase the value of property are added to the basis of the property and not deducted as a tax. This may include improvements such as streets, sidewalks, water mains, sewers, and public parking facilities. The amount of an assessment may be a depreciable asset. For example, the cost of a mall enclosure paid for by a business through an assessment is depreciable. Assessments for maintenance or repairs, or for meeting interest charges on the improvements, are currently deductible as a real property tax, although the burden is on the taxpayer to show the allocation of the amounts assessed to the different purposes (Code Sec. 164(c)(1); Reg. § 1.164-4; Rev. Rul. 70-62). Legal fees for obtaining a decrease in an assessment levied against property to pay for local improvements are added to the basis of the property and are not a deductible business expense.

Taxes. Any tax paid in connection with the acquisition of a property is treated as part of the cost of the property. A tax paid in connection with the disposition of a property reduces the amount realized on the disposition (Code Sec. 164(a)).

In computing the cost of real property, the buyer cannot take into account any amount paid to the seller as reimbursement for real property taxes which are treated as imposed upon the purchaser (¶ 1032). This rule applies whether or not the sales contract calls for the buyer to reimburse the seller for real estate taxes paid or to be paid by the seller. However, where the buyer pays or assumes liability for real estate taxes imposed upon the seller, the taxes are considered part of the cost of the property. It is immaterial whether or not the sales contract specifies that the sale price has been reduced by, or is in any way intended to reflect, real estate taxes allocable to the seller (Reg. § 1.1012-1(b)).

1614. Additions to Basis for Carrying Charges. A taxpayer may elect to treat taxes or other carrying charges (such as interest) on some property as capital charges rather than as an expense of the tax year (Code Sec. 266; Reg. § 1.266-1). The items chargeable to the capital account are:

(1) in the case of unimproved and unproductive real property: annual taxes, interest on a mortgage, and other carrying charges;

(2) in the case of real property, whether improved or unimproved and whether productive or unproductive: interest on a loan, taxes of the owner of such property measured by compensation paid to the owner's employees, taxes of the owner on the purchase of materials or on the storage, use, or other consumption of materials, and other necessary expenditures paid or incurred for the development or improvement of the property up to the time the development or construction work has been completed;

(3) in the case of personal property: taxes of an employer measured by compensation for services rendered in transporting machinery or other fixed assets to the plant or installing them, interest on a loan to buy such property or to pay for transporting or installing it, and taxes of the owner imposed on the purchase of such property or on the storage, use, or other consumption, paid or incurred up to the date of installation or the date when the property is first put to use by the taxpayer, whichever is later; and

(4) any other taxes and carrying charges, otherwise deductible, which are chargeable to the capital account under sound accounting principles.

The election must be made by filing a statement with the taxpayer's original return indicating which items the taxpayer elects to treat as chargeable to the capital account. The election in (1) above is effective only for the year in which it is made. The election in (2) is effective until the development or construction work has been completed. The election in (3) is effective until the property is installed or first put to use, whichever date is later. The IRS determines whether the election in (4) is effective.

1617. Reductions in Basis of Property. In order to determine the amount of gain or loss realized on the sale, exchange, or other disposition of property (or for figuring allowable depreciation, depletion, or amortization), the unadjusted basis of property (¶ 1601) must be decreased by any items that represent a return of capital for the period during which the property has been held by the taxpayer (Code Sec. 1016(a)). These include in part:

• deductions previously allowed or allowable for depreciation, depletion, or amortization (¶ 1201 and following);

- the Code Sec. 179 expense deduction for certain depreciable business assets (¶ 1208), as well as the expense deduction for energy efficient commercial business property (¶ 1286);

- any loss recognized from an involuntary conversion, as well as any money received that was not invested in replacement property (¶ 1687);

- gain from the sale of qualified small business stock (¶ 1907) or publicly traded securities before 2018 (¶ 1909) excluded from gross income and rolled over to the basis of qualified replacement stock;

- casualty or theft loss deductions, as well as the amount of any insurance or other recovery for the loss (¶ 1127);

- tax-free dividends by corporations (¶ 733A) and nonliquidating distributions by a partnership to a partner (¶ 447); and

- the investment credit (except for 50 percent of the energy credits) (¶ 1465A).

Depreciation. The basis of property is reduced by the amount of depreciation claimed, or if greater, the depreciation which should have been claimed under the method chosen (Code Sec. 1016(a)(2); Reg. § 1.1016-3). If no depreciation or insufficient depreciation was claimed, the basis is nonetheless reduced by the full amount of depreciation that should have been claimed. In order to mitigate the effect of this rule, the IRS has issued procedures that allow the taxpayer to change to a proper method of accounting for depreciation and claim a downward adjustment to income that reflects the additional amount of depreciation that should have been claimed (¶ 1221). If excess depreciation was claimed on an asset, the basis of the asset is reduced by the amount of depreciation that should have been claimed plus the part of the excess depreciation deducted that actually reduced the taxpayer's tax liability.

Percentage Depletion. Even though a percentage depletion allowance is in excess of cost or other basis, it is not necessary to use a negative basis (less than zero) in computing gain on the sale of mineral property (¶ 1384, ¶ 1386, and ¶ 1388).

Motor Vehicles. The basis of a motor vehicle is reduced by any deduction or tax credit the taxpayer claimed with respect to the purchase, including any applicable credit for new qualified fuel cell motor vehicles purchased before January 1, 2021 (¶ 1446), new qualified plug-in electric drive motor vehicles (¶ 1451), and alternative fuel vehicle refueling property placed in service before January 1, 2021 (¶ 1455). The basis of an automobile must also be reduced by the amount of any gas guzzler tax imposed by Code Sec. 4064 if use of the vehicle begins not more than one year after the first retail sale (Code Sec. 1016(d)).

Easements. The amount received for granting an easement on real property for a limited use or for a limited period generally reduces the basis of the affected part of the property (Rev. Rul. 68-291). Gain is recognized to the extent that the amount received exceeds the basis of the affected part. The granting of a perpetual easement that denies the grantor any beneficial use of the property may be considered a sale of property even though the grantor retains legal title.

Residential Property. The basis of a personal residence or dwelling unit is reduced by certain tax credits the taxpayer claimed with respect to the property. This includes the nonbusiness energy credit for qualified energy efficiency improvements and residential energy property (¶ 1441), and the residential energy efficient property credit for amounts spent on alternative energy equipment such as solar equipment (¶ 1442). An eligible contractor who has constructed and claimed a credit for a qualified new energy-efficient home must also reduce his or her basis in the property to the extent that the credit is claimed (¶ 1465CC). In addition, the basis of a dwelling unit for which an excludable energy conservation subsidy was provided by a public utility must be reduced by the amount of the subsidy (¶ 889).

Homes Purchased Before May 7, 1997. The basis of a home purchased before May 7, 1997, must be reduced to reflect any gain realized on the sale of the prior home but deferred under former Code Sec. 1034.

16

BASIS

Adoption Credit. The basis of a residence must be reduced by the amount of the adoption tax credit that was claimed with respect to improvements that increased the basis of the home (¶ 1407).

Child Care Credit. The basis of facilities acquired, constructed, rehabilitated, or expanded, and with respect to which an employer-provided child care credit (¶ 1465V) is allowed, must be reduced by the amount of the credit. If there is a recapture of the credit on the disposition of such property, the basis of the property is increased by the amount recaptured.

Canceled Debt. A taxpayer must reduce certain tax attributes by an amount excluded from gross income as the result of a discharge of indebtedness in a Title 11 bankruptcy case, a discharge of indebtedness during insolvency, or a discharge of qualified farm indebtedness (¶ 855).

Railroad Track. Eligible small and mid-sized railroad companies must reduce the basis of track on which they have been allowed a railroad track maintenance credit (¶ 1465W).

Substituted Basis. If the basis of the property is a substituted basis (¶ 1607), the same adjustments must be made for the period the property was held by the transferor, donor, or grantor, or during the period the property was held by the person for whom the basis is to be determined (Code Sec. 1016(b)).

1620. Apportionment of Cost or Other Basis. If a sale is made of parts of property purchased as a unit, as in a subdivision of real estate, allocation of the total basis is required (Reg. § 1.61-6). Other instances where allocation of the cost or other basis is necessary include: stock of different classes received as a dividend or pursuant to a reorganization, a split-up, split-off, or spin-off (¶ 2205); stock received as a bonus with the purchase of stock of a different character; stock purchase warrants attached to debenture bonds; and depreciable and nondepreciable property purchased for a lump sum.

Trade or Business Purchased. Applicable asset acquisition rules require the allocation of the purchase price of a trade or business among the assets in proportion to their fair market values in the following classes and in the following order (Code Sec. 1060; Reg. § § 1.338-6 and 1.1060-1):

- Class I asset: Cash and general deposit accounts (including savings and checking accounts), other than certificates of deposits held in banks, savings and loan associations, and other depository institutions.

- Class II asset: Actively traded personal property, as well as certificates of deposit and foreign currency, even if they are not actively traded personal property.

- Class III asset: Assets that the taxpayer marks to market at least annually for federal income tax purposes, including accounts receivable, mortgages, and credit card receivables that arise in the course of business.

- Class IV asset: Stock in trade of the taxpayer or other property of a kind that would properly be included in the inventory of the taxpayer if on hand at the close of the tax year, or property held by the taxpayer primarily for sale to customers in the ordinary course of its trade or business.

- Class V asset: All assets other than Class I, II, III, IV, VI, and VII assets.

- Class VI asset: section 197 intangibles (e.g., work force in place, information bases, patents, copyrights, licenses and covenants not to compete), but not goodwill and going concern value.

- Class VII asset: Goodwill and going concern value whether or not they qualify as section 197 intangibles.

An asset that can be included in more than one class should be assigned to the lower numbered class. For instance, if an asset could be included in Class III or IV, it should go in Class III.

¶1620

Before making the allocation, the purchase price is first reduced by any cash and general deposit accounts (savings and checking) that the acquired business holds as assets. The buyer and seller of the assets of a trade or business are bound by any written agreements allocating consideration to the transferred assets. However, any allocation that is not found to be fair market value will be disregarded. The buyer and seller must attach Form 8594 to their income tax returns for the year of sale to report the allocation.

Land and Buildings. If a building and land are purchased for a lump sum, the purchase price is allocated between the land and building on the basis of their fair market values. If the fair market values are uncertain, the allocation may be based on their assessed values for real estate tax purposes (Reg. §§1.61-6(a) and 1.167(a)-5).

Subdivided Lots. The basis of each lot of a subdivided property is equal to the purchase price of the entire property multiplied by a fraction. The numerator is the fair market value of the lot and the denominator is the fair market value of the entire property. The cost of common improvements is also allocated among the individual lots. A developer who sells subdivided lots before development work is completed may include, with IRS consent, an allocation of the estimated future cost for common improvements in the basis of the lots sold (Rev. Proc. 92-29). There is a special rule relating to the recognition of capital gain on the sale of subdivided lots (¶1762).

1623. Allocation of Basis—Bargain Sale to Charity. If a charitable deduction is available (¶1062), the basis of property sold to charity for less than its fair market value is allocated between the portion of the property sold and the portion donated to charity, based on the fair market value of each portion. Thus, the seller-donor realizes some taxable gain even if the selling price did not exceed the seller-donor's cost or other basis for the entire property (Code Sec. 1011(b); Reg. §1.1011-2). The adjusted basis of the portion of property sold to a charity is computed as:

$$\frac{\text{Amount realized (fair}\\ \text{market value}\\ \text{of part sold)}}{\text{Fair market value}\\ \text{of entire property}} \times \begin{array}{c}\text{Adjusted basis}\\ \text{of}\\ \text{entire property}\end{array}$$

1626. Basis of Residential or Converted Property. If property has been continually occupied by the taxpayer as a residence since its acquisition, no adjustment of basis is made for depreciation because none is allowable. The cost of permanent improvements to the property is added to the basis, as are special assessments paid for local benefits that improve the property (¶1611). Recoveries against a builder for defective construction reduce the basis (Rev. Rul. 81-152).

If residential property is converted to rental property, an adjustment should be made for depreciation from the date of the conversion. Thus, the basis for gain in the case of rented residential property is the taxpayer's cost or other statutory basis, less depreciation allowable while the property was rented or held for rental.

The basis for loss may not exceed the value at the time the residence was converted to rental use, taking into account subsequent basis adjustments, including reduction for allowable depreciation. This is only a limitation. If a smaller loss results from the use of the adjusted cost basis, it must be used (Reg. §1.165-9(b)). The value of the property upon conversion to rental use has no effect on the basis for gain. If converted property is sold for a price that is greater than the basis for loss but less than the basis for gain, there is no gain or loss.

If rental property is converted to a personal residence, adjustments to basis for depreciation end on the date of the conversion. Any gain on the sale of the property is recognized (subject to the exclusion rules at ¶1705) and may be subject to depreciation recapture (¶1779). Loss will not be recognized.

Property Acquired by Gift or Bequest

See CCH® AnswerConnect: *Basis* for more information on this topic.

1630. Basis of Property Acquired by Gift. For property acquired by gift, the basis to the donee is generally the same as it would be in the hands of the donor or the last preceding owner by whom it was not acquired by gift (Code Sec. 1015; Reg. § 1.1015-1). However, the basis for loss is the adjusted basis of the property prior to the date of the gift (¶ 1604) or the fair market value of the property at the time of the gift, whichever is lower. In some cases, there is neither gain nor loss on the sale of property received by gift because the selling price is less than the basis for gain and more than the basis for loss.

If a gift was made on or after September 1, 1958, and before January 1, 1977, the basis of the property is increased by the amount of the gift tax paid (¶ 2903), but not above the fair market value of the property at the time of the gift. For gifts made before September 2, 1958, and held by the donee on that date, the basis is also increased by the amount of the gift tax, but not by more than any excess of the fair market value of the property at the time of the gift over the basis of the property in the hands of the donor at the time of the gift.

In the case of a gift made after 1976 on which the gift tax is paid, the basis of the property is increased by the amount of gift tax attributable to the net appreciation in value of the gift. The net appreciation for this purpose is the amount by which the fair market value of the gift exceeds the donor's adjusted basis immediately before the gift.

Zero basis generally applies to a life estate acquired by gift (¶ 1633).

1633. Basis of Property Acquired from a Decedent. The basis of any real or personal property acquired from a decedent is generally its fair market value on the date of the decedent's death or on the alternate valuation or special use valuation date (¶ 2922) (Code Sec. 1014). If there is no federal estate tax liability, the basis of the property is its fair market value as of the date of the decedent's death for the purpose of state inheritance or transmission taxes (Reg. § 1.1014-3(a); Rev. Rul. 54-97). Fair market value is presumptive, and may be rebutted by clear and convincing evidence. There are certain exceptions to the basis of property acquired from a decedent equaling fair market value, including carryover basis (¶ 1636), appreciated property reacquired by a donor from a decedent (¶ 1639), income in respect of the decedent (¶ 182), and property subject to a qualified conservation easement.

Consistency of Basis. Effective for property with respect to which an estate tax return is filed after July 31, 2015, the basis of property received by reason of a decedent's death must be consistent with the value for estate tax purposes (Code Sec. 1014(f); Prop. Reg. § 1.1014-10). Thus, the basis of any property to which the stepped-up basis rules apply may not exceed the value of the property determined on the decedent's federal estate tax return or the value reported to the taxpayer on Form 8971 (¶ 2938). The consistency in reporting only applies to property that was includible in the decedent's gross estate and resulted in increased estate tax liability (reduced by applicable credits) on the estate. The accuracy-related penalty will be imposed for inconsistent estate basis reporting (Code Sec. 6662(b)(8) and (k)).

Decedents Dying in 2010. Effective for decedents dying in 2010, the executor of the decedent's estate had the option to elect out of the federal estate tax. If the election was made, a modified carryover basis rule applied to property acquired from the decedent (¶ 1636).

Term Interests. In most instances, a zero basis is assigned to a life estate that was acquired by gift or bequest and sold or disposed of after October 9, 1969. Interests covered by this exception include: (1) life interests in property; (2) interests for a term of years in property; and (3) income interests in trusts. The zero basis requirement does not apply if the life tenant and remainderman sell their interests simultaneously so that the entire ownership of the property is transferred to another person or group of persons (Code Sec. 1001(e); Reg. §§ 1.1001-1 and 1.1014-5). Special rules also are provided in determining a beneficiary's basis in a term interest in a charitable remainder trust (CRT) upon a sale or other disposition of all interests in the trust to the extent that the basis consists of a share of adjusted uniform basis.

1634. Basis in Property Held in Joint Tenancy. A decedent's interest in property held in a joint tenancy (with a right of survivorship) or as tenants by the entirety that passes to the other owner by operation of law is considered property acquired from a decedent (Code Sec. 1014(b)(9); Reg. §§1.1014-2(b) and 1.1014-6(a)(1)). Thus, the basis of the property in the hands of the survivor will generally depend upon the amount contributed by each joint tenant toward the original purchase price and, in the case of depreciable property, the manner in which income is divided under local (state) law.

> **Example 1:** Tom and Susan are unmarried and purchased a townhouse for $100,000 that they held as joint tenants with right of survivorship. Tom contributed $30,000 and Susan $70,000. Susan died when the property was worth $200,000. As a result, 70 percent of the fair market value ($140,000) is included in her estate. Tom's basis in the property is $170,000 ($30,000 + $140,000).

> **Example 2:** Assume the same facts as in Example 1, except that Tom and Susan held the townhouse as a rental property and that $25,000 of depreciation was allowed prior to Susan's death. If Tom and Susan are entitled to one-half of the income from the property under local law, Tom's basis would be reduced to $157,500 ($170,000 − $12,500).

For purposes of the federal estate tax, the entire value of jointly held property with the right of survivorship is included in a decedent's gross estate except for the portion of the property that the surviving joint tenant furnished consideration (¶ 2919). If the joint tenants are spouses, then the property is a qualified joint interest and it does not matter who furnished the consideration—one-half of the value is included in the gross estate of the first spouse to die. The surviving spouse's basis in the remaining portion of the qualified joint interest is one-half of the original cost (regardless of the amount that the survivor actually contributed) reduced by any depreciation deductions allocable to the surviving spouse (IRS Pub. 559).

> **Example 3:** Assume the same facts as in Example 1, except that Tom and Susan are married. Tom's basis in the property is $150,000 ($50,000 (one-half of original cost) + $100,000 (one-half of fair market value included in Susan's estate).

1636. Carryover Basis Election for Property Acquired from Decedent. Effective for decedents dying in 2010, the executor of the decedent's estate had the option to elect out of the federal estate tax. If the election was made, a modified carryover basis rule applied to property acquired from the decedent (Code Sec. 1022, prior to P.L. 111-312). Specifically, the property recipient received a basis equal to the lesser of the property's adjusted basis in the hands of the decedent or its fair market value on the date of decedent's death. An executor had the option to elect to increase the basis of estate property by up to $1.3 million (plus an increase for certain carryovers and unrealized losses of the decedent), with an additional basis increase of up to $3 million in the case of property passing to a surviving spouse. The basis of any property could not be increased above its fair market value in the decedent's hands on the date of the decedent's death. The IRS provided optional safe harbor procedures for determining modified carryover basis (Rev. Proc. 2011-41).

Executors and administrators of estates of decedents dying after December 31, 1976, and before November 7, 1978, could elect to determine the basis under the otherwise repealed carryover basis rules (Announcement 80-63). The time for elections expired July 31, 1980, but valid elections will continue to affect computation of gain on dispositions of property to which such elections apply.

1639. Appreciated Property Reacquired by Donor from Decedent. For property acquired from a decedent who dies after December 31, 1981, the basis of the property when reacquired by the donor following the decedent's death is equal to the decedent's adjusted basis in the property immediately before the decedent's death if: (1) appreciated property was acquired by the decedent after August 13, 1981, as a gift; (2) the decedent received the gift within one year before his or her death; and (3) following the decedent's death, the donor of the gift, or the donor's spouse, reacquires the property (Code Sec. 1014(e)).

Property Acquired by Exchange

See CCH® AnswerConnect: *Basis* for more information on this topic.

1648. Basis of Property Transferred to Corporation in a Taxable Exchange. If a corporation acquires property for its stock in an exchange taxable to the transferor, its basis for the property is the fair market value of the stock on the date of the exchange. If the stock has no established market value at that time, it may be considered to be the equivalent of the fair market value of the property received (*Philadelphia Park Amusement Co.*, CtCls, 54-2 USTC ¶ 9697).

1651. Basis of Property Acquired in a Tax-Free Exchange. If property is acquired in an exchange on which no gain or loss is recognized, the basis of the property is the same as that for the property exchanged (Code Sec. 1031(d); Reg. § 1.1031(d)-1). Substitute basis (¶ 1607) applies to:

- like-kind exchange of property held for productive use or investment (¶ 1721), as well as the exchange of government obligations for similar obligations (¶ 1726);

- exchange of stock for stock of the same corporation (¶ 1728);

- exchange of property solely for stock or securities of a controlled corporation (¶ 1731); and

- exchange of stock or securities solely for stock or securities in a reorganization (¶ 2229).

Prior to 2018, trade-in arrangements under where taxpayer sold old equipment used in a trade or business to a dealer and purchased new equipment of like kind from the dealer were like-kind exchanges if the sale and the purchase were mutually dependent transactions, even if they are not simultaneous. (Rev. Rul. 61-119). The basis of the new equipment, for gain or loss or depreciation, is ordinarily the total of the adjusted basis of the trade-in plus whatever additional cash is needed. In effect, the basis of the new property is its purchase price, increased or decreased according to whether the trade-in value of the old equipment is greater or less than its depreciated cost. Special depreciation rules may apply to like-kind exchanges (¶ 1250). Like-kind exchanges are limited to real property after 2017 (Code Sec. 1031(a)).

1657. Basis of Boot Acquired in an Otherwise Tax-Free Exchange. In a like-kind exchange, a taxpayer may receive money or other property (commonly referred to as "boot") that is not of a like-kind (¶ 1721). The taxpayer recognizes gain from the transaction to the extent of the boot's fair market value. In such exchanges, the cost or other applicable basis of the property acquired is the same as that of the property exchanged, decreased by the amount of any money received by the taxpayer in the transaction and increased by the amount of gain or decreased by the amount of loss recognized in the exchange. If boot is received in an exchange that is tax free in part, the cost or other basis of the property disposed of must be allocated between the property received tax free and any other property, assigning to the other property an amount equivalent to its fair market value (Code Sec. 1031(d)).

1660. Basis of Property Transferred to a Corporation. If a corporation acquires property in a Code Sec. 351 transaction (¶ 203), it takes the property with the same basis that the transferor had in the property (Code Sec. 362(a) and (b); Reg. § 1.362-1). The acquiring corporation's basis in the acquired property is increased by any gain recognized by the shareholder on the transfer. The same basis rule applies to property acquired as a paid-in surplus or a contribution to the capital (¶ 1660).

If property is acquired by a corporation in a reorganization, the basis of the transferor (increased by any recognized gain) generally also follows through to the transferee corporation. However, carryover basis will not apply if the property acquired by the corporation consists of stock or securities in another corporation that is a party to the reorganization. This is the case unless the stock or securities were acquired as consideration for the transfer. Rules for property acquired subject to a built-in loss (¶ 1667) and for property acquired upon liquidation of a subsidiary may apply (¶ 2261).

Property contributed to a corporation by nonstockholders has a zero basis. Money contributed by an outsider on or after that date reduces the basis of corporate property acquired with it within 12 months after the contribution is received. To the extent that the contribution is not used to acquire property within this 12-month period, it reduces, as of the last day of the period, the basis of any other property held by the company (Code Sec. 362(c)).

1667. Limitations on Built-In Losses. If a corporation receives property in an exchange with a stockholder who is *not* subject to U.S. tax, and the property's fair market value is less than the transferee's adjusted basis of all property received in the exchange (i.e., there is a built-in loss), the corporate transferee's basis in the property received is its fair market value immediately after the transfer (Code Sec. 362(e)). Thus, the foreign loss is not recognized for U.S. tax purposes. This treatment applies to property acquired by the corporation from a shareholder in exchange for stock in a Code Sec. 351 transaction (¶ 203), as well as the basis of property from a shareholder as paid-in surplus or as a contribution to capital (¶ 1660).

If a corporation acquires property in a section 351 exchange with a shareholder who *is* subject to U.S. tax, and the transferred property's adjusted basis exceeds its fair market value, the corporate transferee's basis in the property is also generally limited to its fair market value immediately after the transaction. Any required basis reduction is allocated among the transferred properties in proportion to their built-in losses immediately before the transaction. The shareholder and corporation can make an irrevocable election to limit the shareholder's basis in the stock received—rather than the corporation's basis in the property—to the aggregate fair market value of the transferred property (Reg. § 1.362-4(d)). If a transaction involves multiple shareholders, the limitation on the transfer of built-in losses is determined separately for each shareholder (Reg. § 1.362-4(b)).

1669. Basis of Property and Assumption of Liabilities. The assumption of liabilities by a shareholder in a Code Sec. 351 exchange with a controlled corporation (¶ 203) or in a reorganization (¶ 2229) is generally not treated as the equivalent of cash or boot (¶ 2233). However, the assumption of a liability is treated as money received for the purpose of determining the basis of the property or stock received in such transfers (Code Secs. 358(d) and 1031(d)). Thus, the corporation's assumption of a liability generally results in a reduction of the basis of the property the shareholder receives in the exchange. An exception applies to an assumption of a liability that would give rise to a deduction, provided the incurrence of such liabilities did not result in the creation or increase of basis of any property.

1672. Basis of Property and Discharge of Debt. Under some conditions, a taxpayer realizes no income from a discharge of debt (¶ 855). Any amount of debt discharged and excluded from gross income reduces the basis of the property securing the debt (Code Sec. 1017). Regulations prescribe the sequence of allocation where the debt is, or must be treated as, a general liability (Reg. §§ 1.108-4 and 1.1017-1).

Other Acquired Property

See CCH® AnswerConnect: *Basis* for more information on this topic.

1678. Basis of Property Transferred in Trust. If property is acquired by a transfer in trust, other than by a transfer in trust by gift, bequest, or devise, its basis is the same as it would be in the hands of the trust's grantor, increased by the gain or decreased by the loss recognized to the grantor under the law in effect as of the date of such transfer (Code Sec. 1015(b)). If an existing charitable remainder trust is split pro rata into separate trusts, one for each beneficiary, the original trust's basis in the assets is split pro rata among the new trusts (Rev. Rul. 2008-41).

1681. Basis of Stock or Other Property Received for Services. If stock or other property is given to an employee as compensation for personal services instead of cash, the fair market value of the property is income to the employee unless the property is subject to a substantial risk of forfeiture (¶ 713). The fair market value of the property included in income is the basis of the property for the employee (Code Sec. 83; Reg.

§ 1.83-4(b)). If the property is sold to the employee for less than its market value, the difference between the amount paid and the value of the property is also income. In this case, the employee's basis for the property is the cash cost, plus the amount reported as income. A taxpayer who receives property subject to a substantial risk of forfeiture may make a section 83(b) election to include the fair market value of the property (less any amount paid for the property) in income in the year that the property is received. The basis for determining gain or loss if the property is sold is the amount included in income in the election year, plus the amount paid for the property (Reg. § 1.83-2).

Corporations may grant their employees the option to purchase stock in the corporation (¶ 1923 and ¶ 1925). For purposes of determining an individual's basis in property transferred in connection with the performance of services, rules similar to the annuity basis rules for nonresident aliens apply (¶ 821).

1682. Basis of Stock Received in Nontaxable Distributions. If a shareholder in a corporation receives stock or stock rights in a nontaxable distribution (¶ 733A), the basis of the old stock is allocated between the old stock and new stock in proportion to the fair market value of each on the date of the distribution (not the record date) (Code Sec. 307; Reg. § 1.307-1). If only part of the stock dividend is nontaxable, the basis of the old stock is allocated between the old stock and the part of the new stock that is not taxable.

This rule applies with respect to stock rights only if such rights are exercised or sold. If exercised, the basis of the stock rights is added to the cost of the stock acquired. If sold, the basis allocable to the stock rights is used to determine the taxpayer's gain or loss. If the stock rights are allowed to expire, the basis of the shares with respect to which the rights were distributed remains intact.

If the fair market value of the stock rights on the date of distribution is less than 15 percent of the fair market value of the stock with respect to which the distribution is made, the basis of the stock rights is deemed to be zero unless the taxpayer elects to make a basis allocation (Code Sec. 307(b); Reg. § 1.307-2). The election must be made in a statement attached to the shareholder's return for the year in which the rights are received. It is irrevocable with respect to the rights for which it is made. The election must be made for all the rights received in a particular distribution by the shareholder on stock of the same class received by the shareholder at the time of the distribution.

Example: Bob bought 100 shares of Yeta Corp. common stock at $125 per share and later received 100 rights entitling him to purchase 20 shares of new common stock in Yeta at $100 per share. When the rights were distributed, the old shares had a fair market value of $120 per share, and the rights had a fair market value of $3 each. Three weeks later, Bob sold his rights for $4 each. He elects to apportion basis.

Cost of old stock on which rights were distributed	$12,500.00
Market value of old stock at date of distribution of rights .	12,000.00
Market value of rights at date of distribution	300.00
Cost apportioned to old stock after distribution of rights (12,000/12,300 of $12,500)	12,195.12
Cost apportioned to rights (300/12,300 of $12,500)	304.88
Selling price of rights	400.00
Gain ($400 – $304.88)	$95.12

In determining gain or loss from any later sale of the stock on which the rights were distributed, the adjusted cost of the old stock is $12,195.12, or $121.95 a share.

The holding period of nontaxable stock rights includes the holding period of the stock on which the rights are distributed. The holding period of the stock acquired by the exercise of the rights begins on the date that the rights are exercised (Code Sec. 1223(4) and (5); Reg. § 1.1223-1(e) and (f)).

1684. Basis of Equipment for Which Medical Deduction Claimed. The basis of equipment whose cost qualifies as a medical expense (¶ 1016) does not include that portion of its cost that has been claimed as an itemized deduction because such amounts are not properly capitalized. However, the equipment's basis includes that portion of the cost that is nondeductible because of the adjusted gross income (AGI) limitation (¶ 1015).

To determine this portion, the total amount of the AGI limitation is multiplied by a fraction. The numerator is the cost of the equipment and the denominator is the total amount of the taxpayer's medical expenses. Similarly, if a taxpayer's total allowable itemized deductions exceed the taxpayer's AGI (or the overall limitation on itemized deductions before 2018 and after 2025 (¶ 1014)), that portion of the equipment's cost attributable to the nondeductible expenses may also be included in the equipment's basis (Reg. § 1.1016-2).

1687. Basis of Property Acquired Through Involuntary Conversion. The basis of property purchased as the result of an involuntary conversion (¶ 1713) on which gain is not recognized is the cost of the replacement property less the amount of gain not recognized on the conversion (Code Sec. 1033(b); Reg. § 1.1033(b)-1). If qualifying replacement property is received as the result of an involuntary conversion, the replacement property's basis is the same as the basis of the involuntarily converted property decreased by any loss recognized on the conversion and any money received and not spent on qualifying replacement property. The basis is increased by any gain recognized on the conversion and any cost of acquiring the replacement property. Special depreciation rules may apply (¶ 1250).

1693. Basis of Property Transferred Between Spouses. No gain or loss is recognized on a transfer of property from an individual to, or in trust for the benefit of, a spouse or a former spouse if the transfer to the former spouse is incident to the divorce of the parties (¶ 1734) (Code Sec. 1041(d)). The basis of the transferred property in the hands of the transferee is the transferor's adjusted basis in the property. The carryover basis rule does not apply to a spouse (or former spouse) who is a nonresident alien.

Nonrecognition of gain is not permitted with respect to the transfer of property in trust to the extent that the sum of the amount of any liabilities assumed, plus the amount of any liabilities to which the property is subject, exceeds the total of the adjusted basis of the property transferred (Code Sec. 1041(e)). The transferee's basis is adjusted to take into account any gain recognized.

Valuation Rules

See CCH® AnswerConnect: *Asset Valuation for Taxes* for more information on this topic.

1695. Indeterminate Fair Market Value. Only in rare and extraordinary cases does property have no determinable fair market value (Reg. § 1.1001-1). If the fair market value of an asset received in an exchange (such as a contract to receive royalties) cannot be determined with fair certainty, gain is not realized on the exchange until after the total payments received under the contract exceed the cost (or other basis) of the property surrendered in exchange (*E.A. Logan*, SCt, 2 ustc ¶ 736). The Tax Court has applied the *Cohan* rule (estimated or approximate value) to estimate the value of patents, patent applications, and stock rights, where the taxpayer could not prove their exact value (*Prosperity Co., Inc.*, CA-2, 53-1 ustc ¶ 66,047).

1697. Valuation of Securities and Real Estate. The fair market value of securities traded on the open market, or on a recognized exchange, is ordinarily the average of the high and low quoted prices on the valuation date. If only a minimal number of shares are traded on the valuation date, or if other abnormal market conditions exist, an alternative valuation method may be necessary (Reg. § 20.2031-2).

If corporate stock is not sold on the open market, its fair market value depends upon many factors, including the nature and history of the business, economic outlook and condition of the industry, book value of stock and financial condition of the business, earning capacity of the company, dividend-paying capacity, goodwill, prior sales, size of the block to be valued, and market price of similar but listed stock. Isolated sales of

16

BASIS

small portions of the stock or forced sales are not considered evidence of fair market value (Code Sec. 2031(b); Rev. Rul. 59-60).

Restrictive sales agreements must be considered in the valuation of stock. If the stock is subject to a repurchase option, its value may not exceed the amount for which it may be repurchased. If there are restrictions making sale of stock impossible, and its value is highly speculative, it does not have a fair market value (*S.A. Salvage*, SCt, 36-1 ustc ¶ 9064).

There are three principal methods used in determining the fair market value of real property:

- the comparable sales method, which involves gathering information on sales of property similar to the subject property and then making adjustments (both positive and negative) for various differences between the *comparables* and the property being appraised (*C.E. Stanton*, Dec. 37,135(M), 40 T.C.M. 885);

- the capitalization of income method, which estimates a property's fair market value based upon future benefits (cash-flow) to be derived from the ownership of the property (*L.J. Vesper*, Dec. 45,858(M), 57 TCM 1035); and

- the replacement cost method, which is based on the principle of substitution and estimates the fair market value of real property based on the assumption that a prudent person (i.e., a willing buyer) would not pay more for a property than it would cost to acquire a similar site and erect a comparable structure (less accrued depreciation) (*J.L. Alioto*, Dec. 37,209(M), 40 TCM 1147).

Other factors that may be appropriate to consider with regard to a fair market value determination of real property include:

- the development potential of the property with regard to its highest and best potential and realistic use;

- the possibility of zoning changes that may either enhance or diminish the marketability of the property;

- the taxpayer's ability to acquire adjacent parcels of property allowing for expanded and, in many cases, enhanced uses;

- leases, debt, and other encumbrances on the property; and

- environmental concerns, restrictions, and hazards.

Appraisal affidavits of a retrospective nature, standing alone, are generally not accorded great weight (*J.C. Blair Co.*, CA-3, 5 ustc ¶ 1509).

Chapter 17

SALES AND EXCHANGES

CAPITAL GAINS

17
SALES

Sales and Exchanges of Property

See CCH® AnswerConnect: *Determining Gain or Loss* for more information on this topic.

1701. Gain or Loss from Sale or Exchange of Property. A taxpayer generally must recognize gain or loss from the sale or exchange of property (Code Sec. 1001(c)). The seller has gain if the amount realized is more than the seller's adjusted basis in the property. The seller has a loss when the adjusted basis of the property is more than the amount realized (Code Sec. 1001(a)). Part of the basis in property generally must be allocated to any portion of that property that is sold or otherwise disposed. However, if basis or fair market value cannot be ascertained or apportioned, the open-transaction doctrine may defer recognition of any gain until the taxpayer's basis in the property has been recovered (*E.A. Fisher*, FedCl, 2008-2 USTC ¶ 50,481).

To determine the tax consequences of a sale or exchange, the following questions must be answered:

- What is the amount realized in the transaction (¶ 1703)?
- What is the taxpayer's adjusted basis in the property (¶ 1604)?
- Is the gain or loss on the transaction recognized (¶ 1719)?
- Do the capital gain and loss provisions apply (¶ 1735)?
- Is any part of the gain attributable to depreciation recapture (¶ 1779)?

Installment Payments. If a nondealer sells real or personal property and part or all of the selling price is to be paid after the year of sale, the recognized gain must be reported on the installment method, unless the taxpayer elects otherwise (¶ 1801).

Gain from Small Business Stock. A noncorporate seller's gain on the sale or exchange of qualified small business stock may qualify for two tax benefits. First, if the stock was issued after August 10, 1993 and the seller held it for more than five years, a percentage of the gain is generally excludable from gross income (¶ 1905). Second, a seller that held the stock for more than six months may defer the gain by rolling it over into other small business stock within 60 days (¶ 1907).

¶1701

Virtual Currency. Convertible virtual currency, such as Bitcoin, that has an equivalent value in or acts as a substitute for real currency is property for federal tax purposes (¶ 785) (Notice 2014-21). Thus, the sale or exchange of virtual currency results in gain or loss, which is capital in nature if the virtual currency was a capital asset in the hands of the seller. The basis of virtual currency that a taxpayer "mines" or receives as payment for goods or services is the fair market value of the virtual currency in U.S. dollars on the date of receipt.

Gift Taxes. A taxpayer who makes a gift of property on condition that the donee pay the resulting gift taxes realizes gain to the extent that the gift taxes paid by the donee exceed the donor's basis in the property (*V.P. Diedrich*, SCt, 82-1 USTC ¶ 9419).

Insurance Company Demutualization. A mutual insurance company is demutualized when it converts into a stock company and issues cash and/or shares to its policyholders in exchange for their equity interests. The IRS has held that a policyholder has zero basis in the surrendered equity interest (Rev. Rul. 71-233), but some courts disagree, and instead treat demutualization proceeds as a return of capital (*E.A. Fisher*, CA-FC, 2010-1 USTC ¶ 50,289).

1703. Amount Realized from Sale or Exchange of Property. The amount realized from the sale or exchange of property is the total of monies received, plus the fair market value of all other property or services received (Code Sec. 1001(b); *International Freighting Corp., Inc.*, CA-2, 43-1 USTC ¶ 9334). Property with no readily determinable fair market value is generally equal in value to the property received in exchange (*Philadelphia Park Amusement Co.*, CtCls, 54-2 USTC ¶ 9697). The amount realized normally includes any liabilities from which the seller is relieved (Reg. § 1.1001-2).

The amount realized on the receipt of an annuity in exchange for property is the fair market value of the annuity contract at the time of the exchange. The entire gain or loss is recognized at the time of the exchange, regardless of the taxpayer's method of accounting (Prop. Reg. § 1.1001-1(j)).

Sale of Principal Residence

See CCH® AnswerConnect: *Exclusion of Gain from the Sale of a Principal Residence* for more information on this topic.

1705. Exclusion of Gain from Sale of Principal Residence. An individual may exclude from gross income up to $250,000 of gain ($500,000 for joint return filers and surviving spouses) realized on the sale or exchange of a principal residence (Code Sec. 121). The individual must meet ownership and use tests for at least two years during the five years preceding the sale or exchange (¶ 1707). The individual also must not have used the exclusion during the two years preceding the sale or exchange. A partial or reduced exclusion may be available for taxpayers who do not meet these requirements (¶ 1709).

Married Individuals. The maximum exclusion is $500,000 for married individuals filing jointly for the tax year of the sale or exchange if:

- either spouse meets the ownership test,
- both spouses meet the use test, and
- neither spouse used the exclusion in the previous two years (Code Sec. 121(b)(2); Reg. § 1.121-2).

A married couple's exclusion is determined on an individual basis. For instance, if Spouse A is eligible for the exclusion, but Spouse B used the exclusion within the previous two years, Spouse A is entitled to a maximum exclusion of $250,000.

Surviving Spouse. A surviving spouse may use the full $500,000 exclusion if the sale or exchange occurs within two years after the other spouse's death and the spouses satisfied all of the requirements listed above immediately before the death (Code Sec. 121(b)(4); Reg. § 1.121-4(a)). A surviving spouse who does not remarry before the sale is treated as having owned and lived in the home for the same period as the deceased spouse (Code Sec. 121(d)(2)).

Gain Allocable to Nonqualified Use. Gain that is allocable to periods of nonqualified use may not be excluded from gross income (Code Sec. 121(b)(5)). Nonqualified use is generally any use other than as a principal residence. Thus, the exclusion for second and vacation homes is significantly limited. However, a period of nonqualified use does not include:

- any portion of the five-year period ending on the date of the sale that is after the last date the home was used as the taxpayer's principal residence;

- any period of 10 years or less if the taxpayer or spouse is serving on qualified duty as a member of the U.S. uniformed services or U.S. Foreign Service, an employee of the intelligence community, or a Peace Corps worker; or

- any period of two years or less for temporary absence due to a change of employment, health conditions, or other unforeseen circumstances.

Like-Kind Exchanges. The exclusion does not apply to a home that was acquired in a like-kind exchange (¶ 1721) if the taxpayer (or any person whose basis in the property is derived from the taxpayer's basis) sells or exchanges the residence within five years after the acquisition (Code Sec. 121(d)(10)).

Gain Recognized to Extent of Depreciation. The exclusion of gain from the sale or exchange of a principal residence does not apply to the extent of any depreciation allowable with respect to the rental or business use of the residence after May 6, 1997 (Code Sec. 121(d)(6); Reg. § 1.121-1(d)(1)). This rule applies to the amount of depreciation allowed if the taxpayer can establish that it was less than the amount allowable (Code Sec. 1250(b)(3)).

Remainder Interests. The exclusion applies to gain on the sale or exchange of a remainder interest in a principal residence, provided the buyer is not a member of the taxpayer's family or another related party (¶ 432 and ¶ 1717) (Code Sec. 121(d)(8)).

Expatriates. The exclusion is not available to nonresident aliens who relinquish U.S. citizenship or long-term resident status and are subject to the mark-to-market rules for covered expatriates (¶ 2412) (Code Sec. 121(e)).

Involuntary Conversions. For purposes of the exclusion, the destruction, theft, seizure, requisition, or condemnation of the property is a sale or exchange (Code Sec. 121(d)(5); Reg. § 1.121-4(d)). In addition, the ownership and use of the replacement property generally includes the ownership and use of the converted property. The amount realized on an involuntary conversion (¶ 1713) is reduced by the excluded gain.

Inherited Property. Estates, heirs and revocable trusts established by a decedent generally cannot exclude any gain on the sale of the decedent's principal residence. However, the exclusion can be used if the decedent died in 2010 and the estate elects to apply the modified carryover basis rules (¶ 1633) (Code Sec. 121(d)(11), prior to repeal by P.L. 111-312)).

Reporting Requirements. If all of the gain from the sale of a home is excludable, the seller does not have to report the sale. If, however, the individual can exclude only part of the gain or receives a Form 1099-S, the sale or exchange is reported on Form 8949. If the home is sold under the installment method and gain is recognized (¶ 1801), the sale is reported on Form 6252. Sale of the business or rental portion of the property (¶ 1707) may have to be reported on Form 4797.

1707. Ownership and Use Requirements for Principal Residence. An individual may exclude gain realized from the sale or exchange of a principal residence (¶ 1705) if, during the five-year period that ends on the date of the sale or exchange, the individual owned and used the property as a principal residence for periods aggregating two years or more (at least 730 days) (Code Sec. 121(a); Reg. § 1.121-1(c)).

A reduced exclusion may be available for a taxpayer who does not meet the ownership and use requirements, or who used the exclusion within two years of the sale or exchange (¶ 1709).

Divorce. If the residence is transferred between spouses, or between former spouses incident to divorce, the period the transferor owned the property is added to the period the transferee owns the property (Code Sec. 121(d)(3); Reg. § 1.121-4(b)). A homeowner also uses the home as a principal residence during the time his or her spouse or former spouse has use of the home under a divorce or separation agreement.

¶1707

Incapacity. A homeowner who becomes physically or mentally incapable of self-care is deemed to use the home as a principal residence while residing in a licensed care facility, such as a nursing home, as long as he or she owned and used the home as a principal residence for periods totalling at least one year during the five years preceding the sale or exchange (Code Sec. 121(d)(7)).

Military, Foreign Service, Peace Corps, and Intelligence Personnel. A homeowner may elect to suspend the running of the five-year ownership and use period for up to 10 years while the homeowner (or spouse) serves on qualified official extended duty as a member of the U.S. uniformed services or U.S. Foreign Service, as an employee of the intelligence community, or outside the United States as a Peace Corps employee on qualified official extended duty or as a Peace Corps enrolled volunteer or volunteer leader (Code Sec. 121(d)(9) and (12); Reg. § 1.121-5). The taxpayer makes the election by not including the gain in gross income for the year of the sale. The election may be made for only one property, but it may be revoked at any time.

Allocation for Partial Use. The exclusion does not apply to any gain that is allocable to any portion of the property that is separate from the actual residence (the dwelling unit) and not used as a residence (Reg. § 1.121-1(e)). The sale is treated as a sale of two properties: the dwelling unit and the nonresidential property. Basis and the amount realized must be allocated under the same method used to determine depreciation adjustments. However, if part of the dwelling unit itself was used for a business, such as a home office, or to produce rental income, these rules do not apply. Instead, the seller must recognize gain only to recapture depreciation (¶ 1705).

Trusts and Single-Owner Entities. An individual is treated as owning a personal residence while it is owned by the individual's grantor trust (¶ 571) or single-member disregarded entity (¶ 402A) (Reg. § 1.121-1(c)(3)).

Cooperatives. A tenant-stockholder in a cooperative housing corporation (¶ 1040) may be able to exclude gain on the sale or exchange of the stock if, for at least two years during the five-year period ending on the date of sale or exchange, the taxpayer owned the stock and lived in the house or apartment as a principal residence (Code Sec. 121(d)(4); Reg. § 1.121-4(c)).

1709. Reduced Exclusion of Gain from Sale of Principal Residence. The maximum exclusion of gain on the sale of a principal residence (¶ 1705) is available only if the homeowner satisfies ownership and use requirements (¶ 1707) and has not used the exclusion for a sale within the previous two years. A reduced exclusion is available for a seller who does not meet these requirements if the primary reason for the sale is a qualified individual's change in place of employment, health reasons, or unforeseen circumstances (Code Sec. 121(c); Reg. § 1.121-3). A qualified individual is the taxpayer, the taxpayer's spouse, a co-owner of the residence, or a person whose principal place of abode is in the same household as the taxpayer, plus certain relatives if the disposition is for health reasons.

Change in Place of Employment. The primary reason test is satisfied if the sale or exchange is due to a change in the location of a qualified individual's employment (Reg. § 1.121-3(c)). The safe harbor applies if the new place of employment is at least 50 miles farther from the residence than was the former place of employment.

Health. The primary reason test is satisfied if the primary reason for the sale or exchange is to obtain, provide, or facilitate the diagnosis, cure, mitigation, or treatment of a qualified individual's disease, illness, or injury; or to obtain or provide medical or personal care for a qualified individual suffering from a disease, illness, or injury (Reg. § 1.121-3(d)). A qualified individual's child, sibling, parent, niece, nephew, in-law, or cousin is also a qualified individual for this purpose (Reg. § 1.121-3(f)).

Unforeseen Circumstances. The primary reason test is satisfied if the sale or exchange is due to an event that the taxpayer could not reasonably anticipate before buying and occupying the residence (Reg. § 1.121-3(e)). The safe harbor applies in the following situations:

- involuntary conversion of the home (¶ 1713);
- damage to the home from natural or man-made disasters or acts of war or terrorism;

- a qualified individual's death, loss of employment that qualifies for unemployment compensation, change in employment status resulting in the taxpayer's inability to pay housing costs and reasonable basic living expenses, divorce or legal separation, or multiple births resulting from a single pregnancy; or

- any other event or situation identified by the IRS.

Computing the Reduced Exclusion. The reduced exclusion is computed by multiplying the maximum allowable exclusion ($250,000 or $500,000) by a fraction (Reg. § 1.121-3(g)). The numerator is the shortest of: (1) the period that the taxpayer owned the property during the five-year period ending on the sale or exchange date; (2) the period that the taxpayer used the property as a principal residence during the five-year period ending on the sale or exchange date; or (3) the period between the current sale and the sale for which the taxpayer last used the exclusion. The denominator of the fraction is either 730 days or 24 months, depending on the whether the numerator is expressed in days or months.

Involuntary Conversions

See CCH® AnswerConnect: *Involuntary Conversions* for more information on this topic.

1713. Gain or Loss from Involuntary Conversion. A taxpayer does not have to recognize gain on an involuntary conversion of property in two circumstances (Code Sec. 1033; Reg. §§ 1.1033(a)-1, 1.1033(a)-2):

- If property is converted involuntarily or by compulsion into other property that is similar or related in service or use, the taxpayer does not recognize gain. The basis of the old property is transferred to the new property (¶ 1687). This nonrecognition rule is mandatory.

- If property is involuntarily converted into money or property that is not similar or related to the converted property in service or use, the taxpayer may elect to postpone recognizing gain that is invested in replacement property within the replacement period (¶ 1715). Thus, an electing taxpayer recognizes gain on the conversion only to the extent that the amount realized exceeds the cost of the replacement property. A taxpayer elects to defer the reinvested gain by simply excluding it from gross income for the tax year in which it is realized, and providing details of the involuntary conversion in a statement attached to the tax return (discussed below).

An involuntary conversion occurs when: (1) property is destroyed, stolen, seized, condemned, or disposed of under threatened or imminent condemnation; and (2) the taxpayer receives other property or money (usually insurance proceeds or a condemnation award) as compensation. To the extent the compensation exceeds the basis of the converted property, the taxpayer realizes gain (¶ 1701).

Loss. Loss from an involuntary conversion is deductible if the converted property was used in a business or for the production of income (¶ 1101). Some casualty or theft losses on personal property may also be deductible (¶ 1121 and ¶ 1123). Some gains and losses from involuntary conversions may be treated as capital gains and losses (¶ 1748).

Conversion of Personal Residence. An individual whose principal residence is involuntarily converted may be able to exclude up to $250,000 of the realized gain ($500,000 for joint return filers and surviving spouses) as if the home had been sold (¶ 1705) (Code Sec. 121(d)(5)). Nonexcludable gain may be deferred if it is used to purchase replacement property. The sale of the underlying land within a reasonable period of time following the destruction of a principal residence can qualify as part of the involuntary conversion of the residence (Rev. Rul. 96-32).

Livestock. Livestock is involuntarily converted if it is destroyed, sold, or exchanged because of disease (Code Sec. 1033(d); Reg. § 1.1033(d)-1). A sale or exchange of livestock (except poultry) that is made solely on account of drought, flood, or other weather-related conditions may also qualify as an involuntary conversion to the extent it exceeds the number of animals that would normally be sold (Code Sec. 1033(e); Reg. § 1.1033(e)-1).

17 | SALES

The general two-year period for purchasing replacement property is extended to four years if the weather-related condition makes the area eligible for assistance from the federal government. The IRS can further extend the replacement period if the weather-related condition continues for more than three years. For instance, the replacement period for livestock that is involuntarily converted due to persistent drought in the taxpayer's region is extended until the end of the taxpayer's first tax year ending after the region's first drought-free year (Notice 2006-82). Each year, the IRS publishes a list of the counties that suffered droughts sufficient to extend the replacement period (Notice 2019-54). The due date for performing certain time-sensitive actions, including the purchase of replacement property within the replacement period, otherwise due on or after April 1, 2020, and before July 15, 2020, is automatically extended to July 15, 2020, in response to the COVID-19 (coronavirus) crisis (Notice 2020-23; Rev. Proc. 2018-58).

Proceeds from an involuntary conversion of livestock can be invested in other property used for farming if, due to drought, flood, other weather-related conditions, or soil or other environmental contamination, it is not feasible for a farmer to reinvest the proceeds in property that is similar or related in service or use (Code Sec. 1033(f)). If the conversion was due to soil or other environmental contamination, even real property can qualify as replacement property.

Severance Damages. If only a portion of a tract of land is appropriated by a government authority, the condemnation award may have two components: compensation for the converted portion and severance damages for the retained portion. Severance damages may be paid if access to the owner's land is impaired, or if the owner must replace fences and plant trees to restore the retained property to its former use. The entire award is considered compensation for the condemned property unless both parties stipulate that a specific amount is severance damages (Rev. Rul. 59-173). The owner's net severance damages (gross severance damages minus legal expenses and other costs) reduce the basis of the retained property. Any excess of the severance damages over the owner's basis is gain (Rev. Rul. 68-37). However, the owner may elect not to recognize gain that is reinvested in replacement property (¶ 1715) (Rev. Rul. 83-49).

Reporting Requirements. Form 4797 is used to report the gain or loss from an involuntary conversion (other than casualty or theft) of business property, as well as capital assets used in a business or in connection with a transaction entered into for profit. Form 4684 is used to report involuntary conversions from casualties and thefts. Gains from involuntary conversions (other than casualty or theft) of capital assets not held for business or profit are reported by individuals, estates, and trusts on Form 8949.

A separate statement that reports all details connected to the involuntary conversion must be attached to the tax return for the year in which gain is realized (Reg. § 1.1033(a)-2(c)(2)). The details must include a description of the property, the date and type of conversion, computation of the gain, the decision to replace the converted property, and expiration of the replacement period.

If the taxpayer elects to defer gain, but then decides not to replace the converted property, or fails to invest all of the deferred gain in replacement property during the replacement period, the taxpayer must recompute the tax liability in an amended return for the year(s) for which the election was made. If the taxpayer elects nonrecognition after filing the return and paying tax for the tax year(s) in which gain is realized but before the replacement period expires, the taxpayer should file a credit or refund claim for each year that gain was reported. The taxpayer must report all of the details of the replacement of converted property in the return for the year of replacement, even if no gain is realized in that year.

The IRS may assess a deficiency attributable to realized gain on an involuntary conversion within three years from the date the taxpayer notifies the IRS of the replacement of the converted property, an intention not to replace, or a failure to replace within the required period (Code Sec. 1033(a)(2)(C); Reg. § 1.1033(a)-2(c)(5)).

1715. Replacement Property for Involuntary Conversions. A taxpayer does not recognize gain on an involuntary conversion of property (¶ 1713) to the extent that the converted property is replaced with qualified replacement property during the replacement period (Code Sec. 1033(a)). Gain that is not invested in replacement property is recognized.

Replacement Property. Replacement property can be (1) property similar or related in service or use to the property converted, or (2) stock with a controlling interest (at least 80-percent control) in a corporation owning such property. If real property used in the taxpayer's trade or business (other than inventory or property held primarily for sale) or held for investment is condemned or disposed of under threat of condemnation, replacement property includes "like-kind" (¶ 1721) property that the taxpayer holds for productive use in trade or business or for investment (Code Sec. 1033(g); Reg. § 1.1033(g)-1). This like-kind rule does not apply to acquisitions of control of a corporation owning such property, or to involuntary conversions by fire, storm, or other casualty.

A taxpayer may elect to treat an outdoor advertising display (billboard) as real property as long as the display was not subject to a Code Sec. 179 expense election (¶ 1208). Business or investment property that is involuntarily converted in a federally declared disaster may be replaced by tangible property held for productive use in a trade or business, even if it is not similar or related in service or use (Code Sec. 1033(h)(2)).

Basis of Replacement Property. If property is compulsorily or involuntarily converted directly into property that is similar or related in service or use, the basis of the acquired property is the same as the basis of the converted property (¶ 1687). If the taxpayer uses conversion proceeds to acquire the replacement property, the basis of the replacement property is its cost, decreased by any unrecognized gain. If the taxpayer purchases more than one piece of replacement property, the basis is allocated to the properties in proportion to their respective costs.

Property Acquired from Related Persons. Certain taxpayers cannot defer the recognition of gain on an involuntary conversion if the replacement property is acquired from a related person (¶ 432 and ¶ 1717), unless the related person obtained the property from an unrelated person during the replacement period (Code Sec. 1033(i)). The prohibition applies to a C corporation, a partnership if more than a 50 percent of its interest is owned by C corporations, and any other taxpayer who realizes gain of more than $100,000 during the year from involuntary conversions.

Replacement Period. The taxpayer must purchase the replacement property within a replacement period that begins on the actual date of the conversion or, if earlier, on the date the threat or imminence of condemnation or requisition begins (Code Sec. 1033(a)(2)(B)). The replacement period generally ends two years after the close of the first tax year in which the taxpayer realizes any gain on the conversion.

The replacement period is three years for real property (other than inventory) used in a trade or business or held for investment (Code Sec. 1033(g)(4)). The replacement period is four years for a principal residence (¶ 1705) in a federally declared disaster area, and insurance proceeds for the residence and its scheduled contents are generally treated as a common pool of funds received for the conversion of a single item of property. The replacement period is also four years for certain involuntarily converted livestock (¶ 1713).

The due date for performing certain time-sensitive actions, including the purchase of replacement property within the applicable replacement period, otherwise due on or after April 1, 2020, and before July 15, 2020, is automatically extended to July 15, 2020, in response to the COVID-19 (coronavirus) crisis (Notice 2020-23; Rev. Proc. 2018-58).

Application for Extension. The IRS also may extend the replacement period upon a written application submitted to the service center where the taxpayer's income tax return is filed (Code Sec. 1033(a)(2)(B); Reg. § 1.1033(a)-2(c)(3)). The IRS does not provide a form for extension requests. The application should explain in detail why the taxpayer is unable to replace the converted property within the replacement period. It should be filed before the statutory replacement period expires, but the IRS may accept a late request if it is made within a reasonable period and there is reasonable cause for the untimely filing. The IRS may grant an extension if the replacement property is being built during the replacement period, but it will not grant an extension based on the scarcity or high price of replacement property (Rev. Rul. 60-69).

17 SALES

¶1715

Related Party Transactions

See CCH® AnswerConnect: *Related Party Transactions* for more information on this topic.

1717. Losses Not Allowed in Transactions Between Related Persons. A loss from a sale or exchange is generally not recognized if the parties to the transaction are related persons (Code Sec. 267(a); Reg. § 1.267(a)-1). However, the loss might be recognized if the buyer subsequently sells or exchanges the property at a gain. Related persons include:

- an individual and members of his or her family (spouse, plus brothers, sisters, ancestors, and lineal descendants);
- an individual and a corporation if the individual owns (directly or indirectly) more than 50 percent in value of the outstanding stock;
- corporations that are members of the same controlled group;
- a grantor and a fiduciary of the same trust;
- fiduciaries of different trusts with the same grantor;
- a fiduciary and a beneficiary of the same trust;
- a fiduciary and a beneficiary of different trusts with the same grantor;
- a trust fiduciary and a corporation, if more than 50 percent in value of the outstanding stock is directly or indirectly owned by or for the trust or its grantor;
- an exempt charitable or educational organization and a person who controls it (including an individual's family members);
- a corporation and a partnership if the same persons own more than 50 percent in value of the outstanding stock of the corporation, and more than 50 percent of the capital interest or profits interest in the partnership;
- S corporations if the same persons own more than 50 percent in value of the outstanding stock of each corporation;
- an S corporation and a C corporation if the same persons own more than 50 percent in value of the outstanding stock of each corporation; and
- an executor and a beneficiary of the same estate, unless the sale or exchange satisfies a pecuniary bequest (Code Sec. 267(b); Reg. § 1.267(b)-1).

Stock Attribution. Stock held by a corporation, partnership, estate, or trust is considered owned proportionately by its shareholders, partners, or beneficiaries. An individual is considered to own stock owned by his or her family members and partners (Code Sec. 267(c)).

Previously Disallowed Loss. The related transferee's gain on a subsequent disposal of the property is generally reduced (but not below zero) by the amount of any loss that was denied to the original transferor because of the related-person rules. However, this gain reduction rule does not apply if the transferor's loss (if allowed) would not have been considered in calculating the transferor's income tax, or any tax computed like an income tax (Code Sec. 267(d)).

Tax-Free Exchanges

See CCH® AnswerConnect: *Like-Kind Exchanges* and *Nonrecognition Transactions* for more information on this topic.

1719. Gain or Loss from Exchanges of Property. Gain and loss from the sale or exchange of property generally must be recognized (Code Sec. 1001(c)). However, some types of exchanges do not result in recognized gain or deductible loss. These include: like-kind exchanges (¶ 1721); exchanges of insurance or annuity contracts (¶ 1724); exchanges of government obligations (¶ 1726); stock exchanged for stock in the same corporation (¶ 1728) or for property (¶ 1729); transfers of property to the transferor's controlled corporation (¶ 1731); exchanges by certain government employees to avoid conflicts of interest (¶ 1732); sales of stock to an employee stock ownership plan (¶ 1733); and transfers between spouses or former spouses (¶ 1734).

1721. Like-Kind Exchanges. No gain or loss is recognized if business or investment real property is exchanged solely for other business or investment real property of a like kind (Code Sec. 1031(a); Reg. § 1.1031(a)-1). An interest in a partnership that has elected out of the partnership rules (¶ 402) is treated as an interest in each of the partnership's assets rather than as interest in the partnership (Code Sec. 1031(e)). Although professional athletes' contracts are not like-kind property, a safe harbor allows professional sports teams to avoid recognizing gain or loss on trades of personnel contracts and draft picks (Rev. Proc. 2019-18). Like-kind exchanges completed before 2018 could involve some types of personal property.

The like-kind exchange rules do not apply to exchanges of property the taxpayer uses for personal purposes (IRS Pub. 544). A vacation home or other dwelling unit may generally be treated as held for business purposes if:

- the taxpayer rented out the unit for at least two weeks in each of the two years before the exchange, and rents out the property received for at least two weeks in each of the first two years after the exchange, and

- the taxpayer's personal use of the units in those years is minimal (Rev. Proc. 2008-16).

The disposition of a home that was converted to business use may be both a like-kind exchange and a sale of a principal residence qualifying for an exclusion of gain (¶ 1705) (Rev. Proc. 2005-14).

Related Persons. If property received in a like-kind exchange between certain controlled partnerships (¶ 432) or related persons (¶ 1717) is disposed of within two years after the last transfer involved in the exchange, the original exchange does not qualify for nonrecognition treatment (Code Sec. 1031(f)). The taxpayer takes the previously unrecognized gain or loss into account on the date of the subsequent disposition of the exchanged property by the taxpayer or the related party. The parties cannot circumvent this rule by using a qualified intermediary. The running of the two-year period may be suspended if the holder of the exchanged property has substantially diminished the risk of loss by the use of a put option (¶ 1921), short sale (¶ 1944), another person's right to acquire the property, or any other transaction (Code Sec. 1031(g)).

The related-person rules do not apply if the avoidance of federal income tax was not a principal purpose of the original exchange or the subsequent disposition. They also do not apply if the disposition was due to the death of either related party or the compulsory or involuntary conversion of the property (¶ 1713).

Like-Kind Property Defined. Properties are of like kind if they are of the same nature or character (Code Sec. 1031(h); Reg. § 1.1031(a)-1(b) and (c)). Most exchanges of real property qualify as like-kind exchanges, except real property located in the United States and real property located outside the United States are not like-kind. Leaseholds with at least 30 years to run are generally like-kind to fee simple interests.

Boot. A taxpayer who receives money or property not of a like kind (boot) as part of a like-kind exchange must recognize gain from the transaction to the extent of the boot's fair market value (Code Sec. 1031(b); Reg. § 1.1031(b)-1). The taxpayer cannot deduct any loss on the exchange (Code Sec. 1031(c); Reg. § 1.1031(c)-1). Boot may consist of cash, relief from debt, property that is not like kind to the property being exchanged, or property excluded from like-kind treatment. Boot is often given to equalize the value of the like-kind properties being exchanged.

A taxpayer who relinquishes mortgaged real estate in a like-kind exchange receives boot equal to the amount of the mortgage from which the taxpayer is relieved (Code Sec. 1031(d); Reg. §§ 1.1031(b)-1(c), 1.1031(d)-2). If mortgaged property is exchanged for mortgaged property, the net reduction of the mortgage is boot, whether the taxpayer transfers or receives property that is subject to a mortgage.

Substituted Basis. The basis of the surrendered property in a like-kind exchange generally carries over to the property received (¶ 1651). If the exchange includes boot, basis is generally decreased by the amount of any money received, and increased by the amount of any gain (or decreased by the amount of any loss) recognized on the exchange (Code Sec. 1031(d); Reg. § 1.1031-1(b)).

Reporting. Like-kind exchanges are reported on Form 8824. If any gain is recognized because the taxpayer transferred and received more than one group of like-properties or boot, then Schedule D is used to report gains on capital assets not held for business or profit, Form 4797 is used to report gains on assets held for business or profit, and Form 6252 is used to report gain from an installment sale.

1722. Deferred Like-Kind Exchanges. A like-kind exchange (¶ 1721) may occur even if the replacement property is received after the relinquished property has been transferred, provided that identification and receipt requirements are satisfied (Code Sec. 1031(a)(3); Reg. § 1.1031(k)-1). In a deferred exchange (sometimes referred to as a "Starker exchange"), the replacement property must be:

- identified within 45 days after the relinquished property is transferred, and

- received within 180 days of the transfer or, if earlier, by the due date (including extensions) of the income tax return for the tax year in which the relinquished property was transferred.

The deadlines may be extended if the parties are affected by a federally declared disaster, including time-sensitive actions otherwise due on or after April 1, 2020, and before July 15, 2020, in response to the COVID-19 (coronavirus) crisis (Rev. Proc. 2018-58; Notice 2020-23). Property not in existence or still under construction may qualify as replacement property in a deferred exchange.

Receipt of Money or Other Property. The taxpayer generally may not actually or constructively receive cash or other property and then use the proceeds to buy the replacement property (Reg. § 1.1031(k)-1(f)). However, there are three safe harbors for holding exchange funds between transactions:

- security or guarantee arrangements in which the taxpayer allows a third party to hold the exchange funds, and the obligation to use the funds to acquire replacement property is secured by a mortgage, deed of trust, or other security interest in property, a standby letter of credit, or a guarantee;

- qualified escrow accounts and qualified trusts in which the cash or a cash equivalent is held in a qualified escrow account or in a qualified trust; and

- qualified intermediaries (accommodators) safe harbor in which the taxpayer contracts with an independent third party who holds the cash and/or transferred property until the exchange is complete (Reg. § 1.1031(k)-1(g)).

A third party that holds exchange funds under any of the safe harbors may agree to pay interest or a "growth factor" on the funds it holds. These amounts are treated and taxed as interest, not taxable boot (non-like-kind property).

Parking Transactions. An additional safe harbor may apply to an exchange in which replacement property is acquired before the relinquished property is transferred (a "parking transaction" or reverse-Starker exchange) (Rev. Proc. 2000-37, modified by Rev. Proc. 2004-51). The replacement property is "parked" with a third party (the accommodation party) until it is transferred to the ultimate transferee in a simultaneous or deferred exchange. The parties use a qualified exchange accommodation arrangement (QEAA) in which a person other than the taxpayer or a disqualified person (a person related to or acting as an agent for the taxpayer) holds title to the property.

The combined time period that the relinquished and replacement properties are held in the QEAA cannot exceed 180 days. If the requirements are met, the IRS will not challenge the qualification of the replacement property or the relinquished property, or the treatment of the exchange accommodation titleholder (EAT) as the beneficial owner of the property.

Interest on Funds Held by Intermediaries. Escrow accounts, trusts, and funds used to facilitate deferred exchanges (exchange funds) are generally treated as loaned by the taxpayer to an exchange facilitator (Reg. § 1.468B-6). An exchange facilitator is a qualified intermediary (QI), transferee, escrow holder, trustee or other party that holds exchange funds for a taxpayer in a deferred exchange under an escrow, trust or exchange agreement. Interest is imputed to the taxpayer under Code Sec. 7872 (¶ 795), unless the exchange facilitator pays sufficient interest. The exchange facilitator is deemed to receive the same amount as compensation for its services, and has an offsetting deduction for its interest "payment" to the taxpayer.

Bankrupt Qualified Intermediaries. The IRS has provided a safe harbor method for reporting gain or loss for a taxpayer undertaking a deferred like-kind exchange if the qualified intermediary defaults on its obligations (Rev. Proc. 2010-14). The taxpayer is generally allowed to defer gain until payment is received.

Direct Deeding of Property. If the replacement property is acquired from a third party, it may be deeded directly to the taxpayer without passing through the hands of the other party to the exchange. For example, if Ann transfers property to Bob, and Bob buys the replacement property from Cal, then Cal may transfer legal title directly to Ann rather than to Bob (Rev. Rul. 90-34).

1724. Exchange of Insurance or Annuity Contracts. A life insurance, endowment, annuity, or qualified long-term care insurance policy is considered property for federal tax purposes, so any gain or loss realized on a sale or exchange of the policy is ordinarily taxable. However, no gain or loss results from an exchange of:

- a life insurance contract for another life insurance contract or an endowment, annuity, or qualified long-term care insurance contract;

- an endowment contract for another endowment contract that provides for regular payment beginning at a date no later than the date payments would have begun under the contract exchanged, or for an annuity or long-term care insurance contract;

- an annuity contract for another annuity contract that is payable over the life of the same annuitant, or for a qualified long-term care insurance contract; or

- a qualified long-term care insurance contract for another qualified long-term care insurance contract (Code Sec. 1035; Reg. § 1.1035-1).

Gain or loss may be recognized if the exchange has the effect of transferring property to any person other than a United States person. Policyholders who surrender life insurance or annuity contracts of a financially troubled insurance company may qualify for nonrecognition treatment if, within 60 days, all cash received is reinvested in another policy or contract issued by another insurance company, or in a single custodial account (Rev. Proc. 92-44; Rev. Proc. 92-44A).

A partial exchange of the cash surrender value of an existing annuity contract for a second annuity contract is a tax-free exchange only if no amount, other than an amount received as an annuity for a period of 10 years or more, or during one or more lives, is received during the 180 days beginning on the date of the transfer (Rev. Proc. 2011-38). A subsequent direct transfer is not taken into account. These rules do not apply to partial annuitizations (¶ 817).

1726. Exchange of Government Obligations. Obligations issued by the United States may be exchanged tax-free for other such obligations, except to the extent that money is received in the exchange (Code Sec. 1037; Reg. § 1.1037-1). Municipal or state bonds may be exchanged under a refunding agreement with no recognized gain or loss, provided that there are no material differences in the terms of the exchanged bonds (Rev. Rul. 81-169).

1728. Stock Exchanged for Stock of the Same Corporation. An exchange of common stock for common stock of the same corporation, or preferred stock for preferred stock of the same corporation, generally does not result in recognized gain or deductible loss (Code Sec. 1036; Reg. § 1.1036-1). Gain (but not loss) may be recognized if cash or other property (boot) is received (¶ 1721). Nonqualified preferred stock is not treated as stock for these purposes.

1729. Stock Exchanged for Property. A corporation does not recognize gain or loss upon the receipt of money or other property in exchange for its own stock, including treasury stock, regardless of the nature of the transaction or the facts and circumstances involved (Code Sec. 1032; Reg. § 1.1032-1). The corporation may receive its own stock, as long as it is received in exchange for its own stock. A corporation also does not recognize gain or loss on the lapse or acquisition of an option, or with respect to a securities futures contract, to buy or sell its own stock, including treasury stock. See

¶1729

¶ 736 for discussion of the nonrecognition of gain or loss when a corporation distributes its stock to shareholders.

1731. Tax-Free Transfer of Property to Controlled Corporation. No gain or loss is recognized if one or more persons (individuals, trusts, estates, partnerships, or corporations) transfer property to a corporation solely in exchange for its stock if, immediately after the transfer, the transferors are in control of the transferee corporation (Code Sec. 351; Reg. § 1.351-1). See ¶ 203 for further discussion of tax-free contributions of property to a corporation in exchange for stock. See ¶ 1660 for discussion of the basis of the property transferred to the controlled corporation.

1732. Dispositions of Property to Avoid Conflicts of Interest. An officer or employee of the executive branch, or a judicial officer of the federal government, who sells property in order to comply with conflict-of-interest requirements may elect to recognize gain only to the extent that the amount realized is more than the adjusted basis of any permitted property that the taxpayer purchases during the 60-day period beginning on the sale date (Code Sec. 1043). Permitted property includes any U.S. obligation or diversified investment fund approved by the Office of Government Ethics. The nonrecognized gain reduces basis in the permitted property. This option is also available to any spouse, minor, or dependent child whose ownership of property is attributable to the federal officer or employee under applicable conflict-of-interest laws. The deferral rules apply to sales by a trustee if any person subject to the rules has a beneficial interest in the trust's principal or income. Form 8824 is used to report conflict-of-interest sales.

1733. Tax-Free Sale of Stock to ESOP. A taxpayer other than a C corporation may elect to sell qualified securities to an employee stock ownership plan (ESOP) (¶ 2103) or worker-owned cooperative and replace them with other securities without recognizing gain (Code Sec. 1042; Temp. Reg. § 1.1042-1T). The taxpayer makes the election by attaching a statement to its original or amended return for the tax year of the sale. The taxpayer must purchase the qualified replacement property within three months before, or 12 months after, the sale to the ESOP or cooperative. However, the due date for performing certain time-sensitive actions, including purchasing replacement property, otherwise due on or after April 1, 2020, and before July 15, 2020, is automatically extended to July 15, 2020, in response to the COVID-19 (coronavirus) crisis (Notice 2020-23; Rev. Proc. 2018-58).

1734. Transfers of Property Between Spouses or Former Spouses. No gain or loss is recognized on transfers of property between spouses, or between former spouses incident to a divorce (Code Sec. 1041; Temp. Reg. § 1.1041-1T). The transferor's basis in the transferred property carries over to the transferee. A transfer to a former spouse must occur within one year after the date on which the marriage ceased, or must be related to the cessation of the marriage. The nonrecognition rule does not apply if the transferee is a nonresident alien.

Capital Gains and Losses

See CCH® AnswerConnect: *Capital Gains* for more information on this topic.

1735. Characterization of Gains or Loss. Gain or loss realized from the sale or disposition of property generally is recognized for federal income tax purposes (¶ 1701), with its tax treatment determined by its character. Capital gain or loss arises only from a sale or exchange of a capital asset (¶ 1741 and ¶ 1742). Taxpayers must follow specific procedures in calculating recognized capital gain or loss (¶ 1739). Gain or loss from the sale or exchange of property that is not a capital asset is ordinary income or ordinary loss (Code Secs. 64 and 65). Capital gain on certain financial conversion transactions may be recharacterized as ordinary income (¶ 1740).

Capital gain or loss is long-term if the taxpayer held the capital asset for more than one year (¶ 1737). Individuals, estates, and trusts may be eligible for lower tax rates on their net long-term capital gain (¶ 1736). Corporate taxpayers must include both net long-term and short-term capital gains in gross income (¶ 1738). Deductions for capital losses that exceed capital gains may be limited for all taxpayers (¶ 1752).

Reporting Requirements. Taxpayers report the details of the sale and disposition of capital assets on Form 8949, and then carry the relevant dollar amount totals to Schedule D of their tax returns.

1736. Tax on Capital Gains—Individual, Estate, Trust. For individuals, estates, and trusts, a number of different tax rates can apply to net capital gains for regular income tax and alternative minimum tax (AMT) purposes. The tax rates on net capital gains and qualified dividend income are 0, 15, or 20 percent, based on taxable income (Code Sec. 1(h)(1) and (j)(5)). The capital gains tax rate is 25 percent for unrecaptured Code Sec. 1250 gain (¶ 1779), and 28 percent for gain on collectibles and qualified small business stock (¶ 1905).

For tax years beginning in 2019, net capital gains and qualified dividends are taxed as follows (Rev. Proc. 2018-57; Rev. Proc. 2019-44):

- 0 percent if taxable income is $78,750 or less ($80,000 for 2020) if married filing jointly or surviving spouse, $52,750 or less ($53,600 for 2020) if head of household, $39,375 or less ($40,000 for 2020) if single or married filing separately, and $2,650 or less ($2,650 for 2020) for estates or trusts;

- 15 percent if taxable income is $488,850 or less ($496,600 for 2020) if married filing jointly or surviving spouse, $461,700 or less ($469,050 for 2020) if head of household, $434,550 or less ($441,450 for 2020) if single, $244,425 or less ($248,300 for 2020) if married filing separately, and $12,950 or less ($13,150 for 2020) for an estate or trust;

- 20 percent if taxable income is more than $488,850 ($496,600 for 2020) if married filing jointly or surviving spouse, more than $461,700 ($469,050 for 2020) if head of household, more than $434,550 ($441,450 for 2020) if single, more than $244,425 ($248,300 for 2020) if married filing separately, and more than $12,950 ($13,150 for 2020) for an estate or trust.

To calculate net capital gain (or loss), a noncorporate taxpayer must first net short-term and long-term capital gains and losses for each of the rate groups separately (¶ 1739). Capital gain or loss is long-term only if the taxpayer held the property for more than one year before its sale or disposition (¶ 1737). Net capital gain that the taxpayer elects to treat as investment interest (¶ 1057) is subtracted from the total net capital gain that is subject to the maximum capital gains rate (Code Sec. 1(h)(2)).

Depreciable Real Estate. A 25-percent tax rate may apply to long-term capital gain attributable to depreciation that was claimed on real property (Code Sec. 1(h)(1)(E) and (6)(A)). This depreciation, known as unrecaptured section 1250 gain, is the excess of:

- long-term capital gain (not otherwise treated as ordinary income) that would be treated as ordinary income if Code Sec. 1250(b)(1) included all depreciation and the applicable percentage under Code Sec. 1250(a) were 100 percent, over

- the excess of 28-percent rate loss over 28-percent rate gain.

Even under these capital gains rules, Code Sec. 1250 still treats some prior claimed depreciation as ordinary income (¶ 1779) (usually the amount claimed in excess of the amount allowable under the straight-line method).

Under the Modified Accelerated Cost Recovery System (MACRS), all depreciation on residential rental property and nonresidential real property must be computed under the straight-line method (¶ 1780). Thus, depreciation is not recaptured upon a disposition of the property.

Collectibles. Gain on collectibles, such as stamps, antiques, gems, and most coins, is generally taxed at a 28-percent rate even if the seller held the collectible for more than 12 months (Code Sec. 1(h)(4)(A)(i) and (5)).

Small Business Stock. Noncorporate taxpayers may exclude from gross income a percentage of capital gain from the sale or exchange of qualified small business stock issued after August 10, 1993, and held for more than five years (¶ 1905). This excluded capital gain is not used in computing the taxpayer's long-term capital gain or loss, and it is not investment income for purposes of the limit on investment interest deductions (¶ 1057). However, the capital gain that is not excluded (section 1202 gain) is taxed at a 28-percent capital gains rate (Code Sec. 1(h)(4)(A)(ii) and (7)).

17

CAPITAL GAINS

Pass-Through Entities. A pass-through entity—including an S corporation, partnership, estate, trust, regulated investment company (RIC), and real estate investment trust (REIT)—allocates capital gains to its shareholders or beneficiaries (Code Sec. 1(h)(10)). Capital gain distributions from a RIC are taxed as long-term capital gains regardless of how long the shareholder owned the shares (¶ 2311). If capital gain distributions are automatically reinvested in the RIC, the reinvested amount is the basis of the additional shares (IRS Pub. 550).

1737. Holding Period for Capital Assets. The holding period for a capital asset (¶ 1741) is the length of time that the taxpayer owns the property before disposing of it. The tax treatment of recognized gain or loss (¶ 1736 and ¶ 1739, respectively) depends, in part, on whether the taxpayer's holding period is short-term or long-term. Long-term gain or loss arises from assets held for more than one year; anything else is short-term gain or loss (Code Secs. 1222 and 1223; Reg. § 1.1223-1).

Calculating the Holding Period. When determining how long an asset was held, the taxpayer generally begins counting on the date after the day the property was acquired. The same date of each following month is the beginning of a new month regardless of the number of days in the preceding month (Rev. Rul. 66-7). The date the asset is disposed of is part of the holding period.

Tax-Free Exchange. If property is received in a tax-free exchange (¶ 1719), the holding period of the property given up by the taxpayer is added ("tacked on") to the holding period of the property that the taxpayer receives (Code Sec. 1223).

Gift. The holding period of property acquired by gift or transfer in trust generally includes the time the property was held by both the donor and the donee if the donee takes the donor's basis (Code Sec. 1223(2)). If the fair market value at the time of the gift is used as the donee's basis (¶ 1630), the holding period starts the day after the gift was made (IRS Pub. 544).

Inheritance. If property is acquired from a decedent, its basis in the hands of the heir or beneficiary is stepped up to its fair market value, and it is automatically deemed to have been held for more than one year (Code Sec. 1223(9)). If the decedent died in 2010 and the executor elected to have the carryover basis rule (¶ 1633) rather than the estate tax apply, the taxpayer's holding period of the property is the same as the decedent's, whether or not the executor allocates any basis increase to the property (Rev. Proc. 2011-41).

Involuntary Conversion. The holding period of involuntarily converted property (¶ 1713) is added to the holding period of qualified replacement property if the basis of the replacement property is determined by reference to the basis of the converted property (Code Sec. 1223(1)(A)).

Stock. The holding period for stock and securities purchased on an exchange begins on the day following the purchase (the trade date), and ends on, and includes, the date of sale, rather than the day when payment is received and delivery is made (the settlement date) (Rev. Rul. 66-97; Rev. Rul. 93-84). The holding period for stock received in a nontaxable stock distribution or in a "spin-off" includes the holding period of the related stock on which the distribution is made (Code Sec. 1223(1) and (4)).

Options. If a taxpayer acquires assets by exercising a purchase option, the holding period starts the day after the option is exercised (IRS Pub. 550).

Partnerships. A partner's holding period for property distributed by the partnership includes the period the partnership held the property (Code Sec. 735(b)). A three-year holding period applies to a taxpayer's net long-term capital gain from the sale or disposition of an "applicable partnership interest" (i.e., carried interest) (¶ 442).

Treasury Obligations. In determining the holding period of U.S. Treasury notes and bonds sold at auction on the basis of yield, the acquisition date is the date the Secretary of Treasury identifies the successful bidder in a news release (Rev. Rul. 78-5). The acquisition date of U.S. Treasury notes sold through an offering on a subscription basis at a specified yield is the date the subscription is submitted.

1738. Corporate Capital Gains. A corporation must include both long-term and short-term capital gains in gross income to the extent they exceed capital losses for the year. Thus, a corporation's capital gains are generally taxed at ordinary corporate income tax rates (¶ 219) (Code Sec. 1221). See ¶ 1752 and ¶ 1756 for treatment of corporate capital losses.

1739. Netting of Capital Gains and Losses. Noncorporate taxpayers must use netting procedures to calculate their recognized capital gain or loss for the tax year (Code Sec. 1(h)(1); Notice 97-59). The gains and losses within each tax rate group are netted in order to arrive at a net gain or loss for the group. There are three tax rate groups—the 0, 15, and 25 percent group for net capital gains and qualified dividends, the 25 percent group for unrecaptured section 1250 gain, and the 28 percent group for gain on collectibles and small business stock (¶ 1736). Once each group has been netted, the following ordering rules apply:

- *Short-term capital gains and losses.* Short-term capital losses (including short-term capital loss carryovers (¶ 1754)) are applied first to reduce short-term capital gains that would otherwise be taxable at ordinary income tax rates. If the losses exceed the gains, the net short-term capital loss is applied first against any net long-term capital gain from the 28-percent group, then against the 25-percent group, and last against the lowest rate group (the 0, 15, and 20 percent group).

- *Long-term capital gains and losses.* A net loss from the 28-percent group (including long-term capital loss carryovers) is used first to reduce gain from the 25-percent group, then to reduce net gain from the lowest rate group. A net loss from the lowest rate group is used first to reduce net gain from the 28-percent group, and then to reduce gain from the 25-percent group.

1740. Capital Gain from Financial Conversion Transactions. Capital gain from the disposition or termination of a position that is part of a financial conversion transaction may be recharacterized as ordinary income (Code Sec. 1258). A conversion transaction is generally a transaction in which a taxpayer's return on an investment is attributable to the time value of money, but appears to be attributable to market risk so that it seems to be capital gain rather than ordinary income. The recharacterization rule applies if:

- the taxpayer acquires property and on a substantially contemporaneous basis enters into a contract to sell it or substantially identical property at a predetermined price,

- the transaction qualifies as a tax straddle (¶ 1948), or

- the transaction is marketed or sold as producing capital gains from a transaction in which the taxpayer's expected return is substantially from the time value of the net investment.

The capital gain treated as ordinary income is equal to the interest that would have accrued on the taxpayer's net investment at a yield equal to 120 percent of the applicable federal rate (AFR) compounded semiannually (or of the federal short-term rates compounded daily if the term of the conversion transaction is indefinite) (¶ 83).

Transactions of options dealers and commodities traders in the normal course of their trade or business of dealing in options or trading section 1256 contracts (¶ 1947) are not conversion transactions. This exception does not apply to certain gains allocated to limited partners and limited entrepreneurs as defined in Code Sec. 461(k)(4).

Constructive Ownership Transactions. The amount of long-term capital gains that a taxpayer may recognize from certain constructive ownership transactions that arise from specified financial assets may be limited (Code Sec. 1260). These financial assets include any equity interest in a pass-through entity (a partnership, S corporation, regulated investment company (RIC), or real estate investment trust (REIT)). The long-term gain is limited to the amount of gain that the taxpayer would have recognized if the taxpayer had directly held the financial asset during the term of the derivative contract. Any additional gain is recognized as ordinary income. Tax liability is increased by the amount of interest that would have accrued on the underpayment that would have arisen if the recharacterized ordinary income had been included in gross income.

1741. Capital Asset Defined. A capital gain or loss arises from the sale or exchange of a capital asset. A capital asset is generally any property, whether or not connected with a trade or business (Code Sec. 1221; Reg. § 1.1221-1). The following items are *not* capital assets:

- stock in trade, inventory, and property held primarily for sale to customers in the ordinary course of the taxpayer's trade or business;

- a note or account receivable acquired in the ordinary course of trade or business for services or from the sale of stock in trade or property held primarily for sale in the ordinary course of business;

- depreciable business property;

- real property used in the taxpayer's trade or business;

- a copyright, a literary, musical or artistic composition, a letter or memorandum, or similar property, or a patent, invention, model, secret formula, or process held by the taxpayer who created it, or by a taxpayer whose basis in the property is determined by reference to the basis of the person who created it, or, in the case of a letter, memorandum or similar property, a taxpayer for whom such property was prepared or produced;

- a U.S. government publication (including the *Congressional Record*) held by a taxpayer who received it (or by another taxpayer whose basis in the publication is determined in whole or in part by reference to the original recipient's basis) other than by purchase at the price at which the publication is offered to the public;

- commodities derivative financial instruments held by commodities derivatives dealers;

- hedging transactions (¶ 1949) entered into in the normal course of the taxpayer's business; and

- supplies of a type regularly used or consumed by the taxpayer in the ordinary course of business.

Although creative works are generally not capital assets in the hands of their creators, a musical composition or a copyright in a musical work may be treated as a capital asset by a taxpayer whose personal efforts created it, or whose basis is determined by the reference to the creator's basis (Code Sec. 1221(b)(3); Reg. § 1.1221-3). The taxpayer may elect capital gains treatment separately for each composition or copyright sold by reporting the transaction as a sale of a capital asset on Form 8949.

Personal Property. Gain from the sale of an individual's household furnishings, personal residence, or automobile is generally taxed as capital gain. Loss from the sale is not recognized unless the property was held for the production of income (¶ 1001 and ¶ 1101) (Reg. § 1.262-1(b)(4)). For example, an individual who sells a residence that was partially used as rental property must allocate the original cost of the building, the selling price, depreciation (applicable to the rental portion only), and selling expenses between the personal and rental portions of the building as if there were two separate transactions (¶ 1707). The loss allocable to the rental portion of the home may be a recognized capital loss. See ¶ 1705 for the exclusion of gain from the sale of a personal residence. See ¶ 1103 for the deductibility of a loss from the sale of a personal residence.

Securities. Stock and securities generally are held for production of income so a loss on their sale is a capital loss, except for a dealer who holds them for sale to customers (¶ 1903). Gain or loss from the sale, exchange, or termination of a securities futures contract may be eligible for capital gain treatment (Code Sec. 1234B).

Noncapital Assets. The sale or exchange of noncapital assets results in ordinary income or loss. The definition of "capital asset" is interpreted broadly, so a noncapital asset must come within one of the noncapital statutory categories listed above. A capital asset remains a capital asset even if the taxpayer acquires it for business purposes. For example, bank stock that a holding company acquired to prevent damage to its own business reputation was a capital asset even though it was acquired for a business purpose, because it did not fall within any of the exclusion categories (*Arkansas Best Corp.*, SCt, 88-1 USTC ¶ 9210).

Special Rules. Special rules apply when a sale involves section 1231 property (¶ 1747), patents (¶ 1767), depreciable property (¶ 1779), farm property (¶ 1797), or partnership interests (¶ 434).

¶1741

1742. Sale or Exchange Requirement for Capital Gains and Losses. The capital gain and loss rules (¶ 1735) apply to the sale or exchange of a capital asset (¶ 1741) (Code Sec. 1222; Reg. § 1.1222-1). A sale or exchange of real estate occurs on the conveyance date or, if earlier, the date when the burden and benefits of ownership pass to the purchaser (Rev. Rul. 69-93). A sale or exchange occurs when a corporation liquidates (¶ 2253), when securities become worthless (¶ 1916), and upon any failure to exercise a privilege or option on property that would have been a capital asset if acquired (¶ 1919).

If bonds with past-due interest are purchased "flat" (that is, with none of the price allocated to the past-due interest), aggregate interest payments are capital gains if they are (1) for the prepurchase period, and (2) more than the purchase price but less than the face value of the bonds. These amounts are considered to be received on retirement of the bonds (Rev. Rul. 60-284). However, ordinary income arises from the sale of (1) an endowment insurance policy before its maturity, or (2) a paid-up annuity contract before the annuity starting date (*E.J. Arnfeld*, CtCls, 58-2 USTC ¶ 9692).

1743. Sale of Trade or Business. The sale of a trade or business is generally treated as if each asset of the business was sold separately (Code Sec. 1060(a); Reg. § 1.1060-1(a); Rev. Rul. 55-79). The purchase price must be allocated among the assets by the seller to determine the amount and character of any recognized gain or loss. It must also be allocated by the buyer to determine basis and allowable depreciation or amortization. The buyer and seller may agree in writing to allocations of part or all of the consideration involved in the transaction and the fair market value of any assets transferred. The allocation is binding on both parties, unless the IRS determines that it is inappropriate (¶ 1620).

Reporting. The purchaser and the seller each must file Form 8594 to report the sale of assets used in a trade or business if the purchaser's basis in the assets is determined wholly by the amount paid. The form is attached to the tax return for the year in which the sale took place.

1744. Sale of Depreciable Assets Between Related Taxpayers. Capital gain treatment (¶ 1735) is denied when depreciable property (including patent applications) is sold or exchanged between related taxpayers (Code Sec. 1239; Reg. § 1.1239-1). This rule applies to sales or exchanges between: (1) a person and all entities that the person controls; (2) a taxpayer and any trust in which the taxpayer or the taxpayer's spouse has a beneficiary interest that is not a remote contingent interest; or (3) an executor and a beneficiary of the same estate, unless the sale or exchange is in satisfaction of a pecuniary bequest.

Entities that are controlled by a taxpayer include:

- a corporation if the taxpayer owns (directly or indirectly) more than 50 percent of the value of its stock;

- a partnership if the taxpayer owns (directly or indirectly) more than 50 percent of the capital or profits interest; and

- certain entities that are related persons with respect to the taxpayer, including: two corporations that are members of the same controlled group; a corporation and a partnership if the same persons own more than 50 percent of each; and two S corporations, or an S corporation and a C corporation, if the same persons own more than 50 percent of the stock of each.

Section 1231 Assets

See CCH® AnswerConnect: *Section 1231 (Hotchpot) Assets* for more information on this topic.

1747. Section 1231 Property Used in Trade or Business. Business real estate and depreciable business property generally is not a capital asset (¶ 1741). However, if the business property is section 1231 property, gain or loss realized from its sale, exchange, or involuntary conversion may qualify as capital gain or ordinary loss. Specifically, if section 1231 gains exceed section 1231 losses, all of the section 1231 gains and losses are generally treated as long-term capital gains and losses (¶ 1736) (Code Sec. 1231; Reg. §§ 1.1231-1 and 1.1231-2). On the other hand, if section 1231 losses exceed section 1231 gains, all of the section 1231 gains and losses are treated as ordinary income and losses. The sale or exchange of section 1231 property is reported on Form 4797.

Section 1231 property includes:

- depreciable property used in the taxpayer's trade or business and held more than one year, other than (i) property includible in inventory, (ii) property held primarily for sale to customers, (iii) a copyright, a literary, musical or artistic composition, or a letter, memorandum, or similar property, and a patent, invention, model, design, secret formula, or process, and (iv) certain federal government publications;

- real property used in the trade or business and held for more than one year, other than property that is includible in inventory or held primarily for sale to customers;

- trade or business property held for more than one year and compulsorily or involuntarily converted (¶ 1748);

- capital assets held for more than one year in connection with a trade or business or a transaction entered into for profit, and compulsorily or involuntarily converted;

- an unharvested crop on land used in the trade or business and held for more than one year, if the crop and land are sold, exchanged, or involuntarily converted at the same time to the same person;

- certain livestock, but not poultry (¶ 1750); and

- timber, domestic iron ore, and coal (¶ 1772).

If section 1231 property is subject to depreciation recapture, the section 1231 gain is the amount by which the total gain exceeds the amounts recaptured and taxed at ordinary income rates (¶ 1779). The recapture of certain farmland expenses may also reduce section 1231 gain (¶ 1797). A gain or loss that is disallowed by other rules, such as a loss on a sale between related parties (¶ 1717), is not taken into account in determining section 1231 gains and losses.

Recapture of Net Section 1231 Losses. Net section 1231 losses must be recaptured by treating the current year's net section 1231 gain (section 1231 gain that exceeds current-year section 1231 loss) as ordinary income to the extent of the unrecaptured net section 1231 losses for the five previous tax years. The losses are recaptured on a first-in, first-out (FIFO) basis (IRS Pub. 544).

1748. Compulsory or Involuntary Conversion of Section 1231 Property. The capital gain and ordinary loss rules of Code Sec. 1231 (¶ 1747) can apply to gains and losses from the compulsory or involuntary conversion of section 1231 property unless the nonrecognition rules for involuntary conversions (¶ 1713) apply (Code Sec. 1231(a)(3)(A)(ii); Reg. § 1.1231-1(d)(4) and (e)). Gains and losses from a theft, seizure, requisition, or condemnation are section 1231 gains or losses. However, if casualty or theft gains and losses result in a net loss, the transactions are not grouped with other section 1231 transactions. Instead, the net loss is an ordinary loss. Since personal assets (those not used in a trade or business or for investment) are not section 1231 property, casualty and theft losses on personal assets are excluded from Code Sec. 1231. See ¶ 1129 and ¶ 1131 for taxation of personal casualty gains and losses.

1750. Livestock as Section 1231 Property. Capital gain and ordinary loss treatment under Code Sec. 1231 (¶ 1747) applies to the sale, exchange, or involuntary conversion of livestock (not including poultry) held for draft, breeding, dairy or sporting purposes (Code Sec. 1231(b)(3); Reg. § 1.1231-2). The taxpayer must have held the livestock for at least 12 months (24 months for horses and cattle). The holding period begins on the date the animal is acquired rather than the date it is put to an allowed use. Livestock includes fur-bearing animals such as chinchillas, mink, and foxes (Rev. Rul. 57-588). See ¶ 1713 for involuntary conversions of livestock due to disease or weather conditions and ¶ 767 for forced sales due to weather conditions, such as flood or drought.

1751. Canceled Leases and Distributor's Agreements. An amount received by a lessee for cancellation of a lease is received in exchange for the lease. This rule also applies to amounts that a distributor of goods receives for the cancellation of a distributor's agreement if the taxpayer has a substantial capital investment in the distributorship (Code Sec. 1241; Reg. § 1.1241-1). If the lease or agreement is section 1231 property (¶ 1747), the taxpayer has a section 1231 gain or loss (Rev. Rul. 2007-37).

Capital Loss Limitation, Carryover, Carryback

See CCH® AnswerConnect: *Capital Gains* for more information on this topic.

1752. Limitation on Capital Losses. To determine the deductibility of capital losses (¶ 1735), the taxpayer totals all capital gains and losses, both long term and short term, incurred during the year.

For a noncorporate taxpayer, capital losses are deductible only to the extent of capital gains, plus $3,000 of ordinary income (Code Sec. 1211(b); Reg. § 1.1211-1(b)). Thus, both net long-term capital losses and net short-term capital losses may be used to offset up to $3,000 of an individual's ordinary income ($1,500 for married individuals filing separate returns). Special rules apply to married individuals, whether filing joint or separate returns (¶ 1757). Unused losses are carried forward (¶ 1754).

> **Example:** Pat is a single individual with $30,000 of ordinary income, a net short-term capital loss of $3,500, a net long-term capital loss of $300, and no capital gain. Pat's capital loss deduction is limited to $3,000 for the current tax year. The remaining $800 is carried forward.

A corporation may use capital losses to offset only capital gains and not ordinary income (Code Sec. 1211(a); Reg. § 1.1211-1(a)). However, a corporation may carry capital losses back or forward (¶ 1756).

1754. Capital Loss Carryover of Noncorporate Taxpayers. An individual, estate, and trust may carry over a net capital loss (¶ 1739) to future tax years until the loss is used (Code Sec. 1212(b)). The carried-over loss retains its long-term or short-term character. In determining the amount of the carryover, short-term capital gain is increased by the lesser of:

- the ordinary income offset by the loss, or

- taxable income increased by the offset, with any excess of allowable deductions over gross income for the loss year treated as negative taxable income.

A short-term capital loss carryover first offsets short-term gain in the carryover year. Any remaining net short-term capital loss first offsets net long-term capital gain, and then up to $3,000 of ordinary income ($1,500 if married filing separately) (¶ 1752). A long-term capital loss carryover first reduces long-term capital gain in the carryover year, then net short-term capital gain, and finally up to $3,000 of ordinary income.

Code Sec. 1256 Contract Loss. An individual (but not an estate, trust, or corporation) may elect to carry back a net section 1256 contract loss (¶ 1947) to the three prior tax years (Code Sec. 1212(c)).

1756. Corporate Capital Loss Carryover and Carryback. A corporation may carry back a net capital loss (¶ 1738) to the three tax years preceding the loss year (Code Sec. 1212(a); Reg. § 1.1212-1(a)). Any excess may be carried forward for five years following the loss year. However, the carryback cannot cause or increase a net operating loss (¶ 1145) in the carryback year. Any carryback or carryover is a short-term capital loss for the carryover year that is grouped with other capital losses for that year and used to offset any capital gains. Any undeducted loss remaining after the three-year carryback and the five-year carryover is not deductible.

Foreign expropriation losses can be carried forward for 10 years but are ineligible for the three-year carryback. A foreign expropriation capital loss is the sum of the capital losses sustained (either directly or on securities that become worthless) because of a foreign country's expropriation, intervention, seizure, or similar taking of property.

A regulated investment company (RIC) (¶ 2301) can carry forward net capital losses indefinitely, with the carried over losses maintaining their long-term or short-term character (Code Sec. 1212(a)(3)).

A quick refund procedure is available for corporate net operating loss carrybacks or capital loss carrybacks (¶ 2773).

1757. Capital Gains and Losses of Spouses. Married individuals who file a joint return compute their aggregate capital gains and losses (¶ 1735) as if they were the gains and losses of one person (Reg. § 1.1211-1(b)(6)). If the spouses file separate returns, the capital loss deduction (¶ 1752) for each is limited to $1,500 (one-half of the limit for a joint return) (Code Sec. 1211(b)(1)). If they file separate returns for a year after a net capital loss was reported on a joint return, any carryover is allocated on the basis of the individual net capital loss of the spouses for the prior year (Reg. § 1.1212-1(c)).

1758. Capital Gains and Losses of Partnerships and S Corporations. The capital gains and losses of a partnership or S corporation are generally segregated from its ordinary net income and carried separately into the income of the partners or shareholders. The distributive shares of the capital gain or loss are treated as if they were the partners' (¶ 431) or shareholders' (¶ 309) own capital gain or loss. The same rule applies for Code Sec. 1231 transactions (¶ 1747) (Code Secs. 702(a) and 1366(a)). An S corporation may be taxed on capital gains in very limited situations (¶ 337).

Reporting. A partnership or S corporation uses Form 8949 to report capital gains and losses that are not required to be reported on any other form. A partnerships then uses Schedule D (Form 1065) to determine the overall gain or loss from the transactions reported on Form 8949. The net gains and losses from Schedule D are entered on Schedule K, and each partner's share is entered on Schedule K-1 (Form 1065). An S corporation similarly uses Schedule D (Form 1120-S) to determine the overall gain or loss from the transactions reported on Form 8949. The net gains and losses from Schedule D are entered on Schedule K, and each shareholder's share is entered on Schedule K-1 (Form 1120-S).

1760. Gains and Losses of Investors, Dealers, and Traders. Gains or losses on securities are either ordinary or capital in nature (¶ 1735) depending on whether the taxpayer entered into the transaction as an investor, dealer, or trader.

Investors. Investors' activities are limited to occasional transactions for their own accounts. The level of activity is less than that associated with a trade or business (*F.R. Mayer*, FedCl, 94-2 USTC ¶ 50,509). An investor's gains and losses are capital (¶ 1736).

Dealers. A dealer regularly purchases securities from, and sells securities to, customers in the ordinary course of a trade or business. Because dealers are in the business of buying and selling, their gains and losses are ordinary unless the securities are held primarily for personal investment (Code Sec. 1236). Securities held for personal investment must be clearly identified in the dealer's records before the close of the day on which they are acquired, and must never be held primarily for sale to the dealer's customers. Similarly, capital gain and loss treatment does not apply to real estate sales by a dealer in real property unless the property was held as an investment (¶ 1762). See ¶ 1903 for discussion of the mark-to-market requirement for dealers in securities.

Traders. Securities traders, including "day traders," buy and sell securities for their own accounts. A trader seeks to profit from short-term changes in value rather than long-term investments. A trader's trading activity must be substantial, frequent, regular, and continuous (IRS Pub. 550). Because a trader's securities are not held primarily for sale to customers (¶ 1741), the gains and losses are generally capital in nature, and are reported on Form 8949. However, traders that make a mark-to-market election report their gains and losses on Form 4797. Traders claim their business expenses on Schedule C (Form 1040) because they are in the business of trading. See ¶ 1983 for the rules concerning the commissions paid by traders when buying and selling securities.

Real Property Subdivided for Sale

1762. Real Property Subdivided for Sale. Individuals, estates, trusts, and S corporations are not treated as real estate dealers solely because they subdivide a tract of land for sale (Code Sec. 1237; Reg. § 1.1237-1). At least part of the gain on the sale of a lot or parcel is capital gain if:

¶1757

- the taxpayer has not previously held the tract, or any lot or parcel of it, for sale in the ordinary course of business and, in the tax year of the sale, does not hold any other real estate for sale in the ordinary course of business (this rule automatically disqualifies a real estate dealer);

- no substantial improvements are made while the tract is held by the taxpayer or under a sale contract between the taxpayer and the buyer; and

- the taxpayer either held the lot for at least five years, or acquired it by inheritance or devise.

Certain improvements, such as water, sewage, drainage, or road installations, are not considered substantial improvements if: (1) the property (including inherited property) is held for at least 10 years; (2) the property would not have been marketable at the prevailing local price for similar building sites without such improvements; and (3) the taxpayer elects not to adjust the basis of the property (or other property) for the improvement costs or deduct them as expenses. The election is reported with the tax return for the year in which the lots covered by the election are sold. The election must include additional information, including a plat of the subdivision and a list of all the improvements.

The profits realized on the sales of the first five lots or parcels from the same tract are capital gains. However, beginning in the year in which the sixth sale or exchange is made, gain on each sale is ordinary income to the extent of five percent of the selling price. Selling expenses are deducted first from this ordinary income, and then are used to reduce the capital gain on the sale or exchange. The selling expenses cannot be deducted from other income as ordinary business expenses.

If five years pass without the taxpayer selling or exchanging any other lots from the parcel, the taxpayer can sell another five lots without any of the gain taxed as ordinary income.

A taxpayer that buys a tract of land with the intent to subdivide and sell it as separate lots or parcels must measure gain or loss on every lot or parcel sold on the basis of an equitable (not ratable) apportionment (such as their relative assessed valuations for real estate tax purposes) of the cost of the subdivision (Reg. § 1.61-6(a)).

Patents, Royalties, and Franchises

See CCH® AnswerConnect: *Intellectual Property Rights: Patents, Trademarks, Trade Names, Franchises and Copyrights* for more information on this topic.

1767. Sale or Exchange of Patents. The transfer of all substantial rights to a patent, or an undivided interest in such rights, is treated as the sale of a capital asset (¶ 1741) held for more than 12 months (Code Sec. 1235; Reg. §§ 1.1235-1 and 1.1235-2). The payment for the patent may be a lump-sum, a periodic payment, or contingent upon the productivity or use of the property transferred. These rules do not apply to transfers by gift or inheritance. The rules do apply to a transfer by the original inventor or another individual who acquired the patent from the original inventor before the invention was tested successfully under operating conditions. The inventor's employer and certain related persons are not eligible for long-term capital gain treatment if they acquire the patent from the inventor.

1772. Timber, Coal or Iron Ore. A taxpayer may elect to treat the cutting of timber for sale or for use in a trade or business as a sale or exchange of the timber. The taxpayer must have owned the timber or held the contract right to cut it for more than one year (Code Sec. 631; Reg. § 1.631-1). The timber is property used in the trade or business, so it is section 1231 property and the gain may be treated as long-term capital gain under certain conditions (¶ 1747). An electing taxpayer must generally file Form T with the tax return for the year in which the election is effective.

Timber, coal, and domestic iron ore royalties are generally subject to section 1231 treatment if the owner or holder (including a lessee) disposes of the timber, coal, or ore while retaining an economic interest in it (Code Sec. 631(b) and (c); Reg. §§ 1.631-2 and 1.631-3). An outright sale of timber also qualifies. This treatment is not available for iron ore mined outside the United States, or for coal or iron ore dispositions between related parties or persons owned and controlled by the same interests.

1774. Transfers of Franchises, Trademarks, or Trade Names. Amounts received from the transfer of a franchise, trademark, or trade name are generally ordinary income if the transferor retains any significant power, right, or continuing interest over the transferred asset (Code Sec. 1253). Ordinary income treatment also applies to amounts received from the transfer, sale, or other disposition that are contingent on the transferred asset's productivity, use, or disposition. Amounts paid or incurred on account of the transfer of a franchise, trademark, or trade name are amortized over 15 years under Code Sec. 197 (¶ 1362). Amortization is claimed on Form 4562.

Contingent serial payments paid or incurred on account of a transfer, sale, or other disposition of a trademark, trade name, or franchise may be a deductible business expense (¶ 901) if: (1) the payments are contingent on the asset's productivity, use, or disposition; and (2) the contingent amounts are paid as part of a series of payments that are payable at least annually throughout the term of the transfer agreement, and are substantially equal in amount or payable under a fixed formula.

Depreciation Recapture

See CCH® AnswerConnect: *Recapture of Depreciation and Similar Allowances* for more information on this topic.

1779. Depreciation Recapture Rules. A taxpayer that sells or disposes of certain depreciable or amortizable section 1245 property (¶ 1785) and section 1250 property (¶ 1786) must treat realized gain as ordinary income (rather than capital gain) to the extent of depreciation or amortization deductions previously allowed or allowable. The recapture rules apply notwithstanding any other Code provision (Reg. § § 1.1245-6 and 1.1250-1(c)).

Section 1245 Property. Gain realized from the disposition of section 1245 property is ordinary income to the extent the adjusted basis of the property is exceeded by the lowest of: (1) the recomputed basis of the property; (2) the amount realized upon a sale, exchange, or involuntary conversion of the property; or (3) the fair market value of the property in any other disposition (Code Sec. 1245(a)).

Recomputed basis is the property's adjusted basis plus previously allowed or allowable depreciation or amortization. Amortization deductions include amounts expensed for the following: Code Sec. 179 property (¶ 1208); capital costs of compliance with EPA sulfur regulations; refinery property; energy efficient commercial buildings (¶ 1286); mine safety equipment (¶ 989A); film, television production, and live theatrical production costs (¶ 1229); and expenditures for removing architectural and transportation barriers to the handicapped and elderly, reforestation (¶ 1360), and tertiary injectants.

Section 1250 Property. Gain on the sale or other disposition of section 1250 property is treated as ordinary income to the extent of the excess of post-1969 depreciation allowances over the depreciation that would have been available under the straight-line method (¶ 1780) (Code Sec. 1250). However, if section 1250 property is held for one year or less, all depreciation (and not just the excess over straight-line depreciation) is recaptured. See ¶ 1736 for capital gains treatment of unrecaptured Section 1250 gain. In a sale to a related party (¶ 1717), gain that is not recaptured may still be treated as ordinary income (¶ 1744). Different holding periods and recapture percentages may apply to substantial improvements made to section 1250 property that are considered separate property for recapture purposes, and also to property that consists of more than one element.

For residential rental property, certain types of government assisted housing, subsidized housing, section 1250 property for which rapid depreciation of rehabilitation expenditures was claimed, and property mortgaged under the Housing Act of 1949, depreciation recapture is reduced by one percent for each full month the property is held over a specified period.

Dispositions. Depreciation recapture is triggered by the disposition of depreciable property, including sales, exchanges, and involuntary conversions. Special rules apply for transfers by gift or at death (¶ 1788), certain tax-free corporate or partnership transactions (¶ 1789), disposal in a like-kind exchange or involuntary conversion where gain is not recognized (¶ 1790), and property distributed by a partnership (¶ 1792). A disposition of section 1245 property includes a sale in a sale-and-leaseback transaction and a transfer upon the foreclosure of a security interest, but it does not include a mere transfer of title between a debtor and creditor upon the creation or termination of a security interest (Reg. § 1.1245-1).

Installment Sale. In an installment sale of section 1245 or section 1250 property, gain recaptured as ordinary income is recognized in the year of the disposition, and gain in excess of the recapture income is reported under the installment method (¶ 1823).

Investment Credit Basis Reductions. For recapture purposes, the amount of an investment credit downward basis adjustment is treated as a deduction allowed for depreciation (¶ 1465A).

Additional Recapture for Corporations. For C corporations, the amount treated as ordinary income on the sale or other disposition of section 1250 property is increased by 20 percent of the additional amount that would be treated as ordinary income if the property were subject to recapture under the rules for section 1245 property (Code Sec. 291(a)(1)).

Reporting Recapture. Form 4797 is used to calculate and report the amount of depreciation recaptured. A taxpayer subject to recapture of an investment credit downward basis adjustment must file Form 4255.

1780. Depreciation Subject to Recapture. Depreciation on tangible property placed in service after 1986 is generally determined under the Modified Accelerated Cost Recovery System (MACRS). Property placed in service after 1980 and before 1987 is subject to the Accelerated Cost Recovery System (ACRS). See ¶ 1216 and following for the methods of computing allowable depreciation deductions.

MACRS. Gain on the disposition of tangible personal property is ordinary income to the extent of previously-allowed MACRS deductions (¶ 1779). If a taxpayer disposes of property from a general asset account, the proceeds are ordinary income to the extent the unadjusted depreciable basis of the account (increased by amounts allowed as deductions under Code Secs. 179 and 190 for assets in the account) exceeds previously recognized ordinary income from prior dispositions (Code Sec. 168(i)(4); Reg. § 1.168(i)-1(e)).

Residential rental property and nonresidential real property that is placed in service after 1986 and is subject to MACRS must be depreciated under the straight-line MACRS method (¶ 1243). Thus, depreciation is not recaptured on disposition of such property because no depreciation in excess of straight-line depreciation could have been taken.

ACRS. Gain on the disposition of personal recovery property and nonresidential real recovery property is treated as ordinary income to the extent of previously allowed ACRS deductions (¶ 1779). Gain on the disposition of residential rental real recovery property is ordinary income to the extent that ACRS deductions exceed straight-line ACRS depreciation over the recovery period applicable to the property. Thus, there is no recapture if the taxpayer elected straight-line ACRS for real property.

Proceeds from the disposition of assets from mass asset accounts are ordinary income to the extent of the unadjusted basis in the account less any amounts previously included in income. Any excess proceeds are capital gain, unless a nonrecognition provision applies. Regarding the recovery of depreciation, the mass asset account is treated as though there was no disposition of the asset, and the unadjusted basis of the property is left in the capital account until fully recovered in future years (Prop. Reg. § 1.168-2(h)).

Amounts Excluded from Depreciation Adjustments. In determining the amount of additional depreciation taken before the disposition of section 1250 property, depreciation adjustments do not include: amortization of emergency facilities, pollution control facilities, railroad grading and tunnel bores, and child care facilities; expenditures to remove architectural and transportation barriers to the handicapped and elderly; or tertiary injectant expenses (Code Sec. 1250(b)(3)).

1785. Code Sec. 1245 Property. Code Sec. 1245 property is property that is or has been depreciable (or subject to amortization under Code Sec. 197) and is either:

- personal property (tangible and intangible); or

- other tangible property (not including a building or its structural components) used as an integral part of: (1) manufacturing, production, or extraction; or (2) the furnishing of transportation, communications, electrical energy, gas, water, or sewage disposal services (Code Sec. 1245(a)(3); Reg. § 1.1245-3).

Other tangible property includes research facilities or facilities for the bulk storage of fungible commodities used in connection with the activities listed above. A leasehold of section 1245 property is also treated as section 1245 property. Livestock is section 1245 property, and depreciation on purchased draft, breeding, dairy and sporting livestock is recaptured as ordinary income when sold. Raised livestock generally has no basis for depreciation, but to the extent that it does have a basis and is depreciated, it is subject to recapture (IRS Pub. 225).

Section 1245 property also includes any real property that has an adjusted basis reflecting adjustments for special amortization for the following: Code Sec. 179 property (¶ 1208); capital costs of compliance with EPA sulfur regulations; refinery property; energy efficient commercial buildings (¶ 1286); mine safety equipment (¶ 989A); railroad grading and tunnel bores; child care facilities; and expenditures for removal of architectural and transportation barriers to the handicapped and elderly, reforestation (¶ 1360), or tertiary injectants. Section 1245 property also includes single purpose agricultural and horticultural structures, and storage facilities used in connection with the distribution of petroleum products.

1786. Code Sec. 1250 Property. Code Sec. 1250 property is real property that is or has been depreciable under Code Sec. 167 but is not subject to recapture under Code Sec. 1245. This includes intangible real property (such as leases of land or section 1250 property), buildings and their structural components, and all other tangible real property except section 1245 property (Code Sec. 1250(c); Reg. § 1.1250-1(e)). See ¶ 1785 for real property that is section 1245 property rather than section 1250 property.

1788. Disposition of Depreciable Property by Gift or Death. The recapture of depreciation as ordinary income upon the sale or disposition of section 1245 or section 1250 property (¶ 1779) does not apply to dispositions by gift or transfers at death, other than taxable transfers of section 1245 or section 1250 property in satisfaction of a specific bequest of money (Code Secs. 1245(b) and 1250(d); Reg. §§ 1.1245-4 and 1.1250-3). However, upon a later sale the donee realizes the same amount of ordinary income that the donor would have realized had the donor retained the property and sold it unless the donee is tax-exempt. Also, if a taxpayer contributes section 1245 or section 1250 property to a charitable organization, the allowable charitable contribution deduction is reduced by the amount that would have been treated as ordinary income had the taxpayer sold the asset at its fair market value (¶ 1062).

1789. Disposition of Depreciable Property in Tax-Free Corporate or Partnership Transaction. If section 1245 or section 1250 property is disposed of in certain tax-free transactions (i.e., Code Secs. 332, 351, 361, 721, or 731), the transferor takes into account the depreciation recapture treated as ordinary income (¶ 1779) only to the extent that gain is recognized under those sections (Code Secs. 1245(b)(3) and 1250(d)(3); Reg. §§ 1.1245-4(c) and 1.1250-3(c)). However, if there is an otherwise tax-free transfer to a tax-exempt organization (other than a cooperative described in Code Sec. 521), the gain is recognized in full to the transferor. On a later sale of section 1245 or section 1250 property received in a tax-free transaction, the transferee realizes depreciation recapture to the extent of the transferor's unrecognized unrecaptured section 1245 or section 1250 gain, plus depreciation deducted by the transferee (not to exceed the actual gain).

1790. Disposition of Depreciable Property in Like-Kind Exchange or Involuntary Conversion. If section 1245 or section 1250 property is exchanged for like-kind property (¶ 1721) or is involuntarily converted (¶ 1713), depreciation recapture (¶ 1779) is recognized to the extent of any gain recognized on the exchange or conversion, plus the fair market value of any property received in the exchange or acquired as replacement property that is not section 1245 or section 1250 property (Code Secs. 1245(b)(4) and 1250(d)(4); Reg. §§ 1.1245-4(d) and 1.1250-3(d)). The basis of the acquired property is

¶1786

determined under the like-kind exchange or involuntary conversion rules (Reg. §§ 1.1245-5 and 1.1250-3(d)).

1792. Partnership Distribution of Depreciable Property. The basis of section 1245 or section 1250 property that a partnership distributes to a partner for purposes of the depreciation recapture rules (¶ 1779) is determined by reference to the partnership's adjusted basis in the property (Code Secs. 1245(b)(5) and 1250(d)(5); Reg. §§ 1.1245-4(f) and 1.1250-3(f)). For recomputing the partner's basis in the property, the amount of the depreciation or amortization adjustments for section 1245 property, or the additional depreciation for distributed section 1250 property, attributable to pre-distribution periods is equal to:

- the amount of gain that would have been treated as ordinary income under the recapture rules had the partnership sold the property at fair market value immediately before the distribution, less

- any gain treated as ordinary income under the partnership rules for distributions of receivables or inventory items (¶ 436).

1793. Corporate Distribution of Depreciable Property. A corporation that distributes a dividend consisting of section 1245 or section 1250 property may have to recognize ordinary income under the depreciation recapture rules (¶ 1779), even though it would not normally recognize gain under the corporate distribution rules (¶ 736) (Reg. §§ 1.1245-1(a), 1.1245-6(b), and 1.1250-1(c)).

If a corporation transfers section 1245 property or section 1250 property to a shareholder in a sale or exchange for less than fair market value, the disposition is not treated as a sale, exchange, or involuntary conversion for depreciation recapture purposes (Reg. §§ 1.1245-1(c) and 1.1250-1(a)). Accordingly, the corporation's gain for recapture purposes is the excess of the property's adjusted basis over the lower of the property's fair market value on the disposition date or the property's recomputed basis.

If the transferee's basis in the property is determined solely by the corporate distribution rules (¶ 735), no depreciation adjustments are reflected in the adjusted basis of section 1245 property, and no additional depreciation is reflected in the adjusted basis of section 1250 property, on the date that the transferee acquires the property (Reg. §§ 1.1245-2(c) and 1.1250-2(e)).

1797. Recapture on Gain from Sale of Farm Land. A taxpayer that deducts soil and water conservations expenses (¶ 982) must recapture as ordinary income on Form 4797 part of the gain from the sale or other disposition of the underlying farmland held for less than 10 years (Code Sec. 1252; Reg. § 1.1252-2). The amount recaptured is the lesser of the gain realized from the disposition or a percentage of the deductions claimed for soil and water conservation expenses. The recapture percentage is 100 percent if the land is held for five years or less, and declines 20 percent for each additional year (80 percent in the sixth year, 60 percent in the seventh year, 40 percent in the eighth year, and 20 percent in the ninth year). There is no recapture after the ninth year. The recapture rule does not apply to transfers by gift, transfers at death, and transfers in certain tax-free transactions.

Empowerment and Opportunity Zones

1799B. Empowerment Zones. Geographic areas may be designated as empowerment zones for purposes of enhanced tax benefits before January 1, 2021 (Code Sec. 1391(d)(1)(A)(i), as amended by the Taxpayer Certainty and Disaster Tax Relief Act of 2019 (P.L. 116-94)). The locations of qualifying empowerment zones and renewal communities are listed in the instructions to Form 8844.

Work Opportunity Credit. Employers may claim the work opportunity credit for certain first-year wages paid or incurred to "designated community residents" and "qualified summer youth employees" who begin work before January 1, 2021, and live in certain economically distressed areas (¶ 1465G) (Code Sec. 51(c)(4), as amended by the Taxpayer Certainty and Disaster Tax Relief Act of 2019 (P.L. 116-94)).

Code Sec. 179 Expense Deduction. The section 179 expense dollar limitation (¶ 1208) for any tax year is increased by $35,000 for property placed in service in a designated empowerment zone by an enterprise zone business (Code Sec. 1397A).

60-Percent Gain Exclusion for Small Business Stock. A noncorporate taxpayer may exclude 60 percent of the gain on the sale or exchange of qualified small business stock if (1) the small business corporation is an empowerment zone business, (2) the taxpayer acquired the stock after December 21, 2001, and (3) the taxpayer held the stock for more than five years (Code Sec. 1202(a)(2)(C)). However, the gain attributable to periods after 2018 is not excludable. The exclusion is still relevant for qualified small business stock acquired after December 21, 2001, and before February 18, 2009, because the exclusion rate is 100 percent for any qualified small business stock acquired after September 27, 2010; and 75 percent for any qualified small business stock acquired after February 17, 2009, and before September 28, 2010 (¶ 1905). The corporation must qualify as an enterprise zone business during substantially all of the time the taxpayer held the stock, without regard to the end of the empowerment zone designation. The District of Columbia enterprise zone is not an empowerment zone for this purpose.

1799E. Qualified Opportunity Zones. A taxpayer may elect to exclude gain realized from the sale or exchange of property to an unrelated party that is reinvested in a qualified opportunity fund (QOF) within 180 days (Code Secs. 1400Z-1 and 1400Z-2; Reg. § 1.1400Z2(a)-1; Prop. Reg. § 1.1400Z-2(a)-1; Prop. Reg. § 1.1400Z2(a)-1). The election is made on Form 8949 and filed with the income tax return for the tax year in which the sale or exchange of the capital occurred. The deferred gain continues to be reported as usual on the appropriate return (e.g., Form 8949, Schedule D, Form 4797) and as a negative adjustment entered on Form 8949. Only one election may be made with respect to a sale or exchange. The due date for performing certain time-sensitive actions, including the 180 investment period in QOFs, otherwise due on or after April 1, 2020, and before July 15, 2020, is automatically extended to July 15, 2020, in response to the COVID-19 (coronavirus) crisis (Notice 2020-23; Rev. Proc. 2018-58).

The election allows the taxpayer to defer gain on the QOF investment until the investment is sold or exchanged (or other inclusion event), or December 31, 2026, whichever is earlier. If deferred gain is recognized in gross income on December 31, 2026, before the fund investment is sold, the recognized gain increases the basis in the fund for purposes of determining any gain that will be recognized on a subsequent sale. Gain included in gross income is the excess of the lesser of the amount of gain excluded or the fair market value of the property on the date of the sale or exchange, over the taxpayer's basis in the investment. Basis is generally treated as zero, but it is increased if the taxpayer held the property for at least five years (Reg. § 1400Z2(b)-1; Prop. Reg. § 1.1400Z2(b)-1). If the investment in the QOF is held at least ten years, any appreciation in the value of the investment attributable to the deferred gain is not taxed (Reg. § 1.1400Z2(c)-1).

A QOF is a corporation, partnership, or limited liability company (LLC) taxed as a corporation or partnership that invests at least 90 percent of its assets in qualified opportunity zone (QOZ) property. The 90-percent requirement is determined using the average percentage of qualified zone property held by the fund on the last day of the first six-month period of the fund's tax year and on the last day of the fund's tax year. There is no application or approval process for an entity to become a QOF. The entity elects QOF status (i.e., self certifies) by filing Form 8996 with its annual income tax return (Reg. § 1.1400Z2(d)-1; Prop. Reg. § 1.1400Z-2(d)-1).

QOZ property is QOZ stock, QOZ partnership interest, or QOZ business property (Reg. § 1.1400Z2(d)-2; Rev. Rul. 2018-29). A population census tract that is a low-income community (¶ 1465T) may be designated as a qualified opportunity zone. The IRS provides a list of population census tracts designated as qualified opportunity zones (Notice 2018-48, amplified by Notice 2019-42).

Chapter 18

INSTALLMENT SALES

DEFERRED PAYMENTS

Installment Method

See CCH® AnswerConnect: *Installment Sales* for more information on this topic.

1801. Installment Sales of Property. A taxpayer generally must use the installment method of accounting to report gain (but not losses) from an installment sale of property (Code Sec. 453). An installment sale occurs if at least one payment for the property is received in a tax year after the tax year of sale (i.e., deferred payments). Under the installment method, gain from the sale is prorated and recognized over the years in which payments are received. As a result, each payment received usually consists of interest, return of basis, and gain on the sale.

The installment method of reporting is mandatory for installment sales unless the taxpayer elects out (¶ 1803). It applies to the sale of a single asset, multiple assets in a single transaction, or the sale of a trade or business, and regardless whether the taxpayer uses the cash or accrual method of accounting (¶ 1515). Installment sale treatment generally may not be used for:

- sales of publicly-traded stock or securities, or personal property sold under a revolving credit plan,
- dealer sales (¶ 1808),
- sales of inventory related to personal property (¶ 1553), and
- depreciable property sold to a related person (¶ 1835).

Payments for such sales are treated as if they are received in the year of disposition, even if the taxpayer expects to receive some payments in future years. Also, gain from installment sales of depreciable property subject to recapture under Code Sec. 1245 or Code Sec. 1250 must be reported fully in the year of the sale, not when payments are received (¶ 1823).

Gain Calculation. The taxpayer calculates the amount of gain from an installment sale that is taxable in a given year by multiplying the payments received in that year by the gross profit ratio for the sale (Code Sec. 453(c)). The gross profit ratio is equal to the anticipated gross profit divided by the total contract price (¶ 1813).

Example: On December 1, 2018, Bob Smith sells vacant land that he has held for investment purposes for a number of years. His basis in the land is $12,000. The total contract price is $15,000. Bob receives a $5,000 down payment, with the

18
INSTALLMENT SALE

$10,000 balance due in monthly installments of $500 each, plus interest at the applicable federal rate, beginning on January 1, 2019. His anticipated gross profit from the sale is $3,000. His gross profit percentage is 20% ($3,000 gross profit ÷ $15,000 contract price). Under the installment method, Bob must report $1,000 ($5,000 × 20%) as long-term capital gain in 2018, $1,200 ($6,000 × 20%) in 2019, and $800 ($4,000 × 20%) in 2020. The interest is reported as ordinary income.

Although use of the installment method determines when gain from an installment sale is reported, it does not affect the characterization of the gain as capital gain or ordinary income. The proper characterization depends on the nature of the asset sold (¶ 1735 and ¶ 1741).

Reporting Requirements. Gain from an installment sale is reported on Form 6252, which must be filed with the tax return in the year of sale and in each year payments are received. The gain calculated on Form 6252 is carried over and entered on Schedule D of the taxpayer's return, Form 4797, or both, as appropriate.

1803. Election Out of Installment Method. If a taxpayer elects not to use the installment method (¶ 1801), the entire gain is reported in the year of the sale, even if not all of the sale proceeds are received in that year (Code Sec. 453(d); Temp. Reg. § 15A.453-1(d)). The election is made by an individual, estate, trust, corporation, or partnership by simply reporting the gain on Form 8949 or Form 4797, or both. The election must be made by the due date, including extensions, of the tax return for the year in which the installment sale occurs. The due date for filing any federal income tax return otherwise due on or after April 1, 2020, and before July 15, 2020, is automatically extended to July 15, 2020 (¶ 2505).

If a taxpayer files a timely return without an election out of the installment method, the taxpayer can elect out by filing an amended return within six months of the due date of the return (excluding extensions) (Reg. § 301.9100-2). The IRS will otherwise permit late elections only in rare circumstances where the taxpayer can show good cause for not making the election by the due date. An election out can be revoked only with IRS approval, but revocation is not allowed if one of its purposes is to avoid federal income tax, or if the tax year in which any payment was received has closed.

1808. Dealer Dispositions by Installment Sale. Dealers in real or personal property cannot use the installment method of accounting for installment sales (¶ 1801) to report the gain from dealer dispositions (Code Sec. 453(b)(2)(A) and (l)(1)). A dealer disposition includes:

- any disposition of personal property by a person who regularly sells or otherwise disposes of such property on an installment plan; and

- any disposition of real property that is held by the taxpayer for sale to customers in the ordinary course of the taxpayer's trade or business.

Certain types of installment transactions by a dealer are not considered dealer dispositions and the installment method of reporting can be used (Code Sec. 453(l)(2)). These include:

- the disposition of any property used or produced in the trade or business of farming;

- the disposition to an individual in the ordinary course of the taxpayer's trade or business of:

— any residential lot, provided that the dealer or any related person is not obligated to make any improvements to the lot; or

— a timeshare right to use or own residential real property for not more than six weeks per year, or a right to use specified campgrounds for recreational purposes.

A timeshare right to use or own property held by an individual's spouse, children, grandchildren, or parents is treated as held by the individual.

Payment of Interest. To use the installment method for the sale of residential lots and timeshares, the taxpayer must elect to pay interest on the amount of tax attributable to the installment payments received during the year. The interest is calculated for the period beginning on the date of sale and ending on the date the payment is received (Code Sec. 453(l)(3)). The amount of interest is based upon the applicable federal rate in effect at the time of sale, compounded semiannually (¶ 1875).

Computation of Gain

See CCH® AnswerConnect: *Installment Sales* for more information on this topic.

1813. Calculating Gain from Installment Sale. The amount of gain reported from an installment sale (¶ 1801) in any tax year (including the year of sale) generally is equal to the payments received during the year multiplied by the gross profit ratio for the sale (Code Sec. 453(c); Temp. Reg. § 15A.453-1(b)(2)). Payments include all amounts actually or constructively received in the tax year under the installment obligation (¶ 1819). Different computations are required for installment sales of property that are not subject to the depreciation recapture rules for section 1245 property or section 1250 property (¶ 1823).

The gross profit ratio is the gross profit on the installment sale divided by the total contract price. The gross profit is the selling price of the property minus its adjusted basis. The selling price of the property is not reduced by any existing mortgage or encumbrance, or by any selling expenses. It is reduced by any imputed interest (¶ 1859).

The total contract price (denominator of gross profit ratio) is the selling price minus that portion of qualifying debt (¶ 1815) the buyer assumes or takes the property subject to that does not exceed the seller's basis in the property (adjusted to reflect commissions and other selling expenses). In the case of an installment sale that is a partially nontaxable like-kind exchange (¶ 1721), the gross profit is reduced by that portion of the gain that is not recognized, and the total contract price is reduced by the value of the like-kind property received (Code Sec. 453(f)(6)).

For certain nondealer sales of property over $150,000, a special interest charge may apply (¶ 1825).

1815. Qualifying Debt for Installment Sales. Qualifying debt for purposes of determining the total contract price of an installment sale of property (¶ 1813) includes:

- any mortgage or other debt encumbering the property; and
- any debt not secured by the property but incurred or assumed by the purchaser incident to the acquisition, holding, or operation of the property in the ordinary course of business or investment (Temp. Reg. § 15A.453-1(b)(2)(iv)).

Qualifying debt does not include an obligation of the seller incurred incident to the *disposition* of the property, or an obligation functionally unrelated to the acquisition, holding, or operation of the property. Any obligation incurred or assumed in contemplation of disposition of the property is not qualifying debt if recovery of the seller's basis is accelerated.

Wrap-Around Mortgage. If property encumbered by an outstanding mortgage is sold in exchange for an installment obligation equal to the mortgage, the installment obligation is considered to "wrap around" the mortgage. The seller generally uses the payments received from the installment obligation to pay the wrapped mortgage. In this situation, the IRS will follow the Tax Court's position and will not treat the buyer as having taken the property subject to, or as having assumed, the seller's mortgage (*Professional Equities, Inc.*, Dec. 44,064, 89 TC 165 (Acq.)). As a result, the seller does not have to reduce the total contract price by the amount of the wrapped mortgage.

1819. Definition of Payments Under Installment Sale. An installment payment for purposes of determining the amount of gain recognized under the installment method of accounting (¶ 1813) includes all amounts actually or constructively received in the tax year under an installment obligation, as well as:

18

INSTALLMENT SALE

- evidence of debt of a person other than the buyer;

- evidence of debt of the buyer that is payable on demand or readily tradable, including a bond issued with coupons or in registered form;

- a bank certificate or treasury note;

- qualifying debt (¶ 1815) assumed or taken subject to by the buyer, to the extent it exceeds the seller's basis for the sold property as adjusted for selling expenses;

- seller's debt to the buyer that is canceled; and

- debt on the sold property (for which the seller is not personally liable) when the buyer is the obligee of the debt (Code Sec. 453(f)(3), (f)(4), and (f)(5); Temp. Reg. § 15A.453-1(b)(3)).

Debt instruments in registered form that the seller can establish are not readily tradable are not considered payments. In addition, like-kind property received in a partially tax-free exchange (¶ 1721) that is part of an installment sale transaction is not treated as a payment for determining the amount of income to be reported under the installment method (Code Sec. 453(f)(6)).

1821. Contingent Payment Sales. A contingent payment sale must be reported on the installment method (¶ 1801) unless the seller elects not to use the installment method (Temp. Reg. § 15A.453-1(c)). A contingent payment sale is a sale or other disposition of property that the total selling price cannot be determined by the close of the tax year in which the sale or disposition occurs. It does not include transactions in which the installment obligation represents, under applicable tax law principles: (1) a retained interest in the subject property of the transaction; (2) an interest in a joint venture or partnership; (3) an equity interest in a corporation; or (4) similar transactions, regardless of whether a stated maximum selling price or a fixed payment term exists.

The basis of the property sold (including selling expenses unless the taxpayer is a real estate dealer) in a contingent payment sale is allocated to payments received in each tax year and recovered as follows:

- for sales with a stated maximum selling price, basis is recovered according to a profit ratio based on the stated maximum selling price;

- for sales with a fixed payment period, basis is recovered ratably over the fixed period; and

- for sales with neither a maximum selling price nor a fixed payment period, basis is recovered ratably over a 15-year period.

Alternate methods of basis recovery may be required when the normal method would substantially and inappropriately accelerate or defer the recovery of basis.

1823. Installment Sale of Property Subject to Depreciation Recapture. For installment sales of section 1245 or section 1250 property to which the depreciation recapture rules apply (¶ 1779), any recapture income must be reported in the year of disposition, whether or not an installment payment is received in that year (Code Sec. 453(i)). The amount of ordinary income reported in the year of sale is added to the property's basis, and the adjusted basis is used in determining the remaining profit on the disposition. The remaining profit amount is used to compute the gross profit percentage to be applied to each installment payment.

Example: On December 1, 2019, Bob sells a rental building for a total contract price of $100,000, plus interest at the applicable federal rate. He receives a note due in yearly installments of $20,000, plus interest, beginning January 1, 2020. Bob's adjusted basis in the building is $20,000. Assume that $10,000 of the total $80,000 gain is attributable to depreciation that must be recaptured as ordinary income. The $10,000 must be included in Bob's ordinary income for 2019. The $10,000 is added to his $20,000 adjusted basis for determining the gross profit on the remaining gain. Therefore, gross profit is $70,000 ($100,000 − $30,000). Of each $20,000 payment received in the following years, $14,000 is includible in income ($20,000 × ($70,000 ÷ $100,000)).

¶**1821**

If a portion of the capital gain from an installment sale of depreciable real property consists of unrecaptured section 1250 gain, and another portion consists of other capital gains (¶ 1736), the taxpayer is required to take the unrecaptured section 1250 gain into account before the other capital gains are received (Reg. § 1.453-12).

1825. Interest Charge for Installment Sales by Nondealers. A special interest charge may apply to an installment obligation that arises from a nondealer disposition of real or personal property (¶ 1813) under the installment method if the sales price is over $150,000 (Code Sec. 453A). The interest charge does not apply to nondealer dispositions of property used in the business of farming or personal use property. Personal use property for this purpose is property that is not substantially used in connection with the taxpayer's trade or business, or in an investment activity. The interest charge also does not apply to dispositions of timeshares and residential lots, but the interest payment rule for dealer dispositions applies (¶ 1808).

The interest charge is generally imposed on the tax deferred under the installment method with respect to outstanding installment obligations. However, the interest charge will not apply unless the face amount of all obligations held by the taxpayer that arose during and remain outstanding at the close of the tax year exceeds $5 million.

If any debt is secured by a nondealer installment obligation that arises from the disposition of any real or personal property having a sales price over $150,000, the net proceeds of the secured debt is treated as a payment received on the installment obligation as of the later of the date that the debt is secured or the date that the seller receives the net proceeds.

The interest is not reported on Form 6252, but rather is entered as an additional tax on the taxpayer's return. For individuals, it is included on the line for "Other taxes" on Schedule 2 (Form 1040). For estates and trusts, it is included on the line for "Other Taxes and Amounts Due" on Schedule G (Form 1041). For corporations, it is entered on Schedule J (Form 1120).

Related-Party Sales

See CCH® AnswerConnect: *Installment Sales* for more information on this topic.

1833. Installment Sale to Related Persons. If a person makes an installment sale of property (¶ 1801) to a related person who sells the property before the installment payments are made in full, the amount realized by the related person from the second sale is treated as being received by the initial seller at the time of the second sale (Code Sec. 453(e)). The resale rule generally does not apply if the second sale takes place more than two years after the first sale.

The two-year cutoff does not apply to marketable securities. Further, the two-year period is suspended during any period the related purchaser's risk of loss is substantially lessened by: (1) the holding of a put on the property or on similar property; (2) another person holding a right to acquire the property; or (3) a short sale or other transaction having the requisite effect.

A related person for this purpose is defined in Code Sec. 267(b) (¶ 1717) and Code Sec. 318(a) (¶ 743), but without regard to the stock option rules. It includes the seller's spouse, child, grandchild and other lineal descendants, parent, grandparent and other ancestors, brother, sister, controlled corporation, partnership, certain trusts, estate, or executor (Code Sec. 453(f)(1)).

In applying the resale rule, the amount treated as received by the initial seller is limited to:

- the *lesser* of (1) the total amount realized from the second disposition before the close of the tax year of disposition, or (2) the total contract price for the first disposition;

- *minus* the sum of the (1) total amount received from the first disposition before the close of the year of the second disposition, and (2) the total amount treated as received for prior years under the resale rule.

18

INSTALLMENT SALE

¶1833

There are several exceptions to the resale rule. Any sale or exchange of stock to the issuing corporation is not treated as a first disposition. An involuntary conversion (¶ 1713), and any subsequent transfer, is not treated as a second disposition if the first disposition occurred before the threat or imminence of the conversion. Any transfer after the earlier of the death of the person making the first disposition or the death of the person acquiring the property in the first disposition, and any subsequent transfer, is not treated as a second disposition. Further, the resale rule does not apply if it is established to the IRS's satisfaction that neither disposition had federal income tax avoidance as one of its principal purposes.

1835. Installment Sale of Depreciable Property Between Related Persons. The installment method (¶ 1801) generally cannot be used for installment sales of depreciable property between related persons. As a result, all payments are deemed received in the year of sale. However, the installment method can be used if the IRS is satisfied that tax avoidance was not one of the principal purposes of the sale (Code Sec. 453(g)). For this purpose, a related person is defined in Code Sec. 1239(b) (¶ 1744) and includes corporations and partnerships that are more than 50-percent owned, either directly or indirectly, by the same person.

Repossessions of Property

See CCH® AnswerConnect: *Installment Sales* for more information on this topic.

1838. Repossession of Personal Property Sold Under Installment Method. If personal property that was sold in an installment sale (¶ 1801) is repossessed, the repossession is treated as a disposition of the installment obligation (¶ 1846) (IRS Pub. 537). Gain or loss is measured by subtracting the seller's basis in the obligation and any repossession expenses from the sum of (1) the fair market value of the property on the date of repossession, and (2) the value of any other property received from the buyer.

If the seller did not use the installment method to report the gain on the original sale, the seller's basis in the obligation is equal to the face value of the obligation minus all principal payments that the seller received on the obligation. If the seller used the installment method to report the gain on the original sale, the seller's basis in the obligation is determined by multiplying the unpaid balance of the obligation by the seller's gross profit percentage, and then subtracting that amount from the unpaid balance. The character of the gain or loss, if any, on the repossession is the same as on the original sale.

If the installment obligation is not completely satisfied by repossession of the property, and the seller is unable to collect the balance of the debt, the seller may be able to claim a bad debt deduction for the portion of the obligation that is not satisfied through repossession (¶ 1135 and ¶ 1143).

1841. Repossession of Real Property Sold Under Installment Method. If real property is sold on the installment method (¶ 1801) and the seller accepts an installment debt secured by the property, the seller will recognize only a limited amount of gain and no loss upon repossession of the property (Code Sec. 1038; Reg. § 1.1038-1). Gain on the repossession is limited to the lesser of:

- the amount by which the amount of money and the fair market value of other property (other than obligations of the purchaser) received, prior to the reacquisition, with respect to the sale of such property, exceeds the amount of the gain on the sale of such property returned as income for periods prior to the reacquisition (Reg. § 1.1038-1(b)); or

- the amount by which the price at which the real property was sold exceeded its adjusted basis, reduced by the sum of: (1) the amount of the gain on the sale of such property returned as income for periods prior to the reacquisition of such property; and (2) the amount of money and the fair market value of other property (other than obligations of the purchaser received with respect to the sale of such property) paid or transferred by the seller in connection with the reacquisition of such property (Reg. § 1.1038-1(c)).

¶1835

The same rules apply if an estate or beneficiary repossesses real property that had been sold by a decedent on the installment method (Code Sec. 1038(g)).

Repossession of Principal Residence. Special rules apply if a seller repossesses a principal residence that was sold under the installment method and gain realized from the sale was excluded from gross income (¶ 1705). If the seller resells the residence within one year of repossession, the original sale and the resale are treated as one transaction and realized gain is determined on the combined sale and resale (Code Sec. 1038(e); Reg. § 1.1038-2). If the resale does not take place within one year, the general rules for repossessions of real property apply.

1843. Basis of Real Property After Repossession. The seller's basis in the repossession of real property under the installment method (¶ 1841) is generally the adjusted basis of the debt secured by the property (determined at the time of the repossession), increased by any gain recognized at the time of the repossession and by the seller's repossession costs. If the debt to the seller is not discharged as a result of the repossession, the basis of the debt is zero (Code Sec. 1038(c)). If, before repossession, the seller has treated the secured debt as having become worthless or partially worthless, then, upon repossession, the seller is considered to have received an amount equal to the amount that was treated as worthless. However, the seller's adjusted basis in the debt is increased by the same amount (Code Sec. 1038(d)).

Dispositions of Installment Obligations

See CCH® AnswerConnect: *Installment Sales* for more information on this topic.

1846. Sale or Disposition of Installment Obligations. Gain or loss is generally recognized when an installment obligation (¶ 1801) is sold, disposed, or satisfied other than at face value (Code Sec. 453B). The character of any resulting gain or loss on the disposition of an installment obligation is determined by the character of the original asset that was sold (¶ 1735). The amount of gain or loss is the difference between the basis of the obligation and either:

- the amount realized, if the obligation is satisfied other than at face value or is sold or exchanged; or

- the fair market value of the obligation, if the obligation is distributed or disposed of other than by sale or exchange.

The basis of the obligation to the transferor for this purpose is the excess of the face value of the obligation over the income that would have been returnable had the obligation been satisfied in full. To determine the basis, the unpaid balance of the installment obligation is multiplied by the gross profit percentage, and the result is subtracted from the unpaid balance. The result is the basis in the installment obligation (IRS Pub. 537).

The cancellation or lapse of an installment obligation is treated as a disposition other than a sale or exchange. This includes a self-canceling installment note that is extinguished at the death of the holder (*R.E. Frane Est.*, CA-8, 93-2 USTC ¶ 50,386). Therefore, gain or loss is computed based on the fair market value of the obligation.

Transfers Between Spouses. The transfer of an installment obligation between married individuals or former spouses incident to divorce (other than a transfer in trust) does not trigger recognition of gain (Code Sec. 453B(g)). Thus, the same tax treatment applies to the transferee spouse that would have applied to the transferor spouse.

Transfers at Death. The transfer of an installment obligation at the death of the obligee (other than to the buyer) is not a taxable disposition requiring the recognition of any gain or loss (Code Sec. 453B(c)). Instead, the gain from any installment obligation acquired from a decedent is considered income in respect of a decedent (¶ 182). The taxpayer who receives the installment payments (estate, beneficiary, etc.) must report as income the same portion of the payments that would have been taxable income to the decedent. The amount considered to be an item of gross income in respect of the decedent is the excess of the face value of the obligation over its basis in the hands of the decedent.

¶1846

While the transfer of an installment obligation upon a seller's death is generally not a taxable disposition, the seller's estate is deemed to have made a taxable disposition if the obligation is transferred by bequest, devise, or inheritance to the obligor, or if the estate allows the obligation to become unenforceable. If the decedent and obligor-recipient were related persons (¶ 1833), the fair market value of the obligation cannot be determined at less than its face amount (Code Sec. 691(a)(5)).

Corporate Liquidations

1856. Installment Obligations Received in Corporate Liquidations. Liquidating corporations, other than certain liquidating S corporations (¶ 1858), that distribute installment obligations to shareholders in exchange for their stock must currently recognize gain or loss from the distribution (¶ 1846). However, a shareholder that receives a qualifying installment obligation can treat the exchange as though it were an ordinary sale of stock for an installment obligation. Thus, the shareholder may be able to use the installment method (¶ 1801) to report the gain from the exchange (Code Sec. 453(h)(1)(A); Reg. § 1.453-11(a)(1)).

If the liquidating corporation is traded on an established securities market, installment sale treatment is generally not available. A shareholder *can* use the installment method if the stock of the liquidating corporation is not traded on an established market, even if the obligation arose from the sale by the liquidating corporation of securities that are traded on an established market. For this rule to apply, the liquidating corporation must not have been formed or used to avoid the prohibition against using the installment method for publicly traded stock (Reg. § 1.453-11(c)(5)).

Gain on the transfer of a qualifying installment obligation to a shareholder during a liquidation is not immediately taxed to the shareholder. Instead, the payments received under the installment obligation are treated as payments for the stock, and any gain is included in the shareholder's income as payments are received. This rule applies when:

- stockholders exchange their stock in the corporation in a Code Sec. 331 liquidation (¶ 2253);

- the corporation, during the 12-month period beginning with the adoption of the plan of liquidation, had sold some or all of its assets in exchange for an installment note;

- the corporation, within that 12-month period, distributes the installment notes acquired in connection with those sales to the shareholders in exchange for their stock; and

- the liquidation is completed within that 12-month period.

This rule does not apply to obligations arising from a sale of inventory, stock in trade, or assets held for sale to customers in the ordinary course of business, unless those assets are sold in a bulk sale (Code Sec. 453(h)(1)(B)).

Subsidiary Liquidations. In a complete liquidation of a subsidiary, in which gain or loss on distributions of property is generally not recognized by the parent or the subsidiary (¶ 2261), the distribution of installment obligations will not cause recognition of gain or loss (Code Sec. 453B(d)).

1858. Installment Obligation Received in S Corporation Liquidations. If an installment obligation is distributed by an S corporation in a complete liquidation (¶ 2253), and the receipt of the obligation is not treated as payment for stock in a complete 12-month liquidation (¶ 1856), then the corporation generally does not recognize gain or loss on the distribution. This is true even for an S corporation using the accrual-method of accounting (Code Sec. 453B(h)).

Imputed Interest

See CCH® AnswerConnect: *Interest Income: Deferred Payment Property Sales* for more information on this topic.

1859. Inadequate or Unpaid Interest on Deferred Payments. If a sale or exchange of property involves the issuance of a debt instrument with deferred payments such as an installment sale (¶ 1801), the instrument generally should provide for the payment of adequate interest. If the instrument does not provide for the payment of adequate stated interest, interest income must be imputed to the seller or holder of the debt under the original issue discount (OID) rules of Code Sec. 1274 (¶ 1954) or the unstated interest rules of Code Sec. 483 (¶ 1868). The unstated interest rules will apply only if the transaction does not come within the scope of the OID rules (Code Sec. 483(d)(1)).

If neither the unstated interest rules nor OID rules apply, interest might be imputed under other Code sections (Reg. § 1.483-1(a) and (c)(3); Reg. § 1.1274-1(b)). For example, interest is imputed to certain obligations given in exchange for services or for the use of property under Code Secs. 404 and 467 (¶ 906 and ¶ 1541). Further, the interest imputation rules of Code Sec. 7872 apply to certain below-market demand loans (¶ 795).

The unstated interest rules and OID rules also do not apply to transfers of property between spouses or incident to divorce (¶ 778) or to a purchaser who gives debt when buying personal use property. Special rules apply to cash method debt instruments (¶ 1954).

The following steps should be taken with respect to deferred contracts:

- determine whether the transaction is covered by either the unstated interest rules or the OID rules (¶ 1868 and ¶ 1954);

- test for unstated interest or OID;

- compute the total unstated interest or OID under the contract; and

- apportion the unstated interest or OID over the payments.

1868. Scope of Unstated Interest Rules of Code Sec. 483. The unstated interest rules of Code Sec. 483 impute interest income (¶ 1872) on any payments on the sale or exchange of property that are due more than six months after the sale or exchange if any payments are due more than one year after the sale or exchange (Code Sec. 483(c)). The Code Sec. 483 rules do not apply in the following situations:

- debt instruments for which an issue price is determined under Code Sec. 1273(b)(1), (2) or (3), or Code Sec. 1274;

- sales for $3,000 or less;

- with respect to the buyer, any purchase of personal property or educational services (under Code Sec. 163(b)) on an installment basis if the interest charge cannot be ascertained and is treated as six percent; and

- sales or exchanges of patents (¶ 1767) to the extent of any payments that are contingent on the productivity, use or disposition of the property transferred (Code Sec. 483(d)).

1872. Testing for and Imputing Unstated Interest. The imputed interest rules of Code Sec. 483 apply (¶ 1868) when there is "unstated interest," which is the excess of the total payments (excluding any interest payments) due more than six months after the date of sale over the total of their present values (including the present values of any interest payments). Present value is generally determined by using a discount rate equal to the applicable federal rate (AFR) determined under Code Sec. 1274(d) (¶ 1875) (Code Sec. 483(b); Reg. § § 1.483-2 and 1.483-3). However, the discount rate cannot exceed six percent, compounded semiannually, for transfers of land between family members. This rule only applies if the aggregate sales price of all land sales between the family members does not exceed $500,000, and if no party to the sale is a nonresident alien (Code Sec. 483(e); Reg. § 1.483-3(b)). In addition, a discount rate not in excess of nine percent (if less than the AFR), compounded semiannually, applies to most debt instruments given in consideration for the sale or exchange of property if the stated principal amount does not exceed a certain inflation-adjusted amount (¶ 1954).

1875. Adequate Stated Interest. A debt instrument with deferred payments is considered to have adequate stated interest under the unstated interest rules of Code Sec. 483 (¶ 1868) if the stated principal amount is less than or equal to its imputed principal amount (Code Secs. 483(b), 1274(b) and (c); Reg. §§1.483-2(b) and 1.1274-2(c)). The imputed principal amount is determined by totaling the present values of all principal and interest payments due on the instrument discounted at the applicable federal rate (AFR) (¶83). Payments within six months after the sale are taken into account.

The AFR is the lowest rate in effect for any month in the three-calendar-month period ending with the first calendar month in which there is a binding written contract. It is determined by reference to the term of the debt instrument, including renewal and extension options, as shown in the following table (Code Sec. 1274(d); Reg. §§1.483-3(a) and 1.1274-4(a)).

Term of Debt Instrument:	*Applicable Federal Rate:*
Not over 3 years	Federal short-term rate
Over 3 years but not over 9 years .	Federal mid-term rate
Over 9 years	Federal long-term rate

For sale and leaseback transactions, the discount rate is 110 percent of the AFR, compounded semiannually (Code Sec. 1274(e); Reg. §1.1274-4(a)(2)). For transactions in which a debt instrument is given in consideration for the sale or exchange of property (other than new Code Sec. 38 property) and the stated principal amount of the instrument does not exceed an inflation-adjusted amount ($5,944,600 for 2019 and $6,039,100 in 2020), a rate of up to nine percent can be substituted for the AFR (Code Sec. 1274A; Rev. Proc. 2018-57; Rev. Proc. 2019-44). The discount rate will not exceed six percent, compounded semiannually, in the case of certain transfers of land between family members (¶1872).

1881. Effect of Assumptions of Debt on Unstated Interest. If any person in connection with the sale or exchange of property assumes any debt instrument or acquires any property subject to any debt instrument, the assumption or acquisition is not generally taken into account in determining whether the unstated interest rules apply. However, if the instrument's terms and conditions are modified in a manner that would constitute an exchange (¶1701), the unstated interest rules apply (Reg. §1.483-1(d)).

Treatment of Interest

See CCH® AnswerConnect: *Interest Income: Deferred Payment Property Sales* for more information on this topic.

1883. Treatment of Imputed Interest. The amount of unstated interest determined under Code Sec. 483 (¶1868) is classified as interest for tax purposes (Reg. §1.483-1(a)(2)). As a result, it may be deductible by the buyer. Unstated interest is not deductible by the issuer of a debt instrument given in consideration for the sale or exchange of personal use property (Reg. §1.483-1(c)(3)). Instead, the unstated interest must be accrued by the holder. Personal use property means any property substantially all the use of which by the taxpayer is not in connection with the taxpayer's trade or business or activities engaged in for profit (Code Sec. 1275(b)(3)).

Reporting Requirements. The reporting of unstated interest depends upon whether the seller uses the cash or accrual method of accounting. Cash basis sellers include unstated interest as interest income in the year payments are received. Sellers on the accrual basis include unstated interest in income in the year payments are due (Reg. §1.446-2(a)).

Chapter 19

SECURITIES TRANSACTIONS

Taxation of Securities Transactions

See CCH® AnswerConnect: *Financial Transactions: Securities, Commodities, Section 1256 Contracts and Investment Property* and *Mark-to-Market Accounting Method for Dealers and Traders of Securities and Commodities* for more information on this topic.

1901. Securities Transactions. Securities such as stocks and bonds held for investment are generally capital assets. Gain or loss from the sale of securities is calculated as it is for other capital assets (¶ 1701). There are, however, a number of special rules that apply to the sale or exchange of certain securities, including securities held by dealers (¶ 1903), worthless securities (¶ 1916), options to buy securities (¶ 1919), wash sales (¶ 1935), short sales (¶ 1944), tax straddles (¶ 1948), and a corporation dealing in its own stocks or bonds (¶ 1729). In addition, gain on the sale of qualified small business stock may be excluded from gross income (¶ 1905) or rolled over to other small business stock (¶ 1907). A taxpayer may also roll over gain from the sale of publicly traded securities before 2018 to an interest in a specialized small business investment company (¶ 1909). Losses from the sale of stock in certain small businesses may be treated as ordinary losses (¶ 1911 and ¶ 1913).

1903. Dealer in Securities. Securities held by a dealer for sale to customers in the ordinary course of a trade or business are not capital assets (¶ 1741). Thus, gain or loss realized from the sale or disposition is ordinary gain or loss unless the dealer holds the securities primarily for personal investment (Code Sec. 1236; Reg. § 1.1236-1). Securities held for personal investment must be clearly identified in the dealer's records before the close of the day they are acquired, and must never be held primarily for sale to customers. See ¶ 1760 for a discussion of the differences between a dealer, trader, and investor.

Mark-to-Market Requirements. A dealer in securities must use the mark-to-market method of accounting to report gains and losses from the disposition of securities (Code Sec. 475(a)). Under the mark-to-market rules, any security that is inventory in the hands of the dealer must be included in inventory at its fair market value. The dealer may use the fair market value reported on its financial statements (Reg. § 1.475(a)-4).

Any security that the dealer holds at the close of the tax year and does not classify as inventory is treated as if it were sold at its fair market value on the last business day of the year. The dealer must recognize any gain or loss that would result from the deemed sale and take it into account when calculating gain or loss on the actual sale or exchange of the security.

The mark-to-market rules generally apply to all securities held by a dealer, other than those held as investments or not for sale to customers in the ordinary course of the dealer's trade or business (Code Sec. 475(b)). The rules also do not apply to debt instruments acquired in the ordinary course of a trade or business or securities that are

¶1903

hedges of certain positions (¶ 1949). In order for a security to be exempt from the mark-to-market requirements, it must be clearly identified in the dealer's records before the close of the day on which it is acquired, originated, or entered into.

A dealer in commodities, or a trader in securities or commodities, may elect to apply the mark-to-market rules to noninvestment positions (Code Sec. 475(e) and (f)). The election applies to commodities held by a commodities dealer in the same manner as securities held by a dealer. A trader in securities or commodities that elects mark-to-market treatment must recognize gain or loss on any security or commodity held in connection with the trading business as if the security or commodity were sold at fair market value on the last business day of the tax year.

A trader must make the mark-to-market election by the original due date (not including extensions) of the tax return for the year prior to the year for which the election becomes effective. For example, the election must be made by April 15, 2020, to be effective for 2020. The election is made by attaching a statement to the taxpayer's timely filed return or request for a filing extension. A taxpayer that is not required to file a tax return makes the election by placing a statement in its books and records no later than March 15 of the election year.

Taxpayers may obtain automatic consent to change their methods of accounting to comply with the election. A securities or commodities trader may make a separate election for each trade or business. The election generally applies to the current and all subsequent tax years, but may be revoked by using automatic consent procedures for accounting method changes (Rev. Proc. 99-17; Rev. Proc. 2015-13; Rev. Proc. 2018-31; Rev. Proc. 2019-43).

Gains and Losses on Small Business Stock

See CCH® AnswerConnect: *Small Business Stock* for more information on this topic.

1905. Exclusion of Gain from Small Business Stock. A noncorporate taxpayer can exclude from gross income 100 percent of gain from the sale or exchange of qualified small business stock acquired after September 27, 2010, and held for more than five years (Code Sec. 1202). The exclusion is only 75 percent for qualified small business stock acquired after February 17, 2009, and before September 28, 2010; 50 percent for qualified stock acquired before February 18, 2009; and 60 percent for gain attributable to periods before 2019 on a disposition of stock issued by a corporation in an empowerment zone (¶ 1799B) that was acquired after December 21, 2000, and before February 18, 2009. For stock acquired before September 28, 2010, seven percent of the excluded gain is a tax preference item for alternative minimum tax (AMT) purposes (¶ 194). The sale or exchange of qualified small business stock is reported on Form 8949.

Excludable gain on dispositions of stock from any single issuer for any given tax year is limited to the greater of: (1) $10 million reduced by the aggregate amount of eligible gain on the issuer's stock that the taxpayer excluded in prior years ($5 million for married individuals filing separately); or (2) 10 times the taxpayer's adjusted basis in all of the issuer's qualified stock disposed of during the tax year.

Qualified Small Business Stock. Qualified small business stock is stock issued after August 10, 1993, and acquired by the taxpayer at its original issue, directly or through an underwriter, in exchange for money or property, or as compensation for services provided to the corporation (Code Sec. 1202(c) and (d); Reg. § 1.1202-2). Qualified stock acquired by exercising options or warrants, or by converting debt, is deemed acquired at original issue. The issuing corporation must be a domestic C corporation other than a regulated investment company (RIC) (¶ 2301), cooperative, or other similar pass-through corporation.

Both before and immediately after the qualified stock is issued, the corporation's aggregate gross assets must not exceed $50 million, with all corporations in the same parent-subsidiary controlled group treated as one corporation. In addition, during substantially all of the taxpayer's holding period, at least 80 percent of the value of the corporation's assets must be used in the active conduct of qualified trades or businesses (Code Sec. 1202(e)). The performance of services in the fields of health, law, engineering, architecture, etc., is not a qualified trade or business, nor are the hospitality, farming, insurance, finance or mineral extraction industries. However, a specialized small business investment company (SSBIC), licensed under section 301(d) of the Small Business Investment Act of 1958, meets the active business test. Small business stock is not qualified if it has been the subject of certain redemptions that are more than *de minimis*.

Qualified stock that is converted to other stock of the corporation, such as preferred stock, remains qualified stock (Code Sec. 1202(f)). If stock is transferred by gift or inheritance, the transferee is treated as having acquired the stock in the same manner as the transferor, and the transferor's holding period tacks on to the transferee's (Code Sec. 1202(h)). Gain on dispositions of qualified stock held by a pass-through entity (partnership, S corporation, RIC, or common trust fund) for more than five years is excludable when it is passed through to partners, shareholders, and participants who held interests in the entity when it acquired the stock and at all times thereafter. However, the exclusion cannot reflect any increase in that person's share of the entity after the entity acquired the stock (Code Sec. 1202(g)).

1907. Rollover of Gain from Small Business Stock. A noncorporate taxpayer may elect to roll over capital gain from the sale of qualified small business stock (¶ 1905) held for more than six months if other qualified small business stock is purchased during the 60-day period beginning on the date of sale (Code Sec. 1045; Reg. § 1.1045-1). The due date for performing certain time-sensitive actions, including the 60-day rollover period, otherwise due on or after April 1, 2020, and before July 15, 2020, is automatically extended to July 15, 2020, in response to the COVID-19 (coronavirus) crisis (Notice 2020-23; Rev. Proc. 2018-58). The replacement stock must meet the active business requirement for the six-month period following its purchase.

Except for purposes of applying the six-month active business test, the holding period of the stock purchased includes the holding period of the stock sold. Gain is recognized only to the extent that the amount realized on the sale exceeds the cost of the replacement stock. The basis of the newly purchased stock is reduced by the amount of gain rolled over. Special rules apply for partnerships that roll over gain from a business that is held in the form of qualified small business stock. The sale of the stock is reported on Form 8949.

1909. Rollover of Gain from Publicly Traded Securities. An individual or C corporation can elect to defer recognition of capital gain on the sale of publicly traded securities before 2018 that is used within 60 days to purchase common stock or a partnership interest in a specialized small business investment company (SSBIC) (Code Sec. 1044, prior to repeal by the Tax Cuts and Jobs Act (P.L. 115-97); Reg. § 1.1044(a)-1). The exclusion is subject to both annual and lifetime limits. An SSBIC is a corporation or partnership licensed under section 301(d) of the Small Business Investment Act of 1958 to finance small business concerns owned by disadvantaged persons. The election to defer recognition of capital gain is repealed for sales after 2017.

1911. Losses on Small Business Stock (Section 1244 Stock). An individual's loss on the sale, exchange, or worthlessness of small business stock (section 1244 stock) may be treated as an ordinary loss, even if the stock is a capital asset (Code Sec. 1244). The maximum amount deductible as an ordinary loss in any tax year is $50,000 ($100,000 for married individuals filing a joint return).

The ordinary loss is treated as a loss from the taxpayer's trade or business in computing a net operating loss (NOL) for the tax year (¶ 1145) and is reported on Form 4797. Any loss that exceeds the annual limit is treated as a capital loss and reported on Form 8949. Gain on the disposition of section 1244 stock is capital gain if the stock was a capital asset in the taxpayer's hands (¶ 1741).

Section 1244 stock is stock of a domestic corporation, including preferred stock, issued after November 6, 1978, that meets the following requirements (additional requirements apply to stock issued after June 30, 1958, and before November 7, 1978):

- The stock must have been issued to the taxpayer, or a partnership in which the taxpayer was a partner, in exchange for money or property other than stock or securities.

19

SECURITIES

- The issuing corporation must be a small business corporation, meaning that at the time the stock was issued the aggregate amount of money and other property, taken into account at its adjusted basis, received by the corporation as contributions to capital and as paid-in surplus (for the stock in question and also any previously issued stock) did not exceed $1 million. S corporation stock does not automatically qualify as section 1244 stock.

- During the corporation's five most recent tax years ending before the taxpayer sells the stock, more than 50 percent of its gross receipts must have been derived from sources other than royalties, rents, dividends, interest, annuities, and gains from the sales of securities (Reg. § § 1.1244(c)-1 and -2). Since the corporation must be largely an operating company, stock in a corporation with little or no gross receipts is not eligible.

1913. Losses on Small Business Investment Company Stock (SBIC). A loss on the sale, exchange, or worthlessness of stock in a small business investment company (SBIC) (¶ 2392) may be treated as an ordinary loss on Form 4797, even if the stock is a capital asset in the taxpayer's hands (Code Sec. 1242; Reg. § 1.1242-1(b)). The SBIC must be licensed to operate as an SBIC when the loss is sustained. The loss is not subject to the limitations on the allowance of nonbusiness deductions in computing net operating losses (NOLs) (¶ 1145). If a taxpayer has several transactions involving SBIC stock, each transaction is considered separately; they are not netted to determine if the taxpayer has an overall gain or loss. A loss on a short sale of SBIC stock (¶ 1944) with other SBIC stock acquired only for the purpose of closing the short sale is a capital loss under the short sale rules, rather than an ordinary loss (Rev. Rul. 63-65).

Worthless Securities

1916. Worthless Securities. A security is treated as sold or exchanged on the last day of the tax year in which it becomes completely worthless (Code Sec. 165(g); Reg. § 1.165-5). If the security is a capital asset (¶ 1741), the loss is generally a capital loss subject to the limits on capital losses (¶ 1752). If the security is not a capital asset, the loss is an ordinary loss subject to the limits on ordinary losses (¶ 1101). The amount of the loss is the taxpayer's adjusted basis in the security, less any compensation from insurance.

> **Example:** On December 10, Year 1, Judy bought shares of Xetco Corp. for $5,000. On May 1, Year 2, she received formal notification that the shares were worthless. In claiming a capital loss for the worthless shares on her Year 2 tax return, Judy must treat the shares as becoming worthless on December 31, Year 2. As a result, her $5,000 capital loss is a long-term loss even though she did not own the shares for more than 12 months before they became worthless.

A security becomes totally worthless when it has no value or potential value as the result of an identifiable event. The abandonment of a security establishes its worthlessness to the taxpayer. To abandon a security, the taxpayer must permanently surrender and relinquish all rights in it and receive no consideration for the exchange. Deductions for partial worthlessness are generally not allowed.

A security includes stock and the right to subscribe for or receive stock. It also includes bonds, debentures, notes, certificates, or other evidence of debt issued with interest coupons or in registered form by a corporation or government to pay a fixed or determinable sum of money. A worthless debt that does not meet the definition of a security (e.g., because it was not issued by a corporation or government) is a bad debt (¶ 1135 and ¶ 1143).

Securities held by a securities dealer as inventory are not capital assets, so a dealer's loss from worthlessness is an ordinary loss (¶ 1903). An ordinary loss may also be claimed for losses from worthless securities that are section 1244 stock (¶ 1911), securities issued by a small business investment company (SBIC) (¶ 1913), securities held by an SBIC (¶ 2392), securities in an affiliated corporation, and securities held by a bank or other financial institution (¶ 2383).

Options

See CCH® AnswerConnect: *Options, Puts and Calls Using Securities and Commodities* and *Incentive Stock Options for Employees* for more information on this topic.

1919. Options to Buy or Sell Property. Gain or loss from the sale or exchange of an option to buy or sell property, including a cash settlement option and an option on a section 1256 contract (¶ 1947), is considered gain or loss from the sale or exchange of the underlying property (Code Sec. 1234; Reg. §1.1234-1). Thus, the gain or loss is capital only if the option covers property that would be a capital asset in the taxpayer's hands (¶ 1741). The length of time the taxpayer held the option determines whether a capital gain or loss is short term or long term unless the sale or exchange is part of a hedging transaction (¶ 1949). If the underlying property is section 1231 property, gain or loss on the sale or exchange of the option may be section 1231 gain or loss (¶ 1747).

If a loss arises from an option holder's failure to exercise an option, the option is deemed to have been sold or exchanged on the date it expired. For the grantor of an option for stock, securities, commodities, or commodity futures (including an option granted as part of a straddle (¶ 1948)), gain or loss from any closing transaction and gain on the lapse of the option is a short-term capital gain or loss. See ¶ 1921 for a discussion of holders and writers of options on securities (i.e., puts and calls).

These characterization rules do not apply to gain or loss realized on the sale or exchange of an option by a dealer who holds options primarily for sale to customers (¶ 1903). They also do not apply to gain realized from the sale or exchange of an employee stock option (¶ 1925 and ¶ 1927), an option to lease property, an option to buy or sell inventory, an option equivalent to a dividend, an option involving section 306 stock (¶ 739), or an option included as part of a short sale (¶ 1944).

1921. Puts and Calls. Puts are options to sell, and calls are options to buy, stock, securities, or commodities at a set price on or before a specified date. Puts and calls are issued by writers (grantors) to holders for premiums. They end when the holder exercises the option, the option lapses, or the option is effectively terminated at its current fair market value in a closing transaction (Rev. Rul. 78-182; IRS Pub. 550).

Holders of Puts and Calls. The purchase of a put option or call option is not a taxable event. The cost of purchasing the put or call is a nondeductible capital expenditure (Rev. Rul. 71-521). If the holder sells a put or call without exercising it, the difference between its cost and the amount received is either a long-term or short-term capital gain or loss, depending on how long it was held (¶ 1919). If the option expires, its cost is either a long-term or short-term capital loss, depending on the taxpayer's holding period, which ends on the expiration date. If the holder exercises a call, its cost is added to the basis of the security purchased. If the holder exercises a put, the amount realized on the sale of the underlying security is reduced by the cost of the put when computing gain or loss on the sale of the security. That gain or loss is long-term or short-term depending on the taxpayer's holding period for the underlying security (Rev. Rul. 78-182; IRS Pub. 550). The acquisition of a put is considered a short sale, and the exercise, sale, or lapse of the put is a closing of the short sale (¶ 1944).

Writers of Puts and Calls. If a taxpayer writes or grants a call or put option, the premium received is not included in income at the time of receipt. Instead it is deferred until the option expires, the taxpayer buys or sells the underlying security when the option is exercised, or the taxpayer engages in a closing transaction.

If the option expires, the premium can then be treated as a short-term capital gain. If a call is exercised and the taxpayer sells the underlying security, the premium is added to the amount realized on the sale and any gain or loss is long-term or short-term depending on how long the taxpayer held the security. If a put is exercised and the taxpayer buys the underlying security, then the premium reduces its basis in the security. The taxpayer's holding period on the security begins on the date of the purchase, not on the date the put was written.

The taxpayer can also terminate a put or call through a closing transaction—such as repurchasing the option or substituting the original option by purchasing another option with identical terms. The difference between the premium originally received and the amount paid in the closing transaction is short-term capital gain or loss.

> **Example 1:** Ten call options were issued on April 8 for $4,000. The options expired in December without being exercised. The holder (buyer) of the options recognizes a short-term capital loss of $4,000. The writer of the options recognizes a short-term capital gain of $4,000.

> **Example 2:** Assume the same facts as in Example 1, except that on May 10, the options were sold for $6,000. The holder (buyer) of the options who sold them recognizes a short-term capital gain of $2,000. If the writer of the options bought them back, he or she would recognize a short-term capital loss of $2,000.

> **Example 3:** Assume the facts as in Example 1, except that the options were exercised on May 27. The holder (buyer) adds the $4,000 cost of the options to the basis of the stock bought through the exercise of the options. The writer adds the $4,000 received from writing the options to the amount realized from selling the stock. The gain or loss is short term or long term, depending on the holding period of the stock.

1923. Nonstatutory Stock Options. An employee or independent contractor who receives a stock option as compensation for services rendered is generally subject to the Code Sec. 83 rules regarding restricted property transfers (¶ 713) when the option is granted or exercised, unless it is an incentive stock option (ISO) (¶ 1925) or an option granted under an employee stock purchase plan (ESPP) (¶ 1929) (Code Sec. 83(e)(1); Reg. § 1.83-7).

If a nonstatutory stock option has a readily ascertainable fair market value (FMV) when it is granted, the restricted property rules apply on the grant date. The taxpayer has ordinary income equal to the stock's fair market value on the grant date, less any amount paid. If a nonstatutory stock option does not have a readily ascertainable FMV when it is granted, the restricted property rules apply when the taxpayer exercises or disposes of the option, even if the FMV becomes ascertainable before then. A taxpayer who exercises the option has ordinary income equal to the stock's FMV at the exercise date or when substantially vested, less the exercise price.

If a nonstatutory stock option is sold or disposed of in an arm's-length transaction, the taxpayer is considered to have exercised the option and has income equal to the money or property received, less the exercise price. If the sale or disposition is not an arm's-length transaction, the taxpayer is not considered to have exercised the option, but must still treat the money or property received as compensation that is included in income. In addition, when the transferee exercises the option, the taxpayer (transferor) has additional income equal to the FMV of stock acquired by the transferee, less the exercise price and any amount the taxpayer received from the sale of the option. A sale or disposition to a related person is not an arm's-length transaction. If the holder of an option incurs a loss on failure to exercise the option, it is deemed to have been sold or exchanged on the date it expired (¶ 1919).

Readily Ascertainable Market Value. A stock option generally has a readily ascertainable FMV if it is actively traded on an established securities market (Reg. § 1.83-7(b)). An option that is not actively traded on an established securities market has a readily ascertainable value if the taxpayer can demonstrate that the option is transferable and immediately exercisable, there is no condition or restriction on the underlying property that would have a significant effect on its FMV, and the FMV of the option privilege is readily ascertainable.

Sale of Stock. Stock acquired through the exercise of a nonstatutory stock option is treated as any other investment property when sold or exchanged (IRS Pub. 525). The taxpayer's basis is the amount paid for the stock, plus any amount included in income upon grant or exercise of the option. The taxpayer's holding period begins when the option was acquired if it had a readily ascertainable value, or the date the option was exercised if it did not.

Employer's Deduction. An employer may deduct the value of a nonqualified stock option as a business expense for the tax year in which the option is included in the employee's gross income (Code Sec. 83(h); Reg. § 1.83-6(a)). If the employer and the employee have different tax years, the employer generally claims the deduction in the tax year in or with which the employee's tax year ends. If the option's market value, however, is not readily ascertainable at the time of grant, and the employee's rights in the stock are substantially vested upon exercise, the employer may take the deduction in accordance with its usual method of accounting.

Reporting Requirements. In most situations, when an employee exercises a nonqualified stock option, the employer must report the excess of the FMV of the stock received over the amount that the employee paid for that stock ("the spread") on the employee's Form W-2.

1925. Incentive Stock Option (ISO). An incentive stock option (ISO) is an option granted by an employer corporation (or related corporation) that gives an employee the right to purchase stock of the employer, often at a discount. Unlike with a nonstatutory stock option (¶ 1923), the employee generally does not realize gain or loss when an ISO is granted or exercised if certain requirements are met (Code Sec. 421(a)). Instead, the employee realizes gain or loss when the shares acquired by the exercise of the option are sold. See ¶ 1927 for a discussion of ISO plan requirements.

Gain or loss from the sale of the stock received in an ISO is a capital gain or loss if the taxpayer holds the stock for at least two years after the option is granted and for at least one year after the option is exercised (Code Sec. 422(a); Reg. § 1.422-1(a)). The amount of gain or loss is the difference between the amount the taxpayer paid for the stock (the option price) and the amount received when the taxpayer sold the stock. The taxpayer must remain an employee of the corporation from the time the option is granted until three months before the option is exercised (one year if employment ends because of the taxpayer's permanent and total disability). If the holder of an ISO dies, his or her executor, administrator, or representative may exercise the option and receive the same treatment but does not have to do so within three months after the death of the employee (Reg. § 1.421-2(c)).

If the employee sells the stock before the required holding period ends (a disqualifying disposition), gain on the sale is ordinary income to the extent that the fair market value of the stock when the option was exercised exceeds the exercise price (Code Sec. 421(b); Reg. § 1.421-2(b)). Any additional gain is capital gain, and any loss is a capital loss. The gain is recognized for the tax year in which the sale occurs. Gain from a disqualifying disposition is excluded from wages for FICA and FUTA tax purposes and is not subject to income tax withholding (Code Secs. 3121(a)(22) and 3306(b)(19)).

Basis of ISO. An employee's basis in an ISO is the amount that the employee paid for the option. If the employee did not pay for the option and the option lapses, the employee does not have a deductible loss because there is no basis. An employee's basis in stock purchased through an ISO is the amount paid for the stock when the option was exercised, plus any amount paid for the option.

Annual Dollar Limit. The maximum value of stock with respect to which ISOs may first become exercisable in any one year is $100,000. Stock is valued when the option is granted. Options are taken into account in the order in which they are granted, and options issued under ISO plans of any parent, subsidiary, or predecessor corporation are taken into account (Code Sec. 422(d)).

Alternative Minimum Tax. The favorable tax treatment of ISOs does not apply for purposes of the alternative minimum tax (AMT). Instead, the *excess* of the (1) fair market value of the stock received upon the exercise of the option, over (2) the amount paid for the stock, plus any amount paid for the ISO, must generally be recognized as an AMT adjustment (¶ 196). As a result, individuals who have exercised ISOs to purchase stock with a high fair market value that declined before they were able to sell it may be left with large AMT liabilities and no cash to pay them.

1927. Incentive Stock Options (ISO) Plan Requirements. A stock option that an employer grants to an employee must satisfy several requirements to qualify for favorable tax treatment as an incentive stock option (ISO) (¶ 1925) (Code Sec. 422(b); Reg. § 1.422-2). ISOs must be granted under a plan adopted by the granting corporation that sets out the total number of shares that may be issued under options and the

19

SECURITIES

employees who may receive them. The plan must be approved by the stockholders within 12 months before or after the corporation adopts it.

The options must be granted within 10 years from the date the plan is adopted or approved, whichever is earlier, and they must be exercisable within 10 years from the date of the grant. The option price may not be less than the fair market value of the stock at the time the option is granted, and the option may be transferable only at the grantee's death. The option may be exercised only by the employee. In addition, at the time the option is granted, the employee may not own stock with more than 10 percent of the total combined voting power of all classes of stock of the employer corporation or its parent or any subsidiary. For options exercised after 2017, the employee may elect to treat the transfer of stock as a qualified equity grant (¶ 1933) rather than the exercise of an incentive stock option.

1929. Employee Stock Purchase Plans. An employee stock purchase plan (ESPP) (¶ 1931) may grant an employee the option to purchase stock in the employer or the employer's parent or subsidiary. Unlike with a nonstatutory stock option (¶ 1923), the employee generally does not realize gain or loss when an option is granted or exercised under an ESPP if certain requirements are met (Code Sec. 421(a)). Instead, the employee realizes gain or loss only when the shares acquired by the exercise of the option are sold.

Gain or loss from the sale of stock received in an ESPP is a capital gain or loss if the taxpayer holds the stock for at least two years after the option is granted and for at least one year after the option is exercised (Code Sec. 423(a)). The amount of gain or loss is the difference between the amount the taxpayer paid for the stock (the option price) and the amount the taxpayer received on the sale of the stock. The taxpayer must remain an employee of the corporation from the time the option is granted until three months before the option is exercised (one year if employment ends because of the taxpayer's permanent and total disability). A deceased employee's executor, administrator, or representative may exercise the option and receive the same treatment but does not have to do so within three months after the employee's death (Reg. § 1.421-2(c)).

If the option price is at least 85 percent, but less than 100 percent of the fair market value of the stock, the favorable tax treatment does not apply when the taxpayer disposes of the stock (Code Sec. 423(c)). Instead, the employee recognizes ordinary income equal to the lesser of the amount by which the fair market value of the shares exceeds the option price (1) when the shares are sold or the employee dies, or (2) when the option was granted. The balance of any gain is capital gain. Any loss from the sale is a capital loss.

If the employee sells the stock before the required holding period ends (a disqualifying disposition), gain on the sale is ordinary income equal to the fair market value of the stock when the option was exercised, less the exercise price (Code Sec. 421(b); Reg. § 1.421-2(b)). Any additional gain is capital gain, and any loss is a capital loss. The gain is recognized for the tax year in which the sale occurs. Gain from a disqualifying disposition is excluded from wages for FICA and FUTA tax purposes and is not subject to income tax withholding (Code Secs. 3121(a)(22) and 3306(b)(19)).

An ESPP is different from an employee stock ownership plan (ESOP) (¶ 2103). While both plans involve employee ownership of company stock, an ESOP is a retirement plan that holds employer stock for the benefit of participating employees.

1931. Employee Stock Purchase Plan Requirements. An employee stock purchase plan (ESPP) must satisfy several requirements in order for options acquired under the plan to qualify for favorable tax treatment (¶ 1929) (Code Sec. 423(b)). ESPPs are written, shareholder-approved plans under which employees are granted options to purchase shares of their employer's stock or the stock of a parent or subsidiary corporation.

An ESPP cannot grant options to any employee who has more than five percent of the voting power or value of stock in the employer or its parent or subsidiary. The plan must include all full-time employees except those with less than two years of employment, highly compensated employees (¶ 2114), part-time employees, and seasonal workers. The plan must be nondiscriminatory, though it may limit the amount of stock any employee can buy, and the amount of stock that each employee may become entitled to buy may be tied to compensation.

The option price must be at least equal to 85 percent of the fair market value of the stock at the time the option is granted or, if less, at the time it is exercised. The option must be exercised within 27 months after it is granted (or within five years if the option price test considers the fair market value of the stock at the time the option is exercised). No employee can acquire the right to buy more than $25,000 of stock per year (valued at the time the option is granted).

Options that the employee elects to treat as a qualified equity grant after 2017 (¶ 1933) are not considered granted under an employee stock purchase plan (Code Sec. 423(d)).

1933. Qualified Equity Grants. A qualified employee of a privately held company may elect to defer recognizing income attributable to qualified stock received from the employer (Code Sec. 83(i)(1); Notice 2018-97). The election is an alternative to being taxed in the year in which the stock vests or in the year it is received (¶ 713) and is available for stock attributable to options exercised, or restricted stock units (RSUs) settled, after December 31 2017.

An employee who makes the election must include the income in his or her gross income for the tax year that includes the earliest of:

- the first date the qualified stock becomes transferable, including transferable to the employer;

- the date the employee first becomes an "excluded employee";

- the first date on which any stock of the employer becomes readily tradable on an established securities market;

- the date five years after the earlier of the first date the employee's right to the stock is transferable or is not subject to a substantial risk of forfeiture; or

- the date on which the employee revokes the election.

Qualified Employee. A qualified employee is any employee who is not an excluded employee and who agrees, in the election, to meet the requirements the IRS deems necessary to ensure that the employer corporation meets its income tax withholding requirements regarding the qualified stock (Code Sec. 83(i)(3)). An excluded employee is any employee who:

(1) is or was a one-percent owner of the corporation at any time during the calendar year or the 10 preceding calendar years;

(2) is or was at any time the chief executive officer or chief financial officer of the corporation, or an individual acting in either capacity;

(3) is a family member of an individual described in (1) or (2); or

(4) is or was one of the corporation's four highest compensated officers for the tax year or for any of the 10 preceding tax years.

Qualified Stock. Qualified stock is any stock in the qualified employee's employer if (1) the employee receives the stock in connection with the exercise of an option or in settlement of a RSU, and (2) the corporation granted the option or RSU in connection with the performance of services as an employee and during a calendar year in which it was an eligible corporation (Code Sec. 83(i)(2); Notice 2018-97). Stock is not qualified if, at the time the employee's right to the stock becomes substantially vested, the employee may sell the stock to, or otherwise receive cash in lieu of stock from, the corporation.

A corporation is an eligible corporation for a calendar year if:

- no stock of the employer corporation or any predecessor is readily tradable on an established securities market during any preceding calendar year; and

- the corporation has a written plan under which, in the calendar year, not less than 80 percent of all employees who provide services to the corporation in the United States or any U.S. possession are granted stock options or RSUs with the same rights and privileges to receive qualified stock.

Election, Notice, and Reporting. The election to defer income with respect to qualified stock is made in a similar manner as the Code Sec. 83(b) election. It must be made no later than 30 days after the first date the employee's right to the stock is substantially vested or is transferable, whichever occurs earlier. However, the due date for performing certain time-sensitive actions, including making the section 83(i) election, otherwise due on or after April 1, 2020, and before July 15, 2020, is automatically extended to July 15, 2020, in response to the COVID-19 (coronavirus) crisis (Notice 2020-23; Rev. Proc. 2018-58).

The election is not allowed for income with respect to nonvested stock that is includible in gross income because of a Code Sec. 83(b) election. The employer must provide notice to its employees that they are eligible for the election at the time (or a reasonable period before) the employee's right to the qualified stock vests and income attributable to the stock would first be includible in gross income absent the deferral election (Code Secs. 83(i)(6) and 6652(p)).

An electing employees' qualified stock is treated as wages received on the earliest income inclusion date (¶ 2604). The employer must report the income covered by an inclusion deferral on the qualified employee's Form W-2 for both (1) the year of deferral and (2) the year the employee must recognize the income. The Form W-2 must also report the aggregate amount of income covered by inclusion deferral elections, determined as of the close of the calendar year (Code Sec. 6051(a)(16) and (17)).

Wash Sales

See CCH® AnswerConnect: *Wash Sales of Stock and Securities* for more information on this topic.

1935. Wash Sales of Stock or Securities. Under the wash sale rule, a loss on a sale or other disposition of stock or securities is not deductible unless it is incurred in the ordinary course of a securities dealer's trade or business (¶ 1903) (Code Sec. 1091; Reg. § 1.1091-1). A wash sale occurs if the taxpayer sells or disposes of stock or securities, and within 30 days before or after the disposition date (the 61-day period), acquires substantially identical stock or securities (¶ 1937). Stock and securities acquisitions include contacts and options to acquire them, as well as acquisitions by the taxpayer's traditional IRA or Roth IRA (Rev. Rul. 2008-5).

Only a portion of the total loss is disallowed if a taxpayer acquires less stock or securities during the 61-day period than the taxpayer sold. The nondeductible loss is allocated to the stock or securities disposed of in the order they were acquired. If the amount of stock and securities acquired during the 61-day period is more than the amount sold, the shares acquired that resulted in the nondeductibility of the loss are determined by the order of their acquisition.

A loss realized on the closing of a short sale of stock or securities (¶ 1944) is disallowed under the wash sale rule if within 30 days before or after the closing, the taxpayer sells, or enters into another short sale of, substantially identical stock or securities. The wash sale rule also applies to a loss realized on the sale, exchange, or termination of a securities futures contract to sell stock or securities. However, it does not apply to losses from sales or trades of commodity futures contracts and foreign currencies.

The disallowance of a loss under the wash sale rule does not apply to stock or securities acquired in a nontaxable exchange (¶ 1719). This includes stock or securities acquired by gift, bequest, or devise, or through a nonrecognition transaction such as an exchange of property for stock, exchange of stock for stock, and transfers between spouses or between former spouses incident to divorce. The wash sale rule also does not apply to any loss attributable to a section 1256 contract (¶ 1947) (Code Sec. 1256(f)(5)).

A loss that is disallowed because of the wash sale rule is added to the cost basis of the new stock or securities unless they are acquired through an IRA. The adjustment postpones the loss deduction until the disposition of the new stock or securities (Code Sec. 1091(d); Reg. § 1.1091-2). The taxpayer's holding period of the new stock or securities includes the holding period of the stock or securities sold (Code Sec. 1223(3)).

¶ 1935

Example: Betty buys 100 shares of Rapid Corp. stock for $1,000 on January 1, Year 1, and sells them on January 2, Year 2, for $750. Less than 30 days later, she buys another 100 shares of Rapid for $800. Because Betty purchased substantially identical stock, she cannot deduct the $250 loss that she realized on the sale. However, she adds the disallowed loss of $250 to the cost of her new shares. As a result, her basis in the new shares is $1,050 ($800 cost, plus the $250 loss she could not claim under the wash sale rule). If she sells the new shares on March 31, Year 2, any gain is long-term capital gain.

The wash sale rule applies without regard to gain or loss realized on the sale of separate lots of the same stock or security. Thus, a disallowed loss on one lot does not reduce gain realized on a separate lot (Rev. Rul. 70-231). The wash sale rule also does not specifically apply when stock is sold at a loss and a related party, such as the seller's spouse, reacquires the stock within the prohibited 61-day period. However, the loss may be disallowed under the related party rules of Code Sec. 267 (¶ 1717) on the ground that there is an indirect sale to the spouse (*J.P. McWilliams*, SCt, 47-1 USTC ¶ 9289).

1937. Substantially Identical Stock or Securities for Wash Sales. Whether stock or securities are substantially identical under the wash sale rule (¶ 1935) depends on all the facts and circumstances. Stocks or securities of one corporation ordinarily are not substantially identical to stocks or securities of another corporation. However, they may be substantially identical in some cases; for instance, in a reorganization, the stocks and securities of the predecessor and successor corporations may be substantially identical (IRS Pub. 550). A corporation's bonds or preferred stock ordinarily are not substantially identical to its common stock. If the bonds or preferred stock are convertible into common stock, the relative values, price changes, and other circumstances may make them substantially identical to common stock (Rev. Rul. 77-201).

1942. Share Lending Agreements. No gain or loss is recognized on an exchange of securities that is part of a qualifying securities lending arrangement in which the taxpayer transfers the securities and later receives identical securities in return (Code Sec. 1058). In effect, the taxpayer is merely lending securities to the other party to the transaction. This provision is intended to mitigate delays that a broker may face in obtaining securities by allowing the broker to borrow securities without creating tax consequences for the lender. However, these rules apply to any taxpayer that lends securities, not just those that lend to brokers. The securities lending agreement must require the borrower to return securities to the taxpayer that are identical to those that were lent. The taxpayer's basis in the securities received is the same as the taxpayer's basis in the securities that were loaned to the borrower.

Short Sales

See CCH® AnswerConnect: *Short Sales of Securities and Commodities* for more information on this topic.

1944. Short Sales. In a short sale, a taxpayer sells shares of stock or property that he or she does not own or wish to transfer at the time of the sale. The taxpayer sells short by: (1) borrowing property (usually from a broker) and delivering it to the buyer; and (2) closing or covering the transaction at a later date by purchasing substantially identical property and delivering it to the lender, or making delivery out of property the taxpayer held at the time of the sale (Code Sec. 1233(a); Reg. § 1.1233-1(a)).

The seller generally does not recognize gain or loss on a short sale until the property is delivered to the lender and the short sale is closed. However, the seller must recognize gain as if the short sale were closed on the date the property that was sold short becomes substantially worthless (Code Sec. 1233(h)). In addition, a short sale of an appreciated financial position may cause the taxpayer to be treated as making a constructive sale at the time that the taxpayer entered into the transaction (¶ 1945). A taxpayer can avoid the prohibition on recognizing losses from a short sale if the position is part of a mixed straddle (¶ 1948).

Gain or loss on a closed short sale is the difference between the amount realized on the sale of the borrowed property and the taxpayer's adjusted basis in the property used to close the transaction. The character of that gain or loss generally depends on the character of the property used to close the sale in the hands of the taxpayer. Thus, a

¶1944

taxpayer has capital gain or loss if the property used to close the short sale is a capital asset (¶ 1741). Hedging transactions, however, generally result in ordinary income or loss (¶ 1949). If a short seller has a gain on the transaction when the replacement property is purchased, the gain is recognized at that time. A loss is not recognized until the replacement property is delivered to the lender (Rev. Rul. 2002-44).

Holding Period. The short-term or long-term nature of a short seller's capital gain or loss generally depends on how long the seller held the property that is delivered to the lender to close out the sale.

> **Example:** On January 2, Mary agrees to sell 100 shares of Niftexo Corp. for $10 a share to Susan. Mary does not own any Niftexo shares, so she borrows the 100 shares from her broker and delivers them to Susan. On May 1, Mary buys 100 shares of Niftexo at a price of $15 a share, and immediately delivers them to her broker to replace the shares she had borrowed. Her recognized loss of $500 is short term because her holding period of the Niftexo shares she delivered to her lender (the broker) is determined by the amount of time she held the shares (i.e., less than one day).

Gain from the short sale of a capital asset is short-term capital gain if the taxpayer owned substantially identical property for one year or less on the date of the short sale, or if the taxpayer acquired substantially identical property after the short sale and by the date the sale is closed (Code Sec. 1233(b); Reg. § 1.1233-1(c)). The holding period of the substantially identical property begins on the closing of the short sale or on the date the property is sold, whichever happens first. Any loss realized on the short sale of a capital asset is a long-term capital loss if the taxpayer owned substantially identical property for more than one year, even when the property used to close the short sale is held by the seller for one year or less (Code Sec. 1233(d)).

Special holding period rules apply to a broker's arbitrage transactions (Code Sec. 1233(f); Reg. § 1.1233-1(f)). Losses on short sales of stock or securities are also subject to the wash sales rule (¶ 1935).

1945. Constructive Sale of Appreciated Positions. Appreciated financial positions are treated as constructively sold when the taxpayer enters into certain transactions (Code Sec. 1259(a)). The taxpayer must recognize gain as if the position were sold, assigned, or otherwise terminated at its fair market value on the date of the constructive sale, and then immediately repurchased. Any gain or loss subsequently realized on the position is adjusted to reflect the gain recognized. A new holding period begins on the date of the constructive sale.

An appreciated financial position is generally any position with respect to any stock, debt instrument, or partnership interest if gain would arise if the position were sold, assigned, or otherwise terminated at its fair market value (Code Sec. 1259(b)). It does not include any position that is subject to mark-to-market requirements (¶ 1903), including section 1256 contracts (¶ 1947). It also does not include any position or hedge of a position with regard to straight debt if:

- the debt unconditionally entitles the holder to receive a specified principal amount;

- interest payments are payable based on a fixed rate or, to the extent provided in regulations, at a variable rate; and

- the debt is not convertible into stock of the issuer or any related person (¶ 432 and ¶ 1717).

A constructive sale generally is one of four specified types of transactions offsetting an appreciated financial position that have the effect of substantially eliminating both the taxpayer's risk of loss and chance for further gain on the position. They include short sales (¶ 1944), notional principal contracts, forward or futures contracts, and the purchase of property to cover the position if the appreciated position is itself a short position (Code Sec. 1259(c)). A contract for the sale of appreciated financial assets that are not publicly traded is not a constructive sale if the contract settles within one year after it was entered. A safe harbor may apply to certain short-term hedges that would otherwise be treated as constructive sales if:

¶1945

- the transaction closes on or before the end of the 30th day after the end of the tax year in which it was entered;

- the taxpayer holds the appreciated financial position throughout the 60-day period beginning on the date the transaction is closed; and

- at no time during that 60-day period is the taxpayer's risk of loss with respect to the position reduced by a circumstance that would be described in Code Sec. 246(c)(4) if the position was treated as stock.

The closed transaction exception also applies to certain reestablished positions.

1946. Payments in Lieu of Dividends on Short Sales. A taxpayer who borrows stock to make a short sale (¶ 1944) may have to make payments to the lender in lieu of dividends distributed during the short position. An individual may treat the payments as an itemized deduction for investment interest expense (¶ 1057) if the short sale is held open for at least 46 days (more than one year if extraordinary dividends are involved). If the short sale is closed by the 45th day after the date of the short sale (one year or less if extraordinary dividends are involved), the short seller cannot claim the deduction and must instead increase the basis of the stock used to close the short sale by the amount of the payment (Code Sec. 263(h)). The 45-day and one-year periods are suspended for any period in which the borrower holds options to buy substantially identical property or holds one or more positions in such property.

Commodities and Related Instruments

See CCH® AnswerConnect: *Section 1256 Contracts for Commodities and the Marked-to-Market Rule* and *Straddles, Mixed Straddles, Hedges and the Loss Deferral Rule* for more information on this topic.

1947. Section 1256 Contracts. Each section 1256 contract held by a taxpayer at the end of the tax year is generally subject to mark-to-market requirements that treat the contract as sold at its fair market value on the last business day of the year (Code Sec. 1256). The mark-to-market rule also applies if the taxpayer's obligations or rights under a section 1256 contract are terminated or transferred during the tax year.

Capital gains or losses resulting from the mark-to-market requirement for section 1256 contracts are 60 percent long-term and 40 percent short-term without regard to the taxpayer's actual holding period. Taxpayers use Form 6781 to report gains and losses from all section 1256 contracts that are open at the end of the year or that were closed during the year. An individual may elect to carry back a net section 1256 contract loss for three years instead of carrying it over to the next year (¶ 1754).

A section 1256 contract includes regulated futures contracts, foreign currency contracts, nonequity options, dealer equity options, and dealer securities futures contracts. The mark-to-market rules do not apply to hedging transactions (¶ 1949) or equity options. The taxpayer may elect out of mark-to-market treatment for section 1256 contracts that are part of a mixed straddle (¶ 1948).

1948. Tax Straddles. A tax straddle is any set of offsetting positions, such as a futures contract, a forward contract, or an option on actively traded stock or personal property, that seeks to diminish an investor's risk of loss (Code Sec. 1092). Loss realized with respect to a straddle position is deductible only to the extent that it exceeds the taxpayer's unrealized gain in the offsetting position. Unused losses are carried forward to the next tax year. The taxpayer uses Form 6781 to report each position in actively traded personal property (whether or not it is part of a straddle) on which the taxpayer has unrecognized gain at the end of the tax year.

The loss deferral rule does not apply if a straddle is identified on the taxpayer's books before the close of the day on which it is acquired. If there is a loss from any position in an identified straddle, the taxpayer must increase the basis of each of the positions that offset the loss position by the same ratio to the loss as the unrecognized gain for the offsetting position bears to the total unrecognized gain for all the offsetting positions. The loss deferral rule also does not apply to hedging transactions (¶ 1949), straddles consisting entirely of qualified covered call options, and straddles consisting entirely of section 1256 contracts (¶ 1947).

19

SECURITIES

Wash Sales and Short Sales. A modified wash sale rule (¶ 1935) applies to any disposition of a position in a straddle and denies a deduction of a loss if there is unrecognized gain in a successor position (Temp. Reg. § 1.1092(b)-1T). A modified short sale rule (¶ 1944) also applies to a straddle suspending the taxpayer's holding period during the time the taxpayer holds offsetting and successor positions (Temp. Reg. § 1.1092(b)-2T).

Mixed Straddles. A mixed straddle is a straddle in which at least one, but not all, of the positions is a section 1256 contract (¶ 1947), with each position being properly identified as part of the straddle. A taxpayer may elect not to have the mark-to-market rules apply to the section 1256 contracts that are a part of the mixed straddle (Code Sec. 1256(d)). If the taxpayer elects out of the mark-to-market rules, the straddle is subject to the loss deferral rule, the modified wash sale rule, and the modified short sale rule. Alternatively, a taxpayer may elect to offset gains and losses from positions that are part of a mixed straddle by (1) separately identifying each mixed straddle to which such treatment applies, or (2) establishing a mixed straddle account with respect to a class of activities for which gains and losses will be recognized and offset on a periodic basis (Code Sec. 1092(b); Temp. Reg. §§ 1.1092(b)-3T and 1.1092(b)-4T).

Interest and Carrying Charges. Interest and carrying charges incurred with respect to a straddle position can be offset only by current income generated by the position. Any excess must be capitalized (Code Sec. 263(g)).

1949. Hedging Transactions. A hedging transaction is a transaction in the normal course of the taxpayer's trade or business that is primarily intended to reduce the risk of changes in interest rates, price changes, or currency fluctuations (Code Sec. 1221(a)(7); Reg. § 1.1221-2). The property involved in a hedging transaction is generally not a capital asset (¶ 1741), so gain or loss is generally ordinary income or loss. This rule also applies when a short sale or option is part of a hedging transaction (¶ 1944). The determination of whether a transaction was intended to manage the taxpayer's business risk is based upon all the facts and circumstances. A transaction that is not a hedging transaction may be a straddle (¶ 1948).

Identification. The hedging transaction must be identified before the close of the day on which the taxpayer entered into the transaction (Reg. § 1.1221-2(f)). Within 35 days after the transaction is entered into, the taxpayer's books and records must unambiguously identify the property that is being hedged.

Corporate Bonds and Other Debt Instruments

See CCH® AnswerConnect: *Original Issue Discount, Acquisition Discount, and Market Discount Bonds* for more information on this topic.

1950. Corporate Bond Discounts, Premiums, and Issue Expenses. The tax effects of a corporation's issuance or reacquisition of bonds depends on whether the bonds are issued at face value, at a discount, or at a premium. A corporation generally does not realize gain or loss upon the issuance of a bond or other debt instrument (Reg. § 1.61-12(c)). However, a corporation that repurchases a bond for less than its adjusted issue price realizes income from the discharge of debt (¶ 855). For bonds repurchased at a discount during 2009 or 2010, the corporation can elect to recognize the discharge of debt income ratably over a five-year period beginning in 2014 (Code Sec. 108(i)).

For bonds issued at a discount, the corporation amortizes the discount and deducts it over the life of the bond. If bonds are issued at a premium on or after March 2, 1998, the premium is amortized as an offset to the corporation's otherwise allowable interest deduction, with the portion of bond premium allocable to the accrual period based on constant yield (Reg. § 1.163-13(a)). Any amount allocable to a bond's conversion feature is not part of the bond premium (Code Sec. 171(b)(1)). See ¶ 1967 for the tax treatment of a premium paid by the buyer of a bond. Any expenses related to issuing the bond (i.e., printing, advertising, legal fees) are amortized over the life of the bond and deducted as business expenses (Reg. § 1.446-5).

1952. Original Issue Discount (OID). If a debt instrument has original issue discount (OID), the holder's gross income must include an amount equal to the sum of the daily portions of the OID for each day during the tax year that the holder held the instrument (Code Sec. 1272). The holder's basis in the instrument is increased by the OID that must be included in gross income. The OID requirement does not apply to short-term obligations with a fixed maturity of less than one year, tax-exempt obligations, U.S. savings bonds, and certain loans between natural persons. It also does not apply if the holder purchased the debt instrument at a premium or if the holder is a life insurance company.

OID on a debt instrument is the excess of the stated redemption price at maturity over the issue price (Code Sec. 1273). Under a *de minimis* rule, if the difference is less than 0.25 percent of the redemption price multiplied by the number of full years from the date of issue to the date of maturity, then the OID is zero.

The stated redemption price at maturity includes all payments provided by the obligation other than qualified interest payments. Qualified interest is stated interest that is actually and unconditionally payable at fixed, periodic intervals of one year or less, based on a fixed interest rate and outstanding principal amount. If debt instruments are publicly offered or issued for money or publicly traded property, their issue price is determined based on those objective features, with additional rules for publicly offered debt instruments that are part of investment units. For debt instruments that are issued for property, services, or the right to use property, but are not publicly traded, the issue price may be the stated principal amount, or the imputed principal amount (¶ 1954).

Interest Deduction. The portion of OID that the issuer may deduct for any tax year is equal to the aggregate daily portions of the OID for days during that tax year (Code Sec. 163(e)). The daily portion of OID is determined by allocating to each day in an accrual period a ratable portion of the increase during the accrual period in the adjusted issue price of the debt instrument (Code Sec. 1272(a)(3)).

Information Statements. An issuer with any outstanding bond or any other evidence of debt in registered form issued at a discount must generally furnish the holder and the IRS with an information statement (Form 1099-OID) for the calendar year if there is OID of at least $10 (Code Sec. 6049).

Stripped Bonds and Stripped Coupons. Special OID rules govern stripped bonds and stripped coupons (Code Sec. 1286(a)). Under this type of arrangement, one taxpayer strips an interest coupon from a bond and sells either the bond or the coupon. The bond and the coupon are treated as separate debt instruments issued with OID. For the buyer of a stripped bond, OID is the bond's value at maturity minus the price paid. For the buyer of a stripped coupon, OID is the interest to be paid on the due date of the coupon minus the price paid.

The seller of stripped bonds or stripped coupons must include in income the interest that accrued before the date of sale that was not previously included in income. Market discount must also be included in the seller's income. Both of these items increase the seller's basis in the bonds and coupons. The seller then allocates the adjusted basis between the item kept (e.g., the bond) and the item sold (e.g., the coupon) based on their fair market values. The difference between the sales price of the item and its adjusted basis is the seller's gain or loss.

Stripped Stock. Preferred stock purchased after April 30, 1993, that has been stripped of some or all of its dividend rights is treated like stripped bonds. OID is equal to the stated redemption price minus the amount paid for the stock (Code Sec. 305(e)).

Tax-Exempt and Stripped Tax-Exempt Bonds. OID on a tax-exempt bond is generally treated as tax-exempt interest (¶ 1956). However, when a tax-exempt bond is stripped, only a portion of the OID is treated as coming from a tax-exempt obligation (Code Sec. 1286(c)). The balance is treated as OID on a taxable obligation. Specific rules apply in determining the tax-exempt portion of the OID.

1954. Original Issue Discount for Debt Instruments Issued for Property. In determining the original issue discount (OID) of certain debt instruments issued for property (¶ 1952), the issue price is the stated principal amount of the instrument if there is adequate stated interest, or the imputed principal amount if there is not adequately stated interest (Code Sec. 1274). This rule applies to debt instruments given in consideration for the sale or exchange of property if: (1) the stated redemption price at maturity exceeds either the stated principal amount (when there is adequate stated interest) or the imputed principal amount; and (2) some or all of the payments due under the instrument are due more than six months after the date of the sale or exchange. This rule does not apply to:

- sales for $250,000 or less;
- sales of principal residences by individuals (¶ 1707);
- sales of farms by individuals, estates, testamentary trusts, or small business corporations or partnerships for $1 million or less;
- certain land transfers between related parties covered by the imputed interest rules of Code Sec. 483(e) (¶ 1872);
- sales of patents for amounts that are contingent on the productivity, use, or disposition of the property transferred (¶ 1767); or
- in the case of the borrower, sales or exchanges of personal use property (Code Sec. 1275(b)).

Certain annuity contracts are also excluded from the definition of debt instrument (Code Sec. 1275(a)(1)(B)). A debt-for-property transaction that is not covered by these rules may be subject to the imputed interest rules of Code Sec. 483 (¶ 1868).

Adequate Stated Interest. A debt instrument generally provides for adequate stated interest if its stated principal amount is less than or equal to the imputed principal amount—the sum of the present value of all principal and interest payments due on the instrument (Code Sec. 1274(c)(2)). Except for potentially abusive situations, the present value of all payments due on the instrument is generally determined based on the lowest applicable federal rate (AFR) (¶ 83) in effect in the three-month period ending with (1) the first month in which there is a binding written contract, or (2) the month in which the sale or exchange occurred (Code Sec. 1274(b)). The AFR is determined by reference to the term of the debt instrument, including renewal and extension options. If the imputed interest rules of Code Sec. 483 apply to a debt instrument, payments due within six months after the sale are taken into account at face value. For a sale-leaseback transaction, a rate equal to 110 percent of the AFR is used to determine the present value of payments (Code Sec. 1274(e)).

The discount rate may not exceed nine percent, compounded semiannually, if a debt instrument is given in consideration for the sale or exchange of property (other than new Code Sec. 38 property) and the stated principal amount of the instrument does not exceed an inflation-adjusted amount ($5,944,600 for 2019 and $6,039,100 for 2020) (Code Sec. 1274A; Rev. Proc. 2018-57; Rev. Proc. 2019-44). The discount rate may not exceed six percent, compounded semiannually, when determining unstated interest on deferred payments in a transfer of land between family members if the aggregate sales price of all prior land sales between the family members during the calendar year is $500,000 or less. This limit does not apply if any party to the sale is a nonresident alien (Code Sec. 483(e); Reg. § 1.483-3(b)).

Joint Election. The lender and borrower may jointly elect out of the OID rules on debt issued for a sale or exchange of property (other than new Code Sec. 38 property), and take the interest on the debt instrument into account under the cash method of accounting (Code Sec. 1274A(c); Rev. Rul. 2018-11). The election can be made only if:

- the stated principal amount of the instrument does not exceed an inflation-adjusted amount ($4,246,200 for 2019 and $4,313,600 for 2020);
- the lender is on the cash-basis method of accounting and is not a dealer with respect to the property sold or exchanged; and
- these rules would otherwise have applied to the transaction.

1956. Original Issue Discount on Tax-Exempt Bonds. Original issue discount (OID) for tax-exempt obligations is accrued like OID on obligations issued by corporations and other entities under the constant yield method (¶ 1952) when determining the interest expense deduction and the holder's adjusted basis (Code Sec. 1288). For purposes of determining the interest expense deduction, the reduction normally required where a subsequent holder pays an acquisition premium is disregarded. For tax-exempt obligations with a maturity of less than one year, interest is computed as it is for short-term taxable obligations. The tables at ¶ 84 show applicable federal interest rates that are adjusted to account for tax-exempt interest.

1958. Market Discount Bonds. Gain from the sale of a market discount bond is ordinary interest income to the extent of the accrued market discount (Code Sec. 1276(a)). If the bond is disposed of in a transaction other than a sale, exchange, or involuntary conversion, the amount realized is equal to its fair market value. A partial payment of principal on the bond is also included in gross income as ordinary income to the extent of the accrued market discount. The payment of principal that is included in gross income reduces the amount of the accrued market discount.

A bond has market discount if its stated redemption price at maturity exceeds its basis immediately after its acquisition (Code Sec. 1278(a)). However, market discount bonds do not include a bond acquired at its original issue, an obligation that matures within one year of issuance, a U.S. savings bond, certain installment obligations, and a tax-exempt bond purchased before May 1, 1993. The amount of accrued market discount on a bond is generally determined under a ratable accrual method, but the taxpayer can make an irrevocable election to determine the discount under a constant interest method (Code Sec. 1276(b); Rev. Proc. 92-67).

Except for certain tax-exempt bonds acquired after July 18, 1994, net direct interest expense with respect to a market discount bond is not deductible until the holder has net interest income or disposes of the bond (Code Sec. 1277). The taxpayer can elect to deduct disallowed interest expense before disposing of the bond, but only up to the net interest income accrued from the bond during the tax year of the deduction. Any remaining deferred interest expense is deducted in the year of disposition.

Election to Include Market Discount Currently. A taxpayer may elect to include the market discount of any market discount bond in gross income as interest for the tax year it accrues (Code Sec. 1278(b); Rev. Proc. 92-67). If the election is made, the rules requiring recognition of ordinary interest income upon disposition of a market discount bond and disallowing a deduction for net direct interest expense do not apply. The election generally applies to the current and all subsequent tax years, but may be revoked by using automatic consent procedures for accounting method changes (Rev. Proc. 2018-31; Rev. Proc. 2019-43).

1961. Discount on Short-Term Obligations. Certain holders of a short-term obligation must include in gross income: (1) an amount equal to the sum of the daily portions of the acquisition discount for each day during the tax year that the holder held the obligation; and (2) any other interest payable on the obligation (Code Sec. 1281). The amounts included in gross income increase the holder's basis in the obligation. An obligation can include a bond, debenture, note, certificate, or other evidence of debt (but not a tax-exempt obligation) with a fixed maturity date not more than one year from the date of issue (Code Sec. 1283(a)(1)). For a short-term nongovernmental obligation, the accrual requirement applies to original issue discount (OID), as opposed to acquisition discount.

Acquisition discount on a short-term obligation must be accrued by: accrual method taxpayers; banks; brokers and dealers who hold short-term obligations for sale to customers in the ordinary course of a trade or business; regulated investment companies (RICs) (¶ 2301) and common trust funds (¶ 2389); persons who identify short-term obligations as part of a hedging transaction (¶ 1949); persons who strip a short-term bond of its interest coupons (¶ 1952); and any person whose basis in the instrument is determined by reference to the basis in the hands of any other listed person. Accrual of acquisition discount and interest is also mandatory for an obligation held by a pass-through entity (i.e., partnership, S corporation, or trust) that acquires the obligation during the required accrual period or acquires the obligation to avoid mandatory accrual.

Net direct interest expense incurred with respect to a short-term obligation is deductible only to the extent that it exceeds the sum of: (1) acquisition discount (excess of stated redemption price over basis) for each day during the year that the taxpayer holds the obligation, and (2) any interest payable on the obligation that accrues during the year but is not included in gross income because of the taxpayer's accounting

19

SECURITIES

method. The daily portion of the acquisition discount is equal to the total discount divided by the number of days from the acquisition date to the maturity date (Code Secs. 1282(a) and 1283(b)(1)). The interest deduction is deferred in a manner similar to that applicable to market discount bonds (¶ 1958).

1963. Unregistered Debt Obligations. Most corporate and government debt obligations must be in registered form for the payor to deduct interest (Code Sec. 163(f)(1); Prop. Reg. § 1.163-5). An excise tax applies to issues of registration-required obligations (other than tax-exempt bonds) that are not in registered form (Code Sec. 4701). The excise tax is equal to one percent of the principal amount of the obligation multiplied by the number of calendar years (or portions thereof) during the period beginning on the issue date of the obligation and ending on the date of maturity.

If a registration-required obligation is not in registered form, any gain realized on its sale or other disposition is ordinary income (Code Sec. 1287) and any loss is not deductible (Code Sec. 165(j)) unless the issuance of the obligation was subject to the excise tax or certain other specified exceptions apply. The issuer cannot reduce earnings and profits by the amount of any interest on the obligation (Code Sec. 312(m)).

1965. Exchanges of U.S. Obligations. Some types of U.S. savings bonds may be exchanged tax free for other types of U.S. savings bonds (¶ 730) (Code Sec. 1037). If the original bond was issued at a discount, an amount equal to what would have been ordinary income from original issue discount (OID) (¶ 1952) if the exchange had been taxable is treated as ordinary income when the bond received in exchange is disposed of or redeemed at a gain.

1967. Amortized Bond Premium. A bond owner who pays a premium over the face amount of a taxable bond has the option of (1) amortizing the premium by deducting it over the life of the bond, or (2) adding the premium to the basis of the bond (Code Sec. 171(a); Reg. § 1.171-4). A holder elects to amortize the premium by reporting the amortization on the tax return for the first year the election applies and attaching an election statement to the return. Premiums paid for tax-exempt bonds cannot be amortized; instead, the premium reduces the basis of the bond (Code Sec. 1016(a)(5)). See ¶ 1970 for rules municipal bond dealers.

The amount of bond premium that can be amortized for the tax year (and deducted currently) is calculated under a constant yield method (Code Sec. 171(b); Reg. § 1.171-2). Under this method, the amount of the amortizable bond premium and the amount attributable to a particular tax year must be determined on the basis of the taxpayer's yield to maturity, using the taxpayer's basis in the obligation and compounding at the close of each accrual period. If the basis of a bond that is received in an exchange is determined at least in part from the basis of the surrendered property, the basis of the bond cannot exceed its fair market value immediately after the exchange. This rule generally does not apply to an exchange of securities in a reorganization.

Premium on Convertible Bond. Amortization is not allowed for any part of a premium that is paid for the conversion feature in a convertible bond. A corporation's deduction for the premium it pays to repurchase its own convertible debt is generally limited to the amount of the normal call premium (Code Sec. 249(a)).

1970. Dealer in Tax-Exempt Bonds. A dealer in tax-exempt obligations must amortize any premiums just as if the interest on the bonds had been taxable. A dealer who does not inventory securities or who inventories them at cost must reduce the adjusted basis of any municipal bonds sold during the year by the total amortization for the period they were held. A dealer who values inventories other than at cost (for example, market value) must annually reduce the cost of securities sold by the amortization on municipal bonds held during the year (Code Sec. 75; Reg. § 1.75-1).

If a purchased tax-exempt obligation is sold or otherwise disposed of within 30 days after acquisition, matures, or is callable more than five years after it is acquired, an amortization adjustment must be made unless the bond is sold or disposed of at a gain. Thus, a dealer who inventories securities other than at cost and, at the end of the year, holds a tax-exempt bond maturing or callable more than five years after acquisition, does not have to reflect amortization in the bond in the cost of securities sold. If the bond is sold at a gain, no amortization adjustment is made. If it is not sold at a gain, the cost of securities sold is reduced by the amortization for the entire period it was held.

Accounting Issues

1973. Time of Sale for Publicly Traded Securities. A cash or accrual method taxpayer other than a dealer (¶ 1903) who sells stock or securities traded on an established securities market generally must recognize gains and losses on the trade date, rather than the settlement date (Rev. Rul. 93-84). The holding period for the stock or securities is also measured by using the trade date as the date sold (¶ 1737). Gain or loss on a short sale of securities, however, is recognized on the settlement date as set by exchange rules (¶ 1944). The installment method of reporting is not available for sales of stock or securities traded on an established securities market (¶ 1801).

1975. Identification of Securities Sold. If a seller can adequately identify the shares of securities sold or exchanged, basis is the cost or other basis of the particular shares of stock or bond. Shares are adequately identified if the taxpayer can show the certificates representing shares of stock from a lot that the taxpayer acquired on a certain date or for a certain price, and delivered to the taxpayer's broker or other transferee. If a taxpayer buys and sells securities at various times in varying quantities and cannot adequately identify the shares that are sold, the basis and holding period of the shares sold are generally determined on a first-in, first-out (FIFO) basis (Reg. § 1.1012-1(c)). For a sale, exchange, or other disposition of a specified security (¶ 1980), the basis reported by the broker on Form 1099-B must be calculated on an account by account basis (Code Sec. 1012(c)). Thus, the broker may be required to use different basis computation methods for different accounts.

A shareholder in a regulated investment company (RIC) (¶ 2301) may elect to figure gain or loss on identical shares using an average basis if the shareholder (1) acquired the shares at various times and prices, and (2) left the shares on deposit in an account handled by a custodian or agent who acquires or redeems shares of the RIC (Code Sec. 1012(d); Reg. § 1.1012-1(e)). Shares are identical if they have the same Committee on Uniform Security Identification Procedure (CUSIP) number or other security identifier number permitted by the IRS. The option to use average basis is limited to RIC shares and dividend reinvestment plans. Average basis is determined by averaging the basis of all shares of identical stock in an account regardless of the taxpayer's holding period.

1980. Basis and Holding Period Reporting for Securities. If a broker is required to file a return on Form 1099-B to report the gross proceeds from the sale of a covered security (¶ 2565), the broker must also report the customer's adjusted basis in the security and whether any gain or loss with respect to the security is long-term or short-term (Code Sec. 6045(g); Reg. § 1.6045-1). A covered security is any specified security that was acquired through a transaction in the account in which the security was held, or was transferred to that account from an account in which the security was a covered security if the broker receiving custody of the security receives a statutory statement with respect to the transfer. A specified security includes:

- a share of stock in a corporation;

- a note, bond, debenture or other evidence of debt, other than certain interests in a real estate mortgage investment conduit (REMIC) (¶ 2343), a debt instrument where payments may be accelerated, and pools of debt instruments affected by prepayments;

- a commodity, or a contract or a derivative with respect to a commodity;

- a securities futures contract;

- an option on one or more specified securities, or a warrant or stock right; and

- other financial instruments as determined by the IRS.

Special rules apply to broker reporting on sales by S corporations, short sales (¶ 1944), certain stock held in connection with a dividend reinvestment plan, and options transactions. However, a security acquired before January 1, 2016, may not be a specified security if it is a debt instrument with more complex features (e.g., variable rate, inflation-indexed, or contingent payment), convertible debt, stripped bond or coupon, tax credit bond, or a debt instrument issued by a non-U.S. issuer or requiring payment in a foreign currency; an option, stock right, or warrant issued as part of an investment unit; or an option if the underlying property is a debt instrument issued by a non-U.S. person or providing for payments in a foreign currency.

The broker must generally determine adjusted basis of a covered security under the first-in, first-out (FIFO) method (¶ 1975) unless the taxpayer adequately identifies the stock sold. For stock that is eligible for an average basis method, such as stock in a regulated investment company (RIC) acquired in connection with a dividend reinvestment plan, the customer's adjusted basis is determined according to the broker's default method, unless the customer notifies the broker of an election to use another acceptable method regarding the account that holds the stock. Basis is determined without regard to the wash sale rule (¶ 1935) unless the acquisition and sale transactions resulting in a wash sale involve identical securities and occur in the same account.

Securities Transfers Between Accounts. Every broker (and any other person specified in regulations) that transfers a covered security to another broker must furnish to the transferee broker a written statement that lets the transferee broker satisfy the basis and holding-period reporting requirements (Code Sec. 6045A; Reg. § 1.6045A-1). The transferor may be subject to a penalty if the written statement is not furnished (¶ 2823).

Organizational Actions Affecting Basis. Issuers of specified securities must file Form 8937 describing any organizational action (e.g., stock split, merger, acquisition) that affects the basis of the security, the quantitative effect on basis from the action, and any other information required by the IRS (Code Sec. 6045B; Reg. § 1.6045B-1). A copy of Form 8937 must also be given to each security holder of record or the holder's nominee as of the date of the organizational action.

An issuer does not have to file Form 8937 if, by the filing due date, the issuer posts a completed and signed Form 8937 in a readily accessible format in a dedicated area of its primary public website and keeps that form accessible on its website (or its successor's primary public website) for 10 years. An issuer that satisfies these public reporting requirements is treated as having furnished a copy of Form 8937 to all holders and nominees. Form 8937 also does not have to be filed if: (1) the issuer reasonably determines that all recipients of the securities are exempt recipients; or (2) the issuer is an S corporation that reports the information on a timely filed Schedule K-1 (Form 1120-S). Penalties may be imposed for failure to file correct information returns in connection with organizational actions, failure to furnish correct statements to holders or nominees, or failure to provide required publicly available information (¶ 2823).

1983. Commissions Paid on Securities. Commissions and other transaction costs paid to facilitate the sale of securities generally must be capitalized (Reg. § 1.263(a)-1(e)). For securities dealers, however, commissions and other amounts paid to facilitate the sale of a security are ordinary and necessary business expenses. For traders and investors, the amounts capitalized reduce the amount realized from the sale and are taken into account in either the tax year the sale occurs, or the tax year the sale is abandoned if a loss deduction is permitted. The capitalized amount is not added to the basis of the property. See ¶ 1760 for information concerning the proper classification of a taxpayer as a trader, dealer, or investor. Ordinary and necessary expenses for investment advice, including a "wrap fee" on a brokerage account paid by an investor in lieu of commissions on individual trades, are deductible investment expenses and are claimed as miscellaneous itemized deductions in the year paid (¶ 1085) (Reg. § 1.212-1(g)).

Chapter 20

HEALTH AND EMPLOYEE BENEFITS

Employer Health Insurance Mandate

See CCH® AnswerConnect: *Employer Shared Responsibility Payments (Play or Pay)* for more information on this topic.

2001. Employer Health Insurance Mandate. An applicable large employer may be assessed a nondeductible penalty known as a shared responsibility payment for any month if:

- the employer fails to offer at least 95 percent of its full-time employees and their dependents the opportunity to enroll in minimum essential coverage under an eligible employer-sponsored plan (¶ 2003); or

- the employer offers its full-time employees and their dependents the opportunity to enroll in minimum essential coverage under an eligible employer-sponsored plan but the coverage is unaffordable to the employee or does not provide minimum value (¶ 2005) (Code Sec. 4980H; Reg. § § 54.4980H-4 and 54.4980H-5).

An applicable large employer may be liable for either type of assessable payment in any calendar month, but not both. Minimum essential coverage for this purpose means coverage under an employer-sponsored plan offered in the small or large group market within a state and which meets the requirements for group health plans or group health insurance coverage under section 2791 of the Public Health Service Act (Code Sec. 5000A(f); Reg. § 54.4980H-1(a)(27)).

Applicable Large Employer. An applicable large employer is any employer that employed on average at least 50 full-time employees, full-time equivalents (FTEs), or some combination on business days during the preceding calendar year (Code Sec. 4980H(c)(2); Reg. § § 54.4980H-1(a)(4) and 54.4980H-2). An individual who has medical coverage through the military, including TRICARE or a Department of Veterans Affairs program, is not considered an employee in determining whether an employer meets the 50-employee threshold.

FTEs are determined by adding all hours of service for the month for employees who were not full-time employees (but no more than 120 hours per employee), and dividing by 120. An employer not in existence during an entire preceding calendar year is an applicable large employer for the current year if it is reasonably expected to employ an average of 50 or more full-time employees (including FTEs) on business days during the current calendar year.

An exemption to the 50-employee threshold applies if the employer has more than 50 employees for 120 days or less during the preceding calendar year, but the employees in excess of 50 are seasonal workers. A seasonal worker is an employee who performs labor or services on a seasonal basis including, but not limited to, certain agricultural workers and retail workers employed during the holiday season.

In applying the 50-employee threshold, an employer means all common law employers, including for-profit businesses, tax-exempt organizations, and government entities (federal, state, local, and Indian tribes). Employers with common ownership such as controlled groups under Code Sec. 414(b) or (c), or related employers such as an affiliated service group under Code Sec. 414(m), are combined for the 50-employee threshold. Moreover, any references to an employer include references to the employer's predecessors and successors.

Full-Time Employee. A full-time employee for purposes of determining applicable large employer status is an employee who was employed on average at least 30 hours of service per week or 130 hours of service in a calendar month (Code Sec. 4980H(c)(4); Reg. §§ 54.4980H-1(a)(21) and 54.4980H-3). Employee is defined under the common law standard (i.e., right to control, direct, etc.). It does not include a leased employee, sole proprietor, partner in partnership, or two-percent or more S corporation shareholder, unless services are provided as both an employee and nonemployee.

An hour of service includes each hour for which the employee is paid or entitled to be paid for services performed in the United States for the employer, including periods of paid leave. For an hourly employee, the employer calculates hours of service using records of hours worked and for which payment is made or due. For a non-hourly employee, an employer can count actual hours worked and for which payment is due, or apply a days-worked equivalency (8 hours of service) or weeks-worked equivalency (40 hours of service). An employer may use different methods for different classifications of non-hourly employees as long as the categories are reasonable and consistently applied.

Safe harbors are provided allowing an employer the option of using either a look-back method or monthly measurement method to determine full-time employee status. Look-back measurements are provided for ongoing employees, new employees, and employees with a change in employment status.

Offer of Coverage. An employer is treated as offering coverage for a calendar month if it offers the coverage for that month to at least 95 percent of its full-time employees and their dependents (Reg. §§ 54.4980H-4(b) and 54.4980H-5(b)). An offer occurs if the employee has the opportunity to elect to enroll in or decline coverage at least once during the plan year. Failure to offer coverage for any day of a calendar month is treated as failure to offer coverage for the entire month.

A full-time employee is treated as having been offered coverage only if the employer also offers coverage to the employee's dependents. A dependent is the employee's child who is under the age of 26. It does not include anyone other than children, such as the employee's spouse. If an employee or dependent enrolls in coverage but fails to pay his or her share of premiums on a timely basis, the employer is nonetheless treated as offering coverage for that coverage period.

Reporting Requirements. Employers and insurers are required to file an annual information return with the IRS reporting health care coverage provided to employees and other individuals (¶ 2567).

2003. Penalty for Employers Not Offering Health Care Coverage. An applicable large employer (¶ 2001) is liable for a shared responsibility payment (assessable payment) if:

- the employer fails to offer to its full-time employees and their dependents the opportunity to enroll in minimum essential coverage under an eligible employer-sponsored group health plan for any month, and
- at least one full-time employee is certified as having enrolled in a qualified health plan through a Health Insurance Exchange and eligible to receive a premium tax credit (¶ 1431) or cost-sharing reduction payment (Code Sec. 4980H(a); Reg. § 54.4980H-4).

The assessable payment for an employer not offering coverage with respect to any calendar month equals the number of the employer's full-time employees reduced by 30, multiplied by 1/12 of $2,500 for 2019 ($2,570 for 2020) (Code Sec. 4980H(c)(1) and (c)(5)). The 30-employee reduction applies only for purposes of calculating the assessable payment (Code Sec. 4980H(c)(2)(D)). It does not apply for determining if the employer is an applicable large employer (i.e., 50-employee threshold). Also, a full-time employee does not include a full-time equivalent (FTE) employee for purposes of the payment calculation (Code Sec. 4980H(c)(2)(E)). Employers with common ownership or otherwise related are allowed only one 30-employee reduction which is allocated ratably among all the related employers.

An employer must pay the assessable payment upon notice and demand by IRS; it is not required to be included with the employer's tax return (Code Sec. 4980H(d)). The payment is assessed and collected in the same manner as an assessable penalty. However, it is not deductible as a business expense (Code Sec. 4980H(c)(7)).

2005. Penalty for Employers Offering Health Care Coverage. An applicable large employer (¶ 2001) is liable for a shared responsibility payment (assessable payment) if:

- the employer offers minimum essential coverage under an eligible employer-sponsored group health plan to its full-time employees and their dependents for any month, but

- at least one full-time employee is certified as having enrolled in a qualified health plan through a Health Insurance Exchange and eligible to receive an applicable premium tax credit (¶ 1431) or cost-sharing reduction payment because the coverage is not affordable to the employee or does not provide minimum value (Code Sec. 4980H(b); Reg. § 54.4980H-5).

Affordability. Coverage for an employee is affordable if the employee's share of the premium for self-only coverage, not family coverage, does not exceed a percentage of the employee's annual household income (9.86 percent for 2019, 9.78 percent for 2020) (Rev. Proc. 2018-34; Rev. Proc. 2019-29). The affordability test applies to the lowest-cost option available to the employee that also meets the minimum value requirement.

Safe harbors are provided for an employer to determine if coverage is affordable to an employee based on the employee's Form W-2 wages, the employee's rate of pay, or the federal poverty line. An employer may choose one or more safe harbors for all of its employees or any reasonable category of employees, so long as it is done on a uniform and consistent basis. The safe harbors only apply for purposes of the assessable payment; they do not affect an employee's eligibility for a premium tax credit.

Minimum Value. An employer-sponsored group health plan fails to provide minimum value if the plan's share of the total allowed costs of benefits provided under the plan is less than 60 percent of the costs, and generally fails to offer substantial coverage for in-patient hospitalization and physician services (Prop. Reg. § 1.36B-6). An eligible employer-sponsored plan may determine whether it provides minimum value by: (1) a minimum value calculator provided by the IRS and the Department of Health and Human Services (HHS); (2) actuarial certification; (3) certain safe harbor plan designs; or (4) for plans in the small group market, meeting the requirements for bronze, silver, gold, or platinum level coverage.

Calculation of Assessable Payment. The assessable payment for an employer offering health care coverage with respect to any calendar month equals the number of the employer's full-time employees who receive a premium tax credit or cost-sharing reduction, multiplied by 1/12 of $3,750 for 2019 ($3,860 for 2020) (Code Sec. 4980H(b) and (c)(5); Reg. § 54.4980H-5). The assessable payment for any calendar month is capped at the number of the employer's full-time employees for the month reduced by 30, multiplied by 1/12 of $2,500 for 2019 ($2,570 for 2020). The cap ensures that the payment for an employer that offers coverage can never exceed the assessable payment the employer would owe if it did not offer coverage (¶ 2003).

An employer must pay the assessable payment upon notice and demand by the IRS; it is not required to be included with the employer's tax return (Code Sec. 4980H(d)). The payment is assessed and collected in the same manner as an assessable penalty. However, it is not deductible as a business expense (Code Sec. 4980H(c)(7)).

Health and Welfare Benefits

See CCH® AnswerConnect: *Employee Welfare Benefit Plans* and *Employer Provided Life Insurance* for more information on this topic.

2011. Welfare Benefit Plans. A welfare benefit plan or welfare benefit fund is any fund through which an employer provides welfare benefits to employees, independent contractors, or their beneficiaries (Code Sec. 419). Welfare benefits are benefits other than deferred compensation or transfers of restricted property, such as accident or health benefits, disability or death benefits, unemployment benefits, severance benefits, vacation, or similar benefits.

An employer may deduct contributions paid or accrued to a welfare benefit fund to the extent that the contributions do not exceed the qualified cost of the fund for the tax year, reduced by the after-tax income of the fund. If the employer's contributions to the fund are more than its qualified cost, the excess is carried over to the next tax year. Welfare benefits provided directly by an employer to an employee are deductible only in the tax year the employee includes the benefits in gross income or would include such benefits in gross income if they were taxable to the employee (¶ 906) (Code Sec. 404(b)(2)(A)). An employer may not accrue and deduct unpaid welfare benefits.

A welfare benefit fund's qualified cost is the direct cost the employer would have been able to deduct using the cash method of accounting if it paid for the benefits directly (Code Sec. 419(c)). It also includes any addition to a qualified asset account—a reserve set aside for the payment of disability benefits, medical benefits, supplemental unemployment benefits (SUB) or severance pay benefits, and life insurance or death benefits (Code Sec. 419A).

The allowable addition to a qualified asset account for a tax year is the amount that will bring the account to a level (the account limit) that is reasonably and actuarially necessary to fund the payment of incurred but unpaid benefits. In the case of post-retirement medical and life insurance benefits, the allowable addition is the amount required to fund the payment of such benefits on a level basis over the working lives of the covered employees based on current medical costs. For employers who do not support higher additions to a qualified asset account by actuarial certifications, there are safe harbor additions for the various benefits. Limits are placed on the level of disability, SUB, and severance pay benefits that may be considered in establishing the account limit for such benefits.

VEBAs. Collectively bargained voluntary employees' beneficiary associations (VEBAs) are exempt from the account limits applicable to welfare benefit funds (Code Sec. 419A(f)(5)). Thus, employer contributions to VEBAs are deductible and earnings are tax exempt. In addition, VEBAs that are funded solely with employee contributions are also exempt from the account limits if: (1) the VEBA covers at least 50 employees; and (2) no employee is entitled to a refund with respect to amounts in the fund, other than a refund based on the experience of the entire fund. VEBAs are tax-exempt trusts that provide life, sickness, accident, and other benefits to members, or their dependents or beneficiaries, and meet certain nondiscrimination requirements (Code Secs. 501(c)(9) and 505).

2013. Employer Contributions to Accident and Health Plans. Contributions by an employer to an accident or health plan that provides coverage for personal injuries or sickness incurred by the employee and his or her spouse, dependent, or child under the age of 27, are excluded from the employee's gross income (Code Sec. 106; Reg. § 1.106-1). If a plan provides other benefits in addition to accident and health benefits, the exclusion applies only to the part of the employer's contributions that is allocable to accident and health benefits. See ¶ 2015 for a further discussion of accident and health plans. See ¶ 322 and ¶ 421 for a discussion of accident and health insurance premiums paid by a partnership and S corporation.

An employer generally contributes to an accident or health plan by paying a portion of the premium for accident and health insurance, or by contributing to a separate trust or fund that provides benefits directly or through insurance. A qualified long-term care insurance contract is generally treated as an accident and health insurance contract for this purpose (¶ 2019). Employer contributions for the cost of long-term care insurance provided through a flexible spending account (FSA) or similar arrangement (¶ 2041) are included in the employee's wages for income tax purposes, but they are excluded from wages for FICA and FUTA purposes (Code Sec. 106(c)).

Employer contributions to an employee's health savings account (HSA) (¶ 2035) or Archer medical savings account (MSA) (¶ 2037) may be excluded from an employee's gross income as employer-provided coverage for medical expenses under an accident or health plan to the extent they do not exceed the HSA or MSA limits (Code Sec. 106(b) and (d)). If an employer makes such contributions, it must make comparable contributions on behalf of all employees with comparable coverage during the same period (Code Secs. 4980E and 4980G). Payments or reimbursements made under a qualified small employer health reimbursement account (QSEHRA) (¶ 2039) are includible in an employee's gross income if in the month of which the medical expense is incurred the individual does not have minimal essential coverage (Code Sec. 106(g)). Employer contributions paid for COBRA continuation coverage of a former employee (¶ 2021) may also be excluded as coverage under an accident or health plan (IRS Pub. 15-B).

2015. Accident and Health Benefits Provided By Employer Plans. Amounts received by an employee under an employer-financed accident and health plan are generally excluded from gross income if received as:

- reimbursements for medical care of the employee, his or her spouse, dependent, or child under the age of 27 to the extent the medical expenses were not deducted by the employee in a prior tax year (Code Sec. 105(b); Reg. § 1.105-2); or

- payments for permanent injury or loss of bodily function (i.e., disability) of the employee, spouse, or dependent, so long as the payments are based on the nature of the injury rather than length of time the employee is absent from work (Code Sec. 105(c); Reg. § 1.105-3).

Amounts received by an employee through an accident and health plan that are not reimbursements of medical expenses, but are instead payments for personal injuries or sickness, generally are included in gross income if they are attributable to contributions by the employer that were not included in the employee's gross income or paid directly by the employer (¶ 2013) (Code Sec. 105(a); Reg. § 1.105-1). Amounts the employee receives that are not attributable to employer contributions, such as benefits attributable to the employee's own contributions, are not included in gross income. Payments or reimbursements made under a qualified small employer health reimbursement account (QSEHRA) (¶ 2039) are includible in gross income if in the month of which the medical expense is incurred the individual does not have minimal essential coverage (Code Sec. 106(g)).

Employee. An employee for this purpose includes any current, retired, and former employee, as well as a widow or widower of a retired employee and any individual who died while an employee. It also includes a leased employee who provides services on a substantially full-time basis (IRS Pub. 15-B). A self-employed individual is not considered an employee and the cost of employer-provided accident and health insurance is included in gross income (Code Sec. 105(g); Reg. § 1.105-5(b)). However, a self-employed individual may deduct from gross income 100 percent of amounts paid for health insurance coverage (¶ 908). Partners in a partnership and two-percent or greater shareholders of an S corporation who are employees are considered to be self-employed.

Dependents. A dependent for this purpose is a qualifying child and qualifying relative (¶ 137), but without regard to whether the dependent claims dependent on his or her return, files a joint return, or has gross income in excess of a threshold amount for the year. If certain conditions are met, the IRS will treat the child of divorced or separated parents as a dependent of both parents under an employer accident and health plan (Code Sec. 105(b)).

Accident and Health Plan. An accident and health plan is any arrangement of an employer that provides benefits to employees and their spouses, dependents, and children under age 27 in the event of personal injury or sickness (Code Sec. 105(e); Reg. § 1.105-5(a)). The plan may be insured or not insured, and does not need to be in writing. A qualified long-term care insurance contract is generally treated as an accident and health insurance contract for this purpose (¶ 2019). A sickness and disability fund for employees maintained by a state, the District of Columbia, or Indian tribal government is also treated the same as an employer accident and health plan (Code Sec. 7871(a)(6)(A)). Qualified health care benefits provided by an Indian tribal government may also be excluded from gross income (¶ 2027). An employer's accident and health plan must not discriminate in favor of highly compensated individuals (¶ 2017).

COBRA Coverage. A group health plan provided by an employer must offer each qualified beneficiary who would otherwise lose coverage as a result of a qualifying event, an opportunity to elect continuation coverage referred to as COBRA continuation coverage (¶ 2021).

Railroad Unemployment Insurance. Benefits paid to an employee under the Railroad Unemployment Insurance Act for sick days are included in the employee's gross income unless an illness is due to an on-the-job injury (Code Sec. 105(i)).

Annuity Rules. Amounts received as accident or health benefits are generally not taxable under the annuity rules of Code Sec. 72 (Reg. § 1.72-15). However, some employer-established plans pay participants both amounts taxable under the annuity rules (¶ 817) and amounts excludable from gross income as payments under an accident or health plan. Specific rules are provided for determining which amounts are excludable in these cases. Benefits attributable to the employee's contributions are excludable from gross income under the rules at ¶ 851.

2017. Nondiscrimination Requirements for Employer Health Plans. An employer's self-insured medical reimbursement plan must not discriminate in favor of highly compensated individuals in terms of eligibility for coverage or benefits offered under the plan (Code Sec. 105(h); Reg. § 1.105-11). For plan years beginning on or after September 23, 2010, similar nondiscrimination requirements apply to group health plans other than self-insured plans. However, compliance for group health plans will not be required until additional guidance is issued (Code Sec. 9815; Notice 2011-1). See ¶ 2039 for a discussion of employer health reimbursement arrangements (HRAs).

Excess reimbursements paid to a highly compensated individual under a plan that fails to meet the nondiscrimination requirements are includible in the individual's gross income. A highly compensated employee for this purpose is an employee who is one of the five highest paid officers, among the highest paid 25 percent of all employees, or a shareholder owning more than 10 percent in value of the company's stock.

The entire amount of a reimbursement with respect to a benefit that is available only to highly compensated individuals is treated as an excess reimbursement includible in income. In the case of a plan that discriminates in terms of eligibility, the includible excess reimbursement is equal to all the medical expenses for which the highly compensated individual was reimbursed times a fraction. The numerator is the total amount reimbursed to all participants who are highly compensated individuals. The denominator is the total amount reimbursed to all employees under the plan for the plan year. If the plan discriminates in terms of eligibility *and* benefits, any amount which is included in income by reason of the benefits not being available to all other participants is not to be taken into account in determining the excess reimbursements that result from the plan being discriminatory in terms of eligibility.

There is no eligibility discrimination if the plan benefits: (1) at least 70 percent of all employees or 80 percent of all eligible employees if at least 70 percent of all employees are eligible; or (2) a class of employees found by the IRS not to be discriminatory in favor of highly compensated individuals. Certain employees, such as part-time workers, employees with less than three years of service, employees under age 25, and employees excluded as a result of a collective bargaining agreement, may be excluded from coverage. There is no benefits discrimination if the self-insured medical expense plan provides the same benefits for non-highly compensated employees as it does for highly compensated employees.

2019. Long-Term Care Insurance. A qualified long-term care insurance contract is treated as an accident and health insurance contract, and any employer plan providing coverage under a qualified long-term care insurance contract is treated as an accident and health plan (Code Sec. 7702B). Amounts received under the contract other than dividends and refunds are excluded from the recipient's gross income as amounts received for personal injuries and sickness (¶ 2015). The exclusion does not apply to long-term care insurance coverage provided under a cafeteria plan (¶ 2045) or flexible spending arrangement (¶ 2041) (Code Secs. 106(c) and 125(f)). Premiums paid by an individual for a qualified long-term care insurance contract may be deducted as a medical expense (¶ 1019).

A qualified long-term care insurance contract is an insurance contract that only provides coverage of qualified long-term care services, including necessary diagnostic, preventive, and treatment services, or personal care services required by a chronically ill individual and prescribed by a licensed health care practitioner (Code Sec. 7702B(b) and (c)). In addition, the contract must be guaranteed renewable, must not provide a cash surrender value, and must meet certain consumer protection provisions.

2021. COBRA Continuation Coverage. A group health plan provided by an employer with 20 or more employees must offer each covered employee, as well as his or her spouse and dependent, who would lose coverage as a result of a qualifying event, an opportunity to elect to continue coverage referred to as COBRA coverage (Code Sec. 4980B). A qualifying event with respect to a covered employee includes death, termination of employment or reduction of hours, divorce or legal separation, eligibility for Medicare, a dependent child ceasing to be a dependent, or bankruptcy of the employer. Group health plans that fail to provide COBRA coverage to qualified beneficiaries are subject to an excise tax.

The option to elect COBRA coverage must allow the qualified beneficiary to purchase medical coverage under the company plan at group, rather than individual, rates for at least 18 months for most qualified beneficiaries (36 months in limited circumstances). The plan may require the beneficiary to pay premiums for the continuation coverage not to exceed 102 percent of the applicable premium for the coverage period. The continuation coverage must be identical to the coverage provided to similarly situated beneficiaries under the plan for whom no qualifying event has occurred.

2023. Wellness Programs; Employee Assistance Programs. Wellness programs or employee assistance programs (EAPs) are generally part of an employer's overall health promotion for employees and may be one of several methods used to reduce health care costs. Although many EAPs are initiated to deal with drug and alcohol abuse, EAPs may also address family problems, stress, job termination, finances, and retirement. Because EAPs commonly provide treatment for drug and alcohol abuse and other similar health and medical problems, they often qualify as employee welfare benefit plans (¶ 2011). If an EAP merely provides referrals and does not pay for any services or benefits, the EAP will not be deemed to be an employee welfare benefit plan (Pension Welfare Benefits Administration (PWBA) Opinion Letter 91-26A).

2025. Disability Benefits Under Employer Insurance Plan. Disability income plans are employer plans, some mandated by state law, that provide full or partial income replacement for employees who become disabled. To the extent an employer offers such coverage under an accident and health plan, whether benefits received by employees are taxable depends on who pays for the premiums and whether they are paid on an after-tax basis (¶ 2015) (Code Sec. 105(a)).

2027. Indian Health Care Benefits. Qualified health care benefits provided by an Indian tribal government to a member of an Indian tribe, or to a member's spouse or dependent, are excluded from the beneficiary's gross income (Code Sec. 139D). A qualified health care benefit includes:

- any health service provided or purchased by the Indian Health Service through a grant, contract or compact with an Indian tribe or tribal organization, or through a program funded by the Indian Health Service;

- medical care provided or purchased, or reimbursements for medical care, by an Indian tribe or tribal organization for a member of an Indian tribe, the member's spouse or dependent;

- coverage under an accident or health insurance plan provided by an Indian tribe or tribal organization for medical care to a member of an Indian tribe, the member's spouse or dependent; and

- any other medical care provided by an Indian tribe or tribal organization that supplements, replaces or substitutes for medical care programs and services provided by the federal government to Indian tribes or their members.

The exclusion does not apply to Indian health care benefits that are not includible in the beneficiary's gross income under another provision in the Code or to any benefit for which the beneficiary may claim a deduction.

2028. Indian General Welfare Benefits. Indian general welfare benefits provided to, or on behalf of, a member of an Indian tribe, the member's spouse, or dependents are excluded from the recipient's gross income (Code Sec. 139E). An Indian general welfare benefit is any payment made, or service provided, under an Indian tribal government program administered under specific guidelines and which does not discriminate in favor of members of the governing body of the Indian tribe. A program will not fail to be treated as an Indian tribal government program solely by reason of it being established by tribal custom or government practice. Benefits under the program must be available to any tribal member and must be for the promotion of general welfare. In addition, benefits must not be lavish or extravagant, and not provided as compensation for services. Any items of cultural significance, reimbursement of costs, or cash honorarium for participation in cultural or ceremonial activities for the transmission of tribal culture will not be treated as compensation.

2029. Subsidies for Retiree Prescription Drug Plans. An employer that provides a qualified retiree prescription drug plan to its retired employees is eligible for a special subsidy payment each year from the federal government based on the cost of providing the coverage to qualified retirees (Social Security Act, §1860D-22). The subsidy payment is excludable from the employer's gross income for both regular income tax and alternative minimum tax (AMT) purposes (Code Sec. 139A). The amount otherwise allowable as a deduction to the employer for retiree prescription drug costs is reduced by the amount of the excludable subsidy received by the employer.

2031. Medical Loss Ratio Rebates. Health insurance issuers may be required to pay medical loss ratio (MLR) rebates to policyholders in the form of either cash payments or premium reductions. For policies purchased on the individual insurance market, MLR rebates are taxable or nontaxable depending on whether the individual deducted the premium payments (Internal Revenue Service, Medical Loss Ratio (MLR) FAQs). If the individual did not deduct the premiums for the year, an MLR rebate received in the following year is excluded from income whether received as cash or premium reduction. If the individual deducted the premiums, then an MLR rebate received in the following year is treated as the recovery of an itemized deduction under the tax benefit rule (¶ 799).

For policies purchased by an employee through an employer-sponsored group health plan, MLR rebates are taxable or nontaxable depending on whether the employee used pre-tax or after-tax dollars to pay the health insurance premiums. If the employee used pre-tax dollars, then any MLR rebate received is subject to income and employment taxes. If the employee used after-tax dollars and MLR rebates are paid only to employees who participated in the plan both in the year the premiums were paid and in the year the rebates are received, then a rebate is not included in income if the employee did not deduct the premiums. If, however, MLR rebates are provided to all employees participating in the group health plan in the year the rebates are paid, regardless of whether the employee participated in the plan in the year the premiums were paid, then the rebates are not included in income if the employee used after-tax dollars.

HSAs, HRAs, and FSAs

See CCH® AnswerConnect: *Health Savings Accounts (HSA), Health Reimbursement Arrangements (HRA),* and *Flexible Spending Account* for more information on this topic.

2035. Health Savings Accounts (HSAs). A health savings account (HSA) is a trust or custodial account established for the exclusive purpose of paying for qualified medical expenses of the account beneficiary (Code Sec. 223). HSAs can be established through an employer's cafeteria plan (¶ 2045) or by an individual outside the employment context. The HSA itself is exempt from paying income tax, except on unrelated business income (¶ 655). Contributions are either deductible or excluded from income, but the amount that may be contributed each year is limited. Distributions are excluded from gross income as long as they are used exclusively to pay for qualified medical expenses.

Eligibility. An individual is eligible to establish an HSA in any month if:

- he or she is covered by high-deductible health plan (HDHP) on the first day of the month;
- is generally not covered by any other health plan or enrolled in Medicare; and
- cannot be claimed as a dependent on another taxpayer's return.

Certain insurance coverage that is not an HDHP is permitted without jeopardizing an individual's eligibility including insurance for accidents, disability, dental care, vision care, long term care, or prescription drugs. Permitted coverage also includes insurance for a specified disease or illness, insurance paying a fixed amount per day (or other period) for hospitalization, and insurance if substantially all the coverage relates to liabilities for workers' compensation, ownership or use of property (for example, auto insurance), or torts. An individual will not fail to be treated as an eligible individual solely because he or she receives hospital care or medical services under any law administered by the Department of Veterans Affairs for a service-connected disability.

For plan years beginning on or before December 31, 2021, a health plan is treated as a HDHP even if it does not impose a deductible for telehealth or other remote care services (Code Sec. 223(c)(2)(E), added by the Coronavirus Aid, Relief, and Economic Security (CARES) Act (P.L. 116-136)). Telehealth and remote care are also added to the list of coverage items that are disregarded for purposes of determining HDHP deductibles (Code Sec. 223(c)(1)(B)(ii), amended by P.L. 116-136). Furthermore, an HDHP may cover testing and treatment of COVID-19 (coronavirus) prior to the satisfaction of the minimum deductible (Notice 2020-15).

An HDHP is a health plan with (1) an annual deductible of at least $1,350 for 2019 ($1,400 for 2020) for self-only coverage, or $2,700 for 2019 ($2,800 for 2020) for family coverage; and (2) an annual out-of-pocket expenses limit of $6,750 for 2019 ($6,900 for 2020) for self-only coverage or $13,500 for 2019 ($13,800 for 2020) for family coverage. Out-of-pocket expenses include deductibles, co-payments and other amounts (other than premiums) that must be paid for plan benefits (Notice 2008-59; Rev. Proc. 2018-30; Rev. Proc. 2019-25).

While covered by an HSA, an individual generally may not be covered by a health flexible spending arrangement (FSA) (¶ 2041) or health reimbursement account (HRA) (¶ 2039) sponsored by the individual's employer or spouse's employer unless it is a limited purpose FSA or HRA, a suspended HRA, a post-deductible health FSA or HRA, or a retirement HRA. Coverage under a general purpose health FSA during a grace period is disregarded in determining if tax deductible contributions can be made to an HSA for that period if the balance in the health FSA at the end of the plan year is zero or the entire remaining balance in the health FSA at the end of the plan year is contributed to an HSA in a qualified HSA distribution.

A taxpayer who is an eligible individual for an HSA on the first day of the last month of a tax year is treated as eligible during every month of the year. If the taxpayer ceases to be eligible during the period beginning with the last month of the tax year and ending on the last day of the 12th month following that month, he or she must include in gross income an amount equal to the amount actually contributed minus the sum of the monthly contribution limits to which the individual would otherwise have been entitled. An additional 10-percent tax is imposed on this amount. Recapture does not apply if the taxpayer is ineligible due to death or disability (Code Sec. 223(b)(8); Notice 2008-52).

Contributions. Cash contributions may be made to an HSA by the eligible individual, the individual's employer, or any other person on behalf of the eligible individual. Contributions made by an individual outside the employment context are deductible as an above-the-line deduction in calculating adjusted gross income (AGI) (Code Secs. 62(a)(19) and 223(a)). Employer contributions to an employee's HSA may be excluded from the employee's gross income (¶ 2013).

The maximum amount that can be contributed for 2019 is $3,500 for self-only coverage or $7,000 for family coverage. The maximum contribution for 2020 is $3,550 for self-only coverage or $7,100 for family coverage. The annual contribution limit is increased $1,000 if the individual reaches age 55 by the end of the tax year. The annual limit applies to all HSAs of the eligible individual combined, and all contributions made by anyone to the accounts. The limit is decreased for any month the participant is not an eligible individual. Excess contributions are subject to a six-percent excise tax. Contributions cannot be made after the participant attains age 65 or is enrolled in Medicare (Notice 2008-59; Notice 2004-50; Rev. Proc. 2018-30; Rev. Proc. 2019-25).

An individual must report all contributions to his or her HSA on Form 8889. Contributions may be made at any time during a tax year or by the due date for filing a return for that year (not including extensions). For example, this means that deductible contributions by individuals generally must be made by April 15 if the following year. However, the due date for filing federal tax returns, as well as making HSA contributions for the tax years, otherwise due on or after April 1, 2020, and before July 15, 2020, is

¶2035

automatically extended to July 15, 2020, in response to the COVID-19 (coronavirus) crisis (¶ 2505).

Married Taxpayers. For married individuals, if either spouse has family coverage under any health plan, then both will be treated as having family coverage under the plan. If each spouse has family coverage under different plans, then both spouses are treated as having coverage under the plan with the lowest deductible (Code Sec. 223(b)(5)). If only one spouse is an eligible individual, only that spouse may contribute to an HSA (Notice 2004-50). If one or both spouses have family coverage, the contribution limit is the lowest deductible amount, divided equally between the spouses unless they agree on a different division, and further reduced by any contribution to an Archer medical savings account (MSA) (¶ 2037). Both spouses may make the catch-up contributions for individuals age 55 or over without exceeding the family coverage limit (Notice 2008-59, amplifying Notice 2004-2).

If a husband and wife are each eligible to make catch-up contributions, each spouse can make such contributions only to his or her own HSA. The maximum annual contribution limit for a married couple is the statutory maximum for family coverage where: (1) one spouse has family coverage and the other spouse has self-only coverage, regardless of whether the family coverage includes the spouse with self-only coverage; or (2) both spouses have family coverage, regardless of whether each spouse's family coverage covers the other spouse. A married taxpayer covered under an HDHP can contribute to an HSA for use with qualifying out-of-pocket medical expenses even if his or her spouse's coverage is nonqualifying family coverage, as long as the taxpayer is not covered by the spouse's policy (Rev. Rul. 2005-25).

Distributions. Distributions from an HSA are excluded from the account beneficiary's gross income if used to pay or be reimbursed for qualified medical expenses incurred during the coverage period (Code Sec. 223(f)). Qualified medical expenses are those specified in the plan that would generally qualify as an itemized deduction and incurred by the account beneficiary, his or her spouse, or dependents (¶ 1016). Nonprescription medicines (other than insulin) are not considered qualified medical expenses under an HSA for amounts paid before 2020. Over the counter medicines or drugs are considered qualified medical expenses under an HSA for amounts paid after 2019. In addition, menstrual care products paid or incurred after 2019 are eligible medical care expenses for purposes of an HSA (Code Sec. 223(d)(2), amended by P.L. 116-136).

Health insurance premiums are not qualified medical expenses under an HSA unless for long-term care insurance, COBRA continuation coverage, health care coverage while receiving unemployment compensation, or Medicare. Distributions from an HSA not used for qualified medical expenses are included in the account beneficiary's gross income and subject to a 20 percent additional tax, unless made after the beneficiary reaches age 65, dies, or becomes disabled. The additional tax is not treated as a tax liability for purposes of the alternative minimum tax (¶ 1415).

The definition of a dependent for purposes of an HSA is a qualifying child or qualifying relative (¶ 137), but determined without regard to whether the dependent claims a dependent on his or her return, files a joint return, or has gross income in excess of a threshold amount for the year (Code Sec. 223(d)(2)(A)). If certain conditions are met, the IRS will treat the child of divorced or separated parents as a dependent of both parents, without a declaration by the custodial parent releasing the claim to the dependency exemption (¶ 139A) (Rev. Proc. 2008-48).

Contributions by Partnership or S Corporation. Contributions made by a partnership or S corporation to a partner's or shareholder's HSA are generally treated as payments to the partner or shareholder and includible in gross income. The individual partner or shareholder may treat the contribution as an above-the-line deduction (an adjustment to gross income). However, a contribution to the partner's HSA by the partnership for services rendered is treated as a guaranteed payment, and the partnership may deduct the contribution as a business expense. Similarly, a contribution by a S corporation to a two-percent shareholder's HSA for services rendered is deductible by the S corporation and included in the shareholders income (Notice 2005-8).

Distributions to Fund HSAs. An eligible individual can make a one-time qualified HSA distribution directly from an IRA to his or her HSA (¶ 2165). The amount that can otherwise be contributed to the HSA for the tax year of the distribution is reduced by the amount contributed from the IRA, and the individual cannot deduct the distribution amount as an HSA contribution (Code Sec. 223(b)(4)(C); Notice 2008-51). An eligible individual can also roll over distributions from another HSA or Archer MSA into an HSA. The taxpayer does not have to be an eligible individual to make a rollover contribution from an existing HSA to a new HSA (Code Sec. 106(e)).

2037. Archer Medical Savings Accounts (MSAs). An Archer medical savings account (MSA) is a trust or custodial account established for the exclusive purpose of paying for qualified medical expenses of the account beneficiary, his or her spouse, or dependents (Code Sec. 220). Archer MSAs operate almost exactly the same as health savings accounts (HSAs) (¶ 2035), except that new Archer MSAs may *not* be established after 2007. An individual can still utilize an Archer MSA if he or she was an active participant in the MSA before 2008, or he or she became an active participant for a tax year ending after 2007 by reason of coverage under a high deductible health plan (HDHP) of an Archer MSA participating employer.

To qualify for an Archer MSA, an individual or spouse must be either an employee of a small employer or self-employed person that maintains an HDHP. A small employer for this purpose is generally an employer who had an average of 50 or fewer employees during either of the last two calendar years. Like HSAs, the individual can have no other health care coverage, including under Medicare.

An HDHP under an Archer MSA has higher annual deductibles and lower out-of-pocket limits than under an HSA:

- for self-only coverage, the minimum deductible is $2,350 for 2019 ($2,350 for 2020), the maximum deductible is $3,500 for 2019 ($3,550 for 2020), and the maximum out-of-pocket limitation is $4,650 for 2019 ($4,750 for 2020); and

- for family coverage, the minimum deductible is $4,650 for 2019 ($4,750 for 2020), the maximum deductible is $7,000 for 2019 ($7,100 for 2020), and the maximum out-of-pocket limitation is $8,550 for 2019 ($8,650 for 2020) (Rev. Proc. 2018-57; Rev. Proc. 2019-44).

Contributions. Cash contributions may be made to an Archer MSA by the eligible individual or the individual's employer. Contributions made by the individual outside of the employment contact are deductible as an above-the-line deduction in calculating adjusted gross income (AGI) (Code Secs. 62(a)(16) and 220(a)). Employer contributions to an employee's MSA may be excluded from the employee's gross income (¶ 2013). An individual must report all contributions to an MSA on Form 8853. Annual contributions to an Archer MSA are limited to 75 percent of the deductible of the required health insurance plan (65 percent if a self-only plan). Contributions are also limited by an employee's compensation or the income earned from a self-employed individual's business (Code Sec. 220(b)). Excess contributions are subject to an excise tax.

Distributions. Distributions from an Archer MSA are excluded from the account beneficiary's gross income only if used to pay or be reimbursed for qualified medical expenses incurred during the coverage period (Code Sec. 220(f)). Qualified medical expenses are those specified in the plan that would generally qualify as an itemized deduction and incurred by the account beneficiary, his or her spouse, or dependents (¶ 1016). Nonprescription medicines (other than insulin) are not considered qualified medical expenses under an Archer MSA for amounts paid before 2020. Over the counter medicines or drugs are considered qualified medical expenses under an MSA for amounts paid after 2019. In addition, menstrual care products paid or incurred after 2019 are eligible medical care expenses for purposes of an MSA (Code Sec. 220(d)(2), amended by the Coronavirus Aid, Relief, and Economic Security (CARES) Act (P.L. 116-136) P.L. 116-136).

Health insurance premiums are not qualified medical expenses under an MSA unless for long-term care insurance, COBRA continuation coverage, and health care coverage while receiving unemployment compensation. Distributions from an MSA not used for qualified medical expenses are included in the account beneficiary's gross income and subject to a 20 percent additional tax, unless made after the beneficiary reaches age 65, dies, or becomes disabled. The additional tax is not treated as a tax liability for purposes of the alternative minimum tax (¶ 1415).

¶2037

Medicare Advantage MSAs. Medicare Advantage MSAs are medical savings accounts that are used in conjunction with a high deductible Medicare Advantage MSA health plan (Code Sec. 138). Individuals eligible for Medicare are permitted to have their Medicare benefits deposited directly into a Medicare Advantage MSA and can make trustee-to-trustee transfers from Archer MSAs to these MSAs. Income earned on the account and withdrawals used to pay health care expenses are not included in the individual's income.

2039. Health Reimbursement Arrangements (HRAs). A health reimbursement arrangement (HRA) is an employer-funded plan that reimburses employees for qualified medical care expenses (Notice 2002-45, amplified by Rev. Rul. 2006-36). An HRA is funded solely by employer contributions and may not be funded through employee salary deferrals under a cafeteria plan (¶ 2045). The plan must provide reimbursements up to a maximum dollar amount for a coverage period. Any unused amounts in an HRA can be carried forward for reimbursements in later years. To the extent an HRA constitutes an employer-provided accident or health plan (¶ 2015), coverage and reimbursements of qualified medical care expenses are generally excludable from the employee's gross income.

An HRA may be offered in conjunction with other provided health benefits, such as a group health plan or health flexible spending arrangement (FSA) (¶ 2041). An HRA is generally subject to an excise tax for failing to meet group health plan requirements unless it is integrated with an employer's minimum essential coverage, and reimbursements cannot be used to obtain individual coverage on a health exchange. Exceptions are provided for stand-alone retiree plans and plans with fewer than two participants (Notice 2013-54; Notice 2015-87).

An exception is also provided for a qualified small employer health reimbursement arrangement (QSEHRA) (Code Sec. 9831(d); Notice 2017-67). As a result, a small employer may offer a stand-alone HRA and reimburse employees with pre-tax dollars for the cost of individual health care coverage through a QSEHRA without incurring the penalty for failing to meet the group health plan requirements. A QSEHRA must limit payments or reimbursements for the year to $5,150 for employee-only coverage or $10,450 for family coverage for 2019 ($5,250 and $10,600, respectively, for 2020) (Rev. Proc. 2018-57; Rev. Proc. 2019-44). An eligible employer must furnish a written notice to its eligible employees at least 90 days before the beginning of a year for which the QSEHRA is provided.

Distributions from an HRA can only be used to reimburse the employee for his or her qualified medical expenses incurred during the coverage period. Qualified medical expenses are those specified in the plan that would generally qualify as an itemized deduction and incurred for the employee, spouse, dependent, or child under the age of 27 (¶ 1016). Nonprescription medicines (other than insulin) are not considered qualified medical expenses under an HRA for amounts paid before 2020. Over the counter medicines or drugs are considered qualified medical expenses under an HRA for amounts paid after 2019. In addition, menstrual care products paid or incurred after 2019 are eligible medical care expenses for purposes of an HRA (Code Sec. 106(f), amended by the Coronavirus Aid, Relief, and Economic Security (CARES) Act (P.L. 116-136)).

2041. Flexible Spending Arrangements (FSAs). A flexible spending arrangement (FSA) is an employer-established benefit program under which amounts credited to an employee's account may be used to reimburse the employee for health care, dependent care, or adoption expenses that would otherwise be excludable from the employee's gross income if paid by the employer (Prop. Reg. § 1.125-5). An FSA may be funded by employer contributions or by a salary reduction agreement with pre-tax dollars as part of a cafeteria plan (¶ 2045).

The plan must provide either a maximum dollar limit or maximum percentage of compensation that can be contributed through a cafeteria plan. In the case of a health FSA, the maximum contribution is limited to $2,700 for 2019 ($2,750 for 2020) (Code Sec. 125(i); Rev. Proc. 2018-57; Rev. Proc. 2019-44). If the plan allows salary reduction contributions to a health FSA in excess of the annual dollar amount, then the employee will be subject to tax on distributions from the health FSA. In the case of an adoption or dependent FSA, the maximum contribution is limited to the amount the employee could exclude under a adoption assistance program (¶ 2063) or dependent care assistance program (¶ 2065).

An FSA may not be used to defer compensation and any balance remaining in the account at the end of the plan year is generally forfeited (use-it-or-lose-it rule) (Prop. Reg. § 1.125-5(c); Notice 2005-42). However, a plan may permit a grace period of up to 2½ months after the end of the plan year (March 15 for calendar year plans) during which qualified expenses incurred during the period can be paid from any amounts left in the account at the end of the previous year. The employer is not permitted to refund any balance in an FSA account to an employee.

A cafeteria plan may also allow up to $500 of any balance remaining in a health FSA at the end of the year to be carried over to pay or reimburse qualified medical expenses incurred in the next year (Notice 2013-71). The carried over amount does not count against the maximum contribution an employee can make to the health FSA. Any unused amount in a health FSA at the end of the year in excess of $500 (or lower amount specified in the plan) is forfeited. A plan that adopts the carryover option may not also provide the 2½ month grace period.

Special Rules for Health FSAs. Health FSA plans must comply with the rules applicable to other accident and health plans, including the nondiscrimination requirements for highly compensated employees (¶ 2017). Distributions from a health FSA can only be used to reimburse the employee for qualified medical expenses incurred during the coverage period. Qualified medical expenses are those specified in the plan that would generally qualify as an itemized deduction and incurred for the employee, spouse, dependent, or child under the age of 27 (¶ 1016). Nonprescription medicines (other than insulin) are not considered qualified medical expenses under a health FSA for amounts paid before 2020. Over the counter medicines or drugs are considered qualified medical expenses under a health FSA for amounts paid after 2019. In addition, menstrual care products paid or incurred after 2019 are eligible medical care expenses for purposes of a health FSA (Code Sec. 106(f), amended by the Coronavirus Aid, Relief, and Economic Security (CARES) Act (P.L. 116-136)).

Qualified Reservist Distribution. A cafeteria plan may allow for distribution of any remaining balance of a health FSA for any reason to a participant who is called to active duty for a period of at least 180 days due to his or her membership in a reserve unit of the military (Code Sec. 125(h)). The distribution must be made between the date of the order and the last day for which reimbursements can be made during the plan year.

Family and Medical Leave Act. The Family and Medical Leave Act (P.L. 103-3) (FMLA) imposes certain requirements on employers regarding coverage, including family coverage, under group health plans for employees taking FMLA leave and regarding the restoration of benefits to employees who return from FMLA leave. Reg. § 1.125-3 provides guidance on the effect of the FMLA on the operation of cafeteria plans.

Cafeteria Plans

See CCH® AnswerConnect: *Cafeteria Plans* for more information on this topic.

2045. Cafeteria Plans. Cafeteria plans are employer-sponsored benefit packages that offer employees a choice between taking cash and receiving qualified benefits that may be excluded from gross income (Code Sec. 125; Prop. Reg. § 1.125-1). If a participant chooses cash, it is includible in gross income as compensation. If qualified benefits are chosen, they are excludable to the extent allowed under the Code. A cafeteria plan cannot offer anything other than cash or qualified benefits. An employer who maintains a cafeteria plan is required to file an information return, but the reporting requirement has been suspended indefinitely (Code Sec. 6039D; Notice 2002-24).

Cafeteria plan elections must be made before the start of the plan year and are generally irrevocable unless the employee experiences a change in status (i.e., marital status, number of dependents, etc.). However, an employer may permit elections regarding health care coverage to be revoked for (1) employees expected to average less than 30 hours of service per week who nevertheless are still eligible for coverage under the employer plan, and (2) employees who would like to cease employer coverage and buy health care coverage through an American Health Benefit Exchange (see later) without a period of duplicate or no coverage (Notice 2014-55).

A cafeteria plan may include any of the following qualified benefits: accident and health benefits (¶ 2015) including benefits under a flexible spending arrangement (FSA) (¶ 2041), adoption assistance benefits (¶ 2063), dependent care assistance benefits (¶ 2065), disability coverage (¶ 2025), group-term life insurance (¶ 2055), and health savings accounts (HSAs) (¶ 2035). A qualified benefit does *not* include benefits under an Archer medical savings accounts (MSAs) (¶ 2037), scholarships and fellowship grants (¶ 865), educational assistance benefits (¶ 2067), long-term care insurance (¶ 2019), or statutory fringe benefits under Code Sec. 132 (¶ 2085). A plan that provides deferred compensation is generally *not* included in the definition of a cafeteria plan. However, elective contributions under a qualified cash or deferred arrangement, profit-sharing plan, stock bonus plan, such as a 401(k) plan (¶ 2121), or contributions by an educational institution for post-retirement group life insurance are permitted.

Highly compensated employees (¶ 2114) are not entitled to exclude any benefit under a cafeteria plan attributable to a plan year in which the plan discriminates in favor of the highly compensated employees with respect to participation, contributions, and benefits. Key employees (¶ 2132) are not entitled to exclude any benefit attributable to a plan year in which the statutory qualified benefits provided to all key employees exceed 25 percent of the total of such benefits provided to all employees under the plan. In such cases, the benefits must be included in the gross income of the highly compensated employees or key employees for the tax year in which the plan year ends (Code Sec. 125(b)).

American Health Benefit Exchange Plans. An American Health Benefit Exchange (otherwise known as a Marketplace Exchange) and Small Business Health Options Program (SHOP) Exchange, run either by a state or the federal government, are generally available in every state and provide qualified individuals and small businesses with access to health plans, possibly at subsidized prices. Qualified health plans offered through such an exchange cannot be provided by employers through a cafeteria plan unless the employer is exchange-eligible (Code Sec. 125(f)(3)). An exchange-eligible employer is a small employer electing to make all of its full-time employees eligible for one or more qualified health plans offered in the small group market through an exchange (Act Sec. 1312(f)(2)(A) of the Patient Protection and Affordable Care Act (P.L. 111-148)).

A small employer is an employer who employed an average of at least one, but not more than 50, employees on business days during the preceding plan year and employs at least one employee on the first day of the current plan year. States have the option to treat employers with 51 to 100 employees as small employers (Act Sec. 1304(b)(2) of P.L. 111-148, as amended by Act Sec. 2(a) of the Protecting Affordable Coverage for Employees (PACE) Act (P.L. 114-60)). The small group market is the health insurance market that employees obtain health insurance coverage through a group health plan maintained by a small employer (Act Sec. 1304(a)(3) of P.L. 111-148). A state may expand the definition of an exchange-eligible employer to include large employers in addition to small employers (Act Sec. 1312(f)(2)(B) of P.L. 111-148).

2047. Simple Cafeteria Plans. Certain small employers can establish simple cafeteria plans under which the nondiscrimination requirements applicable to regular cafeteria plans (¶ 2045), as well as the nondiscrimination rules applicable to group-term life insurance (¶ 2055), accident and health plans (¶ 2015), and dependent care assistance programs (¶ 2065), are considered satisfied (Code Sec. 125(j)). A simple cafeteria plan is a cafeteria plan established and maintained by an eligible employer that meets certain contribution, eligibility, and participation requirements.

Eligible Employers. To be eligible to establish a simple cafeteria plan, an employer must have employed an average of 100 or fewer employees on business days during either of the two preceding years. An employer that was not in existence throughout the preceding year may be considered as an eligible employer if it reasonably expects to average 100 or fewer employees on business days during the current year. If an employer has 100 or fewer employees for the year and establishes a simple cafeteria plan, then it is treated as an eligible employer for any subsequent year even if the employer employs more than 100 employees in the subsequent year, unless the employer employs an average of 200 or more employees during the subsequent year.

¶2047

For purposes of determining the qualification of a business that has changed ownership, the fact that the previous owner had 100 or fewer employees in a preceding year is used to determine eligibility of the current ownership to establish a simple cafeteria plan. Also, all persons treated as a single employer for purposes of the work opportunity credit (¶ 1465G) or the deferred compensation rules for leased employees under Code Sec. 414(n) or (o) are treated as one person for purposes of simple cafeteria plans.

Contribution Requirements. The contribution requirements of a simple cafeteria plan are met if the employer is required by the plan to make a contribution to provide qualified benefits on behalf of each qualified employee in an amount equal to: (1) a uniform percentage of at least two percent of the employee's compensation for the year; or (2) at least six percent of the employee's compensation for the plan year or twice the amount of the salary reduction contributions of each qualified employee, whichever is less (Code Sec. 125(j)(3)). If the employer bases the satisfaction of the contribution requirements on the second option, it will not be treated as met if the rate of contributions with respect to any salary reduction contribution of a highly compensated (¶ 2114) or key employee (¶ 2132) is greater than that with respect to any other employee.

Employee Eligibility and Participation Requirements. The minimum eligibility and participation requirements of a simple cafeteria plan are met if all employees who had at least 1,000 hours of service for the preceding plan year are eligible to participate. In addition, each employee eligible to participate may elect any benefit under the plan, subject to terms and conditions applicable to all participants (Code Sec. 125(j)(4)). An employer may elect to exclude from the plan, regardless of the satisfaction of the 1,000 hour requirement, employees: (1) who have not attained the age of 21 before the close of the plan year; (2) who have less than one year of service with the employer; (3) who are covered under a collective bargaining agreement; or (4) who are nonresident aliens working outside the United States whose income did not come from a U.S. source.

Other Employee Benefits

See CCH® AnswerConnect: *Compensation and Benefits* for more information on this topic.

2055. Group-Term Life Insurance. An employee may exclude from gross income the cost of the first $50,000 of group-term life insurance on his or her life provided under a policy carried directly or indirectly by the employer (Code Sec. 79(a) and (c); Reg. §§ 1.79-1 and 1.79-3). The cost of coverage in excess of $50,000 is included in the employee's gross income and subject to employment taxes, reduced by any amount the employee paid toward the insurance. The cost in excess of $50,000 is not the employer's actual cost in providing coverage. Instead, the cost is determined under a Uniform Premium Table (see below) which provides a per-month premium cost for $1,000 of insurance based on the employee's age as of the end of the employee's tax year. The $50,000 limit relates to the group-term life insurance coverage which the employee receives during any part of the tax year.

In the case of a disabled or retired employee, the full cost of employer-provided group-term life insurance coverage is excluded from the employee's income (Code Sec. 79(b) and (d); Reg. § 1.79-2; Temp. Reg. § 1.79-4T). A full exclusion is also available if the employer or a charity is the beneficiary of the insurance benefits. On the other hand, a key employee (¶ 2132) must include the cost of all benefits he or she receives under a plan that does not satisfy nondiscrimination requirements. In addition, coverage on the life of the employee's spouse or dependents is not excluded unless it qualifies as a *de minimis* fringe benefit (¶ 2089).

Group-term life insurance is insurance that provides for a general death benefit that is excluded from gross income (¶ 803) and provided to a group of at least 10 full-time employees at some time during the year (Reg. § 1.79-1; IRS Pub. 15-B). An employee includes any current common-law employee, former employee, or leased employee, as well as a statutory employee who is a full-time salesperson. An employee does not include a self-employed person, partner, or two-percent or more S corporation shareholder. The amount of insurance provided to each employee must be computed under a formula that precludes individual selection. In addition, the policy must not provide any permanent benefits.

Table 1

Cost Per $1,000 of Protection for One-Month Period

Age	Cost
Under 25	5 cents
25 through 29	6 cents
30 through 34	8 cents
35 through 39	9 cents
40 through 44	10 cents
45 through 49	15 cents
50 through 54	23 cents
55 through 59	43 cents
60 through 64	66 cents
65 through 69	$1.27
70 and above	$2.06

Example: X Corp. pays the premiums on a $70,000 group-term insurance policy on the life of its president, Fox, who is 51 years old at the end of 2019. The IRS-established uniform cost for $1,000 of group-term coverage for twelve months is $2.76 ($0.23 × 12) (Reg. § 1.79-3(d)(2)). The cost of the policy includible in Fox's gross income is computed as follows:

Total insurance coverage	$70,000.00
Tax-free insurance	50,000.00
Insurance coverage subject to tax	$20,000.00
Taxable cost of policy includible in Fox's gross income ($2.76 × 20)	$55.20

2057. Split-Dollar Life Insurance. A split-dollar life insurance arrangement is an arrangement where the premiums, cash-surrender value, or death benefits are split between an owner and nonowner of a life insurance policy (Reg. § 1.61-22). Ownership and benefits are most often split between an employer and an employee, but they may also be split between a corporation and shareholder, or between family members. A split-dollar arrangement entered into, or materially modified after, September 17, 2003, is taxed under either the economic benefit rule or the loan rule depending upon which party owns the contract, and the relationship of the owner to the nonowner.

Owner of the Contract. The owner of a contract is generally the person named as the policy owner (Reg. § 1.61-22(c)). If two or more persons are named as policy owners and each has an undivided interest in every right and benefit, those persons are treated as owners of separate contracts. However, an employer is treated as the owner of the policy if the only benefit available under the arrangement is the value of the current life insurance protection (i.e., non-equity arrangement).

Economic Benefit Rule. Under the economic benefit rule, the owner of the life insurance contract is treated as transferring economic benefits to the nonowner (Reg. § 1.61-22(d)). Depending on the relationship between the parties, the economic benefits may constitute compensation, a distribution under Code Sec. 301, a gift, or another type of income. Both the owner and nonowner must account for the economic benefits fully and consistently, reduced by any consideration paid by the nonowner for the economic benefits. The economic benefit rule generally applies to compensatory arrangements in which the employer is the owner of the contract—for example, endorsement split-dollar arrangements, in which the employer is formally designated as the owner of the insurance contract and endorses the contract to specify the portion of the insurance proceeds payable to the employee's beneficiary (Reg. § 1.61-22(b)(3)(ii)). The value of the benefit provided under such an arrangement is the cost of any current life insurance protection provided to the employee (Reg. § 1.61-22(d)).

Loan Rule. Under the loan rule, the nonowner is treated as lending premium payments to the owner (Reg. § 1.7872-15). The rule generally applies to collateral assignments in which the employee is designated as the owner of the contract and the employer pays all or a portion of the premiums, the payment is a loan under general principals of federal tax law, and repayment is secured by the insurance policy's death benefits or cash surrender value. If a split-dollar loan does not provide for sufficient interest, the loan is a below-market split-dollar loan and is subject to the below market interest rules (¶ 795).

Deferred Compensation. Because certain types of split-dollar life insurance arrangements provide for deferred compensation, the requirements of Code Sec. 409A may apply (¶ 2197).

Pre-September 18, 2003, Arrangements. For a split-dollar arrangement entered into on or before September 17, 2003, or not materially modified thereafter, an employee is taxed on the value of economic benefits received. The economic benefit primarily consists of the value of the protection the employee receives over the premiums the employee pays. Certain other benefits might also be taxed, such as policy dividends received by the employee. The value of the economic benefit is determined using the P.S. 58 rate table contained in Rev. Rul. 55-747, the insurance company's lower published term rates, or the Table 2001 group-term rates (¶ 2055) (Notice 2002-8).

2059. Employer-Provided Vehicle. An employee who uses an employer-provided vehicle for more than *de minimis* personal use receives a taxable fringe benefit from his or her employer (Reg. § 1.61-21(a)). The fair market value (FMV) of the fringe benefit is included in the employee's wages for income and employment tax purposes, and may be deducted by the employer as compensation. The FMV is generally the cost to the employee of leasing a comparable car at a comparable price for a similar period in an arms-length transaction (Reg. § 1.61-21(b)(4)). Under certain conditions, the employer may elect to use one of the following special valuation rules: cents-per-mile valuation, commuting valuation, or automobile lease valuation (Reg. § 1.61-21(c)). Separate rules are used for valuing flights by an employee on employer-provided noncommercial aircraft.

Cents-Per-Mile Valuation. The value of the personal use of an employer-provided vehicle may be determined by multiplying personal use mileage by the standard mileage rate (58 cents per mile in 2019 and 57.5 cents per mile in 2020) (Reg. § 1.61-21(e); Rev. Proc. 2019-46; Rev. Proc. 2010-51; Notice 2019-2; Notice 2020-5). To use this rule, the employer must reasonably expect the vehicle to be regularly used in its business throughout the calendar year, and it is driven at least 10,000 miles during the year. Fuel provided by the employer must be valued separately, at either its FMV or at 5.5 cents per mile for miles driven in North America (Reg. § 1.61-21(d)(3)(ii)(B)). The maximum FMV of a vehicle for cents-per-mile valuation is limited to $50,400 for calendar year 2019 (there is no separate maximum value for trucks and vans for 2019) (Notice 2019-34).

Commuting Valuation. If certain requirements are met, the use of an employer-provided commuting vehicle is valued at $1.50 each way (i.e., to and from work), per employee (Reg. § 1.61-21(f)). Even if two or more employees commute in the vehicle such as a car pool, each employee includes $1.50 each way in income. To qualify, personal use of the vehicle must be *de minimis* and the employer must require the employee or employees to commute to and/or from work in the vehicle for bona fide noncompensatory business reasons.

Automobile Lease Valuation. The value of the personal use of an employer-provided car may be computed under annual lease value tables (Reg. § 1.61-21(d); Prop. Reg. § 1.61-21(d)). The annual lease value of an automobile is computed by first determining the FMV of the automobile on the first date it was made available to any employee for personal use. Under a safe-harbor, the employer's cost can be substituted for FMV provided certain conditions are met. FMV is reduced if an employee contributes an amount toward the purchase or lease of the automobile.

In addition, an employer with 20 or more vehicles may average the FMV of all vehicles and apply the fleet-average value to each vehicle. Recalculation of the fleet-average value is required every two years. All qualified vehicles added to the fleet must use the fleet-average value. The maximum FMV of a vehicle for fleet-averaging valuation is limited to $50,400 for calendar year 2019 (there is no separate maximum value for trucks and vans for 2019) (Notice 2019-34).

Once the FMV is established, the annual lease value table prepared by the IRS and reproduced below, is used to determine the annual lease value that corresponds to the FMV. The annual lease values include the FMV of maintenance and insurance for the automobile but do not include the cost of gasoline provided by the employer. The fuel provided can be valued either at its FMV or at 5.5 cents per mile for all miles driven within the United States, Canada, or Mexico by the employee. If continuous personal use of a company car is for less than a year, but at least 30 days, the employee may prorate the car's annual lease value. The values in the table are based on an assumed four-year lease term.

Automobile fair market value (1)	Annual Lease Value (2)
$ 0 to 999	$600
1,000 to 1,999	850
2,000 to 2,999	1,100
3,000 to 3,999	1,350
4,000 to 4,999	1,600
5,000 to 5,999	1,850
6,000 to 6,999	2,100
7,000 to 7,999	2,350
8,000 to 8,999	2,600
9,000 to 9,999	2,850
10,000 to 10,999	3,100
11,000 to 11,999	3,350
12,000 to 12,999	3,600
13,000 to 13,999	3,850
14,000 to 14,999	4,100
15,000 to 15,999	4,350
16,000 to 16,999	4,600
17,000 to 17,999	4,850
18,000 to 18,999	5,100
19,000 to 19,999	5,350
20,000 to 20,999	5,600
21,000 to 21,999	5,850
22,000 to 22,999	6,100
23,000 to 23,999	6,350
24,000 to 24,999	6,600
25,000 to 25,999	6,850
26,000 to 27,999	7,250
28,000 to 29,999	7,750
30,000 to 31,999	8,250
32,000 to 33,999	8,750
34,000 to 35,999	9,250
36,000 to 37,999	9,750
38,000 to 39,999	10,250
40,000 to 41,999	10,750
42,000 to 43,999	11,250
44,000 to 45,999	11,750
46,000 to 47,999	12,250
48,000 to 49,999	12,750
50,000 to 51,999	13,250
52,000 to 53,999	13,750
54,000 to 55,999	14,250
56,000 to 57,999	14,750
58,000 to 59,999	15,250

For vehicles having a fair market value in excess of $59,999, the Annual Lease Value is equal to: (0.25 × the fair market value of the automobile) + $500.

Employer-Provided Transportation Due to Unsafe Conditions. If it is unsafe for an employee, who would normally do so, to walk or use public transportation to get to work and certain other requirements are met, the employee includes only $1.50 per one-way commute ($3.00 per round trip commute) in income with respect to cab fare or an employer-provided vehicle (Reg. § 1.61-21(k)).

Chauffeur Services. The FMV of chauffeur services is determined separately from the value of the availability of an employer-provided automobile (Reg. § 1.61-21(b)(5)). The services of a chauffeur may generally be valued by reference to either (1) the FMV of these services as determined in an arm's-length transaction, or (2) the compensation of the chauffeur.

¶2059

Noncommercial Aircraft Flights. The value of personal flights, domestic or international, on employer-provided noncommercial aircraft is determined under the base aircraft valuation formula by multiplying the Standard Industry Fare Level (SIFL) flight mileage for the applicable period by an aircraft multiple based on weight, and adding a terminal charge (Reg. §1.61-21(g); Rev. Rul. 2019-10; Rev. Rul. 2019-22; Rev. Rul. 2020-10).

If a trip made primarily for business purposes includes business and personal flights, the excess of the value of all the actual flights over the value of the flights that would have been taken if there had been no personal flights is includible in gross income. If the trip is primarily personal, the value of the personal flights that would have been taken if there had been no business flights is includible in gross income. No amount is included in income if the employee takes a personal trip on a noncommercial aircraft and at least one-half of the aircraft's seating capacity is occupied by employees whose flights are primarily business related and excludable from income.

Frequent Flyer Miles. The IRS will not tax the personal use of airline frequent flyer miles or other in-kind promotional benefits attributable to the taxpayer's business or official travel. This relief does not apply to travel or other promotional benefits that are converted to cash, to compensation that is paid in the form of travel or other promotional benefits, or to other circumstances where these benefits are used for tax-avoidance purposes (Announcement 2002-18).

2063. Adoption Assistance Programs. An employee may exclude from gross income any payments or reimbursements received under an employer's written adoption assistance program for qualified adoption expenses paid or incurred by the employee for the adoption of an eligible child (Code Sec. 137). An adoption assistance program is a written plan that:

- benefits employees who qualify under rules set up by the employer which do not favor highly compensated employees (¶ 2114) or their dependents (¶ 137);

- does not pay more than five percent of its payments each year to shareholders or owners of more than five percent of the employer;

- provides for adequate notice to employees of their eligibility; and

- requires employees to provide reasonable substantiation of qualified expenses that are to be paid or reimbursed.

The rules for the exclusion generally parallel the rules for the adoption expense credit. Thus, an eligible child and qualified adoption expenses are defined as they are for purposes of the credit (¶ 1407). The aggregate amount of payments that may be excluded from income (for both special needs adoptions and other adoptions) is $14,080 for 2019 ($14,300 for 2020) (Rev. Proc. 2018-57; Rev. Proc. 2019-44). The exclusion is phased out for higher income taxpayers the same as for the adoption credit when modified adjusted gross income is between $211,160 and $251,160 for 2019 ($214,520 and $254,520 for 2020). The exclusion is calculated on Form 8839.

2065. Dependent Care Assistance Benefits. An employee may exclude from gross income amounts paid or incurred by an employer for dependent care assistance services provided to the employee under a written plan (Code Sec. 129). The maximum amount excluded cannot exceed $5,000 for the tax year ($2,500 if married filing separately). Any amount exceeding the limit is includible in the employee's gross income for the year in which the services are provided, even if the payment for the services is received in a subsequent year. The exclusion also cannot exceed the employee's earned income if unmarried, or earned income of the lower-earning spouse if married.

Dependent care assistance means the payment for services (or providing services) which if paid by the employee would entitle him or her to claim the child and dependent care credit (¶ 1401). Thus, the expenses must be incurred for household services for care of a child or other dependent to enable the employee to work. A dependent care assistance plan generally must not discriminate in favor of employees who are highly compensated (¶ 2114). If a plan would qualify as a dependent care assistance program except for the fact that it fails to meet discrimination, eligibility, or other requirements, it may still be treated as a dependent care assistance program in the case of employees who are not highly compensated.

The exclusion of dependent care assistance benefits does not apply unless the name, address, and taxpayer identification number (i.e., employer identification number) of the person performing the child or dependent care services are included on the return of the employee benefiting from the exclusion. The exclusion may be claimed even though the information is not provided if it can be shown that the taxpayer exercised due diligence in attempting to provide this information.

2067. Educational Assistance Programs. An employee may exclude from gross income up to $5,250 of educational assistance benefits received from his or her employer provided under an educational assistance program (Code Sec. 127, as amended by the Coronavirus Aid, Relief, and Economic Security (CARES) Act (P.L. 116-136); Reg. §§ 1.127-1 and 1.127-2). Educational assistance benefits include payments for tuition, fees and similar expenses, books, supplies, and equipment. Effective for payments made after March 27, 2020, and before January 1, 2021, it also includes payments by an employer to either an employee or a lender to be applied toward the principal or interest on any qualified student loan incurred by the employee for his or her education.

The exclusion is available for both undergraduate and graduate-level courses. Excludable assistance payments may not cover tools or supplies that the employee retains after completion of the course or the cost of meals, lodging, or transportation. Although the courses covered by the plan need not be job related, an exception applies to courses involving sports, games, or hobbies. These courses may only be covered if they involve the employer's business or are required as part of a degree program.

An educational assistance program is a separate written plan that provides educational assistance only to employees, subject to various limitations. An employee for this purpose includes a current employee, as well as a former employee who retired, left on disability, or was laid off. It also includes a partner who performs services for a partnership and a leased employee who has provided services on a substantially full-time basis for at least a year (Rev. Rul. 96-41). A program that provides benefits to a spouse or dependent of an employee is not a qualified program.

Reports and Records. An employer who maintains an educational assistance plan must maintain records and file an information return for the plan, but the reporting requirement has been suspended indefinitely (Code Sec. 6039D; Notice 2002-24).

2069. Employee Achievement Awards Excluded from Gross Income. An employee achievement award is excludable from an employee's gross income to the extent the cost of the award is deductible by the employer ($400 for nonqualified awards or $1,600 for qualified awards) (Code Sec. 74(c); Prop. Reg. § 1.74-2). See ¶ 919 for a discussion of the employer's deduction and the definition of an employee achievement award. If the cost of an award exceeds the dollar limitation, then the employee must include in gross income the greater of excess of the fair market value or the cost to the employer of the award over the dollar limitation, but not in excess of the fair market value of the award. The exclusion is not available for any award made by a sole proprietorship to the sole proprietor.

2071. Vacation Pay. A vacation pay plan is an employer plan that provides compensation to employees for specified periods of vacation, including vacation time that has been earned but not actually taken. Such a plan also generally includes compensation for specified holidays, whether or not those days are actually taken. Vacation pay plans, like other employee benefit plans, can take a wide variety of forms: the benefits may be vested or unvested; the plan may be funded or unfunded; and the plan may be a single-employer plan or a multiemployer plan.

Vacation pay received by an employee is included in gross income and subject to income tax withholding (Code Sec. 61; Reg. § 31.3401(a)-1(b)(3)). It is also subject to FICA and FUTA taxes (Code Secs. 3121(a) and 3306(b)). Vacation pay is generally deductible by an employer as reasonable compensation for prior services rendered (Code Sec. 162; Reg. § 1.162-7). See ¶ 1549 for a discussion of the accrual of vacation and sick leave pay. See ¶ 2073 for a discussion of employer-sponsored leaving programs.

2073. Leave Sharing Programs. An employee who deposits accrued leave in an employer-sponsored leave-sharing program for use by other employees adversely affected by a major disaster does not realize income or wages with respect to the deposited leave, provided the plan treats the amounts paid to the leave recipient as wages subject to income tax withholding and employment taxes (Notice 2006-59). The employee may not claim a charitable contribution, business expense, or loss deduction on account of the deposit of the leave or its use by a leave recipient.

Similarly, if an employee participates in a leave donation program under which he or she may elect to forgo vacation, sick, or personal leave in exchange for employer making cash contributions to charitable organizations, the contributing employee may not claim charitable contribution, business expense, or loss deduction for the contributed leave. However, the IRS will not assert that such cash payments constitute gross income or wages of the employee with respect to donations made to a charitable organization:

- before January 1, 2020, for relief of victims of Hurricane Michael in 2018;

- before January 1, 2019, for relief of victims of the California wildfires that began on October 8, 2017;

- before January 1, 2019, for relief of victims of Hurricane Harvey, Hurricane Irma, or Hurricane Maria in 2017;

- before January 1, 2018, for relief of victims of Hurricane Matthew; and

- before January 1, 2018, for relief of victims of severe storms and flooding in Louisiana that began on August 11, 2016 (Notice 2018-89; Notice 2017-70; Notice 2017-62; Notice 2017-52; Notice 2017-48; Notice 2016-69; Notice 2016-55).

Amounts deposited in a leave bank to be used by employees experiencing medical emergencies are not taxable to contributing employees but they are included in the gross income of the recipients subject to income tax withholding and employment taxes (Rev. Rul. 90-29). The IRS has not granted favorable tax treatment to other leave-sharing plans.

2075. Severance Pay. A severance pay plan is a plan that provides payments to employees upon termination of employment. Depending upon the facts and circumstances, severance pay arrangements can qualify as a welfare benefit plan (¶ 2011) or retirement plan (¶ 2111), or may be exempt from certain federal requirements. Generally, the payments are proportionate to length of employment. The plan may be a permanent program or a limited program—for example an "open-window" program that offers a group of employees cash payments, increased pension benefits, or both as inducements to voluntarily retire or to separate from employment within a certain time period. The plan may cover voluntary separations, involuntary separations, or both, and may place conditions on payment of benefits—for example no benefits are provided if the employee goes to work for a competitor or successor employer. In addition, the plan may deny benefits if the employee is terminated for cause.

Golden Parachutes. In a golden parachute agreement, a corporate employer states that it will pay a key employee (¶ 2132) or a number of key employees an amount over and above other compensation in the event of a change in ownership or control of the corporation or a substantial portion of the corporation's assets (¶ 907). The tax consequences applicable to golden parachute payments are triggered merely by the payment of the requisite amount of compensation, and a termination of employment is not literally required. As a practical matter, however, golden parachute payment provisions in an employment agreement or employer's benefits plan usually are designed to be triggered upon loss of employment within a designated period of time following the acquisition of the employer.

2077. Domestic Partner Benefits. Employers may offer benefits to an employee's domestic partner, including health care insurance (medical, dental, vision), access to an employee assistance plan, and dependent life insurance. Employers often require a written affidavit affirming the relationship and may require various documentation, such as joint mortgage or lease, proof of registration under a local ordinance, drivers' license, tax returns, bank statements, or joint credit statements.

A marriage of two individuals is recognized for federal tax purposes if the marriage would be recognized by the state, possession, or territory of the United States in which the marriage was entered into, regardless of where the individuals are domiciled (¶ 152). A marriage for federal tax purposes does not include a registered domestic partnership, civil union, or other similar relationship recognized under state law that is

20

HEALTH/BENEFITS

not denominated as a marriage under that state's law (Reg. § 301.7701-18). Thus, while employer-provided health benefits are tax free for spouses (including same-sex spouses) and dependents of an employee (¶ 2015), the cost of providing the benefit to a domestic partner who is not legally married to the employee or cannot be claimed as the employee's dependent (¶ 137) is included in the employee's gross income. Additionally, if a domestic partner is not the employee's spouse or dependent, contributions for a partner's coverage must be on an after-tax basis, and the domestic partner is not eligible for reimbursement from health care FSAs.

Fringe Benefits Under Code Sec. 132

See CCH® AnswerConnect: *Statutory Fringe Benefits Under Section 132* for more information on this topic.

2085. Fringe Benefits Under Code Sec. 132. Certain fringe benefits provided by an employer to an employee are excluded from an employee's gross income for income tax purposes, and from wages for purposes of income tax withholding and FICA and FUTA taxes (Code Sec. 132). These include: no-additional-cost services (¶ 2087), qualified employee discounts (¶ 2088), *de minimis* fringe benefits (¶ 2089), working condition fringe benefits (¶ 2090), qualified transportation fringe benefits (¶ 2091), qualified moving expense reimbursements (¶ 2092), qualified retirement planning services (¶ 2093), on-premises athletic facilities (¶ 2094), and qualified military base realignment and closure fringe benefits (¶ 2095). Employers providing fringe benefits must meet certain nondiscrimination requirements in order for such benefits to apply to favored groups.

Any fringe benefit that does not qualify for exclusion under Code Sec. 132, or any other Code provision, is includible in the recipient's gross income and wages at the excess of its fair market value over any amount paid by the employee for the benefit (unless excluded under another specific statutory provision) (¶ 713). Employers are generally allowed a trade or business expense deduction for the value, or a portion of the value, of the fringe benefit provided to employees (¶ 906).

For purposes of no-additional-cost services, qualified employee discounts, and on-premise athletic facilities, the exclusion under Code Sec. 132 applies to benefits provided to: (1) employees, their spouses, and dependent children; (2) former employees who separated from service because of retirement or disability, as well as their spouses and dependent children; (3) the widow or widower of a deceased employee; and (4) the dependent children of deceased employees (Code Sec. 132(h); Reg. § 1.132-1(b)). For purposes of working condition fringe benefits, the exclusion applies to benefits provided to employees, independent contractors, directors, and partners who perform services for a partnership.

2087. No-Additional-Cost Services. No-additional-cost services provided by an employer to employees are excluded from gross income and wages as a fringe benefit (¶ 2085) (Code Sec. 132(b); Reg. § 1.132-2). No-additional-cost services are free services provided to all employees by an employer where the employer incurs no substantial additional cost in providing the service, and the service is normally offered to the employer's customers in the line of business, such as free travel on a standby basis for airline employees. The exclusion is available only if the service is available to employees on a nondiscriminatory basis.

2088. Qualified Employee Discounts. Discounts provided to employees on their purchase of qualified property or services of their employer are excluded from gross income and wages as a fringe benefit (¶ 2085) (Code Sec. 132(c); Reg. § 1.132-3). Qualified employee discounts are discounts provided to all employees on the selling price of certain property or services in the ordinary line of business. In the case of merchandise, the discount cannot exceed the gross profit percentage of the price at which the property is offered to customers. For services, the discount cannot exceed 20 percent of the price at which the service is offered to customers. In order to be excluded, the discounts must be available to employees on a nondiscriminatory basis. Moreover, employees do not receive income if they pay at least fair market value for damaged, distressed, or returned property.

2089. *De Minimis* Fringe Benefits. If the value of any property or service provided to an employee is so minimal that accounting for the property or service would be unreasonable or administratively impracticable for an employer, it is a *de minimis* fringe benefit that is excluded from the employee's gross income and wages (¶ 2085) (Code Sec. 132(e); Reg. § 1.132-6). Examples include limited use of copy machines, occasional parties or picnics, meal money or transit fare due to overtime work, holiday gifts with a small market value, tickets occasionally provided for entertainment events, and employer-furnished coffee and doughnuts.

In determining whether the *de minimis* exclusion applies, the frequency with which similar fringe benefits are provided by an employer to its employees is taken into account. A subsidized eating facility operated by an employer for the benefit of employees is treated as a *de minimis* fringe benefit if the eating facility is located on or near the employer's business premises, and the revenue derived from such facility normally equals or exceeds the direct operating costs of such facility (Reg. § 1.132-7).

Meals and Lodging. Meals are excluded from an employee's gross income and wages as a *de minimis* fringe benefit if furnished on the business premises of the employer for the convenience of the employer (Code Sec. 119; Reg. § 1.119-1). Lodging is also excluded from an employee's gross income and wages if furnished for the convenience of the employer on the business premises of the employer, and as a condition of employment.

Meals are regarded as furnished for the convenience of the employer if they are furnished for a substantial noncompensatory business reason of the employer (even if the meals also serve a compensatory purpose). If more than one-half of the employees who are furnished meals by the employer are furnished meals for the convenience of the employer, then all meals furnished on the premises of the employer are considered to be for the convenience of the employer. Therefore, the meals are fully deductible by the employer, instead of possibly being subject to the 50-percent limit on business meal deductions, and excludable by the employees (¶ 916). The business premises of the employer for this purpose generally means the place of employment of the employee. It can include a camp located in a foreign country if an employee is furnished lodging (¶ 2406).

Faculty Housing. The value of campus lodging furnished to employees by educational or medical research institutions is excludable from the employee's gross income and wages if an adequate rental is charged. A rental is considered *inadequate* and thus the exclusion will not apply to the extent of the excess of: (1) the lesser of (a) five percent of the appraised value of the lodging or (b) an amount equal to the average of the rentals paid by nonemployees or nonstudents during the year for comparable lodging provided by the institution; over (2) the rent paid by the employee for the calendar year (Code Sec. 119(d)). The appraised value of lodging will be determined as of the close of the calendar year in which the tax year begins or, in the case of a rental period not greater than one year, at any time during the calendar year in which such period begins.

2090. Working Condition Fringe Benefits. Working condition fringe benefits provided to an employee may be excluded from gross income and wages as a fringe benefit (¶ 2085) provided the cost of the property or service would have been deductible by the employee as a business expense or depreciation had the employee paid for it on his or her own (Code Sec. 132(d); Reg. § 1.132-5). The general nondiscrimination rules applicable to fringe benefits do not apply to working condition fringes; therefore, they can be provided exclusively, or on more favorable terms, to executives. Examples of working condition fringes include use of a company vehicle, airplane transportation, travel expenses including meals and lodging, allowances for business use of cell phones, computers, internet service, entertainment, and club dues. Denial of a deduction to an employer for its payment of travel expenses of a spouse, dependent, or other individual accompanying an employee on business travel does not preclude those items from qualifying as working condition fringe benefits.

Employer-Provided Cell Phones. An employer-provided cell phone and similar equipment provided to an employee for noncompensatory business purposes is excluded from an employee's gross income and wages as a working condition fringe benefit (Notice 2011-72). In addition, the business substantiation requirements for the working condition fringe exclusion are automatically satisfied for a employer-provided cell-phone. A noncompensatory business purpose is any substantial reason relating to the employer's business, other than providing compensation, such as the employer's need to contact employees during work-related emergencies, or the employer's requirement that the employee be available to speak with clients away from the office or outside normal workday hours.

Personal use of an employer-provided cell-phone, provided primarily for noncompensatory business purposes, is excluded from an employee's gross income and wages as a *de minimis* fringe benefit (¶ 2089). Employers that require employees to use their personal cell phones primarily for noncompensatory business reasons may treat reimbursements of the employees' reasonable expenses as nontaxable. This does not mean, however, that cell phones used for primarily personal reasons are exempt from tax or from the substantiation requirements.

Employer-Provided Vehicles. The value of an employee's *business use* of an employer-provided automobile is excludable from the employee's gross income and wages as a working condition fringe benefit. The value of employee's *personal use* of an employer-provided automobile is generally included in the employee's income and wages (¶ 2059). The employer, however, may elect not to withhold income tax on the value of the employee's personal use (Code Sec. 3402(s)). The employer must notify the employee of the election, and must include the value of the benefit on a timely filed Form W-2. An employer who elects not to withhold income tax for an employer-provided automobile is still required to withhold FICA taxes.

2091. Qualified Transportation Fringe Benefits. Commuting expenses to and from a place of business and home are generally not deductible. However, qualified transportation fringe benefits provided by an employer to an employee may be excluded from the employee's gross income and wages as a fringe benefit (¶ 2085) (Code Sec. 132(f); Reg. § 1.132-9). A qualified transportation fringe benefit includes employer-provided transit passes, qualified parking, van pooling, and qualified bicycle commuting reimbursement for tax years beginning before 2018. The exclusion for qualified bicycle commuting reimbursements is suspended for tax years beginning in 2018 through 2025. An employer may not deduct expenses paid or accrued for qualified transportation fringe benefits after 2017; however, the fringe benefit exclusion rules still apply and the payments may continue to be excluded from an employee's wages (¶ 945).

For 2019, the maximum that may be excluded for qualified parking, transit passes, and van pooling is $265 per month (Rev. Proc. 2018-57). For 2020, the maximum that may be excluded for qualified parking, transit passes, and van pooling is $270 per month (Rev. Proc. 2019-44). The exclusion for qualified bicycle commuting reimbursement before 2018 is limited to a per employee limitation of $20 per month, multiplied by the number of qualified bicycle commuting months during the calendar year.

An employer may simultaneously provide an employee with a transit pass, qualified parking, and van pooling. However, an employee may not receive a bicycle commuting expense reimbursement for any month in which he or she receives any other qualified transportation fringe benefit. An employer who provides any qualified transportation fringe benefits to its employees may offer them a choice between cash and one or more qualified transportation benefits without causing the employees to lose the exclusion from income for noncash transportation fringe benefits. The amount of cash offered is includible in the employee's income only to the extent that the employee chooses the cash option.

Qualified parking for this purpose is parking provided on or near the business premises of the employer, or on or near a location from which the employee commutes to work by mass transit, in a commuter highway vehicle, or by car pool. It does not include parking on or near property used by the employee for residential purposes. Van pooling is transportation in a qualifying commuter highway vehicle if that transportation is in connection with travel between the employee's residence and the place of employment. A qualifying commuter vehicle must seat at least six adults (excluding the driver) and at least 80 percent of its mileage use must be reasonably expected to be for employees' commuting purposes and for trips when the vehicle is at least one-half full (excluding the driver).

2092. Qualified Moving Expenses Reimbursements. An employee generally may exclude any qualified moving expenses reimbursement from gross income and wages as a fringe benefit for tax years beginning before 2018 (¶ 2085) (Code Sec. 132(g)). The exclusion is not permitted in tax years 2018 through 2025 unless the taxpayer is a member of the U.S. Armed Forces on active duty who moves pursuant to a military order and incident to a permanent change. Reimbursements of qualified moving expenses received after December 31, 2017, for expenses that would have been deductible by the employee for a move occurring prior to January 1, 2018 may still be excluded by the employee (Notice 2018-75).

A qualified moving expense reimbursement includes any amount received, directly or indirectly, by the employee from the employer as payment or reimbursement of expenses that would be deductible as moving expenses if directly paid or incurred by the employee (¶ 1073). It does not include a payment for, or a reimbursement of, an expense actually deducted by the employee in a prior tax year. Expenses that would be deductible if paid directly or incurred by the employee include the reasonable expenses of moving household goods and personal effects from a former residence to a new residence, as well as the expense of traveling to the new residence, including lodging during the period of travel. Any nonqualified reimbursement of moving expenses received or accrued from an employer is included in the employee's gross income and wages (Code Secs. 82 and Code Sec. 3401(a)(15)).

2093. Qualified Retirement Planning Services. Qualified retirement planning services provided to an employee and his or her spouse by an employer that maintains a qualified plan are excludable from the employee's gross income and wages as fringe benefits (¶ 2085) (Code Sec. 132(m)). Qualified retirement planning services consist of retirement planning advice and information. The exclusion applies to a highly compensated employee (¶ 2114) only if retirement planning services are available on substantially the same terms to each member of the group of employees that is normally provided with education and information about the employer's qualified plan. In determining the exclusion's application to highly compensated employees, the IRS may allow employers to take into account employee circumstances other than compensation and position in providing advice to classifications of employees.

2094. Athletic Facilities. The value of an on-premises athletic facility provided by an employer is a fringe benefit (¶ 2085) that is excluded from an employee's gross income (Code Sec. 132(j)(4); Reg. § 1.132-1(e)(3)). The athletic facility must be located on the employer's premises, operated by the employer, and be used on a substantially exclusive basis by employees, their spouses, and dependent children. The athletic facility need not be located on the employer's business premises, only on premises owned or leased by the employer. However, the exclusion does not apply to any athletic facility that is a facility for residential use. In addition, employer-paid country club or health club memberships are not qualifying athletic facilities unless owned (or leased) and operated by the employer and substantially all the use of the facility is by employees, their spouses, and dependent children.

2095. Military Base Realignment and Closure Benefits. Qualified military base realignment and closure payments are excluded from an individual's gross income and wages as a fringe benefit (¶ 2085) (Code Sec. 132(n)). The exclusion applies to payments made under the Department of Defense Homeowners Assistance Program (HAP) as in effect February 17, 2009, where: (1) there was a base closure or realignment; (2) the property was purchased before July 1, 2006, and sold between July 1, 2006, and September 30, 2012; (3) the property is the owner's primary residence; and (4) the owner has not previously received benefits under HAP. The payments are intended to compensate military personnel and certain civilian employees for a reduction in the fair market value (FMV) of their homes resulting from military or Coast Guard base closure or realignment.

20 HEALTH/BENEFITS

Chapter 21

RETIREMENT PLANS

Types of Retirement Plans

See CCH® AnswerConnect: *Retirement Plans* for more information on this topic.

2101. Retirement Plans—Introduction. An employer may establish a pension, profit-sharing, or stock bonus plan that qualifies for certain benefits (Code Sec. 401). A qualified plan is entitled to certain tax benefits, including: (1) a tax exemption for the trust established to provide benefits (Code Sec. 501(a); Reg. § 1.401(f)-1(c)(1)); (2) a current deduction by the employer for contributions made to the trust (¶ 2117) and (3) tax deferral for the employee on the employer's contributions and earnings (¶ 2123). To receive these benefits, an employer-provided retirement plan must meet the qualification requirements of Code Sec. 401 (¶ 2111).

There are two broad categories of qualified retirement plans: defined contribution plans and defined benefit plans. Defined contribution plans include profit-sharing, stock bonus, and money purchase plans in which a separate account is provided for each employee covered by the plan. The employee's retirement benefit is based on the contributions to the account, as well as any income, expenses, gains, losses, and any forfeitures of other accounts that may be allocated to the account (Code Sec. 414(i)). Defined benefit plans include pension and annuity plans that offer a specific retirement benefit to employees, usually in the form of a monthly retirement pension based on a formula that takes the employee's wages and years of service into account (Code Sec. 414(j)). An employer's annual contributions to the plan are based on actuarial assumptions and are not allocated to individual accounts maintained for the employees (Reg. § 1.401-1(b)(1)(i)).

As an alternative to a qualified plan, an employer may establish and contribute to an individual retirement account (IRA) based plan such as a savings incentive match plan for employees (SIMPLE IRA) (¶ 2181) or simplified employee pension (SEP) (¶ 2189), or an employer may merely enable employees to choose to make direct contributions via payroll deductions to an IRA they have established. An eligible small business with 100 or fewer employees may claim a credit for the start-up costs incurred in establishing certain benefit plans (¶ 1465U). Outside the employment relationship, individuals who have compensation during a year may contribute to a traditional IRA (¶ 2155) or a Roth IRA (¶ 2171) to save for retirement. Educational employers (¶ 2191) and tax exempt and government employers (¶ 2193) may establish specialized plans. All of these plans and accounts mirror the tax treatment accorded to qualified plans: current deduction for the employers, tax-free accumulation of earnings, and deferral of tax for the participant until the benefits are received. Rules vary, but they tend to favor nondiscriminatory benefits that reach rank and file employees.

Nonqualified deferred compensation plans are different. In general, the employer's deduction is matched to the tax year of the service provider's inclusion in income. These plans are typically aimed narrowly at executives or directors rather than rank and file employees, and are often conditioned on performance (¶ 2197).

2102. Profit-Sharing and Money Purchase Plans. A profit-sharing retirement plan is a type of defined contribution plan (¶ 2101) to which the employer makes discretionary contributions, so long as the plan provides a definite formula for allocating the contributions among participants and distributing accumulated funds (Code Sec. 401(a)(27); Reg. §1.401-1(b)(1)(ii)). The term "profit-sharing plan" is a misnomer because the employer does not have to make a profit for the year in order to make a contribution (unless the individual is self-employed) and the plan may be maintained by a tax-exempt organization. In fact, the employer is not required to contribute every year or any particular percentage of profits or other particular amount, but contributions must be substantial and recurring. A profit-sharing plan can also be coordinated with the employer's paid time off plan so that the cash value of each employee's unused time off, either at the end of each year or at the termination of the employee's employment, is contributed to the employee's account under the plan as an employer contribution or as an elective deferral by the employee (¶ 2104). In either case, the contributions are subject to the generally applicable nondiscrimination rules (¶ 2114) and limits on contributions (¶ 2115).

A money purchase plan is a type of defined contribution plan that operates like a profit-sharing plan except that the employer's annual contributions are fixed under the terms of the plan (Reg. §1.401-1(b)(1)(i)). For example, under a money purchase plan, the employer may be required to contribute five percent of each participating employee's wages, regardless of whether the employer shows a profit for the year.

2103. Stock Bonus Plans and ESOPs. A stock bonus plan is a defined contribution plan (¶ 2101) that must generally follow the same rules as a profit-sharing plan (¶ 2102) except that distributed benefits usually are in the form of employer stock (Reg. §1.401-1(b)(1)(iii)). An employee stock ownership plan (ESOP) is a special type of stock bonus plan that provides special tax advantages including the following (Code Secs. 409 and 4975(e)(7)):

- An ESOP will qualify for an exemption from certain prohibited transaction rules that apply in the case of loans made by disqualified persons to qualified plans (¶ 2136) (Code Sec. 4975(d)(3)).

- Under some circumstances, a shareholder, other than a C corporation, may elect not to recognize gain on the sale of qualified securities to an ESOP (Code Sec. 1042). Nonrecognition depends upon the shareholder purchasing qualified replacement property within a specific period of time.

- A C corporation is entitled to a deduction for dividends on its stock held by an ESOP that are: (1) paid in cash directly to participants in the ESOP, (2) paid to the ESOP and subsequently distributed to the participants in cash no later than 90 days after the end of the plan year in which the dividends are paid to the ESOP, or (3) used to repay an ESOP loan (Code Sec. 404(k)). In addition, a C corporation may deduct dividends that are, at the election of plan participants or their beneficiaries, paid to an ESOP and reinvested in qualified employer securities.

- Contributions to an ESOP that are used to pay the principal on loans that were incurred to purchase employer securities may be deducted to the extent that they do not exceed 25 percent of the compensation paid to participants (Code Sec. 404(a)(9)). This contribution rule does not apply to S corporations.

2104. 401(k) Plans (Cash or Deferred Arrangements). A profit-sharing (¶ 2102) or stock-bonus (¶ 2103) retirement plan can include a cash or deferred arrangement (CODA) under which each participating employee has the option of receiving an amount of their compensation in cash or having it contributed pre-tax to the plan (Code Secs. 401(k), as amended by the Setting Every Community Up for Retirement Enhancement (SECURE) Act of 2019 (P.L. 116-94) and 402(e)(3); Reg. §§1.401(k)-1 and 1.402(a)-1(d)). The contribution is referred to as an elective contribution or elective deferral. A profit-sharing or stock-bonus plan with this type of arrangement is known as a 401(k) plan. If the plan meets certain requirements, the normal constructive receipt rules are preempted and the employees do not have to recognize the deferred amounts immediately in gross income. Certain eligible employers (¶ 2187) may also adopt a savings incentive match plan for employees (SIMPLE) option as part of a 401(k) plan. Generally, a SIMPLE 401(k) must meet the same requirements that apply to other 401(k) plans except for the nondiscrimination and top-heavy rules. It is also subject to special rules on contributions, deductions, and vesting (¶ 2185).

A partnership may maintain a 401(k) plan and individual partners may make elective deferrals to the plan based on their compensation for the services they provide to the partnership (Reg. §1.401(k)-1(a)(6)(i)). A sole proprietor is also permitted to maintain a 401(k) plan with elective deferrals based on net earnings from the business. In fact, many self-employed individuals will find that their tax deductible contributions to a 401(k) plan will be greater than those allowed to other types of self-employed retirement plans (¶ 2107). The Federal Thrift Savings Plan provides federal employees with the same savings and tax benefits that private employers offer their employees with 401(k) plans (¶ 2110).

A 401(k) plan must meet the following specific requirements, in addition to the general requirements for all qualified plans (¶ 2111):

- the plan must not require as a condition of participation that an employee complete more than one year of service with the employer, generally at least 1,000 hours during a 12-month period but for plan years beginning after 2020 the plan must offer participation to employees who work at least 500 hours in three consecutive 12-month periods and who are at least age 21 by the close the third 12-month period (Code Sec. 401(k)(2)(D) and (k)(15)(C), as added and amended by P.L. 116-94);

- the plan must not condition any other employee benefit (apart from matching contributions) upon an employee's election to make contributions to the 401(k) plan;

- the plan must provide that the participant's right to the value of his or her account that is attributable to elective contributions be fully vested at all times;

- the plan must not provide for distributions merely by reason of a stated period of participation or the lapse of a fixed number of years; and

- the plan must be prohibited from distributing amounts attributable to elective contributions of a plan participant *earlier* than:

  — the participant' severance from employment, death, or disability;

  — termination of the plan without establishment or maintenance of another defined contribution plan (¶ 2101) (Code Sec. 401(k)(10));

  — attainment of age 59½ by the plan participant;

  — hardship of the participant (¶ 2129), except that distributions after age 59½ or for hardship are not permitted in the case of a money purchase pension plan; or

  — for plan years beginning after 2019, 90 days prior to the date that any lifetime income investment may no longer be held as an investment option (¶ 2125).

A 401(k) plan that includes a qualified Roth contribution program (¶ 2121) may permit a qualified rollover contribution from a participant's non-Roth account to the participant's designated Roth account within the same plan (¶ 2147) (Code Sec. 402A(c)(4)(B)).

2105. Pension and Annuity Plans. A pension or annuity plan is a employer-provided defined benefit plan (¶ 2101) providing specific benefits to an employee or beneficiaries generally in the form of an annuity based on a formula reflecting the compensation and years of service of the employee. For example, under a flat benefit plan, the benefit for each participant is a fixed dollar amount, as long as a minimum number of years of service is reached. A formula for this type of plan could base a monthly retirement benefit upon a flat percentage of monthly compensation. On the other hand, under a unit benefit plan, greater benefits are generally provided for a long-service employee than for a short-term employee with the same average compensation. A formula for this type of plan could be a monthly retirement benefit based on a percentage of monthly compensation multiplied by years of service.

In either case, the employer (or other sponsor) must make required minimum contributions to the plan based on actuarial assumptions and calculations of the amount necessary to fund the promised benefits (¶ 2133). Employee contributions are sometimes required or voluntary. Instead of funding the plan directly, an employer may buy an insurance policy or annuity contract to fund the plan (Code Secs. 403(a)(1) and 404(a)(2)). Employers with 500 or fewer employees may establish a plan that combines a defined benefit plan with a 401(k) plan (¶ 2109).

2106. IRA-Based Retirement Plans. In addition to individuals being able to set up an individual retirement account (IRA) (¶ 2155 and ¶ 2171), an employer may also establish and contribute to an IRA-based plan for providing retirement benefits to employees. In these arrangements, a separate IRA account is established and maintained on behalf of each participating employee. The employer's contributions to the accounts are deductible as compensation, but generally are not recognized as income by the employee until distributed. There are three types of IRA-based plans. Under a simplified employee pension (SEP) plan, the employer makes contributions directly to a traditional IRA (called a SEP-IRA) set up by or for each eligible employee (¶ 2189). Certain eligible employers may also establish a savings incentive match plan for employees (SIMPLE) in which employees are allowed salary reduction contributions to an IRA and the employer makes matching or nonelective contributions to the account (¶ 2181). Under a payroll deduction IRA, an employer may establish a traditional or Roth IRA to which an employee authorizes a payroll deduction to be contributed to the account.

2107. Retirement Plans Covering Self-Employed Participants. No distinction is generally made between pension, profit-sharing, and other retirement plans (¶ 2101) established by corporations and those established by partnerships and sole proprietors. Retirement plans maintained by self-employed individuals are generally referred to by the name used for that particular plan type—SEP-IRA (¶ 2189), self-employed 401(k) plan (¶ 2104), or SIMPLE IRA (¶ 2181).

Even though there is general parity between retirement plans established by a self-employed individual and plans established by other business entities, special rules have to be considered. For example, the term "employee" generally includes a participant in a plan of an unincorporated enterprise who is a partner or a sole proprietor (Code Sec. 401(c)). When references are made to the employer, a sole proprietor is treated as his or her own employer. A partnership is considered to be the employer of each partner. As a result, sole proprietors may establish their own retirement plans. Only a partnership may establish a retirement plan for its partners.

Contributions and deductions for a self-employed participant covered by a qualified plan are subject to the same basic rules that apply to participants who are common law employees. However, a special computation must be made to figure the maximum deduction for contributions made by a self-employed taxpayer as an employer for himself or herself. Generally, the deduction limits are based, in part, on the compensation paid to eligible employees participating in the plan. For this purpose, a self-employed individual's compensation is his or her earned income, defined as the net earnings from self-employment (¶ 2670) reduced by: (1) the deduction allowed for contributions made on behalf of the self-employed participant, and (2) the deduction from gross income that is allowed for 50 percent of the self-employment tax paid by the self-employed participant (¶ 923) (Code Sec. 401(c)(2)(A)).

Since a self-employed individual's deductions for contributions on his or her own behalf and his or her net earnings are dependent on each other, the deduction for the taxpayer's own contributions must be determined indirectly by reducing the contribution rate provided in the plan (referred to as the percentage equivalent adjustment). IRS Pub. 560 provides a rate table or rate worksheet to determine the reduced contribution rate for this purpose, depending on whether the plan's contribution rate is a whole percentage or not. For example, under the rate table, if the maximum plan contribution rate is 15 percent, the maximum deduction percentage for contributions to the self-employed individual's own plan is 13.0435 percent, while the 15 percent rate applies to other employees. Similarly, if the plan's maximum contribution rate is 25 percent, a 20 percent rate applies to the self-employed individual, and the 25 percent rate applies to other employees.

401(k) Plan for the Self Employed. The same rules that apply to 401(k) plans established by other businesses generally apply to the 401(k) plans of self-employed individuals (¶ 2104) (Reg. § 1.401(k)-1(a)(6)(i)). This makes a 401(k) plan more advantageous than other types of self-employment plans because the taxpayer may make both employer contributions and elective employee contributions subject to the general limit for additions to defined contributions plans (¶ 2115). Self-employed 401(k) plans may also offer the possibility of being able to make loans to participating employees (¶ 2152).

Retirement Contribution for Partner. A partnership's deduction for retirement contributions on behalf of a partner must be allocated solely to that partner (Reg. §1.404(e)-1A(f)). It cannot be allocated among all of the partners pursuant to the partnership agreement (¶ 428).

Deduction of Contributions. Contributions to a qualified plan on behalf of a self-employed individual who is treated as an employee are considered to be ordinary and necessary expenses. They are deductible to the extent of the individual's earned income from the trade or business and not allocated to the purchase of life, accident, health, or other insurance (Code Sec. 404(a)(8)(C)). The contributions are not deductible on Schedule C (Form 1040) or Form 1065, and are also not deductible in calculating self-employment tax (¶ 2670). For a sole proprietorship, the contribution is deducted from gross income in calculating adjusted gross income (AGI) on Form 1040 (an above-the-line deduction) (Code Sec. 62(a)(6)). For a partnership, the contribution is shown on Schedule K-1 (Form 1065) and deducted from gross income on the partner's Form 1040 (¶ 431).

2108. Hybrid Benefit Plans. There are several types of hybrid plans that combine elements of defined contribution plans and defined benefit plans (¶ 2101).

Cash Balance Plans. Cash balance plans are hybrid defined benefit plans that provide guaranteed benefits for employees that are insured by the Pension Benefit Guaranty Corporation (PBGC). These plans establish a separate hypothetical account for each employee. The employer credits a specified percentage of compensation to each account, as well as interest earned to mimic the allocations of actual contributions under a defined contribution plan such as a money purchase plan. The amounts to be contributed are actuarially determined to ensure sufficient funds to provide the promised benefit. If at retirement the balance in a participant's account is less than the amount promised by the employer, the participant will receive the promised amount. A participant may elect to receive his or her benefit in a lump-sum or as an annuity. Since benefits are not based solely on actual contributions and forfeitures allocated to an employee's account and the actual investment experience and expenses of the plan allocated to the account, the arrangement is treated as a defined benefit plan rather than as a defined contribution plan. Accordingly, the plan is required to provide definitely determinable benefits, use a fixed interest rate, and adhere to the minimum funding standards.

Floor Offset Plans. A floor offset plan is a defined contribution plan with a defined benefit floor. Under such a plan, an employee who leaves employment before retirement age receives the amount in his or her individual account. An employee who continues to work until retirement receives the greater of the defined contribution accumulation or the promised defined benefit pension. The defined contribution and defined benefit portions of the combined floor-offset plan must comply with statutory requirements applicable to both plans (i.e., the actuarial equivalence rule governing lump-sum distributions of accrued benefits).

Pension Equity Plans. Under a pension equity plan (PEP plan), benefits accrue on a level basis. An employee earns credits for each year he or she worked. Upon termination, the employee receives a lump-sum payment or annuity based on accumulated credits and final average pay.

Target Benefit Plan. A target benefit plan is a plan under which an employer establishes a target benefit for its employees but where each employee's actual benefit is based on the amount in his or her individual account. The IRS defines a target benefit plan as a money purchase pension plan (¶ 2102) in which:

(1) the plan indicates a stated benefit commencing at the plan's normal retirement date;

(2) contributions necessary to fund the stated benefit with respect to a participant are determined under the individual level premium funding method using actuarial assumptions or factors stated in the plan;

(3) the contributions, and any forfeitures reducing those contributions, are allocated and separately accounted for with respect to each such participant; and

(4) the benefits provided under the plan are provided solely from the contribution amounts allocated in item (3), employee contributions and any income, expenses and gains, reduced by any losses.

Because it is a money purchase pension plan, it is considered a defined contribution plan. However, the employer contributions are determined actuarially, as though the plan were a defined benefit plan. The employer does not guarantee the targeted amount; its only obligation is to pay whatever benefit can be provided by the amount in the participant's account.

Small Employer Combined Plans. Small employers may establish a combined qualified retirement plan that consists of a defined benefit plan and a defined contribution plan incorporating a cash or deferred arrangement (401(k) plan) (¶ 2109).

2109. Defined Benefit and 401(k) Plans (DB/K Plans). Small employers may establish a combined defined benefit/401(k) plan (a "DB/K" plan) under which the relevant Code provisions are applied separately to the defined benefit (¶ 2101) portion of the plan and the 401(k) portion (¶ 2104) (Code Sec. 414(x)). A small employer for this purpose is an employer who employed an average of at least two but not more than 500 employees on business days during the preceding calendar year, and who employs at least two employees on the first day of the plan year.

The assets of the DB/K plan must be held in a single trust and must be clearly identified and allocated to the defined benefit plan and the applicable defined contribution plan to the extent necessary for the separate application of the Code and ERISA. Thus, for example, the Code Sec. 415 limitations apply separately to contributions under the 401(k) plan and to benefits under the defined benefit plan, both of which are part of the DB/K plan (¶ 2115). Similarly, the spousal protection rules apply to the defined benefit plan but not to the 401(k) plan. The DB/K plan must also meet certain benefit, contribution, vesting, and nondiscrimination requirements.

Defined Benefit Plan Requirements. A defined benefit plan that is part of a DB/K plan must provide each participant with a benefit of not less than the applicable percentage of the participant's final average pay. For this purpose, final average pay is determined using the consecutive-year period (not exceeding five years) during which the participant has the greatest aggregate compensation. The applicable percentage is the lesser of one percent multiplied by the participant's years of service or 20 percent (Code Sec. 414(x)(2)(B)(i) and (ii)). Any benefits provided under a defined benefit plan that is part of a DB/K plan (including any benefits provided in addition to required benefits) must be fully vested after three years of service (Code Sec. 414(x)(2)(D)(i)).

Cash Balance Plans. A special rule applies to an applicable defined benefit plan, under which the accrued benefit is calculated as the balance of a hypothetical account or as an accumulated percentage of the participant's final average compensation, and which meets certain interest credit requirements (Code Sec. 414(x)(2)(B)(iii) and (iv)). The plan is treated as meeting the benefit requirement if each participant receives a pay credit for each plan year of not less than a certain percentage of compensation that is determined based on the participant's age. If the participant is age 30 or less, then the percentage is two percent; if the participant is over age 30 but less than age 40, then the percentage is four percent; if the participant is age 40 or over but less than age 50, then the percentage is six percent; and if the participant is age 50 or over, the percentage is eight percent. A defined benefit plan that is part of a DB/K plan must provide the required benefit to each participant, regardless of whether the participant makes elective deferrals to the applicable defined contribution plan that is part of the DB/K plan.

Defined Contribution Plan Requirements. Certain automatic enrollment and matching contribution requirements must be met with respect to a 401(k) plan that is part of a DB/K plan. First, the qualified cash or deferred arrangement under the plan must constitute an automatic contribution arrangement (Code Sec. 414(x)(2)(C)(i)(I)). It generally must provide that each employee eligible to participate in the arrangement is treated as having elected to make elective contributions in an amount of four percent of the employee's compensation. The employee, however, may elect not to make the contributions or to make contributions at a different rate. The automatic contribution arrangement must also meet certain notice requirements (Code Sec. 414(x)(5)(B)).

Second, the employer must make matching contributions on behalf of each employee eligible to participate in the arrangement in an amount equal to 50 percent of the employee's elective deferrals, but no more than four percent of the compensation. The rate of matching contributions with respect to any elective deferrals for highly compensated employees (¶ 2114) must not be greater than the matching contribution rate for non-highly compensated employees. Matching contributions in addition to the required matching contributions can also be made (Code Sec. 414(x)(2)(C)(i)(II)).

The employer can also make nonelective contributions under the 401(k) plan. These contributions, however, are not taken into account in determining whether the matching contribution requirement is met (Code Sec. 414(x)(2)(C)(ii)). Matching contributions under the 401(k) plan (including contributions in excess of the required matching contributions) are fully vested when made, while nonelective contributions are fully vested after three years of service.

2110. Federal Thrift Savings Plan. The Federal Thrift Savings Plan (TSP) provides employees of the federal government with the same savings and tax benefits that private employers offer their employees with 401(k) plans (¶ 2104) (Code Sec. 7701(j)). However, nondiscrimination rules that apply to cash or deferred arrangements do not apply to the TSP.

Qualified Plan Requirements

See CCH® AnswerConnect: *Retirement Plans* for more information on this topic.

2111. Qualified Retirement Plan Requirements—Introduction. A qualified retirement plan is a pension plan that features a tax-exempt trust to which employers contribute. The contributions are currently deductible, earnings accumulate tax-free, and participants are taxed on the payment of benefits. To be a qualified plan, the plan must be written, permanent, and for the exclusive benefit of employees and their beneficiaries. In addition, the plan must satisfy the requirements of Code Sec. 401 regarding:

- participation and coverage (¶ 2112);
- minimum vesting standards (¶ 2113);
- nondiscrimination requirements for contributions and benefits (¶ 2114);
- limitations on contributions and benefits (¶ 2115);
- deduction of employer contributions (¶ 2117);
- elective deferrals to 401(k) and other plans (¶ 2121);
- distributions of benefits (¶ 2125);
- minimum distribution requirements (¶ 2127);
- payment of joint and survivor annuities (¶ 2130);
- anti-assignment of benefits (¶ 2131);
- top-heavy plans (¶ 2132);
- minimum funding standards (¶ 2133); and
- prohibited transactions of retirement plans (¶ 2136).

The annual accounting period adopted by the plan is called the plan year and it may or may not coincide with the employer's tax year. If there is a trust associated with plan, then it must be a valid written domestic trust established by the employer. A plan that is out of compliance risks losing its qualified status causing, among other things, participants to be taxed immediately for current and past employer contributions, the trust income becoming taxable, and rollovers being prohibited (¶ 2101).

A defective retirement plan or a plan with a disqualifying provision may be cured by the adoption of a retroactive remedial amendment, whether the defect was in the plan as originally adopted or was the result of a later amendment that caused the plan to fail to satisfy the requirements of Code Sec. 401. Effective for plan years beginning after December 31, 2019, an employer that adopts a qualified plan after the close of a tax year but before the due date for filing its return for the tax year (including extensions) may treat the plan as having been adopted as of the last day of the tax year (Code Sec. 401(b), as amended by Setting Every Community Up for Retirement Enhancement (SECURE) Act of 2019 (P.L. 116-94)).

Not all employer-sponsored pension plans are Code Sec. 401 qualified plans. Such plans include Code Sec. 403(b) annuity plans for educational employers (¶ 2191), Code Sec. 457 plans for government and tax-exempt employers (¶ 2193), and IRA-based plans for small employers (¶ 2181 and ¶ 2189). These plans are taxed similarly to qualified plans, and they are subject to similar though simplified participation, coverage, and nondiscrimination requirements.

2112. Participation and Coverage Requirements for Retirement Plans. A qualified retirement plan (¶ 2111) must satisfy minimum participation and coverage requirements (Code Sec. 410).

Participation. The minimum participation requirement provides that a qualified plan may generally not condition an employee's participation in the plan on the completion of more than one year of service or being older than age 21, whichever occurs later (Code Sec. 410(a)). Once these conditions are met, an employee must be eligible to participate within six months or, if earlier, by the first day of the plan's next accounting year. Participation may be conditioned on completion of two years of service if, after no more than two years of service, each participant has a vested right to their entire accrued benefit under the plan

Coverage. The minimum coverage requirement limits the ability of a plan to adopt employee classification standards that disproportionately favor highly compensated employees (¶ 2114) in comparison to non-highly compensated employees. The requirement may be met in one of two ways:

- *Ratio percentage test*—The percentage of rank-and-file employees who benefit from the plan divided by the percentage of highly compensated employees who benefit must equal at least 70 percent (Code Sec. 410(b)(1); Reg. § 1.410(b)-2(b)(2)).

- *Average benefit test*—The plan must benefit employees under a classification set up by the employer and found by the IRS not to discriminate in favor of highly compensated employees. In addition, the average benefit percentage for non-highly compensated employees must be at least 70 percent of the average benefit percentage for highly compensated employees. An employee's benefit percentage comprises the employer-provided contributions (including forfeitures) or benefits under all qualified plans of the employer, expressed as a percentage of the employee's compensation (Code Sec. 410(b)(2); Reg. § § 1.410(b)-2, 1.410(b)-4, and 1.410(b)-5).

A defined benefit plan (¶ 2101) must also benefit at least the lesser of: 50 employees, or the greater of 40 percent of all employees or two employees (one employee if there is only one employee) (Code Sec. 401(a)(26)).

2113. Vesting Requirements for Retirement Plans. A qualified retirement plan (¶ 2111) must satisfy minimum vesting requirements (Code Sec. 411(a)). Employee contributions must be vested (i.e., nonforfeitable) at all times, including those made through elective deferral of compensation (¶ 2121).

For defined contribution plans (¶ 2101), employer contributions (including matching contributions) must be vested at least as quickly as they would be under one of the following methods:

- *Graded Vesting*—20 percent of an employee's accrued benefit derived from employer contributions must vest after two years of service and an additional 20 percent must vest after each additional year of service; after six years of service, the employee must be 100 percent vested;

- *Cliff Vesting*—an employee has no vested interest in the accrued benefit derived from employer contributions until the employee has completed three years of service, but then must be 100 percent vested.

For defined benefit plans (¶ 2101), all employees' interests in their accrued benefits derived from employer contributions must vest at least as quickly as they would under either a three-to-seven-year graded vesting schedule or a five-year cliff vesting schedule.

2114. Nondiscrimination Requirements for Retirement Plans. A qualified retirement plan (¶ 2111) must provide either contributions or benefits that do not discriminate in favor of highly compensated employees (Code Sec. 401(a)(4)). This is satisfied if: (1) either the contributions or benefits provided are nondiscriminatory in amount; (2) the benefits, rights, and features under the plan are available in a nondiscriminatory manner; and (3) the plan is nondiscriminatory in effect, including plan amendments, terminations, and grants of past service credit.

Highly Compensated Employees. An employee is generally considered highly compensated for this purpose if he or she: (1) was a five-percent owner at any time during the current or preceding year, or (2) had compensation from the employer for the preceding year in excess of $125,000 for 2019 ($130,000 for 2020) (Code Sec. 414(q)(1); Notice 2018-83; Notice 2019-59). The employer may elect to limit employees treated as highly compensated employees under item (2) to those who are in the top 20 percent of employees when ranked on the basis of compensation paid during the year. Part-time employees, minors, union members, and employees who work less than six months during the year may be excluded from the top-paid group.

Actual Contribution Percentage (ACP) Test. A special nondiscrimination test applies to employee contributions and matching contributions by employers to a qualified plan (Code Sec. 401(m); Reg. § 1.401(m)-1). Matching contributions are those made by the employer on account of a contribution by a participant or because of an elective contribution by a participant under a 401(k) plan. The test is satisfied if the actual contribution percentage (ACP) for the group of eligible highly compensated employees for the plan year does not exceed the greater of: (1) 125 percent of ACP for all other eligible employees for the preceding plan year, or (2) the lesser of 200 percent of ACP for all other eligible employees for the preceding plan year or ACP for all other eligible employees for the preceding plan year, plus two percentage points. The ACP test can be satisfied by the plan adopting one of the alternative safe harbors for meeting the actual deferral percentage (ADP) test for 401(k) plans (¶ 2123).

Failure to satisfy the ACP test will not result in disqualification of the plan if the excess contributions (plus earnings) are distributed within 12 months following the plan year in which they arose (Code Sec. 401(m)(6)). However, the employer is subject to a 10-percent tax on the excess contributions unless distributed to the highly compensated employees within 2½ months after the plan year (Code Sec. 4979(f)). The corrective distribution is included in the employee's gross income but the 10-percent tax on early distributions (¶ 2151) does not apply (Code Sec. 401(m)(7)). The due date for performing certain time-sensitive actions, including distributing excess contributions, otherwise due on or after April 1, 2020, and before July 15, 2020, is automatically extended to July 15, 2020, in response to the COVID-19 (coronavirus) crisis (Notice 2020-23; Rev. Proc. 2018-58).

Closed or Frozen Plans. A defined benefit plan with a closed or frozen class of participants may be eligible for special rules regarding cross-testing and aggregation to meet the nondiscrimination requirements (Code Sec. 401(a)(26) and Code Sec. 401(o), added and amended by the Setting Every Community Up for Retirement Enhancement (SECURE) Act of 2019 (P.L. 116-94)).

2115. Contribution and Benefit Limits for Retirement Plans. A qualified retirement plan (¶ 2111) must limit the contributions and benefits that may be provided to each individual plan participant (Code Sec. 415). See ¶ 2117 and ¶ 2119 for the limits imposed on the deduction of employer contributions.

Defined Contribution Plan. The maximum annual addition that may be made to a participant's account in a defined contribution plan (¶ 2101) may not exceed the *lesser* of $56,000 for 2019 ($57,000 for 2020) or 100 percent of the participant's compensation (earned income if self-employed) (Code Sec. 415(c), as amended by the Setting Every Community Up for Retirement Enhancement (SECURE) Act of 2019 (P.L. 116-94); Notice 2018-83; Notice 2019-59). The term "annual addition" includes employer and employee contributions, as well as forfeitures allocated to the account under the plan. For plan years beginning after 2015, compensation or earned income may be increased by the amount of any qualified foster care payment that is a difficulty of care payment (¶ 883) that the taxpayer excludes from gross income for the tax year.

Defined Benefit Plan. The maximum annual retirement benefit for any participant of a defined benefit plan (¶ 2101) may not exceed the *lesser* of 100 percent of the participant's average compensation for the participant's three consecutive calendar years of highest compensation or $225,000 for 2019 ($230,000 for 2020) (Code Sec. 415(b); Notice 2018-83; Notice 2019-59). The maximum annual benefit is actuarially reduced when retirement benefits are paid before age 62 and increased when benefits are not paid until after age 65. If certain requirements are met, an annual benefit of up to $10,000 may be provided by the plan even if that exceeds the 100 percent of compensation limit.

The benefit limit and the compensation limit are reduced in the case of individuals with less than 10 years of service with the employer.

Compensation Limit. The maximum compensation that may be taken into account when determining the limit on contributions and benefits of an employee, and when applying the nondiscrimination rules (¶ 2114), is $280,000 for 2019 ($285,000 for 2020) (Code Sec. 401(a)(17); Reg. § 1.401(a)(17)-1(a); Notice 2018-83; Notice 2019-59). For purposes of the limitation on contributions to a defined contribution plan, an employee's compensation includes any compensation received from the employer maintaining the plan included in gross income or net earnings from self-employment. It also includes any elective deferrals (¶ 2121) or other amounts contributed by the employer at the employee's election that may be excluded from an employee's gross income such as cafeteria plan benefits (¶ 2045) (Code Sec. 415(c)(3)).

2117. Deduction of Employer Contributions to Retirement Plans. Subject to annual limits (¶ 2119), an employer is allowed to deduct its contributions to a qualified retirement plan (¶ 2111) to the extent they are otherwise deductible under the Code as an ordinary and necessary business expense, or paid for the production of income (Code Sec. 404(a)). The deduction is allowed whether or not the rights of the employees to the contributions are forfeitable. Contributions are generally deductible only for the tax year when paid regardless of whether the employer uses the cash or accrual method of accounting, unless contributions in excess of the annual limits must be carried over to later years.

A deductible contribution is deemed made on the last day of the tax year if it is paid no later than the due date (including extensions) of the employer's income tax return. However, the due date for performing certain time-sensitive actions, including making contributions to a qualified plan, otherwise due on or after April 1, 2020, and before July 15, 2020, is automatically extended to July 15, 2020, in response to the COVID-19 (coronavirus) crisis (Notice 2020-23; Rev. Proc. 2018-58).

In the case of a defined benefit plan, the minimum required contribution for a plan year generally must be paid (¶ 2133) within 8½ months after the close of the plan year (Code Sec. 430(j)). As a result, the required funding date may actually come before the last day for making deductible contributions. Payments made on a date other than the valuation date for the plan year of a defined benefit plan must be adjusted for interest accruing for the period from the valuation date to the payment date. Elective and matching contributions under a 401(k) plan (¶ 2121) and other types of defined contribution plans are not deductible by the employer for a tax year if they are attributable to compensation earned by participants after the end of that tax year (Rev. Rul. 90-105; Rev. Rul. 2002-46).

S Corporations. A retirement plan established by an S corporation is generally governed by the same rules that apply to plans established by other corporations. As a result, S corporation shareholders are not entitled to claim retirement plan deductions based on their pro rata share of pass-through income from the S corporation. The Ninth Circuit has ruled that this income is not treated as earnings from self-employment for retirement plan purposes (*A.R. Durando*, CA-9, 95-2 USTC ¶ 50,615).

2119. Deduction Limits of Employer Contributions to Retirement Plans. There are limits on the annual deductions that may be claimed for an employer's contributions to a qualified retirement plan (¶ 2117).

Defined Contribution Plans. The maximum deduction allowed for contributions to a defined contribution plan (¶ 2101), including a profit-sharing, stock-bonus, and money purchase plan (except as provided otherwise in regulations), is 25 percent of the compensation of all the participants in the plan (Code Sec. 404(a)(3)). Contributions that are in excess of the maximum amount allowed (¶ 2115) may not be deducted (Code Sec. 404(j)). See ¶ 2181 and ¶ 2185 for the deduction limits that apply to SIMPLE IRAs and SIMPLE 401(k) plans, respectively.

Defined Benefit Plans. The maximum deduction allowed for contributions to a defined benefit plan (¶ 2101) generally is determined actuarially based on the expected costs of the plan (Code Sec. 404(a)(1)). The deduction is subject to both a floor of the annual contributions necessary to satisfy the minimum funding standard (¶ 2133) and a ceiling of the full funding limitation for the plan. The amount that can be deducted for any year cannot exceed the greater of the following.

- *Level Funding Method*—The limit is an amount necessary to provide, for all participants under the plan, the remaining unfunded cost of their past and current service credits distributed as a level amount or level percentage of compensation over the remaining service of each participant. Under this method, the past service liability for each participant is deducted ratably over the employee's projected years of service until retirement.

- *Normal Cost Method*—The limit is an amount equal to the normal ("current") cost of the plan plus, if past service or other supplementary credits are provided, an amount not in excess of that necessary to amortize the credits in equal payments over 10 years. However, all defined benefit plans may deduct 100 percent of their unfunded current liability.

Employer Maintaining More Than One Type of Plan. If an employer makes contributions to a defined contribution plan and defined benefit plan, there is an overall limit on the deduction of these contributions. The deduction is limited to the *greater* of: (1) 25 percent of the compensation paid or accrued for that year to the participants in all such plans, or (2) the amount necessary to satisfy the minimum funding standards. The overall limitation does not apply when no individual is a participant in more than one plan maintained by the employer (Code Sec. 404(a)(7)). Also, the overall deduction limit does not apply when only elective deferrals are made to any of the employer's defined contribution plans during the tax year.

Elective Deferrals. Elective deferrals (¶ 2121) made by employees are not taken into account when determining deduction limits for stock bonus and profit-sharing plans, combined defined benefit and defined contribution plans, and ESOPs (Code Sec. 404(n)).

Compensation. In applying the annual deduction limits, the amount of an employee's compensation that may be taken into account is limited in the same manner as for determining contributions and benefits (¶ 2115) (Code Sec. 404(l)). However, compensation for purposes of the deduction limits includes certain amounts that are generally excluded from gross income such as elective deferrals and certain disability benefits (Code Sec. 404(a)(12)).

Carryovers. If an employer's contribution exceeds the maximum deductible amount for the year, the excess amount may be carried over and deducted in later tax years. The total of the carryovers and the regular contributions in the carryover year may not exceed the deductible limit for that year (Code Sec. 404(a)(1)(E) and (3)(A)(ii)). Similarly, if the 25 percent overall limit for contributions to different types of plans is exceeded, the excess may be carried over. The combination of carryovers and regular deductions for any succeeding year may not exceed 25 percent of the compensation paid to participants in that year (Code Sec. 404(a)(7)(B)).

2121. Elective Deferrals to 401(k) Plans. A qualified retirement plan (¶ 2111) may include a cash or deferred arrangement (i.e., 401(k) plan) under which a participating employee has the option of receiving compensation in cash or having it contributed on a pre-tax basis to the plan (¶ 2104). The contribution is referred to as an elective contribution or elective deferral and is subject to an annual limit ($19,000 for 2019 and $19,500 for 2020) (Code Sec. 402(g); Notice 2018-83; Notice 2019-59).

The limit applies to the aggregate amount of all the elective deferrals made by the employee for the year to all plans which permit such contributions, including other 401(k) plans, SIMPLE-IRAs (¶ 2181), and 403(b) annuity plans (¶ 2191), but not 457 plans (¶ 2193). Special nondiscrimination rules for 401(k) plans may further limit the amount of elective deferrals (but not catch-up contributions) that can be made by highly compensated employees (¶ 2123).

Example: Tony, age 45, works for two employers. Each of the employers offers a 401(k) plan and Tony participates in both plans. In 2019, Tony deferred $12,000 of his wages into the 401(k) plan of Employer A and $7,500 of his wages into the 401(k) plan of Employer B. Tony has made an excess deferral of $500 for the year.

Catch-Up Contributions. An individual who will be at least 50 years of age by the end of the tax year may make additional "catch-up" contributions to a qualified plan allowing elective deferrals including 401(k) plan, 403(b) annuity plan, 457 plan, SIMPLE 401(k), SIMPLE IRA, and certain SEPs. The maximum amount of the catch-up contribution depends upon the type of plan involved. The maximum catch-up contribution to a 401(k), 403(b) annuity plan, 457 plan, and certain SEPs is $6,000 for 2019 ($6,500 for 2020). The maximum catch-up contribution to a SIMPLE 401(k) or SIMPLE IRA is $3,000 for 2019 ($3,000 for 2020) (Code Sec. 414(v); Notice 2018-83; Notice 2019-59). Catch-up contributions may only be made if the plan permits them.

Excess Deferrals. Elective deferrals that exceed the annual limit are included in the employee's gross income and subject to a 10-percent penalty (Code Secs. 402(g) and 4979). The employee may generally withdraw the excess contribution from the plan before April 15 of the following tax year along with any attributable income. The due date for performing certain time-sensitive actions, including withdrawing excess deferrals, otherwise due on or after April 1, 2020, and before July 15, 2020, is automatically extended to July 15, 2020, in response to the COVID-19 (coronavirus) crisis (Notice 2020-23; Rev. Proc. 2018-58).

If the employee has made elective deferrals to more than one plan, then the employee can designate the amount of the excess that is to be withdrawn from each plan. Excess deferrals that remain in the plan past the required distribution date are taxed a second time when distributed (Reg. § 1.402(g)-1(e)(8)(iii)). The 10-percent penalty will not apply if the excess is distributed within 2½ months following the plan year in which the excess contribution was made.

Matching Contributions. Matching contributions made to a 401(k) plan by the employer are not treated as an employee's elective contributions and therefore, not subject to the annual limit on deferrals. In addition, matching contributions made by a self-employed person to a 401(k) plan are not treated as part of the individual's elective contributions (Code Sec. 402(g)(8)).

After-Tax Roth Contributions. Plans that allow employees to make pre-tax elective deferrals may also allow participating employees to designate all or part of their elective deferrals to the plan to be treated as after-tax Roth contributions (Code Sec. 402A). The designated Roth contributions are generally treated the same as pre-tax elective deferrals under the plan for purposes of limits on deferrals and nondiscrimination requirements, except that the plan must account for them separately. While the employee must include the Roth contributions in gross income, distributions are subject to rules similar to the rules applicable to distributions from a Roth IRA (¶ 2173). However, unlike a Roth IRA, amounts held in a Roth 401(k) account are subject to the required minimum distribution (RMD) rules (¶ 2127).

2123. Nondiscrimination Requirements for 401(k) Plans. A special nondiscrimination requirement applies to elective deferrals made to a 401(k) plan, but not catch-up contributions (¶ 2121) (Code Sec. 401(k)(3); Reg. § 1.401(k)-2). The plan will not be treated as qualified unless the actual deferral percentage (ADP) for eligible highly compensated employees (¶ 2114) for the plan year bears a relationship to the ADP for all other eligible employees for the preceding plan year that meets either of the following tests:

- the ADP for the group of eligible highly compensated employees is not more than the actual ADP of all other eligible employees multiplied by 1.25, or

- the excess of the ADP for the group of eligible highly compensated employees over that of all other eligible employees is not more than 2 percentage points, and the ADP for the group of eligible highly compensated employees is not more than the ADP of all other eligible employees multiplied by 2.

The employer may elect to calculate the ADP test for rank-and-file employees with reference to the current year rather than the preceding year. The election once made may not be revoked without IRS consent. In the case of a test year which is the first year of the plan (other than a successor plan), the ADP of rank-and-file employees for the preceding plan year will be deemed to be three percent or, if the employer elects, the ADP calculated on the basis of rank-and-file employees for the first plan year. If the 401(k) plan provides for matching employer contributions or allows employees contributions to be made on an after-tax basis, then a separate nondiscrimination test generally applies to those contributions.

A plan can avoid failing to satisfy the ADP test by having the employer make qualified nonelective contributions (QNECs) or qualified matching contributions (QMACs) that are treated as elective contributions under the plan and that, in combination with the elective deferrals, satisfy the nondiscrimination requirements. Alternatively, the plan may limit the elective deferrals by highly compensated employees to prevent any excess contributions or allow the highly compensated employees the option to have any excess contributions distributed back to them or recharacterized (Code Sec. 401(k)(8); Reg. §1.401(k)-2(b)(1)).

An employer may also adopt one of three designed-based safe harbors to satisfy the ADP test for its 401(k) plan. The ADP test will be deemed satisfied if:

- a prescribed level of matching or nonelective contributions are made under the plan on behalf of all eligible non-highly compensated employees and if employees are provided a timely notice describing their rights and obligations under the plan, except that notice is not required for plan years beginning after 2019 for nonelective contributions or a nonelective feature for plans using automatic enrollment safe harbor (Code Sec. 401(k)(12), as amended by the Setting Every Community Up for Retirement Enhancement (SECURE) Act of 2019 (P.L. 116-94) and (m)(11); Reg. §1.401(k)-3);

- the plan meets the requirements for a qualified automatic contribution arrangement (QACA) where eligible employees are uniformly treated as having elected to have the employer make elective contributions equal to a qualified percentage of compensation: not in excess of 15 percent (10 percent for plan years beginning before 2020) and at least three percent in the first year, four percent for the second year, five percent for the third year, and six percent for the fourth year (Code Sec. 401(k)(13), as amended by P.L. 116-94 and (m)(12)); or

- the plans meets the contribution and vesting requirements applicable to SIMPLE 401(k) plans (¶ 2185).

2125. Distribution Requirements for Retirement Plans. A qualified retirement plan (¶ 2111) must provide that the payment of benefits under the plan will begin, unless the participant elects otherwise, no later than the 60th day after the *latest* of the close of the plan year in which:

- the participant attains the earlier of age 65 or the normal retirement age specified in the plan;

- the participant marks the 10th anniversary of enrollment in the plan; or

- the participant terminates service with the employer (Code Sec. 401(a)(14)).

See ¶ 2141 for a discussion of the taxation of distributions from retirement plans.

Mandatory Cash-Outs. A qualified plan is generally restricted from distributing any portion of a participant's accrued benefits in any form without the participant's (or surviving spouse's) consent. However, the plan may pay out the balance of a participant's account without the participant's consent if the present value of the benefit does not exceed $5,000 (Code Sec. 411(a)(11)(A)). If the present value of the benefit exceeds $1,000, and the participant does not elect otherwise, a mandatory distribution must be transferred directly to a traditional IRA (¶ 2155) established by the plan for the benefit of the participant (Code Sec. 401(a)(31)(B); Notice 2005-5).

Phased Retirement Arrangements. A qualified plan is allowed to provide that a distribution may be made to an employee who has attained age 59½ (age 62 for plan years beginning before 2020) and who is not separated from employment at the time of the distribution but instead is in a phased retirement program (i.e., working retirement) (Code Sec. 401(a)(36), as amended by the Bipartisan American Miners Act of 2019 (P.L. 116-94)).

Death Benefits for Participants Serving in the Military. Survivors of a participant who has died while performing qualified military service are entitled to any benefits that would have been provided under the plan (other than benefit accruals relating to the period of military service) had the participant returned from service and then terminated employment on account of death (Code Sec. 401(a)(37)). Thus, survivor benefits such as accelerated vesting or ancillary life insurance benefits that are contingent upon a participant's termination of employment on account of death must be provided to the beneficiaries of a participant who has died during qualified military service. This requirement applies to qualified plans, 403(b) annuity plans (¶ 2191), and 457 plans (¶ 2193).

Portability of Lifetime Income. For plan years beginning after 2019, a defined contribution plan may allow qualified distributions of a lifetime income investment, or distributions of a lifetime income investment in the form of a qualified plan distribution annuity contract on or after the date that is 90 days prior to the date on which such lifetime income investment is no longer authorized to be held as an investment option under the plan (Code Sec. 401(a)(38), as added by the Setting Every Community Up for Retirement Enhancement (SECURE) Act of 2019 (P.L. 116-94)). A qualified distribution is a direct trustee-to-trustee transfer to an eligible retirement plan. A lifetime income investment is an investment option designed to provide an employee with election rights to a lifetime income feature available under the plan that is not uniformly available with respect to other investment options under the plan.

2127. Required Minimum Distributions (RMDs). A required minimum distribution (RMD) is the amount a participant or beneficiary of a qualified retirement plan must withdraw from his or her account annually over the court of their life expectancy after a required beginning date. Failure to take the RMD for the year will result in a penalty. The RMD rules apply to all types of qualified retirement (¶ 2101), as well as traditional IRAs (¶ 2155), 403(b) annuity plans (¶ 2191), and 457 plans (¶ 2193) (Code Sec. 401(a)(9), as amended by the Setting Every Community Up for Retirement Enhancement (SECURE) Act of 2019 (P.L. 116-94); Reg. § 1.401(a)(9)-1).

Waiver of RMDs for 2020. The minimum distribution rules do not apply to the 2020 calendar year for any defined contribution plan (including under 401(a) plan, 403(a) or 403(b) annuity plan, or 457(b) government plan) and IRA. As a result, a plan participant or beneficiary is not required to take any RMD for the 2020 calendar year in response to the COVID-19 (coronavirus) emergency (Code Sec. 401(a)(9)(I), as added by the Coronavirus Aid, Relief, and Economic Security (CARES) Act (P.L. 116-136)). Any distributions that would have been RMDs for the calendar year 2020 are not treated as eligible rollover distributions for certain purposes (¶ 2145).

Required Beginning Date. The required beginning date is generally April 1 of the calendar year following the later of: (1) the calendar year in which the participant reaches age 72 (age 70½ for individuals attaining that age before 2020), or (2) the calendar year in which the participant retires. In the case of a five-percent owner (¶ 2132) or IRA owner, the required beginning date is April 1 of the year following the year in which the individual reaches age 72 (age 70½ for individuals attaining that age before 2020). The change from age 70½ to age 72 applies to distributions required to be made after December 31, 2019. The IRS has provided relief to financial institutions that provided incorrect RMD statements to plan participants as a result of the change (Notice 2020-6). The required beginning date for calendar years after 2020 is determined without regard to the waiver of the RMD requirements for the 2020 calendar year.

The RMD rules vary depending upon whether distributions begin before or after the employee's death. Distributions made to a participant or the beneficiary of a participant must satisfy the RMD rules in each calendar year. The RMD for a particular year is generally equal to the participant's accrued benefit or account balance as of the end of the prior year, divided by the appropriate distribution period (Reg. §§ 1.401(a)(9)-5 and 1.401(a)(9)-6). A plan participant may exclude the value of a qualifying longevity annuity contract (QLAC) from the account balance used to determine RMDs prior to annuitization. QLACs are permissible for qualified plans, as well as for Code Sec. 403(b) annuity plans and IRAs (Reg. §§ 1.403(b)-6(e)(9) and 1.408-8, Q&A 12).

Distributions Before Participant's Death. If RMDs begin while the participant is alive, the distribution period is derived from one of two tables (Reg. § 1.401(a)(9)-9). The *Uniform Lifetime Table* reproduced below is used to determine the distribution period for lifetime distributions to an unmarried individual or married individual if his or her spouse is either: (1) not the sole designated beneficiary; or (2) the sole designated beneficiary and not more than 10 years younger than the participant. The *Joint and Last Survivor Table* is used to determine the distribution period for lifetime distributions to a married individual whose spouse is the sole beneficiary and is more than 10 years younger than the participant. The IRS has proposed updated life expectancy and distribution tables under the RMD rules to reflect longer life expectancies than the tables in the existing regulations. The proposed tables generally would apply for distribution calendar years beginning on or after January 1, 2021 (Prop. Reg. § 1.401(a)(9)-9, NPRM REG-132210-18).

Distributions After Participant's Death. If RMDs have been made to the participant before his or her death, then any remaining benefit payable to a beneficiary is generally payable over the longer of the life expectancy of the beneficiary or the participant (but see 10-year rule below). If RMDs have not been made to the participant before his or her death, then the participant's entire interest must be distributed to the beneficiary within five years after his or her death. However, the five-year period is determined without regard to calendar year 2020 (Code Sec. 401(a)(9)(B), as amended by P.L. 116-94 and 401(a)(9)(I)(iii), as added by P.L. 116-136; Reg. § 1.401(a)(9)-5).

Most beneficiaries may able to take advantage of one of two exceptions to the five-year distribution rule. First, the five-year rule does not apply if:

- any portion of the participant's interest is payable to, or for the benefit of, a designated beneficiary;

- the portion of the participant's interest to which the beneficiary is entitled will be distributed over the life of the beneficiary or over a period not extending beyond the life expectancy of the beneficiary (using the *Single Life Table* provided in Reg. § 1.401(a)(9)-9 and reproduced below); and

- the distributions commence no later than one year after the date of the participant's death.

Second, the five-year rule does not apply if:

- the designated beneficiary is the participant's surviving spouse;

- the portion of the participant's interest to which the surviving spouse is entitled will be distributed over the life expectancy of the spouse; and

- the distributions commence no later than the date on which the participant would have attained age 72 (70½ for individuals attaining that age before 2020).

If the surviving spouse dies before payments are required to begin, the five-year rule is applied as if the surviving spouse were the plan participant. Payments to a surviving spouse under a qualified joint and survivor annuity (¶ 2130) will satisfy this second exception.

10-Year Distribution Period. Distributions to a nonspouse designated beneficiary from a qualified retirement plan made after the death of the plan participant who dies after December 31, 2019, must generally be completed within a 10-year period beginning in the year following the year the participant or IRA owner dies (Code Sec. 401(a)(9)(H), as added by P.L. 116-94). The 10-year rule replaces the life expectancy rule for designated beneficiaries. It applies to all beneficiaries except a surviving spouse, minors, beneficiaries that are disabled or chronically ill, and beneficiaries that are not more than 10 years younger than the plan participant (Code Sec. 401(a)(9)(E), as amended by P.L. 116-94). The 10-year rule does not replace the life expectancy rule for collectively bargained plans, certain governmental plans, and for existing annuity contracts.

Final Determination of Beneficiary. A beneficiary must be designated as of the date of the employee's death. The final determination of who is a beneficiary is not made until September 30 of the year following the calendar year of death (Reg. § 1.401(a)(9)-4, Q&A-4(a)). As a result, if an individual does not remain a beneficiary on the September 30 deadline, the individual is not taken into consideration when determining the RMDs that must be made from the retirement account. For example, an individual who is a named beneficiary as of the time of the participant's death may not be a beneficiary by the September 30 deadline because he or she has disclaimed the right to any portion of the retirement account.

Penalty for Failure to Receive RMDs. An excise tax is imposed on a plan participant or beneficiary who does not take a RMD. The tax is 50 percent of the amount by which the RMD exceeds the distribution actually made (Code Sec. 4974). Part or all of the tax may be waived if any of the RMD shortfall is due to reasonable error and if steps are taken to correct it. The penalty is reported on Form 5329. If the individual believes that part or all of the tax should be waived due to reasonable error, a statement of explanation should be attached along with Form 5329. Any tax due must be paid at the time Form 5329 is filed.

¶2127

Uniform Lifetime Table

Age of employee	Distribution period	Age of employee	Distribution period
70	27.4	92	10.2
71	26.5	93	9.6
72	25.6	94	9.1
73	24.7	95	8.6
74	23.8	96	8.1
75	22.9	97	7.6
76	22.0	98	7.1
77	21.2	99	6.7
78	20.3	100	6.3
79	19.5	101	5.9
80	18.7	102	5.5
81	17.9	103	5.2
82	17.1	104	4.9
83	16.3	105	4.5
84	15.5	106	4.2
85	14.8	107	3.9
86	14.1	108	3.7
87	13.4	109	3.4
88	12.7	110	3.1
89	12.0	111	2.9
90	11.4	112	2.6
91	10.8	113	2.4
		114	2.1
		115+	1.9

Single Life Table (for use by beneficiaries)

Age	Life Expectancy	Age	Life Expectancy	Age	Life Expectancy	Age	Life Expectancy
0	82.4	27	56.2	55	29.6	83	8.6
1	81.6	28	55.3	56	28.7	84	8.1
2	80.6	29	54.3	57	27.9	85	7.6
3	79.7	30	53.3	58	27.0	86	7.1
4	78.7	31	52.4	59	26.1	87	6.7
5	77.7	32	51.4	60	25.2	88	6.3
6	76.7	33	50.4	61	24.4	89	5.9
7	75.8	34	49.4	62	23.5	90	5.5
8	74.8	35	48.5	63	22.7	91	5.2
9	73.8	36	47.5	64	21.8	92	4.9
10	72.8	37	46.5	65	21.0	93	4.6
11	71.8	38	45.6	66	20.2	94	4.3
12	70.8	39	44.6	67	19.4	95	4.1
13	69.9	40	43.6	68	18.6	96	3.8
14	68.9	41	42.7	69	17.8	97	3.6
15	67.9	42	41.7	70	17.0	98	3.4
16	66.9	43	40.7	71	16.3	99	3.1
17	66.0	44	39.8	72	15.5	100	2.9
18	65.0	45	38.8	73	14.8	101	2.7
19	64.0	46	37.9	74	14.1	102	2.5
20	63.0	47	37.0	75	13.4	103	2.3
21	62.1	48	36.0	76	12.7	104	2.1
22	61.1	49	35.1	77	12.1	105	1.9
23	60.1	50	34.2	78	11.4	106	1.7
24	59.1	51	33.3	79	10.8	107	1.5
25	58.2	52	32.3	80	10.2	108	1.4
26	57.2	53	31.4	81	9.7	109	1.2
		54	30.5	82	9.1	110	1.1
						111+	1.0

2129. Hardship Distributions from 401(k) Plans. A 401(k) plan may allow a hardship distribution to an employee if the distribution (1) is made due to an immediate and heavy financial need of the employee and (2) it does not exceed the amount necessary to satisfy that need (Code Sec. 401(k)(14)); Reg. §1.401(k)-1(d)(3)). The maximum amount available for a hardship distribution generally is the employee's total elective contributions (¶2121), reduced by the amount of any previous distributions of elective contributions. For plan years beginning after 2018, an employer may allow a hardship distribution to include account earnings and certain employer contributions (nonelective contributions to profit sharing or stock bonus plan, qualified nonelective contributions (QNECs), and qualified matching contributions (QMACs)).

Types of expenses that satisfy the requirement of immediate and heavy financial need include:

- medical expenses of the employee, spouse, and dependents;

- expenditures (excluding mortgage payments) to purchase a principal residence for the employee;

- post-secondary tuition, related fees, and room and board for up to 12 months for the employee, spouse, or dependents;

- expenditures to stave off eviction or foreclosure with respect to the employee's principal residence;

- burial or funeral expenses for the employee's deceased parent, spouse, or dependents;

- expenses for the repair of casualty damage to the employee's principal residence; and

- effective for distributions after 2019, expenses and losses incurred by the employee due to a federally-declared disaster, provided that the employee's principal residence or principal place of employment at the time of the disaster was in the designated disaster area.

An immediate and heavy financial need also includes any amount necessary to pay any income taxes or penalties reasonably anticipated to result from the distribution. To the extent allowed under the plan, if medical, tuition, or funeral expenses incurred on behalf of the employee's spouse or dependent are deemed to be an immediate and heavy financial need, the same expenses with regard to the employee's beneficiary under the plan can also be considered an immediate and heavy financial need.

A distribution is deemed necessary to satisfy the employee's immediate and heavy financial need if:

- the employee has obtained all other currently available distributions (including ESOP dividends, but not hardship distributions) under the plan and all other plans of the employer; and

- the employee represents in writing that he or she has insufficient cash or other liquid assets to satisfy the need, and the plan administrator does not have actual knowledge that is contrary to the representation

A plan may, but is not required to, provide for additional conditions for plan years beginning after 2018, such as having to use up other readily available resources. For example, a plan may provide that, before a hardship distribution may be made, an employee must obtain all nontaxable loans available under the plan and all other plans of the employer. A plan may not provide for a suspension of an employee's elective contributions or employee contributions as a condition of obtaining a hardship distribution.

A hardship distribution is included in the employee's income and subject to the 10-percent additional tax on early distributions unless an exception applies (¶2151). A hardship distribution generally may *not* be rolled over into an IRA or other type of retirement plan (Code Sec. 402(c)(4)(C)).

Disaster Relief. A hardship distribution received to buy or build a principal residence in a qualified disaster area may be recontributed to the plan as a rollover contribution if the residence was not purchased or constructed due to the disaster. The hardship distribution must be received within 180 days before and 30 days after the incident period of the disaster for any qualified federal disaster declared between January 1, 2018, and February 18, 2020. It must be received after March 31, 2017, and before January 15, 2018, for the California wildfires and after February 28, 2017, and before September 21, 2017, for Hurricanes Harvey, Irma, or Maria. Any recontribution must occur between

¶2129

21
RETIREMENT

the first day of the incident period and June 17, 2020, for a qualified federal disaster. The amount recontributed must be made between October 8, 2017, and June 30, 2018, for the California wildfires and between August 23, 2017, and February 28, 2018, for the hurricanes.

Qualified distributions and repayments for any qualified federal disaster declared between January 1, 2018, and February 18, 2020, are reported on Form 8915-A. Qualified 2017 distributions and repayments are reported on Form 8915-B (Act Secs. 201 and 202(b) of the Taxpayer Certainty and Disaster Tax Relief Act of 2019 (P.L. 116-94); Act Secs. 20101 and 20102(c) of the Bipartisan Budget Act of 2018 (P.L. 115-123); Act Secs. 501 and 502(c) of the Disaster Tax Relief and Airport and Airway Extension Act of 2017 (P.L. 115-63), as amended by P.L. 115-123; IRS Pub 976).

The IRS has also provided relief from certain verification procedures that may be required under retirement plans with respect to loans and hardship distributions for individuals affected by the California wildfires or Hurricanes Harvey, Irma, or Maria. The relief applies to participants in 401(k) plans, 403(b) annuity plans, and 457 plans (Announcement 2017-11; Announcement 2017-13, Announcement 2017-15).

2130. Joint and Survivor and Pre-Retirement Annuities. A qualified retirement plan (¶ 2111) that pays benefits in the form of an annuity generally must provide for the payment in the form of a joint and survivor annuity for the participant and his or her surviving spouse (Code Secs. 401(a)(11)(A)(i) and 417). The annuity must be the actuarial equivalent of an annuity for the single life of the employee, and the survivor portion may not be less than 50 percent of the annuity paid during the joint lives of the employee and spouse. A pre-retirement survivor annuity must be provided for the surviving spouse of a vested participant who dies prior to the earliest retirement age. An employee may elect out of either the joint and survivor or pre-retirement survivor annuity. The election may only be made with the written consent of the spouse and the consent must be witnessed by a notary public or plan representative. The spouse's consent cannot be given in a prenuptial agreement (Reg. § 1.401(a)-20).

2131. Anti-Assignment of Retirement Plan Benefits. A qualified retirement plan (¶ 2111) must provide that benefits under the plan may not be assigned or otherwise transferred (Code Secs. 401(a)(13) and 414(p)). An exception is made for assignments ordered by a qualified domestic relations order (QDRO) issued under a state's domestic relations law (¶ 2144). In addition, a participant's benefits may be reduced when the individual has committed a breach of fiduciary duty or committed a criminal act against the plan.

2132. Top-Heavy Retirement Plans. More stringent qualification requirements must be met by qualified retirement plans (¶ 2111) and 403(b) annuity plans (¶ 2191) that primarily benefit an employer's key employees. These plans are referred to as "top-heavy plans" (Code Sec. 416(a)). Most qualified plans must include language stating that they will comply with the top-heavy rules if they become top heavy. However, the top-heavy requirements do not apply to SIMPLE IRAs (¶ 2181) or SIMPLE 401(k) (¶ 2185). A plan is top heavy if the accrued benefits or account balances of key employees are more than 60 percent of the total benefits or balances under the plan.

Accelerated Vesting. For any plan year in which a plan is top heavy, the benefits of each employee for that year must be *either*: (1) 100 percent vested if the employee has at least three years of service, or (2) 20 percent vested after two years of service with a 20 percent increase for each later year of service (Code Sec. 416(b)). See ¶ 2113 for the general vesting requirements.

Minimum Benefits and Contributions. In any plan year in which a defined benefit plan is top heavy, each participating non-key employee must be provided with a retirement benefit that is not less than two percent of average annual compensation (¶ 2115) for the employee's five consecutive years of highest compensation, multiplied by years of service (up to a maximum of ten years of service) (Code Sec. 416(c)(1)). In any plan year in which a defined contribution plan is top heavy, each participating non-key employee must be provided with a contribution that is not less than three percent of such employee's compensation for that year. Employer matching contributions are taken into account when determining if this contribution requirement has been met. If the contribution rate for the key employee receiving the largest contribution is less than three percent, then the contribution rate for that key employee is used to determine the minimum contribution for non-key employees (Code Sec. 416(c)(2)).

Key Employee Defined. A key employee is defined as an employee who, at any time during the plan year, is:

- an officer with compensation in excess of $180,000 for 2019 ($185,000 for 2020) (Code Sec. 416(i)(1); Notice 2018-83; Notice 2019-59);
- a more-than-five-percent owner, or
- a more-than-one-percent owner who received more than $150,000 (not subject to inflation adjustment) in compensation.

In the case of a corporate employer, an employee is a five-percent owner when the employee owns more than five percent of the employer's outstanding stock or stock possessing more than five percent of the total combined voting power of all of the employer's stock. If the employer is not a corporation, a five-percent owner is any employee who owns more than five percent of the capital or profits interest in the employer. An employee is also treated as owning stock owned by certain members of the employee's family or, in the case of any employer that is not a corporation, by partnerships, estates, trusts, or corporations in which the employee has an interest (Code Sec. 416(i)(1)(B)). The same rules apply to determine whether an individual owner is a one-percent owner.

2133. Minimum Funding Standards of Defined Benefits Plans. Employers maintaining single-employer defined benefit plans (¶ 2101) are required to make minimum contributions to the plan each year based on the plan's assets (reduced by credit balances), funding target, and target normal cost (Code Secs. 412, 430, and 436). However, minimum required contributions to a single-employer retirement plan otherwise due in calendar year 2020 (including any quarterly contributions) are delayed until January 1, 2021, in response to the COVID-19 (coronavirus) crisis (Act Sec. 3608 of Coronavirus Aid, Relief, and Economic Security (CARES) Act (P.L. 116-136)). Full funding of plans is required, with existing shortfalls generally required to be eliminated over seven years, unless a special funding schedule has been elected. Multiemployer collectively bargained plans and cooperative and small employer charity (CSEC) plans operate under different sets of rules (substantially the same rules under which all plans operated prior to 2008) that require a funding standard account (Code Secs. 431 and 433).

Failure to meet minimum funding requirements or correct shortfalls will generally subject the employer to an excise tax (Code Sec. 4971). A temporary waiver of the minimum funding requirements may be provided to an employer that is unable to satisfy the minimum funding standard for a plan year without substantial business hardship. The employer may be required to provide security to the plan as a condition for the waiver. In addition, no plan amendment that has the effect of increasing plan liabilities may generally be adopted during the waiver period.

A sponsor of a defined benefit plan may make a qualified transferred of excess assets of the plan before 2026 to a health benefit account or applicable life insurance account within the plan to fund retiree health benefits (Code Sec. 420).

2136. Prohibited Transactions of Retirement Plans. Certain transactions between a qualified employees' trust (¶ 2101) and a plan fiduciary or other "disqualified person" are prohibited (Code Sec. 4975(c)). The disqualified person who engages in the prohibited transaction is liable for excise taxes based upon the amount of the prohibited transaction. The basic excise tax rate is 15 percent. If the prohibited transaction is not corrected before the IRS assesses the tax or mails a notice of deficiency regarding the transaction, the excise tax rate is 100 percent (Code Sec. 4975(b)).

Plan Loans. Loans of plan assets to owners of the employer, including owner-employees, are generally prohibited transactions. Loans of IRA assets to the account owner are always prohibited, but a loan from an employer plan may qualify for an exception to the rule (Code Sec. 4975(f)(6)(B)(iii)). Loans from employer plans to disqualified persons are not prohibited if (Code Sec. 4975(d)(1)):

- loans are available to all participants on a reasonably equivalent basis;
- the plan explicitly provides for such loans;

- the loans have a reasonable rate of interest; and
- the loans are adequately secured.

For this purpose, an owner-employee is: (1) a self-employed person who owns the entire interest in an unincorporated trade or business (i.e., a sole proprietor), or (2) an individual who owns more than a 10-percent capital or profits interest in a partnership (Code Sec. 401(c)(3)).

2137. Retirement Plan Returns (Form 5500). An employer or plan administrator of a qualified retirement plan (¶ 2111) generally must file Form 5500 (and accompanying schedules) each tax year to report detailed information with respect to qualification, financial condition, and operations of the plan (Code Sec. 6058). Small plans meeting certain eligibility requirements (generally plans with less than 100 participants) must file Form 5500-SF. One-participant plans may file a simpler Form 5500-EZ if a plan's only participants are an individual and spouse who together own the business (whether or not incorporated) for which the plan is established. Form 5500-EZ may also be used by the plan of a partnership if the only participants are partners and their spouses. Form 5500-SF or 5500-EZ need not be filed if certain conditions are met (for example, the plan and any other plan of the employer had total assets of $250,000 or less at the end of the plan year, unless it is the plan's final year).

If a Form 5500 series return must be filed, the form and its required schedules generally have to be filed no later than the last day of the seventh month after the plan year ends (July 31 for calendar year plans). A one-time extension of up to 3½ months (November 15 for calendar year plans) may be obtained by filing Form 5558 (Reg. § 1.6081-11). An automatic extension for filing will be granted if certain conditions are met (for example, the plan year and the employer's tax year are the same and the employer has been granted an extension to file its income tax return). In addition, the due date for performing certain time-sensitive actions, including filing Form 5500 series, otherwise due on or after April 1, 2020, and before July 15, 2020, is automatically extended to July 15, 2020, in response to the COVID-19 (coronavirus) crisis (Notice 2020-23; Rev. Proc. 2018-58).

Form 5500 and Form 5500-SF are filed with the Department of Labor (DOL) and must be filed electronically if the plan administrator and employer are required in the aggregate to file at least 250 returns during the calendar year that includes the first day of the plan year. Form 5500-EZ can only be filed on paper with the IRS. A one-participant plan that is eligible to file may elect to file Form 5500-SF electronically through the DOL's system rather than filing a Form 5500-EZ on paper with the IRS. For returns required to be filed for plan years beginning after 2019, a consolidated Form 5500 that a group of identical plans is allowed to file is treated as a separate return for each plan for purposes of applying the 250 return requirement for electronic filing (Code Sec. 6011(e)(6), as added by the Setting Every Community Up for Retirement Enhancement (SECURE) Act of 2019 (P.L. 116-94); Reg. § 301.6058-2).

A plan may also be required to file Form 8955-SSA to report certain information regarding separated participants with deferred vested benefits under the plan. The form must be filed with the IRS by the last day of the seventh month following the last day of that plan year, plus extensions. It should not be filed with Form 5500 or Form 5500-SF. A extension of up to 3½ months may be obtained by filing Form 5558. In addition, the due date for performing certain time-sensitive actions, including filing Form 8955-SSA. otherwise due on or after April 1, 2020, and before July 15, 2020, is automatically extended to July 15, 2020, in response to the COVID-19 (coronavirus) crisis (Notice 2020-23; Rev. Proc. 2018-58). Form 8955-SSA must be filed electronically if the plan administrator is required to file at least 250 returns during the calendar year that includes the first day of the plan year. The IRS will provide hardship waiver of the electronic filing requirements for Form 8955-SSA only in limited circumstances (Reg. § 301.6057-3; Rev. Proc. 2015-47).

Various penalties may be imposed for the failure to timely file the required Form 5500 series form, schedules, reports, or Form 8955-SSA (Code Secs. 6652 and 6692).

The IRS has implemented a permanent program to grant administrative and certain penalty relief to plan sponsors of one-participant and certain foreign plans for failure to timely file their annual reports on Form 5500-EZ (Rev. Proc. 2015-32; Rev. Proc. 2014-32).

2138. Retirement Plans Terminations. An employer that establishes a qualified retirement plan (¶ 2111) can terminate the plan when it has sufficient assets to satisfy benefit liabilities or in a distress situation. On termination, partial termination, or complete discontinuance of contributions to plan, all affected employees have certain nonforfeitable rights. Depending on type of plan being terminated and whether termination is standard termination or distress termination, the plan administrator must comply with specific requirements. For this purpose, whether a partial termination has occurred is determined on a case-by-case basis (Reg. § 1.411(d)-2(b)).

A special rule applies where a defined benefit plan ceases or reduces future benefit accruals. In this case, a partial termination occurs if a potential reversion to the employer or employees who maintain the plan is created or increased. Multiemployer plans are subject to the vesting, participation, and benefit accrual rules that generally apply to all qualified plans. However, there are special funding and termination rules for multiemployer plans regarding special amortization periods (Code Sec. 412(b)(2)).

A defined contribution plan (¶ 2101) is considered terminated on the date when it is voluntarily terminated by the employer or employers who maintain it. A defined benefit plan is terminated when it is voluntarily terminated by the plan administrator or when it is terminated by the Pension Benefit Guaranty Corporation (PBGC) (Reg. § 1.411(d)-2(c)). The PBGC is a corporation operated under the Department of Labor whose primary purpose is to administer a pension plan termination insurance program for beneficiaries provided in ERISA.

Voluntary Termination. A qualified defined benefit plan may be voluntarily terminated through either a standard termination or a distress termination. The type of termination that the plan administrator uses depends on whether there are, or appear to be, assets sufficient to satisfy PBGC guaranteed benefits. In determining if there are sufficient plan assets to pay benefits in a standard termination, claims are divided into six categories: (1) voluntary employee contributions that are nonforfeitable; (2) mandatory employee contributions, plus interest; (3) annuities provided with employer contributions that have been, or could have been, in pay status at least three years prior to plan termination; (4) the participant's basic-type benefits that do not exceed the guarantee limits; (5) all other nonforfeitable benefits; and (6) all plan benefits not allocated to the other categories (29 CFR § 4044, Secs. 11-16).

On the other hand, a distress termination of a defined benefit plan may be initiated by the plan administrator or the PBGC. Initiating a distress termination requires several steps: notice of intent to terminate given to participants, filing forms with PBGC, PBGC review, determination of whether requirements are met, notice of benefit distribution, issuances of notices, distribution of benefits, and filing of post-distribution certificate (ERISA § 4041).

Involuntary Terminations. A defined benefit may be involuntarily terminated by the PBGC if it makes a determination that: (1) the plan has not met the minimum funding standard; (2) the plan will be unable to pay benefits when due; (3) there has been a distribution under the plan to a participant who is a substantial owner, the distribution has a value of $10,000 or more, the distribution is not made by reason of the death of the participant, and, immediately after the distribution, the plan has nonforfeitable benefits that are not funded; or (4) the possible long-run loss to the PBGC may be expected to increase unreasonably if the plan is not terminated (ERISA § 4042(a)). When a termination occurs, (1) the termination must not have the effect of discriminating in favor of highly compensated employees (¶ 2114), (2) the plan administrator must notify the IRS, (3) all benefits or contributions that are not allocated to employees must be so allocated, (4) benefits must become nonforfeitable, and (5) the plan's assets must be distributed as soon as administratively feasible.

2139. Employee Plan Compliance Resolution System (EPCRS). The Employee Plan Compliance Resolution System (EPCRS) is a comprehensive system of correction programs for sponsors of plans intended to be qualified retirement plans (¶ 2111), 403(b) annuity plans (¶ 2191), SIMPLE IRAs (¶ 2181), and SEPs (¶ 2189) that have not met the qualification requirements for a period of time. Plan sponsors should follow the correction procedures in Rev. Proc. 2019-19. EPCRS includes the following correction programs.

Self-Correction Program (SCP). The SCP is available to correct operational failures for qualified plans and 403(b) annuity plans, as well as SEPs and SIMPLE IRAs provided the SEP or SIMPLE IRA is established and maintained on a document approved by the IRS. In addition, in the case of a qualified plan that is the subject of a favorable determination letter or in the case of a 403(b) annuity plan, the plan sponsor generally may correct significant and insignificant operational failures without payment of any fee or sanction. SEPs and SIMPLE IRAs are eligible for SCP only to correct insignificant operational failures. SCP may also be used to correct significant operational failures for qualified plans or 403(b) annuity plans. A plan can self correct an operational failure if the failure is insignificant. Self correction is available even if the plan or sponsor is under examination or the operational failure is discovered on examination.

Voluntary Correction Program (VCP). The VCP provides general procedures for correction of operational, plan document, demographic, and employer eligibility qualification failures for qualified plans, 403(b) annuity plans, SEPs, and SIMPLE IRAs. A plan sponsor may, at any time prior to audit, pay a limited fee and receive the IRS's approval for a correction. Under VCP, there are special procedures for anonymous submissions and group submissions. If the plan or plan sponsor is under examination, VCP is not available. However, while the plan or plan sponsor is under examination, insignificant operational failures can be corrected under the SCP and, if correction has been substantially completed before the plan or plan sponsor is under examination, significant operational failures can be corrected under SCP. VCP is for correction of failures raised by the plan sponsor or failures identified by the IRS in processing the application. Consideration under VCP does not preclude a subsequent examination of the plan or plan sponsor by the IRS with respect to the tax year(s) involved with respect to matters outside the compliance statement. Absent unusual circumstances, a plan that has been properly submitted under VCP will not be examined while the submission is pending. This does not preclude concurrent examination of the plan sponsor's other plan.

Closing Agreements Programs (Audit CAP). If a failure is identified on audit and has not been corrected through the SCP or the VCP, the plan sponsor may correct the failure and pay a sanction. The sanction imposed will take into account the nature, extent and severity of the failure as well as the extent to which correction occurred before audit. The Audit Closing Agreement Program (Audit CAP) is available for qualified plans for correction of all failures found on examination that have not been corrected in accordance with SCP or VCP. If the IRS and the plan sponsor cannot reach an agreement regarding the correction, the failure(s), or the amount of the sanction, the plan will be disqualified or, in the case of a 403(b) annuity plan, SEP, or SIMPLE IRA, the plan cannot rely on the effect of EPCRS. The sanction under Audit CAP is a negotiated percentage of the maximum payment amount. For 403(b) annuity plans, SEPs and SIMPLE IRAs, the sanction is a negotiated percentage of the total sanction amount.

Taxation of Distributions and Rollovers

See CCH® AnswerConnect: *Retirement Distributions* for more information on this topic.

2141. Taxation of Distributions from Retirement Plans. Distributions from a qualified retirement plan (¶ 2111) are generally taxed to the recipient unless the distribution is an eligible rollover distribution (¶ 2145) or attributable to designated Roth contributions (¶ 2121). The tax treatment of a distribution depends on the form of the distribution.

If the plan distribution takes the form of an annuity, it is taxable under the annuity rules (¶ 817 and ¶ 839) (Code Secs. 402(a) and 403(a)(1)). For this purpose, the benefits derived from the employee's contributions to a defined contribution plan and the earnings on them may be treated as a separate contract from benefits derived from the employer's contributions (Code Sec. 72(d)(2)). A participant's separate account in a defined benefit plan is treated as a defined contribution plan if the plan provides a benefit derived from employer contributions that is based partly on the balance of the separate account (Code Sec. 414(k)(2)).

If a plan distribution is not in the form of an annuity, the following rules apply (Code Sec. 72(e); Reg. § 1.72-11):

- If a distribution is made *before* the annuity starting date, it is treated in much the same way as an annuity distribution. The recipient may exclude from gross income the portion of the distribution that bears the same ratio to the distribution as the investment in the contract bears to the value of the contract. The total amount excluded cannot exceed the employee's investment in the contract.

- A non-annuity distribution made *on or after* the annuity starting date is generally included in full in gross income unless it reduces the dollar amount of subsequent annuity payments.

An individual who receives a retirement distribution check is taxed in the year of receipt even if the check is not cashed. This rule applies whether or not the individual keeps the check, sends it back, destroys it, or cashes it in a later tax year. Note that the operation of this rule is limited to situations where the individual "could cash" the check in the year of receipt (Rev. Rul. 2019-19).

U.S. Civil Service Retirement Benefits. Retired federal employees generally receive annuity payments under the Civil Service Retirement System (CSRS) or the Federal Employee Retirement System (FERS). The portion of the payment that represents the employee's after-tax contributions to the retirement plan is not taxed. Form 1099-R will generally show the nontaxable portion of the CSRS or FERS payment as calculated under the simplified method (¶ 839) (IRS Pub. 721).

Death In Line of Duty. The amount paid as a survivor annuity to the spouse, former spouse, or child of a public safety officer killed in the line of duty is generally excludable from the recipient's gross income if the annuity is provided under a governmental retirement plan (Code Sec. 101(h)). A public safety officer includes law enforcement officers, firefighters, and members of an ambulance crew, or public rescue squad (Act Sec. 1204 of the Omnibus Crime Control and Safe Streets Act of 1968 (P.L. 90-351)). A chaplain killed in the line of duty may also be classified as a public safety officer for purposes of this exclusion.

Victims of Terrorism. If certain requirements are met, death benefits paid by an employer due to the death of an employee who was a victim of a terrorist act may be excluded from income (Code Sec. 101(i)). For this purpose, a self-employed individual may be considered an employee.

Employer Securities. Distributions of an employer's securities under circumstances not involving a lump-sum distribution (¶ 2143) are subject to the above rules except for unrealized appreciation attributable to shares that were purchased with the employee's own contributions (Code Sec. 402(e)(4)(A)). The appreciation is not taxed until the securities are sold.

Loss. For tax years beginning before 2018 and after 2025, an employee may claim a loss deduction if he or she receives a cash distribution that exceeds his or her basis in the qualified plan (Rev. Rul. 72-305). The deduction is claimed as a miscellaneous itemized deduction subject to the two-percent-adjusted gross income limitation. The deduction may not be claimed for tax years beginning in 2018 through 2025 (¶ 1079).

2143. Lump-Sum Distributions from Retirement Plans. Special rules apply in determining the taxable portion of a lump-sum distribution from a qualified retirement plan (¶ 2111). A lump-sum distribution is a distribution of a participant's entire interest in a qualified plan within a single tax year of the recipient due to one of the following circumstances:

- the death of the employee,
- the employee has attained age 59½,
- on account of the employee's separation from service from the employer (as common-law employee), or
- after a participant who is a self-employed individual becomes totally and permanently disabled (Code Sec. 402(e)(4)(D)).

The rules applicable to lump-sum distributions are applied without regard to community property laws. As a result, a lump-sum distribution is considered to belong entirely to the participant, rather than half to the participant and half to his or her spouse (*R.L. Karem*, Dec. 49,091, 100 TC 521). However, a spouse may acquire an interest in retirement plan assets by means of a qualified domestic relations order (QDRO) (¶ 2144).

¶2143

Determining Taxable Amount. The entire amount of the lump-sum distribution is not always subject to taxation. To determine the taxable portion of the lump-sum distribution, the following items must be subtracted from the total amount of the distribution:

- nondeductible amounts contributed to the plan by the participant (less any previous distributions the participant received that were excluded gross income),

- any premiums paid by the plan to furnish a participant with life insurance protection that were included in gross income,

- any repayments of loans from the plan that were included in gross income (¶ 2152),

- the current actuarial value of any annuity contract that was included in the lump-sum distribution, and

- net unrealized appreciation in any employer securities that were distributed as part of the lump-sum distribution (unless the taxpayer elects to be taxed on this appreciation).

If the net unrealized appreciation is excluded from gross income upon distribution of the securities, tax is deferred until the securities are sold or exchanged. The cost or other basis of the employer securities is included in the taxable portion of the distribution (Code Sec. 402(e)(4)(B)).

Born Before January 2, 1936. Employees born before January 2, 1936, may elect to have their lump-sum distributions from a qualified plan taxed under favorable rates. The election is also available to the employee's beneficiaries, including a spouse or former spouse who was named as an alternate payee under a QDRO. The recipient (employee, beneficiary, or alternate payee) must elect to use this special tax treatment for all such amounts received during the tax year (Code Sec. 402(d)(4)(B), prior to amendment by the Small Business Job Protection Act of 1996 (P.L. 104-188)). This special treatment is *not* available if any portion of the lump-sum distribution is rolled over into another plan (Code Sec. 402(d)(4)(K), prior to amendment by P.L. 104-188).

2144. Retirement Plan Distributions Incident to Divorce or Separation. A distribution made by a qualified retirement plan (¶ 2111) to an alternate payee (e.g., spouse, ex-spouse, child, or other dependent of the participant) under the terms of a qualified domestic relations order (QDRO) is taxable to the alternate payee and not to the plan participant (Code Secs. 402(e)(1)(A) and 414(p)). A QDRO is a judgment, decree, or order (including approval of a property settlement agreement) made under a state's domestic relations or community property law. The QDRO must relate to child support, alimony, or marital property rights of a spouse, former spouse, child, or other dependent of the plan participant. In order to be qualified, the order must meet specified requirements as to content and generally may not require the plan to pay benefits that are not otherwise payable under the terms of the plan.

Payment of the entire amount due the spouse or ex-spouse under a QDRO is eligible for special tax averaging treatment for lump-sum distributions if it would be eligible had it been paid to the participant (¶ 2143). All qualified plans must permit a participant, or spouse or ex-spouse of a participant who is an alternate payee under a QDRO, to elect to have any distribution that is eligible for rollover treatment transferred directly to an eligible transferee plan specified by the participant (¶ 2145). The participant's investment in the contract is allocated between the participant, spouse, or ex-spouse, pro rata on the basis of the present value of all benefits awarded to the spouse or ex-spouse, and the present value of all benefits reserved to the participant (Code Sec. 72(m)(10)).

Rollover Distributions. If a participant's spouse or former spouse is awarded all or part of the participant's interest in a qualified retirement plan by a QDRO, the distribution of any part of that interest to the spouse or former spouse may be rolled over on the same terms that would apply if the distribution were made to the participant (¶ 2145) (Code Sec. 414(p)(10)).

Transfers of IRAs. The transfer of all or a portion of an IRA to a spouse or former spouse under a divorce or separation instrument (¶ 772) is a nontaxable transaction as to both parties, and the IRA is thereafter treated as that of the spouse or former spouse (Code Sec. 408(d)(6)). Accordingly, the spouse or former spouse may roll over to another IRA all or any part of the interest transferred to him or her (¶ 2167).

2145. Rollover Distributions from Retirement Plans. A distribution from an qualified retirement plan (¶ 2111) may be excluded from gross income if the recipient rolls over the distribution to another qualified plan or IRA (Code Sec. 402(c)). All distributions from a qualified plan are eligible for rollover treatment except:

- a distribution that is one of a series of substantially equal periodic payments, made over the life (or life expectancy) of the participant or the joint lives (or joint life expectancies) of the participant and his or her beneficiary;

- a distribution that is one of a series of substantially equal periodic payments made over a specified period of 10 years or more;

- required minimum distributions (RMDs) (¶ 2127); and

- hardship distributions from 401(k) plans (¶ 2129).

The minimum distribution rules do not apply for the 2020 calendar year for any defined contribution plan or IRA. Any portion of a distribution in 2020 that otherwise would have been a RMD is not treated as an eligible rollover distribution for the direct transfers, mandatory rollovers, withholding, and written explanation requirements described below (Code Sec. 402(c)(4), as amended by the Coronavirus Aid, Relief, and Economic Security (CARES) Act (P.L. 116-136)).

Eligible rollover distributions from a qualified plan, 403(b) annuity plan, and 457 plan may be rolled over to any type of plan. Similarly, distributions from a traditional IRA generally are permitted to be rolled over into any type of plan (¶ 2167). A distribution from a designated Roth account in a qualified plan may be rolled over only to another designated Roth account in a qualified plan or Roth IRA (¶ 2175). Special rules apply for rollover distributions by successors after the death of the plan participant (¶ 2148) and incident to divorce or separation (¶ 2144). SIMPLE IRA plans can receive rollover distributions from a qualified plan, 403(b) annuity plan, 457 plan, or traditional IRA after an initial period of two years (¶ 2183).

A rollover generally must be made within 60 days of receipt of the distribution. The IRS has the authority to grant a waiver of the 60-day rule in situations involving equity, good conscience, or situations beyond the control of the individual. Acceptable excuses might include: (1) military service in a combat zone or during a Presidentially declared disaster; (2) errors committed by a financial institution; or (3) inability to complete a rollover due to death, disability, hospitalization, incarceration, restrictions imposed by a foreign country, or postal error (Code Sec. 402(c)(3)). The due date for performing certain time-sensitive action, including the 60-day rollover requirement, otherwise due on or after April 1, 2020, and before July 15, 2020, is automatically extended to July 15, 2020, in response to the COVID-19 (coronavirus) crisis (Notice 2020-23; Rev. Proc. 2018-58).

The IRS has provided procedures to obtain a waiver of the 60-day requirement, including an automatic waiver in the event of an error by a financial institution (Rev. Proc. 2016-47; Rev. Proc. 2003-16). In addition, taxpayers may qualify for an automatic waiver and a self-certification procedure in the following circumstances:

- an error was committed by the financial institution receiving the contribution or making the distribution to which the contribution relates;

- the distribution, having been made in the form of a check, was misplaced and never cashed;

- the distribution was deposited into and remained in an account that the taxpayer mistakenly thought was an eligible retirement plan;

- the taxpayer's principal residence was severely damaged;

- a member of the taxpayer's family died;

- the taxpayer or a member of the taxpayer's family was seriously ill;

- the taxpayer was incarcerated;

- restrictions were imposed by a foreign country;

- a postal error occurred;

- the distribution was made on account of a levy and the proceeds of the levy have been returned to the taxpayer; or

- the party making the distribution to which the rollover relates delayed providing information that the receiving plan or IRA required to complete the rollover despite the taxpayer's reasonable efforts to obtain the information.

Direct Transfers. A qualified plan must allow an employee to elect to have any distribution that is eligible to be rolled over transferred directly to another qualified plan or traditional IRA unless it reasonably believes that the employee will receive distributions eligible to be rolled over of less than $200 (Code Secs. 401(a)(31)(C) and 402(c)(2), Reg. §1.401(a)(31)-1). Plans that are eligible to receive direct rollovers generally are the same plans that can receive rollovers, except qualified plans are required to allow direct transfers to qualified plans only if they are defined contribution plans (Code Sec. 401(a)(31)(E)). The defined contribution plan that accepts the transfer must agree to separately account for the pre-tax and after-tax portions of the amount that is transferred.

After-tax contributions from qualified retirement plans can also be rolled over in a direct trustee-to-trustee transfer to a defined benefit plan or a 403(b) annuity plan. The transferee plan must separately account for after-tax contributions and earnings. A traditional IRA to which the pre-tax and post-tax amounts are rolled over does not have to separately account for these amounts. A rollover that includes both pre-tax and post-tax amounts is considered as coming first from pre-tax amounts.

Mandatory Rollovers. A qualified plan must provide for a direct rollover (i.e., a trustee to trustee transfer) from the plan into an IRA when the plan makes a mandatory distribution of the participant's benefit (an involuntary cash-out) (Code Sec. 401(a)(31)). The rule applies when a mandatory distribution from a qualified plan exceeds $1,000 and the plan specifies that nonforfeitable benefits that do not exceed $5,000 must be distributed immediately. The employee must have the right to elect to receive the distribution or have it rolled over into another IRA or qualified plan (Notice 2005-5).

Withholding. If a distributee does not elect a direct transfer, and receives the distribution and then transfers the funds to an eligible plan within 60 days, the payor of the distribution must withhold 20 percent of the distribution (Code Sec. 3405(c)). If the distributee does elect a direct transfer, there is no withholding.

Written Explanation. The plan administrator must provide a written explanation to a recipient of the distribution options, including the direct trustee-to-trustee transfer option, within a reasonable period of time before making an eligible rollover distribution (Code Sec. 402(f); Notice 2018-74, modifying Notice 2014-74). The IRS has provided two safe harbor explanations that may be provided to recipients of eligible rollover distributions from a qualified plan.

2147. Rollover Distributions of After-Tax Roth Contributions. A qualified retirement plan (¶ 2111) that allows participating employees to designate part of their elective deferrals as after-tax Roth contributions (¶ 2121) may permit a rollover of a distribution from a participant's non-Roth account to the participant's designated Roth account within the same plan (Code Sec. 402A(c)(4)). The intra-plan non-Roth to Roth rollover rules mirror the eligible retirement plan to Roth IRA rollover rules (¶ 2175). Both kinds of rollovers adopt the traditional IRA to Roth IRA conversion rules. The distribution to be rolled over must be otherwise allowed under the plan; thus, an employer may have to amend its non-Roth plan to allow in-service distributions or distributions prior to normal retirement age. The converted amount is includible in gross income as a distribution for the tax year in which the amount is distributed or transferred. This amount is reduced by any after-tax contributions included in the amount rolled over. Any election for any distribution during a tax year may not be changed after the due date for such tax year.

2148. Rollover Distributions After Death of Participant. A surviving spouse of an employee may rollover a distribution from a qualified plan (¶ 2111) into an account maintained in his or her name under the same terms and conditions that would have applied to the employee if the distribution would have been eligible for rollover treatment if made to the employee (¶ 2145) (Code Sec. 402(c)(9)). A beneficiary other than a surviving spouse who receives a distribution from a qualified plan is not entitled to roll over the distribution to an IRA or to another qualified plan account in his or her own name. Instead, a nonspouse beneficiary can roll a qualified plan distribution into an IRA established in the name of the decedent. The IRA is treated as an inherited IRA. This allows the beneficiary to take distributions from the IRA in accordance with the required minimum distribution rules (¶ 2127) instead of including the entire distribution into gross income in the year of the plan distribution (Code Sec. 402(c)(11)). The surviving spouse of the owner of an IRA is also eligible to roll over any amount received from that IRA to another IRA or qualified plan (¶ 2167). This cannot be done by any other successor to the IRA.

2151. Penalty for Early Distributions from Retirement Plans. Taxable distributions from a qualified retirement plan (¶ 2141) or traditional IRA (¶ 2165) are generally subject to a 10-percent additional tax if made before the participant reaches age 59½ (Code Sec. 72(t), as amended by the Setting Every Community Up for Retirement Enhancement (SECURE) Act of 2019 (P.L. 116-94)). The 10-percent additional tax does *not* apply to:

- eligible distributions that are timely and properly rolled over into an IRA or other qualified plan (¶ 2145);

- distributions upon death or disability of the participant;

- distributions after separation from service that are part of a series of substantially equal periodic payments (not less frequently than annually) over the life (or life expectancy) of the participant or the joint lives (or life expectancies) of the participant and the beneficiary;

- distributions other than from a SEP (¶ 2189) or traditional IRA (¶ 2163) after the participant's separation from service, provided the separation occurred during or after the calendar year in which the participant reached age 55; the age for separation of service is only 50 in the case of distributions from a government plan to a retired police officer, firefighter, emergency medical services provider, specified federal law enforcement officer, customs and border protection officer, air traffic controller, nuclear materials courier, United States Capitol Police, Supreme Court Police, and diplomatic security special agent;

- certain distributions by employee stock ownership plans (ESOPs) of dividends on employer securities;

- distributions made on account of the IRS's levy against the participant's account;

- distributions not exceeding deductible medical expenses, determined without regard to whether deductions are itemized (¶ 1015);

- distributions to a nonparticipant under a qualified domestic relations order (QDRO) (¶ 2144);

- distributions from federal retirement plans that are made under a phased retirement program;

- qualified reservist distributions (¶ 2160);

- qualified birth or adoption distributions of up to $5,000 made after 2019 during the one-year period beginning on the date the child of the participant is born or the legal adoption of an eligible child; and

- qualified disaster and qualified coronavirus-related distributions.

Additional Tax on IRA Distributions. The exceptions to the 10-percent additional tax generally apply to IRA distributions except for distributions to a participant who has reached age 55 and has separated from service. Also, though the transfer of an interest in an IRA under a divorce or separation agreement is not a taxable event, subsequent distributions from a transferred IRA are not excluded from the additional tax. Some additional exceptions to the tax apply for IRA distributions only (¶ 2169).

SIMPLE Plan Penalty. For employees who withdraw any amount from a SIMPLE IRA (¶ 2181) during the first two years of participation, the 10-percent additional tax is increased to 25 percent (Code Sec. 72(t)(6)).

Coronavirus-Related Distributions. The 10-percent additional tax for early withdrawals does not apply to any qualified coronavirus-related distribution from an eligible retirement plan. The aggregate amount of coronavirus-related distributions an individual may receive in any tax year is limited in the aggregate to $100,000. The individual includes the taxable portion of the distribution in gross income over a three-year span unless he or she elects otherwise. The distribution may be recontributed to an eligible retirement plan within three years as a rollover contribution (Act Secs. 2202(a) and (c) of the Coronavirus Aid, Relief, and Economic Security (CARES) Act (P.L. 116-136)).

A qualified coronavirus-related distribution is a distribution from an eligible retirement plan, including an IRA, made on or after March 27, 2020, and before December 31, 2020, to an individual: (1) who is diagnosed with the virus SARS-CoV-2 or with coronavirus disease 2019 (COVID-19) by a test approved by the Centers for Disease Control and Prevention (CDC); (2) whose spouse or dependent is diagnosed with such virus or disease by such a test, or (3) who experiences adverse financial consequences as a result the coronavirus.

Qualified Disaster Distributions. The 10-percent additional tax for early withdrawals does not apply to any qualified disaster distribution, qualified wildfire distribution, or qualified hurricane distribution. A qualified distribution is any distribution from an eligible retirement plan or IRA made to an individual whose principal place of abode was in the qualified disaster area and who sustained an economic loss due to the disaster.

A qualified disaster distribution must be made between the first day of the incident period of the qualified disaster and before June 17, 2020, for any qualified federal disaster declared between January 1, 2018, and February 18, 2020. A qualified wildfire distribution or qualified hurricane distribution must be made before January 1, 2019, for the California wildfires of 2017, or Hurricanes Harvey, Irma, or Maria (Act Sec. 201 and 202(a) of the Taxpayer Certainty and Disaster Tax Relief Act of 2019 (P.L. 116-94); Act Secs. 20101 and 20102(a) of the Bipartisan Budget Act of 2018 (P.L. 115-123); Act Secs. 501 and 502(a) of the Disaster Tax Relief and Airport and Airway Extension Act of 2017 (P.L. 115-63), as amended by P.L. 115-123; IRS Pub 976).

A qualified disaster, wildfire, or hurricane distribution is limited to $100,000, reduced by the amount of qualified distributions received in prior tax years. The $100,000 limit applies separately for qualified disaster distributions made with respect to each qualified federal disaster declared between January 1, 2018, and February 18, 2020. Unless the individual elects otherwise, the portion of any qualified distribution that is includible in income is reported ratably over three years, beginning with the year that the distribution is received. If the individual dies before the distribution has been fully included in income, the remaining amount is included in income for the year of the individual's death. Alternatively, the distribution may be repaid during the three-year period beginning on the date the distribution was received. A qualified distribution does not qualify as an eligible rollover distribution.

Reporting Requirements. The 10-percent additional tax on early distributions is generally reported on Form 5329. If an exception to the tax exists, the individual should provide this information on the form. If no exception exists and distribution "Code 1" (i.e., early distribution) is correctly shown in the Form 1099-R received by the individual from the plan, then Form 5329 does not need to be filed. Instead, the amount of the additional tax should be reported directly on Schedule 2 (Form 1040).

2152. Retirement Plan Loans. A loan to a participant from a qualified retirement plan is treated as a distribution and included in the participant's gross income unless certain requirements are met. A pledge or assignment of any part of a participant's interest in a plan is treated as a loan for this purpose (Code Sec. 72(p), as amended by the Setting Every Community Up for Retirement Enhancement (SECURE) Act of 2019 (P.L. 116-94); Reg. §1.72(p)-1).

Allowable Loans. Subject to specific dollar limits, a loan is not treated as a distribution if it must be repaid within five years or the proceeds are used to acquire a principal residence for the plan participant. The *refinancing* of a home loan does not qualify for this exception, but the repayment of a loan used to acquire the principal residence does qualify. Any plan loan must be subject to an enforceable agreement and repayment must be made with substantially level payments not less than quarterly. Qualified retirement plans are not permitted to make loans to participants through credit cards or other similar arrangements. The due date for performing certain time-sensitive actions, including repayment of loans, otherwise due on or after April 1, 2020, and before July 15, 2020, is automatically extended to July 15, 2020, in response to the COVID-19 (coronavirus) crisis (Notice 2020-23; Rev. Proc. 2018-58).

> **Example 1:** On July 1, 2019, Betty purchased a home that she used as a principal residence. She paid a portion of the purchase price with a $50,000 loan

from Global Bank. On August 1, 2019, Betty borrowed $50,000 from her 401(k) plan. A few days later, Betty used the money from the plan loan to pay the $50,000 she owed Global Bank. Based on these facts, the plan loan would be treated as having been used to acquire Betty's principal residence. As a result, Betty's plan loan would *not* be treated as a taxable distribution.

Loan Limits. A loan from a qualified plan is not considered a distribution to the extent it does not exceed the lesser of $50,000 or 50 percent of the present value (but not less than $10,000) of the plan participant's vested benefits under the plan. The $50,000 limit is reduced by the excess (if any) of: (1) the highest outstanding balance of loans from the plan during the one-year period ending on the day preceding the date of the loan, over (2) the outstanding balance of those loans on the date of the loan.

> **Example 2:** Jane is a participant in her employer's qualified profit-sharing plan. She wishes to borrow the maximum amount subject to the five-year repayment rule on July 1, 2019. On that date, the value of her vested interest in the plan is $120,000. Her highest loan balance during the period July 1, 2018, through June 30, 2019, was $40,000, and her balance on July 1, 2019, is $35,000. The maximum amount that Jane may borrow on July 1, 2019, is $10,000. This is the amount that, when added to her $35,000 loan balance, does not exceed $45,000. The $45,000 amount is determined by reducing the $50,000 loan limit by the excess of her highest loan balance for the past year ($40,000) over the loan balance at the time of the new loan ($35,000).

If an employee fails to abide by the applicable rules, the loan is treated as a taxable distribution of the accrued benefit, and may be subject to the 10-percent penalty for early withdrawals (¶ 2151). Loan distributions can also occur through a reduction (or offset) of the account balance. Typically, these distributions occur when the plan terminates or the employee terminates employment. If the employee does not repay the outstanding balance, it will be deducted from the account and treated as a distribution. The offset loan balance must be included in the employee's gross income and may be subject to the 10-percent additional tax on early distributions. A distribution of a plan loan offset may be rolled over to an eligible retirement plan by the due date (including extensions) of the taxpayer's return for the year of distribution (Code Sec. 402(c)(3)(C)). However, the due date for performing certain time-sensitive action, including a plan loan offset rollover, otherwise due on or after April 1, 2020, and before July 15, 2020, is automatically extended to July 15, 2020, in response to the COVID-19 (coronavirus) crisis (Notice 2020-23; Rev. Proc. 2018-58).

Coronavirus Relief. The limit on loans from an employer-sponsored retirement plan for a qualified individual affected by COVID-19 (coronavirus) is increased to the lesser of $100,000 or 100 percent of the present value (but not less than $10,000) of the plan participant's benefits under the plan. A qualified individual is any individual who receives a qualified coronavirus-related distribution from eligible retirement plan, including an IRA, on or after March 27, 2020, and before December 31, 2020. The distribution must be made to an individual: (1) who is diagnosed with the virus SARS-CoV-2 or with coronavirus disease 2019 (COVID-19) by a test approved by the Centers for Disease Control and Prevention (CDC); (2) whose spouse or dependent is diagnosed with such virus or disease by such a test, or (3) who experiences adverse financial consequences as a result the coronavirus (Act Sec. 2202(b) and (c) of the Coronavirus Aid, Relief, and Economic Security (CARES) Act (P.L. 116-136)).

Disaster Relief. The limit on loans from a qualified employer plan is increased to the lesser of $100,000 or 100 percent of the present value (but not less than $10,000) of the plan participant's benefits for qualified individuals affected by a qualified federal disaster, the California wildfires of 2017, or Hurricanes Harvey, Irma, or Maria. A qualified individual is an individual whose principal place of abode was in the qualified disaster area and who sustained an economic loss due to the disaster.

The loan must be made between the first day of the incident period of the qualified disaster and before June 17, 2020, for any qualified federal disaster declared between January 1, 2018, and February 18, 2020. The loan must be made before January 1, 2019, for the California wildfires of 2017, or Hurricanes Harvey, Irma, or Maria. Any repayment on an outstanding loan is suspended for one year if the due date occurred before June 17, 2020 for a qualified federal disaster, and December 31, 2018, for 2017 California wildfires or Hurricanes Harvey, Irma, or Maria (Act Sec. 201 and 202(c) of the Taxpayer

Certainty and Disaster Tax Relief Act of 2019 (P.L. 116-94); Act Secs. 20101 and 20102(c) of the Bipartisan Budget Act of 2018 (P.L. 115-123); Act Secs. 501 and 502(c) of the Disaster Tax Relief and Airport and Airway Extension Act of 2017 (P.L. 115-63), as amended by P.L. 115-123; IRS Pub 976).

The IRS has also provided relief from certain verification procedures that may be required under retirement plans with respect to loans and hardship distributions for individuals affected by the California wildfires or Hurricanes Harvey, Irma, or Maria. The relief applies to participants in 401(k) plans, 403(b) annuity plans, and 457 plans (Announcement 2017-11; Announcement 2017-13, Announcement 2017-15).

Traditional IRAs

See CCH® AnswerConnect: *Individual Retirement Accounts* for more information on this topic.

2155. Traditional Individual Retirement Accounts (IRAs). An individual may make deductible contributions to a traditional individual retirement account (IRA) if he or she receives taxable compensation and has not attained age 70½ by the end of the tax year. The age limit is eliminated effective for contributions made for tax years beginning after 2019 (Code Sec. 219, as amended by the Setting Every Community Up for Retirement Enhancement (SECURE) Act of 2019 (P.L. 116-94)). Contributions to a traditional IRA may be deducted subject to limits, including whether the taxpayer is an active participant in an employer-sponsored retirement plan (¶ 2157). Amounts earned in a traditional IRA are not subject to tax until distributions are received from the account (¶ 2163 and ¶ 2165). A Roth IRA is generally subject to the same rules as a traditional IRA except that contributions are not deductible and qualified distributions may be excluded from gross income (¶ 2171).

IRA Contributions. The maximum combined contribution that can be made to all of an individual's traditional and Roth IRAs is $6,000 for 2019 ($6,000 for 2020) (Code Sec. 219(b); Notice 2018-83; Notice 2019-59). An individual who will be at least 50 years of age by the end of the tax year may generally make additional "catch-up" contributions to a traditional or Roth IRA of $1,000.

An individual has until the due date of his or her income tax return without regard to extensions (April 15 generally) to make contributions to an IRA for the year. However, the due date for performing certain time-sensitive actions, including making IRA contributions, otherwise due on or after April 1, 2020, and before July 15, 2020, is automatically extended to July 15, 2020 (Notice 2020-23; Rev. Proc. 2018-58). If the contribution is made by the due date, it will be treated as having been made on the last day of the tax year for which the return is filed (Code Sec. 219(f)(3)). A deduction may be claimed for a contribution even though the contribution had not yet been made when the return is filed. However, the contribution must be made by the due date of the tax return (Rev. Rul. 84-18).

If a contribution to a traditional IRA is *less* than the allowable maximum for that year, the individual cannot contribute more in a later year to make up the difference. If a contribution is *more* than the allowable maximum, the excess contribution may be withdrawn by the due date of the taxpayer's return (including extensions), or carried over and deducted in later years to the extent that the actual contributions in those later years are less than the allowable maximum (Code Sec. 219(f)(6)). Any excess contribution is subject to a six percent excise tax each year until it is corrected (Code Sec. 4973(a)). The individual reports the excise tax on Form 5329. An individual may be able to claim a nonrefundable credit based upon his or her contributions to IRAs (traditional and/or Roth), as well as other types of qualified retirement plans (¶ 1404).

Compensation. For purposes of determining an individual's eligibility to make contributions to an IRA, compensation includes wages, salaries, bonuses, tips, and other amounts received for performing personal services. Under a safe-harbor rule, the IRS will accept as compensation the amount properly shown on the individual's Form W-2 as wages, tips, and other compensation, less any amount properly shown for nonqualified plans (Code Sec. 219(f)(1), as amended by P.L. 116-94; Rev. Proc. 91-18). Thus, amounts received from an employer as disability pay, unemployment compensation, accrued annual leave, sick leave, incentive awards and termination pay is considered compensation.

Compensation also includes commissions, self-employment income, nontaxable combat pay (¶ 895), and military differential wages. The compensation of a self-employed person is the individual's earned income (¶ 2107). For tax years beginning after 2019, compensation includes any amount included in the taxpayer's gross income and paid to aid the individual in the pursuit of graduate or postdoctoral study (i.e., fellowships and stipends). Compensation also include taxable alimony and separate maintenance payments received under divorce or separation agreement executed before 2019. Compensation does not include pensions, annuities, or other forms of deferred compensation.

Tax Refunds. A taxpayer may choose to have a refund of federal income taxes directly deposited into up to three separate accounts, including an IRA. The IRA must be established before the request for the direct deposit is made. The deposit counts against the taxpayer's annual contribution limit. Thus, the taxpayer should inform the IRA trustee which year the direct deposit contribution is made. The taxpayer must also verify that the direct deposit is made to the IRA by the due date of his or her return for that year without regard to extensions. A direct deposit request of an entire refund into an IRA should be made on a taxpayer's Form 1040. If a taxpayer chooses to have a refund split and deposited in up to three different accounts, then Form 8888 is used.

Allowable Investments. Although IRAs may hold almost any investment, they are generally prohibited from investing in collectibles (e.g., antiques and stamps). However, certain U.S. gold and silver bullion coins minted since October 1986 may be held by an IRA. An IRA may also hold certain platinum and state-issued coins, as well as gold, silver, platinum, and palladium bullion (Code Sec. 408(m)(3)).

Deemed IRAs. Qualified retirement plans (¶ 2111) may allow employees to make voluntary contributions to a separate account that will be deemed to be a traditional IRA or Roth IRA if the account meets all the requirements of the particular type of IRA (Code Sec. 408(q); Reg. § 1.408(q)-1(a)). The employee must designate the contribution as a deemed IRA contribution. An employee's contributions to the account count against the annual limit on IRA contributions.

2157. Deductible Contributions to IRAs—In General. Contributions to a traditional IRA are generally deductible to the extent that they do not exceed the lesser of the individual's compensation for the year or the maximum contribution limit for the year (¶ 2155). The maximum allowable deduction may be reduced if the individual or spouse is an active participant in an employer-sponsored retirement plan (Code Sec. 219(g); Reg. § 1.219-2). This includes a qualified plan (¶ 2111), SIMPLE IRA (¶ 2181), and SEP (¶ 2189), but not a 457 plan (¶ 2193). If an individual or spouse is an active participant in an employer's plan, then the amount deductible may be phased out based on the taxpayer's filing status and modified adjusted gross income (AGI). See ¶ 2158 for phaseout of deduction for married individuals filing jointly. See ¶ 2159 for phaseout for married individuals filing separately and single filers. See ¶ 2160 for discussion of nondeductible contributions.

Active Participant Defined. The determination on active participant status is made without regard to whether an individual's rights under an employer-sponsored plan are nonforfeitable. In the case of a defined benefit plan, an individual who is not excluded under the eligibility provisions of the plan is considered to be an active participant if he or she is (1) eligible to participate for any part of the plan year ending with or within the tax year, even though the individual has elected not to do so, (2) has failed to make a mandatory contribution, or (3) has failed to meet the minimum service requirements. In the case of a defined contribution plan, an individual is considered an active participant if contributions or forfeitures are allocated to the individual's account for the plan year that ends with or within that tax year. An individual is also is an active participant for any tax year in which the individual makes a voluntary or mandatory employee contribution (Notice 87-16).

Social Security and Railroad Retirement (Tier I or Tier II) are not retirement arrangements for purposes of determining active participation. If an individual receives benefits from a previous employer's plan, the individual is not covered by the plan. An individual is also *not* considered an active participant in an employer-sponsored plan merely because the individual's spouse is an active participant (Code Sec. 219(g)(7)). An employer should have marked the box labeled "Retirement Plan" on the employee's Form W-2 if the employee participated in an employer plan for the year.

Modified AGI. A taxpayer's modified AGI for purpose of the limits on deductible IRA contributions is the taxpayer's AGI modified by taking into account the inclusion in income of Social Security and Railroad Retirement benefits (¶ 716) and the disallowance of passive activity losses (¶ 1169). It does not take into account the exclusion of interest on educational U.S. savings bonds (¶ 863), the exclusion of employer-paid adoption assistance (¶ 2063), the deduction for student loan interest (¶ 1011), the deduction for tuition and related expenses before 2021 (¶ 1011A), the deduction for domestic production activities before 2018 (¶ 980A), the foreign earned income and housing exclusions (¶ 2402 and ¶ 2403), and the deduction for contributions to IRAs (¶ 2157) (Code Sec. 219(g)(3)(A)).

Social Security Recipients. An employed individual, either the taxpayer or the spouse, who is covered by a retirement plan, currently receiving Social Security benefits, and wants to determine the allowable deduction for contributions to a traditional IRA must compute taxable Social Security benefits twice. The first computation is for the purpose of determining the tentative amount of Social Security benefits that must be included in gross income if the individual did not make any IRA contribution. This computation determines the amount of hypothetical AGI for purposes of the IRA phaseout provision. The second computation determines the actual amount of taxable Social Security benefits by taking into account the deductible IRA contribution that was determined under the first computation. The worksheets necessary for these computations are found in IRS Pub. 590-A (¶ 716).

2158. Deductible IRA Contribution Limits—Married Filing Jointly. If married individuals file a joint return, each spouse may make deductible contributions to his or her own traditional IRA. The spouse with the greater amount of compensation ("higher-paid spouse") may claim deductible contributions for 2019 of up to the *lesser* of: (1) $6,000, or $7,000 if catch-up contributions are allowable ($6,000 and $7,000, respectively, for 2020), as reduced for active participation, or (2) his or her compensation (Code Sec. 219(c); Notice 2018-83; Notice 2019-59). The spouse with the lesser amount of compensation ("lower-paid spouse") may claim deductible contributions for 2019 equal to the *lesser* of:

- $6,000, or $7,000 if catch-up contributions are allowable ($6,000 and $7,000, respectively, for 2020), as reduced for active participation, or
- the sum of:
  - the compensation of the lower-paid spouse, and
  - the compensation of the higher-paid spouse, reduced by: (i) the deduction allowed to the higher-paid spouse for IRA contributions, (ii) the amount of any designated nondeductible IRA contribution on behalf of the higher-paid spouse, and (iii) the amount of any contribution on behalf of the higher-paid spouse to a Roth IRA (¶ 2171).

AGI Limits for Joint Filers. If both individuals on a joint return are active participants in an employer's qualified retirement plan, their ability to claim a deduction for contributions made to traditional IRAs depends upon the amount of their modified adjusted gross income (AGI) (¶ 2157). The allowable IRA deduction for joint filers will be reduced when modified AGI is between $103,000 and $123,000 for 2019 ($104,000 and $124,000 for 2020) (Notice 2018-83; Notice 2019-59). See ¶ 2159 for information regarding the IRA deduction limits for married persons filing separately and single filers. See ¶ 2160 for discussion of nondeductible contributions.

Example 1: Ralph and Alice file a joint return for 2019. They are both employed and both are covered by their employers' qualified plans. Their modified AGI for 2019 is $135,000. Since they are both active participants in qualified plans and their modified AGI exceeds the phaseout range ($103,000 to $123,000), they are not allowed to make deductible IRA contributions for the year. They may make nondeductible contributions to traditional IRAs or to Roth IRAs.

An individual will *not* be considered an active participant in an employer-sponsored plan merely because the individual's spouse is treated as an active participant (Code Sec. 219(g)(7)). However, if an individual is not an active participant and is married to someone who is covered, the deductible contribution is phased out if the couple's

¶2158

modified AGI (jointly computed) is between $193,000 and $203,000 for 2019 ($196,000 and $206,000 for 2020).

> **Example 2:** Bob is covered by a 401(k) plan sponsored by his employer. His wife, Betty, is not employed. The couple files a joint income tax return for 2019, with a modified AGI of $135,000. Betty may make a deductible contribution to a traditional IRA for the year because she is not an active participant in an employer-sponsored retirement plan and their combined modified AGI is below the phaseout range for a married couple where only one spouse is an active participant ($193,000 to $203,000). Bob may not make a deductible IRA contribution because their combined modified AGI is above the phaseout range for active participants who are married and filing jointly ($103,000 to $123,000).

> **Example 3:** Assume the same facts as in Example 2 above, except that the couple's modified AGI was $250,000 for 2019. Neither Bob nor Betty can make a deductible contribution to a traditional IRA.

2159. Deductible IRA Contribution Limits—Single or Married Filing Separately. A taxpayer that files as single, head of household, or married filing separately may claim a deduction for contributions to a traditional IRA to the extent they do not exceed the lesser of: (1) the individual's compensation for the year that is includible in gross income, or (2) for 2019, $6,000 or $7,000 if catch-up contributions are allowable ($6,000 and $7,000, respectively for 2020) (Code Sec. 219(b)(1); Notice 2018-83; Notice 2019-59). The maximum allowable deduction may be reduced if the individual is an active participant in an employer-maintained retirement plan (¶ 2157). See ¶ 2158 for information regarding the IRA deduction limits for married individuals filing jointly. See ¶ 2160 for discussion of nondeductible contributions.

Single or Head of Household. If a single individual or head of household is an active participant in an employer's retirement plan, the IRA deduction begins to phase out when modified adjusted gross income (AGI) is between $64,000 and $74,000 for 2019 ($65,000 and $75,000 for 2020) (Code Sec. 219(g); Notice 2018-83; Notice 2019-59).

Married Filing Separately. If an individual files as married filing separately and the individual, or the spouse, is an active participant in an employer's retirement plan, the IRA deduction begins to phase out when the individual's modified AGI exceeds $0. The deduction is completely phased out when modified AGI is $10,000 or more. This phaseout range is not adjusted for inflation. In determining if an individual is married or single for the purpose of determining which IRA deduction limit applies, spouses who file separate returns and live apart at all times during a tax year are *not* considered to be married during that tax year (Code Sec. 219(g)(4)).

2160. Nondeductible Contributions to Traditional IRAs. An individual may make nondeductible contributions to a traditional IRA (¶ 2155). These contributions may not exceed the *excess* of: (1) the maximum allowable contribution for the year, over (2) the amount actually allowed as a deduction for the year (¶ 2157) (Code Sec. 408(o)). In applying this rule, an individual may elect to treat otherwise deductible contributions as nondeductible contributions. The tax advantages of funding a Roth IRA should be considered before making nondeductible contributions to a traditional IRA (¶ 2171).

> **Example:** In 2019, Bill, age 48 and single, had earned income of $54,000 and a modified adjusted gross income (AGI) of $66,000. He is an active participant in his employer's 401(k) plan. Since his modified AGI exceeds $64,000, a maximum contribution to a traditional IRA would not be fully deductible. Bill determines that his maximum deductible contribution would be $4,900. As a result, he could make an additional $1,100 nondeductible IRA contribution.

Nondeductible contributions may be made up to and including the due date of the return for the tax year without regard to extensions (April 15 generally) (Code Sec. 219(f)(3)). The due date for performing certain time-sensitive actions, including making IRA contributions, otherwise due on or after April 1, 2020, and before July 15, 2020, is automatically extended to July 15, 2020, in response to the COVID-19 (coronavirus) crisis (Notice 2020-23; Rev. Proc. 2018-58). The same deadline applies to deductible IRA contributions and Roth IRA contributions. Nondeductible contributions to a traditional IRA must be reported on Form 8606, which is attached to the individual's return.

Difficulty of Care Payments. For contributions made after December 20, 2019, an individual may elect to increase the limit on nondeductible contributions for the tax year if he or she excludes from gross income for the year a qualified foster care payment that is a difficulty of care payment (¶ 883). The limit is increased by the lesser of the amount of the difficulty of care payment excluded from gross income or the excess of the taxpayer's deductible IRA contributions for the year, over the amount of compensation included in gross income (Code Sec. 408(o)(5), as added by the Setting Every Community Up for Retirement Enhancement (SECURE) Act of 2019 (P.L. 116-94)).

Reservist Contributions. Qualified reservist distributions are not subject to the tax on early distributions and may be recontributed to an IRA as a nondeductible contribution without counting against the dollar limits applicable to IRA contributions (Code Sec. 72(t)(2)(G)). A qualified reservist distribution is a distribution that is made:

- from an IRA or from an individual's elective deferrals under an employer plan such as a 401(k) plan or 403(b) annuity plan (¶ 2121);

- to an individual who is a reservist who was called to active duty for a period of more than 179 days or for an indefinite period; and

- during the period beginning on the date the reservist was called to active duty and ending on the date the active duty ended.

The distribution may be recontributed at any time within the two years after the end of the active duty period. However, the due date for performing certain time-sensitive actions, including recontribution of reservist distribution within two years, otherwise due on or after April 1, 2020, and before July 15, 2020, is automatically extended to July 15, 2020, in response to the COVID-19 (coronavirus) crisis (Notice 2020-23; Rev. Proc. 2018-58). A reservist who took a distribution after being called up and paid the early distribution penalty may file a claim for refund of the penalty.

2161. Excess Contributions to IRAs. Annual contributions to a traditional IRA (¶ 2155) and/or Roth IRA (¶ 2171) in excess of the allowable amount are subject to a cumulative six percent excise tax, which is reported on Form 5329 (Code Sec. 4973). See ¶ 2155 for a discussion on contributions to a traditional IRA.

2163. Distribution Requirements of Traditional IRAs. Traditional IRAs (¶ 2155) are subject to the same required minimum distribution (RMD) rules that apply to qualified employer-provided retirement plans (¶ 2127) (Code Sec. 408(a)(6) and (b)(3); Reg. § 1.408-8). This means that distributions to the owner or beneficiary of a traditional IRA must begin no later than April 1 following the calendar year in which the owner reaches age 72 (age 70½ for individuals attaining that age before 2020). In addition, the minimum distribution rules do not apply to the 2020 calendar year. A few special rules also apply to RMDs from IRAs.

Inherited Traditional IRA: Spouse. A surviving spouse may elect to treat an inherited traditional IRA as his or her own IRA by having the account redesignated as an account belonging to the surviving spouse as owner rather than beneficiary. Alternatively, the surviving spouse may be treated as having made this election if: (1) any amounts in the IRA are not distributed within the time period that applied to the decedent, or (2) the surviving spouse makes contributions (including rollover contributions) to the inherited IRA that are subject, or are deemed subject, to the lifetime distribution requirements. In order to make the election, the surviving spouse must be the sole beneficiary of the IRA and have an unlimited right to withdraw amounts from it (Reg. § 1.408-8, Q&A-5). If a trust is named as the beneficiary of the IRA, this requirement has not been satisfied even if the spouse is the sole beneficiary of the trust. If the surviving spouse makes the election, he or she is treated as the owner of the IRA for all purposes. If the election is not made, then the RMDs are determined as though the spouse was the beneficiary of the IRA.

Inherited Traditional IRA: Nonspouse. A nonspouse beneficiary who inherits an IRA cannot treat it as his or her own account but must take RMDs determined under the rules applicable to beneficiaries receiving distributions from a qualified plan. If an individual other than the decedent's spouse receives a lump sum distribution from an IRA, then the individual may generally not roll over that distribution into another IRA. Instead, it must be distributed within a certain period (Code Sec. 408(d)(3)(C); Rev. Rul. 92-47). The distribution, minus the aggregate amount of the owner's nondeductible IRA contributions, is taxed as ordinary income in the year the distribution is received.

Trust Named as Beneficiary. If a trust is named as the beneficiary of the IRA, the beneficiaries of the trust will be treated as the deceased individual's beneficiaries if certain requirements are met (Reg. § 1.401(a)(9)-4, Q&A-5). The requirements include validity of the trust, identification of the trust's beneficiaries, and the delivery of proper documentation to the plan administrator (Reg. § 1.401(a)(9)-4, Q&A-6).

More Than One IRA. If an individual is required to receive an RMD from more than one traditional IRA in a calendar year, the amount of the minimum distribution from each IRA must be calculated separately and the separate amounts totalled. However, the total may be withdrawn from one or more of the IRAs in whatever amounts the individual chooses (Reg. § 1.408-8, Q&A-9).

Planning and Due Diligence Considerations. For families that are not in immediate need of inherited IRA funds, it can make sense to stretch out the RMD period as long as possible in order to protect the IRA assets from tax. Careful designation of beneficiaries can help to peg the RMD period to the life expectancy of an individual beneficiary. Inherited IRAs are subject to a number of special rules and deadlines in the year following the owner's death, including rules for identifying designated beneficiaries, disclaiming interests, providing the IRS with trust information, and slicing an inherited IRA into multiple IRAs.

2165. Taxation of Distributions from Traditional IRAs. If an individual made only deductible contributions to a traditional IRA (¶ 2157), then any distributions from the IRA are included in gross income as ordinary income unless it is rolled over to another IRA or qualified retirement plan (¶ 2167) (Code Sec. 408(d)(1) and (2); Reg. § 1.408-4(a)).

If nondeductible contributions were made (¶ 2160), the owner has a *cost basis* in the IRA equal to the sum of the nondeductible contributions made, minus any prior withdrawals or distributions of nondeductible contributions (Notice 87-16). The recovery of this basis is not recognized as taxable income. As a result, the individual must determine how much of the IRA distribution is nontaxable. The nontaxable portion of the distribution is generally determined under the same rules that apply to annuity payments (¶ 817). When applying these rules:

• all traditional IRAs of an individual, including SIMPLE IRAs (¶ 2181) and SEPs (¶ 2189), are treated as a single contract;

• all distributions during the individual's tax year are treated as one distribution;

• the value of the contract, the income on the contract, and the investment in the contract are calculated (after adding back distributions made during the year) as of the close of the calendar year in which the tax year of the distribution begins; and

• total withdrawals excludable from income in all tax years cannot exceed the taxpayer's investment in the contract in all tax years.

Pro Rata Rule. The amount representing a nontaxable return of basis for any traditional IRA distribution is a pro rata amount based on the ratio between the owner's total basis in all of the owner's IRAs to the total value of all of the owner's IRAs.

> **Example:** Walt has two IRAs—IRA-1 is worth $50,000 with $10,000 in nondeductible contributions, and IRA-2 is worth $50,000 with no nondeductible contributions. Collectively, Walt's IRAs are worth $100,000 with $10,000 in basis. If he withdraws $10,000 from IRA-1, either to use or to roll over, $1,000 is treated as a nontaxable return of basis. The same would hold true for a $10,000 distribution from IRA-2.

The pro rata rule does not apply to distributions from an employer plan that includes both taxable and nontaxable amounts. These amounts can be separately allocated to different destinations (for example, a nontaxable basis amounts can go to a Roth IRA while taxable amounts to a traditional IRA) (¶ 2175). In addition, in a rollover from an IRA with basis to a qualified employer plan (such as a 401(k) plan) the basis remains in the IRA and only taxable amounts are rolled over (Reg. § 1.402(c)-2, Q&A 3(b)(3)). The basis in an inherited IRA is also not aggregated either with the basis in the IRAs the beneficiary holds as an owner, or with the basis of any other inherited IRA from a different decedent (though if the beneficiary is a spouse who treats the IRA as his or her own, then basis is aggregated) (IRS Pub. 590-B).

Qualified Charitable Distributions (QCDs). An individual age 70½ or older may distribute up to $100,000 tax-free from his or her IRAs to certain charitable organizations without including the distribution in gross income (Code Sec. 408(d)(8), as amended by the Setting Every Community Up for Retirement Enhancement (SECURE) Act of 2019 (P.L. 116-94)). The entire distribution must otherwise be deductible as a charitable contribution, disregarding the percentage limitations, even though the individual cannot claim a charitable deduction for the donation (¶ 1058).

For QCDs made for tax years beginning after 2019, the amount excluded from gross income is reduced by the excess of the deductions allowed to the taxpayer for all tax years ending on or after he or she attains age 70½, over any reductions for all tax years preceding the current tax year. The $100,000 limit is the maximum amount that may be excluded from gross income each year, regardless of the number of the IRAs the taxpayer maintains. For married individuals filing a joint return, the limit is $100,000 per individual IRA owner.

A QCD will count toward an individual's required minimum distributions (RMDs) (¶ 2127). Note that the minimum age for QCDs is 70½ and the minimum age for RMDs is 72 for an individual attaining that age after 2019. Thus, an individual who attains age 70½ after 2019 may take QCDs that are not RMDs for tax years prior to the year he or she turns age 72. Alternatively, such an individual may delay making a QCD until the tax year he or she turns age 72 for the distribution to qualify as a RMD.

HSA Funding Distributions. An individual may make a one-time transfer of funds from his or her IRA directly to his or her health savings account (HSA) without recognizing income on the distribution (Code Sec. 408(d)(9); Notice 2008-51). The transfer can only be made if it would otherwise be a taxable distribution. The dollar amount excluded cannot exceed the annual limitation on the individual's HSA contribution for the year (¶ 2035). The exclusion is lost if the individual ceases to be eligible to contribute to an HSA during the twelve months after the contribution. In such a case, the distribution is includible in gross income and subject to a 10-percent penalty.

Reporting Requirements. Form 8606 is used to report the taxable portion of an IRA distribution if the individual ever made nondeductible contributions to an IRA. Income tax withholding is optional.

Estate Tax. If the distributee of an IRA distribution is the beneficiary of the IRA owner and the value of the IRA is included in the owner's estate for federal estate tax purposes, the distributee is entitled to deduct the estate tax allocable to the IRA (¶ 186) (Rev. Rul. 92-47).

Return of Contributions. A distribution from a traditional IRA that represents the return of a contribution made for a particular tax year will not be included in the individual's income if (Code Sec. 408(d)(4)):

- the distribution is made before the due date, including extensions, of the individual's tax return for that year;
- no deduction is allowed with respect to the contribution; and
- the distribution includes any net income earned by the contribution.

The net income earned by the contribution is included in income for the tax year in which the contribution was made even if the distribution is received in the following year.

Recognizing Loss on an IRA. For tax years beginning before 2018 and after 2025, an IRA owner may claim a loss deduction on traditional IRA investments if the amounts from all the owner's traditional IRAs have been distributed and total distributions are less than any unrecovered basis. If the individual has no tax basis in the IRAs, then no loss may be recognized. Any loss deduction is claimed as a miscellaneous itemized deduction subject to the two-percent-adjusted gross income limitation. The deduction may not be claimed for tax years beginning in 2018 through 2025 (¶ 1079).

2167. Rollover Distributions from IRAs. A distribution from a traditional IRA (¶ 2163) may be excluded from gross income if the recipient rolls over the distribution to another traditional IRA or returns it to the same IRA (Code Sec. 408(d)(3); Rev. Proc. 2016-47; Rev. Proc. 2003-16). A distribution from a traditional IRA may also be rolled over into a qualified plan (¶ 2111), 403(b) annuity plan (¶ 2191), or 457 plan (¶ 2193) provided that the plan accepts rollover contributions. All distributions from a traditional IRA are eligible for rollover treatment except for required minimum distributions (RMDs) and any portion of a distribution in 2020 that otherwise would have been a RMD except for the waiver the RMD requirements (¶ 2145). A rollover of after-tax Roth contributions can be made from one IRA to another IRA. However, after-tax Roth contributions in an IRA cannot be rolled over into an employer's qualified plan. See ¶ 2175 regarding a rollover from a traditional IRA into a Roth IRA. See ¶ 2181 regarding rollovers from a SIMPLE IRA.

The rollover or return of an IRA distribution must generally be accomplished within 60 days after the withdrawal. The IRS has the authority to grant a waiver of the 60-day rule in situations involving equity, good conscience, or situations beyond the control of the individual. The due date for performing certain time-sensitive action, including the 60-day rollover requirement, otherwise due on or after April 1, 2020, and before July 15, 2020, is automatically extended to July 15, 2020, in response to the COVID-19 (coronavirus) crisis (Notice 2020-23; Rev. Proc. 2018-58). It is not necessary that the entire amount withdrawn be transferred, but only the amount that is transferred during the rollover period will be excluded from gross income. Any portion of the withdrawal that is not rolled over within the required time period is includible in gross income and may be subject to the 10-percent additional tax for early distributions (¶ 2169).

Once-Per-12-Month Rule. Once an individual has made a tax-free rollover, he or she must wait at least one year from the date of receipt of the amount withdrawn before becoming eligible to engage in another rollover (Code Sec. 408(d)(3)(B)). The once-per-12-month rule applies on a taxpayer-by-taxpayer basis. Thus, if a taxpayer has multiple IRAs, a rollover from one prevents the taxpayer from rolling over again within 12-months from any of the taxpayer's IRAs. The once-per-12-month rule does not apply to trustee-to-trustee direct transfers.

2169. Penalty for Early Distributions from IRAs. If an individual is under age 59½, a distribution from a traditional IRA (¶ 2165) or nonqualified distribution from a Roth IRA (¶ 2173) is generally subject to the 10-percent additional tax on early distributions. Many of the exceptions to the tax on early distributions that apply to distributions from qualified employer-provided retirement plans (¶ 2151) also apply to early distributions from an IRA with the exception for early retirements (Code Sec. 72(t)(3)(A)). In addition, the following exceptions apply to early distributions from an IRA but not to distributions from a qualified retirement plan. If an exception applies, it may be necessary to file Form 5329.

Medical Insurance Premiums of Unemployed Individuals. Distributions from an IRA, SIMPLE IRA (¶ 2181), or SEP (¶ 2189) to an unemployed individual for use in paying qualified medical insurance premiums are *not* subject to the 10-percent additional tax (Code Sec. 72(t)(2)(D)). An eligible unemployed individual is someone who has received federal or state unemployment compensation for 12 consecutive weeks. A self-employed individual is treated as having received unemployment compensation if, under federal or state law, the individual would have received unemployment compensation but for being self-employed.

Qualifying premiums are deductible premiums for the medical care of the unemployed individual, spouse, and dependents. The distributions must be received in the tax year during which unemployment compensation is received or in the following year. In determining whether the premiums are deductible, the adjusted gross income (AGI) floor for claiming medical expenses as an itemized is ignored (¶ 1015). This exception to the 10-percent additional tax ceases to apply after the individual has been reemployed for 60 days (not necessarily consecutive) after initial unemployment.

Education Expenses. The 10-percent additional tax does not apply if the individual uses the IRA distribution to pay for qualified higher education expenses for the individual, the individual's spouse or child, or a grandchild of the individual or the individual's spouse. Qualified expenses include tuition at a post-secondary educational institution, books, fees, supplies, and equipment (Code Sec. 72(t)(2)(E)).

First-Time Homebuyer Expenses. The 10-percent additional tax does not apply if the individual uses the IRA distribution within 120 days for certain expenses of a first-time homebuyer. The due date for performing certain time-sensitive actions, including the

120-day requirement for first-time homebuyer distributions, otherwise due on or after April 1, 2020, and before July 15, 2020, is automatically extended to July 15, 2020, in response to the COVID-19 (coronavirus) crisis (Notice 2020-23; Rev. Proc. 2018-58).

Only $10,000 during the individual's lifetime may be withdrawn without a penalty for this purpose. Qualified expenses include acquisition costs, settlement charges, and closing costs of a principal residence of the individual or the individual's spouse, child or grandchild, or an ancestor of the individual or the individual's spouse. In order to be considered a first-time homebuyer, the person buying the residence (and spouse, if married) must not have had an ownership interest in a principal residence during the two-year period ending on the date that the new home is acquired (Code Sec. 72(t)(2)(F)).

Return of Nondeductible Contributions. The 10-percent additional tax does not apply to the portion of the distribution that represents a return of nondeductible IRA contributions (¶ 2165).

Roth IRAs

See CCH® AnswerConnect: *Individual Retirement Accounts* **for more information on this topic.**

2171. Roth IRAs. A Roth individual retirement account (IRA) is a type of IRA consisting of after-tax contributions (Code Sec. 408A). A Roth IRA generally is treated like a traditional IRA (¶ 2155) except that contributions to a Roth IRA cannot be deducted from income. On the other hand, qualified distributions from the Roth IRA are excludable from gross income (¶ 2173).

Roth IRA Contributions. The maximum contribution that can be made to individual's Roth and traditional IRAs is $6,000 for 2019 ($6,000 for 2020) (Code Sec. 408A(c); Reg. § 1.408A-3; Notice 2018-83; Notice 2019-59). The limit is the amount that may be contributed to *both* types of IRAs combined, not the amount that may be contributed to each type. An individual who will be at least 50 years of age by the end of the tax year may generally make additional catch-up contributions to a traditional or Roth IRA of $1,000 (Code Sec. 219(b)(5)). Rollover contributions into a Roth IRA are not counted against the annual contribution limit. An individual may make contributions to a Roth IRA regardless of their age.

Income Limits. The limit on contributions to Roth IRAs is phased out if the taxpayer's modified adjusted gross income (MAGI) exceeds a threshold amount.

- For 2019, the MAGI phaseout range is between $193,000 and $203,000 if married filing jointly, and between $122,000 and $137,000 if single, head of household, or married filing separately if the spouses did not live with each other at any time during the tax year (Notice 2018-83).

- For 2020, the MAGI phaseout range is between $196,000 and $206,000 if married filing jointly, and between $124,000 and $139,000 if single, head of household, or married filing separately if the spouses did not live with each other at any time during the tax year (Notice 2019-59).

For any tax year, the MAGI phaseout range is between $0 and $10,000 if married filing separately and the taxpayer lived with his or her spouse at anytime during the year. MAGI is generally calculated as it is for traditional IRAs (¶ 2157), except that for Roth IRAs it does not include the income reported from the conversion of a traditional IRA into a Roth IRA (¶ 2175).

Deemed Roth IRAs. Qualified employer-provided retirement plans may allow employees to make voluntary contributions to an account that will be deemed to be a Roth IRA if the account meets all the requirements of a Roth IRA (Code Sec. 408(q)). An employee's contribution to this account counts towards the maximum annual contribution that may be made to a Roth IRA.

Losses in Roth IRA. For tax years beginning before 2018 and after 2025, a Roth IRA owner may claim a loss deduction on Roth IRA investments if the amounts from all the owner's Roth IRAs have been distributed and total distributions are less than any unrecovered basis. If the individual has not tax basis in the Roth IRAs, then no loss may be recognized. Any loss deduction is claimed as a miscellaneous itemized deduction subject to the two-percent-adjusted gross income limitation. The deduction may not be claimed for tax years beginning in 2018 through 2025 (¶ 1079).

Military Death Gratuity. An individual who receives a military death gratuity or payment under the Servicemembers' Group Life Insurance (SGLI) program may contribute an amount up to the sum of the gratuity and SGLI payments received to a Roth IRA, notwithstanding the annual contribution limit and the phaseout of the contribution limit that otherwise apply. The contribution must be made within one year of the receipt of the payment (Code Sec. 408A(e)). These contributions are generally treated as though they were a rollover from another Roth IRA.

2173. Taxation of Distributions from Roth IRAs. Qualified distributions from a Roth IRA (¶ 2171) are not included in the recipient's gross income nor are they subject to the 10-percent additional tax for early withdrawals (¶ 2169) (Code Sec. 408A(d); Reg. § 1.408A-6). To be treated as a qualified distribution, the Roth IRA distribution, including distributions allocable to rollover contributions, may not be made before the end of the five-year period beginning with the first tax year for which the individual made a contribution to the Roth IRA. The five-year holding period ends on the last day of the individual's fifth consecutive tax year after the holding period started. Each Roth IRA owner generally has only one five-year period for all of the Roth IRAs that the individual owns.

> **Example:** Jack made his first contribution to a Roth IRA on September 15, 2015. He made additional contributions on December 27, 2016, and December 30, 2017. The five-year holding period for all of Jack's Roth IRAs is considered to have started on January 1, 2015. Distributions made after December 31, 2019, will have satisfied the five-year holding period.

In addition to satisfying the five-year holding period, a distribution will constitute a qualified distribution only if it is (Code Sec. 408A(d)(2)):

- made on or after the date on which the individual attains age 59½,
- made to a beneficiary (or the individual's estate) on or after the individual's death,
- attributable to the individual being disabled, or
- a distribution to pay for qualified first-time homebuyer expenses (¶ 2169).

Pre-Death Requirements. The *pre-death* required minimum distribution (RMD) rules (¶ 2127) that apply to qualified retirement plans and traditional IRAs do *not* apply to Roth IRAs (Code Sec. 408A(c)(4)). Thus, owners of Roth IRAs are not required to take distributions by April 1 of the year following the calendar year in which they attain age 72 (age 70½ for individuals attaining that age before 2020). The *post-death* RMD rules also generally do apply to Roth IRAs (Reg. § 1.408A-6, Q&A-14). If the sole beneficiary is the decedent's spouse, the spouse may delay distributions until the decedent would have attained age 72 (age 70½ for individuals attaining that age before 2020) or may treat the Roth IRA as his or her own.

Nonqualified Distributions. If an individual receives a nonqualified distribution from a Roth IRA, a portion of the distribution may be includible in gross income. In order to determine the amount that is includible in gross income, specific ordering rules are applied under which regular Roth contributions are deemed to be withdrawn first, then amounts transferred from traditional IRAs starting with amounts first transferred (Code Sec. 408A(d)(4)). Withdrawals of transferred amounts are then treated as coming first from amounts that were included in income. Earnings are treated as withdrawn after contributions (Reg. § 1.408A-6, Q&A-8). Thus, no amount is includible in gross income until all the after-tax contributions have been distributed. If an individual receives a nonqualified distribution from a Roth IRA that is includible in gross income, then the 10-percent additional tax for early distributions will apply. However, the same exceptions that apply to early distributions from traditional IRAs (¶ 2169) will also apply to the nonqualified Roth IRA distributions.

Reporting Roth IRA Distributions. Distributions from Roth IRAs are reported on Form 8606. If the 10-percent additional tax on early distributions applies, it is reported on Form 5329.

2175. Rollovers and Conversions of Roth IRAs. Taxpayers can make qualified rollover contributions to a Roth IRA (¶ 2171) from another Roth IRA, a traditional IRA (¶ 2155), and from certain qualified retirement plans (Code Sec. 408A(c)(5) and (e)). However, unlike rollovers to traditional IRAs (¶ 2145), qualified rollovers to Roth IRAs may result in the rollover being included in gross income equal to the amount that would be includible if it were not part of a qualified rollover distribution.

Rollovers from Roth IRAs. In the case of a qualified rollover from another Roth IRA, amounts distributed from the Roth IRA must be contributed either to the same or to another Roth IRA within 60 days of receiving the distribution. The IRS has the authority to grant a waiver of the 60-day rule in situations involving equity, good conscience, or situations beyond the control of the individual. The due date for performing certain time-sensitive action, including the 60-day rollover requirement, otherwise due on or after April 1, 2020, and before July 15, 2020, is automatically extended to July 15, 2020, in response to the COVID-19 (coronavirus) crisis (Notice 2020-23; Rev. Proc. 2018-58). Once a qualified rollover has been made, any other distributions received within the twelve months after the distribution rolled over is received cannot also be rolled over.

Conversions of Traditional IRAs. A taxpayer can convert a traditional IRA to a Roth IRA as long as the amount contributed to the Roth IRA satisfies the definition of a qualified rollover contribution for a traditional IRA (¶ 2167) (Code Sec. 408A(e); Reg. § 1.408A-4). Amounts transferred or converted from a traditional IRA into a Roth IRA generally must be included in gross income for the tax year in which the amount is distributed or transferred to the extent it does not represent a return of basis.

The 10-percent additional tax on early distributions does not apply to the taxable conversion amount. However, if within the five-year period starting with the year in which an individual made a conversion contribution of an amount from a traditional IRA to a Roth IRA, the individual takes a distribution from a Roth IRA of an amount that is attributable to the portion of the conversion contribution that was included in income, then the individual will be liable for the 10-percent additional tax unless one of the exceptions to the tax applies (¶ 2169) (Reg. § 1.408A-6, Q&A-5). The five-year period is separately determined for each conversion contribution made to a Roth IRA. Individuals can correct a failed Roth conversion by making a proper recharacterization election (¶ 2177).

Rollovers from Qualified Plans. Distributions from qualified retirement plans (¶ 2145), 403(b) annuity plans (¶ 2191), or 457 plans (¶ 2193) can be rolled over directly into a Roth IRA. Such rollovers are treated the same as under the conversion rules for traditional IRAs, though rollovers from designated Roth accounts are treated as rollovers from another Roth IRA (Notice 2009-75). The rollover contribution must meet the rollover requirements applicable to the specific type of retirement plan.

A plan participant who rolls over a distribution that includes both pre-tax and after-tax contributions may allocate the pre-tax amounts to a different destination than the post-tax amounts. For example, a plan participant may allocate pre-tax amounts to a traditional IRA and post-tax amounts to a Roth IRA as long as the participant re-contributes the amounts within the rollover period. This rule applies to direct trustee-to-trustee transfers as well, so plan participants can take advantage of it without having to pay withholding (Notice 2014-54).

2177. Recharacterization of IRA Contributions. An individual who has made contributions to a traditional IRA (¶ 2155) or Roth IRA (¶ 2171) may later recharacterize the contribution as a contribution to the other kind of IRA. In that case, the contribution is treated as having been originally made to the desired type of IRA (Code Sec. 408A(d)(6)); Reg. § 1.408A-5). Recharacterizing an IRA contribution requires transferring amounts previously contributed to a traditional or Roth IRA (plus any resulting net income or minus any resulting net loss) to a new IRA of the opposite type and electing to have the amounts treated as having been transferred to the second IRA at the time they actually were contributed to the first IRA. The transfer must be from trustee to trustee.

An individual generally has until the due date (including extensions) of the tax return for the year in which the contribution was made to make the recharacterization. The due date for performing certain time-sensitive actions, including recharacterizing contributions, otherwise due on or after April 1, 2020, and before July 15, 2020, is automatically extended to July 15, 2020, in response to the COVID-19 (coronavirus) crisis (Notice 2020-23; Rev. Proc. 2018-58). A recharacterization must be reported on the taxpayer's tax return as directed by Form 8606, along with a statement explaining the nature of the recharacterization (IRS Pub. 590-A).

A taxpayer is prohibited from reconverting a Roth IRA back to a traditional IRA, as well as recharacterizing qualified rollover contributions to a Roth IRA from other retirement plans (e.g., 401(k) or 403(b) plans). For tax years beginning before 2018, however, if a Roth IRA is recharacterized as a traditional IRA, the IRA may be converted back to a Roth IRA provided certain eligibility requirements are met in the reconversion year (¶ 2179).

2179. Roth IRA Reconversions. For tax years beginning before 2018, an IRA owner who converts an amount from a traditional IRA (¶ 2155) to a Roth IRA (¶ 2171) during any tax year and then transfers that amount back to a traditional IRA by means of a recharacterization (¶ 2177) may not reconvert that amount from the traditional IRA to a Roth IRA before the *later* of:

- the beginning of the tax year following the tax year in which the amount was converted to a Roth IRA; or

- the end of the 30-day period beginning on the day on which the IRA owner transfers the amount from the Roth IRA back to a traditional IRA by means of a recharacterization (regardless of whether the recharacterization occurs during the tax year in which the amount was converted to a Roth IRA or the following tax year) (Reg. § 1.408A-5, Q&A-9(a)(1)).

For tax years beginning after 2017, a reconversion is not allowed for amounts converted from a traditional IRA to a Roth IRA (Code Sec. 408A(d)(6)(B)(iii)). The IRA owner is also prohibited from recharacterizing qualified rollover contributions to a Roth IRA from other retirement plans (e.g., 401(k) or 403(b) plans).

SIMPLE Plans and SEPs

See CCH® AnswerConnect: *Retirement Plans for Small Employers and Self-Employed* for more information on this topic.

2181. SIMPLE IRA Plans. An eligible small employer (¶ 2187) may adopt a SIMPLE (Savings Incentive Match Plan for Employees) IRA retirement plan for its employees (Code Sec. 408(p)). A SIMPLE IRA plan is a written salary reduction agreement that lets eligible employees elect to have the employer make payments as elective contributions to a SIMPLE IRA of the employee or to the employee directly in cash. The plan may be designed so that elective contributions are made only if the employee affirmatively elects to have them made or as an automatic contribution unless the employee affirmatively opts out (Notice 2009-66).

The employer is required to make contributions to its employees' SIMPLE IRAs as either matching contributions of up to three percent of compensation or as nonelective contributions. No contributions other than the employee's salary reduction contributions and employer contributions may be made to a SIMPLE IRA. However, a rollover from another SIMPLE IRA may be received (Code Sec. 408(d)(3)(G)). See ¶ 2183 for a discussion of employee and employer contributions to a SIMPLE IRA.

All contributions under a SIMPLE IRA plan must be made to a SIMPLE IRA set up by the employer for each eligible employee. A SIMPLE IRA must meet the same requirements that apply to traditional IRAs (¶ 2155). It may not be designated as a Roth IRA (¶ 2171), but contributions to a SIMPLE IRA are not taken into account in determining the Roth IRA contribution limit (Code Sec. 408A(f)). Each eligible employee must have the right to elect during the 60-day period preceding the beginning of any calendar year (and the 60-day period preceding the employee's first day of eligibility) to participate in the plan for that calendar year or to modify the amount of his or her elective contributions for that calendar year (Code Sec. 408(p)(5)). An employee may terminate participation in the SIMPLE plan at any time during a calendar year, but the plan may prohibit reentry until the beginning of the following calendar year.

Distributions from a SIMPLE IRA are taxable to the employee (or the beneficiary or estate of the employee) under the same rules that govern distributions from traditional IRAs (¶ 2163) (Code Sec. 402(h)(3) and (k)). This includes the 10-percent additional tax that applies to early distributions from an IRA (¶ 2169) except that the tax is 25 percent if the employee takes an early distribution within two years after the employee's first participation in the plan (Code Sec. 72(t)(6); Notice 98-4). The two-year period begins on the first day that contributions made by the individual's employer are deposited in the individual's SIMPLE IRA. If the employee has participated in the SIMPLE IRA for at·

least two years, a distribution may be rolled over (¶ 2167) into other types of retirement plans including qualified employer-provided retirement plans (¶ 2111), 403(b) annuity plans (¶ 2191), and 457 plans (¶ 2193). If the employee has not participated in the SIMPLE plan for two years, the distribution may only be rolled over into another SIMPLE plan (Code Sec. 408(d)(3)(G)).

Establishing SIMPLE IRAs. The IRS has issued two model forms that may be used by an employer that wants to establish a SIMPLE IRA for its employees. Form 5304-SIMPLE is used if the employer permits each employee to choose the financial institution that will receive the SIMPLE IRA contributions. Form 5305-SIMPLE is used if the employer designates the financial institution that will receive the contributions. In that case, an employee must be given a reasonable period of time each year in which to transfer his or her SIMPLE IRA balance without cost or penalty from the designated financial institution to a SIMPLE IRA at another financial institution. Both forms also contain information that can be used to notify employees of the existence of the plan. Although the completed forms do not have to be filed with the IRS, they must be kept in order to show that the plan was adopted by the employer.

2183. SIMPLE IRAs—Employee and Employer Contributions. Contributions to an employee's SIMPLE IRA (¶ 2181) are limited to: (1) employee contributions made under a salary reduction agreement, and (2) employer contributions that are made as either matching contributions or nonelective contributions (Code Sec. 408(p)(2)). However, a rollover from another SIMPLE IRA may be received (Code Sec. 408(d)(3)(G)). A rollover may also be received from another plan (including traditional IRAs, simplified employee pensions (SEPs), qualified plans, tax-favored annuity plans, and nonqualified deferred compensation plans for state and local government employees) after an initial period of two years (Code Sec. 408(p)(1)).

Employee Contributions. An employee's elective contributions to a SIMPLE IRA under a salary reduction agreement are limited to $13,000 for 2019 ($13,500 for 2020) (Code Sec. 408(p)(2); Notice 2018-83; Notice 2019-59). An employee who will be at least age 50 by the end of the year is allowed to make additional catch-up contributions of $3,000 for 2019 ($3,000 for 2020) (Code Sec. 414(v)). The maximum dollar limit is the only limit on employee contributions. An employer may not place a limit on the percentage of salary an employee may elect to defer in the plan except in order to comply with the annual dollar limit. The employer must deposit the employee's elective contributions into the SIMPLE IRA within 30 days after the end of the month in which the amounts would have been paid to the employee. Elective contributions by an employee are fully vested when made (Code Sec. 408(p)(3)).

Matching Contributions If an employee makes an elective contribution to a SIMPLE IRA, then the employer generally must make a matching contribution in an amount not exceeding three percent of the employee's compensation for the calendar year (¶ 2185). An employer may elect to limit its matching contribution to a smaller percentage of compensation but not less than one percent. The election may *not* be made by an employer in more than two out of every five years. If the SIMPLE account did not exist during the full five-year period, the election may still be made in up to two of the years in which it did exist. Employees must be notified of the employer's election to contribute less than three percent a reasonable time before the beginning of the 60-day period at the end of each calendar year during which employees designate the amount of their election contributions for the following calendar year. Matching contributions to SIMPLE IRAs that are made on behalf of self-employed individuals are not treated as elective contributions made by the individuals (Code Sec. 408(p)(9)).

> **Example 1:** Ralph, age 52, participates in his employer's SIMPLE IRA plan and for 2019 his salary will be $50,000. He elects to defer the maximum amount into the plan $16,000 ($13,000 plus $3,000 catch-up). Under the plan, the employer makes a maximum matching contribution for each participating employee, up to the three percent limit. Therefore, the employer will make a $1,500 ($50,000 × three percent) matching contribution to Ralph's SIMPLE IRA.

Nonelective Contributions. Instead of making matching contributions, an employer may elect to make nonelective contributions of two percent of the compensation for each employee who is eligible to participate in the plan and who has at least $5,000 of compensation from the employer for the calendar year (Code Sec. 408(p)(2)(B)).

> **Example 2:** Assume the same facts as in Example 1 above, except that Ralph's employer decided to base its contributions on the nonelective contributions option. In this situation, Ralph would still be allowed to contribute $16,000 to his SIMPLE IRA. However, the employer's contribution would be $1,000 ($50,000 × two percent).

Vesting. The employee's right to both matching contributions and nonelective contributions of the employer (and the earnings on these contributions) in a SIMPLE IRA must be fully vested at all times (Code Sec. 408(p)(3)).

Employer's Deduction. An employer can deduct SIMPLE IRA contributions in the tax year with or within which the calendar year for which the contributions were made ends. Contributions for a particular tax year may be deducted if they are made for that tax year and are made by the due date (including extensions) of the employer's tax return for that year (Code Sec. 404(m)). However, the due date for performing certain time-sensitive actions, including making contributions to a SIMPLE IRA, otherwise due on or after April 1, 2020, and before July 15, 2020, is automatically extended to July 15, 2020, in response to the COVID-19 (coronavirus) crisis (Notice 2020-23; Rev. Proc. 2018-58).

2185. SIMPLE 401(k) Plans. An eligible small employer (¶ 2187) may adopt a SIMPLE (Savings Incentive Match Plan for Employees) retirement plan as part of a 401(k) plan (¶ 2104). A SIMPLE 401(k) is a simplified plan that generally must meet the same requirements that apply to other 401(k) plans except that in lieu of satisfying the nondiscrimination test for elective deferrals and matching contributions (¶ 2123) and the top-heavy rules (¶ 2132), a SIMPLE 401(k) plan must satisfy the following requirements.

Employee Contributions. Each employee eligible to participate in the SIMPLE 401(k) plan must have the right to make annual elective contributions, expressed as a percentage of compensation but not exceeding $13,000 for 2019 ($13,500 for 2020) (Code Sec. 401(k)(11)(B); Notice 2018-83; Notice 2019-59). An employee age 50 or over may make an additional catch-up contribution of $3,000 for 2019 ($3,000 for 2020) (Code Sec. 414(v)). Nondeductible employee contributions and rollover contributions may not be made to a SIMPLE 401(k).

Employer Contributions. The employer generally must make matching contributions for each participant in a SIMPLE 401(k) in an amount not exceeding three percent of the employee's compensation (Code Sec. 401(k)(11)(B)). Instead of making matching contributions, an employer may elect to make nonelective contributions of two percent of compensation for each employee who is eligible to participate in the plan and who has at least $5,000 of compensation. Employees must be notified that the employer has chosen to make the two-percent contribution within a reasonable period of time before the 60th day before the beginning of the calendar year.

Compensation. An employee's compensation for SIMPLE plan requirements is the sum of wages, tips, and other compensation from the eligible employer subject to federal income tax withholding. It also includes the employee's elective contributions made under any other qualified plan, including a SIMPLE IRA plan, a salary reduction simplified employee pension (SARSEP), a 403(b) annuity plan, and compensation deferred under a section 457 plan required to be reported by the employer on Form W-2. For self-employed individuals, SIMPLE compensation means net earnings from self-employment determined prior to subtracting any contributions made under the SIMPLE 401(k) plan on behalf of the individual (Reg. § 1.401(k)-4(e)(5)).

Employer's Deduction. An employer's deduction for contributions to a defined contribution plan is generally limited to the *greater* of: (1) 25 percent of the compensation paid or accrued during the tax year to beneficiaries under a stock bonus or profit-sharing plan, or (2) the amount that the employer is required to contribute to a SIMPLE 401(k) plan for the year (Code Sec. 404(a)(3)(A)(i)). Thus, an employer's deduction for its contributions to a SIMPLE 401(k) may be greater than the general limit of 25 percent of compensation paid (¶ 2119).

Vesting. All contributions to a SIMPLE 401(k) must be fully vested when made, and the plan cannot impose any restrictions on withdrawals (Code Sec. 401(k)(11)(A)).

Establishing a SIMPLE 401(k). The IRS has issued a model amendment that may be used by an employer that wants to adopt a plan that contains a SIMPLE 401(k) plan

(Rev. Proc. 97-9). The model amendment includes provisions for employee contributions, employer options concerning its contributions, and notification to employees.

2187. SIMPLE Plans—Eligible Employers and Employees. A SIMPLE IRA plan (¶ 2181) or SIMPLE 401(k) (¶ 2185) may only be established by an employer that has 100 or fewer eligible employees who received at least $5,000 in compensation during the preceding tax year (Code Secs. 401(k)(11)(D) and 408(p)(2)(C)(i)). Any type of employer can establish a SIMPLE plan, including a tax-exempt entity, governmental entity, and employer of domestic workers even though the compensation of domestic workers may not be subject to income tax withholding. The employer may generally not make contributions to any other qualified plan starting with the year the SIMPLE plan goes into effect. However, employers may adopt a SIMPLE plan for noncollectively bargained employees and at the same time maintain a qualified plan for collectively bargained employees (Code Sec. 408(p)(2)(D)).

If the employer has established a SIMPLE plan, an employee must be eligible to participate in any calendar year if he or she received at least $5,000 of compensation from the employer during *any* of the *two* preceding calendar years and is reasonably expected to receive at least $5,000 in compensation during the current calendar year (Code Sec. 408(p)(4)). An employee who is a nonresident alien or covered by a collective bargaining agreement may be excluded from participation.

If an individual is not self-employed, compensation means the amount of wages, tips, and other compensation from the employer subject to income tax withholding (¶ 2604), and the total amount of elective deferrals to qualified retirement plans (¶ 2121) including deferrals to 401(k) plans, 403(b) annuity plans, and salary reduction SEP (SARSEP), as well as elective contributions made under a SIMPLE IRA plan and section 457 plan (Code Sec. 408(p)(6); Notice 98-4). Compensation does not include amounts deferred under a cafeteria plan (¶ 2045).

A self-employed individual is treated as an employee and may participate in a SIMPLE plan if the minimum compensation requirement is met (Code Sec. 408(p)(6)). For this purpose, compensation means net earnings from self-employment from Schedule SE (Form 1040) before subtracting any contributions made to a SIMPLE IRA. A self-employed individual who has elected out of the self-employment tax on religious grounds (¶ 2667) may base his or her retirement plan contributions, including contributions to SIMPLE IRAs, on his or her self-employment income that is exempt from self-employment tax.

2189. Simplified Employee Pensions (SEPs). A simplified employee pension (SEP) is an arrangement under which an employer makes contributions to the IRAs of each of its employees (Code Sec. 408(k)). Annual contributions by an employer to a SEP are excluded from the employee's gross income to the extent that the contributions do not exceed the *lesser* of 25 percent of the participant's compensation or $56,000 for 2019 ($57,000 for 2020) (Code Sec. 402(h); Notice 2018-83; Notice 2019-59). The maximum amount of compensation that may be considered is $280,000 for 2019 ($285,000 for 2020). If the employer exceeds the annual limit on contributions, the employee is generally taxed on the amount of the excess contribution and subject to a six-percent excise tax if not withdrawn (¶ 2161). In the case of a SEP established by an unincorporated employer, the compensation of a self-employed participant (partner or proprietor) is earned income.

The employer must decide each year whether and how much to contribute to a SEP plan. If any contribution is made to a plan, nondiscriminatory employer contributions must be made for each employee who has reached age 21, performed services for the employer during at least three of the immediately preceding five years, and received at least $600 for 2019 ($600 for 2020) (Code Sec. 408(k)(2); Notice 2018-83; Notice 2019-59). Unlike traditional IRAs, the account owner of a SEP-IRA can make contributions regardless of their age (Code Sec. 219(b)(2)).

In order to deduct its SEP contributions for a particular year, the employer must make the contributions by the due date (including extensions), of its tax return for that tax year (Code Sec. 404(h)). However, the due date for performing certain time-sensitive actions, including making contributions to a SIMPLE IRA, otherwise due on or after April 1, 2020, and before July 15, 2020, is automatically extended to July 15, 2020, in response to the COVID-19 (coronavirus) crisis (Notice 2020-23; Rev. Proc. 2018-58). The contributions are made to the SEP-IRAs that have been established by, or for, each eligible employee. Although the employer's deduction cannot exceed 25 percent of the employee's compensation (¶ 2119), any excess can be carried over and deducted in later years subject to the percentage limitation. In addition, if an employer maintains another type of defined contribution plan, the contributions to a SEP must be taken into account when determining compliance with the annual limit imposed on deductible contributions to the plans.

Employee Contributions. In plan years beginning before 1997, an employer could include a salary reduction agreement (cash or deferred arrangement) as part of its SEP—commonly know as SARSEP. New SARSEPs cannot be established after 1996 (Sec. 1421(c) of Small Business Job Protection Act of 1996 (P.L. 104-188)). SARSEPs established before 1997 are allowed to continue and take on new participants. SARSEPs are generally subject to the same elective contribution rules as 401(k) plans (¶ 2121) after an initial period of two years.

Establishing a SEP-IRA. Most employers are able to establish a SEP plan by completing a Form 5305-SEP. The form is *not* filed with the IRS, but it is retained by the employer as evidence that a SEP plan has been established. All eligible employees must be given a copy of Form 5305-SEP. Certain employers should not use Form 5305-SEP (for example, employers that are currently maintaining another qualified plan or use the services of leased employees). An employer may establish a SEP-IRA for a particular year as late as the due date, including extensions, for its income tax return for that year.

Distributions. Distributions from a SEP are taxed under the rules that apply to distributions from a traditional IRA (¶ 2163) (Code Secs. 402(h)(3) and 408(d)).

Top-Heavy SEP. If a SEP is top heavy (¶ 2132), each participant who is not a key employee must be provided with a contribution that is not less than three percent of his or her compensation. If the rate for the key employee receiving the largest contribution is less than three percent, the contribution rate for that employee is used to determine the minimum contribution for non-key employees (Code Sec. 408(k)(1)(B)).

Sec. 403(b), Sec. 457, and Nonqualified Plans

See CCH® AnswerConnect: *Government and Nonprofit Employer Plans* and *Nonqualified Deferred Compensation Plans* for more information on this topic.

2191. Sec. 403(b) Annuity Plans (Tax Sheltered Annuities). A public school system or tax-exempt educational, charitable, or religious organization may provide retirement benefits for its employees through the purchase of annuities or by contributing to a custodial account invested in regulated investment companies (RICs) (Code Sec. 403(b)). This type of retirement plan is commonly referred to as a 403(b) annuity plan or tax-sheltered annuity (TSA). The employee's rights in the annuity or account generally must be nonforfeitable.

Limit on Annual Addition. A limit imposed on the total amount of the annual addition that may be made to an employee's 403(b) account. This annual limit is sometimes called the maximum amount contributable (MAC). The annual addition or MAC is made up of three types of contributions:

- elective contributions made by the employee,
- nonelective contributions made by the employer, and
- after-tax contributions made by the employee.

The annual addition generally cannot be more than the *lesser* of 100 percent of the employee's compensation or $56,000 for 2019 ($57,000 for 2020) (¶ 2115). There are also limits on the amount of elective deferrals that generally apply to all of an employee's deferrals (¶ 2121) under any 403(b) annuity plan, 401(k) plan, SIMPLE 401(k) (¶ 2185), and SEP (¶ 2189). Employees are not required to coordinate their maximum deferral under a 457 plan (¶ 2193) with their contributions made to a 403(b) annuity plan.

An employee who will be at least age 50 by the end of the year may make catch-up contributions to a 403(b) annuity plan. The maximum catch-up contribution to a 403(b) annuity plan is $6,000 for 2019 ($6,500 for 2020) (Code Sec. 414(v)). A qualified employee of certain organizations (for example, schools, hospitals, churches, and home health service organizations) who is covered by an annuity contract under a 403(b) annuity plan may defer additional amounts of his or her compensation (Code Sec.

402(g)(7)). For this purpose, a qualified employee is one who has completed 15 years of service with the organization.

Distributions. Payments to an employee from a 403(b) annuity plan are taxed under the annuity rules (¶ 817). Any employee contributions that were excluded from wages are not treated as part of the employee's investment in the contract. Distributions may generally be made because of the employee's death, disability, severance from employment, attainment of age 59½, or financial hardship (Code Sec. 403(b)(7)(A) and (b)(11), as amended by the Setting Every Community Up for Retirement Enhancement (SECURE) Act of 2019 (P.L. 116-94)). For plan years beginning after 2019, qualified distributions may also be made 90 days prior to the date that any lifetime income investment may no longer be held as an investment option (¶ 2125). Distributions that do not meet these requirements are subject to the 10-percent additional tax on early distributions (¶ 2151). The required minimum distribution (RMD) rules also apply, except that the minimum distribution rules do not apply to the 2020 calendar year (¶ 2127) (Code Sec. 403(b)(10)).

Rollovers. Distributions from a 403(b) annuity plan may be rolled over into an IRA or another 403(b) annuity plan, as well as to other types of qualified employer-provided retirement plans to the extent they accept rollover contributions (Code Sec. 403(b)(8)). The spousal rollover rules that apply to other types of employer sponsored plans and the written explanation requirements also apply to a beneficiary under a qualified annuity plan (Code Sec. 403(a)(4)(B)). A 403(b) annuity plan that includes a qualified Roth contribution program may permit a qualified rollover contribution from a participant's non-Roth account to the participant's designated Roth account within the same plan (Code Sec. 402A(c)(4)(B)).

2193. Sec. 457 Plans (Deferred Compensation Plans of Exempt Employers). Special rules apply to a deferred compensation plan sponsored by a state and local government, or private tax-exempt organization, commonly referred to as a 457 plan (Code Sec. 457(a)). Under a state or local government plan, compensation deferred under the plan is only included in income when it is paid to the employee. Under the plan of a tax-exempt organization, deferred compensation is includible when paid or made available. As with other types of qualified retirement plans, special requirements have to be met by a 457 plan.

Availability of Benefits. Compensation is deferred for any calendar month under a 457 plan only if an agreement providing for deferral is entered into before the beginning of that month (Code Sec. 457(b)(4); Reg. § 1.457-7(c)). Benefits are not considered to be made available under the plan if the participant or beneficiary may elect, before any benefits become payable, to defer payment of some or all of them to a fixed or determinable future time. In addition, amounts deferred under an eligible plan are not considered to be made available to the participant solely because the individual may choose among various investment options under the plan, whether before or after benefit payments have commenced. After benefits have become payable but before payments have commenced, the participant or beneficiary may elect to defer them to a date later than that originally elected. Only one such election may be made (Code Sec. 457(e)(9)(B)).

Limitation on Deferral. The maximum amount that can be deferred under a 457 plan is the *lesser* of 100 percent of the participant's includible compensation or $19,000 for 2019 ($19,500 for 2020) (Code Sec. 457(e)(15); Notice 2018-83; Notice 2019-59). A participant in a 457 plan is permitted to make additional deferrals of income for one or more of the last three tax years that end before normal retirement age (Code Sec. 457(b)(3)). The allowable deferral for the participant is increased, up to a limit of twice the standard dollar amount for the year, by the amount of allowable deferrals not made in previous plan years. Alternatively, an employee covered by a 457 plan who will be at least 50 years of age by the end of the year may make special catch-up contributions to the plan (Code Sec. 414(v)). The maximum catch-up contribution is $6,000 for 2019 ($6,500 for 2020). However, during the last three years of employment that end before attaining normal retirement age, a special formula is used to determine the maximum contribution (Code Sec. 457(e)(18)).

Other Requirements. A 457 plan must satisfy the required minimum distribution (RMD) rules that are generally imposed on qualified plans, except that the minimum distribution rules do not apply to the 2020 calendar year (¶ 2127) (Code Sec. 457(d), as amended by the Bipartisan American Miners Act of 2019 (P.L. 116-94) and the Setting Every Community Up for Retirement Enhancement (SECURE) Act of 2019 (P.L. 116-94)). Distributions of deferred amounts must not be made available before the calendar year that the participant attains age 70½ (age 59½ in the case of a state employer plans for plan years beginning after 2019), is severed from employment, or is faced with an unforeseen emergency as defined in the plan. For plan years beginning after 2019, qualified distributions may also be made 90 days prior to the date that any lifetime income investment may no longer be held as an investment option (¶ 2125).

Hardship withdrawals may not be made to the extent that the financial hardship can be relieved by insurance, liquidation of the participant's assets (if liquidation would not cause financial hardship), or by stopping deferrals under the plan. Withdrawal of amounts for unforeseeable emergencies is permitted only to the extent reasonably needed to satisfy the emergency (Reg. § 1.457-6(c)). The need for funds to purchase a new home or to meet the college expenses of the participant's children is *not* an unforeseeable emergency. To the extent allowed under the plan, if the occurrence of an event with regard to the employee's spouse or dependent would be a hardship, the occurrence of the same event with regard to the employee's beneficiary under the plan would also be a hardship (Notice 2007-7, Q&A-5).

Rollovers. An employee participating in a 457 plan may roll over distributions into an IRA, 401(k) plan, or 403(b) annuity plan (Code Sec. 457(e)(16)). Similarly, in some circumstances, assets may be rolled over into another 457 plan. A 457 plan that includes a qualified Roth contribution program may permit a qualified rollover contribution from a participant's non-Roth account to the participant's designated Roth account within the same plan (Code Sec. 402A(c)(4)(B)).

Roth 401(k) Plans. A 457 plan may allow participants to designate elective deferrals as Roth contributions. An applicable retirement plan for purposes of offering a qualified Roth contribution program includes eligible deferred compensation plans offered by a state and local government (Code Sec. 402A(e)(1)(C)). Elective deferrals include any elective deferral of compensation by an individual under an eligible deferred compensation plan of an eligible employer that is a state or local government (Code Sec. 402A(e)(2)(B)).

Exceptions. The Code Sec. 457 rules do not apply to plans providing bona fide vacation leave, sick leave, compensatory time, severance pay, disability pay, or death benefits (Code Sec. 457(e)(11)). They also do not apply to plans that pay length-of-service awards to bona fide volunteers or their beneficiaries on account of firefighting, emergency medical, or ambulance services if the total amount of awards accrued for any year of service of any volunteer exceeds $6,000 ($3,000 for tax years beginning before 2018). Compensation deferred under a nonqualified deferred compensation plan (¶ 2197) of a state or local government or other tax-exempt organization that is not an eligible 457 plan is includible in the income of a participant or beneficiary for the first tax year in which there is no substantial risk of forfeiture (Code Sec. 457(f)).

2195. Sec. 457A Plans (Tax-Indifferent Parties). Compensation which is deferred under a nonqualified deferred compensation plan (¶ 2197) of a nonqualified entity is includible in the service provider's gross income when there is no substantial risk of forfeiture of the rights to the compensation (Code Sec. 457A). If the amount of any compensation is not determinable at the time that it is otherwise includible in gross income, then additional taxes apply to the compensation when the amount is determinable and includible in gross income. The additional tax is 20 percent of the amount of the compensation, plus an interest charge.

A nonqualified entity for this purpose includes a foreign corporation unless substantially all its income is effectively connected with the conduct of a U.S. trade or business (¶ 2429) or it is subject to a comprehensive foreign income tax. It also includes a partnership (domestic or foreign) unless substantially all its income is allocated to persons other than: (1) foreign persons with respect to whom such income is not subject to a comprehensive foreign income tax; and (2) organizations that are exempt from U.S. income tax.

A nonqualified deferred compensation plan of a nonqualified entity is defined in the same manner as for purposes of Code Sec. 409A (¶ 2193), except that it also includes any arrangement under which compensation is based on the increase in value of a specified number of equity units of the service recipient. Thus, a nonstatutory stock option to purchase service recipient stock is not included, as well as a stock appreciation rights that at all times by its terms is settled in service recipient stock (Rev. Rul. 2014-18). Nonqualified deferred compensation includes earnings with respect to previously deferred amounts. Compensation is not treated as deferred if the service provider receives payment of the compensation not later than 12 months after the end of the first tax year of the service recipient during which the right to the payment of such compensation is no longer subject to a substantial risk of forfeiture.

2197. Nonqualified Deferred Compensation Plans. An employer may maintain a retirement or other deferred compensation plan for a group of select employees that is not a qualified retirement plan (¶ 2111). Unless certain plan design and funding requirements are met, all compensation deferred under a nonqualified plan for the current year and all preceding tax years is includible in income of plan participants to the extent they are not subject to a substantial risk of forfeiture (¶ 713) and not previously included in gross income (Code Sec. 409A(a)(1)). Any amount included in gross income is also subject to a penalty of 20 percent of the deferred compensation, plus interest. See ¶ 2199 for a discussion of funding rules for nonqualified plans.

Distributions. To avoid immediate inclusion of deferrals and the penalty, a nonqualified plan must allow distributions only if they are permissible payments triggered by the employee's separation from service from the employer, the employee's death or disability, a time specified under the plan, upon a change in the effective ownership or control of the employer, or in the event of an unforeseeable emergency (Code Sec. 409A(a)(2)). Distributions to key employees (¶ 2132) resulting from a separation from service must also not be allowed until six months after the separation, unless the former employee dies in the interim.

Actual distributions from a nonqualified plan are included in the income of the employee in the year in which the distributions are made in accordance with the rules applicable to annuities (¶ 817) (Code Secs. 402(b) and 403(c)). If the distributions do not take the form of an annuity, they are considered to be derived first from plan earnings and asset appreciation (taxable gain), rather than from the employee's investment (basis) in the plan. The participant's basis in a nonqualified plan is increased by any amounts included in his or her income for contributions, if any, made by the plan sponsor.

Acceleration of Benefits. A nonqualified plan generally cannot permit the acceleration of the time or schedule of any payment under the plan (Code Sec. 409A(a)(3)). Exceptions are permitted for: domestic relations orders; *de minimis* cash-out provisions; payment of employment taxes; cancellations of deferrals due to a disability, hardship, or unforeseen circumstances; and as an offset of debts.

Election Rules. A nonqualified plan must meet certain requirements regarding the participants' elections to defer compensation and to receive distributions (Code Sec. 409A(a)(4)). Compensation for services performed during a tax year generally can be deferred only if the participant's election to defer is made before the close of the preceding tax year. In the case of any performance-based compensation that is based on services performed over a period of at least 12 months, the election may be made no later than six months before the end of the period. For new employees, a deferral election may be made within 30 days after the date the participant becomes eligible to participate. A participant is "new" for this purpose if at least 24 months have passed since the employee was an active participant in the plan or the plan aggregated with the plan.

Reporting. The total amount of deferrals under a nonqualified deferred compensation plan are required to be shown on an individual's Form W-2 or Form 1099-MISC even if the amount of deferred compensation is not currently taxable (Code Secs. 6041(g) and 6051(a)(13)).

2199. Nonqualified Deferred Compensation Plans—Funding Rules. The income tax treatment of contributions to a nonqualified deferred compensation plan (¶ 2197) depends on whether the plan is funded or unfunded. If an employer funds a nonqualified plan with contributions or the payment of premiums for an annuity, it is transferring restricted property to the plan participant under Code Sec. 83 in connection with the performance of services (¶ 713). The plan participant generally must include the contributions or amount of the premiums in gross income in the first year that the rights to the contributions or premium amounts are transferable or are not subject to a substantial risk of forfeiture (Code Secs. 402(b)(1) and 403(c)).

If, however, one of the reasons the deferred compensation plan fails to be a qualified deferred compensation plan is the failure to satisfy the minimum participation or coverage requirements (¶ 2112), then highly compensated employees (¶ 2114) must include their vested accrued benefits, reduced by their own investment, in gross income for the tax year with or within which the tax year of the trust ends (Code Sec. 402(b)(4)). Contributions to unfunded deferred compensation plans are discussed at ¶ 723 and ¶ 906.

Employer's Deduction. The employer is entitled to a deduction for contributions to, or premiums paid under, a nonqualified deferred compensation plan on behalf of an employee in the tax year of the employer in which an amount attributable to the contribution is includible in the gross income of the employee (Code Sec. 404(a)(5)). If more than one employee participates, this rule applies only if separate accounts are maintained for each employee.

Plan Income. In the case of a nonqualified plan funded through a trust, the trust is not tax-exempt and the plan's earnings are generally taxable to the trust (Code Sec. 641). The grantor trust rules (¶ 571) ordinarily do not apply to a nonqualified plan. Therefore, the participant is not usually treated as the owner of his or her share of the trust's assets and is not subject to tax on the trust's income. However, if a participant's contributions as of any date exceed the employer's contributions on behalf of the participant, the participant is treated as the owner of the portion of the trust attributable to his or her contributions and is subject to tax on the income from that portion (Reg. § 1.402(b)-1(b)(6)).

Other Funding Rules. If a nonqualified deferred compensation plan uses an offshore trust, or places assets outside the United States, the plan will generally *not* defer the compensation (Code Sec. 409A(b)). Also, if the plan provides that its assets will become restricted to the payment of benefits under the plan if there is a change in the employer's financial health, or if the assets actually become so restricted, the plan will not defer compensation. These rules apply to all deferred compensation, regardless of when it was deferred.

A nonqualified plan will also not defer compensation to the extent of contributions made on behalf of or restricted to benefits for certain employees at a time when the employer or its defined benefit plan are experiencing financial difficulties. This provision applies if the plan is in at-risk status under Code Sec. 430(i), if the plan sponsor is in bankruptcy, and if, during the 12-month period beginning six months before the plan terminates, the plan is underfunded.

Chapter 22

CORPORATE ACQUISITIONS

REORGANIZATIONS

LIQUIDATIONS

Corporate Division

See CCH® AnswerConnect: *Corporate Reorganizations: Sec. 355 Spin-Offs, Split-Offs, and Split-Ups* for more information on this topic.

2201. Spin-Off, Split-Off, Split-Up, and Splint-Off Exchanges. No gain or loss is recognized by shareholders or security holders upon the receipt of stock or securities of a corporation controlled by the distributing corporation (at least 80-percent stock ownership) in certain distributions known as "spin-offs," "split-offs," "split-ups," or "splint-offs" (Code Sec. 355; Reg. § 1.355-1).

Spin-Off. A spin-off occurs when a corporation distributes pro rata stock or securities in a controlled corporation. Shareholders do not typically surrender any of their stock in the controlling corporation. A new or existing corporation may be used for the spin-off.

Split-Off. In a split-off, a parent corporation distributes to some or all of its shareholders stock in a newly formed or pre-existing controlled corporation, under the same conditions as in a "spin-off," except that the shareholders surrender a part of their stock in the parent corporation for the stock in the controlled corporation. The distribution may be pro rata but usually is not.

Split-Up. In a split-up, the distributing corporation's shareholders surrender all shares held in the distributing corporation and in return receive new shares in two or more subsidiaries the distributing corporation controlled immediately before the distribution. The subsidiaries may be pre-existing or newly formed.

Splint-Off. In a splint-off, some of the distributing corporation's shareholders surrender their shares of the corporation in exchange for stock of a controlled corporation (as in a split-off). Other shareholders receive stock of the controlled corporation pro rata without surrendering any of their stock of the distributing corporation (as in a spin-off).

To attain nonrecognition treatment in a spin-off, split-off, split-up, or splint-off, the distributing and controlled corporations must immediately after the transaction be engaged in the active conduct of a trade or business (Code Sec. 355(b); Reg. § 1.355-3). This requirement does not apply to the distributing corporation if immediately before the distribution, it had no assets other than stock in the controlled corporation. The trade or business must have been actively conducted throughout the five-year period immediately preceding the date of the distribution.

In addition to the active business requirement, the transaction must have a valid corporate business purpose, and it cannot be primarily a tax-avoidance device (Reg. § 1.355-2(b)). If, however, a corporate business purpose can be achieved through a nontaxable transaction that does not involve the distribution of stock of a controlled corporation and that is neither impractical nor unduly expensive, then the separation is not carried out for that corporate business purpose. Other limitations relate to continuity of interest on the part of the owners (Reg. § 1.355-2(c)), the amount of securities distributed, taxable acquisitions within five years, and receipt of other property or "boot" (Code Sec. 355(a)(3)).

Basis Rules. With an exchange of stock or securities, the basis of the old stock or securities becomes the basis of the new stock or securities ("substituted basis") (Code Sec. 358). If the exchange is partially taxable, the basis of the old stock or securities is decreased by the sum of the money and fair market value of other property or boot received and increased by the amount of gain recognized and the amount treated as a dividend. If any loss is recognized, the basis of the property received is decreased by that amount. If some old stock is retained, the basis is allocated as though the stock were first surrendered and then received in the exchange.

Morris Trust Rules. Restrictions are imposed on certain spin-offs that follow the fact pattern of *Morris Trust*, SCt, 66-2 USTC ¶ 9718 (Code Sec. 355(e); Reg. §§ 1.355-7 and 1.355-8). If either the controlled or distributing corporation is acquired pursuant to a plan or arrangement in existence on the date of the distribution, gain is generally recognized by the distributing corporation as of the date of the distribution. Recognition can be avoided if more than 50 percent of the historical shareholders retain ownership in the distributing and acquiring corporations. Acquisitions occurring within the four-year period beginning two years before the date of distribution are presumed to have occurred pursuant to a plan or arrangement.

Real Estate Investment Trusts. Nonrecognition treatment generally does not apply if either the distributing corporation or controlled corporation is a real estate investment trust (REIT) (¶ 2326). However, this limitation does not apply if both corporations are REITs. It also does not apply if at all times during a three-year period ending on the date of distribution, the distributing corporation was a REIT, the controlled corporation is a taxable REIT subsidiary (¶ 2340), and the distributing corporation had control of the controlled corporation (Code Sec. 355(h)).

Reporting Requirements. The distributing corporation in a Code Sec. 355 distribution is required to file a statement with its tax return for the year of the distribution (Reg. § 1.355-5). A shareholder or security holder of the distributing corporation that is a significant distributee must also file an information statement with its return for the tax year in which the distribution is received. A significant distributee is any shareholder of the distributing corporation who received stock in the distribution and owned, immediately before the distribution (1) at least five percent (by vote or value) of the stock of the distributing corporation if the stock owned by the shareholder is publicly traded, or (2) at least one percent (by vote or value) of the distributing corporation's stock if the stock owned by the shareholder is not publicly traded.

The distributing corporation and its shareholders and security holders who are required to file information statements in connection with the Code Sec. 355 distribution must keep records that contain information regarding the amount, basis, and fair market value of all property distributed or exchanged in the transaction, and any liabilities assumed or extinguished as part of the transaction.

Corporate Reorganizations

See CCH® AnswerConnect: *Corporate Reorganizations* **for more information on this topic.**

2205. Tax-Free Exchange in Reorganization. A corporation that is a party to a reorganization (¶ 2221), as well at its shareholders and security holders, are eligible for nonrecognition of gain or loss on the reorganization exchange. To achieve the favorable tax treatment, reorganization transactions must satisfy strict statutory and nonstatutory requirements (¶ 2209).

A corporation generally recognizes no gain or loss on the exchange of property solely for stock or securities of another corporation if the corporation is a party to the reorganization and the exchange is made pursuant to a plan of reorganization (Code Sec.

361). If the corporation receives other property or money ("boot") in addition to the stock or securities, it does not recognize gain on the exchange if the boot is distributed pursuant to the plan of reorganization. The transferee corporation does not recognize gain or loss on the receipt of property in exchange for its own stock (Code Sec. 1032).

No gain or loss is generally recognized by shareholders or security holders who exchange, pursuant to a plan of reorganization, stock or securities of a corporation that is a party to the reorganization solely for stock or securities of that corporation or another corporation that is a party to the reorganization (Code Sec. 354). However, gain (but not loss) may be recognized on the receipt of boot (Code Sec. 356). The recognized gain equals the lesser of the amount of gain realized on the exchange or the amount of boot received. Gain on the boot is typically capital gain, unless the exchange has the effect of the distribution of a dividend, in which case the boot is taxed as ordinary income (¶ 2237).

Basis Rules. The basis of stock and securities received by a corporate transferor in a reorganization is generally the same as the basis of the property transferred to the acquiring corporation, adjusted for any gain or loss recognized on the exchange and the value of any boot received (Code Sec. 358(a)). The basis of boot received by the transferor corporation from the acquiring corporation is its fair market value at the time of the exchange. Property received by the transferee corporation has the same basis in the hands of the transferee as it had in the hands of the transferor ("carryover basis"), increased by the amount of gain recognized by the transferor on the transfer (Code Sec. 362(b)). However, the property acquired by the transferee corporation does not take a carryover basis if it consists of stock or securities in a corporation that is a party to the reorganization.

The basis of stock or securities received by shareholders in the reorganization exchange is the same as the basis of stock or securities surrendered in the exchange (Code Sec. 358(a)). If boot is received, the basis of the nonrecognition property received by shareholders is equal to the basis of the stock or securities exchanged in the reorganization, increased by the amount of gain recognized and any amount treated as a dividend (¶ 2237), and decreased by the amount of boot received and the amount of any loss recognized on the exchange. The basis determined for nonrecognition stock and securities must be allocated among all classes of stock or securities involved in the transaction. The basis in any boot received is its fair market value.

2209. "Reorganization" Defined. A qualified reorganization must fall within one of seven categories—each referred to by a letter corresponding to the statutory provisions of Code Sec. 368. In each category, there cannot be a tax-free reorganization unless there is an exchange of properties as distinguished from a sale (Code Sec. 368; Reg. § 1.368-2).

Type A reorganization: a statutory merger or consolidation (that is, a merger or consolidation accomplished pursuant to state law or the laws of a foreign jurisdiction, including certain mergers involving disregarded entities) (Reg. § 1.368-2(b));

Type B reorganization: the acquisition by one corporation of the stock of another corporation, in exchange solely for all or a part of its own or its parent's voting stock (¶ 2211), if the acquiring corporation has control of the other corporation immediately after the acquisition, whether or not it had control before the acquisition (Reg. § 1.368-2(c));

Type C reorganization: the acquisition by one corporation of substantially all of the properties of another corporation (¶ 2217) in exchange solely for all or a part of its own voting stock or its controlling parent's voting stock (¶ 2211), followed by the acquired corporation's distribution of all its property pursuant to the plan of reorganization (unless this requirement is waived by the IRS) (Reg. § 1.368-2(d));

Type D reorganization: a transfer by a corporation of all or a part of its assets to another corporation if, immediately after the transfer, the transferor and/or one or more of its shareholders (who were shareholders immediately before the transfer) are in control of the corporation to which the assets are transferred, but only if the stock or securities of the corporation to which the assets are transferred are distributed under

¶2209

the plan of reorganization in a transaction described at ¶ 2201 or ¶ 2205 (Reg. § 1.368-2(l));

Type E reorganization: a recapitalization (¶ 2225);

Type F reorganization: a mere change in the identity, form, or place of organization of one corporation (Reg. § 1.368-2(m)); or

Type G reorganization: a transfer by a corporation in bankruptcy of all or part of its assets to another corporation, but only if stock or securities of the transferee corporation are distributed to the shareholders tax free or partially tax free (¶ 2247).

80-Percent Control Test. For purposes of the corporate reorganization rules, the term "control" means the ownership of stock possessing at least 80 percent of the combined voting power of all classes of stock entitled to vote and at least 80 percent of the total number of shares of all other classes of stock of the corporation (Code Sec. 368(c)). The control requirement is 50 percent in the case of nondivisive D reorganizations (i.e., a D reorganization that does not involve a Code Sec. 355 distribution) (Code Secs. 304(c) and 368(a)(2)(H)(i)).

In order for the control requirement to be satisfied, it is not necessary that the acquiring corporation acquire 80 percent (or 50 percent) of the target's stock in the reorganization, or that control be attained in the transactions that constitute the reorganization. Rather, it is sufficient that the acquiring corporation is in control of the target corporation immediately after the transaction (Code Sec. 368(a)(1)(B)). Thus, a corporation can acquire stock in one of its subsidiaries in a tax-free reorganization.

S Corporation Reorganization Using QSubs. If an S corporation merges into a newly formed corporation in a transaction qualifying as a Type F reorganization, the newly formed surviving corporation meets the requirements of an S corporation, and the acquiring corporation elects to treat the transferor S corporation as a qualified subchapter S subsidiary (QSub), the reorganization does not terminate the S election (Rev. Rul. 64-250; Rev. Rul. 2008-18). The QSub must retain and use its employer identification number (EIN) if it is treated as a separate corporation for federal tax purposes.

Triangular Reorganizations. Tax-free reorganizations are often structured as triangular reorganizations that involve use of a subsidiary to acquire the target corporation. There are five types of triangular reorganizations (Reg. § 1.358-6(b)(2)):

- triangular B reorganizations;

- triangular C reorganizations;

- triangular G reorganizations;

- forward triangular mergers (the acquiring corporation uses the stock of its parent to acquire substantially all the properties of the target corporation); and

- reverse triangular mergers (parent stock is used to acquire the target corporation, but an acquisition subsidiary of the parent merges into the target, and the target becomes an 80-percent-owned subsidiary of the parent).

2211. Exchange of Stock or Property Solely for Voting Stock. In a B reorganization (¶ 2209), the exchange of stock "solely for voting stock" means that the acquiring corporation cannot use cash or nonvoting stock in the exchange, or the reorganization becomes taxable (Reg. § 1.368-2(c)).

The "solely" requirement is relaxed for a C reorganization (¶ 2209) in that "substantially all the assets" (¶ 2217) must be acquired solely for voting stock. If at least 80 percent of the value of all the property of the transferor corporation is acquired solely for voting stock, the remaining properties may be acquired for money or other property (Code Sec. 368(a)(2)(B)). If the acquiring corporation does transfer money or property in addition to voting stock, then for the purpose of determining if at least 80 percent of the assets are acquired for voting stock, the amount of any liability assumed by the acquiring corporation or the amount of any liability to which the property acquired is subject is also treated as money paid for the property.

2217. "Substantially All" Requirement in C Reorganizations. What constitutes "substantially all" of the properties of a corporation for purposes of a C reorganization (¶ 2209) is not precisely defined in the Code or regulations. A special rule provides that a reorganization may still qualify as a C reorganization if the acquiring corporation acquires at least 80 percent of all of the target corporation's property solely for voting stock of the acquiring corporation or its parent (Code Sec. 368(a)(1)(C) and (a)(2)(B)). Some courts have held that a transfer of approximately two-thirds in value of the assets, or 68 percent or even 75 percent of all the corporate property, is not "substantially all." Other courts have held that 85.2 percent or even 90 percent, which included all property except cash, is substantially all. The IRS interprets the substantially all requirement, for the purpose of issuing ruling letters, as requiring a transfer of assets representing at least 90 percent of the fair market value of the net assets and at least 70 percent of the fair market value of the corporation's gross assets held immediately before the transfer (Rev. Proc. 77-37).

2221. Party to a Reorganization—Plan of Reorganization. The reorganization provisions provide for the nonrecognition solely of the gains and losses of the parties to reorganization, and their shareholders and security holders (¶ 2205 and ¶ 2229). A party to a reorganization includes a corporation resulting from a reorganization and both corporations in a reorganization resulting from the acquisition by one corporation of stock or properties of another (Code Sec. 368(b); Reg. § 1.368-2(f)). In an A, B, C, or G reorganization (¶ 2209), a party to a reorganization includes a controlling corporation if its stock is exchanged and likewise includes a controlled subsidiary that receives any of the assets or stock exchanged.

A plan of reorganization is required in connection with a tax-free exchange (Reg. § 1.368-2(g)). The plan does not need to be a formal written document. However, the safest practice is to incorporate the plan into the corporate records. The plan may be amended as circumstances change so long as the reorganization remains in compliance with the reorganization requirements (¶ 2209).

2225. Recapitalization. For a transaction to qualify as a recapitalization or E reorganization (¶ 2209), there must be a reshuffling of the capital structure of a corporation (*Southwest Consolidated Corp.*, SCt, 42-1 USTC ¶ 9248). For example, an E reorganization occurs if a corporation discharges outstanding bond indebtedness by issuing preferred stock to the shareholders in exchange for the bonds instead of paying them off in cash, if 25 percent of a corporation's preferred stock is surrendered for cancellation and no-par-value common stock is issued, or when previously authorized but unissued preferred stock is issued in exchange for outstanding common stock (Reg. § 1.368-2(e)).

2229. Receipt of Stock, Securities or Other Property in Reorganization. No gain or loss is generally recognized by a shareholder or security holder if stock or securities in a corporation that is party to a reorganization (¶ 2221) are exchanged solely for stock or securities of another corporation that is also a party to the reorganization, and the exchange is made pursuant to a plan of reorganization (¶ 2209) (Code Sec. 354). Nonrecognition treatment also applies to shareholders or security holders who receive stock or securities of a controlled corporation in a corporate division (¶ 2201) (Code Sec. 355; Reg. § 1.355-1).

An exchange of securities in a reorganization or corporate division is tax free only to the extent that the principal amount received does not exceed the principal amount surrendered. Nonrecognition treatment also does not apply if securities are received and no securities are surrendered. The term "securities" is not defined by the Code or regulations for this purpose. However, the courts have held that securities are instruments representing unconditional obligations of a corporation to pay specified sums of money. The term includes only obligations representing a debt of the distributing corporation. Bonds, debentures, and like instruments of other corporations are "property" (*Camp Wolters Enterprises, Inc.*, CA-5, 56-1 USTC ¶ 9314).

If a shareholder or security holder receives money or other property ("boot") in the exchange, it can result in gain recognition, dividend treatment (¶ 2237), or in the case of a corporate division, treatment as a corporate distribution (Code Sec. 356). Securities received in a Code Sec. 351 exchange are treated as boot for this purpose (¶ 1731). In addition, nonqualified preferred stock is treated as boot (Code Sec. 351(g)). Any liabilities of the shareholder or security holder assumed by a party to the organization are not considered boot (¶ 2233).

If no boot is received in a corporate reorganization or division, the shareholders or security holders retain the same basis in the stock or securities they receive that they had in the stock or securities they surrendered in the exchange (Code Sec. 358). If boot is received, the basis of the nonrecognition property received by a shareholder or security holder is equal to the basis of the stock or securities exchanged in the reorganization, increased by the amount of gain recognized and any amount treated as a dividend (¶ 2237), and decreased by the amount of boot received and the amount of any loss recognized on the exchange. The basis determined for nonrecognition stock and securities must be allocated among all classes of stock or securities involved in the transaction. The basis of any boot is its fair market value.

2233. Assumption of Liabilities in Reorganizations. A release from liabilities assumed by a transferee or a disposition of property subject to liabilities in a reorganization (¶ 2209), a transfer of property to a controlled corporation (¶ 1731), or certain bankruptcy reorganizations or foreclosures (¶ 2247) is not money or other property ("boot") received by the taxpayer and does not prevent the transaction from being tax free (Code Sec. 357). However, if the principal purpose of the assumption of liabilities is to avoid income tax, or the purpose is not a bona fide business purpose, the liability assumed is treated as boot (unless the taxpayer can prove to the contrary).

If the liabilities assumed, or to which the property is subject, exceed the total basis of all the properties transferred in a Code Sec. 351 exchange or divisive D reorganization involving a corporate division (¶ 2201), the excess is treated as gain from a sale or exchange of a capital asset or a noncapital asset, depending on the nature of the asset transferred. See ¶ 1669 for the basis of property after an assumption of liabilities. A liability is excluded from this exception if the payment of the liability by the transferor would give rise to a deduction or would be basically the equivalent of a payment made in liquidation of the interest of a retiring or deceased partner, unless such liability resulted in the creation of, or the increase in, the basis of any property.

2237. Dividend Distribution in Reorganization. A distribution of money or other property ("boot") to a shareholder as part of a plan of reorganization or in a corporate division (¶ 2229) may be taxed as a dividend if it has the effect of a taxable dividend, even if the money or other property is received in an exchange which is, in part, tax free (Code Sec. 356; Reg. § 1.356-1). The constructive ownership rules (¶ 743) are applied in determining dividend equivalency. For this purpose, a distribution is taxable as a dividend, not to exceed the recognized gain, to the extent the distributing corporation has earnings and profits sufficient to cover the distribution.

2241. Liquidation as Part of Reorganization. Under a plan of reorganization (¶ 2209), a corporation often acquires for all or part of its stock, all of the stock in another corporation from the shareholders of the latter. As a final step in the reorganization, the acquiring corporation may liquidate the latter corporation, acquiring those assets by surrendering its own stock. This last step in the reorganization may be accomplished tax free under Code Sec. 332 (¶ 2261).

2247. Reorganizations of Bankrupt or Insolvent Corporations. Corporate restructurings ordered pursuant to certain bankruptcy, foreclosure, or similar proceedings may qualify as G reorganizations (¶ 2209) (Code Sec. 368(a)(1)(G)). To qualify for nonrecognition treatment, a G reorganization must meet six requirements:

- the debtor/target corporation must transfer all or part of its assets to an acquiring corporation;
- the transfer must take place in a Title 11 or similar case;
- the stock or securities of the acquiring corporation must be distributed as part of a plan of reorganization;

- there must be continuity of interest;
- there must be continuity of business enterprise; and
- there must be a business purpose for the transaction.

2249. Reporting Requirements for Corporate Reorganizations. Each corporation that is a party to a reorganization (¶ 2221) must file a statement with its tax return for the tax year of the reorganization exchange (Reg. § 1.368-3(a)).

Certain shareholders and security holders of the target corporation ("significant holders") must also file an information statement with their return for the tax year of the reorganization exchange (Reg. § 1.368-3(b) and (c)). A target shareholder is a significant holder if the shareholder receives stock in the reorganization exchange and owns, before the exchange, (1) at least five percent (by vote or value) of the target's total outstanding stock if the stock owned by the shareholder is publicly traded, or (2) at least one percent (by vote or value) of the target's total outstanding stock if the stock owned by the shareholder is not publicly traded. A security holder in the target corporation who receives stock or securities in the exchange is a significant holder and is required to file a statement if, immediately before the exchange, the security holder owned securities in the target with a basis of $1 million or more.

Corporate parties and shareholders and security holders who are required to file information statements in connection with a reorganization must keep records that contain information regarding the amount, basis, and fair market value of all property transferred or exchanged in the transaction. They must also keep records of any liabilities assumed or extinguished as part of the transaction (Reg. § 1.368-3(d)).

Corporate Liquidations

See CCH® AnswerConnect: *Corporate Liquidations* and *Stock Purchases Treated as Asset Acquisitions (Section 338 Election)* for more information on this topic.

2253. Gain or Loss to Shareholders in Corporate Liquidations. Amounts distributed in a complete liquidation of a corporation are usually treated as full payment in exchange for the stock (Code Sec. 331; Reg. § 1.331-1). The shareholder's gain or loss from a liquidating distribution is determined by comparing the amount distributed to the cost or other basis of the stock. Assuming that the stock is a capital asset, the gain or loss to the shareholder is capital.

If property is received in a distribution in a complete liquidation and gain or loss is recognized on receipt of the property, the basis of the property in the hands of the person receiving it is the fair market value of the property at the time of the distribution (Code Sec. 334(a)). If a parent corporation liquidates an 80-percent controlled subsidiary, the parent corporation's basis in the property received is generally the same as the liquidating subsidiary's basis in the property unless the subsidiary recognizes gain from the transfer (¶ 2261). If property received in a complete liquidation is subject to a liability, the recipient's recognition of gain or loss is adjusted accordingly (¶ 1672).

A distribution that is one of a series of distributions in redemption of all of a corporation's stock pursuant to a plan is treated as a complete liquidation (Code Sec. 346(a)). If a distribution is made as one of a series of distributions intended eventually to result in a complete liquidation of the corporation, no gain is realized by the shareholder until the entire cost of the stock is recovered. If a complete liquidation covers two or more consecutive tax years, the distribution first offsets the shareholder's basis for the stock and the excess is gain in the year received. The gain is not allocable to all of the years in which distributions were received (Rev. Rul. 85-48).

Partial Liquidation. A distribution of corporate assets to a *noncorporate* shareholder is treated as made in exchange for stock (whether or not stock is actually surrendered) if the distribution is in a partial liquidation of the corporation. The distribution must not be essentially equivalent to a dividend (determined by reference to the effect on the corporation rather than the effect on the shareholders), but rather must be made pursuant to a plan and must occur within the tax year in which the plan is adopted or within the succeeding tax year. A distribution qualifies as a partial liquidation if it is attributable to the corporation ceasing to conduct a trade or business that it actively conducted for at least five years ending with the date of the distribution and if the corporation continues to conduct at least one other trade or business immediately after the distribution (Code Sec. 302(b)(4) and (e)). A corporation may also rely on the common law doctrine of "corporate contraction"—contraction of the business of the corporation—to establish a partial liquidation.

2257. Recognition of Gain or Loss by Liquidating Corporation. Property distributed in a complete liquidation of a corporation is generally deemed to have been sold by the corporation at its fair market value and any gain or loss is recognized by the liquidating corporation (Code Sec. 336). If the distributed property is subject to a liability or if the distributee assumes a liability upon the distribution, the fair market value of the property is deemed to be no less than the amount of the liability. The following exceptions to this general recognition rule apply:

- No gain or loss is recognized upon any distribution of property to shareholders in a tax-free reorganization (¶ 2205 and ¶ 2209), except that gain may be recognized on the distribution of appreciated property that is not a qualified property (Code Secs. 336(c) and 361(c)(4)).

- No gain or loss is generally recognized in connection with the complete liquidation of a controlled subsidiary into its parent corporation, except that gain (but not loss) is recognized with respect to any property distributed to minority shareholders (¶ 2261).

- No loss is recognized with respect to a distribution of property to a related person within the meaning of Code Sec. 267 (¶ 1717), unless the property (1) is distributed to all shareholders on a pro rata basis, and (2) was not acquired by the liquidating corporation in a Code Sec. 351 transaction or as a contribution to capital during the five years preceding the distribution (Code Sec. 336(d)(1)).

- Recognition of loss may be limited if the distributed property was initially acquired by the liquidating corporation, either by tax-free transfer to a controlled corporation or as a contribution to capital, as part of a plan a principal purpose of which was the recognition of loss on the property in connection with the liquidation. In these circumstances, the basis of the property for purposes of determining loss is reduced, but not below zero, by the excess of the adjusted basis of the property on the date of contribution over its fair market value. There is a presumption of a tax-avoidance purpose with respect to any such transfer within the two-year period prior to the adoption of the plan of liquidation (Code Sec. 336(d)(2)).

- No gain or loss is recognized if a corporation owning 80 percent or more of the voting power and value of another corporation elects to treat any disposition (sale, exchange, or distribution) of the subsidiary's stock as a disposition of all of the subsidiary's assets (¶ 2263) (Code Sec. 336(e); Reg. § § 1.336-0—1.336-5).

2259. Reporting Requirements for Complete Liquidations. Certain shareholders of a liquidating corporation who transfer stock to the liquidating corporation in exchange for property must file a statement with their return for the tax year of the liquidating exchange (Reg. § 1.331-1(d)). The statement must include the fair market value and basis of the transferred stock and a description of the property received in the exchange.

The reporting requirement applies to a "significant shareholder." This is a shareholder who owns (1) at least five percent (by vote or value) of the liquidating corporation's total outstanding stock if the stock owned by the shareholder is publicly traded, or (2) at least one percent (by vote or value) of the liquidating corporation's total outstanding stock if the stock owned by the shareholder is not publicly traded. A shareholder need not file a statement if the property is part of a distribution made pursuant to a resolution providing that the distribution is made in a complete liquidation, and the liquidating corporation is completely liquidated and dissolved within one year after the distribution.

¶2257

The liquidating corporation must file Form 966 within 30 days after it adopts a plan of liquidation (Code Sec. 6043(a); Reg. §§ 1.6043-1 and 1.6043-2). The liquidating corporation must also file a separate Form 1099-DIV for each shareholder to whom a liquidating distribution of $600 or more is made and furnish a copy to the shareholder.

2261. Complete Liquidation of Subsidiary. If distributions in a complete liquidation are made by a subsidiary to a parent corporation (owning at least 80 percent by value and voting power of the subsidiary), then no gain or loss on the distributions is recognized by either the parent corporation or the liquidating subsidiary (Code Secs. 332 and 337). For this purpose, the 80-percent control requirement must be met by direct ownership and not by reason of the aggregation rules. In addition, property distributed to a controlling domestic corporation in satisfaction of a debt owed by the liquidating subsidiary is treated as a distribution in a complete liquidation for these purposes. However, the distribution of earnings by a U.S. holding company to a foreign corporation in a complete liquidation is treated as a taxable dividend if the U.S. holding company was in existence for less than five years.

If a minority shareholder receives property in such a liquidation, the shareholder may recognize gain or loss on the distribution (¶ 2253), while the liquidating corporation may recognize gain, but not loss (¶ 2257). Gain or loss also is recognized on distributions to 80-percent distributees that are foreign corporations (¶ 2492), as well as tax-exempt organizations unless the property is used by a tax-exempt organization in a trade or business unrelated to its exempt purpose.

Basis. After a complete liquidation of a subsidiary, the parent corporation usually holds the distributed assets with the same basis that the assets formerly had in the hands of the subsidiary. However, the basis of the property in the hands of the parent corporation is the fair market value at the time of the distribution if: (1) the subsidiary recognizes gain or loss with respect to the property; or (2) the parent's aggregate adjusted basis in the property exceeds its fair market value immediately after the liquidation in the case of a loss importation transaction where the built-in loss property was not subject to tax in the hands of the subsidiary but is subject to tax in the hands of the parent (Code Sec. 334(b); Reg. § 1.334-1(b)).

Reporting Requirements. The parent corporation must include a statement with its tax return for the year in which it receives a distribution from the liquidating subsidiary (Reg. § 1.332-6(a)). The liquidating subsidiary must timely file Form 966 and its final income tax return (Code Sec. 6043(a); Reg. §§ 1.332-6(b) and 1.6043-1). Both the liquidating subsidiary and the parent corporation must also retain permanent records regarding the liquidation (Reg. § 1.332-6(d)). These records must specifically include information regarding the amount, basis, and fair market value of the distributed property, and any liability assumed or extinguished as part of the liquidation.

2263. Code Sec. 336(e) Election for Qualified Stock Dispositions. A corporation may make an election to treat a sale, exchange, or distribution of stock of a subsidiary (target corporation) as a sale, exchange, or distribution of all the subsidiary's underlying assets (a section 336(e) election) (Code Sec. 336(e); Reg. §§ 1.336-1 and 1.336-2). The corporation must own subsidiary stock possessing at least 80 percent of the total voting power of the subsidiary stock and having a value equal to at least 80 percent of the total value of the subsidiary stock. If the section 336(e) election is made, the corporation does not recognize gain or loss on the sale, exchange, or distribution of the subsidiary stock.

A qualified stock disposition is any disposition or series of dispositions in which the seller sells, exchanges, or distributes—or any combination thereof—stock equal to 80 percent or more of the voting power and 80 percent or more of the total value of a domestic target corporation during the 12-month disposition period. Thus, the seller may retain a portion of the target stock. The 12-month disposition period is the 12-month period beginning with the date of the first sale, exchange, or distribution of stock included in a qualified stock disposition. However, the due date for performing certain time-sensitive actions, including completion of qualified stock disposition within 12 months, otherwise due on or after April 1, 2020, and before July 15, 2020, is automatically extended to July 15, 2020, in response to the COVID-19 (coronavirus) crisis (Notice 2020-23; Rev. Proc. 2018-58).

A disposition is any sale, exchange, or distribution of stock, but only if:

- the basis of the stock in the hands of the purchaser is not determined by reference to the adjusted basis of the stock in the hands of the person from whom the stock is acquired or from a decedent;

- the stock is not sold, exchanged, or distributed in a transaction to which Code Sec. 351, 354, 355, or 356 applies and is not sold, exchanged, or distributed in any transaction described in regulations that the transferor does not recognize the entire amount of the gain or loss realized in the transaction (an exception applies to a distribution of stock to an unrelated person in which the full amount of stock gain would be recognized in certain Code Sec. 355 transactions); and

- the stock is not sold, exchanged, or distributed to a related person.

Stock disposed of by the seller to another person that is reacquired by the seller during the 12-month disposition period is not considered as disposed of by the seller. If a seller retains any target stock after the 12-month disposition period, the seller is treated as purchasing the retained stock from an unrelated person on the day after the disposition date for its fair market value. The holding period for the retained stock starts on the day after the disposition date. For this purpose, the fair market value of all the target stock equals the grossed-up amount realized on the sale, exchange, or distribution of recently disposed stock of the target corporation.

A seller for this purpose is any domestic corporation that makes a qualified stock disposition of stock of another corporation. A seller includes both a transferor and a distributor of target stock. A purchaser is one or more persons that receive the stock of another corporation in a qualified stock disposition. A target corporation is any domestic corporation the stock of which is sold, exchanged, or distributed by another domestic corporation in a qualified stock disposition.

The seller (or in the case of an S corporation target, all of the S corporation shareholders) and the target must enter into a written, binding agreement to make a section 336(e) election. They also must attach a section 336(e) election statement to the relevant tax returns for the year of the disposition.

2265. Acquisition of Stock Treated as Acquisition of Assets. If a corporation (the acquiring corporation) purchases 80-percent control of a second corporation (the target) within a 12-month period, the acquiring corporation may irrevocably elect to have the target treated as if it had sold and purchased its own assets (a section 338 election) (Code Sec. 338; Reg. § 1.338-3). Once the election is made, the target is treated as a new corporation after the date of acquisition of 80-percent control, holding its assets with a stepped-up basis.

The purchasing corporation makes the section 338 election on Form 8023. The election must be made no later than the 15th day of the *ninth month* following the month in which the acquisition date occurs. The due date for performing certain time-sensitive actions, including the election and completion of qualified stock purchase, otherwise due on or after April 1, 2020, and before July 15, 2020, is automatically extended to July 15, 2020, in response to the COVID-19 (coronavirus) crisis (Notice 2020-23; Rev. Proc. 2018-58).

The hypothetical sale is deemed to occur on the date of acquisition of control. The target's tax year as the "selling corporation" ends on that date, and its carryovers and other tax attributes disappear. As the "purchasing corporation," the target is treated as if it had purchased the assets on the day following the acquisition date. The target becomes a member of the affiliated group including the acquiring corporation on the day following the acquisition date.

Gain or loss is recognized by the target as though it had sold all of its assets at fair market value in a single transaction on the acquisition date. Gain or loss from the deemed asset sale is reported, and recapture items are typically taken into account, on the final return of the "selling corporation." The acquiring corporation is not required to liquidate the target, but if it does, it succeeds to the basis of the target's assets, as increased by the hypothetical purchase.

There are detailed rules to ensure consistency of treatment for acquisitions of stock or assets by and from members of an affiliated group of corporations (Reg. § § 1.338-4(h) and 1.338-8). A consolidated group may treat a sale of its 80-percent-controlled target as a sale of the target's underlying assets. The assets receive a stepped-up basis to fair market value, and the selling consolidated group recognizes gain or loss attributable to the assets, but there is no separate tax on the seller's gain attributable to the stock. This treatment also applies in situations where the selling affiliated group owns 80 percent of the target's stock by value and voting power but does not file a consolidated return (Code Sec. 338(h)(10)).

Carryforwards

See CCH® AnswerConnect: *NOL Limits in Corporate Acquisitions and Reorganizations* for more information on this topic.

2277. Carryovers in Certain Corporate Acquisitions. In a tax-free asset acquisition, certain tax attributes may be transferred or are carried over to the acquiring corporation (Code Sec. 381; Reg. § 1.381(a)-1). This applies to a parent after a complete liquidation of a subsidiary (¶ 2261), as well as to an acquiring corporation after a tax-free A, C, D, F, or G reorganization (¶ 2209). In the case of D and G reorganizations, however, the carryover of certain tax attributes only applies to acquisitive reorganizations, where substantially all of the assets are acquired and distributed, not to divisive reorganizations.

The carryover provisions are mandatory, even though in some cases they work to the disadvantage of the successor. They do not apply after a split-up, split-off, spin-off, or splint-off type of divisive reorganization (¶ 2201) or a partial liquidation. The tax-attribute items covered are listed in Code Sec. 381(c) and include, but are not limited to, net operating losses (NOLs), unused general business credits, capital loss carryovers, carryover of disallowed business interest, method of computing depreciation, and method of accounting. Even if a tax attribute properly carries over to an acquiring corporation, the acquiring corporation's ability to use the attribute may be limited (¶ 2281). If an acquiring corporation makes a section 338 election to treat the target corporation as having purchased its own assets (¶ 2265), there is no carryforward of attributes of the subsidiary for the periods prior to the parent's acquisition.

Carrybacks. Carrybacks of NOLs for certain farming losses and nonlife insurance company losses (other NOLs may be carried back only if arising in tax years ending before 2018) (¶ 1149) and net capital losses (¶ 1756) are permitted from one corporate entity to another only in the case of an F reorganization—a mere change in identity, form, or place of organization (¶ 2209).

2281. Limitations on Use of Carryforwards in Corporate Acquisitions. After a reorganization or other change in corporate ownership, the use of certain carryforwards may be limited or prohibited (¶ 2277). The carryforwards involved concern:

- net operating losses (NOLs);
- carryforward of disallowed business interest under Code Sec. 163(j) (¶ 937);
- unused general business credit;
- corporate minimum tax credit;
- foreign tax credit; and
- capital loss carryovers (Code Secs. 382 and 383).

After an ownership change, the amount of *income* that a corporation may offset each year by any pre-change losses is generally limited to an amount determined by multiplying the value of the equity of the corporation just prior to the ownership change by the federal long-term tax-exempt rate (¶ 85) in effect on the date of the change (Code Sec. 382). A pre-change loss for this purposes includes NOLs for the year of the ownership change that are allocable to the period on or before the change date, NOL carryforwards, and carryforwards of disallowed business interest. Any unused limitation may be carried forward and added to the next year's limitation. Carryforwards are disallowed completely unless the business continuity requirements for reorganizations are satisfied for the two-year period following the ownership change. The annual income limitation is reduced by the recognition of any built-in losses and increased by the recognition of built-in gains. An exception to the limitations on NOL carryforwards is provided in bankruptcy situations, with certain restrictions.

Two kinds of ownership changes can trigger the income limitation: a change involving a five-percent shareholder, and any tax-free reorganization other than divisive and F reorganizations (¶ 2209). In either case, one or more of the five-percent shareholders must have increased their percentage of ownership in the corporation by more than 50 percent over their lowest pre-change ownership percentage (generally within three years of the ownership change).

Similar rules apply to the other carryforwards, including those for net capital losses, unused general business credit, and foreign taxes (Code Sec. 383; Reg. § 1.383-1).

Pre- and Post-change Allocation. A loss corporation must allocate NOLs or taxable income and net capital loss or gain for the change year between the pre-change period and the post-change period either by: (1) ratably allocating an equal portion to each day in the change year; or (2) electing to treat its books as closed on the date of the change (Reg. § 1.382-6). If a "closing of the books" election is made, the amounts allocated to either period may not exceed the NOL or taxable income and net capital loss or gain for the change year. Any disallowed business interest under Code Sec. 163(j) is treated as a pre-change loss and must also be allocated under these rules (Code Sec. 382(d)(3)).

Worthless Stock. In order to prevent a double tax benefit, the NOLs of a corporation may not be carried forward after an ownership change if a shareholder with 50-percent-or-more control (prior to the ownership change) claims, within three years, a worthless stock deduction with respect to the stock (Code Sec. 382(g)(4)(D)).

Tax Avoidance Purpose. NOLs and other carryforwards may be disallowed if an acquisition is made with a tax avoidance purpose (¶ 1575).

2285. Limitation on Preacquisition Losses. A corporation (or any member of its affiliated group) may not use its preacquisition losses (net operating losses (NOLs), net built-in losses, net capital losses, and credit carryforwards, ¶ 2281) against the built-in gains of a corporation:

- whose assets are acquired in an A, C, or D reorganization (¶ 2209); or

- that becomes directly or indirectly controlled (80-percent ownership of its stock by vote and value) by the acquiring corporation.

The restriction generally applies to built-in gains recognized within five years of the acquisition date, unless 50 percent or more of the gain corporation has been owned by the loss corporation (or a member of its group) for five years prior to the acquisition (Code Sec. 384).

The unrealized built-in gains of either the acquired or acquiring corporation are subject to the restriction. It applies to any successor corporation to the same extent as to its predecessor, and all members of the same affiliated group before the acquisition are treated as one corporation.

¶2285

Chapter 23

SPECIAL CORPORATE STATUS

Regulated Investment Companies

2301. Qualification as Regulated Investment Company (RIC). A regulated investment company (RIC) is a domestic corporation that acts as an investment agent for its shareholders, typically investing in corporate and government securities and distributing income earned from the investments as dividends (for example, a mutual fund or exchange-traded fund). A RIC may escape corporate taxation because, unlike an ordinary corporation, it is entitled to claim a deduction for dividends paid (¶ 259) to shareholders against ordinary income and net capital gain. A corporation qualifies as a RIC if it makes an irrevocable election to be treated as such by filing Form 1120-RIC, and it meets all of the following requirements (Code Sec. 851; Reg. § § 1.851-1—1.851-7).

- The corporation must be registered under the Investment Company Act of 1940 as a management company, unit investment trust, business development company, or as a type of common trust fund.

- At least 90 percent of its gross income must be derived from dividends, interest, payments with respect to certain securities loans, gains from the sale or disposition of stock, securities, or foreign currencies, or other income derived from the business of investing, including the net investment income of qualified publicly traded partnerships.

- At the close of each quarter of the tax year, at least 50 percent of its total assets must be invested in cash, government securities, securities of other RICs, or securities of other issuers (so long as the securities of any given issuer do not exceed five percent of the value of the RIC's assets or 10 percent of the issuer's outstanding voting securities).

- At the close of each quarter of the tax year, no more than 25 percent of the total value of its assets may be invested in securities of any one issuer (other than government securities or securities of other RICs), securities of two or more issuers controlled by the RIC and engaged in a related trade or business, or securities of one or more qualified publicly traded partnerships.

- The corporation must distribute at least 90 percent of its annual investment company taxable income (¶ 2303) and its net tax-exempt interest income (¶ 2307) to its shareholders (there is no threshold for net capital gains) (Code Sec. 852(a)).

2303. Taxation of Regulated Investment Companies (RICs). A regulated investment company (RIC) (¶ 2301) is subject to tax at regular corporate income tax rates (21 percent for tax years beginning after 2017) on its investment company taxable income (Code Sec. 852(b); Reg. § 1.852-3). A RIC with a fiscal year that includes January 1, 2018, pays federal income tax using a blended tax rate under the Code Sec. 15 tax proration rules. More specifically, a RIC determines its federal income tax for the fiscal year by (1) calculating its tax for the entire tax year using the graduated corporate income tax rates in effect for tax years beginning before 2018, (2) calculating its tax for the tax year using the 21-percent rate for tax years beginning after 2017, (3) proportioning each tax amount in (1) and (2) based on the number of days in the tax year when the different rates were in effect, and (4) adding the two amounts determined in (3). The sum of these two amounts is the RIC's income tax for the fiscal year that includes January 1, 2018 (Notice 2018-38).

Investment company taxable income is computed on Form 1120-RIC in the same manner as the taxable income of an ordinary corporation (¶ 221) with the following adjustments:

- gross income is the corporation's ordinary income (net capital gains are not included);

- a deduction is allowed for any ordinary dividends paid (¶ 259), but no deduction is allowed for dividends of capital gains or tax-exempt interest;

- no deduction is allowed for dividends received;

- no deduction is allowed for net operating losses (NOLs);

- taxable income of a short tax year is not annualized;

- if the corporation elects, taxable income is computed by disregarding the short-term discount obligation rules of Code Sec. 454(b); and

- a deduction is allowed for the tax imposed on the corporation if it fails to meet the asset test or gross income test (¶ 2301).

For purposes of the dividends-paid deduction, dividends declared and payable by a RIC in October, November, or December of a calendar year are treated as paid on December 31 of that year if they are actually paid in January of the following calendar year (Code Sec. 852(b)(7)). See ¶ 2323 for the treatment of certain dividends declared after the close of the RIC's tax year.

A RIC, other than a publicly offered RIC, generally may not claim a deduction for dividend distributions if it singles out one class of shareholders or one or more members of a class of shareholders for special dividend treatment, unless such treatment was originally intended when the dividend rights were created (Code Sec. 562(c); Rev. Rul. 89-81). The IRS has issued guidance describing the conditions under which distributions to RIC shareholders may vary and nevertheless be deductible, including the treatment of distributions to shareholders that differ as a result of the allocation and payment of fees and expenses (Rev. Proc. 99-40).

Excise Taxes. A nondeductible excise tax is generally imposed on a RIC that does not satisfy minimum distribution requirements (Code Sec. 4982). The tax is four percent of the excess of any required distribution for the calendar year over the amount actually distributed for the calendar year. For this purpose, the required distribution is the sum of 98 percent of the corporation's ordinary income for the year, plus 98.2 percent of its net capital gain income for the one-year period ending October 31 of the calendar year. Special rules apply for how a RIC treats post-October 31 capital gains and foreign currency losses.

Built-in Gains Tax. A RIC may be subject to a modified version of the built-in gains tax imposed on an S corporation (¶ 337) if property owned by a C corporation becomes property of the RIC when the corporation qualifies as a RIC, or if property of a C corporation is transferred to the entity (Reg. § 1.337(d)-7). The tax does not apply if the corporation makes a deemed sale election to recognize gain and loss as if it sold the converted property to an unrelated person at fair market value. The tax also does not apply if the corporation otherwise recognizes gain or loss on the conversion transaction, or if the corporation's gain is not recognized in a like-kind exchange or involuntary conversion.

2305. Capital Gains and Losses of Regulated Investment Companies (RICs). A regulated investment company (RIC) (¶ 2301) may avoid corporate level tax on its net capital gains by distributing such gains to shareholders. If the corporation elects to retain some of its net capital gains, then it is subject to tax at the 21-percent corporate income tax rate for tax years beginning after 2017 or at the alternative tax rate on net capital gains for tax years beginning before 2018 (¶ 1738) on the excess of its net capital gains for the tax year over the amount of any capital gains dividends paid during the year (Code Sec. 852(b)(3)).

Form 2438 is used to figure and report the RIC's capital gains. Although the fund is taxed on its undistributed net capital gains, it may elect to designate to its shareholders some or all of its undistributed gains and the tax paid on those gains. Form 2439 is used to notify each shareholder of his or her portion of the undistributed capital gains and tax paid for the year (¶ 2309 and ¶ 2311). The RIC must also report any undistributed long-term capital gains not designated to shareholders and any net short-term capital gain on Form 8949 and Schedule D (Form 1120).

Capital Loss Carryovers. If a RIC has a net capital loss for a tax year, any excess of the net short-term capital loss over the net long-term capital gain is treated as a short-term capital loss arising on the first day of the next tax year. Any excess of the net long-term capital loss over the net short-term capital gain is treated as a long-term capital loss arising on the first day of the next tax year (Code Sec. 1212(a)(3)(A)). There is no limit to the number of tax years that a net capital loss of a RIC may be carried over.

If a net capital loss under the general corporate capital loss carryback and carryover rules (¶ 1756) is carried over to a tax year of a RIC, amounts treated as a long-term or short-term capital loss arising on the first day of the next tax year under the capital loss carryover rules for RICs are determined without regard to amounts treated as a short-term capital loss under the general corporate capital loss carryover rule. Further, in determining the reduction of a carryover by capital gain net income for a prior tax year under the general corporate capital loss carryover rule, any capital loss treated as arising on the first day of the prior tax year under the capital loss carryover rules for RICs is taken into account in determining capital gain net income for the prior year (Code Sec. 1212(a)(3)(B)). Capital gain net income is the excess of gains from the sale or exchange of capital assets over losses from such sales or exchanges (Code Sec. 1222(9)).

2307. Tax-Exempt Interest of Regulated Investment Companies (RICs). A regulated investment company (RIC) (¶ 2301) may pay tax-exempt interest earned on state or local bonds to its shareholders in the form of exempt-interest dividends, but only if the bonds represent at least 50 percent of the value of the corporation's assets at the close of each quarter of its tax year (Code Sec. 852(b)(5)). Form 1099-INT is used to inform shareholders of dividends identified as tax-exempt interest dividends (¶ 2309 and ¶ 2311).

An upper-tier RIC that is a qualified fund of funds may pass through exempt-interest dividends to its shareholders without having to meet the 50-percent asset requirement (Code Sec. 852(g)). A qualified fund of funds is a RIC if, at the close of each quarter of the tax year, at least 50 percent of the value of its total assets is represented by interests in other RICs.

If a RIC shareholder receives an exempt-interest dividend with respect to any share of the corporation held for six months or less, then any loss on the sale or exchange of the share is generally disallowed to the extent of the exempt-interest dividend (Code Sec. 852(b)(4)). However, the disallowance of a loss does not apply, except as otherwise provided by regulations, to a regular dividend paid by a RIC that declares exempt-interest dividends on a daily basis in an amount not less than 90 percent of its net tax-exempt interest and distributes such dividends on a monthly or more frequent basis.

2309. Designation of Regulated Investment Companies (RICs) Distributions. A regulated investment company (RIC) (¶ 2301) must report in written statements furnished to its shareholders the portions of distributions made during the tax year that are capital gains dividends (¶ 2305) and exempt-interest dividends (¶ 2307), as well as any foreign tax credits (¶ 2320), tax credit bond credits (¶ 2320), dividends that qualify for the dividends-received deduction (¶ 223), and passed-through ordinary dividends eligible for the reduced tax rate for qualified dividends (¶ 2311) (Code Secs. 852(b)(3)(C) and (5), 853(c), 853A(c), and 854(b)). Capital gain dividends, dividends received from a tax-exempt corporation, and dividends received from a qualified real estate investment trust (REIT) (¶ 2326) are not eligible for the dividends-received deduction (Code Sec. 854(a) and (b)(2)).

The aggregate amount that the RIC can report as dividends eligible for the dividends-received deduction is limited to its aggregate dividends received from domestic corporations for the tax year. The aggregate amount that the RIC can report as qualified dividend income is limited to its qualified dividend income for the tax year (Code Sec. 854(b)(1)(C)). Additionally, within 60 days after the close of its tax year, a RIC must report and notify its shareholders of the portion of distributions made during the tax year that is designated as undistributed capital gain (Code Sec. 852(b)(3)(D)).

2311. Taxation of Regulated Investment Company (RIC) Distributions. The tax treatment of a distribution received from a regulated investment company (RIC) (¶ 2301) depends on how the distribution is designated (¶ 2309). Distributions not designated as capital gain dividends are generally included in gross income by shareholders as ordinary income to the extent of the fund's earnings and profits. However, all or a portion of the distribution of an ordinary dividend may be a qualified dividend eligible to be taxed at capital gains rates (¶ 733) if the aggregate amount of qualified dividends received by the fund during the year is less than 95 percent of its gross income (Code Sec. 854(b)(1)(B)). Distributions reported as tax-exempt interest dividends may generally be excluded from the shareholder's gross income (Code Sec. 852(b)(5)(B)). Exempt-interest dividends derived from private activity bonds constitute tax preference items for alternative minimum tax (AMT) purposes (¶ 239).

If a publicly offered RIC (¶ 2315) makes a qualifying distribution of its stock to shareholders who have the option to receive cash or stock, the distribution is treated as a Code Sec. 301 distribution that generally results in a dividend (Rev. Proc. 2017-45). This treatment applies to distributions declared on or after August 11, 2017, if, among other requirements, each shareholder has a cash or stock election with respect to part or all of the distribution and at least 20 percent of the aggregate declared distribution consists of money. The value of the stock received by any shareholder in lieu of cash is considered to be equal to the amount of cash for which the stock is substituted. If a shareholder participates in a dividend reinvestment plan, the stock received by that shareholder pursuant to the reinvestment plan is treated as received in exchange for cash received in the distribution.

Distributions received from a RIC reported as capital gain dividends may be treated as long-term capital gains by the shareholder for income and AMT purposes, regardless of how long the shareholder held the shares (Code Sec. 852(b)(3)(B)). Similarly, capital gains that the fund elects to pass through to the shareholder are treated as long-term capital gains (¶ 2305). The shareholder is entitled to a credit or refund for its portion of any capital gain taxes paid by the RIC on the undistributed capital gains (Code Sec. 852(b)(3)(D)). In addition, the shareholder may increase the basis of its shares by the difference between the undistributed capital gains and its deemed portion of taxes paid. The RIC must designate distributions as undistributed capital gain dividends, reporting the designation and providing shareholders a written notice within 60 days of the end of its tax year (¶ 2309).

If a shareholder receives a capital gain dividend or has capital gain passed through by the fund with respect to any share or beneficial interest, and holds the share for six months or less, then any loss on the sale of that share is treated as a long-term capital loss to the extent of any long-term capital gain (Code Sec. 852(b)(4)). The amount of loss that may be claimed must also be reduced by the amount of any exempt-interest dividend received on the shares. These rules do not apply to losses incurred on the disposition of RIC shares or beneficial interests pursuant to a plan that provides for the periodic liquidation of such shares or interests. For purposes of determining whether a taxpayer has held RIC shares for six months or less, rules similar to those for the dividends-received deduction are applied (¶ 223). A RIC shareholder may also not claim a loss from the sale or exchange of shares if the wash sale rules apply (¶ 1935).

A distribution that is not out of a RIC's earnings and profits is a return of the shareholder's investment. Return-of-capital distributions are generally not subject to tax and reduce the shareholder's basis in the RIC shares. On the other hand, distributions that are automatically reinvested by the shareholder into more shares of the fund are taxed as if they had actually been received by shareholder in cash. Thus, reinvested ordinary dividends and reinvested capital gain distributions are generally includible in gross income, reinvested exempt-interest dividends are not reported as income, and reinvested return-of-capital distributions are reported as a return of capital (IRS Pub. 550).

Deferral of Late-Year Losses. A RIC can elect to defer certain post-October capital losses for a tax year, as well as certain late-year ordinary losses for that year, to the first day of the following tax year (Code Sec. 852(b)(8); Notice 2015-41). The corporation makes the election by giving effect to the deferral in computing its capital gains and losses for the tax year in question, and completing its income tax return (including any necessary schedules) for that year according to the instructions for those items that apply to the election.

Capital Gains Tax Rates. The IRS has provided guidance that a RIC and its shareholders must use in applying the net capital gain tax rates (¶ 1736) to capital gain dividends (Notices 97-64, 2004-39, and 2015-41).

2313. Earnings and Profits of Regulated Investment Companies (RICs). Dividends from a regulated investment company (RIC), just like dividends from most other corporations, must be paid out of earnings and profits (¶ 747—¶ 757) (Code Secs. 301, 312, 316, 561, 562(a), and 852(a)(1)). Thus, a RIC must maintain sufficient current or accumulated earnings and profits to satisfy annual dividend distribution requirements. There should also be enough earnings and profits to avoid the excise tax on the undistributed income (¶ 2303).

A RIC's earnings and profits are generally computed under the rules that apply to an ordinary corporation. However, a RIC does not reduce its current earnings and profits by any amount it is unable to claim as a deduction from taxable income in that year (Code Sec. 852(c)(1)). A net capital loss for the tax year is also not taken into account in determining earnings and profits. Deductions disallowed in computing the RIC's taxable income with respect to tax-exempt interest are allowed in calculating its current earnings and profits (but not accumulated earnings and profits).

If a RIC that is not a calendar-year taxpayer makes distributions to its shareholders with respect to any class of stock of the company in excess of the sum of its current and accumulated earnings and profits (i.e., a portion of the distribution constitutes return of capital or capital gain), its current earnings and profits must be allocated first to distributions during the RIC's tax year that are made before January 1 (Code Sec. 316(b)(4)). If a RIC has more than one class of stock, this rule applies separately to each class of stock, so that distributions made during the RIC's tax year are considered to be made to the shares with higher priority before they are made to shares with lower priority (Rev. Rul. 69-440).

A company that has failed to qualify as a RIC because it has not purged itself of non-RIC earnings and profits may still qualify if it distributes those earnings and profits with interest to its shareholders (Code Sec. 852(e)). In order to qualify, distributions must be specifically designated as non-RIC distributions and take place within the 90-day period that begins on the date the corporation is determined not to be a RIC (¶ 2317). This option is not available if the corporation was determined not to be a RIC because it engaged in fraudulent tax evasion.

2315. Redemption of Regulated Investment Company (RIC) Stock. A redemption of stock by a corporation, including a regulated investment company (RIC) (¶ 2301), is generally treated as an exchange of stock if the redemption falls within one of four categories of transactions (Code Sec. 302): (1) a redemption that is not essentially equivalent to a dividend; (2) a substantially disproportionate redemption; (3) a redemption that terminates the shareholder's interest in the corporation; or (4) a partial liquidation, in the case of a noncorporate shareholder. Redemptions of corporate stock are discussed in ¶ 742—¶ 745. Because transactions that fall within one of these four categories are treated as exchanges of stock, they normally result in capital gain treatment to the shareholder. If the redemption does not fall within any of these categories, it is treated as a Code Sec. 301 distribution of property that generally results in dividend treatment.

Special rules apply to redemptions of RIC shares. A distribution in redemption of stock of a publicly offered RIC is treated as an exchange for stock if the redemption is upon the demand by the stockholder and the RIC issues only stock that is redeemable upon the demand of the stockholder. A publicly offered RIC is a fund whose shares are: (1) continuously offered pursuant to a public offering; (2) regularly traded on an established securities market; or (3) held by or for no fewer than 500 persons at all times during the tax year (Code Sec. 67(c)(2)(B)). Additionally, the loss disallowance and deferral rules for transactions between related persons (¶ 1717) do not apply to any redemption of stock of a fund-of-funds RIC if the RIC issues only stock that is redeemable upon the demand of the stockholder and the redemption is upon the demand of another RIC (Code Sec. 267(f)(3)(D)).

2317. Deficiency Dividends of Regulated Investment Companies (RICs). A regulated investment company (RIC) (¶ 2301) may avoid being disqualified as a RIC for the tax year by making deficient distributions to its shareholders if there is a determination that certain adjustments could otherwise cause the entity to lose its status as a RIC (Code Sec. 860; Reg. §§ 1.860-1—1.860-5). A deficiency dividend is a distribution of property (including money) that would have been includible in calculating the entity's dividends-paid deduction had the property been distributed during the tax year. The distribution must be made within 90 days after the determination date, and before the entity files a deficiency dividend deduction claim on Form 976. The entity may claim a deduction for deficiency dividends paid.

For a RIC, an adjustment can be: (1) an increase in its investment company taxable income, determined without regard to the dividends-paid deduction; (2) an increase in the amount of the excess of its net capital gain over its deduction for capital gain dividends paid; or (3) a decrease in its dividends-paid deduction (determined without regard to capital gains dividends). A determination is a final decision by a court, a closing agreement, an agreement between the IRS and the entity relating to its tax liability, or a statement by the entity attached to its amendment or supplement to a tax return for the relevant tax year. Filing Form 8927 is treated as a self-determination by the entity for these purposes (Rev. Proc. 2009-28).

The deficiency dividend deduction is not available if part of the adjustment is due to fraud with intent to evade tax or willful failure to file a timely income tax return.

2318. Basis in Regulated Investment Company (RIC) Shares. A shareholder's basis in the shares of a regulated investment company (RIC) (¶ 2301) is usually the cost to purchase the shares, including any fees or load charges incurred to acquire or redeem them (¶ 1975). Fees or load charges are not added to the shareholder's original basis if the shareholder acquires a reinvestment right, disposes of the shares within 90 days of being purchased, and acquires new shares in the same (or another) RIC for which the fee or load charge is reduced or waived because of the reinvestment right (Code Sec. 852(f)). In such cases, the omission of the load charge from basis applies to the extent the charge does not exceed the reduction in the load charge for the new investment. To the extent that a load charge is not taken into account in determining the purchaser's gain or loss, it is treated as incurred in connection with the acquisition of the second-acquired shares.

This treatment of load charges applies only if the original RIC stock is disposed of within 90 days after the date it was originally acquired, and the taxpayer acquires stock in the same or another RIC during the period beginning on the date of the disposition of the original stock, and ending on January 31 of the calendar year following the calendar year that includes the date of such disposition.

The original basis of RIC shares acquired by reinvesting distributions (even exempt-interest dividends) is the amount of the distributions used to buy each full or fractional share (¶ 1975). A shareholder's original basis in shares acquired by gift is generally the donor's adjusted basis (¶ 1630). However, if the fair market value of the shares was more than the donor's adjusted basis, then the shareholder's basis is the donor's adjusted basis at the time of the gift, plus all or part of any gift tax paid. A shareholder's basis in RIC shares that are inherited is generally the fair market value of the shares at the decedent's death (or the alternate valuation date if the estate chooses) (¶ 1633). No matter how a shareholder's original basis is determined, it must be adjusted for post-acquisition occurrences such as reinvestment of distributions and return of capital distributions (¶ 2311).

2320. Tax Credit Elections of Regulated Investment Companies (RICs). A regulated investment company (RIC) (¶ 2301) may elect to have its foreign tax credit (¶ 2475) claimed by its shareholders on their tax returns instead of its own. The election can only be made if more than 50 percent of the value of the RIC's total assets at the close of the tax year consists of stock or securities in foreign corporations and it has distributed at least 90 percent of its investment company taxable income (¶ 2303) and net tax-exempt interest (¶ 2307) for the year (Code Sec. 853).

An upper-tier RIC that is a qualified fund of funds may pass through foreign tax credits to its shareholders without having to meet the 50-percent asset requirement (Code Sec. 852(g)). A qualified fund of funds is a RIC at least 50 percent of the total value of whose assets (as measured at the close of each quarter of its tax year) is represented by interests in other RICs.

A RIC may also elect to pass through to its shareholders credits attributable to tax credit bonds (¶ 1471) held by the RIC (Code Sec. 853A).

2323. After-Tax Year Distributions of Regulated Investment Companies (RICs). A regulated investment company (RIC) (¶ 2301) may declare and pay spillover dividends after the close of a tax year that are considered made out of its earnings and profits for that year (Code Sec. 855; Reg. § 1.855-1). Spillover dividends are included in the calculation of the RIC's taxable income for that year and are considered in determining whether the fund met its distribution requirements for the year.

Spillover dividends must be declared no later than the 15th day of the ninth month following the close of the tax year to which the dividend relates, or the extended due date for the RIC's return for the tax year, whichever comes later. The dividend must be paid to shareholders in the 12-month period after the close of the tax year to which the dividend relates, but no later than the date of the first dividend payment *of the same type of dividend* (e.g., capital gains or ordinary) after the declaration.

The shareholder generally must treat such a dividend as received in the tax year in which the distribution is made. This does not apply, however, to dividends declared in October, November, or December that are treated as paid on December 31 of a calendar year even though they are actually paid in January of the following calendar year (¶ 2303).

Real Estate Investment Trusts

See CCH® AnswerConnect: *Real Estate Investment Trusts (REITs)* for more information on this topic.

2326. Qualification as Real Estate Investment Trusts (REIT). A corporation, trust, or association that acts as an investment agent specializing in real estate and real estate mortgages may elect to be a real estate investment trust (REIT) (Code Sec. 856). A REIT may escape corporate taxation because, unlike an ordinary corporation, it is entitled to claim a deduction for dividends paid to shareholders against ordinary income and net capital gains (¶ 259). An entity qualifies as a REIT if it makes an election to be treated as such by filing Form 1120-REIT, and it meets certain requirements as to ownership and organization, source of income, investment of assets, and distribution of income to shareholders. The REIT election may be revoked voluntarily, but the organization will be prohibited from making a new REIT election for the four tax years after revocation. An organization may elect REIT status even if it fails the ownership test in the first year.

Ownership and Organization Requirements. To be eligible for REIT status, an entity must be taxable as a domestic corporation (Code Sec. 856(a)). A foreign corporation, trust, and association, as well as a financial institution such as a bank or insurance company, is not eligible. An eligible entity must be managed by one or more trustees or directors during the entire tax year. It must also adopt a calendar-year accounting period

(Code Sec. 859). An entity making a REIT election may change its accounting period to a calendar year without seeking IRS approval.

Beneficial ownership in a REIT must be evidenced by transferable shares or certificates of interest. The REIT must have at least 100 beneficial owners for at least 335 days of a 12-month tax year (Code Sec. 856(a) and (b)). Ownership cannot be closely held as determined under the personal holding company rules (¶ 285) (Code Sec. 856(h)). However, attribution to another partner in a partnership is ignored. In addition, a pension trust generally is not treated as a single owner, but any REIT shares or certificates of interest held by the trust are treated as directly held by its beneficiaries. The look-through rule does not apply if persons disqualified from dealings with the pension trust own five percent or more of the value of the REIT and the REIT has accumulated earnings and profits attributable to a year it did not qualify as a REIT.

A corporation that was either a distributing or controlled corporation in a Code Sec. 355 distribution (¶ 2201) is generally not eligible to make a REIT election during the 10-year period after the date of distribution (Code Sec. 856(c)(8)).

Income Requirements. An entity must satisfy the following income tests each tax year in order to qualify as a REIT (Code Sec. 856(c)(2) and (3)):

- at least 95 percent of the entity's gross income must be from rents from real property, gain from the disposition of real property, dividends, interest, gains from dispositions of stock and securities, abatements and refunds of real property taxes, income and gain from foreclosure property, consideration received or accrued for agreeing to make loans secured by real property mortgages or interests or to purchase or lease real property, and certain mineral royalty income earned from real property owned by a timber REIT; and

- at least 75 percent of the entity's gross income, excluding income from prohibited transactions (¶ 2329), must be from real property sources, which include rents from real property, interest on real property mortgages, gain from the disposition of a real estate asset (other than a nonqualified publicly offered REIT debt instrument), dividends and gain from the disposition of shares in other qualifying REITs, abatements and refunds of real property taxes, income and gain from foreclosure property, consideration received or accrued for agreeing to make loans secured by real property mortgages or interests, or to purchase or lease real property, and qualified temporary investment income.

For both tests, an entity's gross income does not include the gross income from prohibited transactions, foreign currency gains in the form of passive foreign exchange gains, or real estate foreign exchange gains (Code Sec. 856(n)). It also does not include gains from hedging transactions (including counteracting hedges) entered into by the entity to reduce the risk of debt incurred to acquire or hold real estate or to manage the risk of currency fluctuations (Code Sec. 856(c)(5)(G)). The IRS has the authority to designate income as not constituting gross income for purposes of the REIT income tests. Alternatively, the IRS may designate nonqualified income as qualified income (Code Sec. 856(c)(5)(J)).

Real property is defined for these purposes as land and improvements to land, including inherently permanent structures and structural components of inherently permanent structures (Reg. § 1.856-10). Rents from real property generally include: rents from interests in real property; amounts received for customary services (utilities, maintenance), even if separate charges are made for such services; and rent attributable to personal property incidental to rental of real property if the amount allocable to personal property is 15 percent or less of the total rent (Code Sec. 856(d)).

Rents from real property do *not* include amounts received from: (1) any noncorporate person in which the REIT owns 10 percent or more in that person's assets or profits; (2) a corporation, if the REIT owns 10 percent or more of either the voting stock or the value of all shares issued by the corporation; or (3) amounts received based on income or profits of a tenant or debtor (unless certain conditions are met). Rents from real property also generally do not include rents that depend on income or profits derived by any person from the property.

¶2326

Amounts paid to a REIT by a taxable REIT subsidiary (¶ 2340) are treated as rents from real property if at least 90 percent of the property at issue is rented to unrelated parties at rents comparable to those paid by other tenants for comparable space (Code Sec. 856(d)(8)). In addition, a taxable REIT subsidiary may lease a qualified lodging facility or a qualified health care property, and the rents paid are treated as rents from real property so long as the facility is operated by an eligible independent contractor for a fee.

An entity that fails to meet either of the income tests for any tax year may still qualify as a REIT if it identifies the failure on a statement attached to its return and the failure is due to reasonable cause and not willful neglect (Code Sec. 856(c)(6)). The REIT also must pay a tax equal to the greater of the amount that the entity fails to meet either the 95-percent or 75-percent income test, multiplied by the fraction of the REIT's taxable income over its gross income for the tax year (Code Sec. 857(b)(5)).

Asset Requirements. A REIT must meet the following requirements regarding its assets at the close of each quarter of the tax year:

- at least 75 percent of the value of its total assets must consist of real estate assets (including interests in a REMIC (¶ 2343)), cash items (including receivables), and government securities;

- no more than 25 percent of the value of its total assets can be invested in securities other than those representing real estate assets or government securities;

- no more than 20 percent of the value of its total assets can be invested in securities of taxable REIT subsidiaries (25 percent for tax years beginning before January 1, 2018) (¶ 2340);

- no more than 25 percent of the value of its total assets can be invested in nonqualified publicly offered REIT debt instruments, as defined under Code Sec. 856(c)(5)(L)(ii); and

- except for government securities and securities of taxable REIT subsidiaries, no more than five percent of the value of its total assets can be invested in the securities of any one issuer, and investment in the securities of any one issuer cannot exceed 10 percent of the total value or voting power of that issuer's outstanding securities (Code Sec. 856(c)(4)).

For purposes of the limitation that a REIT may not hold more than 10 percent of the value of the outstanding securities of a single issuer, certain obligations are not treated as securities of an issuer, including straight debt securities, loans to an individual or estate, section 467 rental agreements (¶ 1541), or any obligation to pay rents from real property (Code Sec. 856(m)). A straight debt security is debt payable on demand or on a specified date where the interest rate and interest payments are not contingent on profits, the borrower's discretion, or similar factors, and there is no convertibility (directly or indirectly) into stock (Code Sec. 1361(c)(5)(B)). However, special rules permit certain contingencies of straight debt.

An entity that fails to meet any of the asset requirements for a particular tax quarter (other than the five-percent and 10-percent asset tests) may still qualify as a REIT if:

- it identifies the failure on a statement attached to its return;

- failure is due to reasonable cause and not willful neglect;

- the assets causing the failure are disposed of within six months of the last day of the quarter in which the failure occurred; and

- the REIT pays an excise tax (Code Sec. 856(c)(7)).

The tax is the greater of $50,000 or the tax on the net income generated by the assets during the period of failure at the highest applicable corporate rate (21 percent for tax years beginning after 2017) (¶ 219). A REIT will not lose its exempt status for a *de minimis* failure to meet the five-percent or 10-percent asset requirements if the failure is due to ownership of assets the total value of which does not exceed the lesser of one percent of the total value of the REIT's assets at the end of a tax quarter or $10 million.

The REIT must dispose of the assets causing the failure within six months of the last day of the quarter in which the failure occurred.

Ancillary Personal Property. The 95-percent income test, the 75-percent asset test, and the 75-percent income test can include rents from personal property and gains from the distribution of personal property that is ancillary to real property. Rents may also include obligations secured by mortgages if no more than 15 percent of the total fair market value of all secured property is represented by personal property (Code Sec. 856(c)(9)).

Distribution of Income. To qualify as a REIT, an entity generally must distribute to its shareholders during the tax year the sum of 90 percent of its ordinary taxable income (determined without the deduction for dividends paid and excluding net capital gain) (¶ 2329) and 90 percent of its net income from foreclosure property (less the tax imposed on that income), minus its excess noncash income (Code Sec. 857(a)). The IRS has the authority to waive this requirement if the REIT's failure to meet it is due to distributions necessary to avoid imposition of the excise tax on undistributed REIT income.

Other Failures. If an entity fails to satisfy one or more requirements of REIT qualification other than the income tests or asset requirements, then the entity may still retain REIT qualification if the failure is due to reasonable cause and not willful neglect. However, the REIT must pay a penalty of $50,000 for each failure (Code Sec. 856(g)(5)).

2329. Taxation of REITs. An entity that qualifies as a real estate investment trust (REIT) (¶ 2326) is subject to regular corporate income tax rates on its taxable income (21 percent for tax years beginning after 2017) (Code Sec. 857(b)). A REIT's taxable income is computed on Form 1120-REIT in the same manner as an ordinary corporation with the following adjustments:

- A deduction is allowed for dividends paid (¶ 259), but without regard to dividends attributable to the net income from foreclosure property.

- Net income from foreclosure property or a prohibited transaction is disregarded.

- The special deductions available to corporations (¶ 223—¶ 231), including the dividends-received deduction, are not allowed, but the deduction for organizational expenditures (¶ 237) is allowed.

- Any tax imposed on redetermined rents, redetermined deductions, and excess interest under Code Sec. 857(b)(7), and any tax imposed for failures to meet the income, asset, or other REIT qualification requirements (¶ 2326), are deducted.

- Taxable income is not annualized in the case of a change in accounting periods.

For purposes of the dividends-paid deduction, dividends declared and payable in October, November, or December of a calendar year are treated as paid on December 31 of that year if they are actually paid in January of the following calendar year (Code Sec. 857(b)(9)). See ¶ 2339 for the treatment of dividends declared after the close of the REIT's tax year.

Capital Gains. For tax years beginning after 2017, a REIT is subject to tax of 21 percent on its undistributed capital gain (Code Sec. 857(b)(1) and (b)(3)). The undistributed capital gain is the excess of the net capital gain over the deduction for dividends paid (as defined in Code Sec. 561) determined with reference to capital gain dividends only. For tax years beginning before 2018, if a REIT has any net capital gains in the tax year, the tax imposed on REIT taxable income is the lesser of (1) the regular corporate tax on REIT taxable income, or (2) the regular corporate tax on REIT taxable income, determined by excluding net capital gains and by computing the deduction for dividends paid without capital gain dividends, plus 35 percent on the excess of the net capital gain minus any capital gain dividends paid (Code Sec. 857(b)(3), prior to amendment by the Tax Cuts and Jobs Act (P.L. 115-97)).

¶2329

A REIT may avoid tax on its net capital gains by distributing the gains to its shareholders (¶ 2331). The REIT must designate any distributions as capital gain dividends in a written notice to the shareholders or beneficiaries with its annual report or within 30 days of the end of the tax year. For purposes of determining the maximum amount of capital gain dividends that a REIT may pay for a tax year, the REIT may not offset its net capital gains with the amount of any net operating losses (NOLs) (¶ 1145). In addition, the REIT must increase the amount of any NOL carryover to the extent it pays capital gains dividends in excess of its net income.

If the REIT does retain any net capital gains, it may elect to designate to its shareholders some or all of those undistributed amounts and the tax it paid on those gains. For this purpose, undistributed capital gains is the excess of net capital gain over the deduction for dividends paid for capital gain dividends only. The REIT must make the designation in a written notice to its shareholders at any time before the end of the 60-day period after the close of its tax year, or mailed with its annual report for the tax year. The REIT uses Form 2438 to report and determine its tax on undistributed capital gains, and Form 2439 to inform each shareholder of his or her portion of the undistributed gains and any tax paid. Form 2439 must be provided within 60 days of the close of the REIT's tax year. The REIT must also report any undistributed long-term capital gains not designated to shareholders and any net short-term capital gain on Form 8949 and Schedule D (Form 1120).

Net Operating Losses. NOLs sustained by a REIT in tax years ending after 2017 may not be carried back, but may be carried forward indefinitely. However, NOLs sustained in tax years beginning after 2017 may only reduce 80 percent of the REIT's taxable income (Code Sec. 172(a) and (b)(1)(A)). NOLs sustained by a REIT in tax years ending before 2018 may not be carried back, and only may be carried forward 20 years. NOLs arising from a non-REIT year ending before 2018 cannot be carried back to a REIT year (¶ 1151) (Code Sec. 172(b)(1)(B), prior to being stricken by P.L. 115-97).

Built-in Gains Tax. A REIT may be subject to a modified version of the built-in gains tax imposed on an S corporation (¶ 337) if property owned by a C corporation becomes property of the REIT when the corporation qualifies as a REIT (¶ 2326) or is transferred to the REIT, or if a C corporation engages in a conversion transaction involving a REIT (Reg. § 1.337(d)-7). The tax does not apply if the corporation makes a deemed sale election to recognize gain and loss as if it sold the converted property to an unrelated person at fair market value. The tax also does not apply if the corporation otherwise recognizes gain or loss on the conversion transaction, or if the corporation's gain is not recognized in a like-kind exchange or an involuntary conversion.

Other Taxes. In addition to the tax on its taxable income, a REIT may be subject to the following additional taxes:

- a tax for failure to meet the REIT asset or income requirements for the tax year (¶ 2326);

- a tax at the highest corporate rate (21 percent for tax years beginning after 2017) on net income from foreclosure property (Code Sec. 857(b)(4));

- a 100-percent tax on the net income derived from a prohibited transaction (e.g., disposition of property, other than foreclosure property, that is held for sale to customers in the ordinary course of business) (Code Sec. 857(b)(6));

- a four-percent excise tax on the amount of any taxable income that is undistributed at the end of the tax year, and calculated and paid on Form 8612 (Code Sec. 4981); and

- a 100-percent tax on the excess portion of rents, deductions, and interest that must be reduced to clearly reflect income if a REIT and taxable REIT subsidiary (¶ 2340) engage in transactions other than those at arm's length (Code Sec. 857(b)(7)).

2331. Taxation of REIT Distributions. Distributions received from a real estate investment trust (REIT) (¶ 2326) not designated as capital gain dividends are generally treated by shareholders as ordinary income to the extent of the REIT's earnings and profits. However, all or a portion of the distribution of an ordinary dividend may be a qualified dividend eligible to be taxed at capital gains rates (¶ 733). The amount a REIT can designate as qualified dividend income is limited to the sum of:

- the REIT's qualified dividend income for the tax year;

- the excess of the sum of REIT taxable income for the preceding tax year and the income subject to tax under the Code Sec. 337(d) regulations for that preceding tax year, over the taxes payable by the REIT under the REIT rules (¶ 2329) and the Code Sec. 337(d) regulations for that preceding tax year; and

- the amount of earnings and profits that were distributed by the REIT for the tax year and accumulated in tax years in which the entity was not a REIT (Code Sec. 857(c)(2)).

The amount of qualified dividends must be specified by the REIT in a written notice to shareholders no later than 60 days after the close of the tax year.

If a publicly offered REIT makes a qualifying distribution of stock to shareholders who have the option to receive cash or stock, the distribution is treated as a Code Sec. 301 distribution that generally results in a dividend (Rev. Proc. 2017-45). This treatment applies to distributions declared on or after August 11, 2017, if, among other requirements, each shareholder has a cash or stock election with respect to part or all of the distribution and at least 20 percent of the aggregate declared distribution consists of money. The value of the stock received by any shareholder in lieu of cash is considered to be equal to the amount of cash for which the stock is substituted. If a shareholder participates in a dividend reinvestment plan, the stock received by that shareholder pursuant to the reinvestment plan is treated as received in exchange for cash received in the distribution.

Distributions in excess of the REIT's earnings and profits (other than deficiency dividends (¶ 2337)) constitute a return of the shareholder's basis (¶ 735). Dividends received from a REIT do not qualify for the dividends-received deduction for corporations (¶ 223).

Distributions designated as capital gain dividends are treated as long-term capital gains by the shareholders, regardless of how long they held their interests in the REIT (Code Sec. 857(b)(3)). This includes any undistributed capital gains designated by the REIT (¶ 2329). Shareholders are entitled to a credit or refund for their portion of any capital gain taxes paid by the REIT on the undistributed capital gains. In addition, a shareholder must increase the basis of his or her REIT shares by the difference between his or her portions of the undistributed capital gains and the deemed taxes paid. Certain capital gain distributions from REITs to foreign investors are treated as REIT dividends that are not capital gains.

If a shareholder receives a capital gain dividend or the REIT has designated undistributed capital gains with respect to any share or beneficial interest, and the shareholder holds the share for six months or less, then any loss on the sale of that share is treated as a long-term capital loss to the extent of the long-term capital gain dividend (Code Sec. 857(b)(8)). This rule does not apply to losses incurred on the disposition of REIT stock or a beneficial interest under a plan that provides for the periodic liquidation of such shares or interests. For purposes of determining whether a taxpayer has held REIT stock or a beneficial interest for six months or less, rules similar to those for the dividends-received deduction are applied (¶ 223).

Capital Gains Tax Rates. The IRS has provided guidance that a REIT and its shareholders must use in applying the net capital gain tax rates (¶ 1736) to capital gain dividends (Notices 97-64 and 2004-39).

2337. Deficiency Dividends of REITs. A real estate investment trust (REIT) (¶ 2326) may avoid being disqualified as a REIT for the tax year by making deficient distributions to its shareholders if there is a determination that certain adjustments could otherwise cause the entity to lose its status as a REIT (Code Sec. 860; Reg. §§ 1.860-1—1.860-5). The entity may claim a deduction for deficiency dividends paid. For a REIT, an adjustment can be: (1) an increase in the sum of its taxable income (determined without regard to its dividends-paid deduction and excluding any net capital gain), plus the excess of its net income from foreclosure property minus the tax on the foreclosure property net income; (2) an increase in the amount of the excess of its net capital gain over its deduction for capital gain dividends paid; or (3) a decrease in its dividends-paid deduction (determined without regard to capital gains dividends). See ¶ 2317 for the deficiency dividend procedure, which is the same as that for regulated investment companies (RICs).

2339. After-Tax Year Distributions of REITs. A real estate investment trust (REIT) (¶ 2326) that declares a dividend (including a capital gain dividend) before the due date for filing its return for a tax year (including extensions), but distributes the dividend after the close of the tax year, can treat the dividend as having been paid during the tax year if the entire declared dividend is paid within the 12-month period following the close of the tax year and no later than the date of the first regular dividend payment after the declaration (Code Sec. 858; Reg. § 1.858-1). The shareholder must generally treat the dividend as received in the tax year in which the distribution is made. This rule does not apply, however, to dividends declared in October, November, or December that are treated as paid on December 31 of a calendar year even if they are actually paid in January of the following calendar year (¶ 2329).

2340. REIT Subsidiaries. A real estate investment trust (REIT) (¶ 2326) may own a qualified REIT subsidiary and treat all of the subsidiary's assets, liabilities, and items of income, deduction, and credit as its own (Code Sec. 856(i)). A qualified subsidiary is any corporation other than a taxable REIT subsidiary, all of the stock of which is held by the REIT. A taxable REIT subsidiary is any corporation that is owned, in whole or in part, by the REIT and that both entities jointly elect using Form 8875 to treat as a taxable REIT subsidiary (Code Sec. 856(l)). A taxable REIT subsidiary can be used by the REIT to provide noncustomary services to its tenants or to manage and operate properties without causing the amounts received or accrued to be disqualified as rents from real property. The election to be treated as a taxable REIT subsidiary can only be revoked with the consent of both the REIT and the subsidiary.

Real Estate Mortgage Investment Conduits

See CCH® AnswerConnect: *Real Estate Mortgage Investment Conduits (REMICs)* for more information on this topic.

2343. Qualification as Real Estate Mortgage Investment Conduit (REMIC). A real estate mortgage investment conduit (REMIC) is an entity that holds a fixed pool of mortgages and issues multiple classes of interests to investors (Code Sec. 860D; Reg. § 1.860D-1). A REMIC is treated like a partnership for federal tax purposes with its income passed through to its interest holders (¶ 2344). Thus, a REMIC is not subject to taxation on its income, although it is subject to taxes on prohibited transactions (¶ 2355), income from foreclosure property (¶ 2356), and on certain contributions received after its start-up day (¶ 2357). It also may be required to withhold taxes on amounts paid to foreign holders of regular or residual interests (¶ 2367).

An entity qualifies as REMIC if it makes an irrevocable election to be treated as such by filing Form 1066 during its first tax year of existence, and if it meets certain requirements as to its investors (¶ 2344) and assets (¶ 2345). If an entity ceases to qualify as a REMIC at any time during the tax year, it will not be treated as a REMIC for that or any later tax year. A REMIC is required to file an information return with the IRS on Form 8811 within 30 days of its start-up day (and 30 days from any change of information provided in a previously-filed Form 8811) identifying its representative for reporting tax information (Reg. § 1.6049-7).

2344. Investors' Interests in REMICs. In order to qualify as a real estate mortgage investment conduit (REMIC) (¶ 2343), all of the interests in the entity must be either regular interests or residual interests, and there must be only one class of residual interests (Code Sec. 860D; Reg. § 1.860D-1). However, a *de minimis* interest that is neither a regular nor a residual interest can be created to facilitate the REMIC creation.

¶2344

A regular interest is any interest that is issued on the start-up day of the REMIC with fixed terms and that is designated as a regular interest (Code Sec. 860G(a)(1); Reg. § 1.860G-1). A regular interest may be issued in the form of debt, stock, interest in a partnership or trust, or any other form permitted by state law, as long as it unconditionally entitles the holder to receive a specific principal amount and interest based on a fixed rate (or permitted variable rate). An interest-only regular interest may also be issued that entitles the holder to receive interest payments determined by reference to the interest payable on qualified mortgages, rather than a specified principal amount.

An interest does not fail to qualify as a regular interest merely because the timing of principal payments may be contingent on the prepayments on qualified mortgages or the amount of income from permitted investments (¶ 2345). In addition, an interest does not fail to be a regular interest solely because the specified principal amount may be reduced as a result of a nonoccurrence of a contingent payment with respect to a reverse mortgage loan held by the REMIC if the REMIC's sponsor reasonably believes on the start-up day that all principal and interest due under the regular interest will be paid at or prior to the REMIC's liquidation. The REMIC must file Form 1099-INT for each regular interest holder (and furnish a copy to the interest holder) that has been paid or to which has accrued $10 or more of interest during the calendar year (Reg. § 1.6049-7). If the REMIC is also reporting original issue discount (OID) (¶ 1952), it can report both the interest and OID on Form 1099-OID.

A residual interest is an interest issued on the REMIC's start-up day that is not a regular interest and that is designated as a residual interest (Code Sec. 860G(a)(2)). There may be only one class of residual interests, and any distribution with respect to such interests must be pro rata. A REMIC must have reasonable arrangements to ensure that residual interests are not held by certain disqualified organizations (governments, exempt organizations, cooperatives) (Code Sec. 860D(a)(3) and (6)). For each quarter of its tax year, a REMIC must send a Schedule Q (Form 1066) to residual interest holders reporting their share of the REMIC's income or loss (Reg. § 1.860F-4(e)).

REMIC Interests as Assets in Other Contexts. Regular and residual interests in a REMIC are treated as real estate assets for purposes of determining if an organization qualifies as a real estate investment trust (REIT) (¶ 2326). However, if for any calendar quarter less than 95 percent of the REMIC's assets are real estate assets, the REIT is treated as holding directly its proportionate share of the assets and income of the REMIC (Code Sec. 856(c)(5)(E); Reg. § 1.856-3(b)).

If one REMIC owns interests in another REMIC, then the character of the second REMIC's assets flow through for purposes of making this determination. Any regular or residual interest in a REMIC can also qualify as an asset for purposes of determining whether an organization is a domestic building and loan association (Code Sec. 7701(a)(19); Reg. § 301.7701-13A). If 95 percent or more of REMIC assets qualify as an asset for this purpose, then the entire interest in the REMIC can qualify as an asset.

2345. Qualified Mortgages and Permitted Investments of REMICs. In order to qualify as a real estate mortgage investment conduit (REMIC) (¶ 2343), substantially all of an entity's assets must consist of qualified mortgages and permitted investments at the close of the third month beginning after the start-up day and all times thereafter (Code Sec. 860D(a)(4)). A qualified mortgage is any obligation that is principally secured by an interest in real property and that:

- is transferred to the REMIC on the start-up day in exchange for a regular or residual interest;

- is purchased by the REMIC within three months after the start-up day pursuant to a fixed price contract in effect on the start-up day; or

- represents an increase in the principal under the original terms of the obligation, if the increase (1) is attributable to an advance made to the obligor under the terms of a reverse mortgage or other obligation, (2) occurs after the start-up day, and (3) is purchased by the REMIC pursuant to a fixed price contract in effect on the start-up day (Code Sec. 860G(a)(3)).

¶2345

A qualified mortgage may also include any qualified replacement mortgage, or a regular interest in another REMIC transferred on the start-up day in exchange for a regular or residual interest.

Permitted investments include cash-flow investments of amounts received under qualified mortgages for a temporary period, intangible property held for payment of expenses as part of a qualified reserve fund, and foreclosure property acquired in connection with the default of a qualified mortgage (Code Sec. 860G(a)(5)).

2349. Transfer of Property to REMICs. No gain or loss is recognized if property is transferred to a real estate mortgage investment conduit (REMIC) in exchange for a regular or residual interest (¶ 2344) (Code Sec. 860F(b); Reg. § 1.860F-2(b)). The basis of a regular or residual interest received in the exchange is equal to the total adjusted basis of the property transferred, plus any organizational expenses. If the transferor receives more than one interest in the REMIC (both a regular and residual interest), then the basis must be allocated among the interests in accordance with their respective fair market values. The basis of the property received by the REMIC in exchange for a regular or residual interest is its fair market value immediately after the transfer.

The issue price of a regular or residual interest is generally determined under the same rules as for determining the issue price for the original issue discount (OID) of debt instruments (¶ 1952) (Code Sec. 860G(a)(10)). If the issue price of a regular interest in a REMIC exceeds its adjusted basis, then the excess is included in the transferor's gross income as if it were a market discount bond (¶ 1958) (Code Sec. 860F(b)(1)(C); Reg. § 1.860F-2(b)(4)). If the issue price of a residual interest exceeds its adjusted basis, then the excess is included in the transferor's gross income ratably over the anticipated weighted average life of the REMIC. If the adjusted basis of a regular interest exceeds the issue price, then the excess is allowable as a deduction to the transferor under the rules similar to those governing amortizable bond premiums (¶ 1967) (Code Sec. 860F(b)(1)(D); Reg. § 1.860F-2(b)(4)). If the adjusted basis of a residual interest exceeds the issue price, then the excess is allowed as a deduction to the transferor over the anticipated weighted average life of the REMIC.

2352. Taxable Income or Loss of REMICs. A real estate mortgage investment conduit (REMIC) (¶ 2343) is not generally taxed on its income (Code Sec. 860A). However, its taxable income must still be determined for purposes of the taxation of residual interest holders (¶ 2361). REMIC taxable income is determined in the same manner as that of an individual, except that it must use the accrual method of accounting and make the following adjustments:

• Regular interests in the REMIC are treated as debt.

• Market discount on any bond is included in gross income as the discount accrues.

• No item of income, gain, loss, or deduction from a prohibited transaction is taken into account (¶ 2355).

• The deductions for personal exemptions for tax years beginning before 2018 and after 2025, foreign taxes, charitable contributions, net operating losses (NOLs), itemized deductions for individuals (except ordinary and necessary expenses paid or incurred for the production of income), and depletion are not allowed.

• The amount of any net income from foreclosure property is reduced by the amount of tax imposed on that income.

• Gain or loss from the disposition of assets, including qualified mortgages and permitted investments, is treated as ordinary gain or loss rather than gain or loss from a capital asset.

• Interest expenses (other than the portion allocable to tax-exempt interest) may be deducted without regard to the investment interest limitation, or under proposed regulations on which taxpayers may rely for tax years beginning after 2017, the limitation on business interest (Prop. Reg. § 1.860C-2(b)(2)).

23 SPEC. CORP. STATUS

- Debts owed to the REMIC are not treated as nonbusiness debts for purposes of the bad debt deduction.

- The REMIC is not treated as carrying on a trade or business, and ordinary and necessary operating expenses may only be deducted as expenses incurred for the production of income for tax years beginning before 2018 and after 2025 (¶ 1085) (Code Sec. 860C(b); Reg. § 1.860C-2).

A REMIC's net loss is determined by subtracting its gross income from allowable deductions, taking into account the same modifications listed above.

2355. Prohibited Transactions of REMICs. A real estate mortgage investment conduit (REMIC) (¶ 2343) is required to pay a 100-percent tax on its *net income* from a prohibited transaction (Code Sec. 860F(a)). Losses are not taken into account for this purpose. The disposition of any qualified mortgage is considered a prohibited transaction unless the disposition is due to:

- the substitution of a qualified replacement mortgage for a qualified mortgage (or the repurchase in lieu of substitution of a defective obligation);

- the bankruptcy or insolvency of the REMIC;

- a disposition incident to foreclosure or default of a mortgage; or

- a qualified liquidation.

A significant modification of a mortgage is considered a disposition (Reg. § 1.860G-2(b)). The IRS has issued procedures under which modifications of certain mortgage loans, as well as subprime mortgage loans, will not be considered a disposition of a qualified mortgage and a prohibited transaction of a REMIC or investment trust that holds the loans (Rev. Proc. 2010-30; Rev. Proc. 2009-45; Rev. Proc. 2009-23).

Prohibited transactions of a REMIC also include: the receipt of any income from an asset that is neither a qualified mortgage nor a permitted investment (¶ 2345); the receipt of any amount that represents a fee or compensation for services; and the receipt of gain from the disposition of any cash flow investment, unless the disposition is made pursuant to a qualified liquidation. A disposition is not treated as a prohibited transaction if it is required to prevent default on a regular interest where the threatened default results from a default on one or more qualified mortgages, or is undertaken to facilitate a cleanup call.

2356. Net Income from Foreclosure Property of REMICs. A real estate mortgage investment conduit (REMIC) is subject to tax at the highest applicable corporate income tax rate (21 percent for tax years beginning after 2017) (¶ 219) on its *net income* from foreclosure property for the tax year (Code Sec. 860G(c)). For this purpose, net income from foreclosure property is the excess of gain from the sale or other disposition of foreclosure property as described in Code Sec. 1221(a)(1) (i.e., stock in trade or property held by the REMIC for sale to customers in the ordinary course of trade or business), plus the gross income derived from foreclosure property during the tax year, over deductions derived from the production of such income (Code Sec. 857(b)(4)(B)).

Foreclosure property is any interest in real property, and personal property incident to the real property, acquired by a REMIC as a result of a default of a lease on the property or a debt securing the property. A REMIC must elect to treat property as foreclosure property by the due date (including extensions) of its annual return for the year in which it acquires the property. Property ceases to be foreclosure property: (1) as of the close of the third tax year after the tax year in which it is acquired, unless an extension is granted, or (2) if the property's foreclosure property status terminates prior to that date (Code Sec. 856(e)).

2357. Post-Startup Contributions to REMICs. A real estate mortgage investment conduit (REMIC) (¶ 2343) that receives contributions of property after its start-up day is subject to a tax equal to the full value of the contribution (Code Sec. 860G(d)). Exceptions to the tax are provided for cash contributions that are: made to facilitate a cleanup call or a qualified liquidation; in the nature of a guarantee; made during the three-month period that begins on the start-up day; made by a holder of a residual interest in the REMIC to a qualified reserve fund; or permitted under regulations.

2358. Taxation of Regular Interests in REMICs. Holders of regular interests in a real estate mortgage investment conduit (REMIC) (¶ 2344) are taxed as if their interests were debt instruments, except that income derived from their interests must be computed under the accrual method of accounting (Code Sec. 860B). Gain on the disposition of a regular interest is treated as ordinary income to the extent of unaccrued original issue discount (OID) (¶ 1952), computed at 110 percent of the applicable federal rate (AFR) effective at the time the interest was acquired. The REMIC must report interest payments of $10 or more to regular interest holders and the IRS on Form 1099-INT.

2361. Taxation of Residual Interests in REMICs. A holder of a residual interest in a real estate mortgage investment conduit (REMIC) (¶ 2344) must take into account daily portions of the taxable income or net loss of the REMIC (¶ 2352) for each day during the tax year on which the interest is held (Code Sec. 860C; Reg. § 1.860C-1). The daily portion is determined on the basis of quarterly computations of the REMIC's taxable income or net loss with such amounts being allocated among all residual interests in proportion to their respective holdings on each day during the quarter (reported on Schedule Q (Form 1066)).

The holder treats the daily portion of taxable income and net loss as ordinary income or loss. However, the amount of loss that the holder may take into account in any calendar quarter cannot exceed the holder's adjusted basis in the residual interest (as determined without regard to any required basis decreases for the daily portions of the REMIC's net loss). Any allocated loss that is disallowed may be carried forward to succeeding calendar quarters indefinitely, but it may only be used to offset income from the same REMIC.

Distributions made by the REMIC to a holder of a residual interest are received tax free to the extent that they do not exceed that holder's adjusted basis in his or her interest. Any excess is treated as gain from the sale or exchange of the interest. The basis of a holder's residual interest is increased by the daily portion of REMIC taxable income allocated to the interest. The holder's basis is decreased, but not below zero, by the amount of any distribution received and the daily portion of the REMIC net loss allocated to the interest holder. If a residual interest in a REMIC is disposed of by the holder, these adjustments are treated as occurring immediately before the disposition.

Income in Excess of Daily Accruals. A holder of a residual interest may not reduce taxable income (or alternative minimum taxable income (AMTI)) for the tax year below his or her excess inclusion for the year (Code Sec. 860E; Reg. § 1.860E-1). A holder's excess inclusion is equal to the excess of the net income passed through to the holder each calendar quarter over a deemed interest component referred to as the "daily accrual." The effect is to prevent a holder from offsetting his or her excess inclusion by any net operating losses (NOLs) (¶ 1145) or in calculating alternative minimum tax (AMT) (¶ 190). Excess inclusions are also treated as unrelated business taxable income for tax-exempt holders (¶ 655). If a residual interest is held by a regulated investment company (RIC), real estate investment trust (REIT), common trust fund, or cooperative, a portion of the dividends paid by the organization to its shareholders are treated as excess inclusions.

Application of Wash Sale Rules. The wash sale rules (¶ 1935) generally apply to dispositions of residual interests where a seller of the interest acquires any residual interest in any REMIC (or any interest in a taxable mortgage pool (¶ 2368) that is comparable to a residual interest) within a period beginning six months before the date of sale or disposition and ending six months after that date (Code Sec. 860F(d)).

Residual Interests Held by Disqualified Organizations. If a disqualified organization (government, exempt organization, cooperative) holds a residual interest in a REMIC at any time during the tax year, then an excise tax is imposed against the person or entity that has transferred the interest to the organization (Code Sec. 860E(e); Reg. § 1.860E-2). The tax is the highest applicable corporate income tax rate (21 percent for tax years beginning after 2017) (¶ 219) imposed on the present value of the total excess inclusion that is anticipated for the interest after the transfer takes place. If the transfer is through an agent of the disqualified organization, the agent must pay the tax.

Noneconomic Interests. The transfer of a noneconomic residual interest is disregarded for federal tax purposes if a significant purpose of the transfer was to impede the assessment or collection of tax (Reg. § 1.860E-1(c)). A noneconomic residual interest is one for which anticipated distributions are insufficient to meet anticipated tax liabilities.

2367. Foreign Holders of REMIC Interests. If the holder of a residual interest in a real estate mortgage investment conduit (REMIC) (¶ 2361) is a nonresident alien or foreign corporation, then for withholding and income tax purposes (¶ 2425): (1) amounts includible in the holder's gross income are taken into account when paid or distributed, or when the interest is disposed; and (2) no exemption from the 30-percent tax imposed on U.S.-source income not effectively connected with a U.S. business applies to any excess inclusion (¶ 2431) (Code Sec. 860G(b)).

2368. Taxable Mortgage Pools. If a mortgage pool does not elect to be or qualify as a real estate mortgage investment conduit (REMIC) (¶ 2343) or as a financial asset securitization investment trust (FASIT) formed prior to January 1, 2005 (¶ 2394), it may qualify as a taxable mortgage pool. An entity is a taxable mortgage pool if:

> (1) substantially all the assets of which consist of debt obligations (or interests therein) and more than 50 percent of the obligations (or interests) consist of real estate mortgages;

> (2) the entity is the obligor under debt obligations with two or more maturities; and

> (3) under the terms of the entity's debt obligations, payments on the obligations referred to in (2) are related to payments on the obligations or interests referred to in (1) (Code Sec. 7701(i)).

A taxable mortgage pool is taxed as a separate corporation and may not join with any other corporation in filing a consolidated return. Any portion of an entity that meets the requirements above is treated as a taxable mortgage pool. However, no domestic savings and loan association can qualify to be a taxable mortgage pool.

Insurance Companies

2370. Taxation of Life Insurance Companies. For tax years beginning after 2017, a life insurance company is generally taxed on its life insurance company taxable income, including any net capital gains, at the 21-percent corporate income tax rate (¶ 219) (Code Sec. 801). A life insurance company with a fiscal year that includes January 1, 2018, pays federal income tax using a blended tax rate under the Code Sec. 15 tax proration rules. More specifically, a life insurance company determines its federal income tax for the fiscal year by (1) calculating its tax for the entire tax year using the graduated corporate income tax rates in effect for tax years beginning before 2018, (2) calculating its tax for the tax year using the 21-percent rate for tax years beginning after 2017, (3) proportioning each tax amount in (1) and (2) based on the number of days in the tax year when the different rates were in effect, and (4) adding the two amounts determined in (3). The sum of these two amounts is the life insurance company's income tax for the fiscal year that includes January 1, 2018 (Notice 2018-38).

In tax years beginning before 2018, if a life insurance company has net capital gains, the company is taxed at the 35-percent corporate capital gain rate (¶ 1738) on its net capital gain, and at regular corporate tax rates on the excess of its life insurance company taxable income minus the net capital gain, if this results in a lower tax amount (Code Sec. 801(a)(2), prior to being stricken by the Tax Cuts and Jobs Act (P.L. 115-97)).

Life insurance company taxable income for this purpose is the sum of the life insurance company's net premiums, net decreases in reserves, and other items of income, minus deductions for the following: claims, benefits, and losses accrued; net increases in various reserves (¶ 2372); policyholder dividends (¶ 2373); dividends received (subject to limitations); operational losses in tax years beginning before 2018

(¶ 2377); net operating losses in tax years beginning after 2017; consideration paid for another person's assumption of the company's insurance and annuity liabilities; and dividend reimbursements paid to another insurance company (Code Secs. 803, 804, and 805). All other deductions allowed to a corporation are also permitted, subject to some modifications. A life insurance company uses Form 1120-L to figure and report its taxable income.

For tax years beginning before 2018, small life insurance companies with gross assets of less than $500 million at the close of a tax year may claim an additional deduction based on their tentative taxable income (Code Sec. 806, prior to being stricken by P.L. 115-97).

A business entity qualifies as a life insurance company if: (1) more than half of its business activities consist of issuing life insurance or annuity contracts, or reinsuring risks underwritten by other insurance companies; and (2) more than half of its total reserves for paying off insurance obligations consist of life insurance reserves, plus unearned premiums, and unpaid losses on noncancellable life, accident, or health policies that are not included in life insurance reserves (Code Sec. 816).

2372. Net Change in Reserves of Life Insurance Companies. A life insurance company (¶ 2370) may deduct the net increase in certain reserves and must include in income the net decrease in such reserves that have occurred during the tax year (Code Sec. 807). The net increase or decrease is generally computed by comparing the closing balance for the company's reserves to the opening balance of the reserves. The closing balance is reduced by the policyholders' shares of tax-exempt interest and shares of the increase in cash values of insurance and annuity contracts for the year.

Items that must be taken into account in determining whether reserves have had a net increase or decrease include:

- life insurance reserves;

- unearned premiums and unpaid losses (Code Sec. 846; Reg. § 1.846-1);

- discounted amounts necessary to satisfy obligations arising under contracts that did not involve life, accident, or health contingencies;

- dividend accumulations and other amounts held in connection with insurance and annuity contracts;

- advanced premiums and liabilities for premium deposit funds; and

- reasonable special contingency reserves for group term life insurance or group accident and health contracts.

For tax years beginning before 2018, insurance companies that are required to discount unpaid losses could claim an additional deduction up to the excess of undiscounted unpaid losses over related discounted unpaid losses (Code Sec. 847, prior to being stricken by the Tax Cuts and Jobs Act (P.L. 115-97)).

2373. Policyholder Dividends of Life Insurance Companies. A life insurance company (¶ 2370) may claim a deduction in calculating taxable income for dividends or similar distributions paid or accrued to policyholders during the tax year (Code Sec. 808). A policyholder dividend includes excess interest, premium adjustments, experience-rated refunds, and any amount paid or credited to policyholders not based on a fixed amount in the contract but dependent on the experience rate of the company or the discretion of management. The policyholder dividends deduction must be reduced by the amount by which the deduction was accelerated due to a change in the life insurance company's business practice.

2377. Net Operating Loss (NOL) Deduction of Life Insurance Companies. A life insurance company (¶ 2370) is allowed a net operating loss (NOL) deduction for losses arising in tax years beginning after 2017 the same as any other corporation (¶ 1145). However, NOLs are not taken into account in determining a life insurance company's limitation on the its' dividends-received or charitable contribution deductions (Code Sec. 805).

For losses arising in tax years beginning before 2018, a life insurance company could claim an operations loss deduction in calculating taxable income, which equaled the sum of operations loss carryovers and carrybacks to the tax year. The company's loss from operations for a tax year was the excess of its life insurance deductions over its life insurance gross income (subject to limitations). An operations loss could be carried back three years and carried forward 15 years (Code Sec. 810, prior to being stricken by the Tax Cuts and Jobs Act (P.L. 115-97)).

2378. Taxation of Other Insurance Companies. An insurance company that does not meet the definition of a life insurance company (¶ 2370) (property and casualty companies) is subject to taxation at regular corporate income tax rates (¶ 219) on its taxable income (Code Secs. 831(a) and 832). However, the company is exempt from tax if its gross receipts for the tax year do not exceed $600,000 and more than 50 percent of gross receipts consist of premiums ($150,000 and 35 percent, respectively, for a mutual insurance company) (Code Sec. 501(c)(15)).

A property and casualty insurance company may elect to be taxed only on its taxable investment income if it has net written premiums for the tax year (or direct written premiums if greater) that do not exceed $2.3 million for 2019 ($2.35 million for 2020). The company's net written premiums is its gross investment income less deductions for tax-free interest, investment expenses, real estate expenses, depreciation, paid or accrued interest, capital losses, trade or business deductions, and certain corporate deductions (Code Secs. 831(b) and 834(e); Rev. Proc. 2018-57; Rev. Proc. 2019-44).

A property and casualty insurance company must also meet a diversification requirement to be eligible to be taxed on only its taxable investment income. There are two methods of meeting this requirement. The primary method—the "risk diversification test"—is to have no more that 20 percent of the company's net written premiums (or direct written premiums if greater) attributable to one policyholder in a tax year.

A small insurance company that fails to meet this test may be able to meet the alternative "relatedness test." This requires that no person who holds (directly or indirectly) an interest in the company be a "specified holder" with aggregate interests in the company (held directly or indirectly) that are a higher percentage of the entire interests in that insurance company than a *de minimis* percentage of interests in the relevant specified assets with respect to the company held (directly or indirectly) by the specified holder.

A small insurance company with an election in effect to be taxed on its taxable investment income is required to meet any information and substantiation reporting requirements regarding the diversification test as may be established by the IRS (Code Sec. 831(d)).

2380. Foreign Insurance Companies. A foreign company carrying on an insurance business within the United States that would otherwise qualify as an insurance company if it were a domestic company is taxable as an insurance company on its income effectively connected with the conduct of any U.S. trade or business (¶ 2429) and is taxable on its remaining income from U.S. sources (¶ 2431) (Code Sec. 842).

Other Special Entities

2383. Banks and Other Financial Institutions. A bank or other financial institution is generally subject to the same tax rules as a corporation except that a bank is not subject to capital loss limitations with respect to the worthlessness of debt securities (¶ 1916). Instead, a bank may treat these losses as bad debt losses. In addition, if one bank directly owns at least 80 percent of each class of stock of another bank, the first bank's losses on worthless stock and stock rights in the second bank are not treated as losses from the sale or exchange of capital assets (Code Sec. 582).

The method that is used to deduct bad debts of a bank depends on the type and size of the institution in question (Code Sec. 585; Reg. § § 1.585-1—1.585-8). A small bank (average adjusted basis of all assets of $500 million or less) may add to its bad debt reserves an amount based on its actual experience as shown by losses for the current and preceding five tax years. A thrift institution that would be treated as a small bank may utilize this method as well. A large bank is generally required to use either a specific charge-off method in which its debt reserves are recaptured over a four-year period, or the cutoff method in which recoveries and losses are reflected as adjustments to the bank's reserve account.

Definition of a Bank. For this purpose, a bank is defined as a corporation with a substantial part of its business consisting of either receiving deposits and making loans or exercising fiduciary powers similar to those permitted to national banks. This includes a commercial bank and trust company, mutual savings bank, building and loan association, cooperative bank, and federal savings and loan association (Code Sec. 581; Reg. § 1.581-2). However, a corporation that is one of these other type of entities is allowed a deduction for dividends paid or credited to depositors (Code Sec. 591).

Sale or Exchange of Securities. In the case of certain financial institutions, the sale or exchange of a bond, debenture, note, certificate, or other evidence of indebtedness is not considered a sale or exchange of a capital asset (Code Sec. 582(c)). Instead, net gains and losses from such transactions are treated as ordinary income and losses. A financial institution includes a commercial bank, mutual savings bank, domestic building and loan association, cooperative bank, business development corporation, and small business investment company (¶ 2392).

2389. Common Trust Funds. A common trust fund is an investment vehicle established by a bank in the form of a state-law trust to handle the investment and reinvestment of money contributed to it in its capacity as a trustee, executor, administrator, guardian, or as a custodian of a Uniform Gifts to Minors account (Code Sec. 584). For tax purposes, a common trust fund is treated in a manner similar to that of a partnership. Instead of the trust being subject to tax, each participant that invests in the trust fund must include his or her proportionate share of the trust fund's income or loss on his or her own return. This includes a participant's share of dividends received by the fund that are eligible for the reduced tax rate on qualified dividends (¶ 733). The admission and withdrawal of a participant does not result in a gain or loss to the common trust fund.

2392. Small Business Investment Companies. A small business investment company (SBIC) is a private corporation that operates under the Small Business Investment Act of 1958 to provide capital to small business concerns through the purchase of convertible debentures. An SBIC is generally treated as a corporation for federal tax purposes with a few exceptions. First, an SBIC may claim an ordinary loss deduction for any loss on the sale or exchange of stock of a small business concern if the stock was received under the conversion privilege of a debenture acquired on the providing of equity capital to small business concerns (Code Sec. 1243). Second, an SBIC may deduct 100 percent of the dividends it receives from taxable domestic corporations (Code Sec. 243(a)(2)). See ¶ 1913 for the treatment of losses on SBIC stock and ¶ 1909 for the rollover of gain from the sale of publicly traded securities before 2018 into stock or a partnership interest in a specialized SBIC.

2394. Financial Asset Securitization Investment Trusts. Prior to January 1, 2005, a qualified entity could elect to be treated as a financial asset securitization investment trust (FASIT) (Code Secs. 860H—860L, prior to repeal by the American Jobs Creation Act of 2004 (P.L. 108-357)). A FASIT is a pass-through entity used to securitize debt obligations such as credit card receivables, home equity loans, and auto loans. A FASIT must be entirely owned by a taxable C corporation. Any residual income of the FASIT is passed through and taxed to the owner. The advantage offered by a FASIT is that asset-backed securities issued by a FASIT are treated as debt for federal tax purposes. Thus, interest paid to investors is deductible. The rules regarding FASITs are repealed as of January 1, 2005, but the repeal does not apply to any FASIT in existence on October 22, 2004, to the extent that regular interests already issued by the FASIT remain outstanding in accordance with their original terms.

2396. Alaska Native Corporations and Settlement Trusts. Alaska Native Settlement Trusts (ANSTs) established to promote the health, education and welfare of its beneficiaries and preserve heritage and culture by Alaska Native Corporations under the

Alaska Native Claims Settlement Act (43 U.S.C. § 1601) can elect to have special rules apply to the taxation of the trust and its beneficiaries (Code Sec. 646). The Native Corporations were initially established to receive claims settlements from the U.S. government. The electing ANST pays tax on its income at the lowest rate specified for ordinary income and capital gains of an unmarried individual. No amount is included in the gross income of the beneficiaries by reason of a contribution to the electing ANST. Electing ANSTs are subject to reporting requirements (Code Sec. 6039H).

Native Corporations are not required to recognize income for the amount of certain payments assigned to ANSTs, provided that the payments are assigned in writing to an ANST, and were not received by the Native Corporation before it made the assignment to the ANST. In turn, the ANST is required to include in income any payment received pursuant to the assignment, and those payments retain the same character as if received by the Native Corporation. The assignment may be a percentage or a fixed amount, but must be described with reasonable particularity and must specify if the assignment is in perpetuity or for a period of time and whether the assignment in revocable (Code Sec. 139G).

Alternatively, a Native Corporation may claim a deduction (regardless of whether it elects the applicability of the special rules under Code Sec. 646) for contributions to an ANST, equal to the amount of a cash contribution or, in the case of other form a contribution, equal to the lesser of the Native Corporation's basis in the contributed property or the fair market value of the contributed property (Code Sec. 247(a) and (b)). The deduction is subject to limitations and carryover rules, as well as special holding period and basis rules. A Native Corporation cannot claim the deduction for any amounts excluded from income by the ANST (Code Sec. 139G(e)). In the case of non-cash contributions, the ANST can elect to defer recognition of income on any or all properties received until the property is sold or exchanged (Code Sec. 247(g)).

Chapter 24

FOREIGN INCOME AND TRANSACTIONS

U.S. Citizens and Residents Living Abroad

See CCH® AnswerConnect: *U.S. Citizens and Residents Abroad* for more information on this topic.

2402. Foreign Earned Income Exclusion. A qualifying individual (¶ 2404) who lives and works abroad may elect (¶ 2408) to exclude from gross income a certain amount of foreign earned income attributable to his or her residence in a foreign country during the tax year (Code Sec. 911(a)(1) and (b)(2)). The maximum amount of foreign earned income that may be excluded is $105,900 for 2019 ($107,600 for 2020) (Rev. Proc. 2018-57; Rev. Proc. 2019-44). The exclusion is reported on Form 2555.

The exclusion is calculated on a daily basis. Therefore, the maximum limit must be reduced ratably for each day during the calendar year that the taxpayer does not qualify for the exclusion. The exclusion is also limited to the excess of the individual's foreign earned income for the year over his or her foreign housing exclusion (¶ 2403). In the case of married taxpayers, each spouse may compute the limitation separately and without regard to community property laws (if otherwise applicable). Thus, it is possible for a married couple to exclude up to $211,800 for 2019 ($215,200 for 2020) if each spouse is qualified to claim the exclusion (Reg. § 1.911-5).

> **Example 1:** Andy is a U.S. citizen who qualified as a bona fide resident of Costa Rica for all of 2018 and who received $78,000 in salary for work he did in Costa Rica. Assuming he claimed no foreign housing exclusion, Andy was able to exclude all of the salary from his gross income for 2018. Andy continues to work in Costa Rica until October 31, 2019, when his employer permanently reassigns him to the United States. During this time, Andy received a salary of $90,000 for his work in Costa Rica in 2019. Assuming he claimed no foreign housing exclusion, the maximum amount of foreign earned income he can exclude from his gross income in 2019 is $88,202 ($105,900 multiplied by ratio of the number of days he was a bona fide resident of Costa Rica ($304/365$)).

Foreign Earned Income. Foreign earned income includes wages, salaries, professional fees, and other amounts received as compensation for personal services actually rendered when the taxpayer's tax home is located in a foreign country and the taxpayer meets either the bona fide residence or physical presence test (Code Sec. 911(b)(1) and (d)(2); Reg. § 1.911-3). If the taxpayer engages in a sole proprietorship or partnership where both personal services and capital are material income-producing factors, no more than 30 percent of the taxpayer's share of the net profits can be treated as earned income (30 percent of gross profits if no net profits). Any salary received from a corporation is earned income to the extent it represents reasonable compensation for personal services performed.

Foreign earned income does not include any compensation received after the close of the tax year following the year in which the personal services were performed. It also does not include any reimbursements received under an accountable plan for expenses incurred on an employer's behalf (¶ 952A), the value of meals and lodging that are furnished for the convenience of an employer and excluded from gross income (¶ 2089 and ¶ 2406), employer contributions to a nonqualified retirement plan, or any recaptured moving expenses. Foreign earned income also does not include amounts received as a

24 | FOREIGN

pension, annuity, or social security payments, amounts paid by the United States or its agencies to its employees, or income earned in a country in which the United States imposes travel restrictions.

A taxpayer who elects to claim the foreign earned income exclusion (or foreign housing exclusion) is prohibited from claiming any deduction, exclusion, or tax credit (including the foreign tax credit) that is properly allocable to the excluded amounts (Code Sec. 911(d)(6); Reg. §1.911-6(a)). For example, a taxpayer may not deduct unreimbursed employee business expenses against wages that are excluded as foreign earned income.

Determination of Tax Liability. If an individual elects to exclude foreign earned income or foreign housing expenses (or both), then his or her income tax liability and alternative minimum tax (AMT) liability on the nonexcluded amount is determined using the tax rates that would have applied had the exclusion(s) not been claimed (Code Sec. 911(f)). If the taxpayer's net capital gains exceed his or her taxable income or alternative minimum taxable income (AMTI), then the excess reduces the taxpayer's net capital gains without regard to qualified dividend income, and then qualified dividend income. The excess is also treated as a long-term capital loss in computing the taxpayer's adjusted net capital gain, unrecaptured section 1250 gain, and 28-percent rate gain. The worksheet in Instructions to Form 1040 or Instructions to Form 6251 is used to calculate tax liability for this purpose.

2403. Foreign Housing Exclusion or Deduction. In addition to the election to exclude foreign earned income (¶ 2402), a qualified individual (¶ 2404) may elect (¶ 2408) to exclude from gross income a certain amount of foreign housing expenses paid for with employer-provided amounts included in the taxpayer's foreign earned income (for example, housing allowance or reimbursement) (Code Sec. 911(a)(2)). The amount of foreign housing expenses or foreign earned income excluded from an individual's gross income is used to determine the taxpayer's regular income tax and alternative minimum tax (AMT) liability on his or her nonexcluded income.

The maximum housing amount that may be excluded is limited to 14 percent of the maximum foreign earned income exclusion for the year (Code Sec. 911(c)). This is the excess of: (1) the taxpayer's reasonable foreign housing expenses for the tax year (generally limited to 30 percent of the maximum foreign earned income exclusion for the year), over (2) a base housing amount equal to 16 percent of the maximum foreign earned income exclusion amount for the year. The exclusion is computed on a daily basis and multiplied by the number of days of foreign residence or presence by the taxpayer for the year.

For 2019, the maximum amount of foreign housing expenses that generally may be excluded is $14,826 or $40.62 per day (14 percent of $105,900) (Rev. Proc. 2018-57). For 2020, the maximum amount of foreign housing expenses that generally may be excluded is $15,064 or $41.16 per day (14 percent of $107,600) (Rev. Proc. 2019-44). Foreign housing expenses may be excluded only to the extent of the lesser of the expenses attributable to employer-provided amounts or the individual's foreign earned income for the tax year. The exclusion is calculated on Form 2555.

The reasonable amount of expenses that may be used in calculating the maximum exclusion limit, i.e., the 30 percent of the maximum foreign earned income exclusion, may be adjusted annually by the IRS for specific geographic locations that have higher housing costs relative to the United States (Notice 2020-13). For this purpose, the taxpayer must actually reside within the geographic limits of the high-cost location identified by the IRS to claim the adjusted limit. The taxpayer cannot reside in a suburb of the location. The limits for high-cost localities are listed in the Instructions for Form 2555.

Housing Expenses. An individual's foreign housing expenses are the reasonable costs paid or incurred during the tax year to provide housing in a foreign country for the taxpayer and for his or her spouse and dependents if they reside with the taxpayer (Reg. §1.911-4). This may include reasonable expenses related to a second foreign household for the taxpayer's spouse and dependents if they do not reside with the taxpayer due to adverse conditions near the taxpayer's tax home. Eligible expenses include rent or the fair rental value of housing provided in kind by an employer, utilities (other than telephone charges), real or personal property insurance, household repairs, rental of furniture and accessories, and residential parking. Excluded are expenses that are otherwise deductible (depreciation, interest, taxes) or that are extravagant. Also excluded is the cost of buying property (including mortgage payments), capital improvements to property, purchased furniture or accessories, or the cost of domestic labor. If a husband and wife are both qualified individuals with foreign earned income, special rules apply which may allow them both to claim the foreign housing exclusion or deduction, depending on whether separate households are maintained (Reg. § 1.911-5).

Self-Employment. A self-employed individual is entitled to deduct from gross income a certain amount of foreign housing expenses in lieu of the exclusion for employer-provided amounts (Code Sec. 911(c)(4); Reg. § 1.911-4(e)). The deduction is limited to the amount by which the taxpayer's foreign earned income for the tax year exceeds his or her foreign earned income and housing exclusion. Any amount that exceeds the deduction limit can be carried forward one tax year. If the taxpayer has foreign earned income that consists of both employer-provided amounts and self-employment amounts, then the taxpayer may elect to exclude the part of the housing expenses that are paid for with employer-provided amounts and may claim a deduction for any remaining housing expenses attributed to self-employment income.

2404. Eligibility for Foreign Earned Income and Housing Exclusions. In order to qualify for the foreign earned income exclusion (¶ 2402) or foreign housing exclusion (¶ 2403), an individual's tax home must be in a foreign country and he or she must satisfy either the bona fide residence test or the physical presence test (Code Sec. 911(d)(1); Reg. § 1.911-2). A foreign country is any territory, including airspace and territorial waters, under the sovereignty of a government other than the United States. A foreign country does not include Antarctica or U.S. possessions such as Puerto Rico, Guam, the Commonwealth of the Northern Mariana Islands, the U.S. Virgin Islands, and Johnston Island. A bona fide resident of American Samoa (¶ 2414) or Puerto Rico (¶ 2415) may be eligible to exclude income from the possession for U.S. tax purposes. The foreign earned income and housing exclusions are denied if the taxpayer is present in a foreign country in which travel is generally restricted (Code Sec. 911(d)(8)).

Tax Home. A tax home for this purpose generally has the same meaning as it does for determining the deductibility of travel expenses away from home (¶ 950). An individual's tax home is where his or her principal place of business is located, regardless of where he or she maintains a family home (Code Sec. 911(d)(3)). The location of a taxpayer's tax home often depends on whether a work assignment is temporary or indefinite. An individual is not considered to have a tax home in a foreign country for any period during which his or her abode is in the United States. However, an individual serving in support of the Armed Forces of the United States in a designated combat zone is considered to have a tax home outside the United States for purposes of the exclusion. Temporary presence or maintenance of a dwelling in the United States does not necessarily mean that an abode is in the United States during that time, even if the taxpayer's spouse or dependents use the dwelling.

Bona Fide Residence. A U.S. citizen (or resident alien subject to a U.S. income tax treaty) may qualify for the foreign earned income or housing exclusions if he or she is a bona fide resident of a foreign country for an uninterrupted period that includes a full tax year (Code Sec. 911(d)(1)(A) and (d)(5)). This determination is based on all of the facts and circumstances, including the taxpayer's intentions regarding the length and nature of the stay. It is not determined by the taxpayer's status under the laws of the foreign country, nor by merely living in a foreign country for a year. The taxpayer does not have to be a bona fide resident of the same foreign country for the entire period and the foreign country in which the taxpayer is a bona fide resident does not have to be the primary place of employment. Once the bona fide residence requirement is met, the taxpayer is permitted the exclusions for any tax year in which the period of residence began or ended.

> **Example 1:** Barney is a calendar-year taxpayer whose salary is $120,000 per year. On January 1, 2018, he establishes bona fide residence in Canada. His residence lasts until March 31, 2019. Assuming he claims no foreign housing exclusion, he qualifies in 2018 for the maximum exclusion of $103,900 for his foreign earned income because he established residence for the full year in a

foreign country. He also qualifies for the exclusion of $26,112 of his foreign earned income ($105,900 × $^{90}/_{365}$) for the portion of the 2019 tax year he was a resident in Canada.

Physical Presence. A U.S. citizen or resident alien may qualify for the foreign income or housing exclusions if he or she is present in a foreign country (or countries) for 330 full days out of any consecutive 12-month period (Code Sec. 911(d)(1)(B)). The taxpayer does not have to be present in the foreign country solely for business purposes and the 330 days do not have to be consecutive. In addition, the taxpayer can select any 12-month period in which he or she meets the physical presence test.

> **Example 2:** Betty is a U.S. citizen who leaves New York on February 3, 2019, and arrives in Spain on that same day. During December 2019, Betty vacations in France for 10 days. She leaves Spain to move back to the United States on January 10, 2020. Betty meets the 330-day test during either the 12-month period beginning February 4, 2019, or the 12-month period ending January 10, 2020.

Waiver of Time Requirements. Relief from either the bona fide residence or the physical presence test is provided to an individual if he or she was forced to flee a foreign country because of civil unrest, war, or other adverse conditions (Code Sec. 911(d)(4)). To qualify for the relief, the individual must have been a bona fide resident of, or present in, the foreign country on or prior to the date the IRS determines that adverse conditions exist in the foreign country and individuals are required to leave. In addition, the taxpayer must establish that he or she could reasonably be expected to have satisfied the residency requirement had the adverse conditions not arisen. The IRS publishes annually the names of countries for which the waiver is available (Rev. Proc. 2020-14). A waiver has also been provided for certain individuals for the 2019 and 2020 tax years as a result of adverse conditions in a foreign country caused by the COVID-19 (coronavirus) crisis (Rev. Proc. 2020-27).

2406. Camps Located in a Foreign Country. In addition to the exclusion of foreign earned income (¶ 2402) and foreign housing expenses (¶ 2403), an individual may exclude from gross income and wages as a *de minimis* fringe benefit (¶ 2089) the value of meals and lodging provided by his or her employer in a camp located in a foreign country if three requirements are met (Code Sec. 119(c)). First, the lodging must be provided for the convenience of the employer because the place where the employee's services are performed is in a remote area where satisfactory housing is unavailable. Second, the location of the camp must be as near as practicable to the place where the employee's services are performed. Third, the lodging must be provided in a common area, not open to the public, that normally accommodates 10 or more employees. An employee who works for a U.S. military contractor on a foreign military base cannot exclude from income the value of lodging provided by his or her employer, as the lodging is not considered to be on the employer's business premises (*P.M. Middleton,* Dec. 57,464(M), TC Memo. 2008-150).

2408. Electing the Foreign Earned Income and Housing Exclusions. A qualified individual (¶ 2404) must make a separate election with respect to the foreign earned income exclusion (¶ 2402) and the foreign housing exclusion (¶ 2403). The elections are made by filing Form 2555 with the taxpayer's timely-filed income tax return (including extensions), amended return, or a late-filed return if filed within one year after the due date of the return (not including extensions) (Code Sec. 911(e); Reg. § 1.911-7).

Once made, the election will remain in effect for the current tax year and all subsequent years unless revoked. A taxpayer who revokes the election will be prohibited from making a new election for at least five tax years without IRS approval. If both a taxpayer and his or her spouse qualify for the exclusions, each must file a separate Form 2555 regardless of whether they file a joint return or separate returns. A self-employed taxpayer does not have to make an election in order to claim the foreign housing deduction. An eligible individual must provide Form 673 to his or her employer to claim an exemption from U.S. income tax withholding on foreign earned income that may be excluded from gross income.

An individual who claims either the foreign earned income or foreign housing exclusion may not claim the foreign tax credit or deduction (¶ 2475) for any income excluded. If a taxpayer attempts to claim the foreign tax credit or deduction, then the

¶2406

election for the foreign earned income and foreign housing exclusions is considered revoked (IRS Pub. 54). In addition, a taxpayer cannot claim either of the exclusions and also the earned income tax credit (¶ 1422) or the additional child tax credit (¶ 1405).

2409. Resident Aliens. A resident alien is generally taxed in the same manner as a U.S. citizen. For this purpose, residency is determined under the lawful permanent residence test (green card) or the substantial presence test (Code Sec. 7701(b)(1)). An alien who does not qualify under either test is generally treated as a nonresident alien for federal income, employment, and excise tax purposes (but not estate and gift tax purposes).

Some individuals may be eligible to elect resident status (¶ 2410). In addition, an individual can have a dual-status tax year and be both a resident and nonresident alien during the year (¶ 2411). In the case of an individual who is considered both a U.S. resident and a resident of a foreign country during the year (dual resident taxpayer), a tax treaty may override the normal treatment of the individual as a resident alien for all purposes under the treaty. The green card test and substantial presence test determine whether an alien is a resident of a U.S. possession or territory whose income tax laws mirror those of the United States. They do not determine whether an individual is a bona fide resident of other U.S. possessions or territories (¶ 2414) (Reg. § 301.7701(b)-1(d)).

Green Card Test. An alien who is a lawful permanent resident of the United States under U.S. immigration laws (i.e., receives a "green card") is considered a resident alien for federal tax purposes (Reg. § 301.7701(b)-1(b)). Resident status begins in the first calendar year in which the alien is a lawful resident and is physically present in the United States for at least one day (¶ 2411). Resident status continues until permanent resident status is terminated or abandoned (¶ 2412).

Substantial Presence Test. An alien is considered a U.S. resident if the individual is physically present in the United States for at least 31 days during the calendar year and 183 days for the current and two preceding calendar years (¶ 2411). For purposes of the 183-day requirement, each day present in the United States during the current calendar year counts as a full day, each day in the first preceding year as $1/3$ of a day, and each day in the second preceding year as $1/6$ of a day (Code Sec. 7701(b)(3); Reg. § 301.7701(b)-1(c)).

There are exceptions as to what days an alien is considered to be physically present in the United States, including days for: (1) regular commuters from Canada or Mexico; (2) days in transit between two places outside the United States; (3) medical conditions preventing departure; (4) exempt individuals including teachers, trainees, and students on temporary visas, as well as professional athletes competing in a charitable event; (5) crew members of foreign vessels; and (6) foreign government workers. The IRS has provided relief to individuals affected by travel disruptions arising from the COVID-19 (coronavirus) crisis to claim the medical condition travel exception for the 2020 tax year (Rev. Proc. 2020-20). Form 8843 must be completed to exclude days of physical presence in the United States due to a medical condition or as an exempt individual. Presence in U.S. territories or possessions does not count as presence in the United States.

An individual who otherwise meets the substantial presence test may still be treated as a nonresident alien if the individual has a tax home in a foreign country during the tax year, has a closer connection to the foreign country, and was physically present in the United States for less than 183 days during the year. An alien must fully complete Form 8840 and attach it to his or her return for the relevant tax year to prove that he or she satisfies the closer connection exception.

2410. Elective Resident Status. There are two ways alien individuals are permitted to elect resident status if they do not otherwise qualify as a resident alien (¶ 2409). First, an individual who otherwise fails to meet the green card or substantial presence test may elect to be a resident alien for part of the current year (Code Sec. 7701(b)(4); Reg. § 301.7701(b)-4(c)(3)). To qualify for the election, the individual:

- must not be a resident alien in the prior calendar year;
- must meet the substantial presence test in the calendar year following the election year;

24 FOREIGN

¶2410

- must be present in the United States for at least 31 consecutive days in the election year; and

- must be present in the United States for at least 75 percent of the days during the period from the first day of the 31-day presence period through the end of the election year.

If these requirements are met, the individual's election to be treated as a U.S. resident alien is effective for that portion of the year that begins on the first day of the earliest testing period that the 31-day and 75 percent requirements are met. The election is made by attaching a signed statement to the individual's tax return for the election year indicating that the individual meets the election requirements. The election cannot be made before the individual has met the substantial presence test for the calendar year following the election year. Once made, the election can be revoked only with IRS consent.

The second way an alien may elect resident status is if the individual is married to a U.S. citizen or resident alien at the end of the tax year—then the election may be made in order to file a joint return (Code Sec. 6013(g) and (h)). The taxpayer may be either a nonresident or resident alien at the end of the tax year for the election to be made. Both spouses must join in the election by attaching a statement to a joint return for the first tax year for which the election applies. It is effective for the entire tax year and all subsequent tax years for federal income tax and withholding purposes, unless neither spouse is a U.S. citizen or resident alien at any time during the year. The election may also be jointly revoked by the couple or terminated by reason of death, separation, divorce, or by the IRS for failure of the couple to keep adequate records. Once terminated, the election may not be made again by the couple.

2411. Dual-Status Tax Years. An individual can be both a resident and nonresident alien during the same tax year (¶ 2409). This usually occurs the year of arrival in, or departure from, the United States. An individual who is a dual-status alien has a dual-status tax year. Thus, the individual's income tax liability is computed as a resident alien for the period of residence and as a nonresident alien for the period of nonresidence (¶ 2425) (Reg. § 1.871-13).

If an alien individual is filing a tax return for a dual-status year, then head of household filing status may not be used, the standard deduction cannot be claimed, and the deduction for personal and dependency exemptions for tax years beginning before 2018 and after 2025 cannot exceed taxable income for the period the individual is a resident alien. A married individual may also not use joint filing status and tax rates for joint filers for the period of residency unless he or she is married to a U.S. citizen or resident alien and the election to be treated as a resident alien for the year is made (¶ 2410) (IRS Pub. 519). The education credits, earned income credit, and the elderly or disabled credit may also not be claimed unless the individual is married and elects to be treated as a resident alien by filing a joint return.

Residency Starting Date and Termination Date. If an alien meets the green card test, residency starts the first day the individual is physically present in the United States while a lawfully admitted resident. If an alien meets the substantial presence test, residency starts the first day the individual is physically present in the United States during the calendar year. A *de minimis* exception allows up to 10 days to be disregarded in determining the residency starting date under the substantial presence test if the individual has a closer connection to a foreign country. For an alien that satisfies both tests, residency starts on the earlier date when either test is satisfied (Reg. § 301.7701(b)-4).

If the individual was a resident alien in the previous tax year, then residency begins on the first day of the current tax year regardless of whether residency status is determined under the green card test or substantial presence test. Residency status may terminate before the end of the tax year under either test, but only if the individual is not a U.S. resident alien at any time during the following tax year.

Departure Requirements. No alien (whether resident or nonresident) is generally permitted to depart the United States or a U.S. possession without first obtaining a certificate of compliance from the IRS (i.e., sailing or departure permit). The certificate is proof that the individual has discharged all of his or her U.S. income tax liability (Code

¶2411

Sec. 6851(d); Reg. § 1.6851-2). The certificate must be obtained at least two weeks before the individual leaves the United States. A resident alien (whether he or she has taxable income or not) and a nonresident alien having no taxable income for the tax year must file Form 2063 to obtain the certificate. A nonresident alien with taxable income for the tax year must file Form 1040-C to obtain the certificate. The forms do not constitute an individual's final tax return and Form 1040 or Form 1040-NR must still be filed after the individual's tax year ends. Payment of any tax is not required prior to departure if it is determined that tax collection will not be jeopardized by the alien's departure. An individual who abandons U.S. citizenship or long-term residency for tax avoidance purposes is subject to special rules (¶ 2412).

2412. Expatriation to Avoid Tax. An individual who is a covered expatriate is subject to a mark-to-market tax regime under which he or she is taxed on the unrealized gain in his or her property to the extent it exceeds $725,000 for 2019 ($737,000 in 2020) (Code Sec. 877A; Notice 2009-85; Rev. Proc. 2018-57; Rev. Proc. 2019-44). For this purpose, a covered expatriate is considered to own any interest in property that would generally be taxable as part of his or her gross estate for federal estate tax purposes (¶ 2912) if the individual died on the day before the expatriation date. For example, an installment obligation held by a covered expatriate is property subject to tax because it would be included in the expatriate's estate (*G. Topsnik*, Dec. 60,501, 146 TC No. 1). Special rules apply for deferred compensation items, specified tax deferred accounts, and interests in nongrantor trusts (¶ 566). A U.S. citizen or resident alien is also subject to a special transfer tax upon receipt of property by gift, devise, bequest, or inheritance from a covered expatriate (¶ 2948).

The exclusion amount must be allocated among all built-in gain property that is subject to the mark-to-market regime and is owned by the covered expatriate on the day before the expatriation date. Gain is determined as if a sale of the property for fair market value had taken place on the day before the expatriation date without regard to other Code provisions. Losses from the deemed sale are generally taken into account as otherwise provided in the Code, except that the wash sale rules do not apply (¶ 1935). The taxpayer must make adjustments to the basis of any property by the amount of gain or loss taken into account.

Covered Expatriate. A covered expatriate is any U.S. citizen who relinquishes citizenship or any long-term U.S. resident who ceases to be a lawful permanent resident of the United States (¶ 2409), if the individual: (1) has an average annual net income tax liability for the five preceding years ending before expatriation that exceeds $168,000 for 2019 ($171,000 in 2020); (2) has a net worth of $2 million or more on the expatriation date; or (3) fails to certify under penalties of perjury that he or she has complied with all U.S. tax obligations for the preceding five years or fails to submit evidence of compliance required by the IRS on Form 8854 (Code Sec. 877A(g); Notice 2009-85; Rev. Proc. 2018-57; Rev. Proc. 2019-44). Dual citizens and minors may be excepted from the tax liability and net worth requirements.

Election to Defer Tax. A covered expatriate may make an irrevocable election to defer payment of the mark-to-market tax that would otherwise be imposed on the deemed sale of property (Code Sec. 877A(b); Notice 2009-85). The election cannot be made without providing adequate security such as a bond or letter of credit to ensure payment of the tax. In addition, no election can be made unless the individual makes an irrevocable waiver of any rights under an income tax treaty that would preclude assessment or collection of the tax.

The election is made on an asset-by-asset basis. The tax for each piece of property is determined by multiplying the total mark-to-market tax by the ratio of the gain on the deemed sale of the property over the total gain taken into account with respect to all property deemed sold. The election defers payment of the tax until the due date for the return for the tax year in which the property is disposed of or the taxpayer's death. Payment may not be extended beyond the due date for the return for the tax year in which the covered expatriate dies.

Reporting Requirements. A covered expatriate must file an information return on Form 8854 in each tax year he or she is subject to the mark-to-market tax (Code Sec. 6039G; Notice 2009-85). The return is also to be used to provide notice that the individual has relinquished his or her U.S. citizenship or long-term residency status.

The IRS has provided procedures that allow expatriated individuals to come into compliance with their U.S. tax and filing obligations, if certain requirements are met (IR-2019-151).

2414. Resident of U.S. Possessions. An individual who is a bona fide resident of a U.S. possession during the tax year is generally subject to U.S. taxation as a U.S. citizen or resident alien (¶ 2409), rather than as a nonresident alien (Code Sec. 876). A U.S. possession for this purpose includes American Samoa, Guam, the Northern Mariana Islands, and Puerto Rico. Separate rules apply to a bona fide resident of the U.S. Virgin Islands (¶ 2416).

An individual is a bona fide resident of a U.S. possession if the person is physically present in the possession for a certain number of days during the tax year, does not have a tax home outside the possession, and does not have a closer connection to the United States or a foreign country than to the possession during the tax year (Code Sec. 937; Reg. § 1.937-1). An individual with worldwide gross income of more than $75,000 must file Form 8898 for the tax year in which the individual becomes or ceases to be a bona fide resident of a U.S. possession. A spouse's income is not included when calculating an individual's worldwide gross income for this purpose. Thus, if married individuals are each required to file Form 8898, a separate Form 8898 must be filed by each spouse regardless of whether a joint return is filed.

A U.S. citizen or resident alien who is a bona fide resident of American Samoa for the entire tax year may exclude from gross income for U.S. tax purposes any income derived from sources within the possession or that is effectively connected with a trade or business by the individual in the possession (Code Sec. 931). The exclusion does not apply to income that is received for services performed as an employee of the United States. The individual may also not claim a tax credit or deduction that is attributable to the amount of excluded income. Form 4563 is used to claim the exclusion and must be attached to a Form 1040 filed with the IRS. A similar rule applies to a bona fide resident of Puerto Rico (¶ 2415).

2415. Resident of Puerto Rico. A U.S. citizen or resident alien (¶ 2409) who is also a bona fide resident of Puerto Rico (¶ 2414) during the entire tax year may exclude from gross income for U.S. tax purposes any income derived from sources within Puerto Rico (Code Sec. 933). If the taxpayer gives up Puerto Rican residence after having been a bona fide resident for at least two years, then the taxpayer may claim a partial exclusion for the tax year of the residence change. In either case, the exclusion does not apply to income received for services performed as an employee of the United States. The taxpayer may also not claim any tax credit or deduction (except a personal exemption before 2018 and after 2025) which is attributable to the amount of excluded income.

A U.S. citizen or resident alien who has income from Puerto Rican sources is liable for the payment of taxes to Puerto Rico and may have to file a tax return with the United States as well. A U.S. citizen or resident alien who is a bona fide resident of Puerto Rico for the entire tax year generally must pay taxes to Puerto Rico on income from worldwide sources. If U.S. source income is also reported on an individual's Puerto Rican tax return, a credit may be claimed up to the amount allowable for income taxes paid to the United States.

2416. Resident of U.S. Virgin Islands. A U.S. citizen or resident alien (other than a bona fide resident of the U.S. Virgin Islands (¶ 2414)) who has income from sources within the U.S. Virgin Islands or effectively connected with a trade or business in the U.S. Virgin Islands is required to file an income tax return with both the United States and the U.S. Virgin Islands (Code Sec. 932). The tax owed to the U.S. Virgin Islands is determined on Form 8689 by multiplying the total tax owed on the United States return (after certain adjustments) by the ratio of adjusted gross income (AGI) from the U.S. Virgin Islands to worldwide AGI. The U.S. Virgin Islands' tax liability (if paid) is credited against the individual's total U.S. tax liability. An individual who qualifies as a bona fide resident of the U.S. Virgin Islands (or who files a joint U.S. return with a U.S. citizen or resident with U.S. Virgin Islands income) will generally have no U.S. tax liability so long as the taxpayer reports all income from all sources on the return filed with the U.S. Virgin Islands.

Nonresident Aliens and Foreign Corporations

See CCH® AnswerConnect: *Tax Filing Requirements for Nonresident Aliens* and *Foreign Corporations and Other Foreign Entities* for more information on this topic.

2425. Taxation of Nonresident Aliens and Foreign Corporations. A nonresident alien (¶ 2409) or a foreign corporation are generally taxed in the same manner as a U.S. citizen or domestic corporation on all income that is effectively connected with the conduct of a trade or business in the United States (¶ 2429). For this purpose, gain or loss from the disposition of a U.S. real property interest is treated as effectively connected income (¶ 2442). If any U.S. source income (¶ 2427) received by a nonresident alien or foreign corporation is not effectively connected with a U.S. trade or business, such as fixed, determinable, annual, or periodical (FDAP) income (¶ 2431), then it will generally be taxed at a flat 30-percent rate, absent a lower treaty rate. A nonresident alien and foreign corporation may generally only claim deductions and credits related to effectively connected income (¶ 2446). A flat 30-percent tax rate also applies to the profits (and certain interest amounts) of a U.S. branch of a foreign corporation that are remitted to the foreign corporation during the tax year (¶ 2433).

A nonresident alien or foreign corporation that engages in trade or business in the United States at any time during the tax year or that has taxable income must generally file an income tax return (Code Secs. 6012 and 6072(c)). Form 1040-NR or Form 1040-NR-EZ is used by a nonresident alien, and Form 1120-F is used by a foreign corporation. Nonresident aliens and foreign corporations do not need to file a return in certain circumstances, including if the taxpayer's full U.S. tax liability was withheld at the source.

The returns of nonresident aliens and foreign corporations are generally due on or before the 15th day of the *sixth month* following the close of the tax year (June 15 for calendar year taxpayers). The due date is generally the 15th day of the *fourth month* following the close of the tax year (April 15 for calendar year taxpayers) if the nonresident alien has wages subject to income tax withholding or the foreign corporation has an office or place of business in the United States. The IRS may grant a taxpayer an extension of the due date for filing a return (¶ 2509). The filing deadline may also be postponed for a taxpayer affected by a federally declared disaster or a military or terrorist action. Under this authority, the due date for filing federal tax returns and tax payments, including estimated taxes, otherwise due on or after April 1, 2020, and before July 15, 2020, is automatically extended to July 15, 2020, due to the COVID-19 (coronavirus) emergency (Notice 2020-23).

2427. Source of Income Rules. The U.S. taxation of nonresident aliens and foreign corporations (¶ 2425), as well as the application of the foreign tax credit limitations (¶ 2479), is dependent on the determination of the source of a taxpayer's income. Income is generally derived from U.S. sources or foreign sources in the following manner (Code Secs. 861, 862, 863, and 865).

- Interest income is generally sourced to the residence or country of incorporation of the obligor. The method and place of payment are irrelevant (see exceptions below). Interest for the guarantee of a debt is analogous to interest paid on a loan and is U.S. source income if paid by a noncorporate U.S. resident, domestic corporation, or any foreign person if effectively connected with a U.S. trade or business (¶ 2429).

- Dividend income, scholarships, grants, prizes, and awards are sourced to the residence of the payor (see exceptions following).

- Compensation for personal services is sourced to the place where the services are rendered. The location of the payor's residence, where the services are contracted for, and place of payment are irrelevant. If services are performed only partly within the United States, compensation is generally sourced on the basis of time spent working in each location.

- Rents and royalties are sourced to the location of the property.

- Gain on the sale of real property is sourced to the location of the property (¶ 2442).

24 | FOREIGN

• Gain on the sale of inventory is sourced solely on the basis of the production activities, with respect to the property, for tax years beginning after December 31, 2017.

• Gain on the sale of personal property that is not inventory is sourced to the residence of the seller (except for depreciable personal property, intangible property, or stock of an affiliate).

Special source rules apply to income that is derived from transportation, space, ocean, and communications activities. Other items of income are allocated or apportioned to sources within or without the United States as provided in regulations or other IRS rulings (for example, mixed-source income). Where allocation of an item of income is not provided, then it must be construed.

Interest Income Exceptions. Interest paid by a foreign corporation or foreign partnership engaged in a U.S. trade or business is treated as U.S. source income rather than foreign source income if paid by the U.S. trade or business (Code Secs. 861(a)(1) and 884(f)). However, interest on deposits in foreign branches of U.S. commercial banks is treated as foreign source income. A qualified fails charge is also treated similarly to interest but is sourced to the residence of the recipient or the taxpayer's qualified business unit (QBU), unless the income is effectively connected with a U.S. trade or business. Qualified fails charges are amounts paid for the failure to deliver designated securities on the settlement date in a delivery-versus-payment transaction (Reg. § 1.863-10).

Dividend Exceptions. A portion of the dividends paid by a foreign corporation are U.S. source income rather than foreign sourced if: (1) 25 percent or more of the corporation's gross income for a three-year period is effectively connected with a U.S. trade or business, or (2) it is required to figure the dividends received deduction by a U.S. corporation (¶ 223) (Code Sec. 861(a)(2)).

Allocation of Expenses. U.S. taxpayers are allowed deductions directly related to U.S. source or foreign source income to determine taxable income. Deductions are generally first allocated to the activity or property from which the class of income is derived. If any expense or loss is not directly related to any specific item of income, then it is apportioned ratably between certain statutory and residual groupings (Code Secs. 861(b) and 862(b); Reg. § 1.861-8; Temp. Reg. § 1.861-8T). Special apportionment rules are provided for interest expenses, research and experimentation expenses, losses from the disposition of property, net operating losses, income taxes, legal, accounting, and stewardship fees, charitable contribution deductions, Code Sec. 250 deductions, and partnership deductions.

Interest expenses are considered related to all income-producing activities and assets of a taxpayer. They are generally allocated to all gross income that the assets of the taxpayer generate. A taxpayer must allocate and apportion interest expenses using the adjusted basis of the assets, for tax years beginning after December 31, 2017. The use of the fair market value may no longer be used. The use of gross income to allocate and apportion interest expense continues to be disallowed. For tax years beginning after December 31, 2020, a one-time election may be made to determine foreign source taxable income of an affiliated group, by allocating and apportioning interest expense of the domestic members of the affiliated group on a worldwide basis, as if all members of the group were a single corporation. Separate rules apply for individuals, partnerships and corporations (Code Sec. 864(e) and 864(f); Reg. § § 1.861-9 and 1.861-11; Temp. Reg. § § 1.861-9T and 1.861-11T).

2429. Income Effectively Connected With U.S. Trade or Business. A nonresident alien (¶ 2409) and foreign corporation are taxed in the same manner as a U.S. citizen or domestic corporation on income that is effectively connected with the conduct of a trade or business in the United States (Code Secs. 871(b) and 882(a)). All income, gain, or loss from U.S. sources is generally treated as effectively connected with the conduct of a trade or business in the United States (Code Sec. 864(c)(3)). This includes gain from the disposition of U.S. real property interests (¶ 2442) and any scholarship or fellowship grant of a visiting student, teacher, or trainer (¶ 2448).

Special rules apply to fixed, determinable, annual, or periodical (FDAP) income, as well as certain income, gain, or loss from foreign sources, and gain or loss from the sale of a partnership interest by a foreign person (¶ 434). No withholding is generally required on income that is effectively connected with the conduct of a trade or business in the United States if Form W-8ECI is provided to the withholding agent or payer of the income (¶ 2455).

FDAP Income from U.S. Sources. FDAP income (¶ 2431) from *U.S. sources*, as well as capital gains from U.S. sources (¶ 2435) are treated as income effectively connected with a U.S. trade or business only if: (1) the income, gain, or loss is derived from assets used or held for use in the conduct of a U.S. trade or business, or (2) the activities of a U.S. trade or business are a material factor in the realization of the income, gain, or loss. In applying these factors, consideration is given to whether or not the asset or income involved was separately accounted for by the trade or business.

A nonresident alien or foreign corporation who is a member of a partnership or the beneficiary of an estate or trust, which at any time within the tax year is engaged in a trade or business within the United States, is considered to be engaged in a U.S. trade or business (Code Sec. 875). A nonresident alien and foreign corporation may elect to treat investment income from U.S. real property interests as effectively connected income (¶ 2432).

Income from Foreign Sources. Income, gain, or loss from *foreign sources* is treated as effectively connected with the conduct of a U.S. trade or business if the nonresident alien or foreign corporation maintains an office or other fixed place of business in the United States at any time during the tax year to which the income, gain, or loss is attributable (Code Sec. 864(c)(4)). Under these circumstances, the following foreign source income (or the economic equivalent of such income) is treated as effectively connected with a U.S. trade or business:

- rents and royalties derived from the use of intangible property;
- dividends, interest, or amounts received for the guarantees of debt that is either (1) derived from the active conduct of a banking, financial, or similar business through securities or debt obligations, or (2) received by a corporation the principal business of which is trading in stocks or securities for its own account; or
- income from the disposition of inventory or personal property held for sale in the normal course of business through a U.S. office.

Trade or Business. Whether a nonresident alien or foreign corporation is conducting a trade or business within the United States is a facts and circumstances test determined on a yearly basis (Reg. § 1.864-2(e)). The conduct of a U.S. trade or business denotes a considerable, continuous, and regular course of activity by the taxpayer or through an agent, partnership, estate, or trust. Thus, the taxpayer need not be present in the United States to be engaged in a U.S. trade or business.

For this purpose, a trade or business includes the performance of personal services within the United States at any time during the tax year unless the services are performed by a nonresident alien who is temporarily present in the United States for a period of 90 days or less, compensation received for the services does not exceed $3,000, and the services are performed for another nonresident alien, foreign corporation, or foreign partnership (Code Sec. 864(b)). A trade or business also does not generally include the trading of stocks, securities, or commodities through a resident broker, commission agent, custodian, or other independent agent unless the individual or foreign corporation is a dealer.

Certain U.S. business activities conducted by a nonresident alien or foreign corporation will not be counted for up to 60 consecutive calendar days beginning on or after February 1, 2020, and on or before April 1, 2020 in determining whether the individual or entity is engaged in a U.S. trade or business or has a U.S. permanent establishment, if those activities would not have been conducted in the United States but for travel disruptions arising from the COVID-19 emergency (IRS FAQs for Nonresident Aliens and Foreign Businesses).

2431. Fixed, Determinable, Annual, or Periodical (FDAP) Income. Fixed, determinable, annual, or periodical (FDAP) income of a nonresident alien or foreign corporation received from U.S. sources is generally taxed at a flat 30-percent rate (or lower rate permitted under a tax treaty) if the income is not effectively connected with the conduct of a U.S. trade or business (¶ 2429). To ensure collection and payment, the tax must be withheld from the payment of FDAP income by a withholding agent (¶ 2455).

FDAP income includes interest, dividends, rents, salaries, wages, premiums, annuities, compensation, remunerations, emoluments, and any other item of annual or periodical gain, profit, or income (Code Secs. 871(a) and 881(a)). It also includes royalties for timber, coal, and iron ore, as well as payments contingent on the productivity, use, or disposition of patents, copyrights, secret processes and formulas, and other like property. A nonresident alien and foreign corporation may elect to treat income from U.S. real property interests as effectively connected income (¶ 2432).

A dividend equivalent payment is treated as a dividend from U.S. sources in determining FDAP income (Code Sec. 871(m); Reg. § 1.871-15; Notice 2017-42; Notice 2018-5; Notice 2018-72; Notice 2020-2). A dividend equivalent payment is any payment (or substantially similar payment) that references a dividend from an underlying security pursuant to a securities lending or sale-repurchase transaction, a specified notional principal contract (NPC), or a specified equity linked index (ELI). Both specified NPCs and ELIs are described based on the delta of the contract.

Social Security Benefits. For purposes of computing a nonresident alien's taxable income (as well as for withholding purposes), 85 percent of any Social Security benefits received is considered FDAP income (Code Sec. 871(a)(3)).

Original Issue Discount. For a sale or exchange of an original issue discount (OID) obligation (¶ 1952), the amount of OID accruing while the obligation is held by a nonresident alien or foreign corporation is considered FDAP income. A payment on an OID obligation is also subject to tax to the extent that the payment reflects OID accruing while the obligation is held by the nonresident alien or foreign corporation (Code Secs. 871(a)(1)(C) and 881(a)(3)). For this purpose, an OID obligation includes any bond or other evidence of indebtedness having OID (Code Sec. 871(g)). It does not include any obligation payable 183 days or less from its date of original issue or any tax-exempt obligation.

Portfolio Interest. U.S. source portfolio interest is generally not considered FDAP income. Exempt portfolio interest includes any interest (including OID) accrued on an obligation that is in registered form and held by the nonresident alien or foreign corporation (Code Secs. 871(h) and 881(c); Reg. § 1.871-14). For registered obligations, the exception is generally available only if the beneficial owner has provided the withholding agent with Form W-8BEN or other statement certifying that the beneficial owner is not a U.S. person (with exceptions for certain foreign-targeted obligations issued before January 1, 2016). For obligations issued on or before March 18, 2012, the portfolio interest exemption applies if the obligation is in bearer or registered form.

Exempt portfolio interest does not include contingent interest or interest received by a nonresident alien or foreign corporation that is a 10-percent shareholder. Interest is generally contingent if it is determined by reference to any receipts, income, or change in value of property of the debtor or a related person (¶ 432 and ¶ 1717). Other types of contingent interest may be identified by the IRS to prevent tax avoidance. A 10-percent shareholder is any person who owns 10 percent or more of the total combined voting power of all classes of stock in a corporation or 10 percent or more of a capital or profits interest in a partnership.

Other Interest and Dividend Income. FDAP does not include a portion of any dividend received by a nonresident alien or foreign corporation paid by a U.S. corporation primarily engaged in an active trade or business in a foreign country (80/20 company), but only if the corporation was an 80/20 company before 2011 (Code Secs. 871(i), (l), and 881(d)). Payments made by a corporation not in existence as of January 1, 2011, are not eligible for the exemption. A grandfathered corporation must meet a modified 80-percent foreign business requirement for each subsequent tax year (rather than over a three year period). The grandfathered corporation must also not have a substantial new line of business after August 10, 2010.

FDAP income of a nonresident alien and foreign corporation does not include other types of interest and dividends, including: (1) interest paid on bank deposits not effectively connected with a U.S. trade or business; (2) income derived by a foreign bank of central issue from bankers' acceptances; and (3) the portion of a dividend that is paid by a foreign corporation and treated as U.S. source income (¶ 231) (Code Secs. 871(i)(2) and 881(d)). It also does not include certain interest-related dividends and short-term capital gain dividends received from a regulated investment company (RIC) (¶ 2301) (Code Sec. 871(k)).

U.S. Possession Corporations. A corporation created or organized in, or under the laws of, Guam, American Samoa, the Northern Mariana Islands, or the U.S. Virgin Islands is not considered a foreign corporation and thus is not subject to the tax on FDAP income if certain requirements are met. However, U.S. source dividends paid to a Puerto Rico corporation are considered FDAP income and subject to U.S. taxation and withholding at a 10-percent rate (Code Sec. 881(b)).

2432. Election to Treat Real Property Income as Effectively Connected Income. A nonresident alien (¶ 2409) and foreign corporation may elect to treat income from U.S. real property interests (¶ 2442) held for investment purposes as effectively connected with the conduct of a U.S. trade or business (Code Secs. 871(d) and 882(d)). The election is available where the income would not otherwise qualify as effectively connected income (¶ 2429), thus allowing the taxpayer to claim deductions associated with the property (¶ 2446).

The election applies to all income of the taxpayer from all U.S. real property interests, including rents or royalties from mines, wells, or other natural deposits, as well as certain timber, iron ore, and coal royalties. It does not include mortgage interest, dividends from a real estate investment trust (¶ 2331), income from personal property, and income of a nonresident alien from real property which is not held for the production of income, such as a personal residence (Reg. § § 1.871-10 and 1.882-2).

The election is made by attaching a statement to the taxpayer's timely filed return or amended return (¶ 2505). Once made, the election applies to the current tax year and all subsequent tax years until revoked by filing a timely amended return for all affected years. If the election is revoked, the taxpayer may not make a new election for five years without the IRS's consent.

2433. Branch Profits Tax. A foreign corporation that operates a trade or business in the United States may be required to pay a branch profits tax and a branch-level interest tax in addition to the tax on income effectively connected with the conduct of a U.S. trade or business (¶ 2429). The branch profits tax is 30 percent (or lower if permitted by a tax treaty) of the foreign corporation's dividend equivalent amount (Code Sec. 884). This is the amount of the foreign corporation's effectively connected after-tax earnings that are not reinvested in a U.S. trade or business by the close of the tax year or disinvested in a later tax year. The branch interest tax is 30 percent (or lower if permitted by a tax treaty) of the amount of interest paid by a U.S. branch of a foreign corporation with respect to a liability and notional excess interest amounts. If there is a conflict between the branch profits tax or branch-level interest tax with any U.S. income tax treaty, special rules are provided to determine the extent to which the treaty takes priority.

2435. Capital Gains of Nonresident Aliens and Foreign Corporations. U.S. sourced capital gains of a nonresident alien (¶ 2409) or foreign corporation may be completely exempt from U.S. taxation if they are *not*:

- effectively connected with the conduct of a U.S. trade or business (¶ 2429);

- gains from the sale of U.S. real property interests (¶ 2442); or

- fixed, determinable, annual, or periodical (FDAP) income (¶ 2431) (Code Secs. 871(a)(2) and 881(a)).

In the case of a nonresident alien, net capital gains that do not fall into one of these three categories are exempt from U.S. tax if the individual is not present in the United States for at least 183 days (whether or not consecutive) during the tax year. If the 183-day limitation is exceeded, the individual's net capital gains not effectively connected to conduct of a U.S. trade or business are subject to a flat 30-percent tax rate, or lower treaty rate. For purposes of this rule, gains and losses are determined without regard to the exclusion of gain from the sale of qualified small business stock (¶ 1905) or the carryover of capital losses (¶ 1754).

24 | FOREIGN

2438. Community Income of Nonresident Aliens. If a nonresident alien (¶ 2409) is married to a U.S. citizen or resident and does not elect to be treated as a resident (¶ 2410), then any community income is to be treated as follows:

- earned income (other than from a trade or business or the distributive share of partnership income) is treated as income of the spouse who earned it;

- trade or business income (other than from a partnership) is treated as the separate income of the spouse carrying on the trade or business (unless carried on jointly);

- a distributive share of partnership income is treated as the income of the spouse who is the partner with no portion attributed to the other spouse; and

- all other community income from separate property of one spouse is treated as the income of that spouse (Code Sec. 879).

2442. Sale or Disposition of U.S. Real Property Interest. The gain or loss derived by a nonresident alien (¶ 2409) or foreign corporation from the sale, exchange, or other disposition of a U.S. real property interest (USRPI) is treated as gain or loss effectively connected with the conduct of a U.S. trade or business (¶ 2429) (Code Sec. 897). Income from a USRPI held for investment purposes is not considered income effectively connected with a U.S. trade or business. However, a nonresident alien and foreign corporation may elect to treat income from a USRPI held for investment purposes as effectively connected income in order to claim deductions associated with the property (¶ 2446). A foreign corporation that holds a USRPI may also elect to be treated as a domestic corporation for this purpose if, under any treaty obligation of the United States, it is entitled to nondiscriminatory treatment for USRPIs.

Cash or property received by a nonresident alien or foreign corporation in exchange for an interest in a partnership, trust, or estate is considered received from the sale or disposition of USRPIs to the extent attributable to the sale or disposition of USRPIs by the entity (Code Sec. 897(g)). Similarly, special look-through rules apply for distributions by qualified investment entities attributable to dispositions of USRPIs (¶ 2444). USRPIs held by qualified foreign pension funds (or any entity that has all of its interests held by a qualified pension fund) are not subject to these rules (Code Secs. 897(l) and 1445(f); Reg. § 1.1445-2(b)(2); Prop. Reg. § 1.897(l)-1).

U.S. Real Property Interests Defined. A USRPI is any interest in real property (including a mine, well, or other natural deposit) located in the United States or the U.S. Virgin Islands (Code Sec. 897(c); Reg. § 1.897-1). Real property includes land and improvements, personal property associated with the use of the real property, and unsevered timber, crops, and minerals. The nonresident alien's or foreign corporation's interest can be any interest (other than solely as a creditor), such as a direct ownership, fee-ownership, co-ownership, as well as any leasehold or option to acquire the property.

An interest in U.S. real property also includes any interest (other than solely as a creditor) in a U.S. real property holding corporation (USRPHC), unless the corporation was not a USRPHC during the shorter of the five-year period ending on the date of disposition, or the period the taxpayer held the interest in the corporation. A corporation is a USRPHC if the fair market value of its USRPIs is at least 50 percent of the fair market value of all of its real property interests and any other property used in its business (Reg. § 1.897-2). For this purpose, a corporation is considered to own a proportionate share of the assets held through a partnership, trust, or estate, as well as a domestic or foreign corporation in which it holds a controlling interest.

Whether a corporation is a USRPHC is generally determined as of the last day of the corporation's tax year, the date on which the corporation acquires a USRPI, *and* the date on which the corporation disposes of a real property interest located outside the United States or disposes of other assets used in a trade or business during the calendar year. The IRS has issued simplified procedures for a taxpayer to request relief for late filings establishing that a domestic corporation is not a USRPHC or that nonrecognition of gain or treaty provisions apply (Rev. Proc. 2008-27).

A USRPI does not include any interest in a USRPHC if, as of the date of disposition, the corporation has already disposed of all of its USRPIs in a transaction in which it recognized gain (the cleansing rule) (Code Sec. 897(c)(1)(B); Reg. § 1.897-2(f)(2)). The cleansing rule will not apply if the corporation or its predecessor was a regulated investment company (RIC) or real estate investment trust (REIT) during the testing period. In addition, if a corporation has a class of stock that is regularly traded on an established securities market, then the stock is treated as a USRPI only in the hands of a taxpayer who owns more than five percent of the total fair market value of that class of stock.

A USRPI generally does not include the stock of a REIT held directly, or indirectly through partnerships, by a publicly traded qualified shareholder entity. Additionally, distributions to the qualified shareholder will not be treated as gain from the sale or exchange of a USRPI to the extent that the stock of the REIT held by the qualified shareholders is not treated as a USRPI under this rule (Code Sec. 897(k)(2)).

Distributions of USRPIs. If a foreign corporation distributes a USRPI with respect to its stock, then the corporation recognizes gain (but not loss) to the extent the fair market value of the property at the time of distribution exceeds its adjusted basis (Code Sec. 897(d); Temp. Reg. §1.897-5T(c)). A foreign corporation may avoid recognizing gain if at the time of the distribution, the distributee would be subject to U.S. taxation on a subsequent disposition of the property and if the fair market value of the distributed property in the hands of the distributee is no greater than its basis increased by any amount of gain recognized by the distributing corporation. The foreign corporation is required to file a U.S. income tax return to report the distribution, even if it has no tax liability.

Nonrecognition Exchanges. Nonrecognition provisions of the Code apply to the exchange of a USRPI by a nonresident alien or foreign corporation if the property is exchanged for another USRPI that would be subject to U.S. tax upon its subsequent disposition and the transferor meets certain filing requirements (Code Sec. 897(e); Temp. Reg. §1.897-6T). Nonrecognition provisions for this purpose include like-kind exchanges (¶1721), involuntary conversions (¶1713), contributions and distributions related to partnerships (¶443 and ¶453), and corporate liquidations and reorganizations (¶2205 and ¶2253). The transfer of a USRPI in exchange for stock in a foreign corporation may also qualify for nonrecognition treatment. This includes contributions to capital or as paid in surplus (Code Sec. 897(j)).

Withholding. In order to ensure that a foreign investor will pay taxes on gain realized on the sale or disposition of a USRPI, the transferee is generally required to withhold and deduct a tax equal to 15 percent of the amount realized on the disposition (Code Sec. 1445; Reg. §1.1445-1; Reg. §1.1445-2). Special rules and withholding rates apply for distributions and other transactions by corporations, partnerships, estates, trusts, and qualified investment entities.

There are certain exemptions and exceptions from withholding. For example, an exemption from withholding applies if the amount realized on the disposition of a residence does not exceed $300,000. The withholding rate is 10 percent for amounts realized in excess of $300,000, but not in excess of $1 million, and 15 percent for amounts in excess of $1 million.

If the transferee fails to withhold the required tax, then it may be held liable for the tax, as well as any applicable penalties or interest. The transferee must file Form 8288 and Form 8288-A to report and transmit the amount withheld to the IRS within 20 days of the transfer of the property. However, the due date for performing certain time-sensitive actions, including reporting and transmitting withheld taxes on Form 8288 and Form 8288-A, otherwise due on or after April 1, 2020, and before July 15, 2020, is automatically extended to July 15, 2020, in response to the COVID-19 (coronavirus) crisis (Notice 2020-23; Rev. Proc. 2018-58).

2444. Look-Through Rules for Disposition of U.S. Real Property Interests. Any distribution by a qualified investment entity to a nonresident alien (¶2409), foreign corporation, or other qualified investment entity to the extent attributable to gain from the sale or exchange of a U.S. real property interest (USRPI) (¶2442), is treated by the recipient as gain from the sale or exchange of a USRPI (Code Sec. 897(h)). A qualified investment entity includes any real estate investment trust (REIT) (¶2326) and any regulated investment company (RIC) (¶2301) that is a U.S. real property holding company (USRPHC). However, in determining whether a RIC is a USRPHC, the regularly traded stock exception in defining a USRPHC does not apply. In addition, the

RIC must include its interest in any other domestically controlled REIT or RIC that is a USRPHC.

The look-through rule does not apply to any distribution from a qualified investment entity with respect to a class of stock that is regularly traded on an established securities market in the United States if the foreign distributee did not own more than 10 percent of the class of stock at any time within one year of the distribution (Code Sec. 897(k)(1)). To the extent this exception applies, the distribution from the qualified investment entity is treated as a dividend, and not as income effectively connected with a U.S. trade or business.

An interest in a domestically controlled qualified investment entity (less than 50 percent of the stock's value is held by foreign persons) is not treated as a USRPI and any gain from the sale of the interest does not pass through to a nonresident alien or foreign corporation. However, the gain is passed through if a wash sale transaction is involved. For this purpose, a wash sale transaction is one in which: (1) the interest in a domestically controlled qualified investment entity is disposed of within 30 days prior to a distribution by the qualified entity that would be treated as gain from the sale or exchange of a USRPI; and (2) a substantially identical interest is reacquired within 61 days of the distribution. For purposes of the exception for domestically controlled qualified investment entities, a number of rules and presumptions are applied to determine if the stock owner is a U.S. or foreign person (Code Sec. 897(h)(4)(E)).

2446. Taxable Income of Nonresident Aliens and Foreign Corporations. A nonresident alien (¶ 2409) and foreign corporation are subject to U.S. income tax on income effectively connected with a U.S. trade or business (¶ 2429) and fixed, determinable, annual, periodical (FDAP) income from U.S. sources (¶ 2431). All exclusions from gross income permitted to a U.S. citizen and domestic corporation generally may also be excluded by a nonresident alien and foreign corporation (Code Secs. 872 and 883). Earnings on certain categories of cross-border transactions may also be excluded, such as compensation paid by a foreign employer to an exchange student, teacher, trainee, or specialist (¶ 2448), gambling winnings derived from a legal wager initiated outside the United States, and earnings from the international operation of a ship or aircraft.

A nonresident alien or foreign corporation may only claim deductions and tax credits related to effectively connected income in determining taxable income (Code Secs. 873, 874 and 882(c)). This includes the foreign tax credit subject to the same limitations that apply to U.S. citizens and domestic corporations (¶ 2479) (Code Sec. 906). Deductions and credits are generally not allowed in determining the tax on U.S. sourced FDAP income. However, a charitable contribution deduction can be claimed whether or not related to effectively connected income. Similarly, a nonresident alien may deduct one personal exemption for tax years beginning before 2018 and after 2025 (with certain exceptions) and casualty or theft losses (so long as the property is located in the United States). A nonresident alien and foreign corporation may elect to treat income from U.S. real property interests as effectively connected income in order to claim the deductions associated with the property (¶ 2432).

A nonresident alien and foreign corporation must file an accurate and timely return to claim any allowable deduction or credit. If a return is not filed, then the IRS may prepare one for the taxpayer but no deductions and credits will be allowed other than the credits for withheld taxes, gasoline and special fuels, and for nonresident aliens for taxes paid by a regulated investment company on undistributed capital gains (¶ 2305).

2448. Foreign Students, Teachers, or Trainees. A nonresident alien (¶ 2409) who is not otherwise engaged in a U.S. trade or business but who is temporarily present in the United States under immigration laws on a F, J, M, or Q visa as a visiting student, teacher, trainee, or specialist is considered to be engaged in a U.S. trade or business (Code Sec. 871(c)). This means that any portion of a scholarship or fellowship grant from U.S. sources (including incidental expenses) that is not excludable from gross income (¶ 865) is income effectively connected with the conduct of a U.S. trade or business (¶ 2429). The income is subject to a special withholding rate of 14 percent (¶ 2455) (Code Sec. 1441(b); Reg. § 1.1441-4(c)). Compensation paid by a foreign employer to a person in the United States as a visiting student, teacher, trainee, or specialist is exempt from tax (Code Sec. 872(b)(3)).

¶2446

2450. Tax Treaties. The United States has negotiated a network of tax treaties with other countries to avoid the double taxation of taxpayers on the same income and to prevent taxpayers from evading taxation. In addition, the United States has enacted strict anti-abuse rules to prevent individuals from treaty shopping, and has incorporated exchange of information clauses in many tax treaties to facilitate the enforcement of these rules. These anti-abuse rules deny treaty benefits to nonresidents of either the United States or its treaty partner that funnel income through the treaty country only to take advantage of reduced tax rates.

The Code generally is to be applied to a taxpayer with "due regard" to treaty obligations of the United States (Code Sec. 894). In instances where a U.S. taxpayer takes the position that a treaty overrules or modifies the Code or regulations, disclosure of the position must generally be made with the taxpayer's tax return on Form 8833 (Code Sec. 6114; Reg. § 301.6114-1). If a return is not otherwise required to be filed, a return must nevertheless be filed for purposes of making the required disclosure. The determination of whether a treaty-based return position is required to be reported is made by comparing the taxpayer's tax liability under current law to that same tax liability as it would exist if the relevant treaty positions did not exist. Any difference must be reported. Failure to disclose the difference may result in a penalty (Code Sec. 6712).

Tax treaties between the United States and foreign countries generally reduce the tax rate for income paid. Some countries allow the withholding of tax at the treaty-reduced rate. Other countries withhold tax at their statutory tax rate and refund any difference upon receiving proof of residency. To apply for certification of U.S. residency to receive the benefits under a tax treaty, a taxpayer must file Form 8802 at least 45 days before the certificate is needed. If the application is approved, the IRS will provide the residency certification to the taxpayer on Form 6166.

A nonresident alien or foreign corporation is not entitled under any U.S. income tax treaty to any reduced rate of withholding on an item of income derived through an entity treated as a partnership (or other fiscally transparent entity) if: (1) the income is not treated by the treaty partner as an item of income of such foreign person; (2) the foreign country does not impose tax on a distribution of the item by the U.S. entity to the foreign person; and (3) the treaty does not contain a provision addressing its applicability in the case of an item of income derived through a partnership (Code Sec. 894(c)).

2452. Corporate Inversions. Special rules apply for the tax treatment of corporate inversion transactions where a U.S. corporation reincorporates in a foreign jurisdiction and thereby replaces the U.S. parent corporation of a multinational corporate group with a foreign parent corporation. Inversion transactions may take many different forms, including stock inversions, asset inversions, and various combinations.

In any case, if former shareholders of a U.S. corporation hold 80 percent or more (by vote or value) of the stock of a foreign corporation after the transaction, the foreign corporation will be treated as a domestic corporation for U.S. tax purposes (Code Sec. 7874). If the former shareholders hold at least 60 percent but less than 80 percent of the stock of the foreign corporation after the transaction, then the inversion transaction is respected but any applicable corporate-level tax imposed as a result of the transaction cannot be offset by tax attributes such as a net operating loss (NOL) or foreign tax credit.

An inversion transaction for this purpose is a transaction in which, pursuant to a plan or a series of related transactions, the following requirements are met:

- the foreign corporation (surrogate corporation) must acquire substantially all of the properties of the domestic corporation or that constitute the trade or business of a domestic partnership;

- the former U.S. shareholders must hold 60 percent or more (by vote or value) of the stock of the foreign corporation after the transaction (ownership fraction); and

- the expanded affiliated group (EAG) must not conduct substantial business activities in the foreign country in which the foreign acquiring entity is created or organized, compared to the total business activities of the expanded affiliated group (Reg. § 1.7874-12).

24

FOREIGN

¶2452

An EAG has substantial business activities in the relevant foreign country only if at least 25 percent of the group employees, group assets, and group income are located or derived in the relevant country, and the foreign acquiring country corporation is subject to tax as a resident of the relevant foreign country (Reg. § 1.7874-3).

Dividends paid by surrogate foreign corporations after December 22, 2017, that are not treated as domestic corporations are ineligible for the reduced rate of tax on qualified dividends (¶ 1736) (Code Sec. 1(h)(11)(C)(iii)).

Stock compensation received by insiders in an expatriated corporation is subject to a 20 percent excise tax, effective for corporations that first became expatriated after December 22, 2017 (Code Sec. 4985(a)(1)).

A number of rules apply to disregard certain stock of the foreign acquiring corporation in determining the ownership fraction. For example, the stock may be disregarded under a modified statutory public offering rule or if it is attributable to passive assets (Reg. §§ 1.7874-4 and 1.7874-7). Rules also describe the effect of transfers of the foreign acquiring corporation stock after the foreign corporation has acquired substantially all of the properties of a domestic corporation or of a trade or business of a domestic partnership (Reg. § 1.7874-5).

2455. Withholding of Tax on Nonresident Aliens and Foreign Corporations. A foreign person is generally subject to U.S. tax on U.S. source income received during the tax year (¶ 2425). To ensure collection and payment, the tax must be withheld from the payment of the U.S. source income to the foreign person by a withholding agent (Code Secs. 1441 and 1442).

Most types of U.S. source income received by a foreign person are subject to a 30-percent withholding rate. However, different rates may apply to wages paid to a nonresident alien employee (including pensions paid for personal services), scholarship or fellowship grants of a foreign exchange student (¶ 2448), dispositions of U.S. real property interests (¶ 2442), a foreign partner's distributive share of effectively connected income of a partnership, gross investment income paid to foreign private foundations (¶ 631), and dividends paid to a Puerto Rican corporation. Reduced rates of withholding may also apply, including an exemption, under a tax treaty or convention with the foreign person's country of residence (¶ 2450).

Persons Subject to Withholding. All nonresident aliens and foreign corporations, foreign partnerships, foreign trusts, and foreign estates are subject to withholding on U.S. source income. Withholding also applies to the foreign branch of a U.S. financial institution that furnishes an intermediary withholding certificate on Form W-8IMY to the withholding agent (Reg. § 1.1441-1(b) and (c)). A nonresident alien is any individual who is not a U.S. citizen or resident alien and includes any bona fide resident of Puerto Rico, Guam, the Northern Mariana Islands, the U.S. Virgin Islands, or American Samoa. A nonresident alien who elects resident status for income tax purposes (¶ 2410) is still considered a foreign person for nonresident alien withholding purposes on all income except wages. Withholding may also be required for payments made to certain foreign financial institutions (FFIs) (¶ 2469) and nonfinancial foreign entities (NFFEs) (¶ 2473) if certain requirements are not met. Under coordination rules, withholding does not apply if there is withholding under these provisions.

Income Subject to Withholding. U.S. source income subject to the withholding requirements includes: (1) fixed, determinable, annual, or periodical (FDAP) income (¶ 2431); (2) certain gains on the disposal of timber, coal, or domestic iron ore; and (3) gains relating to contingent payments received from the sale or exchange of patents, copyrights, and similar intangible property. If the source of the income cannot be determined at the time of payment (¶ 2427), it is treated as U.S. source income (Code Sec. 1441(b); Reg. § 1.1441-2(a)). In addition, income payable for personal services performed in the United States is treated as from sources within the United States, regardless of where the location of the contract for the services was entered, the place of payment, or residence of payer.

Income effectively connected with the conduct of a U.S. trade or business is not subject to the withholding requirements for foreign persons, including income received as wages (¶ 2429). Instead, such income is generally subject to the tax and withholding rules as if the foreign person were a U.S. citizen, resident, or domestic entity. However,

¶2455

special rules require withholding by a partnership on the effectively connected income of the partnership (foreign or domestic) that is allocable to its foreign partners, including withholding upon the disposition of certain partnership interests (¶ 434) (Code Sec. 1446). The withholding tax is a partnership item for purposes of partnership-item adjustments (*Ya Global Investments, LP*, Dec. 61,237, 151 TC No. 2).

Withholding Agent. The withholding agent is the person or entity required to deduct, withhold, and pay any tax on income paid to a foreign person (Reg. § 1.1441-7; Prop. Reg. § 1.1441-7). The duty is imposed on all persons (acting in whatever capacity) that have control, receipt, custody, disposal, or payment of any items of income which are subject to withholding. Thus, the withholding agent may be any individual, corporation, partnership, trust, or other entity (including a foreign intermediary or partnership). A withholding agent may designate an authorized agent on its behalf.

The withholding agent is personally liable for any tax required to be withheld except in the case of certain conduit financing arrangements (Code Sec. 1461). This liability is independent of the tax liability of the foreign person for whom the tax was withheld from a payment of income. Even if the foreign person pays the tax, the withholding agent may still be liable for any interest, penalty, or addition to tax for failure to withhold (Code Sec. 1463). A refund or credit of any overpayment is made to the withholding agent unless the tax was actually withheld (Code Sec. 1464). The withholding agent is indemnified against any person claiming any tax properly withheld.

A withholding agent is not required to withhold any amount if the payee is a U.S. person or a foreign person that is the beneficial owner of the income and is entitled to a reduced rate of withholding. Absent actual knowledge or reason to know, the withholding agent must obtain valid documentation from the payee that it is either a U.S. payee or beneficial owner. A U.S. payee is generally any person required to furnish Form W-9. While such persons are not subject to withholding as a foreign person, they may be subject to Form 1099 reporting and withholding requirements. A beneficial owner is any foreign person or entity that is required to furnish Form W-8BEN, Form W-8BEN-E, Form W-8ECI or Form W-8EXP. Payment to an intermediary (whether qualified or not), flow-through entity, or U.S. branch of a foreign entity may be treated as a payee for these purposes so long as valid documentation is provided on Form W-8IMY. In all cases in which valid documentation cannot be provided, the withholding agent may presume a person to be a U.S. payee or beneficial owner under specified rules.

Returns. A withholding agent must file an annual information return on Form 1042-S to report income paid to a foreign person during the tax year that is subject to withholding, unless an exception applies (Reg. § § 1.1461-1 and 1.6302-2). A separate Form 1042-S must be filed for each recipient, as well as for each type of income that is paid to the same recipient. A copy of Form 1042-S must also be provided to the recipient and may be provided electronically, if certain requirements are met. Form 1042 is used by the withholding agent to report and pay the taxes withheld from the payments of income. The forms are also used by withholding agents making payments to foreign financial institutions (FFIs) (¶ 2469) and non-financial foreign institutions (NFFEs) (¶ 2473).

Both forms must be filed by March 15 of the year following the calendar year the income was paid. An automatic six-month extension for filing Form 1042 can be obtained by filing Form 7004. The extension of time to file does not extend the time to pay the withheld tax. An automatic 30-day extension for filing Form 1042-S can be obtained by filing Form 8809. A second extension request may be submitted by filing a second Form 8809 before the end of the initial extended due date. Form 1042-S *must* be filed electronically if 250 or more returns are filed or if the returns are filed by a financial institution (¶ 2503) (Reg. § § 1.1461-1(c)(5) and 301.1474-1(a)). Paper Forms 1042-S must be accompanied by Form 1042-T.

The amount of tax required to be withheld will determine whether the withholding agent must deposit the taxes prior to the due date for filing the returns and how frequently such amounts must be deposited. Penalties may be imposed for failure to file, failure to provide complete and correct information, as well as failure to pay any taxes.

24 | FOREIGN

Reporting Foreign Assets of U.S. Taxpayers

2465. FBAR Reporting (Foreign Financial Assets). A U.S. person is required to disclose any financial interests in, signature authority, or other authority over foreign financial accounts if the aggregate value of the accounts exceeds $10,000 at any time during the calendar year (31 CFR Reg. § 1010.350). The information is reported electronically on FinCEN Report 114 (commonly referred to as FBAR) through the Treasury's Financial Crimes Enforcement Network (FinCEN) BSA E-Filing System. The filing of the FBAR does not relieve a taxpayer of the requirement to file Form 8938 to report specified foreign financial assets (¶ 2570 and ¶ 2572).

2467. FATCA Reporting of Specified Foreign Financial Assets (Form 8938). Under the Foreign Account Tax Compliance Act (FATCA), an individual is required to disclose his or her interest in a specified foreign financial asset during the tax year if the aggregate value of all of the assets exceeds an applicable threshold amount. The reporting requirement also applies to any domestic entity that is "formed or availed of" for purposes of holding, directly or indirectly, specified foreign financial assets (¶ 2572) (Code Sec. 6038D; Reg. § § 1.6038D-2 and 1.6038D-6). The information is reported on Form 8938.

The filing of Form 8938 does not relieve an individual of the requirement to file the FBAR or FinCEN Report 114 (¶ 2570) for disclosing foreign financial accounts. Similarly, the filing of the FBAR does not relieve an individual of the requirement to file Form 8938. An individual may be required to file both Form 8938 and FBAR to report the same information on certain foreign accounts. The FBAR, however, is not filed with the individual's federal income tax return.

2469. FATCA Reporting and Withholding Obligations for Foreign Financial Institutions (FFIs). Under the Foreign Account Tax Compliance Act (FATCA), a foreign financial institution (FFI) is required to report to the IRS certain information about financial accounts held by U.S. taxpayers or by foreign entities in which U.S. taxpayers hold substantial ownership interests (Code Sec. 1471; Reg. § 1.1471-2(a)). If an FFI fails to meet the FATCA requirements, a U.S. withholding agent must deduct and withhold a tax equal to 30 percent on any withholdable payment made to the FFI, unless the withholding agent can reasonably rely on documentation that the payment is exempt from withholding. The withholding requirement applies without regard to whether the FFI receives a withholdable payment as a beneficial owner or as a qualified intermediary (QI). No withholding is required if an FFI enters into an agreement with the IRS to provide the required information (participating FFI). An FFI may also be deemed to meet the requirements of the agreement (deemed-compliant FFI) (¶ 2471).

Foreign Financial Institutions. An FFI is a foreign entity that accepts deposits in the ordinary course of a banking business, holds financial assets for the account of others as a substantial part of its business (i.e., mutual fund), or is an entity whose gross income is primarily attributable to investing, reinvesting, or trading in financial assets (i.e., hedge fund, private equity fund) (Code Sec. 1471(d)(4); Reg. § 1.1471-5(d) and (e)). In the case of an entity that is resident in a country that has in effect a Model 1 or Model 2 Intergovernmental Agreement with the United States (Model 1 IGA or Model 2 IGA), an FFI is any entity that is treated as an FFI pursuant to the Model 1 or Model 2 IGA.

Withholdable Payment. A withholdable payment includes any payment of U.S. source fixed or determinable, annual or periodical (FDAP) income (¶ 2431) (Code Sec. 1473(1); Reg. § 1.1473-1(a); Prop. Reg. § 1.1473-1(a)). Withholdable payments do not include items of income effectively connected with a U.S. trade or business (¶ 2429), payments of interest or original issue discount (OID) on short-term obligations, and other specified nonfinancial payments, such as payments for services, leases of property, and interest payable from the acquisition of goods and services. Withholding is not required with respect to any payment under a grandfathered obligation or from any gross proceeds from the disposition of a grandfathered obligation (Code Sec. 1471(f); Reg. § § 1.1471-2(b) and 1.1471-6).

Withholding Agent. A withholding agent for FATCA reporting purposes includes any U.S. or foreign person, in whatever capacity having the control, receipt, custody, disposal, or payment of any withholdable payment or foreign pass-through payment (Code Sec. 1473(4); Reg. § 1.1473-1(d)). A U.S. withholding agent, participating FFI,

¶2465

qualified intermediary, or any other person that fails to withhold and deposit tax as required is liable for the tax and penalties, but is indemnified against claims and demands of anyone for the amount of the payments (Code Sec. 1474; Reg. §§1.1474-1 and 301.1474-1; Prop. Reg. §1.1474-1). Form 1042 is used to report and pay taxes withheld during the tax year. In addition, an annual information return must be filed on Form 1042-S and a copy furnished to the recipient of the withholdable payment, including any qualified intermediaries, withholding foreign partnerships, and withholding foreign trusts. Both forms are due by March 15 of the calendar year following the year the withholdable payment was made to the recipient.

2471. Foreign Financial Institution (FFI) Agreements. A foreign financial institution (FFI) meets its reporting requirements under the Foreign Account Tax Compliance Act (FATCA) (¶ 2469) by: (1) entering into an FFI agreement with the IRS (participating FFI); (2) being deemed to comply with the FATCA requirements without the need to enter into an FFI agreement (deemed-compliant FFI); or (3) being a resident in a country that has in effect a Model 1 or Model 2 Intergovernmental Agreement with the United States (Model 1 IGA or Model 2 IGA). The reporting requirements the FFI must meet include:

- identifying U.S. accounts it maintains in accordance with certain verification and due diligence procedures;

- reporting certain information to the IRS regarding the U.S. accounts and accounts held by a U.S. person who is unwilling to provide the required information (recalcitrant account holder); and

- deducting and withholding tax on any payment of U.S. source income by the FFI to a recalcitrant account holder or nonparticipating FFI (Code Sec. 1471(b); Reg. §1.1471-4; Prop. Reg. §1.1471-4).

An FFI (including a reporting Model 2 FFI) may register itself and its branches on the IRS's FATCA registration website (or on a paper copy of Form 8957) to enter into an FFI agreement as a participating FFI (Rev. Proc. 2017-16). A registered FFI and its branches will receive a Global Intermediary Identification Number (GIIN) from the IRS to identify that it is registered and approved to withholding agents and the IRS. The IRS publishes a list of registered and approved FFIs and their GIINs monthly that withholding agents may rely on to verify an FFI's GIIN and not withhold on payments made to the FFI.

Identification Requirement. A participating FFI is required to identify and document the status of each holder of an account maintained by the FFI to determine if the account is a U.S. account, non-U.S. account, or an account held by a recalcitrant account holder or nonparticipating FFI (Reg. §1.1471-4(c)). A U.S. account is a financial account held by one or more specified U.S. persons or U.S.-owned foreign entities, including any depository or custodial account maintained by the FFI, and any equity or debt interest in the FFI other than an interest regularly traded on an established securities market (Code Sec. 1471(d); Reg. §§1.1471-5(a) and 1.1473-1(c)). A specified U.S. person is any U.S. person *other than* a: dealer in securities, commodities, or derivative financial instruments; broker; publicly traded corporation; tax exempt organization, trust, or individual retirement plan; bank, real estate investment trust (REIT), regulated investment company (RIC), common trust fund or charitable remainder trust; or government entity.

An FFI must follow due diligence procedures for identifying and documenting account holders based on the value and risk profile of the account. FFIs in many cases are permitted to rely on information they already collect (Reg. §1.1471-4(c)). For example, accounts with a balance or value of more than $50,000 ($250,000 for a cash value insurance or annuity contract) but less than $1 million generally are only subject to electronic review of searchable data for indicia of U.S. status.

Reporting Requirement. A participating FFI is required to report annually to the IRS the name, address, and taxpayer identification number (TIN) of each holder of a U.S. account which is a specified U.S. person. In the case of any account holder which is a U.S.-owned foreign entity, the participating FFI must report the name, address, and TIN of each substantial U.S. owner of the entity (Code Sec. 1471(c); Reg. §1.1471-4(d) and (i)). The FFI must also report the account number, the year-end account balance or value in U.S. dollars, and the gross amount and character of dividends, interest, or other income paid or credited to the account. Special rules apply for a participating FFI to report information regarding its recalcitrant account holders. If an FFI is prohibited by foreign law from reporting the required information with respect to an account, then it must close the account within a reasonable period of time or must otherwise block or transfer the account.

A participating FFI reports the required information on Form 8966 with respect to each account maintained at any time during the calendar year. The form generally must be filed electronically with the IRS by March 31 of the year following the end of the calendar year to which it relates but the deadline is extended to July 15, 2020, for the 2019 calendar year. Form 8809-I is used to request an automatic 90-day extension. As an alternative to filing Form 8966, the FFI may elect to be subject to the same reporting requirements of U.S. institutions. Thus, the institution must provide a full Form 1099 reporting for every account with a U.S. person or U.S. foreign entity as an account holder.

Withholding Requirement. A participating FFI is required to deduct and withhold 30 percent from any withholdable payment (¶ 2469) made by the FFI to an account held by a recalcitrant account holder or to a nonparticipating FFI (Reg. § 1.1471-4(b)(1)). If an FFI is prohibited by foreign law from withholding as required with respect to an account, then it must close the account within a reasonable period of time or must otherwise block or transfer the account (Reg. § 1.1471-4(a)(1)). A participating FFI is not required to deduct and withhold tax on a foreign pass-through payment made by the FFI to an account held by a recalcitrant account holder or to a nonparticipating FFI before the later of January 1, 2019, or the date final regulations are issued defining foreign pass-through payments. A participating FFI may elect not to withhold on any withholdable payments, but instead have a U.S. withholding agent withhold tax on payments the electing FFI receives which are allocable to a recalcitrant account holder or a nonparticipating FFI (Code Sec. 1471(b)(3); Reg. § 1.1471-4(b)(3) and (b)(4)).

2473. FATCA Reporting and Withholding Obligations for Non-Financial Foreign Entities (NFFEs). Under the Foreign Account Tax Compliance Act (FATCA), if a non-financial foreign entity (NFFE) is the beneficial owner of a withholdable payment (¶ 2469) made to the NFFE , then the NFFE is required to report certain information to the withholding agent (Code Sec. 1472(b); Reg. § 1.1472-1). The reporting requirement is satisfied if the NFFE reports the name, address, and taxpayer identification number (TIN) of each substantial U.S. owner or if it certifies that it does not have any substantial U.S. owners. If the NFFE or other payee fails to meet the reporting requirement, then the withholding agent must deduct and withhold a tax of 30 percent from the withholdable payment.

An NFFE for this purpose is any foreign entity that is not a financial institution, meaning the entity does not accept deposits in the ordinary course of a banking business, does not hold financial assets for the account of others as a substantial part of its business, and is not engaged primarily in investing. A substantial U.S. owner is:

- in the case of a corporation, a U.S. person that owns, directly or indirectly, more than 10 percent of the corporate stock by vote or value;

- in the case of a partnership, a U.S. person that owns directly or indirectly, more than 10 percent of the capital or profits interests of the partnership; and

- in the case of a trust, a U.S. person treated as an owner of any portion of the trust under the grantor trust rules and any U.S. person holding more than 10 percent of the beneficial interests (Code Sec. 1473(2); Reg. § 1.1473-1(b)).

A withholding agent that receives information about substantial U.S. owners of an NFFE must report the information to the IRS on or before March 15 of the calendar year following the year in which the withholdable payment is made. If withholding is required, Form 1042 is used to report and pay taxes withheld during the tax year. In addition, an annual information return must be filed on Form 1042-S and a copy furnished to the recipient of the withholdable payment (Code Sec. 1472(b); Reg. § 1.1472-1(e)).

If the NFFE and the withholding agent satisfy their reporting requirements, withholding is not required unless the withholding agent knows or has reason to know that any information provided about substantial U.S. owners is incorrect. A withholding agent is also not required to withhold taxes if the withholding agent may treat the payment as beneficially owned by an excepted NFFE. An excepted NFFE includes a publicly traded corporation and its related entities, territory entities, the government of a foreign country or U.S. possession, an international organization, or any foreign central bank of issue. Additionally, active NFFEs, direct reporting NFFEs, and sponsored direct reporting NFFEs are excepted NFFEs (Code Sec. 1472(c); Reg. § 1.1472-1(c)).

Foreign Tax Credit or Deduction

See CCH® AnswerConnect: *Foreign Tax Credit* for more information on this topic.

2475. Foreign Tax Credit or Deduction. A U.S. taxpayer may elect a credit or deduction against U.S. income liability for foreign taxes paid or accrued to a foreign country or U.S. possession during the tax year subject to certain limits (¶ 2479) (Code Sec. 901; Reg. § 1.901-1). The credit and deduction are intended to relieve a U.S. taxpayer of double taxation on foreign source income. The election is made on an annual basis (¶ 2476) and is applicable to all creditable foreign taxes paid or incurred during the tax year (¶ 2477). A separate foreign tax credit can be claimed against alternative minimum tax liability (AMT) (¶ 190).

A taxpayer eligible to claim the foreign tax credit or deduction includes a U.S. citizen, resident alien (¶ 2409), bona fide resident of Puerto Rico for the entire tax year (¶ 2415), domestic corporation, and nonresident alien and foreign corporation with respect to foreign taxes paid or accrued on foreign source income effectively connected with the conduct of a U.S. trade or business (¶ 2429). A taxpayer who is a partner in a partnership, shareholder in an S corporation, or beneficiary of an estate or trust may claim the credit or deduction with respect to the taxpayer's proportionate share of creditable foreign taxes paid or accrued by the entity (Code Secs. 901(b) and 1373(a)). Similarly, a shareholder of a regulated investment company (RIC) may be able to claim the credit or deduction based on the shareholder's share of creditable foreign taxes paid by the entity (¶ 2320).

Income Matching. If there is a foreign tax credit splitting event, the foreign tax credit or deduction may not be claimed by a taxpayer until the related income is taken into account for U.S. income tax purposes (Code Sec. 909; Reg. § 1.909-2). A foreign tax credit splitting event occurs with respect to a foreign income tax if in connection with a splitter arrangement the related income is (or will be) taken into account by a covered person. A covered person is a person or entity that has a specified relationship with the taxpayer—at least 10 percent ownership interest, related party, or otherwise specified by the IRS. In the case of a partnership, S corporation, or trust, the matching requirement is applied at the partner, shareholder, or beneficiary level. Special rules apply to a foreign tax credit splitting event involving a Code Sec. 902 corporation (¶ 2485), effective for tax years of foreign corporations beginning before January 1, 2018, and to tax years of U.S. shareholders in which or with which such tax years of foreign corporations end (Reg. §§ 1.909-5 and 1.909-6).

The special matching rule applies to specified 10-percent owned foreign corporations for tax years of foreign corporations beginning after December 31, 2017, and tax years of U.S. shareholders in which or with which such tax years of foreign corporations end (Code Sec. 909(b)). Under the rule, if there is a foreign tax credit splitting event, a foreign income tax paid or accrued by a specified 10-percent owned foreign corporation is not taken into account for purposes of the deemed-paid credit and the determination of earnings and profits under the Subpart F rules (¶ 2487) before the tax year in which the related income is taken into account by the corporation or a domestic corporation which is a U.S. shareholder of the corporation.

2476. Election of Foreign Tax Credit or Deduction. The election to claim the foreign tax credit or deduction (¶ 2475) is made on an annual basis. It may be made or changed anytime within 10 years from the due date for filing a return for the year in which the taxes were actually paid or accrued, unless the period is extended by agreement with the IRS (Code Sec. 6511(d)(3); Reg. § 1.901-1(d) and (e)). For partnerships and S corporations, the election is made by the individual partners and shareholders, respectively (Code Secs. 702(a)(6), 703(b)(3), and 1366(a)(1)). Corporations in an

24 FOREIGN

affiliated group make the election and compute the credit on a consolidated basis for a consolidated return year (Reg. § 1.1502-4).

A taxpayer claims the foreign tax credit by filing Form 1116 (for individuals, estates, and trusts) or Form 1118 (for corporations) with the taxpayer's income tax return. An individual may elect to claim the foreign tax credit without filing Form 1116 by entering the credit directly on his or her tax return if: (1) all of the individual's foreign source income is passive income; (2) all of the income and any foreign taxes paid on the income is reported on a qualified payee statement (i.e., Form 1099); and (3) the total creditable foreign taxes is less than $300 ($600 if married filing jointly) (Code Sec. 904(j)). If an individual makes the election, then the foreign tax credit limitations do not apply, but the individual cannot carry over any excess credit to another tax year (¶ 2479). The election is not available to estates, trusts, or corporations. An election to take the credit or deduction on a joint return applies to the qualifying foreign taxes paid or accrued by both spouses. If married taxpayers file separate returns, either may take the credit or deduction without regard to the other.

Credit vs. Deduction. Generally, it is more advantageous for a U.S. taxpayer to elect the foreign tax credit rather than the deduction because the credit is taken against the taxpayer's U.S. liability on a dollar-for-dollar basis. In contrast, a deduction for foreign taxes merely reduces a taxpayer's income subject to tax. In addition, an individual who deducts foreign taxes must claim the taxes as an itemized deduction.

The election to claim the credit or deduction applies to all creditable foreign taxes paid or incurred by the taxpayer during the tax year for which a U.S. return is required (¶ 2477). A taxpayer cannot claim a credit for some creditable foreign taxes and a deduction for other creditable foreign taxes in the same tax year. Partial credits and partial deductions are not permitted except in limited circumstances (Code Sec. 275(a)(4)).

2477. Creditable Foreign Taxes. A U.S. taxpayer is allowed a foreign tax credit or deduction (¶ 2475) against U.S. income tax liability for any income tax, including war profits, and excess profits taxes, paid or accrued to a foreign country or U.S. possession during the tax year on foreign source income. This includes taxes paid or accrued in lieu of income taxes imposed by the foreign country or U.S. possession (Code Secs. 901 and 903; Reg. § 1.901-2). For tax years beginning before January 1, 2018, a U.S. corporation is also allowed a foreign tax credit for creditable foreign taxes paid by a foreign subsidiary in which it owns at least 10 percent of the voting stock and from which it receives a dividend (¶ 2485).

A creditable foreign tax is a levy the predominant character of which is that of a compulsory income tax according to U.S. tax principles. A penalty, fine, interest payment, customs duty, or similar obligation is not a tax; nor is any payment to a foreign government in exchange for a specific economic benefit that is not available on substantially the same terms to all persons. A foreign tax paid for retirement, unemployment, or disability benefits is generally not a payment for a specific economic benefit. However, no credit or deduction is allowed for social security taxes paid or accrued to a foreign country with which the United States has a social security agreement. The IRS may disallow foreign tax credits generated in transactions it views as abusive such as structured passive investment arrangements. The foreign tax credit or deduction is also not available for the withholding of otherwise creditable foreign taxes on dividends and other items of gain or income from property unless certain holding period requirements are met (Code Sec. 901(k) and (l)).

The foreign tax credit or deduction can only be claimed by the taxpayer upon whom the foreign law imposes legal liability, and who actually pays or accrues the tax. In the case of combined income of two or more persons, foreign law is considered to impose legal liability on each person on a pro rata basis (Reg. § 1.901-2(f)). This includes the combined income of a husband and wife, or a corporation and one or more of its subsidiaries. However, income which is subject to a special tax rate, exempt from tax, or for which certain deductions or credits are allowed under the foreign law must be allocated only to the person(s) with that type of income. The income subject to preferential treatment must be computed separately and the tax on that income allocated separately.

¶2477

A U.S. taxpayer may not claim the foreign tax credit or deduction for any foreign taxes paid or accrued on income excluded from U.S. gross income. This includes income excluded under the foreign earned income or foreign housing exclusions (¶ 2402 and ¶ 2403), or income from a U.S. possession (¶ 2414). The taxpayer may also not claim a credit or deduction for foreign taxes paid or accrued to the extent that: (1) the taxpayer is certain to receive a refund or credit, or the tax is used as a subsidy; (2) the liability is dependent on the availability of a foreign tax credit in another jurisdiction; (3) the taxes are paid or accrued to a country with which the United States does not conduct diplomatic relations or which is designated as supporting acts of international terrorism; or (4) the taxes are attributable to boycott income (¶ 2496). The amount of foreign taxes a taxpayer may claim is reduced if the taxpayer controls a foreign corporation (CFC) or partnership that fails to file Form 5471 or Form 8865, respectively (¶ 2487 and ¶ 2494).

Covered Asset Acquisitions. In the case of a covered asset acquisition, a taxpayer may not take into account in determining the foreign tax credit the disqualified portion of any foreign income tax determined with respect to income or gain attributable to the relevant foreign assets (Code Sec. 901(m); Reg. § 1.901(m)-2). A covered asset acquisition includes: (1) a qualified stock purchase under Code Sec. 338 (¶ 2265); (2) any transaction that is treated as the acquisition of assets for U.S. tax purposes and as the acquisition of stock (or is disregarded) for foreign tax purposes; (3) any acquisition of an interest in a partnership that has an election in effect under Code Sec. 754 (¶ 459); and (4) any other transaction as determined by the IRS. Transactions determined by the IRS include: (1) transactions treated as an acquisition of assets for U.S. tax purposes and as an acquisition of an interest in a fiscally transparent entity for foreign tax purposes; (2) certain transactions treated as a partnership distribution of one or more assets, if the transaction results in an increase in the U.S. basis of one or more assets; and (3) transactions treated as an acquisition of assets for both U.S. and foreign tax purposes, if there is an increase in the U.S. basis, without a decrease in the foreign basis of one or more assets.

The disqualified portion of any covered asset acquisition for any tax year is generally the aggregate basis difference allocable to the tax year with respect to all relevant foreign assets (RFAs), divided by the income on which the foreign income tax is determined (Code Sec. 901(m)(3); Reg. § § 1.901(m)-4 and 1.901(m)-5(c)). The basis difference with respect to any RFA is taken into account for a U.S. tax year (allocated basis difference), under an applicable U.S. cost recovery method or as a result of a disposition. If an asset is an RFA with respect to more than one foreign income tax, basis difference with respect to each foreign income tax is separately taken into account. Except as provided in regulations, upon a disposition of an RFA, the basis difference allocated to the U.S. tax year of the disposition is the excess of the basis difference of the RFA over the total amount of such basis difference that has been allocated to all prior U.S. tax years (unallocated basis difference).

2479. Foreign Tax Credit Limitations. The foreign tax credit or deduction (¶ 2475) is subject to a two-part limitation calculated on Form 1116 or Form 1118 that prevents the use of foreign taxes to reduce U.S. income tax liability on U.S. source income. First, an overall limitation provides that the total amount of a taxpayer's foreign tax credit may not exceed the taxpayer's entire U.S. income tax liability (determined without regard to the credit), multiplied by a fraction equal to the taxpayer's foreign source taxable income over worldwide taxable income from all sources (Code Sec. 904(a); Reg. § 1.904-1). Second, the limitation must be calculated separately for certain categories or baskets of foreign source income (¶ 2481). Special rules also apply if the taxpayer has an overall foreign loss or an overall domestic loss (¶ 2483). The IRS may recharacterize the income of an affiliated group of corporations or modify the consolidated return regulations to the extent necessary to prevent avoidance of the foreign tax credit limitation rules (Code Sec. 904(i); Reg. § 1.904(i)-1).

Foreign source taxable income is the taxpayer's gross income from all geographic sources outside the United States (regardless of the country), less any applicable deductions that properly relate to the income and an allocation of deductions unrelated to any specific item of income (Code Sec. 904(b); Reg. § § 1.904(b)-1 and 1.904(b)-2). An individual, estate, or trust may not claim deductions for personal exemptions for tax

24 FOREIGN

years beginning before 2018 and after 2025 in calculating taxable income. For all taxpayers, foreign source capital gains and losses are subject to (1) a capital gain net income limitation adjustment (i.e., U.S. capital loss adjustment), and (2) a capital gain rate differential adjustment. Adjustments must also be made for the participation exemption deduction (¶ 231) (Reg. § 1.904(b)-3).

De Minimis Exemption. An individual with $300 or less of creditable foreign taxes ($600 if married filing jointly) is exempt from the overall foreign tax credit limitation provided he or she has no foreign source income other than qualified passive income (¶ 2476). The exemption is not automatic and an individual must elect to take the exemption for the tax year directly on Form 1040.

U.S.-Owned Foreign Corporations. Certain amounts derived from U.S.-owned foreign corporations that would otherwise be treated as foreign source income are treated as U.S. source income for purposes of the foreign tax credit limitations (Code Sec. 904(h); Reg. § 1.904-5(m)). The sourcing rule applies to subpart F income inclusions from a controlled foreign corporation (CFC) (¶ 2488), income from a qualified electing fund (¶ 2490), and interest and dividends paid by a foreign corporation where not less than 10 percent of the corporation's earnings and profits for the tax year are attributable to U.S. sources. A U.S.-owned foreign corporation is generally any foreign corporation if 50 percent or more of the total combined voting power of all classes of stock in the corporation entitled to vote or of the total value of the stock of the corporation is held by U.S. persons.

Carryover of Unused Foreign Taxes. If the amount of creditable foreign taxes paid or accrued by a taxpayer during the tax year exceeds the overall limitation for that year (as well as the separate limitation for each separate basket of foreign source income other than GILTI), the unused portion may be carried back one year and then forward ten years (Code Sec. 904(c)); Reg. § § 1.904-2 and 1.904-3). The amount that may be carried back and forward is limited to the amount by which the credit limitation in the carryback or forward year exceeds the amount of foreign taxes paid or accrued in that year. In addition, any unused foreign tax must be carried back and forward to its own separate basket of income. It cannot offset other taxes imposed on income in another basket.

If any unused foreign tax credit is carried back or forward to a tax year in which a foreign tax deduction is claimed (¶ 2476), the taxpayer must compute a foreign tax credit limit as if the credit was elected for that year. Any excess generated in the deduction year cannot be deducted or claimed as a credit for any year, but reduces the amount of unused foreign taxes that can be carried over to another tax year. Alternatively, an amended return may be filed within 10 years from the due date of the return of the deduction year to claim the foreign tax credit rather than the deduction (¶ 2475). For any portion of a foreign tax credit carryback from a tax year attributable to the carryback of a net operating loss or capital loss from a later tax year, the carryback stops the running of interest until the filing date for the later tax year (Code Sec. 6601(d)). An individual electing the *de minimis* exemption may not carryback or carryforward any excess foreign taxes to an election year.

Transition rules are provided to take into account the post-2017 additional foreign tax credit limitation categories for foreign branch income and global intangible low-taxed income (GILTI) (¶ 2481) (Reg. § 1.904-4(j)).

2481. Separate Foreign Tax Limitation Categories. A taxpayer is generally required to compute the foreign tax credit limitation (¶ 2479) separately for the following baskets or categories of foreign source income: passive category income, foreign branch category income, global intangible low-taxed category income (GILTI), and general category income (i.e., income not in the other baskets) (Code Sec. 904(d)(1) and (d)(2); Reg. § 1.904-4; Prop. Reg. § 1.904-4).

The passive category income basket includes investment income such as dividends, interest, rents, royalties, annuities, net gain from the sale of non-income producing investment property or property that generates passive income, and income from a qualified electing fund (¶ 2490) (Reg. § 1.904-4(b)). It also includes distributive shares of partnership income treated as passive category income (Reg. § 1.904-4(n)). It does not include gains or losses from the sale of inventory or property held mainly for sale to customers in the ordinary course of a trade or business, any rents or royalties that are derived in the active conduct of a trade or business, certain export financing interest, and highly taxed income.

Foreign branch category income is a separate basket effective for tax years beginning after December 31, 2017, and includes the business profits of a U.S. person that are attributable to one or more qualified business units (QBU) in one or more foreign countries (Reg. § 1.904-4(f)). A QBU is any separate and clearly identified unit of a trade or business of a taxpayer that maintains separate books and records (Code Sec. 989(b); Reg. § 1.989(a)-1). The foreign branch foreign tax credit limitation basket does not apply to income of the foreign branch that is passive category income.

GILTI is a separate basket effective for tax years of foreign corporations beginning after December 31, 2017, and to tax years of U.S. shareholders in which or with which such tax years of foreign corporations end. GILTI is the excess (if any) of a U.S. shareholder's net controlled foreign corporation (CFC) tested income for the tax year, over the U.S. shareholder's net deemed tangible income return for the tax year (¶ 2488B) (Reg. § 1.904-4(g)).

To determine taxable income in each basket, a taxpayer must allocate expenses, losses, and other deductions directly related to the foreign source income allocated to each basket (¶ 2427). Similarly, foreign taxes paid or accrued may only include those taxes that are related to income in that basket (Reg. § 1.904-6). If a tax is related to more than one basket, the taxpayer must apportion the tax.

Look-Through Rules. Foreign source income received by a U.S. shareholder from a controlled foreign corporation (CFC) is treated as passive category income only to the extent the amounts are allocable to the passive category income of the CFC (¶ 2487) (Code Sec. 904(d)(3) and (4); Reg. § 1.904-5). Tracing rules prescribe classification of subpart F income (¶ 2488), global intangible low-taxed income (GILTI) (¶ 2488B), interest, rents, royalties, and dividends to various limitation categories. The look-through rules also apply in the case of payments made by certain noncontrolled corporations (¶ 2485), and domestic corporations, partnerships, and related look-through entities. In the case of a partner in a partnership, the look-through rule will apply with respect to the partner's distributive share of partnership income unless the partner owns less than 10 percent of the partnership, in which case the income is treated as passive income.

Other Limitations. In addition to the separate foreign tax credit limitation baskets or categories, separate foreign tax credit limitations must also be determined for certain special categories of income (Reg. § 1.904-4(m)). This includes: (1) any income sourced under a tax treaty as foreign source income including any income derived from foreign sources; (2) income from sanctioned countries; (3) dividends received from a corporation that qualifies for the possession tax credit if the dividends-received deduction is disallowed under the alternative current earnings (ACE) rules in calculating alternative minimum tax (AMT) liability before 2018; (4) dividends received from 10-percent owned foreign corporations (¶ 231); (5) gain from the sale of stock in a foreign corporation or intangible property that is treated as foreign source under a tax treaty; (6) lump-sum distributions from retirement plans for which the special averaging treatment is used to figure tax; and (7) combined foreign oil and gas income including foreign oil and gas extraction income (FOGEI) and foreign oil-related income (FORI) (Code Sec. 907).

2483. Recapture of Foreign and U.S. Losses. An overall foreign loss (OFL) is subject to recapture to prevent a double tax benefit from using the OFL to reduce U.S. tax liability on U.S. source income and claiming the foreign tax credit (¶ 2475) on the same income. If a taxpayer has an OFL in any tax year, then a portion of the taxpayer's foreign source income earned in a subsequent year is recharacterized as U.S. source income (Code Sec. 904(f); Reg. § 1.904(f)-1). For this purpose, an OFL is the amount by which gross income from foreign sources is exceeded by the sum of expenses, losses, and other deductions properly allocable to such income, but without taking into account any net operating losses (NOL), foreign expropriation losses, and uncompensated casualty or theft losses. A foreign loss must be determined for each separate foreign tax credit basket or category (¶ 2481), referred to as a separate limitation loss (SLL). Thus, a taxpayer can have an OFL, an SLL for passive income, an SLL for foreign branch income, an SLL for global low-taxed income, and an SLL for general income in any given

24

FOREIGN

tax year. Foreign losses in one separate foreign tax credit basket must be offset against income in other foreign categories before offsetting U.S. income.

The amount of foreign source income that must be recaptured and recharacterized as U.S. source income is generally limited to the lesser of the taxpayer's OFL (to the extent not used in prior tax years) or 50 percent of the taxpayer's foreign source taxable income for the tax year. If a taxpayer disposes of assets used in its trade or business predominantly outside the United States in a taxable disposition, or disposes of stock in a controlled foreign corporation (CFC) (¶ 2487) in which it owns more than 50 percent, then 100 percent of the gain must be recaptured. Fifty percent of the recognized gain is recaptured under the general rule above and the remainder recaptured to the extent of the taxpayer's OFL balance. Special recapture rules also apply if the disposition is nontaxable. Similar recapture rules apply to an overall domestic loss (ODL) requiring U.S. source income earned in a subsequent year to be recharacterized as foreign source income (Code Sec. 904(g); Reg. § 1.904(g)-1). Special ordering rules are used to allocate NOLs, net capital losses, U.S. source losses and SLLs, and for the recapture of SLLs, OFLs, and ODLs (Reg. § 1.904(g)-3).

Recapture of ODLs Accelerated. Effective for tax years beginning after December 31, 2017, and before January 1, 2028, a taxpayer who claims the foreign tax credit and has an ODL may elect to recapture the ODL by recharacterizing up to 100 percent of U.S. source taxable income earned in subsequent years as foreign source taxable income. The amount that is recharacterized each year is limited to the lesser of the aggregate amount in the ODL account or up to 100 percent of the taxpayer's U.S. source taxable income for the year (Code Sec. 904(g)(5)). The increased recapture amount applies to the pre-2018 unused ODL, meaning a loss that arises in a qualified tax year beginning before January 1, 2018.

Transition Rules. Transition rules are provided to take into account the post-2017 additional foreign tax credit limitation categories for foreign branch income and global intangible low-taxed income (GILTI) (¶ 2481) (Reg. § 1.904(f)-12).

2485. Deemed Paid or Indirect Foreign Tax Credit. A domestic corporation and U.S. shareholder is allowed an "indirect" or "deemed paid" credit for foreign income taxes of a controlled foreign corporation (CFC) associated with: (1) a subpart F inclusion (¶ 2488), (2) a global intangible low-taxed income (GILTI) inclusion (¶ 2488B), and (3) certain distributions of previously taxed earnings and profits (PTEP) (Code Sec. 960; Reg. § 1.960-1). The deemed paid credit is determined on an annual basis. To compute the credit, the CFC's gross income for the tax year is assigned to foreign tax credit limitation categories and then to an income group within a category. Foreign taxes are associated with an income group. PTEP groups must also be established and maintained within an annual PTEP account and PTEP are assigned to those groups (Reg. § § 1.960-2 and 1.960-3).

A corporation electing to take the deemed paid credit must increase or "gross up" its tax base by including the tax deemed paid by the foreign corporation as a dividend (Code Sec. 78).

For tax years beginning before January 1, 2018, and tax years of U.S. shareholders in which or with which such tax years of foreign corporations end, the foreign tax credit (¶ 2475) was available to a U.S. corporate shareholder that owned 10 percent or more of the voting stock in a foreign corporation from which it received a dividend (or deemed to receive a dividend through an affiliated group or a partnership) ("Code Sec. 902 deemed paid credit") (Code Sec. 902, prior to repeal by the Tax Cuts and Jobs Act (P.L. 115-97)). The amount of the deemed paid or indirect credit was determined by reference to the portion of the foreign corporation's foreign income taxes that the dividend received by the domestic corporation bore to the foreign corporation's undistributed earnings. A deemed paid credit was also allowed for subpart F inclusions under the same rules (Code Sec. 960(a)(1), prior to amendment by P.L. 115-97).

U.S. Shareholders of Foreign Corporations

See CCH® AnswerConnect: *Controlled Foreign Corporations* and *Passive Foreign Investment Company* for more information on this topic.

2487. Controlled Foreign Corporations (CFCs). A U.S. shareholder of a foreign corporation that is a controlled foreign corporation (CFC) for an uninterrupted period of

30 days or more during the tax year must include in gross income its pro rata share of the CFC's subpart F income (¶ 2488) (whether distributed or not) and earnings invested in U.S. property during the year (Code Sec. 951(a)). The required 30-day period is eliminated for tax years of foreign corporations beginning after December 31, 2017, and to tax years of U.S. shareholders with or within which such tax years end. Thus, if the foreign corporation is a CFC at any time during the tax year, U.S. shareholders must include in gross income their pro rata share of subpart F income.

A foreign corporation is a CFC if more than 50 percent of its total voting power or value is owned by U.S. shareholders (Code Sec. 957). A U.S. shareholder is any U.S. person (U.S. citizen, resident, domestic corporation partnerships, estate, or trust) who owns or is considered as owning: (1) 10 percent or more of the total combined voting power of all classes of voting stock of a foreign corporation; or (2) 10 percent or more of the total value of all classes of stock of the foreign corporation for tax years of foreign corporations beginning after December 31, 2017, and for tax years of U.S. shareholders with or within which such tax years end (Code Secs. 951(b) and 958; Rev. Proc. 2019-40). The expanded definition applies for all purposes of the Internal Revenue Code and not just the subpart F rules.

The U.S. shareholder includes subpart F income and earnings in gross income in its tax year in which the CFC's tax year ends but only if it is a shareholder on the last day of the CFC's tax year. In addition, the shareholder only includes income from that portion of the year that the corporation qualifies as a CFC. The income is treated as a deemed dividend (¶ 733). Actual distributions are excluded from gross income to the extent they have already been accounted for by the shareholder (Code Sec. 959). To prevent double taxation, the basis of the U.S. shareholder's CFC stock and property the shareholder is considered owning through the CFC is increased by the amount of subpart F income required to be included in income and decreased by any distribution that is excluded from income (Code Sec. 961).

If a domestic corporation and U.S. shareholder of a CFC includes amounts in gross income under subpart F (subpart F inclusion), then it is allowed a foreign tax credit (¶ 2475) for foreign taxes deemed paid, based on the amount of the CFC's foreign taxes that are properly attributable to items of income in the subpart F income group of the CFC giving rise to the subpart F income inclusion (Code Sec. 960; Reg. §§ 1.960-1(d)(2)(ii)(B) and 1.960-2(b)). The credit is determined on a current year basis according to the amount of foreign taxes attributable to the inclusion, rather than by reference to the rules of Code Sec. 902, effective for tax years of foreign corporations beginning after December 31, 2017, and to tax years of U.S. shareholders with or within which such tax years of foreign corporations end. A deemed paid credit is also available to any individual U.S. shareholder who elects to be taxed at the domestic corporate income tax rate on amounts included in gross income (Code Sec. 962).

A deemed paid tax credit is allowed for eligible domestic corporations with respect to inclusions under the transition tax rules for accumulated earnings (¶ 2488C). The Code Sec. 902 deemed paid credit rules (¶ 2485) apply because the transition tax applies to the last tax year of a foreign corporation beginning before January 1, 2018, and to tax years of U.S. shareholders in which or with which such tax years of foreign corporations end (Code Sec. 965; Reg. § 1.965-6). A deemed paid credit is also allowed for domestic corporations with respect to inclusions of global intangible low-taxed income (GILTI) (¶ 2488B). A corporation electing to take the deemed paid credit must increase or "gross up" its tax base by including the tax deemed paid by the foreign corporation as a dividend (Code Sec. 78).

Investment of Earnings. U.S. shareholders of a CFC are taxed on their pro rata share of the CFC's earnings that are invested in U.S. property during the tax year and not distributed or otherwise taxed (Code Sec. 956; Reg. §§ 1.956-1, 1.956-2, 1.956-4). The amount of earnings invested in U.S. property is the economic equivalent of a dividend deemed to have been paid, but it is not a qualified dividend eligible to be taxed at capital gains rates because it is not actually distributed (*O. Rodriguez*, CA-5, 2013-2 USTC ¶ 50,420). A CFC acquires a direct interest in U.S. property when it acquires an adjusted basis in the property. U.S. property can also be held indirectly by the CFC through a trustee or nominee, or through another foreign corporation or partnership. U.S. property includes tangible real or personal property located in the United States, stock of

24 | FOREIGN

domestic corporations, obligations of U.S. persons, and the right to use a patent, copyright, invention, etc., in the United States. Certain properties acquired in normal commercial transactions without the intention that they remain in the United States indefinitely are not to be treated as U.S. property.

Sales and Exchanges. Any gain recognized by a U.S. shareholder from the sale, exchange, or redemption of stock in a CFC is included in gross income as an ordinary dividend to the extent of the corporation's earnings and profits allocable to the stock (Code Sec. 1248). Any gain exceeding the CFC's earnings and profits is treated as capital gain. The shareholder may claim a foreign tax credit for the taxes paid by the CFC on the income. However, the credit may be less than the indirect credit (¶ 2485) because it does not apply to as many tiers of foreign corporations. If a domestic corporation sells or exchanges stock in a foreign corporation held for one year or more, any amount received by the domestic corporation that is treated as a dividend is treated as a dividend for purposes of the 100-percent participation dividends-received deduction (DRD) (¶ 2488A).

Solely for purposes of determining loss on any disposition of stock of a specified 10-percent owned foreign corporation, a domestic corporation's basis of the stock is reduced by the amount of the participation DRD allowable for dividends received with respect to that stock (Code Secs. 961(d) and 964(e)(4)). In the case of a sale by a CFC of a lower-tier CFC, the foreign-source portion of the amount that is treated as a dividend is treated as subpart F income. A U.S shareholder of the selling CFC includes in income a pro rata share of that amount and is allowed a participation DRD. Also, a loss recapture rule requires a domestic corporation that transfers after December 31, 2017, substantially all of the assets of a foreign branch to a specified 10-percent owned foreign corporation in which it is a U.S. shareholder after the transfer, to include in income the amount of transferred losses, subject to certain limitations (Code Sec. 91(a)).

Returns. Every U.S. person (U.S. citizen, resident alien, domestic corporation, domestic partnership, or domestic estate or trust) who is a U.S. shareholder of a CFC must file an information return on Form 5471 with their income tax return (Code Sec. 6038). Failure to timely file the form may result in penalties and a reduced foreign tax credit. The taxpayer must include information on acquisitions, reorganizations, and dispositions of ownership interests in a CFC during the tax year (Code Sec. 6046). U.S. shareholders of controlled foreign partnerships are subject to similar reporting requirements using Form 8865. The due date for filing any federal tax return, including Form 5471 and Form 8865 with the taxpayer's return, otherwise due on or after April 1, 2020, and before July 15, 2020, is automatically extended to July 15, 2020, in response to the COVID-19 (coronavirus) crisis (Notice 2020-23).

2488. Subpart F Income. Subpart F income of a controlled foreign corporation (CFC) (¶ 2487) is the sum of the corporation's insurance income, foreign base company income, boycott income (¶ 2496), illegal payments (¶ 2497), and income from countries not diplomatically recognized by the U.S. government (Code Sec. 952; Reg. § 1.952-1). It does not include income from sources within the United States that is effectively connected with the conduct of a trade or business by the corporation (¶ 2429) unless that income is exempt from tax or taxed at a reduced rate pursuant to a tax treaty. Subpart F income for the tax year is also limited to the CFC's total earnings and profits for that year, and may be reduced in certain circumstances to accumulated deficits of earnings and profits.

Subpart F insurance income is any income that is attributable to the issuance or reissuance of any insurance or annuity contract (Code Sec. 953). The income must be of a type that would be taxed (with some modifications) under the rules that apply to domestic insurance companies. It does not include insurance income in connection with risks located outside of the United States.

Foreign base company income of a CFC is made up of income from a foreign personal holding company (FPHC), as well as foreign base company sales services and oil-related income. However, foreign base company oil-related income is eliminated for tax years of foreign corporation beginning after December 31, 2017, and to tax years of U.S. shareholders in which or with which such tax years of foreign corporations end (Code Sec. 954; Reg. § 1.954-1). FPHC income is generally the major component of foreign base company income and includes dividends, interest (including otherwise tax-exempt interest), rents, royalties, and annuities. It also includes: amounts received under a contract to furnish personal services; any item of income, gain, deduction, or loss from a notional principal contract; and the excess of gains over losses from the sale or exchange of property (including foreign currency and commodities) unless the CFC is a regular dealer. FPHC income does not include rents and royalties from an active trade or business, certain income from related persons, and export financing interest. It also does not include income derived in the active conduct of a banking, financing or similar business (active financing income), income derived in the active conduct of an insurance business (active insurance income), or qualified insurance investment income.

For purposes of determining FPHC income, the sale of a partnership interest by a CFC with at least a 25-percent ownership interest is treated as a sale of the proportionate share of partnership assets attributable to that interest, including subpart F income (Code Sec. 954(c)(4)). On the other hand, for tax years beginning before January 1, 2021, dividends, interest, rents and royalties received by a CFC from a related CFC are not treated as FPHCI to the extent attributable to income of the related CFC that is neither subpart F income nor effectively connected income (Code Sec. 954(c)(6), as amended by the Taxpayer Certainty and Disaster Tax Relief Act of 2019 (P.L. 116-94)).

2488A. Participation Exemption Deduction. A 100-percent deduction is allowed for the foreign-source portion of dividends received from a specified 10-percent owned foreign corporation by a domestic corporation that is a U.S. shareholder of the foreign corporation, effective for distributions made after December 31, 2017 (Code Sec. 245A) (¶ 231). No foreign tax credit or deduction is allowed for any taxes paid or accrued with respect to a dividend that qualifies for the participation dividends-received deduction (DRD). The participation DRD is available only to a C corporation that is not a regulated investment company (RIC) or real estate investment trust (REIT).

2488B. Global Intangible Low-Taxed Income (GILTI). A U.S. shareholder of any controlled foreign corporation (CFC) (¶ 2487) is required to include its global intangible low-taxed income (GILTI) in gross income for the tax year in a manner generally similar to that for subpart F inclusions (Code Sec. 951A; Reg. § 1.951A-1). A U.S. shareholder calculates GILTI on Form 8992. The inclusion applies to tax years of foreign corporations beginning after December 31, 2017, and to tax years of shareholders in which or with which such tax years of foreign corporations end.

GILTI is the excess (if any) of: (1) the U.S. shareholder's net CFC tested income for that tax year, over (2) the U.S. shareholder's net deemed tangible income return for that tax year. A CFC's tested income for any tax year is the gross income of the corporation, subject to certain exclusions, in excess of the properly allocated deductions. A CFC's tested loss for any tax year is the excess of the properly allocated deductions over the CFC's tested income. Net CFC tested income is the aggregate of the U.S. shareholder's pro rata share of tested income of each CFC, over the aggregate of the U.S. shareholder's pro rata share of tested loss of each CFC (Code Sec. 951A(c); Reg. § 1.951A-2).

Net deemed tangible income return with respect to any U.S. shareholder for the tax year is the excess (if any) of: (1) 10 percent of the aggregate of its pro rata share of the qualified business asset investment (QBAI) of each tested income CFC in which it is a U.S. shareholder, over (2) the aggregate of its pro rata share of certain interest expense of each CFC (Code Sec. 951A(b)(2); Reg. § 1.951A-1(c)(3)). QBAI is defined by reference to specific tangible property used in a trade or business that is depreciable under Code Sec. 167. Specified tangible property is tangible property used in the production of tested income, except as provided for dual use property. Specifically, QBAI is the CFC's average aggregate adjusted bases as of the close of each quarter of the tax year in the property. The adjusted basis of the property is determined using the alternative depreciation system under Code Sec. 168(g) and allocating depreciation deductions for the property ratably to each day during the period in the tax year to which the depreciation relates (Code Sec. 951A(d); Reg. § 1.951A-3).

Foreign tax credits are allowed for foreign income taxes deemed paid on GILTI included in the gross income of a domestic corporation. The foreign income taxes paid are restricted to 80 percent of the domestic corporation's inclusion percentage multiplied by the aggregate tested foreign income taxes paid or accrued by CFCs. The inclusion percentage is the ratio of the corporation's GILTI divided by the aggregate

¶2488B

amounts of the shareholder's pro rata share of the tested income of each CFC where the shareholder is a U.S. shareholder for their tax year (Code Sec. 960(d); Reg. § 1.960-2(c)).

Deduction for FDII and GILTI. For tax years beginning after December 31, 2017, and before January 1, 2026, a domestic corporation is generally allowed a deduction equal to 37.5 percent of its foreign-derived intangible income (FDII), plus 50 percent of its GILTI and the amount treated as a dividend received by the corporation and attributable to its GILTI. The deduction is calculated on Form 8993 (Code Sec. 250; Prop. Reg. § 1.250(a)-1). For tax years beginning after December 31, 2025, the deduction for FDII is 21.875 percent and 37.5 percent for GILTI. The amount of the deduction is limited based on taxable income. If the sum of a domestic corporation's FDII and GILTI amounts exceeds its taxable income, then the amount of the deduction is similarly reduced by the excess.

FDII is the portion of its intangible income derived in connection with property that is sold by the taxpayer to any person who is not a U.S. person for foreign use, consumption, or disposition that is not within the United States. A domestic corporation's FDII is generally its deemed intangible income multiplied by the percentage of its deduction-eligible income that is foreign derived: FDII = Deemed Intangible Income × Foreign-Derived Deduction Eligible Income over Deduction Eligible Income. Deduction eligible income means the excess of the gross income of the domestic corporation over deductions (including taxes) properly allocated to gross income (Prop. Reg. § 1.250(b)-1).

2488C. Transition Tax for Accumulated Foreign Earnings. A transition tax is generally imposed on accumulated foreign earnings, without requiring an actual distribution, upon the transition to the participation exemption system (Code Sec. 965; Reg. § 1.965-1). Under the transition rule, for the last tax year beginning before January 1, 2018, any U.S. shareholder of any deferred foreign income corporation (DFIC) that is at least 10-percent owned by a domestic corporation must include in income its pro rata share of the accumulated post-1986 foreign earnings of the corporation as of November 2, 2017, or December 31, 2017, whichever amount is greater (mandatory inclusion). Form 965 is used to calculate the inclusion amount. The mandatory inclusion also applies to partners, shareholders, owners, and beneficiaries of pass-through entities that are U.S. shareholders of DFICs. A DFIC is a specified foreign corporation (i.e., controlled foreign corporation (CFC) (¶ 2487) or other foreign corporation other than a PFIC that is not a CFC that has positive amounts of accumulated post-1986 deferred foreign income on the measurement dates.

A portion of the mandatory income inclusion is deductible. The deduction results in a reduced rate of tax of 15.5 percent for the included deferred foreign income held in liquid form (i.e., aggregate foreign cash position) and eight percent for the remaining deferred foreign income. A U.S. shareholder's aggregate foreign cash position is the U.S. shareholder's pro rata share of the cash position of each specified foreign corporation of the U.S. shareholder. The aggregate foreign cash position is the greater of the aggregate cash position as of the last day of the last tax year beginning before January 1, 2018, and the average aggregate cash position as of the last day of each of the last two years ending before November 2, 2017 (Code Sec. 965(c); Reg. § 1.965-3). No foreign tax credit or deduction is allowed for a portion (referred to as an applicable percentage) of any foreign income taxes paid or accrued (or deemed paid or accrued) with respect to any mandatory inclusion amount for which a deduction is allowed (Code Sec. 965(g); Reg. § 1.965-5).

A U.S. shareholder takes the net liability for the transition tax into account on its 2017 tax return if the end of the DFIC's tax year is during or ends with the U.S. shareholder's 2017 tax year. If the end of the DFIC's tax year is during or ends with the U.S. shareholder's 2018 tax year, the inclusion is taken into account on the U.S. shareholder's 2018 tax return. Alternatively, the taxpayer may elect to pay the net liability in installments over an eight-year period. An election to pay the net tax liability from the mandatory inclusion in installments must be made by the due date of the tax return. A special rule permits deferral of a portion of the transition net tax liability for shareholders of a U.S. shareholder that is an S corporation. Form 965 is used to calculate the inclusion (Code Sec. 965(h) and (i); Reg. § 1.965-7; IRS Pub. 5292). The due

¶2488C

date for paying any federal income tax, including installment payments of net liability for the transition tax, otherwise due on or after April 1, 2020, and before July 15, 2020, is automatically extended to July 15, 2020, in response to the COVID-19 (coronavirus) crisis (Notice 2020-23).

2489. Base Erosion and Anti-Abuse Tax (BEAT). A base erosion minimum tax is imposed on an applicable corporation with annual average annual gross receipts of at least $500 million over the previous three tax years (Code Sec. 59A; Reg. § 1.59A-1). The tax is referred to as a base erosion and anti-abuse tax (BEAT) and is effective for base erosion payments paid or accrued in tax years beginning after December 31, 2017. The BEAT for any tax year generally is 10 percent of the taxpayer's modified taxable income (five percent for 2018), less the taxpayer's regular tax liability reduced by certain tax credits. For tax years beginning after December 31, 2025, the BEAT rate is increased to 12.5 percent and the taxpayer's regular tax liability is reduced by the aggregate amount of allowable credits. Form 8991 is used to calculate the tax and filed with the taxpayer's return. The due date for filing any federal tax return, including Form 8991 with the taxpayer's return, otherwise due on or after April 1, 2020, and before July 15, 2020, is automatically extended to July 15, 2020, in response to the COVID-19 (coronavirus) crisis (Notice 2020-23).

The applicable taxpayer's modified taxable income is its taxable income without regard to (1) any base erosion tax benefit with respect to any base erosion payment, or (ii) the base erosion percentage of any net operating loss deduction for the tax year. A base erosion payment is any amount paid or accrued by a taxpayer to a foreign person that is a related party and with respect to which a deduction is allowable, including the acquisition of depreciable property and reinsurance. Base erosion payments generally do not include any amount that constitutes reductions in gross receipts including payments for costs of goods sold (COGS). In addition, there is an exception for qualified derivative payments made in the ordinary course of a trade or business.

2489A. Related Party Payments Involving Hybrid Entities or Hybrid Transactions. For tax years beginning after December 31, 2017, a deduction is disallowed for a disqualified related party amount paid or accrued pursuant to a hybrid transaction. A deduction is also disallowed for a disqualified related party amount paid or accrued by, or to, a hybrid entity (Code Sec. 267A; Reg. § 1.267A-1).

Any interest or royalty paid or accrued to a related party is a "disqualified related party amount" to the extent that under the tax law of the country where the related party is a resident for tax purposes or is subject to tax: (1) the amount is not included in the income of the related party, or (2) the related party is allowed a deduction for the amount. A disqualified related party amount does not include any payment that is included in the gross income of a U.S. shareholder under subpart F.

A "related party" is a person related with respect to a controlled foreign corporation (CFC) under Code Sec. 954(d)(3), except that the person is related to the payor rather than the CFC. Thus, a related person includes any individual, corporation, partnership, trust, or estate, that directly or indirectly, controls or is controlled by the payor or is controlled by the same person that controls the payor. Control is ownership of more than 50 percent (by vote or value) of the corporation's stock or more than a 50 percent (by value) of the beneficial interests in a partnership, trust or estate.

A hybrid transaction means any transaction, series of transactions, agreement, or instrument, if one or more payments are treated as interest or royalties for federal income tax purposes, but are not treated as such for purposes of the tax law of the foreign country where the recipient of the payment is resident for tax purposes or is subject to tax. A hybrid entity is an entity that is either: (1) treated as fiscally transparent for federal income tax purposes, but not under the tax law of the foreign country where the entity is resident for tax purposes or is subject to tax, or (2) treated as fiscally transparent under the tax law of the foreign country where the entity is resident for tax purposes or is subject to tax, but not for federal income tax purposes.

2490. Passive Foreign Investment Company. A U.S. shareholder of a passive foreign investment company (PFIC) that receives an excess distribution with respect to its stock or disposes of its PFIC stock must allocate the income or gain pro rata over the shareholder's holding period for the stock unless the shareholder elects to treat the

PFIC as a qualifying electing fund (QEF) or makes a mark-to-market election (Code Sec. 1291). The amount allocated to the shareholder's current tax year, and to the tax years in its holding period before the foreign corporation qualified as a PFIC (pre-PFIC years), are taxed as ordinary income. The amount allocated to any other tax year in the shareholder's holding period is taxed at the highest income tax rate applicable for that year, plus interest from the due date for the taxpayer's return for that year. For this purpose, an excess distribution is any part of a distribution received from the PFIC which is greater than 125 percent of the average distribution received by the shareholder during the shorter of the three preceding tax years or the period the shareholder held the stock.

A PFIC is any foreign corporation that derives 75 percent or more of its gross income for the tax year from passive investments or for which at least 50 percent of its average total assets held for the year produce passive income or are held for the production of passive income (Code Sec. 1297; Prop. Reg. § 1.1297-1). In applying the asset test, the period over which the average percentage is calculated is at least quarterly, but taxpayers are allowed to use a shorter period, such as a monthly or daily measurement of asset values. Passive income generally is the type of income that would be foreign personal holding company income (¶ 2488).

Miscellaneous rules apply regarding stock attribution, start-up companies and business changes, the leasing of tangible personal property, intangible assets, and the interaction of the PFIC rules with the taxation of accumulated earnings and subpart F income (Code Sec. 1298). Even if a foreign corporation ceases to qualify as a PFIC, a U.S. shareholder is subject to the PFIC rules for any period stock is held that the corporation was a PFIC. To avoid the PFIC rules, the shareholder can purge PFIC stock by making a deemed sale or deemed dividend election.

A U.S. person that is a direct or indirect shareholder of a PFIC generally must file Form 8621 with its tax return for each tax year in which the person receives an excess distribution, disposes of its PFIC stock, or makes an election to purge its PFIC stock, including a QEF or mark-to-market election. The reporting requirement may also meet the FATCA requirements for disclosing information with respect to specified foreign financial assets on Form 8938 (¶ 2572). A separate Form 8621 must be filed for each PFIC in which stock is held, directly or indirectly (Reg. § 1.1298-1). The due date for filing any federal tax return, including Form 8621 with the taxpayer's return, otherwise due on or after April 1, 2020, and before July 15, 2020, is automatically extended to July 15, 2020, in response to the COVID-19 (coronavirus) crisis (Notice 2020-23).

Qualified Electing Fund. Instead of paying the additional tax on deferrals (or deemed sale or deemed dividend elections), a U.S. shareholder of a PFIC may elect to treat the corporation as a QEF. If the election is made, the shareholder must include in gross income each year as ordinary income its pro rata share of earnings of the corporation, and as long-term capital gain, its pro rata share of the net capital gain of the corporation (Code Secs. 1293 and 1295). The inclusions are made for the shareholder's tax year in which, or with which, the QEF's tax year ends. Once made, the QEF election is revocable only with IRS consent and is effective for the current tax year and all subsequent tax years. Under certain circumstances, the U.S. shareholder can elect to defer payment of the tax on any undistributed earnings of the QEF (Code Sec. 1294).

Mark-to-Market Election. A U.S. shareholder of a PFIC may also avoid the additional tax on the deferral of income by making a mark-to-market election with respect to its PFIC stock that is marketable (Code Sec. 1296). If the election is made, the shareholder annually includes in gross income as ordinary income an amount equal to the excess of the fair market value of the PFIC stock as of the close of the tax year over its adjusted basis. If the stock has declined in value, an ordinary loss deduction is allowed, limited to the net amount of gain previously included in income.

2491. Sale or Exchange of Patent, Etc. to Foreign Corporations. A U.S. person who controls a foreign corporation (more than 50 percent of voting power of all stock) directly or indirectly must recognize gain from the sale or exchange of a patent, invention, model, design, copyright, secret formula or process, or any other similar property right to the foreign corporation as ordinary income rather than capital gain (Code Sec. 1249).

¶2491

2492. Reorganization Involving Foreign Corporations. A U.S. person is generally required to recognize gains (but not losses) on the transfer of appreciated property to a foreign corporation (outbound transfers) that would otherwise be tax-free under the corporate organization (¶ 203), reorganization (¶ 2205), and liquidation rules (¶ 2253) (Code Sec. 367(a); Reg. § 1.367(a)-1; Temp. Reg. § 1.367(a)-1T). Similarly, transfers by a foreign corporation to a U.S. corporation (inbound transfers) or transfers by a foreign corporation to another foreign corporation (foreign-to-foreign transfers) may require U.S. shareholders to recognize income currently, or defer recognition of gain by making basis, and earnings and profits adjustments (Code Sec. 367(b); Reg. § 1.367(b)-3; Reg. § 1.367(b)-4).

Active Trade or Business. For tax years beginning before December 31, 2017, recognition of gain on outbound transfers does not apply to certain eligible property transferred for use by the foreign corporation in the active conduct of a trade or business outside the United States, provided the U.S. person transferring the property complies with the reporting requirements of Code Sec. 6038B by filing Form 926 (Code Sec. 367(a)(3), prior to repeal by the Tax Cuts and Jobs Act (P.L. 115-97)); Reg. § 1.367(a)-2). Eligible property includes tangible property, a working interest in oil and gas property, financial assets, commodities positions, and notional principal contracts. It does not include inventory, installment obligations, accounts receivable, property that gives rise to certain nonfunctional currency transactions, and certain leased property. The exception also does not apply in the case where a U.S. person transfers assets of a foreign branch with previously deducted losses to a foreign corporation (Reg. § 1.367(a)-6; Temp. Reg. § 1.367(a)-6T).

Transfers of Stock or Securities. Recognition of gain on outbound transfers does not apply to any transfer of stock or securities of a party to the exchange (Code Sec. 367(a)(2); Reg. § 1.367(a)-3). An outbound transfer of foreign stock or securities is not subject to tax if the U.S. person owns less than five percent of the transferee foreign corporation or enters into a five-year gain recognition agreement (GRA) with the IRS (Reg. § 1.367(a)-8). An outbound transfer of domestic stock or securities is *not* subject to tax if:

- the U.S. person receives 50 percent or less of the voting power and stock value of the transferee;

- U.S. officers, directors, five percent or more shareholders of U.S. corporation do not own more than 50 percent of voting power and stock value of the transferee;

- the U.S. person is not a five-percent or more shareholder of the transferee or must enter into a GRA with the IRS; and

- the transferee has been actively engaged in business for at least three years.

Code Sec. 361 Exchanges. If a U.S. person transfers property to a foreign corporation in a Code Sec. 361 exchange (¶ 2205), the exceptions above will generally not apply and the transferor will recognize gain under the outbound transfer rules (Code Sec. 367(a)(5); Reg. § 1.367(a)-3(e)). However, recognition of gain only applies if the transferring corporation is controlled by five or fewer domestic corporations, and basis adjustment and other conditions provided in the regulations are met.

Transfers of Intangible Property. A U.S. person is generally required to recognize income on outbound transfers of intangible property to a foreign corporation if the transfer occurs in a Code Sec. 351 or Code Sec. 361 exchange (Code Sec. 367(d)). For this purpose, intangible property includes:

- patent, invention, formula, process, design, pattern, or know-how;

- copyright or literary, musical, or artistic composition;

- trademark, trade name, or brand name;

- franchise, license, or contract;

- method, program, system, procedure, campaign, survey, study, forecast, estimate, customer list, or technical data;

- any goodwill, going concern value, or workforce in place (including its composition and terms and conditions (contractual or otherwise) of its employment), for transfers in tax years beginning after 2017; or

- any other item the value or potential value of which is not attributable to tangible property or the services of any individual.

2493. Transfers of Property to Foreign Trusts. Any U.S. person that transfers property to a foreign trust (other than the trust of an employee benefits plan or tax-exempt organization) with a U.S. beneficiary (¶ 588) is treated as the owner of the portion of the trust attributable to the property (Code Sec. 679; Reg. § 1.679-1). If the transferor and another person would be treated as owner of the same portion of the trust, then the U.S. transferor will be treated as the owner. Thus, any income received by the trust with respect to the property is taxable to the transferor under the grantor trust rules (¶ 571).

This rule applies without regard to whether the transferor retains any power or interest in the property. It also applies regardless of whether the transfer is direct or indirect. Exceptions exist for foreign trusts established by a will, transfers made by reason of death of the U.S. person (transferor), or transfers of property to the foreign trust in exchange for consideration equal to its fair market value. A U.S. person who is treated as the owner of any portion of a foreign trust under the grantor trust rules is required to ensure that the trust files an annual information return on Form 3520-A and furnishes the required annual statements to its U.S. owners and beneficiaries, or be subject to a penalty (Code Secs. 6048(b) and 6677(a)). Certain exceptions from reporting may apply, including transactions with, or ownership of, a tax-favored foreign trust (Rev. Proc. 2020-17).

2494. Information Reporting on Foreign Partnerships. A number of reporting requirements apply with respect to foreign partnerships. First, a foreign partnership must file a U.S. partnership return (Form 1065) if it has gross income that is either U.S. source income (¶ 2427) or income effectively connected with a U.S. trade or business (¶ 2429) (Code Sec. 6031(e)). A U.S. partner cannot claim distributive shares of any partnership deduction, loss, or credit if a partnership return is not filed, generally applicable for returns filed for partnership tax years beginning on or before December 31, 2017 (Code Sec. 6231(f), prior to amendment by P.L. 114-74).

Second, every U.S. person that controls a foreign partnership (more than 50 percent interest) is required to file an annual information return on Form 8865 with their income tax return (¶ 2487). Additionally, any U.S. person that owns at least a 10-percent interest in a foreign partnership must report on Form 8865 any changes to his or her ownership in the partnership during the tax year (Code Secs. 6046A and 6679). Failure to file Form 8865 will result in a $10,000 penalty per occurrence.

A U.S. person who transfers property to a foreign partnership in a nontaxable transfer must report the transaction on Form 8865 if the U.S. person has a at least a 10-percent interest in the partnership or the value of the property transferred exceeds $100,000 (Code Sec. 6038B; 1.6038B-2). A U.S. person must report on Form 8865 any transfer of property with built-in gain to a foreign partnership with a foreign partner if the gain deferral method is applied (¶ 443). The U.S. person also must report for each subsequent tax year to which the gain deferral method is applied, even if the gain deferral contributions with respect to that property occurred before 2018 (Reg. § 1.721(c)-6).

Other Foreign Tax Rules

2495. Foreign Currency Transactions. All federal income tax determinations must be made in the taxpayer's functional currency (Code Sec. 985). The functional currency of a U.S. taxpayer generally is the U.S. dollar. In the case of a qualified business unit (QBU), the functional currency is the currency in which the taxpayer conducts a significant part of its activities and which is used in keeping books and records. For this purpose, a QBU is any separate and clearly identified unit of a trade or business of the taxpayer which maintains its own books and records (for example, a foreign subsidiary of a U.S. corporation or a foreign corporation) (Code Sec. 989). Special rules apply in determining when foreign earnings and profits and foreign income taxes must be translated into U.S. dollars, as well as the use of a foreign branch of a U.S. taxpayer (Code Secs. 986 and 987; Reg. § 1.987-1).

Foreign currency gain or loss attributable to a nonfunctional currency transaction is treated separately from the underlying transaction. It is generally treated as ordinary gain or loss but is not treated as interest income or expenses (Code Sec. 988). However, gain of an individual from the disposition of foreign currency in a personal transaction is not taxable, provided that the gain realized does not exceed $200. A personal transaction is any transaction other than one with respect to which properly allocable expenses are deductible as trade or business expenses or expenses incurred in the production of income. It also refers to an individual's currency exchange transactions that are entered into in connection with business travel but do not affect tax treatment of capital losses (¶ 1754).

2496. International Boycotts. Participation by a taxpayer in, or cooperation with, an international boycott will result in the reduction or denial of the foreign tax credit (¶ 2475), the deferral of tax allowed to foreign subsidiaries (¶ 2485), and the deferral of tax allowed to domestic international sales corporation (DISC) shareholders (¶ 2498) (Code Secs. 908 and 999; Temp. Reg. § 7.999-1). The amount of the benefits to be denied is determined from the ratio of the value of the sales or purchases of goods and services (or other transactions) arising from the boycott activity to the total value of the foreign sales or purchases of goods and services (or other transactions).

Participation in or cooperation with an international boycott occurs when a person, in order to do business in a certain country, agrees not to do business with a specified second country or with other countries doing business in specified countries. An agreement not to hire employees of, or to do business with, other companies whose employees are of a specified nationality, race, or religion is also boycott activity. The following countries may require participation in, or cooperation with, an international boycott: Iraq, Kuwait, Lebanon, Libya, Qatar, Saudi Arabia, Syria, United Arab Emirates, and the Republic of Yemen (Instructions to Form 5713; Boycott Notice, April 8, 2020). Taxpayers who participate in or cooperate with a boycott and derive income from such activities must report such information to the IRS by filing Form 5713 when their income tax return is due, including extensions.

2497. Illegal Payments. If an illegal bribe, kickback, or other payment is made by, or on behalf of, a controlled foreign corporation (CFC) (¶ 2487) or domestic international sales corporation (DISC) (¶ 2498) either directly or indirectly to an official, employee, or agent-in-fact of a foreign government, the amount of the bribe, kickback or other payment will affect shareholders. In the case of a CFC, the amount is included as subpart F income for the year (¶ 2488) and thus is included in the shareholder's income (Code Sec. 952(a)(4)). In the case of a DISC, the amount is considered a constructive dividend and must be included in the shareholder's income (Code Sec. 995(b)(1)(F)(iii)). However, such payments may be deductible in certain circumstances, despite their possible illegality (¶ 972).

2498. IC-DISCs. A percentage of income generated through an interest-charge domestic international sales corporation (IC-DISC) can be deferred for U.S. tax purposes. The IC-DISC provisions, which are geared toward small businesses, limit the income deferred by shareholders and require that an interest charge be paid on the deferred amounts (Code Sec. 995). The election to be treated as an interest-charge DISC is made on Form 4876-A.

2499. Information from Foreign Sources. The IRS may make a formal document request for foreign records if the normal summons procedure fails to produce the requested documentation (Code Sec. 982). The request for formal documentation supplements the administrative summons procedure and does not prevent the use of any other Code provisions to obtain documents.

24 FOREIGN

Chapter 25

RETURNS □ PAYMENT OF TAXES

Filing Returns

See CCH® AnswerConnect: *Filing Returns and Paying Taxes* for more information on this topic.

2501. Income Tax Returns—Types of Returns. Individuals who must file income tax returns generally use Form 1040 along with any appropriate schedules. The following specialized income tax return forms for individuals also exist: Form 1040-SR for an individual age 65 or older; Form 1040-C for a departing alien; Form 1040-NR or Form 1040-NR-EZ for a nonresident alien; Form 1040-SS (self-employment) for a resident of the Virgin Islands, Guam, American Samoa or the Northern Mariana Islands; and Form 1040-PR or 1040-SS (self-employment) for a resident of Puerto Rico.

Fiduciaries of estates and trusts who must file income tax returns use Form 1041. Partnerships must file information returns on Form 1065. Corporations must file income tax returns on Form 1120, and entities covered by an S corporation election must file Form 1120-S.

Specialized forms for certain types of corporations also exist, including: Schedule PH, attached to Form 1120 for a U.S. personal holding company; Schedule UTP, attached to the Form 1120 series return for a corporation with at least $10 million in assets that has taken an uncertain tax position; Form 1120-C for a cooperative association; Form 1120-F for a foreign corporation; Form 1120-FSC for a foreign sales corporation; Form 1120-H for a homeowners association; Form 1120-IC-DISC for an interest charge domestic international sales corporation; Form 1120-L for a life insurance company; Form 1120-ND for a nuclear decommissioning fund; Form 1120-PC for a property and casualty insurance company; Form 1120-POL for a political organization; Form 1120-REIT for a real estate investment trust; Form 1120-RIC for a regulated investment company; Form 1120-SF for a settlement fund.

Rules for determining which individuals must file an income tax return are at ¶ 101; rules for determining which individuals must pay estimated tax are at ¶ 125; rules for corporation returns are at ¶ 211; rules for S corporations are at ¶ 351; rules applicable to partners and partnerships are at ¶ 406; and rules for estates and trusts are at ¶ 510.

Employers must file quarterly returns on Form 941 to report (1) wages paid to employees and income tax withheld on the wages and tips employees have received, (2) both the employer's and the employee's share of Social Security and Medicare taxes, and (3) additional Medicare taxes withheld from employees (¶ 2650). Certain small employers with an estimated employment tax liability of $1,000 or less may instead file an annual return on Form 944. Employers who pay wages for agricultural labor must file Form 943. In addition, employers must file Form 940 annually to report and pay federal unemployment taxes.

Individuals who pay annual cash wages of at least $2,100 in 2019 ($2,200 in 2020) to a household employee for domestic services in their private homes must file Schedule H (Form 1040) to report and pay both the employer and employee share of Social Security and Medicare taxes, and any income tax withheld at the employee's request. Individuals also use Schedule H to pay and report federal unemployment taxes if they paid total cash wages of $1,000 or more to all household employees in any calendar quarter of the current or previous year (¶ 2652) (IRS Pub. 926).

2503. Electronic Filing of Returns. The IRS is required to promote electronic filing and is authorized to issue regulations providing standards for determining which returns must be filed electronically (i.e., magnetic media) (Code Sec. 6011(e), as amended by the Taxpayer First Act (P.L. 116-25); Code Sec. 6011(f)). The regulations may require any person to file returns electronically (e-file) if the person is required to file at least the applicable number of returns during the calendar year: 250 returns for calendar years before 2021, 100 returns for calendar year 2021, 10 returns for calendar years after 2021. The regulations generally may not require e-filing of income tax returns of individuals, trusts, or estates, but an exception is provided for specified tax return preparers that expect to file 11 or more income tax returns during the calendar year. Additional rules apply to partnerships, corporations, and tax-exempt organizations.

Electronic filing is the only acceptable method to file returns when required. A taxpayer can e-file using commercial tax preparation software, a paid preparer, or an authorized e-file provider. Individual taxpayers who meet certain adjusted gross income requirements may prepare and e-file their returns for free through the Free File program (https://www.irs.gov/filing/free-file-do-your-federal-taxes-for-free). A Fillable Tax Forms option is also available that allows all taxpayers to fill out and file their tax forms electronically. Form 8453 is used to transmit certain forms and supporting paper documents that are required to be submitted to the IRS with e-filed returns.

Specified Tax Return Preparers. Any income tax return prepared by a specified tax return preparer for an individual, estate, or trust must be filed electronically if the return is filed by the preparer (Code Sec. 6011(e)(3), as amended by P.L. 116-25; Reg. §301.6011-7). A specified tax return preparer is any tax return preparer (¶2517) unless he or she reasonably expects to file 10 or fewer individual income tax returns during the calendar year. A return is considered "filed" if the preparer submits the return to the IRS on the taxpayer's behalf. A return is not considered filed if the preparer obtains a hand-signed and dated statement from the taxpayer that the taxpayer chooses to file the return on paper and that the taxpayer, and not the preparer, will submit the paper return to the IRS.

Effective July 1, 2019, the IRS may waive the e-filing requirement for a specified tax return preparer unable to file electronically due to limited internet availability in the geographic location where the preparer's business is operated. The IRS may also grant waivers of the e-filing requirement in cases of undue hardship (Reg. §301.6011-7(c); Rev. Proc. 2011-25). Requests for a hardship waiver are made by filing Form 8944 before the preparer would otherwise be required to file. Additional automatic exemptions from the e-filing requirement are available to certain classes of specified tax return preparers (for example, members of certain religious groups, foreign preparers without Social Security numbers, returns currently not accepted electronically, etc.) (Notice 2011-26). Form 8948 is used to explain why an individual tax return that was able to be filed electronically was filed in a paper format.

Partnerships. IRS regulations may require a partnership to file Form 1065 electronically (¶406) if the partnership files:

- 200 or more returns for calendar year 2018,

- 150 or more returns for calendar year 2019,

- 100 or more returns for calendar year 2020,

- 50 or more returns for calendar year 2021, and

- 10 or more returns for calendar years after 2021 (Code Sec. 6011(e)(5), as added by P.L. 116-25).

Notwithstanding these thresholds, a partnership with more than 100 partners is required to file Form 1065 electronically, along with the corresponding Schedule K-1s and all other related forms and schedules (Code Sec. 6011(e)(6), as added by P.L. 116-25; Reg. §301.6011-3). A partnership has more than 100 partners if, over the course of the partnership's tax year, the partnership had more than 100 partners, regardless of whether a partner was a partner for the entire year or whether the partnership had over 100 partners on any day during the year. The IRS may waive the electronic filing requirement if a partnership can demonstrate undue economic hardship.

Corporations. A corporation (C or S corporation) with assets of $10 million or more must file Form 1120 or Form 1120-S electronically (¶211 and ¶351) if the corporation is required to file at least 250 returns during a calendar year before 2021 (Reg. §§301.6011-5 and 301.6037-2). This requirement generally applies to all forms in the 1120 and 1120-S series, including amended and superseding returns. A corporation's assets are determined based on the total assets at the end of the tax year as reported on the return. The determination of whether a corporation is required to file electronically is made by aggregating all returns, regardless of type, that the corporation is required to file during the calendar year (for example, income tax returns, information returns, excise tax returns, and employment tax returns). The IRS may waive the electronic filing requirement if the corporation can demonstrate undue economic hardship (Notice 2010-13).

Tax-Exempt Organizations. For tax years beginning after July 1, 2019, a tax-exempt organization must file its annual information return (¶ 625) on Form 990 or Form 990-PF electronically (Code Sec. 6033(n), as added by P.L. 116-25; Reg. §301.6033-4). For tax years beginning on or before July 1, 2019, a tax-exempt corporation with assets of $10 million or more that files Form 990, and a private foundation or charitable trust that files Form 990-PF (regardless of assets), must file its return electronically. For tax years beginning after July 1, 2019, a tax-exempt organization subject to tax on its unrelated business taxable income must file Form 990-T electronically (¶ 658) (Code Sec. 6011(h), as added by P.L. 116-25).

Information Returns. Any person that is required to file certain information returns (¶ 2565) with the IRS must file them electronically if it is required to file at least 250 returns during a calendar year before 2021 (Reg. §301.6011-2; IRS Pub. 1220). The 250-return threshold applies separately to each type of return and separately to each type of corrected return. All persons that use the same taxpayer identification number (TIN) are treated as one filer for this purpose. Form 8508 is used to request a waiver from the e-filing requirement for information returns. E-filing of information returns is done on the Filing Information Returns Electronically (FIRE) system, at https://fire.irs.gov. A filer must request IRS authorization to file electronically by submitting Form 4419 at least 45 days before the due date of the return.

Withholding on Foreign Transfers. A financial institution must electronically file returns with respect to withheld taxes for which the institution is liable as a withholding agent under the nonresident alien and foreign corporation withholding rules (¶ 2455), or under the foreign account withholding rules (¶ 2469). This rule applies even if the financial institution does not file the applicable number of returns normally required for electronic filing during the calendar year (Code Sec. 6011(e)(4)).

2504. Signatures on Returns. Any return, document, or statement required to be made under the Internal Revenue Code must be signed in accordance with the appropriate forms or regulations, except for corporation and partnership returns (Code Sec. 6061; Reg. §1.6061-1). Thus, an individual return generally must be signed personally by the taxpayer. In the case of married individuals filing a joint return, both spouses must sign. If the taxpayer did not prepare the return, the return must be signed by the taxpayer and the tax return preparer (¶ 2517). If a decedent's return is filed by a representative, the representative should sign the return on the line indicated for the taxpayer and attach a written power of attorney. A taxpayer who files his or her tax return electronically must use an electronic signature (¶ 2503). All returns filed with the IRS must contain a declaration that they are made under the penalties of perjury (Code Sec. 6065).

2505. Income Tax Returns—When to File. Every taxpayer subject to federal income tax must file an income tax return by the required due date listed below. The IRS may grant a taxpayer an extension of the due date for filing an income tax return (¶ 2509). The due date is extended if it falls on Saturday, Sunday or legal holiday (¶ 2549). The filing deadline also may postponed for a taxpayer affected by a federally declared disaster or a military or terrorist action.

The due date for filing federal income tax returns and tax payments, including estimated taxes, otherwise due on or after April 1, 2020, and before July 15, 2020, is extended to July 15, 2020, due to the COVID-19 (coronavirus) crisis (Notice 2020-23, amplifying Notice 2020-18). The extension applies not only the taxpayer's income tax return, but also any schedule, return, or other form that is either required to be filed as an attachment or filed by the due date of the form. Any election that is required to be made on any the return is will be considered timely made if filed with the form or attachment by July 15, 2020. The extension is automatic and the taxpayer does not need to file any form or otherwise contact the IRS to receive it. Any penalty, addition to tax, or interest for failure to file a return will not accrue until July 16, 2020, as a result of the extension.

Individuals, Estates, and Trusts. The income tax return of an individual (Form 1040), or an estate or a trust (Form 1041) is due on or before the 15th day of the *fourth* month following the close of the tax year (April 15 for a calendar-year taxpayer) (Code Sec. 6072(a); Reg. § 1.6072-1). The final income tax return of a decedent for a fractional part of a year is due on the same date as would apply had the taxpayer lived the entire year (i.e., the 15th day of the fourth month following the close of the 12-month period that began on the first day of the fractional year).

Partnerships. A partnership's income tax return (Form 1065) is generally due on or before the 15th day of the *third* month following the close of the tax year (March 15 for a calendar-year partnership) (Code Sec. 6072(b); Reg. § 1.6031(a)-1).

S Corporations. An S corporation's income tax return (Form 1120-S) is due on or before the 15th day of the *third* month following the close of the tax year (March 15 for a calendar-year S corporation) (Code Sec. 6072(b); Reg. § 1.6072-2(a)).

C Corporations. A domestic C corporation or a foreign C corporation having a U.S. office generally must file its U.S. income tax return (Form 1120) on or before the 15th day of the *fourth* month following the close of the tax year (April 15 for a calendar-year corporation) (Code Sec. 6072; Reg. § 1.6072-2(a)). However, for tax years beginning before January 1, 2026, the return of a C corporation with a fiscal tax year ending on June 30 must be filed on or before the 15th day of the *third* month following the close of the tax year (Act Sec. 2006(a)(3)(B) of the Surface Transportation and Veterans Health Care Choice Improvement Act of 2015 (P.L. 114-41)). If the last day of a C corporation's tax year does not end on the last day of a month (as in the case of a dissolved corporation whose tax year ends on the date of dissolution), the return is due on or before the 15th day of the third or fourth full month (depending on the tax year) following the date of dissolution. These due date rules also apply to a corporation whose foreign sales corporation election is still in effect (Instructions for Form 1120-FSC).

The return of an interest charge domestic international sales corporation (IC-DISC), an exempt farmers' cooperative, or other cooperative organization is due on or before the 15th day of the *ninth* month following the close of the tax year (September 15 for a calendar-year taxpayer) (Reg. § 1.6072-2(d) and (e)).

Tax-Exempt Organizations. The due date for the return of a tax-exempt organization (other than an employees' trust under Code Sec. 401(a)) subject to the unrelated business income tax (¶ 655 and ¶ 658) is the 15th day of the *fifth* month following the close of the tax year (May 15 for a calendar-year organization) (Reg. § 1.6072-2(c)).

Nonresident Aliens and Foreign Corporations. The due date for an income tax return of a nonresident alien who is not subject to income tax withholding on wages (¶ 2601), and a foreign corporation not having an office or place of business in the United States, is the 15th day of the *sixth* month after the close of the tax year (June 15 for a calendar-year taxpayer) (Code Sec. 6072(c); Reg. §§ 1.6072-1(c) and 1.6072-2(b)). A nonresident alien who has wages subject to income tax withholding is required to file a return on or before the 15th day of the *fourth* month following the close of the tax year (April 15 for a calendar-year taxpayer).

Amended Returns. A taxpayer may correct an error in a return, without incurring penalties and interest, by filing an amended return and paying any additional tax due on or before the last day prescribed for filing the original return. An amended return filed after the due date may be accepted, rejected, or ignored by the IRS in its sole discretion. In the absence of an abuse of discretion, the courts will not grant relief to the taxpayer for the IRS's action (*G. Colvin*, CA-5 (unpub. op.), 2005-1 USTC ¶ 50,192). A taxpayer claiming a credit or refund generally must file an amended return within the applicable limitations period (¶ 2763) (Instructions for Form 1040-X).

2509. Extension of Time to File Returns. The IRS may grant a taxpayer an extension of the due date for filing a tax return, declaration, statement, or other document (¶ 2505) (Code Sec. 6081; Reg. § 1.6081-1). The filing deadline may also be postponed for a taxpayer affected by a federally declared disaster or a military or terrorist action. An extension to file a return generally does not extend the time to pay the tax (¶ 2529), and penalties and interest may apply (¶ 2805). Exceptions apply if the taxpayer elects to have the IRS compute the tax, the taxpayer resides outside the United States, or payment of tax on the return due date would result in undue hardship.

The due date for filing federal tax returns otherwise due on or after April 1, 2020, and before July 15, 2020, is extended to July 15, 2020, due to the COVID-19 (coronavirus) crisis. The extension applies to any schedule, return, or other form that is filed as attachment with the taxpayer's return (Notice 2020-23, amplifying Notice 2020-18). The extension is automatic and applies to all taxpayers including individuals, trusts and estates, corporations and other non-corporate entities. A taxpayer does not need to file any form or otherwise contact the IRS to receive the extension. Any taxpayer who needs additional time to file a return after July 15, 2020, may file the appropriate extension form by July 15, 2020. Any additional extension will not go beyond the original extension due date (for example, October 15, 2020, for an individual). Any penalty, addition to tax, or interest for failure to file will not accrue until July 16, 2020, as a result of the extension.

Individuals. An individual obtains an automatic extension of *six months* to file an income tax return by filing Form 4868 on or before the normal due date of his or her return (Reg. § 1.6081-4). The filing extension can be obtained without making tax payments, so long as the taxpayer properly estimates his or her tax liability. Otherwise, the extension request will be denied and penalties and interest may apply for any late payment. If the amount of tax included with the extension request is less than sufficient to cover the taxpayer's liability, the taxpayer will be charged interest on the overdue amount. No late-payment penalty is imposed if the income tax paid through withholding and estimated tax payments. The penalty also does apply if any payment accompanying Form 4868 is at least 90 percent of the total tax due on the taxpayer's return and if the remaining unpaid balance is paid with the return within the extension period (¶ 2805). An automatic extension should not be requested if the taxpayer has asked the IRS to compute the tax or if the taxpayer is under a court order to file the return by the original due date.

Corporations. A corporation obtains an automatic extension of *six months* to file its income tax return (Form 1120) by filing Form 7004 on or before its normal due date of the return, provided it pays the full amount of estimated tax liability on the return (Code Sec. 6081(b); Reg. § 1.6081-3). Although the statutory language provides only a *five-month* automatic extension for a C corporation with a tax year ending on December 31 and beginning before January 1, 2026, the IRS will grant a *six-month* extension to the corporation. In the case of a C corporation with a fiscal year ending on June 30 and beginning before January 1, 2026, the maximum extension allowed is *seven months*.

Partnerships, Estates, and Trusts. A partnership obtains an automatic extension of *six months* to file its income tax return on Form 1065, as well as Form 8804 to report the withholding of tax for a foreign partner, by filing Form 7004 on or before the normal due date of the return (Reg. § 1.6081-2).

An estate or a trust obtains an automatic extension of *five-and-a-half months* to file its income tax return on Form 1041 by filing Form 7004 on or before the normal due date of the return (Reg. § 1.6081-6).

Taxpayers Outside the United States. Certain taxpayers outside the United States are granted an automatic extension of *six months* following the close of the tax year (June 15 for a calendar-year taxpayer) for filing income tax returns *and* payment of income tax. The extension applies to: (1) a U.S. citizen or resident living outside the United States and Puerto Rico, including individuals in military or naval service, (2) certain partnerships and domestic corporations that keep records outside of the United States and Puerto Rico, (3) domestic corporations whose principal income is from sources within U.S. possessions, and (4) foreign corporations that maintain an office or place of business within the United States (Reg. § 1.6081-5).

To qualify for the extension, a statement must be attached to the taxpayer's return showing that the person is eligible for the extension. The extension must be requested on or before the 15th day of the sixth month following the close of the tax year and the appropriate box must be checked on Form 4868 or Form 7004. The extension runs concurrently with the automatic extension normally allowed to the taxpayer. For example, the maximum extension for an individual is only six months (October 15 for a calendar-year individual), unless the individual files Form 2350 because he or she needs extra time to qualify for the foreign earned income exclusion or the foreign housing exclusion or deduction.

Other Entities. Any entity required to file the following returns obtains an automatic filing extension of *six months* by filing Form 8868 on or before the normal due date of the return: Form 990 series, Form 1041-A, Form 4720, Form 5227, Form 6069, and Form 8870 (Reg. § 1.6081-9). Any entity required to file the following returns obtains an automatic filing extension of *six months* by filing Form 7004 on or before the normal due date of the return: Form 1120-POL, Form 1066, and Form 8831 (Reg. § 1.6081-7; Reg. § 1.6081-9(b)).

2513. Place for Filing Paper Returns. An individual, estate, or trust that elects to file a paper return must file it with the IRS service center indicated in the instructions to the taxpayer's return, except for certain charitable and split-interest trusts and pooled-income funds (Instructions for Form 1040; Instructions for Form 1041).

A corporation, S corporation, or partnership that files a paper return must file it with the IRS service center indicated in the instructions to the entity's return (Instructions for Form 1120; Instructions for Form 1120-S; Instructions for Form 1065).

The place to file certain elections, statements, returns and other documents can be found at the IRS website, at https://www.irs.gov/filing/where-to-file-certain-elections-statements-returns-and-other-documents (Notice 2010-53).

2517. Tax Return Preparers. A person who prepares for compensation, or employs other persons to prepare for compensation, all or a substantial portion of *any* tax return or refund claim is a "tax return preparer" (Code Sec. 7701(a)(36); Reg. § 301.7701-15). Preparers are divided into two categories for purposes of the return preparer penalties (¶ 2807): signing tax return preparers and nonsigning tax return preparers. A signing tax return preparer is the individual preparer with primary responsibility for the overall substantive accuracy of the preparation of tax returns or refund claims. A nonsigning tax return preparer is any preparer who is not a signing tax return preparer but who prepares a substantial portion of a return or refund claim regarding events that have occurred at the time advice is rendered.

In addition to the prohibition against disclosure of return information (¶ 2894), a tax return preparer is subject to the following rules:

- The signing tax return preparer must sign a tax return electronically using a Self-Select Personal Identification Number (PIN) or a Practitioner PIN (IRS Pub. 1345). The preparer need not sign an electronic return before presenting a completed copy to the taxpayer, but must furnish all information that will be transmitted as the electronically signed return to the taxpayer at the same time that the preparer furnishes Form 8878, Form 8879, or a similar IRS e-file signature form. The signing tax return preparer must actually sign a paper return after its completion but before its presentation to the taxpayer for signature (Code Sec. 6695(b); Reg. § 1.6695-1(b)). Paper returns require the preparer to manually sign the return or use any of three alternative methods that include either a facsimile of the preparer's signature or the individual preparer's printed name: rubber stamp, mechanical device, or computer software program (Notice 2004-54; Notice 2007-79).

- The signing tax return preparer must include his or her identifying number on the taxpayer's return after its completion but before its presentation to the taxpayer. The identifying number is the individual's preparer tax identification number (PTIN) or other number prescribed by the IRS. If the preparer is employed by another person, the employer must furnish the identifying numbers of both the employer and the employee-preparer (Code Sec. 6109(a)(4); Reg. § 1.6109-2; Notice 2011-6).

- The signing tax return preparer must provide the taxpayer with a completed copy of the prepared return, in either paper or electronic form, no later than the time the original return is presented for signing. The copy must be in any media acceptable to both the taxpayer and the preparer, and must include all information submitted to the IRS to enable the taxpayer to determine what schedules, forms, electronic files, and other supporting materials have been filed. The copy need not contain the identification number of the paid tax return preparer. The signing tax return preparer must also keep, for three years following the close of the return period, a copy of the return (in either paper or electronic form) or a list of the names, identification numbers, and tax years of taxpayers for whom returns were prepared, and the name of the individual tax return preparer required to sign the return (Code Sec. 6107; Reg. § 1.6107-1). The preparer need not sign the taxpayer's copy of the return.

- If a tax return preparer, or any person, employs any signing tax return preparer to prepare returns for other persons (i.e., not the employer's return), the preparer must keep a record, for three years following the close of the return period to which the record relates, of the name, taxpayer identification number (TIN), and principal place of work of each tax return preparer employed by the preparer at any time during the return period (Code Sec. 6060; Reg. § 1.6060-1). Any individual signing tax return preparer who is not employed by another preparer is treated as his or her own employer. The return period is the 12-month period beginning on July 1 of each year.

PTIN Requirement. All tax return preparers must have a PTIN or other prescribed identifying number that was applied for and received in the manner prescribed by the IRS. To obtain a PTIN, a tax return preparer must be an attorney, certified public accountant (CPA), enrolled agent, or registered tax return preparer authorized to practice before the IRS (Reg. § 1.6109-2(d); Notice 2011-6). The IRS also allows individuals who are 18 years old or older, but are not one of these specific types of professionals, to obtain a PTIN if:

- the individual is supervised by an attorney, CPA, enrolled agent, enrolled retirement plan agent, or enrolled actuary authorized to practice before the IRS under Circular 230 § 10.3(a)-(e);

- the supervising attorney, CPA, enrolled agent, enrolled retirement plan agent, or enrolled actuary signs the tax returns or refund claims prepared by the individual;

- the individual is employed at the law firm, CPA firm, or other recognized firm of the tax return preparer who signs the tax return or refund claim; or

- the individual passes the requisite tax compliance check and suitability check when available.

The IRS was barred from continuing its registered tax return preparer program because it lacked the statutory authority to regulate tax return preparers. The injunction does not affect the requirement for all paid tax return preparers to obtain a PTIN (*S. Loving,* CA D.C., 2014-1 ustc ¶ 50,175).

The PTIN can be obtained or renewed online at http://www.irs.gov/Tax-Professionals/PTIN-Requirements-for-Tax-Return-Preparers. Alternatively, a paper application may be submitted on Form W-12. A U.S. citizen or foreign person without a Social Security number must also submit Form 8945 or Form 8946 with their application. All PTINs must be renewed on a calendar year basis. The renewal period begins after October 15 and runs through December 31 of the calendar year. PTINs obtained or renewed during the calendar year will expire on December 31 of the calendar year. The IRS requires tax return preparers to pay a user fee to obtain and renew a PTIN. A federal appeals court has ruled that the IRS has the authority to charge a user fee to obtain or renew a PTIN (*B. Montrois,* CA-D.C. 2019-1 ustc ¶ 50,164).

Voluntary Certification Program. The IRS has established a voluntary certification program, the Annual Filing Season Program (AFSP), designed to encourage unenrolled tax preparers to complete continuing education courses for the purpose of increasing his or her knowledge of relevant federal tax law necessary for preparation of tax returns (Rev. Proc. 2014-42, modifying and superseding Rev. Proc. 81-38). The voluntary program neither restricts any individual from preparing and signing tax returns or claims for refund, nor changes the requirement that paid tax return preparers must obtain a PTIN. Upon successful completion each year of certain requirements, the IRS will issue a Record of Completion that is only valid for tax returns or claims for refund prepared and signed during the calendar year for which it has been issued. Thus, a Record of Completion is valid from the later of January 1 of the year covered by the Record of Completion or the date the Record of Completion is issued until December 31st of that year. The application for a Record of Completion is made on Form W-12 and all applications must be received no later than April 15th of the year for which it is sought.

Unenrolled tax return preparers who obtain an AFSP Record of Completion are permitted to represent taxpayers before the IRS during examination of tax returns and refund claims that he or she prepared and signed, or prepared if there is no signature space on the form, provided the individual had a valid Record of Completion for the year the return or claim of refund was prepared and a valid Record of Completion for the year or years in which the representation occurs. The representation is limited to exams, and the individual may not appear before an appeals officer, a revenue officer, Counsel, or similar IRS officer or employee.

2523. Requirement to Keep Books and Records. Taxpayers are required to keep accurate, permanent books and records to be able to determine the various types of income, gains, losses, costs, expenses, and other amounts that affect their income tax liability for the year (Reg. § 1.6001-1(a)). The records must be retained for as long as they may be, or may become, "material" for any federal tax purpose. Records that support an item of income or a deduction on a tax return generally should be kept at least for the period of limitation for that return. See ¶ 2726 for the general statute of limitations, as well as ¶ 2732 for limitations period for false returns, ¶ 2733 for limitation period for listed transactions, and ¶ 2734 for limitations period for omissions over 25 percent of income.

Payment of Taxes

See CCH® AnswerConnect: *Installment Payment Agreements* and *Extensions to File Returns and Pay Taxes* for more information on this topic.

2525. Place for Paying Tax. The amount of tax owed as shown on a return of an individual, estate, or trust must be paid to the IRS service center indicated in the instructions to the return (¶ 2513). The IRS requests that an individual use a payment voucher, Form 1040-V, for any balance due on any Forms 1040. See ¶ 2545 regarding electronic funds withdrawal. In the case of a corporation, the tax must be deposited using electronic funds transfer (Code Sec. 6151(a); Reg. § 1.6302-1).

2529. Time for Paying Tax. The tax shown on an income tax return generally must be paid, without assessment or notice and demand, at the time fixed for filing the return (¶ 2505) (Code Sec. 6151; Reg. § 1.6151-1). An extension of time for filing a tax return ordinarily does not postpone the time for payment. Exceptions apply when:

- a taxpayer shows that payment on the return due date will result in undue hardship (¶ 2537);

- a taxpayer is residing outside the United States on the return due date (¶ 2509); or

- a taxpayer elects to have the IRS compute the tax (¶ 105), in which case payment is due within 30 days after the IRS mails a notice and demand.

The due date for filing federal income tax returns and tax payments, including estimated taxes, otherwise due on or after April 1, 2020, and before July 15, 2020, is extended to July 15, 2020, due to the COVID-19 (coronavirus) crisis (Notice 2020-23, amplifying Notice 2020-18). The extension applies not only the taxpayer's income tax return, but also any schedule, return, or other form that is either required to be filed as an attachment or filed by the due date of the form. Any election that is required to be made on the return is considered timely made if filed with the form or attachment by July 15, 2020. The extension is automatic and the taxpayer does not need to file any form or otherwise contact the IRS to receive it. Any penalty, addition to tax, or interest for failure to file a return will not accrue until July 16, 2020, as a result of the extension.

Installment Agreements. The IRS is authorized to enter into a written agreement with the taxpayer, allowing for the full or partial payment of any tax in installments, if such an agreement will facilitate the collection of a tax liability (Code Sec. 6159). For a taxpayer with $50,000 or less in combined tax liability, penalties, and interest, an interactive Online Payment Agreement (OPA) application is available on the IRS website for requesting an installment agreement. Otherwise, a taxpayer can request an installment agreement by filing Form 9465.

For installment agreements entered into on or after January 1, 2017, the IRS charges a taxpayer a $225 user fee, reduced to $107 for a taxpayer who pays the agreement by direct debit from their bank account. Alternatively, the user fee is $149 for a taxpayer who applies for an installment agreement through the OPA application process. The user fee is only $31 for a taxpayer who applies through the OPA process and pays by direct debit. The user fee for a low-income taxpayer is $43, but is reduced to $31 if the taxpayer applies through the OPA process and pays by direct debit (Reg. § 300.1(b)). The user fee for restructuring and reinstating an installment agreement is $89 (Reg. § 300.2(b)). The IRS is prohibited from increasing user fees for installment agreements entered into on or after April 10, 2018. The user fee is also waived for a low-income taxpayer who agrees to make automated installment payments through a debit account. A low-income taxpayer unable to make automatic payments through a debit account will be reimbursed for the user fee upon completion of the installment agreement (Code Sec. 6159(f)).

There are four types of installment agreements. The first type is the *guaranteed installment agreement,* which must be accepted by the IRS if an individual taxpayer's tax liabilities, without regard to interest, penalties, additions to tax, and any other additional amounts, total $10,000 or less and certain other conditions are met (Code Sec. 6159(c)). The second type is the *streamlined installment agreement,* which may be used by an individual who does not qualify for the guaranteed agreement, or by a business. The taxpayer must owe no more than $50,000, without regard to interest, penalties, additions to tax, or any other additions, and agree to pay the amount due in full within six years (IRM 5.14.5.2). For liabilities of $25,000 or less, the IRS generally will not require taxpayers to disclose any financial information. For liabilities greater than $25,000 but not more than $50,000, the IRS requires taxpayers to disclose certain information. To qualify for the streamlined agreement for amounts owed of $25,001 to $50,000, a taxpayer must agree to make payments via direct debit from a bank account.

The third type of installment agreement is the *in-business trust fund express agreement,* which is available to a business with trust fund liabilities, such as employment taxes. The total balance may not exceed $25,000 and generally must be paid within 24 months. No financial statement is required, and the IRS does not determine any trust fund recovery penalty. The fourth type of installment agreement is available to a taxpayer owing more than $50,000 of income taxes. The taxpayer must file an installment agreement request on Form 9465 and attach a completed collection information statement. These agreements are accepted on a case-by-case basis if the IRS determines the taxpayer can eventually pay off the debt, and the agreement will facilitate the collection of the debt.

2533. Taxes of Armed Forces Member upon Death. The tax liability of a member of the U.S. Armed Forces is forgiven in the tax year the individual dies: (1) while in active service in a combat zone (¶ 895), (2) from wounds, disease, or injury incurred while serving in a combat zone, or (3) from wounds or injury incurred in a terrorist or military action (IRS Pub. 3). Any unpaid taxes of the individual that relate to tax years prior to service in a combat zone may also be abated. In the case of a joint return, only the decedent's portion of joint tax liability is forgiven. A similar tax forgiveness rule applies to U.S. military and civilian employees who die as the result of wounds or injury occurring outside the United States in a terroristic or military action against the United States or any of its allies (Code Sec. 692).

2537. Extension of Time for Payment of Tax. An extension of time for filing a tax return ordinarily does not postpone the time for payment (¶ 2509). The IRS may extend the time for payment of the tax shown on the return for up to six months, or longer if the taxpayer is abroad, upon a showing of undue hardship. A taxpayer applying for an extension of the time to pay tax must file Form 1127 on or before the original due date for payment of the tax. The application must be accompanied by evidence showing the undue hardship that would result if the extension were refused, a statement of the taxpayer's assets and liabilities, and a statement of the taxpayer's receipts and disbursements for the three months preceding the original due date for payment of tax (Code Sec. 6161(a); Reg. § 1.6161-1). If an extension of time for payment of tax is granted, interest on the tax liability will accrue (¶ 2838) from the original due date until the date on which the balance is fully paid. The taxpayer may also be required to furnish a bond (Code Sec. 6165; Reg. § 1.6165-1).

Military and Government Personnel. A taxpayer who is a U.S. Armed Forces member or civilian serving in support of the U.S. Armed Forces who serves in a designated combat zone (¶ 895) or in a contingency operation, or is hospitalized outside the United States as a result of an injury received while serving in a combat zone/contingency operation, qualifies for an extension for filing returns and paying tax for the period of combat/contingency operation service or hospitalization plus 180 days (Code Sec. 7508). This extension is also available to the taxpayer's spouse who wishes to file a joint return.

Disaster Areas. A taxpayer affected by a federally declared disaster is granted an automatic 60-day extension for federal tax deadlines, including those related to qualified retirement plans, effective for a federal disaster declared after December 20, 2019 (Code Sec. 7508A, as amended by the Tax Certainty and Disaster Tax Relief Act (Division Q of P.L. 116-94)). In addition, the IRS is authorized to postpone deadlines for filing returns and paying taxes for up to one year for taxpayers affected by a federally declared disaster. This includes taxpayers affected by terroristic or military actions. A list of recent federally declared disaster areas may be found on the IRS website at https://www.irs.gov/newsroom/tax-relief-in-disaster-situations. The due date for filing federal income tax returns and tax payments, including estimated taxes, otherwise due on or after April 1, 2020, and before July 15, 2020, is extended to July 15, 2020, due to the COVID-19 (coronavirus) crisis (¶ 2529).

2541. Extension of Time for Payment of Deficiency in Tax. The IRS may grant an extension of time to pay a tax deficiency for a period of not more than 18 months if timely payment of the deficiency would result in undue hardship. The extension may be applied for according to the procedure for an extension of time for payment of tax (¶ 2537). An additional period of not more than 12 months may be granted in an exceptional case. A request for an extension will be refused if the deficiency was due to negligence, intentional disregard of income tax rules and regulations, or fraud (Code Sec. 6161(b); Reg. § 1.6161-1(a)(2) and (c)).

2545. Forms and Methods of Tax Payments. Payment of taxes must be made by a commercially acceptable means deemed appropriate by the IRS, including personal or cashier's check, money order, credit, debit or credit card, or electronic funds withdrawal (Code Sec. 6311; Reg. § 301.6311-2). Payments can be made online, by phone, or by mail whether the taxpayer files electronically or on paper. Payments made by credit card, debit card, or digital wallet are processed by a payment processor that will charge a convenience fee (IRS Pub. 17). For tax years beginning before 2018 and after 2025, the convenience fee may be deductible by an individual as a miscellaneous itemized deduction subject to the two-percent of adjusted gross income limitation (¶ 1079).

Electronic funds withdrawal is free and allows taxpayers to schedule payments to be withdrawn directly from their bank accounts. Additionally, taxpayers may use the Electronic Federal Tax Payment System (EFTPS) to pay online or via telephone (IRS Pub. 966). EFTPS must be used for all federal tax deposits, including deposits of employment taxes, corporate income and corporate estimated taxes, unrelated business income taxes paid by tax-exempt organizations, private foundation excise taxes, taxes withheld on nonresident aliens and foreign corporations, estimated taxes on certain trusts, railroad retirement taxes, nonpayroll taxes, FUTA taxes, and excise taxes reported on Form 720 (Reg. § § 1.6302-1, 1.6302-2, 1.6302-3, and 1.6302-4).

Individual taxpayers may use the IRS web-based Direct Pay system, which allows individuals with Social Security numbers or eligible IRS-issued individual taxpayer identification numbers (ITINs) (¶ 2579) to pay tax bills or make estimated tax payments directly from their checking or savings accounts without fees or, unlike EFTPS, pre-registration (IRM 21.2.1.48.1).

Deadlines

See CCH® AnswerConnect: *Filing and Paying Due Dates on Weekends and Holidays* and *Filing Timely Returns by Mail and Electronically* for more information on this topic.

2549. Deadlines Falling on a Weekend or Holiday. If the last day for performing any act such as filing a return, paying tax, or filing a claim for credit or refund, falls on Saturday, Sunday, or a legal holiday, the act is timely if it is performed on the next day that is not a Saturday, Sunday, or legal holiday (Code Sec. 7503; Reg. § 301.7503-1). A "legal holiday" means a legal holiday in the District of Columbia, including Emancipation Day. If a legal holiday in the District of Columbia falls on a Sunday, the next Monday is

25 RETURNS

treated as a legal holiday. If a legal holiday in the District of Columbia other than Inauguration Day falls on a Saturday, the preceding Friday is treated as a legal holiday (DC Code § 28-2701; Rev. Rul. 2015-13 clarifying and amplifying Notice 2011-17). For the 2020 calendar year, Emancipation Day in the District of Columbia falls on Thursday, April 16, 2020. Thus, the filing deadline for all tax forms and payments required to be filed or completed by an individual for the 2019 tax year is generally Wednesday, April 15, 2020.

In the case of a return, statement, or other document required to be filed with an IRS office, a legal holiday also includes a statewide legal holiday in the state in which the office is located, such as Patriots' Day in Massachusetts and Maine. This extension for filing a return, statement, or other document required to be filed with an IRS office for statewide legal holidays does not include the payment of estimated taxes if the designated depository is located in another non-celebrating state. Thus, if the first payment of estimated taxes for a resident of Massachusetts falls on the statewide holiday of Patriots' Day, the first payment must still be made on that day since the designated depository for estimated payments for residents of Massachusetts is in Connecticut, which does not celebrate Patriots' Day.

2553. Timely Mailing as Timely Filing and Paying (Mailbox Rule). Any return, claim, statement, or document that must be filed with the IRS or the Tax Court, or any payment required to be made, is timely filed or paid if, on or before the due date (including extensions), it is deposited in the mail in the United States in an envelope or other appropriate wrapper, postage prepaid and properly addressed, and the date of the U.S. postmark falls on or before the due date (Code Sec. 7502(a); Reg. § 301.7502-1). The postmark date is deemed the date of delivery or payment. Federal tax returns, including claims, statements, or other documents, mailed from outside the United States are timely if they bear the official timely dated postmark of the foreign country (Rev. Rul. 2002-23). The timely-mailed-is-timely-filed rule applies to designated private delivery services. The designated private delivery services are listed on the IRS website, at https://www.irs.gov/uac/private-delivery-services-pds.

Documents or payments properly sent by registered mail are considered to have been filed on time if the registration date falls on or before the due date of the document. Documents or payments properly sent by certified mail are timely filed if the certified mail sender's receipt is postmarked on or before the due date of the document. Delivery by properly registered or certified mail is presumed to have occurred if the envelope or package was properly addressed to the appropriate agency, officer, or office for filing or payment. Proof of use of a designated private delivery service under criteria established by the IRS is entitled to a similar presumption of delivery. The timely-mailed-is-timely-filed rule also covers documents filed electronically. The date of an electronic postmark that is given by an authorized electronic return transmitter and is on or before the filing due date is deemed to be the filing date.

A tax deposit received by an authorized depository after the due date for the deposit is timely if it has been properly mailed at least two days before the prescribed due date. However, if any person is required to deposit tax more than once a month and the deposit amounts to $20,000 or more, the deposit must be received on or before the prescribed due date to be timely (Code Sec. 7502(e); Reg. § 301.7502-2).

Information Returns and Payment at Source

See CCH® AnswerConnect: *Information Returns* for more information on this topic.

2565. Information Return Reporting. Every person engaged in a trade or business must file an information return for each calendar year that certain payments are made or received during the year in the course of the payor's trade or business (Code Secs. 6041—6050Y). In many cases, the return must be filed with the IRS electronically through the Filing Information Returns Electronically (FIRE) system at https://fire.irs.gov, if the person is required to file 250 or more returns during a calendar year before 2021 (¶ 2503) (Reg. § 301.6011-2; IRS Pub. 1220). Form 8508 is used to request a waiver from the e-filing requirement. The filer also must furnish a statement to the payee or other recipient, either on paper or electronically, that contains the information provided to the IRS in the information return.

¶2553

The information returns described below are among those required to be filed. See ¶ 64 for a chart that includes due dates for filing the returns with the IRS and for providing statements to a payee or other person. Unless otherwise specified, information returns for a calendar year are filed with the IRS by February 28 of the following year if filed on paper, or March 31 if filed electronically. The due date for filing information returns reporting nonemployee compensation is January 31 of the following year. The due date for furnishing statements to payees and other recipients for a calendar year is generally January 31 of the following year, whether furnished on paper or electronically (Code Sec. 6071). See ¶ 2549 for discussion of due dates falling on a weekend or holiday. Form 8809 is used to request an 30-day extension of time to file most information returns with the IRS. Form 8809 *cannot* be used to request an extension of time to furnish required statements to recipients (Reg. § 1.6081-8).

Form 1098. Persons file this form if they receive $600 or more in mortgage interest from an individual in the course of a trade or business. Points paid directly by a borrower, including seller-paid points, for the purchase of a principal residence must be reported on Form 1098. Refunds and reimbursements of overpaid mortgage interest, and mortgage insurance premiums of $600 or more must also be reported. In addition, Form 1098 is used to report: (1) the amount of outstanding principal of the mortgage as of the beginning of the calendar year, (2) the address of the property securing the mortgage, and (3) the loan origination date (Code Sec. 6050H; Reg. § 1.6050H-2).

Form 1098-C. A charitable organization must file this form for each contribution received of a qualified vehicle that has a claimed value of more than $500 (¶ 1070A).

Form 1098-E. Financial institutions, governmental units, and educational institutions must file this form if in the course of a trade or business they receive interest of $600 or more in a calendar year on a student loan that is used solely to pay for qualified higher education expenses (Code Sec. 6050S; Reg. § 1.6050S-3).

Form 1098-F. Any federal, state, or foreign government or governmental entity uses this form to report settlements of fines and penalties paid or incurred after December 21, 2017, due to the violation of a law or an inquiry into the potential violation of a law (¶ 972) (Code Sec. 6050X).

Form 1098-MA. A state housing finance agency (HFA) uses this form for calendar years through 2021 to report mortgage payments made by homeowners and mortgage assistance payments funded through allocations from the Treasury Department's Housing Finance Agency Innovation Fund for the Hardest Hit Housing Markets (Notice 2018-63).

Form 1098-Q. Persons that issue a contract intended to be a qualifying longevity annuity contract (QLAC) purchased or held under any qualified employer-sponsored retirement plan or traditional IRA must file this form to report contributions, premiums, fair market value, and the annuity payment amount and start date of the contract (Reg. § 1.6047-2).

Form 1098-T. An educational institution must file this form with respect to each individual enrolled for an academic period, to report payments received for qualified tuition and related expenses. Also, any person engaged in a trade or business of making payments to any individual under an insurance arrangement as reimbursements or refunds of qualified tuition and related expenses must file this form for each individual for whom reimbursements or refunds are made during the calendar year (Code Sec. 6050S; Reg. § § 1.6050S-1 and 1.6050S-2).

Form 1099-A. Persons that lend money in connection with their trade or business and, in full or partial satisfaction of the debt, acquire an interest in property that is security for the debt, must file this form. The form must also be filed if the person has reason to know that the property securing the debt has been abandoned (Code Sec. 6050J).

Form 1099-B. Brokers are required to use this form to report sales, including short sales, of stock, bonds, commodities, regulated futures contracts, foreign currency contracts, forward contracts, and debt instruments. For a "covered security," brokers must also report the customer's adjusted basis in the security (¶ 1980). Brokers that hold shares for a customer in a corporation that the broker knows or has reason to know has engaged in a transaction of acquisition of control or substantial change in capital structure must also file this form. The form is also used to report barter exchanges of

¶2565

property or services (Code Sec. 6045; Reg. §§ 1.6045-1 and 1.6045-3). Trustees and middlemen of widely held fixed investment trusts (WHFITs) must use Form 1099-B to report the *non-pro rata* partial principal payments, trust sales proceeds, redemption asset proceeds, redemption proceeds, sales asset proceeds, and the sales proceeds that are attributable to a trust interest holder (TIH) for the calendar year.

Form 1099-C. Financial institutions, credit unions, federal agencies, and other organizations that lend money on a regular and continuing basis must file this form for each debtor for whom a debt of $600 or more was cancelled. Multiple discharges of debt of less than $600 during a year need not be aggregated unless the separate discharges occurred with the purpose of evading the reporting requirements. The return must be filed regardless of whether the debtor is subject to tax on the discharged debt (e.g., debt discharged in bankruptcy) (Code Sec. 6050P; Reg. § 1.6050P-1).

Form 1099-DIV. Corporations and regulated investment companies generally file this form for each person:

- to whom payments of $10 or more in distributions, such as dividends, capital gains, or nontaxable distributions, were made on stock;

- for whom any foreign tax was withheld and paid on dividends and on other distributions on stock if the recipient can claim a credit for the tax;

- for whom any federal income tax was withheld under the backup withholding rules; or

- to whom payments of $600 or more were made as part of a liquidation (Code Sec. 6042).

S corporations use this form only to report distributions made during the calendar year out of accumulated earnings and profits (¶ 323).

Form 1099-G. Government units use this form to report payments of $10 or more for unemployment benefits, state and local tax refunds, credits, or offsets, payments of $600 or more in taxable grants or alternative trade adjustment assistance payments, and agricultural subsidy payments made during the year (Code Secs. 6050B and 6050E).

Form 1099-H. Health insurance providers are required to file this return to report any advance payments made before January 1, 2021, of the credit for health insurance costs they are entitled to receive on behalf of individuals under Code Sec. 7527 (¶ 1432) (Code Sec. 6050T).

Form 1099-INT. Payors file this form for each person to whom payments of $10 or more in interest were paid, including interest on bearer certificates of deposit and interest on U.S. Savings Bonds, Treasury bills, Treasury notes, and Treasury bonds (Code Sec. 6049). Interest of $600 or more is also reportable if paid to a person in the course of a trade or business, such as interest on delayed death benefits paid by a life insurance company, interest received with damages, or interest on a state or federal income tax refund. Form 1099-INT must also be filed to report interest of $10 or more (other than original issue discount) accrued to a real estate mortgage investment conduit (REMIC), a holder of a regular interest in a financial asset securitization investment trust (FASIT), and a holder of a collateralized debt obligation (CDO). Additionally, trustees and middlemen of WHFITs must report the gross amount of interest exceeding $10 that is attributable to a trust interest holder (TIH) for the calendar year on this form. Form 1099-INT is not required for payments to certain exempt payees, including corporations, tax-exempt organizations, individual retirement arrangements, the U.S. government, and states (Reg. § 1.6049-4). Further, Form 1099-INT is not required for certain types of interest, including interest on debt issued by an individual, interest on amounts from sources outside the United States paid outside the United States by a non-U.S. payer, and certain portfolio interest (Reg. § 1.6049-5).

Form 1099-K. Banks and other processors of merchant payment card transactions (e.g., credit and debit cards and internet payment systems) must use this form to report a merchant's annual gross payment card receipts to the IRS and to the merchant (Code Sec. 6050W; Reg. §§ 1.6050W-1 and 1.6050W-2). A third-party settlement organization must report information concerning a merchant's third-party network transactions only if for the calendar year the aggregate value of reportable payment transactions for the merchant exceeds $20,000 and the aggregate number of transactions exceeds 200.

Form 1099-MISC. This form is filed by payors for each person to whom the payor has paid, in the course of a trade or business, at least $10 in gross royalty payments or broker payments in lieu of dividends or tax-exempt interest, or at least $600 for rents, services, or other payments. Some of the items reported on this form include:

- payments for real estate, machine and pasture rentals;
- royalties paid to authors;
- prizes and awards that were not paid for services rendered;
- amounts withheld as backup withholding;
- payments by medical and health care insurers to each physician or health care provider under health, accident and sickness insurance programs;
- compensation such as fees, commissions and awards, and golden parachute payments paid to a nonemployee for services, including payments to attorneys for legal services (Code Sec. 6045(f));
- notification of sales of $5,000 or more of consumer products to a person on a buy-sell or commission basis for resale anywhere other than in a permanent retail establishment;
- fishing boat proceeds;
- fish purchases of $600 or more paid in cash for resale (Code Sec. 6050R);
- crop insurance proceeds of $600 or more; and
- any deferrals for the year under a nonqualified deferred compensation plan (Code Sec. 6041(g)).

Form 1099-MISC is not required for payments to certain exempt payees, including corporations, tax-exempt organizations, individual retirement arrangements, the U.S. government, and states (Instructions for Form 1099-MISC).

The form generally must be furnished to recipients by January 31 of the following calendar year, but it may be furnished to recipients by February 15 if substitute payments in lieu of dividends or tax-exempt interest are being reported in box 8 or gross proceeds paid to an attorney are being reported in box 14. The form is generally required to be filed with the IRS by February 28 of the following calendar year, but it must be filed with the IRS by January 31 if nonemployee compensation is reported in box 7 for payments made before 2020.

Form 1099-NEC. For payments made after 2019, this form is used to report $600 or more in nonemployee compensation in the course of the payer's business for services performed (including parts and materials), as well as certain payments to an attorney and cash payments for fish or other aquatic life purchased from a anyone engaged in the trade or business of catching fish. The form must be filed by January 31 electronically or by paper.

Form 1099-OID. Issuers of bonds or certificates of deposit, and trustees and middlemen of WHFITs use this form to report original issue discount of $10 or more (Code Sec. 6049(d); Reg. § 1.6049-4).

Form 1099-PATR. Cooperatives use this form to report patronage dividends and other distributions of $10 or more to patrons (Code Sec. 6044).

Form 1099-Q and Form 5498-ESA. Persons maintaining a qualified tuition program (QTP or 529) or Coverdell education savings accounts (ESAs) for beneficiaries use Form 1099-Q to report distributions from the accounts, as well as earnings and certain other information. Persons that maintain a Coverdell ESA for beneficiaries use Form 5498-ESA to report contributions made to the account during the year, including rollovers. A copy of Form 5498-ESA generally must be provided to the beneficiary by April 30 of the following year and filed with the IRS by May 31 but the deadlines are extended to July 15, 2020, for the 2019 calendar year in response to the COVID-19 (coronavirus) crisis (Notice 2020-23; Rev. Proc. 2018-58).

Form 1099-QA and Form 5498-QA. Any state or its agency or instrumentality that establishes and maintains a qualified ABLE program (¶ 870) must file these forms to report contributions and distributions from an ABLE account, as well as if the account was terminated during the tax year. A copy of Form 5498-QA must be provided to the beneficiary by March 15 of the following calendar year and filed with the IRS by May 31 but the due date for filing Form 5498-QA with the IRS is extended to July 15, 2020, for the 2019 calendar year (Notice 2020-23; Rev. Proc. 2018-58).

Form 1099-R and Form 5498. Payors file Form 1099-R to report any distributions of $10 or more from retirement or profit-sharing plans, individual retirement arrangements (IRAs), simplified employee pensions (SEPs), annuities, or insurance contracts. Reports must be furnished to the participants by January 31 following the year of distribution. Persons maintaining an IRA, including a deemed IRA, file Form 5498 to report contributions to the IRA during the tax year, including rollovers. A copy of Form 5498 must be provided to the beneficiary by March 15 of the following year to report the fair market value of the account and required minimum distributions, and by May 31 to report contributions. Form 5498 generally must be filed with the IRS by May 31 but the due date is extended to July 15, 2020, for the 2019 calendar year (Notice 2020-23; Rev. Proc. 2018-58).

Form 1099-S. This form is used to report the sale or exchange of real estate, as well as the real property taxes imposed on the purchaser of a residence. Included are sales or exchanges of residences, land (including air space), commercial buildings, condominium units, stock in cooperative housing corporations, and noncontingent interests in standing timber (Reg. § 1.6045-4). The form must be filed by the person responsible for closing the real estate transaction or, if no such person exists, by the mortgage lender, the transferor's broker, the transferee's broker or the transferee, in that order. Payments of timber royalties under a "pay-as-cut" contract are also reported on the form. The form must be furnished to recipients by February 15 of the following year.

Form 1099-SA and Form 5498-SA. Persons that maintain a health savings account (HSA) (¶ 2035), Archer medical savings account (MSA), or Medicare Advantage MSA (¶ 2037) for beneficiaries use these forms to report contributions and distributions related to the account. Form 5498-SA is required to be filed with the IRS and a copy provided to the beneficiary by May 31 of the following year but the due date is extended to July 15, 2020, for the 2019 calendar year (Notice 2020-23; Rev. Proc. 2018-58).

Form 3921 and Form 3922. These forms are filed by a corporation to report certain stock transfers to an employee. Form 3921 is used to report a transfer of stock pursuant to an employee's exercise of an incentive stock option. Form 3922 is used to report a transfer of stock pursuant to an employee's exercise of an option granted under an employee stock purchase plan where the exercise price is less than 100 percent of the value of the stock, or is not fixed or determinable, on the date of grant (Code Sec. 6039).

Form 8027. Each employer that runs a large food or beverage establishment (¶ 2605) must file an annual return of the receipts from food or beverage operations and tips reported by employees (Code Sec. 6053; Rev. Proc. 2012-37). In addition, in certain circumstances, the employer is required to allocate amounts as tips to employees. Establishments must file Form 8027 electronically if they file 250 or more Forms 8027 during a calendar year before 2021 (¶ 2503).

Form 8300. Each person engaged in a trade or business who, in the course of such trade or business, receives more than $10,000 in cash in one transaction (or two or more related transactions) must file this form. The form must be filed with the IRS by the 15th day after the transaction, but the due date is extended to July 15, 2020, if otherwise due on or after April 1, 2020, and before July 15, 2020 (Notice 2020-23; Rev. Proc. 2018-58). A written or electronic statement must be provided to each person named on the form on or before January 31 of the year following the calendar year of receipt (Code Sec. 6050I).

Form W-2. Employers use this form to report wages, tips, other compensation, and withheld income and FICA taxes to both the recipient (¶ 2655) and the Social Security Administration (SSA) (Code Sec. 6051). Bonuses, vacation allowances, severance pay, moving expense payments, some kinds of travel allowances and third-party payments of sick pay are included. Certain employers must use Form W-2 to report the aggregate cost of certain employer-sponsored health coverage provided to employees (¶ 2567). Form W-3 must be filed along with Form W-2 if submitting a paper copy of the form to the SSA.

Other Information Returns. Other information returns are required with respect to the following:

- issuers of certain tax credit bonds must report each tax credit distributed on Form 1097-BTC (¶ 1471) (Code Sec. 6049);

¶2565

- U.S. persons that own at least a 10-percent interest in a foreign partnership must report on Form 8865 any changes in ownership during the tax year (¶ 2494) (Code Sec. 6046A);

- in cases of liquidation or dissolution of a corporation, including an exempt organization, Form 966 must be filed (¶ 2259) (Code Sec. 6043(a) and (b));

- corporate mergers, acquisitions, and recapitalization are reported on Form 8806 and Form 1099-CAP (Code Sec. 6043(c); Code Sec. 6043A);

- formations or reorganizations of foreign corporations are reported on Form 5471 (¶ 2487) (Code Sec. 6046);

- U.S. persons and executors of estates of U.S. decedents must file Form 3520 to report transactions with or affecting a foreign trust; foreign trusts with at least one U.S. owner must file an annual information return on Form 3520-A (¶ 588) (Code Sec. 6048);

- U.S. persons that own interests in foreign partnerships or foreign corporations must file Form 5471 (¶ 2487) (Code Sec. 6038);

- U.S. persons that transfer property to foreign partnerships or foreign corporations report the transaction on Form 8865 or Form 926, respectively (Code Sec. 6038B);

- payors of long-term care benefits must file Form 1099-LTC (Code Sec. 6050Q);

- U.S. persons, other than tax-exempt organizations, that receive large foreign gifts during the tax year—gifts totaling more than $100,000 from a nonresident alien individual or a foreign estate, or more than $16,388 in 2019 ($16,649 in 2020) from a foreign partnership or a foreign corporation—report the gifts on Form 3520 (Code Sec. 6039F; Rev. Proc. 2018-57; Rev. Proc. 2019-44);

- individuals who lose citizenship and long-term residents who terminate residency in the United States are required to file Form 8854 annually (¶ 2412) (Code Sec. 6039G);

- Alaska Native Settlement Trusts may elect to have special rules apply to the trust and its beneficiaries using Form 1041-N (¶ 2396) (Code Sec. 6039H);

- donors making noncash donations must file Form 8283 if the amount of the charitable deduction for all noncash gifts is more than $500 (¶ 1070A);

- dispositions by charitable donees within three years of donated property with a value in excess of $5,000 are reported on Form 8282 by the donee (¶ 627) (Code Sec. 6050L(a));

- charitable organizations that receive or accrue net income from a qualified intellectual property contribution must file Form 8899 and provide a copy to the donor (¶ 1062A) (Code Sec. 6050L(b));

- employer-owned life insurance contracts (also known as company-owned life insurance (COLI) contracts) must be reported by the policyholder on Form 8925 (¶ 804) (Code Sec. 6039I);

- acquisitions of life insurance contracts in reportable policy sales and payments of reportable death benefits under the contracts are reported on Form 1099-LS and Form 1099-SB (¶ 807) (Code Sec. 6050Y);

- charges or payments made for qualified long-term insurance contracts under combined arrangements are reported on Form 1099-R (Code Sec. 6050U); and

- federal executive agencies must report information about persons with whom they have entered certain contracts for products or services on Form 8596 and Form 8596-A, as well file Form 1099-MISC if in the course of a trade or business they pay remuneration of $600 or more in a calendar year to any person for services provided by that person (Code Secs. 6041A and 6050M).

2567. Health Care Coverage Reporting. A employer is required to disclose the aggregate cost of employer-sponsored health insurance coverage provided to an employee on Form W-2 (Code Sec. 6051(a)(14); Notice 2012-9). The aggregate cost of the coverage reported includes both the portion of coverage paid by the employer and the employee, as well as any portion of the cost of coverage that is includible in the employee's gross income for the employee's spouse, dependent, or child under the age of 27. It does not include salary reduction contributions to a health savings account (HSA) (¶ 2035), Archer medical savings account (MSA) (¶ 2037), or flexible spending arrangement under a cafeteria plan (¶ 2041).

Reporting the cost of health care coverage on Form W-2 does not mean that the coverage is taxable. An employer is not required to provide Form W-2 solely to report the value of the coverage for retirees or former employees. Pending further guidance, the reporting requirement is optional for an employer who is required to file fewer than the applicable number of Forms W-2 for the preceding calendar year, based on the rule for the electronic filing of returns (¶ 2503). Transitional relief is also available for certain other types of coverage and situations.

Offers of Coverage. An applicable large employer (¶ 2001) must report on Form 1094-C and Form 1095-C whether full-time employees and their dependents are offered the opportunity to enroll in minimum essential coverage under an eligible employer-sponsored plan, along with other related information (Code Sec. 6056; Reg. §§ 301.6056-1 and 301.6056-2; Notice 2013-45). The returns must be filed with the IRS on or before February 28 (March 31 if filed electronically) of the year following the calendar year to which they relate. A copy of Form 1095-C is generally required to be furnished to each full-time employee by January 31 of the following calendar year, except the due date is extended to March 2, 2020, for the 2019 year (Notice 2019-63). An applicable large employer that is self-insured may combine this reporting with an insurer's reporting (discussed below) on Form 1095-C. Failure to file the returns may subject the employer to a penalty (¶ 2816 and ¶ 2823).

Insurer Reporting. Every insurer who provides minimum essential health care coverage to an individual during a calendar year, including an employer who self-insures, is required to file Form 1094-B and Form 1095-B reporting such coverage (Code Sec. 6055; Reg. § 1.6055-1; Prop. Reg. § 1.6055-1; Notice 2013-45). The returns must be filed with the IRS on or before February 28 (or March 31 if filed electronically) of the year following the calendar year to which they relate. Self-insured employers that are also applicable large employers subject to shared responsibility reporting can instead combine insurance provider reporting. A copy of Form 1095-B is generally required to be furnished to each full-time employee by January 31 of the following calendar year, except the due date is extended to March 2, 2020, for the 2019 year (Notice 2019-63). The statement may be furnished electronically if affirmative consent is given. Failure to file the returns may subject the employer to a penalty (¶ 2816 and ¶ 2823).

2570. Reporting Foreign Financial Accounts (FBAR). A U.S. person is required to disclose any financial interests in, or signature authority or other authority over, foreign financial accounts if the aggregate value of the accounts exceeds $10,000 at any time during the calendar year (31 CFR §§ 1010.306(c) and 1010.350). The information is reported electronically on FinCEN Report 114 (commonly referred to as the FBAR) through the Treasury's Financial Crimes Enforcement Network (FinCEN) BSA E-Filing System. The filing of the FBAR does not relieve a taxpayer of the requirement to file Form 8938 to report specified foreign financial assets (¶ 2572).

The FBAR for a calendar year is required to be filed by the due date for filing federal income tax returns (i.e., April 15 of the succeeding year), with a maximum extension of six months. Any penalty for failure to timely file a request for an extension to file the FBAR may be waived by the IRS for first-time filers (Act Sec. 2006(b)(11) of the Surface Transportation and Veterans Health Care Choice Improvement Act of 2015 (P.L. 114-41)). FinCEN allows all FBAR filers an automatic filing extension to October 15, and does not require specific requests for this extension (FinCEN Form 114 Instructions, Release Date January 2017 (v. 1.4)). Relief from FBAR reporting is provided for certain individuals who have signature authority over, but no financial interest in, one or more foreign financial accounts. Under this relief, the deadline for filing the FBAR for signature authority held during the 2019 calendar year (as well as the reporting deadlines previously extended for 2011 through 2018) is extended to April 15, 2021 (FinCEN Notice 2019-1).

U.S. persons subject to FBAR reporting are U.S. citizens, resident aliens, and entities created, organized, or formed under U.S. laws, including but not limited to domestic corporations, partnerships, limited liability companies (LLCs), trusts, and estates. The federal tax treatment of a person or entity does not determine whether an FBAR filing is required. For example, an entity disregarded for federal tax purposes must still file an FBAR if otherwise required. Participants and beneficiaries in qualified retirement plans, including individual retirement accounts (IRAs), are not required to file FBARs with respect to a foreign financial account held by or on behalf of the plan. A beneficiary of a trust in which a U.S. person has a greater than 50 percent present beneficial interest in the assets or income of the trust for the calendar year is not required to file FBAR if the trust, trustee, or agent of the trust is a U.S. person that files an FBAR for the trust's foreign financial assets.

FinCEN Form 114a, Record of Authorization to Electronically File FBARs, is used by a U.S. person to authorize a third party preparer (i.e., CPA, enrolled agent, or attorney) to file the FBAR on his or her behalf, or to jointly file the FBAR with his or her spouse. Form 114a is not filed with Treasury, but must be maintained by the foreign account holder and the filer and made available upon request by Treasury or the IRS.

2572. Reporting Specified Foreign Financial Assets (Form 8938). Under the Foreign Account Tax Compliance Act (FATCA), any individual who holds an interest in a specified foreign financial asset during the tax year must attach Form 8938 to his or her tax return to report certain information for each asset if the total value of all such assets exceeds an applicable threshold amount (Code Sec. 6038D). The requirement applies to any U.S. citizen, and any individual who is a resident alien of the United States for any part of the tax year. A nonresident alien who elects to be treated as a resident alien (¶ 2410) must also file Form 8938, as well as a nonresident alien who is a bona fide resident of American Samoa or Puerto Rico. Form 8938 must also be filed by any domestic entity that is formed or used to hold, directly or indirectly, specified foreign financial assets. Specified domestic entities subject to the reporting requirement include certain closely-held domestic corporations or partnerships, as well as certain domestic trusts (Reg. § 1.6038D-6).

A "specified foreign financial asset" includes (1) a depository, custodial, or other financial account maintained by a foreign financial institution, (2) a stock or security issued by a person other than a U.S. person, (3) a financial instrument or contract held for investment that has an issuer or counterparty other than a U.S. person, and (4) an interest in an entity that is not a U.S. person. Filing Form 8938 does not relieve the filer of the requirement to file the FBAR or FinCEN Report 114 (¶ 2570) for disclosing foreign financial accounts. Similarly, filing the FBAR does not relieve the filer of the requirement to file Form 8938. An individual or entity may be required to file both Form 8938 and the FBAR to report the same information on certain foreign accounts.

The value of a specified foreign financial asset for determining whether the individual or entity has met the applicable threshold for filing Form 8938 is the asset's fair market value as determined in U.S. dollars using the Treasury's currency exchange rate on the last day of the tax year (Reg. § 1.6038D-5). A specified domestic entity must file Form 8938 if the total value of specified foreign financial assets is more than $50,000 on the last day of the tax year or more than $75,000 at any time during the tax year.

For an individual, the applicable threshold amount depends on the individual's filing status and whether he or she lives in the United States or abroad (Reg. § 1.6038D-2; Instructions for Form 8938). The applicable threshold amounts for individuals are as follows:

- Unmarried individuals living in the United States, and married individuals living in the United States and filing separate income tax returns, must file Form 8938 if the total value of specified foreign financial assets is more than $50,000 on the last day of the tax year or more than $75,000 at any time during the tax year.

- Married individuals living in the United States and filing a joint income tax return must file Form 8938 if the value of specified foreign financial assets is more than $100,000 on the last day of the tax year or more than $150,000 at any time during the tax year.

- Unmarried individuals living abroad, and married individuals living abroad and filing a separate return, must file Form 8938 if the total value of specified foreign assets is more than $200,000 on the last day of the tax year or more than $300,000 at any time during the year.

• Married individuals living abroad and filing a joint return must file Form 8938 if the value of specified foreign assets is more than $400,000 on the last day of the tax year or more than $600,000 at any time during the year.

The filer must disclose the asset's maximum value during the tax year and provide specific information based on the asset type. For a financial account, the filer must provide the name and address of the financial institution in which the account is maintained, and the account number. For stock or security, the filer must provide the issuer's name and address, and any other information needed to identify the asset's class or issue. For any other instrument, contract, or interest, the filer must provide any information needed to identify the asset, and the names and addresses of all issuers and counterparties. An individual or entity that fails to furnish the required information in timely manner will be subject to a penalty. Additionally, a 40-percent accuracy-related penalty (¶ 2864) may be imposed for any underpayment of tax attributable to an undisclosed foreign financial asset, and the statute of limitations for tax assessment may be extended or suspended depending on the circumstances (¶ 2726 and ¶ 2734).

2579. Taxpayer Identification Numbers (TINs). A taxpayer or other entity required to file a return, statement, or other document with the IRS must include their taxpayer identification number (TIN) on such items (Code Sec. 6109(a); Reg. §301.6109-1). A person may also be required to furnish a TIN to another person or request an identifying number from another person using Form W-9 for filing information returns (¶ 2565). Where permitted, a person can use a truncated taxpayer identification number (TTIN) to identify any other person on a statement or document that must be furnished to another person, but cannot truncate its own TIN. A TTIN cannot be used on any form filed with the IRS or the Social Security Administration (Reg. § 301.6109-4).

An individual generally uses his or her Social Security number (SSN) as the TIN. An executor of a decedent's estate who must file Form 706 uses both the executor's SSN and the decedent's SSN on the form. An individual who needs a SSN must file an application on Form SS-5 with the Social Security Administration. A prospective adoptive parent can apply for an adoption taxpayer identification number (ATIN) for a child who is in the process of being adopted (Reg. § 301.6109-3; Prop. Reg. § 301.6109-3). Application for an ATIN must be made on Form W-7A.

Individual Taxpayer Identification Numbers. A foreign individual or other person who does not have, and is ineligible to obtain a SSN may use an IRS-issued individual taxpayer identification number (ITIN) (Code Sec. 6109(i); Reg. §301.6109-1(d)(1)). Form W-7 is used to apply for an ITIN and generally must be filed with the individual's original tax return for which the ITIN is needed. The individual must include with the application original or certified copies of documents proving his or her identity, foreign status, and U.S. residency. Form W-7 packets may be submitted by mail or in person to an employee of the IRS. Individuals may also submit the Form W-7 packets to an acceptance agent (AA) or a community-based certifying acceptance agent (CAA). Until further guidance is issued, all applicants may continue to submit their Form W-7 packets to CAAs under existing procedures (Notice 2016-48; Rev. Proc. 2006-10). ITINs that are not used on a federal tax return at least once in the last three tax years will expire and must be renewed by the taxpayer.

Employer Identification Number (EIN). The TIN of a corporation, partnership, nonprofit association, estate, trust, and other business entity is the employer identification number (EIN). An individual who is engaged in a trade or business as a sole proprietor uses both his or her SSN and EIN of the business when supplying a TIN on returns, statements, or other documents, depending on which number is required by the IRS. Any person needing an EIN must file an application on Form SS-4 (Reg. § 301.6109-1(d)(2)).

Penalties. A penalty of $50 per failure applies to a person that omits its own TIN from a required return, statement, or document. Failure to furnish one's TIN to another person when so required or to include another person's TIN in any document for information reporting purposes will also give rise to a $50 penalty. The maximum penalty per calendar year for failure to include TINs is $100,000 (Code Secs. 6723 and 6724(d)(3)).

¶2579

Reportable Transactions and Tax Shelters

See CCH® AnswerConnect: *Tax Shelter Penalties* for more information on this topic.

2591. Reportable Transactions. Reporting and disclosure requirements apply to taxpayers (¶ 2592) and material advisors (¶ 2593) with respect to reportable transactions. A reportable transaction is any transaction for which information must be included with a return or statement because the IRS has determined under regulations that this type of transaction has a potential for tax avoidance or evasion (Code Sec. 6707A(c)(1)).

There are five categories of reportable transactions: listed transactions, confidential transactions, transactions with contractual protection, loss transactions, and transactions of interest (Reg. § 1.6011-4(b)). A transaction is not considered a reportable transaction, or is excluded from any individual category of reportable transaction, if the IRS determines in published guidance that the transaction is not subject to the reporting requirements. The IRS may make a determination by individual letter.

2592. Disclosure of Reportable Transactions by Taxpayers. Every taxpayer that is required to file a tax return and has participated directly or indirectly in a reportable transaction (¶ 2591) must disclose its participation in the transaction (Reg. § 1.6011-4(a)). The fact that a transaction is a reportable transaction does not affect the legal determination of whether the taxpayer's treatment of the transaction is proper.

Form 8886 is used to disclose information for each reportable transaction in which the taxpayer has participated. A taxpayer generally must file a separate Form 8886 for each reportable transaction, but a single form can be filed for transactions that are the same or substantially similar. The form must be attached to the taxpayer's tax return for each tax year for which the taxpayer participates in a reportable transaction. A copy must be sent to the Office of Tax Shelter Analysis (OTSA) at the same time that any disclosure statement is first filed with the taxpayer's tax return (Reg. § 1.6011-4(d) and (e)). If a reportable transaction results in a loss that is carried back to a prior year, Form 8886 is attached to the taxpayer's application for tentative refund or amended tax return for the prior year.

In the case of a taxpayer that is a partnership, S corporation, or trust, Form 8886 must be attached to the partnership's, S corporation's, or trust's tax return for each tax year in which the entity participates in the transaction. A taxpayer who is a partner, S corporation shareholder, or beneficiary of a trust who receives a Schedule K-1 less than 10 calendar days before the due date of its return, including extensions, has a 60-day extension to file Form 8886 with the OTSA if the taxpayer determines from the Schedule K-1 that it has participated in a reportable transaction.

A taxpayer that fails to file Form 8886 regarding a reportable transaction is subject to a penalty (¶ 2594). Special reporting rules apply to listed transactions and transactions of interest. Also, in some cases, taxpayers must make multiple disclosures of a reportable transaction (Reg. § 1.6011-4(e)).

A taxpayer may submit a request to the IRS for a ruling as to whether a transaction is subject to the disclosure requirements (Reg. § 1.6011-4(f)). If a taxpayer requests a ruling on the merits of a specific transaction on or before the date that disclosure would otherwise be required and receives a favorable ruling, the disclosure rules are satisfied. The ruling request must fully disclose all relevant facts relating to the transaction. If a taxpayer is uncertain whether a transaction must be disclosed, the taxpayer may make a protective disclosure. The taxpayer must disclose the transaction and indicate on the disclosure statement that the taxpayer is uncertain whether the transaction is required to be disclosed and that the disclosure statement is being filed on a protective basis. The taxpayer must retain a copy of all documents and other records related to a transaction subject to disclosure (Reg. § 1.6011-4(g)). The retained documents and records are those that are material to an understanding of the tax treatment or tax structure of the transaction.

2593. Disclosure of Reportable Transactions by Material Advisors. Each material advisor is required to timely file an information return with the IRS for any reportable transaction (¶ 2591) (Code Sec. 6111; Reg. § 301.6111-3). The disclosure is made on Form 8918 and generally must be filed with the Office of Tax Shelter Analysis (OTSA) by the last day of the month that follows the calendar quarter in which the advisor became a material advisor with respect to the reportable transaction or in which circumstances occur to require an amended disclosure statement.

The material advisor's disclosure on Form 8918 must include: (1) information identifying and describing the transaction; (2) information describing any potential tax benefits expected to result from the transaction; and (3) any other information the IRS may require. This includes enough information about the transaction to identify if any other person that the material advisor knows or has reason to know acted as a material advisor with respect to the transaction. A single Form 8918 may be filed for transactions that are the same or substantially similar. An amended form must be filed if information previously provided is no longer accurate, additional information becomes available, or there are material changes to the transaction. If a potential material advisor is uncertain whether a transaction must be disclosed, a protective disclosure may be made. Any material advisor that fails to file Form 8918 when required or files a false or incomplete form is subject to a penalty (¶ 2595).

A material advisor is any person that: (1) provides material aid, assistance, or advice with respect to organizing, managing, promoting, selling, implementing, insuring, or carrying out any reportable transaction; and (2) directly or indirectly derives gross income in excess of $250,000 ($50,000 in the case of a reportable transaction that provides substantially all of the tax benefits to individuals) for that aid, assistance, or advice. If more than one material advisor is required to disclose a reportable transaction, the material advisors may designate by written agreement a single material advisor to disclose the transaction.

2594. Penalty for Failure to Disclose Reportable Transaction. A penalty is imposed on any taxpayer that fails to disclose its participation in a reportable transaction that is required to be included on the taxpayer's return (¶ 2592) (Code Sec. 6707A; Reg. § 301.6707A-1). The penalty is generally equal to 75 percent of the decrease in tax shown on the return as a result of the transaction, or that would have resulted from the transaction if the transaction had been respected for federal tax purposes. The *minimum* penalty is $10,000 ($5,000 in the case of an individual). The maximum penalty is $50,000 ($10,000 in the case of an individual), but in circumstances involving listed transactions, the maximum penalty is $200,000 ($100,000 in the case of an individual). The penalty for failure to disclose is imposed in addition to any other penalty, including a special accuracy-related penalty for an understatement of tax resulting from a reportable transaction (¶ 2870).

For reportable transactions other than listed transactions, the penalty can be rescinded or abated only in exceptional circumstances, and abatement of the penalty must promote compliance with the tax laws and effective tax administration. Factors considered in deciding whether to grant rescission include:

- the taxpayer filed a complete and proper, although untimely, Form 8886 upon becoming aware of the failure to properly disclose a reportable transaction;

- the failure to properly disclose was due to an unintentional mistake of fact that existed despite the taxpayer's reasonable attempts to determine the correct facts;

- the taxpayer generally has an established history of properly disclosing reportable transactions and complying with tax laws;

- the failure to file was beyond the taxpayer's control;

- the taxpayer cooperates with the IRS; and

- assessment of the penalty weighs against good conscience, and the taxpayer demonstrates that it acted in good faith with respect to the failure.

Any person seeking rescission of a penalty must make a written request within 30 days after the date that the IRS sends notice and demand for payment of the penalty. If the penalty is paid (not including interest) prior to the date that notice and demand is sent, the written request must be made within 30 days from the date of payment. In order to request rescission, the person must have either exhausted the administrative remedies available within the IRS Independent Office of Appeals or agreed in writing to the assessment of the penalty and not to file or prosecute a claim for refund or credit of the penalty. The IRS has provided guidance on the information required to be included with any rescission request, as well as factors considered in granting or denying the request (Rev. Proc. 2007-21; Announcement 2016-1). The IRS's collection efforts are not suspended because a rescission request has been made.

2595. Material Advisor Penalty for Reportable Transactions. A penalty is imposed on any material advisor who fails to file an information return or who files a false or incomplete information return regarding a reportable transaction (¶ 2593) (Code Sec. 6707; Reg. § 301.6707-1). A $50,000 penalty is generally assessed for failure to furnish required information with respect to a reportable transaction. In the case of the failure to file an information return with respect to a listed transaction, the penalty assessed is the greater of $200,000 or 50 percent of the gross income derived by the person required to file the return with respect to aid, assistance, or advice that is provided. The 50-percent limit is raised to 75 percent in cases involving an intentional failure to act.

Only one penalty applies in the case of a transaction that is both a listed transaction and a reportable transaction. The penalty that applies in these cases is the higher penalty for listed transactions. If there is a failure with respect to more than one reportable or listed transaction, a material advisor will be subject to a separate penalty for each transaction. The penalty with respect to reportable transactions other than listed transactions may be rescinded only in exceptional circumstances similar to those for rescission of the penalty for failure to disclose reportable transactions by taxpayers (¶ 2594). The penalty with respect to a listed transaction cannot be waived.

Each material advisor must maintain a list that identifies each person with respect to whom that advisor acted as a material advisor with respect to a reportable transaction, and contains any other information required by the IRS (Code Sec. 6112; Reg. § 301.6112-1). Regulations set forth the requirements for preparing and maintaining advisee lists, such as the persons required to be included on lists, the contents of the list, definitions, and the requirements for retention and furnishing of the lists. Information that is required to be included in the advisee lists must be retained for seven years. Any person required to maintain advisee lists that receives a written request from the IRS, but fails to make the lists available within 20 business days, may be assessed a $10,000 penalty for each day of failure after the 20th business day (Code Sec. 6708; Reg. § 301.6708-1).

2597. Abusive Tax Shelters Penalty. A penalty is imposed against any person that organizes, assists in organizing, or participates in the sale of any interest in a tax shelter if the person makes or furnishes, or causes another person to make or furnish: (1) a statement concerning the allowability of any tax benefit obtained through participation in the tax shelter that the person knows or has reason to know is false or fraudulent; or (2) a gross valuation overstatement concerning any matter that is material to the tax shelter (Code Sec. 6700). The penalty is 50 percent of the gross income derived, or to be derived, from the abusive plan or arrangement activities engaged in, other than promotion activities involving gross valuation overstatements. The penalty for promotion of activities involving gross valuation overstatements is equal to the lesser of $1,000 or 100 percent of the gross income derived, or to be derived, by the promoter from the activity.

In applying the penalty, promotion of each entity or activity is a separate activity, and each sale of an interest in the shelter is a separate activity. The penalty is imposed in addition to all other penalties that may be imposed, except with respect to any documents if an aiding and abetting penalty is imposed on that person with respect to the same document (¶ 2807).

2598. Injunctions Related to Tax Shelters. An injunction may be obtained with respect to the following acts: (1) promoting an abusive tax shelter (¶ 2597); (2) aiding someone in understating a tax liability in a return or other document (¶ 2807); (3) failing to furnish information about a reportable transaction (¶ 2593); or (4) failing to maintain a list of advisees (¶ 2595) (Code Sec. 7408). Once a court has enjoined a person from engaging in one or more of these activities, the court may expand the injunction to include any other activity that is subject to a penalty under tax law.

25 RETURNS

¶2598

Chapter 26

WITHHOLDING ☐ SELF-EMPLOYMENT TAX

Withholding on Wages

See CCH® AnswerConnect: *Withholding—Employment Taxes: Income Tax Withholding on Wages* for more information on this topic.

2601. Withholding of Income Tax on Wages. An employer generally must deduct and withhold income taxes from wages actually or constructively paid to each employee (Code Sec. 3402(a); Reg. § 31.3402(a)-1). Wages include all remuneration (other than fees paid to a public official) for services performed by an employee for an employer, including the cash value of all remuneration (including benefits) paid in any medium other than cash (¶ 2604). Thus, salaries, fees, bonuses, commissions on sales or insurance premiums, taxable fringe benefits, pensions, and retirement pay (unless taxed as an annuity) are subject to income tax withholding if paid as compensation for services.

An "employer" is generally any person for whom an individual has performed any service as an employee, regardless of the nature of the service. If the person for whom services are performed does not have legal control over the payment of wages, then the employer is the person actually controlling the payment of the wages (Code Sec. 3401(d); Reg. § 31.3401(d)-1). The services do not need to be continuing at the time the wages are paid in order for employer status to exist. An employer includes not only individuals and organizations engaged in trade or business, but also tax-exempt organizations and federal, state, and local government units, including the District of Columbia and Puerto Rico. An employer also includes any person paying wages on behalf of a nonresident alien individual, foreign partnership, or foreign corporation not engaged in trade or business within the United States or Puerto Rico.

An individual is an employee if the employer for whom the services are performed has the right to control and direct the individual not only as to the result to be accomplished by the work, but also as to the details and the means by which that result is accomplished (Code Sec. 3401(c); Reg. § 31.3401(c)-1). An employee also includes any officer, employee, or elected official of a federal, state, or local government unit, as well as an officer of a corporation, but not a director. Professionals such as physicians, lawyers, contractors, and others who follow an independent trade, business, or profession in which they offer their services to the public generally are not employees. If an employer-employee relationship exists, it does not matter what the parties call it (independent contractor, agent, etc.). It also does not matter how wages are measured, or whether the employee works full time or part time (¶ 2602).

An employer that is required to deduct and withhold income taxes from an employee's wages is generally liable for paying the taxes, even if the taxes are not withheld (Code Sec. 3403). If an employer's agent pays or controls the payment of wages, both the agent and the employer are liable (Code Sec. 3504). Any third party who pays wages directly to employees of an employer or to the employee's agent is liable for any required withholding on those wages (Code Sec. 3505). A certified professional employer organization (CPEO) is treated as the sole employer of an employee performing services for a customer of the CPEO (¶ 2660).

2602. Employee v. Independent Contractor. Employees must be distinguished from independent contractors, because an employer does not generally have employment tax obligations for independent contractors. The IRS examines three main categories to determine whether individuals are employees or independent contractors: behavioral control, financial control, and relationship of the parties (IRS Pub. 15-A). The previous 20-factor test in Rev. Rul. 87-41 can be still used for reference purposes (IRM 4.23.5.7.1). A worker who may be an independent contractor under this analysis may nevertheless be treated as an employee for FICA and FUTA tax purposes if the worker is classified as a statutory employee (¶ 941B). Either an employer or employee, with or without the other's knowledge or assent, may file Form SS-8 to request that the IRS determine whether or not a particular worker is an employee.

If an employer erroneously classifies an employee as an independent contractor and has no reasonable basis for doing so, the employer is liable for taxes under the income tax withholding (¶ 2601), FICA (¶ 2648), and FUTA (¶ 2649) tax provisions. An employer may be eligible for reduced rates with respect to income tax withholding (1.5 percent of employee's wages) and the employee's share of FICA taxes (20 percent of the amount otherwise due) (Code Sec. 3509). These rates are doubled if the employer failed to file forms consistent with the employer's treatment of the worker as an independent contractor. The reduced rate for FICA taxes is not available for statutory employees. If the employer had a reasonable basis for not treating an individual as an employee, the employer may be relieved of liability for employment taxes for that individual if the employer has consistently treated the worker as a nonemployee (Section 530 of the Revenue Act of 1978).

The IRS's Voluntary Classification Settlement Program allows an eligible business to voluntarily reclassify some or all of its workers as employees for future tax periods while limiting employment tax liability for past nonemployee treatment (Announcement 2012-45, modifying Announcement 2011-64). Form 8952 is used to apply for the program.

An employee who has been misclassified as an independent contractor uses Form 8919 to figure and report the employee's share of uncollected Social Security and Medicare taxes due on his or her compensation.

2604. Wages Subject to Income Tax Withholding. Wages subject to income tax withholding (¶ 2601) generally include all remuneration (other than fees paid to a public official) for services performed by an employee for an employer (Code Sec. 3401(a); Reg. § 31.3401(a)-1(a)). It includes salaries, fees, bonuses, and commissions. Withholding is based on *gross* wage payments before deductions such as those for federal or state unemployment insurance, pensions (except deductible contributions to IRAs), insurance, etc., or liabilities of the employee paid by the employer. An employer must withhold income tax from wages paid for employment regardless of the circumstances under which the employee is employed or the frequency or size of the individual wage payments (Rev. Rul. 57-12). Tax must be withheld from wages paid for *each* payroll period (Code Sec. 3402(a)).

If an employee works on two jobs for the same employer, and only a part of the remuneration is wages—for example, a construction worker who also works on his employer's farm (exempt employment)—all of the remuneration is treated alike. Thus, either: (1) all of the wages are subject to withholding if more than one-half of the time is spent performing services for which wages are received; or (2) all the remuneration is excluded from wages if more than one-half of the time spent is in exempt services, provided the payroll period is no longer than 31 consecutive days (Code Sec. 3402(e); Reg. § 31.3402(e)-1).

Compensation. Other forms of compensation are subject to withholding, including tips and other gratuities (¶ 2605), reimbursed employee expenses paid through a nonaccountable plan (¶ 2607), other supplemental wages such as fringe benefits

(¶ 2606), employee expenses in excess of per diem rates (¶ 2608), and payments for the stoppage of work such as severance payments and strike benefits (Reg. § 31.3401(a)-1). Some types of compensation are specifically excluded from the definition of wages for income tax withholding purposes (¶ 2609).

Supplemental unemployment compensation benefit (SUB) payments are treated as wages for income tax withholding purposes, but withholding applies only to the extent that such benefits are includible in the employee's gross income (Code Sec. 3402(o)). SUB payments are also wages for FICA purposes, but may be excluded from wages for FICA (¶ 2648) and FUTA (¶ 2649) tax purposes if payable based upon state unemployment benefits (*In re Quality Stores, Inc.*, SCt, 2014-1 USTC ¶ 50,228; Rev. Rul. 90-72). Guaranteed annual wage payments made during periods of unemployment under a collective bargaining agreement are wages subject to withholding (Rev. Rul. 73-22). Strike benefits paid in fixed amounts by a union to its members, regardless of whether the members perform services for the union, are not subject to withholding (Rev. Rul. 68-424). However, strike benefits paid by a union only to members who actually perform strike-related services and at an hourly rate are wages subject to withholding (Rev. Rul. 75-475).

Although the value of noncash compensation generally must be included in wages, if a retail commission salesperson is occasionally paid other than in cash, then the employer is not required to withhold income tax for the noncash payments (Code Sec. 3402(j); Reg. § 31.3402(j)-1). However, the fair market value of the noncash payments (such as prizes) must be included on the Form W-2 furnished to the employee as part of the total pay earned during the calendar year.

Withholding is available if the payee requests it for sick pay (i.e., wage continuation payments) received from a third party under a health or accident plan in which the employer participates (Code Sec. 3402(o); Reg. § 31.3402(o)-3). Payments of sick pay made directly by employers to their employees are automatically subject to withholding. Employers who are third-party payors of sick pay are not required to withhold income taxes from payments unless the employee has requested withholding on Form W-4S. Sick pay is exempt for FICA and FUTA tax purposes after six calendar months following the month the employee last worked for the employer (Code Secs. 3121(a)(4) and 3306(b)(4)).

Wages subject to withholding include amounts received under a nonqualified deferred compensation plan that are includible in an employee's gross income under Code Sec. 409A for the year of inclusion (¶ 2197) (Code Sec. 3401(a)).

Differential Wage Payments. Differential wage payments are treated as wages for federal income tax withholding purposes (Code Sec. 3401(h)). A differential wage payment is any payment that: (1) is made by an employer to an individual for any period during which the individual is performing service in the uniformed services while on active duty for a period of more than 30 days, and (2) represents all or a portion of the wages the individual would have received from the employer if the individual were performing services for the employer. Differential wage payments are considered supplemental wages and subject to the special rules that apply to such payments (¶ 2606). They are not treated as wages for FICA and FUTA tax purposes (Rev. Rul. 2009-11).

Qualified Equity Grants. Qualified stock for which a Code Sec. 83(i) election is made (¶ 1933) is treated as wages received on the earliest date possible under Code Sec. 83(i)(1)(B), and in the amount included as income for the tax year which includes that date. If the employee must include the deferred amount in gross income, tax must be withheld at the maximum income tax rate (37 percent for tax years 2018 through 2025), and the stock is treated as a noncash fringe benefit for tax collection purposes (Code Secs. 3401(i) and 3402(t); Notice 2018-97).

2605. Tips and Gratuities Subject to Withholding. An employee must account for cash tips paid directly to him or her by a customer and charged tips paid over to the employee (¶ 717). The employee must furnish a written statement to the employer on or before the 10th day of the month following the month when the tips are received (Code Sec. 6053(a)). The employee reports the tips on Form 4070 or similar statement. If tips received in the course of his or her employment for a single employer are less than $20 in a calendar month, then the employee is not required to report the tips.

¶ 2605

The employer uses the employee's report to figure the amount of income tax to withhold for the pay period on both wages and reported tips (Code Sec. 3401(a)(16)). The report is also used to figure the amount of FICA and FUTA taxes to withhold for the pay period (Code Secs. 3121(a)(12) and 3306(s)). A service charge added to a bill or fixed by the employer that the customer must pay is not a tip. A payment is a tip rather than wages only if it is made free from compulsion, the amount is freely determined by the customer, the payment is not negotiated or dictated by the employer, and the customer decides who receives the payment (Rev. Rul. 2012-18).

A large food and beverage establishment (one normally with more than 10 employees on a typical business day and in which tipping is customary) must file an annual information return using Form 8027 (¶ 2565). The return must report gross food and beverage sales receipts, employee-reported tip income, total charge receipts, and total charge tips (Code Sec. 6053(c); Reg. § 31.6053-3). The employer must allocate during the payroll period among its employees who customarily receive tip income an amount equal to the excess of eight percent of gross receipts over reported tips. The allocation is not required if the employees voluntarily report total tips equal to at least eight percent of gross sales. If it can be shown that average tips are less than eight percent of gross sales, the employer or a majority of its employees may apply to the IRS to have the allocation reduced, but not to below two percent.

2606. Supplemental Wages Subject to Withholding. Special withholding rules apply if an employee is paid supplemental wages (e.g., bonus, overtime pay, back pay, commissions, vacation allowance, taxable fringe benefits, etc.). If supplemental wages are paid at the same time as regular wages, the two are added together and income tax withholding is computed on the total as a single wage payment. If the supplemental wages are not paid at the same time as the regular wages, the supplemental wages may be added either to the regular wages for the preceding payroll period or for the current payroll period within the same calendar year (Reg. § 31.3402(g)-1).

Under an alternative method, the employer may treat supplemental wages as wholly separate from regular wages, and withhold at a flat rate equal to the third lowest income tax rate (22 percent in 2018 through 2025) without regard to any allowances or reference to any regular payment of wages. Once the total of supplemental wage payments made to an employee within a calendar year exceeds $1 million, the excess is subject to withholding at the highest income tax rate (37 percent in 2018 through 2025). This rule applies regardless of the method otherwise used to withhold supplemental wages paid to the employee (IRS Pub. 15; IRS Pub. 505; Notice 2018-92).

An employer must collect both income tax and an employee's share of Social Security or railroad retirement tax on tips reported by the employee from wages due the employee or other funds that the employee makes available. Tips may be treated as if they were supplemental wages subject to the flat withholding rate (22 percent in 2018 through 2025) without regard to any allowances, provided that income tax has been withheld on the employee's regular wages. Otherwise, the tips must be treated as part of the current or preceding wage payment of the same calendar year and are subject to the regular graduated withholding rates (Rev. Rul. 66-190).

2607. Employee Expense Reimbursements Subject to Withholding. An employer's withholding obligations for amounts paid to employees under an expense allowance or reimbursement arrangement depend on whether the amounts are paid under an accountable plan or a nonaccountable plan (¶ 943 and ¶ 952A). Amounts paid under an accountable plan may be excluded from an employee's gross income to the extent of the employee's substantiated expenses, and are not required to be reported on the employee's Form W-2. Thus, the payments are exempt from employment tax obligations (income tax withholding, FICA, FUTA, railroad retirement, and railroad unemployment taxes) (Reg. §§ 1.62-2 and 31.3401(a)-4).

Amounts paid under a nonaccountable plan are included in the employee's gross income, reported on Form W-2, and are subject to withholding as supplemental wages (¶ 2606). If expenses are reimbursed under an accountable plan, but either the expenses are not substantiated within a reasonable time period or amounts in excess of substantiated expenses are not returned within a reasonable time period, the unsubstantiated or excess amounts are treated as paid under a nonaccountable plan and are subject to withholding no later than the first payroll period following the end of the reasonable time period.

Expense reimbursements that are subject to withholding may be added to the employee's regular wages for the appropriate payroll period, and withheld taxes may be computed on the total. Alternatively, the employer may withhold at the flat rate that applies to supplemental wages (¶ 2606) if the expense reimbursement or allowance is separately paid or separately identified (Reg. § 31.3401(a)-4(c)).

2608. Per Diem Allowances Subject to Withholding. If an employee's business expenses are substantiated using an IRS-approved per diem allowance, any amounts paid by the employer to the employee exceeding the amounts deemed substantiated are treated as paid under a nonaccountable plan (¶ 2607) and subject to income tax withholding and other employment taxes (Reg. § § 1.62-2(h)(2)(i)(B) and 31.3401(a)-4(b)(1)(ii)). See ¶ 947 for standard mileage rate and FAVR allowances for automobile expenses, and ¶ 954 for per diem methods relating to meal and lodging expenses.

For per diem or mileage allowances paid in advance, withholding on any excess must occur no later than the first payroll period following the payroll period in which the employee substantiates the expenses paid (i.e., the days or miles of travel). For a per diem or mileage allowance paid as a reimbursement, the excess amounts reimbursed are subject to withholding when paid.

2609. Compensation Not Subject to Withholding. Some types of compensation are excluded from the definition of wages for income tax withholding purposes (¶ 2601). This includes amounts paid for or for the services of:

- newspaper carriers under age 18 delivering to customers;
- newspaper and magazine vendors who buy at fixed prices and retain the excess from sales to customers;
- agricultural workers who are not subject to FICA withholding;
- household employees;
- cash or noncash tips of less than $20 per month;
- certain employer contributions to IRAs and deferred compensation plans;
- individuals not working in the course of the employer's business (less than $50 paid and less than 24 days worked during the current or preceding quarter);
- employees of foreign governments and international organizations;
- armed forces personnel serving in a combat zone;
- foreign earned income if excludable from gross income; and
- members of a religious order performing services for the order or associated institution (Code Sec. 3401(a)).

Fringe benefits are generally included in supplemental wages (¶ 2606). However, certain qualified employee fringe benefits—such as no-additional-cost services, qualified employee discounts, working condition fringe benefits, *de minimis* fringe benefits, qualified transportation fringe benefits, qualified moving expense reimbursements (generally before 2018 and after 2025 (¶ 2092)), qualified retirement planning services, qualified military base realignment and closure fringe benefits, and certain employer-provided cell phones—are not subject to income tax withholding if it is reasonable to believe the recipient will be able to exclude them from gross income (¶ 2085) (Code Sec. 3401(a)(19); IRS Pub. 15-B). Accident and health insurance premiums paid by a partnership on behalf of a partner, and premiums paid by an S corporation on behalf of a two-percent shareholder-employee, are not excludable from gross income (Rev. Rul. 91-26). Thus, they are wages subject to income tax withholding, but not for FICA and FUTA purposes (Code Secs. 3121(a)(2)(B) and 3306(b)(2)(B)).

An employer's cost of group-term life insurance, including any amount in excess of $50,000 coverage that is taxable to the employee as compensation (¶ 2055), is exempt from income tax withholding (Code Sec. 3401(a)(14); Reg. § 31.3401(a)(14)-1). However, the employer must report the cost of the insurance coverage includible in the employee's gross income on Form W-2 (Code Sec. 6052; Reg. § 1.6052-1). An employer's reimbursement of an employee's moving expenses is exempt from income tax withholding if it is reasonable to believe a moving expense deduction will be allowable to the employee (generally before 2018 and after 2025) (¶ 1073) (Code Sec. 3401(a)(15)). Certain moving expense reimbursements that an employee received in 2018 for a move occurring in 2017 may be exempt (Notice 2018-75). In addition, the value of any meals or lodging excludable by the employee from gross income (¶ 2089) is exempt from income tax withholding (Reg. § 31.3401(a)-1(b)(9)). See ¶ 2607 and ¶ 2608 for information concerning amounts paid to employees as advances or reimbursements for traveling, meals, etc.

Benefits provided by an employer to an employee in the form of certain educational assistance (¶ 2067), dependent care assistance (¶ 2065), fellowship or scholarship grants (¶ 865), National Health Service Corps loan repayments, employee achievement awards (¶ 2069), or qualified military benefits for dependent care assistance and for certain travel (¶ 896) are not subject to income tax withholding if it is reasonable to believe that the employee is entitled to exclude the payment from income (Code Sec. 3401(a)(18) and (19)). Benefits provided by the employer in the form of medical care reimbursement made to, or for the benefit of, an employee under a self-insured medical reimbursement plan are excluded from wages for withholding purposes (¶ 2015) (Code Sec. 3401(a)(20)). Benefits paid under workers' compensation laws (other than nonoccupational disability benefits) are not taxable compensation for services performed and are not subject to withholding for income, FICA, or FUTA tax purposes (Code Secs. 104, 3121(a)(2)(A), and 3306(b)(2)(A)).

An employee's elective contributions to a traditional Code Sec. 401(k) retirement plan, simplified employee pension (SEP), Code Sec. 403(b) annuity plan, or SIMPLE retirement account are not included in wages for income tax withholding purposes, but they are wages for FICA and FUTA tax purposes (Code Secs. 3401(a)(12), 3121(a)(5), and 3306(b)(5)).

Death benefit payments to beneficiaries or to the estates of deceased employees, and payments to such persons of compensation due but unpaid at the time of the decedent's death, are not subject to withholding (Rev. Rul. 59-64).

Withholding is not required on a disqualifying disposition of stock acquired through exercise of an incentive stock option (¶ 1925) or through an employee stock purchase plan (ESPP) (¶ 1929) (Code Sec. 421(b)). Further, no withholding is required if compensation is recognized in connection with an ESPP discount (Code Sec. 423(c)).

Voluntary Withholding. If remuneration is taxable to the employee but exempt from withholding, the employee may voluntarily request that the employer increase the amount withheld from the employee's other compensation. In many cases, the employee and employer may enter into a mutual agreement for the employer to withhold from remuneration that would be otherwise exempt from withholding (¶ 2629).

Computation of Withholding on Wages

See CCH® AnswerConnect: *Withholding—Employment Taxes: Income Tax Withholding on Wages* for more information on this topic.

2612. Calculation of Income Tax Withholding. To calculate an employee's income tax withholding (¶ 2601), an employer should follow a few basic steps:

- determine the payroll period, such as weekly, biweekly, or monthly (¶ 2621);

- calculate the employee's wages for the applicable payroll period (¶ 2604);

- determine the employee's withholding allowance based on his or her filled-out Form W-4 (¶ 2634); and

- choose the withholding method (¶ 2614).

Other factors to consider include whether the employee is a recent hire or only works part-time, whether the employee has more than one employer, and whether the employee receives any supplemental wage payments (¶ 2606).

2614. Methods of Income Tax Withholding. An employer will generally elect to use one of the two primary methods of computing income tax to be withheld from

26 | WITHHOLDING

wages: the percentage method (¶ 2616) or the wage bracket method (¶ 2619) (Code Sec. 3402; Reg. § 31.3402(a)-1). See ¶ 2627 for other permissible withholding methods. Regardless of which method is used, the amount of withholding depends upon the amount of wages paid (¶ 2604), the information provided by the employee on his or her Form W-4 (¶ 2632 and ¶ 2634), and the employee's payroll period (¶ 2621) (IRS Pub. 15; IRS Pub. 15-T).

2616. Percentage Method of Income Tax Withholding. An employer that uses the percentage method of withholding (¶ 2614) calculates the amount of income tax to be deducted and withheld using the applicable percentage method withholding table published by the IRS (Reg. § 31.3402(b)-1; Prop. Reg. § 31.3402(b)-1; IRS Pub. 15-T). If the employee has submitted a redesigned Form W-4 for 2020 or later (¶ 2634), the employer determines the withholding amount as follows:

(1) divide the amount, if any, of other income (not from any jobs) listed on Step 4(a) of the employee's Form W-4 by the number of pay periods for the year;

(2) add to the amount in (1) the employee's taxable wages for the payroll period;

(3) divide the amount, if any, on Step 4(b) of the Form W-4 (i.e., calculation from Deductions Worksheet in the Form W-4 instructions) by the number of pay periods for the year;

(4) subtract (3) from (2) to determine the "adjusted wage amount";

(5) for the adjusted wage amount in (4), apply the appropriate percentage rate table, based on pay frequency, the employee's filing status, and whether the employee has checked the optional box in Step 2 of the Form W-4 (indicating there are only two jobs in the household), to determine the "tentative withholding amount";

(6) divide the amount, if any, on Step 3 of the Form W-4 (i.e., the total amount claimed for the child tax credit, the credit for other dependents, and other tax credits) by the number of pay periods for the year;

(7) subtract (6) from the amount determined in (5); and

(8) add to the amount in (7) the additional withholding amount, if any, listed on Step 4(c) of the Form W-4.

If the employee has submitted a Form W-4 in a year before 2020 and does not need to submit a new form, the employer determines the withholding amount as follows:

(1) multiply the amount for one withholding allowance for the payroll period by the number of allowances claimed on the employee's Form W-4;

(2) subtract the amount in (1) from the employee's taxable wages for the payroll period;

(3) for the amount in (2), apply the appropriate percentage rate table, based on pay frequency and the employee's marital status, to determine the "tentative withholding amount"; and

(4) add to the amount determined in (3) the additional withholding amount listed on line 6 of the Form W-4.

Withholding is determined based on the amount by which the wages exceed the taxpayer's withholding allowance, prorated to the payroll period (¶ 2621) (Code Sec. 3402(a)(2)). For tax years beginning before 2018, one withholding exemption was equal to one personal exemption for the year, prorated to the payroll period. For tax years beginning in 2018 through 2025, the personal exemption amount is zero (¶ 133).

For Forms W-4 from before 2020, each payroll period has a separate percentage method table for single individuals (including heads of household) and married individuals. For Forms W-4 redesigned for 2020 and after, each payroll period has two withholding rate schedules—one for standard withholding, one for withholding if the optional box in Step 2 of the Form W-4 is checked—and each schedule has a separate percentage method table based on filing status (single, head of household, and married filing jointly).

¶2616

2619. Wage Bracket Method of Income Tax Withholding. For Forms W-4 from before 2020 (¶ 2634), the wage bracket method of withholding (¶ 2614) is based on the employee's marital status, pay period, and claimed withholding allowances. Unlike the percentage method (¶ 2616), the wage bracket method generally does not require the employer to make separate computations. Instead, the tentative withholding amounts are pre-calculated in wage bracket tables covering daily, weekly, biweekly, semimonthly, and monthly payroll periods (Code Sec. 3402(c); IRS Pub. 15-T). Separate tables for each period are provided for single individuals (including heads of household) and married individuals. The proper columns for the employer to use are determined by the total number of allowances claimed on the employee's withholding certificate. The employer adds to the tentative withholding amount any additional withholding amount listed on line 6 of the employee's Form W-4.

For redesigned Form W-4 for 2020 or later, the employer must make calculations similar to those for the percentage method to compute the "adjusted wage amount" to be used in the appropriate wage bracket table. There is a separate wage bracket table for each payroll period, each with separate columns based on filing status (single, head of household, married filing jointly). Each column has two subcolumns: one for standard withholding, one for withholding if the optional box in Step 2 of the Form W-4 is checked (IRS Pub. 15-T).

The wage bracket method tables produce results similar to those of the percentage method tables, and are designed to accommodate different payroll systems. If the wage bracket tables cannot be used because wages are more than the amount shown in the last bracket of the table (or, for a pre-2020 Form W-4, the employee has claimed more than 10 withholding allowances), the employer should use the percentage method tables (IRS Pub. 15-T).

2621. Payroll Period. For calculating income tax withholding (¶ 2612), the employee's payroll period, or the period of service for which a payment of wages is ordinarily made to an employee, determines the correct withholding table that the employer uses under the percentage method (¶ 2616) or the wage bracket method (¶ 2619). There are separate tables for weekly, biweekly, semimonthly, monthly, and daily payroll periods; for Forms W-4 from before 2020 (¶ 2634), there are also separate percentage method tables for quarterly, semiannual, and annual payroll periods. Any other payroll period is a miscellaneous payroll period. Wages may also be paid for periods that are not payroll periods (¶ 2624).

2624. Calculation of Income Tax Withholding Allowance. If an employee has an established payroll period (¶ 2621), the amount of the withholding allowance for the percentage method (¶ 2616) is determined by the payroll period, without regard to the time the employee is actually engaged in performing services during such period. If the payment is for a period that is not a payroll period, such as when wages are paid upon completion of a particular project, the withholding allowance under the percentage method or the amount withheld under the wage bracket method (¶ 2619) is computed based on a miscellaneous payroll period containing a number of days (including Sundays and holidays) equal to those in the period covered by the payment (Code Sec. 3402(b); Reg. § 31.3402(c)-1(c)). If the wages are paid without regard to any period, the tax to be withheld is the same as for a miscellaneous payroll period containing the number of days equal to the days (including Sundays and holidays) that have elapsed since the later of: (1) the first day after the last payment of wages by the employer during the calendar year, (2) the date employment began with the employer during such year, or (3) January 1 of such year.

2627. Alternative Methods of Income Tax Withholding. An employer may withhold income taxes based on average wages (using estimated quarterly wages paid to an employee), annualized wages, cumulative wages, or any method which produces substantially the same withholding amount as the percentage method or the wage bracket method (¶ 2614) (Code Sec. 3402(h); Reg. § 31.3402(h)(4)-1; IRS Pub. 15-T).

2629. Voluntary Income Tax Withholding. An employee may request on Form W-4 that the employer withhold additional amounts of income from the employee's wages. An employer must comply with the request, but only to the extent the additional withholding amount does not reduce the employee's net pay (after other deductions required by law) below zero (Code Sec. 3402(i); Reg. §§ 31.3402(i)-1 and 31.3402(i)-2; Prop. Reg. § 31.3402(i)-1).

An employee and employer may also enter into an agreement for the employer to withhold from certain types of income that are not subject to mandatory withholding (¶ 2609). For example, magazine vendors, domestic workers, etc., may enter into an agreement with their employer to have income tax withheld. To effectuate this agreement, the employee must submit Form W-4 to the employer, and the employer must begin withholding (Code Sec. 3402(p); Reg. § 31.3402(p)-1). Taxpayers may use Form W-4V to request voluntary withholding from certain federal payments, including Social Security benefits, crop disaster payments, Commodity Credit Corporation loans, and unemployment compensation.

2632. Claiming Withholding Allowance. An employee must furnish his or her employer with a Form W-4 (¶ 2634) showing information for the withholding allowance the employee is claiming (Code Sec. 3402(f); Reg. § 31.3402(f)(1)-1). An employee's withholding allowance is determined based on:

(1) whether the employee is an individual for whom a personal exemption deduction is allowable to another taxpayer (¶ 137);

(2) if the employee is married, whether the employee's spouse is entitled to an allowance under (1) above or (4) below (or would be if the spouse were an employee), but only if the spouse does not have a withholding certificate in effect claiming the allowance;

(3) the number of individuals for whom the employee may reasonably be expected to be allowed a child tax credit for the tax year (and a credit for other dependents, for tax years 2018 through 2025) (¶ 1405);

(4) any additional amounts the employee elects to claim under Code Sec. 3402(m), but only if his or her spouse does not have a withholding certificate in effect making the election;

(5) the standard deduction allowable to the employee (one-half of the standard deduction if the employee is married and the spouse is an employee receiving wages subject to withholding) (¶ 131); and

(6) whether the employee has withholding certificates in effect with more than one employer (Code Sec. 3402(f)(1)).

For tax years beginning before 2018, every employee was entitled to a withholding exemption for himself or herself, as well as one for each dependent (¶ 137). A married employee could claim a withholding exemption for his or her spouse if the latter did not claim one. An employee who could be claimed as a dependent on another individual's tax return, such as a parent's return, could not claim an exemption for himself or herself. No exemption was allowed for unborn children, even if the birth was expected to occur within the same tax year. Employees with more than one job could not claim an exemption that was currently in effect with another employer. An employee could claim a standard deduction allowance equal to one withholding exemption if the employee: (1) did not have a spouse who was receiving wages subject to withholding; and (2) did not have withholding certificates in effect with more than one employer. These restrictions did not apply if the wages earned by the spouse or by the employee from another employer were $1,500 or less, combined.

Additional Allowances. An employee can claim an additional withholding allowance or additional reductions in withholding based on the additional standard deduction for age or blindness, estimated itemized deductions, the estimated deduction for qualified business income (QBI), alimony payments (generally for divorce or separation instruments executed before January 1, 2019), moving expenses (generally before 2018 and after 2025), employee business expenses, retirement contributions, net losses from Schedule C, Schedule D, Schedule E, and Schedule F of Form 1040, certain tax credits, and estimated tax payments (Code Sec. 3402(m); Reg. § 31.3402(m)-1).

2634. Employee's Withholding Certificate (Form W-4). Before an employee is allowed a withholding allowance (¶ 2632), he or she must furnish the employer with a

¶ 2632

withholding certificate on Form W-4, showing information on the withholding allowance to which the employee claims he or she is entitled (Code Sec. 3402(f)(2); Reg. § 31.3402(f)(2)-1). If the employee does not submit a Form W-4, the employer must compute withholding as if the employee were single and claiming no withholding allowance. A widow or widower may claim married status for withholding purposes if he or she qualifies as a surviving spouse (¶ 175) (Code Sec. 3402(l)(3)).

The Form W-4 for 2020 and after has been redesigned, so that employees will no longer be able to request adjustments to their withholding using withholding allowances. Instead, the employee uses the redesigned Form W-4 to provide the employer with amounts to increase or reduce withholding, and amounts to increase or decrease the income that is subject to withholding. Employees who have submitted a Form W-4 in a year before 2020 are not required to submit a new form merely because of the redesign (IRS News Release IR-2019-98).

An employee who certifies to the employer that he or she had no income tax liability for the preceding tax year and anticipates none for the current tax year may be exempt from wage withholding (Code Sec. 3402(n); Reg. § 31.3402(n)-1). An employee claiming exemption from withholding for a tax year must give the employer a new Form W-4 by February 15 each year to continue the exemption (Reg. § 31.3402(f)(4)-2(c); Prop. Reg. § 31.3402(f)(4)-1(b); Notice 2018-92).

A $500 civil penalty may be assessed against any individual who decreases his or her withholding by claiming allowances on Form W-4 without a reasonable basis (Code Sec. 6682). In addition, a criminal penalty may be imposed against any individual who willfully supplies false or fraudulent withholding information, or willfully fails to supply information that would increase the amount withheld (Code Sec. 7205).

Most Forms W-4 are retained by the employer and only need to be submitted to the IRS if directed to do so. The IRS may issue a notice to the employer ("lock-in letter") that specifies the maximum withholding allowance a particular employee may claim. The employer is generally bound by this determination until otherwise advised by the IRS (Reg. § 31.3402(f)(2)-1(g)).

2637. Changes to Withholding Allowance. An employee furnishes his or her employer with a new withholding certificate (¶ 2634) to alter the amount of the withholding allowance claimed (¶ 2632). An employee may provide a new Form W-4 at any time that he or she becomes eligible for an increase in the allowance. However, an employee must furnish a new certificate within 10 days if a "change in status" event occurs that decreases the allowance to which the employee is entitled for the current calendar year (Code Sec. 3402(f)(2)(B); Reg. § 31.3402(f)(2)-1(b); Prop. Reg. § 31.3402(f)(2)-1(b)). If the event that decreases the allowance affects the next calendar year, the employee must furnish a new Form W-4 by the later of December 1 of the year when the change occurs or within 10 days after the change occurs (Reg. § 31.3402(f)(2)-1(c); Prop. Reg. § 31.3402(f)(2)-1(e)).

Proposed regulations that employers and employees may apply on and after January 1, 2020, list the following events that may reduce the withholding allowance (Prop. Reg. § 31.3402(f)(2)-1(b)):

- an employee's filing status changes from married filing jointly (or qualifying widow(er)) to head of household, married filing separately, or single; or from head of household to married filing separately or single;

- an employee, his or her spouse, or both, no longer have only one Form W-4 in effect, and higher withholding rate tables were selected on the additional Form W-4 but not on the previously furnished Form W-4;

- an employee has multiple Forms W-4 in effect on which higher withholding rate tables are not selected, and the employee or his or her spouse reasonably expects a wage increase of more than $10,000;

- an employee has claimed a child tax credit on a Form W-4, but reasonably expects the number of qualifying children to decrease;

- an employee has claimed any tax credit on a Form W-4, but reasonably expects the tax credits to be claimed on his or her return to decrease by more than $500;

26 | WITHHOLDING

- an employee has claimed additional withholding allowances on a Form W-4, but reasonably expects the deductions to be claimed on his or her return to decrease by more than $2,300; or

- an employee has claimed exemption from withholding, but reasonably expects to incur an income tax liability for either the current or previous year.

Under temporary relief, if an employee experienced a change of status, on or before April 30, 2019, that reduced the number of withholding allowances to which he or she was entitled, and if that change was due solely to changes made by the Tax Cuts and Jobs Act (P.L. 115-97), the employee was generally required to furnish a new Form W-4 to the employer by May 10, 2019 (Notice 2018-92).

A Form W-4 furnished to the employer that replaces an existing certificate can be effective for the first payment after the form is received if so elected by the employer. The replacement certificate must be effective for the first payroll period that ends on or after the 30th day after the day on which the new Form W-4 is furnished (Code Sec. 3402(f)(3)(B); Reg. § 31.3402(f)(3)-1(b)).

Withholding on Non-Wage Payments

See CCH® AnswerConnect: *Withholding—Backup Withholding and Other Nonwage Withholding* for more information on this topic.

2642. Withholding on Certain Gambling Winnings. Income tax withholding is required at a flat rate of 24 percent for tax years beginning in 2018 through 2025 for winnings of more than $5,000 from sweepstakes, wagering pools, and lotteries. Withholding is required on winnings from other types of gambling (including pari-mutual pools on horse races, dog races, and jai alai) if the winnings are at least 300 times the wager. No withholding is required on winnings from bingo, keno, or slot machines (Code Secs. 1(j)(2)(F) and 3402(q)).

The payor must report gambling winnings to the taxpayer and the IRS on Form W-2G if the winnings are subject to withholding or if the winner receives: $1,200 or more from a bingo game or slot machine; $1,500 or more from keno; more than $5,000 from a poker tournament; or for other gambling winnings of $600 or more and at least 300 times the amount of the wager (Reg. § 1.6041-10). If reporting is required, backup withholding must occur if the winner does not furnish his or her taxpayer identification number (TIN) to the payor (¶ 2645). All withheld income reported on Form W-2G must also be reported on Form 945.

2643. Withholding on Pensions, Annuities, and Certain Deferred Income. For taxable payments from an employer-sponsored pension, annuity, profit-sharing, stock bonus, or other deferred compensation plan, income tax withholding is required unless the recipient elects not to have tax withheld (Code Sec. 3405). The same rule applies to an IRA or an annuity, endowment, or life insurance contract issued by a life insurance company. The recipient's election not to have withholding apply remains in effect until revoked. The payor must notify the recipient of his or her right to make or revoke such election. The election is generally not available for payments delivered outside the United States or a U.S. possession, unless the recipient certifies to the payor that he or she is not a U.S. citizen, a U.S. resident alien, or a tax-avoidance expatriate.

The amount withheld depends on whether the distributions are periodic payments or nonperiodic payments. For periodic payments (annuity and similar periodic payments), withholding is made as though the payment were a payment of wages for the appropriate payroll period. If a withholding certificate (Form W-4P) is not in effect for a periodic payment, the amount withheld is to be calculated under IRS rules.

For 2019 and 2020, the payee is treated as a married individual claiming three withholding allowances if no withholding certificate is furnished (Notice 2018-92; Notice 2020-3). For tax years beginning before 2018, a payee who did not have a withholding certificate in effect was treated as a married individual claiming three exemptions. The payee is treated as single with no withholding allowances if the payee fails to provide his or her social security number to a payor, or if the IRS notifies the payor that the payee's social security number is incorrect (Instructions for Form W-4P; IRS Pub. 505).

¶2642

The withholding rate on nonperiodic distributions is 10 percent. The withholding rate on distributions that were eligible for rollover but not directly transferred from the distributing plan to an eligible transferee plan is 20 percent. Withholding is mandatory, and distributees cannot elect to forego withholding on rollover eligible distributions.

IRA Payment to Unclaimed Property Fund. A trustee's payment of an individual's interest in a traditional IRA to a state unclaimed property fund, as required by state law, is a designated distribution subject to federal income tax withholding and IRA reporting requirements. The IRS has provided transition relief to the withholding and reporting requirements for payments made before January 1, 2020 (Rev. Rul. 2018-17, as modified by Notice 2018-90).

2645. Backup Withholding. The backup withholding system requires a payor to deduct and withhold income tax at a flat rate of 24 percent for tax years beginning in 2018 through 2025 from reportable payments, such as interest or dividends, if:

- the payee fails to furnish a correct taxpayer identification number (TIN) to the payor in the manner required;
- the IRS notifies the payor that the TIN furnished by the payee is incorrect;
- the IRS notifies the payor that the payee has underreported reportable payments; or
- the payee is required, but fails, to certify that he or she is not subject to withholding (Code Sec. 3406).

Backup withholding is reported on Form 945.

FICA and FUTA Taxes

See CCH® AnswerConnect: *Withholding—Employment Taxes: FICA Taxes* and *Withholding—Employment Taxes: FUTA Tax* for more information on this topic.

2648. FICA Tax. Under the Federal Insurance Contributions Act (FICA), an employer must withhold an employee's share of Social Security and Medicare taxes from FICA wages paid to the employee during the year, and pay a matching amount as the employer's share of these taxes (Code Secs. 3101, 3111, and 3121(a)). Even if an employee claims exemption from income tax withholding, the employer must withhold FICA taxes. The employer must report FICA taxes withheld (¶ 2650) and deposit the amounts paid and withheld (¶ 2651).

FICA Tax Rate and Base. The employee and employer are each subject to a 7.65-percent FICA tax on wages paid, consisting of a 6.2-percent tax for old-age, survivors, and disability insurance (OASDI) (i.e., Social Security) and a 1.45-percent tax for hospital insurance (HI) (i.e., Medicare). The Social Security tax applies only to wages paid up to the Social Security wage base limit for the year ($132,900 in 2019; $137,700 in 2020). The wage base applies separately to each common-law employer, with exceptions for successor employers and common paymasters, as well as certain motion picture project employers (Code Sec. 3512).

COVID-19 (Coronavirus) Employee Retention Credit. An eligible employer may claim a refundable credit for 50 percent of qualified wages paid from March 13, 2020, through December 31, 2020 (limited to $10,000 in wages per employee) against the *employer's portion* of OASDI (or Railroad Retirement Tax Act (RRTA), as applicable). For employers with 100 or fewer full-time employees (FTEs), all wages paid qualify for the credit. For employers with more than 100 FTEs, only wages paid to employees when not providing services for the employer qualify for the credit. An eligible employer is immediately reimbursed for the credit by reducing their required deposits of payroll taxes that have been withheld from employees' wages by the amount of the credit. The IRS has provided relief from the penalty for failure to deposit employment taxes to employers entitled to credit (Act Sec. 2301 of the Coronavirus Aid, Relief, and Economic Security (CARES) Act (P.L. 116-136); Notice 2020-22).

COVID-19 (Coronavirus) Paid Sick Leave and Family Leave Credits. An eligible employer with fewer than 500 employees may also claim a refundable credit for 100 percent of qualified sick leave wages and qualified family leave wages against the *employer's portion* of OASDI or RRTA taxes. The credits are only for qualified leave wages paid for the period that begins on April 1, 2020, and ends on December 31, 2020.

26 | WITHHOLDING

The IRS has provided relief from the penalty for failure to deposit employment taxes to employers entitled to the credits (Act Secs. 7001, 7003, and 7005 of the Families First Coronavirus Response Act (P.L. 116-127) as amended by Act Sec. 3606 of P.L. 116-136; Notice 2020-21; Notice 2020-22).

The credit for qualified sick leave is limited to $511 per day in the case of an employee who is subject to a federal, state, or local quarantine or isolation order related to COVID-19, has been advised by a health care provider to self-quarantine due to COVID-19-related concerns, or is experiencing symptoms of COVID-19 and is seeking a medical diagnosis. The limitation is reduced to $200 per day if the employee is caring for an individual who is subject to a quarantine or isolation order or has been advised to self quarantine, is caring for a child whose school or place of care has been closed, or a substantially similar condition specified by the Department of Health and Human Services. The credit for paid family leave is also limited to $200 per day (or $10,000 for all calendar quarters) where the paid leave is due to the closure of a child's school or care provider (or the unavailability of the child's care provider) due to a declared public health emergency related to COVID-19. Similar credits are available for a self-employed individual (¶ 2664).

COVID-19 (Coronavirus) Deferral of Employer Payroll Taxes. An employer may defer payment of the *employer's share* of OASDI or RRTA taxes that they otherwise are responsible for paying on wages normally required to be paid from March 27, 2020, through December 31, 2020. The deferred taxes must be paid over the following two years, with half to be paid by December 31, 2021, and the other half to be paid by December 31, 2022 (Act Sec. 2302 of P.L. 116-136). The deferral is also available for 50 percent of these taxes required to be paid by a self-employed individual (¶ 2664).

0.9% Additional Medicare Tax. The employee's portion of the Medicare component of FICA taxes is increased by an additional 0.9 percent (to 2.35 percent) for wages in excess of $200,000 ($250,000 if married filing jointly, $125,000 if married filing separately). For a joint return, the additional tax is imposed on the couple's combined wages (Code Sec. 3101(b)(2); Reg. §31.3102-4). There is no limit on wages subject to the Medicare tax.

Although the employer is generally required to withhold the employee's portion from the employee's wages, the employer is not obligated to withhold the Additional Medicare Tax unless (and until) the employee receives wages from the employer in excess of $200,000. For this purpose, the employer is permitted to disregard the amount of wages received by the employee's spouse. Thus, because an employee may receive wages from more than one employer, or because the employee's spouse may receive wages, an employee may be subject to the Additional Medicare Tax without the tax being withheld from the employee's wages. The employee is responsible for any portion of the additional 0.9-percent tax that is not withheld.

If an employer fails to withhold the Additional Medicare Tax and the employee pays it, the employer is not obligated to pay the tax but may be subject to penalties and additions to tax for failing to withhold (Code Sec. 3102(f)). If the tax is overwithheld, the employee may claim a credit against income tax. The employee takes any underwithheld or overwithheld amount into account in calculating the tax on Form 8959.

Multiple Employers. If an individual works for more than one employer, each employer must withhold and pay FICA taxes on the wages paid. In such instances, the employee's FICA tax withheld for the year might exceed the maximum employee portion of the tax for the year. If this happens, the employee must take the excess as a credit against income tax liability. If the employee is not required to file an income tax return, then he or she may file a special refund claim (¶ 1421) (Reg. §§1.31-2 and 31.6413(c)-1). The same rule applies to taxes withheld under the Railroad Retirement Tax Act.

If an individual is concurrently employed by two or more related corporations and all remuneration is disbursed to the individual through a common paymaster for the group, the common paymaster is responsible for the reporting and payment of FICA and FUTA taxes. However, the other related corporations remain jointly and severally liable for their appropriate share of the taxes (Reg. §31.3121(s)-1).

¶2648

FICA Wages. Wages for FICA tax purposes generally has the same meaning as for income tax withholding, and includes all remuneration for services performed by an employee for the employer with certain exceptions (¶ 2604). For employees performing domestic services in a private home of the employer or performing agricultural labor, if the employer pays the employee's liability for FICA taxes or state unemployment taxes without deduction from the employee's wages, those payments are not wages for FICA purposes (Code Sec. 3121(a)(6)). Other special rules apply to domestic workers (¶ 2652).

2649. FUTA Tax. The Federal Unemployment Tax Act (FUTA) imposes a tax on employers: (1) who employed one or more individuals in covered employment (10 or more individuals for agricultural labor) for at least part of one day in any 20 or more different weeks during the current or preceding calendar year; or (2) who paid wages (in covered employment) of at least $1,500 ($20,000 for agricultural labor, $1,000 for household employees) in any calendar quarter in the current or preceding calendar year (Code Secs. 3301, 3302, and 3306). The FUTA tax on wages is 6 percent, but the employer is allowed a partial credit against the tax based on its state unemployment insurance tax liability. The tax applies only to the first $7,000 of wages paid to each employee in the calendar year. The wage base applies separately to each common-law employer, with exceptions for successor employers and common paymasters, as well as certain motion picture project employers (Code Sec. 3512).

FUTA Wages. Wages for FUTA tax purposes generally has the same meaning as for income tax withholding, and includes all remuneration for services performed by an employee for the employer with certain exceptions (¶ 2604). For employees performing domestic services in a private home of the employer or performing agricultural labor, if the employer pays the employee's liability for FICA taxes or state unemployment taxes without deducting those taxes from the employee's wages, the amounts paid by the employer are not wages for FUTA purposes (Code Sec. 3306(b)(6)). Other special rules apply to domestic workers (¶ 2652).

Return and Payment by Employer

See CCH® AnswerConnect: *Withholding—Employment Taxes: Deposits and Reporting* for more information on this topic.

2650. Employer Returns for Employment Taxes. An employer that is required to withhold federal income tax on wages (¶ 2601) or pays wages subject to FICA taxes (¶ 2648) generally must file a quarterly return on Form 941 (Reg. § 31.6011(a)-1; Reg. § 31.6011(a)-4). The employer uses the form to report wages paid, tips employees have received, federal income tax withheld, both the employer's and the employee's shares of FICA taxes, the Additional Medicare Tax withheld, and any adjustments to FICA taxes for sick pay, tips, and group-term life insurance.

Small employers with an estimated annual employment tax liability of $1,000 or less can report employment taxes annually using Form 944 (discussed below). Taxes on wages for agricultural employees, including domestic services on a farm operated for profit, are reported annually on Form 943. Nonpayroll items, such as pension and annuity payments (¶ 2643), are reported annually on Form 945. Employers who must pay FUTA tax (¶ 2649) generally must file an annual return using Form 940.

Form 941 is due on or before the last day of the month following the quarter involved. Forms 940, 943, 944, and 945 are all due by January 31 of the year following the calendar year for which the return is made. All of these forms, including Form 941, can be filed by or before the 10th day of the second month following the close of the calendar quarter if the employer timely deposited in full payment its taxes due for the period (Reg. § 31.6071(a)-1).

The employer must file Forms W-2 and W-3 with the Social Security Administration (SSA) by January 31 of the year following the year included in the return, whether filed electronically or on paper (Code Sec. 6071(c); Reg. § 31.6071(a)-1). The SSA transmits the income tax information on the return to the IRS.

Form 944 Program. The Form 944 Program allows certain small employers to file an annual Form 944 rather than quarterly on Form 941. Form 944 is generally due January

31 of the year following the year for which the return is filed (Reg. §§ 31.6011(a)-1(a)(5) and 31.6011(a)-4(a)(4)).

Eligibility for the Form 944 Program is limited to employers with an annual estimated employment tax liability of $1,000 or less, who are notified in writing by the IRS that they must file Form 944. An employer that believes it is qualified for the program can contact the IRS to request to file Form 944 instead of Form 941, but cannot file Form 944 unless it receives written notice from the IRS that it is eligible to do so (Rev. Proc. 2009-51). Employers can opt out of filing Form 944 for any reason by calling or writing the IRS before the applicable due date.

Most participating employers can pay their employment taxes annually with their Form 944, rather than making monthly or semiweekly deposits (¶ 2651). However, a participating employer might not discover that its actual annual employment tax liability exceeded the $1,000 threshold until it files its Form 944 on the following January 31. These employers can avoid the penalty for failing to make a timely monthly deposit of their January taxes, so long as they deposit their January employment taxes in full by March 15 (Reg. § 31.6302-1).

A modified lookback period applies for determining whether a participating employer that eventually discovers that it is not eligible for the Form 944 Program is a monthly or semiweekly depositor. For those employers, the lookback period is the second calendar year preceding the current calendar year. For instance, the lookback period for 2020 is calendar year 2018 (Reg. § 31.6302-1(b)(4)).

An employer in the Form 944 Program whose actual total employment tax liability exceeds the $1,000 threshold but whose employment tax liability for a quarter is less than $2,500 is eligible for the *de minimis* deposit rules that apply to quarterly Form 941 filers (¶ 2651). The employer can apply the *de minimis* rules if it deposits the employment taxes that accumulated during a quarter by the last day of the month following the close of the quarter. If an employer's tax liability for a quarter does not qualify for *de minimis* treatment, the employer must make deposits either monthly or semiweekly, whichever is appropriate, in order to avoid the failure-to-deposit penalty (¶ 2828).

2651. Employer Deposit of Withheld Taxes. An employer generally must deposit withheld income taxes (¶ 2601) and FICA taxes (¶ 2648) on either a monthly or semiweekly basis. An employer's status as a monthly or semiweekly depositor for a given calendar year is based on the employer's employment tax reporting history during a lookback period. An employer must also deposit FUTA taxes quarterly (¶ 2649).

All employers must make deposits by electronic funds transfer (EFT) using the Electronic Federal Tax Payment System (EFTPS) unless the IRS authorizes an exemption, such as for a small business that would suffer a hardship if required to make EFT deposits (Reg. § 31.6302-1). A deposit of taxes by EFT is deemed made when the amount is withdrawn from the employer's account. Employers that fail to deposit the full amount of taxes in a timely manner or fail to use EFT may be subject to penalties (¶ 2828). The IRS has provided relief from the penalty for failure to deposit FICA taxes to employers entitled to the employee retention credit, as well as paid sick leave or paid family leave credits, provided in response to the COVID-19 (coronavirus) crisis (¶ 2648).

Depositing Income Taxes and FICA Taxes. For calendar year 2020, an employer generally must deposit withheld income and FICA taxes on a monthly basis if, during the 12-month lookback period from July 1, 2018, through June 30, 2019, the amount of the aggregate employment taxes reported was $50,000 or less. For new employers, during the first calendar year of business, the tax liability for each quarter of the lookback period is considered to be zero. Therefore, the employer is a monthly depositor for the first calendar year of business. Monthly depositors must deposit each month's taxes on or before the 15th day of the following month. If the 15th day is a Saturday, Sunday, or legal holiday in the District of Columbia (¶ 2549), the employer has until the next succeeding business day to make the deposit.

An employer that reported more than $50,000 in aggregate employment taxes during the lookback period from July 1, 2018, through June 30, 2019, must deposit withheld taxes on a semiweekly basis for calendar year 2020. Semiweekly depositors generally must deposit their taxes by the Wednesday after payday, if the payday falls on a Wednesday, Thursday, or Friday. For all other paydays, the deposit is due by the Friday following payday. Semiweekly depositors always have at least three business days after the payday to make the deposit.

For agricultural employers filing Form 943, the lookback period used to determine monthly or semiweekly depositing status is the second calendar year preceding the current calendar year. For example, the lookback period for calendar year 2020 is calendar year 2018.

Notwithstanding these general requirements, under the next-day rule, employers with $100,000 or more of accumulated liability on any day during a monthly or semi-weekly period must deposit the funds by the next day that is not a Saturday, Sunday, or legal holiday in the District of Columbia. Monthly depositors subject to the next-day rule must switch to making deposits semiweekly.

As a safe harbor, employers that fail to deposit the full amount of employment taxes will not be penalized (¶ 2828) if the shortfall does not exceed the greater of $100 or two percent of the amount of taxes required to be deposited, provided that the shortfall is deposited on or before a prescribed makeup date. For a monthly depositor, the makeup date is the due date of the return for the period in which the shortfall occurred. For a semiweekly depositor, the makeup date is the earlier of the due date of the return for the period of the shortfall, or the first Wednesday or Friday (whichever comes first) that falls on or after the 15th of the month following the month in which the shortfall occurred. Penalties may also be abated if an employer shows that a failure to deposit the full amount of taxes was due to reasonable cause.

Amounts withheld under the backup withholding requirements (¶ 2645) are treated as employment taxes subject to the deposit rules. Employers can treat the backup withholding amounts separately from other employment taxes for purposes of the deposit rules (Reg. § 31.6302-3). Different monthly and semimonthly deposit require-ments apply to taxes withheld from nonresident aliens and foreign corporations (Reg. § 1.6302-2).

Depositing FUTA Taxes. Although Form 940 is an annual return, an employer generally must deposit FUTA taxes quarterly. For deposit purposes, the employer determines the FUTA tax for each of the first three calendar quarters by multiplying the amount of wages paid during the quarter by 0.006. If at the end of the quarter the employer owes, but has not yet deposited, more than $500 in FUTA tax for the year, the employer must make a deposit by the last day of the month following the end of the quarter (Reg. § 31.6302(c)-3(a)(1)). For example, for the quarter ending March 31, deposits of FUTA are due by April 30. If the last day of the month is a Saturday, Sunday, or legal holiday in the District of Columbia, the employer has until the next succeeding business day which is not a Saturday, Sunday, or legal holiday to make the deposit.

De Minimis Exceptions. Two *de minimis* rules allow small employers to make payments with Form 941 or Form 943 rather than make deposits (Reg. § 31.6302-1(f)(4)). First, deposits are not required if the employer's accumulated employ-ment taxes for the current quarter are less than $2,500. Secondly, deposits are not required if the total accumulated employment taxes for the preceding quarter were less than $2,500 and the next-day rule does not require a deposit at the close of the next business day. An additional exception to the deposit requirement exists for employers in the Form 944 program (¶ 2650).

2652. Household Employees (Nanny Tax). An employer generally must withhold and pay FICA taxes (¶ 2648) for a household employee only if the employer has paid the employee cash wages during the calendar year at least equal to the threshold amount for that year ($2,100 in 2019; $2,200 in 2020) (Code Sec. 3121(a)(7)(B) and (x)). An employer must pay FUTA taxes for a household employee if the employer has paid aggregate cash wages of $1,000 or more to the employee in any calendar quarter of the current or preceding calendar year (Code Sec. 3306(c)(2)).

An employer must report and pay required employment taxes for household employees on Schedule H (Form 1040). While withheld amounts do not have to be deposited on a monthly basis, the employer does need an employer identification number (EIN) to include on the employee's Form W-2 (¶ 2655) and the employer's Schedule H. To obtain an EIN, an employer should complete Form SS-4.

An employer must increase either his or her quarterly estimated tax payments or the income tax withholding on his or her own wages in order to satisfy employment tax obligations regarding household employees. Failure to withhold results in liability for the penalty for underpayment of estimated tax (¶ 125).

2654. Withholding for Disregarded Entities. A disregarded entity (¶ 402A) is treated as a separate entity responsible for employment tax liabilities (Reg. § 301.7701-2(c) (2) (iv)). Thus, an otherwise disregarded entity is liable for employment taxes on wages paid to its employees, and is responsible for other employment tax obligations such as making timely tax deposits, filing returns, and providing Forms W-2 to employees. This rule applies to disregarded entities such as a qualified subchapter S subsidiary (QSub) and a single-member limited liability company (LLC). The entity continues to be disregarded for other federal tax purposes, including self-employment taxes (¶ 2667) for which the owner of the entity is personally liable.

2655. Employee Wage Statements (Form W-2). An employer must furnish Form W-2 to each employee for a calendar year, reporting taxable compensation, as well as withheld income taxes and FICA taxes (Code Sec. 6051(a); Reg. § 31.6051-1). Information on certain nontaxable items must also be reported, such as certain retirement and health plan contributions. The employer must furnish Form W-2 to the employee by January 31 of the succeeding calendar year. With the employee's consent, the employer may elect to furnish the form electronically. If employment terminates before the end of the calendar year, there is no reasonable expectation of reemployment, and the employee submits a written request for the information, the employer must furnish Form W-2 within 30 days of the written request if the 30-day period ends before January 31.

Form W-2 is a multiple-part wage statement with several copies: Copy A is sent to the Social Security Administration (SSA), Copy 1 is sent to the state where the employee resides, Copy B is kept by the employee and attached to his or her federal tax return, Copy C is retained for the employee's records, Copy 2 is attached to the employee's state, city, or local tax return, and Copy D is kept in the employer's records. Employers must file Form W-2 electronically if they are required to file at least the "applicable number" of Forms W-2 during the calendar year: 250 for calendar years before 2021, 100 for calendar year 2021, 10 for calendar years after 2021 (¶ 2503). Hardship waivers may be requested (Reg. § 301.6011-2(c)).

If the FICA tax imposed on tips reported by the employee exceeds the tax that has been collected by the employer, the employer must furnish the employee with a statement showing the amount of the excess (Code Sec. 6053(b)).

An employer may voluntarily truncate employees' Social Security numbers on copies of Form W-2 furnished to employees after December 31, 2020, to report wages, withheld taxes, and correct errors. A employer may not truncate employees' Social Security numbers on copies of Form W-2 filed with SSA (Reg. § § 31.6051-1 and 31.6051-2).

2660. Certified Professional Employer Organizations. Employers sometimes contract with professional employer organizations (PEOs), also called employee-leasing organizations, to help the employer lower health and worker's compensation insurance costs or to provide other employee benefits. PEOs also complete and file returns, and pay and withhold employment taxes on wages paid to employees. Under an employee-leasing arrangement, a PEO provides payroll, worker's compensation, human resources, and employee benefits administration to employer-customers. The PEO essentially becomes the workers' employer for tax and insurance purposes, while the lessee-employer retains control of the workers' day-to-day activities.

A certified professional employer organization (CPEO) is treated as the sole employer of a work-site employee performing services for a customer of the CPEO with respect to remuneration paid to the employee. A CPEO is a legal entity that is certified by the IRS as meeting certain requirements (Code Secs. 3511 and 7705; Reg. § § 31.3511-1 and 301.7705-1). For the CPEO to qualify as the sole employer of a particular individual, at least 85 percent of the individuals performing services for the

CPEO's customer at the work site where the individual works must be employed under contract with the CPEO.

A CPEO is considered the employer with respect to remuneration paid to an individual (other than a work-site employee or an individual with net earnings from self-employment derived from the trade or business of the CPEO's customer) who is performing services covered by a contract that meets the service contract requirements for purposes of liability for the CPEO's employment tax obligations. The exceptions, exclusions, definitions, and other rules that are based on type of employer and would otherwise apply to the taxes imposed on the individual's remuneration still apply to the remuneration.

User Fee. A annual fee of no more than $1,000 per year may be imposed on a CPEO in connection with the certification program (Code Sec. 7528(b)(4)).

Application and Certification. The IRS has provided detailed procedures for applying to become a CPEO, and for maintaining, suspending, and revoking CPEO certification (Code Sec. 7705(h); Reg. § 301.7705-2; Rev. Proc. 2016-33; Notice 2016-49; Rev. Proc. 2017-14). As part of the certification process, the IRS will: (1) complete background, credit, and tax compliance checks; (2) verify that the CPEO has an active and approved surety bond; (3) verify that the CPEO satisfies the service agreement and financial review requirements; (4) collect a user fee; and (5) provide public disclosure of CPEOs and of any person whose certification has been suspended or revoked. To qualify for and maintain IRS certification, CPEOs must adhere to bonding and independent financial review requirements, and observe ongoing reporting and recordkeeping responsibilities. Certification is not intended to create any inference in determining who is an employee or employer for federal tax purposes (Code Sec. 7705(g)).

Tax on Self-Employment Income

See CCH® AnswerConnect: *Self-Employment Tax* for more information on this topic.

2664. Self-Employment Tax Rate. Every individual who has self-employment income (¶ 2667 and ¶ 2670) for a tax year must pay a self-employment tax in addition to any other applicable taxes. The combined tax rate on self-employment income generally is 15.3 percent, consisting of a 12.4-percent Social Security tax (old-age, survivors, and disability insurance (OASDI)) and a 2.9-percent Medicare tax (hospital insurance (HI)) (Code Sec. 1401).

If net earnings from self-employment are less than $400, no self-employment tax is payable. The amount of self-employment income subject to the Social Security tax rate in a tax year is limited to the amount of the Social Security wage base for the year ($132,900 for 2019; $137,700 for 2020). If the taxpayer receives wages subject to FICA or railroad retirement tax during the year, the Social Security wage base is reduced by the amount of wages on which these taxes were paid (Code Sec. 1402(b)). There is no cap on self-employment income subject to the Medicare tax.

COVID-19 (Coronavirus) Paid Sick Leave and Family Leave Credits. An eligible self-employed individual may claim a refundable income tax credit for 100 percent of qualified sick leave and qualified family leave equivalent amount paid for the period beginning April 1, 2020, and ending December 31, 2020. The credits are "equivalent" to those available to an eligible employer who pays required paid sick leave or family leave to an employee who cannot work due to COVID-19 (¶ 2648) (Act Secs. 7002 and 7004 of the Families First Coronavirus Response Act (P.L. 116-127) as amended by Act Sec. 3606 of the Coranvirus Aid, Relief, and Economic Security (CARES) Act (P.L. 116-136); Notice 2020-21).

The qualified sick leave equivalent amount is generally limited to the lesser of $511 per day or 100 percent of daily self-employment income if the paid sick leave is due to an individual who is subject to a federal, state, or local quarantine or isolation order related to COVID-19, has been advised by a health care provider to self-quarantine due to COVID-19-related concerns, or is experiencing symptoms of COVID-19 and is seeking a medical diagnosis. The qualified family leave equivalent amount is generally limited to the lesser of $200 per day or 67 percent of daily self-employment income if the paid sick leave is because the individual is caring for an individual who is subject to a quarantine or isolation order or has been advised to self quarantine, is caring for a child whose school or place of care has been closed, or a substantially similar condition specified by the Department of Health and Human Services.

COVID-19 (Coronavirus) Deferral of Employer Payroll Taxes. A self-employed individual may also defer the payment of 50 percent of the 12.4-percent OASDI tax on self-employment income for the payroll tax deferral period from March 27, 2020 through December 31, 2020. For estimated tax purposes for any tax year which includes the deferral period, 50 percent of the OASDI tax on self-employment income for the deferral period is treated as subject to the required installment payment rules of Code Sec. 6654 (Act Sec. 2302 of P.L. 116-136).

0.9% Additional Medicare Tax. The Medicare portion of the self-employment tax rate is increased by an additional 0.9 percent (to 3.8 percent) for self-employment income in excess of $200,000 ($250,000 if married filing jointly, $125,000 if married filing separately). For a joint return, the Additional Medicare Tax is imposed on the combined self-employment income of the taxpayer and his or her spouse. If a taxpayer, or a taxpayer and his or her spouse, receives both self-employment income and wages that may be subject to the Additional Medicare Tax for FICA purposes (¶ 2648), then the threshold amount for determining the Additional Medicare Tax for self-employment purposes is reduced by the taxpayer's wages, but not below zero (Code Sec. 1401(b)(2); Reg. § 1.1401-1(d)).

Under these rules, a taxpayer's self-employment tax rate is 15.3 percent (12.4 percent + 2.9 percent) of the taxpayer's self-employment income up to the Social Security wage base in effect for the year, 2.9 percent of self-employment income above the Social Security wage base not in excess of the threshold amount for the 0.9-percent Additional Medicare Tax, and 3.8 percent (2.9 percent + 0.9 percent) of any self-employment income above that threshold amount.

> **Example:** Carl, a single filer, has $130,000 in wages and $145,000 in self-employment income. His wages are not in excess of the $200,000 threshold for single filers, so he is not liable for the Additional Medicare Tax on these wages for FICA purposes. Before calculating the Additional Medicare Tax on self-employment income, the $200,000 threshold for single filers is reduced by Carl's $130,000 in wages, resulting in a reduced self-employment income threshold of $70,000. Carl is liable to pay the Additional Medicare Tax on $75,000 of self-employment income ($145,000 minus $70,000).

Reporting Requirements. The self-employment tax is computed on Schedule SE (Form 1040), is treated as part of the taxpayer's income tax liability, and must be taken into account for estimated tax purposes (¶ 125). A married couple filing a joint return must file separate Schedules SE if each spouse is self-employed. An individual subject to the Additional Medicare Tax must also complete Form 8959. The forms must be attached the individual's income tax return for the year. The due date for filing any federal tax return, including Schedule SE and Form 8959 with the taxpayer's return, otherwise due on or after April 1, 2020, and before July 15, 2020, is automatically extended to July 15, 2020, in response to the COVID-19 (coronavirus) crisis (Notice 2020-23).

2667. Persons Subject to Self-Employment Tax. An individual who is self-employed is subject to self-employment tax (¶ 2664) if he or she earns $433.13 or more of self-employment income in a year (¶ 2670). An individual is generally self-employed if he or she carries on a trade or business as a sole proprietor or independent contractor (¶ 2602), or is a member of a partnership that carries on a trade or business (Code Sec. 1402(a)). A trade or business does not include the performance of services by an employee, but certain employee services are treated as a trade or business and are therefore subject to self-employment tax (Code Sec. 1402(c)).

Members of religious orders who have taken vows of poverty are not subject to self-employment tax when they perform duties connected with their religious order (Code Sec. 1402(c)(4) and (5)). Also, a duly ordained, commissioned, or licensed minister of a church, a member of a religious order (who has not taken a vow of poverty), or a Christian Science practitioner may elect not to be covered by Social Security by filing an exemption certificate on Form 4361 indicating that he or she is opposed by conscience or religious principle to the acceptance of any public insurance. The statement must include a declaration that the individual has informed the church's ordaining, commissioning, or licensing body of his or her opposition to such insurance. A qualified individual must apply for the exemption on or before the due date of the income tax return for the second tax year that the individual had net earnings from self-employment of $400 or more from religious activities (Code Sec. 1402(e)). An individual who has conscientious objections to accepting private or public insurance due to an adherence to established tenets or teachings of a religious sect of which he or she is a member may also be exempt from the self-employment tax (Code Sec. 1402(g)).

Services performed by employees for a church or church-controlled organization may be excluded from Social Security coverage if the church or organization makes a valid election under Code Sec. 3121(w) to be exempt from the employer portion of FICA taxes. However, the employees remain liable for FICA or self-employment tax on remuneration paid for such services unless the remuneration is less than $100 per year (Code Sec. 1402(a)(14) and (j)).

A U.S. citizen who works for an employer that is exempt from the Social Security tax because it is either a foreign government or instrumentality, or an international organization, is treated as self-employed (Code Sec. 1402(c)(2)). Nonresident aliens are not subject to self-employment tax, but the tax may apply to a resident of Puerto Rico, the Virgin Islands, Guam, the Commonwealth of the Northern Mariana Islands, or American Samoa who is not a U.S. citizen (Code Sec. 1402(b); IRS Pub. 334).

2670. Self-Employment Income. The self-employment tax (¶ 2664) is imposed on self-employment income derived by an individual during the tax year. Self-employment income is generally defined as net earnings from self-employment which consists of: (1) the gross income derived from any trade or business, less allowable deductions attributable to the trade or business, and (2) the taxpayer's distributive share of the ordinary income or loss of a partnership engaged in a trade or business (Code Sec. 1402(b); Reg. § 1.1402(a)-1). A trade or business does not include services performed as an employee other than services relating to certain newspaper and magazine sales, sharing of crops, foreign organizations, and sharing of fishing catches (Code Sec. 1402(c)(2)).

There are special rules for computing net earnings from self-employment, including a special optional method for nonfarm self-employment (¶ 2673) (Code Sec. 1402(a)). Rents from real estate and personal property leased with the real estate, and the attributable deductions, are also excluded from net earnings from self-employment unless the individual receives the rents in the course of his or her business as a real estate dealer. Rental real estate income that is otherwise excludable does not become self-employment income merely because it is held in a qualified joint venture (¶ 402) (CCA 200816030). A taxpayer who is in the farming business, either as an individual or as a general partner in a farm partnership, may be able to use the farm optional method to determine his or her earnings from farm self-employment (¶ 2676).

Dividends and interest from any bond, debenture, note, certificate or other evidence of indebtedness issued with interest coupons or in registered form by any corporation are excluded from net earnings from self-employment income unless received by a dealer in stocks and securities in the course of his or her business (Code Sec. 1402(a)(2)). Other interest received in the course of any trade or business is not excluded. Gain or loss from the sale or exchange of property that is not stock in trade or held primarily for sale is excluded, as is gain or loss from the sale or exchange of a capital asset (Code Sec. 1402(a)(3)).

Termination payments received by former insurance salespersons are excludable from net earnings from self-employment if the amount is received after the termination of the individual's agreement to perform services for the company, and the individual performs no services for the company after the termination and before the close of the tax year. In addition, the payment must be conditioned upon the salesperson agreeing not to compete with the company for at least one year following termination. The payment also must depend primarily on policies sold by or credited to the individual during the last year of the agreement and/or the extent to which the policies remain in force for some period after the termination, and must not depend on the length of

26 WITHHOLDING

¶2670

service or overall earnings from services performed for the company (Code Sec. 1402(k)).

Even though the rental value of a parsonage (¶ 875) and the value of meals and lodging furnished for the convenience of the employer (¶ 2089) are not included in a minister's gross income for income tax purposes, they are taken into account in calculating net earnings from self-employment (Code Sec. 1402(a)(8)). The same is true of amounts excluded from gross income as foreign earned income (¶ 2402). However, self-employment income does not include a minister's retirement benefits received from a church plan or the rental value of a parsonage allowance, as long as each was furnished after the date of retirement.

One business deduction that cannot be taken in calculating net earnings from self-employment for the tax year is the deduction allowed for self-employment tax paid during the year (¶ 923). However, a substitute is provided for that deduction. This is an amount determined by multiplying net earnings from self-employment (calculated without regard to the substitute deduction) by one-half of the self-employment tax rate (¶ 2664) (Code Sec. 1402(a)(12)). Thus, the deduction equals 7.65 percent of the net earnings from self-employment. Taxpayers who reduce self-employment income by an amount equal to one-half of the combined self-employment tax rate do not include the 0.9-percent Additional Medicare Tax in the rate used to make such computation.

> **Example:** Aileen, a self-employed individual, has $40,000 of net earnings from self-employment during the year (determined without regard to the substitute deduction). Her self-employment tax is computed as follows:
>
> | | |
> |---|---:|
> | Self-employment net earnings . . . . | $40,000 |
> | Less: $40,000 × 7.65% . . . . | 3,060 |
> | Reduced self-employment net earnings . . . . | $36,940 |
> | Tax rate on self-employment income | × 15.3% |
> | Self-employment tax | $5,652 |

2673. Optional Method for Nonfarm Self-Employment. A taxpayer may be able to use an optional method to compute net earnings from self-employment if the net earnings from nonfarm self-employment for 2019 are less than $5,891 and less than 72.189 percent of gross nonfarm income. In addition, the nonfarm optional method may only be used if the taxpayer had net earnings from self-employment of $400 or more in at least two of the three years immediately preceding the year in which the nonfarm optional method is elected (Code Sec. 1402(a) and (l)).

If the taxpayer is eligible to use the nonfarm optional method for 2019, he or she may report two-thirds of the gross income from the nonfarm business as net earnings from self-employment, provided the gross income from all nonfarm trades or businesses is less than 72.189 percent of gross nonfarm income. If, however, the gross income from all nonfarm trades or businesses is more than $5,440, the individual may report $5,440 as net earnings from nonfarm self-employment. The nonfarm optional method may not be used to report an amount less than actual net earnings from self-employment.

The purpose of the nonfarm optional method is to permit taxpayers to pay into the Social Security system and obtain or increase their benefits, even though they are not otherwise eligible because the amount of their net earnings from self-employment is under $400. The nonfarm optional method may not be used more than five times by any individual. Note that the $5,440 amount for 2019 refers to net earnings after reduction by the 7.65-percent deduction amount (¶ 2670).

2676. Farmer's Self-Employment Income. A special method for determining self-employment net earnings is provided for farm operators whether they own the land they farm, rent on a fixed rental basis, or rent under a share-farming arrangement. Rentals received by the owner or tenant of the land under a share-farming arrangement—where the farm is operated by a third party such as a share-farmer who may be a subtenant—are treated as self-employment income (¶ 2670) if the owner or tenant materially participates with the share-farmer working the land in the production, or management of the production, of an agricultural or horticultural commodity. There is no material participation if the owner or tenant does not participate in operations and has turned over management of the land to an agent, such as a professional farm management company. The share-farmer is also considered a self-employed farmer (Code Sec. 1402(a)(1); Reg. §§ 1.1402(a)-4 and 1.1402(a)-13; IRS Pub. 225).

Payments made by the U.S. Department of Agriculture under its Conservation Reserve Program (CRP) are considered earnings from a trade or business, and are includible in a farmer's self-employment income regardless of whether the farmer actively engages in farming or ceases all farming activities (Notice 2006-108). However, authorities are split on whether CRP payments to a nonfarmer are included in net earnings from self-employment as rental income from real estate (*F.J. Wuebker*, CA-6, 2000-1 USTC ¶ 50,254; *R.J. Morehouse*, CA-8, 2014-2 USTC ¶ 50,471 (Nonacq.)). Regardless of the recipient's farming activities, CRP payments are excluded from an individual's net earnings from self-employment if the individual is receiving retirement or disability benefits from Social Security.

A self-employed farmer has to pay the self-employment tax if his or her net earnings from self-employment are $400 or more (Code Sec. 1402(b)). However, an optional method for reporting income from farming, providing for greater credit toward benefits under Social Security old-age and survivors insurance, is available to a farmer. If the farmer's gross income for 2019 is not more than $8,160 ("upper limit"), he or she can report two-thirds of gross income as net earnings from self-employment (Code Sec. 1402(a)). If the farmer has more than $8,160 of gross income from farm operations in 2019, he or she may report either actual net earnings or, if net earnings are less than $5,440 ("lower limit"), $5,440 as net earnings. As in the case of the nonfarm optional method (¶ 2673), the $5,440 amount refers to net earnings after reduction by the 7.65-percent deduction (¶ 2670). There is no limit on the number of times a taxpayer may use the farm optional method.

> **Example:** Breanna owns and operates her own farm. She receives all her income from the operation of the farm. Her gross income (receipts minus cost of goods sold) for 2019 is $8,310, but her net earnings for that year are only $4,000. She cannot simply report $5,540 (⅔ of $8,310) because her gross income is over $8,160, but she can report $5,440 as her net earnings from self-employment even though her actual net earnings are only $4,000. In electing to pay the self-employment tax on $5,440 rather than on $4,000, she will pay a greater tax. The positive effect, however, is that she will theoretically receive a greater credit toward Social Security benefits.

Chapter 27

EXAMINATION OF RETURNS

COLLECTION OF TAX

Organization of IRS

2701. IRS Organization and Functions. The Internal Revenue Service (IRS) is the bureau of the Treasury Department responsible for determining, assessing, and collecting federal taxes and enforcing the Internal Revenue Code. The IRS is organized into four operating divisions serving groups of taxpayers with similar needs. These operating divisions are:

- Wage and Investment—serving individual taxpayers with wage and investment income;

- Small Business/Self-Employed—serving self-employed individuals and small businesses with assets of $10 million or less;

- Large Business and International—serving C corporations, S corporations and partnerships with assets of greater than $10 million; and

- Tax-Exempt and Government Entities—serving employee plans, exempt organizations, and government entities.

IRS field offices also include a number of IRS service centers. These service centers currently receive and process tax and information returns, manage accounts, and conduct simple audits. In addition, a nine-member IRS Oversight Board helps ensure that the IRS is organized and operated to carry out its mission to place a greater emphasis on serving the public and meeting taxpayers' needs (Code Sec. 7802).

2703. IRS Personnel. The administration and enforcement of the federal tax system is required by law to be performed by, or under the supervision of, the Secretary of the Treasury (Code Sec. 7801). In the Department of the Treasury, the official immediately in charge of the IRS is the Commissioner of Internal Revenue, whose duties and powers are determined by the Secretary of the Treasury. The Commissioner's duties are to administer, manage, direct, and supervise the execution and application of the tax laws, as well ensure that IRS employees are familiar with certain taxpayer rights. There are a number of key personnel of the IRS that report directly the Commissioner (Code Sec. 7803, as amended by the Taxpayer First Act (P.L. 116-25)).

The IRS Chief Counsel is the counsel and legal adviser to the Commissioner in all matters pertaining to the administration and enforcement of internal revenue laws. The Treasury Inspector General for Tax Administration conducts independent audits of the IRS for evaluation of compliance with internal revenue laws. Effective July 1, 2019, the Chief Information Officer (CIO) is responsible for development, implementation, and maintenance of information technology for the IRS. Effective July 1, 2019, the Chief of Appeals supervises and directs the IRS Independent Office of Appeals to resolve tax controversies without litigation in court (¶ 2705). The National Taxpayer Advocate assists taxpayers in resolving problems with the IRS and has the authority to issue a

¶2701

taxpayer assistance order if a taxpayer is suffering, or is about to suffer, significant hardship as a result of the IRS's actions (¶ 2707).

2705. IRS Appeals. A taxpayer who does not agree with the result of an IRS examination may seek administrative review through the IRS Independent Office of Appeals (Code Sec. 7803(e), added by the Taxpayer First Act (P.L. 116-25); Reg. § 601.106). Independent Appeals is established by the Code and is under the supervision and direction of the Chief of Appeals.

Once the IRS has issued a preliminary 30-day letter, the taxpayer has the right to appeal to a local Appeals Office by filing a written request for appellate consideration. This is the only level of appeal within the IRS, disregarding the functions of the National Taxpayer Advocate (¶ 2707). Appeals conferences are conducted in an informal manner. A taxpayer who requests a conference may also need to file a formal written protest. However, if the protested amount is $25,000 or less for any tax period, a taxpayer may make a small case request instead of a formal written protest (IRS Pub. 556). A taxpayer who wishes to forego the right to submit a protest to the Appeals Office after receiving a 30-day letter can file a petition in the Tax Court within 90 days after the receipt of a statutory notice of deficiency.

The IRS is required to develop certain appeals dispute resolution procedures (Code Sec. 7123). Accordingly, the IRS procedures are provided under which any taxpayer may request early referral of issues from the examination or collection division to the Office of Appeals (Rev. Proc. 99-28). Additionally, procedures have been developed under which either a taxpayer or the Office of Appeals may request nonbinding mediation of any unresolved issue at the conclusion of the appeals procedure or an unsuccessful attempt to enter into a closing agreement or an offer in compromise (Rev. Proc. 2014-63).

The Secretary of the Treasury is also required to establish procedures under which an organization that is exempt from tax under Code Sec. 501(a) because of its status as a Code Sec. 501(c) organization (or because it believes that it qualifies as a 501(c) organization) can request an administrative appeal—together with a conference related to that appeal, if so desired—in response to receiving an adverse determination (Code Sec. 7123(c)). For this purpose, an adverse determination is one that is adverse to the organization's exempt status, regardless of whether that involves the organization's initial qualification or the continuing classification of the organization, concerning whether the organization is an organization described in Code Sec. 170(c)(2), exempt from tax under Code Sec. 501(a), a private foundation under Code Sec. 509(a), or a private operating foundation under Code Sec. 4942(j)(3).

Small business and self-employed taxpayers can resolve certain tax disputes through fast-track mediation (Rev. Proc. 2016-57). Disputes are resolved through this expedited process within 30 to 40 days, compared to several months using the regular appeals process.

Large- and mid-size businesses can resolve their tax disputes through a fast-track settlement program (Rev. Proc. 2003-40). The goal for this program is to reach settlement within 120 days. A similar fast-track settlement program exists for small businesses and self-employed taxpayers as well (Announcement 2011-5). A fast-track settlement program for tax-exempt and government entities is also available (Announcement 2012-34). The goal for both this program and the small business and self-employed taxpayer program is to reach settlement within 60 days. Additional criteria may be found on the Appeals Mediation Programs webpage on the IRS website.

2707. National Taxpayer Advocate. The National Taxpayer Advocate assists taxpayers in resolving problems with the IRS and has the authority to issue a taxpayer assistance order if a taxpayer is suffering, or is about to suffer, significant hardship as a result of the IRS's actions (Code Secs. 7803(c) and 7811; Reg. § 301.7811-1). "Significant hardship" means any serious privation caused to the taxpayer as the result of the IRS's administration of revenue laws. Mere economic or personal inconvenience to the taxpayer does not constitute significant hardship. The following factors, among other things, must be considered by the Advocate when determining whether there is a significant hardship:

- whether there is an immediate threat of adverse action;

- whether there has been a delay of more than 30 days in resolving the taxpayer's account problems;

- whether the taxpayer will incur significant costs, including fees for professional representation, if relief is not granted; and

- whether the taxpayer will suffer irreparable injury, or a long-term adverse impact, if relief is not granted.

An application for a taxpayer assistance order may be filed by the taxpayer or a duly authorized representative, who may request remedial action, such as the release of the taxpayer's property from IRS levy or the immediate reissuance of a lost refund check. Form 911 is used for this purpose. Any relevant limitations period is suspended from the date on which the application is filed until the Advocate makes a decision on the application, unless the order provides for the suspension to be continued beyond the date of the order. These orders are binding on the IRS unless modified or rescinded by the Advocate, IRS Commissioner, or Deputy Commissioner. The Advocate can take independent action and issue an assistance order without an application by the taxpayer. The statute of limitations is not suspended when the Advocate issues an order independently.

Examination

2708. Examination of Return. The IRS examines a taxpayer's books and records either at the place of business where the books and records are maintained (i.e., a field examination) or at an IRS office (Reg. § 601.105).

The Taxpayer Bill of Rights requires the IRS to provide a written statement detailing the taxpayer's rights and the IRS's obligations during the audit, appeals, refund, and collection process. At or before the first in-person interview with a taxpayer relating to the determination of any tax, the IRS must provide the taxpayer with an explanation of the audit process and the taxpayer's rights under the process (Code Sec. 7521).

The taxpayer has the right to make an audio recording of any in-person interview conducted by the IRS upon 10 days' advance notice. Moreover, a taxpayer is guaranteed the right to be represented by any individual currently permitted to practice before the IRS, unless the IRS notifies the taxpayer that the representative is responsible for unreasonable delay or hindrance. Any interview must be suspended when the taxpayer clearly requests the right to consult with a representative. Further, unless it issues an administrative summons, the IRS cannot require the taxpayer to accompany the representative to the interview.

The IRS may provide administrative relief to taxpayers in hostage situations or in a combat zone (or qualified hazardous duty area) who are continuously hospitalized as a result of injuries received in a combat zone (or qualified hazardous duty area) by suspending tax examination and collection actions for a period of time (Code Sec. 7508; Act Sec. 11026 of the Tax Cuts and Jobs Act (P.L. 115-97)). Examination and collection actions that may be precluded or suspended include tax return audits, mailings of notices, and other actions involving the collection of overdue taxes. The collection period for taxpayers hospitalized for combat zone injuries may not be suspended for any period of continuous hospitalization or 180 days thereafter. As a result, the collection period expires 10 years after assessment, plus the actual time spent in a combat zone, regardless of the length of the postponement period available for hospitalized individuals to comply with their tax obligations.

A taxpayer affected by a federally declared disaster is granted an automatic 60-day extension for federal tax deadlines, effective for a federal disaster declared after December 20, 2019 (Code Sec. 7508A, as amended by the Tax Certainty and Disaster Tax Relief Act (P.L. 116-94)). The IRS is also authorized to postpone deadlines for filing returns and paying taxes for up to one year for taxpayers affected by a federally declared disaster, as well as terroristic or military actions. The due date for filing any federal income tax return and federal income tax payer otherwise due on or after April 1, 2020, and before July 15, 2020, is automatically extended to July 15, 2020, in response to the COVID-19 (coronavirus) crisis (Notice 2020-23). A list of other recent federally declared disaster areas may be found on the IRS website at https://www.irs.gov/newsroom/tax-relief-in-disaster-situations.

2708A. Power of Attorney. A taxpayer generally may choose a person to represent him or her before the IRS by filing a power of attorney (Reg. § 601.501(a)). A power of attorney is a written authorization for an individual to act on behalf of another individual or an entity in tax matters. Form 2848 can be used to grant a power of attorney, or another equivalent form can be used. If the authorization is not limited, the individual can generally perform all acts that the taxpayer granting the power can perform. However, the holder of a power of attorney cannot represent the taxpayer before the IRS unless the holder is a person authorized to practice before the IRS (CCA 200321017).

A taxpayer may change his or her representative by filing a new power of attorney (Reg. § 601.505(a)). The new power revokes any prior power that the taxpayer granted to someone else concerning the same matter unless the new power contains a clause stating that it does not revoke the prior power. A taxpayer may also revoke a power of attorney without authorizing a new representative.

A taxpayer who only wants to have someone answer any questions that may arise regarding his or her income tax return does not have to file a power of attorney. Instead, the taxpayer can designate anyone to do this, not just a person qualified to practice before the IRS, by checking the appropriate box on his or her tax return (Instructions to Form 1040).

2709. Third-Party Summonses. The IRS may issue summonses to third-party recordkeepers (attorneys, enrolled agents, banks, brokers, accountants, etc.) and other third parties for the production of records concerning the business transactions or affairs of a taxpayer (Code Sec. 7609, as amended by the Taxpayer First Act (P.L. 116-25)). The taxpayer is to be notified of the summons within three days of service of the summons, but no later than 23 days before the examination of the summoned person or records is scheduled to take place. Notice is not required with respect to any summons:

- served on the person with respect to whose liability the summons is issued, or any officer or employee of the person;
- issued to determine whether or not records of the business transactions or affairs of an identified person have been made or kept;
- issued solely to determine the identity of any person having a numbered account or similar arrangement with a bank or similar institution;
- issued to aid the collection of (1) an assessment or judgment against the person with respect to whose liability the summons is issued, or (2) the liability of that person's transferee or fiduciary; or
- issued in certain criminal investigations.

Any person who is entitled to notice may intervene in any proceeding for the enforcement of the summons in question. The person also has the right to begin a proceeding to quash the summons if, within 20 days after the day the notice of summons was served on or mailed, the person files a petition to quash the summons in a federal district court having jurisdiction and notifies the IRS and the third party by mailing a copy of the petition by certified or registered mail to each one. If a person intervenes and the dispute is not resolved within six months, the statute-of-limitations period will be suspended beginning on the date that is six months after the summons is served and continuing until the dispute is resolved.

The IRS may issue a summons to a third party that does not identify the person with respect to whose liability the summons ("John Doe" summons). The summons may be issued only after the IRS has shown adequate grounds for serving the summons, and an ex parte court proceeding is held to determine its validity. Effective for John Doe summons served after August 15, 2019, the summons must be "narrowly tailored" to information that pertains to failure of the person or group of persons to comply with internal revenue laws.

Effective August 15, 2019, the IRS must provide written notification to a taxpayer that it intends to contact third parties regarding the determination or collection of the taxpayer's tax liability at least 45 days prior to the beginning of a one-year contact period (Code Sec. 7602(c), as amended by P.L. 116-25; Reg. § 301.7602-2). Prior this date, the IRS was simply required to provide reasonable notice in advance to a taxpayer before contacting third parties with respect to examination or collection activities regarding the taxpayer. Notice is not required if the taxpayer has authorized the contact, it would jeopardize the collection of tax, or it relates to a pending criminal investigation.

Assessment and Collection of Tax

2711. Assessment of Deficiency. The IRS is authorized to assess taxes but there are certain procedures that must be followed before assessing a deficiency (Code Sec. 6201; Reg. § 301.6201-1). A deficiency is the excess of (1) the correct tax liability, over (2) the tax shown on the return, if any, plus amounts previously assessed or collected without assessment as a deficiency, and minus any rebates made to the taxpayer such as the earned income credit, the refundable portion of the child tax credit, and the recovery rebate credit (Code Sec. 6211, as amended by the Coronavirus Aid, Relief, and Economic Security (CARES) Act (P.L. 116-136)). For this purpose, the tax shown on the return is the amount of tax before application of credits for estimated tax paid, withheld tax, or amounts collected under a termination assessment.

The deficiency process begins when a notice of deficiency is sent to the taxpayer's last known address by registered or certified mail (Code Sec. 6212). In each deficiency notice, the IRS must provide a description of the basis for the assessment, an identification of the amount of tax, interest, and penalties assessed, and the date determined to be the last day on which the taxpayer may file a petition with the Tax Court (Code Secs. 6213(a) and Code Sec. 7522). Failure by the IRS to specify the last day on which to file a petition will not invalidate an otherwise valid deficiency notice if the taxpayer was not prejudiced by the omission (*V.B. Elings*, CA-9, 2003-1 USTC ¶ 60,461).

Within 90 days after notice of the deficiency is mailed (or within 150 days if the notice is mailed to an address outside the United States), the taxpayer may file a petition with the Tax Court for a redetermination of the deficiency (Code Sec. 6213; Reg. § 301.6213-1(b)(3)). Payment of the assessed amount after the deficiency notice is mailed does not deprive the Tax Court of jurisdiction over the deficiency.

If the taxpayer does not file a Tax Court petition within the required time period, the tax may be assessed. After giving notice and demand for payment of the tax, the IRS may take action to collect (¶ 2735). A taxpayer's property may be seized to enforce collection if there is a failure to pay an assessed tax within 30 days after notice of intent to levy (Code Sec. 6331). However, the notice and waiting period does not apply if the IRS finds that the collection of tax is in jeopardy (¶ 2713). Notices of levy must provide a description of the levy process in simple and nontechnical terms.

Last Known Address. A taxpayer's last known address for purposes of sending the deficiency notice is the address that appears on the taxpayer's most recently filed federal tax return. If the taxpayer gives the IRS clear and concise notice of a different address, that address is the taxpayer's last known address (Reg. § 301.6212-2). The IRS uses the National Change of Address database maintained by the U.S. Postal Service to update a taxpayer's last known address.

A taxpayer can change his or her last known address with the IRS through any of several means (Rev. Proc. 2010-16). First, the taxpayer can file a return with new address information. Second, the taxpayer can provide clear and concise written notice to the appropriate IRS address using Form 8822 (Form 8822-B for employers), or other written notice satisfying the requirements including returning IRS correspondence with corrections marked (IRS Pub. 15). Next, the taxpayer can provide clear and concise written or oral notice of a change of address to an IRS employee who contacts the taxpayer regarding the filing of a return or an adjustment in his or her account. Finally, the taxpayer can provide the IRS with clear and concise electronic notification through one of the secure applications found on the IRS website.

Mathematical or Clerical Errors. A notice of tax due because of mathematical or clerical errors is not a deficiency notice, and the taxpayer has no right to file a petition with the Tax Court for redetermining the deficiency. A taxpayer who receives notice of additional tax due to mathematical or clerical error has 60 days after the notice is sent in which to file a request for abatement of any part of the assessment. Any reassessment must be made under the regular notice-of-deficiency procedures. During the 60-day period, the IRS cannot proceed to collect upon the summary assessment (Code Sec. 6213(b)(1) and (f)).

¶2711

Criminal Restitution. Criminal restitution for a failure to pay tax, ordered by a court pursuant to 18 USC § 3556, is assessed and collected as if it were a tax (Code Sec. 6201(a)(4)(A)). The restitution assessment is not subject to the general restrictions on assessments and filing Tax Court petitions for deficiency redetermination. The restitution amount may be assessed, or a court proceeding for its collection may begin without assessment, at any time.

2712. Waiver of Deficiency Restrictions. A taxpayer has the right to waive the restrictions on assessment and collection of all or part of a deficiency at any time, whether or not a notice of deficiency has been issued (Code Sec. 6213(d); Reg. § 301.6213-1(b)(3)). This is done by executing Form 870. Execution of a waiver of the restrictions on assessment and collection of the entire deficiency in advance of the statutory (90-day) notice relieves the IRS of sending such a notice and precludes appeal to the Tax Court. However, an appeal to the Tax Court is not precluded if the waiver covers only part of the deficiency or is executed after receipt of the 90-day deficiency notice. Payment of an amount of tax before the statutory notice is issued has the effect of a waiver and, if the amount paid equals or exceeds the amount of a subsequently determined deficiency, it deprives the Tax Court of jurisdiction.

2713. Jeopardy and Termination Assessments. The IRS can immediately determine and assess income tax in a termination assessment if it finds that tax collection is in jeopardy because a taxpayer is leaving the country, or seeking to hide assets, or doing any other act that tends to render collection ineffective (Code Sec. 6851). Similarly, the IRS can immediately assess a deficiency if tax assessment or collection would be jeopardized by delay (Code Sec. 6861). If a jeopardy assessment is made prior to the mailing of the notice of deficiency, the notice must be mailed to the taxpayer within 60 days after the assessment.

If a termination assessment is made, the assessment ends the taxpayer's tax year only for purposes of computing the amount of tax that becomes immediately due and payable. It does not end the tax year for any other purpose. In the case of a termination assessment, the IRS must issue the taxpayer a notice of deficiency within 60 days of the later of (1) the due date, including extensions, of the taxpayer's return for the full tax year, or (2) the day on which the taxpayer files the return.

The IRS may presume that the collection of tax is in jeopardy if an individual is in physical possession of more than $10,000 in cash or its equivalent, and does not claim either ownership of the cash or that it belongs to another person whose identity the IRS can readily ascertain and who acknowledges ownership of the cash. In this case, the IRS may treat the entire amount as gross income taxable at the highest income tax rate. The possessor of the cash is entitled to notice of, and the right to challenge, the assessment. If the true owner appears, he or she will be substituted for the possessor and all rights will vest in the true owner (Code Sec. 6867).

2719. Injunction to Restrain Collection. The Code prohibits a suit to restrain the assessment or collection of any tax or to restrain the enforcement of liability against a transferee or fiduciary (Code Sec. 7421). Nevertheless, injunctive relief may be available in rare cases if irreparable harm would be done to the taxpayer and the taxpayer shows, at the outset of the suit, that the government could not collect the tax under any circumstances (*Standard Nut Margarine Co. of Florida*, SCt, 3 USTC ¶ 878). Injunctive relief may be obtained for assessment or collection actions (other than jeopardy or termination assessments) if a notice of deficiency has not been mailed to the taxpayer, the period for filing a Tax Court petition has not expired, or a Tax Court proceeding with respect to the tax is pending (Code Sec. 6213(a)).

2721. Closing Agreement. The IRS is authorized to enter into a written agreement with a taxpayer in order to determine conclusively the tax liability for a tax period that ended prior to the date of the agreement (Form 866) or to determine one or more separate items affecting the tax liability for any tax period (Form 906). A closing agreement may also be entered for tax periods that end subsequent to the date of the agreement.

Closing agreements may be entered into in order to finally resolve questions of tax liability (Code Sec. 7121; Reg. § § 301.7121-1 and 601.202). For example, a fiduciary may desire a final determination before an estate is closed or trust assets distributed. Closing agreements are final, conclusive, and binding upon both parties. They cannot be reopened or modified except upon a showing of fraud or malfeasance or the misrepresentation of a material fact (*Wolverine Petroleum*, CA-8, 35-1 USTC ¶ 9098). Generally, the IRS is not precluded from later determining additions to tax absent terms in the agreement that specifically address the issue of additions to tax.

2723. Offers-In-Compromise. The IRS may generally compromise a tax liability before it has been referred to the Department of Justice for prosecution or defense. The Attorney General or a delegate may compromise any case after the referral. Interest and penalties, as well as tax, may be compromised (Code Sec. 7122; Reg. § 301.7122-1). Offers-in-compromise based on doubt as to collectibility or effective tax administration are submitted on Form 656, and must be accompanied by a financial statement on Form 433-A (OIC) for an individual or Form 433-B (OIC) for a business. Offers-in-compromise based on doubt as to liability are submitted on Form 656-L (Reg. § 601.203(b)).

If the IRS accepts an offer-in-compromise, and the terms of the offer (and collateral agreement, if any) provide for the allocation of payments, the payments will be allocated under the terms of the agreement. If the offer or agreement do not provide for the allocation of payments, the IRS will apply payments, whether paid in installments or in a lump sum, to the periods in the order of priority that the IRS determines will best serve the government's interest (Rev. Proc. 2002-26).

A user fee is generally required to be paid when an offer-in-compromise is submitted ($205 for offers submitted on or after April 27, 2020, and $186 for offers submitted before April 27, 2020) (Reg. § 300.3). No user fee is imposed with respect to offers that are based solely on doubt as to liability or that are made by certain low-income taxpayers. For offers submitted after July 1, 2019, a low income taxpayer is an individual with adjusted gross income for the most recent tax year that does not exceed 250 percent of the applicable poverty level (Code Sec. 7122(c)(3), as added by the Taxpayer First Act (P.L. 116-25)). For offers submitted on or before July 1, 2019, a low income taxpayer is an individual who falls at or below the poverty guidelines set by the Department of Health and Human Services.

The user fee is applied to the amount of the offer or refunded to the taxpayer (if requested) if the offer is accepted to promote effective tax administration or is accepted based on doubt as to collectibility and a determination that collecting more than the amount offered would create economic hardship. The fee will not be refunded if an offer is withdrawn, rejected, or returned as nonprocessable. Offers received with less than the required user fee will be treated as nonprocessable, unless the low-income certification box on Form 656 is checked (SBSE-05-0817-0045). The IRS treats offers received by taxpayers in bankruptcy as nonprocessable. The IRS has issued detailed procedures for the submission and processing of offers-in-compromise (Rev. Proc. 2003-71).

Partial Payment Requirement. Taxpayers are required to make nonrefundable partial payments with the submission of any offer-in-compromise based on doubt as to collectibility or effective tax administration (Code Sec. 7122(c)). Taxpayers who submit a lump-sum offer (any offer that will be paid in five or fewer installments) must include a payment of 20 percent of the amount offered. Taxpayers who submit a periodic payment offer must include payment of the first proposed installment with the offer and continue making payments under the terms proposed while the offer is being evaluated. Offers that are submitted to the IRS without the required partial payments will be returned to the taxpayer as nonprocessable. Partial payments are not required for offers based solely on doubt as to liability or filed by low-income taxpayers (Notice 2006-68).

The required partial payments are applied to the taxpayer's unpaid liability and are not refundable. Taxpayers may specify the liability to which they want their payments applied. Additionally, the user fee is applied to the taxpayer's outstanding tax liability. Any offer that is not rejected within 24 months of the date it is submitted is deemed to be accepted. However, any period during which the tax liability to be compromised is in dispute in any judicial proceeding is not taken into account in determining the expiration of the 24-month period (Code Sec. 7122(f)).

The IRS will return any filed offer in compromise application if the taxpayer has not filed all required tax returns.

2724. Partial Payments. Specific written directions from a taxpayer regarding the application of partial payments of assessed federal income taxes, penalties, and interest made by the taxpayer generally will be respected by the IRS (Rev. Proc. 2002-26). A partial payment on deficiencies received without instructions for its application will be applied to tax, penalties, and interest, in the order of priority that best serves the government's interest.

2726. Statute of Limitations for Assessment. All income taxes generally must be assessed within three years after the original return is filed (the last day prescribed by law for filing if the return was filed before the last day) (Code Sec. 6501; Reg. § 301.6501(a)-1). In the case of passthrough entities, the three-year period begins to run at the time the passthrough entity's shareholder or other beneficial owner files an individual income tax return. A return filed prior to its due date is deemed to have been filed on the due date. A return executed by an IRS official or employee for a taxpayer that has not filed a return will not start the running of the statute of limitations. A proceeding in court without assessment for collection of the tax must commence within the same period. The period can be extended by a written agreement between the taxpayer and the IRS. Interest on any tax may be assessed and collected at any time during the period within which the tax itself may be collected (Code Sec. 6601(g); Reg. § 301.6601-1(f)).

If, within the 60-day period ending on the last day of the assessment period, the IRS receives an amended return or written document from the taxpayer showing that additional tax is due for the year in question, the period to assess such additional tax is extended for 60 days after the day on which the IRS receives the amended return or written document (Code Sec. 6501(c)(7)). The assessment period is extended an additional 30 days if the taxpayer files an amended return or written statement, as well as submit payments, during the period on or after April 6, 2020, and ending before July 15, 2020, in response to the COVID-19 (coronavirus) crisis (Notice 2020-23).

If unused foreign tax credits have been carried back, the statute of limitations on assessment and collection for the year to which the carryback is made will not close until one year after the expiration of the period within which a deficiency may be assessed for the year from which the carryback was made (Code Sec. 6501(i); Reg. § 301.6501(i)-1). Deficiencies attributable to carryback of a net operating loss, a capital loss, or the general business and research credit, may be assessed within the period that applies to the loss or credit year. Deficiencies attributable to the carrying back of one of those credits as a result of the carryback of another credit, a net operating loss or a capital loss, may be assessed within the period that applies to the loss or other credit year (Code Sec. 6501(h) and (j)).

2728. Request for Prompt Assessment. A corporation that is contemplating dissolution, is in the process of dissolving, or has actually dissolved, or the fiduciary representing the estate of a decedent (for taxes other than the estate tax imposed by chapter 11), may request a prompt assessment (Code Sec. 6501(d); Reg. § 301.6501(d)-1). If such a request is made, an assessment or a proceeding in court without assessment for the collection of any tax must begin within 18 months after the receipt of a written request for a prompt assessment.

In the case of a corporation, the 18-month period does not apply unless the corporation has completed or will eventually complete its dissolution at or before the end of the 18-month period. This provision does not apply in the case of false or no returns (¶ 2732) or listed transactions (¶ 2734). It also does not apply for personal holding company taxes in certain instances or where a waiver filed by the taxpayer extends the assessment period beyond the 18-month period.

2732. Assessment Period for False Returns or No Return. There is no limitation period on an assessment or a court proceeding to collect tax if the return is false or fraudulent, there is a willful attempt to evade tax, or no return is filed (Code Sec. 6501(c); Reg. § 301.6501(c)-1). In addition, in the case of a fraudulent return, the government may impose additional taxes at any time, without regard to statutes of limitations, although the burden of proof falls on the government to prove fraud by the taxpayer (Code Sec. 7454(a)).

2733. Assessment Period for Listed Transactions. If a taxpayer fails to include with a return any information required relating to a listed transaction (¶ 2591), the statute of limitations with respect to that transaction will not expire before one year after the earlier of: (1) the date on which the information is furnished to the IRS, or (2) the date that a material advisor to the listed transaction satisfies certain list maintenance requirements (¶ 2595) with respect to the transaction (Code Sec. 6501(c)(10)).

2734. Assessment Period for Omission of Over 25 Percent of Income. If the taxpayer omits from gross income (total receipts, without reduction for cost) an amount in excess of 25 percent of the amount of gross income stated in the return, a six-year limitations period on assessment and collection of tax applies. An item will not be considered as omitted from gross income if information sufficient to apprise the IRS of the nature and amount of such item is disclosed in the return or in any schedule or statement attached to the return (Code Sec. 6501(e); Reg. § 301.6501(e)-1(a)). A taxpayer's overstatement of its basis in an asset that resulted in an understatement of gross income from the asset's sale will trigger the six-year limitations period as an omission from gross income.

2735. Statute of Limitations on Collection After Assessment. After assessment of tax is made within the statutory period of limitations (¶ 2726), the tax may be collected by levy or a proceeding in court commenced within 10 years after the assessment or within any period for collection agreed upon in writing between the IRS and the taxpayer before the expiration of the 10-year period (Code Sec. 6502(a); Reg. § 301.6502-1). The period agreed upon by the parties may be extended by later written agreements, so long as they are made prior to the expiration of the period previously agreed upon. The IRS has to notify taxpayers of their right to refuse an extension each time one is requested (Code Sec. 6501(c)(4)). If a timely court proceeding has commenced for the collection of the tax, then the period during which the tax may be collected is extended until the liability for tax, or a judgment against the taxpayer, is satisfied or becomes unenforceable.

The 10-year limitations period on collections is generally suspended for any period during which the IRS is prohibited from levying on the taxpayer's property. The collection period may also be extended by agreement between a taxpayer and the IRS. If the taxpayer entered into an installment agreement with the IRS, then the 10-year limitations period may be extended for the period that the limitations period was extended under the original terms of the installment agreement plus 90 days.

Interest accrues on a deficiency from the date the tax was due (determined without regard to extensions) until the date payment is received at the underpayment rate (¶ 2838) (Code Sec. 6601(g); Reg. § 301.6601-1(a)(1)). Interest may be assessed and collected during the period in which the related tax may be collected.

2736. Suspension of Assessment or Collections Period. The statue of limitations for assessment (¶ 2726) and collection (¶ 2735) of any deficiency of income, estate, or gift taxes is suspended for 90 business days after the mailing of a notice of deficiency (150 days for a deficiency notice mailed to persons outside the United States) (Code Sec. 6503; Reg. § 301.6503(a)-1). If a petition is filed with the Tax Court, the running of the period of limitations is suspended until the Tax Court's decision becomes final and for an additional 60 days thereafter.

The 10-year statute of limitations for collections is also suspended if the taxpayer is outside the United States, the taxpayer's assets are in the control or custody of a state or federal court, the IRS wrongfully seizes or places a federal tax lien on property of a third party, the taxpayer obtains an extension of time to pay tax attributable to a estate tax, undistributed passive foreign investment company earnings, and foreign expropriation losses. The three-year statute of limitations on assessments is suspended with respect to any tax return by a corporation that is the subject of a designated summons in a court proceeding (Code Sec. 6503(j), as amended by the Taxpayer First Act (P.L. 116-25)).

For federal bankruptcy cases, the running of the period of limitations is suspended during the period of the automatic stay on collection of taxes and for an additional period ending 60 days after the day the stay is lifted for assessments and for six months thereafter for collection (Code Sec. 6503(h)). Additionally, in receivership and bankruptcy cases where a fiduciary is required to give written notice to the IRS of an

¶2733

appointment or authorization to act, the assessment period is suspended from the date the proceedings are instituted and ending 30 days after the day of notice to the IRS of such appointment. The extension period cannot exceed two years (Code Sec. 6872).

If the taxpayer and the IRS agree to the rescission of a deficiency notice, the statute of limitations again begins to run as of the date of the rescission and continues to run for the period of time that remains on the date the notice was issued (Code Sec. 6212(d)).

2738. Suit for Recovery of Erroneous Refund. The government may sue to recover an erroneous refund, including one made after the applicable refund period (¶ 2763), within two years after such refund was paid. However, a suit may be commenced within five years if any part of the refund was induced by fraud or misrepresentation of a material fact (Code Sec. 6532(b); Reg. § 301.6532-2).

2740. Criminal Prosecution. A criminal prosecution must generally be started within three years after the offense is committed (Code Sec. 6531). A six-year period applies in a case where there is:

- fraud or an attempt to defraud the United States or an agency thereof, by conspiracy or otherwise;

- a willful attempt to evade or defeat any tax or payment;

- willful aiding or assisting in the preparation of a false return or other document;

- willful failure to pay any tax or make any return (except certain information returns) at the time required by law;

- a false statement verified under penalties of perjury or a false or fraudulent return, statement or other document;

- intimidation of a U.S. officer or employee;

- an offense committed by a U.S. officer or employee in connection with a revenue law; or

- a conspiracy to defeat tax or payment.

2743. Collection from Transferee of Property. The liability of a transferee of property is generally assessed and collected in the same manner as is any other deficiency imposed by the IRS (Code Sec. 6901; Reg. § 301.6901-1(a)). A transferee includes an heir, legatee, devisee, distributee of an estate of a deceased person, the shareholder of a dissolved corporation, the assignee or donee of an insolvent person, the successor of a corporation, a party to a Code Sec. 368(a) reorganization, and a member of any other class of distributees. It also includes, with respect to the gift tax, a donee (without regard to the solvency of the donor) and, with respect to the estate tax, any person who, under Code Sec. 6324(a)(2), is personally liable for any part of the tax.

2745. Transferee Assessment and Collection Period. Unless a taxpayer has filed a false return with intent to evade tax (¶ 2732), an assessment against a transferee or fiduciary must be made within the following periods:

- in the case of an initial transferee, within one year after the expiration of the period of limitations for assessment against the taxpayer;

- in the case of a transferee of a transferee, within one year after the expiration of the period of limitations for assessment against the preceding transferee or three years after the expiration of the period of limitations for assessment against the taxpayer, whichever of these two periods expires first;

- if a timely court proceeding has been brought against the taxpayer or last preceding transferee, within one year after the return of execution in such proceeding; or

- in the case of a fiduciary, within one year after the liability arises or within the limitations period for collection of the tax (¶ 2726), whichever is the later (Code Sec. 6901; Reg. § 301.6901-1(c)).

2747. Collection from Fiduciary. In order to receive advance notice from the IRS with respect to assessments, every fiduciary must give written notice to the IRS of his or her fiduciary capacity using Form 56. If the notice is not filed, the IRS may proceed against the property in the hands of the fiduciary after mailing notice of the deficiency or other liability to the taxpayer's last known address, even if the taxpayer is then deceased or is under legal disability. The fiduciary may be relieved of any further liability by filing with the IRS written notice and evidence of the termination (Reg. § 301.6903-1).

2750. Assessment in Bankruptcy or Receiverships. If a taxpayer's assets are taken over by a receiver appointed by the court, the IRS may immediately assess the tax if it has not already been lawfully assessed. The IRS may also assess the tax on: (1) the debtor's estate under U.S. Code Title 11 bankruptcy proceedings; or (2) the debtor if the tax liability has become *res judicata* pursuant to a Title 11 bankruptcy determination (Code Sec. 6871). Tax claims may be presented to the court before which the receivership or a Title 11 bankruptcy is pending, despite the pendency of proceedings in the Tax Court. However, in the case of a receivership proceeding, no petition may be filed with the Tax Court after the appointment of the receiver. The trustee of the debtor's estate in a Title 11 bankruptcy proceeding may intervene on behalf of the debtor's estate in any Tax Court proceeding to which the debtor is a party (Code Sec. 7464).

Liens and Levies

2751. Property Subject to Liens. If a taxpayer fails to pay an assessed tax after notice and demand for payment, the United States acquires a lien for the amount due, including interest and penalties, against all the taxpayer's property (real, personal, tangible, and intangible), including after-acquired property and rights to property (Code Sec. 6321; Reg. § 301.6321-1). Whether the taxpayer owns or has an interest in property is determined under the appropriate state law. Once the taxpayer's rights in the property are established, federal law determines priorities among competing creditors (Code Sec. 6323). Federal law also controls whether specific property is exempt from levy (¶ 2753). Once a tax lien arises, it continues until the tax liability is paid or the lien becomes unenforceable due to a lapse of time (Code Sec. 6322). The lien period generally coincides with the statutory period for collection, which is 10 years from the date of assessment, but the collection period may be suspended or extended (Code Sec. 6502(a)).

2753. Property Subject to Levy. A tax lien attaches to all of the debtor's property (¶ 2151), but some property is exempt from levy. The following are among the items that are exempt from levy to some extent:

- wearing apparel and school books;
- fuel, provisions, furniture, and personal effects: up to $9,540 for 2019 ($9,690 for 2020);
- unemployment benefits;
- books and tools of a trade, business, or profession: up to $4,770 for 2019 ($4,850 for 2020);
- undelivered mail;
- certain annuity and pension payments;
- workers' compensation;
- judgments for support of minor children;
- certain public assistance payments, supplemental security income for the aged, blind, and disabled, state and local welfare payments, and Job Training Partnership Act payments;
- certain amounts of wages, salary, and other income; and
- certain service-connected disability payments (Code Sec. 6334; Rev. Proc. 2018-57; Rev. Proc. 2019-44).

Certain specified payments are not exempt from levy if the Secretary of the Treasury approves a continuous levy. Under the Federal Payment Levy Program (FPLP), the IRS can generally approve a continuous levy up to 15 percent on any federal payment. The continuous levy may be up to 100 percent for payments due to a vendor of goods and services, sales or leases of real property, and payments owed to a Medicare provider. The continuous levy may not be applied to: a payment for which eligibility is not based on the income or assets or both of the payee; unemployment benefits, worker's compensation payments, wages, or salary; Social Security disability payments; welfare and public assistance payments; and annuity or pension payments or benefits under the Railroad Retirement Act or Railroad Unemployment Insurance Act (Code Sec. 6331(h)).

The IRS may not seize any real property used as a residence by the taxpayer or any real property of the taxpayer (other than rental property) that is used as a residence by another person in order to satisfy a liability of $5,000 or less (including tax, penalties, and interest). In the case of the taxpayer's principal residence, the IRS may not seize the residence without written approval of a federal district court judge or magistrate (Code Sec. 6334(a)(13) and (e)). Unless collection of tax is in jeopardy, tangible personal property or real property (other than rented real property) used in the taxpayer's trade or business may not be seized without written approval of an IRS district or assistant director. The approval may not be given unless it is determined that the taxpayer's other assets subject to collection are not sufficient to pay the amount due and the expenses of the proceedings. If a levy is made on tangible personal property essential to the taxpayer's trade or business, the IRS must provide an accelerated appeals process to determine whether the property should be released from levy (¶ 2755) (Code Sec. 6343(a)(2)).

Levies are prohibited if the estimated expenses of the levy and sale exceed the fair market value of the property (Code Sec. 6331(f)). Also, unless the collection of tax is in jeopardy, a levy cannot be made on any day on which the taxpayer is required to respond to an IRS summons (Code Sec. 6331(g)). Further, financial institutions are required to hold amounts garnished by the IRS for 21 days after receiving notice of the levy to provide the taxpayer time to notify the IRS of any errors (Code Sec. 6332(c)).

2754. Recording and Priority of Tax Liens. Until notice of a tax lien has been properly recorded, it is not valid against any bona fide purchaser for value, mechanic's lienor, judgment lien creditor, or holder of a security interest (e.g., a mortgagee or pledgee) (Code Sec. 6323(a)). Also, even a properly recorded tax lien may not be valid against so-called superpriorities, which include purchases of securities and automobiles, retail purchases, casual sales of less than $1,590 for 2019 ($1,620 for 2020), certain possessory liens securing payment for repairs to personal property, real property taxes and special assessment liens, mechanic's liens for repairs and improvements of not more than $7,970 for 2019 ($8,100 for 2020) to certain residential property, attorneys' liens, certain insurance contracts and deposit secured loans (previously referred to as passbook loans) (Code Sec. 6323(b); Rev. Proc. 2018-57; Rev. Proc. 2019-44). In addition, security interests arising from commercial financing agreements may be accorded superpriority status (Code Sec. 6323(c)).

Notice of a federal tax lien must be filed in one office designated by the state in which the property is situated (Code Sec. 6323(f); Reg. § 301.6323(f)-1). Personal property is generally considered situated in the state where the taxpayer resides, rather than where domiciled; for real property, the situs is its physical location. If, in the case of either real or personal property, the state designates more than one office or does not designate an office where notice must be filed, notice of the lien must be filed with the federal district court for the jurisdiction where the property is situated. If state law provides that a notice of lien affecting personal property must be filed in the county clerk's office located in the taxpayer's county of residence and also adopts a federal law that requires a notice of lien to be filed in another location in order to attach to a specific type of property, the state is deemed to have designated only one office for the filing of the notice. Thus, to protect its lien, the IRS need only file its notice in the county clerk's office located in the taxpayer's home county. Notice regarding property located in the District of Columbia is filed with the Recorder of Deeds of the District of Columbia. Special rules apply in a state that requires public indexing for priority liens against realty.

A forfeiture under local law of property seized by any law enforcement agency or other local governmental branch relates back to the time the property was first seized, unless, under local law, a claim holder would have priority over the interest of the government in the property (Code Sec. 6323(i)(3)).

The IRS may not levy against property while a taxpayer has a pending offer in compromise or installment agreement (Code Sec. 6331(k)). If the offer in compromise or installment agreement is ultimately rejected, the levy prohibition remains in effect for 30 days after the rejection and during the pendency of any appeal of the rejection, providing the appeal is filed within 30 days of the rejection. No levy may be made while the installment agreement is in effect. If the installment agreement is terminated by the IRS, no levy may be made for 30 days after the termination and during the pendency of any appeal.

2754A. Notice and Opportunity for Hearing. The IRS must notify any person subject to a lien of the existence of the lien within five days of the lien being filed (Code Sec. 6320; Reg. § 301.6320-1). Among other requirements, the notice must address the person's right to request a hearing during the 30-day period beginning on the sixth day after the lien is filed. Similarly, at least 30 days prior to levying on any person's property or right to property, the IRS must provide the taxpayer with notice of its intent to levy and of the taxpayer's right to a hearing, commonly referred to as a Collection Due Process (CDP) hearing (Code Sec. 6330; Reg. § 301.6330-1).

The hearing is held by the IRS Independent Office of Appeals whether in connection with the notice of lien or notice of intent to levy. At the hearing, the taxpayer may raise any issue relevant to the appropriateness of the proposed collection activity if such issue was not raised at a previous hearing. The taxpayer has 30 days after the hearing determination to appeal the determination to the Tax Court, which has exclusive jurisdiction over appeals of hearing determinations. A taxpayer subject to a levy for the collection of employment taxes cannot request a hearing if the taxpayer already requested a hearing regarding unpaid employment taxes arising in the two-year period before the beginning of the tax period at issue.

2755. Release of Tax Liens and Levies. Taxpayers may appeal the filing of a notice of lien in the public record and petition for release (Code Sec. 6326; Reg. § 301.6326-1). If filed in error, the IRS must release the lien and state that the lien was erroneous. The request for relief must be based on one of the following grounds:

- the tax liability had been satisfied before the lien was filed;
- the assessing of the tax liability violated either the notice of deficiency procedures or the Bankruptcy Code; or
- the limitations period for collecting the liability had expired prior to the filing of the lien.

Further, the IRS may withdraw a public notice of tax lien before payment in full if:

- the filing of the notice was premature or not in accord with administrative procedures;
- the taxpayer has entered into an installment agreement to satisfy the tax liability;
- withdrawal of the notice would facilitate the collection of the tax liability; or
- withdrawal of the notice would be in the best interest of the taxpayer and the government, as determined by the National Taxpayer Advocate (Code Sec. 6323(j)).

The withdrawal of a notice of tax lien does not affect the underlying tax lien; rather, the withdrawal simply relinquishes any lien priority the IRS had obtained when the notice was filed.

The IRS is required to release a levy if:

- the underlying liability is satisfied or becomes unenforceable due to lapse of time;
- the IRS determines that the release of the levy will facilitate the collection of tax;
- an installment payment agreement has been executed by the taxpayer with respect to the liability;
- the IRS determines that the levy is creating a financial hardship; or
- the fair market value of the property exceeds the liability, and the partial release of the levy would not hinder the collection of tax (Code Sec. 6343(a)).

A taxpayer may also request that the IRS sell the levied property (Code Sec. 6335(f); Reg. § 301.6335-1(d)).

The IRS may return property that has been levied upon if:

- the levy was premature or not in accordance with administrative procedure;
- the taxpayer has entered into an installment agreement to satisfy the tax liability, unless the agreement provides otherwise;
- the return of the property will facilitate collection of the tax liability; or
- with the consent of the taxpayer or the Taxpayer Advocate, the return of the property would be in the best interests of the taxpayer and the government (Code Sec. 6343(d)).

Property is returned in the same manner as if the property had been wrongfully levied upon, except that the taxpayer is not entitled to interest. Effective for tax years after 2017, amounts returned to an individual from the IRS, including any applicable interest, due to an improper or wrongful levy upon the taxpayer's individual retirement account (IRA) (¶ 2155) or other employer-sponsored retirement account, may be contributed to the IRA or retirement account without regard to any contribution limits (¶ 2115) (Code Sec. 6343(f)).

A taxpayer may bring a suit in federal district court if an IRS employee knowingly or negligently fails to release a tax lien on the taxpayer's property after receiving written notice from the taxpayer of the IRS's failure to release the lien (Code Sec. 7432; Reg. § 301.7432-1). The taxpayer may recover actual economic damages plus the costs of the action. Injuries such as inconvenience, emotional distress, and loss of reputation are not compensable damages unless they result in actual economic harm. Costs of the action that may be recovered are limited generally to certain court costs and do not include administrative costs or attorney's fees, although attorney's fees may be recoverable (¶ 2796). A two-year statute of limitations, measured from the date on which the cause of action accrued, applies.

Third-Party Owners. A third-party owner of property against which a federal tax lien has been filed may obtain a certificate of discharge with respect to the lien on such property (Code Sec. 6325(b)(4); Reg. § 301.6325-1(b)(4)). The certificate is issued if (1) the third-party owner deposits with the IRS an amount of money equal to the value of the government's interest in the property as determined by the IRS, or (2) the third-party owner posts a bond covering the government's interest in the property in a form acceptable to the IRS. A third-party owner who is a co-owner of property with the taxpayer against whom the underlying tax was assessed may no longer be automatically barred from obtaining a certificate of discharge with respect to a lien on the property. A third-party owner may request the discharge of a tax lien on property they own with the person whose tax liability gave rise to the lien.

The IRS will refund, with interest, the amount deposited and release the bond applicable to any property if the IRS determines that (1) the liability to which the lien relates can be satisfied from other sources, or (2) the value of the government's interest in the property is less than the IRS's prior determination of the government's interest in the property. Within 120 days after a certificate of discharge is issued, the third-party owner may file a civil action against the United States in a federal district court for a determination of whether the government's interest in the property, if any, has less value than that determined by the IRS (Code Sec. 7426(a)(4) and (b)(5)).

Mitigation of Effect of Statute of Limitations

2756. Correction of Errors in Certain Cases. Relief is provided from some of the inequities caused by the statute of limitations and other provisions that would otherwise prevent equitable adjustment of various income tax hardships (Code Secs. 1311–1314; Reg. §§ 1.1311(a)-1–1.1314(c)-1). Adjustments are permitted, even though the limitations period for assessment or refund for the year at issue may have otherwise expired, if a determination under the income tax laws:

- requires the inclusion in gross income of an item that was erroneously included in the income of the taxpayer for another tax year or in the gross income of a related taxpayer (e.g., spouse, beneficiary, partner, member of affiliated group of corporations, etc.);
- allows a deduction or credit that was erroneously allowed to the taxpayer for another tax year or to a related taxpayer;

- requires the exclusion from gross income of an item included in a return filed by the taxpayer or with respect to which tax was paid and which was erroneously excluded or omitted from the gross income of the taxpayer for another tax year or from the gross income of a related taxpayer for the same or another tax year;

- allows or disallows, in certain situations, deductions or inclusions for a trust or an estate, and there has been no appropriate corresponding change in the income of beneficiaries, heirs, or legatees;

- establishes the basis of property by making adjustments to such basis for items that should have been added to, or deducted from, income of preceding years;

- requires the allowance or disallowance of a deduction or credit to a corporation where a correlative deduction or credit was erroneously allowed, or disallowed, to a related taxpayer that is a member of an affiliated group of corporations where there is an 80 percent common ownership;

- requires the exclusion from gross income of an item not included in a return filed by the taxpayer and with respect to which the tax was not paid but which is includible in the gross income of the taxpayer for another tax year or in the gross income of a related taxpayer; or

- disallows a deduction or credit that should have been allowed, but was not allowed, to the taxpayer for another tax year or to a related taxpayer for the same or another tax year (Code Sec. 1312).

Refunds and Credits

2759. Claim for Refund or Credit. The IRS may credit overpayments of federal tax against any type of outstanding federal tax liability. Any remaining balance may be refunded to the taxpayer unless it must be applied to outstanding child support, government-agency debts, or state income tax debt (¶ 2764) (Code Sec. 6402, as amended by the Taxpayer First Act (P.L. 116-25); Reg. § 301.6402-2). A taxpayer must file a claim for a credit or refund within the applicable statute of limitations (¶ 2763). This is also a precondition to filing a civil action for refund (Code Sec. 7422). Interest is allowed on a refund from the date of overpayment to a date preceding the date of the refund by not more than 30 days (¶ 2765). A separate claim for credit or refund must be filed for each taxable year or period.

A claim for a credit or refund for an overpayment of income taxes is generally made on the appropriate income tax return. Once the return has been filed, the claim is made on an amended return. Form 843 is used to file a claim for refund of taxes other than income taxes. Generally, a claim for a credit or refund of taxes must be made within three years after the date the taxpayer filed their original return, or within two years after the taxpayer paid the tax, whichever is later. However, the due date for filing any claim for credit or refund of taxes otherwise due on or after April 1, 2020, and before July 15, 2020, is automatically extended to July 15, 2020, in response to the COVID-19 (coronavirus) crisis (Notice 2020-23).

Most taxpayers may elect on their return to have the IRS deposit their refunds directly deposited into one account in a financial institution provided it accepts direct deposits. Taxpayer may also have their refunded directly deposited in up to three financial accounts, such as checking, savings and retirement accounts using Form 8888. Direct deposit must be requested separately each tax year. The IRS is authorized to provide procedures for identification and recovery of a misdirected direct deposit refunds.

2760. Amendment of Refund Claim. A timely claim for refund based upon one or more specific grounds may not be amended to include other and different grounds after the statute of limitations has expired (Reg. § 301.6402-2(b)).

2761. Refund or Credit After Appeal to Tax Court. If the taxpayer has been mailed a notice of deficiency and has filed a petition with the Tax Court, the taxpayer may not bring a separate refund suit in any other court for recovery of any part of the tax at issue in the Tax Court (Code Sec. 6512). The taxpayer is permitted to institute a claim for credit or refund in another court for the same tax year to recover:

- an overpayment determined by a decision of the Tax Court that has become final;

- any amount collected in excess of an amount computed in accordance with a final decision of the Tax Court;

- any amount collected after the expiration of the period of limitations upon the beginning of levy or a proceeding in court for collection;

- overpayments attributable to partnership items;

- any amount that was collected within the period following the mailing of a notice of deficiency during which the IRS is prohibited from collecting by levy or through a court proceeding; and

- any amount that is not contested on an appeal from a Tax Court decision.

The Tax Court can order the refund of a tax overpayment plus interest if the IRS has not made a refund to the taxpayer within 120 days after the decision fixing the amount of the refund has become final.

The Tax Court is empowered to resolve disputes regarding the amount of interest to be charged on a tax deficiency redetermined pursuant to a Tax Court order. The action must be brought within one year from the date on which the decision ordering the redetermination of taxes became final. Further, the taxpayer must pay the entire redetermined deficiency, plus the entire amount of interest, before the Tax Court can hear the case (Code Sec. 7481(c)).

2763. Limitations on Credit or Refund. A taxpayer may generally file a claim for refund within three years from the time the return was filed or within two years from the time the tax was paid, whichever is later. If no return was filed by the taxpayer, the claim must be filed within two years from the time the tax was paid (Code Sec. 6511(a)). The due date for filing any claim for credit or refund of taxes otherwise due on or after April 1, 2020, and before July 15, 2020, is automatically extended to July 15, 2020, in response to the COVID-19 (coronavirus) crisis (Notice 2020-23). For this purpose, a return filed before the due date is treated as filed on the due date (Code Sec. 6513(a)). A taxpayer who fails to file a return as of the date the IRS mails a deficiency notice may recover in the Tax Court taxes paid during the three years preceding the IRS mailing date (Code Sec. 6512(b)(3)).

If the claim relates to the deductibility of bad debts or worthless securities, the period is seven years; if it relates to the credit for foreign taxes, the period is 10 years. If the refund claim relates to a net operating loss (NOL) carryback or a capital loss carryback, the period is that period which ends three years after the time prescribed by law for filing the return, including extensions, for the tax year of the NOL or capital loss carryback. To the extent that an overpayment is due to unused credit carrybacks that arise as the result of the carryback of an NOL or capital loss, the claim may be filed during the period that ends three years after the time prescribed by law for filing the return, including extensions, for the tax year of the unused credit that results in the carryback (Code Sec. 6511(d); Reg. § 301.6511(d)-2).

The statute of limitations on refund claims is suspended during any period that an individual is financially disabled—under a medically determinable mental or physical impairment that: (1) can be expected to result in death or that has lasted or can be expected to last for a continuous period of not less than one year, and (2) renders the person unable to manage his or her financial affairs (Code Sec. 6511(h)). The suspension of the limitations period does not apply for any period during which the taxpayer's spouse or another person is authorized to act on behalf of the individual in financial matters.

Retired Military Personnel. The time period for retired military personnel to file claims for credits or refunds related to disability determinations by the Department of Veterans Affairs (e.g., determinations after the tax return is filed) is extended until one year after the date of the disability determination if that period is later than the normal three-year period of limitations (Code Sec. 6511(d)(8)). This provision does not apply to any tax year that began more than five years before the date of the disability determination.

2764. Refund Reduction for Past-Due, Legally Enforceable Debts. The Treasury Department's Financial Management Service (FMS) will reduce the amount of any tax refund payable to a taxpayer by the amount of any past-due, legally enforceable nontax debt that is owed to any federal agency. Debts that are less than $25 are exempt. In most cases, the creditor federal agencies must have first attempted to collect the debt by using salary offset and administrative procedures. The federal agency is also required to notify the taxpayer that a debt will be referred to the FMS for refund offset if the debt remains unpaid after 60 days or if there is insufficient evidence that the debt is either not past due or not legally enforceable (31 CFR § 285.2).

Rules are provided governing the offset of tax refunds against past-due child and spousal support (31 CFR § 285.3) and against state income tax debts reduced to judgment (31 CFR § 285.8). Tax refunds may also be offset against past-due debts owed to a state for (1) erroneous payment of unemployment compensation due to fraud or failure to report earnings, or (2) failure to make contributions to a state's unemployment fund for which the state has determined the person to be liable (Code Sec. 6402(f)).

2765. Interest on Refund. If a return has been properly filed in processable form, interest is allowed on a refund from the date of overpayment to a date preceding the date of the refund by not more than 30 days (Code Sec. 6611(b)(2) and (3)). If a return is filed late, no interest is allowed for any day before the date on which it is filed. No interest is payable on a refund arising from an original tax return if the refund is issued by the 45th day after the later of the due date for the return, determined without regard to any extensions, or the date the return is filed (Code Sec. 6611(e)). Similarly, if a refund claimed on an amended return or claim for refund is issued within 45 days after the date the amended document was filed, interest is not payable for that period, although interest is payable from the due date of the original return to the date the amended document was filed. If a refund is not issued within the 45-day grace period, interest is payable for the period from the due date of the original return to the date the refund is paid.

The interest rate the IRS must pay for overpayment of taxes by noncorporate taxpayers is equal to the federal short-term rate (¶ 83) plus three percentage points (which is equal to the interest rate on underpayments of tax). The interest rate on overpayments by corporate taxpayers is the short-term federal rate plus two percentage points (Code Sec. 6621). For large corporate overpayments (i.e., any portion that exceeds $10,000) the rate is reduced to the sum of the short-term federal rate plus one-half of one percentage point. These rates are adjusted quarterly, with each successive rate becoming effective two months after the date of each quarterly adjustment.

Overlapping Overpayments and Underpayments. The interest rates for overpayments and underpayments have been equalized (also referred to as "global interest netting") for any period of mutual indebtedness between a taxpayer and the IRS (Code Sec. 6621(d)). No interest is imposed to the extent that underpayment and overpayment interest run simultaneously on equal amounts. The net zero interest rate applies regardless of whether an underpayment otherwise would be subject to the increased interest rate imposed on large corporate underpayments or an overpayment otherwise would be subject to a reduced interest rate because it was a corporate overpayment in excess of $10,000. Although global interest netting is available to both corporate and noncorporate taxpayers, its effect on noncorporate taxpayers is mitigated due to the equalization of the underpayment and overpayment interest rates for such taxpayers.

2768. Refunds Disregarded for Means-Tested Assistance Programs. Any federal tax refund, or advance payment with respect to a refundable federal tax credit made to any individual cannot be taken into account as income or as resources for a period of 12 months from receipt, for purposes of determining the individual's eligibility (or that of any other individual) for benefits or assistance, or for the amount or extent of benefits or assistance, under (1) any federal program, or (2) any state or local program financed in whole or in part with federal funds (Code Sec. 6409).

2773. Quick Carryback Refund and Postponement of Tax Payment. A corporation other than an S corporation that has an overpayment of tax as a result of a net operating loss (NOL), capital loss, business and research credits, or a claim-of-right adjustment can file an application on Form 1139 for a tentative adjustment or refund of taxes for a year affected by the carryback of such loss or credits or by such adjustment. A noncorporate taxpayer can apply for similar adjustments on Form 1045 (Code Sec. 6411; Temp. Reg. §5.6411-1). See ¶ 1145 for discussion of the quick refund from a NOL carryback.

The application itself is not a formal refund claim and its rejection in whole or in part cannot be made the basis of a refund suit. However, the taxpayer can file a regular claim for refund within the limitations period (¶ 2763), and this claim can be made the basis for a suit. For losses and credits, the IRS must allow or disallow the refund or credit within 90 days from the later of (1) the date the application is filed or (2) the last day of the month in which the return for the loss or unused credit year is due (giving effect to extensions of time). For claim-of-right adjustments, the IRS must allow or disallow the refund or credit within 90 days from the later of the date the application is filed or the date of the overpayment.

If a corporation expects a NOL carryback from the current (unfinished) tax year, it can, subject to certain limitations, extend the time for payment of all or a part of the tax still payable for the immediately preceding year by filing a statement on Form 1138 (Reg. § 1.6164-1).

The Courts

2776. Organization of Tax Court. The primary function of the U.S. Tax Court is to review deficiencies asserted by the IRS for additional income, estate, gift, or self-employment taxes or special excise taxes (Code Secs. 6512 and 7442). The Tax Court is not an agency of, and is independent of, the Executive Branch of the Government (Code Sec. 7441). The Tax Court is the only judicial body from which relief may be obtained without the payment of tax. The Tax Court also may issue declaratory judgments on the initial or continuing qualification of a retirement plan under Code Sec. 401, a tax-exempt organization under Code Sec. 170(c)(2), Code Sec. 501(c), Code Sec. 501(d), a private foundation under Code Sec. 509(a), a private operating foundation under Code Sec. 4942(j)(3), or a tax-exempt farmers' cooperative under Code Sec. 521. However, a revocation of tax-exempt status for failure to file an annual information return or notice is not subject to an action for declaratory judgment relief. The Tax Court also may rule on the tax-exempt interest status of a government bond issue (Code Secs. 7428, 7476, and 7478; Tax Court Rule 210). Declaratory judgment powers are also provided for estate tax installments, gift tax revaluations, and employment status determinations.

The Tax Court may establish procedures for filing complaints with respect to the conduct of any judge or special trial judge (Code Sec. 7466). The Tax Court has the same general management, administrative and expenditure authorities that are available to other courts and may conduct annual judicial conferences and charge reasonable registration fees (Code Sec. 7470 and Code Sec. 7470A). All fees received by the Tax Court, except for annual conference registration fees and periodic practice fees, must be deposited into a Treasury special fund (Code Sec. 7473).

The Tax Court's offices and trial rooms are located in Washington, D.C., but trials are also conducted in principal cities throughout the country. At the time of filing a petition, the taxpayer should file a request indicating where he or she prefers the trial to be held. The court imposes a filing fee of $60 (Code Sec. 7451).

In any Tax Court case, other than small tax cases (¶ 2784), the findings of fact and opinion must generally be reported in writing. In appropriate cases, a Tax Court judge may state orally, and record in the transcript of the proceedings, the findings of fact or opinion in the case (Code Sec. 7459). In these cases, the court must provide to all parties in the case either a copy of the transcript pages, which record the findings or opinion, or a written summary of such findings or opinion (Tax Court Rule 152).

2782. Burden of Proof. The IRS has the burden of proof in the Tax Court with respect to a factual issue that is relevant to determining a taxpayer's tax liability if the taxpayer presents credible evidence with respect to that issue *and* satisfies three applicable conditions (Code Sec. 7491):

- the taxpayer must comply with the substantiation and recordkeeping requirements of the Code and regulations;

¶2782

- the taxpayer must cooperate with reasonable requests by the IRS for witnesses, information, documents, meetings and interviews; and

- the taxpayer, *other than an individual*, must meet the net worth limitations that apply for awarding attorneys' fees under Code Sec. 7430, but a taxpayer whose tax worth exceeds $7 million cannot benefit from this provision.

Further, in any court proceeding where the IRS solely uses statistical information from unrelated taxpayers to reconstruct an item of an *individual* taxpayer's income, such as the average income for taxpayers in the area in which the taxpayer lives, the burden of proof is on the IRS with respect to that item of income. Also with respect to individuals, the IRS must initially come forward with evidence that it is appropriate to apply a penalty, addition to tax, or additional amount before the court can impose the penalty.

The IRS bears the burden of proof with respect to any new matter, increase in deficiency, or affirmative defenses raised in its answer. Further, the burden of proving fraud and liability as a transferee is upon the IRS (Code Secs. 6902 and 7454). The IRS also has the burden of proof in proceedings involving a manager of a private foundation where the manager knowingly participated in an act of self-dealing, participated in an investment that jeopardizes the carrying out of an exempt purpose, or agreed to the making of a taxable expenditure.

2784. Small Tax Cases. The Tax Court maintains relatively informal procedures for the filing and handling of cases where neither the tax deficiency in dispute (including additions to tax and penalties) nor the amount of claimed overpayment exceeds $50,000. Usually taxpayers represent themselves, although they may be represented by anyone admitted to practice before the Tax Court. Each decision is final and cannot be appealed by either the taxpayer or the government (Code Sec. 7463). The filing fee for all Tax Court petitions is $60 (¶ 2776).

2786. Appeal from Tax Court Decision. A taxpayer who loses in the Tax Court may appeal the case (unless the case was tried as a small tax case (¶ 2784)) to the proper U.S. Court of Appeals by filing a notice of appeal with the clerk of the Tax Court. The notice must be filed within 90 days after the Tax Court decision is entered. If one party to the proceeding files a timely notice of appeal, any other party to the proceeding may take an appeal by filing a notice of appeal within 120 days after the decision of the Tax Court is entered (Code Sec. 7483). A taxpayer who wants the assessment postponed pending the outcome of the appeal must file an appeal bond with the Tax Court guaranteeing payment of the deficiency as finally determined (Code Sec. 7485).

2788. Acquiescence and Nonacquiescence by Commissioner. The IRS may announce in the Internal Revenue Bulletin if it has decided to acquiesce or not acquiesce in a regular decision of the Tax Court. Any acquiescence or nonacquiescence may be withdrawn, modified, or reversed at any time and any such action may be given retrospective, as well as prospective, effect (*H.B. Quinn*, CA-7, 75-2 USTC ¶ 9764).

An acquiescence or nonacquiescence relates only to the issue or issues decided adversely to the government. Acquiescence means the IRS accepts the conclusion reached and does not necessarily mean acceptance and approval of any or all of the reasons assigned by the court for its conclusions. Acquiescences are to be relied on by IRS officers and others concerned as conclusions of the IRS only with respect to the application of the law to the facts in the particular case.

2790. Suits for Refund of Tax Overpayments. After the IRS rejects a refund claim for an alleged tax overpayment, a suit can be maintained in the U.S. Court of Federal Claims or a U.S. District Court. A suit may be brought in the Court of Federal Claims against the United States to recover any overpayment of tax, regardless of amount (Judicial Code Sec. 1491). Final decisions of the U.S. Court of Federal Claims are appealable to the U.S. Court of Appeals for the Federal Circuit (Judicial Code Sec. 1295). All civil actions against the United States for the recovery of any internal revenue tax alleged to have been erroneously or illegally assessed or collected may be brought against the United States as defendant in a U.S. District Court with right of trial by jury in any action if either party makes a specific request for a jury trial (Judicial Code Secs. 1346 and 2402). Filing a proper claim for refund or credit (¶ 2759) is a condition precedent to a suit for recovery of overpaid taxes (Code Sec. 7422(a)).

¶2784

If, prior to the hearing on a taxpayer's refund suit in a District Court or the Court of Federal Claims, a notice of deficiency is issued on the subject matter of the taxpayer's suit, then the District Court or Court of Federal Claims proceedings are stayed during the period of time in which the taxpayer can file a petition with the Tax Court (¶ 2792) and for 60 days thereafter. If the taxpayer files a petition with the Tax Court, then the District Court or the Court of Federal Claims loses jurisdiction as to any issues over which the Tax Court acquires jurisdiction. If the taxpayer does not appeal to the Tax Court, the United States may then counterclaim in the taxpayer's suit within the period of the stay of proceedings even though the time for such pleading may otherwise have expired (Code Sec. 7422(e)).

2792. Time to Bring Suit. A suit or proceeding based upon a refund claim must be brought within two years from the date the IRS mails, by registered or certified mail, notice of disallowance of the part of the claim to which such suit or proceeding relates or within two years from the date the taxpayer waives notification of disallowance of his or her claim (Code Sec. 6532(a)). The two-year period of limitations for filing suit may be extended by written agreement between the taxpayer and the IRS. Unless a bankruptcy proceeding has begun, no action can be brought before the expiration of six months from the date of filing the refund claim unless the IRS renders a decision on the claim before the six months are up. In bankruptcy proceedings, the six-month period is reduced to 120 days.

2794. Supreme Court. Either party may seek a review of a U.S. Court of Appeals decision by the U.S. Supreme Court through a petition for a writ of certiorari (Code Sec. 7482(a); Judicial Code Sec. 2101).

2796. Attorneys' Fees and Court Costs. A "prevailing party"—any party, other than the United States or a creditor of the taxpayer— who has substantially prevailed with respect to the amount in controversy or the most significant issue or issues, may be awarded reasonable litigation costs in most civil tax litigation, including declaratory judgment proceedings (Code Sec. 7430). In addition, a prevailing party can recover reasonable administrative costs incurred in connection with such administrative proceeding with the IRS.

These awards may be made if the taxpayer meets certain net worth limitations and the IRS fails to prove that its position was substantially justified. If litigation costs are involved, the IRS's position is the position taken in the litigation or administrative proceeding by the IRS District Counsel. In the case of administrative costs, the IRS's position is the position taken as of the earlier of the date the taxpayer received a decision notice from the IRS Independent Office of Appeals or the date of the deficiency notice.

Reasonable administrative costs include (1) administrative fees or similar charges imposed by the IRS, and (2) the reasonable expenses incurred with respect to compensating expert witnesses, financing necessary studies and reports, and paying attorneys' fees. The costs can only be awarded if incurred after the earlier of:

- the date the taxpayer received the decision notice from the IRS Independent Office of Appeals;

- the date of the deficiency notice; or

- the date on which the first letter of proposed deficiency is sent that allows the taxpayer an opportunity for administrative review in the IRS Independent Office of Appeals.

Reasonable litigation costs include:

- expenses of expert witnesses;

- costs of any study, analysis, engineering report, test, or project, which was found by the court to be necessary for the preparation of its case;

- fees of an individual authorized to practice before the court or the IRS, whether or not an attorney (generally not in excess of $200 per hour for 2019 and $210 per hour for 2020), unless an affidavit is presented that establishes a special factor for a higher rate, such as the unavailability of qualified representatives at the customary rate (Rev. Proc. 2018-57; Rev. Proc. 2019-44); and

- court costs.

To be recoverable, litigation costs must generally be paid or incurred by the taxpayer. The taxpayer may recover costs paid by a third party if the taxpayer assumes either a noncontingent obligation to repay the advanced fees or a contingent obligation to repay the fees in the event of their eventual recovery *(B.F. Morrison*, CA-9, 2009-1 USTC ¶ 50,387).

For purposes of both reasonable administrative costs and reasonable litigation costs, reasonable attorneys' fees may be awarded to attorneys and specified persons who represent prevailing parties on a pro bono basis or for a nominal fee. Thus, the amount awarded may be more than the amount of fees actually paid or incurred. The award must be paid to the attorney or the attorney's employer.

In order to establish that the taxpayer was a prevailing party, the taxpayer needs to establish that he or she has substantially prevailed with respect to the amount in controversy or with respect to the most significant issue or set of issues presented (Code Sec. 7430(c)(4); Reg. § 301.7430-5). A taxpayer who meets the timely filing and net worth requirements may be treated as a prevailing party if the taxpayer's liability is determined to be equal to or less than it would have been had the government accepted the taxpayer's last qualified offer to settle the case (including interest). A qualified offer is a written offer made at any time during the time from the issuance of the 30-day letter to a date 30 days before the date the case is first set for trial (Code Sec. 7430(g); Reg. § 301.7430-7).

No costs will be awarded where the prevailing party failed to exhaust all of the administrative remedies within the IRS (Code Sec. 7430(b); Reg. § 301.7430-1). The tender of a qualified settlement offer does not satisfy the requirement to exhaust all administrative remedies *(Haas & Associates Accounting Corporation*, CA-9, 2003-1 USTC ¶ 50,253). Further, costs will be denied for any portion of the proceeding if the prevailing party caused unreasonable delay. A taxpayer who prevails in an IRS proceeding must apply to the IRS for administrative costs before the 91st day after the date the final IRS determination of tax, interest or penalty was mailed to the taxpayer. If the IRS denies the application for costs, the taxpayer must petition the Tax Court within 90 days of the IRS mailing of the denial.

An order granting or denying an award for litigation costs becomes part of the decision or judgment in the case and is subject to appeal in the same manner as the decision or judgment (Code Sec. 7430(f)).

2798. Suit for Damages in Connection with Collection of Tax. A taxpayer may bring a suit in federal district court for damages sustained in connection with the collection of any federal tax because an IRS employee recklessly or intentionally disregarded any provision of the Internal Revenue Code, any IRS regulations or certain provisions of the Bankruptcy Code (Code Sec. 7433; Reg. § 301.7433-1). A suit may also be brought for negligent disregard of the Internal Revenue Code or any IRS regulations. Except as provided in Code Sec. 7432 relating to damage awards for failure to release liens (¶ 2755), this action is the taxpayer's exclusive remedy for recovering damages caused by reckless, intentional or negligent disregard of such provisions and regulations by IRS employees. The suit must be brought within two years after the right of action accrues.

The award is limited to the costs of the action plus any actual direct economic damages sustained by the taxpayer, up to a maximum award of $1 million for reckless or intentional actions and $100,000 for acts of negligence. The IRS must comply with certain provisions of the Fair Debt Collection Practices Act so that the treatment of tax debtors by the IRS is at least equal to that required of private sector debt collectors (Code Sec. 6304). A taxpayer may bring a damages action under Code Sec. 7433 against the IRS for violations of these provisions.

Chapter 28

PENALTIES □ INTEREST

Failure to File Returns or Pay Tax

See CCH® AnswerConnect: *Delinquency-Related Penalties* for more information on this topic.

2801. Penalty for Failure to File Returns. A penalty (i.e., addition to tax) is imposed for a failure to file any tax return within the time prescribed, including extensions, unless the failure is due to reasonable cause and not willful neglect (Code Sec. 6651(a)(1)). The due date for filing federal income tax returns and making federal income tax payments otherwise due on or after April 1, 2020, and before July 15, 2020, is automatically extended to July 15, 2020, in response to the COVID-19 (coronavirus) crisis (¶ 2505). Any penalty, addition to tax, or interest for failure to file or pay taxes during this period will not begin to accrue until July 16, 2020 (Notice 2020-23).

The penalty for failure to file is five percent of the unpaid tax shown on the return for one month and an additional five percent for each month or part of a month that the failure continues, up to maximum of 25 percent. If an income tax return is not filed within 60 days of the prescribed due date (including extensions), the minimum penalty is the lesser of 100 percent of the tax required to be shown on the return or $210 for returns required to be filed in 2019 ($435 for returns required to be filed in 2020) (Code Sec. 6651(a) and (j), as amended by the Setting Every Community Up for Retirement Enhancement (SECURE) Act of 2019 (P.L. 116-94) and the Taxpayer First Act (P.L. 116-25); Rev. Proc. 2018-18).

The late-filing penalty runs for the period up to the date the IRS actually receives the late return (Rev. Rul. 73-133). The penalty is computed only on the net amount of tax due on the return after application of credits for payments of tax through withholding and estimated tax, as well as any other tax credits claimed on the return (Code Sec. 6651(b); Reg. § 301.6651-1(d)). The fraud and accuracy-related penalties (¶ 2854) do not apply in the case of a fraudulent failure to file a return. Instead, the failure-to-file penalty ranges from 15 percent to 75 percent of the unpaid tax shown on the return (Code Sec. 6651(f)).

If both the failure to file penalty and failure to pay taxes apply (¶ 2805), the failure to pay penalty offsets the failure to file penalty for any month or part of a month that both penalties apply (Code Sec. 6651(c)). However, the failure to file penalty may not be reduced below the minimum penalty for a failing to file an income tax return within 60 days of the due date (including extensions).

The failure-to-file penalty is not imposed if the taxpayer can show that the failure was due to reasonable cause and not willful neglect. Reasonable cause is if the taxpayer exercised ordinary business care and prudence and was nevertheless unable to file the return within the prescribed time (Reg. § 301.6651-1(c)). In assessing ordinary business care and prudence, the IRS will examine the taxpayer's reason for failure to comply, whether the taxpayer has a history of complying with the tax law, the length of time

¶2801

between the event and the cited reason for the failure to comply, and whether the circumstances were beyond the taxpayer's control.

Reliance on a tax return preparer generally is not reasonable cause for failure to file as the duty to file is on the taxpayer (IRM 20.1.1.3 (11-21-2017); *R.W. Boyle*, SCt, 85-1 USTC ¶ 13,602). Mistaken reliance on erroneous substantive advice from a tax professional may constitute reasonable cause, as long as the taxpayer gave the professional complete information and did not otherwise have reason to believe that a return might be required (*Paula Construction Co.*, Dec. 31,555, 58 TC 1055).

2805. Penalty for Failure to Pay Tax. A penalty or addition to tax is imposed for failure to pay taxes shown on a return within the time prescribed (including extensions), unless the failure is due to reasonable cause and not willful neglect (Code Sec. 6651(a)(2)). A penalty is also imposed for failure to pay a deficiency of tax required to be shown on the return within 21 calendar days of IRS demand and notice (10 business days if the amount assessed and demanded is $100,000 or more) (Code Sec. 6651(a)(3)). In the case of the failure to pay tax shown on the return, the penalty is imposed on the amount shown on the return less amounts that have been withheld, estimated tax payments, partial payments, and other applicable credits.

The due date for filing federal income tax returns and making federal income tax payments otherwise due on or after April 1, 2020, and before July 15, 2020, is automatically extended to July 15, 2020, in response to the COVID-19 (coronavirus) crisis (¶ 2505). Any penalty, addition to tax, or interest for failure to file or pay taxes during this period will not begin to accrue until July 16, 2020 (Notice 2020-23).

The penalty for failure to pay tax is 0.5 percent of the tax not paid, for each month or part of a month the tax remains unpaid, up to a maximum of 25 percent. The penalty increases to one percent per month beginning with either the 10th day after notice of levy is given or the day that notice and demand is made by the IRS in the case of a jeopardy assessment (¶ 2713). If a taxpayer enters into an installment agreement with the IRS (¶ 2529), the penalty for failure to timely pay taxes is reduced to 0.25 percent of the unpaid tax (Code Sec. 6651(h); Reg. § 301.6651-1(a)(4)). If both the failure to file penalty and failure to pay taxes shown on a return apply, the failure to file penalty may offset the failure to file penalty (¶ 2801).

The failure-to-pay penalty is not imposed if the taxpayer can show that the failure was due to reasonable cause and not willful neglect. Reasonable cause is if the taxpayer exercised ordinary business care and prudence and was nevertheless either unable to pay the tax within the prescribed time or would suffer an undue hardship (Reg. § 301.6651-1(c)). In assessing ordinary business care and prudence, the IRS will consider the nature of the tax that the taxpayer has failed to pay. It will also examine the taxpayer's reason for failure to comply, whether the taxpayer has a history of complying with the tax law, the length of time between the event and the cited reason for the failure to comply, and whether the circumstances were beyond the taxpayer's control. Reliance on a tax return preparer generally is not reasonable cause for failure to pay taxes as the duty is on the taxpayer (IRM 20.1.1.3 (11-21-2017); *R.W. Boyle*, SCt, 85-1 USTC ¶ 13,602).

An automatic extension of time to file a tax return (¶ 2509) is *not* an extension of time to pay the tax due on the return. However, an individual taxpayer can avoid a failure-to-pay penalty by making an estimate of the tax due and paying that estimate with the request for extension of time to file. The estimate may be reduced by any amounts already paid through withholding or estimated tax payments over the course of the tax year. If the balance of tax due is remitted when the income tax return is filed by an individual or corporation, no penalty for failure to pay will apply unless the unpaid amount is more than 10 percent of the total tax liability (Reg. § 301.6651-1(c)(3) and (4)).

2807. Tax Return Preparer Penalties. Several penalties may be imposed on a tax return preparer (¶ 2517) in addition to the prohibition against disclosure of return information (¶ 2894) and promoting abusive tax shelters (¶ 2597).

Understatement of Taxpayer's Liability. A penalty is imposed against a tax return preparer for each tax return or claim for refund that understates the taxpayer's liability due to an unreasonable position that the preparer knew, or reasonably should have known. The penalty is the greater of $1,000 or 50 percent of the income derived, or to be derived, by the preparer with respect to the return or refund claim (Code Sec. 6694(a); Reg. §§ 1.6694-1 and 1.6694-2; Rev. Proc. 2019-42).

The penalty is not imposed if the preparer shows that there was reasonable cause for the understatement and the preparer acted in good faith. Modified rules apply to nonsigning preparers. A position is treated as unreasonable unless:

- there is or was substantial authority for the position (¶ 2858);

- the position is adequately disclosed and has a reasonable basis; or

- the position pertains to a tax shelter (¶ 2870) or a reportable transaction (¶ 2591), and it is reasonable to believe that the position would more likely than not be sustained on its merits (Notice 2009-5).

The understatement penalty increases to the greater of $5,000 or 75 percent of the income derived, or to be derived, by the preparer with respect to the return or refund claim if the understatement is willful or reckless (Code Sec. 6694(b); Reg. § 1.6694-3; CCA 201519029). A preparer willfully attempts to understate liability if he or she disregards information furnished by the taxpayer in an attempt to wrongfully reduce the taxpayer's liability.

A preparer recklessly or intentionally disregards a rule or regulation if he or she takes a position on the return or claim for refund that is contrary to a rule or regulation the preparer knows of, or is reckless in not knowing of the rule or regulation in question. A preparer is not considered to have recklessly or intentionally disregarded a rule or regulation if the position contrary to the rule or regulation is adequately disclosed and has a reasonable basis.

Aiding or Abetting Understatement. A penalty of $1,000 may also be imposed on persons for aiding or abetting in an understatement of tax liability on a return, claim, or other document. The penalty increases to $10,000 for aiding or abetting an understatement of liability on a corporate return (Code Sec. 6701). Only one penalty may be imposed per taxpayer per period, but the tax period may not necessarily be a tax year. For instance, understatements on quarterly employment tax returns may give rise to four separate penalties for a calendar year. According to the Sixth and Eighth Circuit Court of Appeals, no statute of limitations applies to bar the penalty. This penalty generally may be imposed in addition to other penalties. It will not be imposed if either the tax return preparer penalty for understatements due to unreasonable positions or the penalty for promoting abusive tax shelters has been applied with respect to the same tax return or refund claim.

Administrative Penalties. A tax return preparer who fails to meet certain administrative requirements with respect to a taxpayer's return (¶ 2517) may be assessed the following penalties, unless the failure is due to reasonable cause and not to willful neglect:

- $50 for returns filed in 2019 or 2020 for each failure to sign a return, to furnish an identifying number, or to furnish the taxpayer with a copy of the prepared return, up to a maximum penalty per calendar year of $26,000 for returns filed in 2019 or $26,500 for returns filed in 2020;

- $50 for returns filed in 2019 or 2020 for each failure to retain and make available a copy of prepared returns or a list of taxpayers for whom returns were prepared, and the name of the individual preparer required to sign the return, up to a maximum penalty per return period of $26,000 for returns filed in 2019 or $26,500 for returns filed in 2020; and

- $50 for returns filed in 2019 or 2020 for each failure to retain and make available a record of preparers employed, or each failure to include an item required in such record, up to a maximum penalty per return period of $26,000 for returns filed in 2019 or $26,500 for returns filed in 2020.

A preparer who endorses or negotiates a taxpayer's refund check is also subject to a penalty of $520 for returns filed in 2019 or $530 for returns filed in 2020. The penalty will

28

PENALTIES

not apply to a bank preparer who negotiates customers' refund checks for bank account deposits (Code Sec. 6695; Reg. § 1.6695-1; Rev. Proc. 2018-18; Rev. Proc. 2018-57).

Lack of Due Diligence. A tax return preparer must comply with due diligence requirements for returns or refund claims asserting eligibility for the earned income credit (EIC), the child tax credit (CTC), the additional child tax credit (ACTC), American Opportunity tax credit (AOTC), as well as head of household filing status (Code Sec. 6695(g); Reg. § 1.6695-2). Among the requirements, a tax return preparer is required to file, or submit to the taxpayer for filing, Form 8867 with any federal return claiming any of the credits or head or household filing status. Each failure to meet the requirements regarding the amount of, or eligibility for, the credits or filing status will result in a penalty of $520 for returns filed in 2019 or $530 for returns filed in 2020 (Rev. Proc. 2018-18; Rev. Proc. 2018-57). The penalty is in addition to any other penalty imposed.

2811. Frivolous Return Penalty. A $5,000 penalty is imposed upon any person (including an individual, trust, estate, partnership, association, company, or corporation) who files a purported tax return (income or otherwise) if: (1) the return fails to contain sufficient information from which the substantial correctness of the amount of tax liability can be judged, or contains information that on its face indicates that the amount of tax shown is substantially incorrect; and (2) such conduct arises from a frivolous position or from a desire to delay or impede administration of the tax laws. The penalty is imposed in addition to any other penalties imposed on the taxpayer (Code Sec. 6702; Notice 2010-33).

A $5,000 civil penalty may also be imposed on any person who files a specified frivolous submission. A specified submission is a request for a collection due process hearing or an application for an installment agreement, offer in compromise, or taxpayer assistance order. The submission is frivolous if either it is based on a position that has been identified as frivolous by the IRS or reflects a desire to delay or impede the administration of federal tax laws. If a person withdraws a submission within 30 days after receiving notice that the return is a specified frivolous submission, the penalty will not be imposed.

The IRS has issued procedures outlining limited circumstances under which a frivolous return penalty, along with a frivolous submission penalty may be reduced to $500, regardless of the number of penalties assessed (Rev. Proc. 2012-43). A person must satisfy all eligibility criteria under the procedure, including filing all tax returns and paying all outstanding taxes, penalties (other than the frivolous return penalty), and related interest. Any employer applying for relief must deposit all employment taxes for the current quarter and the prior two quarters.

A list of frivolous positions may be found in Notice 2010-33. The list is not conclusive and is periodically revised. Returns or submissions that contain positions not described in the Notice, but that on their face have no basis for validity in existing law, or which have been deemed frivolous in a published opinion by the U.S. Tax Court or other court of competent jurisdiction may also be subject to the $5,000 penalty.

The Tax Court may assess a penalty (up to $25,000) against a taxpayer who institutes or maintains proceedings primarily for delay or on frivolous grounds, or who unreasonably fails to pursue available administrative remedies. Other courts may require a taxpayer to pay a penalty of up to $10,000 if the taxpayer's action against the IRS for unauthorized collection activities appears to be a frivolous or groundless proceeding (Code Sec. 6673).

2813. Abatement of Penalties and Interest. The IRS must abate certain penalties that result from reliance on incorrect IRS advice if: (1) the advice was furnished in writing in response to a specific written request from the taxpayer, and (2) the taxpayer reasonably relied upon the advice (Code Sec. 6404(f); Reg. § 301.6404-3). Penalties will be abated only if the taxpayer furnished adequate and accurate information in making the request. A taxpayer entitled to abatement should file Form 843 with copies of the relevant written documents attached.

The IRS also will abate the interest that would otherwise accrue if the due date for filing any income, estate, gift, employment, or excise tax return and paying any tax due for a taxpayer located in a federally declared disaster area is extended (Code Secs. 6404(i) and 7508A, as amended by the Tax Certainty and Disaster Tax Relief Act (P.L. 116-94)). The due date for filing federal income tax returns and making federal income tax payments otherwise due on or after April 1, 2020, and before July 15, 2020, is automatically extended to July 15, 2020, in response to the COVID-19 (coronavirus) crisis (¶ 2505). Any penalty, addition to tax, or interest for failure to file or pay taxes during this period will not begin to accrue until July 16, 2020 (Notice 2020-23).

The accrual of penalties and interest is also suspended after 36 months unless the IRS sends the taxpayer a notice of the penalty following the later of: (1) the original due date of the return (without regard to extensions), or (2) the date on which a timely return is filed (Code Sec. 6404(g)). The suspension of penalties and interest is available only for individuals and only for income taxes. The suspension does not apply to the failure-to-file (¶ 2801) and failure-to-pay (¶ 2805) penalties. It also does not stop the accrual of any interest, penalty, or other addition to tax in a case involving fraud, with respect to any liability shown on the return, any gross misstatement, any reportable transaction or listed transaction (¶ 2591), or any criminal penalty (¶ 2598).

Although the suspension pertains only to tax that is related to timely filed returns, the IRS has expanded this rule to cover additional tax voluntarily reported by a taxpayer, after a timely original return has been filed, on an amended return, or in correspondence with the IRS (Rev. Rul. 2005-4). The suspension begins on the day after the end of the 36-month period and ends on the day that is 21 days after the date on which the notice is made.

Document and Information Return Penalties

See CCH® AnswerConnect: *Information Returns: Penalties* for more information on this topic.

2816. Failure to File Correct Information Returns. A three-tier penalty structure is imposed for: (1) any failure to file correct information returns (¶ 2565) with the IRS on or before the required filing date (other than a failure due to reasonable cause and not to willful neglect); (2) any failure to include all the information required to be shown on a return; and (3) the inclusion of incorrect information (Code Sec. 6721). The penalty also applies to any failure to file electronically when required (¶ 2503) (Code Sec. 6724(c)).

The total amount of each penalty that may be imposed during a calendar year is subject to a maximum limit. The annual maximum is reduced for small businesses whose average annual gross receipts for the three most recent tax years before the calendar year are $5 million or less. The penalty amounts and maximum limits are adjusted annually for inflation and are as follows:

• If a person files a correct information return after the required filing date but on or before the date that is 30 days after the required filing date, the amount of the penalty is (first-tier penalty):

— for returns required to be filed in 2019, $50 per return, with a maximum penalty of $545,500 (for small businesses the maximum penalty is $191,000), and

— for returns required to be filed in 2020, $50 per return, with a maximum penalty of $556,500 (for small businesses the maximum penalty is $194,500) (Code Sec. 6721(b)(1) and (d)(1)(B); Rev. Proc. 2018-18; Rev. Proc. 2018-57).

• If a person files a correct information return after the date that is 30 days after the prescribed filing date but on or before August 1 of the calendar year in which the required filing date occurs, the amount of the penalty is (second-tier penalty):

— for returns required to be filed in 2019, $100 per return, with a maximum penalty of $1,637,500 (for small businesses the maximum penalty is $545,500), and;

— for returns required to be filed in 2020, $110 per return, with a maximum penalty of $1,669,500 (for small businesses the maximum penalty is $556,500) (Code Sec. 6721(b)(2) and (d)(1)(C); Rev. Proc. 2018-18; Rev. Proc. 2018-57).

• If a correct information return is not filed on or before August 1 of the calendar year in which the required filing date occurs, the amount of the penalty is (third-tier penalty):

— for returns required to be filed in 2019, $270 per return, with a maximum penalty of $3,275,500 (for small businesses the maximum penalty is $1,091,500), and

— for returns required to be filed in 2020, $270 per return, with a maximum penalty of $3,339,000 (for small businesses the maximum penalty is $1,113,000) (Code Sec. 6721(a)(1) and (d)(1)(A); Rev. Proc. 2018-18; Rev. Proc. 2018-57).

The IRS will not impose the penalty for failure to file a correct information return by:

• a mortgage servicer that reports on Form 1098 payments received under a financially distressed homeowner program designed by a state housing finance agency during calendar years 2011 through 2021 (Notice 2017-40);

• a state housing finance agency that fails to file Form 1098 regarding payments under a financially distressed homeowner program for calendar years 2011 through 2021 (Notice 2017-40);

• a partnership or other entity that fails to file Form 1065 by the due date for the partnership's first tax year that began after 2015 and before 2017 (Notice 2017-47; Notice 2017-71);

• an eligible educational institution that fails to provide the taxpayer identification number (TIN) on the information return if it certifies that they requested and were unable to obtain the required information (Code Sec. 6724(f)); and

• an eligible educational institution that reports the aggregate amount billed, instead of the aggregate amount of payments received, for qualified tuition and related expenses on Form 1098-T for the 2016 or 2017 calendar year (Announcement 2016-17; Announcement 2016-42).

De Minimis Errors. No penalty is imposed for inconsequential errors or omissions that do not prevent or hinder the IRS from adequately processing the return. Errors and omissions that relate to a taxpayer identification number (TIN) or to the surname of a person required to receive a copy of the information provided are never considered inconsequential (Code Sec. 6721(c); Reg. § 301.6721-1(c)). A certain *de minimis* number of returns timely filed with incorrect or omitted information that are corrected on or before August 1 of the calendar year in which the returns are due will be treated as having been filed correctly, and no penalty will be imposed. This exception is limited to the greater of 10 returns or 0.5 percent of the total number of information returns required to be filed during the calendar year.

A safe harbor is also provided for an incorrect dollar amount that is a *de minimis* error (Code Secs. 6721(c)(3) and 6722(c)(3); Notice 2017-9). An information return that is otherwise correct will be treated as filed or furnished with all correct required information if no single erroneous dollar amount differs from the correct amount by more than $100, and no single amount reported for tax withheld differs from the correct amount by more than $25. The safe harbor does not apply to an information return if the person to whom a related payee statement must be furnished elects to not have the safe harbor apply to the payee statement. A broker must determine the adjusted basis in a covered security by treating as correct any incorrect dollar amount that does not need to be corrected due to the *de minimis* safe harbor (Code Sec. 6045(g)(2)(B)(iii)).

¶2816

Intentional Disregard. If the failure to file an information return or to include all the required correct information is due to intentional disregard of the filing requirements, neither the three-tier penalty nor the *de minimis* exception will apply (Code Sec. 6721(e); Rev. Proc. 2018-18; Rev. Proc. 2018-57). Instead, the penalty for each failure is the greater of $540 per return for returns required to be filed in 2019 ($550 per return for returns required to be filed in 2020), or:

- 10 percent of the aggregate amount of the items required to be reported correctly in the case of a return *other than* a return required under Code Sec. 6045 (brokers' transactions with customers), Code Sec. 6041A (payments of remuneration for direct sales), Code Sec. 6050H (information on mortgage interest received in a trade or business from individuals), Code Sec. 6050I (information on cash receipts from a trade or business), Code Sec. 6050J (information on foreclosures and abandonments of security), Code Sec. 6050K (information on exchanges of certain partnership interests), or Code Sec. 6050L (information on certain dispositions of donated property);

- five percent of the aggregate amount of the items required to be properly reported under Code Secs. 6045, 6050K, or 6050L;

- for informational returns required under Code Sec. 6050I(a) (cash receipts of more than $10,000 in a trade or business) for returns required to be filed in 2019, the greater of $27,290 or the amount of cash received in the transaction or related transactions, up to a maximum of $109,000 ($27,820 and $111,000, respectively for returns required to be filed in 2020); or

- in the case of a return filed under Code Sec. 6050V, 10 percent of the value of the benefit of any contract with respect to which information is required to be include on the return.

The intentional disregard penalties are not considered in figuring the yearly maximum penalty for the third-tier penalty for failures not attributable to intentional disregard.

2823. Failure to Furnish Correct Payee Statement. A three-tier penalty structure is imposed for (1) any failure to furnish a payee statement to the appropriate person on or before the required date, or (2) any failure to include all of the information required to be shown on a payee statement or the inclusion of incorrect information (Code Sec. 6722). The total amount of each penalty that may be imposed during a calendar year is subject to a maximum limit. The annual maximum is reduced for small businesses whose average annual gross receipts for the three most recent tax years before the calendar year are $5 million or less. The penalty amounts and maximum limits are adjusted annually for inflation and are as follows:

- If a person furnishes a correct payee statement up to 30 days after the date prescribed for furnishing such statement, the amount of the penalty is (first-tier penalty):

  — for statements required to be furnished in 2019, $50 per statement, with a maximum penalty of $545,500 (for small businesses the maximum penalty is $191,000), and

  — for statements required to be furnished in 2020, $50 per statement, with a maximum penalty of $556,500 (for small businesses the maximum penalty is $194,500) (Code Sec. 6722(b)(1) and (d)(1)(B); Rev. Proc. 2018-18; Rev. Proc. 2018-57).

- If a person furnishes a correct payee statement more than 30 days after the prescribed filing date but on or before August 1 of the calendar year in which the date prescribed for furnishing such statement occurs, the amount of the penalty is (second-tier penalty):

  — for statements required to be furnished in 2019, $100 per statement, with a maximum penalty of $1,637,500 (for small businesses, the maximum penalty is $545,500), and

— for statements required to be furnished in 2020, $110 per statement, with a maximum penalty of $1,669,500 (for small businesses, the maximum penalty is $556,500) (Code Sec. 6722(b)(2) and (d)(1)(C); Rev. Proc. 2018-18; Rev. Proc. 2018-57).

• If a correct payee statement is not furnished on or before August 1 of the calendar year in which the date prescribed for furnishing such statement occurs, the amount of the penalty is (third-tier penalty):

— for statements required to be furnished in 2019, $270 per statement, with a maximum penalty of $3,275,500 (for small businesses the maximum penalty is $1,091,500), and

— for statements required to be furnished in 2020, $270 per statement, with a maximum penalty of $3,339,000 (for small businesses the maximum penalty is $1,113,000) (Code Sec. 6722(a)(1) and (d)(1)(A); Rev. Proc. 2018-18; Rev. Proc. 2018-57).

The IRS will not impose the penalty for failure to furnish payee statements by:

• a mortgage servicer that reports on Form 1098 payments received under a financially distressed homeowner program designed by a state housing finance agency during calendar years 2011 through 2021 (Notice 2017-40);

• a state housing finance agency that fails to furnish Form 1098 regarding payments under a financially distressed homeowner program for calendar years 2011 through 2021 (Notice 2017-40);

• a partnership that fails to timely furnish to a partner a Schedule K-1 (Form 1065) that includes the partner's negative tax basis capital account information (Notice 2019-20);

• a partnership or other entity required to file Form 1065 that failed to timely furnish Schedule K-1s for by the due date for the partnership's first tax year that began after 2015 and before 2017 (Notice 2017-47; Notice 2017-71);

• an eligible educational institution that fails to provide the taxpayer identification number (TIN) on the payee statement if it certifies that they requested and were unable to obtain the required information (Code Sec. 6724(f)); and

• an eligible educational institution that reports the aggregate amount billed, instead of the aggregate amount of payments received, for qualified tuition and related expenses on Form 1098-T for the 2016 or 2017 calendar year (Announcement 2016-17; Announcement 2016-42).

De Minimis Errors. No penalty is imposed for inconsequential errors or omissions that can reasonably be expected to prevent or hinder the payee from timely receiving correct information and reporting it on his or her return. Errors and omissions that are never considered inconsequential include significant items in the address of the payee, the appropriate form provided, and the manner of furnishing certain payee statements (Code Sec. 6722(c); Reg. § 301.6722-1(b)). A certain *de minimis* number of failures that are corrected on or before August 1 of the calendar year that the payee statements are required to be provided will be treated as filed correctly. The de minimis exception is limited to the greater of 10 payee statements or 0.5 percent of the total number of payee statements required to be furnished during the calendar year.

A safe harbor is also provided for an incorrect dollar amount that is a *de minimis* error (Code Sec. 6722(c)(3); Notice 2017-9). A payee statement that is otherwise correct will be treated as furnished with all correct required information if no single erroneous dollar amount differs from the correct amount by more than $100, and no single amount reported for tax withheld differs from the correct amount by more than $25. The person to whom a payee statement must be furnished may elect that the safe harbor does not apply to the payee statement.

Intentional Disregard. If the failure to furnish a payee statement or to include all the required correct information is due to intentional disregard, neither the three-tier penalty nor the de minimis exception will apply (Code Sec. 6722(e)). Instead, the penalty is identical to that for failure to file information returns due to intentional disregard (¶ 2816).

2828. Employment Tax Penalty for Employers. An employer is primarily liable for deducting and paying employment taxes whether or not the taxes are actually collected from the employee (¶ 2601). The employer may be subject to civil and criminal penalties for failing to deduct and withhold employment taxes.

Trust Fund Recovery Penalty. Any responsible person who willfully fails to withhold, account for, or pay over employment taxes to the IRS is subject to a penalty equal to 100 percent of such tax, as well as a criminal fine of up to $10,000 and up to five years imprisonment (Code Secs. 6672 and 7202). A responsible person is any individual who had sufficient authority to pay over the taxes—generally officers and employees responsible for paying the taxes. The civil penalty is a collection device, usually assessed only if the tax cannot be collected from the employer, and results in a personal liability not dischargeable by bankruptcy.

The 100-percent penalty only applies to the failure to collect, account for, and pay over third-party taxes (i.e., employee's share). It does not apply to taxes that are directly paid, such as the employer's share of employment taxes, or to delinquency penalties or interest owed on the delinquent trust fund taxes. Civil and criminal penalties can also be imposed if an employer willfully fails to furnish, or furnishes a false or fraudulent, Form W-2 statement (¶ 2655) to an employee (Code Secs. 6674 and 7204).

Failure to Make Timely Deposits. A graduated penalty applies to failures to make timely tax deposits of employment taxes (¶ 2651) unless the failure is due to reasonable cause and not willful neglect (Code Sec. 6656). Also, the IRS has provided penalty relief for failure to deposit employment taxes to employers entitled to the employee retention, paid sick leave, and paid family tax credits provided in response to the COVID-19 (coronavirus) crisis (¶ 2648). The relief is provided the extent that the amounts not deposited are equal to or less than the amount of refundable tax credits to which the employer is entitled (Notice 2020-22).

If the penalty applies, it varies based on how long it takes the taxpayer to correct the failure. The penalty is assessed as follows:

- two percent of the underpayment amount if the failure is for not more than five days;

- five percent of the underpayment amount if the failure is for more than five days but not more than 15 days; and

- 10 percent of the underpayment amount if the failure is for more than 15 days.

The penalty imposed is 15 percent of the underpayment amount if a required deposit is not made on or before the earlier of (1) the day that is 10 days after the date of the first delinquency notice to the taxpayer, or (2) the day on which notice and demand for immediate payment of tax is given in cases of jeopardy. A failure to deposit includes a failure to make deposits electronically when required to do so.

Deposits are generally applied to the most recent tax liability within the quarter. Any depositor to whom the IRS mails a penalty notice may, within 90 days of the date of the notice, designate how the payment is to be applied to minimize the penalty amount. The due date for performing certain time-sensitive actions, including designating deposits within 90 days, otherwise due on or after April 1, 2020, and before July 15, 2020, is automatically extended to July 15, 2020, in response to the COVID-19 (coronavirus) crisis (Notice 2020-23; Rev. Proc. 2018-58).

2833. Failure to Comply with Other Information Reporting Requirements. A penalty of $50 is imposed for each failure to comply with any specified information reporting requirement on or before the prescribed time, up to a maximum of $100,000 for a calendar year (Code Sec. 6723). The penalty will *not* be imposed if it can be shown that the failure was due to reasonable cause and not to willful neglect. Specified information reporting requirements include the requirement that:

• a transferor of an interest in a partnership promptly give notice to the partnership concerning the transfer;

• a person include his or her taxpayer identification number (TIN) on any return, statement, or other document (other than an information return or payee statement), furnish his or her TIN to another person, or include the TIN of another person on any return, statement, or other document made with respect to that person;

• returns reporting alimony payments for divorce or separation instruments (¶ 771) generally executed before January 1, 2019, the payee's TIN be furnished to the payor or included on the payor's return;

• a person include the TIN of any dependent on his or her return; and

• a person who deducts home mortgage interest (¶ 1047) on any seller-provided financing include the name, address, and TIN of the person to whom such interest is paid or accrued (Code Sec. 6724(d)(3)).

Interest on Underpayments

See CCH® AnswerConnect: *Interest on Underpayments* for more information on this topic.

2838. Interest on Underpayment of Tax. If any amount of tax imposed under the Internal Revenue Code is not paid on or before the last date prescribed for payment, the taxpayer must pay interest on the unpaid amount at the underpayment rate (Code Sec. 6601; Reg. § 301.6601-1). Exceptions exist for underpayments of estimated taxes by individuals or corporations, and any failure to pay federal unemployment taxes (FUTA) for a calendar quarter. Underpayment interest also does not accrue on late payments of FICA taxes or withheld income taxes if adjustments are made by the employer.

The due date for filing federal income tax returns and making federal tax income payments otherwise due on or after April 1, 2020, and before July 15, 2020, is automatically extended to July 15, 2020, in response to the COVID-19 (coronavirus) crisis (¶ 2505). Any penalty, addition to tax, or interest for failure to file or pay taxes during this period will not begin to accrue until July 16, 2020 (Notice 2020-23).

Underpayment interest accrues from the date the payment was due, determined without regard to any extensions of time. If a carryback of a net operating loss, net capital loss, or other credit carryback eliminates or reduces a deficiency otherwise due for such earlier year, the taxpayer remains liable for interest on unpaid income taxes, including deficiencies later assessed by the IRS, for the carryback year. The entire amount of the deficiency is subject to interest from the last date prescribed for payment of the income tax of the carryback year up to the due date, excluding extensions, for filing the return for the tax year in which the loss or credit occurred.

Underpayment interest is generally assessed, collected, and paid in the same fashion as the underlying tax. The principal amount due includes any tax unpaid, as well as most penalties, additions, to tax, and additional amounts unless paid within 21 calendar days of IRS notice and demand (10 business days if the amount in the notice and demand equals or exceeds $100,000). Interest on penalties for failure to file a return (¶ 2801), accuracy-related (¶ 2854), and fraud (¶ 2866) is imposed for the period beginning on the due date of the return with respect to the penalty is imposed, including extensions. If any part of an underpayment is satisfied by credit of an overpayment (for another year, or of a tax other than income tax), interest does not accrue on the portion of the underpayment so satisfied for any period for which interest would have been allowed on the overpayment if it had been refunded instead of credited. This rule does not apply if a net interest of zero applies (¶ 2765).

Underpayment Interest Rate. Interest on underpayment of tax for most taxpayers is imposed at the federal short-term rate, plus three percentage points. Interest on large underpayments by a C corporation is imposed at the federal short-term rate, plus five percentage points. A large corporate underpayment is any tax underpayment by a C corporation that exceeds $100,000 for any tax period. The interest rates, which are adjusted quarterly, are determined during the first month of a calendar quarter and become effective for the following quarter. Underpayment interest is compounded daily (Code Secs. 6621 and 6662). Special rules apply with respect to estate tax attributable to a closely held business when an estate elects to extend the time for the payment of the tax (¶ 2939).

Abatement of Interest. The IRS may abate interest in cases where the additional interest was caused by IRS errors or delays (Code Sec. 6404(e)). The IRS may act only if there was an error or delay in performing either a ministerial act or a managerial act, including loss of records by the IRS, transfers of IRS personnel, extended illness, extended personnel training, or extended leave, and only if the abatement relates to a tax of the type for which a notice of deficiency is required. These taxes would be those relating to income, generation-skipping transfers, estate, gift, and certain excise taxes, but not employment taxes or other excise taxes.

A taxpayer requesting an abatement of interest generally must file a separate Form 843 for each tax period for each type of tax with the IRS Service Center where their tax return was filed or, if unknown, with the Service Center where their most recent tax return was filed. A taxpayer may file a petition to review a claim for interest abatement with the Tax Court in cases in which the IRS has failed to issue a final determination within the 180-day period following the filing of claim (Code Sec. 6404(h)). The due date for performing certain time-sensitive actions, including filing a petition with the Tax Court to review an interest abatement, otherwise due on or after April 1, 2020, and before July 15, 2020, is automatically extended to July 15, 2020, in response to the COVID-19 (coronavirus) crisis (Notice 2020-23).

The Tax Court also has jurisdiction over interest abatement actions in cases to be conducted using small tax case procedures where the total amount of interest abatement sought does not exceed $50,000 (Code Sec. 7463(f)).

Suspension of Interest. In order to avoid the accrual of underpayment interest, a taxpayer may make a cash deposit with the IRS for future application against an underpayment of income, gift, estate, generation-skipping, or certain excise taxes that have not been assessed at the time of the deposit (Code Sec. 6603; Rev. Proc. 2005-18). To the extent that a deposit is used by the IRS to pay a tax liability, the tax is treated as paid when the deposit is made, and no underpayment interest is imposed. Furthermore, if the dispute is resolved in favor of the taxpayer or the taxpayer withdraws the deposited money before resolution of the dispute, interest is payable on the deposit at the federal short-term rate. See ¶ 2723 and ¶ 2724, respectively, for rules governing the allocation of interest on tax liabilities paid pursuant to a compromise or partial payment.

Penalties on Underpayments

See CCH® AnswerConnect: *Accuracy-Related Penalties* for more information on this topic.

2854. Accuracy-Related Penalties. An accuracy-related penalty of 20 percent is imposed on the portion of any underpayment of tax that is due to:

- negligence or disregard of rules or regulations (¶ 2856),
- substantial understatement of income tax (¶ 2858),
- substantial valuation misstatement (¶ 2860),
- substantial overstatement of pension liabilities (¶ 2862),
- substantial estate or gift tax valuation understatement (¶ 2862A),
- transactions lacking economic substance (¶ 2863), and
- inconsistent estate basis reporting, and (¶ 2863A) (Code Sec. 6662).

A 40-percent accuracy-related penalty is also imposed for an underpayment of tax due to an undisclosed foreign financial asset understatement (¶ 2864). If any part of an underpayment of tax required to be shown on a return is due to fraud, a separate penalty equal to 75 percent of that portion of the underpayment is imposed (¶ 2866).

28

PENALTIES

The accuracy-related penalty is entirely separate from the failure-to-file penalty (¶ 2801) and will not be imposed if no return is filed, other than a return prepared by the IRS when a person fails to make a required return (Code Sec. 6664(b)). In addition, the accuracy-related penalty will not apply to any portion of a tax underpayment on which the fraud penalty is imposed. Also, with the exception of the penalty for underpayments attributable to transactions lacking economic substance, no penalty is imposed with respect to any portion of any underpayment if the taxpayer shows that there was reasonable cause for the underpayment and that the taxpayer acted in good faith (Code Sec. 6664(c)).

2856. Penalty for Negligence or Disregard of Rules and Regulations. A 20-percent accuracy-related penalty (¶ 2854) is imposed on any portion of the underpayment of tax attributable to the negligence or intentional disregard of rules and regulations (Code Sec. 6662(c); Reg. § 1.6662-3). Negligence includes the failure to reasonably comply with tax laws, to exercise reasonable care in preparing a tax return, to keep adequate books and records, or to substantiate items properly. Negligence occurs if the taxpayer is careless, reckless, or acts with intentional disregard of rules or regulations. A taxpayer may not avoid the negligence penalty by adequately disclosing a return position that is "not frivolous" on Form 8275 or Form 8275-R.

2858. Penalty for Substantial Understatement of Income Tax. A 20-percent accuracy-related penalty (¶ 2854) is imposed on a taxpayer for any substantial understatement of income tax for the tax year (Code Sec. 6662(d); Reg. § 1.6662-4). A substantial understatement exists if the understatement exceeds the greater of $5,000 or 10 percent of the tax required to be shown on the return (five percent of the tax required to be shown if the taxpayer claims the qualified business income (QBI) deduction (¶ 980P)). In the case of a corporation (other than an S corporation or personal holding company), a substantial understatement exists when the understatement exceeds the lesser of 10 percent of the tax required to be shown on the return (or, if greater, $10,000) or $10 million.

A taxpayer generally may avoid all or part of the penalty by showing:

- that the taxpayer acted in good faith and there was reasonable cause for the understatement;

- that the understatement was based on substantial authority; or

- if there was a reasonable basis for the tax treatment of an item, the relevant facts affecting the item's tax treatment were adequately disclosed on Form 8275 or Form 8275-R.

Substantial authority is an objective standard that the taxpayer's position is correct based on an analysis of the law and relevant facts. It is less stringent than the "more likely than not" standard (greater than 50-likelihood of the position being upheld), but more stringent than the reasonable basis standard for the negligence penalty (¶ 2856).

The disclosure exception does not apply to a tax shelter item, if the taxpayer's return is not properly substantiated, or the taxpayer failed to keep adequate books and records. Further, a corporation does not have a reasonable basis for its tax treatment of an item attributable to a multiple-party financing transaction if the treatment does not clearly reflect the income of the corporation. Some items may be disclosed on the taxpayer's return, instead of on Form 8275 or Form 8275-R (Rev. Proc. 2019-42).

Only the following are authority for purposes of determining whether a position is supported by substantial authority:

- the Internal Revenue Code and other statutory provisions;

- proposed, temporary, and final regulations construing the statutes;

- revenue rulings and procedures;

- tax treaties and the regulations thereunder, and Treasury Department and other official explanations of such treaties;

- court cases;

¶2856

- Congressional intent as reflected in committee reports, joint explanatory statements of managers included in conference committee reports, and floor statements made prior to enactment by one of a bill's managers;

- General Explanations of tax legislation prepared by the Joint Committee on Taxation (the Blue Book);

- private letter rulings and technical advice memoranda issued after October 31, 1976;

- actions on decisions and general counsel memoranda issued after March 12, 1981, as well as general counsel memoranda published in pre-1955 volumes of the Cumulative Bulletin;

- IRS information and press releases; and

- notices, announcements, and other administrative pronouncements published by the IRS in the Internal Revenue Bulletin.

2860. Penalty for Substantial Valuation Misstatement. A 20-percent accuracy-related penalty (¶ 2854) is imposed on any portion of an underpayment of tax resulting from any substantial income tax valuation misstatement (Code Sec. 6662(e); Reg. § 1.6662-5; Temp. Reg. § 1.6662-5T). There is a substantial valuation misstatement if:

- the value or adjusted basis of any property claimed on a tax return is 150 percent or more of the amount determined to be the correct amount of the valuation or adjusted basis;

- the price for any property, use of property, or services in connection with any transaction between persons described in Code Sec. 482 is 200 percent or more (or 50 percent or less) of the correct Code Sec. 482 valuation; or

- the net Code Sec. 482 transfer price adjustment exceeds the lesser of $5 million or 10 percent of the taxpayer's gross receipts.

The penalty is doubled to 40 percent in cases of gross valuation misstatements if:

- the value or adjusted basis of any property claimed on a tax return is 200 percent or more of the amount determined to be the correct amount of the valuation or adjusted basis;

- the price for any property, use of property, or services in connection with any transaction between persons described in Code Sec. 482 is 400 percent or more (or 25 percent or less) of the correct Code Sec. 482 valuation; or

- the net Code Sec. 482 transfer price adjustment exceeds the lesser of $20 million or 20 percent of the taxpayer's gross receipts.

No penalty is imposed unless the portion of the underpayment attributable to the substantial valuation misstatement exceeds $5,000 ($10,000 in the case of corporations other than S corporations or personal holding companies). This limitation is applied separately for each tax year. The penalty will not be imposed if it is shown that there was reasonable cause for an underpayment and the taxpayer acted in good faith. However, there generally is no reasonable cause exception for underpayments due to gross valuation misstatements on charitable deduction property. The exception still exists for substantial valuation misstatements on charitable deduction property and for gross valuation misstatements on property for which a charitable deduction is not being claimed (Code Sec. 6664(c)).

2862. Penalty for Substantial Overstatement of Pension Liabilities. A 20-percent accuracy-related penalty (¶ 2854) is imposed on any portion of any underpayment of tax resulting from a substantial overstatement of pension liabilities (Code Sec. 6662(f) and (h)). A substantial overstatement occurs if the actuarial determination of pension liabilities is 200 percent or more of the amount determined to be correct. The penalty is doubled to 40 percent of the underpayment if a portion of the substantial overstatement to which the penalty applies is attributable to a gross valuation misstatement of 400 percent or more. The penalty applies only if the portion of the underpayment attributable to the overstatement exceeds $1,000. The penalty will not be imposed if it is shown that there was a reasonable cause for an underpayment and the taxpayer acted in good faith (Code Sec. 6664(c)).

2862A. Penalty for Substantial Estate or Gift Tax Valuation Understatements. A 20-percent accuracy-related penalty (¶ 2854) is imposed on the portion of an underpayment of tax that is due to a substantial estate or gift tax valuation understatement (Code Sec. 6662(g) and (h)). There is a substantial estate or gift tax valuation understatement if the value of any property claimed on any estate or gift tax return is 65 percent or less of the amount determined to be the correct amount of the valuation. The penalty will not be imposed unless the portion of the underpayment attributable to the valuation understatements for the taxable period or for the estate of the decedent exceeds $5,000. The penalty is increased to 40 percent if the valuation understatement is a gross valuation misstatement. A valuation understatement is a gross valuation understatement if the value of any property claimed on any estate or gift tax return is 40 percent or less of the amount determined to be the correct amount of the valuation. The penalty will not be imposed if it is shown that there was a reasonable cause for an underpayment and the taxpayer acted in good faith (Code Sec. 6664(c)).

2863. Penalty for Underpayment Attributable to Transactions Lacking Economic Substance. A 20-percent accuracy-related penalty (¶ 2854) is imposed for an underpayment of tax attributable to any disallowance of claimed tax benefits by reason of a transaction lacking economic substance, or failing to meet the requirements of any similar rule of law (Code Sec. 6662(b)(6)). A transaction is treated as having economic substance if: (1) apart from the federal income tax effects, it changes in a meaningful way the taxpayer's economic position; and (2) the taxpayer has a substantial purpose for entering into the transaction (Code Sec. 7701(o); Notice 2014-58, amplifying Notice 2010-62).

A "transaction," including related transactions, generally includes all the factual elements relevant to the expected tax treatment of any investment, entity, plan, or arrangement, and any and all steps that are carried out as part of the plan. Whether a plan's steps should be aggregated or separated is a facts and circumstances analysis. The phase "similar rule of law" means a rule or doctrine that disallows the tax benefits in the Code related to a transaction because the taxpayer's economic position does not change in a meaningful way apart from the Federal income tax effects, or the taxpayer does not have a substantial purpose, apart from the Federal income tax effects, for entering into the transaction.

Although the IRS will continue to rely on relevant case law handed down prior to the codification of the economic substance doctrine for transactions entered into after March 30, 2010, when applying the two-prong test, taxpayers may not rely on case law that treats a transaction as having economic substance unless the transaction satisfies *both* prongs of the test.

The penalty is increased to 40 percent for an underpayment attributable to an undisclosed noneconomic substance transaction (Code Sec. 6662(i)). An undisclosed noneconomic substance transaction is any portion of a transaction lacking economic substance with respect to which the relevant facts affecting the tax treatment are not adequately disclosed in the return or in a statement attached to the return. The determination of whether a position is an undisclosed noneconomic substance transaction is generally be based on the return as originally filed or as amended by the taxpayer prior to being contacted by the IRS. To satisfy the adequate disclosure requirements, the taxpayer must: (1) disclose the relevant facts on a timely filed original return or a qualified amended return; (2) file Form 8275 or Form 8275-R; and (3) if the transaction is a reportable transaction (¶ 2591), satisfy all disclosure requirements for such transactions (¶ 2592).

No exceptions, including the reasonable cause exception, are available to the imposition of a penalty for any underpayment or reportable transaction understatement attributable to a transaction lacking economic substance (Code Sec. 6664(c)(2) and (d)(2)).

¶2862A

2863A Penalty for Inconsistent Estate Basis Reporting. A 20-percent accuracy-related penalty (¶ 2854) is imposed for inconsistent estate basis reporting, applicable to property with respect to which an estate tax return is filed after July 31, 2015 (Code Sec. 6662(b)(8) and (k)). Inconsistent estate basis reporting is defined as any portion of an underpayment attributable to the failure to comply with Code Sec. 1014(f) (¶ 1633).

2864. Penalty for Underpayment Attributable to Undisclosed Foreign Financial Assets. A 40-percent accuracy-related penalty (¶ 2854) is imposed for underpayment of tax that is attributable to an undisclosed foreign financial asset understatement (Code Sec. 6662(j)). An undisclosed foreign financial asset understatement for any tax year is the portion of the understatement for the year that is attributable to any transaction involving undisclosed foreign financial assets. An undisclosed foreign financial asset includes any asset for which information was not reported as required with respect to:

- persons who control foreign corporations and partnerships, under Code Sec. 6038 (¶ 2487);

- transfers to foreign corporations or foreign partnerships, and certain corporate distributions to non-U.S. persons, under Code Sec. 6038B (¶ 2492);

- individuals who own more than $50,000 of foreign financial assets, under Code Sec. 6038D (¶ 2572);

- persons who acquire or dispose of an interest in a foreign partnership, under Code Sec. 6046A (¶ 2494); and

- transactions involving foreign trusts, under Code Sec. 6048 (¶ 588).

2866. Penalty for Fraud. A 75-percent penalty is imposed on the portion of any underpayment of tax that is attributable to fraud (Code Sec. 6663; *R.W. Bradford*, CA-9, 86-2 USTC ¶ 960). The IRS has the burden of proving fraud by clear and convincing evidence that the taxpayer engaged in intentional wrongdoing with the specific intent to avoid a tax that he or she knew to be owing. If the IRS establishes that any portion of the underpayment is attributable to fraud, then the entire underpayment is treated as attributable to fraud unless the taxpayer can establish otherwise by preponderance of the evidence.

The fraud penalty applies only to a filed return or a return prepared by the IRS when a person fails to make a required return (Code Sec. 6664(b)). If married taxpayers file a joint return, the penalty does not apply to a spouse unless some part of the underpayment is due to the fraud of that spouse. Although the failure-to-file penalty is entirely separate from the fraud penalty, in cases of a fraudulent failure to file, the failure-to-file penalty will be imposed at a higher rate (¶ 2801). The accuracy-related penalty will not apply to any portion of an underpayment on which the fraud penalty is imposed (¶ 2854).

2870. Penalty for Tax Shelters. An accuracy-related penalty is imposed for under-statement of tax attributable to any listed transaction and any reportable transaction with a significant tax avoidance purpose (¶ 2591) (Code Sec. 6662A). The penalty is generally 20 percent of the understatement if the taxpayer adequately disclosed the transaction, and 30 percent if the transaction was not adequately disclosed. The 20-percent accuracy-related penalty on understatements attributable to reportable transactions will not be imposed if the 40-percent penalty is imposed on an underpayment attributable to one or more undisclosed noneconomic substance transactions (¶ 2863).

Erroneous Refund Claims

See CCH® AnswerConnect: *Penalty for Erroneous Refund Claims* for more information on this topic.

2891. Erroneous Refund or Credit Claims. An income tax refund or credit claims made for an excessive amount is subject to a penalty equal to 20 percent of the excessive amount (Code Sec. 6676). An excessive amount is the amount by which the refund or credit claim exceeds the amount allowable under the Code for the tax year. The penalty is not imposed it can be shown that the claim for the excessive amount has a reasonable basis. In addition, the penalty does not apply to any portion of the excessive amount of a refund claim or credit that is subject to an accuracy-related penalty (¶ 2854 and ¶ 2870) or the fraud penalty (¶ 2866).

Unauthorized Return Disclosures or Inspections

2892. Disclosure of Return Information by Government Employees. Returns and tax return information are confidential and may not be disclosed to federal or state agencies or employees except as provided in Code Sec. 6103. A return is defined as any tax return, information return, declaration of estimated tax, or claim for refund filed under the Internal Revenue Code. Return information includes the taxpayer's identity, the nature, source or amount of income, payments, receipts, deductions, net worth, tax liability, deficiencies, closing (and similar) agreements, and information regarding the actual or possible investigation of a return.

All officers and employees of the United States, of any state, and of any local child support enforcement agency are prohibited from disclosing tax returns and return information. The prohibition also applies to most other persons who have had access to returns or return information by virtue of permitted disclosures of such returns or information under Code Sec. 6103. A taxpayer may bring a civil action in federal court against a person who knowingly or negligently makes an unauthorized disclosure or inspection of any return or return information of the taxpayer (¶ 2893).

The IRS may disclose returns and return information to a person (or persons) designated by the taxpayer in a request for or consent to disclosure. It may also disclose to any other person at the taxpayer's request to the extent necessary to comply with a request for information or assistance made by the taxpayer to the other person. Disclosure may also be made to the duly authorized attorney in fact of the person with a material interest making the disclosure request. Disclosure is permitted subject to the requirements and conditions prescribed by IRS regulations.

Agreements and information received under a tax convention with a foreign government, including a U.S. possession, are also confidential and generally cannot be disclosed (Code Sec. 6105).

2893. Remedies for Unauthorized Disclosures or Inspections of Return Information. A taxpayer may bring a civil action against the United States if a government employee knowingly or negligently discloses or inspects any return or return information with respect to the taxpayer under Code Sec. 6103 (¶ 2892) without authorization. A taxpayer may also bring a civil action against any person who is *not* a United States employee who knowingly or negligently discloses or inspects any return or return information with respect to the taxpayer under Code Sec. 6103 or a tax-exempt organization under Code Sec. 6104 (¶ 625) (Code Sec. 7431).

Upon a finding of liability, the taxpayer may recover the greater of $1,000 for each unauthorized disclosure or the amount of the actual damages sustained as a result of the disclosure. Punitive damages, as well as litigation costs, may be recovered if the disclosure was willful or grossly negligent. Criminal penalties can also be brought against individuals who have made unauthorized and willful disclosures of any return or return information including present and former federal employees, and any other person who obtains returns and return information in the course of processing, storing, and reproducing returns and return information (Code Sec. 7213).

Criminal penalties for unauthorized inspections also may be imposed against any federal employee, as well as any state employee or other person who acquires the return or return information under Code Sec. 6103 or Code Sec. 6104. These provisions permit the use of federal return information for other government purposes, such as state tax and child support collection, law enforcement, social welfare program administration, and statistical use (Code Sec. 7213A).

It is permissible for the IRS to release information regarding investigations of unauthorized disclosure or inspection of return information, to the person making the allegation of a violation of privacy, or that person's designee (Code Sec. 6103(e)(11)).

¶2892

2894. Disclosure of Return Information by Return Preparers. A return preparer who uses return information for any purpose other than to prepare a return, or who makes an unauthorized disclosure of return information, is subject to a $250 penalty for each disclosure, up to a maximum of $10,000. If the action is undertaken knowingly or recklessly, the preparer may be subject to criminal penalties or a fine of up to $1,000, or up to a year in jail, or both, together with the cost of prosecution. Additional penalties apply for disclosures or improper uses occurring after July 1, 2019, related to the misappropriation of a person's identity (Code Secs. 6713 and 7216, as amended by the Taxpayer First Act (P.L. 116-25)). A taxpayer may bring a civil action for damages against the U.S. government if an IRS employee offers the taxpayer's representative favorable tax treatment in exchange for information about the taxpayer (Code Sec. 7435).

Criminal Penalties

2898. Criminal Penalties. Criminal penalties may be incurred if a taxpayer: (1) willfully fails to make a return, keep records, supply required information, or pay any tax or estimated tax; (2) willfully attempts in any manner to evade or defeat the tax; or (3) willfully fails to collect and pay over the tax. In addition to the felony charges listed in the preceding sentence, misdemeanor charges can be brought for making fraudulent statements to employees, filing a fraudulent withholding certificate, or failing to obey a summons. The criminal penalties are in addition to the civil penalties (Code Secs. 7201—7212). A good faith misunderstanding of the law or a good faith belief that one is not violating the law negates the willfulness element of a tax evasion charge (*J.L. Cheek*, SCt, 91-1 USTC ¶ 50,012).

28

PENALTIES

Chapter 29

ESTATE, GIFT AND GENERATION-SKIPPING TRANSFER TAX

Transfer Tax System

2901. Estate, Gift, and Generation-Skipping Transfer Tax System. The estate, gift, and generation-skipping transfer (GST) taxes are designed to form a unified transfer tax system on the transfer of property at death (estate tax), during life (gift tax), and on transfers that skip a generation (GST tax). The maximum marginal tax rate is 40 percent for the estates of decedents dying and gifts and GSTs made after December 31, 2012 (¶ 40). An applicable credit amount (previously known as the unified credit) applies to estate, gift, and GST taxes. It is the amount of tentative tax that would be imposed on an amount equal to the applicable exclusion amount, adjusted annually for inflation. The applicable exclusion amount is $10 million and adjusted annually for inflation, for decedents dying and gifts made after 2017 and before 2026 (¶ 41).

The applicable exclusion amount is $11.4 million for 2019 and $11.58 million for 2020 (Rev. Proc. 2018-57; Rev. Proc. 2019-44). A decedent's estate may elect to allow the unused portion of the decedent's applicable exclusion amount to be available to his or her surviving spouse or the spouse's estate (referred to as "portability"). As a result, the applicable exclusion amount of a surviving spouse may include the predeceased spouse's unused exclusion amount, potentially allowing the spouse to transfer up to $22.8 million for 2019 and $23.16 million for 2020 (¶ 2934 and ¶ 2938).

Gift Tax

See CCH® AnswerConnect: *Gift Tax* for more information on this topic.

2903. Transfers Subject to Gift Tax. A federal gift tax applies to the transfer of property by gift, whether the gift is direct or indirect, and whether the transfer is in trust or otherwise. The property transferred may be real, personal, tangible, or intangible (Code Sec. 2511; Reg. § 25.2511-1(a)). The donor makes a gift to the extent that the value of the property transferred exceeds the consideration received in return for the transfer (Code Sec. 2512(b)). The transferred property or evidence of it must be delivered to the donee and the donor must relinquish all control over the property for the gift to be completed (Reg. § 25.2511-2). Transfers to qualifying political organizations are not considered gifts (Code Sec. 2501(a)(4)). Transfers to organizations that are described in Code Sec. 501(c)(4), (5), or (6) (¶ 692) and are exempt from tax under Code Sec. 501(a) are not subject to federal gift tax (Code Sec. 2501(a)(6)).

Indirect gifts, such as transfers in trust and the cancellation of indebtedness, are subject to the gift tax (Code Sec. 2511). Other examples of indirect gifts include certain assignments of benefits, permission to withdraw funds deposited by a donor from a joint account, and below-market interest rate loans (Reg. § 25.2511-1(c) and (h)). A waiver of the right to a joint and survivor annuity in a qualified plan is not a gift (Code Sec. 2503(f)).

A gratuitous transfer of property by a corporation is considered to be a gift by the shareholders to the donee, while a gift to a corporation is considered to be a gift to its shareholders (Reg. §25.2511-1(h)). In addition, a gift may occur at the creation of a family limited partnership or when transferring control of a closely held company (*J.C. Shepherd*, CA-11, 2002-1 USTC ¶ 60,431; *M. Senda*, CA-8, 2006-1 USTC ¶ 60,515). Transfers of stock or securities are gifts, even if the securities are exempt from tax. The transfer of an option is a gift. Also, gratuitous transfers made by guardians or conservators under court orders are gifts. Conversely, a transfer pursuant to a will contest settlement entered into at arm's length is generally not a gift. The treatment of income earned by domestic partners as community property by operation of state law is also not considered a gift (Rev. Rul. 55-461).

Valuation. Generally, the value of property for gift tax purposes is its fair market value on the date of the gift. That is, the price at which the property would change hands between a willing buyer and a willing seller, both having reasonable knowledge of relevant facts (Code Sec. 2512; Reg. §25.2512-1). Special valuation rules apply for determining the amount of a gift if the transferor retains (1) an equity interest in a corporation or partnership transferred to a family member, or (2) an interest in a trust to or for the benefit of a family member (Code Secs. 2701, 2702, and 2704).

Qualified Disclaimers. The donee of a gift may make a qualified disclaimer of the entire interest or a portion of it without making a taxable gift. To be a qualified disclaimer:

- the disclaimer must be in writing;
- the disclaimer must be received by the transferor or the transferor's representative within nine months of the date of the transfer;
- the beneficiary may not accept any of the benefits from the transferred property; and
- the property being disclaimed must pass to someone other than, and without direction from, the disclaiming beneficiary (Code Sec. 2518).

The due date for performing certain time-sensitive actions, including receipt of a qualified waiver within nine months, otherwise due on or after April 1, 2020, and before July 15, 2020, is automatically extended to July 15, 2020, in response to the COVID-19 (coronavirus) crisis (Notice 2020-23; Rev. Proc. 2018-58).

Nonresident Alien Donors. A donor who is a nonresident alien is subject to gift tax on transfers of real and tangible property situated in the United States (Code Sec. 2501(a); Reg. §25.2501-1). Transfers of intangible property by a nonresident alien generally are not subject to gift tax. A donor who relinquishes his or her U.S. citizenship or terminates his or her long-term residency is subject to special expatriation rules (Code Sec. 2501(a)(3)). See ¶ 2948 for the transfer tax imposed on recipients of gifts from "covered expatriates." Taxable gifts are taxed at the same rates that apply to U.S. citizens (Code Sec. 2501(a)(1)).

2905. Gift Tax Annual Exclusion. The first $15,000 of gifts of a present interest made by a donor during calendar year 2019 ($15,000 for 2020) to each donee is not included in the total amount of the donor's taxable gifts during that year (Code Sec. 2503(b); Rev. Proc. 2018-57; Rev. Proc. 2019-44). Therefore, these amounts are not taxed and do not use up any of the donor's lifetime gift tax applicable credit amount. Also, spouses who consent to split their gifts may transfer a total of $30,000 per donee for 2019 ($30,000 for 2020), free of gift and generation-skipping transfer (GST) tax (Code Sec. 2513(a)).

If the donor's spouse is not a U.S. citizen, an annual exclusion of $155,000 for 2019 ($157,000 for 2020) is allowed for present interest gifts to the spouse that would qualify for the marital deduction if the spouse were a U.S. citizen (Code Sec. 2523(i)(2); Rev. Proc. 2018-57; Rev. Proc. 2019-44). The annual exclusion is available to all donors, including nonresident citizens.

The annual exclusion is allowed for gifts of present interests, but not for gifts of future interests in property. Present interests include any interests, whether vested or contingent, that are available for the donee's immediate use, possession, or enjoyment (Reg. § 25.2503-3(b)). A transfer of property for the benefit of a minor pursuant to the Uniform Transfers to Minors Act (UTMA), the Uniform Gifts to Minors Act (UGMA), or the Gifts of Securities to Minors Act (GSMA) is considered to be a completed gift of the full fair market value of the property.

Transfers in Trust. The number of annual exclusions available for a gift in trust is determined by the number of trust beneficiaries who have a present interest in the gifted property. A transfer to a trust that allows a beneficiary the unrestricted right to the immediate use, possession, or enjoyment of the transferred property or the income from the property, such as a life estate or term certain, is a present interest gift that qualifies for the annual exclusion (Reg. § 25.2503-3(b)). However, such unrestricted gifts through a trust are rarely made. Normally, limits are placed on the beneficiary's right to use, possess, or enjoy the trust property.

A gift of the right to demand a portion of a trust corpus is a gift of a present interest, so long as the donee-beneficiary is aware of his or her right to make the demand. Typically, the beneficiary of such a trust (known as a *Crummey* trust) is given the right to demand an amount of corpus equal to the annual gift tax exclusion for a limited period of time, such as 60 days. If the persons who have a right of withdrawal do not have a present income interest in the trust or a vested remainder interest, the IRS may question the claimed annual exclusion (TAM 9628004).

Gifts to Minors. Gifts to minors may qualify for the annual exclusion if they meet certain requirements (Code Sec. 2503(c); Reg. § 25.2503-4(a)). The property and income from the property must be expended by or for the benefit of the minor. Any income and principal not expended must be paid to the minor at age 21, or to his or her estate if the minor dies before age 21. If a transfer of property is made under a parent's legal obligation to support a minor, the transfer is not a gift, as is the case with child support (Reg. § 25.2516-2).

2907. Exclusion for Educational or Medical Payment. An unlimited gift tax exclusion is allowed for amounts paid on behalf of a donee *directly* to an educational organization, provided such amounts constitute tuition payments (Code Sec. 2503(e)). Amounts paid for books, dormitory fees, or board on behalf of the donee are not eligible for the exclusion. Likewise, amounts paid *directly* to health care providers for medical services on behalf of a donee also qualify for the unlimited gift tax exclusion. Medical expense payments are excludable without regard to the percentage limitations imposed for income tax purposes. Both the medical and tuition exclusions are in addition to the annual exclusion (¶ 2905) and available without regard to the relationship between the donor and donee.

2908. Gifts to Spouse. A marital deduction is allowed in computing the taxable gifts of a married donor for property that passes to the donor's spouse (Code Sec. 2523; Rev. Proc. 2018-57; Rev. Proc. 2019-44). As a result, an unlimited amount of property, other than certain terminable interests, can be transferred between spouses. The gift tax marital deduction may not be claimed if the donor's spouse is not a U.S. citizen at the time of the gift. Instead, gifts to a noncitizen spouse are eligible for a annual gift tax exclusion of up to $155,000 for 2019 ($157,000 for 2020).

A gift tax marital deduction also is not allowed for transfers of terminable interests in property. A terminable interest in property is an interest that will terminate or fail on the lapse of time or on the occurrence or failure to occur of some contingency. For example, terminable interests include life estates, terms for years, and annuities. A gift tax marital deduction is allowed if the donee spouse is given a life estate with a general power of appointment or a qualified terminable interest property (QTIP). The deduction is also allowed if the donor and spouse are named as the only noncharitable beneficiaries of a qualified charitable remainder trust (¶ 2926).

2909. Gifts to Charity. A gift tax charitable deduction is allowed in determining a donor's taxable gifts for transfers to: federal, state, and local governmental entities; charitable organizations; fraternal societies (if the property is used for charitable purposes); or veterans' organizations (Code Sec. 2522). The charitable deduction is not limited to gifts for use within the United States, unless the donor is a nonresident alien at the time of the gift. A deduction may also be allowed for the value of the charitable interest in a split-interest transfer (a transfer in which there are both charitable and noncharitable beneficiaries) provided the charitable interest is in a qualified form (i.e., charitable remainder annuity trust, charitable remainder unitrust, charitable lead annuity trust, charitable lead unitrust, or a pooled income fund) (¶ 2932).

2910. Computing the Gift Tax Liability. The gift tax is calculated by first determining the total value of the donor's gifts for the current calendar year. The value of a gift is its fair market value on the date of the gift (¶ 2903). This amount is reduced by any exclusions—annual (¶ 2905), and educational and medical (¶ 2907)—and deductions—marital (¶ 2908) and charitable (¶ 2909). The sum of all taxable gifts made by the donor in all prior years is then added to the current year's taxable gifts to arrive at the total taxable gifts. The donor's tentative gift tax liability is then determined by (1) calculating a tentative tax on the sum of all taxable gifts made in the calendar year and in preceding calendar periods, (2) calculating a tentative tax on only the taxable gifts in preceding calendar periods, and (3) then subtracting the tentative tax determined in step (2) from the tentative tax determined in step (1) (Code Sec. 2502).

The donor is allowed an applicable credit (or unified credit) against gift tax, equal to (1) the estate tax applicable credit amount in effect for the calendar year of the gift (¶ 2934), minus (2) the sum of all applicable credits allowable to the donor for gifts made in all prior calendar periods. For 2019, the basic exclusion amount is $11.4 million ($11.58 million for 2020), and the gift tax applicable credit amount is $4,505,800 for 2019 ($4,577,800 for 2020) (Code Secs. 2010(c) and 2505(a); Rev. Proc. 2018-57; Rev. Proc. 2019-44). The applicable credit amount might be higher for any year if the donor is a surviving spouse and the estate of his or her predeceased spouse has elected portability of the deceased spouse's unused exclusion (DSUE) amount (¶ 2934 and ¶ 2938).

For gifts made after 2009, any unified credit allocated to prior periods must be redetermined using current gift tax rates, rather than the rates that were in effect when the prior gifts were made (Code Sec. 2505(a)). In addition, the tax rates in effect at the time of the decedent's death are to be used rather than the rates that were in effect at the time the gifts were made, with respect to the computation of gift tax payable in the case of prior gifts, for the estates of decedents dying and gifts made after 2017 and before 2026 (Code Sec. 2010(c)(3)(C)). Thus, for gifts made in 2019, the $11.4 million and first dollar (that is, the first dollar that becomes taxable) is taxed at the rate that would apply to gifts in the amount of $11,400,001 (40 percent) rather than the rate that would apply to a gift of $1 (18 percent).

If a gift is adequately disclosed on the gift tax return and the gift tax statute of limitations has expired, the IRS may not revalue the donor's lifetime gifts when computing the estate tax liability upon the donor's death (Code Sec. 2001(f)). There is a three-year statute of limitations for gift tax returns (Code Sec. 2504(c)).

Filing Requirements. Form 709 is used for federal gift tax purposes and must be filed and any gift tax must be paid, on an annual basis. The due date for filing the annual gift tax return is generally the same as the due date for the income tax return (April 15). For the calendar year in which the donor dies, the gift tax return is due on the earlier of the due date (with extensions) for filing the donor's estate tax return or the "normal" due date with respect to the gifts (Code Sec. 6075(b)).

The due date for filing and payment obligations for estate, gift, and generation-skipping transfer (GST) taxes otherwise due between April 1, 2020, and July 15, 2020, is extended to July 15, 2020, in response to the COVID-19 (coronavirus) crisis. The extension is automatic, and a taxpayer does not need to file any form or contact the IRS to receive it. A taxpayer that needs more time to file his or her return after July 15, 2020, may request an additional extension by filing the appropriate extension form by July 15, 2020, but the extension may not go beyond the original statutory or regulatory extension date. Penalties, additions to tax, and interest for failure to file the return or pay the taxes will not accrue until July 16, 2020 (Notice 2020-23, amplifying Notice 2020-20 and Notice 2020-18).

2911. Donor Is Primarily Liable to File Return and Pay Gift Tax. Gift tax returns must be filed by individual donors of gifts of more than $15,000 for 2019 ($15,000 for 2020) that do not qualify for an exclusion. Gift tax returns must be filed on Form 709. The donor is primarily liable for the payment of the gift tax (Code Sec. 6019).

Estate Tax

See CCH® AnswerConnect: *Estate Tax* for more information on this topic.

2912. Gross Estate. A federal estate tax is imposed on the transfer of a person's property at the time of that person's death. The amount of the tax is determined by applying the relevant tax rates to the taxable estate—the gross estate reduced by any deductions. The gross estate of a U.S. citizen or resident decedent includes the value of all property described in Code Sec. 2033 through Code Sec. 2044, whether real or personal, tangible or intangible, wherever situated. Effectively executed disclaimers prevent the property subject to the disclaimer from being included in the disclaimant's gross estate (Code Secs. 2046 and 2518).

Qualified terminable interest property (QTIP) for which an election was made to qualify it for the marital deduction in the estate of the first spouse to die (¶ 2926), or on the gift tax return of the donor spouse, is included in the gross estate of the surviving or donee spouse (Code Sec. 2044(a)).

Form 706 is used to figure the estate tax and includes specific schedules on which the estate must provide details for specific types of property included in the decedent's gross estate (¶ 2938). Real estate that the decedent owned or had contracted to purchase is reported on Schedule A. Stocks and bonds included in the gross estate are reported on Schedule B. Mortgages and notes payable to the decedent at the time of death, as well as cash that the decedent possessed on the date of death, are reported on Schedule C. Other Form 706 schedules are specifically designated for other types of property. If an asset in the gross estate is not required to be reported on any other schedule, it must be reported on Schedule F.

2913. Transferred Property in Which Decedent Retained an Interest. If a decedent retains some control over gifts of property made during life, the property may be added back to the decedent's gross estate. For example, gifts in which the decedent retains a life estate or the right to the income, possession, or enjoyment, or the right to designate who will enjoy the property, are includible in the gross estate (Code Sec. 2036). Also, includible in the gross estate are gifts in which the decedent retains a right to a reversionary interest that exceeds five percent of the value of the transferred property, and possession or enjoyment of the property can be obtained only by surviving the decedent (Code Sec. 2037(a)). Finally, gifts in which the decedent holds a power to alter, amend, revoke, or terminate the gift are included in the gross estate (Code Sec. 2038(a)(1); Reg. § 20.2038-1(a)).

An estate valuation freeze is a technique used to limit the value of closely held business interests owned by an individual by transferring the future appreciation in value of the business to the next generation of the owner's family while retaining certain interests in the business. This technique has been severely limited by the special valuation rules (Code Secs. 2701—2704), which treat transfers of family business interests unfavorably for gift tax purposes by assigning a value of zero to certain types of interests retained by the donor in such exchanges (¶ 2903).

If a lifetime transfer with a retained interest is a sale for adequate and full consideration, the property that is transferred is not included in the transferor's gross estate (Code Sec. 2036(a); Reg. § 20.2036-1(c)). If the transfer is not for adequate and full consideration, the amount included in the decedent's estate is the full value of the property subject to the decedent's retained interest. If the interest or right is reserved over only part of the property transferred, only the reserved portion is included in the gross estate.

2914. Gifts Made Within Three Years of Death. Gifts made within three years of the donor's death generally are not includible in the donor's gross estate unless the gift consists of interests in property that would otherwise be included in the gross estate because of the donor's retained powers, such as the power to alter, amend, revoke, or terminate the gift (¶ 2913) (Code Sec. 2035(a)). Gifts made from a decedent's revocable trust within three years of death are not included in the decedent's gross estate, but instead are treated as if made directly by the decedent (Code Secs. 2035(e) and 2038). Gift tax paid on all transfers made within three years of death is included in the gross estate (Code Sec. 2035(b)). Such transfers are generally reported on Schedule G (Form 706).

2915. Life Insurance Proceeds Includible in Gross Estate. Proceeds of insurance on a decedent's life payable to or for the benefit of his or her estate, and insurance payable to other beneficiaries in which the decedent retained incidents of ownership, are included in the decedent's gross estate (Code Sec. 2042; Reg. § 20.2042-1). Insurance that is paid to a named beneficiary, but that must be used to satisfy a legal obligation to meet expenses of the decedent's estate, such as debts and taxes, is also included in the decedent's gross estate.

Incidents of Ownership. If proceeds of insurance on the life of a decedent are payable to a beneficiary other than the decedent's estate, they are included in the decedent's gross estate if the decedent has retained an incident of ownership in the life insurance policy on the date of death. The term "incidents of ownership" is not limited in its meaning to ownership of the policy. It refers to the right of the insured or the insured's estate to the economic benefits of the policy. If the decedent transfers a life insurance policy or an incident of ownership in the policy within three years of his or her death, the proceeds are included in the decedent's gross estate (Code Sec. 2035(a)). However, only one-half of the proceeds of life insurance purchased with community property is generally included in the estate of the insured spouse, even if the decedent possessed an incident of ownership.

A person insured under a key-employee insurance arrangement usually has no interest in the insurance. None of its proceeds are included in the insured's gross estate. The arrangement will be taken into account in determining a value for any stock that the insured may have owned in the company.

In the case of split-dollar life insurance, death proceeds from the employee's portion of the policy are included in the employee's estate if: (1) the proceeds are payable to, or for the benefit of, the employee's estate or (2) the employee holds an incident of ownership in the policy at death or transfers an incident of ownership to a third party within three years before death. Gift tax liability for employer-paid premiums may arise if a co-owner of the policy is neither the employer nor the employee.

Life insurance that is included in a decedent's gross estate is generally reported on Schedule D (Form 706). For each policy listed, a separate Form 712 must be completed and attached to Schedule D.

2917. Annuities and Retirement Benefits Includible in Gross Estate. The value of an annuity or other payment received by any beneficiary by reason of surviving the decedent is generally included in the decedent's gross estate (Code Sec. 2039). The annuity or other payment is not taxable under the rules unless it is payable under a contract by agreement entered into after March 31, 1931, and the following factors exist: the contract or agreement is not a policy of insurance on the decedent's life; the decedent possessed the right to receive the payments during his or her lifetime; and payments under the contract are determined by reference to the decedent's life or life expectancy.

The value of an annuity or other payment included in a decedent's gross estate is the portion of its value attributable to the portion of the purchase price contributed by the decedent. Any contribution made by a decedent's employer or former employer by reason of his or her employment is considered to be made by the decedent. Annuities that are included in a decedent's gross estate are generally reported on Schedule I (Form 706).

With respect to the estate tax valuation of a qualified account such as an individual retirement account (IRA), the value of the account is the fair market value of the assets in the account without any discount for the income tax liability that would be triggered if the estate or beneficiary was to take a distribution of the assets in order to sell them (Reg. § 20.2031-1(b); *D. Kahn Est.*, Dec. 56,195, 125 TC 227).

2918. Powers of Appointment. Property subject to a general power of appointment is included in the gross estate of the holder of the power if the power exists at the holder's death (Code Secs. 2041 and 2514). The exercise or release of a general power during the life of the holder is a transfer subject to gift tax.

A power of appointment is the right to dispose of the property given to someone other than the donor of the property. The holder of the power of appointment has a general power if the holder may exercise it in favor of himself or herself, the holder's creditors, the holder's estate, or the creditors of the holder's estate. Powers that expressly cannot be exercised in favor of any of these persons are special or limited powers (Reg. § 20.2041-1(c)(1)). A power is not general if its exercise is limited by an ascertainable standard. A power is not general if the creator of the power must join in its exercise or if a co-holder of the power has a substantial adverse interest.

The power holder's incompetence or lack of capacity to exercise the power does not affect whether the power is taxable to the power holder (*N.E. Rosenblatt Est.*, CA-10, 80-2 USTC ¶ 13,374; *A.L. Gilchrist Est.*, CA-5, 80-2 USTC ¶ 13,378). Property subject to a power of appointment that is included in a decedent's gross estate is generally reported on Schedule H (Form 706).

2919. Estate and Gift Tax on Jointly Held Property. The entire value of jointly held property with the right of survivorship, including joint bank accounts and U.S. savings bonds registered in two names, is included in a decedent's gross estate except for the portion of the property for which the surviving joint tenant furnished consideration (Code Sec. 2040). If the joint property was received by the decedent and the other joint tenants as a gift or bequest, the decedent's fractional share of the property is included in the decedent's gross estate. If the joint tenants are spouses, it generally does not matter who furnished the consideration for the property; one-half of the value of a qualified joint interest is included in the gross estate of the first spouse to die. Jointly held property that is included in a decedent's gross estate is generally reported on Schedule E (Form 706).

The creation of a joint interest in property results in a taxable gift by the person supplying the consideration to the noncontributing joint tenant. Creation of a joint bank account or joint brokerage account is not a taxable gift until a joint owner withdraws funds (Reg. § 25.2511-1(h)). If a donor purchased property and conveyed title to himself or herself and another as joint tenants with rights of survivorship, and those rights may be defeated by either owner severing his or her interest, the donor made a gift to the other joint owner in the amount of one-half of the property's value.

2921. Estate Tax and Community Property. Community property is all property acquired by means other than gift, devise, bequest, and inheritance by spouses domiciled in community property jurisdictions. Separate property is property other than community property.

Laws in community property states differ greatly, but generally limit the extent of a person's interest in community property to one-half of the value of the property (Code Sec. 2033; Reg. § 20.2033-1). The federal estate tax law recognizes these differences in state law by not providing a distinct, specific method of treating community property. For community property, the application of the federal estate tax is governed by state law. As a result, only one-half of the value of each item of community property held by a decedent and the decedent's spouse may be included in the decedent's gross estate.

2922. Valuation of Gross Estate. The value of property that is included in the gross estate is its fair market value on the decedent's date of death (Code Sec. 2031; Reg. § 20.2031-1(b)). The fair market value of property includible in the gross estate is the price at which it would change hands between a willing buyer and a willing seller, both having reasonable knowledge of relevant facts.

Alternate Valuation. Instead of valuing property as of the date of death, the executor may elect to value the gross estate at the fair market value of the property on the alternate valuation date, which is the date six months after the date of the decedent's death (Code Sec. 2032; Reg. § 20.2032-1). The use of this method is limited to situations in which the election would reduce both the value of the decedent's gross estate and the federal estate and generation-skipping transfer (GST) tax liability of the estate.

The alternate valuation date may be elected on Part 3, line 1 of Form 706. Once elected, the use of the alternate valuation date is irrevocable. The amount of any marital or charitable deduction is adjusted based on the alternate value of assets passing to charity or the surviving spouse. If the alternate valuation election is made, all property included in the gross estate is valued as of the alternate valuation date. If property is sold, exchanged, distributed, or otherwise disposed of during the six-month period, it is valued on the date of disposition rather than the alternate valuation date.

Special Use Valuation. If a farm or real property used in a closely held business is included in the gross estate, the executor may elect to value the property at its "current use" rather than at its "highest and best use" (Code Sec. 2032A; Reg. § 20.2032A-8). Special use valuation is obtained pursuant to an irrevocable election by an executor to value real property used in a farm, trade, or business. The limitation on the reduction in value resulting from special use valuation is $1.16 million for 2019 ($1.18 million for 2020) (Rev. Proc. 2018-57; Rev. Proc. 2019-44).

Special use valuation is elected on the estate tax return (Part 3, line 2 of Form 706) by, among other things, completing the notice of election (Schedule A-1 (Form 706)) and submitting a recapture agreement. If the qualified heir ceases to use the farm property for farming or sells the property to a non-family member within 10 years of the decedent's date of death, an additional estate tax, the recapture tax, is due and Form 706-A must be filed.

2925. Deductions from Gross Estate—Expenses. A deduction from the gross estate is allowed for funeral expenses, administration expenses, claims against the estate, certain taxes, and unpaid mortgages or other indebtedness allowable under the local law governing the administration of the decedent's estate (Code Sec. 2053; Reg. § 20.2053-1). For expenses that are not paid before filing the estate tax return, an estimated amount may be deducted if the amount is ascertainable and there is reasonable certainty that the amount will be paid. Contested and contingent claims and expenses cannot be ascertained with reasonable certainty. Estate administration expenses may generally be deducted on either the decedent's estate tax return or the estate's income tax return, but not on both (¶ 529).

Funeral and Administrative Expenses. Expenses incurred in connection with the decedent's funeral, including reasonable expenses for a tombstone, mausoleum, or burial lot, are deductible (Code Sec. 2053(a)(1)). Administration expenses are deductible if actually and necessarily incurred in the administration of the estate. Administration expenses include fees paid to surrogates, appraisers, and accountants. Reasonable attorney's fees that meet the requirements of Reg. § 20.2053-1 are deductible (Code Sec. 2053(a)(2); Reg. § 20.2053-3(c)). Fees incurred by beneficiaries incident to litigation with regard to their interests are not deductible, unless the litigation is essential to the proper settlement of the estate. An executor or administrator may deduct the amount of his or her commissions from the decedent's gross estate in an amount actually paid or an amount that is reasonably ascertainable and will be paid (Reg. § 20.2053-3(b)). Miscellaneous expenses necessarily incurred in preserving and distributing estate assets are also deductible as administration expenses (Reg. § 20.2053-3(d)). Funeral and administrative expenses are generally reported on Schedule J (Form 706).

Debts, Mortgages, and Liabilities. Claims that are a personal obligation of the decedent are deductible, provided that they are existing and enforceable against the decedent at the time of his or her death, are allowable under local law, and have actually been paid or meet the requirements of Reg. § 20.2053-1(d)(4). Liabilities imposed by law or arising out of torts committed by the decedent are also deductible. In certain circumstances, an executor may deduct the current value of a claim or claims that

29

ESTATE—GIFT

concern the same or similar issue or asset, even if the claim has not yet been paid (Reg. § 20.2053-4). The full value of any unpaid mortgage or other indebtedness charged against property for which the decedent is personally liable, plus interest accrued on the debt to the date of death, is deductible if the property's entire value undiminished by the mortgage or debt is included in the gross estate (Code Sec. 2053(a)(4); Reg. § 20.2053-7). Debts, mortgages, and liabilities of the decedent are generally reported on Schedule K (Form 706).

Taxes and Losses. Federal estate taxes are not deductible. State estate, succession, legacy, or inheritance taxes actually paid to any state or the District of Columbia from the value of the gross estate are deductible (¶ 2933), as are unpaid gift taxes on gifts made before death. Unpaid income taxes are deductible if they are on income properly includible in an income tax return of a decedent for a period before his or her death (Reg. § 20.2053-6). A deduction is also allowed for losses arising from fires, storms, shipwrecks, or other casualties or thefts that are incurred during estate administration and not compensated for by insurance (Code Sec. 2054). Such losses and taxes, except for the state death tax deduction (¶ 2933), are generally reported on Schedule L (Form 706).

2926. Estate Tax Marital Deduction. In determining a married decedent's taxable estate, an unlimited deduction is allowable for property that passes to the decedent's surviving spouse (Code Sec. 2056). In order to qualify for the deduction, the decedent must be married and survived by his or her spouse, the spouse must be a U.S. citizen, the property must be included in the decedent's gross estate and pass to the surviving spouse, and the property must not be a nondeductible terminable interest. The estate tax marital deduction is not available if the decedent's surviving spouse is not a U.S. citizen unless the spouse becomes a citizen before the estate tax return is filed or the property passes to a qualified domestic trust (QDOT) (Code Secs. 2056(d) and 2056A). Estates of decedents who are in a same-sex marriage may claim the estate tax marital deduction.

Passing Requirement. Property must pass from the decedent to a surviving spouse for a transfer to be deductible (Code Sec. 2056(a)). Bequests and inheritances, dower and curtesy interests, joint property, property received under antenuptial agreements, annuities, and life insurance may pass from the decedent to the surviving spouse. Property received by a spouse under a state law right of election against the will satisfies the passing requirement (Code Sec. 2056(c); Reg. § 20.2056(c)-2(c)). Property passing to the spouse as a result of another person's qualified disclaimer (¶ 2903) is considered to pass from the decedent (Reg. § 20.2056(d)-2(b)).

Terminable Interest Rule. The terminable interest rule bars a deduction for any nondeductible terminable interest. A terminable interest in property is an interest that terminates or fails because of the lapse of time or the occurrence of an event (Code Sec. 2056(b)(1) and (3); Reg. § 20.2056(b)-3). A nondeductible terminable interest is an interest in which a person, other than the surviving spouse, receives an interest in property from the decedent and, upon the termination of the spouse's interest in the same property, the other person may possess or enjoy the property. Property interests passing to a spouse that are conditioned on the spouse's survival of a period of six months or less, or on the spouse's survival in a common disaster, are not subject to the terminable interest rule.

Qualified Terminable Interest Property. Qualified terminable interest property (QTIP) is excluded from the terminable interest rule. To qualify as QTIP, the surviving spouse must have the right to all the income from the property for life, payable no less frequently than annually (Code Sec. 2056(b)(7); Reg. § 20.2056(b)-7(a)). A surviving spouse's income interest may be contingent upon the executor's QTIP election and still be considered a qualifying income interest for life. In addition, no person may have a power to appoint any of the property to any person other than the surviving spouse during the surviving spouse's life. An election on Schedule M (Form 706) is necessary to designate property as QTIP. Once the QTIP election is made, the surviving spouse must include the property remaining at death in his or her gross estate, even though the surviving spouse has no control over its disposition (Code Sec. 2044). However, the estate tax that is attributable to the QTIP included in the spouse's estate may be recovered from the QTIP (Code Sec. 2207A).

Life Estate with Power of Appointment. A life estate with a power of appointment qualifies for the marital deduction if: (1) the surviving spouse is entitled to all the income from the entire interest or a specific portion of the interest for life; (2) the income is payable at least annually; (3) the spouse has the power to appoint the property, or the specific portion, to himself or herself or to his or her estate; (4) the power is exercisable by the spouse alone and in all events; and (5) no other person has the power to appoint property to anyone but the surviving spouse (Code Sec. 2056(b)(5)). There is a similar exception to the terminable interest rule for life insurance proceeds held by an insurer in which the spouse has a right to all payments and a power of appointment (Code Sec. 2056(b)(6); Reg. § 20.2056(b)-6(c)).

Amount of the Marital Deduction. The marital deduction is limited to the net value of property passing to the spouse. Death taxes, debts, and administration expenses payable from the marital bequest, mortgages on property passing to the spouse, and insufficient estate assets to fund the marital bequest all reduce the amount of the deduction (Code Sec. 2056(b)(4); Reg. § 20.2056(b)-4). However, administration expenses allocable to an estate's income do not necessarily reduce the amount of the marital deduction (*O. Hubert Est.*, SCt, 97-1 USTC ¶ 60,261). Transfers for which an estate is taking the estate tax marital deduction are generally reported on Schedule M (Form 706).

2932. Estate Tax Charitable Deduction. An unlimited estate tax charitable deduction is available for transfers to: federal, state, and local governmental entities; charitable organizations; fraternal societies (if the property is used for charitable purposes); veterans' organizations; or an employee stock ownership plan if the transfer qualifies as a qualified gratuitous transfer. The bequest must have a public rather than a private purpose (Code Sec. 2055; Reg. § 20.2055-2).

Transfers of Partial Interests. If an interest in property passes from a transferor to a charity and an interest in the same property passes to a noncharitable recipient, the transfer must take a certain form. One acceptable form is a charitable remainder annuity trust, which provides for a fixed-dollar amount to be paid to the noncharitable income beneficiary annually, or charitable remainder unitrust, which provides for a fixed percentage of trust assets, valued annually, to be paid to the noncharitable income beneficiary annually. A charitable lead trust with guaranteed annuity or unitrust amount paid to charity is allowed. The decedent could transfer a remainder interest in a farm or personal residence. A decedent can also transfer a copyrighted work of art separate from its copyright. Finally, a qualified conservation contribution is a permissible method to transfer an interest to both charitable and noncharitable recipients.

The amount of the estate tax charitable deduction must be reduced by the administration expenses and death taxes paid from the property transferred to charity (Code Sec. 2055(c); Reg. § 20.2055-3(a)). However, administration expenses allocable to an estate's income do not necessarily reduce the amount of the charitable deduction (*O. Hubert Est.*, SCt, 97-1 USTC ¶ 60,261). Transfers for which an estate is taking the estate tax charitable deduction are generally reported on Schedule O (Form 706).

2933. State Death Tax Deduction. A deduction from the gross estate is allowed for estate, inheritance, legacy, or succession taxes actually paid to any state or the District of Columbia as a result of the decedent's death (Code Sec. 2058). A limitations period is imposed that allows a deduction only for those state death taxes paid and a deduction claimed before the later of:

- four years after filing the estate tax return;

- if a timely petition for redetermination has been filed with the Tax Court, 60 days after the Tax Court decision becomes final;

- if an extension of time has been granted for payment of estate tax or of a deficiency, the date the extension expires; or

- if a timely refund claim has been filed, then the latest of the expiration of (1) 60 days from the mailing of a notice to the taxpayer of a disallowance of the refund claim, (2) 60 days after a court decision on the merits of the claim becomes final, or (3) two years after a notice of waiver of disallowance is filed under Code Sec. 6532(a)(3).

A refund based on the deduction may be made if the refund claim is filed within the above-defined period. Any refunds made will be without interest. The state death tax deduction is taken on Part 2, line 3b of Form 706.

2934. Credits Against the Estate Tax. A number of credits are available to offset a decedent's federal estate tax liability. The most important credit is the applicable credit amount (previously known as the unified credit), that is determined by calculating a tentative estate tax on the basic exclusion amount (adjusted annually for inflation) (Code Sec. 2010(c); Reg. § 20.2010-1). For 2019, the basic exclusion amount is $11.4 million, and the applicable credit amount is $4,505,800 (Rev. Proc. 2018-57). For 2020, the basic exclusion amount is $11.58 million, and the applicable credit amount is $4,577,800 (Rev. Proc. 2019-44).

Applicable Exclusion Amount After 2025. The basic exclusion amount is temporarily increased for the estates of decedents dying and gifts made in 2018 through 2025. Final regulations have been issued to reconcile when a donor makes a gift during the period the basic exclusion amount is increased and then dies after it reverts back to pre-2018 levels (Reg. § 20.2010-1(c)). In that situation, the portion of the credit against the net tentative estate tax that is attributable to the basic exclusion amount is based upon the greater of those two amounts.

Portability of Unused Applicable Exclusion Amount. The applicable exclusion amount for a surviving spouse whose predeceased spouse's estate elected portability is the sum of (1) the basic exclusion amount ($11.4 million for 2019 and $11.58 million for 2020), plus (2) the aggregate deceased spousal unused exclusion (DSUE) amount (Code Sec. 2010(c)(2) and (4); Reg. §§ 20.2010-2 and 20.2010-3). The DSUE amount is the lesser of (1) the basic exclusion amount in effect in the year of the deceased spouse's death, or (2) the last deceased spouse's applicable exclusion amount minus the amount with respect to which the tentative tax is determined on the last deceased spouse's estate. To take advantage of this special provision, the predeceased spouse must have died after December 31, 2010, and the predeceased spouse's estate must have made an election on Form 706 (¶ 2938).

If portability is elected, the surviving spouse can apply the predeceased spouse's unused exclusion amount toward lifetime gifts, and any remaining unused exclusion amount can generally be applied by the surviving spouse's estate upon his or her death. Special rules limit the use of unused exclusion amounts by a surviving spouse with multiple predeceased spouses. Guidance has been issued on the interplay between the portability election and the qualified terminable interest property (QTIP) election, where the QTIP election was unnecessary to reduce the estate tax to zero but was done to maximize the DSUE amount portable to the surviving spouse (Rev. Proc. 2016-49).

Federal Estate Tax Paid on Prior Transfers. A credit is available for federal estate tax paid on prior transfers to the decedent from a person who died within 10 years before or two years after the decedent (Code Sec. 2013). The credit is limited to the lesser of the estate tax attributable to the transferred property in the transferor's estate or the estate tax attributable to the transferred property in the decedent's estate. If the transferor predeceased the decedent by more than two years, the allowable credit is reduced by 20 percent for each full two-year period by which the death of the transferor preceded the transferor's death. The credit is claimed on Schedule Q (Form 706).

Foreign Death Taxes. A credit against estate tax is available for foreign death taxes paid on property located in a foreign country, but included in the gross estate of a U.S. citizen or resident (Code Sec. 2014). The credit is limited to the lesser of the foreign or the U.S. tax attributable to the property. If a treaty exists with the foreign country, the credit provided for under the treaty or Code Sec. 2014 may be used, whichever results in the lower amount of estate tax. The credit cannot be allowed until the foreign tax has been paid. The credit is claimed on Schedule P (Form 706) and Form 706-CE must be attached to support any credit claimed.

¶2934

Credit for Gift Taxes on Pre-1977 Gifts. For gifts made before 1977, the gift tax paid on gifts included in the gross estate is a credit against the estate tax (Code Sec. 2012). The credit is limited to the lesser of the gift tax paid or the estate tax attributable to inclusion of the gift in the gross estate.

2937. Computing the Estate Tax Liability. The estate tax computation begins with a calculation of the gross estate (¶ 2912—¶ 2921). The gross estate is valued at the fair market value on the decedent's date of death or, if elected, on the alternate valuation date, which is six months after the date of death (¶ 2922). Deductions for charitable (¶ 2932) and marital bequests (¶ 2926), state death taxes (¶ 2933), and estate administration expenses (¶ 2925), as well as other allowable deductions are subtracted from the gross estate to determine the taxable estate (Code Sec. 2051). The amount of adjusted taxable gifts made after 1976 is added to the taxable estate.

A tentative tax is computed by applying the applicable tax rates from the unified rate schedule (¶ 40) to the sum of the amount of the taxable estate and the adjusted taxable gifts. The tentative tax is then reduced by the amount of gift tax payable on the post-1976 gifts. The resulting amount is the gross estate tax, which is reduced by any allowable credits (¶ 2934), including the applicable credit amount, credits for foreign death taxes paid, the credit for tax on prior transfers, and the credit for gift tax paid on pre-1977 gifts included in the gross estate. The estate tax rates in effect at the time of the decedent's death are used to recompute (1) the gift tax imposed on post-1976 gifts made in prior years and (2) the unified credit allowed against such gift taxes (Code Sec. 2001(g)(1)).

An estate tax reduction is available for the estates of U.S. citizens or residents who are active members of the Armed Forces and who are killed in action while serving in a combat zone (Code Sec. 2201). This special treatment has been extended to include specified terrorist victims (¶ 2533), any astronaut whose death occurs in the line of duty, and certain members of the military serving in the Sinai Peninsula of Egypt.

2938. Filing Estate Tax Return and Liability for Payment. Form 706 must be filed for every U.S. citizen or resident decedent whose gross estate exceeds the basic exclusion amount (¶ 2934) for the year of the decedent's death or whose executor makes the portability election (discussed below) regardless of the size of the gross estate.

Filing the Return. The estate tax return must be filed by the executor, administrator, or person in possession of the estate's assets (Code Secs. 2203 and 6018(a)). The return is due within nine months of the decedent's date of death, but a six-month extension of time to file is available (Code Sec. 6075(a); Reg. § 20.6075-1). The six-month extension is automatic if: (1) Form 4768 is filed on or before the due date for the estate tax return; (2) the application is filed with the IRS office designated in the application's instructions; and (3) an estimate of the amount of estate and generation-skipping transfer tax liability is included.

The due date for filing and payment obligations for estate, gift, and generation-skipping transfer (GST) taxes otherwise due between April 1, 2020, and July 15, 2020, is extended to July 15, 2020, in response to the COVID-19 (coronavirus) crisis. The extension is automatic and the taxpayer does not need to file any form or contact the IRS to receive it. A taxpayer that needs more time to file a return after July 15, 2020, may request an additional extension by filing the appropriate extension form by July 15, 2020, but the extension may not go beyond the original statutory or regulatory extension date. Penalties, additions to tax, and interest for failure to file the return or pay the taxes will not accrue until July 16, 2020 (Notice 2020-23, amplifying Notice 2020-20 and Notice 2020-18).

Basis Reporting Requirement. Executors and beneficiaries who are required to file an estate tax return after July 31, 2015, must provide the IRS and each person acquiring an interest in property included in the decedent's gross estate a statement that identifies the value of each interest in property as it was reported on the estate tax return (Code Sec. 6035; Prop. Reg. § 1.6035-1; Reg. § 1.6035-2). The information is reported on Form 8971 and each beneficiary receiving property from the estates should be given Schedule

29 ESTATE—GIFT

A of Form 8971. See ¶ 1633 for discussion of rules requiring consistent basis reporting between a decedent's estate and a person who acquires property from the decedent.

Paying the Tax. The estate tax must be paid within nine months after the decedent's date of death (Code Secs. 6075(a) and 6151(a)) by the executor or person in possession of the estate's property (Code Sec. 2002; Reg. § 20.2002-1). The tax may be paid by check, money order, draft, credit card, or debit card (Code Sec. 6311(a)). The time for payment of the estate tax may be extended, upon reasonable cause, for a period of one year after the due date (Code Sec. 6161(a)). If reasonable cause exists, the time for payment may be extended for up to 10 years. The due date for filing and payment obligations for estate, gift, and generation-skipping transfer (GST) taxes otherwise due between April 1, 2020, and July 15, 2020, is automatically extended to July 15, 2020, in response to the COVID-19 (coronavirus) crisis.

Portability Election for Unused Applicable Exclusion Amount. Executors can make an election allowing the decedent's surviving spouse to use the unused portion of the decedent spouse's applicable exclusion amount (¶ 2934) (Code Sec. 2010(c)(4) and (5)). The executor of the predeceased spouse's estate must file Form 706 within the required filing period, including extensions actually granted, to make the election, even if Form 706 is not otherwise required to be filed (Reg. § 20.2010-2(a)). Simplified procedures for requesting an extension of time to make a portability election apply for estates that otherwise are not required to file an estate tax return, effective June 9, 2017, through the later of January 2, 2018, or the second anniversary of a decedent's date of death (Rev. Proc. 2017-34).

2939. Election to Pay Estate Tax in Installments. If an estate includes a farm or closely held business whose value exceeds 35 percent of the adjusted gross estate, the executor may elect to pay the estate and generation-skipping transfer (GST) taxes in 10 annual installments following a deferral period of five years (Code Sec. 6166). The amount of tax that may be deferred is limited to the tax attributable to the business interest. A *two-percent* interest rate applies to that portion of the estate tax deferred on the first $1.55 million in taxable value of the closely held business for estates of decedents dying in 2019 ($1.57 million for decedents dying in 2020) (Code Sec. 6601(j); Rev. Proc. 2018-57; Rev. Proc. 2019-44).

A closely held corporation may redeem stock from the estate of a decedent or from the beneficiaries of the estate to pay estate taxes and administrative expenses if the stock comprises 35 percent of the gross estate. This redemption of stock is generally not treated as a disqualifying disposition for purposes of the installment payment of the estate tax.

The election to pay the estate and GST taxes in installments is made by checking "Yes" on Part 3, line 3 of Form 706 and attaching a statement as described in the instructions to Form 706.

2940. Estate Taxation of Nonresident Aliens. A decedent who is a nonresident alien is subject to estate tax on real, tangible, and intangible property situated in the United States (Code Secs. 2101 and 2103). Intangible property situated in the United States includes stock in domestic corporations, bonds, and debt obligations of U.S. obligors, U.S. partnership assets, and U.S. property owned by a trust in which the nonresident alien has an interest. The value of such property in a nonresident alien's gross estate is not reduced by indebtedness secured by the property if the decedent was personally liable for the debt, even though the personal debt deduction allowed a nonresident alien may be less than the amount actually owed (*H.H. Fung Est.,* CA-9 (unpub. op.), 2003-1 USTC ¶ 60,460).

The estate of a nonresident alien is taxed at the same estate tax rates that apply to U.S. citizens' estates (Code Sec. 2101(b); Reg. § 20.2101-1). Except where provided by treaty, the unified credit is $13,000 (Code Sec. 2102(b)). The estate may claim deductions for a pro rata share of expenses, debts, and losses, a marital deduction if the surviving spouse is a U.S. citizen, and a charitable deduction (Code Sec. 2106(a)(1); Reg. § 20.2106-2(a)(2)). An estate tax return must be filed if a nonresident alien's gross estate situated in the United States exceeds $60,000 (Code Sec. 6018(a)(2)). The estate must file Form 706-NA.

If a former citizen or long-term resident who is subject to the alternative tax regime of Code Sec. 877(b) dies within 10 years of relinquishing citizenship or residency, an estate tax is imposed on the transfer of U.S.-situs property, including the decedent's pro rata share of the U.S. property held by a foreign corporation. The estate tax is computed on the taxable estate using the same estate tax rate schedule used for the estate of a U.S. citizen or resident (Code Secs. 2107(a) and 2501(a)(3)(B); Reg. §§20.2107-1(a) and 25.2511-1(b)).

The estate and gift tax Code provisions may be affected by provisions contained in foreign tax treaties (Code Sec. 7852(d)).

Generation-Skipping Transfer Tax

See CCH® AnswerConnect: *Generation-Skipping Transfer Tax* for more information on this topic.

2942. Transfers Subject to Tax. To ensure that property transfers are subject to transfer tax at least once at each generation, a generation-skipping transfer (GST) tax is imposed on certain transfers (Code Sec. 2601). The GST tax rate is 40 percent (¶2901).

A GST may take one of three forms: a direct skip, a taxable termination, or a taxable distribution to a skip person. A direct skip is a transfer to a skip person that is also subject to estate or gift tax (Code Sec. 2612(c)). A skip person is defined as (1) a person two generations or more younger than the transferor or (2) a trust for the benefit of one or more skip persons (Code Sec. 2613(a); Reg. §26.2612-1(d)). If the parent of the skip person predeceases the transferor, a gift to the skip person is not a GST (Code Sec. 2651(e)(1)).

A taxable termination occurs when an interest in property held in trust terminates and trust property is held for or distributed to a skip person (Code Sec. 2612(a)). A taxable distribution is any distribution from a trust to a skip person that is not a taxable termination or a direct skip (Code Sec. 2612(b)). Transfers that are not subject to gift tax because of the unlimited exclusion for direct payment of medical and tuition expenses (¶2907), certain transfers to the extent that the property transferred was previously subject to the GST tax, as well as direct skips and certain transfers to trusts that qualify for the annual gift tax exclusion (¶2905) or the medical and tuition expense payment exclusion, are not subject to GST tax (Code Secs. 2611(b) and 2642(c)(2)).

2943. Allocation of GST Exemption and Tax Rate Computation. An individual is entitled to a lifetime exemption from generation-skipping transfer (GST) tax equal to the estate and gift tax basic exclusion amount (¶2942) (Code Sec. 2631). The GST exemption is $11.4 million for GSTs occurring in 2019 ($11.58 million for GSTs occurring in 2020) (Rev. Proc. 2018-57; Rev. Proc. 2019-44). The exemption amount is not transferable between spouses, but married couples may elect to "split" a transfer and treat it as being made one-half by each spouse, pursuant to the rules applicable to split gifts (¶2905) (Code Sec. 2652(a)(2); Reg. §26.2652-1(a)(4)). Special procedures are provided for certain taxpayers to recalculate the remaining GST exemption to the extent that an allocation of the exemption was made to certain transfers while the taxpayer was married to a person of the same sex (Notice 2017-15).

The GST tax is computed by multiplying the taxable amount of the transfer by the applicable rate (Code Sec. 2602). The applicable rate is a flat rate equal to the product of the maximum estate tax rate (¶40) and the "inclusion ratio" with respect to the transfer (Code Sec. 2641(a); Reg. §26.2641-1). The inclusion ratio represents the portion of the transfer that is *not* exempted from the GST tax by the transferor's exemption amount. It is the excess, if any, of 1 over the "applicable fraction" determined for the trust from which a GST is made or, in the case of a direct skip, the applicable fraction determined for such a skip.

Conversely, the applicable fraction represents the proportion of the transfer, whether in trust or as a direct skip, that is free of tax due to an allocation of the transferor's exemption amount. The numerator of the applicable fraction is the amount of the GST exemption allocated to the trust, or to the property transferred in a direct skip. The denominator is the value of the property transferred to the trust or involved in the direct skip, reduced by the sum of any federal estate or state death tax attributable to the property that was recovered from the trust and any estate or gift tax charitable deductions allowed with respect to the property (Code Sec. 2642; Reg. § § 26.2642-1 and 26.2642-2(a)(1)).

The GST tax exemption may be allocated by an individual, or the individual's executor, to any property with respect to which the individual was the transferor (Code Sec. 2632; Reg. § 26.2632-1). In the case of property held in trust, the GST tax exemption is allocated to the entire trust rather than to specific assets. In the case of a lifetime direct skip, any unused GST tax exemption is automatically deemed allocated to the property transferred in an amount necessary to make such property's inclusion ratio equal to zero. An individual may elect out of this automatic allocation for lifetime direct skips.

2944. Filing the Return and Paying the GST Tax. For purposes of the generation skipping transfer (GST) tax, direct skips occurring at death are reported on Schedule R (Form 706) and Schedule R-1 (Form 706) and pay the tax. The transferor is responsible for filing the return (Form 709) and paying the tax on lifetime direct skips. The trustee is responsible for filing the return (Form 706-GS(T)) and paying the tax on taxable terminations. The transferee is responsible for filing the return (Form 706-GS(D)) and paying the tax on taxable distributions (Code Sec. 2603(a); Reg. § 26.2662-1(c)(1)).

The due date for filing and payment obligations for estate, gift, and generation-skipping transfer (GST) taxes otherwise due between April 1, 2020, and July 15, 2020, is extended to July 15, 2020, in response to the COVID-19 (coronavirus) crisis. The extension is automatic and a taxpayer does not need to file any form or contact the IRS to receive it. A taxpayer that needs more time to file a return after July 15, 2020, may request an additional extension by filing the appropriate extension form by July 15, 2020, but the extension may not go beyond the original statutory or regulatory extension date. Penalties, additions to tax, and interest for failure to file the return or pay the taxes will not accrue until July 16, 2020 (Notice 2020-23, amplifying Notice 2020-20 and Notice 2020-18).

Transfer Tax on Gifts and Bequests from Expatriates

See CCH® AnswerConnect: *Estate Taxation of Nonresident Aliens* for more information on this topic.

2948. Gifts and Bequests from Expatriates. A U.S. citizen or resident who directly or indirectly receives a gift, devise, bequest, or inheritance from a covered expatriate (¶ 2412) after the date of expatriation must pay a tax equal to the value of the covered gift or bequest multiplied by the highest rate in effect for estates and gifts (40 percent) (Code Sec. 2801). This special transfer tax applies only to the extent that the value of the covered gifts and bequests received by any person during the calendar year exceeds the annual gift tax exclusion amount for the year ($15,000 for 2019 and $15,000 for 2020) (Rev. Proc. 2018-57; Rev. Proc. 2019-44). The tax is reduced by the amount of any gift or estate tax paid to a foreign country with respect to such covered gift or bequest. The IRS has issued proposed regulations affecting taxpayers who received covered gifts or covered bequests from expatriates. The IRS intends to issue Form 708 for reporting the tax once the regulations are finalized (Prop. Reg. § § 28.2801-0—28.2801-7).

A covered gift or bequest made to a domestic trust is subject to tax in the same manner as for a U.S. citizen or resident, and as the recipient, the trust is required to pay the tax imposed. A covered gift or bequest made to a foreign trust is also subject to tax, but only at the time a distribution, whether from income or principal, is made to a U.S. citizen or resident from the trust that is attributable to the covered gift or bequest. The recipient is allowed an income tax deduction for the amount of tax paid or accrued for gifts or bequests from a covered expatriate by reason of a distribution from a foreign trust, but only to the extent the tax is imposed on the portion of the distribution included in the recipient's gross income. For this purpose only, a foreign trust may elect to be treated as a domestic trust.

Topical Index

References are to paragraph (¶) numbers

ANN

DEF

EXE

FIL

INC

INT

TAX